CONTRACT LAW AND THEORY

CONTRACT LAW AND THEORY

Fifth Edition

Robert E. Scott
Alfred McCormack Professor of Law
Director, Center for Contract and Economic Organization
Columbia Law School

Jody S. Kraus
Patricia D. and R. Paul Yetter Professor of Law
Professor of Philosophy
Columbia Law School

CAROLINA ACADEMIC PRESS
Durham, North Carolina

Print ISBN: 978-0-7698-4894-5
eBook ISBN: 978-0-3271-7717-3
Looseleaf ISBN: 978-0-7698-4896-9

Library of Congress Cataloging-in-Publication Data

Scott, Robert E., 1944-
    Contract law and theory / Robert E. Scott, Alfred McCormack Professor of Law, Director, Center
for Contract and Economic Organization, Columbia Law School; Jody S. Kraus, Patricia D. and R.
Paul Yetter Professor of Law, Professor of Philosophy, Columbia Law School. -- Fifth edition.
        p. cm.
    Includes index.
    ISBN 978-0-7698-4894-5
1. Contracts--United States--Cases. I. Kraus, Jody S. II. Title.
    KF801.A7S34 2013
    346.7302'2--dc23
2013010601

Carolina Academic Press, LLC
700 Kent Street
Durham, North Carolina 27701
Telephone (919) 489-7486
Fax (919) 493-5668
www.caplaw.com

Printed in the United States of America
2022 Printing

DEDICATION

To

Madeline, Sam, and Julia

and

Atticus

PREFACE

In the first edition to this casebook, we began with the question: Why do we need another casebook on Contracts? Our claim then, which we believe to be true today, is that this casebook and the approach to the study of contract law that it develops are unique. We began with a belief that colors much of the analysis that follows— theory works. Not only is it more interesting to study legal rules against a background of legal theory, but the effort has practical payoffs as well. There are clear, discernable themes and patterns that underlie much of contract law, and by developing them explicitly we invite the student to develop a working model of contract law. This framework for analyzing and predicting the outcome of contract disputes is then tested through careful case and doctrinal analysis.

Our commitment to the practical uses of theory commits us as well to a functional analysis of contract law. We ask: What discernable purposes are the various legal rules (as announced in cases and statutes) designed to serve? Are the policy goals desirable and how effectively are they implemented through contract doctrine? This functional approach begins with an instrumental analysis that focuses on the incentive effects of contract rules. We often ask a question familiar to students of economics: How are the rules likely to influence the behavior of similarly situated parties in the future? We use this economic perspective as an organizing principle because we believe it does the best job of any contemporary theory in explaining contract law. But we recognize that other perspectives on contract law deserve careful attention as well. In particular, throughout the casebook we use autonomy and related moral theory as an alternative framework for analyzing the law of contracts. In this edition, we add a third, pluralist, perspective that considers claims of fairness along with norms of efficiency and autonomy. In short, we believe that a commitment to a functional analysis of contract law does not demand the acceptance of any particular dogma. Skeptics will find that the organizing themes of the book are sufficiently explicit so as to provide ample opportunity for counter-examples and dissent.

The theoretical perspective of the book also shapes our pedagogical objectives. We begin, in Chapter 1, with a thorough doctrinal and theoretical overview. The chapters that follow are in-depth elaborations of the introductory themes. This approach has several benefits. In particular, once the analytical framework is introduced in Chapter 1, the thick analysis of individual doctrines that follows is more readily digested and integrated by the student learning law for the first time. This allows us to focus in subsequent chapters on the counseling and drafting functions that contract lawyers perform. We remind students that they study past disputes in order to draft contractual provisions that will avoid similar problems in the future. We develop this theme through questions and problems as well as textual notes that explore the underlying objectives of parties entering into various contractual relationships.

In this edition, we have added a few new cases reflecting contemporary developments particularly in the areas of precontractual liability, preliminary agreements and collaborative contracts. Most of our efforts, however, have focused on careful rewriting and editing of text and essays and on shifting a number of principal cases to notes. The

PREFACE

object has been both to condense the book for easier coverage in four-hour courses and to enhance the book's accessibility to students. We continue to work on improving and updating this book because teaching contract law and theory has been so rewarding for us and (apparently) for our students. We hope those of you who try our approach will experience a similar success.

ROBERT E. SCOTT

JODY S. KRAUS

ACKNOWLEDGMENTS

We express our thanks to the authors and publishers for permission to reprint portions of the following copyrighted material:

Restatement, Second, Contracts copyright © 1981 by The American Law Institute. Reprinted with the permission. All rights reserved.

Uniform Commercial Code copyright © 2001 by The American Law Institute and the National Conference of Commissioners on Uniform State Laws. Reprinted with the permission of the Permanent Editorial Board for the Uniform Commercial Code. All rights reserved.

Melvin Eisenberg, *The Principles of Consideration*, 67 CORNELL L. REV. 640 (1982). Copyright © 1982. Reprinted with permission of the author. All rights reserved.

Melvin Eisenberg, *Third-Party Beneficiaries*, 92 COLUM. L. REV. 1358 (1992). Copyright © 1992. Reprinted with permission of the author. All rights reserved.

GRANT GILMORE, THE DEATH OF CONTRACT (1974). Copyright © 1974. Reprinted by permission of The Ohio State University Press. All rights reserved.

Victor Goldberg, *Excuse Doctrine: The Eisenberg Uncertainty Principle*, 2 J. LEGAL ANALYSIS 359 (2010). Copyright © 2010. Reprinted with permission of the author. All rights reserved.

VICTOR GOLDBERG, FRAMING CONTRACT LAW: AN ECONOMIC PERSPECTIVE (2007). Copyright © 2007. Reprinted with permission of the author. All rights reserved.

Anthony Kronman, *Mistake, Disclosure, Information and the Law of Contracts*, 7 J. LEGAL STUD. 1 (1975). Copyright © 1975. Reprinted by permission of the author. All rights reserved.

RICHARD POSNER, ECONOMIC ANALYSIS OF LAW (1992). Copyright © 1992. Reprinted by permission of the author.

Alan Schwartz, *The Case for Specific Performance*, 89 YALE L.J. 271 (1979). Copyright © 1979. Reprinted by permission of Yale Law Journal. All rights reserved.

Maurice Womser, *The True Conception of Unilateral Contracts*, 26 YALE L.J. 136 (1916). Copyright © 1916. Reprinted by permission of Yale Law Journal. All rights reserved.

Many of the cases in this book were downloaded from Lexis. The authors gratefully acknowledge the courtesy of LexisNexis Group for permitting them to download the cases without charge. The authors also thank George Cohen, Michael Dooley, Einer Elhauge, Victor Goldberg, Ed Morrison, and Alan Schwartz for valuable comments on the prior edition which we have endeavored to incorporate into the current text, and Trey Brewer and Will Sears for invaluable research assistance.

TABLE OF CONTENTS

TABLE OF CONTENTS

TABLE OF CONTENTS

TABLE OF CONTENTS

TABLE OF CONTENTS

TABLE OF CONTENTS

TABLE OF CONTENTS

TABLE OF CONTENTS

TABLE OF CONTENTS

TABLE OF CONTENTS

TABLE OF CONTENTS

Chapter 1

AN OVERVIEW OF CONTRACT LAW

A. INTRODUCTION: THE PURPOSES OF CONTRACT LAW

The purpose of this chapter is to present an overview of the issues, methods, theory, and basic doctrines of modern contract law. The chapter thus serves both as a framework for analysis as well as a window to the contents of each of the subsequent chapters of this book. Neither a fully developed conceptual approach to contracts, nor an adequate doctrinal development of the many concepts such as consideration, excuse, or remedies can be fully developed in the space of a single chapter. But the treatment of these and other topics in this chapter will aid students in understanding the ensuing materials. Students should approach this first chapter much like the task of building a jigsaw puzzle. The first goal is to understand the contours and parameters of the puzzle. Thus, this chapter will show how various contract doctrines relate to each other and to prevailing theories that purport to explain and justify contract law. Subsequent chapters will flesh out the balance of the picture in greater detail. Our hope, of course, is that at the end of the course each student will have a coherent and integrated understanding of contract law.

The study of contracts is the study of the legal enforcement of promises. When a person promises to do something in the future but later changes her mind about performing the promised act, will or should the law intervene and "enforce" the promise? If so, what steps are appropriate to "enforce" the promise? These are the fundamental questions of contract law. The answers to these questions determine when and how society, through its legal system, intervenes in private contractual relationships — when it imposes constraints on its members' ability to act inconsistently with a promise or representation.

This inquiry might be easy enough to undertake if the law either enforced *all* promises or, alternatively, enforced *none*. But, in fact, American law shares one central characteristic with every other advanced legal system: some promises are enforced and others are not. Thus, the central challenge of contracts is to explain and justify this *mixed* system of enforcement. This challenge raises two quite distinct concerns. First, it is important for any lawyer to be able to predict which promises will be enforced and which broken promises the law will choose to ignore. The second concern is to justify the *selective* use of the state's coercive power to force some people, under some circumstances, to do what they are currently unwilling to do voluntarily. In this book we will work to answer both questions: What promises are enforced and why?

1

B. THE SOURCES AND FUNCTIONS OF CONTRACT LAW

The study of contract law consists of two inquiries. The first is to *explain* the patterns of promissory enforcement that we observe in contract law. A "descriptive" or "positive" theory of contract law provides a response to this inquiry. The second is to *justify* the exercise of state coercion through the application of contract law. A "normative" theory of contract law provides a response to this inquiry. The source or "data" for both kinds of theories are the various rules, or "doctrines," that comprise the law of contracts. Many of the doctrines that form the foundation of modern contract law were developed and announced by English courts deciding cases over a period of centuries. This common law of contracts was imported into the jurisprudence of colonial America. For the past 200 years, the common law courts in England and in America have developed along parallel lines, frequently being influenced by one another, but each assuming a distinct identity.

Over time, efforts have been made to systematize and/or codify American contract law. These efforts have taken several different forms. One form is the *Restatement of the Law of Contracts.* The Restatement was first published in 1932 by the American Law Institute (ALI), an organization made up of distinguished law professors, practicing attorneys, and judges formed for the purpose of "restating" the law in a variety of subjects. The Restatement was not intended to be enacted as a statute by legislatures. Rather, the Restatement was intended to assist the various state and federal courts in determining the patterns of prior judicial decisions in the developing common law of contracts. Thus, a particular Restatement provision does not carry the force of law unless and until it is adopted as an authoritative statement by courts deciding contested cases. Over the past 30 years, the ALI has revised the original Restatement, adopting the Restatement (Second) of Contracts in 1979.

The second means of systematizing the law is to reduce the common law to statutory form and seek adoption by state legislatures. The most influential of the various efforts to codify the law of contracts is Article 2 of the Uniform Commercial Code (UCC). The UCC was drafted in the 1940s by a group of scholars working under the auspices of the ALI and the National Conference of Commissioners on Uniform State Laws (NCCUSL). Rather than restating the law, Article 2 is an ambitious (and largely successful) effort to simplify, modernize, and standardize the various state laws governing certain kinds of contracts, namely contracts for the sale of goods. Every state except Louisiana has enacted Article 2. Despite the Code's initial success in gaining overwhelming adoption by the states, a several decade-long effort to amend Article 2 concluded in failure in 2011. The ALI and NCCUSL had proposed Amendments to Article 2 in 2003, but they immediately generated considerable controversy and faced interest group opposition in the various state legislatures. Over the next eight years, not a single state adopted the 2003 Amendments to Article 2. Recognizing the inevitable, the ALI withdrew the proposed Amendments in May 2011. Finally, there is a further codification of sales law that affects certain contracting parties in the United States. The United Nations Convention for the International Sale of Goods (CISG) is a self-executing treaty adopted by the United States and (currently) 78 other nations. CISG governs international sales contracts between commercial parties who are from different contracting states *unless* those parties declare their intention to opt out of its provisions and, in the case of United States entities, elect to be governed instead by Article 2 of the UCC.

Despite the statutory provisions that govern certain areas, much of modern contract law is still based on common law decisions. Within these two sources of law (statutes and common law) one finds many specific rules and doctrines. Taken together these rules may often seem confusing and contradictory. A primary goal of the study of contract law, therefore, is to develop a sense of the "patterns" or themes that link these rules together. One useful taxonomy is to classify each rule in terms of four basic functions that the rules and doctrines of contract law serve.

The first function of contract rules is to solve an initial *sorting problem*: Our legal system does not enforce all promises, not even all those that were seriously intended. Thus, at the outset we must identify the criteria for determining the enforceability of promises. This means we need to understand what behavior constitutes a "promise" and which of the acts that fall within that category are subject to state coercion. The so-called "objective" theory of contract and the doctrines of consideration and promissory estoppel are central to this first inquiry.

Second, contract law serves a *gap-filling* function.[1] Let's assume that we have identified the set of enforceable promises and we know that these are obligations that the law will require individuals to perform even when subsequent events make performance burdensome. But frequently, parties to these enforceable promises will not have specified in advance *all* of the details and contingencies under which performance may be required in the future. In short, promises made to others are invariably *incomplete.* Contract rules thus fill in, by default, many parts of an agreement that the parties do not expressly stipulate in their negotiations. One frequently litigated illustration of the gap-filling function arises in the case of changed circumstances. For example, contingencies can arise that the parties did not foresee — a fire, an oil embargo, or unprecedented inflation rates — and one party will be faced with a large loss when she originally thought she made a very profitable deal. In such cases, the contracting parties may dispute who should bear the risk of the changed circumstances, since they failed to negotiate explicit contractual provisions to cover the particular contingency. The need to fill gaps so as to resolve cases of changed circumstances is explored in subsequent chapters under various doctrinal headings, including mistake, excuse, and impossibility.

It is important to spend a few minutes thinking about this gap-filling function. Contract rules differ from many other legal rules in several respects. Most contract rules may be altered by agreement between the contracting parties. Thus, these rules are defaults. Similar to the default settings on a computer software program, they can be varied by explicit agreement to the contrary. There is a reason why there are default rules in contract law and not elsewhere. Contracting parties often have direct contact with each other and therefore are in a position to negotiate their legal obligations. Indeed, the costs of negotiating a variation from the legal rule that would otherwise apply are often quite low because the parties are already communicating and seeking to reach an initial agreement. In contrast, it is often

---

[1] The following discussion of the functions of contract law builds on the analysis in ALAN SCHWARTZ & ROBERT E. SCOTT, SALES LAW AND THE CONTRACTING PROCESS 29–30 (2d ed. 1991).

impractical, if not impossible, for individuals to renegotiate their legal liabilities in other areas of the law. For example, it is impractical (if not impossible) for the driver of an automobile to gather together all the parties (pedestrians, property owners, other drivers, etc.) who might be affected by a change in her legal obligation to drive reasonably. Moreover, contracting parties are usually the persons directly and substantially affected by their contract terms,[2] thus the rights and responsibilities of third parties often do not complicate the issue.

The gap-filling function of contract law points to a third function. Even when parties explicitly set out terms in a contract, the terms may be ambiguous and open to interpretation. Thus, contract law also provides rules for determining the meaning of the promises the parties have made to each other. For example, contracts commonly contain promises that serve to allocate future risks — such as the occurrence of an unanticipated event like a war or environmental disaster — to one party or the other. But when the war breaks out or the crops are embargoed, the party on whom the resulting loss initially falls sometimes will claim that, properly understood, the contract actually imposed the risk on the other party. The other party is likely to respond that, to the contrary, she never agreed to such an imposition under these particular circumstances. The legal system must now decide on whom the contract imposed the risk; that is, the law must determine the meaning of the promises made by the parties. This third function of contract law thus provides rules that enable courts to determine what the parties meant (or are assumed to have meant) by their promises. Legal rules that guide the courts in resolving these questions include the parol evidence rule and rules that govern the interpretation of language and of customary understandings.

The ability of parties to alter the default rules in contract necessarily raises the question of *when* they should be allowed to do so. The fourth function of contract rules thus seeks to solve a line-drawing problem: which rules should be treated as default rules (where the parties are free to opt out) and which ones should be mandatory and not subject to variation by mutual consent? Some contract rules are so fundamental to the underlying justification for contract law that they must be taken as given. Other rules can be varied by agreement under certain conditions but not others. For example, attempts to vary some rules are thought to produce results that offend widely held social values or that are grossly unfair to one of the parties. This final function of contract rules, then, is to define the outer boundaries of acceptable bargaining behavior and outcomes, and to deny enforcement of agreements that fall outside of those bounds. The wisdom of making some rules mandatory is the concern of the doctrines of duress, fraud, and unconscionability.

C. ENFORCING PROMISES

[1] What is a Promise?

Read Restatement (Second) of Contracts §§ 1, 2, and 4. Can you now answer the question: what is a contract? Notice that the Restatement's definition of a contract leaves open the question of precisely which promises the law will enforce. More

---

[2] There is a sense in which all contracts affect third parties, but that issue is not dealt with here.

fundamentally, however, it points out the central importance of the definition of promise in Restatement § 2. Before we examine the issue of which promises the law will enforce, therefore, we need first to give meaning to the concept of promise itself. Consider the following case.

BAILEY v. WEST
Rhode Island Supreme Court
105 R.I. 61, 249 A.2d 414 (1969)

court of last resort (state court)

PAOLINO, J.

This is a civil action wherein the plaintiff alleges that the defendant is indebted to him for the reasonable value of his services rendered in connection with the feeding, care and maintenance of a certain race horse named "Bascom's Folly" from May 3, 1962 through July 3, 1966. The case was tried before a justice of the superior court sitting without a jury, and resulted in a decision for the plaintiff for his cost of boarding the horse for the five months immediately subsequent to May 3, 1962, and for certain expenses incurred by him in trimming its hoofs. The cause is now before us on the plaintiff's appeal and defendant's cross appeal from the judgment entered pursuant to such decision.

The facts material to a resolution of the precise issues raised herein are as follows. In late April 1962, defendant, accompanied by his horse trainer, went to Belmont Park in New York to buy race horses. On April 27, 1962, defendant purchased "Bascom's Folly" from a Dr. Strauss and arranged to have the horse shipped to Suffolk Downs in East Boston, Massachusetts. Upon its arrival defendant's trainer discovered that the horse was lame, and so notified defendant, who ordered him to reship the horse by van to the seller at Belmont Park. The seller refused to accept delivery at Belmont on May 3, 1962, and thereupon, the van driver, one Kelly, called defendant's trainer and asked for further instructions. Although the trial testimony is in conflict as to what the trainer told him, it is not disputed that on the same day Kelly brought "Bascom's Folly" to plaintiff's farm where the horse remained until July 3, 1966, when it was sold by plaintiff to a third party.

While "Bascom's Folly" was residing at his horse farm, plaintiff sent bills for its feed and board to defendant at regular intervals. According to testimony elicited from defendant at the trial, the first such bill was received by him some two or three months after "Bascom's Folly" was placed on plaintiff's farm. He also stated that he immediately returned the bill to plaintiff with the notation that he was not the owner of the horse nor was it sent to plaintiff's farm at his request. The plaintiff testified that he sent bills monthly to defendant and that the first notice he received from him disclaiming ownership was ". . . maybe after a month or two or so" subsequent to the time when the horse was left in plaintiff's care.

In his decision the trial judge found that defendant's trainer had informed Kelly during their telephone conversation of May 3, 1962, that ". . . he would have to do whatever he wanted to do with the horse, that he wouldn't be on any farm at the defendant's expense. . . ." He also found, however, that when "Bascom's Folly" was brought to his farm, plaintiff was not aware of the telephone conversation between

Kelly and defendant's trainer, and hence, even though he knew there was a controversy surrounding the ownership of the horse, he was entitled to assume that ". . . there is an implication here that, I am to take care of this horse." Continuing his decision, the trial justice stated that in view of the result reached by this court in a recent opinion[3] wherein we held that the instant defendant was liable to the original seller, Dr. Strauss, for the purchase price of this horse, there was a contract "implied in fact" between the plaintiff and defendant to board "Bascom's Folly" and that this contract continued until plaintiff received notification from defendant that he would not be responsible for the horse's board. The trial justice further stated that ". . . I think there was notice given at least at the end of the four months, and I think we must add another month on there for a reasonable disposition of his property."

In view of the conclusion we reach with respect to defendant's first two contentions, we shall confine ourselves solely to a discussion and resolution of the issues necessarily implicit therein, and shall not examine other subsidiary arguments advanced by plaintiff and defendant.

I

The defendant alleges in his brief and oral argument that the trial judge erred in finding a contract "implied in fact" between the parties. We agree.

The following quotation from 17 C.J.S. *Contracts* § 4 at pp. 557-560, illustrates the elements necessary to the establishment of a contract "implied in fact":

> . . . A "contract implied in fact," . . . or an implied contract in the proper sense, arises where the intention of the parties is not expressed, but an agreement in fact, creating an obligation, is implied or presumed from their acts, or, as it has been otherwise stated, where there are circumstances which, according to the ordinary course of dealing and the common understanding of men, show a mutual intent to contract.

It has been said that a contract implied in fact must contain all the elements of an express contract. So, such a contract is dependent on mutual agreement or consent, and on the intention of the parties; and a meeting of the minds is required. A contract implied in fact is to every intent and purpose an agreement between the parties, and it cannot be found to exist unless a contract status is shown. Such a contract does not arise out of an implied legal duty or obligation, but out of facts from which consent may be inferred; there must be a manifestation of assent arising wholly or in part from acts other than words, and a contract cannot be implied in fact where the facts are inconsistent with its existence.

Therefore, essential elements of contracts "implied in fact" are mutual agreement, and intent to promise, but the agreement and the promise have not been made in words and are implied from the facts. Power-Matics, Inc. v. Ligotti, 79 N.J. Super. 294, 191 A.2d 483 (1963); St. Paul Fire & M. Ins. Co. v. Indemnity Ins. Co. of No. America, 32 N.J. 17, 158 A.2d 825 (1960); St. John's First Lutheran Church

---

[3] [1] *See Strauss v. West*, 100 R.I. 388, 216 A.2d 366.

v. Storsteen, 77 S.D. 33, 84 N.W.2d 725 (1957).[4]

In the instant case, plaintiff sued on the theory of a contract "implied in law." There was no evidence introduced by him to support the establishment of a contract "implied in fact," and he cannot now argue solely on the basis of the trial justice's decision for such a result.

The source of the obligation in a contract "implied in fact," as in express contracts, is in the intention of the parties. We hold that there was no mutual agreement and "intent to promise" between the plaintiff and defendant so as to establish a contract "implied in fact" for defendant to pay plaintiff for the maintenance of this horse. From the time Kelly delivered the horse to him plaintiff knew there was a dispute as to its ownership, and his subsequent actions indicated he did not know with whom, if anyone, he had a contract. After he had accepted the horse, he made inquiries as to its ownership and, initially, and for some time thereafter, sent his bills to both defendant and Dr. Strauss, the original seller.

There is also uncontroverted testimony in the record that prior to the assertion of the claim which is the subject of this suit neither defendant nor his trainer had ever had any business transactions with plaintiff, and had never used his farm to board horses. Additionally, there is uncontradicted evidence that this horse, when found to be lame, was shipped by defendant's trainer not to plaintiff's farm, but back to the seller at Belmont Park. What is most important, the trial justice expressly stated that he believed the testimony of defendant's trainer that he had instructed Kelly that defendant would not be responsible for boarding the horse on any farm.

From our examination of the record we are constrained to conclude that the trial justice overlooked and misconceived material evidence which establishes beyond question that there never existed between the parties an element essential to the formulation of any true contract, namely, an "intent to contract." Compare Morrissey v. Piette, R.I., 241 A.2d 302, 303.

II

The defendant's second contention is that, even assuming the trial justice was in essence predicating defendant's liability upon a quasi-contractual theory, his decision is still unsupported by competent evidence and is clearly erroneous.

The following discussion of quasi-contracts appears in 12 Am. Jur., *Contracts*, § 6 (1938) at pp. 503 to 504:

. . . A quasi contract has no reference to the intentions or expressions of the parties. The obligation is imposed despite, and frequently in frustration of, their intention. For a quasi contract neither promise nor privity, real or imagined, is necessary. In quasi contracts the obligation arises, not from consent of the parties, as in the case of contracts, express or implied in fact, but from the law of natural immutable justice and equity. The act, or acts, from which the law implies the contract must, however, be voluntary.

---

[4] [2] *Compare Arden Engineering Co. v. E. Turgeon Constr. Co.*, 97 R.I. 342, 347, 197 A.2d 743, 746, and *George Spalt & Sons, Inc. v. Maiello*, 48 R.I. 223, 226, 136 A. 882, 883.

Where a case shows that it is the duty of the defendant to pay, the law imputes to him a promise to fulfill that obligation. The duty, which thus forms the foundation of a quasi-contractual obligation, is frequently based on the doctrine of unjust enrichment. . . .

. . . The law will not imply a promise against the express declaration of the party to be charged, made at the time of the supposed undertaking, unless such party is under legal obligation paramount to his will to perform some duty, and he is not under such legal obligation unless there is a demand in equity and good conscience that he should perform the duty.

Therefore, the essential elements of a quasi-contract are a benefit conferred upon defendant by plaintiff, appreciation by defendant of such benefit, and acceptance and retention by defendant of such benefit under such circumstances that it would be inequitable to retain the benefit without payment of the value thereof. Home Savings Bank v. General Finance Corp., 10 Wis. 2d 417, 103 N.W.2d 117, 81 A.L.R.2d 580.

The key question raised by this appeal with respect to the establishment of a quasi-contract is whether or not plaintiff was acting as a "volunteer" at the time he accepted the horse for boarding at his farm. There is a long line of authority which has clearly enunciated the general rule that ". . . if a performance is rendered by one person without any request by another, it is very unlikely that this person will be under a legal duty to pay compensation." 1A Corbin, Contracts § 234.

The Restatement of Restitution, § 2 (1937) provides: "A person who officiously confers a benefit upon another is not entitled to restitution therefor." Comment a in the above-mentioned section states in part as follows:

Policy ordinarily requires that a person who has conferred a benefit . . . by way of giving another services . . . should not be permitted to require the other to pay therefor, unless the one conferring the benefit had a valid reason for so doing. A person is not required to deal with another unless he so desires and, ordinarily, a person should not be required to become an obligor unless he so desires.

Applying those principles to the facts in the case at bar it is clear that plaintiff cannot recover. The plaintiff's testimony on cross-examination is the only evidence in the record relating to what transpired between Kelly and him at the time the horse was accepted for boarding. The defendant's attorney asked plaintiff if he had any conversation with Kelly at that time, and plaintiff answered in substance that he had noticed that the horse was very lame and that Kelly had told him: "That's why they wouldn't accept him at Belmont Track." The plaintiff also testified that he had inquired of Kelly as to the ownership of "Bascom's Folly," and had been told that "Dr. Strauss made a deal and that's all I know." It further appears from the record that plaintiff acknowledged receipt of the horse by signing a uniform livestock bill of lading, which clearly indicated on its face that the horse in question had been consigned by defendant's trainer not to plaintiff, but to Dr. Strauss's trainer at Belmont Park. Knowing at the time he accepted the horse for boarding that a controversy surrounded its ownership, plaintiff could not reasonably expect remuneration from defendant, nor can it be said that defendant acquiesced in the conferment of a benefit upon him. The undisputed testimony was that defendant, upon receipt of plaintiff's first bill, immediately notified him that he was not the owner of "Bascom's Folly" and would not be responsible for its keep.

It is our judgment that the plaintiff was a mere volunteer who boarded and maintained "Bascom's Folly" at his own risk and with full knowledge that he might not be reimbursed for expenses he incurred incident thereto.

The plaintiff's appeal is denied and dismissed, the defendant's cross appeal is sustained, and the cause is remanded to the superior court for entry of judgment for the defendant.

NOTES

1. ***Why Print Opinions?*** The numbers and letters after the caption "Bailey v. West,"[5] refer to the printed opinions of the Rhode Island state supreme court, the highest appellate court in that state. "R.I." designates volumes printed by the state of Rhode Island, and the "A.2d" designates volumes printed by a privately owned publishing company. Why did the court give reasons for ruling in favor of West? The court could have sent Bailey a letter, saying "Bailey, you lose." If you develop a theory for why the courts give reasons, does it follow that the reasons ought to be published? Again, a letter to Bailey saying, "Bailey, you lose because . . ." ought to suffice. Instead, the reasons are printed up, and appear in countless public and private law libraries throughout the country. Try to come up with as many explanations for this as you can.

2. ***Understanding the Arguments.*** The following quotation from *Continental Forest Prods. v. Chandler Supply Co.*, 95 Idaho 739, 518 P.2d 1201 (1974), may help you understand Bailey's arguments:

> Basically the courts have recognized three types of contractual arrangements. Restatement of Contracts, § 5, comment a, at p. 7 (1932); 3 Corbin on Contracts, § 562 at p. 283 (1960). First is the express contract wherein the parties expressly agree regarding a transaction.

> Secondly, there is the implied in fact contract wherein there is no express agreement but the conduct of the parties implies an agreement from which an obligation in contract exists.

> The third category is called an implied in law contract, or quasi contract. However, a contract implied in law is not a contract at all, but an obligation imposed by law for the purpose of bringing about justice and equity without reference to the intent or the agreement of the parties and, in some cases, in spite of an agreement between the parties. . . .

---

[5] Can you tell which party is Bailey and which is West? Practice is not the same in every state, but a good rule of thumb is that the name of the party filing the lawsuit will appear first at the trial court level, and the name of the party filing the appeal will appear first in the appellate court. When both parties are disappointed with the ruling of the lower court, both may appeal. Ordinarily, the name of the party who files first appears first.

[T]he essence of a contract implied in law lies in the fact that the defendant has received a benefit which it would be inequitable for him to retain. . . .

518 P.2d at 1205.

Consider the following hypothetical:

In 2003, a small-time potato farmer in Idaho named Rick Miles was selling a modest amount of potatoes to what was then an eight-store restaurant chain named Five Guys. Since then, the burger chain has expanded exponentially and, naturally, so has its potato orders. In 2010, Five Guys purchased 150 million pounds of fresh Idaho potatoes — all of them from Miles. While Five Guys does not purchase potatoes from other sources, neither has it ever explicitly represented that it plans to always buy all its potatoes from Miles. The parties have never put any agreement in writing, relying only on a handshake. Nevertheless, Miles has invested heavily in new equipment, employees, and land. Five Guys is aware the extent to which Miles relies upon their relationship.[6]

Although it has never given any indication that it would do so, suppose Five Guys decides, without warning, to switch potato suppliers. Should Miles be able to sue for breach of contract? If so, should he argue express contract, contract implied in fact or contract implied in law? What other information, if any, would it be useful for a court to know?

3. ***The Agency Issue and Other Questions.*** Whose employee was Kelly? Is the answer important? Is it likely that the case would have been decided differently if Bailey and West had an ongoing business relationship? Why? With respect to these questions, how would you decide the following case and why?

John is a wealthy man. His holdings in stocks and bonds are managed by Rhonda, a local stockbroker. For several years, Rhonda has had unlimited power to sell to and from John's account, without seeking prior permission from John. As John's broker, Rhonda has often bought from and sold to Michael. Last week, John called Rhonda and told her not to sell the stock of Leading Aviation because, although it was falling rapidly, John had a special interest in keeping it. Notwithstanding these instructions, Rhonda entered into a written agreement with Michael to sell him John's Leading Aviation stock. The price of Leading Aviation has taken a sudden, major rise. Rhonda does not have the money to recompense either John or Michael for the error. As between John and Michael, who do you think wins? Why?

4. ***The Expectations of Bailey and West.*** Unless he was lying, Bailey thought that he had an agreement with West. Ought it to matter whether that belief was reasonable or idiosyncratic? A "reasonableness" standard is very vague and general — how should the court decide if Bailey's impressions were reasonable? Would a survey of horse owners, horse trainers, lawyers, or random persons be helpful?

---

[6] This hypothetical is based on a true story. *Behind the Counter* (CNBC television broadcast Dec. 15, 2010), http://www.cnbc.com/id/39911155.

Bailey and West each had a different expectation concerning the boarding of the horse and the existence of any agreement between them, and the court chose to support West's expectations. Perhaps the result doesn't turn on the reasonableness of Bailey's expectation, but on the fact that West never said, "I promise," nor made any other verbal or written representation to Bailey. Could a promise be inferred solely from conduct or other nonverbal behavior?

5. ***The Prospective Effects of* Bailey v. West.** What is the loss caused by the misunderstanding between Bailey and West? Why should Bailey bear all the loss? Would it not be "fairer" or more "just" if the court decided to divide the losses between the parties in such cases? This question requires you to focus on the purposes of legal rules. Legal rules that determine liability and/or impose damages have both a redistributive function and a behavior modification function. That is, they redistribute wealth between the immediate parties to any particular dispute (make one richer, the other poorer), and they also influence the behavior of future parties who may be similarly situated.

In that sense, then, contract rules can be evaluated in two ways: whether they do justice between the parties to the particular dispute and whether they appropriately regulate the conduct of other parties likely to have similar disputes in the future. The first perspective looks at contract law *ex post* (after the event that leads to a dispute has occurred). It considers how existing burdens or losses should be allocated. The second perspective looks at contract law *ex ante* (before any disagreement has materialized). It concerns the kind of behavior thought to be desirable for the law to encourage or deter. Both perspectives are influential in shaping rules in all legal fields, but one or the other predominates in particular areas. Which perspective better explains *Bailey v. West*?

6. ***The Puzzle of Quasi-Contract.*** As the court in *Bailey v. West* points out, a person conferring a benefit without a prior promise from the recipient of the benefit typically won't be able to recover in quasi-contract. Generally, the law regards the conferrer of the unbargained for benefit as an officious intermeddler or a mere volunteer for whom recovery is not available. When, then, is quasi-contractual recovery available? One such circumstance occurs when the recipient of the benefit was in the best position to prevent the mistake or error that led to the conferral of the benefit. In other words, where the recipient had the "last clear chance" to prevent a non-bargained-for benefit that was conferred by mistake. Consider, for example, the following quotation:

> If a person saw day after day a laborer at work in his field doing services, which must of necessity enure to his benefit, knowing that the laborer expected pay for his work, when it was perfectly easy to notify him if his services were not wanted, even if a request were not expressly proved, such a request, either previous to or contemporaneous with the performance of the services, might fairly be inferred. But if the fact was merely brought to his attention upon a single occasion and casually, if he had little opportunity to notify the other that he did not desire the work and should not pay for it, or could only do so at the expense of much time and trouble, the same inference might not be made.

Day v. Caton, 119 Mass. 513 (1876) (HOLMES, J.).

How would you expect to see the following hypothetical decided?

Bob is a house painter newly arrived to Marshalltown. A local realtor hires Bob to paint "the two large, white houses at 222 and 224 Rugby Road." Bob doesn't realize that there are both a Rugby Road and a Rugby Circle in Marshalltown, and, having lost the paper on which he wrote down the precise house numbers, he proceeds to paint two white houses on Rugby Circle. One of the houses is owned by McQueen, who is vacationing at the beach. The other house is owned by Randle, who is living across the street while he seeks a renter for the white house. Every day Randle comes home and sips his mint julep on his porch, watching Bob paint the houses, and saying nothing. As Bob finishes his work on the last house, he notices that he has some paint left over, so he decides to paint the garage of the third house in the block. It badly needs the paint, and although the owner is not at home, Bob feels he would want the garage painted. McQueen is delighted with the work done on his house, as are Randle and the garage owner, but each refuses to pay Bob anything.

If Bob seeks quasi-contract from the three owners, who ought to win and why? Are your reasons the same for each owner? Assuming that the quotation from Justice Holmes' opinion in *Day v. Caton, supra,* identifies facts that you, too, think are determinative with respect to the homeowners, it does not tell you why those *ought* to be the determinative facts. Can you speculate about the reasons for this legal rule? The excerpt in the note that follows suggests one scholar's attempt to rationalize the puzzle of quasi-contract.

7. *Restitution in Lieu of Bargain.*

A theme so prevalent in contract and tort law theory that it sometimes passes unmentioned is that legal rules reflect parties' abilities to bargain. Our legal system rests on the belief that citizens generally know what is in their own interests and that it is in society's interest to accept and encourage private agreements.

But an awareness of impediments to bargain is only a first step toward understanding restitution law. The inability to bargain does a fair job of explaining, for instance, restitution in cases of emergency. . . . Restitution in cases of mistake, on the other hand, is not easily explained by the law's fondness for bargains. If, contrary to prevailing law, debtors could not retrieve overrepayments or disbursing agents could not recover payments made for mistaken claims, debtors would protect themselves with more paperwork, and disbursing agents would demand more proof before paying claims. It does not require great faith in the usefulness of economic analysis in law to believe that the flat denial of restitution in these cases would lead to an inefficiently high level of care. Thus, although the general law of restitution seeks to encourage private bargaining rather than to replace it with judicial intervention, a counterforce in the law impels courts [in some cases] to recognize or create missing bargains.

Saul Levmore, *Explaining Restitution,* 71 Va. L. Rev. 65, 68–69 (1985).

Consider the following hypothetical and analysis.

Late one night a bedraggled dog scratched at Lillian's front door. When she let the dog in she recognized it as a bearded collie, a valuable breed, with an injured paw. The dog's collar was torn and the tag that ordinarily identifies the owner was gone. The next day the dog appeared feverish and Lillian took it to the vet. The vet recommended surgery on the paw to prevent infection and possible death. Lillian ordered the surgery and paid the vet $100.

The next day a lost-and-found notice appeared in the paper. Lillian called, and the dog's owner appeared to claim the dog. When Lillian mentioned the $100 she had paid to the vet, the owner said, "I love my dog and I would surely have paid $100 also, but the fact is that I did not authorize the surgery and I shall not recompense you."

Analysis: There is a voluntary transaction — the owner contracting with Lillian to have the dog cared for — that we can be confident would have occurred but for the insuperable transaction cost (*i.e.*, the owner did not know that Lillian had the dog). Therefore, this is not like the case of the officious intermeddler or the mistaken conferrer of a benefit. The best the law can do is to replicate the result of the bargain that would have occurred absent the transaction costs. Lillian will recover in quasi-contract.

Could the same analysis be applied to *Bailey v. West*? What is the transaction cost in that case? Interestingly, the "analysis" supplied above is not predictive of the results courts reach in restitution cases. There is respectable authority that Lillian would not recover.[7]

Where does the analysis go wrong when applied to *Bailey v. West*? Hint (to one possible explanation): what are the facts of the hypothetical that seem crucial to the suggested analysis? Vary those facts and decide if the analysis still holds. Put another way, when Bascom's Folly arrived at Bailey's door, was Bascom's Folly a valuable horse?

Bailey v. West shows that people frequently place differing characterizations on the conduct that they observe. It is tempting to conclude from Bailey's mistake that conduct which may or may not constitute a promise is inherently more ambiguous than oral or written expressions. On the other hand, statements in words are also subject to differing characterizations. A typical example is where one person makes a representation that seems to the other person to be an unequivocal promise to act in a certain way, but the first person does not really intend to be bound by his statement. How should the courts determine whether the representation in question was, in fact, a legal promise? How can a court determine the "true" intent of the parties? Reread Restatement (Second) § 2 and consider the following case.

---

[7] This conclusion will be implicit in the cases in Chapter 2D. For a further discussion of the "puzzle" of restitution and some suggestions as to the predictive theories, see Saul Levmore, *Explaining Restitution*, 71 Va. L. Rev. 65 (1985).

LUCY v. ZEHMER
Supreme Court of Virginia
196 Va. 493, 84 S.E.2d 516 (1954)

Buchanan, J.

This suit was instituted by W. O. Lucy and J. C. Lucy, complainants, against A. H. Zehmer and Ida S. Zehmer, his wife, defendants, to have specific performance of a contract by which it was alleged the Zehmers had sold to W. O. Lucy a tract of land owned by A. H. Zehmer in Dinwiddie county containing 471.6 acres, more or less, known as the Ferguson farm, for $50,000. J. C. Lucy, the other complainant, is a brother of W. O. Lucy, to whom W. O. Lucy transferred a half interest in his alleged purchase.

The instrument sought to be enforced was written by A. H. Zehmer on December 20, 1952, in these words: "We hereby agree to sell to W. O. Lucy the Ferguson Farm complete for $50,000.00, title satisfactory to buyer," and signed by the defendants, A. H. Zehmer and Ida S. Zehmer.

The answer of A. H. Zehmer admitted that at the time mentioned W. O. Lucy offered him $50,000 cash for the farm, but that he, Zehmer, considered that the offer was made in jest; that so thinking, and both he and Lucy having had several drinks, he wrote out "the memorandum" quoted above and induced his wife to sign it; that he did not deliver the memorandum to Lucy, but that Lucy picked it up, read it, put it in his pocket, attempted to offer Zehmer $5 to bind the bargain, which Zehmer refused to accept, and realizing for the first time that Lucy was serious, Zehmer assured him that he had no intention of selling the farm and that the whole matter was a joke. Lucy left the premises insisting that he had purchased the farm.

Depositions were taken and the decree appealed from was entered holding that the complainants had failed to establish their right to specific performance, and dismissing their bill. The assignment of error is to this action of the court. . . .

Mr. and Mrs. Zehmer were called by the complainants as adverse witnesses. Zehmer testified in substance as follows:

He bought this farm more than ten years ago for $11,000. He had had twenty-five offers, more or less, to buy it, including several from Lucy, who had never offered any specific sum of money. He had given them all the same answer, that he was not interested in selling it. On this Saturday night before Christmas it looked like everybody and his brother came by there to have a drink. He took a good many drinks during the afternoon and had a pint of his own. When he entered the restaurant around eight-thirty Lucy was there and he could see that he was "pretty high." He said to Lucy, "Boy, you got some good liquor, drinking, ain't you?" Lucy then offered him a drink. "I was already high as a Georgia pine, and didn't have any more better sense than to pour another great big slug out and gulp it down, and he took one too."

After they had talked a while Lucy asked whether he still had the Ferguson farm. He replied that he had not sold it and Lucy said, "I bet you wouldn't take $50,000.00 for it." Zehmer asked him if he would give $50,000 and Lucy said yes.

Zehmer replied, "You haven't got $50,000 in cash." Lucy said he did and Zehmer replied that he did not believe it. They argued "pro and con for a long time," mainly about "whether he had $50,000 in cash that he could put up right then and buy that farm."

Finally, said Zehmer, Lucy told him if he didn't believe he had $50,000, "you sign that piece of paper here and say you will take $50,000.00 for the farm." He, Zehmer, "just grabbed the back off of a guest check there" and wrote on the back of it. At that point in his testimony Zehmer asked to see what he had written to "see if I recognize my own handwriting." He examined the paper and exclaimed, "Great balls of fire, I got 'Firgerson' for Ferguson. I have got satisfactory spelled wrong. I don't recognize that writing if I would see it, wouldn't know it was mine."

After Zehmer had, as he described it, "scribbled this thing off," Lucy said, "Get your wife to sign it." Zehmer walked over to where she was and she at first refused to sign but did so after he told her that he "was just needling him (Lucy), and didn't mean a thing in the world, that I was not selling the farm." Zehmer then "took it back over there . . . and I was still looking at the dern thing. I had the drink right there by my hand, and I reached over to get a drink, and he said, 'Let me see it.' He reached and picked it up, and when I looked back again he had it in his pocket and he dropped a five dollar bill over there, and he said, 'Here is five dollars payment on it.' . . . I said, 'Hell no, that is beer and liquor talking. I am not going to sell you the farm. I have told you that too many times before.' " . . .

The defendants insist that the evidence was ample to support their contention that the writing sought to be enforced was prepared as a bluff or dare to force Lucy to admit that he did not have $50,000; that the whole matter was a joke; that the writing was not delivered to Lucy and no binding contract was ever made between the parties.

It is an unusual, if not bizarre, defense. When made to the writing admittedly prepared by one of the defendants and signed by both, clear evidence is required to sustain it.

In his testimony Zehmer claimed that he "was high as a Georgia pine," and that the transaction "was just a bunch of two doggoned drunks bluffing to see who could talk the biggest and say the most." That claim is inconsistent with his attempt to testify in great detail as to what was said and what was done. It is contradicted by other evidence as to the condition of both parties, and rendered of no weight by the testimony of his wife that when Lucy left the restaurant she suggested that Zehmer drive him home. The record is convincing that Zehmer was not intoxicated to the extent of being unable to comprehend the nature and consequences of the instrument he executed, and hence that instrument is not to be invalidated on that ground. 17 C.J.S., *Contracts*, § 133 b., p. 483; Taliaferro v. Emery, 124 Va. 674. It was in fact conceded by defendants' counsel in oral argument that under the evidence Zehmer was not too drunk to make a valid contract. The evidence is convincing also that Zehmer wrote two agreements, the first one beginning "I hereby agree to sell." Zehmer first said he could not remember about that, then that "I don't think I wrote but one out." Mrs. Zehmer said that what he wrote was "I hereby agree," but that the "I" was changed to "We" after that night. The agreement that was written and signed is in the record and indicates no such change. Neither are the mistakes in spelling that Zehmer sought to point out readily apparent.

The appearance of the contract, the fact that it was under discussion for forty minutes or more before it was signed; Lucy's objection to the first draft because it was written in the singular, and he wanted Mrs. Zehmer to sign it also; the rewriting to meet that objection and the signing by Mrs. Zehmer; the discussion of what was to be included in the sale, the provision for the examination of the title, the completeness of the instrument that was executed, the taking possession of it by Lucy with no request or suggestion by either of the defendants that he give it back, are facts which furnish persuasive evidence that the execution of the contract was a serious business transaction rather than a casual, jesting matter as defendants now contend.

On Sunday, the day after the instrument was signed on Saturday night, there was a social gathering in a home in the town of McKenney at which there were general comments that the sale had been made. Mrs. Zehmer testified that on that occasion as she passed by a group of people, including Lucy, who were talking about the transaction, $50,000 was mentioned, whereupon she stepped up and said, "Well, with the high-price whiskey you were drinking last night you should have paid more. That was cheap." Lucy testified that at that time Zehmer told him that he did not want to "stick" him or hold him to the agreement because he, Lucy, was too tight and didn't know what he was doing, to which Lucy replied that he was not too tight; that he had been stuck before and was going through with it. Zehmer's version was that he said to Lucy: "I am not trying to claim it wasn't a deal on account of the fact the price was too low. If I had wanted to sell $50,000.00 would be a good price, in fact I think you would get stuck at $50,000.00." A disinterested witness testified that what Zehmer said to Lucy was that "he was going to let him up off the deal, because he thought he was too tight, didn't know what he was doing. Lucy said something to the effect that "I have been stuck before and I will go through with it.' "

If it be assumed, contrary to what we think the evidence shows, that Zehmer was jesting about selling his farm to Lucy and that the transaction was intended by him to be a joke, nevertheless the evidence shows that Lucy did not so understand it but considered it to be a serious business transaction and the contract to be binding on the Zehmers as well as on himself. The very next day he arranged with his brother to put up half the money and take a half interest in the land. The day after that he employed an attorney to examine the title. The next night, Tuesday, he was back at Zehmer's place and there Zehmer told him for the first time, Lucy said, that he wasn't going to sell and he told Zehmer, "You know you sold that place fair and square." After receiving the report from his attorney that the title was good he wrote to Zehmer that he was ready to close the deal.

Not only did Lucy actually believe, but the evidence shows he was warranted in believing, that the contract represented a serious business transaction and a good faith sale and purchase of the farm.

In the field of contracts, as generally elsewhere, "We must look to the outward expression of a person as manifesting his intention rather than to his secret and unexpressed intention. 'The law imputes to a person an intention corresponding to the reasonable meaning of his words and acts.' " First Nat. Bank v. Roanoke Oil Co., 169 Va. 99, 114.

At no time prior to the execution of the contract had Zehmer indicated to Lucy by word or act that he was not in earnest about selling the farm. They had argued about it and discussed its terms, as Zehmer admitted, for a long time. Lucy testified that if there was any jesting it was about paying $50,000 that night. The contract and the evidence show that he was not expected to pay the money that night. Zehmer said that after the writing was signed he laid it down on the counter in front of Lucy. Lucy said Zehmer handed it to him. In any event there had been what appeared to be a good faith offer and a good faith acceptance, followed by the execution and apparent delivery of a written contract. Both said that Lucy put the writing in his pocket and then offered Zehmer $5 to seal the bargain. Not until then, even under the defendants' evidence, was anything said or done to indicate that the matter was a joke. Both of the Zehmers testified that when Zehmer asked his wife to sign he whispered that it was a joke so Lucy wouldn't hear and that it was not intended that he should hear.

The mental assent of the parties is not requisite for the formation of a contract. If the words or other acts of one of the parties have but one reasonable meaning, his undisclosed intention is immaterial except when an unreasonable meaning which he attaches to his manifestations is known to the other party. Restatement of the Law of Contracts, Vol. I, § 71, p. 74.

> The law, therefore, judges of an agreement between two persons exclusively from those expressions of their intentions which are communicated between them. . . .

Clark on Contracts, 4 ed., § 3, p. 4.

An agreement or mutual assent is of course essential to a valid contract but the law imputes to a person an intention corresponding to the reasonable meaning of his words and acts. If his words and acts, judged by a reasonable standard, manifest an intention to agree, it is immaterial what may be the real but unexpressed state of his mind. 17 C.J.S., *Contracts*, § 32, p. 361; 12 Am. Jur., *Contracts*, § 19, p. 515. So a person cannot set up that he was merely jesting when his conduct and words would warrant a reasonable person in believing that he intended a real agreement, 17 C.J.S., *Contracts*, § 47, p. 390; *Clark on Contracts*, 4 ed., § 27, at p. 54.

Whether the writing signed by the defendants and now sought to be enforced by the complainants was the result of a serious offer by Lucy and a serious acceptance by the defendants, or was a serious offer by Lucy and an acceptance in secret jest by the defendants, in either event it constituted a binding contract of sale between the parties.

Defendants contend further, however, that even though a contract was made, equity should decline to enforce it under the circumstances. These circumstances have been set forth in detail above. They disclose some drinking by the two parties but not to an extent that they were unable to understand fully what they were doing. There was no fraud, no misrepresentation, no sharp practice and no dealing between unequal parties. The farm had been bought for $11,000 and was assessed for taxation at $6,300. The purchase price was $50,000. Zehmer admitted that it was a good price. There is in fact present in this case none of the grounds usually urged against specific performance.

Specific performance, it is true, is not a matter of absolute or arbitrary right, but is addressed to the reasonable and sound discretion of the court. But it is likewise true that the discretion which may be exercised is not an arbitrary or capricious one, but one which is controlled by the established doctrines and settled principles of equity; and, generally, where a contract is in its nature and circumstances unobjectionable, it is as much a matter of course for courts of equity to decree a specific performance of it as it is for a court of law to give damages for a breach of it.

The complainants are entitled to have specific performance of the contracts sued on. The decree appealed from is therefore reversed and the cause is remanded for the entry of a proper decree requiring the defendants to perform the contract in accordance with the prayer of the bill.

Reversed and remanded.

NOTES

1. *Reasonable Belief*: **Leonard v. PepsiCo.** Compare the conclusion reached in *Lucy v. Zehmer* to *Leonard v. PepsiCo*, 88 F. Supp. 2d 116 (S.D.N.Y. 1997). The issue in *Leonard* was whether a Pepsi Stuff commercial which encouraged consumers to collect "Pepsi Points" from specially marked packages and redeem these points for merchandise featuring the Pepsi logo constituted an offer of a Harrier Jet. The idyllic commercial featured scenes of a teenager wearing a Pepsi t-shirt accompanied by the subtitle "T-SHIRT 75 PEPSI POINTS," a leather jacket with the subtitle "LEATHER JACKET 1450 PEPSI POINTS," a pair of sunglasses with the subtitle "SHADES 175 PEPSI POINTS," and culminated with the teenager flying a Harrier Jet to school as "HARRIER FIGHTER 7,000,000 PEPSI POINTS" scrolled across the screen. Harrier Jets are used by the United States Military Corps to attack surface targets. At the time, the cost of a Harrier Jet was approximately 23 million dollars.

Inspired by this commercial, plaintiff set out to obtain a Harrier Jet. Plaintiff consulted the Pepsi Stuff Catalog which specified the number of Pepsi Points required to obtain promotional merchandise. Conspicuously absent from the order form was any entry or description of a Harrier Jet. The Catalog noted that in the event that a consumer lacks enough Pepsi Points to obtain a desired item (and to obtain 7,000,000 points, plaintiff would have had to buy 190 Pepsis a day for the next hundred years), additional Pepsi Points could be purchased for ten cents each. Plaintiff submitted an order form and a check for $700,008.50. At the bottom of the order form, plaintiff wrote in "1 Harrier Jet" in the "Item" column and "7,000,000" in the "Total Points" column. Defendant rejected plaintiff's submission and returned his check, explaining that the item was not included in the catalogue and was included in the advertisement for fanciful and humorous effect. In evaluating whether the defendant's commercial constituted an offer, the court said:

> Plaintiff's understanding of the commercial as an offer must . . . be rejected because the Court finds that no objective person could reasonably have concluded that the commercial actually offered consumers a Harrier Jet.

In evaluating the commercial, the Court must not consider defendant's subjective intent in making the commercial, or plaintiff's subjective view of what the commercial offered, but what an objective, reasonable person would have understood the commercial to convey . . . If it is clear that an offer was not serious, then no offer has been made: An obvious joke, of course, would not give rise to a contract.

Id. at 127.

In *Lucy*, the promisors claimed that their promise was in jest, but the court nonetheless enforced their promise to sell the farm. In *Leonard*, the promisors claimed that their promise was in jest and the court released them of any liability to perform. Are these two cases irreconcilable? Can you suggest a principle that harmonizes them? Why was the promisee's belief that a commitment had been made a reasonable belief in *Lucy* but an unreasonable belief in *Leonard?* One possibility, of course, is that Leonard never really believed that there was a promise to exchange a Harrier Jet for 7,000,000 Pepsi points. On the other hand, would he have tendered $700,000 in cash if he believed the offer was only a joke? Isn't Leonard's behavior every bit as "reasonable" as Lucy's? After all, both were trying to grab a "good deal" before their promisor changed his mind.[8]

2. ***Looking Beyond the Record: The Value of the Farm.*** The court in *Lucy* states that the $50,000 price was a fair valuation of the farm. Recent academic scholarship calls this conclusion into question. The Ferguson Farm contained valuable, and long untouched, timber. Timber was a commodity subject to significant price fluctuations, but whose value was increasing in post-war Virginia. The Lucys acted as middle-men: they obtained wooded land from less knowledgeable farmers and then sold the timber rights, for a sizable profit, to lumber companies. Indeed, less than a decade after the sale, the Lucys had earned an estimated $142,000 from the Ferguson Farm. For a detailed historical account, see Barak Richman & Dennis Schmelzer, *When Money Grew on Trees:* Lucy v. Zehmer *and Contracting in a Boom Market,* 61 DUKE L.J. 1511 (2012). Does this change your opinion of the court's decision? Should the parties' subjective valuations trump their objective manifestations?

3. ***Instant Retraction or Why We Enforce Wholly Executory Promises.*** Consider the puzzle of "instant retraction." In *Lucy*, Zehmer changed his mind and tried to retract his promise the next day, but the court held that the attempted retraction came too late. Thus, the court ordered specific performance of the contract despite Zehmer's claim that enforcement would be inequitable under the circumstances. Why can't Zehmer change his mind if he does so the very next day before Lucy has substantially relied? Assume that Zehmer changed his mind about selling the farm while still in the tavern and that he told Lucy this before either had left the place. Under these circumstances, are there any reasons why the law should nonetheless enforce the promise to sell?

As a matter of legal doctrine there is no rule that would excuse Zehmer on the grounds of "instant retraction." If the promise otherwise meets the criteria for

---

[8] For further discussion of these questions and "joke" promises, see Keith A. Rowley, *You Asked for It, You Got It . . . Toy Yoda: Practical Jokes, Prizes, and Contract Law,* 3 NEV. L.J. 526 (2003).

enforceability, the courts will presumably pay no attention (at least not directly) to how soon a change of heart is announced. What explains that rule? Why can't someone in Zehmer's position argue successfully that, "even if I made a contract, it is inequitable to enforce my promise where there has been no substantial reliance by Lucy before I changed my mind." (In other words, why can't Zehmer argue "no harm, no foul"?) On this question, evaluate the following three arguments.

(a) The first argument is found in an excerpt from A. MELDEN, RIGHTS AND PERSONS 47–48 (1977):

> A promise is not, therefore, merely an assurance one gives to help another, just as it is not merely an expression of a resolution to perform an action. It is, in addition, to *underwrite* any endeavor the other party to the transaction may choose to launch, by giving notice to him that he may henceforth regard the performance of the promised action as one which he may be as assured as he is of any action that he, as a moral agent, is capable of performing and as he himself chooses. The failure to keep the promise, therefore, is no mere defeating of an expectation, no mere failure to carry out a professed intention or to make good an expression of one's resolution. It is, as we commonly put it, letting the other person down; it is tantamount to interfering with or subverting endeavors he has a right to pursue. It is thus to subvert the person's status as moral agent, one who relies not only on his own resources as an agent but also, by virtue of the promise he has received and accepted in good faith, on the promised action as a virtual *fait accompli.* It is for this reason that the promisee is entitled to the promised action: he is as entitled to it as he is, as a responsible agent, to conduct his own affairs. He is wronged by a promisor's breaking of a promise as much as he is wronged by any unwarranted interference with his conduct which violates the right that he has freely to go about his affairs. . . . Finally, given the function of the promise locution to provide the sort of formal notice described above, it is now intelligible that an obligation is incurred whether or not the promise was made in good faith. . . .

(b) The second argument could be said to be grounded on an "efficiency analysis."

> To enforce the promise in this case of "instant retraction" would be inefficient. The hypothetical facts show that Zehmer values the land more highly than does Lucy. That is why he "retracted" his promise and sacrificed the $50,000 in exchange. To put the land in the hands of Lucy after Zehmer's retraction moves it to a less highly valued use. The purpose of enforcing contracts should be to promote economic efficiency by cementing an exchange in which resources are more productively used after the exchange than before. Whenever there is an "instant retraction" we have information that the exchange will not accomplish that purpose and thus should not be coerced by the law.

> (Hint: Is it clear that transferring ownership of the land is the ultimate outcome? After the promise is held to be enforceable by the Virginia Supreme Court, is further bargaining between Lucy and Zehmer possible?)

(c) Finally, evaluate a third argument:

Why does anyone make a promise? A moment's reflection provides the answer. A person promises so that the promisee can rely on the promise. If I am going to give you my car next Tuesday, why do I promise to do so, when I could instead just wait until Tuesday and deliver the car to you? I promise so you will have the information and can adjust your life accordingly. If you adjust your life and I keep my promise, then your reliance will have been beneficial. If I do not keep my promise, then your reliance will have been detrimental to you.

Society values beneficial reliance and deplores detrimental reliance, and that is why promises are enforced. Yet in the case of an "instant retraction" there is no reliance whatsoever, and thus no reason to enforce the promise.

(Hint: In evaluating this argument think carefully about the unstated assumptions. In *Lucy*, is the important fact that the promisee did, in fact, rely or that he *could have* relied?)

4. *Objective Versus Subjective Intent.* The court in *Lucy* stated that "[t]he mental assent of the parties is not requisite for the formation of a contract." In *Leonard*, the court seemed to hold a similar view, stating that "we are not concerned with what was going through the heads of the parties at the time." Nevertheless, courts state that both parties must agree in some sense to the proposed bargain before it is binding. How is that mutual assent to be determined? Historically, courts have employed one of two rules to determine mutual assent. At one time they required a "meeting of the minds" or an actual intent by both parties to agree to the proposed bargain. Under this rule, courts would enforce a promise only if the promisor subjectively believed that he had made a firm promise. Later, courts began to bind individuals to their outward, objective manifestations without regard to the potentially conflicting subjective intent of the individual.

The rule at early common law required a subjective agreement between the contracting parties. Thus, a party's alleged acceptance of an offer was void if she could show that she did not intend to contract at the time she seemed to accept.[9] Of course, in the face of compelling circumstantial evidence based on outward manifestations, it might be difficult to convince a court of one's subjective intent not to accept.

In the 20th century, common law decisions shifted to the language of the objective theory. For example, Judge Learned Hand wrote in *Hotchkiss v. National City Bank*, 200 F. 287, 293 (S.D.N.Y. 1911):

A contract has, strictly speaking, nothing to do with the personal, or individual, intent of the parties. A contract is an obligation attached by the mere force of law to certain acts of the parties, usually words, which ordinarily accompany and represent a known intent. If, however, it were proved by twenty bishops that either party, when he used the words, intended something else than the usual meaning which the law imposes upon them, he would still be held, unless there were some mutual mistake, or something else of the sort. Of course, if it appear by other words, or acts,

---

[9] *See, e.g., Cook v. Oxley*, 3 Tenn. R. 653, 100 Eng. Rep. 785 (1790).

of the parties, that they attribute a peculiar meaning to such words as they use in the contract, that meaning will prevail, but only by virtue of the other words, and not because of their unexpressed intent.

Can an autonomy theory account for this result, which may seem morally intuitive to many of us? Professor Fried writes,

> The most likely [principle supporting enforcement of the promise] acknowledges that one party . . . is being forced to bear a loss he had not knowingly assumed, but . . . [h]e should not be disappointed because (1) if a loss is inevitable and both parties are innocent, the careless man should not be able to cast that loss on the prudent, and (2) the chances that the [party denying the fact of the contract has] reservations [that] are an afterthought are too great to warrant a systematic legal inquiry. The first of these reasons may be referred to consideration of fairness or to the encouragement of due care. The second reason is concerned not with the ultimate equities but with problems of administration. Both these considerations rely on grounds distinct from the promissory [autonomy] principle.[10]

An economic analysis seeks to explicate these "grounds distinct." Consider a transaction that is affected by the legal rule, and think about its impact on individuals' future behavior. A speaks to B as if he were making an offer, but A does not intend to make an offer.[11] B, believing that there has been an offer, accepts. In deciding whether to enforce A's promise, the law effectively must choose to support either A's or B's *beliefs*. Suppose the courts in State X follow the subjective approach and thus uphold A's belief that there was no offer. B has now lost a bargain, and presumably in the future he will take steps to reassure himself that the bargains he enters into will be performed. As for A, he has no reason to alter his future behavior, because the courts will not bind him to an offer unless he intends to be bound.

Now assume that in State Y the courts do enforce A's promise in order to support B's objective belief that A's offer was valid. This decision may affect A's future behavior. To avoid entering contracts when he does not intend to, A may take some precautions to attempt to make the objective meaning of his statements conform to his subjective intent. The question of which test to adopt can be considered in terms of alternative future actions. Which actions are preferable — B's efforts to seek reassurances or A's precautionary steps?

One way of answering this question is to choose the action that you think imposes the smallest burden or cost on society. One such cost is a result of the friction or misunderstanding that accompanies human interaction. Would it be less costly for B to seek reassurances or for A to take precautions? This, in turn, may depend upon the "reasonableness" of A's belief that his statement was not a promise. If most people would have regarded A's statement as a promise, then A was idiosyncratic

---

[10] CHARLES FRIED, CONTRACT AS PROMISE 63 (1981).

[11] Perhaps A has his fingers crossed behind his back. For years, A has taken the consistent position that he never intends to make a true promise so long as his fingers are crossed. All of A's friends and relatives know about this, but B is not one of them.

in his beliefs. Perhaps idiosyncratic people are better able to conform their conduct to the beliefs of the majority than are the majority to conform their beliefs to those of the idiosyncratic. Even if this is not true, one could contend that since the idiosyncratic are fewer in number (by definition) than the majority, asking them to take precautions will entail lower total cost. It is less costly for the relatively few idiosyncratic persons to clarify their misleading statements than it is for the "normal" majority to investigate extensively every communication that seems to be a straightforward offer.

Of course, one must acknowledge that we may put the burden on the idiosyncratic just because their beliefs differ from our own, and thus seem "strange."

5. *Reflection and Review.* Evaluate the following statement:

Bailey and *Lucy* share the feature that in each case one party believed there was an agreement while the other did not. In each case the court placed the entire loss caused by the misunderstanding on one party rather than dividing the loss between them according to some principle of proportionate responsibility. Moreover, in each case the court assigned the loss to the party who it (apparently) believed could have more readily reduced the risk of the misunderstanding (or avoided the misunderstanding altogether); that is, the courts seem to have imposed liability on the party with the comparative advantage in reducing the likelihood that such a misunderstanding would result. Obviously, it is too late to undo the costs of the misunderstanding in the litigated cases. Nor does it appear that the parties who lost were venal or deliberately careless in their actions. Thus, it seems from this limited sample that the courts are sending a message to future parties. If it is true that courts commonly reach outcomes consistent with this "comparative advantage" criterion, then we can use the criterion as a tool of positive analysis — in particular, as a principle of explanation — to predict and explain the results in contract cases. Furthermore, if we find the comparative advantage criterion normatively attractive, then we can also use it as a principle of justification and criticism to defend observed legal rules and to criticize those which deviate from the principle.

In *Lucy v. Zehmer*, the alleged promisor does not wish to perform and is willing to incur whatever loss of reputation and good will or internal sense of guilt that this decision might impose. Under such circumstances, what possible justification is there for the law to step in and coerce performance of the promise (whether made in jest or not)? We begin our exploration of this question with the following introductory essay.

Essay: An Introduction to Theories of Contract Law

The Western tradition in moral and political philosophy begins with a presumption in favor of individual liberty, and so it demands a justification for state coercion. The state exercises coercion through legal institutions. When a court enforces a promise, it imposes a legal sanction on a promisor who fails to keep her promise. As we will see, these sanctions can take the form of an order to pay compensatory damages or an order to perform the promise. In either case, if the promisor refuses to comply with the court's order, the state will exercise its coercive power to compel the promisor to comply. In the case of compensatory damages, state law provides procedures for collecting judgments which allow the aggrieved promisee to deliver the judgment to a sheriff. To satisfy the judgment, the sheriff has the authority to seize and sell the promisor's assets, or directly transfer to the promisee any money the promisor has in a bank account. If a court orders a promisor to perform, in some cases it can execute the promise on behalf of the promisor, as when a court transfers a breaching seller's deed to real estate in order to enforce the seller's promise to sell the real estate to a buyer. In other cases, a court might enjoin a promisor from engaging in conduct inconsistent with keeping his promise. And a promisor who resists a court order can be fined and/or jailed pursuant to contempt proceedings. In each of these cases, the state acts through the judicial and executive branches of government to coerce compliance with its orders. Thus, because the state coerces individuals when it legally enforces promises, the law of contract stands in need of justification.

But the task of justification cannot proceed independently of the task of identifying and explaining the doctrines that constitute contract law. Indeed, a considerable portion of the theoretical discussion of contract law during the 20th century concerned the question of whether contract law constitutes a distinct area of law, or instead is conceptually and normatively derivative of tort law. Before contract law can be justified, scholars and lawyers must first agree on which, if any, doctrines are distinctive to contract law and what these doctrines require. Once the doctrines of contract law are identified and fleshed out, we then can ask whether contract law, so understood, is justified. The following provides a brief overview of the kinds of descriptive and normative contract theories that have come to dominate contemporary discussion and analysis.

Autonomy Theories. Contract law enforces promises. A natural first instinct is to attempt to explain and justify contract law on the ground that promisors have a moral obligation to keep their promises, and that promisees have a corresponding moral right to the promisor's performance. This is Charles Fried's claim in *Contract as Promise*, the first and most prominent of several well-developed "autonomy" theories of contract law.[12] Professor Fried explains his view of the moral obligation to keep one's promise:

> The obligation to keep a promise is grounded not in arguments of utility but in respect for individual autonomy and in trust. Autonomy and trust are grounds for the institution of promising as well, but the argument for *individual* obligation is not the same. Individual obligation is only a step away, but that step must be taken. An individual is morally bound to keep his promises because he has intentionally invoked a convention whose function it is to give grounds — moral grounds — for another to expect the promised performance. To renege is to abuse a confidence he was free to invite or not, and which he intentionally did invite. To abuse the confidence now is like (but only *like*) lying: the abuse of a shared social institution that is intended to invoke the bonds of trust. A liar and a promise-breaker each

---

[12] FRIED, *supra* note 10. Other autonomy theories of contract have been developed by Randy Barnett and Peter Benson. For an analysis and comparison of Fried's and Benson's autonomy theories with economic theories of contract, see Jody S. Kraus, *Philosophy of Contract Law, in* THE OXFORD HANDBOOK ON JURISPRUDENCE AND LEGAL THEORY Ch. 18 (Jules L. Coleman & Scott Shapiro eds., Oxford University Press 2002).

use another person. In both speech and promising there is an invitation to the other to trust, to make himself vulnerable; the liar and the promise-breaker then abuse that trust. The obligation to keep a promise is thus similar to but more constraining than the obligation to tell the truth. To avoid lying you need only believe in the truth of what you say when you say it, but a promise binds into the future, well past the moment when the promise is made. There will, of course, be great social utility to a general regime of trust and confidence in promises and truthfulness. But this just shows that a regime of mutual respect allows men and women to accomplish what in a jungle of unrestrained self-interest could not be accomplished. If this advantage is to be firmly established, there must exist a ground for mutual confidence deeper than and independent of the social utility it permits.[13]

At the outset, three problems confront the "moral promise principle" as an account of contractual liability. First, philosophers have long sought to explain why promises create moral obligations. Although most people would agree that they do, it is surprisingly difficult to provide an account of promising that explains how and why this is so. Fried argues that promising is made possible by a social convention of promising that transforms morally optional activity into morally mandatory activity. In his view, breaking a promise therefore constitutes a breach of trust: "This convention provides a way that a person may create expectations in others. By virtue of the Kantian principles of trust and respect, it is wrong to invoke that convention in order to make a promise, and then to break it."[14] Philosophers disagree about the adequacy of this account of the moral obligation to keep a promise.[15]

Second, according to the moral promise principle, contract law enforces promises in order to enforce the moral duties of promisors and protect the moral rights of promisees. But courts do not enforce all promises. Indeed, contract law's policy of selective enforcement is implicit in the common law definition of a contract: "A contract is a promise or a set of promises for the breach of which the law gives a remedy, or the performance of which the law in some way recognizes as a duty." Restatement (Second) of Contracts § 1 (1998). Thus, the objective theory of contract provides one of many examples where contract law declines to enforce some promises: Even if the promisee honestly (*i.e.*, subjectively) believes that she has received a promise, enforcement is denied if a reasonable, objective observer would not have understood that the statement was a "commitment to act." In addition, as we will see, the doctrines of consideration, promissory estoppel, and past material benefit also prevent courts from enforcing certain promises. Thus, on its face, the moral promise principle seems unable to explain why contract law does not enforce all promises.[16]

---

[13] FRIED, *supra* note 10, at 16–17.

[14] *Id.* at 17.

[15] *See, e.g.*, THOMAS SCANLON, PROMISES AND CONTRACTS, The Theory of Contract Law Ch. 3 (Peter Benson, ed., Cambridge Univ. Press 2001); *Promises and Practices*, 19 PHIL. & PUB. AFF. 199 (1990).

[16] For an explanation of how Fried's theory meets this and other objections, see Jody S. Kraus, *supra* note 12.

Third, the moral promise principle can justify contractual obligation only if, as a general principle, the state is justified in using its coercive power to enforce moral obligations and protect moral rights. But few people are prepared to endorse this view, often referred to as "legal moralism," which permits or requires the state to enforce morality as a general matter. Just as the moral duty to remain faithful to one's spouse seems insufficient to justify a legal rule criminalizing or imposing civil fines for infidelity, the moral duty to perform promises by itself seems insufficient to justify legal rules that enforce all promises.

But the idea of contract as promise is just one version of an autonomy theory of contract. Whether or not the promise principle provides a compelling explanatory or normative account of contract, the broader conception of autonomy on which it draws provides a powerful tool for understanding and justifying particular contract doctrines. Thus, autonomy theory might begin by suggesting that the "[l]egal enforcement of contract promotes individual freedom by giving people the power to bind themselves with others."[17] One immediate objection to autonomy as a justification for legal enforcement of promises might be that the freedom to change one's mind and renege on a promise is itself an exercise of autonomous choice. To this objection, the autonomy theorist might respond as follows: The freedom to renege on a promise (what one might call "ex post" autonomy) necessarily forecloses the freedom to make binding commitments (what one might call "ex ante" autonomy). (Do you see why?) Since the freedom to commit includes the freedom to choose not to commit, *ex ante* autonomy is a more robust conception of personal freedom. This is illustrated by the doctrines governing contracts of infants. As we will see in Chapter 5, persons under the age of 18 are legally "infants" and are free to renege on their promises at any time even after they have promised to perform and have enjoyed the fruits of the other's performance. But it is well understood that such a "freedom" is actually a limitation on the autonomy of young persons, who are thus disabled from securing the commitments of others.[18]

In addition to underwriting the infancy doctrine, the idea of autonomy seems central to understanding many other basic contract doctrines, such as duress, fraud, and unconscionability, also discussed in Chapter 5. The concept of autonomy itself ranges over a domain far broader than the law of contract. For example, the concept of autonomy is foundational in John Rawls' famous theory of justice.[19] As Rawls understands it, the value of autonomy generates individuals' right to form, revise, and pursue their own conception of the good. Contract law might be viewed as an institution essential to vindicating this right. As we proceed through each chapter, we will raise the question of how various conceptions of autonomy might be brought to bear on the doctrines we examine.

Economic Theories. Autonomy theories of contract take an *ex post* perspective in adjudication. They view adjudication as an occasion for identifying and vindicating the pre-existing rights of the litigants. Thus, autonomy theories tend to view

---

[17] David Charny, *Hypothetical Bargains: The Normative Structure of Contract Interpretation*, 89 MICH. L. REV. 1815, 1823 (1991).

[18] *See* Elizabeth S. Scott & Robert E. Scott, *Marriage as Relational Contract*, 84 VA. L. REV. 1225, 1246–47 (1998).

[19] JOHN RAWLS, A THEORY OF JUSTICE (1971).

adjudication primarily as a mechanism of resolving a dispute between litigants. In contrast, economic theories take an *ex ante*, and therefore consequentialist, perspective in adjudication. Economic theories view adjudication primarily as a mechanism for creating rules and rights that will provide incentives for individuals in the future. Judicial decisions are then evaluated according to whether their prospective effects are socially desirable. In contract law, economic analysis asks, for example, how enforcement of promises is likely to affect the behavior of promisors and promisees in the future. Cases such as *Lucy v. Zehmer* will influence the behavior of others who may contemplate making and receiving promises in the future. Enforcement of serious promises will encourage promisees to rely on such representations in the future, while a decision not to enforce will lead potential promisees to be more cautious the next time they receive a promise. Thus, a key question is whether it is socially more desirable to encourage or to discourage parties to rely on promises.

One answer to that question is that encouraging parties to rely on promises is socially beneficial when those promises are kept because it permits parties to plan for uncertain future events sooner rather than later. Since uncertainty about the future is a deadweight social loss, reducing that uncertainty enhances social welfare.[20] On the other hand, such reliance is detrimental when a promise is subsequently broken because the broken promise will frustrate the plans of the promisee. Such an outcome is a social cost. If we thought that, as an empirical matter, more promises were broken than kept and that detrimental reliance dominated, then the costs of promise-making would exceed the benefits and society should strictly regulate the activity. (Perhaps, like driving, one would need to get a license in order to make promises or, as an even more extreme response, one would be prohibited from making promises altogether.) But, to the contrary, as a society we believe that the aggregate benefits of promise-making outweigh the aggregate harms, and that belief explains why autonomous individuals (over the age of 18) are currently free to make legally binding promises.

Economic analysis, then, suggests a ground for legal enforcement of promises: promises are enforced, not to do justice between the parties to a particular dispute, but rather to establish rules that will encourage socially desirable promise-making behavior by future parties. Full development of this theory requires an explanation of why legal enforcement is required (is legal enforcement cheaper than enforcement by other means?), and why it isn't the case that all promises are enforced. This analysis is the subject of Chapter 2. The economic analysis of contract law must also determine whether it is more socially desirable to encourage individuals to weigh their options at the time they are considering breaking a promise, or to encourage individuals to weigh their options at the time they are considering making a promise. These considerations affect many contract doctrines, including those rules governing anticipatory repudiation, mitigation, and remedies, each of which are discussed in subsequent chapters.

---

[20] For a normative discussion of social welfare maximization as the objective of contract law as applied to business entities, see Alan Schwartz & Robert E. Scott, *Contract Theory and the Limits of Contract Law*, 113 Yale L.J. 541, 544 (2003).

In sum, economic analysis in general takes an *ex ante* perspective in evaluating judicial decisions and the legal doctrines that drive them. In doing so, it focuses on how legal decisions provide incentives for future actors rather than the identification and vindication of pre-existing rights. To this extent, economic and autonomy theories seem committed to incompatible assumptions about the nature of adjudication. Autonomy theories presuppose that every dispute can be resolved by reference to pre-existing rights of the parties, while economic theories treat adjudication, at least sometimes, as an occasion for prospective regulation — that is, creating legal rights that did not exist prior to the dispute.

Despite this apparent divide, autonomy and economic theories have much in common. Milton Friedman wrote that "[t]he possibility of coordination through voluntary cooperation rests on the elementary — yet frequently denied — proposition that both parties to an economic transaction benefit from it, *provided the transaction is bilaterally voluntary and informed.*"[21] Friedman's claim suggests that economic analysis relies on the assumption that market participants are autonomous actors. Thus, economic analysis must rely on an autonomy theory to flesh out the requirements that market actors are competent, voluntary, and informed. In this regard, economic analysis builds on, rather than conflicts with, autonomy theory. As we consider various contract doctrines, you should both identify how the economic and autonomy perspectives might illuminate them, and consider whether the explanations and justifications they provide are compatible or conflicting.[22]

Pluralist Theories. Finally, one could argue (and many do) that neither efficiency nor autonomy standing alone can explain and justify a legal obligation to keep one's promise.[23] Pluralist scholars hold that each of the suggested grounds lacks internal consistency as a fully developed theory and is contingent on presupposed entitlements and values. Pluralist theories thus attempt to respond to the difficulty that unitary normative theories pose by claiming that courts pursue multiple goals, including efficiency, the protection of individual autonomy *and* fairness. The fairness goal is necessary in order to do justice between the parties to a dispute in particular circumstances such as where one party has superior information or where one party is susceptible to exploitation because of one or more systematic cognitive errors. When such circumstances arise, the pluralist scholars argue that general principles grounded in efficiency or autonomy should give way to the goal of protecting the party who is less capable of protecting herself. Which goal will predominate, under this view, thus depends upon the particular facts and circumstances. In short, the argument goes, there are many different reasons why

---

[21] MILTON FRIEDMAN, CAPITALISM AND FREEDOM 13 (1962).

[22] For a systematic comparison between these two theoretical approaches to contract theory, see MICHAEL TREBILCOCK, THE LIMITS OF FREEDOM OF CONTRACT (1993). For an analysis of the second-order, or meta-theoretical divide between autonomy and economic theories of contract, see Jody S. Kraus, *supra* note 12.

[23] For a criticism of economic analysis as having failed to produce an "economic theory" of contract law despite its contemporary popularity, see Eric A. Posner, *Economic Analysis of Contract Law After Three Decades: Success or Failure?*, 112 YALE L.J. 829 (2003). For a defense of the normative and explanatory value of economic analysis, see Ian Ayres, *Valuing Modern Contract Scholarship*, 112 YALE L.J. 881 (2003).

courts enforce promises and the search for a single, general theory to explain or justify contract law is hopelessly idealistic (or simplistic). Rather, the pluralist might argue, all of the preceding theories are important grounds of explanation and justification in certain contexts but not in others. (Or, put another way, each explains part of the puzzle but not the whole).

Pluralist theories are not without difficulties of their own, however. First, autonomy and economic theorists would deny that pluralists have identified values or concerns that their theories fail to address. For example, autonomy theorists would argue that cognitive error may well undermine autonomy and provide grounds for altering or setting aside otherwise binding contractual obligations. And economic theorists would argue that contract law does and should have doctrines that sometimes alter or set aside contractual obligations when informational asymmetries lead to inefficiency. Second, when multiple values conflict, pluralist theories need, but so far lack, a meta-principle that tells a court or legislator which of these goals should be decisive.[24] Professor Melvin Eisenberg, one of the foremost pluralist scholars, argues, for example, that the domain of freedom of contract should be (and is) restricted by norms of reciprocity, trust, and fairness. Eisenberg then suggests that when conflicts occur, "the lawmaker must make a legal rule that gives a proper weight and role to each of the conflicting values or goals in the context at hand." Eisenberg recognizes, however, that his theory lacks a metric that would tell lawmakers just how to give the proper "weight and role" to each social proposition or value when conflicts occur.[25]

Contract Theory and the Study of Contract Law. The foregoing discussion of possible theories that explain and justify the legal enforcement of promises is crude and incomplete. It does not provide either a complete description of the theories themselves or an account of the differing views of scholars within the schools of analysis set forth. Instead, it is designed merely to familiarize you with the basics of the existing theoretical approaches to understanding contract law. Our emphasis on contract theory throughout this book derives from its utility as a means of explaining and justifying the content of contract law. Contract theory at once addresses the practical perspective of lawyers, judges, and scholars interested in explaining, applying, and justifying the law. Lawyers in particular are interested in explaining contract doctrine in order to predict how courts will rule on questions that affect their clients' interests. Lawyers use these predictions both to advise clients on how to structure their affairs, and to argue on behalf of their clients when contractual disputes arise, both before and during litigation. Explanatory/predictive theories therefore can play a central role in the daily tasks every lawyer must perform.

More important for present purposes, we believe that the principal theories of contract provide sound pedagogical tools for developing a systematic grasp of the

---

[24] For a discussion of the possibility of principled pluralism and a two-tiered ordering of autonomy and efficiency, see Nathan Oman, 2005 *Survey of Books Related to the Law: Unity and Pluralism in Contract Law: Contract Theory*, 103 MICH. L. REV. 1483 (2005).

[25] *See* Melvin Aron Eisenberg, *The Theory of Contracts, in* THE THEORY OF CONTRACT LAW: NEW ESSAYS 206 (Peter Benson ed., 2001); *see also* Melvin Aron Eisenberg, *The Bargain Principle and its Limits*, 95 HARV. L. REV. 741 (1982).

fundamental doctrines and principles of contract law. It is our conviction that the pedagogical value of these theories transcends their substantive merits. Thus, while our treatment of contract law will require students to understand the basic tenets of autonomy and economic analysis, and to consider how to resolve conflicts between these goals when they occur, we do not intend to bias the student toward or against these or any other theoretical perspectives on contract law. Rather, the principal theories of contract can serve as organizing principles to help the student absorb and understand contract doctrine, as well as provide a basis for criticism of particular contract doctrines. If there is a bias to our approach, it lies in our belief that no one — students, lawyers, judges, or scholars — can truly understand contract law without also understanding contract theory.

[2] Indefinite Promises and Open Terms

Assuming that parties have otherwise manifested an intention to promise, a further question arises: must a legally enforceable promise incorporate all the relevant details of each party's prospective undertaking? What is the relationship between incompleteness, specifically the level of uncertainty and indefiniteness as to the precise terms of an undertaking, and the question of intention? Consider the following cases.

TRIMMER v. VAN BOMEL
New York Supreme Court
107 Misc. 2d 201, 434 N.Y.S.2d 82 (1980)

GREENFIELD, J.

Plaintiff is a 67-year-old gentleman, who was earning a modest but respectable living as a travel tour operator, when a person on one of his tours, the defendant, Mrs. Catherine Bryer Van Bomel, a wealthy widow with assets stated to be in excess of $40,000,000, began making demands on his time, and allegedly agreed to support him in luxurious fashion, if he would devote all his time and attention to her. He gave up his business career, in which he admits he was earning no more than $8,900 a year and became the ever-present companion of Mrs. Van Bomel. He moved to larger quarters and modified his wardrobe to suit her tastes. He accompanied her to lunch and dinner, escorted her to the theatre and parties, and travelled with her on her trips to Europe. All this was at the lady's expense, of course. He also acted as her confidante and her friends became his friends.

For five years his life was constantly dominated by the needs, whims and desires of Mrs. Van Bomel. She spent money lavishly on him. Apart from taking care of his rent and his travel expenses, she had his suits hand tailored in Italy and in London, presented him with two Pontiacs and a Jaguar and gave him a monthly stipend. All in all, she expended well over $300,000 for his personal needs. Then, suddenly, it all came to an end. Accustomed to a life of luxury, and now without the means to attain it, plaintiff sues his former benefactress for $1,500,000.

Plaintiff seeks recovery on an alleged express oral agreement, pursuant to which he agreed to give up his business and render services to the defendant, in return for which defendant would pay and provide (a) all his costs and expenses incurred in connection with the performance of his services, (b) all his costs and expenses for sumptuous living during the time the services were rendered, and (c) to pay "within a reasonable time" an amount sufficient to pay for all his costs and expenses for sumptuous living for the rest of his life. The plaintiff further alleges that he fully performed the agreement on his part and that the defendant, in part performance, paid all his costs and expenses during the period of rendition of services, but has failed and refused to provide plaintiff with a sum sufficient to maintain him on a standard of "sumptuous living" for the remainder of his life, which sum plaintiff contends would be $1,500,000.

Defendant has moved for summary judgment contending that the action is without merit and that the purported agreement is too vague and indefinite to be enforceable. . . .

The [plaintiff] alleges an express agreement to pay the plaintiff. For the purposes of this motion for summary judgment, the court must accept as true plaintiff's allegation that defendant agreed to set up a fund which would permit plaintiff to live for the remainder of his life in the sumptuous style to which he had become accustomed. . . . Thus, the principal issue presented is whether such an agreement as alleged in the complaint can be regarded as enforceable. While there is no public policy bar to such an agreement, as an alleged express oral contract, its validity must be tested exactly the same as other contracts.

Unlike the situation in *Morone v. Marone*, 50 NY 2d 481, where the plaintiff alleged an explicit partnership agreement in which she asserted that all the "net profits" from the partnership were to be used and applied to the equal benefit of plaintiff and defendant, so that the specific dollar amount, although not indicated, can be calculated upon an accounting by one partner to another, there is no ready means of arithmetic calculation to determine what amount plaintiff claims as his just dues.

All courts would agree with the doctrine, although not necessarily the application, that as a basic premise of contract law "it is a necessary requirement in the nature of things that an agreement in order to be binding must be sufficiently definite to enable a court to give it an exact meaning. '(1 Williston Contracts (3(d) ed. s 37))'." In *Dombrowski v. Somers*, 41 N.Y.2d 858, 393 N.Y.S.2d 706, 362 N.E.2d 257, a unanimous Court of Appeals found that an alleged oral agreement, pursuant to which the decedent said that in return for plaintiff's services he would "take care of" the plaintiff, was too vague to spell out a meaningful promise.

The question in this case is whether an alleged agreement by defendant to pay an amount sufficient to take care of all of plaintiff's "costs and expenses for sumptuous living and maintenance for the remainder of his life" . . . will enable the court to award plaintiff a judgment in a specific sum of dollars. In his Bill of Particulars, plaintiff asserted that the defendant had agreed "to provide and set up for him a fund, either by giving him a block of stock or cash, or both, which would take care of all his living expenses in the same expensive style for the rest of his life."

. . . .

Plaintiff has attempted to overcome the inherent vagueness of this agreement by trying to spell out, after the fact, what amounts he deems to be required for "sumptuous living." What is "sumptuous" to one person may be merely adequate to another, of course . . . Moreover, sumptuous living "* * * cannot be computed from anything that was said by the parties or by reference to any document, paper or other transaction." (*Varney v. Ditmars*, 217 N.Y. 223, 227, 111 N.E. 822) nor would it be provable by evidence of custom (dissent of Cardozo, J., 217 N.Y. at 233, 111 N.E. 822). Essentially, then the amount was left subject to the will of the defendant or for further negotiation. Courts cannot aid parties who have not specified the terms of their own agreements.

Plaintiff calculates that since he was given an average of $71,672 (tax free) by Mrs. Van Bomel during their five year relationship, that this is the sum he should be given for the rest of his life. That is how he comes to the $1,500,000 set forth in the ad damnum. $1,500,000 in six month certificates would give him $180,000 a year and that same sum in tax free municipals would produce well over $100,000 per year, in which case the principal would be left intact. It appears clear that we are dealing with an alleged agreement which is too vague in any of its material terms to be deemed enforceable. No amount being specified, no time having been set forth, no mechanics for the payments having been spelled out and there being no specification as to what had to be done to qualify or disqualify the plaintiff for the payments, what we have, at best, is some vague but legally unenforceable reassurance that plaintiff "would be taken care of."

Since plaintiff alleges an express agreement which is to be governed by the law applicable to all contracts, it is instructive to compare the kind of agreement upon which plaintiff relies with other, more detailed contracts which the courts have nevertheless found to be unenforceable. Thus, in *Brause v. Goldman*, 10 A.D.2d 328, 199 N.Y.S.2d 606, where negotiations had progressed to a point of much greater detail than what was involved here, the court found that many of the essentials of an agreement were lacking. The court found that even though there were memoranda of agreement prepared after oral negotiations, there was no indication as to the date on which the arrangement was to be commenced nor as to the method of payment, nor as to the rights of the parties in the event of various contingencies coming to pass. The Appellate Division declared, "It is not for the court to dictate such terms to the parties, for its function is to enforce agreements only if they exist, and not to create them by the imposition of such terms as it considers reasonable.

. . . .

In an agreement terminable at will, and with no clear bounds and parameters set forth, an alleged obligation which would continue and survive beyond the termination of employment must appear with specificity. What if the relationship had been terminated for "cause"? Suppose plaintiff had been disloyal or discourteous or had secretly embezzled some of defendant's funds, would the agreement to take care of him for life continue nevertheless? Since this relationship was terminable at will, and the relationship had come to an end, this court can see no legal basis upon which the defendant can be compelled to continue lavishing her favors and her bounty upon the plaintiff. There are no guarantees in life, and good fortune, to be enjoyed while it lasts, does not invariably bring with it a life-long annuity.

Accordingly, defendant is entitled to summary judgment on the First Cause of Action as well as the Second. The complaint should be dismissed.

NOTES

1. **Trimmer** *and the Rationale Underlying Indefiniteness.* The rationale of the common law indefiniteness doctrine as developed in *Trimmer v. Van Bomel* is grounded in the presumed intentions of the parties. Where the parties did not make their intentions clear, the common law presumed that the failure to reach an agreement on material terms, where no terms could be objectively supplied, implied an intention not to be legally bound. Thus, under the common law rule the question of intent to promise is addressed indirectly, by looking at the extent to which material terms were left unspecified by the parties. If the court finds that the terms are sufficiently complete and definite, it infers from that fact the intent to contract; if not, the court infers that the parties did not intend to be bound

In *Varney v. Ditmars,* cited in *Trimmer,* the New York Court of Appeals found that the failure to specify what constituted a "fair share of the profits" in an agreement by an employer to provide a bonus to his employee, an architect, in return for his helping to clear a back log of work required the conclusion that there was no intent to contract as a matter of law. Justice Cardozo in dissent argued that:

> I do not think it is true that a promise to pay an employee a fair share of the profits in addition to his salary is always and of necessity too vague to be enforced . . . The promise must, of course, appear to have been made with contractual intent. . . . But if that intent is present, it cannot be said from the mere form of the promise that the estimate of [this] reward is inherently impossible.

Would Cardozo say the same thing about a promise to establish a fund to maintain Mr. Trimmer in a sumptuous style for the rest of his life? Or is there a difference between a promise to give one employee a "fair share" and a promise to give another a way to maintain a "sumptuous living"?

Suppose that you sign an agreement to sell your 2006 Honda to a friend. The price is set at $5,000 and the delivery date is specified as next Thursday. When Thursday comes, you deliver the Honda but the friend says, "I will pay you the money in two weeks." Your view is that he is bound to pay you now. He points out (correctly) that the written agreement says nothing about the time of payment, and that nothing was said about it in negotiations either.

It probably comes as no surprise to you that the legal rule is that your friend is bound to pay you when the car is delivered. This is an example of a legal rule filling a gap in the agreement between the parties. As was mentioned in the beginning of this chapter, this is a common function of legal rules. There are, however, instances where the gaps are so many, or have to do with terms so central to the agreement, that the court will not to try and fill the gaps.[26] One rationale for this refusal to

---

[26] For a discussion of a proposed methodology where partial agreements may deserve partial performance if the parties so intended, see Omri Ben-Shahar, *"Agreeing to Disagree": Filling Gaps in Deliberately Incomplete Contracts,* 2004 Wis. L. Rev. 389.

enforce is that the court may well err in trying to supplement the parties' expressed intentions. Alternatively, a court could instead be saying, "Although this court is willing to fill gaps in an agreement, there are so many gaps in this alleged agreement, and they relate to such important terms, that we cannot believe the parties thought they had contracted. If one party thought so, it was clearly unreasonable."

Which approach do you think the court was adopting in *Trimmer*?

2. ***Filling the Gaps.*** In *Corthell v. Summit Thread Co.*, 132 Me. 94 (1933), Summit Thread Company promised its employee "reasonable recognition" in return for his promise to turn over all future inventions for development. The employee turned over four inventions to Summit Thread, three of which were patented and developed by the company, but he never received any compensation for these inventions. The court held the employer liable even though the written agreement stipulated "the basis and amount of recognition to rest *entirely* with the Summit Thread Company at all times . . . to be interpreted in good faith on the basis of what is reasonable and intended and not technically." In considering whether the uncertainty of price in the agreement renders it unenforceable, the court said:

> There is no more settled rule of law applicable to actions based on contracts than that an agreement, in order to be binding, must be sufficiently definite to enable the Court to determine its exact meaning and fix exactly the legal liability of the parties. Indefiniteness may relate to the time of performance, the price to be paid, work to be done, property to be transferred or other miscellaneous stipulations of the agreement. If the contract makes no statement as to the price to be paid, the law invokes the standard of reasonableness, and the fair value of the services or property is recoverable. If the terms of the agreement are uncertain as to price, but exclude the supposition that a reasonable price was intended, no contract can arise. . . . the contract of the parties indicates that they both promised with "contractual intent," the one intending to pay and the other to accept a fair price for the inventions turned over. "Reasonable recognition" seems to have meant what was fair and just between the parties, that is, reasonable compensation.

Id. at 99.

Are the conclusions reached in *Corthell* and *Trimmer* reconcilable? Why is one court willing to fill the gap for compensation where the agreement calls for "reasonable recognition" (*Corthell*) and another unwilling to do so where the agreement promises to pay a party "costs and expenses for sumptuous living and maintenance for the remainder of his life." (*Trimmer*)?

Corthell may be seen as an illustration of how courts can escape the indefiniteness doctrine. Where the agreement is indefinite as to material terms it is unenforceable *unless* the parties intend some external reference point to fill the gaps. A market price is a reasonable price. Therefore, the court in *Corthell* could escape the doctrine by filling the "reasonable recognition" gap with the market price. Now apply the argument to *Varney*. What exactly is a "sumptuous living"? In the absence of an external reference point, would a court's attempt to supply a term be sheer speculation as to the parties' intent?[27]

3. ***Reasons for Open Terms.*** Why do parties leave gaps — sometimes important gaps — in their agreement? First, they may think the probability of a particular event occurring is too remote to dicker over its consequences. Second, they may fail to foresee the event at all. Third, when the event is not certain to occur but dickering over it may block the agreement entirely, the parties may leave it open. Fourth, the parties may deliberately leave the terms vague in order to avoid legal enforcement altogether and rely instead on norms of trust and bonds of affection. Why did the parties leave gaps in *Trimmer* and *Corthell?*.[28]

4. ***Important Terms and Necessary Terms.*** Contract terms are sometimes characterized as being "material" to the contract. What might this mean in the context of indefinite terms? Consider one (famous) example: Cameron and Tyler Winklevoss sued Mark Zuckerberg alleging he stole from them the idea of Facebook. Following extensive discovery, the parties agreed to settle the dispute (for a dramatic account, see the Academy Award winning film, "The Social Network"). The Winklevosses later tried to void the settlement agreement, claiming the settlement was incomplete because it lacked material terms. In *Facebook, Inc. v. Pac. Northwest Software, Inc.*, 2011 U.S. App. LEXIS 7430 (9th Cir. Apr. 11, 2011), Judge Alex Kozinski rejected this argument:

> The Winklevosses argue that if these terms really are "required" and "typical," then they must be material, and their absence from the Settlement Agreement renders it unenforceable. But a term may be "material" in one of two ways: It may be a necessary term, without which there can be no contract; or, it may be an important term that affects the value of the bargain. Obviously, omission of the former would render the contract a nullity. *See Citizens Utils. Co. v. Wheeler, 156 Cal.App. 2d 423, 319 P.2d 763, 769–70 (1958)* (arms-length acquisition of a private company's shares couldn't proceed because price was omitted from the contract). But a contract that omits terms of the latter type is enforceable under California law, so long as the terms it does include are sufficiently definite for a court to determine whether a breach has occurred, order specific performance or award damages. This is not a very demanding test, and the Settlement Agreement easily passes it: The parties agreed that Facebook would swallow up ConnectU, the Winklevosses would get cash and a small piece of Facebook, and both sides would stop fighting and get on with their lives.

5. ***Indefiniteness Qualified.*** The indefiniteness doctrine is subject to several qualifications. First, a party who has performed under an agreement that is unenforceable for indefiniteness may recover in *quantum meruit* — an equitable remedy to provide restitution to a person who has rendered services in a

---

[27] For a discussion of *Corthell* and a discussion of how the court managed to escape the plain language of the contract providing that the amount of recognition would be "entirely" within Summit Thread's discretion, see Jody S. Kraus & Robert E. Scott, *Contract Design and the Structure of Contractual Intent*, 84 N.Y.U. L. Rev. 1023, 1085–94 (2009).

[28] For a discussion of reasons why parties might deliberately make their promises indefinite and therefore legally unenforceable, see Robert E. Scott, *A Theory of Self-Enforcing Indefinite Agreements*, 103 COLUM. L. REV. 1641, 1649 (2003).

quasi-contractual relationship. In *Trimmer*, however, the court denied the plaintiffs quasi-contractual claim, stating that:

> In this case, the services for which plaintiff seeks compensation on a quantum meruit basis, like those in a quasi-marital relationship, arise out of the nature of the relationship of the parties to one another. The services involved . . . are of a nature which would ordinarily be exchanged without expectation of pay. The claims of friendship, like the claims of kinship, may be many and varied. To imply an obligation by a wealthy friend to compensate a less wealthy companion for being together, dining together, talking together and accepting tokens of regard stretches the bond[s] of friendship to the breaking point. The implied obligation to compensate arises from those things which, in normal society, we expect to pay for. An obligation to pay for friendship is not ordinarily to be implied — it is too crass. Friendship, like virtue, must be its own reward.

Id. at 205–06.

Recall the elements for quasi-contractual recovery discussed in *Bailey v. West*: 1) a benefit is conferred by the plaintiff; 2) the benefit is appreciated and accepted by the defendant; and 3) the retention of the benefit would unjustly enrich the defendant. Mr. Trimmer performed even though there was no legally enforceable bargain. Do you agree that the nature of the relationship between them precluded quasi-contractual recovery as a matter of law?

As a second qualification, the question whether the facially indefinite words expressing the right to compensation have a definite and enforceable meaning may depend on the subject matter of the agreement. In sales of goods, for example, common law courts held that the words "fair and reasonable value" were a synonym for "market value" and thus a definite promise to pay the fair market value of goods may be inferred by the express agreement of the parties.

Although there are some variations in the cases, two factual patterns typify unenforceable indefinite agreements at common law. The first, illustrated by the decision in *Varney v. Ditmars*, 217 N.Y. 223 (1916), is the indefinite bonus contract. Recall that in *Varney*, the New York Court of Appeals held a bonus agreement for a "fair share of the profits" too indefinite and thus unenforceable. The second archetype is a variation on the first, extending the common law rule to agreements where essential terms were explicitly left to further negotiation. For example, in *Petze v. Morse Dry Dock & Repair Co.*, 109 N.Y.S. 328 (App. Div. 1908), the New York appellate court held that an agreement providing that "the method of accounting to determine the net distributable profits is to be agreed upon later" was unenforceable under the indefiniteness rule. Common law courts thereafter have consistently held that such "agreements to agree" are unenforceable so long as any essential term was open to negotiation.[29] Compare this common law rule to the rule applied in contracts for the sale of goods. Read UCC §§ 2-204, 2-305 and consider the following case.

---

[29] Robert E. Scott, *A Theory of Self-Enforcing Indefinite Agreements*, 103 Colum. L. Rev. 1641, 1658 (2003).

WAGNER EXCELLO FOODS, INC. v. FEARN INT'L, INC.

Illinois Appellate Court

235 Ill. App. 3d 224, 601 N.E.2d 956 (1992)

EGAN, J.

The plaintiff and the defendant entered into a five-year agreement on February 1, 1985. Under the terms of the agreement, the plaintiff agreed to manufacture for the defendant various pasteurized fruit drink concentrates with a juice content of less than 35 percent. The plaintiff was to manufacture the concentrates from formulas supplied by the defendant and was to package the concentrate according to the defendant's specifications. [The agreement specified minimum quantities to be purchased each year under the agreement.]

The agreement did not establish the price at which the concentrate would be sold. Instead, it provided that the plaintiff and the defendant would review the price per case of each product every four months. Thirty days before the end of each four month period, the plaintiff was required to notify the defendant of, and substantiate, any proposed price changes for the upcoming period. If the defendant failed to object to the proposed price change, the new price would go into effect. If the defendant objected, however, the plaintiff and the defendant would seek to "mutually agree" on the price change. If the plaintiff and defendant were unable to agree on a price, the agreement terminated 30 days after the end of the four month period. At the end of five years, the agreement would automatically extend on a year-to-year basis until one party terminated through written notice between 120 and 90 days before the expiration of the agreement or its extension.

After the agreement was signed, the plaintiff hired additional employees and bought equipment, including machinery, necessary to package the concentrate as the defendant instructed. The purchase of the equipment and additional employees cost the plaintiff $900,286. The plaintiff purchased the equipment and hired the additional employees "solely in contemplation of a continuing business relationship" with the defendant.

On April 23, 1990, the plaintiff filed a complaint [alleging] a breach of contract claim which sought in excess of $3,000,000 for profits lost due to the defendant's failure to meet the minimum purchase guarantee over the entire five years of the agreement. . . .

The defendant filed a motion to dismiss the complaint under section 2–615 of the Illinois Code of Civil Procedure. In response to the breach of contract claim the defendant contended that the agreement between the parties was merely an agreement to agree as there was no fixed price and the agreement would terminate in the absence of an agreement on price by the parties. . . .

The defendant maintains that there was no contract . . . because the price was not settled at the time the agreement was made; instead, every four months the parties entered into a new contract when they agreed to a price. In substance, it is the defendant's position that the parties actually entered into an agreement to agree which was not a binding contract.

To be enforceable, a contract must show a manifestation of agreement between the parties and be definite and certain in its terms. When material terms and conditions are not ascertainable there is no enforceable contract, even if the intent to contract is present. Under the Illinois Uniform Commercial Code (the Code), a contract for the sale of goods will not fail for indefiniteness, however, "if the parties have intended to make a contract and there is a reasonably certain basis for giving an appropriate remedy." [UCC 2-204(3)]. The terms of the agreement are definite. All the essential elements of an agreement are present except for the price of the goods. The absence of the price term is the sole basis for the defendant's contention that no contract exists.

The Code, as adopted in Illinois, expressly addresses the situation where the parties deliberately leave the price term open. [UCC 2-305]. Section 2–305(1) of the Code provides that "[t]he parties *if they so intend* can conclude a contract for sale even though the price is not settled." (Emphasis added). In the case of an open price, the Code provides for a reasonable price at the time of delivery if, among other instances, "the price is left to be agreed by the parties and they fail to agree." [UCC 2-305(1)(b)].

Section 2–305(4) provides an exception to the recognition of a contract when there is an open price term. This section provides:

"Where, however, the parties intend not to be bound unless the price be fixed or agreed *and* it is not fixed or agreed there is no contract." (Emphasis added.)

In both section 2–305(1) and section 2–305(4), the intent of the parties is the dispositive factor in determining whether a contract is present. The plaintiff states that the question of the parties' intent as to contract formation is a factual question that cannot be decided on a motion to dismiss. . . .

The Code Comments emphasize that the language of section 2–305(1) "if the parties so intend," must be read together with section 2–305(4). The Comments conclude that whether the parties have intended to enter into a binding agreement "is, in most cases, a question to be determined by the trier of fact." UCC 2–305, Uniform Commercial Code Comment.

We believe that the complaint alleges an agreement that a fact finder could reasonably conclude manifested an intent of both parties to be bound by the agreement for five years, subject only to the condition subsequent of termination by the failure to agree on the price. The agreement provided that the plaintiff would not manufacture for sale nor sell to anyone other than the defendant. It also provided that the plaintiff would indemnify and hold harmless the defendant for any claims made against the defendant; that the plaintiff would carry product liability insurance; and that the agreement could not be assigned without the written consent of either party. Acceptance of the defendant's argument would require that we ignore the other parts of the contract. Most important, the interpretation urged on us by the defendant that, as a matter of law, the parties intended only to enter severable 120 day contracts would render the minimum quantity requirements of the initial agreement meaningless. We agree with Judge Greiman that the complaint alleged a contract.

. . . .

We judge, therefore, that a fact question remains under the amended complaint that could not be resolved on the basis of what was presented to the judge. For that reason, the order dismissing the amended complaint is reversed and the cause is remanded for further proceedings consistent with this opinion.

NOTES

1. *Agreements to Agree:* **Joseph Martin, Jr., Delicatessen, Inc. v. Schumacher.** Compare *Wagner Excello Foods* with *Joseph Martin, Jr., Delicatessen, Inc. v. Schumacher*, 52 N.Y.2d 105 (1981), in which the parties entered into a rental contract with an option to renew at a price to be agreed upon. In 1973, the plaintiff, as tenant, leased a retail store for a five-year term at a rent graduated upwards from $500 per month for the first year to $650 for the fifth. The renewal clause stated that "[the] Tenant may renew this lease for an additional period of five years at annual rentals to be agreed upon; Tenant shall give Landlord thirty (30) days written notice, to be mailed certified mail, return receipt requested, of the intention to exercise such right." Once the landlord made it clear that he would do so only at a rental starting at $900 a month, the tenant engaged an appraiser who opined that a fair market rental value would be $545.41. The tenant then commenced an action for specific performance to compel the landlord to extend the lease for the additional term at the appraiser's figure or such other sum as the court would decide was reasonable. A lower court established a "fair" rent for the renewal period. On appeal, the lower court was reversed on the grounds that, at common law, "an agreement to agree, in which a material term is left for future negotiations, is unenforceable." The court reasoned that a mere agreement to agree, without more, leaves no room for legal construction or resolution of ambiguity.

Why are agreements to agree unenforceable at common law, but potentially enforceable where the agreement is for the sale of goods? Does the "external reference point" argument help explain the difference? Is a rental appraisal a sufficient proxy for market price? What would be a "reasonable price" in the case of a five-year contract to manufacture fruit drinks under the direction of the counterparty?

Agreements to agree over price terms remain unenforceable at common law absent an external reference point (such as market price in sales cases) by which courts can determine a "reasonable price." But in recent years some courts have imposed a duty to bargain in good faith over terms yet to be agreed upon in certain preliminary agreements. The nature and justification for the modern rule imposing an obligation to bargain in good faith are explored in detail in Chapter 4.

2. *Article 2 of the UCC and the Codification of Contract Law.* The first major codification of contract and commercial law came in 1893 when England passed the Sale of Goods Act. In the United States, sales law was first codified in the Uniform Sales Act, drafted by Professor Samuel Williston and promulgated for adoption by the states in 1906. Both of these efforts were designed to reproduce the existing law of sales in a systematic fashion rather than to effect major changes in the law.

The most influential of the various efforts to systematize a portion of the law of contracts is Article 2 of the Uniform Commercial Code (UCC or Code). The UCC was drafted in the 1940s by a group of scholars and practitioners headed by Professor Karl Llewellyn and working under the auspices of the American Law Institute (ALI) and the National Conference of Commissioners on Uniform State Laws (NCCUSL). Rather than simply restating the law, Article 2 was an ambitious effort to simplify, modernize, and standardize the various state laws governing the sale of goods. By 1967, every state, with the partial exception of the civil-law jurisdiction of Louisiana, had adopted Article 2 of the Code, and it has significantly influenced the development of contract law in areas beyond its official limitation to the sale of goods.[30]

In *A Comment on the Jurisprudence of the Uniform Commercial Code*, 27 STAN. L. REV. 621 (1975), Richard Danzig suggested that Karl Llewellyn, in drafting Article 2, was motivated by the legal realist's concept of an "immanent law," that is, a cohesive system of "correct" rules that are inherent in the relationships and mores of the community. Under Llewellyn's view, the role of commercial lawyers and judges was to discover these rules by discovering the nascent rules imbedded in the customs and practices of commercial parties. The court's job, in other words, was to "look for the law in life" and then incorporate that immanent law into the disputed contract. Llewellyn intended that the Code guide courts in a continuous process of discovering the law as revealed through the behavior of commercial parties. This conception has produced a statute, therefore, that requires continuous interpretation and elaboration by courts on a case-by-case basis. One of the central challenges in this course will be for you to evaluate whether (and to what extent) this "incorporation strategy" has worked in the way that Llewellyn envisioned that it could (and should).

For the past 25 years, the ALI and NCCUSL have worked to improve and update the various Articles of the UCC, seeking to adapt them to new conditions. But, as we noted in the Introduction to this Chapter, the attempt to revise Article 2 has been more controversial than the revisions to the other Articles of the Code. In 2003, the ALI and NCCUSL finally approved a modest effort to amend specific sections of Article 2 rather than the comprehensive revision originally contemplated. These amendments were offered to the states for enactment into law but approval was stymied by interest group opposition.[31] After eight years, when not a single state had adopted the proposed Amendments, they were withdrawn by the ALI in May 2011.

3. *The Codification of International Sales Law.* The dramatic growth in international trade over the latter half of the 20th century generated corresponding calls for a uniform law to govern international sales transactions. The effort to devise such a law was led by the United Nations Commission on International Trade

---

[30] It is important to keep in mind a key distinction between the Restatement and the UCC. Once enacted by a state legislature, the UCC is the law and its provisions have the full force of a statute. The various provisions of the Restatement are not law unless and until a court adopts the Restatement formulation in the course of resolving a particular case. Until that occurs, Restatement provisions are merely a (fairly influential) statement of the evolving common law in the United States. Most of the time, Restatement provisions track the rule adopted in the majority of American jurisdictions, but sometimes the restaters have endorsed rules that only a distinct minority of jurisdictions have adopted.

[31] For an explanation of why states have not enacted the Article 2 amendments, see William H. Henning, *Amended Article 2: What Went Wrong?*, 11 DUQ. BUS. L.J. 131 (2009).

Law (UNCITRAL) and led to the United Nations convening a Diplomatic Conference in Vienna in 1980 to debate a draft treaty. The Conference unanimously approved the Convention on Contracts for the International Sale of Goods (CISG). Currently 78 nations, including the United States and most major trading nations (with the notable exceptions of the United Kingdom and Japan), have adopted the CISG. As a self-executing treaty, the CISG is part of the domestic law of every state in the United States and thus, unless the parties elect to opt out of its terms, it applies to any sales contract between commercial parties located in different contracting states. Thus, for example, if Fearn Int'l, Inc., had its principal place of business in Vancouver, Canada, and Wagner Excello Foods was located in Chicago, the dispute in this case would be governed by the terms of the CISG and not by the UCC *unless* the parties in their contract had explicitly signaled their intent to have any dispute governed by Article 2 and not by the terms of the CISG.

Despite the success of the CISG in securing widespread adoption, it has received substantial criticism for the vagueness of many of its provisions. For that reason, and perhaps also because of unfamiliarity, the data show that most American lawyers have chosen to opt out of the CISG in their international contracts. For a discussion of the tensions that threaten the success of a uniform international sales law, see Clayton P. Gillette & Robert E. Scott, *The Political Economy of International Sales Law*, 25 INT'L. REV. L. & ECON. 446 (2005).

4.   *The Scope of Article 2.* Article 2 of the UCC does not apply to real estate transactions, bankruptcy, or the performance and enforcement of contracts for services.[32] The contractual clause in *Trimmer v. Van Bomel* involves an employment contract, so it lies outside the ambit of the UCC. Despite its limitations, however, the Code influences transactions outside its explicit coverage. *See, e.g.*, Allied Disposal, Inc. v. Bob's Home Service, Inc., 595 S.W.2d 417 (Mo. Ct. App. 1980).

As the opinion in *Wagner Excello Foods* reflects, the UCC takes a decidedly broader approach to indefinite price terms than does the common law. In theory, the *Wagner Excello Foods* and *Schumacher* and *Trimmer* decisions could exist in the same jurisdiction, since the UCC governs the former case but not the latter two. Do you think the approaches to open terms in these cases runs deeper than a matter of source of law?

5.   *Extrinsic Evidence.* Courts sometimes look at the standard practices of other participants in the relevant industry in order to determine whether an open-term contract is enforceable, and if so, what are its terms. An example of such a practice can be found in *Metro-Goldwyn-Mayer, Inc. v. Scheider*, 392 N.Y.S.2d 252, 360 N.E.2d 930 (1976). In that case, actor Roy Scheider entered into an oral agreement with MGM Studios to appear in a motion picture as well as a television series which would be based on the movie. After appearing in the pilot and being fully compensated, Scheider refused to appear in the series, claiming that the

---

[32] Article 2 is limited to contracts for the sale of goods. Section 2-105(1) defines goods to mean "all things (including specially manufactured goods) which are movable at the time of identification to the contract for sale other than the money in which the price is to be paid, investment securities . . . and things in action. 'Goods' also includes the unborn young of animals and growing crops." The section also defines as goods certain things which may be severed from realty such as minerals, timber, and structures and their materials.

contract was too indefinite as to the starting date for the series. The court referenced the standard practices of the entertainment industry, noting that both parties were aware of these practices, and concluded that a valid contract had been formed, which was breached by Scheider's refusal to perform.

The same principle was at work in *Lee v. Joseph E. Seagram & Sons, Inc.*, 552 F.2d 447 (2d Cir. 1977), where the court upheld an oral agreement detailing the conditions of the sale of the plaintiffs' liquor distributorship. Seagram had promised to provide a distributorship "in a location acceptable to plaintiffs," with a price roughly equal to that of their current distributorship, in exchange for the plaintiffs' 50% share of a Washington, D.C. Seagram's distributorship. Seagram argued that the contract was invalid because it failed to specify adequately the purchase price, sales volume, or profitability of the new distributorship and that there were no limits to guide the plaintiffs' discretion in choosing an acceptable location. The court rejected these arguments, looking to external evidence which suggested a means of assessing the value and future profitability of the distributorship. The court was also persuaded by an industry-specific valuation of the distributorship at book value plus three times the post-tax net profits of the previous year.

Although courts in each of these cases found the agreements to be valid and enforceable, one might ask why the parties chose not to put the agreements in writing or to come to an agreement explicitly as to significant features of the contract. What advantages do each of the parties enjoy by preserving such ambiguity?

[3]   Which Promises Will Be Enforced?

Once a court determines that there was indeed a promise made, it must decide if the promise is one that it should enforce. In this Section, we begin our study of the factors that go into a court's enforcement decision.

> The essential function of consideration is to determine the types of promises which should not be enforced. The promise which does not purport to exact an exchange is singled out by consideration doctrine as the one least worthy of enforcement, because it may well have been given without the care which an exchange relationship encourages and because it is least likely to serve a useful economic function.

Stanley D. Henderson, *Promissory Estoppel and Traditional Contract Doctrine*, 78 YALE L.J. 343, 346 (1969).

The doctrine of consideration has long been used by courts to distinguish between enforceable and unenforceable promises. The general rule is that contracts that lack consideration are not enforced, while those contracts that are supported by consideration are enforced.

In the simplest terms, existence of consideration in a contract means that an *exchange* has taken place between the parties. Read the definition of consideration in § 71 of the Restatement (Second) of Contracts. Consideration exists in a bargained-for exchange of a promise for a promise, or a promise for a performance. The original Restatement of Contracts (1932) described these exchanges as "bilateral" (promise for promise) or "unilateral" (promise for performance) contracts. The Second Restatement has abandoned this language, but you are likely to come across these terms frequently.

How did the early conception of consideration evolve into the modern formulation of the Restatement (Second)? Consider the following cases.

HAMER v. SIDWAY
Court of Appeals of New York
124 N.Y. 538, 27 N.E. 256 (1891)

Appeal from an order of the general term of the supreme court in the fourth judicial department, reversing a judgment entered on the decision of the court at special term in the county clerk's office of Chemung county on the 1st day of October, 1889. The plaintiff presented a claim to the executor of William E. Story, Sr., for $5,000 and interest from the 6th day of February, 1875. She acquired it through several mesne assignments from William E. Story, 2d. The claim being rejected by the executor, this action was brought. It appears that William E. Story, Sr., was the uncle of William E. Story, 2d; that at the celebration of the golden wedding [anniversary] of Samuel Story and wife, father and mother of William E. Story, Sr., on the 20th day of March, 1869, in the presence of the family and invited guests, he promised his nephew that if he would refrain from drinking, using tobacco, swearing, and playing cards or billiards for money until he became 21 years of age, he would pay him the sum of $5,000. The nephew assented thereto, and fully performed the conditions inducing the promise. When the nephew arrived at the age of 21 years, and on the 31st day of January, 1875, he wrote to his uncle, informing him that he had performed his part of the agreement, and had thereby become entitled to the sum of $5,000.

The uncle received the letter, and a few days later, on the 6th day of February, he wrote and mailed to his nephew the following letter: "Buffalo, Feb. 6, 1875, W. E. Story, Jr. — Dear Nephew: Your letter of the 31st ult. came to hand all right, saying that you had lived up to the promise made to me several years ago. I have no doubt but you have, for which you shall have five thousand dollars, as I promised you. I had the money in the bank the day you was twenty-one years old that I intend for you, and you shall have the money certain. Now Willie, I do not intend to interfere with this money in any way till I think you are capable of taking care of it, and the sooner that times comes the better it will please me. I would hate very much to have you start out in some adventure that you thought all right and lose this money in one year. The first five thousand dollars that I got together cost me a heap of hard work. . . . This money you have earned much easier than I did, besides, acquiring good habits at the same time, and you are quite welcome to the money. Hope you will make good use of it. I was ten long years getting this together after I was your age. . . . Truly yours, W. E. Story. P. S. You can consider this money on interest.

The nephew received the letter, and thereafter consented that the money should remain with his uncle in accordance with the terms and conditions of the letter. The uncle died on the 29th day of January, 1887, without having paid over to his nephew any portion of the said $5,000 and interest.

PARKER, J.

. . . The defendant contends that the contract was without consideration to support it, and therefore invalid. He asserts that the promisee, by refraining from the use of liquor and tobacco, was not harmed, but benefited; that that which he did was best for him to do, independently of his uncle's promise, — and insists that it follows that, unless the promisor was benefited, the contract was without consideration, — a contention which, if well founded, would seem to leave open for controversy in many cases whether that which the promisee did or omitted to do was in fact of such benefit to him as to leave no consideration to support the enforcement of the promisor's agreement. Such a rule could not be tolerated, and is without foundation in the law. The Exchequer Chamber in 1875 defined "consideration" as follows: "A valuable consideration, in the sense of the law, may consist either in some right, interest, profit, or benefit accruing to the one party, or some forbearance, detriment, loss, or responsibility given, suffered, or undertaken by the other." Courts, "will not ask whether the thing which forms the consideration does in fact benefit the promisee or a third party, or is of any substantial value to any one. It is enough that something is promised, done, forborne, or suffered by the party to whom the promise is made as consideration for the promise made to him." Anson. Cont. 63. "In general waiver of any legal right at the request of another party is a sufficient consideration for a promise." Pars. Cont. 444. "Any damage, or suspension, or forbearance of a right will be sufficient to sustain a promise." 2 Kent. Comm. (12th Ed.) 465. Pollock in his work on Contracts (page 166), after citing the definition given by the Exchequer Chamber, already quoted, says: "The second branch of this judicial description is really the most important one. 'Consideration' means not so much that one party is profiting as that the other abandons some legal right in the present, or limits his legal freedom of action in the future, as an inducement for the promise of the first."

Now, applying this rule to the facts before us, the promisee used tobacco, occasionally drank liquor, and he had a legal right to do so. That right he abandoned for a period of years upon the strength of the promise of the testator that for such forbearance he would give him $5,000. We need not speculate on the effort which may have been required to give up the use of those stimulants. It is sufficient that he restricted his lawful freedom of action within certain prescribed limits upon the faith of his uncle's agreement, and now, having fully performed the conditions imposed, it is of no moment whether such performance actually proved a benefit to the promisor, and the court will not inquire into it; but, were it a proper subject of inquiry, we see nothing in this record that would permit a determination that the uncle was not benefited in a legal sense. Few cases have been found which may be said to be precisely in point, but such as have been, support the position we have taken. . . .

The order appealed from should be reversed, and the judgment of the special term affirmed.

ST. PETER v. PIONEER THEATRE CORP.
Supreme Court of Iowa
227 Iowa 1391, 291 N.W. 164 (1940)

MILLER, J.

This controversy involves a drawing at a theatre under an arrangement designated as "bank night," not identical with, but substantially similar to the arrangement involved in the controversy heretofore presented to this court by the case of State v. Hundling, 220 Iowa 1369, 164 N.W. 608, 103 A.L.R. 861. In that case, we held that the arrangement was not a lottery in violation of the provisions of Section 13218 of the Code, 1931, and that the proprietor of the theatre was not subject to criminal prosecution. In this case, we are confronted with the question whether the arrangement is such that one, to whom the prize is awarded, has a cause of action to enforce the payment thereof.

Plaintiff's petition alleges that the Pioneer Theatre Corporation operates a theatre at Jefferson, Iowa, known as the Iowa Theatre, and that the defendant Parkinson was at all times material herein manager of such theatre. The bank night drawing by defendants was conducted on Wednesday evening, at about 9 p.m. On December 21, 1938, the prize or purse was advertised by defendants in the amount of $275. At about 9 p.m., plaintiff and her husband were outside the theatre when an agent of the defendants announced that plaintiff's name had been called. Plaintiff immediately went into the theatre and made demand upon the manager, who refused to pay her the prize or purse, although plaintiff made demand therefor within the three minutes allowed by defendants. Plaintiff demanded judgment for the $275 and costs.

In count II of the plaintiff's petition, plaintiff alleged that her husband's name was drawn, he presented himself within three minutes, demanded the $275 and payment was refused, if he was not within the allotted time it was due to acts of defendants, her husband assigned his claim to plaintiff and plaintiff demanded judgment as such assignee.

Defendants' answer admitted that the Pioneer Theatre Corporation is operating the Iowa Theatre at Jefferson, Iowa, and that the defendant Parkinson is and has been for more than five years manager of said Iowa Theatre for the corporate defendant. The answer denied all other allegations of both counts of the petition.

The only witnesses to testify at the trial were the plaintiff and her husband. Their testimony is not in conflict. Accordingly, no disputed question of fact is presented, only questions of law.

They testified that each had signed the bank night register, plaintiff's number was 6396, her husband's number 212. The husband signed the register at the express invitation and request of Parkinson. Plaintiff signed the register later at the theatre in the presence of an usher. Plaintiff attended every bank night, often accompanied by her husband. Sometimes they attended as patrons of the theatre. Other times they stood on the sidewalk outside. On the occasions when they remained on the sidewalk outside the theatre, one Alice Kafer habitually announced the name that had been drawn inside the theatre. The only other person seen by them to make such announcement was Parkinson.

On the evening of December 21, 1938, plaintiff and her husband were on the sidewalk in front of the theatre. They observed a sign reading "Bank Night $275." About 9 o'clock Alice Kafer came out and said to plaintiff, "Hurry up Mrs. St. Peter, your name is called." Plaintiff entered the theatre and called to Parkinson. He came back and said, "I am sorry, but it was your husband's name that was called, where is your husband?" She said, "He is right behind me," turned around and motioned to him and said, "It's your name that was called." As he started toward them, the lights went out and in the darkness they lost sight of Parkinson. They sent an usher to look for him. When Parkinson came out and approached them he said to plaintiff's husband, "You are too late, just one second too late." Mr. St. Peter said, "You have a pretty good watch." Parkinson replied, "One second is just as good as a week." Mr. St. Peter said, "Why don't you call the name outside like you do inside?" Parkinson replied, "I have a lady hired to call the name out." When asked who she was, he said, "It's none of your business." When told that Mr. St. Peter intended to see a lawyer, Parkinson stated, "That is what we want you to do; the law is backing us up on our side." Plaintiff and her husband then left the theatre. Plaintiff's husband testified that he assigned his claim to the plaintiff before the action was commenced.

At the close of plaintiff's evidence, which consisted solely of her testimony, that of her husband, and defendants' bank night register, defendants made a motion for a directed verdict on [several] grounds, to wit: [1] there was no adequate or legal consideration for the claimed promise to give the alleged purse, [2] the most that could be claimed for plaintiff's alleged cause of action was a mere executory agreement to make a gift upon the happening of certain events without legal or adequate consideration, and no recovery could be had, [and (3)] if there is any legal or sufficient consideration for the promise sought to be enforced, then such consideration would constitute the transaction a lottery and, therefore, an illegal transaction upon which no recovery could be had.

The court sustained the motion generally. A verdict for the defendants was returned accordingly and judgment was entered dismissing the action at plaintiff's costs. Plaintiff appeals, assigning as error the sustaining of the motion and the entry of judgment pursuant thereto.

Since the motion was sustained generally, it is incumbent upon appellant, before she would be entitled to a reversal at our hands, to establish that the motion was not good upon any ground thereof. . . .

We are faced at the outset with our decision in the case of State v. Hundling, 220 Iowa 1369, heretofore referred to, wherein we held that an arrangement such as is involved herein does not constitute a lottery, and that the proprietor of the theatre is not subject to criminal prosecution on account thereof. In defining a lottery, we state as follows: "The giving away of property or prizes is not unlawful, nor is the gift made unlawful by the fact that the recipient is determined by lot. Our statute provides that the recipient of a public office may be determined by lot in certain cases where there is a tie vote. Section 883, Code 1931. To constitute a lottery there must be a further element, and that is the payment of a valuable consideration for the chance to receive the prize. Thus, it is quite generally recognized that there are three elements necessary to constitute a lottery: First, a prize to be given; second, upon a contingency to be determined by chance; and, third, to a person who has paid some valuable consideration or hazarded something of value for the chance."

In applying such definition to the facts presented in that case, we state at page 1371 of 220 Iowa, as follows:

> The term "lottery," as popularly and generally used, refers to a gambling scheme in which chances are sold or disposed of for value and the sums thus paid are hazarded in the hope of winning a much larger sum. That is the predominant characteristic of lotteries which has become known to history and is the source of the evil which attends a lottery, in that it arouses the gambling spirit and leads people to hazard their substance on a mere chance. It is undoubtedly the evil against which our statute is directed. To have a lottery, therefore, he who has the chance to win a prize must pay, or agree to pay, something of value for that chance.

> In the particular scheme under consideration here, there is no question but what two elements of a lottery are present, first, a prize, and, second, a determination of the recipient by lot. Difficulty arises in the third element, namely, the payment of some valuable consideration for the chance by the holder thereof. The holder of the chance to win the prize in the case at bar was required to do two things in order to be eligible to receive the prize, first, to sign his name in the book, and, second, be in such proximity to the theater as that he could claim the prize within two and one-half minutes after his name was announced. He was not required to purchase a ticket of admission to the theater either as a condition of signing the registration book or claiming the prize when his name was drawn. In other words, paying admission to the theater added nothing to the chance. Where there is the payment by the holder of the chance of a valuable consideration for the chance, which is necessary in order to make the scheme a lottery?

In holding that there was not such a valuable consideration as would constitute the arrangement of a lottery, we state at page 1372 of 220 Iowa, as follows:

> It is urged on behalf of the state that the defendant theater manager gained some benefit, or hoped to gain some benefit, from the scheme in the way of increased attendance at his theater, and that this would afford the consideration required. If it be conceded that the attendance at the theater on the particular night that the prize was to be given away was stimulated by reason of the scheme, it is difficult to see how that would make the scheme a lottery. The question is not whether the donor of the prize makes a profit in some remote and indirect way, but, rather, whether those who have a chance at the prize pay anything of value for that chance. Every scheme of advertising, including the giving away of premiums and prizes, naturally has for its object, not purely a philanthropic purpose, but increased business. . . . Profit accruing remotely and indirectly to the person who gives the prize is not a substitute for the requirement that he who has the chance to win the prize must pay a valuable consideration therefor, in order to make the scheme a lottery.

Appellees rely upon the language above quoted to support their contention that the arrangement involved in both cases constitutes merely an offer to make a gift, which is not supported by a valuable consideration and is, therefore, unenforceable.

In 12 American Jurisprudence, pages 564 and 565, in Section 72, it is stated, "It is well settled, however, that ordinarily consideration is an essential element of a simple contract, and want or lack of consideration is an excuse for nonperformance of a promise." It is also stated, "The policy of the courts in requiring a consideration for the maintenance of an action of assumpsit appears to be to prevent the enforcement of gratuitous promises." Such principles have been recognized by this court. In the case of Farlow v. Farlow, 154 Iowa 647, 135 N.W. 1, we held that a promise to make a gift is without consideration and not enforceable.

Appellees contend that the foregoing principles, considered with our statements in State v. Hundling, supra, show that this action is based upon a promise that cannot be enforced. In the Hundling case, we state, "The giving away of property or prizes is not unlawful," and, "profit accruing remotely and indirectly to the person who gives the prize is not a substitute for the requirement that he who has a chance to win the prize must pay a valuable consideration therefor." Appellees contend that these pronouncements commit us to the proposition that the arrangement involved herein constituted nothing more than a promise to make a gift which is not supported by a legal consideration, and, accordingly, is not enforceable. We are unable to agree with the contentions of appellees.

At the outset, it is important to bear in mind that the plaintiff herein seeks to recover on a unilateral contract. A bilateral contract is one in which two promises are made: the promise of each party to the contract is consideration for the promise of the other party. In a unilateral contract, only one party makes a promise. If that promise is made contingent upon the other party doing some act, which he is not under legal obligation to do, or forbearing an action which he has a legal right to take, then such affirmative act or forbearance constitutes the consideration for and acceptance of the promise.

The case of Scott v. People's Monthly Co., 209 Iowa 503, 508, involved an action for a $1,000 prize offered in a "Word-building Contest." We there state:

> An offer of or promise to pay a reward is a proposal merely or a conditional promise, on the part of the offeror, and not a consummated contract. It may be said to be in effect the offer of a promise for an act, and the offer becomes a binding contract when the act is done or the service rendered in accordance with the terms of the offer.

> It is the doing of the act in accordance with the terms and conditions of the offer which completes the contract. In other words, to make a binding and enforceable contract, the act must be done in accordance with the terms and conditions of the offer.

The principles applicable to the question of the adequacy of the consideration are clearly and concisely stated by Chief Justice Wright in the early case of Blake v. Blake, 7 Iowa 46, 51, as follows:

The essence and requisite of every consideration is, that it should create some benefit to the party promising, or some trouble, prejudice, or inconvenience to the party to whom the promise is made. Whenever, therefore, any injury to the one party, or any benefit to the other, springs from a consideration, it is sufficient to support a contract. Each party to a contract may, ordinarily, exercise his own discretion, as to the adequacy of the consideration; and if the agreement be made bona fide, it matters not how insignificant the benefit may apparently be to the promisor, or how slight the inconvenience or damage appear to be to the promisee, provided it be susceptible of legal estimation. Of course, however, if the inadequacy is so gross as to create a presumption of fraud, the contract founded thereon would not be enforced. But, even then, it is the fraud which is thereby indicated, and not the inadequacy of consideration, which invalidates the contract. . . .

Applying the principles above reviewed, it is readily apparent that, in this action on a unilateral contract, it was necessary for the plaintiff to show that a promise had been made which might be accepted by the doing of an act, which act would constitute consideration for the promise and performance of the contract. There is no basis for any claim of fraud herein. Plaintiff had nothing to do with inducing the defendants' promise. That promise was voluntarily and deliberately made. Defendants exercised their own discretion in determining the adequacy of the consideration for their promise. If the plaintiff did the acts called for by that promise, defendants cannot complain of the adequacy of the consideration.

Of course, it is fundamental that the act which is asserted as the consideration for acceptance and performance of a unilateral contract must be an act which the party sought to be bound bargained for, and the acts must have been induced by the promise made. Appellees contend that the facts are wholly insufficient to meet such requirements, contending as follows: "Although the action of Appellant in writing her name or standing in front of the theater might under some circumstances be such an act as would furnish a consideration for a promise, yet under the facts in the case at bar, . . . no reasonable person could say that the requested acts were actually bargained for in a legal sense so as to give rise to an enforceable promise."

We are unable to concur in the contentions of counsel above quoted. We think that the requested acts were bargained for. We see nothing unreasonable in such holdings. If there is anything unreasonable in this phase of the case, it would appear to be the contentions of counsel.

This brings us to the proposition raised by the motion for directed verdict, wherein it is asserted that, if there was a legal consideration for the promise sought to be enforced, then such consideration would constitute the transaction a lottery. To sustain such contention would require us to overrule State v. Hundling, *supra*, and to overrule such contention requires a differentiating of that case from this case. We think that the two questions are different and may be logically distinguished.

In the *Hundling* case, we point out that the source of the evil which attends a lottery is that it arouses the gambling spirit and leads people to hazard their substance on a mere chance. Accordingly, it is vitally necessary to constitute a lottery that one who has the chance to win the prize must pay something of value for that chance. The value of the consideration, from a monetary standpoint, is the essence of the crime. However, in a civil action to enforce the promise to pay a prize, the monetary value of the consideration is in no wise controlling. It is only necessary that the act done be that which the promisor specified. The sufficiency of the consideration lies wholly within the discretion of the one who offers to pay the prize. "It matters not how insignificant the benefit may apparently be to the promisor, or how slight the inconvenience or damage appear to be to the promisee, provided it be susceptible of legal estimation." Blake v. Blake, *supra*. Accordingly, it is entirely possible that the act, specified by the promisor as being sufficient in his discretion to constitute consideration for and acceptance of his promise, might have no monetary value and yet constitute a legal consideration for the promise. Under such circumstances, the arrangement is not a lottery. But, if the act specified is done, the unilateral contract is supported by a consideration, and, having been performed by the party doing the act, can be enforced against the party making the promise. We hold that such is the situation here.

All of appellant's assignments of error are well grounded. No ground of the motion for directed verdict was sufficient to warrant a sustaining of the motion. The court's ruling was erroneous. The judgment entered pursuant thereto must be and it is reversed.

The Chief Justice and all the Justices concur.

NOTES

1. ***Background to* St. Peter v. Pioneer.** *State v. Hundling*, discussed in *St. Peter*, was a criminal prosecution for a violation of Iowa's lottery laws.[33] The court held that the consideration given in a Bank Night contest was insufficient to support a criminal prosecution. The St. Peters argued that valid consideration supported a promise to pay them $275. Do you understand the role that context plays in determining when consideration is present? Would the outcome of the *St. Peter* case change if the defendant showed that the St. Peters were habitual Thursday night patrons?

Bank Night was a promotional idea sold to movie theatres as a device to increase movie attendance and gain publicity. Does this fact change your view of the court's reasoning? Should the court have taken the theatre's reasonable expectation of increased patronage into account?[34]

2. ***Motive and Consideration.*** Why would the theatre owner bargain for the St. Peters to sign their name in a book and stand on the street outside the theatre? Does the answer matter? Consider this excerpt from HOLMES, THE COMMON LAW 293–94 (1887):

---

[33] Bank nights in Iowa were held to be illegal lotteries in *Idea Research & Development Corp. v. Hultman*, 256 Iowa 1381, 131 N.W.2d 496 (1964) (affirmed by an equally divided court). *Hundling* and *St. Peter* were reversed on this point.

[34] For the history of Bank Night litigation, see ANN., 103 A.L.R. 866; 109 A.L.R. 709; 113 A.L.R. 1121.

It is said that consideration must not be confounded with motive. It is true that it must not be confounded with what may be the prevailing or chief motive in actual fact. A man may promise to paint a picture for five hundred dollars, while his chief motive may be a desire for fame. A consideration may be given and accepted, in fact, solely for the purpose of making a promise binding. But, nevertheless, it is the essence of a consideration, that, by the terms of the agreement, it is given and accepted as the motive or inducement of the promise. Conversely, the promise must be made and accepted as the conventional motive or inducement for furnishing the consideration. The root of the whole matter is the relation of reciprocal conventional inducement, each for the other between consideration and promise.

3. **Beyond Consideration.** Consideration is no longer the *sine qua non* for the enforcement of promises. In Chapter 2 we shall consider two other doctrinal bases for enforcement: promissory estoppel (certain promises are enforced without consideration when followed by actions or forbearance by the promisee in reliance on the promise) and the material benefit rule (certain promises are enforced, even without consideration, if made in recognition of a prior material benefit conferred by the promisee on the promisor). The relationship between these additional enforcement doctrines and the doctrine of consideration is complex. For now it is sufficient to keep in mind that the consideration doctrine proved to be insufficiently expansive to accommodate all the cases where common law courts enforced promises. The challenge in Chapter 2, then, will be to search for common themes that link those various doctrines of contractual enforcement.

4. **Benefit/Detriment.** A contemporary perspective on the "benefit/detriment" concept discussed in *Hamer v. Sidway* is offered in *Davies v. Martel Laboratory Services, Inc.*, 545 N.E.2d 475 (1989). Martel promised Janet Davies a permanent position, and ultimately, a position as vice-president of the company, if she entered an MBA program. She accepted the offer and enrolled in the MBA program at Northwestern University, only to be fired a year later. Martel contended that the promise was not supported by consideration, as the MBA degree was a benefit to her future marketability, and not any sort of hindrance or detriment. The appellate court disagreed:

> While this fact may be true, it is not necessarily legally so. The words "benefit" and "detriment" in contract cases involving consideration have technical meanings. "Detriment" as used in determining the sufficiency of consideration to support a contract means " 'legal detriment' as distinguished from detriment in fact. It means giving up something which immediately prior thereto the promisee was privileged to retain, or doing or refraining from doing something which he was then privileged not to do, or not to refrain from doing." (Hamilton Bancshares, Inc. v. Leroy (1985), 131 Ill. App. 3d 907, 913, quoting 1 Williston, Contracts § 102A, at 380-82 (3d ed. 1957).) For example, a promise to give up smoking may be a benefit to the promisee's health, but a promise to give up smoking is also a legal detriment and sufficient consideration to support a contract. *Id.*

In the present case, Davies did not have to obtain an MBA degree and expend her own time and money in doing so in order to continue as an at-will employee of Martel's; she could have continued to perform oil analyses and mapping work rather than enter the ivied walls of Northwestern. Nor does it appear that Davies was obligated to serve as a member on Martel's President's Council and to assume additional duties and responsibilities. In other words, Davies was privileged to refrain from serving on Martel's council and from pursuing an MBA degree. By giving up her privilege to refrain from so acting, Davies clearly could be said to have suffered a legal detriment, which would constitute sufficient consideration to support the alleged oral contract between the parties.

545 N.E.2d at 477.

5. *Contract vs. Gift*. The distinction between an executory contract, where the promise has not yet been performed, and a fully executed gift transaction demarcates the line between contract law and property law. In a contract, the obligation to perform a promise in the future is grounded in the notion of reciprocity, wherein each party receives something of value from the other in return for undertaking an obligation to the other in return. A gift, however, is a one-sided, or non-reciprocal, exchange. Thus, it is enforceable only when it is completed; that is, when the donor transfers legal title to property to the donee. A completed gift is thus enforceable as a property right by the donee just as an executory promise supported by consideration is enforceable by the promisee as a contract right. The key difference is that a mere promise to make a gift, also known as a "donative promise," is generally not legally enforceable. For discussion, see Melvin Aron Eisenberg, *The World of Contract and the World of Gift*, 85 CAL. L. REV. 821 (1997). In *Dougherty v. Salt*, 125 N.E. 94 (1919), for example, the plaintiff's aunt had given him a promissory note for $3,000, payable at her death or before. The gift was memorialized in a printed form, which said it was in exchange for "value received." Judge Cardozo, however, ruled that the "note was the voluntary and unenforceable promise of an executory gift." *Id.* at 95.

[4] Limitations on Enforcement: Unconscionability

Viewed from the perspective of the promisee, the legal enforcement of promises seems entirely benign. As seen in cases such as *Hamer v. Sidway*, the fact that a promise supported by consideration is legally enforceable permits the promisee to rely on the promise from the time it is made. Reliability, in turn, permits promisees to adjust their future actions in light of the promise in ways that better promote their long term interests. If such promises were not enforceable, the promisee would have to wait until the date of the promised performance to see whether or not the promise would be performed. For the promisee, therefore, legal enforcement is a means of bringing the future to the present and thus is an important element in better formulating a life plan.

But the reverse side of enforcement is the risk that the promisor will come to regret the promise. Often this risk will materialize regardless of the good intentions and careful calculation of the promisor at the time the promise is made. When this happens, the decision to enforce the promise anyway is one that imposes costs on the reluctant promisor. This suggests several questions. Why does the law enforce promises in the face of a genuine and understandable change of heart by the promisor? And, more to the point perhaps, why would anyone be motivated to make a promise that the law will subsequently require them to perform regardless of a change of heart? In other words, what does a prospective promisor get out of the "freedom" to make a legally enforceable promise? One answer is to focus on the benefits of precommitment. Just as Ulysses was able, by tying his hands to the mast, to hear the sirens' song without being crushed by the rocks, so too a promisor, by making a legally binding commitment to do a future act, can secure a present benefit from the promisee that he would not otherwise enjoy.

The norm that underlies this conception of promissory enforcement is the idea of *expanded choice*. Enforceable promise making gives the promisor the opportunity to expand his present choices by agreeing to constrain his future actions. The binding character of such a commitment also implies that the law cares about the integrity of the promisor's decision-making process. Ideally, a legally binding commitment should always be the product of a voluntary, rational, and informed choice by the promisor. Thus, the common law has developed doctrines of fraud and duress as defenses against enforcement in circumstances where those conditions are not satisfied. But in a post-industrial world, where many promises are made via standard form contracts, are the traditional common law defenses sufficient protection against involuntary and/or uninformed promises? And, if not, how can courts protect the integrity of the promise making process without undermining the very purposes supporting legal enforcement in the first place? Consider the following case as you begin to grapple with these questions.

WILLIAMS v. WALKER-THOMAS FURNITURE CO. I
District of Columbia Court of Appeals
198 A.2d 914 (1964)

Quinn, J.

Appellant, a person of limited education separated from her husband, is maintaining herself and her seven children by means of public assistance. During the period 1957-1962 she had a continuous course of dealings with appellee from which she purchased many household articles on the installment plan. These included sheets, curtains, rugs, chairs, a chest of drawers, beds, mattresses, a washing machine, and a stereo set. In 1963 appellee filed a complaint in replevin for possession of all the items purchased by appellant, alleging that her payments were in default and that it retained title to the goods according to the sales contracts. By the writ of replevin appellee obtained a bed, chest of drawers, washing machine, and the stereo set. After hearing testimony and examining the contracts, the trial court entered judgment for appellee.

Appellant's principal contentions on appeal are (1) there was a lack of meeting of the minds, and (2) the contracts were against public policy.

Appellant signed fourteen contracts in all. They were approximately six inches in length and each contained a long paragraph in extremely fine print. One of the sentences in this paragraph provided that payments, after the first purchase, were to be prorated on all purchases then outstanding. Mathematically, this had the effect of keeping a balance due on all items until the time balance was completely eliminated. It meant that title to the first purchase remained in appellee until the fourteenth purchase, made some five years later, was fully paid.

At trial appellant testified that she understood the agreements to mean that when payments on the running account were sufficient to balance the amount due on an individual item, the item became hers. She testified that most of the purchases were made at her home; that the contracts were signed in blank; that she did not read the instruments; and that she was not provided with a copy. She admitted, however, that she did not ask anyone to read or explain the contracts to her.

We have stated that "one who refrains from reading a contract and in conscious ignorance of its terms voluntarily assents thereto will not be relieved from his bad bargain." Bob Wilson, Inc. v. Swann, D.C. Mun. App., 168 A.2d 198, 199 (1961). "One who signs a contract has a duty to read it and is obligated according to its terms." Hollywood Credit Clothing Co. v. Gibson, D.C. App., 188 A.2d 348, 349 (1963). "It is as much the duty of a person who cannot read the language in which a contract is written to have someone read it to him before he signs it, as it is the duty of one who can read to peruse it himself before signing it." Stern v. Moneyweight Scale Co., 42 App.D.C. 162, 165 (1914).

A careful review of the record shows that appellant's assent was not obtained "by fraud or even misrepresentation falling short of fraud." Hollywood Credit Clothing Co. v. Gibson, *supra.* This is not a case of mutual misunderstanding but a unilateral mistake. Under these circumstances, appellant's first contention is without merit.

Appellant's second argument presents a more serious question. The record reveals that prior to the last purchase appellant had reduced the balance in her account to $164. The last purchase, a stereo set, raised the balance due to $678. Significantly, at the time of this and the preceding purchases, appellee was aware of appellant's financial position. The reverse side of the stereo contract listed the name of appellant's social worker and her $218 monthly stipend from the government. Nevertheless, with full knowledge that appellant had to feed, clothe and support both herself and seven children on this amount, appellee sold her a $514 stereo set.

We cannot condemn too strongly appellee's conduct. It raises serious questions of sharp practice and irresponsible business dealings. A review of the legislation in the District of Columbia affecting retail sales and the pertinent decisions of the highest court in this jurisdiction disclose, however, no ground upon which this court can declare the contracts in question contrary to public policy. We note that were the Maryland Retail Installment Sales Act, Art. 83 §§ 128-153, or its equivalent, in force in the District of Columbia, we could grant appellant appropriate relief. We think Congress should consider corrective legislation to protect the public from such exploitive contracts as were utilized in the case at bar.

WILLIAMS v. WALKER-THOMAS FURNITURE CO. II
United States Court of Appeals, District of Columbia Circuit
350 F.2d 445, 121 U.S. App. D.C. 315 (1965)

J. SKELLY WRIGHT, J.

Appellee, Walker-Thomas Furniture Company, operates a retail furniture store in the District of Columbia. During the period from 1957 to 1962 each appellant in these cases purchased a number of household items from Walker-Thomas, for which payment was to be made in installments. The terms of each purchase were contained in a printed form contract which set forth the value of the purchased item and purported to lease the item to appellant for a stipulated monthly rent payment. The contract then provided, in substance, that title would remain in Walker-Thomas until the total of all the monthly payments made equaled the stated value of the item, at which time appellants could take title. In the event of a default in the payment of any monthly installment, Walker-Thomas could repossess the item.

The contract further provided that "the amount of each periodical installment payment to be made by (purchaser) to the Company under this present lease shall be inclusive of and not in addition to the amount of each installment payment to be made by (purchaser) under such prior leases, bills or accounts; and all payments now and hereafter made by (purchaser) shall be credited pro rata on all outstanding leases, bills and accounts due the Company by (purchaser) at the time each such payment is made." The effect of this rather obscure provision was to keep a balance due on every item purchased until the balance due on all items, whenever purchased, was liquidated. As a result, the debt incurred at the time of purchase of each item was secured by the right to repossess all the items previously purchased by the same purchaser, and each new item purchased automatically became subject to a security interest arising out of the previous dealings. [. . .]

[O]n April 17, 1962, appellant Williams bought a stereo set of stated value of $514.95.[35] She too defaulted shortly thereafter, and appellee sought to replevy all the items purchased since December, 1957. The Court of General Sessions granted judgment for appellee. The District of Columbia Court of Appeals affirmed, and we granted appellants' motion for leave to appeal to this court.

Appellants' principal contention, rejected by both the trial and the appellate courts below, is that these contracts, or at least some of them, are unconscionable and, hence, not enforceable. . . .

We do not agree that the court lacked the power to refuse enforcement to contracts found to be unconscionable. In other jurisdictions, it has been held as a matter of common law that unconscionable contracts are not enforceable. While no decision of this court so holding has been found, the notion that an unconscionable bargain should not be given full enforcement is by no means novel. In Scott v. United States, 79 U.S. (12 Wall.) 443, 445 (1870), the Supreme Court stated:

---

[35] [1] At the time of this purchase her account showed a balance of $164 still owing from her prior purchases. The total of all the purchases made over the years in question came to $1,800. The total payments amounted to $1,400.

> If a contract be unreasonable and unconscionable, but not void for fraud, a court of law will give to the party who sues for its breach damages, not according to its letter, but only such as he is equitably entitled to. . . .

Since we have never adopted or rejected such a rule, the question here presented is actually one of first impression.

Congress has recently enacted the Uniform Commercial Code, which specifically provides that the court may refuse to enforce a contract which it finds to be unconscionable at the time it was made. 28 D.C. Code § 2-302 (Supp. IV 1965). The enactment of this section, which occurred subsequent to the contracts here in suit, does not mean that the common law of the District of Columbia was otherwise at the time of enactment, nor does it preclude the court from adopting a similar rule in the exercise of its powers to develop the common law for the District of Columbia. In fact, in view of the absence of prior authority on the point, we consider the congressional adoption of § 2-302 persuasive authority for following the rationale of the cases from which the section is explicitly derived. Accordingly, we hold that where the element of unconscionability is present at the time a contract is made, the contract should not be enforced.

Unconscionability has generally been recognized to include an absence of meaningful choice on the part of one of the parties together with contract terms which are unreasonably favorable to the other party. Whether a meaningful choice is present in a particular case can only be determined by consideration of all the circumstances surrounding the transaction. In many cases the meaningfulness of the choice is negated by a gross inequality of bargaining power. The manner in which the contract was entered is also relevant to this consideration. Did each party to the contract, considering his obvious education or lack of it, have a reasonable opportunity to understand the terms of the contract, or were the important terms hidden in a maze of fine print and minimized by deceptive sales practices? Ordinarily, one who signs an agreement without full knowledge of its terms might be held to assume the risk that he has entered a one-sided bargain. But when a party of little bargaining power, and hence little real choice, signs a commercially unreasonable contract with little or no knowledge of its terms, it is hardly likely that his consent, or even an objective manifestation of his consent, was ever given to all the terms. In such a case the usual rule that the terms of the agreement are not to be questioned should be abandoned and the court should consider whether the terms of the contract are so unfair that enforcement should be withheld.

In determining reasonableness or fairness, the primary concern must be with the terms of the contract considered in light of the circumstances existing when the contract was made. The test is not simple, nor can it be mechanically applied. The terms are to be considered "in the light of the general commercial background and the commercial needs of the particular trade or case." Corbin suggests the test as being whether the terms are "so extreme as to appear unconscionable according to the mores and business practices of the time and place." 1 Corbin, *Contracts*. We think this formulation correctly states the test to be applied in those cases where no meaningful choice was exercised upon entering the contract.

Because the trial court and the appellate court did not feel that enforcement could be refused, no findings were made on the possible unconscionability of the contracts in these cases. Since the record is not sufficient for our deciding the issue as a matter of law, the cases must be remanded to the trial court for further proceedings.

So ordered.

DANAHER, J. (dissenting).

The District of Columbia Court of Appeals obviously was as unhappy about the situation here presented as any of us can possibly be. Its opinion in the *Williams* case, quoted in the majority text, concludes: "We think Congress should consider corrective legislation to protect the public from such exploitive contracts as were utilized in the case at bar."

My view is thus summed up by an able court which made no finding that there had actually been sharp practice. Rather the appellant seems to have known precisely where she stood.

There are many aspects of public policy here involved. What is a luxury to some may seem an outright necessity to others. Is public oversight to be required of the expenditures of relief funds? A washing machine, e.g., in the hands of a relief client might become a fruitful source of income. Many relief clients may well need credit, and certain business establishments will take long chances on the sale of items, expecting their pricing policies will afford a degree of protection commensurate with the risk.

I mention such matters only to emphasize the desirability of a cautious approach to any such problem, particularly since the law for so long has allowed parties such great latitude in making their own contracts. I dare say there must annually be thousands upon thousands of installment credit transactions in this jurisdiction, and one can only speculate as to the effect the decision in these cases will have.

I join the District of Columbia Court of Appeals in its disposition of the issues.

NOTES

1. *Understanding the Substantive Law of Secured Transactions.* In evaluating *Walker-Thomas*, it is important for you to understand the legal rights that the law of secured transactions (embodied in Article 9 of the UCC) gives to sellers such as Walker-Thomas.[36] Under Article 9, if a debtor gives a seller a security interest in goods purchased, the seller has the right to repossess the goods upon default. *See* UCC § 9-609. Thereafter, in consumer cases, such as Ms. Williams, the seller *must* offer the goods for sale — after duly notifying the buyer. *See* UCC §§ 9-610-614,

---

[36] In 1984 the Federal Trade Commission enacted a rule that prohibits sellers such as the Walker-Thomas Furniture Company from taking blanket security interests in household goods. *See* 16 C.F.R. § 444.2 (1984). Thus, the UCC provisions governing secured transactions no longer apply to the precise situation presented in *Walker-Thomas*. Retail sellers remain free, however, to take security interests in other consumer goods, such as automobiles. For a discussion of the FTC rule and an argument that it may do little to solve the problem of coercive creditor behavior see Robert E. Scott, *Rethinking the Regulation of Coercive Creditor Remedies*, 89 COLUM. L. REV. 730 (1989).

9-620(e). The proceeds of the sale will be first applied to satisfy the balance of the debt owed, the expenses of repossession, etc., and then the balance (if any) must be returned to the debtor. *See* UCC § 9-615. The effect of a cross-collateral clause (which is explicitly authorized as a general matter in UCC § 9-204(1)) is to ensure that the secured party will be as fully secured as possible. It does not entitle the secured party to retain any goods or money above the amount of security.

If such security clauses are commonly employed in commercial transactions, why are they found objectionable in *Williams*? One symptom of an underlying pattern in consumer cases is that almost inevitably there is no surplus available to the debtor after the goods are resold. Instead, the secured party will typically exercise its right to recover a deficiency. Why do you suppose there is so seldom a surplus? Does this fact suggest that all consumer security interests should be banned, or perhaps just those types involving consumers such as Ms. Williams? Or sellers such as Walker-Thomas?

2. *Fairness.* Is it adequate to argue that a business practice or a contract term ought to be set aside because it is "unfair"?[37] For a moral rights theorist, perhaps, fairness is a meaningful concept; but for the lawyer arguing a case, more is surely needed. Put concretely, if you are arguing to a judge that a contract term is not fair, and the judge says, "The term seems fair to me, what is your problem?," you had better have more to say or you are in trouble.

One inquiry asks: what are the effects of a decision to deny enforcement on the grounds of unconscionability of an otherwise enforceable contract term? In other words, is it "fair" to grant Ms. Williams relief on the grounds of unconscionability if the effect of that decision is to reduce the access to credit to other poor consumers who shop at the same store(s)? For example, in the *Williams* context we might wish that poor people had more money to buy stereos, but that option is not available to the judge. We might also wish that poor people could buy stereos without assuming onerous credit terms, and one question about *Williams* is whether the court has that option available.

Another approach to fairness is to argue that the consequences of a particular judicial outcome in terms of its future effects are not the relevant inquiry. Rather, the question is how best to do justice to persons before the court, such as Ms. Williams. On this analysis you might argue that Ms. Williams has been wronged by the behavior of the Walker-Thomas Furniture Co. This injustice must be corrected, and to do so the court must declare the contract unconscionable. Under this view, the question of whether future consumers would be better off or worse off after this case is decided is a problem for the legislature to address, but ought not to prevent Ms. Williams from securing the "corrective justice" to which she is entitled.

3. *Unequal Bargaining Power.* The court suggests that the contract in

---

[37] For discussion, see Kevin A. Kordana & David H. Tabachnick, *Rawls and Contract Law*, 73 Geo. Wash. L. Rev. 598, 626–29 (2005); Richard L. Barnes, *Rediscovering Subjectivity in Contracts: Adhesion and Unconscionability*, 66 La. L. Rev. 123 (2005); Russell Korobkin, *A "Traditional" and "Behavioral" Law-and-Economics Analysis of* Williams v. Walker-Thomas *Furniture Company*, 26 U. Haw. L. Rev. 441 (2004); Philip Bridwell, *The Philosophical Dimensions of the Doctrine of Unconscionability*, 70 U. Chi. L. Rev. 1513 (2003).

Williams may have been marked by an absence of meaningful choice and that one factor that would be relevant to that conclusion is whether there is gross inequality of bargaining power. "Unequal bargaining power" is a slogan found in more than one area of law, but careful analysis reveals it to be an ambiguous term.

You go to the grocery store to buy a box of a particular kind of cereal. The price on the box is $2.89. You find the store manager and try to bargain down the price of the cereal. What result? The manager will think that you are crazy. If you persist, you'll be fortunate not to be arrested. You go to the store across the street. There, too, the cereal is $2.89, and they won't bargain either.

If you are prepared to call this unequal bargaining power, then the term is trivial, for such situations are commonplace. Nor is the analysis any different with respect to subjects less easily found than a box of cereal. Suppose that you would like to buy my dog "Lucy," and I quote you a take-it-or-leave-it asking price of $1,000. Or suppose that I want to buy your Hasselblad camera and I offer you a take-it-or-leave-it price of $1,500. Again, it would not be helpful to call these instances of unequal bargaining power even though in each case there was no willingness to dicker over the terms of the deal.

Another term used in *Williams,* which may be connected to the judge's notion of unequal bargaining power, is "a commercially unreasonable contract." Was the cross-collateral clause "commercially unreasonable"? Consider this example. I own a furniture store in the city. I sell stereos. There are several other furniture stores in this area, all selling the same stereo that I sell. My brother-in-law makes toasters. To please my spouse, I decide that I will sell a stereo to a customer only if he or she will buy a toaster as well. How many stereos will I sell? Few or none. Unless the stereo customer also happens to want a toaster, all the sales will be by my competitors.

But perhaps I am in the happy (for me) situation of having no competitors. Either I am the only store selling stereos in this part of the city, or the brand that I (exclusively) sell is somehow special. (Were either of these the case in *Williams*? Why didn't Ms. Williams buy the stereo from another local furniture store? If they too demanded a cross-collateral clause, why didn't she take a bus out to Sears and buy the stereo there?) Now I have the "power" to require a buyer also to purchase a toaster. But do I want to? The ordinary monopolist (for that is what I am) is faced with many potential buyers who differ one from another in their desire for the product. Some will pay a great deal for a stereo, but others will not. As a monopolist, I have some calculations to perform. At one extreme, I could price stereos so as to make the most possible money off a sale to the one buyer who would pay the most. But I would have only one sale. If I lower my price to pick up a second sale, I will have forgone a little money from the most anxious buyer, but I will have made money on a second sale. If the money from the second sale more than makes up for the loss of the extra money on the first sale, then I lower my price and sell two stereos.[38] I then go through the same calculations to determine whether to lower

---

[38] What I would really like to do is sell one stereo to the first buyer at a really high price and a second stereo to the second buyer at a lower price (still, the maximum that buyer is willing to pay). Ordinarily, two things make it impossible for the monopolist to price in this fashion. First, there is the danger that

my price a little bit more and sell a third stereo. At some point, I will forgo more money by reducing my price further than I will make up in increased sales. If I have calculated correctly, I will be making the most money possible off the sales of stereos. Now what happens if I try to force my customers to buy a toaster along with their stereo? Some of those customers don't want a toaster, others want to buy their toasters somewhere else. Since I had already calculated precisely what price to charge for stereos, forcing customers to take a toaster with the stereo keeps me from doing as well as I possibly could.

Do I still want to force customers to take a toaster with their stereo? Sure, if my spouse's happiness is worth the loss in revenues. On similar reasoning, would Walker-Thomas force a cross-collateral clause on their customers? Yes, if they had monopoly power and if the owners preferred forcing these clauses on buyers more than the owners preferred greater profits. Neither of these assumptions seems very plausible.

The thrust of this analysis is that the presence of the cross-collateral clause is not explainable as abuse of market power by Walker-Thomas.[39] Thus, we cannot be sure that condemning the clause on grounds of unconscionability will make people in Ms. Williams' position better off. We need to seek another explanation for the presence of the clause.

4. ***The Effect of* Williams *on Credit Availability.*** Why did not Ms. Williams take a bus to Sears and buy the stereo on credit? It may be that Sears would not sell her a stereo on credit. Furniture depreciates very quickly. In a later case involving unconscionability, a welfare recipient bought a refrigerator, a stove, furniture, and an air conditioner, and defaulted after having paid more than two-thirds of the charges.[40] The resale value of the used goods was so low that it failed to cover the remaining debt. What would you (as their business advisor) advise Walker-Thomas to do if the only collateral for their requested extension of credit is the single stereo? This analysis suggests that the effect of a decision (remember, this is not the *holding* in *Williams*) declaring cross-collateral clauses to be unconscionable will be to make credit in the inner-city less available, stereos more expensive, or both. Some inner-city residents who could have purchased stereos before will no longer be able to.[41]

5. ***The Distributional Effects of* Williams.** The argument that the cross-collateral clause in *Williams* ought not to be voided as unconscionable is straight-

---

the "second buyers" will resell to the "first buyers" at just less than my price. (Don't you think this danger would prevent the OPEC oil monopoly from charging different prices for the same oil to different customers?) Second, the potential customers tend to "cheat" the monopolist by disguising their preferences for the product. So, the customer who really has the highest desire for the stereo will pretend that he is far less interested. Unless he does this poorly, he may get the lower price, for if I try to prevent this by insisting on the highest price, I will lose the customers who really are less interested. (Has this ever happened to you? What do you think is going on when you dicker with a car dealer over the price of a new car?)

[39] *See* Alan Schwartz, *A Re-Examination of Nonsubstantive Unconscionability*, 63 VA. L. REV. 1053 (1977).

[40] *Jones v. Star Credit Corp.*, 59 Misc. 2d 189, 298 N.Y.S.2d 264 (Sup. Ct. 1969).

[41] For an elaboration of this argument, see Richard A. Epstein, *Unconscionability: A Critical Reappraisal*, 18 J.L. & ECON. 293 (1975).

forward: the clause makes possible transactions that would otherwise be unavailable or at least more costly. Both the buyer and the seller believe that they are better off entering into the transaction, and there is no reason to substitute a judge's later preferences for the parties' preferences at the time of contracting. The parties are better off with the contract and no one is worse off.

This argument may be unsatisfying in two respects. You may think that as a mother of seven, who is on welfare, Ms. Williams was less capable of knowing what is in her best interests than a judge, who is college-educated, has a law degree, etc. This would suggest that a court might not void such a clause had it been entered into by a person who had been more successful in life than Ms. Williams. Are you comfortable making that argument?[42] Second, you might conclude that while you are willing to allow Ms. Williams to decide this matter for herself, there are others affected by the cross-collateral clause who have no say in the matter. Ms. Williams' seven children were probably adversely affected by the loss of the furniture, and perhaps Ms. Williams inadequately considered their interests when she bought the stereo. Other people may have depended on Ms. Williams as well, such as her parents. In the next cross-collateral case, ought the judge to address that question explicitly?[43]

6. *Procedural Unconscionability.* Unconscionability has been divided by scholars into substantive and procedural branches. Substantive unconscionability usually refers to the terms of the agreement itself, *for example*, an "unreasonable" price or contract term which deprives a party of the "essence of his bargain." The notes have thus far been addressing this category of unconscionability.

Procedural unconscionability, on the other hand, describes a defective bargaining process, *for example*, an "unreasonable" failure of one party to inform the other party about important aspects of the exchange. Generally, procedural unconscionability refers to practices which impermissibly reduce an individual's ability to make rational choices concerning the bargain. As one case notes:

> The procedural element focuses on two factors: "oppression" and "surprise." "Oppression" arises from an inequality of bargaining power which results in no real negotiation and "an absence of meaningful choice." "Surprise" involves the extent to which the supposedly agreed-upon terms of the bargain are hidden in a prolix printed form drafted by the party seeking to enforce the disputed terms. Characteristically, the form contract is drafted by the party with the superior bargaining position.[44]

In *Williams*, the court states that, ordinarily, one who signs a contract is bound by its provisions, whether or not he has actually read them, and, in general, contract

---

[42] For a defense of paternalism as a legitimate grounds for non-enforcement, see Duncan Kennedy, *Distributive and Paternalist Motives in Contract and Tort Law, with Special Reference to Compulsory Terms and Unequal Bargaining Power*, 41 MD. L. REV. 563 (1982).

[43] For a defense of the unconscionability doctrine on the grounds that it reduces these sorts of externalities, see Eric A. Posner, *Contract Law in the Welfare State: A Defense of the Unconscionability Doctrine, Usury Laws, and Related Limitations on the Freedom to Contract*, 24 J. LEGAL STUD. 283 (1995).

[44] A & M Produce Co. v. FMC Corp., 186 Cal. Rptr. 114 (Cal. Dist. Ct. App. 1982).

law is not concerned with the content of a bargain. The procedural unconscionability doctrine is a departure from these rules. What sorts of evidence would you look for to show that Ms. Williams had no reasonable opportunity to understand the cross-collateral clause? After the decision in *Williams*, won't the store more carefully explain the clause to the next customer? Do you think that alone would satisfy Judge Wright? Would it satisfy the persons who brought the *Williams* case — the legal assistance society of the local bar association?[45]

7. *Cognitive Error as the Justification for the Unconscionability Doctrine.* Gullible or careless people certainly are taken advantage of, but why are they not bilked more often? One answer is that competition in the marketplace sometimes takes care of them. First, if Ms. Williams was unaware of the clause in the Walker-Thomas sales agreement, and had she shopped elsewhere for the stereo, another store (out of self-interest, in order to make the sale) might have told her of the "bad clause" in the Walker-Thomas agreement. Second, assume that 10% of stereo shoppers are gullible and the other 90% are not. If the store wants to print up its sales agreement in advance, it has to decide whether to include the "bad clause." If it does, it loses 90% of its potential customers. If it doesn't need to print the agreement in advance, it must find a way to discover which of its shoppers are gullible, otherwise it will again lose some or all of the 90%. Most stores will find it not to be in their profit-making interest to lose the many in order to bilk the few. If the majority of customers shop at only one store and are gullible, the market will not protect them.[46]

There is, in theory, however, a market condition in which striking down a clause for procedural unconscionability unambiguously enhances consumer welfare without harming sellers. Suppose that although every potential buyer of stereos understands the meaning of a cross-collateral clause, they systematically underrate the costs to them of agreeing to such a clause, perhaps to the extent of discounting the cost of the clause to zero. Why might this happen? It could be that the risk of the clause being invoked against any particular buyer is very small, and that buyers ignore entirely clauses that bear only a small risk. Or it might be that buyers do not like to imagine circumstances in which they might default, and so they treat the possibility of default as trivial.[47] If for either or both of these reasons buyers ignore these clauses, sellers lose no sales by including the clauses. Moreover, if potential stereo buyers shop carefully for the best (money) price of a stereo, the resulting

---

[45] Skilton & Helstad, *Protection of the Installment Buyer of Goods Under the UCC*, 65 MICH. L. REV. 1465 (1967).

[46] *See* Alan Schwartz & Louis Wilde, *Intervening in Markets on the Basis of Imperfect Information: A Legal and Economic Analysis*, 127 U. PA. L. REV. 630 (1979); *see also* Alan Schwartz, *Unconscionability and Imperfect Information: A Research Agenda*, 19 CAN. BUS. L.J. 437 (1991).

[47] For a further discussion of the relevance of such cognitive "errors" to promissory enforcement, see Karen E. Francis, *Rollover, Rollover: A Behavioral Law and Economics Analysis of the Payday-Loan Industry*, 88 TEX. L. REV. 611 (2010); Oren Bar-Gill, *The Behavioral Economics of Consumer Contracts*, 92 MINN. L. REV. 749 (2008); Ronald J. Mann, *Boilerplate in Consumer Contract: "Contracting" for Credit*, 104 MICH. L. REV. 899 (2006); Clayton P. Gillette, *Pre-Approved Contracts for Internet Commerce*, 42 HOUS. L. REV. 975 (2005); Oren Bar-Gill, *Seduction by Plastic*, 98 NW. U. L. REV. 1373 (2004). Melvin Eisenberg, *The Limits of Cognition and the Limits of Contract*, 47 STAN. L. REV. 211 (1995); Robert E. Scott, *Error and Rationality in Individual Decision-Making: An Essay on the Relationship Between Cognitive Illusions and the Management of Choices*, 59 S. CAL. L. REV. 329 (1986).

competition among stereo sellers would force those sellers to offer the lowest price they could and still earn a reasonable return to capital. Competition would force sellers to reduce their stated price for stereos, which they can do by including cross-collateral clauses in the sales agreement. Voiding cross-collateral clauses would then raise stereo prices, but since they were being under-evaluated by consumers, the effect would be to enhance consumer welfare. Stereo sellers would still earn the same return to capital.

A pluralist scholar might be inclined to support the use of unconsionability when the probability of consumers suffering from systematic cognitive error seems high while an economic analyst might be inclined to argue that the assumptions supporting the case for intervention on the grounds of systematic cognitive errors are "strong," and probably not very amenable to empirical verification. How should a policy maker decide what legal rule is best when efficiency and fairness values appear to conflict? Is it better to rely on the market and its assumption of rationality even when the market is imperfect or is it better to rely on courts and legislators to make judgments about protecting individuals from themselves even though these institutions also are imperfect? Consider, for example the following hypothetical:

> Your client, Cliff Welcher, after some reluctance, tells you the following facts:[48] Cliff is 67 years old. He has never been married. Feeling that he has gotten less out of life than he should have, Cliff went to the Vanity Dance Studios for dance lessons. Cliff has had a great time. One of the dance instructors, Doris, is Cliff's personal favorite. While their relationship has never been anything other that strictly instructor/pupil, Cliff looks forward to his dance lessons more than anything else.
>
> Over a period of time, Cliff has signed contracts with Vanity for additional dance lessons. Lessons ordinarily cost $15 per hour. At that rate, if you added up all the contracts for future dance lessons that Cliff has signed, he would have to take seven hours of dance lessons per day until age 83 in order to complete the contracts.
>
> Doris has quit the studio. Cliff wants to know if he can get out of the dance contracts with Vanity. After looking at the contracts and listening to the circumstances of their signings, you are forced to conclude the following: First, the contracts are not conditioned on Doris staying at the Vanity studio. Second, no pressure was brought to bear on Cliff to sign the contracts, other than the fact that he thought (correctly) that Doris would get a commission on the contracts. Third, Cliff comes across as being of average intelligence, with a good awareness of what is going on around him. He has little explanation of why he signed the contracts.

What are the arguments for and against voiding the contract on the grounds of unconscionability?[49]

---

[48] Compare the hypothetical with *Vokes v. Arthur Murray, Inc.*, 212 So. 2d 906 (Fla. Dist. Ct. App. 1968) (finding a duty to disclose pupil's lack of talent).

[49] The court in *Jones v. Star Credit Corp., supra* note 40, talked of a "fraud, which 'may be apparent from the intrinsic nature and subject of the bargain itself; such as no man in his senses and not under delusion would make.'" (quoting Lord Hardwicke in an uncited case from Great Britain).

8. *Unconscionability and Arbitration Clauses.* Unconscionability arguments are not merely raised to challenge the substantive terms of agreements, such as prices or financing procedures. In recent years, due to the rising costs of litigation (and a desire to avoid class action lawsuits), many firms have required their customers and/or franchisees to submit to arbitration in lieu of resolving any disputes via the judicial system. Such requirements are often found in preprinted forms, making it difficult for the parties to bargain around them. Many aggrieved parties who fear that they are being deprived of "their day in court" have consequently chosen to challenge such provisions on the ground of unconscionability.

In *We Care Hair Dev., Inc. v. Engen*, 180 F.3d 838 (7th Cir. 1999), a group of franchisees challenged a contractual provision in their lease that required them to pursue arbitration as a necessary prior condition for commencing any legal action arising out of the franchise arrangement. The parent company, however, could directly pursue eviction proceedings through a subsidiary, We Care Hair Realty, without resorting to arbitration. The court rejected an unconscionability challenge, noting that the franchisees were situated far differently from the plaintiff in *Williams.* The court stated:

> The arbitration clauses in the present case cannot be viewed as creating unfair surprise. Before signing the franchise agreement and the sublease, each franchisee was provided with a copy of the uniform offering circular which clearly disclosed that the leasing company could bring eviction proceedings for any breach of the sublease. . . . Furthermore, the franchisees were "not vulnerable consumers or helpless workers," but rather "business people who bought a franchise." *The Original Great Am. Chocolate Chip Cookie Co., Inc. v. River Valley Cookies, Ltd.*, 970 F.2d 273, 281. We cannot conclude that, in acquiring their franchises, the franchisees were "forced to swallow unpalatable terms."

While arbitration requirements are rarely found to be unconscionable on their face, parties must nonetheless be made aware of the arbitration provision in order for the clause to be enforced. In *Rosenberg v. Merrill Lynch, Pierce, Fenner & Smith, Inc.*, 170 F.3d 1 (1st Cir. 1999), the court refused to hold unconscionable a requirement that prospective employees sign an agreement to arbitrate disputes as a precondition for employment. The agreement covered any disputes arising from the rules of several stock exchanges with which the brokerage conducted business. At the same time, however, the court refused to enforce the agreement in this particular instance because the employee never received a copy of the New York Stock Exchange's rules and procedures. What does this case say about the values that courts are seeking to protect through the unconscionability doctrine? Are unconscionability concerns satisfied if the proponent of disputed terms conspicuously highlights the key clauses — using different size print or bold lettering — in a pre-printed form and perhaps requires a separate signature signifying that the consumer has read the form?

A related practice is the inclusion of forum selection clauses in standard-form contracts; these clauses stipulate that a particular court or forum has exclusive jurisdiction to adjudicate any dispute arising under the contract. Typically, the selected jurisdiction is the one preferred by the party who has drafted the standardized form. In *Carnival Cruise Lines v. Shute*, 499 U.S. 585 (1991), the Supreme Court held upheld as reasonable and enforceable the forum selection clause printed on the back of Carnival's cruise tickets. Citing *Walker-Thomas*, Justice Stevens argued in dissent that the clause should be unenforceable because "courts traditionally have reviewed with heightened scrutiny the terms of contracts of adhesion, form contracts offered on a take-or-leave basis by a party with stronger bargaining power to a party with weaker power." *Id.* at 600.

9. *Class Wide Arbitration and Federal Law*. Class actions allow a group of similarly situated individuals to bring a single suit for damages. Often in these cases any individual's harm is not sufficiently large to warrant bringing suit (or to motivate a lawyer to bring a suit on his or her client's behalf). By certifying as a class the damages can be aggregated and any resulting lawyer's fee will be sufficiently large to justify the action. This allows the legal system to redress small but widely shared harms. Class proceedings can also proceed via arbitration. What if a contract specifically requires arbitration but prohibits class arbitration. Could this contract be struck down as unconscionable?

In *Discover Bank v. Superior Court*, 113 P.3d 1100 (Cal. 2005), the California Supreme Court found such "class action waiver" clauses to be unconscionable when "the waiver is found in a consumer contract of adhesion in a setting in which disputes between the contracting parties predictably involve small amounts of damages, and when it is alleged that the party with the superior bargaining power has carried out a scheme to deliberately cheat large numbers of consumers out of individually small sums of money." This rule was abrogated by the United States Supreme Court in *AT&T Mobility LLC v. Concepcion*, 131 S. Ct. 1740 (2011). The Court held that the California rule conflicted with federal law. Specifically, the Federal Arbitration Act prohibited states from declaring that class action waivers were unconscionable per se. How might this decision affect the viability of class action litigation?

10. *Unconscionability Under the UCC: How Should Courts Fix an Unconscionable Term?* Read § 2-302 of the UCC and the comments to that section. Two important questions stand out First, what exactly does "unconscionablity" mean? Note that Comment 1 mentions both "unfair surprise" and "oppression," but it does not elaborate on these concepts. Is it possible to define the meaning of these terms more precisely so as to rebut those scholars who argue that unconscionability is an ambiguous and ill-defined invitation to judicial intervention in private contracts?[50] Second, what should a court do once it finds a particular term unfair? Assume that a particular term (rather than the entire contract) is struck down as unconscionable, what term should be substituted in place of the unfair one? Professor Omri Ben Shahar argues that that courts should (and in fact do) chose the term that preserves the original term as much as is tolerable rather than selecting a "reasonable" term. Do you agree? For more, see Omri Ben Shahar, *Fixing Unfair Contracts*, 63 STAN. L. REV. 869 (2011).

---

[50] For discussion, see Robert A. Hillman, *Debunking Some Myths About Unconscionability: A New Framework for U.C.C. Section 2-302*, 67 CORNELL L. REV. 1 (1981).

D. PERFORMANCE OF THE OBLIGATION

[1] Introduction to the Idiosyncratic Bargainer

We have seen that courts will not enforce a promise if a reasonable person would not consider the representation to be a promise. We have suggested that one argument for placing this burden on the "unreasonable" or idiosyncratic party is that then typical parties can negotiate and bargain without taking any special precautions to make sure that their understanding is shared by others. This result has the advantage of reducing "friction" in the bargaining process. The idiosyncratic party bears the costs of such a system since he must take special care to signal adequately his beliefs to others. When he is making a special contract, what must the idiosyncratic party do to make sure his preferences are clear? The next case raises this issue, and others.

JACOB & YOUNGS, INC. v. KENT
Court of Appeals of New York
230 N.Y. 239, 129 N.E. 889 (1921)

CARDOZO, J.

The plaintiff built a country residence for the defendant at a cost of upwards of $77,000, and now sues to recover a balance of $3,483.46, remaining unpaid. The work of construction ceased in June, 1914, and the defendant then began to occupy the dwelling. There was no complaint of defective performance until March, 1915. One of the specifications for the plumbing work provides that ("all wrought iron pipe must be well galvanized, lap welded pipe of the grade known as 'standard pipe' of Reading manufacture.") The defendant learned in March, 1915, that some of the pipe, instead of being made in Reading, was the product of other factories. The plaintiff was accordingly directed by the architect to do the work anew. The plumbing was then encased within the walls except in a few places where it had to be exposed. Obedience to the order meant more than the substitution of other pipe. It meant the demolition at great expense of substantial parts of the completed structure. The plaintiff left the work untouched, and asked for a certificate that the final payment was due. Refusal of the certificate was followed by this suit.

The evidence sustains a finding that the omission of the prescribed brand of pipe was neither fraudulent nor willful. It was the result of the oversight and inattention of the plaintiff's subcontractor. Reading pipe is distinguished from Cohoes pipe and other brands only by the name of the manufacturer stamped upon it at intervals of between six and seven feet. Even the defendant's architect, though he inspected the pipe upon arrival, failed to notice the discrepancy. The plaintiff tried to show that the brands installed, though made by other manufacturers, were the same in quality, in appearance, in market value and in cost as the brand stated in the contract — that they were, indeed, the same thing, though manufactured in another place. The evidence was excluded, and a verdict directed for the defendant. The Appellate Division reversed, and granted a new trial.

We think the evidence, if admitted, would have supplied some basis for the inference that the defect was insignificant in its relation to the project. The courts never say that one who makes a contract fills the measure of his duty by less than full performance. They do say, however, that an omission, both trivial and innocent, will sometimes be atoned for by allowance of the resulting damage, and will not always be the breach of a condition to be followed by a forfeiture (Spence v. Ham, 163 N.Y. 220; Woodward v. Fuller, 80 N.Y. 312; Glacius v. Black, 67 N.Y. 563, 566; Bowen v. Kimbell, 203 Mass. 364, 370). The distinction is akin to that between dependent and independent promises, or between promises and conditions. Some promises are so plainly independent that they can never by fair construction be conditions of one another. Others are so plainly dependent that they must always be conditions. Others, though dependent and thus conditions when there is departure in point of substance, will be viewed as independent and collateral when the departure is insignificant. Considerations partly of justice and partly of presumable intention are to tell us whether this or that promise shall be placed in one class or in another. The simple and the uniform will call for different remedies from the multifarious and the intricate. The margin of departure within the range of normal expectation upon a sale of common chattels will vary from the margin to be expected upon a contract for the construction of a mansion or a "skyscraper." There will be harshness sometimes and oppression in the implication of a condition when the thing upon which labor has been expended is incapable of surrender because united to the land, and equity and reason in the implication of a like condition when the subject-matter, if defective, is in shape to be returned. From the conclusion that promises may not be treated as dependent to the extent of their uttermost minutiae without a sacrifice of justice, the progress is a short one to the conclusion that they may not be so treated without a perversion of intention. Intention not otherwise revealed may be presumed to hold in contemplation the reasonable and probable. If something else is in view, it must not be left to implication. There will be no assumption of a purpose to visit venial faults with oppressive retribution.

Those who think more of symmetry and logic in the development of legal rules than of practical adaptation to the attainment of a just result will be troubled by a classification where the lines of division are so wavering and blurred. Something, doubtless, may be said on the score of consistency and certainty in favor of a stricter standard. The courts have balanced such considerations against those of equity and fairness, and found the latter to be the weightier. The decisions in this state commit us to the liberal view, which is making its way, nowadays, in jurisdictions slow to welcome it. Where the line is to be drawn between the important and the trivial cannot be settled by a formula. "In the nature of the case precise boundaries are impossible" (2 *Williston on Contracts*, § 841). The same omission may take on one aspect or another according to its setting. Substitution of equivalents may not have the same significance in fields of art on the one side and in those of mere utility on the other. Nowhere will change be tolerated, however, if it is so dominant or pervasive as in any real or substantial measure to frustrate the purpose of the contract. There is no general license to install whatever, in the builder's judgment, may be regarded as "just as good." The question is one of degree, to be answered, if there is doubt, by the triers of the facts, and, if the inferences are certain, by the judges of the law. We must weigh the purpose to be served, the desire to be gratified, the excuse for deviation from the letter, the cruelty of enforced adherence. Then only can we tell whether literal fulfillment is to be implied by law as a condition. This is not to say that the parties are not free by apt and certain words to effectuate a purpose that performance of every term shall be a condition of recovery. That question is not here. This is merely to say that the law will be slow to impute the purpose, in the silence of the parties, where the significance of the default is grievously out of proportion to the oppression of the forfeiture. The willful transgressor must accept the penalty of his transgression. For him there is no occasion to mitigate the rigor of implied conditions. The transgressor whose default is unintentional and trivial may hope for mercy if he will offer atonement for his wrong.

In the circumstances of this case, we think the measure of the allowance is not the cost of replacement, which would be great, but the difference in value, which would be either nominal or nothing. Some of the exposed sections might perhaps have been replaced at moderate expense. The defendant did not limit his demand to them, but treated the plumbing as a unit to be corrected from cellar to roof. In point of fact, the plaintiff never reached the stage at which evidence of the extent of the allowance became necessary. The trial court had excluded evidence that the defect was unsubstantial, and in view of that ruling there was no occasion for the plaintiff to go farther with an offer of proof. We think, however, that the offer, if it had been made, would not of necessity have been defective because directed to difference in value. It is true that in most cases the cost of replacement is the measure. The owner is entitled to the money which will permit him to complete, unless the cost of completion is grossly and unfairly out of proportion to the good to be attained. When that is true, the measure is the difference in value. Specifications call, let us say, for a foundation built of granite quarried in Vermont. On the completion of the building, the owner learns that through the blunder of a subcontractor part of the foundation has been built of granite of the same quality quarried in New Hampshire. The measure of allowance is not the cost of reconstruction. "There may be omissions of that which could not afterwards be supplied exactly as called for by the contract without taking down the building to its foundations, and at the same time the omission may not affect the value of the building for use or otherwise, except so slightly as to be hardly appreciable." Handy v. Bliss, 204 Mass. 513, 519. The rule that gives a remedy in cases of substantial performance with compensation for defects of trivial or inappreciable importance, has been developed by the courts as an instrument of justice. The measure of the allowance must be shaped to the same end.

The order should be affirmed, and judgment absolute directed in favor of the plaintiff upon the stipulation, with costs in all courts.

McLaughlin, J. (dissenting).

I dissent. The plaintiff did not perform its contract. Its failure to do so was either intentional or due to gross neglect which, under the uncontradicted facts, amounted to the same thing, nor did it make any proof of the cost of compliance, where compliance was possible.

Under its contract it obligated itself to use in the plumbing only pipe (between 2,000 and 2,500 feet) made by the Reading Manufacturing Company. The first pipe delivered was about 1,000 feet and the plaintiff's superintendent then called the attention of the foreman of the subcontractor, who was doing the plumbing, to the fact that the specifications annexed to the contract required all pipe used in the plumbing to be of the Reading Manufacturing Company. They then examined it for the purpose of ascertaining whether this delivery was of that manufacture and found it was. Thereafter, as pipe was required in the progress of the work, the foreman of the subcontractor would leave word at its shop that he wanted a specified number of feet of pipe, without in any way indicating of what manufacture. Pipe would thereafter be delivered and installed in the building, without any examination whatever. Indeed, no examination, so far as appears, was made by the plaintiff, the subcontractor, defendant's architect, or any one else, of any of the pipe except the first delivery, until after the building had been completed. Plaintiff's architect then refused to give the certificate of completion, upon which the final payment depended, because all of the pipe used in the plumbing was not of the kind called for by the contract. After such refusal, the subcontractor removed the covering or insulation from about 900 feet of pipe which was exposed in the basement, cellar and attic, and all but 70 feet was found to have been manufactured, not by the Reading Company, but by other manufacturers, some by the Cohoes Rolling Mill Company, some by the National Steel Works, some by the South Chester Tubing Company, and some which bore no manufacturer's mark at all. The balance of the pipe had been so installed in the building that an inspection of it could not be had without demolishing, in part at least, the building itself.

I am of the opinion the trial court was right in directing a verdict for the defendant. The plaintiff agreed that all the pipe used should be of the Reading Manufacturing Company. Only about two-fifths of it, so far as appears, was of that kind. If more were used, then the burden of proving that fact was upon the plaintiff, which it could easily have done, since it knew where the pipe was obtained. The question of substantial performance of a contract of the character of the one under consideration depends in no small degree upon the good faith of the contractor. If the plaintiff had intended to, and had complied with the terms of the contract except as to minor omissions, due to inadvertence, then he might be allowed to recover the contract price, less the amount necessary to fully compensate the defendant for damages caused by such omissions. But that is not this case. It installed between 2,000 and 2,500 feet of pipe, of which only 1,000 feet at most complied with the contract. No explanation was given why pipe called for by the contract was not used, nor was any effort made to show what it would cost to remove the pipe of other manufacturers and install that of the Reading Manufacturing Company. The defendant had a right to contract for what he wanted. He had a right before making payment to get what the contract called for. It is no answer to this suggestion to say that the pipe put in was just as good as that made by the Reading Manufacturing Company, or that the difference in value between such pipe and the pipe made by the Reading Manufacturing Company would be either "nominal or nothing." Defendant contracted for pipe made by the Reading Manufacturing Company. What his reason was for requiring this kind of pipe is of no importance. He wanted that and was entitled to it. It may have been a mere whim on his part, but even so, he had a right to this kind of pipe, regardless of whether some other kind, according to the opinion of the contractor or experts, would have been "just as good, better, or done just as well." He agreed to pay only upon condition that the pipe installed were made by that company and he ought not to be compelled to pay unless that condition be performed. The rule, therefore, of substantial performance, with damages for unsubstantial omissions, has no application.

What was said by this court in Smith v. Brady [17 N.Y. 173] is quite applicable here:

> I suppose it will be conceded that everyone has a right to build his house, his cottage or his store after such a model and in such style as shall best accord with his notions of utility or be most agreeable to his fancy. The specifications of the contract become the law between the parties until voluntarily changed. If the owner prefers a plain and simple Doric column, and has so provided in the agreement, the contractor has no right to put in its place the more costly and elegant Corinthian. If the owner, having regard to strength and durability, has contracted for walls of specified materials to be laid in a particular manner, or for a given number of joists and beams, the builder has no right to substitute his own judgment or that of others. Having departed from the agreement, if performance has not been waived by the other party, the law will not allow him to allege that he has made as good a building as the one he engaged to erect. He can demand payment only upon and according to the terms of his contract, and if the conditions on which payment is due have not been performed, then the right to demand it does not exist. To hold a different doctrine would be simply to make another contract, and would be giving to parties an encouragement to violate their engagements, which the just policy of the law does not permit.

I am of the opinion the trial court did not err in ruling on the admission of evidence or in directing a verdict for the defendant.

NOTES

1. ***Conditions and Dependent Promises.*** Justice Cardozo writes on the one hand about conditions and on the other hand about dependent and independent promises. A simple example may help you to begin to understand these categories. Suppose that I contract to sell you my Hasselblad camera on October 1st for $1,500. I show up on October 1st without the camera, saying "I didn't have time to pick up the camera, but give me the money." Do you breach if you don't give me the money? If not, it is because the promises are dependent. Your duty to perform (pay) is dependent on my performing (delivering the camera). Also, my duty to perform is dependent on your performance. Alternatively, the result could be put in terms of conditions. Your duty to perform (pay) is conditioned on my performing my part of the bargain.

It is said that the doctrine of "substantial performance" is applicable to construction contracts. Does Cardozo think so? How does substantial performance fit into the categories of conditions and dependent/independent promises?

2. ***Standards of Performance.*** "Perfect tender" and "substantial performance" are two standards of performance used for different kinds of contracts. For sales of goods, the "perfect tender" rule applies; that is, a buyer of goods can "reject" the goods (and thereby avoid having to pay for them) for any defect, however minor. *See*

UCC § 2-601. Perfect tender thus purports to provide the promisee a clear and definitive yardstick against which to measure the seller's performance.[51] On the other hand, the substantial performance doctrine, which typically applies to service and construction contracts, embodies a general standard rather than a bright-line rule. It permits a party to withhold his own performance only when the defect *materially impairs* the essence of what was contracted for. Or put another way, under the substantial performance test, a promisee is required to tender the return performance if the promisor has provided a "substantial performance" together with damages for any unsubstantial omissions.

Is there something special about contracts for the sale of goods that warrants this difference in treatment? Since "perfect tender" is much easier to apply in any particular case than "substantial performance," why not use it as the default rule in all contracts? Cardozo tries to explain the distinction this way: "There will be harshness sometimes and oppression in the implication of a condition when the thing upon which labor has been expended is incapable of surrender because united to the land, and equity and reason in the implication of a like condition when the subject matter, if defective, is in shape to be returned." What is the "harshness and oppression" Cardozo fears if a perfect tender rule were applied in construction contracts generally? For one explanation, see Charles J. Goetz & Robert E. Scott, *The Mitigation Principle: Toward a General Theory of Contractual Obligation*, 69 VA. L. REV. 967, 995–97, 1009–11 (1983).

3.   *Substantial Performance and Strategic Behavior.* In his opinion, Justice Cardozo emphasizes the high cost that Jacob & Youngs would incur to replace the piping in the house after construction. He says nothing, however, about the cost of *preventing* the mistake in the first place. When the piping was first being installed, it was cheap — and more importantly, efficient — to avoid breach of the contract. All Jacob & Youngs had to do was inspect the pipe. Should courts, in determining the remedy, look at this preliminary cost rather than the cost to fix the mistake ex-post? In fact, doesn't the doctrine of "economic waste" encourage builders to shirk their contractual duties when breach will only lead to a trivial loss in value but a high ex-post replacement cost? Some scholars have argued for alternative remedies:

> In the cases that courts commonly see, it is efficient to take the contractually required action assuming the precaution is taken, but it is inefficient to take the action otherwise. Courts that strive to avoid ex post wealth transfers award low damages [difference in market value] . . . in these cases . . . Current law thus exacerbates the parties' problem rather than relieves it: The law should impose a high sanction for breach when the buyer cannot fully help himself [by ensuring that the precaution is taken], but the law instead imposes a low sanction.

Alan Schwartz & Robert E. Scott, *Market Damages, Efficient Contracting, and the Economic Waste Fallacy*, 108 COLUM. L. REV. 1610, 1656 (2008).

---

[51] Even the perfect tender rule is subject to some qualifications that limit the buyer's freedom to reject nonconforming goods. See, e.g., § 2-508 which describes the seller's right to "cure" its defective tender in two limited circumstances.

Cardozo's solution for preventing such strategic behavior is to award to the buyer the difference in value only when the builder's breach is not willful. Yet how does a court determine whether or not a breach is willful? Unless someone is constantly monitoring the builder (and such monitoring is costly), evidence may be sparse. Nevertheless, is any other solution better? Schwartz and Scott suggest awarding the buyer the cost of completion. While their solution will discourage strategic breaches, does it offer any protection for builders who make an honest mistake? Note that in this case the architect refused to give the builders a certificate of completion. Is that because the architect believed that the breach was willful? Why doesn't Cardozo consider this? For further analysis of how contract law controls such strategic behavior by the parties, see George Cohen, *The Fault Lines in Contract Damages*, 80 VA. L. REV. 1225 (1994).

4. ***Default Rules, "Presumed Intentions," and Opting Out.*** Cardozo holds that, in the case of construction contracts, the parties will be presumed to have agreed to measure the contractor's performance by the standard of substantial performance rather than the more exacting standard that prevails in other contexts, such as the sale of goods. But he also states that "this is not to say that the parties are not free by apt and certain words to effectuate a purpose that performance of *every* term shall be a condition of recovery." In order to resolve cases such as *Jacobs & Youngs*, therefore, two key issues must be addressed. The first question is what default rule should the court select to fill the gap whenever the parties have not specifically agreed on the standard of performance that should govern their contract. Is the best default in construction contracts the rule of substantial performance, or the sales law rule of perfect tender (*see, e.g.*, UCC § 2-601), or perhaps a third alternative?[52] How does Cardozo answer this question? The second issue is whether the parties have "opted out" of the default rule by "apt and certain words" that signify a contrary understanding. In other words, did the parties sufficiently specify that supplying Reading Pipe is "a condition of recovery"? How are these two issues different? Consider the following three cases.

a. Ken signs a contract for a special order Erick Carlson SAAB 900 Turbo, 5-speed, racing cam, oversize pistons, sunroof, Pirelli tires, etc. When the car arrives, it has Michelin tires on it. Michelin tires cost the same as Pirelli tires do, and they have the same performance ratings. The Pirelli tires are hard to get because of troubles in Italy. Can Ken refuse delivery? If not,[53] the promise to provide Pirelli tires and his promise to pay for the car are independent.

b. Christy hires a painter to paint a portrait of her dog, Jack, a bearded collie. The finished picture looks like a miniature schnauzer. The painter insists that Christy must pay for the portrait because the market price for a schnauzer portrait is higher than for a portrait of Jack. If Christy does not have to pay, it is because her promise to pay is conditioned on receiving a portrait that looks like her dog.

c. Mr. and Mrs. Kant contracted with a builder for a new house. The Kants

---

[52] For an argument that courts should often fill the gap with the term that is most favorable to the party with the greater bargaining power, see Omri Ben-Shahar, *A Bargaining Power Theory of Default Rules*, 109 COLUM. L. REV. 396 (2009).

[53] Do not presume that this is the result that a court would reach.

specified that all the pipe in the house must carry a "union-made" label because Mr. Kant's late father was president of the pipefitters union. The builder hears the reason and agrees to install only union-label pipe. When there is $5,000 still owing on the price of the house, the Kants learn that half the pipe is nonunion made. The Kants refuse to pay the remainder of the price. If the Kants don't have to pay, it is because their promise to pay is conditioned on union-label pipe being installed.

How would you analyze these three cases? Are they the same? How do they differ?

How would Cardozo decide the case of the Kants' union-label pipe? How important is it that the Kants told the builder why union-label pipe was important to them? In *Jacob & Youngs*, Kent cared enough to specify Reading pipe, yet he is forced to be content with Cohoes. Cardozo wrote, "Intention not otherwise revealed may be presumed to hold in contemplation the reasonable and probable. If something else is in view, it must not be left to implication." Why does he say this?

5.   *How Difficult Is it to Signal Intensity of Preference by Opting Out?* Suppose Kent intended to make this house a "Reading pipe showcase." Write the contract language for the pipe specification to replace the one reproduced by Cardozo in his opinion. Would the following language suffice?

> Any work furnished by the Contractor, the material or workmanship of which is defective or which is not fully in accordance with the drawings and specifications, in every respect, will be rejected and is to be immediately torn down, removed and remade or replaced in accordance with the drawings and specifications, whenever discovered. . . . The Owner will have the option at all times to allow the defective or improper work to stand and to receive from the Contractor a sum of money equivalent to the difference in value of the work as performed and as herein specified.

According to the record on appeal in *Jacob & Youngs*, this clause was in the contract in that case. Would a reasonable contractor believe that this clause meant that any defect could be used to force him to tear out nonconforming materials? If the clause does not mean that, presumably it doesn't have any effect at all. Would that be proper? Can you draft a clause that is more likely to accomplish the Kents' purpose?

In denying a motion for rehearing in *Jacob & Youngs*, the court of appeals ruled:

> PER CURIAM.

> The court did not overlook the specification which provides that defective work shall be replaced. The promise to replace, like the promise to install, is to be viewed, not as a condition, but as independent and collateral, when the defect is trivial and innocent. The law does not nullify the covenant, but restricts the remedy to damages.

230 N.Y. 656 (1921).

6.   *The Justification for Default Rules in Contract.* What is the justification for a court "presuming the intentions" of the parties when the parties have not, in fact, indicated what their intentions are? When we discussed the problem of indefinite agreements earlier, we saw that courts are reluctant to fill in gaps in agreements where they have no plausible grounds for knowing what the parties would have agreed to had they been required to negotiate over the issue in dispute. If that is so, on what basis can courts fill gaps in contracts with legal default rules that presumably apply to large populations of contracting parties?

[2]   Allocating Risks

One way of addressing the question of why people exchange promises as opposed to simply exchanging goods, services and the like, is to think about the question in terms of risk. Suppose that you want to go on vacation at the beach for a week. Among other things, you have to board your dog at a kennel and find a rental cottage at the beach. Why will you call the kennel in advance to make a reservation, and call the rental cottage owner as well? The risks inherent in waiting for the first day of vacation and buying space in the kennel and in the cottage are that the kennel may be full, the cottage rented, or the prices may be greater than you anticipated. The risks of contracting in advance for the kennel and the cottage include the possibility that something will come up and you will be unable to go, or that at the time the vacation begins, the prices are lower than what you contracted for. When you enter into contracts with the kennel and the cottage owner, you are exchanging risks with each of them. If a regret contingency materializes (e.g., something comes up and you can't go), and you forfeit your deposit on the cottage, the resulting loss is the cost to you of making an executory contract.

If contracts sometimes cause parties to suffer losses, why do we permit parties to make and enforce them? The answer, of course, is that the risks of contracting are believed to be less than the risks the parties would bear in the absence of any contract. Before entering into the contract you were subject to a batch of risks, after entering into the contract you had a slightly different, and presumably less onerous, set of risks.

This section, and the next, take up the questions of why contracting parties exchange some risks but not others, and how courts approach questions of risk allocation when the parties have not signaled explicitly what risks have been exchanged.

STEES v. LEONARD
Supreme Court of Minnesota
20 Minn. 494 (1874)

[The defendants entered into a sealed contract with the plaintiffs "to build, erect and complete" a building on the plaintiffs' lot, located in St. Paul on Minnesota Street between Third and Fourth Streets, The contract provided detailed specifications and plans for the building. The builders commenced work and had raised the structure to a height of three stories when it collapsed. They began construction again and had progressed to the third story when the building fell to the ground again. Their difficulties were caused by soft soil at the construction site. The ground was composed of quicksand and became unstable whenever water flowed into it. The builders did not discover the problem with the soil until after they had completed the written contract and had begun excavation for the cellar and foundation. The builders abandoned the project after the second collapse of the building and refused to perform the contract.

The plaintiffs sued the builders, seeking $5,215 damages for payments already made to the defendants and for losses caused by the fall of the building as well as an unreported amount of damages for the builders' failure to complete construction. The builders responded that they had carefully followed the specifications in the contract and that the structure's collapse was caused by the soil rather than by any fault of their own. The defendants also argued that the plaintiffs selected the precise spot on the lot for construction, and therefore they had a duty to act reasonably and select a spot that could support the proposed structure. The jury found for the plaintiffs, and the builders appealed from an order of the district court denying their motion for a new trial.]

Young, J.

The general principle of law which underlies this case is well established. If a man bind himself, by a positive, express contract, to do an act in itself possible, he must perform his engagement, unless prevented by the act of God, the law, or the other party to the contract. No hardship, no unforeseen hindrance, no difficulty short of absolute impossibility, will excuse him from doing what he has expressly agreed to do. This doctrine may sometimes seem to bear heavily upon contractors; but, in such cases, the hardship is attributable, not to the law, but to the contractor himself, who has improvidently assumed an absolute, when he might have undertaken only a qualified liability. The law does no more than enforce the contract as the parties themselves have made it. . . .

The rule has been applied in several recent cases, closely analogous to the present in their leading facts. In Adams v. Nichols, 10 Pick. 275, the defendant, Nichols, contracted to erect a dwelling house for plaintiff on plaintiff's land. The house was nearly completed, when it was destroyed by accidental fire. It was held that the casualty did not relieve the contractor from his obligation to perform the contract he had deliberately entered into. The court clearly states and illustrates the rule, as laid down in the note to Walton v. Waterhouse, 2 Wms. Saunders, 422, and add: "In these and similar cases, which seem hard and oppressive, the law does no more than enforce the exact contract entered into. If there be any hardship, it arises from the indiscretion or want of foresight of the suffering party. It is not the province of the law to relieve persons from the improvidence of their own acts."

School Trustees v. Bennett, 3 Dutcher, 513, is almost identical, in its material facts, with the present case. The contractors agreed to build and complete a school-house, and find all materials therefor, according to specifications annexed to the contract; the building to be located on a lot owned by plaintiff, and designated in the contract. When the building was nearly completed it was blown down by a sudden and violent gale of wind. The contractors again began to erect the building, when it fell, solely on account of the soil on which it stood having become soft and miry, and unable to sustain the weight of the building; although, when the foundations were laid, the soil was so hard as to be penetrated with difficulty by a pickax, and its defects were latent. The plaintiff had a verdict for the amount of the installments paid under the contract as the work progressed. The verdict was sustained by the supreme court, which held that the loss, although arising solely from a latent defect in the soil, and not from a faulty construction of the building, must fall on the contractor.

In the opinion of the court, the question is fully examined, many cases are cited, and the rule is stated "that where a party by his own contract creates a duty or charge upon himself he is bound to make it good if he may, notwithstanding any accident by inevitable necessity, because he might have provided against it by his contract. . . . If, before the building is completed or accepted, it is destroyed by fire or other casualty, the loss falls upon the builder; he must rebuild. The thing may be done, and he has contracted to do it. . . . No matter how harsh and apparently unjust in its operation the rule may occasionally be, it cannot be denied that it has its foundations in good sense and inflexible honesty. He that agrees to do an act should do it, unless absolutely impossible. He should provide against contingencies in his contract. Where one of two innocent persons must sustain a loss, the law casts it upon him who has agreed to sustain it; or, rather, the law leaves it where the agreement of the parties has put it. . . . Neither the destruction of the incomplete building by a tornado, nor its falling by a latent softness of the soil, which rendered the foundation insecure, *necessarily* prevented the performance of the contract to build, erect, and complete this building for the specified price. It can still be done, for aught that was opened to the jury as a defense, and overruled by the court."

In Dermott v. Jones, 2 Wall. 1, the foundation of the building sank, owing to a latent defect in the soil, and the owner was compelled to take down and rebuild a portion of the work. The contractor having sued for his pay, it was held that the owner might recoup the damages sustained by his deviation from the contract. The Court refer with approval to the cases cited, and say: "The principle which controlled them rests upon a solid foundation of reason and justice. It regards the sanctity of contracts. It requires a party to do what he has agreed to do. If unexpected impediments lie in the way, and a loss ensue, it leaves the loss where the contract places it. If the parties have made no provision for a dispensation, the rule of law gives none. It does not allow a contract fairly made to be annulled, and it does not permit to be interpolated what the parties themselves have not stipulated."

Nothing can be added to the clear and cogent arguments we have quoted in vindication of the wisdom and justice of the rule which must govern this case, unless it is in some way distinguishable from the cases cited. [. . .]

It is argued that the spot on which the building is to be erected is not designated with precision in the contract, but is left to be selected by the owner; that, under the contract, the right to designate the particular spot being reserved to plaintiffs, they must select one that will sustain the building described in the specifications, and if the spot they select is not, in its natural state, suitable, they must make it so. . . .

The contract does not, perhaps, designate the site of the proposed building with absolute certainty; but in this particular it is aided by the pleadings. . . . The [defendants'] answer expressly admits that the defendants entered into a contract to erect the building, according to the plans, etc., "on that certain piece of land in said complaint described," and that they "entered upon the performance of said contract, and proceeded with the erection of said building," etc. This is an express admission that the contract was made with reference to the identical piece of land on which the defendants afterwards attempted to perform it, and leaves no foundation in fact for the defendants' argument.

It is no defense to the action that the specifications directed that "footings" should be used as the foundation of the building, and that the defendants, in the construction of these footings, as well as in all other particulars, conformed to the specifications. The defendants contracted to "erect and complete the building." Whatever was necessary to be done in order to complete the building, they were bound by the contract to do. If the building could not be completed without other or stronger foundations than the footings specified, they were bound to furnish such other foundations. If the building could not be erected without draining the land, then they must drain the land, "because they have agreed to do everything necessary to erect and complete the building." 3 Dutcher, 520. . . .

[The court rejected defendants' other assignments of error.]

There was, therefore, no error in the exclusion of the evidence offered, and the order appealed from is affirmed.

NOTES

1. ***Allocating the Risks in*** **Stees.** According to the court, the builders should have reinforced the building's foundation and drained the land, although the contract only expressly required the builder to conform with the plaintiffs' plans and specifications. In this result, does the owner get more than he "deserves"? On the one hand, if the builder is released, the owner is not getting his building at the price at which he contracted to pay. On the other hand, if the builder is not excused, the owner is getting a building at a price at which he could not have contracted for had the facts of the quicksand been known.

The decision of what steps each party must take to perform a contract is thus a risk allocation question. The issue at stake is who should bear the risk of the unanticipated circumstances that cause one or both parties to regret having entered into the contract. Why does the court impose the risk of a defect in the soil on the builders? The court suggests that the builders bear the risk because they could have provided otherwise in the contract by qualifying or limiting their liability. If the court had decided the case in favor of the builders, could it have said the same thing about the plaintiffs' ability to write in terms limiting the losses they bear? Consider these same questions in the context of the following note case.

2. **Paradine v. Jane.** The defendant in *Paradine v. Jane*, Aleyn 26, 82 Eng. Rep. 897 (K.B. 1647), leased a house from the plaintiff for a term of four years. During the term of the lease, the armies of Prince Rupert invaded the region and expelled the lessee from the property. Consequently, the lessee stopped paying rent, and the lessor brought suit to recover three years of back payments. There was no provision in the contract expressly allocating the risk. The issue before the court was whether the lessee's duty to pay rent was dependent upon his possession of the property. In answering that question, the court said:

> [W]hen the party by his own contract creates a duty or charge upon himself, he is bound to make it good, if he may, notwithstanding any

accident by inevitable necessity, because he might have provided against it by his contract. And therefore if the lessee covenant to repair a house, though it be burnt by lightning, or thrown down by enemies, yet he ought to repair it. Dyer 33.a. 40 E.3. 6. h. . . . Another reason was added, that as the lessee is to have the advantage of casual profits, so he must run the hazard of casual losses, and not lay the whole burthen of them upon his lessor; and Dyer 56.6 was cited for this purpose, that though the land be surrounded, or gained by the sea, or made barren by wildfire, yet the lessor shall have his whole rent: and judgment was given for the plaintiff.

Id. at 27–28, 82 Eng. Rep. at 897–98.

The court in *Paradine* implied into the contract a covenant (promise) to pay rent which was not dependent on the lessee's possession of the house. As in *Stees*, the court provided a term that was lacking in the parties' express promises. Why did the court imply an independent covenant in *Paradine*? (Think of this again in terms of risk allocation.) The court also said in an earlier part of the opinion, "[I]f a house be destroyed by tempest, or by enemies, the lessee is excused." *Id.* at 27, 82 Eng. Rep. at 897. Why is destruction of the house sufficient to excuse the lessee from paying rent while an invasion is not?

3. ***The* Spearin *Doctrine.*** *Stees* suggests that, when a contracting party has expressly agreed to perform a task, ordinarily it must do so, regardless of what hardships may arise. If the performing party is distressed with that prospect, it can (and should) allocate expressly the risks of such potential hardships while negotiating the contract. But what happens if one party is contractually bound to perform according to the detailed specifications of the other party and the specifications themselves are defective? Such a situation occurs when a private party contracts with the government according to government specifications. Consider *United States v. Spearin*, 248 U.S. 132 (1918), where a contractor agreed to build a dry-dock in a naval yard, subject to governmental specifications. The work was jeopardized by a sewer which burst from increased water pressure due to a dam within the sewer. Government officials were aware that the sewer had overflowed in the past, but did not inform the contractor. Governmental maps did not indicate the presence of the dam within the sewer; instead, they presented the sewer as unobstructed. The damage from the sewer forced the contractor to withdraw from the project until the sewer problem was remedied.

The Supreme Court, in finding for the contractor, emphasized the fact that the contractor was required to follow the government's specifications. Justice Brandeis noted:

[I]f the contractor is bound to build according to plans and specifications prepared by the owner, the contractor will not be responsible for the consequences of defects in the plans and specifications . . . [T]he sewer, as well as the other structures, was to be built in accordance with the plans and specifications furnished by the Government. . . . The risk of the existing system proving adequate might have rested upon Spearin, if the contract for the dry-dock had not contained the provision for relocation of the 6-foot sewer. But the insertion of the articles prescribing the character, dimensions and location of the sewer imported a warranty that, if the specifications were complied with, the sewer would be adequate. This implied warranty is not overcome by the general clauses requiring the contractor to examine the site, to check up the plans, and to assume responsibility for the work until completion and acceptance. The obligation to examine the site did not impose upon him the duty of making a diligent enquiry into the history of the locality with a view to determining, at his peril, whether the sewer specifically prescribed by the Government would prove adequate.

Id. at 136–37.

For contemporary applications of the *Spearin* doctrine, see *Blake Constr. Co. v. United States*, 987 F.2d 743 (Fed. Cir. 1993) (differentiates between design specifications, which indicate in precise detail the manner in which the work is to be performed, and thus carry a *Spearin* implied warranty, and performance specifications, which merely specify the ultimate objective); *USA Petroleum Corp. v. United States*, 821 F.2d 622 (Fed. Cir. 1987) (contractor not liable for complying with contractual terms requiring it to use defective strapping tables provided by government); and *Rhone Poulenc Rorer Pharms. v. Newman Glass Works*, 112 F.3d 695 (3d Cir. 1997) (contractor liable because provision in contract creating express warranty that work would be free from defects trumps implied *Spearin* warranty).

4. ***Reasons for Explicit Risk Allocation.*** Parties allocate risks explicitly in their contracts, in part to protect against unforeseen contingencies, and partly to protect themselves against potentially opportunistic behavior by their contractual partners. Thus, clauses that allocate risks often serve as incentives designed to motivate or constrain certain types of behavior.

For an illustration of this effect, see *Industrial Representatives v. CP Clare Corp.*, 74 F.3d 128 (7th Cir. 1996). IRI entered into a contract to promote CP Clare's electronic products. The contract contained a termination clause requiring CP Clare to give 30 days notice prior to terminating the contract. Under the clause, IRI was entitled to a commission on all products ordered before the termination date that were delivered within 90 days. CP Clare's profits greatly exceeded expectations, and, pursuant to the contractual terms, they terminated the contract. IRI sued for compensation above and beyond the contractually specified commissions for its role in boosting CP Clare's sales. Judge Easterbrook rejected this claim, noting:

No one, least of all IRI, could have thought that a contract permitting termination on 30 days' notice, with payment of commissions for deliveries within 90 days thereafter, entitled the representative to the entire future value of the goodwill built up by its work. Goodwill (beyond the 90-day residual) was allocated to the manufacturer. The terms on which the parties would part ways were handled expressly in this contract, and IRI got what it bargained for. Contracts allocate risks and opportunities. If things turn out well, the party to whom the contract allocates the upper trail of outcomes is entitled to reap the benefits.

Allocating risks by contract is no easy matter, and only a long process of experimentation in the marketplace reveals the best terms. Consider the variables in a sales agency such as this one. The parties must select the length of the relationship, the commission rate, any bonuses for meeting objectives, and post-termination compensation. A long term, with termination only for cause, will assure the agent that it can reap the benefits of success in procuring repeat buyers for the goods — but disputes about "cause" may lead to costly litigation, and the longer term eventually may stifle effort. As the end of the term approaches, the agent cannot obtain much of the gain and may begin to take it easy, the "last-period problem" well known to contracting parties. Instead of rewarding the agent through a longer term, the parties may choose a higher commission rate. This increases the agent's incentive to work hard, but the higher rate also may over reward the agent for sales that would have occurred without the agent's efforts; and a high commission rate gives the principal a greater reason to replace the agent. That incentive may be alleviated by paying the agent a bonus for defined levels of success, such as landing a big contract, but a bonus is risky for both sides — and as most people want to avoid risk, the prospect of a large bonus may be worth less to the agent than the cash outlay to the principal. Thus the parties may prefer to compensate the agent by a share of the profits over time, even after the agency is over. Stock options may do this; so do posttermination commissions. But back-loading of the compensation, like a long-term contract, creates incentives to shirk; for if the agent makes a big sale he can collect his residuals and invite the principal to fire him so that he can turn to other projects. All of the provisions for creating incentives and allocating risks have their advantages and disadvantages; all are well known to professionals such as IRI and CP Clare; no one combination of these terms is right for all people at all times.

CP Clare and IRI addressed most of these issues explicitly in their contract. IRI received a minimum term of one year; either party could walk away on 30 days' notice thereafter. The contract did not provide for bonuses, and it tackled residuals by providing that IRI got its full commission on all deliveries within 90 days following its termination. This agreement provides explicitly for what has come to pass: termination with substantial outstanding business. It allocates to IRI three months' worth of commissions. By demanding five years' worth after the fact, IRI has behaved opportunistically.

Id. at 130–31.

5. *Allocating Risks by Default: A General Approach.* Both *Jacob & Youngs v. Kent* and *Stees v. Leonard* involve disputes between parties to an executory contract whose terms are silent about the particular issue that produced the dispute. Note that, in each case, the parties could have dickered over the risk that ultimately produced the litigation, but they remained silent. At this point the law might do one of two things. A court could simply dismiss any dispute on the grounds that the parties failed to provide for this eventuality in their contract, and the law has no choice but to leave the loss where it currently lies. Alternatively, a court could fill in the gap in the contract by default. As we have seen in the preceding cases, contract law seems consistently to choose the second option. The problem for contract law, then, is to determine how a risk can be *justly* allocated by default in cases where the parties could have assigned it but failed to do so. Justice Cardozo supplied one possible answer: "Intention not otherwise revealed may be presumed to hold in contemplation the reasonable and probable." That is to say, Cardozo believed that it is just and proper to assign the risk in the present case to the party that "reasonable" bargainers facing a similar situation would "probably" have chosen.

But how can it be just to allocate a risk to someone who never agreed to the burden and possibly never even thought about the problem before the dispute arose? Suppose that we assume (just for argument) that contracting parties are capable, with a reasonable amount of effort, of "opting out" of any default rule and allocating explicitly every possible contracting risk. Under these conditions, contract default rules have primarily a facilitative function; they serve as standardized risk allocations that operate only in the absence of a contrary agreement. To the extent that these default rules direct the risk allocation that most contracting parties would have agreed to anyway, they serve the important purpose of saving those bargainers the cost of negotiating and writing down every possible contingency in their contracts. On the other hand, if the default rule fails to suit the purposes of any particular parties, then those bargainers are free to negotiate an alternative allocation of risks. As long as the default rules are adequately publicized in advance, then it might be said that those parties who remain silent implicitly *consent* to being governed by these legally supplied contract terms.

Even if you accept this argument (provisionally) there still remains a vexing problem. In Cardozo's words, what risk allocation rule would "reasonable" parties "probably" adopt? One way to begin thinking about this question is to focus on the question *ex ante* (when the parties are negotiating), rather than *ex post* (at the time of the dispute). At the time the parties are concluding their contract, it is to the benefit of *both* parties to assign a particular risk to that party who best appreciates the magnitude of the risk, can more cheaply take cost-effective precautions against its occurrence, or can purchase insurance to cover the contingency should it occur. That party who had the "comparative advantage" would presumably agree to bear the risk in return for an appropriate compensation in the contract. Can you see why, if these conditions hold, both parties are better off assigning the risk that way rather than the other way around? But is it clear to you why an "all or nothing" assignment of the risk is preferable to a 50/50 split of all such contingencies?

Essay: The Puzzle of Incomplete Contracts

The contractor and homeowner in *Stees v. Leonard* entered into a written contract with detailed plans and specifications. Yet, as we have seen, the contract was seriously incomplete in the sense that the parties did not reach an express understanding about who should bear the risk of soft soil that could not support the structure specified in the contract.[54] Why would parties in such a position ever leave

---

[54] Note that a contract can be incomplete in two distinct senses of the word. First, a contract may be incomplete in that it contains a genuine gap — it fails to describe the obligations of the parties in a state of the world that materializes. When a state of the world materializes that falls within the gap, the enforcing court must choose either to decline to enforce the contract or to fill the gap with a default obligation. Parties can easily make such a contract *obligationally complete*, however, by specifying that

such an important question unresolved in their contract?

One possible answer is that contracting parties systematically will fail to write complete contracts (that is to specify the consequences of all possible contingencies that may affect their performance) because the *transaction costs* of writing complete contracts are simply too onerous. Let's think about those costs. One cost of writing complete contracts is the resource costs of negotiating and reducing to a written form the agreed upon allocation of risk. Those resource costs, in turn, include not only the time and effort to negotiate and draft the clauses in question, but also the possibility that in doing so the parties might make a mistake in their written contract. A clause that they regard as perfectly clear may, upon subsequent examination, appear ambiguous or vague. This "formulation error" may then lead to costly litigation over the appropriate meaning that should be given to the clause in question.[55]

Another significant transaction cost is the burden of adequately identifying in advance all the possible contingencies that might occur and then specifying the appropriate outcome for each one. Given the limits of human cognition, parties may simply be unable to identify and foresee all of the uncertain future conditions or may be incapable of characterizing adequately the complex adaptations required to accommodate all the possibilities that *might* materialize. One way to visualize these two problems of *uncertainty* and *complexity* is to imagine that you represent a homeowner who wants you to write a contract providing for the care of his fine home garden during a summer when he is out of town. Your first task is to deal with an uncertain future, that is, to specify in advance all the relevant risks that the gardener must account for: the climatic conditions, possible incursions of the gypsy moth, wind-borne powdery mildew, etc. Assuming you can overcome the uncertainty problem, you must then resolve the complexity problem; that is, you must specify to the gardener exactly what responses should be made in each case: how much to spend on sprays, whether and when to water, when a diseased plant should be cut down to prevent infection of adjacent ones, and so on.[56]

Fortunately, as we have seen in *Jacob & Youngs* and *Stees*, you do not have to write your hypothetical contract on a blank slate. Rather, the law of contracts will start you out with a (hopefully complete) set of *default rules*. Putting aside for the moment the separate question of how the law chooses the right default, when would

---

the obligation in question applies to a broadly defined set of contingencies. For example, a contract term that states "the seller shall under all circumstances deliver a blue widget on September 1, 2006 for a price of $10,000" completely defines the parties obligations, even if the contract is not the best the parties could do in every situation that might occur. Such a contract may be incomplete in a second sense, however. It is *informationally incomplete* if it fails to provide the optimal set of obligations for each possible state of the world. Thus, in our example above, there may be circumstance in which the widget costs the seller more to produce than it is worth to the buyer. If so, the contract is incomplete in that it would require the performance of an inefficient contract. In which sense is the contract incomplete in *Stees v. Leonard*?

[55] For a more complete discussion of the different ways that parties can err in expressing their mutual understanding as to who bears what risk and how, see Charles J. Goetz & Robert E. Scott, *The Limits of Expanded Choice: An Analysis of the Interactions Between Express and Implied Contract Terms*, 73 CAL. L. REV. 261 (1985).

[56] For an elaboration of the ways in which contracting parties cope with the problems of uncertainty and complexity, see Charles J. Goetz & Robert E. Scott, *Principles of Relational Contracts*, 67 VA. L. REV. 1089 (1981).

you "opt out" and write a more complete contract for your client? A plausible answer is that you would compare the resource costs of an expressly dickered clause against the possible gains of a tailor-made or designer contract term that was a better fit for your particular situation.

If high transactions costs are the primary reasons why parties write incomplete contracts, then the law properly should fill the gaps with default terms that solve those problems, assuming that the state's contracting costs are lower than the sum of the costs to contracting parties. This might be the case if, for example, the state can benefit from economies of scale not available to individual contractors. But this argument rests on the crucial assumption that courts (and/or legislatures) are capable of devising useful default rules that would be widely suitable for many parties. Many scholars who study this problem argue, to the contrary, that in a complex economy with many heterogeneous contracting parties it is increasingly unlikely that the state is more capable than the parties themselves in devising rules that solve particular contracting problems.[57]

There is a second reason why parties may choose to write incomplete contracts. Suppose that the ideal contract would provide the gardener with optimal incentives by providing a bonus of $5,000 for extra care and attention to the plants over the summer. But now assume that your client, the homeowner, is unable to monitor and observe the amount of care the gardener provides in nurturing young plants in the garden. Under those conditions, it would be foolish for you to specify a compensation scheme that provided the bonus because it is conditioned on acts by the promisor that are difficult or impossible either for the promisee to observe or for either the promisor or promisee subsequently to verify to a court. This is an example of the effects of *asymmetric information* on the contracting process. When conditions of private or hidden information exist, one party cannot either *observe* (discover himself) or *verify* (prove to a court) whether the actions or events specified in the contract took place. Asymmetric information thus leads parties to specify a contract that falls short of the theoretical ideal. In this sense, parties may prefer contracts that are incomplete — they do not contain all the terms an ideal contract for structuring their transaction would contain. To do otherwise would require parties either to disclose information that they wish to keep private or to have enforcement turn on facts that one or both could not observe or verify in court. Writing an incomplete contract is preferable to these unpalatable alternatives.[58]

The possibility that contracts are incomplete because of hidden information or other related factors urges even greater modesty about the role of courts in creating useful default rules for contracting parties. If the parties themselves will not choose to base contractual contingencies on information that is unobservable or unverifiable, they will always elect to opt out of any such legally supplied default rules. Under these conditions, the law simply cannot fill gaps in contracts with

---

[57] See Alan Schwartz & Robert E. Scott, *Contract Theory and the Limits of Contract Law*, 113 YALE L.J. 541 (2003); Robert E. Scott, *The Case for Formalism in Relational Contract*, 94 Nw. U. L. REV. 847 (2000); Alan Schwartz, *The Default Rule Paradigm and the Limits of Contract Law*, 3 S. CAL. INTERDISC. L.J. 389 (1994).

[58] *See* ALAN SCHWARTZ, *Incomplete Contracts* in 2 NEW PALGRAVE DICTIONARY OF ECONOMICS AND LAW 277 (1997).

useful defaults that will solve the informational contracting problem the parties are confronting.

The preceding analysis doesn't resolve the puzzle of incomplete contracting. But it does suggest that the gap-filling role that common law courts — such as the courts in *Jacob & Youngs* and *Stees* — have traditionally assumed may be much less useful today in the context of complex commercial contracting.

Assuming that filling gaps with default rules often (sometimes) is problematic, there remains the question of what alternative is open to a court asked to resolve a dispute over the terms of an incomplete contract. One alternative we suggested earlier was to do nothing and leave the parties where they are. A further alternative is to urge courts to adopt an *ex post* rather than an *ex ante* approach. If courts can't develop prospective default rules to aid future parties, maybe they should just concentrate on filling in the "right" result for the particular parties in litigation. Thus, a court could impose an "equitable adjustment" of the disputed contract that takes into account all of the factors as they appear at the time of adjudication (rather than focusing on the factors as they appeared to the parties at the time of contracting). After all, at the time of adjudication the court has the advantage of hindsight; it presumably is in possession of information that the parties did not have at the time of contracting. Under these conditions, why shouldn't courts focus on filling in the gaps in order to reach a "fair" or "just" outcome in the particular case being litigated? In *Stees*, for example, it seems clear that the contractor did not fully charge the homeowner for the risk of quicksand in the original contract price. Wouldn't it be fairer or more just to divide the losses of the unanticipated soil problems on a 50/50 basis (or some other equitable formula) rather than assigning all of the losses to the contractor?

You will notice as you continue to read contract cases that the *ex post* solution of equitable adjustment is only rarely adopted by common law courts. Why do you suppose that contract law seems to strongly favor "all or nothing" outcomes over a system of proportional sharing of losses from unanticipated circumstances? You should consider the merits of the three possible approaches to incomplete contracts — assigning default rules ex ante, imposing equitable adjustment ex post, or keeping judicial "hands-off" and letting the losses lie where they fall — as you read the following case.

[3] Excuse for Nonperformance

As *Stees v. Leonard* demonstrates, one of the reasons why parties breach contracts is because performance of a promise becomes more costly than it appeared at the time of contract. In general, where those cost increases arise from the occurrence of a foreseeable risk associated with performance, the promisor is required to perform despite the increase in costs. Assume, however, that the increase in the costs of performance can be attributed to changed circumstances that arise between time of contract and the time of performance. Under what conditions, if any, will the claim of changed circumstances permit the promisor to be excused from performance? In general, contract law treats the claim of changed conditions the same as the claim of unanticipated costs: the foreseeable risks associated with performance are assigned by default to the promisor and thus nonperformance will not be excused. But there are exceptions to this rule, and the following case illustrates one of them.

TAYLOR v. CALDWELL
King's Bench
3 B. & S. 826, 122 Eng. Rep. 309 (1863)

BLACKBURN, J.

In this case the plaintiffs and defendants had, on the 27th May, 1861, entered into a contract by which the defendants agreed to let the plaintiffs have the use of The Surrey Gardens and Music Hall on four days then to come, viz., the 17th June, 15th July, 5th August and 19th August, for the purpose of giving a series of four grand concerts, and day and night f/Fetes at the Gardens and Hall on those days respectively; and the plaintiffs agreed to take the Gardens and Hall on those days, and pay £ 100 for each day.

The parties inaccurately call this a "letting," and the money to be paid a "rent;" but the whole agreement is such as to show that the defendants were to retain the possession of the Hall and Gardens so that there was to be no demise of them, and that the contract was merely to give the plaintiffs the use of them on those days. Nothing however, in our opinion, depends on this. The agreement then proceeds to set out various stipulations between the parties as to what each was to supply for these concerts and entertainments, and as to the manner in which they should be carried on. The effect of the whole is to show that the existence of the Music Hall in the Surrey Gardens in a state fit for a concert was essential for the fulfillment of the contract, — such entertainments as the parties contemplated in their agreement could not be given without it.

After the making of the agreement, and before the first day on which a concert was to be given, the Hall was destroyed by fire. This destruction, we must take it on the evidence, was without the fault of either party, and was so complete that in consequence the concerts could not be given as intended. And the question we have to decide is whether, under these circumstances, the loss which the plaintiffs have sustained is to fall upon the defendants. The parties when framing their agreement evidently had not present to their minds the possibility of such a disaster, and have made no express stipulation with reference to it, so that the answer to the question must depend upon the general rules of law applicable to such a contract.

There seems no doubt that where there is a positive contract to do a thing, not in itself unlawful, the contractor must perform it or pay damages for not doing it, although in consequence of unforeseen accidents, the performance of his contract has become unexpectedly burdensome or even impossible. But this rule is only applicable when the contract is positive and absolute, and not subject to any condition either express or implied: and there are authorities which, as we think establish the principle that where, from the nature of the contract, it appears that the parties must from the beginning have known that it could not be fulfilled unless when the time for the fulfillment of the contract arrived some particular specified thing continued to exist, so that, when entering into the contract, they must have contemplated such continuing existence as the foundation of what was to be done; there, in the absence of any express or implied warranty that the thing shall exist, the contract is not to be construed as a positive contract, but as subject to an implied condition that the parties shall be excused in case, before breach, performance becomes impossible from the perishing of the thing without default of the contractor.

There seems little doubt that this implication tends to further the great object of making the legal construction such as to fulfill the intention of those who entered into the contract. For in the course of affairs men in making such contracts in general would, if it were brought to their minds, say that there should be such a condition. . . .

There is a class of contracts in which a person binds himself to do something which requires to be performed by him in person; and such promises, e.g. promises to marry, or promises to serve for a certain time, are never in practice qualified by an express exception of the death of the party; and therefore in such cases the contract is in terms broken if the promisor dies before fulfillment. Yet it was very early determined that, if the performance is personal, the executors are not liable; Hyde v. The Dean of Windsor, Ore. His. 552, 553. See 2 Wms. Exors. 1560, 5th ed., where a very apt illustration is given. "Thus," says the learned author, "if an author undertakes to compose a work, and dies before completing it, his executors are discharged from this contract: for the undertaking is merely personal in its nature, and, by the intervention of the contractor's death, has become impossible to be performed." For this he cites a dictum of Lord Lyndhurst in Marshall v. Broad-hurst, 1 Tyr. 348, 349, and a case mentioned by Patteson J. in Wentworth v. Cock, 10 A. & E. 42, 45-46. In Hall v. Wright, E. B. & E. 746, 749, Compton J., in his judgment, puts another case. "Where a contract depends upon personal skill, and the act of God renders it impossible, as, for instance, in the case of a painter employed to paint a picture who is struck blind, it may be that the performance might be excused."

It seems that in those cases the only ground on which the parties or their executors, can be excused from the consequences of the breach of the contract is, that from the nature of the contract there is an implied condition of the continued existence of the life of the contractor, and, perhaps in the case of the painter of his eyesight. In the instances just given, the person, the continued existence of whose life is necessary to the fulfillment of the contract, is himself the contractor, but that does not seem in itself to be necessary to the application of the principle; as is illustrated by the following example. In the ordinary form of an apprentice deed the apprentice binds himself in unqualified terms to "serve until the full end and term of seven years to be fully complete and ended," during which term it is covenanted that the apprentice his master "faithfully shall serve," and the father of the apprentice in equally unqualified terms binds himself for the performance by the apprentice of all and every covenant on his part. (See the form, 2 Chitty on Pleading, 370, 7th ed. by Greening.) It is undeniable that if the apprentice dies within the seven years, the covenant of the father that he shall perform his covenant to serve for seven years is not fulfilled, yet surely it cannot be that an action would lie against the father? Yet the only reason why it would not is that he is excused because of the apprentice's death.

These are instances where the implied condition is of the life of a human being, but there are others in which the same implication is made as to the continued existence of a thing. For example, where a contract of sale is made amounting to a bargain and sale, transferring presently the property in specific chattels, which are to be delivered by the vendor at a future day; there, if the chattels, without the fault of the vendor, perish in the interval, the purchaser must pay the price and the vendor is excused from performing his contract to deliver, which has thus become impossible.

That this is the rule of the English law is established by the case of Rugg v. Minett (11 East, 210), where the article that perished before delivery was turpentine, and it was decided that the vendor was bound to refund the price of all those lots in which the property had not passed; but was entitled to retain without deduction the price of those lots in which the property had passed, though they were not delivered, and though in the conditions of sale, which are set out in the report, there was no express qualification of the promise to deliver on payment. It seems in that case rather to have been taken for granted than decided that the destruction of the thing sold before delivery excused the vendor from fulfilling his contract to deliver on payment. . . .

It may, we think, be safely asserted to be now English law, that in all contracts of loan of chattels or bailments if the performance of the promise of the borrower or bailee to return the things lent or bailed, become impossible because it has perished, this impossibility (if not arising from the fault of the borrower or bailee from some risk which he has taken upon himself) excuses the borrower or bailee from the performance of his promise to redeliver the chattel.

The great case of Coggs v. Bernard, 1 Smith's L.C. 171, 5th ed.; 2 L. Raym. 909. is now the leading case on the law of bailments, and Lord Holt, in that case, referred so much to the Civil law that it might perhaps be thought that this principle was there derived direct from the civilians, and was not generally applicable in English law except in the case of bailments; but the case of Williams v. Lloyd, W. Jones, 179. above cited, shows that the same law had been already adopted by the English law as early as *The Book of Assises*. The principle seems to us to be that, in contracts in which the performance depends on the continued existence of a given person or thing, a condition is implied that the impossibility of performance arising from the perishing of the person or thing shall excuse the performance.

In none of these cases is the promise in words other than positive, nor is there any express stipulation that the destruction of the person or thing shall excuse the performance; but that excuse is by law implied, because from the nature of the contract it is apparent that the parties contracted on the basis of the continued existence of the particular person or chattel. In the present case, looking at the whole contract, we find that the parties contracted on the basis of the continued existence of the Music Hall at the time when the concerts were to be given; that being essential to their performance.

We think, therefore, that the Music Hall having ceased to exist, without fault of either party, both parties are excused, the plaintiffs from taking the Gardens and paying the money, the defendants from performing their promise to give the use of the Hall and Gardens and other things. Consequently the rule must be absolute to enter the verdict for the defendants.

Rule absolute.

NOTES

1. ***Questions on* Taylor v. Caldwell**. Is it foreseeable that a music hall, constructed primarily with wood, might burn down? If so, why does this case not follow the *Stees* and *Paradine* decisions? In *Taylor*, the court implied a condition that, should the Surrey Gardens Music Hall burn down, there would be no contract, and the defendant would thus be excused from his failure to perform. Who was better able to take precautions against the fire? Would the court have decided the case the same way if the contract was for any music hall, not this particular music hall?

2. ***The Risks of Opting out of Default Rules.*** *Taylor v. Caldwell* establishes a default rule to guide the resolution of certain cases of loss caused by unforeseen circumstances: "in contracts in which the performance depends on the continued existence of a given person or thing, a condition is implied that the impossibility of performance arising from the perishing of the person or thing shall excuse the performance." As we have seen, however, parties are free, if they so desire, to contract around the provisions of this rule. In doing so, however, the parties must take care to appreciate the new set of risks they may be incurring.

RNJ Interstate Corp. v. United States, 181 F.3d 1329 (Fed. Cir. 1999), provides a contemporary perspective on the consequences of opting out of *Taylor v. Caldwell*. In this case, RNJ contracted with the government to renovate a government-owned building at a Naval Air Station. After completing more than half of the renovation work, the building was destroyed by fire. The contractor claimed excuse from further performance and sought recovery for work which was completed before the building was destroyed, citing *Taylor v. Caldwell*.

The court rejected the claim of excuse and denied recovery of work performed before the fire. The resolution of the case turned on a contract clause that stated, "The Contractor shall also be responsible for all materials delivered and work performed *until completion and acceptance of the entire work . . .* (emphasis added)." The court held that the common law doctrine embodied in *Taylor v. Caldwell* was "only a default and does not apply where the parties have agreed by the terms of their contract, to a different allocation of risks." *Id.* at 1331. The contract clause served to allocate all risks to RNJ until the specified condition occurred — the acceptance of the completed building by the government. Since acceptance never occurred, the risks had not shifted from RNJ to the government when the building was destroyed by fire.

3. ***Quantifying Risk Bearing.*** The magnitude of the risk of any occurrence (R) may be analyzed as the product of two separate factors: the impact of the risk should it materialize (I) multiplied by the probability of its occurrence (P). Thus:

$$R = I \times P$$

This simple formulation can help us to think about which of the two parties, Taylor or Caldwell, would have agreed to bear the risk of the fire had they bargained over this issue in advance. The agent, Caldwell, is perhaps better able to know the probability of fire in the music hall. He is more familiar with the structure and its surroundings. On the other hand, Taylor, the performer, knows why it is important to him to perform in this particular music hall; thus, he understands better what the impact of a fire would be. If a particular subject matter was desired, market values are not necessarily a reliable indicator of the value of the hall to Taylor.

This analysis suggests that it is not clear who is the better risk bearer where parties contract for a particular, specialized exchange. In such a case, how should the risk be allocated? Notice that by excusing the defendant, the court in *Taylor* leaves the loss where it falls. That is to say, the court does not attempt to reapportion the loss by awarding a remedy to either party.

To test your understanding of this method of analysis, consider how the parties would have allocated the risk if no particular music hall were specified. In this case, Caldwell, as the booking agent, would have the clear advantage in reducing the probability of nonperformance. He could, for example, book another hall as a back-up in case of fire, or hire special fire protection services. Furthermore, Caldwell could also assess the impact of a fire on Taylor. Thus, he could properly evaluate the choice between any of these (or any other) precautionary actions. Since no particular hall was requested, Caldwell would be safe in assuming that a substitute would be acceptable should the Surrey Gardens burn in the meantime.

For further exploration of the possibilities (and the limits) of this type of analysis, see Anthony Kronman, *Mistake, Disclosure, Information, and the Law of Contracts*, 7 J. LEGAL STUD. 1 (1978); and Subha Narasimhan, *Of Expectations, Incomplete Contracting, and the Bargain Principle*, 74 CAL. L. REV. 1123 (1986).

4. Taylor v. Caldwell *and Modern Law.* As we will consider in detail in Chapter 8, many American jurisdictions now recognize an expanded version of the doctrine of impossibility. Both the Restatement and the UCC excuse performance of a contract when the occurrence of an un-bargained for event makes performance *impracticable* — that is, performance would require extreme and unreasonable difficulty and expense to one of the parties. Both the Restatement and the UCC require, as did the court in *Taylor*, that the non-occurrence of the event be a basic assumption of the contract. Foreseeability of the event is a factor to be weighed in this determination, but it is not conclusive. *See* Restatement (Second) § 261; UCC § 2-615.

Another modern development, closely related to the doctrine of impossibility, is the doctrine of frustration. In many jurisdictions, if a change in circumstances makes one party's performance virtually worthless to the other, then the aggrieved party no longer has to perform. Like impossibility and impracticability, this rule is typically subject to certain conditions: the frustration must be substantial, the object lost must be so essential to the contract that both parties would understand that its loss made the contract worthless, and the non-occurrence of the event must be a basic assumption of the contract. *See* Restatement (Second) § 265, Comment *a*. For example, if a contract is made on the assumption that property will be transferred to an owner who will not have to pay taxes on the property, and the law is changed so that the transferee will have to pay taxes, the doctrine of frustration may apply. *See* W. L.A. Inst. For Cancer Research v. Mayer, 366 F.2d 220 (9th Cir. 1966).

A modern variation of *Taylor v. Caldwell* arose several decades ago involving the band Guns N' Roses. The last concert of the band's 1992 concert tour was scheduled to take place at the Vicente Calderon Stadium in Madrid. Four days before the concert, however, an engineering report found the stadium unsafe and the Spanish government banned use of the stadium. The cancelled concert led to much disappointment among ticketholders, as well as litigation between the band and the stadium promoter. For an in-depth account of the litigation, see Victor Goldberg, *After Frustration: Three Cheers for* Chandler v. Webster, 68 WASH. & LEE L. REV. 1133, 1156–58 (2011).

Essay: More on Default Rules in Contracts

Much of the study of the law of contract is about the methods by which courts go about filling the gaps in contracts. Courts do this when they interpret contract language and when they supply terms to cover contingencies not grounded in a dispute over language. As we have seen, academics (and some courts) call these court-supplied rules "default rules," for they are the rules applied to contracts when the parties do not specify the rules themselves.[59]

A popular technique used by academics, and by courts as well, is to formulate default rules by asking what term the parties would have bargained for had they foreseen the need for a term and bargained over its content. This exercise, which we might call replicating a hypothetical bargain, seems straightforward, if occasionally difficult. In fact, however, it requires some important value choices to be made.

The first choice is whether to customize the default rule to fit the parties before the court. Put differently, we must determine at what level of generality to approach the transaction. Consider the following characterizations of the same contract:

* warranty between the parties to a contract

* warranty between the parties to a contract to build a piece of furniture

* warranty between the parties to a contract to build a custom desk

---

[59] There is a rich literature on the nature of contract default rules. *See* Barry E. Adler, *The Questionable Ascent of* Hadley v. Baxendale, 51 STAN. L. REV. 1547 (1999); Alan Schwartz, *The Default Rule Paradigm and the Limits of Contract Law*, 3 S. CAL. INTERDISC. L.J. 389 (1994); Ian Ayres & Robert Gertner, *Filling Gaps in Incomplete Contracts: An Economic Theory of Default Rules*, 99 YALE L.J. 87 (1989); Ian Ayres & Robert Gertner, *Strategic Contractual Inefficiency and the Optimal Choice of Legal Rules*, 101 YALE L.J. 729 (1992); Randy Barnett, *The Sound of Silence: Default Rules and Contractual Consent*, 78 VA. L. REV. 821 (1992); David Charny, *Hypothetical Bargains: The Normative Structure of Contract Interpretation*, 89 MICH. L. REV. 1815 (1991); Jason Johnston, *Strategic Bargaining and the Economic Theory of Contract Default Rules*, 100 YALE L.J. 615 (1990); Robert E. Scott, *A Relational Theory of Default Rules for Commercial Contracts*, 19 J. LEGAL STUD. 597 (1990); Richard Craswell, *Contract Law, Default Rules, and the Philosophy of Promising*, 88 MICH. L. REV. 489 (1989).

- warranty between the parties to a contract to build a custom desk for $6,000

- warranty between the parties to a contract to build a custom desk for $6,000 where the desk has substantial resale value.

We might reason to one hypothetical term under the first characterization of the case and a different hypothetical term under the last characterization.

The second choice has to do with the characteristics that we are prepared to assign to the parties to our hypothetical bargain. What assumptions will we make about their rationality, their attitude towards risk, and the information available to them? Consider, for example, these alternative statements that might be made by a court:

> "In the situation of this case, a rational, risk-neutral party with adequate information would understand that she is in the better position to take precautions than is her trading partner. She would not bargain for a warranty."

> "In the situation of this case, the buyer showed in negotiating other terms of the contract considerable fear that she might not be protected from loss to her business reputation. She would have negotiated a warranty had the issue been addressed."

The Ex Ante Perspective. How might a court using an ex ante perspective approach default rules? Assuming the parties have not allocated the relevant risks expressly, an important function of default rules from the ex ante perspective is to facilitate contracting for as many future bargainers as is feasible. The provision of widely acceptable default rules saves many (most) parties the time, trouble, and risk of error implicit in crafting their own contract terms. Moreover, parties who do not prefer the majoritarian rules have no cause to complain. Since they are idiosyncratic they could not expect the law to supply their contract terms for them. Such parties remain free to "opt out" and design their own tailor-made contract terms. In sum, the ex ante approach reasons that if the default rule matches the rule that the broadest number of future bargainers would agree to, those parties can leave the gap and save the costs of dickering over the term. An "incorrect" default rule is one with respect to which most future parties will negotiate a different rule in the face of (relatively) low transaction costs. To be sure, as noted above, determining how "most" parties would bargain over the clauses in question is not always an easy matter. Professor Omri Ben-Shahar argues, for example, in *A Bargaining Power Theory of Default Rules*, 109 Coʟᴜᴍ. L. Rᴇᴠ. 396 (2009), that gap-filling must consider the relative bargaining power of each party, mimicking what an actual negotiation could have looked like.

Despite these difficulties, the preference for majoritarian default rules may explain why implicit in the ex ante approach is the assumption that contracting parties are rational (*i.e.*, not operating under a delusion, or out of spite or a desire for revenge), have adequate information *given the context*,[60] and are risk-neutral or modestly risk-averse. Since the objective is to craft rules that are widely-suitable

---

[60] This qualification is necessary because gap-filling rules can be chosen in contexts where we believe there are routinely information barriers and that the parties would choose a rule that deals with the

across many contexts, the analyst may generally assume that, on average, buyers are informed, but not make this assumption when an inexperienced buyer is making the purchase of a complex good from an expert seller.

Professors Ian Ayres and Robert Gertner[61] suggest that sometimes an analyst using the ex ante approach might choose a goal other than selecting the default rule that the broadest number of bargainers would prefer. First, if there was an important reason why parties ought to be forced to negotiate about a particular issue, the court might choose a default rule that one or both of the parties cannot tolerate. Thus, if you want the parties to specify explicitly the damage remedy that will be applied in case of a contract breach, making the default rule twenty times actual loss ought to do the trick. Parties will bargain around a draconian rule.

Second, a court might reason that sometimes having a default rule disfavoring the party with an information advantage will be the best choice. The best example of such a rule is one that forces parties that have superior legal knowledge to inform the other party of the legal rules governing their agreement. For example, in a context where one party knows of a risk that the other party does not know about, the party with information will have no incentive to raise the issue in negotiations if the default rule puts the risk on the party who is ignorant of the issue. Placing the default-rule risk on the party with the information advantage provides that party with an incentive to raise the issue, by requesting a waiver, for instance.

The information-forcing perspective offers a framework for thinking about *Taylor v. Caldwell*. The rule granting excuse from the risk of nonperformance where the contract calls for a specific subject matter that is subsequently destroyed encourages the party with special knowledge — in this case the plaintiff, who has a particular need to rent the Surrey Gardens — to reveal a key fact to the other: how important is it that the Music Hall be available at the designated time. Armed with this information, the Music Hall can quote a higher price in exchange for a guarantee that the Music Hall (or its monetary equivalent) will be available on the day in question. In other words, if the owners of the Music Hall are to assume the risk of nonperformance, they need to know how much more important this particular performance is to the plaintiff than in the typical case where any similar facility would be sufficient. If the information-forcing rule does the job properly, future parties will "opt out" of the rule by negotiating specially tailored agreements under which the special risks of nonperformance are known by the performing party in advance. This permits the performer to adjust his price to account for these risks as well as to plan for special precautions against breach that may now be cost-justified.

The Ex Post Perspective. We have suggested earlier that courts could fill gaps in contracts by adopting an *ex post* perspective. One justification for doing so is that, by focusing on facts known to the court at the time of adjudication, the court can fill in the gaps in a manner more consistent with what the particular parties themselves would have done. Earlier we asked why such an outcome was "fairer" or "more just"

---

information deficiencies. What the instrumentalist is unwilling to assume is a future party who is less informed than ordinary parties in the context.

[61] *See* Ayres & Gertner, *Filling Gaps in Incomplete Contracts, supra* note 59, at 87.

than the ex ante perspective. One answer to that question is to argue that the ex post perspective reinforces the autonomy interests of contracting parties by limiting the exercise of judicial power to a faithful reconstruction of what the parties, themselves, most likely would have done. This conception of autonomy thus would favor a resolution of the dispute that the parties themselves would have chosen rather than one preferred by the judge herself (or perhaps by unknown future bargainers).

But the autonomy principle does not *necessarily* lead a court to adopt the ex post perspective. Professor David Charny argued that a court seeking to reinforce the autonomy interests of the parties might, nevertheless, impose a default rule based upon a hypothetical bargain analysis:

> Consider, for example, the adjudicator who values autonomy because she considers that it serves an important disciplinary function to require persons to specify their arrangements and then live by them. This approach to autonomy would not lead the adjudicator to be sympathetic to careful reconstruction of the individual parties' choices for cases in which they were silent. Indeed, the adjudicator might be inclined to think that for her to "help the parties out in this way" might dilute the disciplinary force of her adherence to express agreements. She might then proceed by other hypothetical bargain rules — for example, she might assume that parties meant to reserve discretion on all issues on which their agreements were silent.

> Most clearly, an autonomy theorist holding to a strong principle of autonomy for situations where there is no express choice would not feel that she compromised her principles: in determining that no strong principle applied where no express choice had been made she would be following her principles rigorously. This is not a case of persons "forced to be free," in Rousseau's infamous phrase. The parties are not being forced here, in the sense of having their express choice overridden; the hypothetical bargain question arises because there is no express choice.

> For hypothetical bargains, then, autonomy theorists do not necessarily find it problematic to impose a bargain different from what these particular parties actually would have done, provided that doing so would enhance autonomy in this other respect. The answer turns on why autonomy seems to be the relevant value.[62]

A Pluralist Perspective. The criteria for choosing default rules for a pluralist requires an initial determination of whether a majoritarian default would be "unfair" to one of the parties because that party justifiably relied on the other's promise. Such a fairness norm is grounded in tort as much as in contract.

Tort law assesses damages according to the loss suffered by the actual victim, not by an average victim. If the rule that the "tortfeasor takes her victim as she finds her" is applicable to contract default rules, then perhaps the pluralist theorist ought to argue for the gap-filler that accords with the hypothetical term the disadvantaged

---

[62] Charny, *supra* note 59, at 1833–34.

party would have thought applied had she considered the matter. But the problem, of course, is that until the court fills the gap with a default, it is not clear which party is the contract breacher and which one is the injured party whose reliance interest must be protected. Take *Stees v. Leonard*, for example. Until the risk of soft soil is allocated, it is not clear that the homeowner has the right to claim "reliance" on the contractor's promise. One could just as easily argue that the contractor "relied" on the homeowner to provide specifications for a building that would be able to be supported by the soil on the homeowner's lot.

In short, a norm of fairness doesn't seem very helpful in giving a lawyer tools to predict with any confidence the outcome of a potential contract dispute such as those presented in *Jacob & Youngs, Stees*, and *Taylor.* Nonetheless, fairness may still have potency as a normative principle.

E. REMEDIES FOR NONPERFORMANCE

[1] Introduction

Recall from Restatement (Second) § 1 that we have defined a contract as a promise or set of promises that the law will enforce. Thus far, however, we have not considered exactly what "enforcement" means. Clearly, one of the most straightforward ways of enforcing a promise is the remedy of *specific performance* that was ordered by the court in *Lucy v. Zehmer.* As you will see, however, the specific performance remedy is rarely available to a plaintiff. Most of the time, therefore, what we mean by enforcing a contract is not that the promisor is *required* to perform, but rather that, after the promisor has failed to perform (either deliberately or inadvertently), a court will order the defendant promisor to pay a specified sum of money.

The question then arises: what is the appropriate monetary damage award that should (will) be imposed on a contract breacher? What should a court do in cases where the parties have failed to specify *any* remedy or damage formulation in their contract? To help you think about this question more carefully, consider the opinion of Justice Oliver Wendell Holmes, Jr. in *Globe Refining Co. v. Landa Cotton Oil Co.*, 190 U.S. 540 (1903).

The plaintiff in *Globe* contracted to buy 10 tank cars of crude cotton oil from defendant whose refinery was located in Texas. Plaintiff sent tank cars from its plant in Louisville, Kentucky according to the contract terms, but the tank cars were turned away at the defendant's refinery and picked up no oil. Assume that the facts establish that on the contracted-for date of delivery there were other refineries in and around Texas from whom plaintiff could have obtained cotton oil but that instead the tank cars returned to Louisville empty. Plaintiff Globe sued Landa for breach of contract asking (among other things) for the difference between the contract price of oil and the market price at the time of the breach and for the cost of sending the tank cars to Texas and back. In holding that Globe could only recover as damages the difference between the contract price of oil and the market price on the date of breach in Texas, Justice Holmes wrote:

Whatever may be the scope of the allegations, it will be seen that none of the items [of damage] was contemplated expressly by the words of the bargain. Those words are before us in writing, and go no further than to contemplate that when the deliveries were to take place the buyer's tank cars should be at the defendant's mill. Under such circumstances the question is how far the express terms of a writing, admitted to be complete, can be enlarged by averment; and, if they can be enlarged, what averments are sufficient?

When a man commits a tort, he incurs, by force of the law, a liability to damages, measured by certain rules. When a man makes a contract, he incurs, by force of the law, a liability to damages, unless a certain promised event comes to pass. But unlike the case of torts, as the contract is by mutual consent, the parties themselves, expressly or by implication, fix the rule by which the damages are to be measured. The old law seems to have regarded it as technically in the election of the promisor to perform or pay damages. It is true that, as people when contracting contemplate performance, not breach, they commonly say little or nothing as to what shall happen in the latter event, *and the common rules have been worked out by common sense, which has established what the parties probably would have said if they had spoken about the matter* (emphasis added).

A man never can be absolutely certain of performing any contract when the time of performance arrives, and, in many cases, he obviously is taking the risk of an event which is wholly, or to an appreciable extent, beyond his control. The extent of liability in such cases is likely to be within his contemplation, and, *whether it is or not, should be worked out on terms which it fairly may be presumed he would have assented to if they had been presented to his mind.* (emphasis added). For instance, in the present case, the defendant's mill and all its oil might have been burned before the time came for delivery. Such a misfortune would not have been an excuse, although probably it would have prevented performance of the contract. If a contract is broken, the measure of damages generally is the same, whatever the cause of the breach. We have to consider, therefore, what the plaintiff would have been entitled to recover in that case, and that depends on what liability the defendant fairly may be supposed to have assumed consciously, or to have warranted the plaintiff reasonably to suppose it assumed, when the contract was made.

[I]t is obvious that the plaintiff was free to bring its tank cars from where it liked — a thousand miles away or an adjoining yard — so far as the contract was concerned. [W]ith regard to the [cost of sending the cars], they were the expenses which the plaintiff was willing to incur for performance. If it had received the oil, these were deductions from any profit which the plaintiff would have made. But, if it gets the difference between the contract price and the market price, it gets what represents the value of the oil in its hands, and to allow these items in addition would be making the defendant pay twice for the same thing.

Holmes' opinion in *Globe* makes it clear that determining the proper remedies for breach of contract is no different from the analysis courts use to allocate any other contractual risks. In the absence of an express agreement between the parties, the contract is incomplete and the court must specify a damages default rule that fills the gap. Moreover, to Holmes' mind, the task of finding the right default asks the same question that Cardozo posed in *Jacob & Youngs:* what damage measure would the parties be fairly presumed to have agreed to if the question had been brought to their mind at the time of contract?

[2]   The Compensation Puzzle

If money damages are the typical remedy for breach of contract, what standard should be used to determine those damages and what purpose are those damages designed to serve? In Holmes' terms "what [is the] liability the defendant fairly may be supposed to have assumed . . . when the contract was made." In beginning to answer this question, read § 344 of the Restatement (Second) of Contracts and then consider the following case.

FREUND v. WASHINGTON SQUARE PRESS, INC.
Court of Appeals of New York
357 N.Y.S.2d 857, 314 N.E.2d 419 (1974)

RABIN, J.

In this action for breach of a publishing contract, we must decide what damages are recoverable for defendant's failure to publish plaintiff's manuscript. In 1965, plaintiff, an author and a college teacher, and defendant, Washington Square Press, Inc., entered into a written agreement which, in relevant part, provided as follows. Plaintiff ("author") granted defendant ("publisher") exclusive rights to publish and sell in book form plaintiff's work on modern drama. Upon plaintiff's delivery of the manuscript, defendant agreed to complete payment of a nonreturnable $2,000 "advance." Thereafter, if defendant deemed the manuscript not "suitable for publication," it had the right to terminate the agreement by written notice within 60 days of delivery. Unless so terminated, defendant agreed to publish the work in hardbound edition within 18 months and afterwards in paperbound edition. The contract further provided that defendant would pay royalties to plaintiff, based upon specified percentages of sales. (For example, plaintiff was to receive 10% of the retail price of the first 10,000 copies sold in the continental United States.) If defendant failed to publish within 18 months, the contract provided that "this agreement shall terminate and the rights herein granted to the Publisher shall revert to the Author. In such event all payments therefore made to the Author shall belong to the Author without prejudice to any other remedies which the Author may have." The contract also provided that controversies were to be determined pursuant to the New York simplified procedure for court determination of disputes.

Plaintiff performed by delivering his manuscript to defendant and was paid his $2,000 advance. Defendant thereafter merged with another publisher and ceased publishing in hardbound. Although defendant did not exercise its 60-day right to terminate, it has refused to publish the manuscript in any form.

Plaintiff commenced the instant action pursuant to the simplified procedure practice and initially sought specific performance of the contract. The Trial Term Justice denied specific performance but, finding a valid contract and a breach by defendant, set the matter down for trial on the issue of monetary damages, if any, sustained by the plaintiff. At trial, plaintiff sought to prove: (1) delay of his academic promotion; (2) loss of royalties which would have been earned; and (3) the cost of publication if plaintiff had made his own arrangements to publish. The trial court found that plaintiff had been promoted despite defendant's failure to publish, and that there was no evidence that the breach had caused any delay. Recovery of lost royalties was denied without discussion. The court found, however, that the cost of hardcover publication to plaintiff was the natural and probable consequence of the breach and, based upon expert testimony, awarded $10,000 to cover this cost. It denied recovery of the expenses of paperbound publication on the ground that plaintiff's proof was conjectural.

The Appellate Division, (3 to 2) affirmed, finding that the cost of publication was the proper measure of damages. In support of its conclusion, the majority analogized to the construction contract situation where the cost of completion may be the proper measure of damages for a builder's failure to complete a house or for use of wrong materials. The dissent concluded that the cost of publication is not an appropriate measure of damages and consequently, that plaintiff may recover nominal damages only. We agree with the dissent. In so concluding, we look to the basic purpose of damage recovery and the nature and effect of the parties' contract.

It is axiomatic that, except where punitive damages are allowable, the law awards damages for breach of contract to compensate for injury caused by the breach — injury which was foreseeable, i.e., reasonably within the contemplation of the parties, at the time the contract was entered into. Money damages are substitutional relief designed in theory "to put the injured party in as good a position as he would have been put by full performance of the contract, at the least cost to the defendant and without charging him with harms that he had no sufficient reason to foresee when he made the contract." (5 Corbin, *Contracts*, § 1002, pp. 31-32; 11 Williston, *Contracts* (3d ed.), § 1338, p. 198.) In other words, so far as possible, the law attempts to secure to the injured party the benefit of his bargain, subject to the limitations that the injury — whether it be losses suffered or gains prevented — was foreseeable, and that the amount of damages claimed be measurable with a reasonable degree of certainty and, of course, adequately proven. But it is equally fundamental that the injured party should not recover more from the breach than he would have gained had the contract been fully performed.

Measurement of damages in this case according to the cost of publication to the plaintiff would confer greater advantage than performance of the contract would have entailed to plaintiff and would place him in a far better position than he would have occupied had the defendant fully performed. Such measurement bears no relation to compensation for plaintiff's actual loss or anticipated profit. Far beyond compensating plaintiff for the interests he had in the defendant's performance of the contract — whether restitution, reliance or expectation (see Fuller & Perdue, *Reliance Interest in Contract Damages*, 46 Yale L.J. 52, 53-56) an award of the cost of publication would enrich plaintiff at defendant's expense.

Pursuant to the contract, plaintiff delivered his manuscript to the defendant. In doing so, he conferred a value on the defendant which, upon defendant's breach, was required to be restored to him. Special Term, in addition to ordering a trial on the issue of damages, ordered defendant to return the manuscript to plaintiff and plaintiff's restitution interest in the contract was thereby protected.

At the trial on the issue of damages, plaintiff alleged no reliance losses suffered in performing the contract or in making necessary preparations to perform. Had such losses, if foreseeable and ascertainable, been incurred, plaintiff would have been entitled to compensation for them.

As for plaintiff's expectation interest in the contract, it was basically two-fold — the "advance" and the royalties. (To be sure, plaintiff may have expected to enjoy whatever notoriety, prestige or other benefits that might have attended publication, but even if these expectations were compensable, plaintiff did not attempt at trial to place a monetary value on them.) There is no dispute that plaintiff's expectancy in the "advance" was fulfilled — he has received his $2,000. His expectancy interest in the royalties — the profit he stood to gain from sale of the published book — while theoretically compensable, was speculative. Although this work is not plaintiff's first, at trial he provided no stable foundation for a reasonable estimate of royalties he would have earned had defendant not breached its promise to publish. In these circumstances, his claim for royalties falls for uncertainty.

Since the damages which would have compensated plaintiff for anticipated royalties were not proved with the required certainty, we agree with the dissent in the Appellate Division that nominal damages alone are recoverable. Though these are damages in name only and not at all compensatory, they are nevertheless awarded as a formal vindication of plaintiff's legal right to compensation which has not been given a sufficiently certain monetary valuation.

In our view, the analogy by the majority in the Appellate Division to the construction contract situation was inapposite. In the typical construction contract, the owner agrees to pay money or other consideration to a builder and expects, under the contract, to receive a completed building in return. The value of the promised performance to the owner is the properly constructed building. In this case, unlike the typical construction contract, the value to plaintiff of the promised performance — publication — was a percentage of sales of the books published and not the books themselves. Had the plaintiff contracted for the printing, binding and delivery of a number of hardbound copies of his manuscript, to be sold or disposed of as he wished, then perhaps the construction analogy, and measurement of damages by the cost of replacement or completion, would have some application.

Here, however, the specific value to plaintiff of the promised publication was the royalties he stood to receive from defendant's sales of the published book. Essentially, publication represented what it would have cost the defendant to confer that value upon the plaintiff, and, by its breach, defendant saved that cost. The error by the courts below was in measuring damages not by the value to plaintiff of the promised performance but by the cost of that performance to defendant. Damages are not measured, however, by what the defaulting party saved by the breach, but by the natural and probable consequences of the breach *to the plaintiff*. In this case, the consequence to plaintiff of defendant's failure to publish is that he is prevented from realizing the gains promised by the contract — the royalties. But, as we have stated, the amount of royalties plaintiff would have realized was not ascertained with adequate certainty and, as a consequence, plaintiff may recover nominal damages only.

Accordingly, the order of the Appellate Division should be modified to the extent of reducing the damage award of $10,000 for the cost of publication to six cents, but with costs and disbursements to the plaintiff.

NOTES

1. **Cataloging the Interests in** Freund. In *Freund*, the author expected to have his book published, earn royalties, get tenure, and enjoy an enhanced reputation. Which of these ought to be included in his "expectancy"?

Wouldn't specific performance of this contract be quite appropriate?[63] There is little or no difficulty in the court having to oversee performance, and if the defendant doesn't have the resources to publish the book, it can subcontract the job to another publisher. Why do you suppose that remedy is not even considered by the court?

Does the return of the manuscript satisfy the restitution interest? Would you treat the passage of time between the making of the promise and the return of the manuscript as part of the restitution interest?

Could Freund have recovered the value of his time spent in writing the book as his reliance interest? How would he compute that value? One might argue that the return of the manuscript undermined the reliance-based argument. Yet, a few additional facts of the case might change your view. Freund was under contract with Washington Square Press to write a book on the life and work of Eugene O'Neill. But during the nine-year-long litigation over this contract, another O'Neill biography, *O'Neill, Son and Artist*, by Louis Sheaffer, was published and it won the Pulitzer Prize for biography in 1974. Thus, by the time the case was decided by the New York Court of Appeals, the manuscript may well have been worthless. In any event, despite Freund's long career as a writer (he published at least eight novels, thirteen plays, nine short story collections, and a four-volume history of the theatre) his book on O'Neill remains unpublished to this day.[64]

Freund cannot prove that he would have earned royalties — they are uncertain. Washington Square Press cannot prove that Freund would not have earned royalties. Who deserves to prevail on this issue? A court might estimate that it was more probable than not that no royalties would have been earned — although there

---

[63] Melvin Eisenberg has proposed an innovative remedial regime where actual specific performance should be awarded unless a special moral, policy, or experiential reason suggests otherwise in a specific class of cases, or the promisee can accomplish virtual specific performance. For discussion, see Melvin A. Eisenberg, *Actual and Virtual Specific Performance, the Theory of Efficient Breach, and the Indifference Principle in Contract Law*, 93 Cal. L. Rev. 975 (2005).

[64] Freund died in 2008 at the age of 98. His obituary in the New York Times listed his many publications. *See* http://www.legacy.com/NYTimes/DeathNotices.asp?Page=LiofeStory&PersonID=100680812.

is no reason to believe that the court has a comparative advantage over the parties, who surely contemplated royalties at the time of contracting — and put the burden of proving otherwise on the author. Or, a court might reason that the breach created the uncertainty and that the burden of showing no royalties is on the promisor. In fact, it is the amount of the royalties, not their existence, that is uncertain. The default rule in the case of uncertainty is zero. Why is that?

2. *Explicitly Negotiating Damages.* Why didn't Freund negotiate a clause in the contract stating explicitly the amount of damages in case of a breach by the publisher? Do you think that Freund could have found another publisher while he was disputing with Washington Square?

3. *Goals of Contract Damages.* Section 344 of the Restatement (Second) of Contracts sets out alternative goals of breach of contract remedies. The relationship among these goals is further elaborated in §§ 347, 349, and 373. At first glance, the goals seem sharply distinguishable one from another. Thus, expectancy damages, the standard "compensatory" recovery, aim to place the promisee in the position she would have been in had the contract been performed. This measure attempts to give the promisee the full gain she anticipated from the breached contract. The second measure, reliance or *status quo ante* damages, attempts to undo the harm that the promisee's reliance on the promise has caused by putting the promisee in the position that she would have been in had the contract not been entered into.[65] In other words, reliance damages represent the "opportunity cost" of the broken promise — the benefits foregone and the costs actually incurred because the promise was made and then breached.[66] To paraphrase Robert Frost, reliance represents the path not taken.

Can anything be said about the theoretical relationship between expectancy and reliance damages?[67] Suppose John wishes to contract to buy 10,000 bushels of wheat for delivery in two months. He orders them from Mary, a seller — but not necessarily a grower — of wheat. The price is $1 per bushel. Mary breaches on the day of delivery, when the price of available wheat is $2 per bushel. What amount of damages satisfies John's expectancy interest? Do you see why John's reliance loss is precisely the same? If you do not, think about what John would have done had he not ordered the wheat from Mary.

4. *The Rationale Behind Expectancy Damages.* In *MCA TV, Ltd. v. Public Interest Corp.*, 171 F.3d 1265, 1271 (11th Cir. 1999), Judge Burkett describes the

---

[65] Restitution damages, the third measure, require the party in breach to repay the value of any advantage or benefit he has received from the injured party — the promisee.

[66] Economic theorists have developed a model of damages which shows that the expectation measure can induce the promisee to over rely on the promise and result in inefficient welfare maximization. For a defense of expectation damages and a critique of overreliance, see Melvin Eisenberg & Brett McDonnell, *Expectation Damages and the Theory of Overreliance*, 54 Hastings L.J. 1335 (2003).

[67] The analysis is "theoretical" because we do not yet have enough data, *that is*, cases, to know what courts actually include as reliance damages. In particular, we have not yet seen whether courts include all opportunity costs in measuring reliance damages. For a sampling of the academic debate over the relationship between expectancy and reliance, see Robert Cooter & Melvin A. Eisenberg, *Damages for Breach of Contract*, 73 Cal. L. Rev. 1432 (1985); Lon L. Fuller & William R. Perdue, Jr., *The Reliance Interest in Contract Damages*, 46 Yale L.J. 52 (1936); Charles J. Goetz & Robert E. Scott, *Enforcing Promises: An Examination of the Basis of Contract*, 89 Yale L.J. 1261 (1981).

role of expectancy damages in the following terms:

> Contract law is designed to protect the expectations of the contracting parties. . . . When a contract is breached, an injured party can look to the legal system for help in achieving the position he or she would have occupied upon the performance of the promise — that is, for his or her "expectation interest," otherwise known as "the benefit of the bargain."[68] Unlike tort law, which permits the imposition of punitive damages as a means to deter disfavored conduct, contract law does not allow for punitive damages unless the breach of contract is also a tort for which punitive damages are recoverable. See id. § 124, at 706-07.
>
> Because damages for breach of contract can be difficult to calculate, parties frequently stipulate in the contract itself to the amount of damages to be paid to the injured party in the event of a breach. Parties may not, however, use such stipulated damages provisions as a way to secure for themselves greater damages in the event of a breach than contract law would normally allow.

Judge Burkett's analysis leaves several key questions unaddressed. Justice Holmes suggested in *Globe v. Landa* that a contract damage rule is merely a default based on an educated guess as to the damage term parties would typically agree to if required to bargain explicitly at the time of contract. If so, then the question is: why wouldn't a promisee, contemplating the possibility of breach, bargain for punitive damages in order to deter the promisor from breaching the contract? Alternatively, why wouldn't the promisor, who contemplates the risk of regret, only agree to nominal damages upon breach? What argument(s) can you devise to suggest how two parties could agree at the time of contract on expectation damages as the best damage rule for both of them?[69]

5. ***Relationship Between Different Measures of Damages.*** Most cases analyze the choice of damage measure in terms of the three traditional categories of expectancy, reliance, and restitution. In general, restitution (which turns on the benefits that were conferred by the promisee) and reliance (which measures the next best alternative for the promisee) will offer a smaller recovery for the promisee than expectancy damages. Do you see why?

In exceptional circumstances, however, a restitutionary claim may exceed the promisee's expectancy. Consider the case of *In re Estate of Montgomery,* 272 N.Y. 323, 6 N.E.2d 40 (1936). In that case, attorney Everett Van Allan contracted with the executrix of the estate of James Montgomery. Van Allan agreed to perform certain legal services for the estate in exchange for $5,000. The executrix, who was "not the easiest kind of client," discharged Van Allan after he had performed approximately 5/6 of the contracted-for services.

---

[68] For further discussion, see David W. Barnes & Deborah Zalesne, *A Unifying Theory of Contract Damage Rules*, 55 SYRACUSE L. REV. 495 (2005); W. David Slawson, *Why Expectation Damages for Breach of Contract Must Be the Norm: A Refutation of the Fuller and Perdue "Three Interests" Thesis*, 81 NEB. L. REV. 839 (2003).

[69] For further discussion of these questions, see Robert E. Scott & George G. Triantis, *Embedded Options and the Case Against Compensation in Contract Law*, 104 COLUM. L. REV. 1428 (2004).

Under the doctrine of *quantum meruit*, Van Allan was allowed to collect for the value of the work he had performed. The appellate court affirmed the decision of the trial court, which held that he was allowed to collect for the reasonable value of his work product, as well as for the work which he had performed earlier for the late Mr. Montgomery without a specified, predetermined fee. A fee of $13,000 — substantially more than the contracted-for fee of $5,000 — was awarded to Van Allan.

The court in *Montgomery's Estate* seems to be using a restitutionary measure of damages, as do all awards under a *quantum meruit* theory. In contrast, payment of the $5,000 contract fee would put Van Allan in the position he expected to be in had he been allowed to fully perform his duties. Is awarding a restitutionary award which greatly exceeds the expected contractual payment equitable? (Or justifiable?). Is such an award contrary to the presumed intent of the parties?

6.   *Uncertain Expectations.* Courts often are reluctant to award full expectancy damages in cases where the expected gains are highly uncertain and speculative. For instance, in *Chicago Coliseum Club v. Dempsey,* 265 Ill. App. 542 (1932), the court refused to award the expected ticket revenues when heavyweight champion Jack Dempsey breached a contract to fight Harry Wills in order to prepare for a subsequent bout against Gene Tunney; instead, the court only allowed the recovery of expenses incurred between the signing of the contract and Dempsey's repudiation of the deal. In allowing a recovery only of reliance, as opposed to the expectation interest, the court noted,

> [I]t would be impossible to produce evidence of a probative character sufficient to establish any amount which could be reasonably ascertainable by reason of the character of the undertaking. The profits from a boxing contest of this character, open to the public, is dependent upon so many different circumstances that they are not susceptible of definite legal determination. . . . Such an entertainment lacks utterly the element of stability which exists in regular organized business.

Id. at 549–50.

For a more contemporary application of this principle, see *Anglia Television Ltd. v. Reed,* 3 All E.R. 690 (C.A. 1971), where actor Robert Reed of "The Brady Bunch" fame was held liable for the organizational costs incurred by the producers of a British television special when he accepted a role and then withdrew prior to the start of filming. The profitability of the special was deemed to be overly speculative; the expectancy interest, in effect, was assumed to be the break-even point.

7.   *Problems.* Suppose a builder contracts to construct a house on an owner's land for $100,000, and the owner pays a deposit of $15,000. The builder anticipates that the project will cost him $90,000. Before construction is complete, however, the owner repudiates the contract. If the builder's costs to date are $60,000 and the value of the owner's land has increased by $40,000 due to the partially completed structure, what is the amount of the builder's expectation, reliance, and restitution interests? *See* Restatement (Second) § 344, illustration 2, for a substantially similar example.

Suppose A contracts to pay an adjacent landowner, B, to drill an oil well on B's land for development and exploration purposes. Both A and B believe that the well will produce oil and will increase the value of A's land by $1,000,000. B then breaks the contract by refusing to drill the well. Later, A learns that there is no oil in the region. What is the value of A's expectation interest? *See* Restatement (Second) § 344, illustration 5.

Essay: Damage Measures and the Theory of Efficient Breach

Holmes' *Globe* opinion argues that, by entering a contract, the parties accept risks that particular events beyond their control may or may not occur. If a risk materializes such that performance now costs more than it is worth, the party who owes performance now faces a disagreeable choice: she can either incur the loss attributable to performance or she can breach and accept the cost of any corresponding sanction. In sum, the choice is to either "perform and lose, or "breach and pay." Presumably the promisor will adopt the cheaper of these options. Contract damage rules obviously play an important role in the breach/performance choice. It is, therefore, appropriate to consider the extent to which any particular damage rule does or should encourage or deter breach of contract. Consider the following excerpt from RICHARD POSNER, ECONOMIC ANALYSIS OF THE LAW (Little, Brown, 4th ed. 1992).[70]

> It makes a difference in deciding which remedy to grant whether the breach was opportunistic. If a promisor breaks his promise merely to take advantage of the vulnerability of the promisee in a setting (the normal contract setting) where performance is sequential rather than simultaneous, we might as well throw the book at the promisor. . . .
>
> Most breaches of contract, however, are not opportunistic. Many are involuntary; performance is impossible at a reasonable cost. Others are voluntary but (as we are about to see) efficient — which from an economic standpoint is the same case as that of an involuntary breach. These observations both explain the centrality of remedies to the law of contracts (can you see why?) and give point to Holmes's dictum that it is not the policy of the law to compel adherence to contracts but only to require each party to choose between performing in accordance with the contract and compensating the other party for any injury resulting from a failure to perform.[71]

---

[70] *See also* Charles J. Goetz & Robert E. Scott, *Liquidated Damages, Penalties and the Just Compensation Principle*, 77 COLUM. L. REV. 554, 558–59 (1977).

[71] Posner here cites to *Holmes, The Path of the Law*, which is found in 10 Harv. L. Rev. 457 (1897), and which reads:

> Nowhere is the confusion between legal and moral ideas more manifest than in the law of contract. Among other things, here again the so called primary rights and duties are invested with a mystic significance beyond what can be assigned and explained. The duty to keep a contract at common law means a prediction that you must pay damages if you do not keep it, — and nothing else. If you commit a tort, you are liable to pay a compensatory sum. If you commit a contract, you are liable to pay a compensatory sum unless the promised event comes to pass, and that is all the difference. But such a mode of looking at the matter stinks in the nostrils of those who think it advantageous to get as much ethics into the law as they can.

This dictum, though over broad, contains an important economic insight. In many cases it is uneconomical to induce completion of performance of a contract after it has been broken. I agree to purchase 100,000 widgets custom-ground for use as components in a machine that I manufacture. After I have taken delivery of 10,000, the market for my machine collapses. I promptly notify my supplier that I am terminating the contract, and admit that my termination is a breach. When notified of the termination he has not yet begun the custom grinding of the other 90,000 widgets, but he informs me that he intends to complete his performance under the contract and bill be accordingly. The custom-ground widgets have no operating use other than in my machine, and a negligible scrap value. To give the supplier a remedy that induced him to complete the contract after the breach would waste resources. The law is alert to this danger and, under the doctrine of mitigation of damages, would not give the supplier damages for any costs he incurred in continuing production after notice of termination.

In [this example] the breach was committed only to avert a larger loss, but in some cases a party is tempted to break his contract simply because his profit from breach would exceed his profit from completion of the contract. If it would also exceed the expected profit to the other party from completion of the contract, and if damages are limited to the loss of that profit, there will be an incentive to commit a breach. But there should be. Suppose I sign a contract to deliver 100,000 custom-ground widgets at 10¢ apiece to A for use in his boiler factory. After I have delivered 10,000, B comes to me, explains that he desperately needs 25,000 custom-ground widgets at once since otherwise he will be forced to close his pianola factory at great cost, and offers me 15¢ apiece for them. I sell him the widgets and as a result do not complete timely delivery to A, causing him to lose $1,000 in profits. Having obtained an additional profit of $1,250 on the sale to B, I am better off even after reimbursing A for his loss, and B is also better off. The breach is Pareto superior. True, if I had refused to sell to B, he could have gone to A and negotiated an assignment to him of part of A's contract with me. But this would have introduced an additional step, with additional transaction costs — and high ones, because it would be a bilateral-monopoly negotiation. On the other hand, litigation costs would be reduced.

Id. at 117–19.

Judge Posner's argument is a version of what academics call the "theory of efficient breach." The argument is that contract damages default rules are (and should be) designed not to coerce performance per se but rather to assure the promisee that either the promise will be performed or she will be awarded its monetary equivalent. Limiting the amount of damages to the "value" of the promise (such as the award in *Globe* of only the difference between the contract price and the market price of cotton oil in Louisville at the date of delivery) motivates the promisor to breach in circumstances where he can both pay off the promisee in damages and still do better economically by reallocating his resources elsewhere. We will critique this theory in the discussion that follows, but for now ask yourselves

---

Id. at 462. — Eds.

whether you are fully comfortable with a default rule that does not focus on deterring a breach of contract but rather on "paying off" the promisee.

One way of understanding the rationale of contract damages is to focus more carefully on the "efficient breach" analysis offered by Judge Posner. First, consider an example much like Judge Posner's. Assume that Seller agrees to sell Buyer 100 widgets for $1000. These widgets are worth $1500 to the buyer. Subsequently, Seller is approached by a foreign consortium that offers him $10,000 if, in lieu of manufacturing widgets, he will manufacture and sell to them 100 gidgets. Assume that Seller can produce either the widgets or gidgets (but not both) at a cost of $500. Posner's argument is that in terms of societal welfare, the optimal solution would be for the seller to breach, compensate the buyer for his contractual expectancy ($1500), and devote his productive energies to manufacturing gidgets for the foreign consortium. Such a result is "efficient"[72] in the sense that the buyer receives the same benefits as performance would have provided, while the seller can do even better. Under these circumstances, the rule of compensatory damages is contended to be preferable to any alternatives since it produces exactly this result.

Consider several of the alternative legal rules. Assume the law imposed penalty damages for breach of contract of 20 times the contract price. Here Seller would owe damages for breach of $20,000. Seller would choose the cheaper (for him) alternative, forego the $10,000 gain obtainable by making gidgets, and instead perform his contract with the buyer. Under these circumstances, the rule of penalty damages would seem to direct an inefficient outcome. While society as a whole would be better off if Seller's productive resources were devoted to making gidgets, he will instead produce widgets in order to avoid the penalty.

Consider instead the effects of a rule which imposed only nominal damages for breach equal to 20% of the contract price. In this case, Seller would certainly breach his contract with Buyer, pay him $200 in damages and manufacture gidgets in exchange for the $10,000. But in other circumstances, this rule too will result in a socially inefficient allocation of resources. Assume that the foreign buyers only offered Seller $1300 for the gidgets. Under the 20% damage rule, he would still have an incentive to breach, pay Buyer $200 in damages and manufacture gidgets, thus pocketing an additional $100. ($1300–$500–$200 = $600 profit v. $1000–$500 = $500 profit.) Social welfare, however, would be improved if the widget contract were, in fact, performed since Buyer values widgets at $1500, which is more than the $1300 value the foreign buyers attach to gidgets. Under a rule of compensatory damages, the widget contract would still be performed in this case since Seller would have to pay Buyer $500 in damages ($1500 value – $1000 contract price), thus making the gidget contract less profitable than his existing obligation to the buyer. In sum, only one legal rule, compensatory damages, appears to satisfy the social welfare

---

[72] Economists have a term for a situation where a change from one state of affairs (Seller performs his contract with Buyer, foregoing his opportunity with the foreign consortium) to another state of affairs (Seller breaches his contract with Buyer, fully compensates Buyer, and makes gidgets for the foreign consortium) will make at least one person better off and no one worse off. The move from one state of affairs to the other is called a *pareto superior* move. The second state of affairs is pareto superior to the first. This is one definition of "efficient."

criterion in every case by directing Seller's productive energies to their most highly valued uses.

This analysis is incomplete and misleading, however. As Judge Posner suggests, but ultimately finds unpersuasive, it ignores the fact that the parties can negotiate around any legal remedies.[73] Thus, in the case where Seller has contracted to manufacture widgets for Buyer at a price of $1,000, is then offered $10,000 by another trading partner to make gidgets, and faces a 20-times-contract-price legal remedy, the Seller will be motivated by the opportunity to earn an additional $9,000. He will buy his way out of the contract with Buyer. The bargaining range will be between $500 (the amount necessary to make Buyer whole), and $9,000 (Seller's potential gain).[74]

Similarly, where the law specifies 20% ("nominal" damages), and the gain to Seller from making gidgets is less than the loss to Buyer from losing widgets, Buyer will "bribe" Seller to perform the widget contract.

Posner disposes of this "rebuttal" to the efficient breach analysis by contending that, because it necessitates a further transaction (in the one case, negotiating out of the first contract; in the other case, bribing Seller to perform the first contract) it is not the best solution.

The efficient breach theory is flawed in a more fundamental respect, however.

The efficient breach hypothesis suffers not only from the objection that, *after* a better opportunity presents itself, contractual partners can renegotiate out of suboptimal legal rules for breach of contract; it also ignores the fact that parties can bargain *in advance* for the most appropriate breach of contract damages rule and can put that rule in their contract.[75] Posner seems to suggest that the renegotiation objection is faulty because it introduces an additional, costly transaction, and so does the *ex ante* specification by the parties in their contract of the optimal damages rule. Yet Posner must have been assuming the absence of transaction costs in his own analysis, for unless low or zero transaction costs are assumed, the efficient breach hypothesis fails. If there are information barriers, such as mis-estimates of the value put on a contract or on a new opportunity by one's contractual partner, or if the costs of litigation are positive (they always are), or if litigation is used

---

[73] Judge Posner's analysis rests on certain unspecified assumptions. Those assumptions are an application of an economic theory first developed by Ronald Coase in his justly famed article, *The Problem of Social Cost*, 3 J.L. & Econ. 1 (1960). Coase's article explored certain long-standing ways of thinking about optimal liability rules and the meaning of causation. Coase began his analysis by (implicitly) making several assumptions. They are: (1) legal rights are well-defined and marketable; (2) "transaction costs" are zero; and (3) the parties are accurately informed of the existence and value of alternative courses of action available to each party. Transaction costs, broadly speaking, are the costs to the parties of initiating and conducting exchange transactions. (Coase did not argue that these are realistic assumptions, or that they describe actual transactions.) Coase then argued that, in a world where these assumptions hold, legal rules will have no allocative effect; a choice of one legal rule over another will not change the mix of goods and services in society.

[74] The range is *not* $500 to $19,000. If Buyer demands more than $9,000, Seller will say, "Don't be silly. At a cost of more than $9,000, I'm not going to breach."

[75] *See* Robert E. Scott, *The Case for Market Damages: Revisiting the Lost Profits Puzzle*, 57 U. Chi. L. Rev. 1155 (1990).

strategically, then no legal rule can be predicted to move goods and services to their most highly valued use. Thus, for Posner to introduce a transaction cost at this point in his analysis is not only inconsistent, it substantially undercuts his analysis.

In one sense this could end the analysis. In a world where transactions costs are low, the breach of contract damages rule is irrelevant. Parties can and will negotiate around a suboptimal legal rule at the time of contracting. In a world of transactions costs, anything can happen, and absent substantial empirical data on the nature of those costs, no rule can be predicted to be better than another.

There is another way of approaching the problem. It is surely uncontroversial that having some rule for treating breaches of contract is preferable to having no rule at all. More controversial, perhaps, is the notion that the law ought to adopt the rule that most parties would adopt were transactions costs low enough to enable contract negotiators to tailor-make their own rules. For situations where transactions costs are low enough to permit such bargaining, a legal rule mirroring what most parties *would* adopt would eliminate the need to negotiate and reduce the rule or rules to writing. Where transaction costs are too high for parties to bargain their own rule, it may be normatively correct to provide them with the rule that they would most probably have chosen for themselves had they been able to bargain.

Deciding on the breach of contract damages rule that most parties would choose for themselves if they could costlessly bargain is not necessarily an easy matter.[76] Why in the widgets/gidgets example might we believe that the parties would have selected a compensatory damage remedy? We draw on our prior analysis. Under a compensatory damages scheme, the seller, who regrets having entered into the contract because he has found a better opportunity, or because his plans have gone awry, need not renegotiate his contract. Instead, he can choose between two options: breach and compensate the buyer for the price of substitute performance, or secure substitute performance himself and perform under the contract. Under this analysis, a breach in these circumstances is not an attempt to renege on a prior commitment. Rather, it is the seller's implicit announcement that the buyer can minimize the costs of the dispute by purchasing substitutes himself and then sending seller the bill. In any case, seller will pay the cost of making sure that buyer's expectation of performance is fulfilled. If, instead, seller is forced to renegotiate, the bargaining costs may be high. The situation is one of a bilateral monopoly, and a game of "chicken" may result. Moreover, it may be in the interest of both parties at the time of contracting to let each one "pay off" the other and then take the entire gain from any opportunity that he or she has discovered after contracting. This will encourage the search for new opportunities which, so long as compensatory damages are paid, is in the interest of both parties.

---

[76] Instead of guessing what breach of contract damage remedy parties would adopt, why not conduct empirical investigations? Predicting the cost-minimizing outcome is less costly than conducting empirical investigations in numerous markets. Our judicial system is not organized in such a way as to make it possible for judges to commission such studies. Litigants in a particular case are unlikely to commission a thorough study for they would absorb all the costs of such a study, with its uncertain results, and one important benefit, a more informed legal rule, would go to other members of society. Suffice it to say that legal academics have little taste for such empirical investigations.

There may be contexts in which we believe that parties would not have chosen a compensatory remedy. Suppose that one party attaches value to the performance of the contract that is likely not to be provable at the time the other side breaches. That person would prefer (at the time of contracting) to specify a damage remedy that did not under-compensate him, as the standard expectation remedy would. Is the better course to have more than one rule — an expectation damages default rule for most parties, but a different rule for those parties whom we believe may attach special or sentimental value to the performance (remember the Kents in *Jacob & Youngs*) — or to adopt a single rule, compensatory (or expectation) damages, and permit idiosyncratic parties to opt out of the rule if they can overcome the transactions costs?

On this analysis, the "true" or "deep" justification for compensatory damages as the best default is not that it encourages efficient breach or performance decisions, but that it is our best guess as to what the parties would have agreed to for themselves had they been able to foresee the contingencies inducing breach and thereafter to bargain over contract remedies. In that sense, the compensation principle of contract damages is no different than the other "off-the-rack" default rules that you have seen in *Jacob & Youngs*, *Stees* and *Taylor*: it directs the result that most parties would be expected to reach if they bargained over the issue in advance.[77]

[3] Specific Performance

The compensation goal of contract law purports to put the promisee in the same position she would have enjoyed had the contract been performed. The preceding case has shown us that it is often quite difficult to measure compensatory damages because it requires the court to answer a hypothetical question: what economic position would the promisee have achieved had the contract been performed? In other words, what exactly did performance require of the promisor? The most straightforward way of avoiding these knotty questions and fully implementing the compensation goal is to require that breached contracts be specifically performed. Yet specific performance is an extraordinary remedy, not generally available to the promisee. A logical question in an analysis of remedies for breach, therefore, is to ask why the law doesn't require specific performance in all cases.

VAN WAGNER ADVER. CORP. v. S&M ENTERS.
Court of Appeals of New York
67 N.Y.2d 186, 492 N.E.2d 756 (1986)

KAYE, J.

By agreement dated December 16, 1981, Barbara Michaels leased to plaintiff, Van Wagner Advertising, for an initial period of three years plus option periods totaling seven additional years, space on the eastern exterior wall of a building on

---

[77] For a recent analysis of the vacuousness of traditional efficient breach theory and a defense of expectation damages on both economic and moral grounds, see Daniel Markovits & Alan Schwartz, *The Myth of Efficient Breach: New Defenses of the Expectation Interest*, 97 VA. L. REV. 1939 (2011).

East 36th Street in Manhattan. Van Wagner was in the business of erecting and leasing billboards, and the parties anticipated that Van Wagner would erect a sign on the leased space, which faced an exit ramp of the Midtown Tunnel and was therefore visible to vehicles entering Manhattan from that tunnel.

In early 1982 Van Wagner erected an illuminated sign and leased it to Asch Advertising, Inc. for a three-year period commencing March 1, 1982. However, by agreement dated January 22, 1982, Michaels sold the building to defendant S & M Enterprises. Michaels informed Van Wagner of the sale in early August 1982, and on August 19, 1982 S & M sent Van Wagner a letter purporting to cancel the lease as of October 18 pursuant to section 1.05, which provided:

"Notwithstanding anything contained in the foregoing provisions to the contrary, Lessor (or its successor) may terminate and cancel this lease on not less than 60 days prior written notice in the event and only in the event of:

a) a bona fide sale of the building to a third party unrelated to Lessor".

Van Wagner abandoned the space under protest and in November 1982 commenced this action for declarations that the purported cancellation was ineffective and the lease still in existence, and for specific performance and damages.

In the litigation the parties differed sharply on the meaning of section 1.05 of the lease. [. . .]

Trial Term concluded that Van Wagner's position on the issue of contract interpretation was correct, either because the lease provision unambiguously so provided or, if the provision were ambiguous, because the parol evidence showed that the "parties to the lease intended that only an owner making a bona fide sale could terminate the lease. They did not intend that once a sale had been made that any future purchaser could terminate the lease at will." Trial Term declared the lease "valid and subsisting" and found that the "demised space is unique as to location for the particular advertising purpose intended by Van Wagner and Michaels, the original parties to the Lease." However, the court declined to order specific performance in light of its finding that Van Wagner "has an adequate remedy at law for damages". Moreover, the court noted that specific performance "would be inequitable in that its effect would be disproportionate in its harm to the defendant and its assistance to plaintiff." Concluding that "[t]he value of the unique qualities of the demised space has been fixed by the contract Van Wagner has with its advertising client, Asch for the period of the contract", the court awarded Van Wagner the lost revenues on the Asch sublease for the period through trial, without prejudice to a new action by Van Wagner for subsequent damages if S & M did not permit Van Wagner to reoccupy the space. On Van Wagner's motion to resettle the judgment to provide for specific performance, the court adhered to its judgment.

On cross appeals the Appellate Division affirmed, without opinion. We granted both parties leave to appeal. [. . .]

Given defendant's unexcused failure to perform its contract, we next turn to a consideration of remedy for the breach: Van Wagner seeks specific performance of the contract, S & M urges that money damages are adequate but that the amount of the award was improper.

Whether or not to award specific performance is a decision that rests in the sound discretion of the trial court, and here that discretion was not abused. Considering first the nature of the transaction, specific performance has been imposed as the remedy for breach of contracts for the sale of real property, but the contract here is to lease rather than sell an interest in real property. While specific performance is available, in appropriate circumstances, for breach of a commercial or residential lease, specific performance of real property leases is not in this State awarded as a matter of course.

Van Wagner argues that specific performance must be granted in light of the trial court's finding that the "demised space is unique as to location for the particular advertising purpose intended". The word "uniqueness" is not, however, a magic door to specific performance. A distinction must be drawn between physical difference and economic interchangeability. The trial court found that the leased property is physically unique, but so is every parcel of real property and so are many consumer goods. Putting aside contracts for the sale of real property, where specific performance has traditionally been the remedy for breach, uniqueness in the sense of physical difference does not itself dictate the propriety of equitable relief.

By the same token, at some level all property may be interchangeable with money. Economic theory is concerned with the degree to which consumers are willing to substitute the use of one good for another (*see*, Anthony T. Kronman, *Specific Performance*, 45 U.Chi.L.Rev. 351, 359 (1978)), the underlying assumption being that "every good has substitutes, even if only very poor ones", and that "all goods are ultimately commensurable" (*id.*). Such a view, however, could strip all meaning from uniqueness, for if all goods are ultimately exchangeable for a price, then all goods may be valued. Even a rare manuscript has an economic substitute in that there is a price for which any purchaser would likely agree to give up a right to buy it, but a court would in all probability order specific performance of such a contract on the ground that the subject matter of the contract is unique.

The point at which breach of a contract will be redressable by specific performance thus must lie not in any inherent physical uniqueness of the property but instead in the uncertainty of valuing it. "What matters, in measuring money damages, is the volume, refinement, and reliability of the available information about substitutes for the subject matter of the breached contract. When the relevant information is thin and unreliable, there is a substantial risk that an award of money damages will either exceed or fall short of the promisee's actual loss. Of course this risk can always be reduced — but only at great cost when reliable information is difficult to obtain. Conversely, when there is a great deal of consumer behavior generating abundant and highly dependable information about substitutes, the risk of error in measuring the promisee's loss may be reduced at much smaller cost. In asserting that the subject matter of a particular contract is unique and has no established market value, a court is really saying that it cannot obtain, at reasonable cost, enough information about substitutes to permit it to calculate an award of money damages without imposing an unacceptably high risk of undercompensation on the injured promisee. Conceived in this way, the uniqueness test seems economically sound." (Kronman, at 362.) This principle is reflected in the case law, and is essentially the position of the Restatement (Second) of Contracts, which lists "the difficulty of proving damages with reasonable certainty" as the first factor affecting adequacy of damages (Restatement [Second] of Contracts § 360[a]).

Thus, the fact that the subject of the contract may be "unique as to location for the particular advertising purpose intended" by the parties does not entitle a plaintiff to the remedy of specific performance.

Here, the trial court correctly concluded that the value of the "unique qualities" of the demised space could be fixed with reasonable certainty and without imposing an unacceptably high risk of undercompensating the injured tenant. Both parties complain: Van Wagner asserts that while lost revenues on the Asch contract may be adequate compensation, that contract expired February 28, 1985, its lease with S & M continues until 1992, and the value of the demised space cannot reasonably be fixed for the balance of the term. S & M urges that future rents and continuing damages are necessarily conjectural, both during and after the Asch contract, and that Van Wagner's damages must be limited to 60 days — the period during which Van Wagner could cancel Asch's contract without consequence in the event Van Wagner lost the demised space. S & M points out that Van Wagner's lease could remain in effect for the full 10-year term, or it could legitimately be extinguished immediately, either in conjunction with a bona fide sale of the property by S & M, or by a reletting of the building if the new tenant required use of the billboard space for its own purposes. Both parties' contentions were properly rejected.

First, it is hardly novel in the law for damages to be projected into the future. Particularly where the value of commercial billboard space can be readily determined by comparisons with similar uses — Van Wagner itself has more than 400 leases — the value of this property between 1985 and 1992 cannot be regarded as speculative. Second, S & M having successfully resisted specific performance on the ground that there is an adequate remedy at law, cannot at the same time be heard to contend that damages beyond 60 days must be denied because they are conjectural. If damages for breach of this lease are indeed conjectural, and cannot be calculated with reasonable certainty, then S & M should be compelled to perform its contractual obligation by restoring Van Wagner to the premises. Moreover, the contingencies to which S & M points do not, as a practical matter, render the calculation of damages speculative. [. . .]

The trial court, additionally, correctly concluded that specific performance should be denied on the ground that such relief "would be inequitable in that its effect would be disproportionate in its harm to defendant and its assistance to plaintiff" (see . . . Restatement [Second] of Contracts § 364[1][b]). It is well settled that the imposition of an equitable remedy must not itself work an inequity, and that specific performance should not be an undue hardship. This conclusion is "not within the absolute discretion of the Supreme Court." Here, however, there was no abuse of discretion; the finding that specific performance would disproportionately harm S & M and benefit Van Wagner has been affirmed by the Appellate Division and has support in the proof regarding S & M's projected development of the property. [. . .]

Accordingly, the order of the Appellate Division should be modified, with costs to plaintiff, and the case remitted to Supreme Court, New York County, for further proceedings in accordance with this opinion and, as so modified, affirmed.

NOTES

1. ***Questions on* Van Wagner Advertising.** The trial court denied Van Wagner's claim for specific performance and, instead, granted damages based on the balance of its rental payments from Asch on its sub-lease with leave to file for future damages should S&M not permit the lease to continue thereafter. Assume that S&M refused to permit Van Wagner to continue to lease the space after the Asch sub-lease had terminated. How then would damages be measured for the balance of the lease term? S&M argued that such a calculation would be entirely speculative. Doesn't that prove the legitimacy of the claim for specific performance? If you were Van Wagner's attorney, what advice would you give as to the risks your client might face in seeking to recover the damages for lost rental payments for the period of the lease following the end of the Asch sub-lease? Could you assure Van Wagner that it will be compensated in full for the losses attributable to the breach by S&M? If not, what does the court mean when it says that "money damages are adequate"? What answer would you give to Van Wagner if it asks you who will pay your firm's fees and the other costs and expenses incurred in litigating the amount of damages incurred by the breach of contract? Note that the Court of Appeals restates the general common law rule that specific performance is customarily granted for breach of contracts for the sale of real property. Why should a lease be treated differently?

The Court of Appeals appears to adopt the view that "uniqueness" is primarily a question of the relative difficulty in accurately fixing appropriate compensatory damages. But isn't the concept broad enough to include the possibility that money is not a substitute because no alternative can reasonably be acquired with the proceeds of the damage award? *See* Restatement (Second) § 360(b). If so, what evidence could Van Wagner introduce in a second trial that would show that, given its proximate location to the mid-town tunnel, the eastern wall on 36th street had a value as billboard space that could not be replicated elsewhere in the city?

2. ***Specific Performance under the UCC.*** In the case of contracts for the sale of goods, the UCC perpetuates the traditional approach to the limitation of specific performance, at least in theory, allowing the remedy to be decreed only when the goods are "unique or in other proper circumstances."[78] See UCC § 2-716 and accompanying comments. The key question is what the phrase "other proper circumstances" adds to the meaning of the word "unique". For two examples of how courts apply the UCC language, consider first *Klein v. PepsiCo, Inc.*, 845 F.2d 76 (4th Cir. 1988). Klein wished to buy a G-II jet from PepsiCo. After much negotiation, the two parties agreed to a deal for the aircraft, only for PepsiCo to back out days before the aircraft was supposed to change hands. Though there were 21 other G-II jets on the market, only three were comparable to PepsiCo's jet. Additionally, the price of G-II jets had started to rise after PepsiCo's withdrawal. Nevertheless, the court found that specific performance was not required. In Klein's case, the existence of comparable aircraft — he made bids on two other G-II's after PepsiCo's withdrawal — made the goods not unique. As for the price increase, they were not enough of an obstacle to qualify as "other proper circumstances." Klein was

---

[78] For an economic analysis of the circumstances in which specific performance should be enforced, see Steven Shavell, *Specific Performance Versus Damages for Breach of Contract: An Economic Analysis*, 84 Tex. L. Rev. 831 (2006).

ultimately awarded damages, and he purchased a G-III jet instead. On the other hand, consider *King Aircraft Sales v. Lane*, 846 P.2d 550 (Wash. Ct. App. 1993). In *King*, the court disagreed with *Klein*, reading "other proper circumstances" broadly to order specific performance in the sale of two small aircraft: "The airplanes, although not necessarily 'unique', were rare enough so as to make the ability to cover virtually impossible. Furthermore, Lane, by its own act of selling the planes, incapacitated itself from performance." *Id.* at 556.

Despite the decision in *Klein*, it is generally assumed that the "other proper circumstances" language is designed to expand the application of specific performance in practice. *See* § 2-716 cmt. 2. An example of the use of this expansive language is *Ace Equip. Co. v. Aqua Chem., Inc.*, 20 U.C.C. Rep. Serv. 392 (1975). In *Ace Equipment*, the court decreed specific performance where the "other proper circumstances" showed that the buyer could not purchase substitute goods in time to meet his third-party commitments.

Essay: Why Isn't Specific Performance Generally Available?

Consider the following justification for the general use of the damages remedy instead of specific performance. Begin by recalling the theory of efficient breach discussed above. That analysis starts with the observation that courts treat a contractual obligation not as an obligation to perform in all circumstances, but rather as an obligation to choose between performance and compensatory damages. The promisor can choose to satisfy her contractual obligation by compensating the promisee with damages and then contract with a third party (presumably at a higher price) to provide the third party the promised performance thereby reaping a greater return. In that case, the law assumes that (1) the promisee is fully compensated through the "breach and pay damages" option, and, therefore, is as well off as if the original contract had been performed; (2) the promisor is better off because, in exercising her breach and pay option, she gains more than she would have otherwise due to the higher return on the third party contract and (3) the third party promisee is also better off because he has now secured a performance that he previously did not have. Economists term this situation *pareto superior*; in laymen's terms, it means somebody is better off, no one is worse off. Moreover, the result is "efficient" in another sense because the party who most dearly values the performance (the third party) obtains it.

Proponents of the efficient breach theory maintain that the remedy of specific performance induces an additional transaction — the promisor must buy her way out of the original contract — that raises transaction costs and jeopardizes the likelihood that an efficient result will be reached. Thus, for example, a seller who is required to specifically perform a contract will instead seek to bargain out of the obligation by offering to share with the buyer some of the gains from the better offer from the third party in order to be released from the contract. To be sure, the alternative of money damages requires a second transaction as well and also necessitates further negotiations. But, the argument goes, negotiations over sharing the spoils of breach are likely to be more complex (and hence more costly) than negotiations over the readily ascertainable contract-market differential. *See* Anthony Kronman, *Specific Performance*, 45 U. Chi. L. Rev. 351 (1978).

This justification for money damages as the preferred remedy is flawed, however. It assumes, incorrectly, that only the buyer can purchase substitute goods in the market. But one of the seller's options is for the *seller* to cover by purchasing goods conforming to the contract on the open market and then supplying them to the buyer in lieu of seller's own performance. When the seller can also cover, neither remedy would generate any post-breach negotiation costs. The seller merely "performs" his contract with the buyer (by supplying the substitute performance) and is free to accept the better offer from the third party.[79]

Thus, in a well-developed market where substitute goods can be purchased as easily by the seller as by the buyer, specific performances do not cause any excessive renegotiation costs. But, the same analysis suggests that in a well-developed market for substitutes, specific performance provides no particular benefits either. An expectancy damages rule is readily enforceable in such environments and presents no risk of measurement inaccuracies because, by definition, market values can be easily established. Specific performance provides no additional security against a breacher who is financially unable to satisfy the damage award. In well-developed markets, therefore, the distinction between the two remedies reduces to whether the buyer receives performance from the original seller or acquires a perfectly fungible performance on the market with the seller's damage payment. The distinction between specific performance and damages is only relevant, therefore, when market alternatives do not provide good substitutes for performance.[80]

This analysis focuses on the relevant issue: which party has the advantage in acquiring substitute goods in an imperfect market? It is tempting to assume that buyers are generally better equipped to purchase substitute goods than are sellers. (Just as it seems fair to assume that sellers are better able to find alternative purchasers for their goods than are buyers.) But, of course, this is not necessarily the case. It is possible that buyers have no advantage over sellers in covering on the market. Since the seller and buyer already have negotiated a contract, the seller may well be as aware of the buyer's particularized needs as is the buyer.

Does this mean that the analysis ends in a stalemate? As an *a priori* matter neither specific performance nor damages seems preferable as the default method of providing the promisee his lost expectancy. But there is a possible resolution that confirms the common law preference for money damages. Once a regret contingency has occurred, the promisor has two principal options: (1) perform the contract notwithstanding the contingency and accept any corresponding losses or (2) breach the contract and pay a compensatory damage award. Since the disappointed promisor will bear the full cost of the choice between "perform and lose" and "breach and pay," she is motivated to choose the least costly option. Thus, if the seller believes that she can cover more cheaply than the buyer, she will simply purchase substitute goods on her own initiative and perform her obligation by

---

[79] *See also* Ian R. Macneil, *Efficient Breach of Contract: Circles in the Sky*, 68 Va. L. Rev. 947 (1982). For a further analysis of the cases and (the limits of) the efficient breach theory, see Richard Craswell, *Contract Remedies, Renegotiation, and the Theory of Efficient Breach*, 61 S. Cal. L. Rev. 629 (1988).

[80] See Charles J. Goetz & Robert E. Scott, *The Mitigation Principle: Toward a General Theory of Contractual Obligation*, 69 Va. L. Rev. 967, 988–89 (1983).

supplying the substitute goods. (In such a case, the buyer may never know there was ever a problem with the seller's performance.) Indeed, there are strong incentives for most sellers to select the "perform and lose" option and not to breach. Breach after all, even if accompanied by a compensatory damage payment, is likely to cause bad feelings, loss of business reputation, good will, etc.

Thus, given the fact that the law requires compensation for breach, why would any seller ever breach? One possible explanation is that the seller might breach when she determines that the buyer is better able to cover on the market and thus reduce the seller's anticipated losses on the contract. Breach, under this conception, is a "cry for help" by the seller. It is a request for the buyer to salvage the broken contract at least cost and to send the seller the damage bill.

To the extent that this "benign" vision of breaching behavior is an accurate one, it supports the general preference for money damages. If specific performance were routinely available, the buyer could decline to mitigate seller's losses and refuse to cooperate. Yet, we have seen that the parties, if considering the question in advance, would incorporate in the contract a mitigation or cooperation responsibility by the buyer-promisee. Retaining the option to "breach and pay damages" is the only way that the disappointed promisor can enlist the promisee's cooperation in minimizing the costs of a regretted contract.

[4]   **Limitations on Compensation**

The preceding discussion has confirmed the centrality of the basic compensation principle of contract damages. Although many difficult questions arise when courts attempt to determine what recovery will be truly compensatory in particular cases, the expectation damages default rule is remarkably robust. As we have seen, the general default is to measure compensation by awarding expectation damages rather than specific performance. In addition, alternative measures such as reliance and restitution damages are awarded in only a narrow range of cases and punitive damages are generally unavailable for breach of contract per se.

In this part we explore the basic compensation principle in greater detail. In certain contexts, contract law limits a promisee's right to recover full compensation even though the promisor has concededly breached the contract. One such limitation on the promisee's damage recovery is the doctrine of avoidable consequences which is a particular manifestation of the pervasive *mitigation principle* that runs throughout contract law. This principle requires the promisee to take cost-justified steps to mitigate (or avoid aggravating) the promisor's damages for breach of the contract. The sanction for failure to mitigate is a reduction in the amount of damages that could reasonably have been avoided by the promisee.

In addition, the *foreseeability* principle seeks to ensure that, at the time of contracting, the promisor has reason to foresee any special or unusual consequences that might enhance the promisee's losses from breach. Consider, as an example, the following celebrated case.

HADLEY v. BAXENDALE
Court of Exchequer
9 Exch. 341, 156 Eng. Rep. 145 (1854)

At the trial before Crompton, J., at the last Gloucester Assizes, it appeared that the plaintiffs carried on an extensive business as millers at Gloucester; and that, on the 11th of May, their mill was stopped by a breakage of the crank shaft by which the mill was worked. The steam-engine was manufactured by Messrs. Joyce & Co., the engineers, at Greenwich, and it became necessary to send the shaft as a pattern for a new one to Greenwich. The fracture was discovered on the 12th, and on the 13th the plaintiffs sent one of their servants to the office of the defendants, who are the well-known carriers trading under the name of Pickford & Co., for the purpose of having the shaft carried to Greenwich. The plaintiffs' servant told the clerk that the mill was stopped, and that the shaft must be sent immediately; and in answer to the inquiry when the shaft would be taken, the answer was, that if it was sent up by twelve o'clock any day, it would be delivered at Greenwich on the following day. On the following day the shaft was taken by the defendants, before noon, for the purpose of being conveyed to Greenwich, and the sum of £ 2, 4s. was paid for its carriage for the whole distance; at the same time the defendants' clerk was told that a special entry, if required, should be made to hasten its delivery. The delivery of the shaft at Greenwich was delayed by some neglect; and the consequence was, that the plaintiffs did not receive the new shaft for several days after they would otherwise have done, and the working of their mill was thereby delayed, and they thereby lost the profits they would otherwise have received.

On the part of the defendants, it was objected that these damages were too remote, and that the defendants were not liable with respect to them. The learned Judge left the case generally to the jury, who found a verdict with £ 25 damages beyond the amount paid into Court.

Whateley, in last Michaelmas Term, obtained a rule nisi for a new trial on the ground of misdirection. . . .

ALDERSON, B.

We think that there ought to be a new trial in this case; but, in so doing, we deem it to be expedient and necessary to state explicitly the rule which the Judge, at the next trial, ought, in our opinion, to direct the jury to be governed by when they estimate the damages.

It is, indeed, of the last importance that we should do this; for, if the jury are left without any definite rule to guide them, it will in such cases as these, manifestly lead to the greatest injustice. The Courts have done this on several occasions; and, in Balke v. Midland Railway Company, 18 Q.B. 93, the Court granted a new trial on this very ground, that the rule had not been definitely laid down to the jury by the learned Judge at Nisi Prius. . . .

Now we think the proper rule in such a case as the present is this — Where two parties have made a contract which one of them has broken, the damages which the other party ought to receive in respect of such breach of contract should be such as may fairly and reasonably be considered either arising naturally, i.e., according to the usual course of things, from such breach of contract itself, or such as may reasonably be supposed to have been in the contemplation of both parties, at the time they made the contract, as the probable result of the breach of it. Now, if the special circumstances under which the contract was actually made were communicated by the plaintiffs to the defendants, and thus known to both parties, the damages resulting from the breach of such a contract, which they would reasonably contemplate, would be the amount of injury which would ordinarily follow from a breach of contract under these special circumstances so known and communicated. But, on the other hand, if these special circumstances were wholly unknown to the party breaking the contract, he, at the most, could only be supposed to have had in his contemplation the amount of injury which would arise generally, and in the great multitude of cases not affected by any special circumstances, from such a breach of contract. For, had the special circumstances been known, the parties might have specially provided for the breach of contract by special terms as to the damages in that case; and of this advantage it would be very unjust to deprive them. Now the above principles are those by which we think the jury ought to be guided in estimating the damages arising out of any breach of contract. It is said, that other cases such as breaches of contract in the non-payment of money, or in the not making a good title to land, are to be treated as exceptions from this, and as governed by a conventional rule. But as, in such cases, both parties must be supposed to be cognizant of that well-known rule, these cases may, we think, be more properly classed under the rule above enunciated as to cases under known special circumstances, because there both parties may reasonably be presumed to contemplate the estimation of the amount of damages according to the conventional rule. Now, in the present case, if we are to apply the principles above laid down, we find that the only circumstances here communicated by the plaintiffs to the defendants at the time the contract were made, were, that the article to be carried was the broken shaft of a mill, and that the plaintiffs were the millers of that mill. But how do these circumstances show reasonably that the profits of the mill must be stopped by an unreasonable delay in the delivery of the broken shaft by the carrier to the third person? Suppose the plaintiffs had another shaft in their possession put up or putting up at the time, and that they only wished to send back the broken shaft to the engineer who made it; it is clear that this would be quite consistent with the above circumstances, and yet the unreasonable delay in the delivery would have no effect upon the intermediate profits of the mill. Or, again, suppose that, at the time of the delivery to the carrier, the machinery of the mill had been in other respects defective, then, also, the same results would follow. Here it is true that the shaft was actually sent back to serve as a model for a new one, and that the want of a new one was the only cause of the stoppage of the mill, and that the loss of profits really arose from not sending down the new shaft in proper time, and that this arose from the delay in delivering the broken one to serve as a model. But it is obvious that, in the great multitude of cases of millers sending off broken shafts to third persons by a carrier under ordinary circumstances, such consequences would not, in all probability, have occurred; and these special circumstances were here never communicated by the plaintiffs to the defendants. It follows, therefore, that the loss of profits here cannot reasonably be considered such a consequence of the breach of contract as could have been fairly and reasonably contemplated by both the parties when they made this contract. For such loss would neither have flowed naturally from the breach of this contract in the great multitude of such cases occurring under ordinary circumstances, nor were the special circumstances, which, perhaps, would have made it a reasonable and natural consequence of such breach of contract, communicated to or known by the defendants. The Judge ought, therefore, to have told the jury, that, upon the facts then before them, they ought not to take the loss of profits into consideration at all in estimating the damages. There must therefore be a new trial in this case.

Rule absolute.

NOTES

1. *The Facts in* Hadley.

In considering the meaning and application of these rules it is essential to bear clearly in mind the facts on which *Hadley v. Baxendale* proceeded. The headnote is definitely misleading insofar as it says that the defendant's clerk, who attended at the office, was told that the mill was stopped and that the shaft must be delivered immediately. The same allegation figures in the statement of facts which are said on page 344 to have 'appeared' at the trial before Crompton J. If the Court of Exchequer had accepted these facts as established, the court must, one would suppose, have decided the case the other way round. . . . But it is reasonably plain from Alderson B.'s judgment that the court rejected this evidence, for on page 355 he says: 'We find that the only circumstances here communicated by the plaintiffs to the defendants at the time when the contract was made were that the article to be carried was the broken shaft of a mill and that the plaintiffs were the millers of the mill.'

Victoria Laundry (Windsor) Ltd. v. Newman Indus. Ltd., 2 K.B. 528, 537 (1949).

2. *Two Propositions.*

[*Hadley*] may be said to stand for two propositions: (1) that it is not always wise to make the defaulting promisor pay for all the damage which follows as a consequence of his breach, and (2) that specifically the proper test for determining whether particular items of damage should be compensable is to inquire whether they should have been foreseen at the time of the contract. The first aspect of the case is much more important than the second. In its first aspect the case bears an integral relation to the very bases of contract liability. It declares in effect that just as it is wise to refuse enforcement altogether to some promises (considerationless, unaccepted, 'social' promises, etc.) so it is wise not to go too far in enforcing those promises which are deemed worthy of legal sanction.

Lon L. Fuller & William R. Perdue, *The Reliance Interest in Contract Damages*, 46 Yale L.J. 52, 84 (1936).

Tortfeasors are said to "take their victims as they find them." Why do different approaches exist in contracts and in tort?[81]

3.   *The Use Value of Goods.* In *Hector Martinez and Company v. Southern Pacific Transportation Co.*, 606 F.2d 106 (5th Cir. 1979), the court allowed an award of consequential damages when a dragline (a type of excavating machine) was damaged when being shipped by train. In declaring that consequential damages would be permissible, even in the absence of the sort of special notice called for in *Hadley v. Baxendale*, the court noted,

> It was not obvious that the shaft in *Hadley* was an indispensable element in a mill. In the instant case, however, it was obvious that the dragline is a machine which of itself has a use value. . . . Capital goods such as machinery have a use value, which may equal the rental value of the machinery or may be an interest value. . . . It might be quite foreseeable that deprivation of the machine's use because of a carriage delay will cause a loss of rental value or interest value during the delay period.

Id. at 109.

4.   *Timing Alone Not Sufficient to Provide Notice of Special Circumstances.* Special notice is not imputed to carriers simply by virtue of the time of year when they agree to transport the products in question. For example, in *B. F. McKernin & Co. v. United States Lines, Inc.*, 416 F. Supp. 1068 (S.D.N.Y. 1976), the court rejected a claim for consequential damages related to the loss of customer goodwill when a Christmas time shipment of brass wares was mistakenly misdirected to Europe. The court noted that the carrier's mere awareness of the contents did not provide adequate notice of the special circumstances of the shipment. Because McKernin did not emphasize the importance of receiving the brass wares in time for the Christmas season, U.S. Lines could not be held liable for any consequential damages resulting from the delay.

Does the distinction between loss of use value in *Hector Martinez and Company* and loss of retail sales in *B. F. McKernin* make sense? Why wouldn't a shipper that has reason to know that a dragline has value in use not also have reason to know that retail goods need to be on the shelves before the annual holiday sales? Is the fact that the carrier only knew it was shipping "brassware" relevant to the foreseeability analysis? If the carrier was transporting inflatable Santas instead, does the case come out differently?

5.   *Custom Designed Equipment.* Certain highly complex products are designed for unique, specialized uses by their purchasers. It often is difficult to project accurately when custom designed equipment will be fully operational. Thus, lengthy delays can prove to be especially costly, as there often are few, if any, viable alternatives. In *Western Industries, Inc. v. Newcor Canada, Ltd.*, 739 F.2d 1198 (7th Cir. 1984), Western ordered several custom-designed welding machines from Newcor which were to be used to design microwave ovens in a manner that was common in Japan, but not used in the United States. Newcor built the machines, but

---

[81] For discussion of the difference between contract and tort with specific focus on *Hadley*, see Melvin A. Eisenberg, *The Principle of* Hadley v. Baxendale, 80 Cal. L. Rev. 563 (1992).

they did not function as intended. Judge Posner noted, "If a custom-built machine is delivered late, or does not work as the buyer had hoped and expected it would, the buyer's business is quite likely to suffer, and may even be ruined; and as the buyers of these welding machines are substantial manufacturers to whose businesses the machines are essential, the potential costs of defective design or late delivery are astronomical." *Id.* at 1203.

Given these risks, many sellers who design and produce custom equipment seek to opt out of the *Hadley* rule and limit their liability, either via express disclaimers of liability, or through liquidated damage clauses which provide a known limit on potential liability. In certain circumstances, however, courts will disregard such contractual limitations and permit buyers to recover full consequential damages notwithstanding the apparent agreement to the contrary. In *Milgard Tempering v. Selas Corp. of Am.*, 902 F.2d 703 (9th Cir. 1990), the parties agreed to limit Selas' liability to repair and replacement of any defective parts in a new type of furnace being purchased by Milgard, and barred liability for consequential damages. Selas was unable to provide a working furnace for nearly three years. The district court ruled that the "repair and replacement" limitation was unenforceable and permitted Milgard to recover consequential damages.

The appellate court noted:

> We agree with the district court's decision to lift the cap on consequential damages. Milgard did not agree to pay $1.45 million in order to participate in a science experiment. It agreed to purchase what Selas represented as a cutting-edge glass furnace that would actually accommodate its needs after two months of debugging. Selas' inability to effect repair despite 2.5 years of intense, albeit injudicious, effort caused Milgard losses not part of the bargained-for allocation of risk. Therefore, the cap on consequential damages is unenforceable.

Id. at 709.

Should courts set aside the provisions that parties have agreed to in the event that one party is unable to perform successfully? How should courts determine what sort of failure is sufficient to justify the invalidation of explicit contractual terms? (For an answer that applies to cases falling within Article 2, see § 2-719(2) cmt. 1.)

6.   *The Value of Secrecy.* Although *Hadley v. Baxendale* creates an incentive for parties to reveal how important performance of the contract is to them, in some commercial contexts parties may be reluctant to reveal such information. Contracting parties understandably may be reluctant to reveal, for example, their costs for materials and labor, the availability of other suppliers, or the identity of other contractual partners. Such information, however, would almost surely be revealed during pretrial discovery if a buyer sought to recover expectation damages based on lost profits.

Omri Ben-Shahar and Lisa Bernstein note that in cases involving a sufficiently strong secrecy interest, the cost of revealing private information may well exceed any expected recovery at trial. Concerns about private information, therefore, skew not only the incentives to bring a case to trial, but also skews the parties incentives to perform contracts. They note:

> In contracting contexts in which the secrecy concern is important, the use of a fully compensatory expectancy measure in a regime with liberal rules of civil discovery may fail to achieve the widely accepted remedial goal of full ex post compensation. It may also fail to induce efficient breach-or-perform decisions because promisors will realize that promisees with a sufficiently strong secrecy interest may not have a credible threat to sue. In addition, the availability of the expectation measure may, in some contexts, lead a promisor to breach solely in the hope that a promisee will sue and that he will be able to obtain valuable information.

For more on the conflicting compensatory and secrecy interests, see Omri Ben-Shahar & Lisa Bernstein, *The Secrecy Interest in Contract Law*, 109 YALE L.J. 1885 (2000).

7. *Foreseeable Emotional Distress Damages.* Damages for emotional distress are permissible under tort law, but only rarely are they recoverable as consequential damages in a breach of contract action. For instance, in *Hatfield v. Max Rouse & Sons Northwest*, 606 P.2d 944 (Idaho 1980), the court used *Hadley v. Baxendale* to reject a plaintiff's claim for damages for emotional distress when an auctioneer sold a piece of lumber equipment for considerably less than the agreed-to price. Similarly, in *Keltner v. Washington County*, 800 P.2d 752 (Or. 1990), a police officer promised a 14-year-old girl that, if she gave him information about the identity of the murderer of a local girl as well as her name and telephone number, the police would not disclose her identity to the accused murderer. Subsequent police reports identified her as the informant; these reports were given by the prosecutor to the defense attorney, who in turn informed his client. The court rejected the promisee's breach of contract claim, holding that such damages were not contemplated by the parties, as they were overly speculative and remote.

Courts are most likely to award damages for emotional distress in contract actions involving items of great sentimental value, such as the purchase of a home. Damages for emotional distress were permitted in *B & M Homes v. Hogan*, 376 So. 2d 667 (Ala. 1979), where the defendant was held liable for selling the plaintiff a house with a series of cracks that could not be repaired. The Supreme Court of Alabama ruled that the plaintiffs could recover, as they lived in fear of their home not being structurally sound. The court noted:

> It was reasonably foreseeable by appellants that faulty construction of appellees' house would cause them severe mental anguish. The largest single investment the average American family will make is the purchase of a home. . . . While one might expect to take the risk of acquiring a defective home if that person bought an older home, he or she certainly would not expect severe defects to exist in a home they contracted to have newly built. Consequently, any reasonable builder could easily foresee that an individual would undergo extreme mental anguish if their newly constructed house contained defects as severe as those shown to exist in this case.

Id. at 672.

Other types of agreements with manifest emotional overtones may have fore-seeable emotional consequences. For example, contracts involving arrangements for weddings or funerals presumably involve emotional considerations which are far more evident than, for instance, a sale of industrial equipment between two large firms. For more on the scope of emotional distress damages in contract law, see John D. McCamus, *Mechanisms for Restricting Recovery for Emotional Distress in Contract*, 42 Loy. L.A. L. Rev. 51 (2008); Douglas Whaley, *Paying for the Agony: The Recovery of Emotional Distress Damages in Contract Actions*, 26 Suffolk U. L. Rev. 935 (1992).

8. *Modern Applicability of* Hadley.

[I]n Hadley v. Baxendale the court spoke as though entrepreneurs were universally flexible enough and enterprises small enough for individuals to be able to serve "notice" over the counter of specialized needs calling for unusual arrangements. But in mass-transaction situations a seller cannot plausibly engage in an individualized "contemplation" of the consequences of breach and a subsequent tailoring of a transaction. In the course of his conversion of a family business into a modern industrial enterprise, Baxendale [the managing director of Pickfords, who was personally liable for its failings] made Pickfords itself into an operation where the contem-plation branch of the rule in Hadley v. Baxendale was no longer viable. Even in the 1820's the Pickfords' operations were "highly complex.". . . . A century later most enterprises fragment and standardize operations. . . . This development — and the law's recognition of it — makes it self-evidently impossible to serve legally cognizable notice on, for example, an airline that scheduled flight is of special importance or on the telephone company that uninterrupted service is particularly vital at a particular point in a firm's business cycle. . . .

The inadequacies of the rule are masked by still more fundamental phenomena which render the case of very limited relevance to the present economy.[82] At least in mass-transaction situations, the modern enterprise manager is not concerned with his corporation's liability as it arises from a particular transaction, but rather with liability when averaged over the full run of transactions of a given type. In the mass-production situation the run of these transactions will average his consequential-damages pay-out in a way far more predictable than a jury's guesses about the pay-out. In other words, for this type of entrepreneur — a type already emerging at the time of Hadley v. Baxendale, and far more prevalent today — there is no need for the law to provide protection from the aberrational customer; his own market and self-insurance capacities are great enough to do the job.

Richard Danzig, Hadley v. Baxendale: *A Study in the Industrialization of the Law*, 4 J. Legal Stud. 249, 279–83 (1975).

---

[82] [For an empirical analysis of the circumstances in which a *Hadley* default rule produces efficient outcomes, see George S. Geis, *Empirically Assessing* Hadley v. Baxendale, 32 Fla. St. U. L. Rev. 897 (2005). —Eds.

9. *The Theory of* Hadley *Limitations on Damages.* Is it possible to construct a justification for the rule in *Hadley v. Baxendale* similar to the analysis suggested for breach of contract damages generally? If the courts were to try to mirror what they thought contracting parties would agree to if they bargained over the *Hadley* issue at the time of contracting, what rule would they adopt? Perhaps the parties' negotiating problems can be ameliorated by a default rule that encourages the kind of information exchange that would give both parties access to all the information necessary to write an optimal contract. Is the rule of *Hadley* an information-forcing rule of the sort we encountered in our previous discussion of *Taylor v. Caldwell*? Consider the following conversation between a transporter of goods and a potential customer.

Customer: How much would you charge to carry this mill-shaft to Liverpool for me?

Carrier: Twenty dollars.

Customer: That sounds good to me. Be especially careful, because a lot rides on the shaft getting there by next week.

Carrier: I can guarantee that, but it will cost you more money.

Customer: Why is that?

Carrier: Because I need to know how many precautions to take to make sure that it gets there on time. Sometimes our equipment breaks down, and we have to decide whether to rent substitute equipment; sometimes another urgent order comes up, and we need to know which goods to "bump" if we can't carry everything. Even if we do our very best, some shipments inevitably get delayed, and we need to know what insurance to carry. All this makes a difference.

Customer: So what will it cost me to have you agree that the shaft either gets there by next week or you will repay all my losses?

Carrier: I can't tell you until you tell me what those losses are likely to be. As a carrier, we know how to take precautions, but you are the one that knows what is at stake if the shaft arrives late. If you tell us what that is likely to be, we can quote you the right price.

Customer: How do you handle this for other people? Surely not everyone needs to go through these complicated calculations.

Carrier: That's right. Most people care, but not to the extent that you do. Our policy is that we quote twenty dollars and we give ordinary care — that's what most people expect — if you have special risks, then you have to tell us, and we will figure the appropriate rate. Other carriers act the same way, so you can check with them if you think our special protection comes at too high a price.

Customer: Suppose that I wanted to send many items over a period of several months. How would we do the charges?

Carrier: We would agree to a schedule of charges for transportation using ordinary care on our part. If you had items needing special precautions, you would have to notify us at the time you brought the goods in and pay the higher price. If you had goods that you could have shipped with less than ordinary care on our part, let us know and we can give you an even lower price on those.[83]

F. BIBLIOGRAPHY AND SUGGESTED READING

[1] The Functions of Contract Rules

PATRICK. S. ATIYAH, AN INTRODUCTION TO THE LAW OF CONTRACT (1971).

Ian Ayres, *Valuing Modern Contract Scholarship*, 112 YALE L.J. 881 (2003).

Randy E. Barnett, *A Consent Theory of Contract*, 86 COLUM. L. REV. 269 (1986).

CHARLES FRIED, CONTRACT AS PROMISE: A THEORY OF CONTRACTUAL OBLIGATIONS (1981).

Clayton P. Gillette & Robert E. Scott, *The Political Economy of International Sales Law*, 25 INT'L. REV. L. & ECON. 446 (2005).

GRANT GILMORE, THE DEATH OF CONTRACT (1974).

William H. Henning, *Amended Article 2: What Went Wrong?*, 11 DUQ. BUS. L.J. 131 (2009).

Duncan Kennedy, *Form and Substance in Private Law Adjudication*, 89 HARV. L. REV. 1685 (1976).

Jody S. Kraus, *Transparency and Determinacy in Common Law Adjudication: A Philosophical Defense of Explanatory Economic Analysis*, 93 VA. L. REV. 287 (2007). Jody S. Kraus, *Philosophy of Contract Law*, THE OXFORD HANDBOOK ON JURISPRUDENCE AND LEGAL THEORY Ch. 18 (Jules L. Coleman and Scott Shapiro, eds., Oxford University Press 2002).

Jody S. Kraus, *Reconciling Autonomy and Efficiency in Contract Law: The Vertical Integration Strategy*, 11 PHIL. ISSUES 420 (2000).

Ian R. Macneil, *The Many Futures of Contract*, 47 S. CAL. L. REV. 691 (1974).

Daniel Markovits, *Contract and Collaboration*, 113 YALE L.J. 1417 (2004).

WILLIAM MITCHELL, AN ESSAY ON THE EARLY HISTORY OF THE LAW MERCHANT (1969).

Nathan Oman, *2005 Survey of Books Related to the Law: Unity and Pluralism in Contract Law: Contract Theory*, 103 MICH. L. REV. 1483 (2005).

Eric A. Posner, *Economic Analysis of Contract Law After Three Decades: Success or Failure?*, 112 YALE L.J. 829 (2003).

Alan Schwartz & Robert E. Scott, *Contract Theory and the Limits of Contract Law*, 113 YALE L.J. 541 (2003).

A.W.B. SIMPSON, A HISTORY OF THE COMMON LAW OF CONTRACT: THE RISE OF THE ACTION OF ASSUMPSIT (1975).

---

[83] For an analysis in the spirit of this note, see Andrew Tettleborn, *Hadley v. Baxendale Foreseeability: A Principle Beyond Its Sell-by Date?* 23 J. CONT. L. 120, 132 (2007).

[2] Enforcing Promises

Oren Bar-Gill, *The Behavioral Economics of Consumer Contracts*, 92 Minn. L. Rev. 749 (2008).

Oren Bar-Gill, *Seduction by Plastic*, 98 Nw. U. L. Rev. 1373 (2004).

Richard L. Barnes, *Rediscovering Subjectivity in Contracts: Adhesion and Unconscionability*, 66 La. L. Rev. 123 (2005).

Omri Ben Shahar, *Fixing Unfair Contracts*, 63 Stan. L. Rev. 869 (2011).

Philip Bridwell, *The Philosophical Dimensions of the Doctrine of Unconscionability*, 70 U. Chi. L. Rev. 1513 (2003).

Colin Camerer, Samuel Issacharoff, George Loewenstein, Ted O'Donoghue, & Matthew Rabin, *Behavioral Economics and the Case for "Asymmetric Paternalism,"* 151 U. Pa. L. Rev. 1211 (2003).

George Cohen, *The Fault Lines in Contract Damages*, 80 Va. L. Rev. 1225 (1994).

Richard Danzig, *A Comment on the Jurisprudence of the Uniform Commercial Code*, 27 Stan. L. Rev. 621 (1975).

Robert C. Ellickson, *Bringing Culture and Human Frailty to Rational Actors: A Critique of Classical Law and Economics*, 65 Chi.-Kent L. Rev. 23 (1989).

Melvin Aron Eisenberg, *The World of Contract and the World of Gift*, 85 Cal. L. Rev. 821 (1997).

Melvin A. Eisenberg, *The Bargain Principle and Its Limits*, 95 Harv. L. Rev. 741 (1982).

Richard Epstein, *Unconscionability: A Critical Reappraisal*, 18 J.L. & Econ. 293 (1975).

E. Allan Farnsworth, *The Past of Promise: An Historical Introduction to Contract*, 69 Colum. L. Rev. 576 (1969).

Clayton P. Gillette, *Pre-Approved Contracts for Internet Commerce*, 42 Hous. L. Rev. 975 (2005).

Grant Gilmore, The Death of Contract (1974).

Charles J. Goetz & Robert E. Scott, *Enforcing Promises: An Examination of the Basis of Contract*, 89 Yale L.J. 1261 (1980).

Gillian Hadfield, *An Expressive Theory of Contract: From Feminist Dilemmas to a Reconceptualization of Rational Choice in Contract Law*, 146 U. Pa. L. Rev. 1235 (1998).

Jon D. Hanson & Douglas A. Kysar, *Taking Behavioralism Seriously: The Problem of Market Manipulation*, 74 N.Y.U. L. Rev. 630 (1999).

Stanley D. Henderson, *Promissory Estoppel and Traditional Contract Docrine*, 78 Yale L.J. 343 (1969).

Christine Jolls, Cass R. Sunstein, & Richard Thaler, *A Behavioral Approach to*

Law and Economics, 50 STAN. L. REV. 1471 (1998).

Duncan Kennedy, *Distributive and Paternalistic Motives in Contract and Tort Law, With Special References to Compulsory Terms and Unequal Bargaining Power*, 41 MD. L. REV. 563 (1982).

Kevin A. Kordana & David H. Tabachnick, *Rawls and Contract Law*, 73 GEO. WASH. L. REV. 598, 626–29 (2005).

Russell Korobkin, *A "Traditional" and "Behavioral" Law-and-Economics Analysis of* Williams v. Walker-Thomas Furniture Company, 26 HAW. L. REV. 441 (2004).

Jody S. Kraus & Robert E. Scott, *Contract Design and the Structure of Contractual Intent*, 84 N.Y.U. L. REV. 1023 (2009).

Anthony Kronman, *Contract Law and Distributive Justice*, 89 YALE L.J. 471 (1980).

Saul Levmore, *Explaining Restitution*, 71 VA. L. REV. 65 (1985).

Ronald J. Mann, *Boilerplate in Consumer Contract: "Contracting" for Credit*, 104 MICH. L. REV. 899 (2006).

A. MELDEN, RIGHTS AND PERSONS (1977).

Gregory Mitchell, *Why Law and Economics' Perfect Rationality Should Not Be Traded for Behavioral Law and Economics' Equal Incompetence*, 91 GEO. L.J. 67 (2002).

Eric Posner, *Contract Law in the Welfare State: A Defense of the Unconscionability Doctrine, Usury Laws, and Related Limitations on the Freedom to Contract*, 24 J. LEGAL STUD. 283 (1995).

Todd Rakoff, *Contracts of Adhesion: An Essay in Reconstruction*, 96 HARV. L. REV. 1173 (1983).

Barak Richman & Dennis Schmelzer, *When Money Grew on Trees:* Lucy v. Zehmer *and Contracting in a Boom Market*, 61 DUKE L.J. 1511 (2012).

Keith A. Rowley, *You Asked for It, You Got It . . . Toy Yoda: Practical Jokes, Prizes, and Contract Law*, 3 NEV. L.J. 526 (2003).

Alan Schwartz, *A Re-Examination of Nonsubstantive Unconscionability*, 63 VA. L. REV. 1053 (1977).

Alan Schwartz & Louis Wilde, *Intervening in Markets on the Basis of Imperfect Information: A Legal and Economic Analysis*, 127 U. PA. L. REV. 630 (1979).

Alan Schwartz, *Unconscionability and Imperfect Information: A Research Agenda*, 19 CAN. BUS. L.J. 437 (1991).

Elizabeth S. Scott & Robert E. Scott, *Marriage as Relational Contract*, 84 VA. L. REV. 1225 (1998).

Robert E. Scott, *A Theory of Self-Enforcing Indefinite Agreements*, 103 COLUM. L. REV. 1641 (2003).

Robert Scott, *Error and Rationality in Individual Decision-making: An Essay on the Relationship Between Cognitive Illusions and the Management of Choices*, 59 S. CAL. L. REV. 329 (1986).

Robert E. Scott, *Rethinking the Regulation of Coercive Creditor Remedies*, 89 COLUM. L. REV. 730 (1989).

Richard E. Speidel, *An Essay on the Reported Death and Continued Vitality of Contract*, 27 STAN. L. REV. 1161 (1975).

[3]   Performance of the Obligation

Ian Ayres & Robert Gertner, *Filling Gaps in Incomplete Contracts: An Economic Theory of Default Rules*, 99 YALE L.J. 87 (1989).

Ian Ayres & Robert Gertner, *Strategic Contractual Inefficiency and the Optimal Choice of Legal Rules*, 101 YALE L.J. 729 (1992).

Randy E. Barnett, *The Sound of Silence: Default Rules and Contractual Consent*, 78 VA. L. REV. 821 (1992).

Omri Ben-Shahar, *A Bargaining Power Theory of Default Rules*, 109 COLUM. L. REV. 396 (2009).

Omri Ben-Shahar, *"Agreeing to Disagree": Filling Gaps in Deliberately Incomplete Contracts*, 2004 WIS. L. REV. 389.

David Charny, *Hypothetical Bargains: The Normative Structure of Contract Interpretation*, 89 MICH. L. REV. 1815 (1991).

Richard Craswell, *Contract Law, Default Rules, and the Philosophy of Promising*, 88 MICH. L. REV. 489 (1989).

Melvin A. Eisenberg, *The Limits of Cognition and the Limits of Contract*, 47 STAN. L. REV. 211 (1995).

Karen E. Francis, *Rollover, Rollover: A Behavioral Law and Economics Analysis of the Payday-Loan Industry*, 88 TEX. L. REV. 611 (2010)

Charles J. Goetz & Robert E. Scott, *Principles of Relational Contracts*, 67 VA. L. REV. 1089 (1981).

Charles J. Goetz & Robert E. Scott, *The Mitigation Principle: Toward a General Theory of Contractual Obligation*, 69 VA. L. REV. 967 (1983).

Victor Goldberg, *After Frustration: Three Cheers for Chandler v. Webster*, 68 WASH. & LEE L. REV. 1133, 1156–58 (2011).

Jason S. Johnston, *Strategic Bargaining and the Economic Theory of Contract Default Rules*, 100 YALE L.J. 615 (1990).

Anthony Kronman, *Mistake, Disclosure, Information, and the Law of Contracts*, 7 J. LEGAL STUD. 1 (1978).

Subha Narasimhan, *Of Expectations, Incomplete Contracting, and the Bargaining Principle*, 74 CAL. L. REV. 1123 (1986).

Dennis Patterson, *The Pseudo Debate over Default Rules in Contract Law*, 3 S. CAL. INTERDISC. L.J. 236 (1993).

Robert E. Scott, *A Relational Theory of Default Rules for Commercial Contracts*, 19 J. LEGAL STUD. 597 (1990).

Alan Schwartz, *The Default Rule Paradigm and the Limits of Contract Law*, 3 S. CAL. INTERDISC. L.J. 389 (1994).

ALAN SCHWARTZ, *Incomplete Contracts*, *in* 2 NEW PALGRAVE DICTIONARY OF ECONOMICS AND LAW 277 (1997).

David Slawson, *The Futile Search for Principles for Default Rules*, 3 S. CAL. INTERDISC. L.J. 29 (1993).

[4]   Remedies for Nonperformance

Barry E. Adler, *The Questionable Ascent of* Hadley v. Baxendale, 51 STAN. L. REV. 1547 (1999).

David W. Barnes & Deborah Zalesne, *A Unifying Theory of Contract Damage Rules*, 55 SYRACUSE L. REV. 495 (2005).

Omri Ben-Shahar & Lisa Bernstein, *The Secrecy Interest in Contract Law*, 109 YALE L.J. 1885 (2000).

Ronald Coase, *The Problem of Social Cost*, 3 J.L. & ECON. 1 (1960).

George Cohen, *The Fault Lines in Contract Damages*, 80 VA. L. REV. 1225 (1994).

Robert Cooter & Melvin A. Eisenberg, *Damages for Breach of Contract*, 73 CAL. L. REV. 1432 (1985).

Richard Craswell, *Contract Remedies, Renegotiation, and the Theory of Efficient Breach*, 61 S. CAL. L. REV. 629 (1988).

Richard Craswell, *Against Fuller and Perdue*, 67 U. CHI. L. REV. 99 (2000).

Richard Danzig, Hadley v. Baxendale: *A Study in the Industrialization of the Law*, 4 J. LEGAL STUD. 249 (1975).

Melvin A. Eisenberg, *Actual and Virtual Specific Performance, the Theory of Efficient Breach, and the Indifference Principle in Contract Law*, 93 CAL. L. REV. 975 (2005).

Melvin A. Eisenberg, *Expectation Damages and the Theory of Overreliance*, 54 HASTINGS L.J. 1335 (2003).

MELVIN A. EISENBERG, *The Principle Of* Hadley v. Baxendale, 80 CAL. L. REV. 563 (1992).

E. Allan Farnsworth, *Legal Remedies for Breach of Contract*, 70 COLUM. L. REV. 1145 (1970).

Lon Fuller & Perdue, *The Reliance Interest in Contract Damages*, 46 YALE L.J. 52 (1936).

George S. Geis, *Empirically Assessing* Hadley v. Baxendale, 32 FLA. ST. U. L. REV. 897 (2005).

Charles J. Goetz & Robert E. Scott, *Liquidated Damages, Penalties and the Just Compensation Principle: Some Notes on an Enforcement Model and a Theory of Efficient Breach*, 77 COLUM. L. REV. 554 (1977).

Oliver Wendell Holmes, Jr., *The Path of the Law*, 10 HARV. L. REV. 457 (1897).

Anthony Kronman, *Specific Performance*, 45 U. CHI. L. REV. 351 (1978).

Daniel Markovits & Alan Schwartz, *The Myth of Efficient Breach, New Defenses of the Expectation Interest*, 97 VA. L. REV. 1939 (2011).

John D. McCamus, *Mechanisms for Restricting Recovery for Emotional Distress in Contract*, 42 LOY. L.A. L. REV. 51 (2008).

RICHARD POSNER, ECONOMIC ANALYSIS OF THE LAW (4th ed. 1992).

Alan Schwartz & Robert E. Scott, *Market Damages, Efficient Contracting, and the Economic Waste Fallacy*, 108 COLUM. L. REV. 1610, 1656 (2008).

Robert E. Scott, *The Case for Market Damages: Revisiting the Lost Profits Puzzle*, 57 U. CHI. L. REV. 1155 (1990).

Robert E. Scott & George G. Triantis, *Embedded Options and the Case Against Compensation in Contract Law*, 104 COLUM. L. REV. 1428 (2004).

Steven Shavell, *Specific Performance Versus Damages for Breach of Contract: An Economic Analysis*, 84 TEX. L. REV. 831 (2006).

W. David Slawson, *Why Expectation Damages for Breach of Contract Must Be the Norm: A Refutation of the Fuller and Perdue "Three Interests" Thesis*, 81 NEB. L. REV. 839 (2003).

Andrew Tettleborn, *Hadley v. Baxendale Foreseeability: a Principle Beyond Its Sell-by Date?* 23 J. CONT. L., 120, 132 (2007).

Douglas Whaley, *Paying for the Agony: The Recovery of Emotional Distress Damages in Contract Actions*, 26 SUFFOLK U. L. REV. 935 (1992).

Chapter 2

ENFORCING PROMISES

A. INTRODUCTION

Contract law is commonly supposed to enforce promises. Why should promises be enforced? . . . [It] is the view of Kantians like Reinach that the duty to keep one's promise is one without which rational society would be impossible. There can be no doubt that from an empirical or historical point of view, the ability to rely on the promises of others adds to the confidence necessary for social intercourse and enterprise. But as an absolute proposition this is untenable. The actual world, which assuredly is among the possible ones, is not one in which all promises are kept, and there are many people — not necessarily diplomats — who prefer a world in which they and others occasionally depart from the truth and go back on some promise. It is indeed very doubtful whether there are many who would prefer to live in an entirely rigid world in which one would be obliged to keep all one's promises instead of the present more viable system, in which a vaguely fair proportion is sufficient. Many of us indeed would shudder at the idea of being bound by every promise, no matter how foolish, without any chance of letting increased wisdom undo past foolishness. Certainly, some freedom to change one's mind is necessary for free intercourse between those who lack omniscience.

At various times it has been claimed that mere promises as such received legal force in Hebrew, Greek, early German, and canon law. None of these claims can be justified.

Morris Cohen, *The Basis of Contract*, 46 Harv. L. Rev. 553, 571, 572–74 (1933).

A contract is a legally enforceable promise. But why are some promises legally binding, while others are not? Chapter 1 introduced this question. The purpose of Chapter 2 is to examine the enforcement doctrines of contract law in more detail. Courts use three principal doctrines to distinguish between enforceable and nonenforceable promises: the consideration doctrine (Restatement (Second) § 71), promissory estoppel (Restatement (Second) § 90), and the material benefit rule (Restatement (Second) § 86). As you consider each below, pay close attention to how courts apply the black letter formulations of these doctrines to the specific facts before them. For each case, ask yourself whether the black letter doctrine explains why the court enforced or refused to enforce the promise at issue. Could you have predicted how the court would have decided the case based on the facts and Restatement alone? What are the relevant factual differences between the cases that explain why they were decided differently or the relevant similarities that explain why they were decided similarly?

B. THE CONSIDERATION DOCTRINE

Read § 71 of the Restatement (Second). Section 71 sets out the so-called "bargain theory" of consideration, which replaced its predecessor, the so-called "benefit-detriment" theory of consideration applied in *Hamer v. Sidway* (in Chapter 1 and below). Consideration is the oldest doctrine used to distinguish between promises that are legally enforceable and those that are not. Unless one of the other enforcement doctrines applies (promissory estoppel or the material benefit rule), courts will enforce only those promises that are "supported by consideration." How do courts determine whether a promise is supported by consideration? The standard answer suggested by § 71 is that "bargained for" promises are supported by consideration, but "gift promises" are not.

[1] Bargain Versus Gift

HAMER v. SIDWAY
Court of Appeals of New York
124 N.Y. 538, 27 N.E. 256 (1891)

See p. 43, *supra.*

KIRKSEY v. KIRKSEY
Supreme Court of Alabama
8 Ala. 131 (1845)

Assumpsit by the defendant, against the plaintiff in error. The question is presented in this Court, upon a case agreed, which shows the following facts:

The plaintiff was the wife of defendant's brother, but had for some time been a widow, and had several children. In 1840, the plaintiff resided on public land, under a contract of lease, she had held over, and was comfortably settled and would have attempted to secure the land she lived on. The defendant resided in Talladega county, some sixty, or seventy miles off. On the 10th October, 1840, he wrote to her the following letter:

> Dear sister Antillico — Much to my mortification, I heard, that brother Henry was dead, and one of his children. I know that your situation is one of grief, and difficulty. You had a bad chance before, but a great deal worse now. I should like to come and see you, but cannot with convenience at present. . . . I do not know whether you have a preference on the place you live on, or not. If you had, I would advise you to obtain your preference, and sell the land and quit the country, as I understand it is very unhealthy, and I know society is very bad. If you will come down and see me, I will let you have a place to raise your family, and I have more open land than I can tend; and on the account of your situation and that of your family, I feel like I want you and the children to do well.

Within a month or two after the receipt of this letter, the plaintiff abandoned her possession, without disposing of it, and removed with her family, to the residence of the defendant, who put her in comfortable houses, and gave her land to cultivate for two years at the end of which time he notified her to remove, and put her in a house, not comfortable, in the woods, which he afterwards required her to leave.

A verdict being found for the plaintiff for two hundred dollars, the above facts were agreed, and if they will sustain the action, the judgment is to be affirmed, otherwise it is to be reversed.

ORMOND, **J.**

The inclination of my mind, is that the loss and inconvenience, which the plaintiff sustained in breaking up, and moving to the defendant's, a distance of sixty miles, is a sufficient consideration to support the promise, to furnish her with a house, and land to cultivate, until she could raise her family. My brothers, however think, that the promise on the part of the defendant, was a mere gratuity, and that an action will not lie for its breach. The judgment of the Court below must therefore be reversed pursuant to the agreement of the parties.

NOTES

1.   *Consideration and Gift.* Since the brother-in-law in *Kirksey* was found not to have made a binding promise, is it appropriate to conclude that he promised to make a gift? If so, the promise is not enforceable under the law of gifts. Consider this language from *Spooner's Adm'r v. Hilbish's Ex'r*, 92 Va. 333, 341, 23 S.E. 751, 753 (1895):

> A gift is a contract without valid consideration, and, to be valid, must be executed. A valid gift is therefore a contract executed. It is to be executed by the actual delivery by the donor to the donee, or to someone for him, of the thing given, or by the delivery of the means of obtaining the subject of the gift, without further act of the donor to enable the donee to reduce it to his own possession. "The intention to give must be accompanied by a delivery, and the delivery must be made with an intention to give." Otherwise there is only an intention or promise to give, which, being gratuitous, would be a mere nullity. Delivery of possession of the thing given, or of the means of obtaining it so as to make the disposal of it irrevocable, is indispensable to a valid gift.

2.   *What was Kirksey's motivation?* Many subsequent readers of *Kirksey v. Kirksey* have speculated about the motives of Issac Kirksey in inviting his sister-in-law to move on his land and then subsequently requiring her to leave. Professors William Castro and Val Ricks claim that

> Issac Kirksey . . . had an ulterior motive. He meant to place Antillico on public land to hold his place . . . so that he could buy the land from the U.S. government at a lucrative discount. . . . Issac evicted Antillico because a change in the laws made Issac ineligible to buy government land at a

discount, but the same law allowed Antillico a right to the land on which Issac placed her. . . . Only by evicting her could Issac hope to retain that land.[1]

3. *Williston's Tramp.* The uncle's promise was enforced in *Hamer*, but the brother-in-law's promise was not enforced in *Kirksey*. Can *Hamer* be distinguished from *Kirksey*? What benefit did the brother-in-law in *Kirksey* receive? What detriment did the widow suffer? Aren't similar benefits and detriments present every time a promise is made and taken seriously? Consider this quotation from a very influential contracts scholar:

> If a benevolent man says to a tramp: "If you go around the corner to the clothing shop there, you may purchase an overcoat on my credit," no reasonable person would understand that the short walk was requested as the consideration for the promise, but that in the event of the tramp going to the shop the promisor would make him a gift. Yet the walk to the shop is in its nature capable of being consideration. It is a legal detriment to the tramp to make the walk, and the only reason why the walk is not consideration is because on a reasonable construction it must be held that the walk was not requested as the price of the promise, but was merely a condition of a gratuitous promise. It is often difficult to determine whether words of condition in a promise indicate a request for consideration or state a mere condition in a gratuitous promise. An aid, though not a conclusive test in determining which construction of the promise is more reasonable is an inquiry whether the happening of the condition will be a benefit to the promisor. If so, it is a fair inference that the happening was requested as a consideration. On the other hand, if, as in the case of the tramp stated above, the happening of the condition will be not only of no benefit to the promisor but is obviously merely for the purpose of enabling the promisee to receive a gift, the happening of the event on which the promise is conditional, though brought about by the promisee in reliance on the promise, will not properly be construed as consideration. In case of doubt where the promisee has incurred a detriment on the faith of the promise, courts will naturally be loath to regard the promise as a mere gratuity and the detriment incurred as merely a condition. But in some cases it is so clear that a conditional gift was intended that even though the promisee has incurred detriment, the promise has been held unenforceable.

1 WILLISTON ON CONTRACTS § 112.

4. *Hey, you never know.* Social promises, such as the one in *Kirksey*, arise often, requiring courts to draw lines about when to enforce them as contracts, and when to cast them aside as merely gratuitous promises. Consider the following puzzle in the context of the court's decision in *Kirksey*:

> A man walks into a convenience store that he frequents and purchases a stack of lottery tickets. He turns to the manager, as well as two fellow

---

[1] William R. Castro & Val D. Ricks, *"Dear Sister Antillico . . .": The Story of* Kirksey v. Kirksey, 94 GEO. L.J. 321, 323–25 (2006).

customers, and says that he will share his winnings if they help him scratch off the tickets. One of the tickets reveals a $100,000 prize, but the man refuses to share the winnings.

In *Fitchie v. Yurko*, 570 N.E.2d 892 (Ill. App. Ct. 1991), the court held for the plaintiffs that there was an enforceable contract. The consideration given by the plaintiffs was that they "expended their time and energy and put forth effort to scratch the tickets." Can this outcome be distinguished from *Kirksey*?

ST. PETER v. PIONEER THEATRE CORP.
Supreme Court of Iowa
227 Iowa 1391, 291 N.W. 164 (1940)

See p. 45, *supra*.

IN RE GREENE
United States District Court, Southern District of New York
45 F.2d 428 (1930)

Woolsey, J.

The petition for review is granted, and the order of the referee is reversed.

I. The claimant, a woman, filed proof of claim in the sum of $375,700, based on an alleged contract, against this bankrupt's estate. The trustee in bankruptcy objected to the claim. A hearing was held before the referee in bankruptcy and testimony taken. The referee held the claim valid and dismissed the objections. The correctness of this ruling is raised by the trustee's petition to review and the referee's certificate.

II. For several years prior to April 28, 1926, the bankrupt, a married man, had apparently lived in adultery with the claimant. He gave her substantial sums of money. He also paid $70,000 for a house on Long Island acquired by her, which she still owns. Throughout their relations the bankrupt was a married man, and the claimant knew it. The claimant was well over thirty years of age when the connection began. She testified that the bankrupt has promised to marry her as soon as his wife should get a divorce from him; this the bankrupt denied. The relations of intimacy between them were discontinued in April, 1926, and they then executed a written instrument under seal which is alleged to be a binding contract and which is the foundation of the claim under consideration.

In this instrument, which was made in New York, the bankrupt undertook (1) to pay to the claimant $1,000 a month during their joint lives; (2) to assign to her a $100,000 life insurance policy on his life and to keep up the premiums on it for life, the bankrupt to pay $100,000 to the claimant in case the policy should lapse for nonpayment of premiums; and (3) to pay the rent for four years on an apartment which she had leased. It was declared in the instrument that the bankrupt had no interest in the Long Island house or in its contents, and that he should no longer be liable for mortgage interest taxes, and other charges on this property. The claimant on her part released the bankrupt from all claims which she had against him. The preamble to the instrument recites as consideration the payment of $1 by the claimant to the bankrupt, "and other good and valuable consideration." The bankrupt kept up the several payments called for by the instrument until August, 1928, but failed to make payments thereafter.

III. In the proof of claim it is alleged that a total of $375,700 was due because of breach of the agreement, made up as follows: $250,000 for failure to pay $1,000 a month; $99,200 for failure to maintain the insurance policy; and $26,500 for failure to pay the rent. The claim was sustained by the referee for the full amount.

It seems clear that the $250,000 allowed as damages for failure to pay $1,000 a month was excessive. The bankrupt's undertaking was to pay $1,000 a month only so long as both he and the claimant should live; it was not an annuity for the claimant's life alone, as she seems to have assumed. There is nothing in the record to indicate the bankrupt's age, and consequently there is a failure of proof as to this element of damage. In view of my conclusion that the entire claim is void, however, the matter of damages is of no present importance.

IV. A contract for future illicit cohabitation is unlawful. There is consideration present in such a case, but the law strikes the agreement down as immoral. *Williston on Contracts*, § 1745. Here the illicit intercourse had been abandoned prior to the making of the agreement, so that the above rule is not infringed. This case is one where the motive which led the bankrupt to make the agreement on which the claim is based was the past illicit cohabitation between him and the claimant. The law is that a promise to pay a woman on account of cohabitation which has ceased is void, not for illegality, but for want of consideration. The consideration in such a case is past. The mere fact that past cohabitation is the motive for the promise will not of itself invalidate it, but the promise in such a case, to be valid, must be supported by some consideration other than past intercourse. *Williston on Contracts*, §§ 148, 1745.

The problem in the present case, therefore, is one of consideration, not of illegality, and it is clear that the past illicit intercourse is not consideration. The cases dealing with situations where there is illegitimate offspring or where there has been seduction are of doubtful authority, for the doctrine that past moral obligation is consideration is now generally exploded. But these cases and others speaking of expiation of past wrong, cited by the referee, are not in point. Here there was not any offspring as a result of the bankrupt's union with the claimant; there was not any seduction shown in the sense in which that word is used in law. Cf. New York Penal Law, art. 195, Sec. 2175. There was not any past wrong for which the bankrupt owed the claimant expiation — *volenti non fit injuria*. Cases involving deeds, mortgages, and the like are not analogous, because no consideration is necessary in an executed transaction.

V. The question, therefore, is whether there was any consideration for the bankrupt's promises, apart from the past cohabitation. It seems plain that no such consideration can be found, but I will review the following points emphasized by the claimant as showing consideration:

(1) The $1 consideration recited in the paper is nominal. It cannot seriously be urged that $1, recited but not even shown to have been paid, will support an executory promise to pay hundreds of thousands of dollars.

(2) "Other good and valuable consideration" are generalities that sound plausible, but the words cannot serve as consideration where the facts show that nothing good or valuable was actually given at the time the contract was made.

(3) It is said that the release of claims furnishes the necessary consideration. So it would if the claimant had had any claims to release. But the evidence shows no vestige of any lawful claim. Release from imaginary claims is not valuable consideration for a promise. In this connection, apparently, the claimant testified that the bankrupt had promised to marry her as soon as he was divorced. Assuming that he did — though he denies it — the illegality of any such promise, made while the bankrupt was still married, is so obvious that no claim could possibly arise from it, and the release of such claim could not possibly be lawful consideration.

(4) The claimant also urges that by the agreement the bankrupt obtained immunity from liability for taxes and other charges on the Long Island house. The fact is that he was never chargeable for these expenses. He doubtless had been in the habit of paying them, just as he had paid many other expenses for the claimant; but such payments were either gratuitous or were the contemporaneous price of the continuance of his illicit intercourse with the claimant. It is absurd to suppose that, when a donor gives a valuable house to a donee, the fact that the donor need pay no taxes or upkeep thereafter on the property converts the gift into a contract upon consideration. The present case is even stronger, for the bankrupt had never owned the house and had never been liable for the taxes. He furnished the purchase price, but the conveyance was from the seller direct to the claimant.

(5) Finally, it is said that the parties intended to make a valid agreement. It is a non sequitur to say that therefore the agreement is valid. A man may promise to make a gift to another, and may put the promise in the most solemn and formal document possible; but, barring exceptional cases, such, perhaps, as charitable subscriptions, the promise will not be enforced. The parties may shout consideration to the housetops, yet, unless consideration is actually present, there is not a legally enforceable contract. What the bankrupt obviously intended in this case was an agreement to make financial contribution to the claimant because of his past cohabitation with her, and, as already pointed out, such an agreement lacks consideration.

V. The presence of the seal would have been decisive in the claimant's favor a hundred years ago. Then an instrument under seal required no consideration, or, to keep to the language of the cases, the seal was conclusive evidence of consideration. In New York, however, a seal is now only presumptive evidence of consideration on an executory instrument. This presumption was amply rebutted in this case, for the proof clearly shows, I think, that there was not in fact any consideration for the bankrupt's promise contained in the executory instrument signed by him and the claimant.

NOTES

1. ***The Shift From "Benefit/Detriment" to "Bargained-for Exchange."*** The *Hamer* court discusses consideration from the perspectives of the benefit to the promisor and the detriment to the promisee. More recent cases, such as *St. Peter*, follow the "bargained-for exchange" language, which is the terminology employed by § 71 of the Restatement (Second). How did this shift in terms occur, and does it signify something deeper than a mere rewording of the test? Professors Grant Gilmore and Richard Speidel each formulated a theory to explain the transformation.

In *The Death of Contract* 19–21 (1974), Professor Gilmore maintained that the modern formulation of consideration emerged, fully developed, from a series of lectures entitled The Common Law, delivered by Oliver Wendell Holmes in 1881. Gilmore contended that the common law, in actions of debt and assumpsit, had defined consideration as consisting of any benefit to the promisor or any detriment to the promisee. But Holmes apparently changed that. According to Gilmore, Holmes was the first legal scholar to promote the idea that consideration existed only when a promise or performance was bargained for in exchange for another promise. That is to say, Holmes added to the traditional benefit-or-detriment formulation the additional requirement that a promisor must seek the purported consideration as a trade for his promise. This idea of bargained-for promises became known as the "bargain theory" of contracts. Holmes' conception of consideration severely limited the range of contractual liability imposed by courts, for a contract would only be enforced when all elements of consideration were satisfied. This "revolutionary" idea, as Gilmore put it, was adopted by Samuel Williston, reporter for the original Restatement of Contracts in 1932, and found expression in § 75. From there it was a small step to § 71 of the Restatement (Second) of Contracts in 1979, the current definition of consideration.

Professor Richard Speidel took issue with Gilmore's explanation of the rise of consideration. In *An Essay on the Reported Death and Continued Vitality of Contract*, 27 STAN. L. REV. 1161 (1975), Speidel presented what he called a more "balanced" approach to the evolution of consideration and the bargain theory of contract. Speidel argued that the bargain theory was the result of historical developments in American economic and legal history and not merely the creation of Justice Holmes. The bargained for exchange is rooted in part in basic human behavior, however history provides further reasons why the bargain theory has emerged as the distinguishing factor between enforceable and unenforceable promises as opposed to other factors.

Speidel built upon Professor Ian Macneil's idea that bargain and exchange behavior is prominent when four conditions exist: "(1) specialization of labor and exchange; (2) a sense by individuals of their capacity for choice and consequences of its exercise; (3) an awareness of the continuum between past, present, and future; and (4) a social matrix which reinforces the exercise of choices made with an eye to the future." While these conditions existed in England prior to the period of colonization, the unique combination of "legal heritage, challenge, opportunity, and individual motivation was irrepressible" in America and resulted in an "explosion of contract behavior." In these circumstances, people turned to bargain-oriented practices rather than following the common law traditions of England, a change in line with Professor Lawrence Friedman's suggestion in *A History of American Law* that colonists brought less of the common law to America than normally presumed. Speidel also referred to Professor J. Willard Hurst's ideas on the development of bargain and exchange. Hurst saw the doctrine of consideration as an emerging method of market control, a legal technique employed by courts to regulate market transactions. Speidel noted that the doctrine performed a formal channeling function, protected and structured market transactions, extended legal protection to the executory exchange (a promise for a promise), and facilitated the development of remedies to protect the plaintiff's expectation interest.

While Hurst and Friedman may have assumed too much intentional employment of contract law by the government to promote economic growth and did not provide a specific explanation of how the bargain theory emerged, Speidel used their ideas to support the contention that Holmes' "announced bargain theory was more evolutionary than revolutionary." In conclusion, Speidel wrote:

> Regardless of defects in the birth announcement or errors in subsequent rearing, the child itself can be viewed as a natural and perhaps inevitable product of the interaction over time of events and ideas in America. It was also a helpful child as courts struggled to develop a framework within which private exchange could occur. These factors, natural development and utility, bespeak a tradition of some durability. Traditions die hard, especially where market ideology and room for its exercise still remain. Since Professor Gilmore has slighted this dimension of the American past, I think that he has branded the new child as illegitimate without taking all of the necessary blood tests.

Id. at 1171.

2.   *The Search for Consideration in* Greene. Read Restatement (Second) § 74. How could you use this provision to argue for the enforceability of Greene's agreement? Didn't Trudel give consideration by agreeing not to pursue any legal action she had against Greene? What if both parties believed that Trudel, in fact, had a valid claim against Greene?[2]

3.   *Consideration and Form: Fuller's Three Functions of Consideration.* Had there been consideration for the promises in *Greene*, they would have been enforceable. We would like to be able to analyze the meaning of the consideration requirement by looking at the justification for imposing the requirement. Unfortunately, there is no widely accepted theory on this question. Consideration is often thought to be a device that distinguishes between enforceable and nonenforceable promises on the basis of form. An exchange between parties to a contract must take place in order to satisfy the requirement of consideration. Once actions have been

---

[2] For a discussion of how the court could have used a "moral obligation" theory to find consideration in *Greene*, see Kevin M. Teeven, *Moral Obligation Promise for Harm Caused*, 39 Gonz. L. Rev. 349, 386–87 (2003).

taken in that specific form, a court is likely to enforce the contract when asked to do so. Consideration, then, provides parties with a set of legal formalities against which each litigated case can be compared.

Professor Lon Fuller discussed this formal aspect of consideration in *Consideration and Form*, 41 Colum. L. Rev. 799, 800–02 (1941). According to Fuller, legal formalities in general, and consideration in particular, serve three functions: an evidentiary function, a cautionary or deterrent function, and a channeling function.

Consideration serves an evidentiary function by providing a court with evidence that an agreement or promise exists when that existence is in dispute. The efforts of parties to reach a binding agreement, through bargaining and negotiation, and the existence of that agreement can be reduced to a shorthand test: Is the contract supported by consideration? Consideration thus is some proof of the existence of a contract.

Legal formalities also perform cautionary or deterrent functions, for they act as a check against rash, impulsive actions. Consideration helps ensure that a hasty, unreasonable promise, made as a joke, for example, or made under adverse circumstances, will not be enforced to the disadvantage of the promisor. Each party to a contract must either perform or promise to perform in order to reap the benefits of the bargain.

Finally, consideration serves a channeling function by providing, as Fuller put it, "a legal framework into which the party may fit his actions, or, to change the figure, it offers channels for the legally effective expression of intention." *Id.* at 801. If parties want to make a binding agreement, they are able to do so according to the set of rules on consideration provided by the legal system. Fuller provided a useful analogy to further explain this channeling idea:

> In seeking to understand this channeling function of form, perhaps the most useful analogy is that of language, which illustrates both the advantages and dangers of form in the aspect we are now considering. One who wishes to communicate his thoughts to others must force the raw material of meaning into defined and recognizable channels; he must reduce the fleeting entities of wordless thought to the patterns of conventional speech. One planning to enter a legal transaction faces a similar problem. His mind first conceives an economic or sentimental objective, or, more usually, a set of overlapping objectives. He must then, with or without the aid of a lawyer, cast about for the legal transaction (written memorandum, sealed contract, lease, conveyance of the fee, etc.) which will most nearly accomplish all these objectives. Just as the use of language contains dangers for the uninitiated, so legal forms are safe only in the hands of those who are familiar with their effect. . . .
>
> The ideal of language would be the word whose significance remained constant and unaffected by the context in which it was used. Actually, there are few words, even in scientific language, which are not capable of taking on a nuance of meaning because of the context in which they occur. So in the law, the ideal type of formal transaction would be the transaction described on the Continent as "abstract," that is, the transaction which is abstracted

from the causes which gave rise to it and which has the same legal effect no matter what the context of motives and lay practices in which it occurs. The seal in its original form represented an approach to this ideal, for it will be recalled that extra-formal factors, including even fraud and mistake, were originally without effect on the sealed promise.

Most of the formal transactions familiar to modern law, however, fall far short of the "abstract" transaction; the channels they cut are not sharply and simply defined.

Id. at 801–02.

If you applied these formal criteria to *Greene*, how would you decide the case? Even if Fuller has identified the correct formal criteria, the cases do not apply the criteria directly. Instead, the criteria produce a "rule" — a promise will be enforced if and only if it is supported by consideration. One feature of a rule is that it will ordinarily be both overinclusive and underinclusive. Some promises will be enforced because they are supported by consideration even though one or more of the underlying criteria are not satisfied (overinclusiveness) — i.e., the promise was made rashly, or was not made at all; other promises will not be enforced because they lack consideration even though the criteria are satisfied (underinclusiveness) — i.e., *Greene*. If a rule, such as that requiring consideration before a promise is enforced, can be overinclusive and underinclusive, why have a "rule" at all? Why not apply the criteria directly to particular promises?

4. *Contracts Under Seal and the Model Written Obligations Act.* The seal referred to in *Greene* and in the excerpt from Professor Fuller is an ancient device that was originally used to identify the maker of a document and to evidence the document's authenticity. English common law has long enforced promises made in sealed documents, even those not supported by consideration, and such is the rule in England today. GUNTHER TREITEL, THE LAW OF CONTRACT 120 (6th ed. 1983). Professor Melvin Eisenberg, in *The Principles of Consideration*, 67 CORNELL L. REV. 640 (1982), discusses the seal in the context of a donative promise:

> Given that unrelied-upon donative promises are normally unenforceable, the question arises whether the law should recognize some special form through which a promisor with the special intent to be legally bound could achieve that objective. "It is something," said Williston, "that a person ought to be able . . . if he wishes to do it . . . to create a legal obligation to make a gift. Why not? . . . I don't see why a man should not be able to make himself liable if he wishes to do so."
>
> At early common law the seal served this purpose. In modern times, most state legislatures have either abolished the distinction between sealed and unsealed promises, abolished the use of a seal in contracts, or otherwise limited the seal's effect. The axiomatic school, however, never rejected the rule that a seal makes a promise enforceable, and that rule is now embodied in § 95(1)(a) of the Restatement Second, which provides that "[i]n the absence of statute a promise is binding without consideration if . . . it is in writing and sealed. . . ."

The Restatement Second makes no attempt to justify this rule. Originally, the seal was a natural formality — that is, a promissory form popularly understood to carry legal significance — which ensured both deliberation and proof by involving a writing, a ritual of hot wax, and a physical object that personified its owner. Later, however, the elements of ritual and personification eroded away, so that in most states by statute or decision a seal may now take the form of a printed device, word, or scrawl, the printed initials "L.S.," [standing for "locus sigilli" — place of the seal] or a printed recital of sealing. Few promisors today have even the vaguest idea of the significance of such words, letters, or signs, if they notice them at all. The Restatement Second itself admits that "the seal has come to seem archaic." Considering this drastic change in circumstances, the rule that the seal renders a promise enforceable has ceased to be tenable under modern conditions. The rule has been changed by statute in about two-thirds of the states, and at least one modern case[3] held even without the benefit of a statute that the rule should no longer be strictly applied.

Id. at 659–60.

Eisenberg notes that the formality of a wax seal was gradually relaxed at common law so that printed or written words or marks were recognized as seals in most American jurisdictions. Perhaps the most extreme example of this is found in *Appeal of Hacker*, 121 Pa. 192, 15 A. 500 (1888), where an ink dash between one-sixteenth and one-eighth of an inch long at the end of a signature was held to be a seal. With the loss of traditional ceremony and formalism, the seal fell under criticism because it no longer served to impress upon a promisor the legal consequences of his act. The New York Law Revision Commission stated its criticism in a 1941 report:

Whatever the historical origin of the seal, the modern justification of its use has been based on the assurance of solemnity and deliberateness arising from the presence of a seal on a promise in writing. Making an impression on wax or adding a seal to an instrument with an adhesive was fairly well designed to impress the sealer with the dignity and importance of the act. The most important objection to the seal as a method of formality is that the seal is [no longer] well adapted for this purpose . . . particularly with the routine printing of the letters "L.S. on law blanks, the solemn effect of the act of sealing was much impaired. It is highly doubtful today whether the presence of the seal on the paper or even the addition of the seal to a writing actually implies greater deliberateness than the signing of the writing by itself. It is quite certain that most laymen and many lawyers have little or no idea of the exact effect of the presence of the seal.

Report of the New York Law Revision Commission 375–76 (1941).

Today, approximately one-half of the states give no special legal effect to a seal.[4] In the remaining states, the seal's principal legal effect is to extend the statute of

---

[3] *Hartford-Connecticut Trust Co. v. Divine*, 97 Conn. 193, 116 A. 239 (1922). [Eds.]

[4] For tables which detail the status of the seal in American jurisdictions, see the passage in the

limitations and/or to raise a rebuttable presumption that the promise was supported by consideration. Though some states have neither enacted statutes nor issued decisions denying the seal's common law power to bind a promisor, the exact status of the seal in these states is uncertain. *See* Restatement (Second) at 255–59 (introductory note). In any event, because of UCC § 2-203, the seal is ineffective in all states (except Louisiana, which never recognized it in the first place) for contracts involving the sale of goods.

A very few states have enacted statutes that provide simple devices other than the seal by which promises without consideration can be made binding. In Mississippi and New Mexico, for example, written promises are binding without consideration, effectively substituting the existence of a writing for the seal. *See* Miss. Code Ann. § 75-10-3 (1972); N.M. Stat. Ann. § 38-7-2 (1978). And Pennsylvania has enacted the Uniform Written Obligations Act (renamed a Model Act in 1943), which was drafted by Professor Williston and approved in 1925 by the National Conference of Commissioners on Uniform State Laws and the American Bar Association. Section One of that act reads:

> A written release or promise hereafter made and signed by the person releasing or promising shall not be invalid or unenforceable for lack of consideration, if the writing also contains an additional express statement, in any form of language, that the signer intends to be legally bound.

While other states have not followed this example, fifteen states have made the existence of writings presumptive evidence of consideration. *See* Holmes, *Stature and Status of a Promise Under Seal as a Legal Formality*, 29 Willamette L. Rev. 617, 647 (1993); 9C U.L.A. 378 (1957).[5]

[2]   Adequacy of Consideration

BATSAKIS v. DEMOTSIS
Court of Civil Appeals of Texas
226 S.W.2d 673 (1949)

[In war-torn Greece of 1942, Eugenia Demotsis borrowed the equivalent of $25 from George Batsakis in exchange for a note which said that she had borrowed $2,000 and would repay him that amount together with eight percent interest on the loan.]

Restatement (Second) cited immediately above; Robert Braucher, *The Status of the Seal Today*, 9 Prac. Law. 97 (May 1963); 1A Williston on Contracts § 219A (3d ed. 1957). On the history and functions of the seal, see Comment, *The Seal in North Carolina and the Need for Reform*, 15 Wake Forest L. Rev. 251, 252–58 (1979).

[5] *See* Pa. Stat. Ann. tit. 33, § 6 (Purdon, 1967). Pennsylvania is an outlier; Utah, the only other state to adopt the act, repealed it in 1933. Other states were concerned that such a statement could become a boilerplate clause in form contracts, and thus not reflect the true intention of the promisor to be legally bound to a donative promise. *See, e.g.*, Holbrook, *The Status of the Common Law Seal Doctrine in Utah*, 3 Utah L. Rev. 73 (1952). For a proposed modification of the act, intended to address these concerns, see Holmes, 29 Willamette L. Rev. at 667. For a criticism of the act, see Steele, *The Uniform Written Obligations Act — A Criticism*, 21 Ill. L. Rev. 185 (1927).

McGILL, J.

This is an appeal from a judgment of the 57th judicial District Court of Bexar County. Appellant was plaintiff and appellee was defendant in the trial court. The parties will be so designated.

Plaintiff sued defendant to recover $2,000 with interest at the rate of 8% per annum from April 2, 1942, alleged to be due on the following instrument, being a translation from the original, which is written in the Greek language:

Peiraeus

April 2, 1942

Mr. George Batsakis
Konstantinou Diadohou #7
Peiraeus

Mr. Batsakis:

I state by my present (letter) that I received today from you the amount of two thousand dollars ($2,000.00) of United States of America money, which I borrowed from you for the support of my family during these difficult days and because it is impossible for me to transfer dollars of my own from America.

The above amount I accept with the expressed promise that I will return to you again in American dollars either at the end of the present war or even before in the event that you might be able to find a way to collect them (dollars) from my representative in America to whom I shall write and give him an order relative to this. You understand until the final execution (payment) to the above amount an eight per cent interest will be added and paid together with the principal.

I thank you and I remain yours with respects.

The recipient,

(Signed) Eugenia The. Demotsis.

Trial to the court without the intervention of a jury resulted in a judgment in favor of plaintiff for $750.00 principal, and interest at the rate of 8% per annum from April 2, 1942 to the date of judgment, totaling $1163.83, with interest thereon at the rate of 8% per annum until paid. Plaintiff has perfected his appeal.

[On appeal, the defendant argued that the agreement lacked consideration because she only received the equivalent of $25 and not $2,000 as stated in the note. The plaintiff responded that the claimed defense of failure of consideration would not lie because defendant received exactly what was agreed to be delivered to her.]

Defendant testified that she did receive 500,000 drachmas from plaintiff. It is not clear whether she received all the 500,000 drachmas or only a portion of them before she signed the instrument in question. Her testimony clearly shows that the understanding of the parties was that plaintiff would give her the 500,000 drachmas if she would sign the instrument. She testified:

Q: . . . who suggested the figure of $2,000.00?

A: That was how he asked me from the beginning. He said he will give
                me five hundred thousand drachmas provided I signed that I would
                pay him $2,000.00 American money.

The transaction amounted to a sale by plaintiff of the 500,000 drachmas in
consideration of the execution of the instrument sued on, by defendant. It is not
contended that the drachmas had no value. Indeed, the judgment indicates that the
trial court placed a value of $750.00 on them or on the other consideration which
plaintiff gave defendant for the instrument if he believed plaintiff's testimony.
Therefore the plea of want of consideration was unavailing. A plea of want of
consideration amounts to a contention that the instrument never became a valid
obligation in the first place.

Mere inadequacy of consideration will not void a contract. Nor was the plea of
failure of consideration availing. Defendant got exactly what she contracted for
according to her own testimony. The court should have rendered judgment in favor
of plaintiff against defendant for the principal sum of $2,000.00 evidenced by the
instrument sued on, with interest as therein provided. We construe the provision
relating to interest as providing for interest at the rate of 8% per annum. The
judgment is reformed so as to award appellant a recovery against appellee of
$2,000.00 with interest thereon at the rate of 8% per annum from April 2, 1942. Such
judgment will bear interest at the rate of 8% per annum until paid on $2,000.00
thereof and on the balance interest at the rate of 6% per annum. As so reformed, the
judgment is affirmed.

WOLFORD v. POWERS
Supreme Court of Indiana
85 Ind. 294 (1882)

[The plaintiff brought suit against the estate of Charles Lehman to obtain
judgment on a promissory note for $10,000. It appears that just prior to his death,
Lehman was a widower, about eighty-seven years old, who had been a friend of the
plaintiff for many years. In April of 1878 a son was born into the plaintiff's family,
and Lehman, whose own son had died many years earlier, promised that if the
plaintiff would name his son Charles Lehman Wolford, that Lehman "would make
[the child's] welfare his chief object in life, and provide for it generously and give it
a good education." During the ensuing months, Lehman visited the plaintiff's home
frequently. At Lehman's request, the plaintiff and his wife cared for Lehman during
some brief illnesses and also hired a carriage to take him out driving several times.

When the boy was five months old, Lehman executed a note to the plaintiff for
$10,000, stating that he preferred this method of carrying out his promise rather
than by making a provision in his will or a present conveyance of property. The trial
court rendered judgment for the defendant, but the Indiana Supreme Court
reversed, holding that the naming of the child and the various services rendered to
Lehman by the plaintiff's family were consideration for Lehman's promise. In
reaching its decision the court said:]

It is the general rule that where there is no fraud, and a party gets all the consideration he contracts for, the contract will be upheld. In Hardesty v. Smith, 3 Ind. 39, it was said: "When a party gets all the consideration he honestly contracted for, he can not say that he gets no consideration, or that it has failed. If this doctrine be not correct then it is not true that parties are at liberty to make their own contracts." The same principle is declared and enforced in many of our own cases. In Pollock's *Principles of Contract*, the author quotes approvingly from a philosophic treatise this statement:

"The value of all things contracted for is measured by the appetite of the contractors, and therefore the just value is that which they be contented to give." An examination of the decided cases will prove this to be an unusually accurate statement of the law. In the case of Sturlyn v. Albany, l Cro. Eliz. 67, it was held that where the defendant promised the plaintiff that if he would show him a lease he would pay him a certain sum, and the contract was held valid. The report of the decision reads thus: "But it was adjudged for the plaintiff: for when a thing is to be done by the plaintiff, be it ever so small, this is a sufficient consideration to ground an action."

. . . [W]here a party contracts for the performance of an act which will afford him pleasure, gratify his ambition, please his fancy, or express his appreciation of a service another has done him, his estimate of value should be left undisturbed unless, indeed, there is evidence of fraud. There is, in such a case, absolutely no rule by which the courts can be guided, if once they depart from the value fixed by the promisor. If they attempt to fix some standard, it must necessarily be an arbitrary one, and ascertained only by mere conjecture. If, in the class of cases under mention, there is any legal consideration for a promise, it must be sufficient for the one made; for, if this be not so, then the result is that the court substitutes its own judgment for that of the promisor, and, in doing this, makes a new contract. Where the purpose of the party is to secure a pecuniary or property benefit, there is much more ground for judicial interference than in a case like this, where the controlling purpose is not gain, but the gratification of a desire or fancy. Even in the former class of cases, courts never do interfere upon the sole ground of inadequacy of consideration, and certainly should not in the class to which the one at bar belongs. No person in the world, other than the promisor, can estimate the value of an act which arouses his gratitude, gratifies his ambition, or pleases his fancy. If there be any consideration at all, it must be allotted the value the parties have placed upon it, or a conjectural estimate, made arbitrarily and without the semblance of a guide, must be substituted by the courts.

NOTES

1. *Comparing* Greene *and* Wolford. The transactions in both *Greene* and *Wolford* were cast in the form of a bargain. The court in *Greene* rejected the argument that the writing's recitation of Trudel's payment of $1 to Greene constitutes consideration, in part because Trudel in fact never paid it. Is that the court's strongest reason for denying that Greene's promise is supported by consideration? The recital of a payment of $1 and "other good and valuable considerations" is common in many agreements. Why do you suppose parties include it in their agreements? Is it the difference in the amount of money paid in

Greene and *Wolford* that explains their different outcomes?

2. **In re Greene *Redux?*** For a modern analogue to *Greene*, consider *Williams v. Ormsby*, 2012 Ohio 690. In May 2004, Frederick Ormsby moved into Amber Williams' house. After Frederick paid the remaining mortgage balance of $310,000, Amber transferred title to the house to him. Although the couple planned to marry, they canceled their plans and, in March 2005, Amber left the house. In June 2005, the parties signed a written agreement and Amber moved back into the house. The agreement stated that "for valuable consideration" the parties agreed that the house, though titled solely in Frederick's name, was owned jointly and that they were equal partners. The agreement provided for Frederick to pay all expenses on the house and that if their relationship ended, and/or the house were sold, they would divide the proceeds after expenses were paid. The Supreme Court of Ohio held that:

> Although the June document states that the agreement was made 'for valuable consideration' it does not specify what that consideration is. . . . The evidence demonstrates that the only consideration offered by Amber for the June 2005 agreement was her resumption of a romantic relationship with Frederick. This agreement amounts to a gratuitous promise by Frederick to give Amber an interest in property based solely on the consideration of her love and affection. Therefore, the June 2005 document is not an enforceable contract.

3. ***The Adequacy and Nominality Doctrines.*** The *Wolford* opinion states the rule that a court will not refuse to enforce a contract on the ground that the value of the consideration is inadequate. The court in *Greene* dismisses the claim in part for the reason that the consideration was "nominal." Professor Corbin rationalizes these two seemingly incongruous rules:

> Parting with a document, the contents of which can in fact render no service, has been held to be a sufficient consideration for a promise to pay a large sum of money. Services or property are sufficient consideration for a promise to pay much more money than anyone else would pay for them. . . .

> The rule that market equivalence of consideration is . . . to be left solely to the free bargaining process of the parties, leads in extreme cases to seeming absurdities. When the consideration is only a "peppercorn" or a "tomtit" or a worthless piece of paper, the requirement of a consideration appeared to Holmes to be as much of a mere formality as is a seal. In such extreme cases, a tendency may be observed to refuse to apply the rule; but it is a tendency that has not been carried very far. Such cases can sometimes be explained on the ground that the stated consideration was a mere pretense.

1 CORBIN ON CONTRACTS § 127 (1963).

Section 79 of the Restatement (Second) adopts the rule that courts ought to honor the values that parties have placed on their respective performances. Comment c to § 79 explains some of the reasoning behind this rule:

To the extent that the apportionment of productive energy and product in the economy are left to private action, the parties to transactions are free to fix their own valuations. The resolution of disputes often requires a determination of value in the more general sense of market value, and such value are commonly fixed as an approximation based on a multitude of private valuations. But in many situations there is no reliable external standard of value, or the general standard is inappropriate to the precise circumstances of the parties. Valuation is left to private action in part because the parties are thought to be better able than others to evaluate the circumstances of particular transactions. In any event, they are not ordinarily bound to follow the valuations of others.

Ordinarily, therefore, courts do not inquire into the adequacy of consideration. This is particularly so when one or both of the values exchanged are uncertain or difficult to measure. But it is also applied even when it is clear that the transaction is a mixture of bargain and gift. . . . Gross inadequacy of consideration may be relevant to issues of capacity, fraud and the like, but the requirement of consideration is not a safeguard against imprudent and improvident contracts except in cases where it appears that there is no bargain in fact.

This rule is known as the adequacy doctrine or, alternatively, as the peppercorn theory, a name that comes from the common law tradition that something as trifling in value as a peppercorn could serve as consideration for a bargain: "A cent or a pepper corn, in legal estimation, would constitute a valuable consideration." *Whitney v. Stearns*, 16 Me. 394, 397 (1839).

The converse of the adequacy doctrine is the "nominality" doctrine. Comment d to § 79 of the Restatement (Second) reflects this idea: "Disparity in value, with or without other circumstances, sometimes indicates that the purported consideration was not in fact bargained for but was a mere formality or pretense. Such sham or 'nominal' consideration does not satisfy the requirement of § 71." Although courts do not "inquire into the adequacy of consideration," they nonetheless refuse to enforce contracts supported by what they consider to be "nominal" or "sham" consideration. As the court in *Greene* states, "[t]he parties may shout consideration to the housetops, yet, unless consideration is actually present, there is not a legally enforceable contract."

What if the promisor intends to make a legally binding donative promise? In most states, the seal is no longer available. Under the nominality doctrine, simply stating the existence of consideration will not suffice to make a promise legally enforceable. Are there circumstances under which courts ought to enforce such promises?[6]

4. *Unconscionability.* Read § 208 of the Restatement (Second) of Contracts. Ought the court in *Batsakis* to have struck down that contract on the ground of

---

[6] For an argument that parties should be able to use nominal consideration to enforce gratuitous promises, see Comment, *The Peppercorn Reconsidered: Why a Promise to Sell Blackacre for Nominal Consideration Is Not Binding, But Should Be*, 97 Nw. U.L. Rev. 1809 (2003).

unconscionability? What is the relationship between the unconscionability doctrine and the consideration doctrine?

Before you conclude that the *Batsakis* contract was unconscionable, you should know more about the context of the agreement. The following is a description of life in Athens under the early days of the German occupation, at which time Mrs. Demotsis borrowed the 500,000 drachmas:

> During the first winter of the occupation, 1941-2, the blockaded cities and the mountain villages, cut off from the plains which had supplied them with grain, salt and oil, suffered the most. Athens became a nightmare landscape of skeletal figures with bellies swollen, shuffling hopelessly in search of food, falling dead and lying unburied in the streets. The children and the elderly died first.
>
> In the first two months of winter, 300,000 people starved to death in the capital. In order to keep the deceaseds' ration cards, families did not report deaths but threw the corpses surreptitiously over the walls of cemeteries. . . .
>
> The ration cards were nearly worthless, since bread was nonexistent, the food shops closed and shuttered. The smallest purchase required sacks of paper money. . . . If a baker happened to find enough flour to bake and sell a loaf of bread, he set the price in British gold sovereigns.
>
> Everyone who could walk spent the entire day until curfew searching for food. The poor stripped the countryside of greens for miles outside of Athens. Trees in the avenues and parks were cut down for firewood. Servants of the wealthy were sent to outlying villages and islands with family treasures in search of a loaf of bread or a chicken. . . .
>
> During the winter of 1941 in Athens, packs of stray dogs howled in the hills below the Acropolis, mass graves were dug in the gardens of the royal palace, and death waited on every street corner.[7]

Given these conditions, Batsakis, it could be said, had slim prospects of ever seeing a penny of his loan repaid. Should the court consider whether the loan actually was repaid in deciding a case such as *Batsakis*?

> It is tempting to rationalize such intervention on fairness grounds, but it is important to examine what degree of intervention would be in the interest of the parties, ex ante. For it may well be that the anticipation of an overly aggressive intervention by the law would backfire and induce the strong party to refrain from any kind of dealings with its counterpart. If the contract is reformed with a term that, while ex post reasonable, does not leave enough of an incentive for the stronger party to enter it, such intervention is not in the ex ante interest of both parties. In *Batsakis*, as in many high-interest loans, the creditor is taking advantage of the borrower's urgent need for funds. But it would be misleading to examine the scenario ex post, when it is already known that the borrower was able to secure the

---

[7] Excerpted from Nicholas Gage, Eleni 65–67 (1983).

loan, and conclude that the price was excessive. Ex ante, the high price was necessary in light of the uncertainty over repayment.

Omri Ben-Shahar, *Fixing Unfair Contracts*, 63 STAN. L. REV. 869, 905 (2011).

5. ***Mutuality of Obligation.*** When one promise is exchanged for another (a "bilateral contract"), courts often apply the doctrine of "mutuality of obligation." The principle of mutuality of obligation is commonly expressed as requiring that "both parties are bound, or neither is bound." Although courts frequently analyze the mutuality principle as though it were a separate requirement for a contract, it can be seen as an application of the test of consideration. The Restatement (Second) of Contracts § 79 adopts the latter approach. The doctrine merits some attention, however, because it still appears in judicial opinions. A federal court has clarified the relation between consideration and mutuality of obligation:

> As a unilateral contract is not founded on mutual promises, the doctrine of mutuality of obligation is inapplicable to such a contract. It is applicable, however, to a bilateral contract containing mutual executory promises because there both parties are bound by reciprocal obligations and the promise of one is the consideration for the promise of the other. If for any reason the promise of one party is not binding upon him, it is not a sufficient consideration for the promise of the other and the contract is void for want of consideration. The terms "consideration" and "mutuality of obligation" are sometimes confused. "Consideration is essential; mutuality of obliga-tion is not unless the want of mutuality would leave one party without a valid or available consideration for his promise. The doctrine of mutuality of obligation appears therefore to be merely one aspect of the rule that mutual promises constitute considerations for each other. Where there is no other consideration for a contract, mutual promises must be binding on both parties. But where there is any other consideration for the contract, mutuality of obligation is not essential." Moreover, a contract does not lack mutuality merely because its terms are harsh or its obligations unequal, or because every obligation of one party is not met by an equivalent counter obligation of the other party.

Meurer Steel Barrel Co. v. Martin, 1 F.2d 687, 688 (3d Cir. 1924).

A paradigmatic case where a problem of mutuality of obligation would arise is where an unenforceable promise (say, a promise to do an illegal act) is given in exchange for a valid promise. Analyze the situation in terms of consideration. Can you articulate the logic behind the "both are bound, or neither is bound" rule of thumb?

6. ***The Problem of the Disgruntled Donees.*** Theresa decided it was time to write her will. She considered whom she wanted to be her beneficiaries, and finally settled on a list of four people. Theresa went to her attorney, explained her wishes, and left him to draw up the will. The final document provided the following: $200 should go to each of three lifelong friends, J. B. Nell, Wendelin Lorenz, and Lorenz's wife, Donata, with the remainder of the estate to go to her husband, Zachariah.

Shortly after her will was witnessed and signed, Theresa died. Her will was entered into probate, but the terms could not be carried out. Theresa's estate consisted entirely of property owned jointly with Zachariah. Upon her death, that property passed directly to Zachariah. Thus, there was no estate from which to pay the $200 legacies.

Knowing how fond his wife had been of her three friends, Zachariah entered into a written agreement with each of them. The documents provided that, in consideration of their mutual desire to honor the memory of Theresa, Zachariah would pay each party $66.67 per year until each had received $200. In return, each party agreed to give Zachariah $1 and to waive any legal claims they might have arising from Theresa's will in consideration for the yearly payments. The documents were signed and sealed by Zachariah and the three would-be legatees. In addition, Nell and the Lorenzs each gave Zachariah $1 as specified in the documents.

Alas, upon surveying his financial situation several months later, Zachariah decided he could not afford to make the yearly payments. When the first payment fell due, Zachariah sent each legatee a note explaining his situation and asking that he be released from his commitment. J.B. Nell and the Lorenzs, upset that they were once again denied their windfall, did not agree to release Zachariah. Instead, they filed suit, asking that the agreement be enforced as a legally binding contract.

You are the judge in this case. What verdict would you render? What policies would you cite in support of your decision? For one court's answer, see *Schnell v. Nell*, 17 Ind. 29 (1861).

Suppose that you are Zachariah's attorney before he encounters financial trouble. How could you draft a document that would give legal effect to his objective?

7. *More Problems.*

a. Carwardine, eager to discover the identity of a murderer, posted an announcement guaranteeing a reward to anyone who could identify the man. Williams, after being beaten by the man she knew to be the murderer and believing herself to be fatally injured, confessed his name and what he had done. Williams recovered from her beating, but Carwardine refused to pay her the reward money, citing the circumstances of her confession. Williams sued him for the money. What result? Was there sufficient consideration? If the courts did not permit Williams to capture the reward, would those with information be more or less willing to come forward with it? Would people still post offers of rewards for information? *See Williams v. Carwardine*, 4 Barnewell & Adolphus 621 (1833).

b. Plaintiff sues for breach of contract. She alleges that she had sexual intercourse with defendant when she was unmarried, that she became pregnant, that defendant acknowledged that the child was his, and that in return for plaintiff's promise not to institute legal proceedings against defendant, defendant promised to pay plaintiff's hospital expenses, doctor bills, and child support of a set amount until the child reached 21 years of age. Defendant alleges that the promise is without consideration because he is not the father of the child. He asks the court to order that the child submit to a blood test to determine whether the defendant can be the father. As a matter of contract law, is this relevant evidence? *See Fiege v. Boehm*, 123 A.2d 316 (Md. 1956); Restatement (Second) of Contracts § 74.

C. PROMISSORY ESTOPPEL

[1] Introduction

Thus far, we have been looking at the doctrine of consideration and bargained-for exchanges as the basis for the imposition of contractual liability. But as the Restatement (Second) § 90 makes explicit, the doctrine of consideration is no longer the sole tenet underlying the enforcement of promises. Courts have expanded the set of enforceable promises to include those that are based on reliance — that is, they have ruled that promises may be enforced if the promisee has incurred costs, or conferred benefits, on the reasonable expectation that the promise would be fulfilled. This "reliance principle" has the advantage of eliminating the need for identifying a bargained-for exchange, and thus has been a convenient doctrinal tool for expanding the scope of enforcement beyond the narrow confines of the common law consideration model.

In this section we turn to the doctrine of promissory estoppel. Begin by reading carefully Restatement (Second) § 90. The foundational question is what is the relationship between the doctrine of consideration as developed in Restatement (Second) § 71 and the doctrine of promissory estoppel (as found in § 90). For example, assume a court finds that a promise is not enforceable under § 71. Is that court free to simply turn to § 90 and enforce the promise according to its quite different standards? If that is so, then what is the point of having a consideration doctrine that serves principally to identify those promises that are *not* enforceable? Before we seek to answer these questions systematically, carefully analyze the following statements and then ask yourself whether promissory estoppel and consideration are facially complementary or fundamentally incompatible doctrines.

> It would cut up the doctrine of consideration by the roots, if a promisee could make a gratuitous promise binding by subsequently acting on it.

Commonwealth by Commissioners of Sav. Banks v. Scituate Sav. Bank, 137 Mass. 301, 302 (1884) (Holmes, J.).

> Certainly some freedom to change one's mind is necessary for free intercourse between those who lack omniscience. For this reason we cannot accept Dean Pound's theory that all promises in the course of business should be enforced. He seems to me undoubtedly right in his insistence that promises constitute modern wealth and that their enforcement is thus a necessity of maintaining wealth as a basis of civilization. . . . Still, business men as a whole do not wish the law to enforce every promise. Many business transactions, such as those on a stock or produce exchange, could not be carried on unless we could rely on a mere verbal agreement or hasty memorandum. But other transactions, like those of real estate, are more complicated and would become too risky if we were bound by every chance promise that escapes us. Negotiations would be checked by such fear. In such cases men do not want to be bound until the final stage, when some formality like the signing of papers gives one the feeling of security, of having taken proper precautions.

Morris Cohen, *The Basis of Contract*, 46 HARV. L. REV. 553, 572–74 (1933).

In fact . . . detrimental reliance is likely to occur even if no visible evidence of it exists. Between the date of the [gratuitous] promise and that of the repudiation, [the promisee] will have modified his consumption habits in adjustment to his suddenly increased expected wealth. If this expectation is disappointed, [the promisee's] excessive consumption will have produced a permanent net loss in welfare; this loss is his reliance injury. Courts rarely acknowledge the existence of such uncompensated reliance when they refuse to enforce gratuitous promises. The absence of bargained-for consideration triggers instead a presumption of nonenforcement.

Charles J. Goetz & Robert E. Scott, *Enforcing Promises: An Examination of the Basis of Contract*, 89 YALE L.J. 1261, 1302 (1980).

Essay: Corbin and the Restatement

Why does the Restatement (Second) include a section on promissory estoppel (§ 90) that conflicts with its own requirement of consideration (§ 71, which was formerly numbered as § 75)? The following explanation is reprinted from GILMORE, THE DEATH OF CONTRACT 60–65 (1974).

[Consider] the Restatement's definition of consideration (§ 75) taken in connection with its most celebrated section, § 90, captioned Promise Reasonably Inducing Definite and Substantial Action. First § 75:

(1) Consideration for a promise is

(a) an act other than a promise, or

(b) a forbearance, or

(c) the creation, modification or destruction of a legal relation, or

(d) a return promise, bargained for and given in exchange for the promise.

(2) Consideration may be given to the promisor or to some other person. It may be given by the promisee or by some other person.

This is, of course, pure Holmes. The venerable Justice took no part in the Restatement project. It is unlikely that he ever looked at the Restatement of Contracts. If, however, § 75 was ever drawn to his attention, it is not hard to imagine him chuckling at the thought of how his revolutionary teaching of the 1880s had become the orthodoxy of a half-century later. Now § 90:

A promise which the promisor should reasonably expect to induce action or forbearance of a definite and substantial character on the part of the promisee and which does induce such action or forbearance is binding if injustice can be avoided only by enforcement of the promise.

And what is that all about? We have become accustomed to the idea, without in the least understanding it, that the universe includes both matter and anti-matter. Perhaps what we have here is Restatement and anti-Restatement or Contract and anti-Contract. We can be sure that Holmes, who relished a good paradox, would have laughed aloud at the sequence of § 75 and § 90. The one thing that is clear is that these two contradictory propositions cannot live comfortably together: in the end one must swallow the other up.

A good many years ago Professor Corbin gave me his version of how this unlikely combination came about. When the Restaters and their advisors came to the definition of consideration, Williston proposed in substance what became § 75. Corbin submitted a quite different proposal. To understand what the Corbin proposal was about, it is necessary to backtrack somewhat. Even after the Holmesian or bargain theory of consideration had won all but universal acceptance, the New York Court of Appeals had, during the Cardozo period, pursued a line of its own. There is a long series of Cardozo contract opinions, scattered over his long tenure on that court. Taken all in all, they express what might be called an expansive theory of contract. Courts should make contracts wherever possible, rather than the other way around. Missing terms can be supplied. If an express promise is lacking, an implied promise can easily be found. In particular Cardozo delighted in weaving gossamer spider webs of consideration. There was consideration for a father's promise to pay his engaged daughter an annuity after marriage in the fact that the engaged couple, instead of breaking off the engagement, had in fact married. There was consideration for a pledge to a college endowment campaign (which the donor had later sought to revoke) in the fact that the college, by accepting the pledge, had come under an implied duty to memorialize the donor's name: "The longing for posthumous remembrance is an emotion not so weak as to justify us in saying that its gratification is a negligible good."[8] Evidently a judge who could find "consideration" in *De Cicco v. Schweizer*[9] or in the *Allegheny College* case [246 N.Y. 369 (1927)] could, when he was so inclined, find consideration anywhere: the term had been so broadened as to have become meaningless. We may now return to the Restatement debate on the consideration definition. Corbin, who had been deeply influenced by Cardozo, proposed to the Restaters what might be called a Cardozoean definition of consideration — broad, vague and, essentially, meaningless — a common law equivalent of *causa*, or cause. In the debate Corbin and the Cardozoeans lost out to Williston and the Holmesians. In Williston's view, that should have been the end of the matter.

Instead, Corbin returned to the attack. At the next meeting of the Restatement group, he addressed them more or less in the following manner: Gentlemen, you are engaged in restating the common law of contracts. You have recently adopted a definition of consideration. I now submit to you a list of cases — hundreds, perhaps or thousands? — in which courts have imposed contractual liability under circumstances in which, according to your definition, there would be no consideration and therefore no liability. Gentlemen, what do you intend to do about these cases?

---

[8] [141] Allegheny College v. National Chautauqua County Bank, 246 N.Y. 369, 377 (1927).

[9] 221 N.Y. 431 (1917). —Eds.

To understand Corbin's point we must backtrack and digress again. I have made the point that Holmesian consideration theory had, as Holmes perfectly well knew, not so much as a leg to stand on if the matter is taken historically. Going back into the past, there was an indefinite number of cases which had imposed liability, in the name of consideration, where nothing like Holmes's "reciprocal conventional inducement" was anywhere in sight. Holmes's point was that these were bad cases and that the range of contractual liability should be confined within narrower limits. By the turn of the century, except in New York, the strict bargain theory of consideration had won general acceptance. But, unlike Holmes, many judges, it appeared, were not prepared to look with stony-eyed indifference on the plight of a plaintiff who had, to his detriment, relied on a defendant's assurances without the protection of a formal contract. However, the new doctrine precluded the judges of the 1900 crop from saying, as their predecessors would have said a half-century earlier, that the "detriment" itself was "consideration." They had to find a new solution, or, at least, a new terminology. In such a situation the word that comes instinctively to the mind of any judge is, of course, "estoppel" — which is simply a way of saying that, for reasons which the court does not care to discuss, there must be judgment for plaintiff. And in the contract cases after 1900 the word "estoppel," modulating into such phrases as "equitable estoppel" and "promissory estoppel," began to appear with increasing frequency. Thus Corbin, in his submission to the Restaters, was plentifully supplied with new, as well as with old, case material.

The Restaters, honorable men, evidently found Corbin's argument unanswerable. However, instead of reopening the debate on the consideration definition, they elected to stand by § 75 but to add a new section — § 90 — incorporating the estoppel idea although without using the word "estoppel." The extent to which the new section § 90 was to be allowed to undercut the underlying principle of § 75 was left entirely unresolved. The format of the Restatement included analytical, discursive, often lengthy comments, interspersed with illustrations — that is, hypothetical cases, the facts of which were frequently drawn from real cases. Section 90 is almost the only section of the Restatement of Contracts which has no Comment at all. Four hypothetical cases, none of them, so far as I know, based on a real case, are offered as "illustrations," presumably to indicate the range which the section was meant to have. An attentive study of the four illustrations will lead any analyst to the despairing conclusion, which is of course reinforced by the mysterious text of § 90 itself, that no one had any idea what the damn thing meant.

[2] Charitable Subscriptions: Consideration or Reliance?

As the introductory statements suggest, the reliance principle embodied in § 90 is not a perfect instrument. The primary difficulty it presents is that reliance is an overly encompassing enforcement rationale. One of the quotations above suggests that all promises that are seriously intended and understood induce some reliance on a promise by the promisee. The argument is that information from a promisor will induce reliance whenever the promisee attaches *any* positive probability to the promised performance. Such responses are beneficial when the promise is kept and detrimental when it is broken. Furthermore, (and here is the deep puzzle) despite the reliance principle, gratuitous promises unsupported by consideration remain presumptively unenforceable to this day. The challenge, then, is to identify those variables that seem to determine which relied-upon promises will be enforced and which will not. A good place to begin is with charitable subscriptions which represent the middle ground between consideration and reliance-based promises.

CONGREGATION KADIMAH TORAS-MOSHE v. DeLEO
Supreme Judicial Court of Massachusetts
405 Mass. 365, 540 N.E.2d 691 (1989)

LIACOS, J.

Congregation Kadimah Toras-Moshe (Congregation), an Orthodox Jewish synagogue, commenced this action in the Superior Court to compel the administrator of an estate (estate) to fulfill the oral promise of the decedent to give the Congregation $25,000. The Superior Court transferred the case to the Boston Municipal Court, which rendered summary judgment for the estate. The case was then transferred back to the Superior Court, which also rendered summary judgment for the estate and dismissed the Congregation's complaint. We granted the Congregation's application for direct appellate review. We now affirm.

The facts are not contested. The decedent suffered a prolonged illness, throughout which he was visited by the Congregation's spiritual leader, Rabbi Abraham Halbfinger. During four or five of these visits, and in the presence of witnesses, the decedent made an oral promise to give the Congregation $25,000. The Congregation planned to use the $25,000 to transform a storage room in the synagogue into a library named after the decedent. The oral promise was never reduced to writing. The decedent died intestate in September, 1985. He had no children, but was survived by his wife.

The Congregation asserts that the decedent's oral promise is an enforceable contract under our case law, because the promise is allegedly supported either by consideration and bargain, or by reliance. *See Loranger Constr. Corp. v. E.F. Hauserman Co.*, 376 Mass. 757, 761, 763, 384 N.E.2d 176 (1978) (distinguishing consideration and bargain from reliance in the absence of consideration). We disagree.

The Superior Court judge determined that "[t]his was an oral gratuitous pledge, with no indication as to how the money should be used, or what [the Congregation] was required to do if anything in return for this promise." There was no legal benefit to the promisor nor detriment to the promisee, and thus no consideration. Furthermore, there is no evidence in the record that the Congregation's plans to name a library after the decedent induced him to make or to renew his promise. *Contrast Allegheny College v. National Chautauqua County Bank*, 246 N.Y. 369, 377–379, 159 N.E. 173 (1927) (subscriber's promise became binding when charity implicitly promised to commemorate subscriber).

As to the lack of reliance, the judge stated that the Congregation's "allocation of $25,000 in its budget[,] for the purpose of renovating a storage room, is insufficient to find reliance or an enforceable obligation." We agree. The inclusion of the promised $25,000 in the budget, by itself, merely reduced to writing the Congregation's expectation that it would have additional funds. A hope or expectation, even though well founded, is not equivalent to either legal detriment or reliance.

The Congregation cites several of our cases in which charitable subscriptions were enforced. These cases are distinguishable because they involved written, as distinguished from oral, promises and also involved substantial consideration or reliance. *See, e.g., Trustees of Amherst Academy v. Cowls*, 6 Pick. 427, 434 (1828) (subscribers to written agreement could not withdraw "after the execution or during the progress of the work which they themselves set in motion"); *Trustees of Farmington Academy v. Allen*, 14 Mass. 172, 176 (1817) (trustees justifiably "proceed[ed] to incur expense, on the faith of the defendant's subscription").

Conversely, in the case of *Cottage St. Methodist Episcopal Church v. Kendall*, 121 Mass. 528 (1877), we refused to enforce a promise in favor of a charity where there was no showing of any consideration or reliance.

The Congregation asks us to abandon the requirement of consideration or reliance in the case of charitable subscriptions. The Congregation cites the Restatement (Second) of Contracts § 90 (2). . . . Assuming without deciding that this court would apply § 90, we are of the opinion that in this case there is no injustice in declining to enforce the decedent's promise. Although § 90 dispenses with the absolute requirement of consideration or reliance, the official comments illustrate that these are relevant considerations. Restatement (Second) of Contracts, *supra* at § 90 comment f. The promise to the Congregation is entirely unsupported by consideration or reliance. Furthermore, it is an oral promise sought to be enforced against an estate. To enforce such a promise would be against public policy.

Judgment affirmed.

NOTES

1. **Charitable Subscriptions and Consideration.** In *Allegheny College v. National Chautauqua County Bank*, 246 N.Y. 369, 159 N.E. 173 (1927), cited in *Congregation Kadimah Toras-Moshe*, the court had less difficulty finding the consideration needed to enforce a charitable promise. In that case, Mary Yates Johnston promised to pay Allegheny College $5,000 from her estate 30 days after her death once other provisions of her will were met. In addition to stating that payment was conditional on her will, Johnston stipulated that the money was to "be known as the Mary Yates Johnston memorial fund, the proceeds from which shall be used to educate students preparing for the ministry, either in the United States or in the Foreign Field." Two years after making the pledge, Johnston paid the college $1,000 toward the pledge. A year later, however, she notified the college that she repudiated the pledge. Thirty days after her death, Allegheny College sued Johnston's executors for the balance of the pledge.

Judge Cardozo wrote the opinion for the New York Court of Appeals. He found for Allegheny College, ordering Johnston's executors to pay the college the remaining $4,000. Cardozo recognized promissory estoppel as a substitute means of enforcing the promise, but stopped short of discussing that doctrine or basing the court's decision on it. Instead, he turned to traditional notions of consideration and contract doctrine to enforce the promise:

> We think the duty assumed by the plaintiff to perpetuate the name of the founder of the memorial is sufficient in itself to give validity to the subscription within the rules that define consideration for a promise of that order. When the promisee subjected itself to such a duty at the implied request of the promisor, the result was the creation of a bilateral agreement. . . .

> There was a promise on the one side and on the other a return promise made, it is true, by implication, but expressing an obligation that had been exacted as a condition of the payment. A bilateral agreement may exist though one of the mutual promises be a promise "implied in fact," an inference from conduct as opposed to an inference from words. . . .

> We think the fair inference to be drawn from the acceptance of a payment on account of the subscription is a promise by the college to do what may be necessary on its part to make the scholarship effective. The plan conceived by the subscriber will be mutilated and distorted unless the sum to be accepted is adequate to the end in view. Moreover, the time to affix her name to the memorial will not arrive until the entire fund has been collected. The college may thus thwart the purpose of the payment on account if at liberty to reject a tender of the residue. It is no answer to say that a duty would then arise to make restitution of the money. If such a duty may be imposed, the only reason for its existence must be that there is then a failure of "consideration." To say that there is a failure of consideration is to concede that a consideration has been promised, since otherwise it could not fail. No doubt there are times and situations in which limitations laid upon a promisee in connection with the use of what is paid by a subscriber lack the quality of a consideration, and are to be classed merely as conditions. . . . "It is often difficult to determine whether words of condition in a promise indicate a request for consideration or state a mere condition in a gratuitous promise. An aid, though not a conclusive test in determining which construction of the promise is more reasonable is an inquiry whether the happening of the condition will be a benefit to the promisor. If so, it is a fair inference that the happening was requested as a consideration." Williston, *supra*, § 112. Such must be the meaning of this transaction unless we are prepared to hold that the college may keep the payment on account, and thereafter nullify the scholarship which is to preserve the memory of the subscriber. The fair implication to be gathered from the whole transaction is assent to the condition and the assumption of a duty to go forward with performance. . . .

> The subscriber does not say: I hand you $1,000 and you may make up your mind later, after my death, whether you will undertake to commemorate

my name. What she says in effect is this: I hand you $1,000 and if you are unwilling to commemorate me, the time to speak is now.

The conclusion thus reached makes it needless to consider whether, aside from the feature of a memorial, a promissory estoppel may result from the assumption of a duty to apply the fund, so far as already paid, to special purposes not mandatory under the provisions of the college charter (the support and education of students preparing for the ministry) — an assumption induced by the belief that other payments sufficient in amount to make the scholarship effective would be added to the fund thereafter upon the death of the subscriber. . . .

The judgment of the Appellate Division and that of the Trial Term should be reversed, and judgment ordered for the plaintiff as prayed for in the complaint, with costs in all courts.

Id. at 246 N.Y. 377–79.

2.   *The Restatements on Charitable Subscriptions.* Read the original Restatement of Contracts (1932), § 90. Note the provision that reliance must be "definite and substantial." Does this requirement translate easily into quantifiable terms? Could this requirement be why Cardozo was reluctant to discuss promissory estoppel in *Allegheny College* and turned instead to the more familiar ground of consideration?

The next group of Restaters began the task of revising the Restatement of Contracts in 1965. Fourteen drafts later, the American Law Institute adopted the Restatement (Second) of Contracts on May 17, 1979. Note that the new § 90 reflects some changes. No longer does reliance have to be definite and substantial. Instead, "the remedy granted for relief may be limited as justice requires." In addition, subsection (2) was added which states that a "charitable subscription . . . is binding under Subsection (1) without proof that the promise induced action or forbearance."

Comment f to § 90, relied on in *Congregation Kadimah Toras-Moshe*, has this to say about the new Subsection:

One of the functions of the doctrine of consideration is to deny enforcement to a promise to make a gift. Such a promise is ordinarily enforced by virtue of the promisee's reliance only if his conduct is foreseeable and reasonable and involves a definite and substantial change of position which would not have occurred if the promise had not been made. In some cases, however, other policies reinforce the promisee's claim. Thus the promisor might be unjustly enriched if he could reclaim the subject of the promised gift after the promisee has improved it.

Subsection (2) identifies . . . cases in which the promisee's claim is similarly reinforced. American courts have traditionally favored charitable subscriptions . . . , and have found consideration in many cases where the element of exchange was doubtful or nonexistent. While recovery is rested on reliance in such cases, a probability of reliance is enough, and no effort is made to sort out mixed motives or to consider whether partial enforcement would be appropriate.

The comment recognizes a tradition of enforcing charitable subscriptions as a result of public policy. Charities rely on the goodwill of people to support them. Many courts, in a desire to promote charitable giving and charities themselves, have fudged traditional contract doctrine to enforce charitable subscriptions. Despite its clarity in adopting a blanket enforcement rule dispensing with the need to prove either consideration or reliance, Section 90(2) has not fared well in the courts. In *Salsbury v. Northwestern Bell Tel. Co.*, 221 N.W.2d 609 (Iowa 1974), the court enforced a promise by defendant to contribute $15,000 to a newly formed college. In expressly adopting § 90(2) the court held:

> It is more logical to bind charitable subscriptions without requiring a showing of consideration or detrimental reliance. Charitable subscriptions often serve the public interest by making possible projects which otherwise could never come about. It is true some fund raising campaigns are not conducted on a plan which calls for subscriptions to be binding. In such cases we do not hesitate to hold them not binding. However where a subscription is unequivocal the pledgor should be made to keep his word.

Most courts, however, have declined to adopt § 90(2) despite the policy arguments advanced by the Iowa court in *Salsbury.* For example, in *Arrowsmith v. Mercantile-Safe Deposit & Trust Co.*, 545 A.2d 674 (Md. 1988), the court, in rejecting the *Salsbury* rationale, held that "the legislative process is more finely and continuously attuned for the societal fact-finding and evaluating required for resolution of this exclusively public policy-based argument."

3. *Oral Promises for Charitable Subscriptions.* The charitable promise in *Salsbury* (note 2, *supra*) was memorialized in a written document. What if the promise is made orally? In *Milligan v. Mueller (In re Estate of Schmidt)*, 723 N.W.2d 454 (Iowa Ct. App. 2006), the court ruled that oral promises should be considered the same way as written ones, subject to an exception:

> [W]hile Salsbury . . . dealt with written pledges, the cases do not restrict application only to written pledges. Generally, a subscription may be oral unless it falls within the provisions of the statute of frauds. . . . There is no allegation in the present case that the statute of frauds should apply. We conclude oral subscriptions are enforceable in the same manner as written subscriptions.

4. *Effects of the Charitable Contribution Cases.* Analysis of the reported charitable contribution cases since 1965 reveals several things. The results are close to being evenly divided between enforcing and not enforcing a charitable promise. Very few state courts have dispensed with a need to show consideration or promissory estoppel in charitable contribution cases. Most interestingly, there are fewer than a half dozen reported cases since 1965. Of course, that the legal rule is clear in a particular state would explain an absence of reported cases. Still, it may also be that the legal rule is not very important in this area. Can you think of reasons why that might be so?

What effect will enforcement have on future charitable promising? The argument often is raised that blanket enforcement of charitable subscriptions protects the social interest by promoting good works. But might such indiscriminate enforcement also result in a decreased number of future charitable promises? There are several conceivable effects that enforcement might have.

- None. Legal enforcement is trivial because donors either don't know or pay no attention to the legal rule, donors usually keep their promises, and donees seldom sue when donors revoke.

- Enforcement enhances charitable treasuries because donees can now enforce against reluctant donors or their estates.

- Enforcement reduces charitable promising but not necessarily giving because donors still give (during their lifetimes or in their wills), but, in order to be able to change their minds, they don't as often promise in advance.

- Enforcement reduces charitable treasuries because some donors who would have promised and kept their promise because they felt morally bound will no longer promise.

How easily do you think parties can bargain and adjust their behavior in a charitable subscription situation? Pledges to give money are generally thought of as falling outside the context where parties can bargain for promises by increasing the value of what they agree to give in return. The would-be promisee (the charitable entity) usually lacks the leverage to compel the promisor to make a legally enforceable promise. But in the case of large charitable gifts — those most worth litigating — do you think bargaining is improbable considering the real benefits, such as having one's name memorialized, that are available to the promisor?

5. *Problem.* Dr. Martin Luther King, an alumnus of Boston University's graduate school program, wrote Boston University Library the following letter:

> On this 16th day of July, 1964, I name the Boston University Library the Repository of my correspondence, manuscripts and other papers, along with a few of my awards and other materials which may come to be of interest in historical or other research.

> In accordance with this action I have authorized the removal of most of the above-mentioned papers and other objects to Boston University, including most correspondence through 1961, at once. It is my intention that after the end of each calendar year, similar files of materials for an additional year should be sent to Boston University.

> All papers and other objects which thus pass into the custody of Boston University remain my legal property until otherwise indicated, according to the statements below. However, if, despite scrupulous care, any such materials are damaged or lost while in custody of Boston University, I absolve Boston University of responsibility to me for such damage or loss.

> I intend each year to indicate a portion of the materials deposited with Boston University to become the absolute property of Boston University as an outright gift from me, until all shall have been thus given to the University. In the event of my death, all such materials deposited with the University shall become from that date the absolute property of Boston University.

Boston University indexed the papers they received from Dr. King, made them available to researchers, provided trained staff to care for the papers and assist researchers, and held a convocation, at which Dr. King spoke, to commemorate receipt of the papers. His widow, Coretta Scott King, as administratrix of her late husband's estate, sued Boston University for conversion, alleging that the estate held title to Dr. King's papers. What are the best arguments for and against Ms. King's position? What doctrines do you think are relevant? *See King v. Trustees of Boston Univ.*, 420 Mass. 52, 647 N.E.2d 1196 (1995).

Essay: The Realist and Neo-Classical Views on Promissory Estoppel

Though promissory estoppel is invoked as a means of enforcement in many different areas of contract law, there are three specific settings — beyond charitable subscriptions — that provide interesting examples of how the doctrine works: intrafamilial promises, employment promises of retirement and other benefits, and promises to insure. Each of these areas has its own distinct pattern of enforcement. Before we begin to examine each setting, however, it is important to understand that from its inception promissory estoppel has been viewed by many as a heresy against the orthodoxy of the consideration doctrine. The great challenge has been to reconcile these two apparently incompatible doctrines within a coherent conception of contract law. As the promissory estoppel doctrine emerged as a challenge to traditional contract law, some scholars argued that promissory estoppel had supplanted the consideration doctrine and thereby effected the absorption of contract into tort. Other scholars pushed back, claiming that the application of promissory estoppel and consideration could be rendered coherent and predictable by taking into account a diverse set of socially desirable ends served exclusively by contract law.

Is Contract Dead? Perhaps the most prominent attack on the coherence of promissory estoppel and consideration doctrine was presented by realist scholars who maintained that contract law is "dead" and that the effort to reconcile consideration and promissory estoppel is a hopeless task. The willingness of courts to move beyond — or to ignore — consideration when deciding cases has left the field of contracts in a muddle of confusion, these scholars contended. No longer does a clear, systematic structure exist in which contractual obligations — as distinct from duties grounded in tort — can be predictably described. Instead, they argued, contract law, increasingly dependent on notions of reliance, will soon be engulfed by the law of torts.

Professor Grant Gilmore was one of the ablest advocates of this thesis. In *The Death of Contract* (1974), he explained how "the theory of contract, as formulated by Holmes and Williston, seems to have gone into its protracted period of breakdown almost from the moment of its birth." *Id.* at 57. "Pure" contract doctrine as pursued by Holmes, Williston, and Professor Christopher Columbus Langdell of Harvard, among others, was, according to Gilmore, too simplistic an idea to survive over time. Basing contractual liability solely on consideration (mutual inducement and bargain) left too many contexts in which enforcement would be denied. To fill in these gaps, courts responded with rules that did not fit the general doctrines of contract, which in turn caused the erosion of the consideration framework as a useful tool for distinguishing between enforceable and unenforceable promises. The final blow was struck, Gilmore concluded, with the rise of the welfare state in the twentieth century. The general, supposedly universal, contract doctrine simply could not withstand the transition from nineteenth century individualism to twentieth century collectivism. Thus, contract law was being absorbed by tort law and that, Gilmore seemed to be saying, is the way it should be.

The Neo-Classical Response. Another group of legal scholars, however — who might be categorized as the "neo-classicists" — recognized the shortcomings of the consideration doctrine but insisted nevertheless that it was premature to toll the bell for contract law. It was still possible, these scholars argued, to specify the underlying logic of contract enforcement and thus determine which promises deserved enforcement.

In defending this position, Professor Lon Fuller argued that what needed abolition was not the doctrine of consideration itself, but a "conception of legal method which assumes that the doctrine can be understood and applied without reference to the ends it services." *Consideration and Form*, 41 COLUM. L. REV. 799, 824 (1941). Fuller analyzed consideration as a legal formality and argued that it served the evidentiary, cautionary, and channeling functions previously mentioned. He also found that the form served the basic rationales — or substantive bases — of contractual liability, four of which he described.

First, there is the desire to protect private autonomy, or "freedom of contract," such that individuals themselves have the power to change their legal relationships. Second, there is the desire of a capitalist system as a whole to promote the exchange of goods and services. Third, reliance should be protected so that a party is compensated for any hardship which results when he changes his position in reliance on a promise which has since been breached. Finally, the legal system should guard against unjust enrichment, so that a party will be paid for conveying a material benefit for which another party had once promised, or should have promised, to pay. When these substantive bases are combined with the formal components discussed above in Section B.1, Fuller maintained that a workable, predictable structure of contract law results.

Summary. Under either the realist or neo-classical approach, then, the fundamental challenge is to identify the principles underlying the application of contract law's enforcement doctrines (i.e., Gilmore's tort principles or Fuller's policy ends). Because the enforcement doctrines have evolved through the common law process, various patterns of promissory enforcement can be discerned in different categories of promises. As we explore them below, ask whether these enforcement patterns compel the conclusion that contract law is an unstructured mosaic of enforcement decisions. Can a coherent enforcement model be pieced together?

[3]   Promises Made in Intrafamilial Contexts

For a number of years following the promulgation of § 90 in the first Restatement of Contracts in 1932, the conventional assumption was that courts would use the doctrine of promissory estoppel to enforce gratuitous promises (such as the promise in *Kirksey v. Kirksey, supra*) that had previously been beyond the reach of the narrow consideration doctrine. But in an important article, *Promissory Estoppel and the Traditional Contract Doctrine*, 78 YALE L.J. 343 (1969), Professor Stanley Henderson exhaustively surveyed the case law and discovered that, in reality, promissory estoppel was not being invoked to enforce gratuitous or benevolent promises. Rather, Henderson claimed, courts use § 90 to expand liability in what are essentially exchange contexts. He cautioned lawyers that the fate of a promisee who presses a § 90 claim turns "on the ability of the court to reconcile the reliance factor implicit in promissory estoppel with a general theory of consideration which is dominated by notions of reciprocity." "Moreover," he continued, "the disposition to treat action in reliance as proof of bargain . . . seriously impairs the reliance principle in the very cases [of gratuitous promises] in which reliance is likely to be the only available ground for relief. . . . [Thus] the risk that action in reliance will be found to be not sufficiently serious to justify application of § 90, or merely the condition of a gratuitous promise, is thereby increased." *Id.* at 345–50.

Consider the following cases that provide, first, an example of Henderson's claim, and then a celebrated exception.

HAASE v. CARDOZA

District Court of Appeal, Third District, California
165 Cal. App. 2d 35, 331 P.2d 419 (1958)

WARNE, J.

Appellant brought this action to recover the sum of $10,000 from respondent as a result of an alleged oral promise made by respondent to and with her deceased husband to pay appellant said sum and also to recover the further sum of $3,000, upon an assigned claim, based upon an alleged oral promise made by respondent to and with her deceased husband to pay to Loretta M. Haase the sum of $3,000. At the close of the appellant's case in chief the trial court granted respondent's motion for a nonsuit and this appeal followed.

On May 17, 1951, the deceased and respondent, as husband and wife, entered into an inter vivos trust on the terms of which the survivor was to receive whatever estate the parties had acquired during their marriage and of which they were then possessed. Sometime later the deceased made a will, leaving the appellant, among other heirs mentioned therein, the sum of $2,500 on the apparent assumption that between said date and the date of his death there would be some additional estate acquired over and above that included in the trust agreement. Approximately two years later deceased died and, although his will was filed with the county clerk of Santa Cruz County, there was no estate subject to probate and the $2,500 bequest to appellant lapsed. However, respondent, desiring to carry out the wishes of her deceased husband, voluntarily and gratuitously gave appellant $2,500 from her own funds because there was no estate from which the bequest could be paid. The appellant is the deceased's sister.

Approximately a year and a half after the death of the respondent's husband, respondent, during a period of illness, arranged through her sister Yvette Harvey to have appellant come to her home. Appellant testified concerning the following conversation which took place between herself and the respondent, Alice I. Cardoza, in the presence of respondent's sister, Mrs. Harvey:

Q: Who was present in the bedroom at the time?

A: Mrs. Harvey and myself and Alice.

Q: What did Alice say to you?

A: She started to cry, and she said, "Rose, I have a confession to make to you. Tony left you $10,000.00 and Loretta Haase $5,000.00, and I didn't give it to you."

Q: Was it $5,000 or $3,000?

A: $3,000. So she said "This will drive me crazy." She was crying all the time. And I said, "Well, why do you cry so? Why don't you do what he told you to do?"

She also testified that in said conversation respondent said, "Rose, I am going to pay you $50.00 a month. Will you accept it?"

Respondent thereafter proceeded to send appellant a check for $50 a month for eight months. These payments ceased when appellant asked for a note to cover the balance alleged to be due on the $10,000.

The assignment of the $3,000 claim of Loretta M. Haase for the purpose of suit was stipulated to.

At the trial no evidence was produced nor was there any claim made by the appellant that respondent's alleged statement was supported by any consideration, by any previous promise between the parties, or by any debt or obligation between any of the parties, including the deceased. . . .

Appellant assumes that the mere statement made by respondent to the effect that respondent's husband had asked her to give the $10,000 was an acknowledgment of an obligation and that, therefore, despite the lack of evidence of any obligation on the part of either the respondent or her husband, and the admissions of the appellant herself that no pre-existing indebtedness existed, respondent's mere statement created a consideration where none prior thereto existed. We feel that there is no merit in this contention. Plaintiff has cited no cases holding that a promise which is without consideration is made actionable by an assumption to carry out such promise where the assumption is without consideration. Nor have we been able to find any cases so holding. While the courts may apply a promise to do something where there is an unjust result, if the promise is not implied we find no cases where the courts will imply consideration. As stated in 1 *Corbin on Contracts*, section 114, at pages 354, 355:

> An informal promise without consideration, in any of the senses of that term, creates no duty and is not enforceable. But this statement is not correct if we limit the definition of consideration so as to require it to be a bargained-for equivalent given in exchange for the promise. There are many informal promises that are enforceable, even though there is no consideration as thus defined. In every case, however, an informal promise

is never enforceable if it stands utterly alone. To be enforceable, there must be some accompanying factor of the past (generally called "past consideration"), or there must be some subsequent changes of position in reliance on the promise. Without any such accompanying factor, an informal promise to make a gift is not binding.

Appellant testified that she had no interest in decedent's business and that neither decedent nor the respondent owed her any money. Nor do we find any evidence of a change of position on the part of the appellant which could give rise to an estoppel as a substitute for consideration. Respondent's promises to pay the $10,000 and the $3,000 stand utterly alone and under such circumstances are not actionable. . . .

In the instant case appellant's own testimony conclusively shows that no good or valuable consideration ever existed between any of the parties.

The judgment is affirmed.

RICKETTS v. SCOTHORN
Supreme Court of Nebraska
57 Neb. 51, 77 N.W. 365 (1898)

SULLIVAN, J.

In the district court of Lancaster county the plaintiff, Katie Scothorn, recovered judgment against the defendant, Andrew D. Ricketts, as executor of the last will and testament of John C. Ricketts, deceased. The action was based upon a promissory note, of which the following is a copy: "May the first, 1891. I promise to pay to Katie Scothorn on demand, $2,000, to be at 6 per cent per annum. J. C. Ricketts." In the petition the plaintiff alleges that the consideration for the execution of the note was that she should surrender her employment as bookkeeper for Mayer Bros., and cease to work for a living. She also alleges that the note was given to induce her to abandon her occupation, and that, relying on it, and on the annual interest, as a means of support, she gave up the employment in which she was then engaged. These allegations of the petition are denied by the administrator. The material facts are undisputed. They are as follows: John C. Ricketts, the maker of the note, was the grandfather of the plaintiff. Early in May — presumably on the day the note bears date — he called on her at the store where she was working. What transpired between them is thus described by Mr. Flodene, one of the plaintiff's witnesses:

A: Well, the old gentleman came in there one morning about nine o'clock, probably a little before or a little after, but early in the morning, and he unbuttoned his vest, and took out a piece of paper in the shape of a note; that is the way it looked to me; and he says to Miss Scothorn, "I have fixed out something that you have not got to work any more." He says, "none of my grandchildren work, and you don't have to."

Q: Where was she?

A: She took the piece of paper and kissed him, and kissed the old
                   gentleman, and commenced to cry.

It seems Miss Scothorn immediately notified her employer of her intention to
quit work, and that she did soon after abandon her occupation. The mother of the
plaintiff was a witness, and testified that she had a conversation with her father, Mr.
Ricketts, shortly after the note was executed, in which he informed her that he had
given the note to the plaintiff to enable her to quit work; that none of his
grandchildren worked, and he did not think she ought to. For something more than
a year the plaintiff was without an occupation, but in September, 1892, with the
consent of her grandfather, and by his assistance, she secured a position as
bookkeeper with Messrs. Funke & Ogden. On June 8, 1894, Mr. Ricketts died. He
had paid one year's interest on the note, and a short time before his death expressed
regret that he had not been able to pay the balance. In the summer or fall of 1892
he stated to his daughter, Mrs. Scothorn, that if he could sell his farm in Ohio he
would pay the note out of the proceeds. He at no time repudiated the obligation.

We quite agree with counsel for the defendant that upon this evidence there was
nothing to submit to the jury, and that a verdict should have been directed
peremptorily for one of the parties. The testimony of Flodene and Mrs. Scothorn,
taken together, conclusively establishes the fact that the note was not given in
consideration of the plaintiff pursuing, or agreeing to pursue, any particular line of
conduct. There was no promise on the part of the plaintiff to do, or refrain from
doing, anything. Her right to the money promised in the note was not made to
depend upon an abandonment of her employment with Mayer Bros., and future
abstention from like service. Mr. Ricketts made no condition, requirement, or
request. He exacted no *quid pro quo*. He gave the note as a gratuity, and looked for
nothing in return. So far as the evidence discloses, it was his purpose to place the
plaintiff in a position of independence, where she could work or remain idle, as she
might choose. The abandonment of Miss Scothorn of her position as bookkeeper
was altogether voluntary. It was not an act done in fulfillment of any contract
obligation assumed when she accepted the note. The instrument in suit, being given
without any valuable consideration, was nothing more than a promise to make a gift
in the future of the sum of money therein named. Ordinarily, such promises are not
enforceable, even when put in the form of a promissory note. . . . But it has often
been held that an action on a note given to a church, college, or other like institution,
upon the faith of which money has been expended or obligation incurred, could not
be successfully defended on the ground of a want of consideration. . . .

In this class of cases the note in suit is nearly always spoken of as a gift or
donation, but the decision is generally put on the ground that the expenditure of
money or assumption of liability by the donee on the faith of the promise constitutes
a valuable and sufficient consideration. It seems to us that the true reason is the
preclusion of the defendant, under the doctrine of estoppel, to deny the consideration.

Under the circumstances of this case, is there an equitable estoppel which ought
to preclude the defendant from alleging that the note in controversy is lacking in
one of the essential elements of a valid contract? We think there is. An estoppel in
pais is defined to be "a right arising from acts, admissions, or conduct which have

induced a change of position in accordance with the real or apparent intention of the party against whom they are alleged." Mr. Pomeroy has formulated the following definition: "Equitable estoppel is the effect of the voluntary conduct of a party whereby he is absolutely precluded, both at law and in equity, from asserting rights which might, perhaps, have otherwise existed, either of property, of contract, or of remedy, as against another person who in good faith relied upon such conduct, and has been led thereby to change his position for the worse, and who on his part acquires some corresponding right, either of property, of contract, or of remedy." 2 Pom. Eq. Jur. 804. According to the undisputed proof, as shown by the record before us, the plaintiff was a working girl, holding a position in which she earned a salary of $10 per week. Her grandfather, desiring to put her in a position of independence, gave her the note, accompanying it with the remark that his other grandchildren did not work, and that she would not be obliged to work any longer. In effect, he suggested that she might abandon her employment, and rely in the future upon the bounty which he promised. He doubtless desired that she should give up her occupation, but, whether he did or not, it is entirely certain that he contemplated such action on her part as a reasonable and probable consequence of his gift. Having intentionally influenced the plaintiff to alter her position for the worse on the faith of the note being paid when due, it would be grossly inequitable to permit the maker, or his executor, to resist payment on the ground that the promise was given without consideration. The petition charges the elements of an equitable estoppel, and the evidence conclusively establishes them. If errors intervened at the trial, they could not have been prejudicial. A verdict for the defendant would be unwarranted. The judgment is right, and is affirmed.

NOTES

1. *Questions on* **Haase.** Was a promise made by the respondent, Alice Cardoza? If so, why does the court refuse to enforce it? Consider Rose Haase's claim from the perspective of Restatement § 90. Why isn't promissory estoppel available as a means of enforcing Alice's promise? The court holds that it doesn't "find any evidence of a change of position . . . which could give rise to an estoppel as a substitute for consideration." Surely it cannot be the case that Rose did not rely at all on this promise. Is this just a case of poor lawyering by her counsel who failed to ask her what actions she took (or failed to take) after the promise was made? If Rose Haase relied on getting $50 every month and, as a result, entered into an installment contract to purchase a new car, should the court consider that in deciding the case? If a showing of reliance would change the result in *Haase*, aren't future promisees well advised to rely substantially on such promises by dramatically changing their consumption habits, in order to secure the enforceability of the promise they received? Is that sound social policy?

Consider these two variations on the *Haase* case. Suppose that when Alice promised to pay the money every month, Rose had said, "and every week, I will light a candle for you at the church." Suppose, instead, that Alice had said, "If you will promise to light a candle for me every week at the church, I will pay you $50 per week until I have paid you $10,000." Would the language of § 71 be satisfied in either or both of these variations?

2. *Reconciling* **Haase** *and* **Ricketts.** Are *Haase v. Cardoza* and *Ricketts v. Scothorn* distinguishable? On what grounds? If the cases cannot be distinguished merely on the basis of relative competence (or incompetence) of the promisees' attorneys, how else would you seek to explain the differing outcomes? If the general reluctance to enforce gratuitous promises (notwithstanding § 90) is a default assumption, can you argue that Mr. Ricketts behaved in a way that rebutted that assumption? Note that the court in *Ricketts* analogizes that case to the charitable subscription cases. Does that mean that the court sees the same possibility of an implicit bargain between Katie Scothorn and her grandfather as some courts have found in the case of enforceable charitable subscriptions?

3. *The Nature of Reliance.* In promissory estoppel doctrine, not all reliance is created equal. Reconsider the "Williston's Tramp" hypothetical, *supra*, page 134. If we applied *Ricketts* to the hypothetical, would the tramp have a right to damages if the promisor changed his mind about the coat after the tramp had walked to the store? Does *Kirksey* now have to be decided differently? Assume that a court hearing the *Kirksey* case finds authoritative precedent in its state approving the doctrine of promissory estoppel as embodied in Restatement (Second) § 90, but the court is unsympathetic to plaintiff's claim. Is there language in § 90 that would permit the court to rule in favor of defendant? How about language in § 90, Restatement (First)?

Comment b to § 90 of the Restatement (Second) describes what sort of reliance § 90 is designed to protect:

> The principle of this Section is flexible. The promisor is affected only by reliance which he does or should foresee, and enforcement must be necessary to avoid injustice. Satisfaction of the latter requirement may depend on the reasonableness of the promisee's reliance, on its definite and substantial character in relation to the remedy sought, on the formality with which the promise is made, on the extent to which the evidentiary, cautionary, deterrent and channeling functions of form are met by the commercial setting or otherwise, and on the extent to which such other policies as the enforcement of bargains and the prevention of unjust enrichment are relevant.

4. *Measuring Damages in Promissory Estoppel Cases.* One possible measure of recovery in promissory estoppel cases is expectancy — the ex ante value of the promise to the promisee. Another is the reliance loss suffered by the promisee, with any gains to the promisee taken into consideration. One might think that since reliance is the basis for recovery, it should also measure the recovery. But the evidence is far from clear.

Reviewing summaries of the results in § 90 cases, Professors Edward Yorio and Steve Thel concluded:[10]

> [T]he remedy routinely granted [in § 90 cases] is either specific perfor-mance or expectation damages. Those rare instances in which courts award reliance damages involve either a problem with the promise or a difficulty

---

[10] Edward Yorio & Steve Thel, *The Promissory Basis of Section 90*, 101 YALE L.J. 111 (1991).

in assessing expectation damages. Some courts explain an expectancy measure by expressly tying the remedy to the promise; more often, courts grant specific performance or expectation damages without analysis or discussion. That courts enforce promises rather than compensate reliance under § 90 is powerful evidence that the basis of the section in the courts is promise.

Id. at 130.

This view has been disputed. In a later study, Professor Hillman found that "[n]ot only do 7 of 14 [§ 90] cases clearly awarding damages appear to grant reliance damages, but those cases are full of language suggesting the widespread acceptance of reliance damages as a remedy." He argues that, contrary to Yorio and Thel's claim, courts are flexible in their damage awards in promissory estoppel cases. The predominance of expectancy damages in some cases may be better explained by the fact that "they may be easier to prove than reliance damages." In *Scothorn*, for example:

> Yorio and Thel assert that the court had "a clear choice" between awarding the granddaughter her lost income of roughly $520 before she began her new job or her expectancy based on the promise of $2000 plus interest. The court's opinion does not mention how much she earned at her new job, however, or whether it was inferior to the original one. If the new job was inferior or the pay was lower, the granddaughter's reliance damages may have been much greater than $520. In short, despite Yorio and Thel's assertions, reliance damages may have been difficult to measure, thereby leading to the expectancy award.

Robert A. Hillman, *Questioning the "New Consensus" on Promissory Estoppel: An Empirical and Theoretical Study*, 98 COLUM. L. REV. 580 (1998).

Yet, Yorio and Thel might have been right all along. A recent study examined nearly 400 promissory estoppel cases that arose between 1981, when the Restatement (Second) was published, and the beginning of 2008. The research suggested that

> with respect to remedies, courts tend to treat promissory estoppel actions as traditional breach of contract actions, in that courts generally tend to award the (usually) more generous expectation measure of damages, which is typical in ordinary breach of contract actions, over the (usually) less generous reliance measure of damages, which is often awarded where non-contractual obligations have been breached (such as in tort law).

Marco Jimenez, *The Many Faces of Promissory Estoppel: An Empirical Analysis Under the Restatement (Second) of Contracts*, 57 UCLA L. REV. 669, 669–70 (2010).

5. *Presumption of Nonenforcement of Intrafamilial or Donative Promises.* Intrafamilial or other "donative" promises generally are not enforced, despite the provision of § 90 and despite the result in *Ricketts*. Professor Melvin Eisenberg, in *Donative Promises*, 47 U. Chi. L. Rev. 1 (1979), confirmed that it takes more than just reliance by the promisee to render a donative promise enforceable. Eisenberg then wrote:

> Reliance may provide some evidence that a promise was actually made, but it seldom provides full evidentiary security, because the kind of reliance involved in a donative context . . . is often consistent with either the existence or the nonexistence of a promise. The prospect of reliance may have a sobering effect on the promisor, but since the motive is donative rather than calculating, a significant danger remains that the promise was made without sufficient deliberation.

Id. at 18–19.

Eisenberg seems to be suggesting that the presumption of non-enforcement is a product of the concern for enforcing improvident promises. But is there any reason to suspect that Mr. Ricketts acted without sufficient deliberation before making his promise to his granddaughter? Can you think of other reasons why such promises are generally not enforceable? Consider, for example the following argument:

> Intrafamilial promises are made in a paradigmatic non-bargaining context. Such promises tend to be made out of love, loyalty, or moral obligation. As such, intrafamilial promisors are unlikely to intend their promises to be given legal effect, and intrafamilial promisees are unlikely to believe such promises are intended to be legally enforceable. Why do we think that is so? One reason is that most such promises are very reliable even without the additional credibility that legal enforcement provides. Thus, legal enforcement may not enhance the reliability of such promises. In addition, given the social context, legal enforcement may actually deter some potential promisors from making (otherwise socially valuable) intrafamilial promises. Family members may simply refrain from promising for fear that their promise may lead to unintended legal liability.

Do you find this argument persuasive? If this analysis suggests reasons why courts are reluctant to enforce such promises, what then explains the result in *Ricketts*? Should the law enforce such promises? Try to marshal as many reasons for or against enforcement as you can.

6.   *The Relevance of Context.* Examine the context in which Alice's promise was made. Was it the kind of environment in which the promisor is likely to have intended the promise to be legally enforceable? Suppose that promises made in this context were enforceable absent clear evidence that the promisor did not intend the promise to have legal effect. How would parties adjust to such a legal enforcement regime? Is it reasonable to suppose that this regime would make it less likely that Alice would promise Rose the $50 per month? Or would this regime just shift the burden of motivating the promise to Rose? How readily could Rose have bargained for such a promise from Alice? Do you think Alice intended her promise to be legally binding?

Many promises are made in a "reciprocal" or bargain context. This does not mean that the parties involved actually dickered over the terms of their agreement, but rather that the environment in which the bargain took place was such that they could have negotiated had they wanted to. That is, if the promisor had been reluctant to make the promise, the promisee nonetheless would have had sufficient leverage to motivate the promisor to make the promise. Most business settings meet this definition. A "donative" or non-bargain context, on the other hand, is an environment in which it is difficult or impossible to imagine the parties bargaining — situations in which the idea of negotiating terms of an agreement is in fact antithetical to the social context. In these contexts, the promisee would have lacked sufficient leverage to motivate a reluctant promisor to make the promise or would have been deterred by powerful informal social norms from seeking to do so. Which context best describes the relationship in *Haase*?

7. *Problems.* Consider each of the following problems. What arguments can you make in each that the promises in question should be enforceable notwithstanding the intrafamilial context that ordinarily leads courts to reject promissory estoppel claims?

a. On September 28, 2006, Mr. James Ortiz wrote to his elderly aunt, Mary Baker, offering to purchase either or both of two large oriental rugs owned by the aunt. Ortiz indicated that he had always greatly admired the rugs in his aunt's house and would be happy to buy them at a price of $10,000 per rug "or perhaps even higher if you do not think that's a fair price."

On October 5, the aunt replied, declining the sale but offering to give the rugs to Ortiz. "I am," she wrote, "only too conscious of my numbered days and would like to pass these rugs on to someone who appreciates their value, as obviously you do." The aunt went on to promise to effect the actual transfer "in May, when I return from Florida," pleading that "I am just too busy planning my departure to bother with the rugs right now."

Ortiz initially rejoiced in his unexpected good fortune, but soon he began to worry. Aunt Mary was known to be in poor health, and the probability of her death before May was not negligible. Also, Ortiz had completed one semester of Contracts during an abortive foray in law school during his youth. ·

As a rug admirer, Ortiz had previously prepared detailed color slides of collector-quality rugs, including those belonging to his aunt. On November 3, Ortiz sold one of the rugs to Salem Deewaise Carpets, Inc. for delivery on June 1, 2007. According to the agreement, Salem Deewaise paid the $10,000 purchase price in advance to Ortiz on November 10.

In late December 2006, Ortiz received a letter from an acquaintance and fellow rug fancier, David Kaye. In the letter, Kaye offered him an opportunity to purchase a beautiful Bokara rug for $8,500. Ortiz was initially excited by the offer because he had frequently admired this rug and only a few days before had resolved to offer Kaye $13,000 for it. Upon reflection, however, he realized that Aunt Mary's remaining rug would complete his design scheme for his home, and he declined to accept the offer, electing instead to send a $5,000 Christmas check to his favorite niece who was a struggling graduate student.

Mary Baker died in St. Petersburg, Florida, on January 23, 2007. Her executor has not only refused to transfer the rugs to Ortiz, but sold them for $42,000 to an Australian rug dealer.

Ortiz has repaid the $10,000 to Salem Deewaise, but is being dunned for an additional $6,500 which, it is alleged, represents the appreciation of the market value of the rug to $16,500.

Ortiz is now suing the Central National Bank, executor of the estate, for damages for the rugs which, he alleges, are rightfully his. What result?

b. Billy and Barbara Ervin were divorced. Shortly before their son Michael's eighteenth birthday, Billy filed a motion to terminate his child-support payments. Barbara responded with a motion to continue child support or in the alternative to increase her alimony to help pay for Michael's college education.

Barbara introduced in court a letter from her ex-husband written some years earlier, in which he wrote: "Concerning saving for Michael's college education — as his father, of course I'll see that he gets to college. How I handle my finances to achieve this is strictly my affair. An inflexible arrangement such as you suggest is unacceptable. As previously described to you I have more than adequately provided for Michael's future in the event of my death. So you have nothing to be concerned about as to Michael's being able to attend college, even if I have to borrow the money."

Is Billy liable for the costs of Michael's education? *See Ervin v. Ervin*, 458 A.2d 342 (R.I. 1983).

c. Even though he knew he was not the father of her child, Bruce Wright promised Kim Newman and her son that he would assume all of the obligations and responsibilities of fatherhood, including that of providing support. He listed himself as the father on the child's birth certificate and gave the child his last name. Wright contends, and Newman does not dispute, that Newman severed the relationship and all ties with Wright when the child was approximately three years old. For approximately the next five years, until the child was eight, Newman and Wright did not communicate. Wright stopped making support payments after three years from making his promise and did not visit with the child again until he was eight years old. However, for ten years following his promise Wright held himself out to others as the father of the child and allowed the child to consider him to be the natural father. When the child turned ten years old, Newman sued Wright for child support. Is Wright's promise enforceable? *See Wright v. Newman*, 266 Ga. 519, 467 S.E.2d 533 (1996).

[4] Promises Made in Employment Contexts

FEINBERG v. PFEIFFER CO.
St. Louis Court of Appeals, Missouri
322 S.W.2d 163 (1959)

DOERNER, COMMISSIONER.

This is a suit brought in the Circuit Court of the City of St. Louis by plaintiff, a former employee of the defendant corporation, on an alleged contract whereby defendant agreed to pay plaintiff the sum of $200 per month for life upon her retirement. A jury being waived, the case was tried by the court alone. Judgment below was for plaintiff for $5,100, the amount of the pension claimed to be due as of the date of the trial, together with interest thereon, and defendant duly appealed.

The parties are in substantial agreement on the essential facts. Plaintiff began working for the defendant, a manufacturer of pharmaceuticals, in 1910, when she was but 17 years of age. By 1947 she had attained the position of bookkeeper, office manager, and assistant treasurer of the defendant, and owned 70 shares of its stock out of a total of 6,503 shares issued and outstanding. Twenty shares had been given to her by the defendant or its then president, she had purchased 20, and the remaining 30 she had acquired by a stock split or stock dividend. Over the years she received substantial dividends on the stock she owned, as did all of the other stockholders. Also, in addition to her salary, plaintiff from 1937 to 1949, inclusive, received each year a bonus varying in amount from $300 in the beginning to $2,000 in the later years.

On December 27, 1947, the annual meeting of the defendant's Board of Directors was held at the Company's offices in St. Louis, presided over by Max Lippman, its then president and largest individual stockholder. The other directors present were George L. Marcus, Sidney Harris, Sol Flammer, and Walter Weinstock, who, with Max Lippman, owned 5,007 of the 6,503 shares then issued and outstanding. At that meeting the Board of Directors adopted the following resolution, which, because it is the crux of the case, we quote in full:

The Chairman thereupon pointed out that the Assistant Treasurer, Mrs. Anna Sacks Feinberg, has given the corporation many years of long and faithful service. Not only has she served the corporation devotedly, but with exceptional ability and skill. The President pointed out that although all of the officers and directors sincerely hoped and desired that Mrs. Feinberg would continue in her present position for as long as she felt able, nevertheless, in view of the length of service which she has contributed provision should be made to afford her retirement privileges and benefits which should become a firm obligation of the corporation to be available to her whenever she should see fit to retire from active duty, however many years in the future such retirement may become effective. It was, accordingly, proposed that Mrs. Feinberg's salary which is presently $350.00 per month, be increased to $400.00 per month, and that Mrs. Feinberg would be given the privilege of retiring from active duty at any time she may elect to see fit so to do upon a retirement pay of $200.00 per month for life, with the distinct understanding that the retirement plan is merely being adopted at the present time in order to afford Mrs. Feinberg security for the future and in the hope that her active services will continue with the corporation for many years to come. After due discussion and consideration, and upon motion duly made and seconded, it was —

Resolved, that the salary of Anna Sacks Feinberg be increased from $350.00 to $400.00 per month and that she be afforded the privilege of retiring from active duty in the corporation at any time she may elect to see fit so to do upon retirement pay of $200.00 per month, for the remainder of her life.

At the request of Mr. Lippman his sons-in-law, Messrs. Harris and Flammer, called upon the plaintiff at her apartment on the same day to advise her of the passage of the resolution. Plaintiff testified on cross-examination that she had no prior information that such a pension plan was contemplated, that it came as a surprise to her, and that she would have continued in her employment whether or not such a resolution had been adopted. It is clear from the evidence that there was no contract, oral or written, as to plaintiff's length of employment, and that she was free to quit, and the defendant to discharge her, at any time.

Plaintiff did continue to work for the defendant through June 30, 1949, on which date she retired. In accordance with the foregoing resolution, the defendant began paying her the sum of $200 on the first of each month. Mr. Lippman died on November 18, 1949, and was succeeded as president of the company by his widow. Because of an illness, she retired from that office and was succeeded in October, 1953, by her son-in-law, Sidney M. Harris. Mr. Harris testified that while Mrs. Lippman had been president she signed the monthly pension check paid plaintiff, but fussed about doing so, and considered the payments as gifts. After his election, he stated, a new accounting firm employed by the defendant questioned the validity of the payments to plaintiff on several occasions, and in the Spring of 1956, upon its recommendation, he consulted the Company's then attorney, Mr. Ralph Kalish. Harris testified that both Ernst and Ernst, the accounting firm, and Kalish told him there was no need of giving plaintiff the money. He also stated that he had concurred in the view that the payments to plaintiff were mere gratuities rather than amounts due under a contractual obligation, and that following his discussion with the Company's attorney plaintiff was sent a check for $100 on April 1, 1956. Plaintiff declined to accept the reduced amount, and this action followed. Additional facts will be referred to later in this opinion. . . .

It is defendant's contention, in essence, that the resolution adopted by its Board of Directors was a mere promise to make a gift, and that no contract resulted either thereby, or when plaintiff retired, because there was no consideration given or paid by the plaintiff. It urges that a promise to make a gift is not binding unless supported by a legal consideration; that the only apparent consideration for the adoption of the foregoing resolution was the "many years of long and faithful service" expressed therein; and that past services are not a valid consideration for a promise. Defendant argues further that there is nothing in the resolution which made its effectiveness conditional upon plaintiff's continued employment, that she was not under contract to work for any length of time but was free to quit whenever she wished, and that she had no contractual right to her position and could have been discharged at any time.

Plaintiff concedes that a promise based upon past services would be without consideration, but contends that there were two other elements which supplied the required element: First, the continuation by plaintiff in the employ of the defendant for the period from December 27, 1947, the date when the resolution was adopted, until the date of her retirement on June 30, 1949. And, second, her change of position, i.e., her retirement, and the abandonment by her of her opportunity to continue in gainful employment, made in reliance on defendant's promise to pay her $200 per month for life.

We must agree with the defendant that the evidence does not support the first of these contentions. There is no language in the resolution predicating plaintiff's right to a pension upon her continued employment. She was not required to work for the defendant for any period of time as a condition to gaining such retirement benefits. She was told that she could quit the day upon which the resolution was adopted, as she herself testified, and it is clear from her own testimony that she made no promise or agreement to continue in the employ of the defendant in return for its promise to pay her a pension. Hence there was lacking that mutuality of obligation which is essential to the validity of a contract.

But as to the second of these contentions we must agree with plaintiff. By the terms of the resolution defendant promised to pay plaintiff the sum of $200 a month upon her retirement. Consideration for a promise has been defined in the Restatement of the Law of Contracts, § 75, as:

(1) Consideration for a promise is

(a) an act other than a promise, or

(b) a forbearance, or

(c) the creation, modification or destruction of a legal relation, or

(d) a return promise, bargained for and given in exchange for the promise.

As the parties agree, the consideration sufficient to support a contract may be either a benefit to the promisor or a loss or detriment to the promisee.

Section 90 of the Restatement of the Law of Contracts states that: "A promise which the promisor should reasonably expect to induce action or forbearance of a definite and substantial character on the part of the promisee and which does induce such action or forbearance is binding if injustice can be avoided only by enforcement of the promise." This doctrine has been described as that of "promissory estoppel," as distinguished from that of equitable estoppel or estoppel in pais, the reason for the differentiation being stated as follows:

It is generally true that one who has led another to act in reasonable reliance on his representations of fact cannot afterwards in litigation between the two deny the truth of the representations, and some courts have sought to apply this principle to the formation of contracts, where, relying on a gratuitous promise, the promisee has suffered detriment. It is to be noticed, however, that such a case does not come within the ordinary definition of estoppel. If there is any representation of an existing fact, it is only that the promisor at the time of making the promise intends to fulfill it. As to such intention there is usually no misrepresentation and if there is, it is not that which has injured the promisee. In other words, he relies on a promise and not on a misstatement of fact; and the term "promissory" estoppel or something equivalent should be used to make the distinction.

Williston on Contracts, Rev. Ed., § 139, Vol. 1.

In speaking of this doctrine, Judge Learned Hand said in Porter v. Commissioner of Internal Revenue, 2 Cir., 60 F.2d 673, 675, that ". . . 'promissory estoppel' is now a recognized species of consideration." . . .

Was there such an act on the part of plaintiff, in reliance upon the promise contained in the resolution, as will estop the defendant, and therefore create an enforceable contract under the doctrine of promissory estoppel? We think there was. One of the illustrations cited under Section 90 of the Restatement is: "2. *A* promises *B* to pay him an annuity during *B*'s life. *B* thereupon resigns a profitable employment, as *A* expected that he might. *B* receives the annuity for some years, in the meantime becoming disqualified from again obtaining good employment. *A*'s promise is binding." This illustration is objected to by defendant as not being applicable to the case at hand. The reason advanced by it is that in the illustration *B* became "disqualified" from obtaining other employment before *A* discontinued the payments, whereas in this case the plaintiff did not discover that she had cancer and thereby became unemployable until after the defendant had discontinued the payments of $200 per month. We think the distinction is immaterial. The only reason for the reference in the illustration to the disqualification of *A* is in connection with that part of Section 90 regarding the prevention of injustice. The injustice would occur regardless of when the disability occurred. Would defendant contend that the contract would be enforceable if the plaintiff's illness had been discovered on March 31, 1956, the day before it discontinued the payment of the $200 a month, but not if it occurred on April 2nd, the day after? Furthermore, there are more ways to become disqualified for work, or unemployable, than as the result of illness. At the time she retired plaintiff was 57 years of age. At the time the payments were discontinued she was over 63 years of age. It is a matter of common knowledge that it is virtually impossible for a woman of that age to find satisfactory employment, much less a position comparable to that which plaintiff enjoyed at the time of her retirement.

The fact of the matter is that plaintiff's subsequent illness was not the "action or forbearance" which was induced by the promise contained in the resolution. As the trial court correctly decided, such action on plaintiff's part was her retirement from a lucrative position in reliance upon defendant's promise to pay her an annuity or pension. . . .

The Commissioner therefore recommends, for the reasons stated, that the judgment be affirmed.

PER CURIAM.

The foregoing opinion by Doerner, C., is adopted as the opinion of the court. The judgment is, accordingly, affirmed.

HAYES v. PLANTATIONS STEEL CO.
Supreme Court of Rhode Island
438 A.2d 1091 (1982)

SHEA, J.

The defendant employer, Plantations Steel Company (Plantations), appeals from a Superior Court judgment for the plaintiff employee, Edward J. Hayes (Hayes). The trial justice, sitting without a jury, found that Plantations was obligated to Hayes on the basis of an implied-in-fact contract to pay him a yearly pension of $5,000. The award covered three years in which payment had not been made. The trial justice ruled, also, that Hayes had made a sufficient showing of detrimental reliance upon Plantations's promise to pay to give rise to its obligation based on the theory of promissory estoppel. The trial justice, however, found in part for Plantations in ruling that the payments to Hayes were not governed by the Employee Retirement Income Security Act, 29 U.S.C.A. §§ 1001-1461 (1975), and consequently he was not entitled to attorney's fees under § 1132(g) of that act. Both parties have appealed.

We reverse the findings of the trial justice regarding Plantations's contractual obligation to pay Hayes a pension. Consequently we need not deal with the cross-appeal concerning the award of attorney's fees under the federal statute.

Plantations is a closely held Rhode Island corporation engaged in the manufacture of steel reinforcing rods for use in concrete construction. The company was founded by Hugo R. Mainelli, Sr., and Alexander A. DiMartino. A dispute between their two families in 1976 and 1977 left the DiMartinos in full control of the corporation. Hayes was an employee of the corporation from 1947 until his retirement in 1972 at age of sixty-five. He began with Plantations as an "estimator and draftsman" and ended his career as general manager, a position of considerable responsibility. Starting in January 1973 and continuing until January 1976, Hayes received the annual sum of $5,000 from Plantations. Hayes instituted this action in December 1977, after the then company management refused to make any further payments.

Hayes testified that in January 1972 he announced his intention to retire the following July, after twenty-five years of continuous service. He decided to retire because he had worked continuously for fifty-one years. He stated, however, that he would not have retired had he not expected to receive a pension. After he stopped working for Plantations, he sought no other employment.

Approximately one week before his actual retirement Hayes spoke with Hugo R. Mainelli, Jr., who was then an officer and a stockholder of Plantations. This conversation was the first and only one concerning payments of a pension to Hayes during retirement. Mainelli said that the company "would take care" of him. There was no mention of a sum of money or a percentage of salary that Hayes would receive. There was no formal authorization for payments by Plantations's shareholders and/or board of directors. Indeed, there was never any formal provision for a pension plan for any employee other than for unionized employees, who benefit from an arrangement through their union. The plaintiff was not a union member.

Mr. Mainelli, Jr., testified that his father, Hugo R. Mainelli, Sr., had authorized the first payment "as a token of appreciation for the many years of [Hayes's] service." Furthermore, "it was implied that that check would continue on an annual basis." Mainelli also testified that it was his "personal intention" that the payments would continue for "as long as I was around."

Mainelli testified that after Hayes's retirement, he would visit the premises each year to say hello and renew old acquaintances. During the course of his visits, Hayes would thank Mainelli for the previous check and ask how long it would continue so that he could plan an orderly retirement.

The payments were discontinued after 1976. At that time a succession of several poor business years plus the stockholders' dispute, resulting in the takeover by the

DiMartino family, contributed to the decision to stop the payments.

The trial justice ruled that Plantations owed Hayes his annual sum of $5,000 for the years 1977 through 1979. The ruling implied that barring bankruptcy or the cessation of business for any other reason, Hayes had a right to expect continued annual payments.

The trial justice found that Hugo Mainelli, Jr.'s statement that Hayes would be taken care of after his retirement was a promise. Although no sum of money was mentioned in 1972, the four annual payments of $5,000 established that otherwise unspecified term of the contract. The trial justice also found that Hayes supplied consideration for the promise by voluntarily retiring, because he was under no obligation to do so. From the words and conduct of the parties and from the surrounding circumstances, the trial justice concluded that there existed an implied contract obligating the company to pay a pension to Hayes for life. The trial justice made a further finding that even if Hayes had not truly bargained for a pension by voluntarily retiring, he had nevertheless incurred the detriment of foregoing other employment in reliance upon the company's promise. He specifically held that Hayes's retirement was in response to the promise and held also that Hayes refrained from seeking other employment in further reliance thereon.

The findings of fact of a trial justice sitting without a jury are entitled to great weight when reviewed by this court. His findings will not be disturbed unless it can be shown that they are clearly wrong or that the trial justice misconceived or overlooked material evidence. After careful review of the record, however, we conclude that the trial justice's findings and conclusions must be reversed.

Assuming for the purpose of this discussion that Plantations in legal effect made a promise to Hayes, we must ask whether Hayes did supply the required consideration that would make the promise binding? And, if Hayes did not supply consideration, was his alleged reliance sufficiently induced by the promise to estop defendant from denying its obligation to him? We answer both questions in the negative.

We turn first to the problem of consideration. The facts at bar do not present the case of an express contract. As the trial justice stated, the existence of a contract in this case must be determined from all the circumstances of the parties' conduct and words. Although words were expressed initially in the remark that Hayes "would be taken care of," any contract in this case would be more in the nature of an implied contract. Certainly the statement of Hugo Mainelli, Jr., standing alone is not an expression of a direct and definite promise to pay Hayes a pension. Though we are analyzing an implied contract, nevertheless we must address the question of consideration.

Contracts implied in fact require the element of consideration to support them as is required in express contracts. The only difference between the two is the manner in which the parties manifest their assent. In this jurisdiction, consideration consists either in some right, interest, or benefit accruing to one party or some forbearance, detriment, or responsibility given, suffered, or undertaken by the other. Valid consideration furthermore must be bargained for. It must induce the return act or promise. To be valid, therefore, the purported consideration must not have been delivered before a promise is executed, that is, given without reference to the promise. Consideration is therefore a test of the enforceability of executory promises, and has no legal effect when rendered in the past and apart from an alleged exchange in the present.

In the case before us, Plantations's promise to pay Hayes a pension is quite clearly not supported by any consideration supplied by Hayes. Hayes had announced his intent to retire well in advance of any promise, and therefore the intention to retire was arrived at without regard to any promise by Plantations. Although Hayes may have had in mind the receipt of a pension when he first informed Plantations, his expectation was not based on any statement made to him or on any conduct of the company officer relative to him in January 1972. In deciding to retire, Hayes acted on his own initiative. Hayes's long years of dedicated service also is legally insufficient because his service too was rendered without being induced by Plantations's promise.

Clearly then this is not a case in which Plantations's promise was meant to induce Hayes to refrain from retiring when he could have chosen to do so in return for further service. Nor was the promise made to encourage long service from the start of his employment. Instead, the testimony establishes that Plantations's promise was intended "as a token of appreciation for [Hayes's] many years of service." As such it was in the nature of a gratuity paid to Hayes for as long as the company chose. In Spickelmier Industries, Inc. v. Passander, 172 Ind. App. 49 (1977), an employer's promise to an employee to pay him a year-end bonus was unenforceable because it was made after the employee had performed his contractual responsibilities for that year.

The plaintiff's most relevant citations are still inapposite to the present case. Bredemann v. Vaughan Mfg. Co., 40 Ill. App. 2d 232 (1963), presents similar yet distinguishable facts. There, the appellate court reversed a summary judgment granted to the defendant employer, stating that a genuine issue of material fact existed regarding whether the plaintiff's retirement was in consideration of her employer's promise to pay her a lifetime pension. As in the present case, the employer made the promise one week prior to the employee's retirement, and in almost the same words. However, Bredemann is distinguishable because the court characterized that promise as a concrete offer to pay if she would retire immediately. In fact, the defendant wanted her to retire. On the contrary, Plantations in this case did not actively seek Hayes's retirement. DiMartino, one of Plantations's founders, testified that he did not want Hayes to retire. Unlike Bredemann, here Hayes announced his unsolicited intent to retire.

Hayes also argues that the work he performed during the week between the promise and the date of his retirement constituted sufficient consideration to support the promise. He relies on Ulmann v. Sunset-McKee Co., 221 F.2d 128 (9th Cir. 1955), in which the court ruled that work performed during the one-week period of the employee's notice of impending retirement constituted consideration for the employer's offer of a pension that the employee had solicited some months previously. But there the court stated that its prime reason for upholding the agreement was that sufficient consideration existed in the employee's consent not to compete with his employer. These circumstances do not appear in our case. Hayes left his employment because he no longer desired to work. He was not contemplating other job offers or considering going into competition with Plantations. Although Plantations did not want Hayes to leave, it did not try to deter him, nor did it seek to prevent Hayes from engaging in other activity.

Hayes argues in the alternative that even if Plantations's promise was not the product of an exchange, its duty is grounded properly in the theory of promissory estoppel. This court adopted the theory of promissory estoppel in East Providence Credit Union v. Geremia, 103 R.I. 597, 601 (1968). . . . In *East Providence Credit Union* this court said that the doctrine of promissory estoppel is invoked "as a substitute for a consideration, rendering a gratuitous promise enforceable as a contract." To restate the matter differently, "the acts of reliance by the promisee to his detriment [provide] a substitute for consideration."

Hayes urges that in the absence of a bargained-for promise the facts require application of the doctrine of promissory estoppel. He stresses that he retired voluntarily while expecting to receive a pension. He would not have otherwise retired. Nor did he seek other employment.

We disagree with this contention largely for the reasons already stated. One of the essential elements of the doctrine of promissory estoppel is that the promise must induce the promisee's action or forbearance. The particular act in this regard is plaintiff's decision whether or not to retire. As we stated earlier, the record indicates that he made the decision on his own initiative. In other words, the conversation between Hayes and Mainelli which occurred a week before Hayes left his employment cannot be said to have induced his decision to leave. He had reached that decision long before.

An example taken from the Restatement provides a meaningful contrast:

> "2. A promises B to pay him an annuity during B's life. B *thereupon* resigns profitable employment, as A *expected* that he might. B receives the annuity for some years, in the meantime becoming disqualified from again obtaining good employment. A's promise is binding." (Emphasis added.)

Restatement Contracts § 90 at 111 (1932).

In Feinberg v. Pfeiffer Co., 322 S.W.2d 163 (Mo. App. 1959), . . . the court held that a pension contract existed between the parties. Although continued employment was not a consideration to [plaintiff's] receipt of retirement benefits, the court found sufficient reliance on the part of the plaintiff to support her claim. The court based its decision upon the above Restatement example, that is, the defendant informed the plaintiff of its plan, and the plaintiff in reliance thereon, retired. *Feinberg* presents factors that also appear in the case at bar. There, the plaintiff had worked many years and desired to retire; she would not have left had she not been able to rely on a pension; and once retired, she sought no other employment.

However, the important distinction between *Feinberg* and the case before us is that in *Feinberg* the employer's decision definitely shaped the thinking of the plaintiff. In this case the promise did not. It is not reasonable to infer from the facts that Hugo R. Mainelli, Jr., expected retirement to result from his conversation with Hayes. Hayes had given notice of his intention seven months previously. Here there was thus no inducement to retire which would satisfy the demands of § 90 of the Restatement. Nor can it be said that Hayes's refraining from other employment was "action or forbearance of a definite and substantial character." The underlying assumption of Hayes's initial decision to retire was that upon leaving the defendant's employ, he would no longer work. It is impossible to say that he changed his position any more so because of what Mainelli had told him in light of his own initial decision. These circumstances do not lead to a conclusion that injustice can be avoided only by enforcement of Plantations's promise. Hayes received $20,000 over the course of four years. He inquired each year about whether he could expect a check for the following year. Obviously, there was no absolute certainty on his part that the pension would continue. Furthermore, in the face of his uncertainty, the mere fact that payment for several years did occur is insufficient by itself to meet the requirements of reliance under the doctrine of promissory estoppel.

For the foregoing reasons, the defendant's appeal is sustained and the judgment of the Superior Court is reversed.

NOTES

1. ***Reconciling* Feinberg *and* Hayes.** In *Feinberg*, the court enforced Pfeiffer Company's promise to pay Anna Feinberg retirement benefits, but in *Hayes*, the court refused to enforce Plantation Steel Company's promise to pay Edward Hayes retirement benefits. Can you reconcile the different outcomes in these cases by distinguishing bargained-for promises from non-bargained-for promises? Are the different outcomes explained by the presence or absence of consideration? In *Feinberg* and *Hayes*, which of the plaintiffs, if any, actually bargained for the promise they received? Are the different outcomes explained by the presence or absence of detrimental reliance? The court in *Feinberg* holds that Feinberg retired "from a lucrative position in reliance upon defendant's promise to pay her an annuity or pension." The court in *Hayes* held that

> the important distinction between *Feinberg* and the case before us is that in *Feinberg* the employer's decision definitely shaped the thinking of the plaintiff. In this case the promise did not. . . . Hayes had given notice of his intention seven months previously. Here there was thus no inducement to retire which would satisfy the demands of § 90 of the Restatement. Nor can it be said that Hayes's refraining from other employment was 'action or forbearance of a definite and substantial character.' . . . Furthermore, . . . the mere fact that payment for several years did occur is insufficient by itself to meet the requirements of reliance under the doctrine of promissory estoppel.

Id. at 1096–97.

If we take the courts at their word, then Edward Hayes would have recovered had his lawyers presented more persuasive evidence of detrimental reliance. Are you convinced that the outcomes in these cases are best explained by bad lawyering? Alternatively, is it really plausible to suppose that Hayes did not rely on the promise made to him by Hugo Mainelli?

2. *Bargaining Contexts and Promissory Estoppel.* If all promises induce reliance, then presumably all promises are potentially enforceable under § 90. But as *Haase* and *Hayes* illustrate, courts often refuse to enforce promises not supported by consideration even though promissory estoppel provides an available theory of enforcement. What then explains when promissory estoppel will lie? If the bargain theory of consideration provides the paradigm case for enforcement, is the presence of a bargain context, if not an actual bargain, relevant to enforcement under promissory estoppel? In which cases were the promises made in a bargain context? If their employers had not promised them retirement benefits, would Anna Feinberg or Edward Hayes have been successful if they had come to their employers and demanded a promise of retirement benefits? In each of these cases, what effect will enforcement have on future promise-making? In which of these cases would the promisor be likely to have intended his or her promise to be legally enforceable?

3. *Relationship Between Promissory Estoppel and Consideration.* Holmes said: "It would cut up the doctrine of consideration by the roots, if a promise could make a gratuitous promise binding by subsequently acting in reliance on it." *Commonwealth by Commissioners of Sav. Banks v. Scituate Sav. Bank*, 137 Mass. 301, 302 (1884). Do not be misled by Judge Hand's statement, which is quoted in *Feinberg*, that " 'promissory estoppel' is now a recognized species of consideration." The term "consideration" has many shades of meaning, but promissory estoppel is foreign to the bargain theory of contract and to the Holmesian concept of consideration.

4. *The Employment Context.* In recent years, the number of reported cases in which employees have raised promissory estoppel claims in discharge cases has far exceeded the number of cases in which retirement benefits were claimed. In many cases, employees rely on oral representations made by their employers regarding job security, only to be released from employment later. Courts have rejected the majority of such claims for various reasons. Professor Robert Hillman has suggested that, among other reasons, "judicial veneration for the employment-at-will rule clearly contributed to the defeat of promissory estoppel claims."[11] What policies support the employment-at-will rule (an employer may release an employee "at any time and for any reason")? Should courts be more willing to find for employees on a theory of promissory estoppel even when employees originally agreed to be employed "at-will"?

Essay: Consideration, Promissory Estoppel, and the Expanded Bargain Theory

The central objective of this chapter is to identify the conditions under which courts will enforce promises. It is tempting to explain the application of promissory estoppel by distinguishing between promises that induce reasonable reliance and those that do not. Section 90 directs courts to do just that, and most courts denying enforcement under promissory estoppel justify their decision by finding insufficient evidence of reasonable reliance. In some cases, reliance by promisees may indeed

---

[11] Robert A. Hillman, *The Unfulfilled Promise of Promissory Estoppel in the Employment Setting*, 31 Rutgers L.J. 1, 25 (1999).

be de minimus. But in the mine run of cases, a serious promise will induce reasonable reliance. Virtually any promise provides a promisee with reasonable grounds for relying to some extent on the promised act. Unless promisees know the promisor is insincere or highly unreliable, it would be irrational for them not to adjust their behavior after they receive a promise. Yet if almost all promises induce some reasonable reliance, then almost every promise should be enforceable under § 90. Instead, many such promises are not enforced. How can this enforcement pattern be explained?

The bargain theory of consideration explains enforcement of promises made as a result of an actual bargain. If we expand the bargain theory to support the enforcement of those promises made in a bargain context, which includes but is not limited to actual bargains, it is possible to explain the various patterns of enforcement in promissory estoppel cases. If the promisee *could have* bargained for the promise, whether or not she did in fact, the promise is more likely to be enforced. If the promisee could not easily have bargained for the promise, because soliciting a promise would have been inappropriate given the social context, the promise is less likely to be enforced. Assuming this expanded bargain theory provides a convincing explanation of the patterns of promissory enforcement under the doctrine of promissory estoppel, what is its underlying rationale?

In most cases, contract law enforces promises when promisors clearly indicate an intention to be legally bound by their promise and refuses to enforce promises when promisors clearly indicate an intention not to be legally bound by their promise. (Can the clarity of intention explain the court's decision in *Ricketts*? Does this theory explain the different outcomes in *Feinberg* and *Hayes*?) But when individuals fail clearly to indicate whether or not they intend to be bound, contract law must have some method for deciding the enforcement question. One solution is to create a presumption in favor or against enforcement in particular circumstances. As we saw in Chapter 1, contemporary contract theory calls such rules "default rules." Default rules dictate a particular result in the absence of evidence that individuals have chosen to "opt out" of the default rule by specifying an alternative result. Enforcement default rules in contract law direct courts to enforce promises in certain kinds of cases, and not to enforce promises in other kinds of cases, unless the promisor clearly indicates a contrary intent. The bargain theory constitutes the promissory enforcement default rule for contract law. By enforcing promises made in bargain contexts, and refusing to enforce promises made in non-bargain contexts, the doctrines of consideration and promissory estoppel enforce only those promises made by promisors who are likely to have intended their promises to be legally enforceable.

Thus, the expanded bargain theory provides a good proxy for determining whether the promisee could have reasonably believed that the promisor intended his promise to be legally binding. In bargain contexts, by hypothesis, the promisee has the leverage necessary to induce the promisor to make a legally enforceable promise (say, by offering a valuable promise in return). Thus, it is reasonable for a promisee in a bargain context to suppose that her promisor intends his promise to be legally binding, even if she has not explicitly bargained for it. It seems reasonable to suppose as well that under these circumstances, a promisor (such as the Pfeiffer Co. in *Feinberg*) would anticipate the need to make a legally enforceable promise, rather than waiting for the promisee to press the issue.

By contrast, in non-bargain contexts, the promisee lacks the leverage necessary to induce the promisor to make a legally enforceable promise. The features of the social context that limit the promisee's leverage over the promisor also make it less likely that the promisor would intend his promise to be legally enforceable. Because promises made in non-bargain contexts are non-reciprocal (i.e., there is no expectation of a return), a promisor has less reason to make his promise legally enforceable. On this analysis, can you explain why the promises in *Haase* and *Hayes* were not enforced? To be sure, this default presumption can be overcome by clear evidence of an intention to be legally bound. In such a case, perhaps *Ricketts* is an example, courts may be motivated to find a theory that justifies enforcement.

Two kinds of theories have been offered to justify contract law's enforcement default rules. Economic analysis provides an *instrumental* justification for enforcing promises. It focuses on the societal benefits of enforcement default regimes. The current enforcement default rules of contract law provided by the bargain theory are justified, according to this view, because they maximize beneficial reliance. On this view, the chief societal benefit advanced by contract law is to maximize the social benefits of reliance on promises. However, such beneficial reliance cannot be maximized simply by enhancing the reliability of promises. In order to increase the reliability of a promise, the negative consequences the promisor bears by breaking the promise must be increased. But any increase in the negative consequences of breaking promises will also deter individuals from making promises in the first place and encourage individuals to add conditions to the promises they do make. Increasing the negative consequences of promise-breaking therefore reduces the quantity and quality of future promises, which in turn decreases the opportunities for beneficial reliance by future promisees. Economists call this phenomenon an "activity level" effect. Here, the activity affected by enhancing the penalties for promise-breaking is the activity of promise-making. The enforcement decision thus implicates a trade-off between enhancing beneficial reliance on promises made and reducing the activity of promising itself. The optimal enforcement default regime enforces promises only when the increase in beneficial reliance that enforcement makes possible offsets the decrease in promising occasioned by legally enforcing such promises. Such a regime maximizes the *net* beneficial reliance made possible by promises.

To see why, consider the incentive effects of this enforcement regime. By enforcing promises when and only when the promisor is likely to have intended his promise to be given legal effect, this expanded bargain theory of contract minimizes the activity level effect of enforcing promises. By hypothesis, legal enforcement of a promise intended by the promisor to be legally enforceable will not deter similar would-be promisors from making such promises in the future. However, if the law enforces promises in contexts where the promisor is not likely to have intended his promise to be legally enforceable, individuals in the future will be less likely to make such promises, and the promises they do make will have to be qualified with an express disclaimer of legal liability. By forcing such promisors to make express disclaimers of legal liability, the promisee may be led to believe that the promisor does not intend the promisee to rely and that the promise is not reliable. But individuals who make promises not intended to be legally enforceable — for example, intra-familial promisors — are often motivated by loyalty, love, morality, or charity. Their promises tend to be very reliable without legal enforcement. A rule that forces such promisors to emphasize their intent not to be bound may undermine their ability to communicate a highly reliable promise. Moreover, because these promises are highly reliable, there is little to be gained by making them legally enforceable.

In sum, enforcing promises in contexts in which promisors are likely to have intended them to be legally enforceable enhances the reliability of such promises without deterring individuals from making such promises in the future. Enforcing promises in contexts in which promisors are likely not to have intended them to be legally enforceable significantly decreases the incentives for individuals in the future to make promises in these contexts, forces individuals who do make promises in these contexts to disclaim legal liability (and thereby undermines their ability effectively to communicate that their promises are highly reliable) and does little to make such promises more reliable than they already are.

Autonomy theory takes a *non-instrumental* approach to justifying the enforcement of promises. At its core, the concept of autonomy embodies the right of individuals to self-determination — to exercise their capacity to form, revise, and pursue their own conception of the good. The right of self-determination entails the capacity to enter into binding agreements to facilitate future planning. Autonomy does not require legal enforcement of all promises, however. It requires legal enforcement only of those promises intended by fully autonomous individuals to be legally enforceable. To do otherwise would fail to respect the promisor's exercise of free will. Thus, autonomy theories require that individuals be free to choose to bind themselves by undertaking a promissory obligation. When individuals make a promise that they intend not to be legally enforceable, they are bound only by morality. But when individuals bind themselves by making a promise that they do intend to be legally binding, then autonomy requires that their promises be enforced by law.

[5] **Promises to Insure**

When one party makes a gratuitous promise to procure insurance for another party, under what conditions will that promise be enforced? This question is the focus of this section.

EAST PROVIDENCE CREDIT UNION v. GEREMIA
Supreme Court of Rhode Island
103 R.I. 597, 239 A.2d 725 (1968)

Kelleher, J.

This is a civil action to collect from the defendants the balance due on a promissory note. The defendants filed a counterclaim. The case was heard by a justice of the superior court. He dismissed the plaintiff's complaint and found for the defendants on their counterclaim. The case is before us on the plaintiff's appeal.

On December 5, 1963, defendants, who are husband and wife, borrowed $2,350.28

from plaintiff for which they gave their promissory note. The payment of the note was secured by a chattel mortgage on defendants' 1962 ranch wagon. The mortgage contained a clause which obligated defendants to maintain insurance on the motor vehicle in such amounts as plaintiff required against loss by fire, collision, upset or overturn of the automobile and similar hazards. This provision also stipulated that if defendants failed to maintain such insurance, plaintiff could pay the premium and ". . . any sum so paid shall be secured hereby and shall be immediately payable." The defendants had procured the required insurance and had designated plaintiff as a loss payee on its policy. The premium therefor was payable in periodic installments.

On October 11, 1965, defendants received a notice from the insurance carrier informing them that the premium then payable was overdue and that, unless it was paid within the ensuing twelve days, the policy would be canceled. A copy of this notice was also sent by the insurer to plaintiff who thereupon sent a letter to defendants. The pertinent portion thereof reads as follows:

We are in receipt of a cancellation notice on your Policy.

If we are not notified of a renewal Policy within 10 days, we shall be forced to renew the policy for you and apply this amount to your loan.

Upon receiving this communication, defendant wife testified that she telephoned plaintiff's office and talked to the treasurer's assistant; that she told this employee to go ahead and pay the premium; that she explained to the employee that her husband was sick and they could not pay the insurance premium and the payment due on the loan; and that the employee told her her call would be referred to plaintiff's treasurer. The employee testified that she told defendant to contact this officer. We deem this difference in testimony insignificant. It is clear from the record that defendants communicated their approval of an acquiescence in plaintiff's promise to pay the insurance due on the car and that this employee notified the treasurer of such fact.

On December 17, 1965, defendants' motor vehicle was demolished in a mishap the nature of which cannot be learned from the record. It is obvious, however, that the loss was within the coverage of the policy. The automobile was a total loss. The evidence shows that at the time of the loss, the outstanding balance of the loan was $987.89 and the value of the ranch wagon prior to the loss exceeded the balance due on the loan.

Sometime after this unfortunate incident, all the parties became aware that the insurer would not indemnify them for the loss because the overdue premium had not been paid and defendants' policy had been canceled prior to the accident.

The defendants had on deposit with plaintiff over $200 in savings shares. The plaintiff, in accordance with the terms of the note, had deducted therefrom certain amounts and applied them to defendants' indebtedness so that at the time this litigation was instituted defendants allegedly owed plaintiff $779.53.

In finding for defendants on their counterclaim, the trial justice awarded them all the moneys which plaintiff had applied after the date of defendants' accident to the then outstanding balance of the loan.21 The justice, at the conclusion of the evidence, made certain findings which were in accordance with the testimony as set forth above. He found from the evidence that plaintiff, in pursuance of its right under the mortgage contract and its letter to defendants, had agreed to renew the policy and charge any premiums paid by it on behalf of defendants to the outstanding balance on their loan.

In reaching this conclusion, the trial justice made the following observation: ". . . it seems to me quite clear that the defendants, having been given notice that the plaintiff would do this (pay the overdue premium), and calling the plaintiff's attention to the fact that they weren't going to renew and that the plaintiff had better do this to protect everybody, seems to me at that point there was agreement on the part of the plaintiff that it would procure this insurance. Or, put it another way, that they are estopped from denying that they were exercising the right that they had under the original mortgage." The superior court further found that defendants were justified in believing in plaintiff's assurance that it would pay the overdue premium.

The sole issue raised by this appeal is whether or not plaintiff is precluded from recovering on its loan contract by reason of its failure to fulfill a promise to defendants to pay the overdue insurance premium. In urging that the trial justice erred in finding for defendants, plaintiff directs our attention to Hazlett v. First Fed. Sav. & Loan Assn., 14 Wash. 2d 124, in which the court refused to apply the doctrine of promissory estoppel to enforce a gratuitous promise made by a mortgagee to procure fire insurance for mortgaged property even though the mortgagor suffered serious detriment in reliance on the mortgagee's promise.

Until recently it was a general rule that the doctrine of estoppel was applied only to representations made as to facts past or present. This doctrine is commonly known as "equitable" estoppel. Over the years, however, courts have carved out a recognized exception to this rule and applied it to those circumstances wherein one promises to do or not to do something in the future. This latter doctrine is known as "promissory" estoppel. Promissory estoppel is defined in the 1 Restatement, Contracts, § 90. . . .

Although this court has not yet applied the doctrine of promissory estoppel as it is expressed in the Restatement, we have in Mann v. McDermott, 77 R.I. 142, implied that in appropriate circumstances we would. Traditionally, the doctrine of promissory estoppel has been invoked as a substitute for a consideration, rendering a gratuitous promise enforceable as a contract. Viewed in another way, the acts of reliance by the promisee to his detriment provided a substitute for consideration. Hoffman v. Red Owl Stores, Inc., 26 Wis. 2d 683.

While the doctrine was originally recognized and most often utilized in charitable subscription cases, it presently enjoys a much wider and more expanded application. Relative to the problem presented in this case, we have discovered several cases in which the theory of promissory estoppel has been invoked. In these cases, courts have held that a gratuitous promise made by one to procure insurance on the promisee's property is made enforceable by the promisee's reliance thereon and his forbearance to procure such insurance himself.

In the instant case, however, after a careful review of the facts, we are of the opinion that plaintiff made more than a mere gratuitous or unrecompensed promise. Instead, we believe that the promise by plaintiff to pay the insurance premium on defendants' car was one made in exchange for valid consideration. The mortgage contract provided that in the event plaintiff paid a premium for defendants, it would add such expended sums to the outstanding balance of defendants' loan. We are satisfied from a close examination of plaintiff's reply to defendants' interrogatories and of the chattel mortgage agreement that plaintiff intended to compute interest on any money it expended in keeping the insurance on defendants' car active. Hence, in our opinion, the interest due on any sums paid out by plaintiff on behalf of defendants for insurance represents valid consideration and converts their promise into a binding contract. The plaintiff's failure to successfully carry out its promise must be deemed a breach of that contract entitling defendants to assert a right of action which would at the very least offset any amount of money found owing to plaintiff on their loan.

We would point out that, even if it could be shown by plaintiff that it never intended to compute any interest on amounts paid by it for insurance premiums on defendants' car and that its promise was truly a pure gratuitous undertaking, we believe such a showing would be of no avail to it since we would not hesitate in finding from this record evidence sufficient to establish a case for the application of promissory estoppel. . . . Promissory estoppel as a legal theory is gaining in prominence as a device used by an increasing number of courts to provide a much needed remedy to alleviate the plight of those who suffer a serious injustice as a result of their good-faith reliance on the unfulfilled promises of others. As the Arkansas supreme court has so appropriately commented in Peoples Nat'l Bank of Little Rock v. Linebarger Constr. Co., 219 Ark. 11, at 17, the law of promissory estoppel exhibits ". . . an attempt by the courts to keep remedies abreast of increased moral consciousness of honesty and fair representations in all business dealings. . . ." We subscribe to those sentiments.

The plaintiff's appeal is denied and dismissed and the judgment appealed from is affirmed.

NOTES

1. ***Liability in the Promise to Insure Cases.*** *Graddon v. Knight*, 138 Cal. App. 2d 577, 292 P.2d 632 (1956), cited in *East Providence*, provides a good example of how a court uses promissory estoppel to enforce a promise to insure. In that case, the Graddons were having a home built for them and the defendant bank was providing the financing. The court found promissory estoppel liability on the following facts:

> The evidence amply supports the jury's implied finding that the bank agreed to procure the insurance, or, at the very least, by its conduct led Graddons to believe that it had done so, and is estopped to deny such agreement. Coppock was a vice president and manager of the bank's Palo Alto branch and was the person with whom Graddons dealt in obtaining the loan on their property and in the execution of the necessary documents. Coppock instructed them about getting appraisers and then stated:

. . . We have to start a file for our own system here, we have to see the plans and get them approved and they have to be approved by the G.I. in San Francisco, and when all those are in and complete, then we can go over this loan. . . .

Coppock also stated that the bank would do the checking of all necessary papers. Graddons were required to sign a letter instructing the bank to pay "any and all expenses in connection with the completion of this loan. . . ."

The bank purchased the title insurance and charged it to Graddons. Coppock stated at the close of the signing of the papers, "'Well, that takes care of everything,'" and then: "When we had finished signing the papers and had gotten up to leave, Mr. Coppock was looking over the papers and he looked up to us and says, 'Do you want the full amount of the insurance?' and I said, 'Yes.'" It should be noted that Coppock denied these statements. The Graddons relied upon this apparent agreement of the bank to do the actual obtaining of the insurance and made no effort to get it themselves. That Coppock intended to convey to Graddons that he would procure the insurance is additionally shown by the fact that the day after the fire he told the architect "he thought the bank held the fire insurance papers."

Coppock testified that he was "dumbfounded" to find no policy in the file, that "just an exception should have gotten by us." However, the jury chose to believe plaintiffs' evidence. The foregoing evidence brings this case well within the rule set forth in section 90, Restatement of Contracts, . . . and in section 1962, subdivision 3, Code of Civil Procedure: "Whenever a party has, by his own declaration, act, or omission, intentionally and deliberately led another to believe a particular thing true, and to act upon such belief, he cannot, in any litigation arising out of such declaration, act, or omission, be permitted to falsify it. . . ."

The evidence here was such that the jury could and did find all the elements necessary for the doctrine of promissory estoppel to apply, namely,

(1) a promise clear and unambiguous in its terms, . . .

(2) reliance by the party to whom the promise is made, . . .

(3) his reliance must be both reasonable and foreseeable, . . .

(4) the party asserting the estoppel must be injured by his reliance. . . .

138 Cal. App. 2d at 582–83, 292 P.2d at 636–37.

Consider also *Spiegel v. Metropolitan Life Ins. Co.*, 6 N.Y.2d 91, 188 N.Y.S.2d 486 (1959). Levy, an agent for the defendant, promised Mrs. Spiegel that he would "take care of" renewing her husband's life insurance policy during the quarter that the Spiegels were unable to make the payment. Two renewal notices were sent to Mrs. Spiegel, and each time Levy assured her that he would see to the renewal of the policy. Levy never rendered payment. When the payment for the next quarter fell due, however, Mrs. Spiegel received the usual notice. Again Mrs. Spiegel was unable to pay. When her husband died two weeks later, Metropolitan refused coverage.

The New York Court of Appeals absolved Metropolitan of liability, but held Levy liable for the full amount of the insurance policy because of his earlier promises to Mrs. Spiegel.

From these cases, it seems that promissory estoppel is often used to impose liability for failure to perform a promise to procure insurance. Comment e to § 90 of the Restatement (Second) of Contracts, however, implies that promissory estoppel is to be used with care because of the magnitude of the liability exposure:

> This section is to be applied with caution to promises to procure insurance. The appropriate remedy for breach of a promise makes the promisor an insurer, and thus may result in a liability which is very large in relation to the value of the promised service. Often the promise is properly to be construed merely as a promise to use reasonable efforts to procure the insurance, and reliance by the promisee may be unjustified or may be justified only for a short time. Or it may be doubtful whether he did in fact rely. Such difficulties may be removed if the proof of the promise and the reliance are clear, or if part performance or a commercial setting or a potential benefit to the promisor provide a substitute for formality.

Consider *East Providence, Graddon* and *Spiegel* in light of this comment. In each case, one party was found to have relied on a promise made by the other party. On what basis do courts decide if reliance is justified? Under what circumstances would the promisor be deemed to promise only to use reasonable efforts to procure insurance? Were the promises in these cases rendered with any formalities? Did the evidence that was presented offer clear and unambiguous proof that the promises were made as stated by the promisees? What was the benefit? Are you satisfied, now, that all three promises rested on reliance supported by clear, uncontradicted proof?

2. *Tort Analogues.* Tort law principles occasionally are invoked to bolster the grounds of enforcement. The voluntary undertaking of an act which the promisor otherwise is not bound to do is covered by the Restatement (Second) of Torts § 323 (1965). That provision reads as follows:

> One who undertakes, gratuitously or for consideration, to render services to another which he should recognize as necessary for the protection of the other's person or things, is subject to liability to the other for physical harm resulting from his failure to exercise reasonable care to perform his undertaking if
>
> (a) his failure to exercise such care increases the risk of harm, or
>
> (b) the harm is suffered because of the other's reliance upon the undertaking.

3. *An Enforcement Variable: The Competitive Market.* One might look to the existence of a competitive market to explain the enforcement of promises to insure, as well as a number of other cases in which promissory estoppel has been successfully invoked. Promises to insure fall within a reciprocal, or bargain, context (in other words, a context in which bargaining between parties could have gone forward whether or not it actually did), but they frequently will not fit within the narrower confines of the consideration model.

Recall that traditional bargain theory does not distinguish between exchange transactions in established markets and exchanges of bespoke promises. In a competitive market, however, alternatives are available to the promisee. Thus, when the promise given to the promisee is not kept, the detriment suffered as a result of reliance on that promise is easily quantifiable — the court need only look at the market alternative to see what the promisee would have received had the promise been kept. When an accurate measure of detrimental reliance is available, courts are more willing to grant enforcement whether the promise was bargained-for or was gratuitous. Promissory estoppel, therefore, is more likely to be successfully invoked for promises that are easily valued by examination of market values. Insurance is one such competitive market with readily available market substitutes. When a party foregoes the opportunity to obtain one insurance policy in favor of a policy that another party promises to procure, upon nonperformance the promisee will be granted a full damages award.

What effect will enforcement of such "promises" have on future promisors in the same position? Will they simply stop promising? Or, will they adjust the quality of the promises by making the terms of the promises more explicit? Perhaps they will take further precautions to ensure their own performance? If so, what will happen to the price they charge?

4. **The "Injustice" Element in Promissory Estoppel.** Section 90 enforces a promise that induces reasonable reliance "if injustice can be avoided only by enforcing the promise." In most cases, courts ignore this third element in promissory estoppel and focus instead on whether a clear and definite promise was made and whether the promisee reasonably relied on the promise. Those few courts that have expressly addressed the "injustice" element have interpreted it as requiring an independent public policy inquiry, often prohibiting enforcement unless necessary to avoid unjust enrichment. For example, in *Faimon v. Winona State Univ.*, 540 N.W.2d 879 (1995), the court found that the University had made a clear and definite promise on which its employee reasonably relied, but refused to enforce the promise because doing so was not necessary to prevent injustice. According to the court, "[n]umerous considerations enter into a judicial determination of injustice, including the reasonableness of a promisee's reliance and a weighing of public policies in favor of both enforcing bargains and preventing unjust enrichment." *Id.* at 883.

The "injustice" prong of promissory estoppel has also been used as a doctrinal "catch-all" device for subjecting promissory enforcement to various matters of public policy. In *Cohen v. Cowles Media Co.*, 457 N.W.2d 199 (1990) (*Cohen* I), and also in *Cohen v. Cowles Media Co.*, 479 N.W.2d 387 (1992) (*Cohen* II), satisfaction of the injustice element turned on whether enforcing a promise violated the First Amendment. In *Cohen* I, the Minnesota Supreme Court refused to apply promissory estoppel to allow an informant, Cohen, to recover for two newspapers' breach of their promise not to reveal Cohen's name. The holding was based on a finding that enforcing the promise would violate the newspapers' First Amendment rights, creating an "injustice." The Supreme Court remanded the case, saying that the First Amendment was not relevant to the injustice element of promissory estoppel as "the First Amendment does not confer upon the press a constitutional right to disregard promises that would otherwise be enforced under state law." 501 U.S. 663, 672 (1991). Upon remand, the Minnesota Supreme Court reversed its previous ruling and held the newspapers' promise enforceable under promissory estoppel. It further noted that "the test is not whether the promise should be enforced to do justice, but whether enforcement is required to prevent an injustice." *Cohen* II, 479 N.W.2d at 391. The ethical importance of protecting confidential sources and the harm to Cohen from the breach were considered great enough to warrant enforcement of the newspapers' promise.

D. THE MATERIAL BENEFIT RULE

Essay: The History and Contemporary Application of the Material Benefit Rule

Recall that the court in *Greene* dismissed a promise to pay for prior cohabitation as void because "[t]he consideration in such a case is past." Section B[1], *supra*. Promises based on past consideration are generally held to be unenforceable for lack of consideration. In past consideration cases, the benefit does not qualify as something given *in exchange for the promise* because the promise is given after the benefit is conferred rather than as a pre-condition of receiving the benefit. However, courts have developed a doctrine that does legally enforce a subset of promises given in recognition of previously conferred benefits. In *Webb v. McGowin*, 27 Ala. App. 82, 168 So. 196 (1935), Webb, a mill worker, was alleged to have diverted the trajectory of a heavy wooden block falling towards McGowin by holding on to the block when it fell from the second floor of the mill. In the course of attempting to save McGowin from being crushed by the block, Webb sustained severe bodily injuries that crippled him for life. McGowin, "in consideration of [Webb] having prevented him from sustaining death or serious bodily harm and in consideration of the injuries [Webb] had received," promised to provide financial support to Webb for the rest of Webb's life. When McGowin died eight years later and his estate refused to pay, the court held that this promise was enforceable even though it was not given in exchange for anything but rather in recognition of a previously conferred benefit.

Courts and commentators have worried that this departure from the consideration doctrine would make the number of enforceable promises almost limitless. *See, e.g., Wennall v. Adney*, 127 Eng. Rep. 137 (K.B. 1840). However, courts have managed to confine the reach of the material benefit rule as an exception to the consideration doctrine. Compare *Webb* to *Mills v. Wyman*, 20 Mass. (3 Pick.) 207 (1825), in which Mills found and cared for Levi Wyman, the 25-year-old son of the defendant, who had fallen ill at sea and was stranded far from home. Mills provided shelter, food, and medicine for the defendant's son, until the young Wyman died. The defendant, whom the court described as having been moved by "a transient feeling of gratitude," made a written promise to pay for the expenses incurred by Mills while caring for Wyman's dying son. The defendant later repudiated this promise and refused to pay. The court held that the promise created a mere moral, not legal, obligation to pay. The court held that because Mills was acting as a Good Samaritan, and thus had not expected compensation at the time he took care of Wyman's son, Wyman's subsequent promise in recognition of the benefit he had received was unenforceable. Thus, despite the holding in *Webb*, courts have limited the enforcement of promises based on past benefits to those in which the benefit was conferred with an expectation of payment. Examples include promises to renew debts that have been discharged by operation of law (e.g., bankruptcy, infancy, statute of limitations, or statute of frauds). However, promises based on past gifts or moral obligations are not enforced.

The material benefit rule is formalized in the Restatement (Second) of Contracts § 86, which allows "promises made in recognition of a benefit previously received" to be legally binding "to the extent necessary to prevent injustice." The provision further states that such a promise is not binding if the previous benefit was conferred gratuitously.

Despite the vague language of § 86, the fear that the material benefit rule would undermine the consideration requirement has largely been proven false. In fact, since the adoption of Restatement (Second) § 86 in 1981, only five reported cases have enforced a subsequent promise made in recognition of a past benefit received. And in the previous twenty years while the Restatement was being drafted, only three cases used the rule to uphold promises based on past consideration.

The relatively few contemporary cases decided under the material benefit rule use the doctrine to overcome a structural impediment to bargaining over ideas and information. Suppose A has an idea or information that might be valuable to B, but once A has disclosed it to B it will be difficult, both legally and practically, to prevent B from benefiting from it. B cannot rationally decide whether to agree to purchase the idea or information, and if so for how much, without A first disclosing it. Yet if A discloses it to B, A takes the risk that B will use the idea or information without paying B for it. In some cases, the solution is for B to promise A to pay the "reasonable value" of the idea or information after A discloses it. But under the common law indefiniteness doctrine, courts will often refuse to enforce A's promise because it is too vague. Informal norms of reputation and morality, though, may lead to a practice of buyers filling in their vague promises with more specific promises after sellers disclose their idea or information to them. Under the past consideration doctrine, such subsequent promises are not enforceable because they are not supported by consideration: because they are made after the seller has voluntarily transferred its idea or information, they are not made as a condition of that transfer and are therefore not "bargained for." The material benefit rule, however, can be used to enforce these subsequent promises because they are made in recognition of a benefit that was previously conferred with the expectation of compensation for the value of the conferred benefit. Sales of creative ideas and informational services are good examples.

For an example of the sale of a creative idea, consider *Desny v. Wilder*, 46 Cal. 2d 715 (1956). In that case, Desny, an aspiring playwright, came up with an idea for a movie based on the life of Floyd Collins, a man who died after being trapped deep in a cave, despite a massive rescue attempt. Collins' tragic death in 1925 had become one of the most celebrated media events of the decade. The plaintiff wrote a screenplay based on the event, which included some fictional scenes created by the plaintiff. He then called the office of Billy Wilder, a prominent movie producer, and asked to speak to him. Wilder's secretary refused to allow Desny to speak directly with Wilder and demanded to know his purpose. Desny told her that he had a great idea for a movie. The secretary refused to allow Desny to explain his idea directly to Wilder insisting that Desny's only option was to convey a synopsis of the idea to her which she would then convey to Wilder if she was impressed by it. Desny provided the synopsis over the phone while the secretary transcribed it. Desny then made it clear to the secretary that he wanted to be paid a reasonable value for the story if it were used. The secretary replied that if Wilder used the story, "naturally we would pay for it." She subsequently submitted the synopsis to Wilder. A few months later, Wilder began making "Ace in the Hole," a movie based on the life of Collins that was very similar to plaintiff's script (even including a scene similar to the fictional one created by the plaintiff). Desny sued for enforcement of the secretary's promise to pay for the reasonable value of his movie idea. The California Supreme Court reversed the trial court's grant of summary judgment in favor of Wilder. Concurring in result, Justice Carter explained his view of the proper analysis of the case:

> When we consider the difference in economic and social backgrounds of those offering such merchandise for sale and those purchasing the same, we are met with the inescapable conclusion that it is the seller who stands in the inferior bargaining position. It should be borne in mind that producers are not easy to contact; that those with authority to purchase for radio and television are surrounded by a coterie of secretaries and assistants; that magazine editors and publishers are not readily available to the average person. It should also be borne in mind that writers have no way of advertising their wares — that, as is *most graphically illustrated by the present opinion*, no producer, publisher, or purchaser for radio or television, is going to buy a pig in a poke. And, when the writer, in an earnest endeavor to sell what he has written, conveys his idea or his different interpretation of an old idea, to such prospective purchaser, he has lost the result of his labor, definitely and irrevocably. And, in addition, there is no way in which he can protect himself. If he says to whomever he is permitted to see, or, as in this case, talk with over the telephone, "I won't tell you what my idea is until you promise to pay me for it," it takes no Sherlock Holmes to figure out what the answer will be! This case is a beautiful example of the practical difficulties besetting a writer with something to sell — he is not permitted even to see the *secretary* in person — he must convey to her over the telephone the result of his efforts.

> . . . In California we have code sections distinctly defining the various types of contracts . . . In the majority opinion we find this statement: "From what has been shown respecting the law of ideas and of contracts we conclude that conveyance of an idea can constitute valuable consideration and can be bargained for before it is disclosed to the proposed purchaser, but once it is conveyed, i.e., disclosed to him and he has grasped it, it is henceforth his own and he may work with it and use it as he sees fit. In the field of entertainment the producer may properly and validly agree that he will pay for the service of conveying to him ideas which are valuable and which he can put to profitable use. Furthermore, where an idea has been conveyed with the expectation by the purveyor that compensation will be

paid if the idea is used, there is no reason why the producer who has been the beneficiary of the conveyance of such an idea, and who finds it valuable and is profiting by it, may not then for the first time, *although he is not at that time under any legal obligation so to do, promise to pay a reasonable compensation for that idea* — that is, for the past service of furnishing it to him — and thus create a valid obligation." (Emphasis added.) It seems to me most obvious that a seller of literary work would not disclose his ideas incorporated in his work to a prospective purchaser of the same without an implied understanding on the part of both that such an idea, if used by the one to whom it was disclosed, would be paid for by the one in a position to use the literary work. The very positions occupied by the buyer and seller would be sufficient to raise an implication that the one offering the literary work, and the one to whom it was disclosed, had agreed, impliedly that if the literary work were used by the one to whom it was shown, or offered, it would be paid for. It should not be necessary to lay down so many cast-iron rules when really the only question involved is the use made of the proffered work without compensation being made therefor. The buyer, or one to whom the literary work was offered, is adequately protected from unfounded claims by the rules defining a protectible literary work and by the fact that the trier of fact must find that the one accused of an unauthorized use of the literary work had access thereto, that the author's work bears a reasonable resemblance to that produced by the defendant. I disagree with the statement in the majority opinion that: "The idea man who blurts out his idea without having first made his bargain has no one but himself to blame for the loss of his bargaining power." It seems to me that in the ordinary situation, when the so-called "idea man" has an opportunity to see, or talk with, the prospective purchaser, or someone in his employ, it is at that time, without anything being said, known to both parties that the one is there to sell, and the other to buy. This is surely true of a department store when merchandise is displayed on the counter — it is understood by anyone entering the store that the merchandise so displayed is for *sale* — it is completely unnecessary for the storekeeper, or anyone in his employ, to *state* to anyone entering the store that all articles there are for sale. I am at a loss to see why any different rules should apply when it is ideas for sale rather than normal run of merchandise. It is quite true that one need not pay for ideas as such which are in the public domain but when those ideas have been so treated that they have worth or value to a prospective purchaser, it is difficult to understand why it is necessary that the seller should definitely state that he is selling his merchandise to a prospective buyer. It appears to me that the positions occupied by the parties should be sufficient to raise the inference that if the literary work is used by the prospective buyer, compensation would be paid therefor regardless of how much time the buyer takes to decide whether he will use it.

Id. at 754–56.

For an example of the sale of information services, consider *Worner Agency, Inc. v. Doyle*, 133 Ill. App. 3d 850 (1985). In that case, at the request of the President of the Institute of Personality and Aptitude Testing ("IPAT"), the Worner Agency assisted IPAT in finding a new location for its headquarters by identifying a tract of real estate, a firm to design a new building, and bidding out the contract to build the new headquarters building for IPAT. At IPAT's suggestion, Worner contacted Doyle to bid on the project. At a subsequent meeting in November of 1980, which Worner arranged between Doyle and IPAT, Doyle agreed to pay Worner a 3% commission on the total cost of the building if Doyle was awarded the bid. After Doyle was awarded the bid, it refused to pay the commission. Worner brought suit. Finding that Doyle had already received the benefit of Worner's services, the Court considered the question of whether Doyle's promise was nonetheless enforceable:

> The general rule is that if the alleged consideration for the promise has been conferred prior to the promise upon which alleged agreement is based, there is no valid contract. As with all general rules, there are exceptions. . . . The question in the instant case is whether it falls within one of the exceptions. The record is clear that any consideration for the defendants' promise was performed before the signing of the agreement: Worner's informing the Doyles of the IPAT project, delivering preliminary plans for the building, and putting the Doyles in touch with IPAT officers. . . . More apropos to the instant case is the exception of "beneficial" or "meritorious" consideration, imposing a moral obligation yielding an implied consideration. . . . In the instant case the defendants admitted that they had benefited from the plaintiff's actions and that they would not have known about the IPAT job if the plaintiff had not arranged the meeting of November 1980. There is sufficient evidence in the record that a benefit was conferred on the defendants, and this benefit is deemed adequate consideration for their promise to pay the finder's fee.

Id. at 857–59.

These cases illustrate how the material benefit rule provides assurance to a party who confers a benefit in absence of a definite agreement for compensation, that a subsequent promise to pay for the benefit received will be legally enforceable. Of course, the material benefit rule provides no guarantee that the beneficiary will make a subsequent promise to pay compensation. However, the cases suggest the practice of providing benefits in advance of a definite bargained-for exchange is common when informational barriers make bargaining in advance impracticable. Reputational and moral norms explain why beneficiaries make the legally enforceable subsequent promises even though they are under no legal obligation to do so.

NOTES

1. _Harmonizing_ Mills _and_ Webb. What facts distinguish *Mills* and *Webb*? These facts are candidates:[12]

 (a) Mills conferred a benefit on Levi Wyman, not on the promisor; Webb conferred a benefit on the promisor.

---

[12] *See* Steve Thel & Edward Yorio, *The Promissory Basis of Past Consideration*, 78 Va. L. Rev. 1045, 1070–72 (1992).

    (b)   McGowin reflected longer on his promise (28 days) than Wyman did (4 days).

    (c)   Wyman himself repudiated the promise, McGowin never did (and, indeed, died without repudiating).

    (d)   McGowin paid for eight years, apparently Wyman never paid anything.

    (e)   McGowin received a substantial benefit, Wyman did not (the son died).

    (f)   Webb incurred substantial detriment (permanent disablement), Mills did not (only the cost of treatment).

Do one or more of these facts satisfactorily explain the difference in results?

    2.   ***The Restatement on the Material Benefit Rule.*** The first Restatement of Contracts, adopted by the American Law Institute in 1932, did not offer a provision by which courts could enforce a subsequent promise that recognized a prior benefit. The Restatement (Second) of Contracts, however, recognizes in § 86 that courts sometimes enforce promises made after a benefit is conferred and includes a section to provide a doctrinal basis for that enforcement.

The commentary provided by the Restaters clarified how this section is to be used. Two comments are particularly instructive. Comment a states:

> Enforcement of promises to pay for benefit received has sometimes been said to rest on "past consideration" or on the "moral obligation" of the promisor, and there are statutes in such terms in a few states. Those terms are not used here: "past consideration" is inconsistent with the meaning of consideration stated in § 71, and there seems to be no consensus as to what constitutes a "moral obligation." The mere fact of promise has been thought to create a moral obligation, but it is clear that not all promises are enforced. Nor are moral obligations based solely on gratitude or sentiment sufficient of themselves to support a subsequent promise.

Comment e reads:

> In the absence of mistake or the like, there is no element of unjust enrichment in the receipt of a gift, and the rule of this Section has no application to a promise to pay for a past gift. Similarly, when a debt is discharged by a binding agreement, the transaction is closed even though full payment is not made. But marginal cases arise in which both parties understand that what is in form a gift is intended to be reimbursed indirectly, or in which a subsequent promise to pay is expressly contemplated. . . . Enforcement of the subsequent promise is proper in some such cases.

Note that a promise to pay for a benefit must have been made before a court will consider whether or not it should be enforced. The promisor must have received the benefit, promised expressly to pay for it, and then breached that express promise before § 86 is invoked as a means of enforcement.

    3.   ***Gilmore's Puzzle.*** Professor Grant Gilmore questioned whether any principle could explain why some courts deny enforcement to promises recognizing past benefits and others enforce the subsequent promise. He focused particularly on § 86:

> The hesitant and cautious text of the new section no doubt reflects the uncertainties of the Reporter and his advisers. . . . [W]hat Subsection (1) giveth, Subsection (2) largely taketh away: the promise . . . will be "binding" only within narrow limits. Furthermore, the use which is made in the Commentary of two of our best known Good Samaritan cases contributes a perhaps desirable confusion:

> A gives emergency care to B's adult son while the son is sick and without funds far from home. B subsequently promises to reimburse A for his expenses. The promise is not binding under this section. [Illustration 1, based on Mills v. Wyman, 20 Mass. 207 (1825).]

> A saves B's life in an emergency and is totally and permanently disabled in so doing. One month later B promises to pay A $15 every two weeks for the rest of A's life, and B makes the payments for eight years until he dies. The promise is binding. [Illustration 7, based on Webb v. McGowin, *supra*].

> The idea that § [86] has succeeded in "codifying" both the nineteenth century Massachusetts case and the twentieth century Alabama case is already sufficiently surprising but we are not yet finished.

> A finds B's escaped bull and feeds and cares for it. B's subsequent promise to pay reasonable compensation to A is binding. [Illustration 6, based on Boothe v. Fitzpatrick, 36 Vt. 681 (1864).]

> Are we to believe that my promise to pay the stranger who takes care of my bull is binding but that my promise to pay the stranger who takes care of my dying son is not? Or that "adult sons" are supposed to be able to take care of themselves while "escaped bulls" are not? Or that, as in maritime salvage law, saving property is to be rewarded but saving life is not?

> Enough has been said to make the point that Restatement (Second), at least in § [86], is characterized by the same "schizophrenic quality" for which Restatement (First) was so notable. This may well be all to the good. A wise draftsman, when he is dealing with novel issues in course of uncertain development, will deliberately retreat into ambiguity. The principal thing is that Restatement (Second) gives overt recognition to an important principle whose existence Restatement (First) ignored and, by implication denied. By the time we get to Restatement (Third) it may well be that § [86] will have flowered like Jack's bean-stalk. . . .

GRANT GILMORE, THE DEATH OF CONTRACT 74–76 (1974).

Can you reconcile the Restatement's illustrations and justify the distinction between Subsection 1 and Subsection 2 of § 86?

4. *Economic Theory and the Material Benefit Rule.* Can you apply the economic analysis of the consideration and promissory estoppel doctrines to the material benefit rule? Does the rule impose liability in cases in which the promisor is likely to have intended his promise to be given legal effect? If promises to compensate for prior non-donative benefits are enforceable, why not impose liability for material non-donative benefits conferred on others in all cases, even those in which the beneficiary does not subsequently promise to reimburse his benefactor? Under such a regime, how would you determine the amount of compensation? Does your answer to this question help explain the material benefit rule?

E. BIBLIOGRAPHY AND SUGGESTED READING

[1] The Consideration Doctrine

Omri Ben Shahar, *Fixing Unfair Contracts*, 63 STAN. L. REV. 869, 905 (2011).

Robert Braucher, *The Status of the Seal Today*, 9 PRAC. LAW. 97 (1963).

William R. Castro & Val D. Ricks, *"Dear Sister Antillico . . . ": The Story of Kirksey v. Kirksey*, 94 GEO. L.J. 321 (2006).

Morris Cohen, *The Basis of Contract*, 46 HARV. L. REV. 553 (1933).

Melvin A. Eisenberg, *The Principles of Consideration*, 67 CORNELL L. REV. 640 (1982).

Lon Fuller, *Consideration and Form*, 41 COLUM. L. REV. 799 (1941).

Grant Gilmore, The Death of Contract (1974).

Donald B. Holbrook, *The Status of the Common Law Seal Doctrine in Utah*, 3 UTAH L. REV. 73 (1952).

OLIVER WENDELL HOLMES, JR., THE COMMON LAW (1881).

Eric Mills Holmes, *Stature and Status of a Promise Under Seal as a Legal Formality*, 29 WILLAMETTE L. REV. 617, 647 (1993).

Richard A. Posner, *Gratuitous Promises in Economics and Law*, 6 J. LEGAL STUD. 411 (1977).

REPORT OF THE NEW YORK LAW REVISION COMMISSION 375–76 (1941).

Richard Speidel, *An Essay on the Reported Death and Continued Vitality of Contract*, 27 STAN. L. REV. 1161 (1975),

Steele, *The Uniform Written Obligations Act — A Criticism*, 21 ILL. L. REV. 185 (1927).

Kevin M. Teeven, *Moral Obligation Promise for Harm Caused*, 39 GONZ. L. REV. 349, 386–87 (2004)

GUNTHER H. TREITEL, THE LAW OF CONTRACT 120 (6th ed. 1983).

[2] Promissory Estoppel

Patrick Atiyah, *Consideration and Estoppel: The Thawing of the Ice*, 38 MOD. L. REV. 65 (1975).

Melvin A. Eisenberg, *Donative Promises*, 47 U. CHI. L. REV. 1 (1979).

Daniel A. Farber & John H. Matheson, *Beyond Promissory Estoppel: Contract Law and the "Invisible Handshake,"* 52 U. Chi. L. Rev. 903 (1985).

Jay M. Feinman, *Critical Approaches to Contract Law*, 30 UCLA L. Rev. 829 (1983).

Jay M. Feinman, *Promissory Estoppel and Judicial Method*, 97 Harv. L. Rev. 678 (1984).

Grant Gilmore, The Death of Contract (1974).

Charles J. Goetz & Robert E. Scott, *Enforcing Promises: An Examination of the Basis of Contract*, 89 Yale L.J. 1261 (1980).

Stanley D. Henderson, *Promissory Estoppel and the Traditional Contract Doctrine*, 78 Yale L.J. 343 (1969).

Lon Fuller, *Consideration and Form*, 41 Colum. L. Rev. 799 (1941).

Robert A. Hillman, *Questioning the "New Consensus" on Promissory Estoppel: An Empirical and Theoretical Study*, 98 Colum. L. Rev. 580 (1998).

Robert A. Hillman, *The Unfulfilled Promise of Promissory Estoppel in the Employment Setting*, 31 Rutgers L.J. 1, 25 (1999).

Marco J. Jimenez, *The Many Faces of Promissory Estoppel: An Empirical Analysis Under the Restatement (Second) of Contracts*, 57 UCLA L. Rev. 669, 669–70 (2010).

Michael B. Metzger & Michael J. Phillips, *The Emergence of Promissory Estoppel as an Independent Theory of Recovery*, 35 Rutgers L. Rev. 472 (1983).

Richard A. Posner, *Gratuitous Promises in Economics and Law*, 6 J. Legal Stud. 411 (1977).

Edward Yorio & Steve Thel, *The Promissory Basis of Section 90*, 101 Yale L.J. 111 (1991).

[3] Material Benefit Rule

John Dawson, *The Self-Serving Intermeddler*, 87 Harv. L. Rev. 1409 (1974).

Charles J. Goetz & Robert E. Scott, *Enforcing Promises: An Examination of the Basis of Contract*, 89 Yale L.J. 1261 (1980).

Grant Gilmore, The Death of Contract (1974).

Stanley D. Henderson, *Promises Grounded in the Past: The Idea of Unjust Enrichment and the Law of Contract*, 57 Va. L. Rev. 1115 (1971).

Saul Levmore, *Waiting for Rescue: An Essay on the Evolution and Incentive Structure of the Law of Affirmative Obligations*, 72 Va. L. Rev. 879 (1986).

Steve Thel & Edward Yorio, *The Promissory Basis of Past Consideration*, 78 Va. L. Rev. 1045 (1992).

Chapter 3

THE BARGAIN CONTEXT

A. INTRODUCTION

In this chapter, we examine those promises that are clearly made within a reciprocal, bargain context. We explore the dynamics of the exchange process, both through common law rules and through the statutory provisions of the Uniform Commercial Code (UCC). Our purpose here is similar to our purpose in Chapter 2: To discover why some exchange promises are binding and others are not, and to identify the variables that are important to that discovery.

The dynamics of the bargain context are governed by a number of rules grouped under the general heading of offer and acceptance. These rules function as defaults; they provide contracting parties a set of ready-made guidelines for determining the precise point during the bargaining process when legal liability attaches. They thus save contracting parties who adopt (either explicitly or implicitly) these ground rules the time-consuming process of specifying all the procedural requirements for reaching a legally-binding agreement. As with any default assumptions, atypical parties remain free to construct their own rules for regulating the sequence of negotiations, and (presumably) a court will enforce or not enforce their bargains accordingly.

We have already seen, however, examples of courts that appear reluctant to adopt the plain meaning of specially designed terms and conditions that purport to contract around the state's default rules. Courts tend to presume that the state's implied terms are fair and may therefore look with disfavor on efforts to vary them. This presumption against the atypical party increases, along with the burden in contracting out of the ready-made rules, as the court's practice of implying terms to contracts becomes more refined.

Nevertheless, despite the difficulties associated with legal default rules, there is a widespread belief that, in the bargain context, any rules at all are generally preferable to no rules. Why should this be so? In economic terms, the Coase Theorem provides an answer. The Coase Theorem was named for Nobel laureate economist Ronald Coase who developed its foundations.[1] The Theorem provides that where (1) the legal rights of the parties are well-defined and marketable; (2) there are no transaction costs to bargaining; and (3) the parties are informed, the parties will bargain to the most efficient outcome (i.e., no further possibilities exist to enhance mutual gains), regardless of where the legal system places liability initially. Note that Coase did not argue that these are realistic assumptions, or that

---

[1] *See* Ronald Coase, *The Problem of Social Cost*, 3 J.L. & Econ. 1 (1960).

they describe actual transactions. Rather, the assumptions are useful because they focus our attention on the key factors in bargaining — particularly transaction costs.

Under the assumptions of the Coase Theorem, where procedural ground rules are in effect, parties can choose whether to contract around them. If contracting parties are not pleased with a judicially created rule, they will bargain between themselves until the optimal rule (and result) is achieved. Under these assumptions, then, it is quite plausible to assume that silence and/or passive acquiescence reflects the parties consent to the state-supplied rule.

If it is true that any rule is better than no rule at all, why are there not more rules concerning offer and acceptance, governing every possible situation? In fact, as we will see, the rules regulating bargaining conduct are quite extensive when compared to the rules of consideration, promissory estoppel, and unjust enrichment that govern enforcement of promises. Nonetheless, there is little doubt that more rules could be generated.

One argument for restraint in rule-making is that society bears much of the cost of formulating default rules. It takes an investment of resources for the judiciary or the legislature to formulate these procedural rules, to integrate them into the existing legal structure, and to resolve conflicts that inevitably arise over the impact and interpretation of the rules. Presumably, the state should undertake this investment only when it is confident that the costs to the state are lower than the costs to the parties of crafting their own arrangements.

For much the same reasons, the rules of offer and acceptance are seldom the subject of litigation. When the parties can devise alternatives fairly easily, only those rules which are significantly off-the-mark generate arguments for, and against, reform. Rather than the rules themselves being litigated, therefore, it is the application of offer and acceptance rules to a given fact situation that ends up on a court's docket.

B. OFFER AND ACCEPTANCE

[1] Subjective and Objective Tests of Mutual Assent

Read Restatement (Second) § 17. Before contractual obligations can be created, both parties to a contract must agree to the terms. In legal jargon, this agreement is known as a manifestation of mutual assent, and generally is reached as a result of offers made and acceptances given. *See* Restatement (Second) § 22.

Knowing precisely when mutual assent to a contract has been achieved is another problem altogether. Traditionally there have been two "tests" for determining mutual assent. *See* Chapter 1. The subjective test, or "actual intent" theory, was dominant in the language of contract cases until about a century ago. That standard required that there be, in fact, a meeting of the minds between parties to a contract before a contract was legally binding. Although outward manifestations of the parties' intent were not completely irrelevant, their relative insignificance under the subjective theory could create difficulties.[2] Judge Frank explained the ramifications of the theory in a concurring opinion in *Ricketts v. Pennsylvania R. Co.*, 153 F.2d 757, 761 (2d Cir. 1946).

> Without doubt the [subjective intent] theory had been carried too far: Once a contract has been validly made, the courts attach legal consequences to the relation created by the contract, consequences of which the parties usually never dreamed — as, for instance, where situations arise which the parties had not contemplated. As to such matters, the "actual intent" theory induced much fictional discourse which imputed to the parties intentions they plainly did not have.

The objective test, in contrast, does not rely on the actual intentions of the parties. Instead, it relies on the outward manifestations of a party's intent: contractual obligation is imposed based on what a party reasonably believed was said and done rather than what was intended. Read § 20 of the Restatement of Contracts (1932). Comment a to § 20 is equally explicit:

> *Comment a.* Mutual assent to the formation of informal contracts is operative only to the extent that it is manifested. Moreover, if the manifestation is at variance with the mental intent, . . . it is the expression which is controlling. Not mutual assent but a manifestation indicating such assent is what the law requires. Nor is it essential that the parties are conscious of the legal relations which their word or acts might give rise to. It is essential, however, that the acts manifesting assent shall be done intentionally. That is, there must be a conscious will to do those acts; but it is not material what induces the will. Even insane persons may so act; but a somnambulist could not.

From an instrumentalist perspective, the objective theory has the attractive feature of putting liability on that party with the comparative advantage in preventing or minimizing the risk that this sort of a misunderstanding would occur in the first place. For example, assume A agrees orally to enter a contract with B, and finalizes the agreement with a nod of her head and a handshake. Suppose further that A thinks to herself that the deal will not be binding until B writes her a letter confirming the details, but A does not mention this further requirement to B. When the agreed-upon time of performance arrives, A refuses to go through with the bargain because B failed to send a written confirmation. Who should bear the liability here?

Under a strict subjective test, there is no deal because A did not intend that there be one. According to the objective test, however, A should bear the liability *if* most people similarly situated would reasonably believe that the deal was already concluded. Under these circumstances, B was justified in believing the bargain was finalized because A's words and actions were consistent with broadly accepted social norms governing human interactions. Presumably it is easier for A, as the atypical party, to either conform her behavior to the prevailing norms or to communicate her special requirements to B, than for B to think of and guard against every peculiar

---

[2] For an amusing case in which a promisor's outward manifestations were reinterpreted by the court, see *Higgins v. Lessig*, 49 Ill. App. 459 (1893).

reaction which might keep *A* from believing that they had reached an agreement. In other words, *given the background assumption that there are widely prevalent norms for signaling assent*, *A* is better able to avoid the problem in the first place. Placing liability on *A* will thus provide incentives for future *A*s to either inform themselves of prevailing customs or explicitly disclose idiosyncratic behaviors that depart from those conventions.

The key to this analysis, therefore, is the claim of *B* that *A should have reason to know that B* would interpret the nod of the head and the handshake as a manifestation of assent. What should be the result if *A* is successfully able to claim to a fact finder that under prevailing conventions her behavior was ambiguous and thus she would have no reason to know that *B* attached a different meaning to her behavior? *See* Restatement (Second) § 20. Is the Restatement's solution to the problem of a genuine misunderstanding consistent with the analysis developed above?

[2]   Offer

Professor Arthur Corbin articulated the principles underlying the rules of offer and acceptance in *Offer and Acceptance, and Some of the Resulting Legal Relations*, 26 YALE L.J. 169, 171 (1917). At this point, we are interested primarily in Corbin's conception of an offer, but you may want to keep his explanation of acceptance in mind for Subsection [3], *infra*.

> An *offer* is an act on the part of one person whereby he gives to another the legal power of creating the obligation called contract. An acceptance is the exercise of the power conferred by the performance of some act or acts. Both offer and acceptance must be acts expressing assent.
>
> The act constituting an offer and the act of constituting an acceptance may each consist of a promise. A promise is an expression of intention that the promisor will conduct himself in a specified way in the future, with an invitation to the promisee to rely thereon. If only one of the acts has this character, the contract is unilateral. If both acts have this character, the contract is bilateral. If neither of the acts has this character, the new set of legal relations, if any exists, is not called obligation. . . . In none of these cases will the expected legal relations be created unless the acts of the parties comply with the rules relating to mutual assent, consideration, form, capacity of parties, and legality of object.

Section 24 of the Restatement (Second) of Contracts defines offer as "the manifestation of willingness to enter into a bargain, so made as to justify another person in understanding that his assent to that bargain is invited and will conclude it."

Thus conceived, an offer is a specific kind of promise, one that is conditioned explicitly (or by implication) on a specified return. As such, it is distinct from a nonreciprocal promise of the sort we examined in Chapter 2 (e.g., I promise to give my son Adam $5,000 on his next birthday), and from a conditional statement of present intention that is not a promise (e.g., in response to your inquiry about whether a house is for sale, the owner responds he plans to sell it *if* he can receive

$70,000 for it). This latter statement is commonly designated as an "invitation to negotiate." *See* Restatement (Second) § 26. At some point in the bargaining process, an invitation to negotiate matures into an offer. How does one determine when that point has been reached? Compare § 26 of the Second Restatement to § 25 of the Restatement of Contracts (1932) and then consider the following cases.

BAILEY v. WEST
Supreme Court of Rhode Island
105 R.I. 61, 249 A.2d 414 (1969)

See p. 5, *supra.*

LUCY v. ZEHMER
Supreme Court of Appeals of Virginia
196 Va. 493, 84 S.E.2d 516

See p. 14, *supra.*

Many of the cases that attempt to draw the line between an offer and an invitation to negotiate involve advertising circulars and price quotations that are sent to a number of potential contracting parties. Consider the following two cases and see if you can discern the key factors that determine the outcome in each case.

COURTEEN SEED CO. v. ABRAHAM
Supreme Court of Oregon
129 Or. 427, 275 P. 684 (1929)

BROWN, J.

This is an action for damages, based upon an alleged contract for the sale of a carload of clover seed. The plaintiff, a corporation organized under the laws of Wisconsin, is engaged in the wholesale seed business. The defendant is a warehouseman and grain dealer at Amity, Or. The plaintiff alleges:

"On October 8, 1927, the defendant, in writing, sold and agreed to deliver to the plaintiff one carload of red clover seed, at 23 cents per pound, f. o. b. Amity, Oregon, such carload containing approximately 50,000 pounds of red clover. * * * [thereafter] plaintiff sold and contracted to sell the seed to others at a profit of 4 cents per pound, after paying freight and charges. Defendant has refused to ship or complete the sale of clover seed to the plaintiff,, and, by reason of the facts set forth, the plaintiff has been damaged in the sum of $2,750."

The defendant assigns error of the court below in overruling his motion for nonsuit: he asserts that the evidence fails to show that defendant ever made a binding offer to plaintiff to sell clover seed. . . .

Contracts in general are reached by an offer on the one side and acceptance on the other. So it becomes necessary to determine whether the defendant actually offered to sell the clover seed to the plaintiff corporation, and whether it was defendant's intention that contractual relations should exist between them on plaintiff's acceptance.

[G]oing back to September 21, 1927, we find that defendant was then mailing out samples of clover seed to divers persons, each sample being enclosed in an envelope on the face of which appeared the following words:

> "Red clover. 50,000 lbs. like sample. I am asking 24 cents per, f. o. b. Amity, Oregon. Amity Seed & Grain Warehouse, Amity, Oregon."

[O]n the envelope the defendant again used the language, "I am asking." The plaintiff acknowledged receipt of the sample received by it, and advised the sender that it had accumulated quite a stock of clover seed and preferred to wait a while "before operating further."

On October 4th, owing to rainy weather, which brought about conditions not favorable for hulling the clover seed, the defendant, in search of buyers, wrote the plaintiff [in the same manner as before].

On October 8th, plaintiff wired defendant as follows:

> "Special delivery sample received. Your price too high. Wire firm offer, naming absolutely lowest f. o. b."

The defendant then wired, in reply:

> "I am asking 23 cents per pound for the car of red clover seed from which your sample was taken. No. 1 seed, practically no plantain whatever. Have an offer 22 3/4 per pound, f. o. b. Amity."

Plaintiff's acceptance of the alleged offer reads: "Telegram received. We accept your offer. Ship promptly, route care Milwaukee Road at Omaha."

A contract should be construed to effect the intention of the parties thereto, as gathered from the entire writings constituting the contract. It is this intent that constitutes the essence of every contract. Giving due consideration to every word contained in the defendant's telegram to plaintiff, we are not prepared to say that that telegram constituted an express offer to sell. It would be poor reasoning to say that the defendant meant to make the plaintiff an offer when he used this language: "I am asking 23 cents per pound for the car of red clover." That does not say, "I offer to you at 23 cents per pound the car of red clover," nor does it say, "I will sell to you the carload of red clover at 23 cents per pound." The writer of the telegram used the word "offer" with reference to some other person when he concluded by saying: "Have an offer 22 3/4 per pound, f. o. b. Amity." Each of the words "offer" and "asking" has its meaning; and we cannot assume that the writer of the telegram meant to use these words in the same sense, nor can we eliminate the word "asking" from the writing.

It is laid down by eminent authority that [an] invitation to negotiate does not constitute an offer. Perhaps one of the most comprehensive discourses on this subject appears in 1 Page on the Law of Contracts; and, for its perspicuity and learning, we set out the following interesting excerpt from section 84: "The commonest examples of offers meant to open negotiations and to call forth offers in the technical sense are the advertisements, circulars and trade letters sent out by business houses. While it is possible that the offers made by such means may be in such form as to become contracts, they are often merely expressions of a willingness to negotiate."

In the following section, the author sets out many illustrations of offers to negotiate: "A statement by A to B of the price at which A will sell certain property is not equivalent to an offer by A to B to sell such property at such price; and B cannot, by accepting such alleged offer, hold A upon a contract. If A writes, asking if certain realty was for sale, and if so 'telegraph lowest cash price;' and B's reply quotes a price, and A replies agreeing to buy at that price; or A writes to B, 'We are authorized to offer Michigan fine salt in full carload lots of 80 to 95 barrels,' B telegraphs, 'Your letter of yesterday received and noted. You may ship me 2,000 barrels of Michigan fine salt as offered in your letter'; no offer has been made in either case, and accordingly the attempted acceptance does not constitute a contract.

[In] Nebraska Seed Co. v. Harsh, 152 N. W. 310 (1915), the defendant wrote the plaintiff company the following:

"Lowell, Nebraska, 4--24--1912.

"Nebraska Seed Co., Omaha, Neb. — Gentlemen: I have about 1,800 bu. or thereabouts of millet seed of which I am mailing you a sample. This millet is recleaned and was grown on sod and is good seed. I want $2.25 per cwt. for this seed, f. o. b. Lowell.

"Yours truly,

"H. F. Harsh."

Upon receipt of this letter, the plaintiff wired defendant as follows:

"4--26--'12.

"H. F. Harsh, Lowell, Nebraska.

"Sample and letter received. Accept your offer Millet like sample $2.25 per cwt. Wire how soon can load.

"The Nebraska Seed Co."

"The Nebraska Seed Company."

The letter was received by defendant at Lowell in due course. After due demand and tender of the purchase price, the defendant refused to deliver the seed. An action followed . . . and the Supreme Court of Nebraska held that the language, "I want $2.25 per cwt. for this seed, f. o. b. Lowell," did not constitute an offer of sale; that the language was general, and, as such, might be used in an advertisement or circular addressed generally to those engaged in the seed business; and that such language was not an offer by which the defendant was bound, if accepted by any or all of the persons addressed.

In the case of Moulton v. Kershaw et al., 59 Wis. 316, the defendant wrote the plaintiff as follows: "In consequence of a rupture in the salt trade, we are authorized to offer Michigan fine salt, in full carload lots of 80 to 95 barrels, delivered at your city, at 85 cts. per barrel, to be shipped per C. & N. W. R. R. Co. only. At this price it is a bargain, as the price in general remains unchanged. Shall be pleased to receive your order."

On the day the plaintiff received this letter, he wired the defendants of his acceptance, and ordered 2,000 barrels of salt. In its disposition of the case, the Supreme Court of Wisconsin held that the letter upon which the plaintiff relied did not constitute an offer, for the reason that neither the word "sell" nor its equivalent was used therein.

There are many cases of record, the great majority of which seem to follow the doctrine announced in the cases hereinabove discussed. From a review of the decisions, and of the law governing the question at issue in the instant case, we are of opinion that the motion for a nonsuit should have been sustained.

This cause is reversed and remanded, with directions to enter a nonsuit.

FAIRMOUNT GLASS WORKS v. CRUNDEN-MARTIN WOODENWARE CO.
Court of Appeals of Kentucky
106 Ky. 659, 51 S.W. 196 (1899)

HOBSON, J.

On April 20, 1895, appellee wrote appellant the following letter:

"St. Louis, Mo., April 20, 1895. Gentlemen: Please advise us the lowest price you can make us on our order for ten car loads of Mason green jars, complete, with caps, packed one dozen in a case, either delivered here, or f. o. b. cars your place, as you prefer. State terms and cash discount. Very truly, Crunden-Martin W. W. Co."

To this letter appellant answered as follows:

"Fairmount, Ind., April 23, 1895. Crunden-Martin Wooden Ware Co., St. Louis, Mo.- Gentlemen: Replying to your favor of April 20, we quote you Mason fruit jars, complete, in one-dozen boxes, delivered in East St. Louis, Ill.: Pints $4.50, quarts $5.00, half gallons $6.50, per gross, for immediate acceptance, and shipment not later than May 15, 1895; sixty days' acceptance, or 2 off, cash in ten days. Yours, truly, Fairmount Glass Works.

"Please note that we make all quotations and contracts subject to the contingencies of agencies or transportation, delays or accidents beyond our control."

[In] reply, appellee sent the following telegram on April 24, 1895:

"Fairmount Glass Works, Fairmount, Ind.: Your letter twenty-third received. Enter order ten car loads as per your quotation. Specifications mailed. Crunden-Martin W. W. Co."

In response to this telegram, appellant sent the following:

"Fairmount, Ind., April 24, 1895. Crunden-Martin W. W. Co., St. Louis, Mo.: Impossible to book your order. Output all sold. See letter. Fairmount Glass Works."

Appellee insists that, by its telegram sent in answer to the letter of April 23d, the contract was closed for the purchase of 10 car loads of Mason fruit jars. Appellant insists that the contract was not closed by this telegram, and that it had the right to decline to fill the order at the time it sent its telegram of April 24. This is the chief question in the case. The court below gave judgment in favor of appellee, and appellant has appealed, earnestly insisting that the judgment is erroneous.

We are referred to a number of authorities holding that a quotation of prices is not an offer to sell, in the sense that a completed contract will arise out of the giving of an order for merchandise in accordance with the proposed terms. There are a number of cases holding that the transaction is not completed until the order so made is accepted. But each case must turn largely upon the language there used. In this case we think there was more than a quotation of prices, although appellant's letter uses the word "quote" in stating the prices given. The true meaning of the correspondence must be determined by reading it as a whole. Appellee's letter of April 20th, which began the transaction, did not ask for a quotation of prices. It reads: "Please advise us the lowest price you can make us on our order for ten car loads of Mason green jars. . . . State terms and cash discount." From this appellant could not fail to understand that appellee wanted to know at what price it would sell it ten car loads of these jars; so when, in answer, it wrote: "We quote you Mason fruit jars . . . pints $4.50, quarts $5.00, half gallons $6.50, per gross, for immediate acceptance; . . . 2 off, cash in ten days,"- it must be deemed as intending to give appellee the information it had asked for. We can hardly understand what was meant by the words "for immediate acceptance," unless the latter was intended as a proposition to sell at these prices if accepted immediately. In construing every contract, the aim of the court is to arrive at the intention of the parties. In none of the cases to which we have been referred on behalf of appellant was there on the face of the correspondence any such expression of intention to make an offer to sell on the terms indicated. In Fitzhugh v. Jones, 6 Munf. 83, the use of the expression that the buyer should reply as soon as possible, in case he was disposed to accede to the terms offered, was held sufficient to show that there was a definite proposition, which was closed by the buyer's acceptance. The expression in appellant's letter, "for immediate acceptance," taken in connection with appellee's letter, in effect, at what price it would sell it the goods, is, it seems to us, much stronger evidence of a present offer, which, when accepted immediately, closed the contract. Appellee's letter was plainly an inquiry for the price and terms on which appellant would sell it the goods, and appellant's answer to it was not a quotation of prices, but a definite offer to sell on the terms indicated, and could not be withdrawn after the terms had been accepted. . . .

Appellant also insists that the contract was indefinite, because the quantity of each size of the jars was not fixed, that 10 car loads is too indefinite a specification of the quantity sold, and that appellee had no right to accept the goods to be delivered on different days. The proof shows that "10 car loads" is an expression used in the trade as equivalent to 1,000 gross, 100 gross being regarded a car load. The offer to sell the different sizes at different prices gave the purchaser the right to name the quantity of each size, and, the offer being to ship not later than May 15th, the buyer had the right to fix the time of delivery at any time before that. . . . The petition, if defective, was cured by the judgment, which is fully sustained by the evidence.

Judgment affirmed.

NOTES

1. ***Questions on* Courteen Seed *and* Fairmont Glass: *The Relevance of Language and Context.*** An offer is easy to recognize when a deal is proposed in which all terms are dickered and are clear and definite. But as *Courteen Seed* and *Fairmont Glass* illustrate, sometimes it is hard to know if an offer has been made. For example, the court in *Courteen Seed* cites a number of cases that held that the quotation of a price when selling goods does not constitute an offer. Yet cases such as *Fairmont Glass* have decided that quoting a price is an offer. If the challenge for the court is to determine when a party has made a promise conditioned on the other's acceptance, then the question, as we learned in Restatement (Second) § 2 is whether the manifestation in question justifies the recipient in believing that "a commitment has been made." What are the social cues that people rely upon in deciding that a manifestation is a "commitment"? The two variables that seem to matter to the courts are the language used by the parties and the context in which the language is used (e.g., how far along are the parties in the sequence of negotiation). Can you use those two factors to distinguish *Courteen Seed* and *Fairmont Glass*? In general, courts appear resolve doubtful cases with a presumption that the communication is an invitation to negotiate and not an offer. Why do you suppose that is so?

2. ***More on Advertising Circulars and Price Quotations.*** It is not the unsolicited nature of the advertisement that renders it generally ineffective as an offer; instead, the very nature of a price quotation has consistently led courts to conclude that the mere act of providing a price does not independently create an offer where none existed before. In *Audio Visual Assocs. v. Sharp Elecs. Corp.*, 210 F.3d 254 (4th Cir. 2000), the court observed:

> Audio Visual cannot maintain that upon its receipt of a price quotation from Sharp, it could have formed a binding contract to purchase, for example, 1.5 million units — a proposition yet more untenable if it turned out that Sharp were unable to deliver 1.5 million units. Price quotations are a daily part of commerce by which products are shopped and commercial transactions initiated. Without more, they amount to an invitation to enter into negotiations, but generally they are not offers that can be accepted to form binding contracts . . . It would bring an end to the competitive practice of shopping products if every quotation exposed the "quoter" to an enforceable contract on whatever terms the "quotee" chose, regardless of product availability.

Id. at 259.

Typically, as the court notes in *Courteen Seed*, a seller's price quotation is only an invitation for an offer, and the offer usually takes the form of a purchase order, providing product choice, quantity, price, and terms of delivery. The UCC provides that the seller can accept such an offer in any of several ways, often determined by custom and practice. *See* §§ 2-204(1), 2-206(1), 2-208. Frequently, the seller accepts the offer of a purchase order by a written acknowledgment, which also provides a shipping date for the product. The seller may also accept simply by performance and delivery of the goods. A seller, however, is also free to reject the terms of the purchase order and/or to propose alternative terms.

Even if they contain proposals with definitive price and quantity terms, unsolicited advertising circulars do not necessarily constitute offers to sell. Often, other essential terms are unstated, thus precluding a court from construing such an advertisement as an offer. For an illustration of this principle, see *Rhen Marshall, Inc. v. Purolator Filter Div, Purolator, Inc.*, 211 Neb. 306, 318 N.W.2d 284 (1982). In this case, Purolator sent Rhen Marshall an advertisement listing prices for their oil filters. Rhen Marshall placed an order, but sought a special truckload discount as well as discounted prices for timely payment. The Supreme Court of Nebraska ruled that no offer was made, noting:

> Rhen Marshall set forth conditions in its order that were not previously discussed by the parties. The sales promotion circular by Purolator did not contain terms with regard to discounts or billing. Rhen Marshall's order requested a 5 percent truckload discount and a 30-60-90-day billing. Rhen Marshall had attached conditions in its order which were usual in its previous dealings with Purolator, but the discounts offered by the promotion were substantial and it could not be assumed by Rhen Marshall that Purolator would also give other, additional discounts. . . . We hold that the brochure was not an offer by Purolator, but that Rhen Marshall's order was itself an offer which Purolator did not accept.

Id. at 309.

3. *Newspaper Advertisements.* Consider the classified ads of your local newspaper. When a person places a for-sale ad in the classifieds, ought a court to rule that she intended to make an offer to sell? If so, what would the result be in the following hypothetical:

> Christy advertises her Honda Civic for sale for $3,000 in the local paper. The first day that the advertisement appears, Steve agrees to buys the car. In the late afternoon of that day, Adam calls Christy. When Christy answers "Hello," Adam says, "I accept your offer to sell the Honda for $3,000."

In deciding whether Adam can sue Christy for breach of contract, consider *Lefkowitz v. Great Minneapolis Surplus Store, Inc.*, 251 Minn. 188, 86 N.W.2d 689 (1957). In *Lefkowitz*, the defendant published the following advertisement in a Minneapolis newspaper on April 6, 1956:

> SATURDAY 9 A.M. SHARP, 3 BRAND NEW FUR COATS: Worth To $100.00. First Come, First Served. $1 Each

On April 13, the defendant again published an advertisement in the same newspaper as follows:

SATURDAY 9 A.M.: 1 BLACK LAPIN STOLE — Beautiful, worth $139.50
. . . . $1.00. FIRST COME, FIRST SERVED.

On both Saturdays, the plaintiff was the first to appear at the defendant's store, demand the coat and the stole and indicate his readiness to pay the sale price of $1. On both occasions, the defendant refused to sell the merchandise to the plaintiff, stating on the first occasion that by a "house rule" the offer was intended for women only, and on the second visit that plaintiff knew defendant's house rules. The Court held that the plaintiff had no claim to the fur coat as the value was too speculative, but granted the plaintiff's claim for the stole, stating that:

> We are of the view on the facts before us that the offer by the defendant of the sale of the Lapin fur was clear, definite, and explicit, and left nothing open for negotiation. The plaintiff having successfully managed to be the first one to appear at the seller's place of business to be served, as requested by the advertisement, and having offered the stated purchase price of the article, he was entitled to performance on the part of the defendant. We think the trial court was correct in holding that there was in the conduct of the parties a sufficient mutuality of obligation to constitute a contract of sale.

Assuming that a court would deny Adam's claim for breach of contract in the hypothetical above, can you discern the distinction between the two cases that might justify a different result. (Hint: Does it matter whether an alleged offeror intends a bilateral or a unilateral contract?)

Think for a moment about the litigation strategy pursued in *Lefkowitz* by the Greater Minneapolis Surplus Store. What possible reason would they have to litigate a case involving less than $100 in controversy all the way to the Supreme Court of Minnesota? Does your answer suggest why they were so adamant in refusing to honor Lefkowitz's demand?[3]

4. ***Two Coats and a Killer.*** Do you see why the *Lefkowitz* court in Note 3 above might have held that the there was an offer to sell Lefkowitz the first coat but not the second? In that connection, how would you decide this case:

> Taft Hyatt, remorseful after numerous sessions with the priest in his church, turned himself in and confessed to a series of murders. The courts found Hyatt guilty and sentenced him to life in prison. Hyatt, seeking money to support his wife and children, now claims reward money that a local newspaper advertised it would give in exchange for any information leading to the arrest of the murderer.

What issues and result?

5. ***Self-Service.*** Many stores feature displays where consumers pick up the merchandise and take it to the checkout counter. Only when they exchange payment for the merchandise is a contract formed between the consumer and the seller. But what rules should govern the interim period between the time the consumer takes

---

[3] For one view as to which party was behaving strategically, see Ian Ayres & Robert Gertnert, *Filling in Gaps in Incomplete Contracts: An Economic Theory of Default Rules*, 99 Yale L.J. 87, 107 (1989).

the item from the store shelf and when she pays for it?

The Supreme Court of Oklahoma explored this question in *Barker v. Allied Supermarket*, 596 P.2d 870 (Okla. 1979). In this case, a Dr. Pepper bottle exploded as the plaintiff placed it in his shopping cart. The court found that there was an implied warranty on the bottle, and that the warranty period did not merely commence upon payment. Instead, the court noted, "A merchant who utilizes the self-service shopping method thereby makes an open invitation to the public to enter his store and to inspect and take possession of any item so displayed. The merchant's act of stocking these self-service displays with goods thereby makes an offer to the shopper to enter a contract for their sale."

6. ***Offer and Acceptance in the Internet Age.*** The contract in question in *Fairmount Glass* was offered and accepted via telegram. Do the same rules apply in the context of the Internet? Should they?

In *Cole v. Sandel Med. Indus., L.L.C.*, 2011 U.S. App. LEXIS 803 (5th Cir. Jan. 12, 2011), the court ruled that no contract existed when a nurse sued a medical supply manufacturer alleging that it based one of its products on an idea she submitted via an online form. The facts established that the company's sales representatives informed healthcare professionals, including Cole, a nurse, that they could submit ideas. A salesman told Cole that if the idea was used, the person who first submitted the idea would receive compensation. The company's standard idea agreement paid $250 upon execution, $500 when the first order is placed, and up to $4,000 per year for five years. The company sold 28 products, 12 of which were inspired by such submissions. However, the online submission form did not specify the compensation and required that the submitter agree to a series of terms, including that the parties "shall have no further obligations to each other, unless a separate agreement is entered into." Cole agreed to the terms and submitted an idea, the "Time Out Towel," and later the company introduced a similar product to the one Cole had suggested. After Cole complained, a company employee told Cole that "it looks like you were the first submitter of the Time Out Towel." The company offered Cole its standard idea agreement, but Cole did not agree to terms and instead made a counter-offer, which the company rejected.

Cole sued for $1 million. The district court granted the company's summary judgment motion, finding that no contract was formed. The Fifth Circuit affirmed: "[B]y using the online submission form, Cole entered into an agreement to agree with Sandel. The agreement left open what price, if any, would be paid to Cole. Accordingly, the online submission form is not an enforceable agreement to compensate Cole for her idea." *Id.* at 686–87. In addition, the court said that although it was not convinced that the salesman's encouragement constituted an offer, "an offeror may revoke an offer prior to acceptance. . . . In our view, the online submission form constituted a new offer." *Id.* at 687. The new offer, therefore, served as an "effective revocation" of the salesman's offer because Cole was well aware that the offer was no longer open. *Id.*

7. ***Offers versus Preliminary Negotiations: Risk Aversion, Precautions and "Cheap Talk."*** One way of characterizing the transformation from invitation to negotiate to offer is in terms of relative degrees of certainty. Recall that in Chapter 2 we analyzed the willingness of parties to incur liability in terms of their relative

certainty (or uncertainty) about the prospects of a mutually beneficial deal materializing.[4] Picture the bargaining context as a continuum with complete uncertainty at one pole and absolute certainty at the other. Invitations to negotiate would fall along the continuum toward uncertainty, while offers would fall nearer the other pole.

What arguments can you make that most parties would prefer not to be bound at the invitation stage? One approach is to assume that most parties are averse to taking risks. If so, they generally would prefer to forego uncertain gains rather than incur equally uncertain losses of the same magnitude. Under these conditions, risk-averse parties would prefer nonenforcement of such preliminary promises. While such a rule would jeopardize the prospect of gain from the deal, it would also reduce each bargainer's potential liability if the deal turned sour. Without assuming risk aversion, an alternative argument can be made based on comparative advantages. In this vein, we might imagine that many (most) bargainers would prefer to walk away when the prospects of a deal are uncertain because at that stage each bargainer can regulate his own reliance (take precautions, make fewer plans) more readily than he can control the reliance of the promisee.

A final way to think about why parties would prefer that preliminary negotiations not be binding is to focus on the distinction between binding commitments which change the opportunities for both parties and non-binding statements which merely alter their expectations. Economists call the latter "cheap talk." "Cheap talk" is a valuable means of bringing the parties together, even though one cannot legally rely upon it. Parties value non-binding preliminary representations because it they are generally informative and truthful. This is because negotiating is costly and parties generally want to determine as quickly as possible whether a deal is forthcoming. Under these assumptions, early enforcement may be counterproductive if it deters valuable communication between the parties.[5]

If self-protection is generally preferred to the risk of liability for another's disappointed reliance, then why would anyone ever agree voluntarily to become legally obligated to perform his promise? One answer to this question is that the promisor places greater value on the return promise of the promisee than he fears regret for his own promise. As parties bargain with each other, reaching tentative understandings over key issues such as price, quality of goods, quantity to be ordered, etc., the outlines of the potential exchange become well-defined. When the prospect of gain measurably outweighs the risk of regret, even risk averse parties would prefer mutual enforcement, thus enhancing the benefits each side expects to receive. At this point the respective representations are relabeled "offer" and "acceptance," thereby signaling that legal liability attaches.

---

[4] *See generally* Charles J. Goetz & Robert E. Scott, *Enforcing Promises: An Examination of the Basis of Contract*, 89 YALE L.J. 1261, 1293–97 (1980). *See also* Avery Katz, *The Strategic Structure of Offer and Acceptance: Game Theory and the Law of Contract Formation*, 89 MICH. L. REV. 215 (1990); Richard Craswell, *Offer, Acceptance, and Efficient Reliance*, 48 STAN. L. REV. 481 (1996).

[5] *See* Jason Scott Johnston, *Communication and Courtship: Cheap Talk Economics and the Law of Contract Formation*, 85 VA. L. REV. 385 (1999).

[3]   Acceptance

Professor Corbin, in *Offer and Acceptance, and Some of the Resulting Legal Relations*, 26 YALE L.J. 169, 199–200 (1917), defined an "acceptance" in the following terms:

> An acceptance is a voluntary act of the offeree whereby he exercises the power conferred on him by the offer, and thereby creates the set of legal relations called a contract. What acts are sufficient to secure this purpose? We must look first to the terms in which the offer was expressed, either by words or by other conduct. The offeror is the creator of the power and at the time of its creation he has full control over both the fact of its existence and its terms. The offeror has, in the beginning, full power to determine the acts that are to constitute acceptance. After he has once created the power, he may lose his control over it, and may become disabled to change or revoke it; but the fact that, in the beginning, the offeror has full control . . . is the characteristic that distinguishes contractual relations from non-contractual ones. After the offeror has created the power [of acceptance], the legal consequences are out of his hands, and he may be brought into numerous consequential relations of which he did not dream, and to which he might not have consented. These later relations are nevertheless called contractual.

Section 50(1) of the Restatement (Second) of Contracts defines acceptance as "a manifestation of assent to the terms thereof made by the offeree in a manner invited or required by the offer." Is this definition consistent with Corbin's statement that acceptance may create obligations "of which the offeror never even dreamed, and to which he might not have assented"?

[a]   Methods of Acceptance

There are a number of ways acceptance can be manifested once an offer has been made. Since the offeror is the creator of the offer, she has the power to invite acceptance by any reasonable means or to limit acceptance to a particular or specified means. Deciding what method of acceptance the offeror has selected often raises difficult questions. Read §§ 30 and 50 of the Restatement (Second), and then consider the following cases.

EVER-TITE ROOFING CORP. v. GREEN
Court of Appeals of Louisiana
83 So. 2d 449 (1955)

AYRES, J.

This is an action for damages allegedly sustained by plaintiff as the result of the breach by the defendants of a written contract for the re-roofing of defendant's residence. Defendants denied that their written proposal or offer was ever accepted by plaintiff in the manner stipulated therein for its acceptance, and hence contended no contract was ever entered into. The trial court sustained defendants' defense and rejected plaintiff's demands and dismissed its suit at its costs. From the judgment thus rendered and signed, plaintiff appealed.

Defendants executed and signed an instrument June 10, 1953, for the purpose of obtaining the services of plaintiff in re-roofing their residence situated in Webster Parish, Louisiana. The document set out in detail the work to be done and the price therefor to be paid in monthly installments. This instrument was likewise signed by plaintiff's sale representative, who, however, was without authority to accept the contract for and on behalf of the plaintiff. This alleged contract contained these provisions:

> This agreement shall become binding only upon written acceptance hereof, by the principal or authorized officer of the Contractor, *or upon commencing performance of the work.* This contract is not subject to cancellation. . . . (Emphasis supplied.)

Inasmuch as this work was to be performed entirely on credit, it was necessary for plaintiff to obtain credit reports and approval from the lending institution which was to finance said contract. With this procedure defendants were more or less familiar and knew their credit rating would have to be checked and a report made. On receipt of the proposed contract in plaintiff's office on the day following its execution, plaintiff requested a credit report, which was made after investigation and which was received in due course and submitted by plaintiff to the lending agency. Additional information was requested by this institution, which was likewise in due course transmitted to the institution, which then gave its approval.

The day immediately following this approval, which was either June 18 or 19, 1953, plaintiff engaged its workmen and two trucks, loaded the trucks with the necessary roofing materials and proceeded from Shreveport to defendants' residence for the purpose of doing the work and performing the services allegedly contracted for the defendants. Upon their arrival at defendants' residence, the workmen found others in the performance of the work which plaintiff had contracted to do. Defendants notified plaintiff's workmen that the work had been contracted to other parties two days before and forbade them to do the work.

Formal acceptance of the contract was not made under the signature and approval of an agent of plaintiff. It was, however, the intention of plaintiff to accept the contract by commencing the work, which was one of the ways provided for in the instrument for acceptance, as will be shown by reference to the extract from the contract quoted hereinabove. Prior to this time, however, defendants had determined on a course of abrogating the agreement and engaged other workmen without notice thereof to plaintiff.

The basis of the judgment appealed was that defendants had timely notified plaintiff before "commencing performance of work." The trial court held that notice to plaintiff's workmen upon their arrival with the materials that defendants did not desire them to commence the actual work was sufficient and timely to signify their intention to withdraw from the contract. With this conclusion we find ourselves unable to agree.

Defendants' attempt to justify their delay in thus notifying plaintiff for the reason they did not know where or how to contact plaintiff is without merit. The contract itself, a copy of which was left with them, conspicuously displayed plaintiff's name, address and telephone number. Be that as it may, defendants at no time, from June 10, 1953, until plaintiff's workmen arrived for the purpose of commencing the work, notified or attempted to notify plaintiff of their intention to abrogate, terminate or cancel the contract.

Defendants evidently knew this work was to be processed through plaintiff's Shreveport office. The record discloses no unreasonable delay on plaintiff's part in receiving, processing or accepting the contract or in commencing the work contracted to be done. No time limit was specified in the contract within which it was to be accepted or within which the work was to be begun. It was nevertheless understood between the parties that some delay would ensue before the acceptance of the contract and the commencement of the work, due to the necessity of compliance with the requirements relative to financing the job through a lending agency. The evidence as referred to hereinabove shows that plaintiff proceeded with due diligence.

The general rule of law is that an offer proposed may be withdrawn before its acceptance and that no obligation is incurred thereby. This is, however, not without exceptions. For instance, Restatement of the Law of Contracts stated:

> (1) The power to create a contract by acceptance of an offer terminates at the time specified in the offer, or, if no time is specified, at the end of a reasonable time.

> What is a reasonable time is a question of fact depending on the nature of the contract proposed, the usages of business and other circumstances of the case which the offeree at the time of his acceptance either knows or has reason to know.

[T]herefore, since the contract did not specify the time within which it was to be accepted or within which the work was to have been commenced, a reasonable time must be allowed therefor in accordance with the facts and circumstances and the evident intention of the parties. A reasonable time is contemplated where no time is expressed. What is a reasonable time depends more or less upon the circumstances surrounding each particular case. The delays to process defendants' application were not unusual. The contract was accepted by plaintiff by commencement of the performance of the work contracted to be done. This commencement began with the loading of the trucks with the necessary materials in Shreveport and transporting such materials and the workmen to defendants' residence. Actual commencement or performance of the work therefore began before any notice of dissent by defendants was given plaintiff. The proposition and its acceptance thus became a completed contract.

By their aforesaid acts defendants breached the contract. They employed others to do the work contracted to be done by plaintiff and forbade plaintiff's workmen to engage upon that undertaking. By this breach defendants are legally bound to respond to plaintiff in damages. . . .

Plaintiff expended the sum of $85.37 in loading the trucks in Shreveport with materials and in transporting them to the site of defendants' residence in Webster Parish and in unloading them on their return, and for wages for the workmen for the time consumed. Plaintiff's Shreveport manager testified that the expected profit on this job was $226. None of this evidence is controverted or contradicted in any manner.

For the reasons assigned, the judgment appealed is annulled, avoided, reversed and set aside and there is now judgment in favor of plaintiff, Ever-Tite Roofing Corporation, against the defendants, G. T. Green and Mrs. Jessie Fay Green, for the full sum of $311.37, with 5 percent per annum interest thereon from judicial demand until paid, and for all costs.

CIARAMELLA v. READER'S DIGEST ASS'N
United States Court of Appeals, Second Circuit
131 F.3d 320 (1997)

OAKES, J.

Plaintiff filed suit against Reader's Digest Association ("RDA") alleging employment discrimination under the Americans with Disabilities Act, and also violations of the Employee Retirement Income Security Act ("ERISA"). Shortly after the commencement of the action, the parties negotiated a settlement which Ciaramella later refused to sign. RDA moved for an order to enforce the settlement agreement. The United States District Court for the Southern District of New York (Charles L. Brieant, J.), granted the motion and dismissed the plaintiff's complaint with prejudice. Ciaramella argues that enforcement of the settlement agreement was improper because he had never signed the written agreement and the parties had specifically agreed that the settlement would not become binding until signed by all the parties. We agree, and reverse.

In November 1995, Ciaramella filed suit against his former employer, RDA, alleging that RDA failed to give him reasonable accommodations for his disability of chronic depression and subsequently terminated his employment in violation of the ADA. Ciaramella also raised a claim under ERISA for failure to pay severance benefits.

Before the exchange of any discovery, the parties entered into settlement negotiations. The negotiations resulted in an agreement in principle to settle the case in May, 1996. RDA prepared a draft agreement and sent it to Ciaramella's then attorney, Herbert Eisenberg, for review. This draft, as well as all subsequent copies, contained language indicating that the settlement would not be effective until executed by all the parties and their attorneys. Eisenberg explained the terms of the settlement to Ciaramella, who authorized Eisenberg to accept it. Eisenberg then made several suggestions for revision to RDA which were incorporated into a revised draft. After reviewing the revised draft, Eisenberg asked for a few final changes and then allegedly stated to RDA's lawyer, "We have a deal." RDA forwarded several execution copies of the settlement to Eisenberg. However, before signing the agreement, Ciaramella consulted a second attorney and ultimately decided that the proposed settlement agreement was not acceptable to him and that he would not sign it. Eisenberg then moved to withdraw as plaintiff's counsel.

RDA, claiming that the parties had reached an enforceable oral settlement, filed a motion to enforce the settlement agreement. . . . The district court, after considering RDA's unopposed motion papers and questioning Ciaramella about the formation of the settlement agreement, granted RDA's motion to enforce the settlement by order dated October 28, 1996. . . .

New York relies on settled common law contract principles to determine when parties to a litigation intended to form a binding agreement. Under New York law, parties are free to bind themselves orally, and the fact that they contemplate later memorializing their agreement in an executed document will not prevent them from being bound by the oral agreement. However, if the parties intend not to be bound until the agreement is set forth in writing and signed, they will not be bound until then. The intention of the parties on this issue is a question of fact, to be determined by examination of the totality of the circumstances. This same standard has been applied by courts relying on federal common law. . . . Even in cases where federal courts can choose the governing law to fill gaps in federal legislation, the Supreme Court has directed that state law be applied as the federal rule of decision unless it presents a significant conflict with federal policy.

This court has articulated four factors to guide the inquiry regarding whether parties intended to be bound by a settlement agreement in the absence of a document executed by both sides. We must consider (1) whether there has been an express reservation of the right not to be bound in the absence of a signed writing; (2) whether there has been partial performance of the contract; (3) whether all of the terms of the alleged contract have been agreed upon; and (4) whether the agreement at issue is the type of contract that is usually committed to writing.

No single factor is decisive, but each provides significant guidance. See R.G. Group, Inc. v. Horn & Hardart Co., 751 F.2d 69, 74-75 (2d Cir. 1984) (granting summary judgment where all four factors indicated that the parties had not intended to be bound by an oral franchise agreement). The district court did not explicitly rely on [this] test, but concluded that based on the evidence the parties intended to enter into a binding oral agreement. Considering the above factors in the context of this case, we are left with the definite and firm conviction that the district court erred in concluding that the parties intended that the unexecuted draft settlement constitute a binding agreement.

We find numerous indications in the proposed settlement agreement that the parties did not intend to bind themselves until the settlement had been signed. We must give these statements considerable weight, as courts should avoid frustrating the clearly-expressed intentions of the parties. For instance, in paragraph 10, the agreement states, "This Settlement Agreement and General Release shall not become effective (the Effective Date") until it is signed by Mr. Ciaramella, Davis & Eisenberg, and Reader's Digest."

RDA argues that the effect of paragraph 10 was simply to define the "Effective Date" of the agreement for the purpose of establishing the time period in which RDA was obligated to deliver payment and a letter of reference to Ciaramella. RDA further urges that Ciaramella's obligation to dismiss the suit was not conditioned on paragraph 10. However, this interpretation is belied by the language of paragraph 2, which addresses RDA's payment obligation. Paragraph 2 states that RDA must proffer payment "within ten (10) business days following the *later* of (a) the

Effective Date of this Settlement Agreement and General Release (as defined by paragraph ten . . .) or (b) entry by the Court of the Stipulation of Dismissal With Prejudice" (emphasis added). Under the terms of the proposed settlement, RDA had no obligation to pay Ciaramella until the agreement was signed and became effective. Likewise, under paragraph 12 of the final draft, RDA was not required to send the letter of reference until the agreement was signed. The interpretation that RDA advances, that Ciaramella had an obligation to dismiss the suit regardless of whether the settlement was signed, leaves Ciaramella no consideration for his promise to dismiss the suit. The more reasonable inference to be drawn from the structure of paragraph 2 is that it provided Ciaramella with an incentive to dismiss the suit quickly because he would receive no payment simply by signing the agreement, but that execution was necessary to trigger either parties' obligations. See, e.g., Davidson Pipe Co., 1986 WL 2201, at *4 (finding that wording in a settlement agreement that placed great significance on the execution date evinced an intent not to create a binding settlement until some formal date of execution).

Similarly, several other paragraphs of the proposed agreement indicate that the parties contemplated the moment of signing as the point when the settlement would become binding. The agreement's first paragraph after the WHEREAS clauses reads, "NOW, THEREFORE, with the intent to be legally bound *hereby*, and in consideration of the mutual promises and covenants contained herein, Reader's Digest and Ciaramella agree to the terms and conditions *set forth below*:. . . ." (emphasis added). This language demonstrates that only the terms of the settlement agreement, and not any preexisting pact, would legally bind the parties. Read in conjunction with paragraph 10, which provides that the settlement agreement is effective only when signed, this paragraph explicitly signals the parties' intent to bind themselves only at the point of signature. See, e.g., R.G. Group, 751 F.2d at 71, 76 (finding an explicit reservation of the right not to be bound absent signature in the wording of an agreement that declared, "when duly executed, this agreement sets forth your rights and your obligations"). In addition to the language of the first paragraph, paragraph 13 of the final draft contains a merger clause which states,

> This Settlement Agreement and General Release constitutes the complete understanding between the parties, may not be changed orally and supersedes any and all prior agreements between the parties. . . . No other promises or agreements shall be binding unless in writing and signed by the parties.

The presence of such a merger clause is persuasive evidence that the parties did not intend to be bound prior to the execution of a written agreement. See, e.g., McCoy v. New York City Police Dep't, 1996 WL 457312 (S.D.N.Y. Aug. 14, 1996) (refusing to enforce a settlement of a § 1983 claim where a signed copy of the settlement agreement containing a merger clause had never been returned by the plaintiff). Other parts of the agreement also emphasize the execution of the document. Paragraph 9 states, in relevant part,

> Mr. Ciaramella represents and warrants that he . . . has executed this Settlement Agreement and General Release after consultation with his . . . legal counsel; . . . that he voluntarily assents to all the terms and

conditions contained therein; and that he is signing the Settlement Agreement and General Release of his own force and will.

Ciaramella's signature was meant to signify his voluntary and informed consent to the terms and obligations of the agreement. By not signing, he demonstrated that he withheld such consent.

The sole communication which might suggest that the parties did not intend to reserve the right to be bound is Eisenberg's alleged statement to RDA's counsel, "We have a deal." However, nothing in the record suggests that either attorney took this statement to be an explicit waiver of the signature requirement. Eisenberg's statement followed weeks of bargaining over the draft settlement, which at all times clearly expressed the requirement that the agreement be signed to become effective. This Court has held in a similar situation that an attorney's statement that "a handshake deal" existed was insufficient to overcome "months of bargaining where there were repeated references to the need for a written and signed document, and where neither party had ever . . . even discussed dropping the writing requirement." R.G. Group, 751 F.2d at 76; see also Davidson Pipe Co., 1986 WL 2201, at *5 (holding that oral statement, "we have a deal," made by one attorney to another did not in and of itself preclude a finding that the parties intended to be bound only by an executed contract).

A second factor for consideration is whether one party has partially performed, and that performance has been accepted by the party disclaiming the existence of an agreement. No evidence of partial performance of the settlement agreement exists here. RDA paid no money to Ciaramella before the district court ordered the settlement enforced, nor did it provide Ciaramella with a letter of reference. These were the two basic elements of consideration that would have been due to Ciaramella under the settlement agreement.

Turning to the third factor, we find that the parties had not yet agreed on all material terms. The execution copy of the settlement agreement contained a new provision at paragraph 12 that was not present in earlier drafts. That provision required RDA to deliver a letter of reference concerning Ciaramella to Eisenberg. The final draft of the settlement contained an example copy of the letter of reference annexed as Exhibit B. Ciaramella was evidently dissatisfied with the example letter. At the October 25, 1996, hearing at which Ciaramella appeared pro se, he attempted to explain to the court that the proposed letter of reference differed from what he had expected. He stated, "The original settlement that was agreed to, the one that was reduced to writing for me to sign had a discrepancy about letters of recommendation. I had requested one thing and the settlement in writing did not represent that." Because Ciaramella's attorney resigned when Ciaramella refused to sign the settlement agreement, and RDA thereafter moved to enforce the agreement, Ciaramella never had an opportunity to finish bargaining for the letter he desired.

This Court [has] found that the existence of even "minor" or "technical" points of disagreement in draft settlement documents were sufficient to forestall the conclusion that a final agreement on all terms had been reached. By contrast, the letter of reference from RDA was a substantive point of disagreement. It was also, from Ciaramella's perspective, a material term of the contract since it was part of

Ciaramella's consideration for dismissing the suit. On this basis, we find that the parties here had not yet reached agreement on all terms of the settlement.

The final factor, whether the agreement at issue is the type of contract that is usually put in writing, also weighs in Ciaramella's favor. Settlements of any claim are generally required to be in writing or, at a minimum, made on the record in open court. As we stated in Winston, "Where, as here, the parties are adversaries and the purpose of the agreement is to forestall litigation, prudence strongly suggests that their agreement be written in order to make it readily enforceable, and to avoid still further litigation." Winston, 777 F.2d at 83.

We have also found that the complexity of the underlying agreement is an indication of whether the parties reasonably could have expected to bind themselves orally. See Reprosystem, B.V. v. SCM Corp., 727 F.2d 257, 262-63 (2d Cir. 1984) (finding that the magnitude and complexity of a four million dollar sale of six companies under the laws of five different countries reinforced the stated intent of the parties not to be bound until written contracts were signed). While this settlement agreement does not concern a complicated business arrangement, it does span eleven pages of text and contains numerous provisions that will apply into perpetuity. For instance, paragraph 6 determines how future requests for references would be handled, and also states that Ciaramella can never reapply for employment at RDA. Paragraph 7 states that Ciaramella will not publicly disparage RDA and agrees not to disclose the terms of the settlement agreement. In such a case, the requirement that the agreement be in writing and formally executed "simply cannot be a surprise to anyone." R.G. Group, 751 F.2d at 77; see also Winston, 777 F.2d at 83 (finding a four-page settlement agreement that contained obligations that would last over several years sufficiently complex to require reduction to writing).

In sum, we find that the totality of the evidence before us clearly indicates that Ciaramella never entered into a binding settlement agreement with his former employer. This conclusion is supported by the text of the proposed agreement and by Ciaramella's testimony at the October 25 hearing. Accordingly, the order enforcing the settlement is vacated and the case remanded for further proceedings. Costs to appellant.

NOTES

1. ***Questions on*** **Ever-Tite** ***and*** **Ciaramella.** Note in *Ever-Tite* that the means by which the offer could be accepted were narrowly limited. Ordinarily, an offer invites acceptance by any reasonable manner or medium (Restatement (Second) § 30(2)). An offeror does, however, have the power to require acceptance to be made in a specified manner (Restatement (Second) § 30(1)). Who is the offeror in *Ever-Tite*? Who placed those limits on the permissible means of acceptance of the offer and what explains them? The offer limited acceptance to a "written acceptance" by an authorized officer or "upon commencing performance of the work." Clearly, the meaning of the phrase "upon commencing performance of the work" is ambiguous on several levels. First, is this an offer that looks to acceptance by performance or acceptance by a return promise? Does it matter? Assuming it is the latter, what is the legal significance of the act of "commencing performance of the

work"? (Hint: Reread Restatement (Second) § 4 and recall the arguments raised in *Bailey v. West, supra*). Second, it is unclear what actions constitute "commencing performance." What construction did the court put on the phrase? What other constructions were available? Assuming the phrase is ambiguous who should bear the risk of ambiguity as between the Greens, the nominal offerors, and the Ever-Tite Corp., the party that formulated the language of the offer?

What fact(s) in *Ciaramella* indicated that there was no acceptance of the offer at the time that the plaintiff's attorney (Eisenberg) said, "we have a deal"? Why do you suppose that individually dickered agreements, such as settlement agreements, large commercial contracts, corporate merger and acquisitions (and many other examples) frequently require a "formal execution" after the "agreement" has been reached. In many of these cases, the trade custom is that legal liability only attaches once the documents are signed and executed and not before. Why do you suppose parties to these transactions prefer to postpone legal liability beyond the time when it might otherwise attach under the default rules of offer and acceptance? Does the four factor test discussed by the court in *Ciaramella* create a clear answer to the question of whether and when parties intend to enter a binding agreement prior to the written agreement being executed? If several of the key factors pull in opposite directions, should certain ones be given priority over the others? For an argument that the test formulated by the Second Circuit impedes the process of communication prior to agreement, see Jason Scott Johnston, *Communication and Courtship: Cheap Talk Economics and the Law of Contract Formation*, 85 VA. L. REV. 385, 449–82 (1999).

2. *When is the Specified Mode of Acceptance Exclusive?* What constructions ought to be put on the language in these two examples?

a. "This purchase order agreement is not binding until accepted. Acceptance should be executed on acknowledgment copy which should be returned to buyer."[6]

b. "The signed acceptance of the proposal shall constitute a contract."[7]

3. *Communication of Acceptance.* Recall the difference between a bilateral and a unilateral contract (promise for promise and promise for performance). According to Restatement (Second) § 54, acceptance of an offer to create a unilateral contract generally does not have to be communicated to the offeror. Instead, acceptance is indicated when the offeree commences performance. In a bilateral contract, on the other hand, acceptance of the offer generally does have to be communicated to the offeror. The promise that serves as acceptance must be given to the offeror (or his agent) to create a contractual obligation. See Restatement (Second) § 56.

How do you explain this distinction? In light of § 56, how do you explain the result in *Ever-Tite* since the revocation of the offer occurred before any acceptance was verbally communicated?

Apply these rules to the following examples:

---

[6] *See Allied Steel & Conveyors, Inc. v. Ford Motor Co.*, 277 F.2d 907 (6th Cir. 1960).

[7] *See Brophy v. Joliet*, 144 N.E.2d 816 (Ill. App. Ct. 1957).

a. Julie says to Gary, "If you run the University cross-country course in 21 minutes or less, I will pay you $50." Gary says, "I'm pretty sure that I can do it, and I will begin training tomorrow."

b. Julie says to Gary, "If you will shoe my horse tomorrow, I will pay you $50." Gary says, "I accept."

c. Julie says to Gary, "If you will paint my garage, I will pay you $500." Gary, saying nothing, picks up a brush and begins painting Julie's garage.

Consider the following problems:

d. The Carbolic Smoke Ball Company purchased an ad in the Illustrated London News in which they offered £100 reward for anyone who used their Smoke Ball for two weeks and thereafter contracted influenza. Subsequently, Ms. Carlill purchased a smoke ball on the facts of the ad, used it as directed for six weeks and then came down with the flu. She sued for £100. Defense: There was no notification of acceptance, and thus no contract. What result?[8]

e. Antonucci ordered a new Chrysler truck from Stevens Dodge, Inc. The salesman filled out a standard order form, which Antonucci signed. The form stated in bold letters, "This order shall not become binding until accepted by dealer or his authorized representative." Although the form was never signed by the dealer or an authorized representative, Stevens Dodge ordered a truck for Antonucci. When it arrived, Antonucci had changed his mind, and he refused to accept the truck, claiming no binding contract had ever been formed. What result?[9]

4. *Making Accommodations.* When one party cannot perform what the other party requests, but they attempt to reach an accommodation, does that accommodation function as an acceptance of the initial offer? This question was addressed in *Corinthian Pharmaceutical Systems, Inc. v. Lederle Laboratories*, 724 F. Supp. 605 (S.D. Ind. 1989). Lederle supplied vaccines to Corinthian. Owing to increasing product liability insurance costs, Lederle was forced to increase its vaccine prices substantially. As a longtime customer, Corinthian had a price list of Lederle's, which warned that prices could be increased at any time. The day before the price increase became effective, Corinthian placed an order for 1,000 vials at the original price. Lederle opted to send them 50 vials at the original price as an accommodation.

The court ruled that the price list was not an offer, but rather functioned as an invitation for offers. Furthermore, it treated the smaller shipment as non-conforming goods, with the buyer being free to accept or reject them. This accommodation was the equivalent of a counteroffer by Lederle. The court noted:

> Thus, as a matter of law, the first offer was made by Corinthian when it phoned in and subsequently confirmed its order for 1,000 vials at the lower price. The next question, then, is whether Lederle ever accepted that offer.
>
> Under the Code, an acceptance need not be the mirror-image of the offer. UCC § 2-207. However, the offeree must still do some act that manifests the

---

[8] *See Carlill v. Carbolic Smoke Ball Co.*, 1 Q.B. 256 (Court of Appeal 1893).

[9] *See Antonucci v. Stevens Dodge, Inc.*, 73 Misc. 2d 173, 340 N.Y.S.2d 979 (1973).

intention to accept the offer and make a contract. Under § 2-206, an offer to make a contract shall be construed as inviting acceptance in any manner and by any medium reasonable in the circumstances. The first question regarding acceptance, therefore, is whether Lederle accepted the offer prior to sending the 50 vials of vaccine.

The record is clear that Lederle did not communicate or do any act prior to shipping the 50 vials that could support the finding of an acceptance. When Corinthian placed its order, it merely received a tracking number from the Telgo computer. Such an automated, ministerial act cannot constitute an acceptance. . . . Thus, there was no acceptance of Corinthian's offer prior to the delivery of 50 vials.

Id. at 610.

The court went on to analyze whether a valid acceptance was made under § 2-206 of the UCC. Under § 2-206 (1) (b), a shipment of non-conforming goods does not constitute acceptance if the seller provides timely notification that the shipment is only an accommodation. The court continued:

An accommodation is an arrangement or engagement made as a favor to another. The term implies no consideration. In this case, then, even taking all inferences favorably for the buyer, the only possible conclusion is that Lederle Labs' shipment of 50 vials was offered merely as an accommodation; that is to say, Lederle had no obligation to make the partial shipment, and did so only as a favor to the buyer. The accommodation letter, which Corinthian is sure it received, clearly stated that the 50 vials were being sent at the lower price as an exception to Lederle's general policy, and that the balance of the offer would be invoiced at the higher price. The letter further indicated that Lederle's proposal to ship the balance of the order at the higher price could be rejected by the buyer. Moreover, the standard terms of Lederle's invoice stated that acceptance of the order was expressly conditioned upon buyer's assent to the seller's terms.

Under these undisputed facts, § 2-206(1)(b) was satisfied. Where, as here, the notification is properly made, the shipment of nonconforming goods is treated as a counteroffer just as at common law, and the buyer may accept or reject the counteroffer under normal contract rules.

Id. at 610–11.

Thus, the end result is that Lederle Lab's price quotations were mere invitations to make an offer, Corinthian's order was an offer to buy 1,000 vials at the lower price, and Lederle's response of shipping 50 vials at the lower price was a mere accommodation and thus constituted a counteroffer and not an acceptance.

5. *Settlement Offers.* Settlement agreements need not always be in writing in order to be enforced. In *Powell v. Omnicom*, 497 F.3d 124 (2d Cir. 2007), the court used the same test as in *Ciaramella* to find an enforceable settlement agreement when the plaintiff assented in open court to the terms of a settlement with her former employee and later sought to renege. The judge reasoned that announcing the terms of an agreement on the record in open court served the same function as a contract in writing. The statement in court functioned as a formal entry memorializing the critical litigation event and performed a "'cautionary function' whereby the parties' acceptance is considered and deliberate." *Id.* at 131.

6. ***Selecting the Permissible Method of Acceptance.*** How is one to know whether a performance or a promise is required as acceptance of the offer? Section 32 of the Restatement (Second) of Contracts states: "In case of doubt an offer is interpreted as inviting the offeree to accept either by promising to perform what the offer requests or by rendering the performance, as the offeree chooses." Hence, in most circumstances, acceptance by either promise or performance is sufficient to create a contract. The UCC has adopted this provision and applied it to the sale of goods. Read UCC § 2-206(1). Where the offeror clearly states a specific method of acceptance, of course, the offeree must then abide by those terms to accept the offer. Section 60 of the Restatement (Second) expresses this idea.

Are these sensible rules? Compare an alternative possibility: "Any suggested method of acceptance is to be presumed exclusive unless the offeror clearly indicates that other methods of acceptance are not precluded."

7. ***Offer and Acceptance in Preliminary Agreements.*** *Ciaramella* raises the issue of *when* the parties agreement is binding. This issue is particularly relevant where the parties appear to have reached agreement but they also have agreed to memorialize their agreement in a formal writing. The question, then, is whether the deal is binding once the preliminary agreement is concluded or whether it is binding only when it is finally memorialized.[10] In answering that question, modern courts begin by distinguishing between two different types of preliminary agreements. This distinction was first proposed by Judge Pierre Leval in a highly influential opinion in *Teachers Ins. & Annuity Asso. v. Tribune Co.*, 670 F. Supp. 491 (S.D.N.Y. 1987). Consider the following explanation of the "Leval Test" from *Adjustrite Sys. v. GAB Bus. Servs.*, 145 F.3d 543 (2d Cir. 1998):

> Parties to proposed . . . transactions often enter into preliminary agree-ments, which may provide for the execution of more formal agreements. When they do so and the parties fail to execute a more formal agreement, the issue arises as to whether the preliminary agreement is a binding contract or an unenforceable agreement to agree. Ordinarily, where the parties contemplate further negotiations and the execution of a formal instrument, a preliminary agreement does not create a binding contract. In some circumstances, however, preliminary agreements can create binding obligations. Usually, binding preliminary agreements fall into one of two categories.
>
> The first is a fully binding preliminary agreement, which is created when the parties agree on all the points that require negotiation but agree to memorialize their agreement in a more formal document. Such an agree-ment is fully binding; it is "preliminary only in form — only in the sense that the parties desire a more elaborate formalization of the agreement." A binding preliminary agreement binds both sides to their ultimate contrac-

---

[10] For a discussion of social concerns arising out of precontractual liability, see Omri Ben-Shahar, *Freedom from Contract*, 2004 Wis. L. Rev. 261, 267.

tual objective in recognition that, "despite the anticipation of further formalities," a contract has been reached. Accordingly, a party may demand performance of the transaction even though the parties fail to produce the "more elaborate formalization of the agreement."

The second type of preliminary agreement, dubbed a "binding preliminary commitment" by Judge Leval, is binding only to a certain degree. It is created when the parties agree on certain major terms, but leave other terms open for further negotiation. The parties "accept a mutual commitment to negotiate together in good faith in an effort to reach final agreement." In contrast to a fully binding preliminary agreement, a "binding preliminary commitment" "does not commit the parties to their ultimate contractual objective but rather to the obligation to negotiate the open issues in good faith in an attempt to reach the . . . objective within the agreed framework." A party to such a binding preliminary commitment has no right to demand performance of the transaction. Indeed, if a final contract is not agreed upon, the parties may abandon the transaction as long as they have made a good faith effort to close the deal and have not insisted on conditions that do not conform to the preliminary writing.

Hence, if a preliminary agreement is of the first type, the parties are fully bound to carry out the terms of the agreement even if the formal instrument is never executed. If a preliminary agreement is of the second type, the parties are bound only to make a good faith effort to negotiate and agree upon the open terms and a final agreement; if they fail to reach such a final agreement after making a good faith effort to do so, there is no further obligation. Finally, however, if the preliminary writing was not intended to be binding on the parties at all, the writing is a mere proposal, and neither party has an obligation to negotiate further.

Courts confronted with the issue of determining whether a preliminary agreement is binding, as an agreement of either the first or the second type, must keep two competing interests in mind. First, courts must be wary of "trapping parties in surprise contractual obligations that they never intended" to undertake. Second, "courts [must] enforce and preserve agreements that were intended [to be] binding, despite a need for further documentation or further negotiation," for it is "the aim of contract law to gratify, not to defeat, expectations."

The key, of course, is the intent of the parties: whether the parties intended to be bound, and if so, to what extent. "To discern that intent a court must look to 'the words and deeds [of the parties] which constitute objective signs in a given set of circumstances.' " Subjective evidence of intent, on the other hand, is generally not considered.

Id. at 549.

    The court in *Ciaramella* considered the first type of preliminary agreement — where the parties agree on all (or almost all) of the terms but also agree to memorialize their agreement in a formal document.[11] What were the parties' intentions in *Ciaramella*? Did the parties intend to be bound once the settlement offer was accepted by Mr. Eisenberg or did Ciaramella signal an intent to postpone acceptance until the formal execution of the written settlement agreement? Can courts reliably recover the parties' intent in those cases where they do not signal intent expressly? If not, what precautions should a drafting attorney take in protecting her client against an adverse outcome?[12]

[b] Silence or Dominion as Acceptance

Only under special circumstances will silence or an act of dominion constitute acceptance of an offer.[13] Read § 69 of the Restatement (Second). These comments follow that section:

> Comment a:
>
> Ordinarily an offeror does not have power to cause the silence of the offeree to operate as acceptance. . . . The mere receipt of an unsolicited offer does not impair the offeree's freedom of action or inaction or impose on him any duty to speak. The exceptional cases where silence is acceptance fall into two main classes: those where the offeree silently takes offered benefits, and those where one party relies on the other party's manifestation of intention that silence may operate as acceptance. . . .
>
> Comment b:
>
> . . . [W]hen the recipient knows or has reason to know that the services are being rendered with an expectation of compensation, and by a word could prevent the mistake, his privilege of inaction gives way; under Subsection (1)(a) he is held to an acceptance if he fails to speak. The resulting duty is not merely a duty to pay for fair value, but a duty to pay or perform according to the terms of the offer.

One of the more common instances where silence constitutes acceptance is described in § 69(1)(c). The practices of a specific business or industry, or the course of dealing between two parties over a period of time may include silence as an established method of acceptance. In such a situation the offeror will be justified in taking silence to mean the offer is accepted.

---

[11] The second type of binding preliminary agreement — binding preliminary commitments — will be explored in detail in Chapter 4, Section B[3], *infra*.

[12] Consider, for example, the following clause:

This Heads of Agreement ("HOA") is intended solely as a basis for further discussion and is not intended to be and does not constitute a legally binding obligation of the parties. No legally binding obligations on the parties will be created, implied, or inferred until appropriate documents in final form are executed and delivered by each or the parties regarding the subject matter of this HOA and containing all other essential terms of an agreed upon transaction. Without limiting the generality of the foregoing, it is the parties intent that, until that event, no agreement binding of the parties shall exist and there shall be no obligations whatsoever based on such things as parol evidence, extended negotiations, "handshakes," oral understandings, or course of conduct (including reliance and changes of position). . . .

[13] For an example of the former, see *Ammons v. Wilson & Co.*, 176 Miss. 645, 170 So. 227 (1936). For an example of the latter, see *Russell v. Texas Co.*, 238 F.2d 636 (9th Cir. 1956).

Many students may be familiar with other sorts of arrangements where silence indicates assent. For instance, some "music clubs" operate by sending their members a CD each month with the understanding that they will later be billed for it; if the recipient chooses not to accept the offer, she has to send it back within a predetermined time. Some commentators have referred to such arrangements as negative option offers. Such offers can occur in two forms: a unilateral negative option and a contracted negative option. A contracted negative option, such as the music club example, occurs after a contractual relationship has already been established between the parties. A unilateral negative option offer, however, occurs without the consent of the recipient. An example of this practice is when a utility company proposes new services for its customers that will automatically be provided unless the customer specifically rejects them. Unlike the contracted negative option, this type of offer did not form the basis for the initial contractual relationship. In contrast, a Cheese-of-the-Month company usually makes the terms of the monthly option explicit prior to the execution of the contract; often, the seller has little to offer beyond the optional product.[14]

[c]   The Mailbox Rule

The clearest manifestation of acceptance occurs when the parties meet face-to-face, make an offer and voice acceptance immediately. Much more often, however, offers and acceptances are transmitted through the mail. Not surprisingly, rules have developed to cover the problems that this method of communication raises.[15]

Acceptance of an offer by mail takes effect as soon as the acceptance is mailed, whether or not it ever reaches the offeror. *See* Restatement (Second) § 63. Section 66 of the Restatement (Second) of Contracts notes, however, that the letter of acceptance must be properly addressed and "such other precautions taken as are ordinarily observed to insure safe transmission" for the acceptance to be effective. Comment a to § 63 explains the rationale behind this rule.

> It is often said that an offeror who makes an offer by mail makes the post office his agent to receive the acceptance, or that the mailing of a letter of acceptance puts it irrevocably out of the offeree's control. Under United States postal regulations however, the sender of a letter has long had the power to stop delivery and reclaim the letter. A better explanation of the rule that the acceptance takes effect on dispatch is that the offeree needs a dependable basis for his decision whether to accept. In many legal systems such a basis is provided by a general rule that an offer is irrevocable unless it provides otherwise. The common law provides such a basis through the rule that a revocation of an offer is ineffective if received after an acceptance has been properly dispatched.

---

[14] For a more extensive discussion of negative option offers, see Dennis D. Lamont, *Negative Option Offers in Consumer Service Contracts*, 42 UCLA L. REV. 1315 (1995). For an economic analysis of silence as acceptance (or assent) in both commercial and consumer contexts, see Avery Katz, *The Strategic Structure of Offer and Acceptance: Game Theory and the Law of Contract Formation*, 89 MICH. L. REV. 215 (1990); Avery Katz, *Transaction Costs and the Legal Mechanics of Exchange: When Should Silence in the Face of an Offer Be Construed as Acceptance?*, 9 J.L. ECON. & ORG. 77 (1993).

[15] *See Adams v. Lindsell*, 1 Burn. & Ald. 681, 106 Eng. Rep. 250 (King's Bench 1818).

We will discuss the rules of revocation in the next section. But consider for a moment the statement that "the offeree needs a dependable basis for his decision whether to accept." Perhaps this is an example of the hypothesis that any rule at all is better than no rule. What would happen to bargaining by mail if the rule were changed so that an acceptance was effective only when received by the offeror? Doesn't that rule provide just as much certainty as the rule presently used?

U.S. Post Office regulations issued in the 1940s presented the possibility for changing the common law mailbox rule.

The new regulation read as follows:

> (c) On receipt of a request for the return of any particle of mail matter the postmaster or railway postal clerk to whom such request is addressed shall return such matter in a penalty envelope, to the mailing postmaster, who shall deliver it to the sender upon payment of all expenses and the regular rate of postage on the matter returned. . . .

39 CFR §§ 10.09, 10.10 (1939 ed.).

Why do you suppose the Reporters of the Restatement (Second) continued to follow the common law mailbox rule in § 63 notwithstanding the fact that current postal regulations permit dispatched mail to be reclaimed by the sender?

Professor Ian Macneil argued that modern bargaining situations are too complex to be governed effectively by a single mailbox rule. Macneil presented his arguments in *Time of Acceptance: Too Many Problems for a Single Rule*, 112 U. PA. L. REV. 947, 978–79 (1964). He argued that while the dispatch (or mailbox) rule is not appropriate for solving every offer and acceptance problem which arises, it is nevertheless a strong foundation upon which to construct a number of workable general rules. "In a great many situations the dispatch rule is a highly functional one," Macneil wrote, "thus its wholesale overruling would be destructive of a satisfactory system of contract formation."

Nevertheless, Macneil asserted that courts need an individualized approach to the problems of "time of acceptance." Concentrating on the functional aspects of each case — how each case can best be regulated to protect the interests of both parties — will "bring more clarity and certainty to the law than it now enjoys with the functional obscurantism dominating time of acceptance' doctrines." Do you agree with Macneil's call for more complex and individually tailored rules governing mailed acceptances?

Even with the growth of modern communications devices, the mailbox rule still plays a significant role in contract litigation. In *University Emergency Med. Found. v. Rapier Invs., Ltd.*, 197 F.3d 18 (1st Cir. 1999), a termination notice was mailed within the contractually specified four-month notification period. The envelope was incorrectly addressed, however, and was returned undelivered; a secondary mailing was received after the four-month deadline. The court held that the contract specifically provided for notification by mail, thus triggering the mailbox rule. Had the contract not specifically mentioned termination via mail, the letters would not have taken effect until receipt, and thus would not have served as a valid termination.

The court also found that the use of the incorrect address did not affect the question of whether timely notice was properly given. The court held that the address given in the contract was not a bargained-for contract term, as it did not confer a benefit on either party, but instead was intended simply as a means of facilitating the sending of the notice. By sending the second letter to the proper address, the plaintiff was able to retain the benefit of the mailbox rule as to the original termination notice.[16]

[4]   Revocation of Offers

Read § 36 of the Restatement (Second) of Contracts, which specifies the methods by which the offeree can lose the power to accept an offer. Counteroffers will be dealt with in Section C. We are interested here in revocation. While it seems straightforward enough as presented by the Restatement (Second), there are a few more rules we need to consider.

[a]   Revocation in General

Once an offer has been made, it generally remains open a reasonable time so the offeree has an opportunity to respond. Nevertheless, the offeror may revoke his offer — manifest the intention not to enter into a contract — without incurring liability, provided the offeree has not already manifested acceptance.[17] One of the more obvious examples of this rule occurs when an offer is made during a conversation. Without an expression to the contrary, such an offer ends at the conclusion of the conversation. Thus, revocation here is automatic, and an acceptance after the end of the conversation will not create contractual obligations. This situation changes when the offeror specifies that the offer will remain open for a certain period of time. In that instance, the offer remains open for the period stated unless it is explicitly revoked before the appointed time.

Revocation is more problematic in the case of a unilateral contract, where an offer is made and can be accepted only by performance. Under the early common law rule, an offer to enter into a unilateral contract was not accepted until full performance had been rendered. An offer could be withdrawn at any time before performance was completed, even after performance had begun. Professor Maurice Wormser provided an example of this rule, and the reasoning behind it in *The True Conception of Unilateral Contracts*, 26 Yale L.J. 136, 136–38 (1916).

> Suppose A says to B, "I will give you $100 if you walk across the Brooklyn Bridge," and B walks — is there a contract? It is clear that A is not asking B for B's promise to walk across the Brooklyn Bridge. What A wants from B is the act of walking across the bridge. When B has walked across the bridge there is a contract, and A is then bound to pay to B $100. At that

---

[16] For a complete discussion of the applicability of the mailbox rule in the Internet age, see Valerie Watnick, *The Electronic Formation of Contracts and the Common Law "Mailbox Rule,"* 56 Baylor L. Rev. 175, 203 (2004).

[17] For a discussion, see Melvin A. Eisenberg, *The Revocation of Offers*, 2004 Wis. L. Rev. 271. *See also* Charles L. Knapp, *An Offer You Can't Revoke*, 2004 Wis. L. Rev. 309.

moment there arises a unilateral contract. A has bartered away his volition for B's act of walking across the Brooklyn Bridge.

When an act is thus wanted in return for a promise, a unilateral contract is created when the act is done. It is clear that only one party is bound. B is not bound to walk across the Brooklyn Bridge, but A is bound to pay B $100 if B does so. Thus, in unilateral contracts, on one side we find merely an act, on the other side a promise.

It is plain that in the Brooklyn Bridge case as first put, what A wants from B is the act of walking across the Brooklyn Bridge. A does not ask for B's promise to walk across the bridge and B has never given it. B has never bound himself to walk across the bridge. A, however, has bound himself to pay $100 to B, if B does so. Let us suppose that B starts to walk across the Brooklyn Bridge and has gone about one-half of the way across. At that moment A overtakes B and says to him, "I withdraw my offer." Has B then any rights against A? Again, let us suppose that after A has said, "I withdraw my offer," B continues to walk across the Brooklyn Bridge and completes the act of crossing. Under these circumstances, has B any rights against A?

In the first of the cases just suggested, A withdrew his offer before B had walked across the bridge. What A wanted from B, what A asked for, was the act of walking across the bridge. Until that was done, B had not given to A what A had requested. The acceptance by B of A's offer could be nothing but the act on B's part of crossing the bridge. It is elementary that an offeror may withdraw his offer until it has been accepted. It follows logically that A is perfectly within his rights in withdrawing his offer before B has accepted it by walking across the bridge — the act contemplated by the offeror and the offeree as the acceptance of the offer.

The more recent common law formulation, however, provides that once the offeree has begun the requested performance, the offer may not be withdrawn until the offeree has had a reasonable opportunity to complete performance. In other words, part performance makes the offer irrevocable subject to completion of the invited performance in accordance with the offer's terms. *See* Restatement (Second) § 45. Judge Wood explained the basis for the modern rule in *Marchiondo v. Scheck*, 432 P.2d 405, 407–08 (N.M. 1967):

> Once partial performance is begun pursuant to the offer made, a contract results. This contract has been termed a contract with conditions or an option contract. This rule avoids hardship to the offeree, and yet does not hold the offeror beyond the terms of his promise. It is true by such terms he was to be bound only if the requested act was done; but this implies that he will let it be done, that he will keep his offer open till the offeree who has begun can finish doing it.

In the case of bargaining by mail, revocation is resolved by a corollary to the mailbox rule. Generally, a revocation of an offer does not become effective until the offeree actually receives the letter communicating the withdrawal. *See* Restatement (Second) § 42. Rather than a "dispatch" rule, then, revocation is governed by a "receipt" rule. It is not hard to imagine the difficulties which can arise when bargaining by mail. It is not unusual for an offeror to mail an offer, reconsider his position, and then mail a revocation before he has actually received the offeree's acceptance, but after that acceptance has been mailed. In such a case, would a contract be formed?

Closely related to the rules of revoking an offer are the rules of revoking an acceptance. While the mailbox rule works to the offeree's advantage in preventing a subsequent revocation of the offer by the offeror, the same rule can operate to bind the offeree to an unwanted contract by preventing revocation of the acceptance. Comment c to Restatement (Second) of Contracts § 63 explains as follows:

> The fact that the offeree has power to reclaim his acceptance from the post office or telegraph company does not prevent the acceptance from taking effect on dispatch. Nor, in the absence of additional circumstances, does the actual recapture of the acceptance deprive it of legal effect, though as a practical matter the offeror cannot assert his rights unless he learns of them. An attempt to revoke the acceptance by an overtaking communication is similarly ineffective, even though the revocation is received before the acceptance is received. After mailing an acceptance of a revocable offer, the offeree is not permitted to speculate at the offeror's expense during the time required for the letter to arrive.

> A purported revocation of acceptance may, however, affect the rights of the parties. It may amount to an offer to rescind the contract or to a repudiation of it, or it may bar the offeree by estoppel from enforcing it. In some cases it may be justified as an exercise of a right of stoppage in transit or a demand for assurance of performance. . . . Or the contract may be voidable for mistake or misrepresentation. . . .

[b] Irrevocable Offers

It is possible to create offers that cannot be revoked for a specific period of time. Option contracts and certain firm offers and construction bids can operate as irrevocable offers.

The most straightforward type of option contract is where one party pays another to make an offer by the latter irrevocable. Stan is unsure whether he wants to buy Graham's business or not. His decision depends on a market survey and on securing a franchise. Stan could accept subject to these contingencies, but they are rather complicated and difficult to reduce to writing. On the other hand, Stan doesn't want to investigate the deal further without being sure of the price. Graham says, "I will sell you the business for $1.7 million, and don't worry, I will keep this offer open for two weeks, while you do your investigation." Because there is no consideration for the promise to hold the offer open for two weeks, this may not be good enough for Stan. If he pays Graham $500 for Graham's promise to keep the offer to sell the business open, that is a (binding) option contract. See Restatement (Second) § 25.

Where the sale of goods is involved, a merchant's "firm offer" is treated as the equivalent of an option contract *if* the offer is in a signed writing in which the merchant gives assurances that the offer will be held open. See UCC § 2-205 and the accompanying comments describing the firm offer under the Code. In addition, bids given by contractors on construction jobs can sometimes function as irrevocable offers. Consider the following case.

PAVEL ENTERPRISES, INC. v. A. S. JOHNSON CO., INC.
Court of Appeals of Maryland
342 Md. 143, 674 A.2d 521 (1996)

KARWACKI, J.

In this case we are invited to adapt the "modern" contractual theory of detrimental reliance, or promissory estoppel, to the relationship between general contractors and their subcontractors. Although the theory of detrimental reliance is available to general contractors, it is not applicable to the facts of this case. For that reason, and because there was no traditional bilateral contract formed, we shall affirm the trial court.

The National Institutes of Health [hereinafter, "NIH"], solicited bids for a renovation project on Building 30 of its Bethesda, Maryland campus. The proposed work entailed some demolition work, but the major component of the job was mechanical, including heating, ventilation and air conditioning ["HVAC"]. Pavel Enterprises Incorporated [hereinafter, "PEI"], a general contractor from Vienna, Virginia and appellant in this action, prepared a bid for the NIH work. In preparing its bid, PEI solicited sub-bids from various mechanical subcontractors. The A. S. Johnson Company [hereinafter, "Johnson"], a mechanical subcontractor located in Clinton, Maryland and the appellee here, responded with a written scope of work proposal on July 27, 1993.[18] On the morning of August 5, 1993, the day NIH opened the general contractors' bids, Johnson verbally submitted a quote of $898,000 for the HVAC component. Neither party disputes that PEI used Johnson's sub-bid in computing its own bid. PEI submitted a bid of $1,585,000 for the entire project.

General contractors' bids were opened on the afternoon of August 5, 1993. PEI's bid was the second lowest bid. The government subsequently disqualified the apparent low bidder, however, and in mid-August, NIH notified PEI that its bid would be accepted.

With the knowledge that PEI was the lowest responsive bidder, Thomas F. Pavel, president of PEI, visited the offices of A. S. Johnson on August 26, 1993, and met with James Kick, Johnson's chief estimator, to discuss Johnson's proposed role in the work. Pavel testified at trial to the purpose of the meeting:

> . . . My company had not performed business with them on a direct relationship, but we had heard of their reputation. I wanted to go out and see where their facility was, see where they were located, and basically just

---

[18] [2] The scope of work proposal listed all work that Johnson proposed to perform, but omitted the price term. This is a standard practice in the construction industry. The subcontractor's bid price is then filled in immediately before the general contractor submits the general bid to the letting party.

sit down and talk to them. Because if we were going to use them on a project, I wanted to know who I was dealing with.

Following that meeting, PEI sent a fax to all of the mechanical subcontractors from whom it had received sub-bids on the NIH job. The text of that fax is reproduced:

> We herewith respectfully request that you review your bid on the above referenced project that was bid on 8/05/93. PEI has been notified that we will be awarded the project as . . . [the original low bidder] has been found to be nonresponsive on the solicitation. We anticipate award on or around the first of September and therefor request that you supply the following information.
>
> 1. Please break out your cost for the "POWERS" supplied control work as we will be subcontracting directly to "POWERS".
>
> 2. Please resubmit your quote deleting the above referenced item. We ask this in an effort to allow all prospective bidders to compete on an even playing field. Should you have any questions, please call us immediately as time is of the essence.

On August 30, 1993, PEI informed NIH that Johnson was to be the mechanical subcontractor on the job. On September 1, 1993, PEI mailed and faxed a letter to Johnson [that stated that PEI was] accepting Johnson's bid . . .

Upon receipt of PEI's fax of September 1, James Kick called and informed PEI that Johnson's bid contained an error, and as a result the price was too low. According to Kick, Johnson had discovered the mistake earlier, but because Johnson believed that PEI had not been awarded the contract, they did not feel compelled to correct the error. Kick sought to withdraw Johnson's bid, both over the telephone and by a letter dated September 2, 1993. . . .

PEI responded to both the September 1 phone call, and the September 2 letter, expressing its refusal to permit Johnson to withdraw.

On September 28, 1993, NIH formally awarded the construction contract to PEI. PEI found a substitute subcontractor to do the mechanical work, but at a cost of $930,000. PEI brought suit against Johnson in the Circuit Court for Prince George's County to recover the $32,000 difference between Johnson's bid and the cost of the substitute mechanical subcontractor. . . .

The trial court made several findings of fact, which we summarize:

1. PEI relied upon Johnson's sub-bid in making its bid for the entire project;

2. The fact that PEI was not the low bidder, but was awarded the project only after the apparent low bidder was disqualified, takes this case out of the ordinary;

3. Prior to NIH awarding PEI the contract on September 28, Johnson, on September 2, withdrew its bid; and

4. PEI's letter to all potential mechanical subcontractors, dated August 26, 1993, indicates that there was no definite agreement between PEI and Johnson, and that PEI was not relying upon Johnson's bid.

The trial court analyzed the case under both a traditional contract theory and under a detrimental reliance theory. PEI was unable to satisfy the trial judge that under either theory that a contractual relationship had been formed.

PEI appealed to the Court of Special Appeals, raising both traditional offer and acceptance theory, and "promissory estoppel." Before our intermediate appellate court considered the case, we issued a writ of certiorari on our own motion.

The relationships involved in construction contracts have long posed a unique problem in the law of contracts. A brief overview of the mechanics of the construction bid process, as well as our legal system's attempts to regulate the process, is in order.

Our description of the bid process in Maryland Supreme Corp. v. Blake Co., 279 Md. 531, 369 A.2d 1017 (1977) is still accurate:

> In such a building project there are basically three parties involved: the letting party, who calls for bids on its job; the general contractor, who makes a bid on the whole project; and the subcontractors, who bid only on that portion of the whole job which involves the field of its specialty. The usual procedure is that when a project is announced, a subcontractor, on his own initiative or at the general contractor's request, prepares an estimate and submits a bid to one or more of the general contractors interested in the project. The general contractor evaluates the bids made by the subcontractors in each field and uses them to compute its total bid to the letting party. After receiving bids from general contractors, the letting party ordinarily awards the contract to the lowest reputable bidder.

Id. at 533-34, 369 A.2d at 1020-21.

The problem the construction bidding process poses is the determination of the precise points on the timeline that the various parties become bound to each other. The early landmark case was James Baird Co. v. Gimbel Bros., Inc., 64 F.2d 344 (2d Cir. 1933). The plaintiff, James Baird Co., ["Baird"], was a general contractor from Washington, D.C., bidding to construct a government building in Harrisburg, Pennsylvania. Gimbel Bros., Inc., ["Gimbel"], the famous New York department store, sent its bid to supply linoleum to a number of bidding general contractors on December 24, and Baird received Gimbel's bid on December 28. Gimbel realized its bid was based on an incorrect computation and notified Baird of its withdrawal on December 28. The letting authority awarded Baird the job on December 30. Baird formally accepted the Gimbel bid on January 2. When Gimbel refused to perform, Baird sued for the additional cost of a substitute linoleum supplier. The Second Circuit Court of Appeals held that Gimbel's initial bid was an offer to contract and, under traditional contract law, remained open only until accepted or withdrawn. Because the offer was withdrawn before it was accepted there was no contract. Judge Learned Hand, speaking for the court, also rejected two alternative theories of the case: unilateral contract and promissory estoppel. He held that Gimbel's bid was not an offer of a unilateral contract that Baird could accept by performing, i.e., submitting the bid as part of the general bid; and second, he held that the theory of promissory estoppel was limited to cases involving charitable pledges.

Judge Hand's opinion was widely criticized, but also widely influential. The effect of the James Baird line of cases, however, is an "obvious injustice." The general contractor is bound to the price submitted to the letting party, but the subcontractors are not bound, and are free to withdraw.

As one commentator described it, "If the subcontractor revokes his bid before it is accepted by the general, any loss which results is a deduction from the general's profit and conceivably may transform overnight a profitable contract into a losing deal." Franklin M. Schultz, The Firm Offer Puzzle: A Study of Business Practice in the Construction Industry, 19 U. Chi. L. Rev. 237, 239 (1952).

The unfairness of this regime to the general contractor was addressed in Drennan v. Star Paving, 51 Cal. 2d 409, 333 P.2d 757 (1958). Like James Baird, the Drennan case arose in the context of a bid mistake. Justice Traynor, writing for the Supreme Court of California, relied upon § 90 of the Restatement (First) of Contracts. Justice Traynor reasoned that the subcontractor's bid contained an implied subsidiary promise not to revoke the bid. As the court stated:

> When plaintiff [a General Contractor,] used defendant's offer in computing his own bid, he bound himself to perform in reliance on defendant's terms. Though defendant did not bargain for the use of its bid neither did defendant make it idly, indifferent to whether it would be used or not. On the contrary it is reasonable to suppose that defendant submitted its bid to obtain the subcontract. It was bound to realize the substantial possibility that its bid would be the lowest, and that it would be included by plaintiff in his bid. It was to its own interest that the contractor be awarded the general contract; the lower the subcontract bid, the lower the general contractor's bid was likely to be and the greater its chance of acceptance and hence the greater defendant's chance of getting the paving subcontract. Defendant had reason not only to expect plaintiff to rely on its bid but to want him to. Clearly defendant had a stake in plaintiff's reliance on its bid. Given this interest and the fact that plaintiff is bound by his own bid, it is only fair that plaintiff should have at least an opportunity to accept defendant's bid after the general contract has been awarded to him.

Drennan, 51 Cal. 2d at 415, 333 P.2d at 760.

The *Drennan* court however did not use "promissory estoppel" as a substitute for the entire contract, as is the doctrine's usual function. Instead, the *Drennan* court, applying the principle of § 90, interpreted the subcontractor's bid to be irrevocable. Justice Traynor's analysis used promissory estoppel as consideration for an implied promise to keep the bid open for a reasonable time. Recovery was then predicated on traditional bilateral contract, with the sub-bid as the offer [followed by the general contractor's] acceptance.

The *Drennan* decision has been very influential. Many states have adopted the reasoning used by Justice Traynor. . . . Despite the popularity of the *Drennan* reasoning, the case has subsequently come under some criticism. The criticism centers on the lack of symmetry of detrimental reliance in the bid process, in that subcontractors are bound to the general, but the general is not bound to the subcontractors. The result is that the general is free to bid shop, bid chop, and to encourage bid peddling, to the detriment of the subcontractors. . . .

The doctrine of detrimental reliance has evolved in the time since *Drennan* was decided in 1958. The American Law Institute, responding to *Drennan*, sought to make detrimental reliance more readily applicable to the construction bidding scenario by adding § 87 to the Restatement (Second) of Contracts. This new section was intended to make subcontractors' bids irrevocable under certain conditions. . . .

. . . [C]ourts and commentators have also suggested other solutions intended to bind the parties without the use of detrimental reliance theory. The most prevalent suggestion is the use of the firm offer provision of the Uniform Commercial Code § 2-205 of that statute provides:

> An offer by a merchant to buy or sell goods in a signed writing which by its terms gives assurance that it will be held open is not revocable, for lack of consideration, during the time stated or if no time is stated for a reasonable time, but in no event may such period of irrevocability exceed three months; but any such term of assurance on a form supplied by the offeree must be separately signed by the offeror.

In this manner, subcontractor's bids, made in writing and giving some assurance of an intent that the offer be held open, can be found to be irrevocable.

The Supreme Judicial Court of Massachusetts has suggested three other traditional theories that might prove the existence of a contractual relationship between a general contractor and a sub: conditional bilateral contract analysis; unilateral contract analysis; and unrevoked offer analysis. Loranger Constr. Corp. v. E. F. Hauserman Co., 376 Mass. 757, 384 N.E.2d 176 (1978). If the general contractor could prove that there was an exchange of promises binding the parties to each other, and that exchange of promises was made before bid opening, that would constitute a valid bilateral promise conditional upon the general being awarded the job. This directly contrasts with Judge Hand's analysis in James Baird, that a general's use of a sub-bid does not constitutes acceptance conditional upon the award of the contract to the general.

Alternatively, if the subcontractor intended its sub-bid as an offer to a unilateral contract, use of the sub-bid in the general's bid constitutes part performance, which renders the initial offer irrevocable under the Restatement (Second) of Contracts § 45 (1979). This resurrects a second theory dismissed by Judge Learned Hand in James Baird.

Finally, the Loranger court pointed out that a jury might choose to disbelieve that a subcontractor had withdrawn the winning bid, meaning that acceptance came before withdrawal, and a traditional bilateral contract was formed.. . . .

If PEI is able to prove by any of the theories described that a contractual relationship existed, but Johnson failed to perform its end of the bargain, then PEI will recover the $32,000 in damages caused by Johnson's breach of contract. Alternatively, if PEI is unable to prove the existence of a contractual relationship, then Johnson has no obligation to PEI. We will test the facts of the case against the theories described to determine if such a relationship existed.

The trial court held, and we agree, that Johnson's sub-bid was an offer to contract and that it was sufficiently clear and definite. We must then determine if PEI made a timely and valid acceptance of that offer and thus created a traditional bilateral contract, or in the absence of a valid acceptance, if PEI's detrimental reliance served to bind Johnson to its sub-bid. We examine each of these alternatives, beginning with traditional contract theory. . . .

The trial judge found that there was not a traditional contract binding Johnson to PEI. . . . The trial judge rejected PEI's claim of bilateral contract for two separate reasons: 1) that there was no meeting of the minds; and 2) that the offer was withdrawn prior to acceptance. Both need not be proper bases for decision; if either of these two theories is not clearly erroneous, we must affirm.

There is substantial evidence in the record to support the judge's conclusion that there was no meeting of the minds. PEI's letter of August 26, to all potential mechanical subcontractors . . . indicates, as the trial judge found, that PEI and Johnson "did not have a definite, certain meeting of the minds on a certain price for a certain quantity of goods. . . ." Because this reason is itself sufficient to sustain the trial judge's finding that no contract was formed, we affirm.

[The court also found that there was sufficient evidence to support the trial court's finding that Johnson withdrew its offer on September 2 prior to the formal acceptance by PEI of the Johnson bid on September 28 after the award of the prime contract by the NIH. The trial court found that the September 1 letter by PEI purporting to accept Johnson's bid was ineffective and did not bind the parties to a bi-lateral contract at that time because "Johnson had made it clear to PEI that they were not going to continue to rely on their earlier submitted bid."]

PEI's alternative theory of the case is that PEI's detrimental reliance binds Johnson to its bid. We are asked, as a threshold question, if detrimental reliance applies to the setting of construction bidding. Nothing in our previous cases suggests that the doctrine was intended to be limited to a specific factual setting. The benefits of binding subcontractors outweigh the possible detriments of the doctrine. . . .

In a construction bidding case, where the general contractor seeks to bind the subcontractor to the sub-bid offered, the general must first prove that the subcontractor's sub-bid constituted an offer to perform a job at a given price. We do not express a judgment about how precise a bid must be to constitute an offer, or to what degree a general contractor may request to change the offered scope before an acceptance becomes a counter-offer. That fact-specific judgment is best reached on a case-by-case basis. In the instant case, the trial judge found that the sub-bid was sufficiently clear and definite to constitute an offer, and his finding was not clearly erroneous. . . .

If the reliance is not "substantial and definite" justice will not compel enforcement . . . [T]he general must prove that the subcontractor reasonably expected that the general contractor would rely upon the offer. The subcontractor's expectation that the general contractor will rely upon the sub-bid may dissipate through time.

In this case, the trial court correctly inquired into Johnson's belief that the bid remained open, and that consequently PEI was not relying on the Johnson bid. The judge found that due to the time lapse between bid opening and award, "it would be unreasonable for offers to continue." This is supported by the substantial evidence. James Kick testified that although he knew of his bid mistake, he did not bother to notify PEI because J.J. Kirlin, Inc., and not PEI, was the apparent low bidder. The trial court's finding that Johnson's reasonable expectation had dissipated in the span of a month is not clearly erroneous. . . .

[Detrimental reliance also requires a general contractor to] prove that he actually and reasonably relied on the subcontractor's sub-bid. We decline to provide a checklist of potential methods of proving this reliance, but we will make several observations. First, a showing by the subcontractor, that the general contractor engaged in "bid shopping," or actively encouraged "bid chopping," or "bid peddling" is strong evidence that the general did not rely on the sub-bid. Second, prompt notice by the general contractor to the subcontractor that the general intends to use the sub on the job, is weighty evidence that the general did rely on the bid. Third, if a sub-bid is so low that a reasonably prudent general contractor would not rely upon it, the trier of fact may infer that the general contractor did not in fact rely upon the erroneous bid.

In this case, the trial judge did not make a specific finding that PEI failed to prove its reasonable reliance upon Johnson's sub-bid. We must assume, however, that it was his conclusion based on his statement that "the parties did not have a definite, certain meeting of the minds on a certain price for a certain quantity of goods and wanted to renegotiate. . . ." The August 26, 1993, fax from PEI to all prospective mechanical subcontractors, is evidence supporting this conclusion. Although the finding that PEI did not rely on Johnson's bid was indisputably a close call, it was not clearly erroneous.

Finally . . . the trial court, and not a jury, must determine that binding the subcontractor is necessary to prevent injustice. This element is to be enforced as required by common law equity courts — the general contractor must have "clean hands." This requirement includes, as did the previous element, that the general did not engage in bid shopping, chopping or peddling, but also requires the further determination that justice compels the result. . . .

Because there was sufficient evidence in the record to support the trial judge's conclusion that PEI had not proven its case for detrimental reliance, we must, and hereby do, affirm the trial court's ruling.

NOTES

1. *Questions about* **Pavel.** PEI asserted two separate grounds for recovery. The first was that it accepted Johnson's offer on September 1 prior to Johnson's attempt to withdraw the next day. The second ground was that they relied on Johnson's offer in submitting their bid to NIH and, therefore, Johnson's offer could not be withdrawn until PEI had a chance to formally accept it on September 28 once they had been awarded the NIH contract. Consider the first ground: The trial court rejected the argument that Johnson's offer was validly accepted by PEI's letter on September 1 which was prior to the attempted withdrawal on September 2. The appellate court held that this finding was supported by evidence that PEI had

indicated to Johnson prior to September 1 that it was no longer relying on Johnson's bid. Why would that fact preclude a subsequent acceptance by PEI? Does Restatement (Second) § 38 provide a possible answer? Now consider the second ground: If PEI had been awarded the prime contract from the outset, would that fact have strengthened its reliance arguments? As a general matter, on what promise does the prime contractor rely? Surely, the prime cannot argue successfully that it relied upon the sub-bid itself? After all, the sub-bid is *conditional*: It says, "we will perform the HVAC work *if* you agree to pay us $898,000." Until the general contractor accepts that offer, there is no unconditional promise on which to rely. Thus, in order to find that the offer is irrevocable, a second promise, "I will not revoke this bid if you use it," must be implied. It is this implied subsidiary promise that is then relied on by the general contractor in using the bid to make its own bid for the prime contract. The issue, then, is whether it is appropriate under these circumstances to imply a promise not to revoke where none is made expressly. In resolving that issue, the court in *Pavel Enterprises* cites extensively from the holdings in two famous prior cases: *James Baird v. Gimbel* and *Drennan v. Star Paving*. Study closely the reasoning of these two quite inconsistent approaches to the firm offer problem. How relevant is the fact that, after being awarded the prime contract, the general contractor faxed all the mechanical subs asking for a new price quote without the "Powers" piece? If PEI did not, in fact, rely on Johnson's bid, is it plausible to believe that they would have instituted suit for $32,000 and pursued the case all the way through the Maryland Court of Appeals?

 2. Baird *and* Drennan. In *James Baird v. Gimbel Bros.* and *Drennan v. Star Paving Co.*, the two cases that were discussed extensively in *Pavel Enterprises*, we see two judicial giants taking opposing positions on the question of the revocability of construction bids.

 In *Baird*, Judge Hand ruled that a subcontractor could revoke his bid at any point prior to a formal acceptance of the offer, even though the general contractor may have relied on the bid in computing his overall bid for the project. Judge Hand first rejected the general contractor's arguments that the use of the bid should, by itself, be seen as an acceptance of the sub's offer. On the central question of whether the court should imply a promise not to revoke the offer, Hand stated "[t]here is not the least reason to believe that the defendant meant to subject itself to such a one-sided obligation." At least as an initial proposition, this rule assigns to the general contractor the risk of a mistake by the subcontractor in calculating his bid. Since, under Hand's approach, a subcontractor is free to revoke his bid in the event of a mistake, is it fair to assume that this rule would make subcontractors less likely to take precautions in submitting bids, as they can rectify their mistakes afterward without penalty?

 Justice Traynor, in *Drennan*, however, decided that "as between the subcontractor who made the bid and the general contractor who reasonably relied on it the loss from the mistake should fall upon the party causing it." Traynor recognized that the initial assignment of this risk was only a default rule. Thus, he continued:

  Had defendant's bid expressly stated or clearly implied that it was revocable at any time before acceptance we would treat it accordingly. It was silent on revocation, however, and we must therefore determine whether there are conditions to the right of revocation *imposed by law or reasonably inferable in fact.*

Drennan, 333 P.2d at 759.

The doctrinal means of assigning the risk by default to the subcontractor was to imply a subsidiary promise not to revoke once the bid was reasonably relied upon by the general contractor. This result seems to give the subcontractor incentives to avoid costly errors, but does it cause general contractors to be less vigilant in comparing aberrant bids against those that are submitted by other subs? As the *Pavel Enterprises* court noted, most jurisdictions that have ruled on this question favor Traynor's approach, but many courts have not taken a position one way or the other so the debate continues.

Compare the discussion of the two opinions carefully. Exactly what point of disagreement separates Justice Traynor and Judge Hand? What result would you reach in *Pavel Enterprises* if you were to follow the analysis of Judge Hand in *James Baird*? Would you reach a different result by following the reasoning of Justice Traynor in *Drennan*? Consider the problem of irrevocable offers in terms of our earlier analysis of offers and preliminary negotiations. Is it to the offeror's benefit to make an offer irrevocable when the offeror receives nothing in return for forfeiting her power of revocation?

In his article *Promissory Estoppel and Traditional Contract Doctrine*, 78 Yale L.J. 343, 356 n.64 (1969), Stanley Henderson states that the effect of *Drennan* has been merely to "keep the power of acceptance alive for a reasonable time after the general contract is awarded. If the general contractor delays acceptance, or reopens negotiations, the protection made available by [reliance] is lost."

3. ***Empirical Assumptions and Contract Default Rules.*** Many of the rules of offer and acceptance analyzed so far could be justified in terms of a "cost-minimizing" criterion; that is, these rules can be justified as the terms that many (if not most) parties would bargain for, if required to do so, because they minimize (or at least reduce) the total cost of the *collective* risks that both parties face if they agree to contract. As we have observed a number of times, these rules are defaults — they apply only if the parties do not choose to design a tailor-made arrangement to suit their particular purposes. Central to the process of choosing contract default rules is the ability to predict which outcome most bargainers would, in fact, prefer. Often we have been able to tentatively resolve that issue by assuming that, other things being equal, parties would prefer to minimize the costs of contracting so as to enhance the size of the "contractual pie" available to be divided between them. It is not always obvious, however, which alternative formulations will best reduce contracting costs. The construction bid/firm offer problem is a case in point. The *Drennan* rule (since incorporated in Restatement (Second) § 87) would initially place the risk of a mistaken bid upon the subcontractor/offeror who would be bound to the bid once the bid was relied on by the general contractor. The traditional common law formulation, as reflected in *James Baird*, initially places the risk of a computation error by the subcontractor on the prime contractor/offeree who relies on the bid even though the sub remains "free" to withdraw. In either case, any two parties could quite easily agree to shift the risk from one to the other.

What default rule best reduces the risk of such errors? One way to answer that question is to ask which party typically enjoys the comparative advantage in guarding against and/or insuring against the risk of a mistake in the bidding process. It is tempting to argue that the subcontractor is better able to take precautions to reduce the likelihood of mistakes such as those occurring in *Baird*, *Drennan*, and *Pavel*. For example, the subcontractor could more readily double check figures, reread correspondence, etc. On the other hand, the general contractor is in the better position — once the mistake has been made — to minimize its impact by comparing bids to those entered by others, confirming unusually low proposals, etc.

In cases such as this — where the best default rule cannot easily be suggested intuitively — it may be wise to undertake more complex, and costly, empirical inquiries to see how the industry operates. One way to avoid excessive costs in rule formulation is simply to observe the terms reached within the industry over a period of time. Frequent efforts to opt out of the default rule are a useful signal that the rule (as applied in that industry) is based on suspect empirical assumptions. In the construction industry, a classic study by Frank Schultz, *The Firm Offer Puzzle: A Study of Business Practice in the Construction Industry*, 19 U. CHI. L. REV. 237 (1952), concluded that even though general contractors were in a position to do so, they did not frequently bargain for an "irrevocable offer" from their subcontractors as a condition for accepting the submission of the bids.

One reason why general contractors may not insist on receiving "firm offers" from their subs may be the presence of powerful extra-legal sanctions in the construction industry that constrain the subcontractors' inclination to revoke except for the most egregious mistakes. Assuming such extra-legal sanctions — loss of goodwill, a refusal to award bids in the future, etc., — are effective, this implies that subcontractors may already be exercising the appropriate level of care in reducing the risk of errors in bids. Retaining the common law default rule under those assumptions might be preferable because *both* parties would then be encouraged to take precautions (the general contractor must guard against the possibility of its own detrimental reliance and the sub against the costs of revoking a mistaken bid), while under the *Drennan* formulation the burden of precautions falls entirely on the subcontractor.

If Schultz's empirical study is valid, therefore, it argues for a return to the *Baird* rule. Despite this analysis, little outcry is heard from any interested parties. Why do you suppose this is so?

4. *The Problem of Bid Shopping.* Under the *Drennan* rule, the general contractor is free to accept or reject the sub's offer, however the sub has made an implied subsidiary promise not to revoke once the bid is reasonably relied upon by the general contractor. In *Southern California Acoustics Co. v. C. V. Holder, Inc.*, 71 Cal. 2d 719, 79 Cal. Rptr. 319, 456 P.2d 975 (1969), another Traynor opinion, a subcontractor mistakenly assumed it was awarded the subcontract and refrained from bidding on other jobs. The general contractor had originally used the sub's bid, however it substituted another subcontractor a month after being awarded the general contract. The court refused to find an analogous subsidiary promise by the general contractor not to reject the sub's bid, claiming that the sub did not demonstrate any promise by the general on which it detrimentally relied. The decision demonstrates one criticism of the *Drennan* rule:

> [I]t allows the general contractor to bid shop, or search for better subcontracting bids, leaving the subcontractor without any guarantee its bid will be accepted but without the option of bidding on other jobs in the meantime.

How can this concern be addressed by courts? How did the *Pavel* court address the bid shopping problem?

5. ***How Important is the Construction Bid Problem?*** The construction bid problem has been a staple in first year Contracts classes ever since the debate between two judicial giants — Hand and Traynor — was fully joined. But how relevant is the problem in the world of construction contracting? In *Traynor* (Drennan) *v. Hand* (Baird): *Much Ado About (Almost) Nothing*, 3 J. Legal Analysis 539 (2011), Professor Victor Goldberg argues, "Not very." Goldberg's analysis of the construction bidding cases shows that:

> Four facts stand out. First, while *Drennan* is the rule in most jurisdictions, application of the reliance qualification is, at best, problematic. Second, *Drennan* doesn't travel well. Aside from the general contractor versus subcontractor context, few opinions rely on *Drennan*. Third, its spawn, Section 87(2), has been a dud. Like *Drennan*, it is rarely cited outside the GC-sub context; but, unlike *Drennan*, it is rarely cited even in that context. Fourth, nearly all GC-sub cases involve a *public* construction project. The fact that the issue rarely seems to get litigated when the project is being done for private owners is the big result. *Drennan* and *Baird* are embedded in regulations of public construction, both of the owner-GC and GC-sub relationships, regulations that have been largely ignored in the contracts discourse. Despite their prominence in contracts casebooks, they are only peripherally contracts cases. The issue they deal with is more usefully framed as one aspect of public competitive bidding law.

Id. at 540–41.

C. OFFER AND COUNTEROFFER

[1] Introduction

Until now, we have talked about the formation of a contract in terms of offer and acceptance. While this characterization is correct, it ignores an intermediate, and often used, step of counteroffer. The Restatement (Second) of Contracts § 39(1) defines a counteroffer as "an offer made by an offeree to his offeror relating to the same matter as the original offer and proposing a substituted bargain differing from that proposed by the original offer." One important consequence of a counteroffer according to the procedural rules that have developed at common law is that it constitutes a rejection of the original offer, *unless* the offeror in her original offer, or the offeree in his counter-offer, expressly opt out of the default rule and provide that the original offer is not so terminated. See Restatement

(Second) § 39(2).

Consider, for example, *Dataserv Equipment, Inc. v. Technology Finance Leasing Corp.*, 364 N.W.2d 838 (Minn. Ct. App. 1985). Dataserv offered to sell computer components to Technology with a proviso that, InDepth, a designated third party, would install the components. Technology replied with a counteroffer in which they agreed to the deal if the proviso was removed. In response, Dataserv offered Technology the right to select any third party installer of their choosing. Finally, (as the price of the components began to fall), Dataserv purported to "accept" Technology's counteroffer by agreeing to delete the installation proviso altogether. The court held that the attempted "acceptance" did not create a contract obligating Technology to buy the components:

> Under familiar principles of contract law, a party's rejection terminates its power of acceptance. Restatement (Second) of Contracts § 38 (1981). Once rejected, an offer is terminated and cannot subsequently be accepted without ratification by the other party.

> The critical issue is whether Dataserv rejected Technology's October 1 counteroffer. Dataserv responded to Technology's October 1 counteroffer by agreeing to delete two of the three objectionable clauses, but insisting that the third be included. By refusing to accept according to the terms of the proposal, Dataserv rejected Technology's counteroffer and thus no contract was formed. Moreover, Dataserv's offer to substitute other third party installation companies, which Technology rejected, operated as a termination of its power to accept Technology's counteroffer. Dataserv's so-called "acceptance," when it offered to delete clause 8 on November 8, 1979, was without any legal effect whatsoever, except to create a new offer which Technology immediately rejected.

Id. at 841.

Can the default rule that a counteroffer operates as a rejection of the original offer be justified? The court noted in *Dataserv* that the price of computer equipment tends to depreciate quickly. Clearly, in such cases there are obvious benefits to a rule that regards a counter offer as a rejection of the original offer. The alternative possibility — a rule that requires offerors to treat a counteroffer as a step in a continuing negotiation process rather than as a rejection — would permit the offeree to play the market and await a fortuitous price adjustment. But should the rule be different for items — such as heavy equipment and other goods in use — that are expected to have a fairly constant value throughout the bargaining process? For cases where the motivation for the parties to contract is to assure a guaranteed source of supply rather than to allocate the risk of future price fluctuations, why shouldn't the rule be that a counteroffer is merely a proposal for addition to the contract and not a rejection of the initial offer? This question asks the analyst to consider the wisdom of courts attempting to develop more "tailored" default rules (such as the one just suggested) so as to more closely fit the market environment that the particular parties are facing. One might be tempted to argue that the "one size fits all" assumption of the common law rules governing offer and acceptance is unrealistic in a modern, complex and heterogeneous economy. On the other hand, as we noted in the Introduction to this Chapter, creating default rules is costly and the operative question should always be whether the state could generate more tailored rules at lower costs than the parties themselves who, after all, have the best information about the economic environments in which they operate.

In any case, given the rule that a counter-offer operates as a rejection of the original offer, the key question then becomes: exactly what kind of response by the offeree constitutes a counteroffer rather than an acceptance? We turn now that that question which has produced a substantial amount of litigation both at common law and under the UCC.

[2]   When is an "Acceptance" a Counteroffer? The Common Law View

[a]   The Mirror Image Rule

According to language found in many common law cases, an offer could only be accepted if the offeree agreed precisely and completely to the terms offered. If the terms of the "acceptance" varied in any way from the terms of the offer, that purported acceptance was deemed a counteroffer. As a counteroffer, the response was a rejection of the terms of the original offer and became the offer "on the table" with which parties had to deal. This exchange continued until the terms proposed by each party were identical. This requirement of a perfect matching of offer and response was termed the "mirror image" rule, for until all the terms mirrored one another, no contract was created. Note that the rule has two parts: the offer and the purported "acceptance" must match, and, if not, the resulting counteroffer has the effect of extinguishing the original offer.

The Restatement of Contracts § 38 (1932) expressed this mirror image rule, and you should read that section. According to § 38, parties could agree to hold an offer open despite disagreement on terms. Creation of an option contract, for example, was one way to keep the main offer open. Parties would then be able to dicker over contract provisions without fear that disagreement over terms would terminate the offer. Remember, however, that unless explicit provisions were made to hold the offer open, the general provisions of the mirror image rule governed.

What justification can be given to support such a strict rule? The mirror image rule provided some certainty to bargaining parties. Under the rule, they knew that they would not be bound to a contract unless each agreed to all terms. It took deliberate action to form a contract under such a system. If the opposite system prevailed — an offer followed by an acceptance "in principle" constitutes a binding agreement even though there is disagreement over certain terms — parties would take costly precautions to avoid being bound to an unfavorable contract. Not only might they want to avoid being bound, but once bound they would be unsure what their contractual obligation involved. In terms of certainty and predictability of contract negotiations, then, the mirror image rule made some sense. It could also be argued, however, that the rule was too rigid, that it was too hard to make a contract under this rule in a world of boilerplate terms and preprinted contracts

While the mirror image rule is generally not followed in its strictest form today, some of its underlying principles still survive. Courts still generally hold that a counteroffer serves to reject the initial offer, and such rejections extinguish the initial offer. In *Ardente v. Horan*, 117 R.I. 254, 366 A.2d 162 (1976), the plaintiff initially accepted the defendants' asking price for their house, but then the plaintiff insisted that certain items had to remain with the house. The defendants refused to part with such items, and they refused to sign the sale agreement and returned the plaintiff's down payment. The Supreme Court of Rhode Island noted that had the plaintiff merely executed and delivered the sale agreement, a valid acceptance would exist. By placing conditions upon his acceptance (the inclusion of the various household items), however, the plaintiff's letter functioned as a counteroffer. Offerees are generally not permitted to add conditions or limitations in their acceptance; a conditional acceptance is valid only if the acceptance is independent of the condition. Since the plaintiff's acceptance letter sought to verify that the items were included in the sale, the conditional acceptance "operated as a rejection of the defendants' offer, and no contractual obligation was created."

[b]   The Last Shot Doctrine

Operating in conjunction with the mirror image rule was a principle known as the "last shot" doctrine. This common law doctrine came into play whenever performance of some contract terms occurred in the absence of an exact agreement on all terms of the contract — that is, where one or both parties performed even though the mirror image rule had not been satisfied. According to the last shot doctrine, both parties were bound to the terms of the last offer (or counteroffer) given by one party to the other before commencement of performance. For example, Beth offers to buy from Sam 10 bushels of wheat at $1.10 per bushel, freight charges included. Sam replies that he will sell 10 bushels at $1.10, freight not included. Sam ships the 10 bushels of wheat and Beth accepts delivery (probably because she didn't pay attention to Sam's different terms). Although the writings are not in agreement, a court under the last shot doctrine would find that Beth's silence plus acceptance of the wheat was an acceptance of Sam's counteroffer and thus a contract was formed on Sam's terms. Beth must therefore pay the freight charges. Sam's terms were the "last shots fired" between the parties while negotiating, and those terms prevail.

Again, the common law provided bargaining parties with a degree of certainty. It was relatively easy under this rule to pinpoint the terms of a disputed contract and to assign liability. Do you sense that formalistic and arbitrary decisions could easily result from this principle? Is there a better way to decide what terms govern when the writings of the parties don't create a contract but they proceed nonetheless with delivery and payment in the belief that they had a deal? If so, would that method be more costly to administer than the mirror image and last shot rules? Consider these questions as you work to understand how the UCC has responded to the mirror image rule and the last shot doctrine.

[3]   UCC Section 2-207

The law governing counteroffers and the effect of responses that purport to accept an offer but have terms that vary from the offer has undergone widespread changes in recent decades. The UCC has changed substantially the common law rules on offers and counteroffers in an effort to deal with the so-called "battle of the forms". The battle is joined when commercial parties buy and sell goods using standardized purchase order and acknowledgment forms whose payment and delivery terms agree but whose boilerplate terms — governing, say, warranties, risk of loss and many other contingencies — are in conflict. To understand the evolution of the drafters' thinking about these issues, we begin by analyzing UCC § 2-207. Read that section carefully. If the subsections of § 2-207 appear to be obscure, ambiguous, or otherwise muddled, keep in mind that state and federal appellate courts have struggled, often with limited success, to provide consistent, comprehensible interpretations of this provision (in other words, you are not alone!).

We will evaluate below the various ways a binding contract can be formed under § 2-207. Consider first the following case:

IONICS, INC. v. ELMWOOD SENSORS
United States Court of Appeals First Circuit
110 F.3d 184 (1997)

Torruella, J.

The facts of the case are not in dispute. Elmwood manufactures and sells thermostats. Ionics makes hot and cold water dispensers, which it leases to its customers. On three separate occasions, Ionics purchased thermostats from Elmwood for use in its water dispensers. Every time Ionics made a purchase of thermostats from Elmwood, it sent the latter a purchase order form which contained, in small type, various "conditions." Of the 20 conditions on the order form, two are of particular relevance:

18. REMEDIES — The remedies provided Buyer herein shall be cumulative, and in addition to any other remedies provided by law or equity. A waiver of a breach of any provision hereof shall not constitute a waiver of any other breach. The laws of the state shown in Buyer's address printed on the masthead of this order shall apply in the construction hereof.

19. ACCEPTANCE — Acceptance by the Seller of this order shall be upon the terms and conditions set forth in items 1 to 17 inclusive, and elsewhere in this order. Said order can be so accepted only on the exact terms herein and set forth. No terms which are in any manner additional to or different from those herein set forth shall become a part of, alter or in any way control the terms and conditions herein set forth.

Near the time when Ionics placed its first order, it sent Elmwood a letter that it sends to all of its new suppliers. The letter states, in part:

The information preprinted, written and/or typed on our purchase order is especially important to us. Should you take exception to this information, please clearly express any reservations to us in writing. If you do not, we will assume that you have agreed to the specified terms and that you will fulfill your obligations according to our purchase order. If necessary, we will change your invoice and pay your invoice according to our purchase order.

Following receipt of each order, Elmwood prepared and sent an "Acknowledgment" form containing the following language in small type:

> THIS WILL ACKNOWLEDGE RECEIPT OF BUYER'S ORDER AND STATE SELLER'S WILLINGNESS TO SELL THE GOODS ORDERED BUT ONLY UPON THE TERMS AND CONDITIONS SET FORTH HEREIN AND ON THE REVERSE SIDE HEREOF AS A COUNTEROFFER. BUYER SHALL BE DEEMED TO HAVE ACCEPTED SUCH COUNTEROFFER UNLESS IT IS REJECTED IN WRITING WITHIN TEN (10) DAYS OF THE RECEIPT HEREOF, AND ALL SUBSEQUENT ACTION SHALL BE PURSUANT TO THE TERMS AND CONDITIONS OF THIS COUNTEROFFER ONLY; ANY ADDITIONAL OR DIFFERENT TERMS ARE HEREBY OBJECTED TO AND SHALL NOT BE BINDING UPON THE PARTIES UNLESS SPECIFICALLY AGREED TO IN WRITING BY SELLER.

Although this passage refers to a "counteroffer," we wish to emphasize that this language is not controlling. The form on which the language appears is labeled an "Acknowledgment" and the language comes under a heading that reads "Notice of Receipt of Order." The form, taken as a whole, appears to contemplate an order's confirmation rather than an order's rejection in the form of a counteroffer.

It is undisputed that the Acknowledgment was received prior to the arrival of the shipment of goods. . . . As we have noted, the Acknowledgment Form expressed Elmwood's willingness to sell thermostats on "terms and conditions" that the Form indicated were listed on the reverse side. Among the terms and conditions listed on the back was the following:

> 9. WARRANTY

> All goods manufactured by Elmwood Sensors, Inc. are guaranteed to be free of defects in material and workmanship for a period of ninety (90) days after receipt of such goods by Buyer or eighteen months from the date of manufacturer [sic] (as evidenced by the manufacturer's date code), whichever shall be longer. THERE IS NO IMPLIED WARRANTY OF MERCHANTABILITY AND NO OTHER WARRANTY, EXPRESSED OR IMPLIED, EXCEPT SUCH AS IS EXPRESSLY SET FORTH HEREIN. SELLER WILL NOT BE LIABLE FOR ANY GENERAL, CONSEQUENTIAL OR INCIDENTAL DAMAGES, INCLUDING WITHOUT LIMITATION ANY DAMAGES FROM LOSS OF PROFITS, FROM ANY BREACH OF WARRANTY OR FOR NEGLIGENCE, SELLER'S LIABILITY AND BUYER'S EXCLUSIVE REMEDY BEING EXPRESSLY LIMITED TO THE REPAIR OF DEFECTIVE GOODS F.O.B. THE SHIPPING POINT INDICATED ON THE FACE HEREOF OR THE REPAYMENT OF THE PURCHASE PRICE UPON THE RETURN OF THE GOODS OR THE GRANTING OF A REASONABLE ALLOWANCE ON ACCOUNT OF ANY DEFECTS, AS SELLER MAY ELECT.

Neither party disputes that they entered into a valid contract and neither disputes the quantity of thermostats purchased, the price paid, or the manner and time of delivery. The only issue in dispute is the extent of Elmwood's liability.

In summary, Ionics' order included language stating that the contract would be governed exclusively by the terms included on the purchase order and that all remedies available under state law would be available to Ionics. In a subsequent letter, Ionics added that Elmwood must indicate any objections to these conditions in writing. Elmwood, in turn, sent Ionics an Acknowledgment stating that the contract was governed exclusively by the terms in the Acknowledgment, and Ionics was given ten days to reject this "counteroffer." Among the terms included in the Acknowledgment is a limitation on Elmwood's liability. As the district court stated, "the terms are diametrically opposed to each other on the issue of whether all warranties implied by law were reserved or waived. . . ."

We face, therefore, a battle of the forms. This is purely a question of law. The dispute turns on whether the contract is governed by the language after the comma in § 2-207(1) of the Uniform Commercial Code, according to the rule laid down by this court in Roto-Lith, Ltd. v. F.P. Bartlett & Co., 297 F.2d 497 (1st Cir. 1962), or whether it is governed by subsection (3) of § 2-207. We find the rule of *Roto-Lith* to be in conflict with the purposes of section 2-207 and, accordingly, we overrule *Roto-Lith* and find that subsection (3) governs the contract. Analyzing the case under section 2-207, we conclude that Ionics defeats Elmwood's motion for partial summary judgment.

In *Roto-Lith*, Roto-Lith sent a purchase order to Bartlett, who responded with an acknowledgment that included language purporting to limit Bartlett's liability. Roto-Lith did not object. This court held that "a response which states a condition materially altering the obligation solely to the disadvantage of the offeror is an 'acceptance . . . expressly . . . conditional on assent to the additional . . . terms.'" Id. at 500. This holding took the case outside of section 2-207 by applying the exception after the comma in subsection (1). The court then reverted to common law and concluded that Roto-Lith "accepted the goods with knowledge of the conditions specified in the acknowledgment [and thereby] became bound." Id. at 500. In other words, the *Roto-Lith* court concluded that the defendant's acceptance was conditional on assent, by the buyer, to the new terms and, therefore, constituted a counter offer rather than an acceptance. When Roto-Lith accepted the goods with knowledge of Bartlett's conditions, it accepted the counteroffer and Bartlett's terms governed the contract. Elmwood argues that Roto-Lith governs the instant appeal, implying that the terms of Elmwood's acknowledgment govern.

Ionics claims that the instant case is distinguishable because in *Roto-Lith* "the seller's language limiting warranties implied at law was proposed as an addition to, but was not in conflict with, the explicit terms of the buyer's form. [In the instant case] the explicit terms of the parties' forms conflict with and reject each other . . ."

We do not believe that Ionics' position sufficiently distinguishes *Roto-Lith*. It would be artificial to enforce language that conflicts with background legal rules while refusing to enforce language that conflicts with the express terms of the contract. Every contract is assumed to incorporate the existing legal norms that are in place. It is not required that every contract explicitly spell out the governing law of the jurisdiction. Allowing later forms to govern with respect to deviations from the background rules but not deviations from the terms in the contract would imply that only the terms in the contract could be relied upon. Aside from being an artificial and arbitrary distinction, such a standard would, no doubt, lead parties to include more of the background rules in their initial forms, making forms longer and more complicated. Longer forms would be more difficult and time consuming to read — implying that even fewer forms would be read than under the existing rules. It is the failure of firms to read their forms that has brought this case before us, and we do not wish to engender more of this type of litigation.

Our inquiry, however, is not complete. Having found that we cannot distinguish this case from *Roto-Lith*, we turn to the Uniform Commercial Code. A plain language reading of section 2-207 suggests that subsection (3) governs the instant case. Ionics sent an initial offer to which Elmwood responded with its "Acknowledgment." Thereafter, the conduct of the parties established the existence of a contract as required by section 2-207(3).

Furthermore, the case before us is squarely addressed in comment 6, which states:

> 6. If no answer is received within a reasonable time after additional terms are proposed, it is both fair and commercially sound to assume that their inclusion has been assented to. Where clauses on confirming forms sent by both parties conflict[,] each party must be assumed to object to a clause of the other conflicting with one on the confirmation sent by himself. As a result[,] the requirement that there be notice of objection which is found in subsection (2) [of § 2-207] is satisfied and the conflicting terms do not become part of the contract. The contract then consists of the terms originally expressly agreed to, terms on which the confirmations agree, and terms supplied by this Act.

This Comment addresses precisely the facts of the instant case. Any attempt at distinguishing the case before us from section 2-207 strikes us as disingenuous.

We are faced, therefore, with a contradiction between a clear precedent of this court, *Roto-Lith*, which suggests that the language after the comma in subsection (1) governs, and the clear dictates of the Uniform Commercial Code, which indicate that subsection (3) governs. It is our view that the two cannot co-exist and the case at bar offers a graphic illustration of the conflict. We have, therefore, no choice but to overrule our previous decision in Roto-Lith, Ltd. v. F.P. Bartlett & Co., 297 F.2d 497 (1st Cir. 1962). Our decision brings this circuit in line with the majority view on the subject and puts to rest a case that has provoked considerable criticism from courts and commentators alike.

We hold, consistent with section 2-207 and Official Comment 6, that where the terms in two forms are contradictory, each party is assumed to object to the other party's conflicting clause. As a result, mere acceptance of the goods by the buyer is insufficient to infer consent to the seller's terms under the language of subsection (1). Nor do such terms become part of the contract under subsection (2) because notification of objection has been given by the conflicting forms. See § 2-207(2)(c).

The alternative result, advocated by Elmwood and consistent with *Roto-Lith*, would undermine the role of section 2-207. Elmwood suggests that "a seller's expressly conditional acknowledgment constitutes a counteroffer where it materially alters the terms proposed by the buyer, and the seller's terms govern the contract between the parties when the buyer accepts and pays for the goods. . . ." Under this view, section 2-207 would no longer apply to cases in which forms have been exchanged and subsequent disputes reveal that the forms are contradictory. That is, the last form would always govern.

The purpose of section 2-207, as stated in *Roto-Lith*, "was to modify the strict principle that a response not precisely in accordance with the offer was a rejection and a counteroffer." 297 F.2d at 500. Under the holding advocated by Elmwood, virtually any response that added to or altered the terms of the offer would be a rejection and a counteroffer. We do not think that such a result is consistent with the intent of section 2-207 and we believe it to be expressly contradicted by Comment 6.

Applied to this case, our holding leads to the conclusion that the contract is governed by section 2-207(3). Section 2-207(1) is inapplicable because Elmwood's acknowledgment is conditional on assent to the additional terms. The additional terms do not become a part of the contract under section 2-207(2) because notification of objection to conflicting terms was given on the order form and because the new terms materially alter those in the offer. Finally, the conduct of the parties demonstrates the existence of a contract, as required by section 2-207(3). Thus, section 2-207(3) applies and the terms of the contract are to be determined in accordance with that subsection.

We conclude, therefore, that section 2-207(3) prevails and "the terms of the particular contract consist of those terms on which the writings of the parties agree, together with any supplementary terms incorporated under any other provisions of this chapter."

The reality of modern commercial dealings, as this case demonstrates, is that not all participants read their forms. To uphold Elmwood's view would not only fly in the face of Official Comment 6 to section 2-207 of the Uniform Commercial Code, and the overall purpose of that section, it would also fly in the face of good sense. The sender of the last form (in the instant case, the seller) could insert virtually any conditions it chooses into the contract, including conditions contrary to those in the initial form. The final form, therefore, would give its sender the power to re-write the contract. Under our holding today, we at least ensure that a party will not be held to terms that are directly contrary to the terms it has included in its own form. Rather than assuming that a failure to object to the offeree's conflicting terms indicates offeror's assent to those terms, we shall make the more reasonable inference that each party continues to object to the other's contradictory terms. We think it too much to grant the second form the power to contradict and override the terms in the first form.

For the reasons stated herein, the district court's order denying Elmwood's motion for partial summary judgment is affirmed and the case is remanded to the district court for further proceedings.

NOTES

1. ***The Drafters' Comment.*** Comment 1 to § 2-207 explained the situations to which the UCC provision applies:

> This section is intended to deal with two typical situations. The one is the written confirmation, where an agreement has been reached either orally or by informal correspondence between the parties and is followed by one or both of the parties sending formal memoranda embodying the terms so far as agreed upon and adding terms not discussed. The other situation is offer and acceptance, in which a wire or letter expressed and intended as an acceptance or the closing of an agreement adds further minor suggestions or proposals such as "ship by Tuesday," "rush," "ship draft against bill of lading inspection allowed," or the like. A frequent example of the second situation is the exchange of printed purchase order and acceptance (sometimes called "acknowledgment") forms. Because the forms are oriented to the thinking of the respective drafting parties, the terms contained in them often do not correspond. Often the seller's form contains terms different from or additional to those set forth in the buyer's form. Nevertheless, the parties proceed with the transaction.

2. ***The Structure of Section 2-207.*** UCC § 2-207 is a significant change from the common law rules governing counteroffers. The section specifies three different ways that a contract can be created when additional terms are present in a counteroffer or acknowledgment.

First. UCC § 2-207(1), clause 1: The first clause of UCC § 2-207(1) maps out the route: "A definite and seasonable expression of acceptance or a written confirmation which is sent within a reasonable time operates as an acceptance even though it states terms additional to or different from those offered or agreed upon." Thus, an acceptance operates here just as it would were there no additional terms — a contract is formed. But what is to be done with the additional terms?

UCC § 2-207(2) provides for the additional terms. Several outcomes are possible, depending on the situation. Generally, between merchants, additional terms that do not materially alter the deal are to be added to the contract, and, absent objection by a party, those terms become part of the contract.[19]

Freedom of contract is retained, however, for parties can prevent the automatic inclusion of additional terms. According to § 2-207(2)(a), parties can limit contractual terms to those put forth in the offer by including such an express provision in the contract. Section 2-207(2)(c) states that a party can reject additional terms by notifying the other party of his objection to those additional terms.

Finally, the additional terms themselves may ensure that they are not included in the contract, according to § 2-207(2)(b). As noted above, additional terms which "materially alter" a contract will not be included in that contract.[20]

---

[19] You should read the definition of "merchant" in UCC § 2-104(1).

[20] Official Comments 4 and 5 to § 2-207 provide examples of terms which do and do not "materially alter" a contract, respectively.

To summarize, a contract is made under § 2-207(1), clause 1, when an offer is tendered and acceptance is given. The resulting contract is based on the terms of the original offer. Additional terms either become part of the contract or are excluded from the contract, depending on how § 2-207(2) deals with them.

Second. UCC § 2-207(1), clause 2: The second route to a contract springs from a negative implication of the second clause in § 2-207(2). That clause affirms the ability of an offeree to make a counteroffer as part of an expression of acceptance as long as the acceptance is expressly made conditional on assent to the new proposals. If the original offeror expressly agrees to those additional terms, a contract is formed, based on the terms of the counteroffer. (Note that clause 2 of § 2-207(1) bypasses § 2-207(2) by providing its own means of dealing with additional terms.)

In brief, a contract is formed under § 2-207(1), clause 2, when an offer is tendered, an expressly conditional acceptance is given, and the offeror expressly agrees to the additional terms.

Third. UCC § 2-207(3): The third and final route to a contract is specified in § 2-207(3). Where a contract has not been formed under subsection (1), conduct of the parties may establish a contract under subsection (3). An example of this situation is the exchange of an order form by the offeror for an acknowledgment form from the offeree. Frequently, the standard printed provisions on each form do not match, but the goods are delivered and accepted anyway. If a contract cannot be established under § 2-207(1) (because the purported acceptance is made expressly conditional on assent to its terms), the additional terms provided by the acknowledgment form are treated as an express counteroffer and are not automatically incorporated into the contract. At this point, if one looks only to the writings, no contract has been formed. But the goods have been shipped and the buyer has accepted and paid for them. Subsequently, if a dispute arises between the parties, its resolution turns on this question: what are the terms of the contract that was formed by their actions? Under § 2-207(3), the contract is based on those terms "on which the writings of the parties agree." In addition, supplementary terms which are covered by other provisions of the UCC (such as place of delivery, § 2-308, and implied warranties, §§ 2-314 and 2-315) are incorporated into the contract. Comment 7 to § 2-207 reveals the drafters' purposes.

> Subsection (3) was, in other words, designed to preempt the "last shot" doctrine. Instead of the last form exchanged establishing the terms of a contract, the provisions on which the writings of both parties agree, together with Code-supplied contract clauses, establish the terms of the contract.

3. *Examining the* Roto-Lith *Decision.* *Roto-Lith*, which was discussed extensively and overruled in *Ionics*, was the first case to examine the impact and effect of § 2-207 on commercial contracts between merchants. The case was widely criticized. The basis for the criticism has been summarized as follows:

> The *Roto-Lith* reasoning has not been well-received. Indeed, the weight of authority uncovered by our research rejects the *Roto-Lith* approach because it permits a result that § 2-207 was designed to avert, i.e., it revives

the "last-shot" technique available to an offeree under the common-law mirror-image rule. Thus, acceptance of the *Roto-Lith* rationale would subvert the very purpose of § 2-207 by binding an offeror to the terms contained in his offeree's "counter-offer" when the offeror takes delivery of the goods and performs his part of the bargain. Nor would the purpose of § 2-207 be well-served by allowing an offeree's responsive document to state additional or different terms, and provide that the terms will be deemed accepted by the offeror's inaction. To permit this . . . seems inconsistent with the objective of Section 2-207, and would allow the offeree . . . almost unilaterally to reinstate the common-law rationale, for the hypothesis of Section 2-207 that businessmen do not read exchanged printed forms assumes that the offeror-buyer would not learn of the term. Furthermore, the clause placing the burden of affirmative objection on the original offeror is itself a modification of the offer to which the offeror should first have to assent, and absent its assent, any shipping and acceptance of the goods should be deemed to constitute the consummation of the contract under (Section 2-207)(3).[21]

4.   *Section 2-207 Comment 6.* The court in *Ionics* concluded that the parties established the existence of a contract through sufficient conduct under § 2-207(3). Then, the court insisted that the facts of the case are squarely addressed by § 2-207 Comment 6. The problem with this analysis is that Comment 6 deals only with contract formation with an agreement and (usually) a writing — i.e., contract formation under § 2-207(1). Notice that Comment 6 addresses how to deal with proposals for additional terms under subsection (2) and, specifically, conflicting terms on *confirming forms* under § 2-207(2)(c). Subsection (2) provides guidance for treatment of additional terms only where a contract has formed with an agreement under subsection (1). Subsection (3), read alone, has its own manner of determining contract terms.

5.   *Additional and Different Terms.* The first sentence of § 2-207 refers to "terms additional to or different from" the offer. The second sentence refers only to "[t]he additional terms." Is this a drafting error? Why might the section distinguish "different" from "additional"? Assuming the distinction is intentional, a harder question is what is supposed to happen to "different" terms under § 2-207(2)? In *Superior Boiler Works v. R.J. Sanders, Inc*, 711 A.2d 628 (R.I. 1998), the Rhode Island Supreme Court addressed the different approaches to this question:

> Courts have taken three divergent approaches to this question. . . . In brief the first approach treats "different" terms as a subgroup of "additional" terms. The result is that such different terms, when material, simply do not become part of the contract and thus the original delivery term offered [by offeror] would control. The second approach reaches the same result by concluding that "the offeror's terms control because the offeree's different terms merely fall out [of the contract]; § 2-207(2) cannot rescue the different terms since that subsection applies only to additional terms." Id. Finally, the third approach, aptly named the "knock-out rule," holds that

---

[21] Deusenberg & King, Sales and Bulk Transfers § 3.06(4) (1977). *See also Uniroyal, Inc. v. Chambers Gasket & Mfg. Co.,* 380 N.E.2d 571 (Ind. Ct. App. 1978).

the conflicting terms cancel one another, leaving a blank in the contract with respect to the unagreed-upon term that would be filled with one of the UCC's "gap-filler" provisions. . . .

After due consideration we conclude that both prudence and the weight of authority favor adoption of the knock-out rule as the law of this jurisdiction. . . . We conclude that this approach best promotes the UCC's aim to abrogate the criticized common-law mirror image rule and its attendant last-shot doctrine and avoids "re-enshrin[ing] the undue advantages derived solely from the fortuitous positions of when a party sent a form." Because of the UCC's gap-filling provisions, we recognize that this approach might result in the enforcement of a contract term that neither party agreed to and, in fact, in regard to which each party expressed an entirely different preference. We note in response to this concern that the offeror and the offeree both have the power to protect any term they deem critical by expressly making acceptance conditional on assent to that term. And as merchants, both parties should have been well aware that their dealings were subject to the UCC and to its various gap- filling provisions.

Professor Victor Goldberg criticizes the knock-out rule in *The "Battle of the Forms": Fairness, Efficiency, and the Best-Shot Rule*, 76 OR. L. REV. 155 (1997). He argues instead for a "best shot" rule under which a court, faced with conflicting terms, must choose one form or the other based on the criterion of overall "fairness." Goldberg suggests that this rule would encourage parties when drafting standard form terms to take the other's interests into account.

6.   *Use of Context.* Some courts interpreting § 2-207 have looked at the broader business context when determining which terms should be controlling. For instance, in *Schulze & Burch Biscuit Co. v. Tree Top, Inc.*, 831 F.2d 709 (7th Cir. 1987), the court, in discussing a questionable mandatory arbitration clause, noted that such clauses are generally regarded as being material alterations to the proposed agreement. The court was careful to note, however, that it would not be a material alteration if the party had reason to know that such a clause would be included. To determine whether or not they had reason to know, the court examined the prior relationship between the two companies (course of dealing) as well as standard practices in the industry (usage of trade).

7.   *Rules versus Standards.* Judge Aldrich in *Roto-Lith* complained that § 2-207 "is not too happily drafted." Indeed, commentators have often noted the problems created by the ambiguous language of § 2-207. One way to think about the evolution from the common law "mirror image" rule to § 2-207 is to evaluate the progression as a movement along a continuum from bright line rules at one pole to broad standards at the other. Many of the provisions of Article 2 are drafted in broad general language that delegates much discretion to courts. In contrast, many of the common law rules governing offer and acceptance — such as the mirror image rule — are bright line rules that are relatively clear and precise.

What difference does it make whether a statutory provision is drafted broadly or precisely? A bright-line rule — e.g., the speed limit is 55 miles per hour — is one that considers only a single easily determined fact. Such a rule is easy for a fact finder to apply, but because of its precision the rule may not accurately reflect the underlying legal norm which the rule is intended to reflect, which in this case is to encourage safe driving behavior. On the other hand, a broad standard — e.g., "drive reasonably" — considers and evaluates many relevant facts. Such a provision better reflects the underlying legal norm that supports the rule. But what is gained in correctly reflecting the legal norm may be lost in the frequency of error in applying the standard to particular cases. Thus, the standard "drive reasonably" is harder for courts (or fact finders) to apply to particular situations consistently. Professors Douglas Baird and Robert Weisberg have pointed out a few of the considerations governing the choice between rules and standards in the drafting of § 2-207 in *Rules, Standards and the Battle of the Forms: A Reassessment of § 2-207*, 68 VA. L. REV. 1217, 1224–25 (1982). They evaluate the trade-off between "rules" and "standards" that is reflected in the Code's formulation of the rule:

> The Code's "standard" approach does have notable virtues. The approach does not create incentives for parties to bargain over contract terms whose benefits are smaller than the cost of negotiating them. Perhaps parties that exchange conflicting forms could easily resolve differences in nondickered terms, if negotiation costs were low enough. Indeed, the Code's off-the-rack terms may give parties the terms they would have settled on if they had negotiated over them. A standard based on the principles of 2-207 may give parties to some transactions what they would have gotten had they spent more time and money bargaining. The standard, therefore, allows these parties to get the terms they want without the costs associated with establishing them through negotiations.

> It is crucial to realize, however, that the Code's off-the-rack terms fit some parties and some transactions better than others, and that parties suffer when off-the-rack terms are imposed that are not in their interest. Where an off-the-rack provision categorically prefers a buyer to a seller or a seller to a buyer, the court may be unable to supply a term in the best interests of both parties. Where the off-the-rack provision works as an open-ended standard, the court may fail to exercise its discretion in the parties' interests.

Id. at 1249–53.

You should continue to evaluate the pros and cons of rules versus standards. We will return to this trade-off many times in the materials that follow.

D.   CONTRACT FORMATION IN THE INTERNET AGE

Traditional contract doctrine presupposes that contracting parties have engaged in some type of bilateral communication prior to the consummation of a deal. With the advent of the "technology revolution" brought on by the widespread use of the personal computer and accelerated by the Internet, people are increasingly able to engage in exchanges without direct communication — instead, sales are often consummated with a few clicks of a mouse. How can contract law adjust to the changed circumstances with which many individuals and firms conduct business? Of particular focus is how the law might respond to the rise in "rolling contracts;" transactions where key terms and conditions of the agreement often follow rather than precede the decision to purchase a product.[22] Frequently, the issue involves the use of soft-ware licensing agreements that are designed to protect the intellectual property rights of the seller of goods in which software is embedded. These transactions are variously termed "shrink wrap," "click wrap" or "browse-wrap" agreements: the common denominator in each instance is that not only are many of the key terms of sale not fully negotiated, but they may not even be presented to the purchaser prior to her decision to buy. The question is whether there should be separate rules for "Internet contracting," or can the traditional rules simply be applied to a contemporary context? Does contemporary commerce involve circumstances that were unforeseen by the courts and legislators who formulated contract doctrine? Consider the following two cases.

STEP-SAVER DATA SYSTEMS, INC. v. WYSE TECHNOLOGY
United States Court of Appeals, Third Circuit
939 F.2d 91 (1991)

WISDOM, J.

The "Limited Use License Agreement" printed on a package containing a copy of a computer program raises the central issue in this appeal. The trial judge held that the terms of the Limited Use License Agreement governed the purchase of the package, and, therefore, granted the software producer, The Software Link, Inc. ("TSL"), a directed verdict on claims of breach of warranty brought by a disgruntled purchaser, Step-Saver Data Systems, Inc. We disagree with the district court's determination of the legal effect of the license, and reverse and remand the warranty claims for further consideration.

The growth in the variety of computer hardware and software has created a strong market for these products. It has also created a difficult choice for consumers, as they must somehow decide which of the many available products will best suit their needs. To assist consumers in this decision process, some companies will evaluate the needs of particular groups of potential computer users, compare those needs with the available technology, and develop a package of hardware and software to satisfy those needs. Beginning in 1981, Step-Saver performed this function as a value added retailer for International Business Machine (IBM) products. It would combine hardware and software to satisfy the word processing, data management, and communications needs for offices of physicians and lawyers. It originally marketed single computer systems, based primarily on the IBM personal computer.

As a result of advances in micro-computer technology, Step-Saver developed and marketed a multi-user system. With a multi-user system, only one computer is required. Terminals are attached, by cable, to the main computer.

From these terminals, a user can access the programs available on the main computer. After evaluating the available technology, Step-Saver selected a program by TSL, entitled Multilink Advanced, as the operating system for the multi-user

---

[22] For discussion, see Robert A. Hillman, *Rolling Contracts*, 71 FORDHAM L. REV. 743 (2002).

system. Step-Saver selected WY-60 terminals manufactured by Wyse, and used an IBM AT as the main computer. For applications software, Step-Saver included in the package several off-the-shelf programs, designed to run under Microsoft's Disk Operating System ("MS-DOS"), as well as several programs written by Step-Saver. Step-Saver began marketing the system in November of 1986, and sold one hundred forty-two systems mostly to law and medical offices before terminating sales of the system in March of 1987. Almost immediately upon installation of the system, Step-Saver began to receive complaints from some of its customers.[23]

Step-Saver, in addition to conducting its own investigation of the problems, referred these complaints to Wyse and TSL, and requested technical assistance in resolving the problems. After several preliminary attempts to address the problems, the three companies were unable to reach a satisfactory solution, and disputes developed among the three concerning responsibility for the problems. As a result, the problems were never solved. At least twelve of Step-Saver's customers filed suit against Step-Saver because of the problems with the multi-user system.

Once it became apparent that the three companies would not be able to resolve their dispute amicably, Step-Saver filed suit . . . alleging breach of warranties by both TSL and Wyse. The district court's actions provide the foundation for this appeal.

On the first day of trial, the district court specifically agreed with the basic contention of TSL that the form language printed on each package containing the Multilink Advanced program ("the box-top license") was the complete and exclusive agreement between Step-Saver and TSL under § 2-202 of the Uniform Commercial Code (UCC). Based on § 2-316 of the UCC, the district court held that the box-top license disclaimed all express and implied warranties otherwise made by TSL. The court therefore granted TSL's motion in limine to exclude all evidence of the earlier oral and written express warranties allegedly made by TSL and dismissed TSL from the case.

Step-Saver appeals [alleging that] Step-Saver and TSL did not intend the box-top license to be a complete and final expression of the terms of their agreement.

The relationship between Step-Saver and TSL began in the fall of 1984 when Step-Saver asked TSL for information on an early version of the Multilink program. TSL provided Step-Saver with a copy of the early program, known simply as Multilink, without charge to permit Step-Saver to test the program to see what it could accomplish. Step-Saver performed some tests with the early program, but did not market a system based on it.

In the summer of 1985, Step-Saver noticed some advertisements in Byte magazine for a more powerful version of the Multilink program, known as Multilink Advanced. Step-Saver requested information from TSL concerning this new version of the program, and allegedly was assured by sales representatives that the new

---

[23] [3] According to the testimony of Jeffrey Worthington, an employee of Step-Saver, twenty to twenty-five of the purchasers of the multi-user system had serious problems with the system that were never resolved.

version was compatible with ninety percent of the programs available "off-the-shelf" for computers using MS-DOS. The sales representatives allegedly made a number of additional specific representations of fact concerning the capabilities of the Multilink Advanced program.

Based on these representations, Step-Saver obtained several copies of the Multilink Advanced program in the spring of 1986, and conducted tests with the program. After these tests, Step-Saver decided to market a multi-user system which used the Multilink Advanced program. From August of 1986 through March of 1987, Step-Saver purchased and resold 142 copies of the Multilink Advanced program. Step-Saver would typically purchase copies of the program in the following manner. First, Step-Saver would telephone TSL and place an order. (Step-Saver would typically order twenty copies of the program at a time.) TSL would accept the order and promise, while on the telephone, to ship the goods promptly. After the telephone order, Step-Saver would send a purchase order, detailing the items to be purchased, their price, and shipping and payment terms. TSL would ship the order promptly, along with an invoice. The invoice would contain terms essentially identical with those on Step- Saver's purchase order: price, quantity, and shipping and payment terms. No reference was made during the telephone calls, or on either the purchase orders or the invoices with regard to a disclaimer of any warranties.

Printed on the package of each copy of the program, however, would be a copy of the box-top license. The box-top license contains five terms relevant to this action:

(1) The box-top license provides that the customer has not purchased the software itself, but has merely obtained a personal, non-transferable license to use the program.

(2) The box-top license, in detail and at some length, disclaims all express and implied warranties except for a warranty that the disks contained in the box are free from defects.

(3) The box-top license provides that the sole remedy available to a purchaser of the program is to return a defective disk for replacement; the license excludes any liability for damages, direct or consequential, caused by the use of the program.

(4) The box-top license contains an integration clause, which provides that the box-top license is the final and complete expression of the terms of the parties' agreement.

(5) The box-top license states: "Opening this package indicates your acceptance of these terms and conditions. If you do not agree with them, you should promptly return the package unopened to the person from whom you purchased it within fifteen days from date of purchase and your money will be refunded to you by that person."

The district court, without much discussion, held, as a matter of law, that the box-top license was the final and complete expression of the terms of the parties' agreement. Because the district court decided the questions of contract formation and interpretation as issues of law, we review the district court's resolution of these questions *de novo.*

Step-Saver contends that the contract for each copy of the program was formed when TSL agreed, on the telephone, to ship the copy at the agreed price. The box-top license, argues Step-Saver, was a material alteration to the parties' contract which did not become a part of the contract under UCC § 2-207. . . . TSL argues that the contract between TSL and Step-Saver did not come into existence until Step-Saver received the program, saw the terms of the license, and opened the program packaging. TSL contends that too many material terms were omitted from the telephone discussion for that discussion to establish a contract for the software. Second, TSL contends that its acceptance of Step-Saver's telephone offer was conditioned on Step-Saver's acceptance of the terms of the box-top license. Therefore, TSL argues, it did not accept Step-Saver's telephone offer, but made a counteroffer represented by the terms of the box-top license, which was accepted when Step-Saver opened each package. Third, TSL argues that, however the contract was formed, Step-Saver was aware of the warranty disclaimer, and that Step-Saver, by continuing to order and accept the product with knowledge of the disclaimer, assented to the disclaimer.

As a basic principle, we agree with Step-Saver that UCC § 2-207 governs our analysis. We see no need to parse the parties' various actions to decide exactly when the parties formed a contract. TSL has shipped the product, and Step-Saver has accepted and paid for each copy of the program. The parties' performance demonstrates the existence of a contract. The dispute is, therefore, not over the existence of a contract, but the nature of its terms. When the parties' conduct establishes a contract, but the parties have failed to adopt expressly a particular writing as the terms of their agreement, and the writings exchanged by the parties do not agree, UCC § 2-207 determines the terms of the contract.

To understand why the terms of the license should be considered under § 2-207 in this case, we review briefly the reasons behind § 2-207. Under the common law of sales, and to some extent still for contracts outside the UCC, an acceptance that varied any term of the offer operated as a rejection of the offer, and simultaneously made a counteroffer. This common law formality was known as the mirror image rule, because the terms of the acceptance had to mirror the terms of the offer to be effective. If the offeror proceeded with the contract despite the differing terms of the supposed acceptance, he would, by his performance, constructively accept the terms of the "counteroffer", and be bound by its terms. As a result of these rules, the terms of the party who sent the last form, typically the seller, would become the terms of the parties' contract. This result was known as the "last shot rule."

The UCC, in § 2-207, rejected this approach. Instead, it recognized that, while a party may desire the terms detailed in its form if a dispute, in fact, arises, most parties do not expect a dispute to arise when they first enter into a contract. As a result, most parties will proceed with the transaction even if they know that the terms of their form would not be enforced. The insight behind the rejection of the last shot rule is that it would be unfair to bind the buyer of goods to the standard terms of the seller, when neither party cared sufficiently to establish expressly the terms of their agreement, simply because the seller sent the last form. Thus, UCC

§ 2-207 establishes a legal rule that proceeding with a contract after receiving a writing that purports to define the terms of the parties' contract is not sufficient to establish the party's consent to the terms of the writing to the extent that the terms of the writing either add to, or differ from, the terms detailed in the parties' earlier writings or discussions. In the absence of a party's express assent to the additional or different terms of the writing, section 2-207 provides a default rule that the parties intended, as the terms of their agreement, those terms to which both parties have agreed, along with any terms implied by the provisions of the UCC.

The reasons that led to the rejection of the last shot rule, and the adoption of section 2-207, apply fully in this case. TSL never mentioned during the parties' negotiations leading to the purchase of the programs, nor did it, at any time, obtain Step-Saver's express assent to, the terms of the box-top license. Instead, TSL contented itself with attaching the terms to the packaging of the software, even though those terms differed substantially from those previously discussed by the parties. Thus, the box-top license, in this case, is best seen as one more form in a battle of forms, and the question of whether Step-Saver has agreed to be bound by the terms of the box-top license is best resolved by applying the legal principles detailed in section 2-207.

TSL advances several reasons why the terms of the box-top license should be incorporated into the parties' agreement under a § 2-207 analysis. First, TSL argues that the parties' contract was not formed until Step-Saver received the package, saw the terms of the box-top license, and opened the package, thereby consenting to the terms of the license. TSL argues that a contract defined without reference to the specific terms provided by the box-top license would necessarily fail for indefiniteness. Second, TSL argues that the box-top license was a conditional acceptance and counter-offer under § 2-207(1). Third, TSL argues that Step-Saver, by continuing to order and use the product with notice of the terms of the box-top license, consented to the terms of the box-top license.

TSL argues that the parties intended to license the copies of the program, and that several critical terms could only be determined by referring to the box-top license. Pressing the point, TSL argues that it is impossible to tell, without referring to the box-top license, whether the parties intended a sale of a copy of the program or a license to use a copy. TSL cites *Bethlehem Steel Corp. v. Litton Industries* in support of its position that any contract defined without reference to the terms of the box-top license would fail for indefiniteness. From the evidence, it appears that the following terms, at the least, were discussed and agreed to, apart from the box-top license: (1) the specific goods involved; (2) the quantity; and (3) the price. TSL argues that the following terms were only defined in the box-top license: (1) the nature of the transaction, sale or license; and (2) the warranties, if any, available. TSL argues that these two terms are essential to creating a sufficiently definite contract. We disagree.

Unlike the terms omitted by the parties in *Bethlehem Steel Corp.*, the two terms cited by TSL are not "gaping holes in a multi-million dollar contract that no one but the parties themselves could fill." First, the rights of the respective parties under the federal copyright law if the transaction is characterized as a sale of a copy of the program are nearly identical to the parties' respective rights under the terms of the box-top license.[24] Second, the UCC provides for express and implied warranties if the seller fails to disclaim expressly those warranties. Thus, even though warranties are an important term left blank by the parties, the default rules of the UCC fill in that blank.

TSL advances two reasons why its box-top license should be considered a conditional acceptance under UCC § 2-207(1). First, TSL argues that the express language of the box-top license, including the integration clause and the phrase "opening this product indicates your acceptance of these terms", made TSL's acceptance "expressly conditional on assent to the additional or different terms". Second, TSL argues that the box-top license, by permitting return of the product within fifteen days if the purchaser does not agree to the terms stated in the license (the "refund offer"), establishes that TSL's acceptance was conditioned on Step-Saver's assent to the terms of the box-top license, citing *Monsanto Agricultural Products Co. v. Edenfield*. While we are not certain that a conditional acceptance analysis applies when a contract is established by performance, we assume that it does and consider TSL's arguments.

To determine whether a writing constitutes a conditional acceptance, courts have established three tests. Under the first test, an offeree's response is a conditional acceptance to the extent it states a term "materially altering the contractual obligations solely to the disadvantage of the offeror". . . . We note that adopting this test would conflict with the express provision of UCC § 2-207(2)(b). Under § 2-207(2)(b), additional terms in a written confirmation that "materially alter [the contract]" are construed "as proposals for addition to the contract," not as conditional acceptances.

A second approach considers an acceptance conditional when certain key words or phrases are used, such as a written confirmation stating that the terms of the confirmation are "the only ones upon which we will accept orders." The third approach requires the offeree to demonstrate an unwillingness to proceed with the transaction unless the additional or different terms are included in the contract.

Although we are not certain that these last two approaches would generate differing answers,[25] we adopt the third approach for our analysis because it best reflects the understanding of commercial transactions developed in the UCC. Section 2-207 attempts to distinguish between: (1) those standard terms in a form

---

[24] [23] The most significant difference would be that, under the terms of the license, Step-Saver could not transfer the copies without TSL's consent, while Step-Saver could do so under the federal copyright law if it had purchased the copy. Even if we assume that federal law would not preempt state law enforcement of this aspect of the license, this difference is not material to this case in that both parties agree that Step-Saver had the right to transfer the copies to purchasers of the Step-Saver multi-user system. We hold that contract was sufficiently definite without the terms provided by the box-top license.

[25] [36] Under the second approach, the box-top license might be considered a conditional acceptance, but Step-Saver, by accepting the product, would not be automatically bound to the terms of the box-top license. *See Diamond Fruit Growers, Inc.*, 794 F.2d at 1444. Instead, courts have applied UCC § 2-207(3) to determine the terms of the parties' agreement. The terms of the agreement would be those "on which the writings of the parties agree, together with any supplementary terms incorporated under any other provisions of this Act." UCC § 2-207(3). Because the writings of the parties did not agree on the warranty disclaimer and limitation of remedies terms, the box-top license version of those terms would not be included in the parties' contract; rather, the default provisions of the UCC would govern.

confirmation, which the party would like a court to incorporate into the contract in the event of a dispute; and (2) the actual terms the parties understand to govern their agreement. The third test properly places the burden on the party asking a court to enforce its form to demonstrate that a particular term is a part of the parties' commercial bargain.

Using this test, it is apparent that the integration clause and the "consent by opening" language is not sufficient to render TSL's acceptance conditional. As other courts have recognized, this type of language provides no real indication that the party is willing to forego the transaction if the additional language is not included in the contract.

The second provision provides a more substantial indication that TSL was willing to forego the contract if the terms of the box-top license were not accepted by Step-Saver. On its face, the box-top license states that TSL will refund the purchase price if the purchaser does not agree to the terms of the license. Even with such a refund term, however, the offeree/counterofferor may be relying on the purchaser's investment in time and energy in reaching this point in the transaction to prevent the purchaser from returning the item. Because a purchaser has made a decision to buy a particular product and has actually obtained the product, the purchaser may use it despite the refund offer, regardless of the additional terms specified after the contract formed. But we need not decide whether such a refund offer could ever amount to a conditional acceptance; the undisputed evidence in this case demonstrates that the terms of the license were not sufficiently important that TSL would forego its sales to Step-Saver if TSL could not obtain Step-Saver's consent to those terms.

TSL asks us to infer, based on the refund offer, that it was willing to forego its sales to Step-Saver unless Step-Saver agreed to the terms of the box-top license. Such an inference is inconsistent with the fact that both parties agree that the terms of the box-top license *did not represent the parties' agreement* with respect to Step-Saver's right to transfer the copies of the Multilink Advanced program. Although the box-top license prohibits the transfer, by Step-Saver, of its copies of the program, both parties agree that Step-Saver was entitled to transfer its copies to the purchasers of the Step- Saver multi-user system. Thus, TSL was willing to proceed with the transaction despite the fact that one of the terms of the box-top license was not included in the contract between TSL and Step-Saver. We see no basis in the terms of the box-top license for inferring that a reasonable offeror would understand from the refund offer that certain terms of the box-top license, such as the warranty disclaimers, were essential to TSL, while others such as the non-transferability provision were not.

Based on these facts, we conclude that TSL did not clearly express its unwillingness to proceed with the transactions unless its additional terms were incorporated into the parties' agreement. The box-top license did not, therefore, constitute a conditional acceptance under UCC § 2-207(1).

When a disclaimer is not expressed until after the contract is formed, UCC § 2-207 governs the interpretation of the contract, and, between merchants, such disclaimers, to the extent they materially alter the parties' agreement, are not incorporated into the parties' agreement.

Under section 2-207, an additional term detailed in the box-top license will not be incorporated into the parties' contract if the term's addition to the contract would materially alter the parties' agreement. Step-Saver alleges that several representations made by TSL constitute express warranties, and that valid implied warranties were also a part of the parties' agreement. Because the district court considered the box-top license to exclude all of these warranties, the district court did not consider whether other factors may act to exclude these warranties. The existence and nature of the warranties is primarily a factual question that we leave for the district court, but assuming that these warranties were included within the parties' original agreement, we must conclude that adding the disclaimer of warranty and limitation of remedies provisions from the box-top license would, as a matter of law, substantially alter the distribution of risk between Step-Saver and TSL. Therefore, under UCC § 2-207(2)(b), the disclaimer of warranty and limitation of remedies terms of the box-top license did not become a part of the parties' agreement.

Based on these considerations, we reverse the trial court's holding that the parties intended the box-top license to be a final and complete expression of the terms of their agreement. Despite the presence of an integration clause in the box-top license, the box-top license should have been treated as a written confirmation containing additional terms. Because the warranty disclaimer and limitation of remedies terms would materially alter the parties' agreement, these terms did not become a part of the parties' agreement. We remand for further consideration the express and implied warranty claims against TSL.

HILL v. GATEWAY 2000
United States Court of Appeals, Seventh Circuit
105 F.3d 1147 (1997)

EASTERBROOK, J.

A customer picks up the phone, orders a computer, and gives a credit card number. Presently a box arrives, containing the computer and a list of terms, said to govern unless the customer returns the computer within 30 days. Are these terms effective as the parties' contract, or is the contract term-free because the order-taker did not read any terms over the phone and elicit the customer's assent?

One of the terms in the box containing a Gateway 2000 system was an arbitration clause. Rich and Enza Hill, the customers, kept the computer more than 30 days before complaining about its components and performance. They filed suit in federal court arguing, among other things, that the product's shortcomings make Gateway a racketeer (mail and wire fraud are said to be the predicate offenses), leading to treble damages under RICO for the Hills and a class of all other purchasers. Gateway asked the district court to enforce the arbitration clause; the judge refused, writing that "the present record is insufficient to support a finding of a valid arbitration agreement between the parties or that the plaintiffs were given adequate notice of the arbitration clause." Gateway took an immediate appeal, as is its right.

The Hills say that the arbitration clause did not stand out: they concede noticing the statement of terms but deny reading it closely enough to discover the agreement to arbitrate, and they ask us to conclude that they therefore may go to court. Yet an agreement to arbitrate must be enforced "save upon such grounds as exist at law or in equity for the revocation of any contract." 9 U.S.C. § 2. Doctor's Associates, Inc. v. Casarotto, 116 S. Ct. 1652, 134 L. Ed. 2d 902 (1996), holds that this provision of the Federal Arbitration Act is inconsistent with any requirement that an arbitration clause be prominent. A contract need not be read to be effective; people who accept take the risk that the unread terms may in retrospect prove unwelcome. Terms inside Gateway's box stand or fall together. If they constitute the parties' contract because the Hills had an opportunity to return the computer after reading them, then all must be enforced.

ProCD, Inc. v. Zeidenberg, 86 F.3d 1447 (7th Cir. 1996), holds that terms inside a box of software bind consumers who use the software after an opportunity to read the terms and to reject them by returning the product. Likewise, Carnival Cruise Lines, Inc. v. Shute, 499 U.S. 585, 111 S. Ct. 1522, 113 L. Ed. 2d 622 (1991), enforces a forum-selection clause that was included among three pages of terms attached to a cruise ship ticket. ProCD and Carnival Cruise Lines exemplify the many commercial transactions in which people pay for products with terms to follow; ProCD discusses others. 86 F.3d at 1451-52. The district court concluded in ProCD that the contract is formed when the consumer pays for the software; as a result, the court held, only terms known to the consumer at that moment are part of the contract, and provisos inside the box do not count. Although this is one way a contract could be formed, it is not the only way: "A vendor, as master of the offer, may invite acceptance by conduct, and may propose limitations on the kind of conduct that constitutes acceptance. A buyer may accept by performing the acts the vendor proposes to treat as acceptance." Id. at 1452. Gateway shipped computers with the same sort of accept-or-return offer ProCD made to users of its software. ProCD relied on the Uniform Commercial Code rather than any peculiarities of Wisconsin law; both Illinois and South Dakota, the two states whose law might govern relations between Gateway and the Hills, have adopted the UCC; neither side has pointed us to any atypical doctrines in those states that might be pertinent; ProCD therefore applies to this dispute.

Plaintiffs ask us to limit ProCD to software, but where's the sense in that? ProCD is about the law of contract, not the law of software. Payment preceding the revelation of full terms is common for air transportation, insurance, and many other endeavors. Practical considerations support allowing vendors to enclose the full legal terms with their products. Cashiers cannot be expected to read legal documents to customers before ringing up sales. If the staff at the other end of the phone for direct-sales operations such as Gateway's had to read the four-page statement of terms before taking the buyer's credit card number, the droning voice would anesthetize rather than enlighten many potential buyers. Others would hang up in a rage over the waste of their time. And oral recitation would not avoid customers' assertions (whether true or feigned) that the clerk did not read term X to them, or that they did not remember or understand it. Writing provides benefits for both sides of commercial transactions. Customers as a group are better off when vendors skip costly and ineffectual steps such as telephonic recitation, and use instead a simple approve-or-return device. Competent adults are bound by such documents, read or unread. For what little it is worth, we add that the box from Gateway was crammed with software. The computer came with an operating system, without which it was useful only as a boat anchor. Gateway also included many application programs. So the Hills' effort to limit ProCD to software would not avail them factually, even if it were sound legally — which it is not.

For their second sally, the Hills contend that ProCD should be limited to executory contracts (to licenses in particular), and therefore does not apply because both parties' performance of this contract was complete when the box arrived at their home. This is legally and factually wrong: legally because the question at hand concerns the formation of the contract rather than its performance, and factually because both contracts were incompletely performed. ProCD did not depend on the fact that the seller characterized the transaction as a license rather than as a contract; we treated it as a contract for the sale of goods and reserved the question whether for other purposes a "license" characterization might be preferable. All debates about characterization to one side, the transaction in ProCD was no more executory than the one here: Zeidenberg paid for the software and walked out of the store with a box under his arm, so if arrival of the box with the product ends the time for revelation of contractual terms, then the time ended in ProCD before Zeidenberg opened the box. But of course ProCD had not completed performance with delivery of the box, and neither had Gateway. One element of the transaction was the warranty, which obliges sellers to fix defects in their products. The Hills have invoked Gateway's warranty and are not satisfied with its response, so they are not well positioned to say that Gateway's obligations were fulfilled when the motor carrier unloaded the box. What is more, both ProCD and Gateway promised to help customers to use their products. Long-term service and information obligations are common in the computer business, on both hardware and software sides. Gateway offers "lifetime service" and has a round-the-clock telephone hotline to fulfil this promise. Some vendors spend more money helping customers use their products than on developing and manufacturing them. The document in Gateway's box includes promises of future performance that some consumers value highly; these promises bind Gateway just as the arbitration clause binds the Hills.

Next the Hills insist that ProCD is irrelevant because Zeidenberg was a "merchant" and they are not. Section 2-207(2) of the UCC, the infamous battle-of-the-forms section, states that "additional terms [following acceptance of an offer] are to be construed as proposals for addition to a contract. Between merchants such terms become part of the contract unless . . .". Plaintiffs tell us that ProCD came out as it did only because Zeidenberg was a "merchant" and the terms inside ProCD's box were not excluded by the "unless" clause. This argument pays scant attention to the opinion in ProCD, which concluded that, when there is only one form, "§ 2-207 is irrelevant." 86 F.3d at 1452. The question in ProCD was not whether terms were added to a contract after its formation, but how and when the contract was formed — in particular, whether a vendor may propose that a contract of sale be formed, not in the store (or over the phone) with the payment of money or a general "send me the product," but after the customer has had a chance to inspect both the item and the terms. ProCD answers "yes," for merchants and consumers alike. Yet again, for what little it is worth we observe that the Hills misunderstand the setting of ProCD. A "merchant" under the UCC "means a person who deals in goods of the kind or otherwise by his occupation holds himself out as having knowledge or skill peculiar to the practices or goods involved in the transaction", § 2-104(1). Zeidenberg bought the product at a retail store, an uncommon place for merchants to acquire inventory. His corporation put ProCD's database on the Internet for anyone to browse, which led to the litigation but did not make Zeidenberg a software merchant.

At oral argument the Hills propounded still another distinction: the box containing ProCD's software displayed a notice that additional terms were within, while the box containing Gateway's computer did not. The difference is functional, not legal. Consumers browsing the aisles of a store can look at the box, and if they are unwilling to deal with the prospect of additional terms can leave the box alone, avoiding the transactions costs of returning the package after reviewing its contents. Gateway's box, by contrast, is just a shipping carton; it is not on display anywhere. Its function is to protect the product during transit, and the information on its sides is for the use of handlers ("Fragile!" "This Side Up!") rather than would-be purchasers.

Perhaps the Hills would have had a better argument if they were first alerted to the bundling of hardware and legal-ware after opening the box and wanted to return the computer in order to avoid disagreeable terms, but were dissuaded by the expense of shipping. What the remedy would be in such a case — could it exceed the shipping charges? — is an interesting question, but one that need not detain us because the Hills knew before they ordered the computer that the carton would include some important terms, and they did not seek to discover these in advance. Gateway's ads state that their products come with limited warranties and lifetime support. How limited was the warranty — 30 days, with service contingent on shipping the computer back, or five years, with free onsite service? What sort of support was offered? Shoppers have three principal ways to discover these things. First, they can ask the vendor to send a copy before deciding whether to buy. The Magnuson-Moss Warranty Act requires firms to distribute their warranty terms on request, 15 U.S.C. § 2302 (b)(1)(A); the Hills do not contend that Gateway would have refused to enclose the remaining terms too. Concealment would be bad for business, scaring some customers away and leading to excess returns from others. Second, shoppers can consult public sources (computer magazines, the Web sites of vendors) that may contain this information. Third, they may inspect the documents after the product's delivery. Like Zeidenberg, the Hills took the third option. By keeping the computer beyond 30 days, the Hills accepted Gateway's offer, including the arbitration clause. The decision of the district court is vacated, and this case is remanded with instructions to compel the Hills to submit their dispute to arbitration.

NOTES

1. *Questions on* **Step-Saver** *and* **Gateway.** In each of these cases, what is the point at which a contract is formed? What are the key terms that led to the resulting litigation, and why were the parties unable to agree on what terms were part of the contract? In each case can you identify the words or conduct that constitute the

offer (and which party is the offeror), and what acts constitute the acceptance of the offer?

In trying to answer these questions, begin first by trying to evaluate the sequence of interactions from the perspective of Judge Easterbrook in *Gateway*. Recall that silence ordinarily does not constitute acceptance. But in *Gateway*, the court held that the buyers' decision not to ship the product back serves as a form of action-by-inaction. In choosing not to return the merchandise, the buyer was held to have engaged in a promissory act of the type envisioned in § 30 of the Restatement. This sort of conduct is also validated in § 2-204(1) of the UCC. In *ProCD Inc. v. Zeidenberg*, which is cited extensively in *Gateway*, Judge Easterbrook outlined the basis for this approach to the problem:

> Must buyers of computer software obey the terms of shrinkwrap licenses? The district court held not [because] they are not contracts because the licenses are inside the box rather than printed on the outside. [W]e disagree with the district judge's conclusion. Shrinkwrap licenses are enforceable unless their terms are objectionable on grounds applicable to contracts in general (for example, if they violate a rule of positive law, or if they are unconscionable).[26] Because no one argues that the terms of the license at issue here are troublesome, we remand with instructions to enter judgment for the plaintiff.

> According to the district court, the UCC does not countenance the sequence of money now, terms later. . . . To judge by the flux of law review articles discussing shrinkwrap licenses, uncertainty is much in need of reduction — although businesses seem to feel less uncertainty than do scholars, for only three cases (other than ours) touch on the subject, and none directly addresses it. [T]hese are not consumer transactions. Step-Saver is a battle-of-the-forms case, in which the parties exchange incompatible forms and a court must decide which prevails. Our case has only one form; UCC § 2-207 is irrelevant.

> What then does the current version of the UCC have to say? We think that the place to start is § 2-204(1): "A contract for sale of goods may be made in any manner sufficient to show agreement, including conduct by both parties which recognizes the existence of such a contract." A vendor, as master of the offer, may invite acceptance by conduct, and may propose limitations on the kind of conduct that constitutes acceptance. A buyer may accept by performing the acts the vendor proposes to treat as acceptance. And that is what happened. ProCD proposed a contract that a buyer would accept by using the software after having an opportunity to read the license at leisure. This Zeidenberg did. He had no choice, because the software splashed the license on the screen and would not let him proceed without indicating acceptance. So although the district judge was right to say that a contract can be, and often is, formed simply by paying the price and walking out of the store, the UCC permits contracts to be formed in other

---

[26] For a criticism of enforcing shrink-wrapped licenses as a limitation on the freedom from contract, see Omri Ben-Shahar, *Freedom from Contract*, 2004 WIS. L. REV. 261, 265.

ways. ProCD proposed such a different way, and without protest Zeidenberg agreed. Ours is not a case in which a consumer opens a package to find an insert saying "you owe us an extra $10,000" and the seller files suit to collect. Any buyer finding such a demand can prevent formation of the contract by returning the package, as can any consumer who concludes that the terms of the license make the software worth less than the purchase price. Nothing in the UCC requires a seller to maximize the buyer's net gains.

86 F.3d 1447 at 1449.

One can conceptualize the interactions differently, however, by changing the roles of offeror and offeree. One could, for example, interpret the sequence in *Gateway* just as Judge Wisdom did in *Step-Saver*, as consisting of an offer to purchase by the buyer with the shipment of the product constituting an acceptance by the seller — together with additional terms provided with the shipment. Under this paradigm, it matters whether the common law or the UCC rules on additional terms govern. Under the common law, the mirror image rule would apply, and there would be no contract as the counteroffer (the additional terms) differs from the initial offer. The buyer's use of the goods, however, would serve as an acceptance of the counteroffer, and under the last shot doctrine, the seller's terms would prevail.

As Judge Wisdom held in *Step-Saver*, however, under the UCC this interaction would be handled under § 2-207. As there has been a "definite and seasonal acceptance," a contract clearly exists under § 2-207(1). If the buyer is a non-merchant consumer, the additional terms would be viewed as mere proposals for addition to the contract. If the buyer is a merchant, the additional terms would be part of the contract unless they materially altered the contract (as Judge Wisdom found that they did in *Step-Saver*). Thus, a contract would exist on the buyer's terms, supplemented by the default rules of the UCC — a marked contrast from the common law approach.

2. *The Controversy Continues.* Should § 2-207 guide the resolution of disputes such as those in *StepSaver* and *Gateway*? Or is Judge Easterbrook's correct in his comment that, in these "shrink wrap" cases, "§ 2-207 is irrelevant" due to the existence of only one form? The issue has generated much academic commentary (most critical of Easterbrook's opinion[27]) and a considerable amount of litigation (most accepting the result if not the reasoning in *Gateway*). In *Klocek v. Gateway, Inc.*, 104 F. Supp. 2d 1332 (D. Kan. 2000), the District Court held, contrary to Easterbrook's opinion, that a consumer was not bound by an arbitration clause that

---

[27] *See* Richard Craswell, *The Sound of One Form Battling*, 98 Mich. L. Rev. 2727 (2000); Clayton Gillette, *Rolling Contracts as an Agency Problem*, 2004 Wis. L. Rev. 679; James J. White, *Contracting Under Amended 2-207*, 2004 Wis. L. Rev. 723; Jean Braucher, *Amended Article 2 and the Decision to Trust the Courts: The Case Against Enforcing Delayed Mass-Market Terms, Especially for Software*, 2004 Wis. L. Rev. 753; Roger Bern, *"Terms Later" Contracting: Bad Economics, Bad Morals, and a Bad Idea for a Uniform Law, Judge Easterbrook Notwithstanding*, 12 J.L. & Pol'y 641 (2004); Robert L. Oakley, *Fairness in Electronic Contracting: Minimum Standards for Non-Negotiated Contracts*, 42 Hous. L. Rev. 1041 (2005); Gregory E. Maggs, *The Waning Importance of Revisions to U.C.C. Article 2*, 78 Notre Dame L. Rev. 595 (2003); William H. Lawrence, *Rolling Contracts Rolling Over Contract Law*, 41 San Diego L. Rev. 1099 (2004); Colin P. Marks, *The Limits of Limiting Liability in the Battle of the Forms: U.C.C. Section 2-207 and the Material Alteration Inquiry*, 33 Pepp. L. Rev. 501 (2005)

was enclosed in the box containing the shipped scanner. The court concluded:

> Disputes under [section] 2-207 often arise in the context of a battle of the forms, but nothing in its language precludes application in a case which involves only one form. . . . By its terms, section 2-207 applies to an acceptance or written confirmation. It states nothing which requires another form before the provision becomes effective. In fact, the official comment to the section specifically provides that sections 2-207(1) and (2) apply where 'an agreement had been reached orally . . . and is followed by one or both of the parties sending formal memoranda embodying the terms so far agreed and adding terms not discussed.

Id. at 1339.[28]

Notwithstanding the (justifiable) criticism of the interpretation of § 2-207 reached in *Gateway*, Judge Easterbrook's argument that consumers simply are not interested in having obscure clauses read to them prior to their purchase of complex computer products appears to have won the day. In *DeFontes v. Dell, Inc.*, 984 A.2d 1061 (R.I. 2009), the Rhode Island Supreme Court undertook a comprehensive review of the case law and concluded that the cases that approved the rolling contract transaction had become the majority rule. The court explained:

> The ProCD line of cases . . . is better reasoned and more consistent with contemporary consumer transactions. It is simply unreasonable to expect a seller to apprise a consumer of every term and condition at the moment he or she makes a purchase.

Id. at 1071.

3. *Should There be Special Rules for E-Commerce?* The special problems raised by rolling contracts were a prime focus of the failed efforts to revise Article 2 during the 1990s. During the process of drafting revisions to Article 2 the reporters proposed a version of § 2-207 that was designed to resolve the so-called "Gateway problem." Owing to strong opposition from industry interest groups, however, the proposal was deleted.

The proposed draft of § 2-207 that was defeated by industry opposition read as follows:

> If a contract for sale is formed in any manner and thereafter the seller in a record proposes terms to the buyer that vary [add to or differ from] terms previously agreed, the following rules apply:
>
> (1) If the seller could have disclosed the varying terms to the buyer in a commercially reasonable manner at the time of contract formation and failed to do so, the terms do not become part of the contract unless expressly agreed to by the buyer.
>
> (2) If the seller could not have disclosed the varying terms to the buyer in a commercially reasonable manner, the seller shall by conspicuous language in a record notify the buyer at the time of contract formation

---

[28] A similar result was reached in *Rogers v. Dell Computer Corp.*, 138 P.3d 826 (Okla. 2005).

that additional or different terms will be proposed.

    (A)   If the seller gives conspicuous notice, the buyer may either accept the proposed terms by any method reasonable under the circumstances or reject the proposed terms and return the goods.

    (B)   If the seller fails to give conspicuous notice, the proposed terms do not become part of the contract unless expressly agreed to by the buyer.

(3)   Upon returning goods to the seller, the buyer has a right to:

    (A)   a refund; and

    (B)   reimbursement of any reasonable expenses incurred related to the return and in compliance with any instructions of the seller for return or, in the absence of instructions, return postage or similar reasonable expenses in returning the goods.

Under this proposed version of § 2-207, how do you believe a court would handle *Step-Saver* and *Gateway*? Is the proposed "cure" that the reporters advocated for the "Gateway problem" worse than the "disease"?

The rolling contract problem was also addressed independently by the NC-CUSL. In 1999, the NCCUSL approved the Uniform Computer Information Transactions Act (UCITA), which provides rules for computer information transactions. UCITA has been submitted to state legislatures across the country in the attempt to create a single uniform statute. In March 2000, Virginia became the first state to adopt UCITA. Maryland followed suit the following year. Some of the key features of UCITA include expressly recognizing the "shrink-wrap" licenses found in *ProCD*, permitting firms to select the forum where disputes are to be litigated, and protecting Internet companies from liability when their networks are used to spread illegal or defamatory information. UCITA has been generally praised by Internet and software companies, but has received criticism from various consumer organizations as being overly merchant-friendly. Continuing opposition by consumer interests has successfully blocked further efforts to adopt UCITA. It is likely that any further attempt to draft uniform legislation to govern these transactions would be stalled by interest group opposition.

In the meantime, the ALI began a project to draft *Principles for the Law of Software Contracts*. These *Principles* were published by the ALI in 2010, and are now offered to courts to aid them in resolving disputes over computer information transactions. The ALI *Principles* do endorse the use of form contracts but they also seek to provide some protection to the unwary customer. Section 2-02 requires that any form contract containing terms and conditions be "reasonably accessible electronically prior to the agreement being concluded" and that the customer have "reasonable notice" of the terms and signify her acceptance by "not exercising the opportunity to return the software unopened for a full refund within a reasonable time after the transfer." Is the rule proposed by the *Principles* a preferable middle ground between the more regulatory approach of the proposed revision of the drafting committee to § 2-207 or the "laissez faire" solution provided in UCITA?

How would a court decide *StepSaver* and *Gateway* under the ALI Principles?

4.   *The Enforceability of Internet Retail Contracting.* Box-top licenses differ from Internet-created contracts in a key aspect: a one-click Internet contract may not really present a § 2-207 issue at all. A common example is when a firm asks a customer to assent to its terms and conditions before it authorizes the contemplated purchase. Anyone who has downloaded a song from Apple's iTunes or purchased anything from Amazon.com is certainly familiar with this increasingly common experience. However, unlike in *Gateway v. Hill*, in Internet retail cases there is no second communication — verbal, written, or otherwise — that can do battle with the company's terms. Nonetheless, courts have struggled with the quandary of the enforceability of such contracts, often using legal tools such as procedural unconscionability. In *Just One Click: The Reality of Internet Retail Contracting*, 108 COLUM. L. REV. 984 (2008), Professors Ronald Mann and Travis Siebeneicher examine the puzzle of so-called "click-wrap" contracts through an empirical study:

> [F]ew retailers — only about 6% in our population — use contracting interfaces sufficiently robust to make it reasonable to expect that their contracts are enforceable against their customers. Even more surprisingly, the contracts found on internet retailers' websites contain the standard, pro-seller boilerplate provisions — arbitration, disclaimers of consequential damages, and the like — much less frequently than would be expected. No such clauses appear in the contracts for more than half of the retailers that we studied. We attribute the appearance of the clauses in almost half of the contracts to the conflict between two motivations: the desire to have terms that appear to be benign and the desire to have terms (albeit not in a binding form) to which consumers will accede in the event of a dispute.

Id. at 1011. In short, while these click wrap contracts might ultimately be unenforceable if a customer were to challenge them in court, many firms have learned that they can "succeed in altering the practical terms of their relations with customers without obtaining enforceable contracts."

5.   *Cognitive Overload in Contractual Bargaining.* Contracts such as the ones in *Gateway* v. *Hill* and *ProCD* may offend the autonomy of consumers because they fail to present the consumer with the choice of purchase only after a review of all the offeror's terms and conditions: the consumer decides whether or not to make a purchase (i.e., to accept) prior to fully understanding the full consequences of the decision. But is it optimal for sellers to fully describe their terms before shipping the product? Would consumers even want a sales representative to recite all the terms of purchase while they are in the store or on the phone? Professor Eric Posner summarizes this puzzle:

> Buyers do not have the time or patience to listen to or read and understand the terms. The optimal terms cannot be disclosed without causing cognitive overload. . . . The nub of the problem is that sellers and buyers need a way for sellers to convey sufficient information about a product prior to the contract, without boring buyers or driving them to distraction. As is always the case with contract, the failure to solve this problem hurts sellers and buyers. If the seller conveys too much information, she will drive away

buyers. If the seller conveys too little information, she will mislead buyers and possibly drive them away as well.

Eric A. Posner, ProCD v. Zeidenberg *and Cognitive Overload in Contractual Bargaining*, 77 U. Chi. L. Rev. 1181 (2010).

One solution to this problem would be what Posner calls a "return rule," which, similar to Judge Easterbrook's reasoning in *ProCD*, allows the full terms of such contracts to be enforceable if consumers can reasonably return a product once they have received it at home and read the complete terms. *Id.* at 1191. A rational consumer can choose to read the terms, accept the risk associated with not reading them, or send the product back. Posner notes that since *ProCD* there have been no appellate cases involving a shrink-wrap license contract with an offensive term that does not include a reasonable return clause, indicating that "sellers either do not use such terms or buyers, relying on branding to protect them, do not object to them." *Id.* at 1194.

5. ***Ritualistic Contracts.*** In *Autistic Contracts*, 45 Wayne L. Rev. 1693 (2000), Professor James J. White suggests that many modern form contracts, such as those discussed in *Gateway* and *Step-Saver*, require inferences of agreement based upon the buyer's ritualistic actions. He notes:

> Parties to modern form contracts sometimes interact with one another in the same way a parent of an autistic child interacts with that child. When a licensor offers a software license with the assertion that it will infer acceptance of all the license terms if the licensee removes the power cord from the plastic wrapper, the licensor is drawing an inference from the licensee's behavior just as doubtful as the inference a hopeful parent draws from an autistic child's apparently knowing response to the parent's statement.

Id. at 1693.

White characterizes such method of assent as "autistic" because it is "non-verbal and subject to differing interpretations, or when verbal, is not directly responsive to what has come before."

The practices of computer companies exemplify the need for tailored rules to govern these kinds of contracts. White cites the example of a consumer who orders a Gateway computer that is loaded with Microsoft software. The customer realizes that some of her payment goes to Microsoft, but never deals directly with the software company. The computer arrives with the software pre-installed, and a statement on the power cord indicates that the consumer will agree to abide by the terms of the Microsoft license by opening the plastic wrapping containing the cord. Thus, the opening of the wrapping serves as a form of ritualistic assent to the terms of Microsoft's license, even though the buyer has not engaged in any communication with Microsoft.

White suggests that such ritualistic affirmations should be considered valid if it is economically efficient for companies to engage in them. To that end, his argument follows the lines of Judge Easterbrook's discussion in *Gateway* of the problems of requiring the seller's representatives to orally read the warranty terms to impatient buyers prior to consummating the sale. White concludes,

> [M]any autistic contracts should be recognized, for in many cases, the reduction in transaction costs made possible by an autistic ritual will easily outweigh the costs imposed on dissenting offerees. This is particularly true where there are many contracts (and so much savings). On the other hand, where a single contract controls a large quantity of goods or services, an autistic ritual is unlikely to be more efficient and so should be questioned. In all cases, the law should insist that the offeree not be bound to an autistic contract until he has had a reasonable opportunity to know the terms offered.

Id. at 1731.

6.   *The Political Economy of the UCC.* The continuing debates over the failure to adopt any amendments to Article 2 raise the issue of whether the ALI and NCCUSL — the unique combination of private law reform organizations that together produce the provisions of the UCC that are then offered to the states on a "take it or leave it" basis — do a good job in formulating commercial law rules. The specific questions that underlie this issue include the following: what does this process do relatively well and what does it do relatively badly in comparison to an appropriate baseline such as the ordinary legislative process? And further, are there structural factors that bias the products of the uniform laws process notwithstanding the good will and effort of those who have worked hard in the law reform process?

In *The Political Economy of Private Legislatures*, 143 U. Pa. L. Rev. 595 (1995), Alan Schwartz and Robert Scott have argued that the uniform laws process works well when it focuses on projects that require technical expertise, but does a poor job when it tackles the legal regulation of complex commercial and economic endeavors about which there are strong and competing views. In their article, Schwartz and Scott predict that the ambitious Article 2 revision that was then underway would fail and that the end result would be a series of vague and inconclusive amendments that largely reinforced the status quo. This prediction would hold, they said, regardless of the dedication and effort of the participants in the process. This is because the outcome of the uniform laws process is the product of powerful structural forces. Whenever there is competition among interest groups with no single group dominating, as is the case in Article 2, the process produces vague and imprecise rules that delegate broad discretion to courts. These rules result, the authors argue, because dedicated academic reformers propose them when they are unable to get clear, bright-line rules enacted. In sum, the argument is that the pressure to formulate rules that will be uniformly adopted distorts the rules themselves in ways that may, quite perversely, undermine the very objective of a uniform law in the first instance.

Why might the uniform laws process perform badly relative to the ordinary legislative process? Schwartz and Scott argue that there are inherent limitations in the uniform laws process that are not found in the ordinary legislative process. These limitations include the lack of standing committees and of standing committee structures for gathering information, providing empirical data and monitoring the efforts of interest groups. They include as well the lack of organized political parties and of the useful practice of log rolling that enables the process of legislative consensus and of harmonizing critical value choices to proceed.

Does the failure of the Article 2 revision process tend to confirm or rebut the arguments of Schwartz and Scott? Consider some of the reasons for the prolonged (and ultimately unsuccessful) adoption process given by Richard Speidel, who was the principal reporter for the Article 2 revision project.

In *Introduction to Symposium on Proposed Revised Article 2*, 54 Smu L. Rev. 787 (2001), Speidel made the following points:

> First, most businesses were content with Article 2 as written and viewed any changes with skepticism. Second, there was great difficulty satisfying both consumer interest groups and businesses. Third, commercial interests threatened to lobby against the adoption of the revision if they were not satisfied, a serious threat given the NCCUSL's goal of universal adoption for the revision.

E.　BIBLIOGRAPHY AND SUGGESTED READING

Ian Ayres & Robert Gertner, *Filling Gaps in Incomplete Contracts: An Economic Theory of Default Rules*, 99 Yale L.J. 87 (1989).

Douglas Baird & Robert Weisberg, *Rules, Standards and the Battle of the Forms: A Reassessment of § 2-207*, 68 Va. L. Rev. 1217 (1982).

Omri Ben-Shahar, *Freedom from Contract*, 2004 Wis. L. Rev. 261, 267.

Roger Bern, *"Terms Later" Contracting: Bad Economics, Bad Morals, and a Bad Idea for a Uniform Law, Judge Easterbrook Notwithstanding*, 12 J.L. & Pol'y 641 (2004).

Jean Braucher, *Amended Article 2 and the Decision to Trust the Courts: The Case Against Enforcing Delayed Mass-Market Terms, Especially for Software*, 2004 Wis. L. Rev. 753.

Arthur Corbin, *Offer and Acceptance and Some of the Resulting Legal Relations*, 26 Yale L.J. 169 (1917).

Richard Craswell, *The Sound of One Form Battling*, 98 Mich. L. Rev. 2727 (2000).

Richard Craswell, *Offer, Acceptance, and Efficient Reliance*, 48 Stan. L. Rev. 481 (1996).

Juanda Daniel, *Electronic Contracting Under the 2003 Revisions to Article 2 of the Uniform Commercial Code: Clarification or Chaos?*, 20 Santa Clara Computer & High Tech. L.J. 319 (2004).

Melvin Eisenberg, *The Revocation of Offers*, 2004 Wis. L. Rev. 271.

Clayton Gillette, *Rolling Contracts as an Agency Problem*, 2004 Wis. L. Rev. 679.

Charles J. Goetz & Robert E. Scott, *Enforcing Promises: An Examination of the Basis of Contract*, 89 Yale L.J. 1261, 1293–97 (1980).

Victor Goldberg, *Traynor* (Drennan*) v. Hand* (Baird*): Much Ado About (Almost)*

Nothing, 3 J. LEGAL ANALYSIS 539 (2011).

Victor Goldberg, *The "Battle of the Forms": Fairness, Efficiency, and the Best Shot Rule*, 76 OR. L. REV. 155 (1997).

Stanley Henderson, *Promissory Estoppel and Traditional Contract Doctrine*, 78 YALE L.J. 343 (1969).

Robert A. Hillman, *Rolling Contracts*, 71 FORDHAM L. REV. 743 (2002).

Jason Scott Johnston, *Communication and Courtship: Cheap Talk Economics and the Law of Contract Formation*, 85 VA. L. REV. 385 (1999).

Avery Katz, *The Strategic Structure of Offer and Acceptance: Game Theory and the Law of Contract Formation*, 89 MICH. L. REV. 215 (1990).

Avery Katz, *Transaction Costs and the Legal Mechanics of Exchange: When Should Silence in the Face of an Offer Be Construed as Acceptance?*, 9 J.L. ECON. & ORG. 77 (1993).

William Noel Keys, *Consideration Reconsidered — The Problem of the Withdrawn Bid*, 10 STAN. L. REV. 441 (1958).

Charles L. Knapp, *An Offer You Can't Revoke*, 2004 WIS. L. REV. 309.

Charles Knapp, *Enforcing the Contract to Bargain*, 44 N.Y.U. L. REV. 673 (1969).

Dennis D. Lamont, *Negative Option Offers in Consumer Service Contracts: A Principled Reconciliation of Commerce and Consumer Protection*, 42 UCLA L. REV. 1315 (1995).

William H. Lawrence, Rolling Contracts *Rolling Over Contract Law*, 41 SAN DIEGO L. REV. 1099 (2004).

Ian Macneil, *Time of Acceptance: Too Many Problems for a Single Rule*, 112 U. PA. L. REV. 947 (1964).

Gregory E. Maggs, *The Waning Importance of Revisions to U.C.C. Article 2*, 78 NOTRE DAME L. REV. 595 (2003).

Ronald Mann & Travis Siebeneicher, *Just One Click: The Reality of Internet Retail Contracting*, 108 COLUM. L. REV. 984 (2008).

Colin P. Marks, *The Limits of Limiting Liability in the Battle of the Forms: U.C.C. Section 2-207 and the Material Alteration Inquiry*, 33 PEPP. L. REV. 501 (2005).

D. O. McGovney, *Irrevocable Offers*, 27 HARV. L. REV. 644 (1914).

John Murray, *The Chaos of the "Battle of the Forms": Solutions*, 39 VAND. L. REV. 1307 (1986).

Robert L. Oakley, *Fairness in Electronic Contracting: Minimum Standards for Non-Negotiated Contracts*, 42 HOUS. L. REV. 1041 (2005).

Eric A. Posner, *ProCD v. Zeidenberg and Cognitive Overload in Contractual Bargaining*, 77 U. CHI. L. REV. 1181 (2010).

Frank Schultz, *The Firm Offer Puzzle: A Study of Business Practice in the Construction Industry*, 19 U. CHI. L. REV. 237 (1952).

Alan Schwartz and Robert E. Scott, *The Political Economy of Private Legislatures*, 1453 U. Pa. L. Rev. 595 (1995).

Richard Speidel, *Introduction to Symposium on Proposed Revised Article 2*, 54 SMU L. REV. 787 (2001).

Gregory M. Travalio, *Clearing the Air After the Battle: Reconciling Fairness and Efficiency in a Formal Approach to U.C.C. Section 2-207*, 33 CASE W. RES. L. REV. 327 (1983).

Valerie Watnick, *The Electronic Formation of Contracts and the Common Law "Mailbox Rule,"* 56 BAYLOR L. REV. 175 (2004).

James J. White, *Autistic Contracts*, 45 WAYNE L. REV. 1693 (2001).

James J. White, *Contracting Under Amended 2-207*, 2004 WIS. L. REV. 723.

Clark B. Whittier, *The Restatement of Contracts and Mutual Assent*, 17 CAL. L. REV. 441 (1929).

I. Maurice Wormser, *The True Conception of Unilateral Contracts*, 26 YALE L.J. 136 (1916).

Chapter 4

CONTRACTUAL RELATIONSHIPS AND CONDUCT

A. AN INTRODUCTION TO RELATIONAL CONTRACTS

The paradigmatic common law notion of a contract is a one-time promissory exchange of goods or services for a price between two parties who may have no future (or previous) dealings. Professor Ian Macneil cites the example of "two strangers at noon come into town from opposite directions, one walking and one riding a horse. The walker offers to buy the horse, and after brief dickering a deal is struck . . . upon the handing over of $10. The two strangers expect to have nothing to do with each other . . . they expect never to see each other thereafter; and each has as much feeling for the other as has a Viking trading with a Saxon." Ian R. Macneil, Contracts: Exchange Transactions and Relations 13 (1977).

If all contractual relationships followed the simple model of the discrete, one-shot exchange of promises, the role of contract law (and contract *lawyers*) would be relatively straightforward. In such an environment, at least in theory, the parties can write a *complete contingent contract*; that is, a contract in which all of the possible contingencies that might affect performance of their respective promises are identified explicitly, together with a specification of the consequences in each case. In such a world, the function of law (as we have seen) is to formulate a menu of default terms for typical bargainers that save formulation and negotiation costs and to enforce the specially-designed contract terms of individual bargainers who wish to opt out of the basic defaults.

Consider, for example, a contract made in February to buy corn in September. Even this simple contract is subject to a number of uncertainties. Will there be enough rain? Will the locusts and other defoliators spare the crop? Will there be too much corn produced nationwide to keep the price at a reasonable level? Will the federal government lift the embargo on sales to Iran, Cuba, and North Korea, thereby creating an increased demand? The future is filled with uncertainties. Nevertheless, in theory, if not in practice, the parties could write a contract that dealt with each of these contingencies. Such a contract would have a price for the corn that is to be delivered in September, and the price clause would be followed by many price-adjustment clauses. There would be a rain clause, an insect clause, and so forth.

But we all recognize that not all contractual agreements are simple, discrete exchanges. Parties often enter contracts knowing that they cannot specify all relevant considerations in advance.

Assume, for example, that we are negotiating a long-term supply contract between an oil company and major airlines for the provision of jet fuel over a

10-year period. As the representative of the airlines purchasing the fuel, will I have any idea of how much fuel we will require five years from now and what will be a favorable price for fuel at that time? If we attempt nonetheless to specify fixed quantity and price terms in the contract, we will inevitably be forced to renegotiate our contractual obligations in light of future events. In such long-term arrangements, therefore, the parties are likely to be motivated by the reality of an uncertain future to reach agreement on flexible terms (such as "output" or "requirements" contracts with price adjustment clauses) that permit price and quantity to be adjusted as circumstances change over time. Allowing flexibility (or discretion) in such "relational" contracts saves parties the transaction costs from continually having to update or renegotiate price and quantity in light of changed external circumstances. One of the advantages of a flexible long-term contract for the supply of a key input — such as jet fuel — is that it permits the parties to "smooth the bumps" in the inevitable variations in supply and demand that otherwise may threaten short-term business disruption. In addition, engaging in long-term contractual relationships engenders trust and goodwill among the contracting parties — factors which can allow them to execute their obligations efficiently, without recourse to the threat of litigation.

Contractual flexibility does not come without a cost, however. One of the benefits of a clear, definitive set of contract terms (e.g., 50 widgets to be delivered in 30 days at $5 per widget) is that subsequent disputes over responsibilities under the contract can be minimized. Flexible contract terms invite disagreements, especially when one of the parties has made a relation-specific investment in the contract. For example, consider how the contracting problem changes in the long-term contract for jet fuel if the refining company agrees at the outset to build a pipeline directly to the airlines hub. Now the parties need to agree in the contract to confine the discretion of the airlines in choosing the quantity of jet fuel that they purchase so as to protect the reliance interest of the oil company in recouping the cost of the pipeline. (If the oil company cannot be assured of recovering their investment costs over the life of the contract they will decline to build the pipeline in the first place. Do you see why?). Under these circumstances, the parties must balance the need for flexibility against the parallel need for a binding commitment from the contracting partner. One way to protect both parties interests in such a contract, for example, is to require the airlines to "take or pay" for a minimum quantity of fuel oil each period. This protects the oil company against the risk of a "holdup" — the risk that once they build the pipeline the airlines will threaten to reduce the quantity of oil purchased unless the price is renegotiated.

This holdup problem is part of a larger concern in relational contracts that arises because each party bears the full cost of her own investments in the contract but must share the resulting contractual benefits with her partner. This separation of cost from benefit is what economists call a *moral hazard* problem. As the name implies, it means that each party to a contract faces a risk that the other party will not perform as promised but rather will (immorally) shirk a portion of his or her responsibility. These moral risks are often minimized in our daily lives by a rich network of social norms. Norms of trust, reciprocity, loyalty, and a desire for esteem bind people to perform obligations even where benefits are shared. But in many arms-length exchange transactions between strangers, these social norms are less effective in reducing moral hazard.

In part because relational contracts often require parties to trade off the benefits of flexibility against the benefits of commitment, there are only a few contract default rules that they can draw upon to define their relationship. Instead, the burden shifts to individual lawyers to draft contract terms (much in the nature of a "private constitution") that regulate the contractual relationship so as to secure the maximum value for the parties from their contract.

The task of the lawyer in drafting relational contracts is first to identify the *purposes* that the parties wish to advance by their contract and then to select from the menu of possible contract terms those that might best serve those purposes. While becoming skilled at this task is a life-long enterprise, the cases and problems that follow provide an introduction to some of the standard ways of dealing with uncertainties about quantity and price and to the contractual mechanisms — such as exclusive dealing arrangements, termination clauses and covenants not to compete — that are designed to reduce moral hazard risk.

B.   COPING WITH UNCERTAINTY: PRELIMINARY NEGOTIATIONS AND PRELIMINARY AGREEMENTS

[1]   Preliminary Negotiations

The agreement process for relational contracts often does not conform to the assumptions underlying the default rules of offer and acceptance that we studied in Chapter 3. While discrete contracts are often formed by the process of offers made and acceptances given, relational exchange typically proceeds instead through an extended process of negotiation prior to reaching any binding agreement. During this negotiation process, each party typically makes certain representations about its respective obligations should a deal ultimately be concluded. Consider then the following problem: assume that two parties are engaged in negotiations and in the course of their deliberations, one party acts in reliance on a representation made by the other as part of the bargaining process. Should the party who has relied be able to recover damages even though the deal is subsequently abandoned?

According to traditional contract doctrine, promises made during negotiations are generally held unenforceable.[1] In *Precontractual Liability and Preliminary Agreements*, Alan Schwartz and Robert Scott report the results of a study of recent litigation.[2] They began with a sample of 30 cases that raised the issue of reliance in the context of on-going negotiations. The underlying question in each case was whether the plaintiff could recover his reliance expenditures if the parties had not yet reached agreement. The courts denied liability, whether premised on

---

[1] *See, e.g., Malaker Corp. Stockholders Protective Committee v. First Jersey Nat'l Bank*, 163 N.J. Super. 463, 395 A.2d 222 (App. Div. 1978); *McMath v. Ford Motor Co.*, 77 Mich. App. 721, 259 N.W.2d 140 (1977).

[2] Alan Schwartz & Robert E. Scott, *Precontractual Liability and Preliminary Agreements*, 120 Harv. L. Rev. 661 (2007).

promissory estoppel, quantum meruit, or negligent misrepresentation, in 87% of these preliminary negotiation cases. Their case data show that, in general, courts will not grant recovery for "early reliance" unless the parties, by agreeing on something significant, have indicated their intention to be bound. In particular, the requirements for recovery under promissory estoppel theory have been strictly construed. For example, In *R.G. Group v. Horn & Hardart Co.*, 751 F.2d 69 (2d Cir. 1984), the court underscored the baseline requirement that a claim for promissory estoppel for early reliance is a "clear and unambiguous promise; a reasonable and foreseeable reliance by the party to whom the promise is made; and an injury sustained by the party asserting the estoppel by reason of his reliance." In denying liability, the court found that

> the entire history of the parties' negotiations made it plain that any promise or agreement at that time was conditional upon the signing of a written contract. . . . Plaintiff manifestly cannot make an end run around the defendant's reservations against undertaking a legal obligation absent a signed contract by recharacterizing the claim as one of promissory estoppel.

The majority approach to precontractual liability and a "celebrated exception" follow.

COLEY v. LANG
Alabama Court of Civil Appeals
339 So. 2d 70 (1976)

HOLMES, J.

This is an appeal from the Circuit Court of Mobile County's action awarding damages to appellee Lang for breach of agreement. The appellant Coley appeals.

The record reveals the following: Lang sued Coley for specific performance. Lang's complaint alleged that Coley and Lang had entered into an agreement whereby Coley was to purchase the stock of Lang's corporation. The price was to be $60,000. The specific performance prayed for was the payment of $60,000. The complaint was later amended to include a claim for damages incurred by Lang in reliance on Coley's promise to buy the stock.

After a hearing *ore tenus* the trial court entered a judgment for Lang in the amount of $7,500 "due to their (Lang's) reliance upon the representation of the agreement by respondent (Coley) that he would purchase the stock. . . ." As noted earlier, Coley appeals from this judgment.

The issues as presented by appellant for this court's consideration are: (1) Did the "letter agreement" entered into by the parties contractually bind the parties? (2) Can the award be supported on the basis of promissory estoppel or reliance on a promise?

Viewing the trial court's decree with the attendant presumption of correctness, our review of the testimony as shown by the transcript of the evidence reveals the following:

Coley, in late August of 1972, entered into discussions with Lang concerning the purchase of IAS Corporation. Lang owned the vast majority of the stock of IAS. Coley did not desire to purchase the assets of IAS, but only desired to purchase the name and good will of IAS. Coley's purpose in acquiring the corporation was to enable Coley to be in a favorable position to bid on government contracts. During the negotiation, the parties contacted an attorney, who represented Coley, and the following document was drafted and signed by each party:

September 1, 1972

Mr. Robert J. Lang, President
International Aerospace Services, Inc.
Post Office Box 9516
Charleston, South Carolina 29410

Dear Bob:

This letter is to express the agreement which we have reached today. Subject to the approval of your Board of Directors and stockholders, you have agreed to sell to nominee to buy, all of the outstanding stock of every kind of International Aerospace Services, Inc. ("IAS"). The purchase price for the stock shall be the sum of Sixty Thousand Dollars ($60,000.00) payable as follows:

$10,000 on the date of sale;
$8,000 on December 31, 1972;
$21,000 on December 31, 1973, and
$21,000 on December 31, 1974.

The unpaid portion of the purchase price shall be represented by a promissory note executed by me, or guaranteed by me for execution by my nominee. Principal payments due on the note shall not bear interest to their stated maturity, but any past due payments shall bear interest at the rate of 10% per annum.

It is our understanding that prior to the sale of the IAS stock to me you will cause IAS to transfer all of its assets and liabilities (other than its corporate name and the right to use that corporate name in foreign jurisdictions, and its corporate franchise) to a new corporation or partnership as you and the other present stockholders of IAS may determine. The new corporation or partnership, herein called IASCO, shall indemnify IAS against all liabilities of IAS which it has assumed. If IASCO fails to perform this indemnity and IAS is required to pay off liabilities assumed by IASCO, then I shall have the right to setoff any such payments against amounts due on the note representing the purchase price of the IAS stock. IAS will, of course, be responsible for any liabilities which it creates or incurs after you sell the stock to me. All work and contracts in progress of IAS shall be transferred to IASCO at the same time as the transfer of assets and liabilities.

I recognize that you must consider the method to complete this transaction to the best advantage of you and the other shareholders of IAS. We agree together that on or before September 18, this letter agreement will be reduced to a definitive agreement binding upon all of the parties hereto and accomplishing the sale and purchase contemplated by this agreement.

You agree that until we reach a definitive agreement I may request bid sets from the government and attend bidding conferences on behalf of and in the name of IAS.

If the foregoing correctly reflects our agreement, please execute and return to me the enclosed copy of this letter.

Yours very truly,
/s/ William H. Coley

Agreed to and accepted.
/s/ R. L. Lang

Both parties testified at great length regarding their understanding of the "letter agreement." Suffice it to say that Lang testified that the agreement was binding and only certain details remained to be done. Additionally, Lang testified that stockholder approval was obtained and further, that the corporation (Lang) had lost $30,000 as a result of the reliance on the "letter agreement." We should note that details of the loss are not spelled out with any degree of specificity.

Coley testified that the letter agreement was only a basic outline of points which had been agreed upon; that there remained many items that had to be worked out; and further, that time was of the essence.

Specifically, Coley testified that Lang had not sought approval of the IRS concerning a pension and profit sharing plan nor had certain details with the government been completed. And that because of this he (Coley) realized that the sale would not work out within the contemplated time frame. Coley, on September 18, 1972, notified Lang of this fact.

We note that Coley did attend certain bid conferences conducted by the U.S. Government and registered with the government as a representative of Lang's corporation. This action occurred after the "letter agreement" had been executed.

The attorney who drafted the "letter agreement" testified that he informed both parties that the document in question was not binding. Lang denied that the attorney so informed him.

The trial court, with the above before it, entered a decree which in pertinent part provided as follows:

THAT the Complainants are the stockholders and owners of the International Aerospace Services, Inc., and that heretofore on, to-wit, September 1, 1972, they, by and through their President, Robert J. Lang, entered into a preliminary agreement with the Respondent, William H. Coley to sell to the Respondent all of the outstanding stock of every kind of International Aerospace Services, Inc., with the purchase price being the sum of $60,000 to be paid in the following manner:

$10,000.00 on the date of the sale;
$8,000 on December 31, 1972;

$21,000.00 on December 31, 1973; and
$21,000.00 on December 31, 1974.

THAT as a part of said preliminary agreement all of the assets and liabilities of International Aerospace Services, Inc., were to be transferred to a new corporation; the said Respondent was to purchase all of the stock, goodwill, and reputation of International Aerospace Services, Inc., a corporation, and the Respondent was authorized to request bids set for the United States Federal Government and attend bidding and conferences on behalf of and in the name of International Aerospace Services, Inc. The Court finds as a matter of fact that the Respondent or his said representative did attend pre-bid conferences and did use the name of International Aerospace Services, Inc.; that the said Respondent has failed and refused and continues to fail and refuse to pay any sum of money or to carry out any of the terms of the above mentioned agreement; that the Complainants have incurred certain expenses and have made certain preparations and plans to transfer all of the said outstanding stock to the Respondent; and to carry out the terms and provisions of the aforesaid preliminary agreement between the Complainants and the Respondent.

The Court finds as a matter of fact, and it is hereby ORDERED, ADJUDGED and DECREED by the Court that the Bill for Specific Performance as filed by the Complainants is hereby denied.

It is further ORDERED, ADJUDGED and DECREED that the Complainants have and recover of the Respondent the sum of $7,500.00 as damages which the Complainants have suffered due to their reliance upon the representation of the agreement by the Respondent that he would purchase the stock of International Aerospace Services, Inc., including certain attorney's fees, accountants fees, loss of business, loss of income, loss of goodwill and reputation by the Complainants.

I

We do not find as a matter of law that the "letter agreement" is an agreement upon which specific performance can be based.

Suffice it to say that the language found in Onyx Oils & Resins v. Moss, 367 Pa. 416, 80 A.2d 815, and quoted to this court by appellant-Coley, in his excellent brief, is a correct statement of the law.

Aside from the intention of the parties to reduce their agreement to writing, it is admitted that there was no full and definite agreement on terms. In Nicholls v. Granger, 1896, 7 App. Div. 113, 40 N.Y.S. 99, 101, the court pertinently stated, "It is undoubtedly true that a stipulation to reduce a valid contract to some other form does not affect its validity, and that although it is in contemplation of the parties that a more formal contract shall be executed. . . . But it is an essential to the enforcement of such an informal contract that the minds of the parties should meet upon all the terms, as well as the subject matter, of the contract; and, if anything is left open for future consideration, the informal paper cannot form the basis of a binding contract.

We cannot enforce a portion of an agreement which failed to materialize; nor can we supply the terms of this contract.

Additionally, we find the language of Elmore, Quillian and Co. v. Parish, Bros., 170 Ala. 499, 54 So. 203, to be appropriate in this instance:

> [A]n agreement to enter into an agreement upon terms to be afterwards settled between the parties, is a contradiction in terms, and amounts to nothing. 170 Ala. at 503, 54 So. at 204.

However, as seen from the above, the trial court did not base its judgment on a finding that the "letter agreement" was a binding agreement upon which specific performance could be enforced.

Therefore, we find no reversible error in this regard.

II

The court decreed complainants recover $7,500 as damages suffered "due to their reliance upon the representation of the agreement by the Respondents." The record viewed in the most favorable light for Mr. Lang does not support such a decree, irrespective of whether premised on a theory of equitable estoppel or promissory estoppel.

The purpose of the former doctrine is to prevent inconsistency and fraud resulting from injustice. "It rests at last for its vindication on the manifest idea that to allow such representation to be gainsaid would be fraud on him who had thus acted, believing it to be true." Cosby v. Moore, 259 Ala. 41, 47. The record in this case shows no misrepresentation or deliberate conduct designed to consciously and unfairly mislead Mr. Lang. The most that can be said is that Mr. Coley and Mr. Lang conducted negotiations which both parties hoped would eventually result in consummation of a contract. That the negotiations proved unfruitful does not warrant application of equitable estoppel. For cases applying the doctrine see Dunn v. Fletcher, 266 Ala. 273; Birmingham Trust and Savings Co. v. Strong, 239 Ala. 118, wherein the facts markedly differ from those herein. As stated by the Alabama Supreme Court in Messer v. City of Birmingham, 243 Ala. 520, 524, "A mere breach of *promise* cannot constitute an estoppel en pais." (Emphasis supplied.)

Neither do we deem promissory estoppel applicable. Restatement (First) of Contracts, § 90 (1932) states:

> A promise which the promisor should reasonably expect to induce action or forbearance of a definite and substantial character on the part of the promisee and which does induce such action or forbearance is binding if injustice can be avoided only by enforcement of the promise. Accord Bush v. Bush, 278 Ala. 244, 245.

Assuming the existence of a promise on the part of Mr. Coley to purchase the name and stock of IAS, the record discloses no "action or forbearance of a definite and substantial character" on the part of Mr. Lang. The total time during which Mr. Lang could have curtailed his profit generating activities due to his reliance on Mr. Coley's promise extended only from September 1, 1972, the date of the signing of the documents by the parties, to September 18, 1972, when the negotiations were terminated. Moreover, Mr. Lang could testify with certainty only that he missed opportunities to bid on two contracts during the period. There was no evidence showing the probability that IAS's bid would have been the lowest in either instance. Furthermore, Mr. Lang attended at least one prebid conference during the eighteen-day period; and, presumably, he could have attended others. The circumstances of this case do not constitute the "substantial" forbearance or action in reliance contemplated by the Restatement. See Hoffman v. Red Owl Stores, Inc., 26 Wis. 2d 683; Wheeler v. White, Tex., 398 S.W.2d 93.

It follows that the trial court misapplied the law to the facts in this case. Disposition of other issues is rendered unnecessary by our resolution of this issue.

The case is due to be and is, accordingly, reversed.

HOFFMAN v. RED OWL STORES, INC.
Supreme Court of Wisconsin
26 Wis. 2d 683, 133 N.W.2d 267 (1965)

The complaint alleged that Lukowitz, as agent for Red Owl, represented to and agreed with plaintiffs that Red Owl would build a store building in Chilton and stock it with merchandise for Hoffman to operate in return for which plaintiffs were to put up and invest a total sum of $18,000; that in reliance upon the above mentioned agreement and representations plaintiffs sold their bakery building and business and their grocery store and business; also in reliance on the agreement and representations Hoffman purchased the building site in Chilton and rented a residence for himself and his family in Chilton; plaintiffs' actions in reliance on the representations and agreement disrupted their personal and business life; plaintiffs lost substantial amounts of income and expended large sums of money as expenses. Plaintiffs demanded recovery of damages for the breach of defendants' representations and agreements.

The action was tried to a court and jury. The facts hereafter stated are taken from the evidence adduced at the trial. Where there was a conflict in the evidence the version favorable to plaintiffs has been accepted since the verdict rendered was in favor of plaintiffs.

Hoffman assisted by his wife operated a bakery at Wautoma from 1956 until sale of the building late in 1961. The building was owned in joint tenancy by him and his wife. Red Owl is a Minnesota corporation having its home office at Hopkins, Minnesota. It owns and operates a number of grocery supermarket stores and also extends franchises to agency stores which are owned by individuals, partnerships and corporations. Lukowitz resides at Green Bay and since September, 1960, has been divisional manager for Red Owl in a territory comprising Upper Michigan and most of Wisconsin in charge of 84 stores. Prior to September, 1960, he was district manager having charge of approximately 20 stores.

In November, 1959, Hoffman was desirous of expanding his operations by establishing a grocery store and contacted a Red Owl representative by the name of Jansen, now deceased. Numerous conversations were had in 1960 with the idea of establishing a Red Owl franchise store in Wautoma. In September, 1960, Lukowitz succeeded Jansen as Red Owl's representative in the negotiations.

Hoffman mentioned that $18,000 was all the capital he had available to invest and he was repeatedly assured that this would be sufficient to set him up in business as a Red Owl store. About Christmastime, 1960, Hoffman thought it would be a good idea if he bought a small grocery store in Wautoma and operated it in order that he gain experience in the grocery business prior to operating a Red Owl store in some larger community. On February 6, 1961, on the advice of Lukowitz and Sykes, who had succeeded Lukowitz as Red Owl's district manager, Hoffman bought the inventory and fixtures of a small grocery store in Wautoma and leased the building in which it was operated.

After three months of operating this Wautoma store, the Red Owl representatives came in and took inventory and checked the operations and found the store was operating at a profit. Lukowitz advised Hoffman to sell the store to his manager, and assured him that Red Owl would find a larger store for him elsewhere. Acting on this advice and assurance, Hoffman sold the fixtures and inventory to his manager on June 6, 1961. Hoffman was reluctant to sell at that time because it meant losing the summer tourist business, but he sold on the assurance that he would be operating in a new location by fall and that he must sell this store if he wanted a bigger one. Before selling, Hoffman told the Red Owl representatives that he had $18,000 for "getting set up in business" and they assured him that there would be no problems in establishing him in a bigger operation. The makeup of the $18,000 was not discussed; it was understood plaintiff's father-in-law would furnish part of it. By June, 1961, the towns for the new grocery store had been narrowed down to two, Kewaunee and Chilton. In Kewaunee, Red Owl had an option on a building site. In Chilton, Red Owl had nothing under option, but it did select a site to which plaintiff obtained an option at Red Owl's suggestion. The option stipulated a purchase price of $6,000 with $1,000 to be paid on election to purchase and the balance to be paid within 30 days. On Lukowitz's assurance that everything was all set plaintiff paid $1,000 down on the lot on September 15th.

On September 27, 1961, plaintiff met at Chilton with Lukowitz and Mr. Reymund and Mr. Carlson from the home office who prepared a projected financial statement. Part of the funds plaintiffs were to supply as their investment in the venture was to be obtained by sale of their Wautoma bakery building.

On the basis of this meeting Lukowitz assured Hoffman: ". . . [E]verything is ready to go. Get your money together and we are set." Shortly after this meeting Lukowitz told plaintiffs that they would have to sell their bakery business and bakery building, and that their retaining this property was the only "hitch" in the entire plan. On November 6, 1961, plaintiffs sold their bakery building for $10,000. Hoffman was to retain the bakery equipment as he contemplated using it to operate a bakery in connection with his Red Owl store. After sale of the bakery Hoffman obtained employment on the night shift at an Appleton bakery.

The record contains different exhibits which were prepared in September and October, some of which were projections of the fiscal operation of the business and others were proposed building and floor plans. Red Owl was to procure some third party to buy the Chilton lot from Hoffman, construct the building, and then lease it to Hoffman. No final plans were ever made, nor were bids let or a construction contract entered. Some time prior to November 20, 1961, certain of the terms of the lease under which the building was to be rented by Hoffman were understood between him and Lukowitz. The lease was to be for 10 years with a rental approximating $550 a month calculated on the basis of 1 percent per month on the building cost, plus 6 percent of the land cost divided on a monthly basis. At the end of the 10-year term he was to have an option to renew the lease for an additional 10-year period or to buy the property at cost on an installment basis. There was no discussion as to what the installments would be or with respect to repairs and maintenance.

On November 22nd or 23rd, Lukowitz and plaintiffs met in Minneapolis with Red Owl's credit manager to confer on Hoffman's financial standing and on financing the agency. Another projected financial statement was there drawn up entitled, "Proposed Financing For An Agency Store." This showed Hoffman contributing $24,100 of cash capital of which only $4,600 was to be cash possessed by plaintiffs. Eight thousand was to be procured as a loan from a Chilton bank secured by a mortgage on the bakery fixtures, $7,500 was to be obtained on a 5 percent loan from the father-in-law, and $4,000 was to be obtained by sale of the lot to the lessor at a profit.

A week or two after the Minneapolis meeting Lukowitz showed Hoffman a telegram from the home office to the effect that if plaintiff could get another $2,000 for promotional purposes the deal could go through for $26,000. Hoffman stated he would have to find out if he could get another $2,000. He met with his father-in-law, who agreed to put $13,000 into the business provided he could come into the business as a partner. Lukowitz told Hoffman the partnership arrangement "sounds fine" and that Hoffman should not go into the partnership arrangement with the "front office." On January 16, 1962, the Red Owl credit manager teletyped Lukowitz that the father-in-law would have to sign an agreement that the $13,000 was either a gift or a loan subordinate to all general creditors and that he would prepare the agreement. On January 31, 1962, Lukowitz teletyped the home office that the father-in-law would sign one or other of the agreements. However, Hoffman testified that it was not until the final meeting some time between January 26th and February 2nd, 1962, that he was told that his father-in-law was expected to sign an agreement that the $13,000 he was advancing was to be an outright gift. No mention was then made by the Red Owl representatives of the alternative of the father-in-law signing a subordination agreement. At this meeting the Red Owl agents presented Hoffman with the following projected financial statement:

Capital required in operation:
Cash	$ 5,000.00
Merchandise	20,000.00
Bakery	18,000.00
Fixtures	17,500.00
Promotional Funds	1,500.00
TOTAL:	$62,000.00

Source of Funds:
Red Owl 7-day terms	$ 5,000.00

Red Owl Fixture contract (Term 5 yr.)	14,000.00
Bank loans (Terms 9 years) Union State Bank of Chilton (Secured by Bakery Equipment)	8,000.00
Other loans (Term No-pay) No interest	13,000.00
Father-in-law (Secured by none) (Secured by Mortgage on Wautoma Bakery Bldg.)	2,000.00
Resale of Land	6,000.00
Equity Capital: $5,000.00 — Cash Amount owner has to invest: $17,500.00 — Bakery Equip.	22,500.00
TOTAL:	$70,500.00

Hoffman interpreted the above statement to require of plaintiffs a total of $34,000 cash made up of $13,000 gift from his father-in-law, $2,000 on mortgage, $8,000 on Chilton bank loan, $5,000 in cash from plaintiff, and $6,000 on the resale of the Chilton lot. Red Owl claims $18,000 is the total of the unborrowed or unencumbered cash, that is, $13,000 from the father-in-law and $5,000 cash from Hoffman himself. Hoffman informed Red Owl he could not go along with this proposal, and particularly objected to the requirement that his father-in-law sign an agreement that his $13,000 advancement was an absolute gift. This terminated the negotiations between the parties.

[The trial court and jury made the following findings: Hoffman and Red Owl engaged in negotiations for a franchise, but did not reach a final agreement; during the negotiations Red Owl represented to Hoffman that if he fulfilled certain requirements he would be established in a franchise; Hoffman reasonably relied on those representations and met all conditions by the time negotiations ended; reasonable compensation for the sale of the Wautoma store fixtures and inventory would be $16,735; for the sale of the bakery building, $2,000; for the option on the Chilton lot, $1,000; for family moving expenses to Neenah, $140; and for house rental in Chilton, $125. On Red Owl's motion, the trial court ordered a new trial on the issue of damages on the sale of the Wautoma store. Red Owl appealed the rest of the decision; Hoffman cross-appealed the vacation of the Wautoma damages.]

CURRIE, C. J.

The instant appeal and cross-appeal present these questions:

(1) Whether this court should recognize causes of action grounded on promissory estoppel as exemplified by sec. 90 of Restatement, 1 Contracts?

(2) Do the facts in this case make out a cause of action for promissory estoppel?

(3) Are the jury's findings with respect to damages evidence?

[Discussion of the first question is omitted.]

Because we deem the doctrine of promissory estoppel, as stated in § 90 of Restatement, 1 Contracts, is one which supplies a needed tool which courts may employ in a proper case to prevent injustice, we endorse and adopt it.

Applicability of Doctrine to Facts of This Case

The record here discloses a number of promises and assurances given to Hoffman by Lukowitz in behalf of Red Owl upon which plaintiffs relied and acted upon to their detriment.

Foremost were the promises that for the sum of $18,000 Red Owl would establish Hoffman in a store. After Hoffman had sold his grocery store and paid the $1,000 on the Chilton lot, the $18,000 figure was changed to $24,100. Then in November, 1961, Hoffman was assured that if the $24,100 figure were increased by $2,000 the deal would go through. Hoffman was induced to sell his grocery store fixtures and inventory in June, 1961, on the promise that he would be in his new store by fall. In November, plaintiffs sold their bakery building on the urging of defendants and on the assurance that this was the last step necessary to have the deal with Red Owl go through.

We determine that there was ample evidence to sustain the answers of the jury to the questions of the verdict with respect to the promissory representations made by Red Owl, Hoffman's reliance thereon in the exercise of ordinary care, and his fulfillment of the conditions required of him by the terms of the negotiations had with Red Owl.

There remains for consideration the question of law raised by defendants that agreement was never reached on essential factors necessary to establish a contract between Hoffman and Red Owl. Among these were the size, cost, design, and layout of the store building; and the terms of the lease with respect to rent, maintenance, renewal, and purchase options. This poses the question of whether the promise necessary to sustain a cause of action for promissory estoppel must embrace all essential details of a proposed transaction between promisor and promisee so as to be the equivalent of an offer that would result in a binding contract between the parties if the promisee were to accept the same.

Originally the doctrine of promissory estoppel was invoked as a substitute for consideration rendering a gratuitous promise enforceable as a contract. See Williston, Contracts (1st ed.), p. 307, § 139. In other words, the acts of reliance by the promisee to his detriment provided a substitute for consideration. If promissory estoppel were to be limited to only those situations where the promise giving rise to the cause of action must be so definite with respect to all details that a contract would result were the promise supported by consideration, then the defendants' instant promises to Hoffman would not meet this test. However, § 90 of Restatement, 1 Contracts, does not impose the requirement that the promise giving rise to the cause of action must be so comprehensive in scope as to meet the requirements of an offer that would ripen into a contract if accepted by the promisee. Rather the conditions imposed are:

(1)   Was the promise one which the promisor should reasonably expect to induce action or forbearance of a definite and substantial character on the part of the promisee?

(2)   Did the promise induce such action or forbearance?

(3)   Can injustice be avoided only by enforcement of the promise?

We deem it would be a mistake to regard an action grounded on promissory estoppel as the equivalent of a breach of contract action. As Dean Boyer points out, it is desirable that fluidity in the application of the concept be maintained. 98 University of Pennsylvania Law Review (1950), 459, at page 497. While the first two of the above listed three requirements of promissory estoppel present issues of fact which ordinarily will be resolved by a jury, the third requirement, that the remedy can only be invoked where necessary to avoid injustice, is one that involves a policy decision by the court. Such a policy decision necessarily embraces an element of discretion.

We conclude that injustice would result here if plaintiffs were not granted some relief because of the failure of defendants to keep their promises which induced plaintiffs to act to their detriment.

Damages

Defendants attack all the items of damages awarded by the jury.

The bakery building at Wautoma was sold at defendants' instigation in order that Hoffman might have the net proceeds available as part of the cash capital he was to invest in the Chilton store venture. The evidence clearly establishes that it was sold at a loss of $2,000. Defendants contend that half of this loss was sustained by Mrs. Hoffman because title stood in joint tenancy. They point out that no dealings took place between her and defendants as all negotiations were had with her husband. Ordinarily only the promisee and not third persons are entitled to enforce the remedy of promissory estoppel against the promisor. However, if the promisor actually foresees, or has reason to foresee, action by a third person in reliance on the promise, it may be quite unjust to refuse to perform the promise. 1A Corbin, Contracts, p. 220, § 200. Here not only did defendants foresee that it would be necessary for Mrs. Hoffman to sell her joint interest in the bakery building, but defendants actually requested that this be done. We approve the jury's award of $2,000 damages for the loss incurred by both plaintiffs in this sale.

Defendants attack on two grounds the $1,000 awarded because of Hoffman's payment of that amount on the purchase price of the Chilton lot. The first is that this $1,000 had already been lost at the time the final negotiations with Red Owl fell through in January, 1962, because the remaining $5,000 of purchase price had been due on October 15, 1961. The record does not disclose that the lot owner had foreclosed Hoffman's interest in the lot for failure to pay this $5,000. The $1,000 was not paid for the option, but had been paid as part of the purchase price at the time Hoffman elected to exercise the option. This gave him an equity in the lot which could not be legally foreclosed without affording Hoffman an opportunity to pay the balance. The second ground of attack is that the lot may have had a fair market value of $6,000, and Hoffman should have paid the remaining $5,000 of purchase price. We determine that it would be unreasonable to require Hoffman to have invested an additional $5,000 in order to protect the $1,000 he had paid. Therefore, we find no merit to defendants' attack upon this item of damages.

We also determine it was reasonable for Hoffman to have paid $125 for one month's rent of a home in Chilton after defendants assured him everything would be set when plaintiff sold the bakery building. This was a proper item of damage.

Plaintiffs never moved to Chilton because defendants suggested that Hoffman get some experience by working in a Red Owl store in the Fox River Valley. Plaintiffs, therefore, moved to Neenah instead of Chilton. After moving, Hoffman worked at night in an Appleton bakery but held himself available for work in a Red Owl store. The $140 moving expense would not have been incurred if plaintiffs had not sold their bakery building in Wautoma in reliance upon defendants' promises. We consider the $140 moving expense to be a proper item of damage.

We turn now to the damage item with respect to which the trial court granted a new trial, i.e., that arising from the sale of the Wautoma grocery store fixtures and inventory for which the jury awarded $16,735. The trial court ruled that Hoffman could not recover for any loss of future profits for the summer months following the sale on June 6, 1961, but that damages would be limited to the difference between the sales price received and fair market value of the assets sold, giving consideration to any goodwill attaching thereto by reason of the transfer of a going business. There was no direct evidence presented as to what this fair market value was on June 6, 1961. The evidence did disclose that Hoffman paid $9,000 for the inventory, added $1,500 to it and sold it for $10,000 or a loss of $500. His 1961 federal income tax return showed that the grocery equipment had been purchased for $7,000 and sold for $7,955.96. Plaintiffs introduced evidence of the buyer that during the first eleven weeks of operation of the grocery store his gross sales were $44,000 and his profit was $6,000 or roughly 15 percent. On cross-examination he admitted that this was gross and not net profit. Plaintiffs contend that in a breach of contract action damages may include loss of profits. However, this is not a breach of contract action.

The only relevancy of evidence relating to profits would be with respect to proving the element of goodwill in establishing the fair market value of the grocery inventory and fixtures sold. Therefore, evidence of profits would be admissible to afford a foundation for expert opinion as to fair market value.

Where damages are awarded in promissory estoppel instead of specifically enforcing the promisor's promise, they should be only such as in the opinion of the court are necessary to prevent injustice. Mechanical or rule of thumb approaches to the damage problem should be avoided. . . .

At the time Hoffman bought the equipment and inventory of the small grocery store at Wautoma he did so in order to gain experience in the grocery store business. At that time discussion had already been had with Red Owl representatives that Wautoma might be too small for a Red Owl operation and that a larger city might be more desirable. Thus Hoffman made this purchase more or less as a temporary experiment. Justice does not require that the damages awarded him, because of selling these assets at the behest of defendants, should exceed any actual loss sustained measured by the difference between the sales price and the fair market value.

Since the evidence does not sustain the large award of damages arising from the sale of the Wautoma grocery business, the trial court properly ordered a new trial on this issue.

Order affirmed. Because of the cross-appeal, plaintiffs shall be limited to taxing but two-thirds of their costs.

NOTES

1. *Questions on* **Hoffman** *and* **Coley.** The court in *Coley* held under the first Restatement § 90 that there was no evidence of a "definite and substantial" reliance by Coley on Lang's representations. Note that Restatement (Second) § 90 eliminates the "definite and substantial" requirement. Would the court in *Coley* reach the same result under Restatement (Second) § 90? In other words, is the "amount" of reliance the key factual difference between these two cases? Or, do the two courts hold fundamentally different views concerning what kinds of preliminary representations should be enforced? Consider again the language of Restatement (Second) § 90(1): "A *promise* which the promisor should reasonably expect to induce action or forbearance on the part of the promisee. . . ." In sum, in order to recover under a theory of promissory estoppel, the Restatement requires a promise. Recall that Restatement § 2 defines a "promise" as a manifestation of an intention to act . . . so made as to justify the promisee in understanding that a commitment had been made." Did Lukowitz, as agent for Red Owl, ever make a promise to Hoffman? The court focused on Lukowitz' assurance that $18,000 would be a sufficient to set Hoffman up in Red Owl store. Is that a promise sufficient to invoke § 90? Consider the following.

> According to the trial transcript of the case, in May 1961, Hoffman said to Lukowitz and his colleague, "Fellows, you know how much money I got — about $18,000. Will this put me in a bigger operation or won't it?"[3] Lukowitz replied that there would be no problem with that level of investment. There was, however, no discussion then (or at any time thereafter) as to the nature of the $18,000 investment. Was it to be all equity, or was it to be part equity and part borrowed cash? Hoffman clearly assumed the latter. At the time, Hoffman had only $10,500 in cash of his own. The balance was to come in the form of a loan to the business by his father-in-law, Simon Van den Heuvel, a prosperous local farmer. By saying he had $18,000, Hoffman presumed that Red Owl would not care whether he funded his financial contribution to the franchise from his own funds or used borrowed funds instead. But a franchisor relies on the franchisee's personal financial stake in the franchise's success as the principal means of assuring the franchisor's best efforts. If a franchisee uses borrowed money as the source of his investment in the franchise, his poor performance risks only his lender's money, not his own. On this view, one could argue that Red Owl regarded

---

[3] Transcript of Record at 86, Hoffmann v. Red Owl Stores, Inc. (Wis. Cir. Ct., Outagamie County, Oct. 21, 1963) (No. 14954) (A.W. Parnell, J.).

a substantial equity contribution from its franchisees as the key to a successful franchise (or to use the colloquial lingo of finance, Hoffman's financial contribution had to represent his own "skin in the game," not someone else's). Although the amount of unencumbered cash Hoffman was supposed to supply was never precisely identified by Red Owl officials, they may reasonably have assumed that by stating he could contribute $18,000, Hoffman meant that he could and would supply his own cash in setting up the business and would not rely on money lent by others.

Robert E. Scott, Hoffman v. Red Owl Stores *and the Myth of Precontractual Reliance*, 68 OHIO STATE L.J. 71 (2007).

2.   *The Debate over the Meaning of* Hoffman *Continues.* If the parties never reached a mutual understanding about the composition of the $18,000 that Hoffman was to contribute, would Lukowtiz's subsequent assurances be enough to constitute a legally enforceable promise? In Hoffman v. Red Owl Stores: *The Rest of the Story*, 61 HASTINGS L.J. 801 (2010), Professors William Whitford and Stewart Macaulay argue that subsequent interviews with Mr. Hoffmann suggest (a) that during the negotiations, the Red Owl Stores corporation made a company-wide decision not to put franchises in small communities and that explains their unwillingness to deal with Mr. Hoffmann, and (b) that the subsequent assurances by Lefkowitz (rather than the statement relied on by the Wisconsin Supreme Court that $18,000 would be a sufficient investment) would justify the result, if not the reasoning, of the Wisconsin court. Professor Scott replied in Hoffman v. Red Owl Stores *and the Limits of the Legal Method*, 61 HASTINGS L. J. 859 (2010), that, while alternative theories of liability might be defended, the use of promissory estoppel was not supported by the law and explains why the theory of the *Hoffman* case adopted by the Wisconsin Supreme Court has not been widely followed by other courts.[4]

2.   *Alternative Theories of Liability.* If Lukowitz never made a promise, are other grounds for liability possible? Consider quasi-contract: Here the argument would be that Hoffman conferred a benefit on Red Owl during the period from May through November when he purchased and then sold his grocery store, sold the bakery building and purchased an option on the lot in Chilton. All these actions gave Red Owl some further indication of the kind of franchisee that Hoffman was likely to be — was he enterprising and resourceful or was he unmotivated and incapable? As we saw earlier in *Bailey v. West*, Chapter 1, quasi-contract claims based on unjust enrichment rarely succeed, however, unless the defendant specifically and wrongfully induced the benefit. What possible motive might Red Owl have for deceiving Hoffman about his prospects for a franchise? Did Hoffman confer a benefit on Red Owl? Was a benefit appreciated by Red Owl?

---

[4] The data show that *Hoffman v. Red Owl, Inc.* has not been followed by most other courts and, as a matter of contract doctrine, it is an outlier. Indeed, even the Supreme Court of Wisconsin has narrowed the scope of the promissory estoppel doctrine in subsequent decisions. *See Beer Capitol Distrib. v. Guinness Bass Imp. Co.*, 290 F.3d 877 (7th Cir. 2002) (denying both promissory estoppel and unjust enrichment claims based on reliance during negotiations on defendant's representation that he would recommend that plaintiff be chosen as the exclusive distributor for southeastern Wisconsin).

Another possible theory of liability that scholars have offered is the tort of negligent misrepresentation.[5] But there are problems applying this theory to arm's length bargaining contexts. Some courts don't recognize this tort at all[6] and the Restatement of Torts requires that the party making the statement owe a duty to the plaintiff to supply correct information to him.[7] Because casual statements and contacts are prevalent in business, under the majority rule in commercial contexts, liability for negligent misrepresentation is imposed only where the party making the statement possesses unique or specialized expertise or is in a special position of trust and confidence with the injured party such that reliance on the negligent misrepresentation is justified.[8] Did Lukowitz misrepresent or conceal information during the process of bargaining with Mr. Hoffman? Did Lukowitz encourage Hoffman to place his trust and confidence in him, or should it have been clear to Hoffman that Lukowitz was dealing with him at "arm's length"?

A final possibility is to ground Red Owl's liability on a duty to bargain in good faith. The problem here is that there was scant factual evidence in the record to support a claim of bad faith by Red Owl. In a portion of the opinion that has been omitted, the court explicitly found that "there is no evidence that would support a finding that Lukowitz made any of the promises . . . in bad faith with any present intent that they would not be fulfilled by Red Owl." To be sure, Lukowitz was careless, especially in making casual assurances in September, that "everything is ready to go. Get your money together and we are set." But wasn't Hoffman equally careless?. Hoffman understood "capital" to mean any combination of debt and equity, and thus thought he had $18,000 in "capital" through his own assets combined with loans he could procure. At trial, Hoffman was asked: "Was there any discussion at any time as to how this $18,000 was to be made up? That is, was it all unencumbered cash or partly to be borrowed cash?" Hoffman answered: "I don't believe there was any discussion on that." Should Hoffman have clarified what *he* meant by having $18,000 to invest?

3. *A Pluralist Analysis of* **Hoffman v. Red Owl.** Perhaps one way of justifying the result reached in *Hoffman v. Red Owl* is through the systematic cognitive error argument discussed in Chapter 1. Recall that pluralist theorists claim that courts pursue multiple goals, including efficiency, autonomy *and* fairness. The fairness

---

[5] For discussion that Red Owl's liability might better rest on misrepresentation, see Richard Craswell, *Taking Information Seriously: Misrepresentation and Nondisclosure in Contract Law and Elsewhere*, 92 VA. L. REV. 565 (2006); *see also* Mark P. Gergen, *Liability for Mistake in Contract Formation*, 64 S. CAL. L. REV. 1, 34–36 (*Hoffman* best explained as liability for negligent misrepresentation); CHARLES FRIED, CONTRACT AS PROMISE 24 (1981) (same).

[6] *See, e.g., Haigh v. Matsushita Electric Corp.*, 676 F. Supp. 1332 (E.D. Va. 1987) (applying Virginia law).

[7] Under Restatement (Second) of Torts § 552, an action for negligent misrepresentation lies only against one "who in the course of his business or profession, or in any other transaction in which he has a pecuniary interest supplies false information for the guidance of others in their business transactions."

[8] *See, e.g., Eternity Global Master Fund Ltd. v. Morgan Guar. Trust Co.*, 375 F.3d 168 (2d Cir. 2004). The key to the tort is that plaintiff must allege and prove that the defendant owes a duty to plaintiff to communicate accurate information. Thus, plaintiff must show that defendant either was in the business of supplying information or that defendant had a pecuniary interest in plaintiff's transaction with a third party. *Continental Leavitt Communications v. Painewebber, Inc.*, 857 F. Supp. 1266 (N.D. Ill 1994); *American Protein Corp. v. AB Volvo*, 844 F.2d 56 (2d Cir. 1988).

goal is necessary in order to do justice where one party has superior information or where one party is susceptible to exploitation because of one or more systematic cognitive errors. When such circumstances arise, the pluralist scholars argue that traditional contract doctrine should give way to the goal of protecting the party who is less capable of protecting herself. In this case, does the bargain context in these franchise negotiations (that typically occur between a large corporate entity and individual entrepreneurs) give rise to "systematic" cognitive error? Perhaps another way of asking the question is to say, would most parties in Hoffman's circumstances make the same mistake? Or is this a case where one party to the bargain should have protected himself by gathering readily available information?

4.   *An Economic Analysis of Non-Enforcement in Preliminary Negotiations.* The economic analysis of liability for relied-upon statements made in preliminary negotiations is premised on the goal of facilitating parties' efforts to invest in valuable projects that create a contractual surplus that they then can share. Courts encourage efficient investment not only by enforcing contracts but also by refusing to protect the interests of parties disappointed by the failure to reach agreement. Freedom from liability for honest expressions of future intention that are later withdrawn encourages parties to negotiate freely without fear that their initial expressions of interest are binding. Suppose, for example, that Bob is interested in purchasing Jody's car. Bob expresses his interest honestly by stating, "I like the car a lot. I'm planning to buy it. I'll come back this afternoon to conclude our negotiations." Jody relies on Bob's statement by declining to negotiate with another prospective buyer later that day. Bob subsequently decides not to purchase the car. Should the law hold Bob liable for Jody's reliance? Jason Johnston argues that the answer should be no.[9] Imposing liability for Jody's precontractual reliance has significant costs, if one believes that, ordinarily, precontractual statements of intention are essentially truthful. Johnston argues that such statements of intention (economists call these statements "cheap talk") should not be the basis of liability in the ordinary case even if though they may change the expectations of the other party. He reasons that delay in reaching a deal is costly to both parties. Thus, negotiators have strong incentives to communicate useful information so as to either reach a deal or move on to other opportunities. Johnson argues, therefore, that liability for precontractual statements should be imposed only when one party misrepresents his relative optimism about the prospects of reaching a deal. Despite this argument, there may be sound reasons to accept the costs of chilling future negotiations in order to prevent exploitation of the weak by the strong. Is there evidence of exploitation in the negotiations between Joseph Hoffman and the representatives of Red Owl Stores?

5.   *Problems.* Consider the following fact situations. How would you resolve each dispute?

a. While serving in the armed services, John Mooney developed skills at handball and racquetball and thus became interested in establishing an athletic club after his retirement to provide facilities and instruction for these and other athletic activities. In March of 1972, Mooney, who was almost eligible for retirement, visited Colorado

---

[9] Jason Scott Johnston, *Communication and Courtship: Cheap Talk Economics and the Law of Contract Formation*, 85 Va. L. Rev. 387, 494–99 (1999).

Springs where he discussed his interest in managing an athletic club with a real estate salesman. At that time, Craddock, an experienced real estate developer, was in the process of constructing an office building which was to include an athletic club. The salesman therefore advised Fred Norton, Craddock's employee, of Mooney's interest.

Mooney returned to his post in Germany. He and Norton communicated thereafter by correspondence and long-distance calls and, based on these communications, Mooney concluded that he and his wife could negotiate a lease for an athletic club. He retired from the service (thus forfeiting certain accrued leave pay) and returned to Colorado Springs to pursue the negotiations.

Discussions followed in Colorado Springs between Mooney, Norton, and Craddock at Craddock's offices. The major points to be resolved were the amount of rental and the erection of an auxiliary building in connection with the main building to house additional handball and squash courts. At the urging of Norton, Mooney was advised to project the type of facilities required to generate $12,000 per year income to Mooney. Upon review of Mooney's proposals as to the number and types of facilities necessary, Craddock replied, "Let's go."

Mooney then moved his wife and children from Germany to Colorado Springs and began preparations for opening an athletic club, such as obtaining sizable loans to purchase equipment, purchasing materials for and installing a sauna in the main building, preparing printed brochures and mailing of same to prospective members of the athletic club, making an extended trip to California to meet with suppliers of equipment and other items utilized in athletic clubs, and joining various organizations to promote the venture. These activities continued through December of 1972.

Craddock's architect was to prepare drawings and blueprints for the auxiliary building, but because of Craddock's other projects, no blueprints or drawings had been completed by October 1972. At that time, Mooney suggested several changes in the auxiliary building, principally for the purpose of substituting two handball courts for the two squash courts originally contemplated.

The printed brochure was mailed to prospective members in December, and within a week thereafter only three responses had been returned. Upon learning of the lack of responses, Norton informed Mooney that the project could not be completed as originally discussed and imposed a minimum membership requirement as a condition for erection of the auxiliary building. The parties failed to reach an agreement.

Can Mooney prevail in a promissory estoppel action against Craddock? If so, would Craddock have a similar claim against Mooney?[10]

b. Bob Fisher and Edward Brill were partners in a flower business. They rented space for their shop from Harry Fried under a three-year lease. About a year into the lease, Fisher decided to open a restaurant in a town several miles away. Brill agreed to buy out Fisher's share of the partnership, as well as to assume responsibility for the lease. Fisher also spoke with Fried, and the latter agreed orally to release him from any further obligations under the lease. Fisher and his

---

[10] *See Mooney v. Craddock*, 35 Colo. App. 20, 530 P.2d 1302 (1974).

family subsequently moved, and Fisher opened a restaurant which was moderately successful.

Several months later, Brill closed up the flower shop and stopped paying rent to Fried. Fried brought suit against Brill and Fisher to recover all outstanding rent through the end of the lease term. Fisher defended against the action on the basis of Fried's promise to release him from any further lease obligations. The court held that the promise to release Fisher from the lease lacked consideration. Is this case a good candidate for applying promissory estoppel?[11]

[2]   Indefinite Agreements

As we suggested in the Introduction to this chapter, parties to relational contracts confront the twin problems of uncertainty and complexity — they are often incapable of specifying the appropriate contractual solution to every possible contingency that may materialize in the future. One possible solution to this problem is to leave certain contingencies unaddressed or describe possible outcomes in broad or general terms. To what extent does this "solution" to the problem of uncertainty expose the parties to the risk of non-enforcement of their respective commitments? As we learned in Chapter 1, one of the core principles of contract law is that the promises of parties to a legally enforceable contract must be certain and definite such that their intention may be ascertained with a reasonable degree of certainty. At common law, parties traditionally have been required to reach agreement on all material terms of their contract or risk a court declining to enforce the contract on the grounds of indefiniteness. Even at common law, however, it was possible for parties to escape the indefiniteness doctrine. In sales of goods, for example, common law courts held the words "fair and reasonable value" to mean "market value" and thus a definite promise to pay the fair market value of goods was inferred from the express agreement of the parties. The drafters of the Uniform Commercial Code followed the line of cases holding that price terms could be supplied from evidence of market prices. But the UCC goes beyond the common law in explicitly authorizing an expansive role for courts in filling open terms in otherwise incomplete agreements.[12] Read UCC §§ 2-204, 2-305 and review the following cases.

---

[11] *See Fried v. Fisher*, 328 Pa. 497, 196 A. 39 (1938).

[12] *See* Robert E. Scott, *A Theory of Self-Enforcing Indefinite Agreements*, 103 COLUM. L. REV. 1641, 1647–49 (2003).

TRIMMER v. VAN BOMEL
New York Supreme Court
107 Misc. 2d 201, 434 N.Y.S.2d 82 (1980)

See p. 29, *supra*.

WAGNER EXCELLO FOODS, INC. v. FEARN INT'L, INC.
Illinois Appellate Court
235 Ill. App. 3d 224, 601 N.E.2d 956 (1992)

See p. 36, *supra*.

NOTES

1. *Filling the Gaps at Common Law*. Two factual patterns typify unenforce-able indefinite agreements at common law. The first, illustrated by *Varney v. Ditmars*, is the indefinite bonus contract. In *Varney*, the New York Court of Appeals held a bonus agreement for "a fair share of the profits" too indefinite and thus not enforceable. The second archetype is a variation on the first, extending the common law rule to agreements where essential terms were explicitly left to further negotiation. Parties often decide to agree in principle, but leave many of the details unresolved, opting instead to bargain over them in subsequent negotiations. This practice, often called making an "agreement to agree," has traditionally been disfavored by courts as yet another example of a contract void for indefiniteness.[13]

As we have seen in previous cases, courts often use legal rules to fill gaps left in agreements. Why are courts unwilling to fill the gaps left in "indefinite bonus contracts" and "agreements to agree"? With respect to this question, consider the following excerpt:

> A contract between two persons, upon a valid consideration, that they will, at some specified time in the future, at the election of one of them, enter into a particular contract, specifying its terms, is undoubtedly binding, and upon a breach thereof the party having the election or option may recover as damages what such particular contract, to be entered into, would have been worth to him, if made. But an agreement that they will in the future make such contract as they may then agree upon amounts to nothing. An agreement to enter into negotiations and agree upon the terms of a contract, if they can, cannot be made the basis of a cause of action. There would be no way by which the court could determine what sort of contract the negotiations would result in; no rule by which the court could ascertain whether any, or, if so, what, damages might follow a refusal to enter into such future contract. So, to be enforceable, a contract to enter into a future

---

[13] For one of the first scholarly arguments that agreements to agree should be legally enforceable, see Charles Knapp, *Enforcing the Contract to Bargain*, 44 N.Y.U. L. Rev. 673 (1969).

contract must specify all its materials and essential terms, and leave none to be agreed upon as the result of future negotiations.

Shepard v. Carpenter, 54 Minn. 153, 155–56, 55 N.W. 906, 906 (1893).

The court in *Shepard v. Carpenter* supplies the rationale of the common law indefiniteness doctrine as applied to "agreements to agree." The court refused to enforce an agreement that lacks material terms because otherwise the court might err in supplementing the parties' expressed intentions. Can the same rationale be applied to "indefinite bonus contracts?" Under what circumstances would a common law court be willing to supply terms left open in an agreement? Consider *Corthell v. Summit Thread Co.*, 132 Me. 94 (1933), where Summit Thread Company promised its employee "reasonable recognition" in return for his promise to turn over all future inventions for development. The court in *Corthell* enforced the agreement and supplied a price term where the agreement called for "reasonable recognition." Would the court in *Corthell* run the risk of erring in supplementing the parties' expressed intentions? This result might be explained by a rule that an agreement with an indefinite material term is unenforceable *unless* the parties intend some external reference point to fill the gap. For example, a market price is a reasonable price, thus allowing the court to objectively supply the price term. In the absence of an external reference point, a court's attempt to supply a term would require speculation as to the parties' intent.

2.   *Indefiniteness Under the UCC.* The justification for the common law rule was that it honored the intent of the parties. That is also the justification for UCC § 2-204: It honors the parties' intent to be bound. The difference, then, is not the purpose of the rule but the presumption that follows from agreements with open or indefinite terms. The UCC shifts from the bright-line rule of the common law to a broad standard, justified primarily by the defects of the common law rule. In many contracting contexts a rule that determines intent by focusing on missing terms is seriously over-inclusive. All contracts are incomplete; thus, the fact of incompleteness does not by itself imply an intention to avoid legal enforcement. Incompleteness may be caused by many factors, including the desire for flexibility and the unwillingness of parties to condition future performance on non-observable or non-verifiable measures of performance.[14] Completeness per se is no longer the key variable in sales contracts. Under the UCC, the key variable is *intent*. If parties want to create a binding contract even though a number of provisions are not expressly agreed upon, courts are instructed to oblige them assuming they can provide a remedy in case of breach.[15]

Consider the following excerpt:

> The basic philosophy of the sales article of the Uniform Commercial Code is simple. Practical business people cannot be expected to govern their actions with references to nice legal formalisms. Thus, when there is basic agreement, however manifested and whether or not the precise moment of agreement may be determined, failure to articulate that agreement in the

---

[14] Scott, *supra* note 12, at 1649–50.

[15] Under UCC § 2-204(3), a binding contract can be formed despite the existence of open terms only where there is "a reasonably certain basis" for calculating damages in the event of breach.

precise language of a lawyer, with every difficulty and contingency considered and resolved, will not prevent formation of a contract. But, of equal importance, if there be no basic agreement, the code will not imply one. . . .

Kleinschmidt Div. of SCM Corp. v. Futuronics Corp., 41 N.Y.2d 972, 973, 363 N.E.2d 701, 702–03 (1977).

3. *Open Price Terms Under the Common Law and the UCC.* Traditionally, as with other indefinite terms, open price terms were disfavored by common law courts. Indefinite price terms met with particular disfavor, since price was regarded as a crucial element of the contract. This reaction to open price terms can be seen in *United Press v. New York Press Co.*, 164 N.Y. 406, 58 N.E. 527 (1900). In that case, the New York Court of Appeals refused to award damages to the plaintiff on the basis of a contract clause which provided for weekly payments "not exceeding three hundred dollars" to be made by the defendant for news provided to it by the plaintiff. The court wrote:

> The appellant claims that, inasmuch as the language of the contract bound the defendant to pay a sum "not exceeding $300 a week" by paying that sum for a period of time it had bound itself through a practical construction of the instrument; and it is also argued that the contract should be construed as one "to recover the reasonable value of the news service for the unexpired term of the contract, less the cost of performance." If this were a case where the contract of the parties was merely ambiguous in its terms, it might be permissible to explain them by evidence of their acts, and thus to show a practical construction; but the difficulty with this instrument lies deeper. It lacked support in one of its essential elements — in the absence of a statement of the price to be paid. That was a defect which was radical in its nature, and which was beyond the reach of oral evidence to supply; for, if the intention of the parties, in so essential a particular, cannot be ascertained from the instrument, neither the court nor the jury will be allowed to make an agreement for them upon the subject. It is elementary in the law that, for the validity of a contract, the promise or the agreement of the parties to it must be certain and explicit, and that their full intention may be ascertained to a reasonable degree of certainty. Their agreement must be neither vague nor indefinite, and, if thus defective, parol proof cannot be resorted to.

164 N.Y. at 409–10.

As we have seen, the UCC permits parties to make a binding contract even if they have not reached agreement on a price term. Section 2-305(1) authorizes courts to provide a reasonable price where the parties have not specified a price but intended nevertheless to be bound to the agreement. This provision, however, simply follows the line of cases at common law holding that price terms in sales contracts could be supplied from evidence of market prices. *See, e.g., Varney v. Ditmars*, 111 N.E. 822 (N.Y. 1916) (positing in dicta that "parties may use the words 'fair and reasonable value' as synonymous with 'market value' ").

An example of the application of § 2-305 can be found in *Alter & Sons, Inc. v. United Eng'rs & Constructors, Inc.*, 366 F. Supp. 959 (S.D. Ill. 1973). In *Alter*, the defendant placed a rush order with the plaintiff for several portable diesel-powered pumps needed as an auxiliary system for the defendant's atomic power plant. Defendant also ordered a primer pump, necessary for the operation of the rest of the system. The order was placed by telephone on the evening of July 6, with the defendant specifying that delivery was required by July 10. (The parties had, on several prior occasions, placed and received orders by phone.) The only material element of the bargain left unspecified was the price. The next day the defendant again telephoned the plaintiff, but this time asked him to stop delivery of the equipment. The defendant maintained that, because of the open price term, no binding contract had ever been formed and refused to reimburse the plaintiff for costs incurred in halting shipment of the pumps. In holding that a sales contract had been formed, the court wrote:

> When the parties so intend, a contract for the sale of goods can be concluded even though the price of the goods sold is not settled. § 2-305. The intention of the parties with reference to the issue whether a contract for sale was made must be determined in the light of the facts and conduct of the parties.

> The salient inference from the actions of defendant's agents on July 6, 1972 is that the imperative factors in their minds were that equipment be obtained and that delivery thereof be effected not later than July 10, 1972. They presented their request to plaintiff in the emergency atmosphere inherent in that almost impossible time limitation. All elements of a sales agreement were mutually agreed between the parties, except that the sales price was left open.

> A sales agreement was concluded between the parties on the early evening of July 6, 1972, when Patton gave Mr. Alter a purchase order number and directed him to order the equipment for July 10 delivery. No other conclusion is consistent with the facts proved. Patton knew and intended that plaintiff would commit itself for the purchase, modification and shipment of the equipment upon the strength of those representations. Defendant's belated concern with the lack of agreement as to sales price is inconsistent with its overriding concern at that critical juncture in time that its equipment needs be filled on an emergency basis. A sales agreement was made, despite the fact that the sales price remained to be determined.

Id. at 965.

4. *Self-Enforcing Indefinite Agreements*. Why do parties write indefinite agreements when they know that courts may not enforce them? Furthermore, when parties could write a complete agreement at a reasonable cost but still leave terms open, should the courts fill in the gaps and enforce the contract?

One response to these questions is that parties often rely on extra-legal norms for the enforcement of their contracts, resulting in "self-enforcing" agreements. Reputational concerns and the possibility of repeated dealings in the future will often motivate contracting parties to perform indefinite promises that would otherwise be unenforceable in a court. However, even when reputation and continued business dealings are not present, as in one-shot transactions between relative strangers, parties still make indefinite agreements. Recent studies in experimental economics provide strong evidence that many people are motivated by sense of "reciprocal fairness," or a desire and willingness to reward generous, "fair-sharing" behavior and to punish unfair, selfish behavior, even if doing so requires them to forego significant financial gains. This suggests that material self-interest is not the only motivating factor in economic decision making. This sense of reciprocity may supply yet another extra-legal factor motivating parties to keep agreements.

Given that many parties behave reciprocally in contracting relationships, should courts seek to make these "self-enforcing" agreements legally enforceable? What result would this have on future contracting parties? Experimental evidence has suggested that indefinite contracts that allow parties to reciprocate may be more beneficial and efficient than legally enforceable contracts. For a more complete analysis of these issues, see Robert E. Scott, *A Theory of Self-Enforcing Indefinite Agreements*, 103 Colum. L. Rev. 1641 (2003).

[3] Binding Preliminary Agreements

As we have seen, negotiating all the terms of a relational contract is not a simple task. To be sure, when parties are entering into a contractual relationship, it makes sense to bargain out the terms and allocate the risks as precisely as possible in the agreement.[16] Yet sometimes the future contingencies are so uncertain or complex that terms are left open, to be negotiated at a later time. Consider the following common commercial pattern: Assume that two commercial parties agree to transact with each other, and agree also on the nature of their respective contributions, but neither the transaction nor what the parties are to do is precisely described. In order for the project ultimately to be realized, however, one or both of the parties must make an investment *before* the uncertainty is resolved. As is typical in such cases, that investment cannot be recovered unless the parties perform their contract and complete their project. In economic parlance, such an investment is termed a "sunk cost." Assume further that after the initial investment and after all the uncertainties are resolved, one party abandons the project, but the party who made the sunk cost investment protests the first party's exit. This pattern has produced extensive litigation and led to the development of legal doctrines that have been subject to recent evolution.

As we have seen, the common law historically has had great difficulty with preliminary agreements that expressed a mutual commitment on agreed terms but failed to specify significant material terms. Typically, the parties agreed to negotiate further over these remaining terms. These "agreements to agree" confronted the indefiniteness doctrine head on. Until recently, courts have held consistently that such "agreements to agree" were unenforceable so long as any

---

[16] For a criticism of negotiating detailed, determinate contract terms at the formation stage of a relational contract on the grounds that bargaining out differences can lead to stalemate and "specification" costs, see William C. Whitford, *Relational Contracts and the New Formalism*, 2004 Wis. L. Rev. 631.

essential term was open to negotiation. But a new rule appears to be emerging. The modern framework for determining intent in agreements to agree was first proposed by Judge Pierre Leval in *Teachers Ins. & Annuity Asso. v. Tribune Co.*[17] The Leval framework is now followed in at least thirteen states, sixteen federal district courts and seven federal circuits.[18] The framework sets out a new default rule for cases in which the parties contemplate further negotiations. This rule relaxes the knife-edge character of the common law, under which agreements were either fully enforceable or not enforceable at all. Consider, for example, the following case.

BROWN v. CARA
United States Court of Appeals, Second Circuit
420 F.3d 148 (2005)

STRAUB, J.

Plaintiff Jeffrey M. Brown ("Brown"), a citizen of Pennsylvania, is CEO of Jeffrey M. Brown Associates, Inc. (collectively "JMB"), a development and construction contractor with its principal place of business in Pennsylvania. Defendant Charles Cara ("Cara"), a citizen and resident of New York, is owner and President of Tracto Equipment, Corp. ("Tracto"), a New York corporation with its principal place of business in New York. During all times relevant to this appeal Tracto owned a parcel of land located at 100 Jay Street, Brooklyn, New York.

In March 2000 the Jay Street Property was in use as a parking lot and was subject to zoning limitations that made it unsuitable for substantial commercial or residential development. At some time prior to March 2000, JMB and Cara together contemplated developing the Jay Street Property for commercial and residential use. The discussions that followed culminated in a two-page Memorandum of Understanding ("MOU"), signed by Brown for "Jeffrey M. Brown Associates, Inc., and his companies, entities, etc.," and by Cara for "Charles Cara and his companies, entities, etc.," on March 27, 2000, by which the parties agreed to "work together to develop, build, market and manage a new real estate venture planned for an existing site at 100 Jay Street in Brooklyn, NY".

The MOU, referring to prior meetings between the parties, sets forth a general working framework for the Project, including basic design parameters and provisions for the division and distribution of future proceeds. According to the stated terms, Cara is to "provide[] the property at no cost to the partnership (or whatever combined entity is formed in the future to develop the project)." Brown is to "provide[] his company and individual experience, lender relationships, architect/ engineering relationships, legal relationships and governmental relationships to lead the development effort . . . [including] the rezoning process, conceptual design of the project, conceptual budgeting, arranging for possible financing avenues and helping to establish an effective marketing plan." The MOU sets forth Cara's responsibility for compensating a named consultant and Brown's responsibility to

---

[17] 670 F. Supp. 491 (S.D.N.Y. 1987).

[18] Schwartz & Scott, *supra* note 2, at 664.

compensate another named consultant. It provides that "Brown will build the project with union labor, if needed," and establishes that "Cara will act in the capacity of an Owner's representative on the project." "Brown agrees to front the costs of development up to an amount not exceeding $175,000," and the parties agree to pursue jointly the provision of necessary financing. Finally, the MOU declares that "time is of the essence," and states the parties' intent to "enter into a formal contract shortly."

In a letter dated April 5, 2000, and addressed to Brown, Cara states his desire to negotiate final terms of the partnership, design, and project financing. None of the proposed terms were settled, however, allegedly because the parties agreed that the costs associated with the negotiations would be wasted if the Property was not suitably rezoned. Consistent with the terms outlined in the MOU, JMB commissioned the design of a multi-use, two-tower, building, which came to be known as the "Light Bridges at Jay Street." JMB subsequently sought, through a process of applications, publicity, community meetings, lobbying, and presentations to community boards, rezoning of the Property to allow construction of the Light Bridges Project. Cara was aware of these efforts and attended some of the meetings. In November and December 2001, the Project received the needed approvals.

Ready to move forward, the parties attempted to negotiate the necessary corporate, financing, construction, and operating agreements. Negotiations proceeded through 2002 and into 2003. During the spring of 2003, Cara requested from JMB a proposed construction management agreement. JMB complied, but Cara was not pleased with the terms described in that document. JMB claims that the wrong document was sent to Cara and that JMB so informed Cara at the time. However, Cara's displeasure and offense were so deep that he refused to continue with negotiations and ceased all communication and collaboration with JMB.

In June 2003 JMB brought this diversity action seeking declaratory judgment, a permanent injunction, specific performance of the MOU, and, in the alternative, damages in *quantum meruit*. . . . The District Court dismissed all causes of action . . . save plaintiffs' claim for relief in *quantum meruit* against Cara, and JMB filed a timely notice of appeal. The first question presented on appeal is whether the MOU is an enforceable preliminary agreement. *See Teachers Ins. & Annuity Ass'n v. Tribune Co.*, 670 F. Supp. 491, 498 (S.D.N.Y. 1987). The District Court found that it is not. We agree that the MOU does not bind the parties to complete the Jay Street Project but disagree insofar as the District Court found that the MOU does not bind the parties to negotiate in good faith open terms that must be settled in order for the development to proceed within the framework described by the MOU.

Ordinarily, where the parties contemplate further negotiations and the execution of a formal instrument, a preliminary agreement does not create a binding contract. There is no dispute that this is the situation here. At the signing of the MOU, JMB and Cara knew that further negotiations would be required. The MOU itself contemplates a "formal contract" to be entered into in the future. Further, only days after the MOU was signed, Cara solicited JMB to enter negotiations toward the execution of significant and necessary agreements, demonstrating the parties' contemporary understanding that, though they had signed the MOU, further negotiations and formal agreements were necessary.

In some circumstances, however, preliminary agreements can create binding obligations. The extent of the obligations created depends on the preliminary agreement in question, though, in general, binding preliminary agreements fall into one of two categories. These two types are most authoritatively described in *Tribune*, where Judge Leval, collecting the relevant New York law, describes Type I preliminary agreements as "complete," reflecting a meeting of the minds on all the issues perceived to require negotiation. Because it is complete, a Type I preliminary agreement binds both sides to their ultimate contractual objective. Type II preliminary agreements, by contrast, are binding only to a certain degree, reflecting agreement on certain major terms, but leaving other terms open for further negotiation. Type II agreements do[] not commit the parties to their ultimate contractual objective but rather to the obligation to negotiate the open issues in good faith in an attempt to reach the objective within the agreed framework. . . .

A. The MOU is not a binding "Type I" preliminary agreement.

The District Court . . . found that the MOU is not a Type I preliminary agreement. We agree. The hallmark of a Type I agreement is that the parties have agreed to all necessary elements of the contract and are, therefore, bound to the ultimate objective despite the fact that a more formal or elaborate writing has yet to be produced. However, there is a strong presumption against finding binding obligation in agreements which include open terms, call for future approvals and expressly anticipate future preparation and execution of contract documents. . . . The category of Type I preliminary agreements is, then, limited to agreements that are "preliminary" in name only.

There are four factors relevant to determining whether a preliminary agreement is enforceable as to the ultimate contractual objective: (1) whether there is an expressed reservation of the right not to be bound in the absence of a writing; (2) whether there has been partial performance of the contract; (3) whether all of the terms of the alleged contract have been agreed upon; and (4) whether the agreement at issue is the type of contract that is usually committed to writing. [After evaluating these factors, the court held that the MOU was not a binding Type I preliminary agreement.]

B. The MOU is a binding "Type II" preliminary agreement.

We agree with the lower courts that the MOU is not a binding Type I preliminary agreement. We hold, however, that the intention of the parties to create a Type II preliminary agreement is patent in the language of the MOU, presenting us with a pure issue of law. We reverse the judgment of the District Court to the extent that it finds to the contrary. . . .

In *Tribune*, Judge Leval identified two core, but often competing, policy concerns relevant to preliminary agreements. The first is to avoid trapping parties in surprise contractual obligations that they never intended. The second is the enforcement and preserv[ation of] agreements that were intended as binding, despite a need for further documentation or further negotiation. The path between this Scylla and

Charybdis is, of course, to enforce a preliminary agreement only to the extent that the parties intend it to be binding. In this regard, giving legal recognition to [Type II agreements] serves a valuable function in the marketplace . . . permit[ting parties] to make plans in reliance upon their preliminary agreements and present market conditions . . . [without] expending enormous sums negotiating every detail of final contract documentation before knowing whether they have an agreement, and if so, on what terms." In our view, this is exactly what these parties did when they signed the MOU.

This flexibility comes with limitations, of course. While a Type I preliminary agreement is fully binding as to the final contractual goal, a Type II agreement does not commit the parties to their ultimate contractual objective but rather to the obligation to negotiate the open issues in good faith in an attempt to reach the . . . objective within the agreed framework. This obligation does not guarantee that the final contract will be concluded if both parties comport with their obligation, as good faith differences in the negotiation of the open issues may prevent a reaching of final contract. Whether the differences that have terminated the parties' working relationship in this case reflect good faith is a question for the District Court on remand.

The considerations relevant to whether a preliminary agreement is a binding Type II agreement are: (1) whether the intent to be bound is revealed by the language of the agreement; (2) the context of the negotiations; (3) the existence of open terms; (4) partial performance; and (5) the necessity of putting the agreement in final form, as indicated by the customary form of such transactions.

While some of these factors are the same as those applied to determine whether a document is a Type I preliminary agreement, they have a somewhat different significance where . . . the nature of the contract alleged is that it commits the parties in good faith to negotiate the open terms. More to the point, if the question posed is whether the parties have agreed to proceed within an open framework toward a contractual goal, leaving necessary terms for later negotiation, rather than whether the parties have agreed to achieve the ultimate contractual goal, then the language of the agreement, its contents and omissions, and the context in which it was negotiated and signed, may lead to different conclusions.

The essence of a Type II preliminary agreement is that it creates an obligation to negotiate the open issues in good faith in an attempt to reach the [ultimate contractual objective] within the agreed framework. Measuring the MOU by the relevant factors in light of this limited contractual goal it is clear that it is a binding preliminary agreement to work toward the goal of developing the Jay Street Property within a defined framework, preserving for later negotiation in good faith business, design, financing, construction, and management terms necessary to achieve the ultimate goal of developing and exploiting the Jay Street Property.

As to the first factor, while the MOU does not disclose an intention by the parties to be bound to the ultimate goal of the contract, it clearly states the parties' agreement to "work together to develop, build, market, and manage [the Jay Street Property]" and to "work together in accordance with the terms and conditions outlined [in the MOU]." We cannot imagine more clear evidence of an intention to be bound to the MOU as a general framework in which the parties will proceed in good faith toward the goal of developing the Property while preserving for later negotiation the specific details of necessary business, design, construction, financing, and management terms.

The second factor also supports a finding that the MOU is a binding Type II agreement. As the parties agree, at the time the MOU was signed, the Jay Street Project was subject to numerous contingencies that had the potential to dramatically affect planning, execution, and management. It was in this context that the parties elected to negotiate a general framework within which they could proceed while preserving flexibility in the face of future uncertainty. While it was possible in the abstract to negotiate a more definitive contract, using determinative methodologies to be applied to open issues, the context of the negotiations did not require derivation of such algorithms if the parties opted instead for a more open arrangement. The MOU is evidence of such an arrangement, and, as a Type II agreement, is consistent with the context of the negotiations.

Turning to the third factor, where the existence of open terms creates a presumption against finding a binding contract as to the ultimate goal, these same omissions may actually support finding a binding Type II agreement. The MOU leaves open terms-critical to every aspect of the Jay Street Project, from design, to business structure, to ownership and management. However, these omissions do not warrant against finding the MOU enforceable as a Type II agreement. In view of indeterminate regulatory and market conditions, JMB and Cara simply elected to pursue rezoning first, leaving finalization of project design and execution for later negotiation within the framework described in the MOU.

Consistent with views expressed in our discussion of the MOU as a Type I agreement, we find that the fourth prong, partial performance, cuts strongly in favor of finding the MOU to be a Type II agreement. JMB provided extensive and valuable performance within the framework described by the MOU. Plaintiffs are entitled to demand defendants' good faith in negotiating remaining open terms.

Finally, while the requirement for a more formal future contract may be terminal to a Type I claim, Type II agreements, by definition, comprehend the necessity of future negotiations and contracts. Here, there can be little debate that creation of the holding corporation, construction, financing, and management of the Property, all required more formal and extensive contracts, both practically and as matters of customary form. The MOU clearly contemplated these future agreements, and, after rezoning, the parties expended considerable effort to negotiate some of these agreements. . . .

For these reasons we reverse the judgment of the District Court to the extent that it dismissed causes of action based on plaintiffs' claim that the MOU is a Type II preliminary agreement. We hold that the MOU is a Type II preliminary agreement binding the parties to negotiate in good faith terms necessary to pursue joint development of the Jay Street Property. We remand for further proceedings consistent with this holding.

NOTES

1. ***Intent to be Bound:*** **Arcadian Phosphates, Inc. v. Arcadian Co.** Compare *Brown v. Cara* to *Arcadian Phosphates, Inc. v. Arcadian Co.*, 884 F.2d 69 (2d Cir. 1989), in which the parties signed a memorandum of understanding outlining the areas of an agreement to sell the defendant's phosphate fertilizer business to a joint venture. When the market for phosphates changed, the defendant informed the plaintiff that it wanted to own more of the joint venture. The plaintiffs — the potential purchasers, consisting of the joint venture and two individuals involved in its formation — claimed that the memorandum was a binding contract. The defendant — the potential seller — argued that the memorandum was an unenforceable "agreement to agree." The court examined whether a preliminary manifestation of assent was a binding preliminary agreement of the second type under the "Leval" framework:

> In applying the *Tribune* test to this case, we need look no further than the first factor. The language of the . . . memorandum — two references to the possibility that negotiations might fail and the reference to a binding sales agreement to be completed at some future date — shows that Arcadian did not intend to be bound. Contrast the language of the November memorandum with the letter[ ] in *Tribune*. . . . In *Tribune*, a letter described itself as a "binding agreement." This fact was critical to Judge Leval's reasoning in *Tribune*: "[A] party that does not wish to be bound, he said, "can very easily protect itself by not accepting language that indicates a 'firm commitment' or 'binding agreement.' " Conversely, a party that *wishes* to be bound can very easily protect itself by refusing to accept language that shows an intent *not* to be bound. . . . In order to prevail on the breach of contract claims, Arcadian needed to show only that API "should have known that [Arcadian] did not intend to be bound before the [final] contract was signed." . . .
>
> As Judge Leval noted in *Tribune*, "There is a strong presumption against finding binding obligation in agreements which include open terms, call for future approvals, and expressly anticipate future preparation and execution of contract documents." In *Tribune*, the language of the agreement argued persuasively for overcoming this presumption; here, the language of the agreement argues persuasively for letting the presumption stand.

Id. at 72–73.

Can *Brown* and *Arcadian Phosphates* be reconciled? The memorandum in *Arcadian* contemplated both the possibility that negotiations might fail and a future binding sales agreement. Even when parties agree to negotiate in good faith, the failure of negotiations and the realization of a binding sales agreement are both realistic possibilities. Do these references to two possible future states of the agreement demonstrate that the parties *did not* intend to be bound to negotiate in good faith? As counsel for Arcadian Phosphates, Inc., how would you draft the memorandum of understanding to protect your client's interests?

2. ***Memoranda of Understanding.*** Memoranda of understanding are particularly common in situations in which at least one party must make an interim

investment during the negotiation stage of bargaining, and yet the parties are unable (or unwilling) at that time to reach an ultimate agreement.[19] MOU's appear under a variety of names, including "letters of intent," "commitment letters," "binders," "agreements in principle," and "heads of agreement." A preliminary agreement to negotiate in good faith may also set out specific substantive terms of the deal, but, in contrast to an agreement with open terms, the parties do not agree to be bound to those terms.[20] The parties' intentions are to go to the next step and convert the agreement into an enforceable contract. Typically, the enforceable contract is complex and final negotiation turns on several variables unknown to the parties at the time the memorandum of understanding is executed. In these cases, therefore, the parties may be learning about each other's competence or waiting to see if their respective investments in pursuing the project make the venture more or less attractive.[21]

3.   *The Duty to Bargain in Good Faith*. The court in *Brown v. Cara* found that the memorandum of understanding was a Type II preliminary agreement binding the parties to negotiate in good faith. But what exactly does it mean to bargain in good faith? Recall that the parties in *Brown* did not intend to be bound, and therefore were not bound, to an ultimate contractual agreement. What is to stop Cara and other similarly situated parties from negotiating the agreement to the point of failure under the guise of good faith?[22] Courts and scholars have differed with regard to the manner in which good faith should be defined. The Restatement (Second) of Contracts § 205, Comment a states: "Good faith performance or enforcement of a contract emphasizes faithfulness to an agreed common purpose and consistency with the justified expectations of the other party." Comment d elaborates further on the duty of good faith: "Subterfuges and evasions violate the obligation of good faith in performance even though the actor believes his conduct to be justified. But the obligation goes further: bad faith may be overt or may consist of inaction." According to the Restatement, bad faith consists of conduct that violates community standards as defined by a judge or jury. The (UCC) defines good faith as honesty in fact and the observance of reasonable commercial standards of fair dealing in trade.[23] Generally, the doctrine of good faith has been defined as requiring reasonableness or fair conduct, but there is no uniformly recognized definition of the duty of good faith that can be utilized in the negotiation

---

[19] For discussion, see Scott, *supra* note 12; Keith E. Witek, *Drafting a More Predictable Letter of Intent — Reducing Risk and Uncertainty in a Risky and Uncertain Transaction*, 9 Tex. Intell. Prop. L.J. 185 (2001).

[20] E. Allan Farnsworth, *Precontractual Liability and Preliminary Agreements: Fair Dealing and Failed Negotiations*, 87 Colum. L. Rev. 217 (1987).

[21] Scott, *supra* note 12, at 1683.

[22] For a discussion that the duty to negotiate in good faith cannot be administered on a meaningful basis because it cannot readily be determined whether a party failed to negotiate in good faith, see Melvin Aron Eisenberg, *Contracts and Property Law: The Emergence of Dynamic Contract Law*, 2 Theoretical Inq. L. 1, 70–72 (2001).

[23] UCC § 2-103(b) (1989). Note that the Article 2 definition of "good faith" in § 2-103(1)(b) that previously applied only between merchants has now been adopted in the Revised Article 1 and applies to all parties. *See* Revised § 1-201(19) (2001).

context.[24]

From the facts of *Brown v. Cara*, Charles Cara seems to be no more than a spiteful bargainer, refusing to proceed with negotiations merely because he was offended. Surely a refusal to negotiate arising out of animus wouldn't pass any standard of "good faith" bargaining. But isn't it more likely that, rather than indulging in spite, Cara had also come to regret the deal, perhaps because he saw more advantage in pursuing his other opportunities? Assume that Brown's efforts to rezone the property to allow construction of the Light Bridges Project failed and the project was now unprofitable. Neither party would then want to pursue the project further, and Cara should be able to make a good faith exit from negotiations. Can Brown reasonably expect Cara to reimburse his sunk costs in the absence of a legally enforceable promise to do so?

Professors Schwartz and Scott argue that awarding the promisee his reliance expenditures if the promisor delays making a promised investment in the project is an important first step in solving this transactional problem. Under their approach, the duty to bargain in good faith is a duty that prohibits parties from strategically delaying their promised investments. Parties that violate this duty must pay their negotiating partners compensation for all verifiable reliance expenditures. On the other hand, on this view parties have no duty to agree to follow through on the deal they contemplated if it becomes unprofitable after they enter into their preliminary agreement but before they conclude a final agreement.[25] Consider the following excerpt:

> Parties make preliminary agreements because they cannot write a complete contract at the outset: they function in a complex environment in which a profitable project can take a number of forms, and just which form will work if any, is unknown at the start. The parties invest in the interim period because early investment accelerates the realization of returns. The sooner the factory is built, the earlier profits will be realized. More

---

[24] For further discussion of the meaning of "good faith" and other conditions relevant to the enforceability of preliminary agreements, see Omri Ben-Shahar, *Mutual Assent Versus Gradual Ascent: The Debate Over the Right to Retract*, 152 U. Pa. L. Rev. 1947 (2004); Jason Scott Johnston, *Investment, Information, and Promissory Liability*, 152 U. Pa. L. Rev. 1923 (2004); Melvin Aron Eisenberg, *Contracts and Property Law: The Emergence of Dynamic Contract Law*, 2 Theoretical Inq. L 1, (2001); Melvin Aron Eisenberg, *The Emergence of Dynamic Contract Law*, 88 Cal. L. Rev. 1743 (2000); Saul Litvinoff, *Good Faith*, 71 Tul. L. Rev. 1645 (1997); Nadia E. Nedzel, *A Comparative Study of Good Faith, Fair Dealing, and Precontractual Liability*, 12 Tul. Eur. & Civ. L.F. 97 (1997); Avery Katz, *When Should an Offer Stick? The Economics of Promissory Estoppel in Preliminary Negotiations*, 105 Yale L.J. 1249 (1996); Nicola W. Palmieri, *Good Faith Negotiations Required During Precontractual Negotiations*, 24 Seton Hall L. Rev. 70 (1993); Harvey L. Temkin, *When Does the Fat Lady Sing?: An Analysis of "Agreements in Principle" in Corporate Acquisitions*, 55 Fordham L. Rev. 125 (1986).

[25] For further discussion of the transactional approach to addressing the problem of incomplete contracts, see Avery W. Katz, *Contractual Incompleteness: A Transactional Perspective*, 56 Case W. Res. 169 (2005); Juliet P. Kostritsky, *Taxonomy for Justifying Judicial Intervention in an Imperfect World; What to Do When Parties Have Not Achieved Bargains or Have Drafted Incomplete Agreements*, 2004 Wis. L. Rev. 323; Kostritsky, *Bargaining with Uncertainty, Moral Hazard, and Sunk Costs: A Default Rule for Pre-Contractual Negotiations*, 44 Hastings L.J. 621 (1993); G. Richard Shell, *Opportunism and Trust in the Negotiation of Commercial Contracts: Toward a New Cause of Action*, 44 Vand. L. Rev. 221 (1991).

importantly, investment clarifies what type of project could succeed. For example, an investment in learning market conditions may reveal which type of widget is likely to sell. . . . Preliminary agreements thus commonly are exploratory; that is, the performance of a preliminary agreement sometimes is a necessary condition for parties to pursue an efficient project later.

To illustrate how a promisee can have a justifiable grievance, realize that in some deals, expected surplus would be maximized if the parties invested sequentially while in other deals surplus would be maximized if the parties invested simultaneously. An efficient preliminary agreement to invest simultaneously may be unstable, however. The promisor has an incentive to defect from any such agreement by delaying her decision whether to invest until *after* the promisee has invested. The promisor benefits from defection if the project turns out to be unprofitable, because she will not have sunk costs in a losing deal. Alternatively, if the project turns out to be profitable, the parties' complete contract will compensate the promisor for the investment costs the contract requires her to make, but the contract will not reimburse the promisee for costs he had already incurred. Defection from a preliminary agreement to invest simultaneously thus disadvantages the promisee. We characterize a promisor's defection as a breach. . . .

It is efficient for contract law to protect the promisee's reliance interest if his promisor deviated from an agreed investment sequence. A reliance recovery will encourage parties to make preliminary agreements and will deter some strategic behavior. Therefore, the new rule governing preliminary agreements — awarding the promisee reliance if the promisor fails to bargain in good faith but not requiring the parties to agree — is a step in the right direction.

Alan Schwartz & Robert E. Scott, *Precontractual Liability and Preliminary Agreements*, 120 HARV. L. REV. 661, 665–67 (2007).

Do the facts in *Brown v. Cara* fit the prototypical transaction that Schwartz and Scott describe? In particular, what investment was Cara required to make in the proposed deal? All he agreed to do was to make the property available. It was Brown who had to make all the subsequent investments. Given those facts, Professor Victor Goldberg argues in Brown v. Cara: *The Type II Preliminary Agreement and the Option to Unbundle* (conference paper presented at Conference on Contractual Innovation, NYU Law School, May 3–4, 2012) that it would have been relatively easy under these circumstances for the parties to write an enforceable contract that would protect Brown's investment and thus they had no need to rely on the preliminary agreement framework created by Judge Leval. Do you agree?

4. ***Lost in Translation: Can E-mail Constitute a Binding Preliminary Agreement?*** In *Rubinstein v. Clark & Green, Inc.*, 2010 U.S. App. LEXIS 21008 (2d Cir. Oct. 12, 2010), the Second Circuit considered whether an exchange of electronic messages could bind the parties to a preliminary agreement. Rubinstein, a homebuilder, sued Clark & Green, an architectural firm, for its purported failure to complete its work on his home. After a series of messages back and forth,

Rubinstein e-mailed Clark, one of the defendant firm's principals:

> I don't have the time or inclination or see the need to get into doing a contract until we are further along. . . . Also by waiting on paperwork we will have some mileage under our belts in terms of a relationship and will have a sense of how specifically we need to document this and that.

Id. at 788. The court analyzed the facts under the same factors as in *Brown v. Cara.* In upholding summary judgment for the defendant, the court said: "three of the four *Adjustrite* factors strongly support a conclusion that the parties did not intend to be bound by the proposed work schedule in the absence of a formal contract. The remaining factor — partial performance — is not sufficiently probative on the issue of the schedule to raise a genuine issue of fact." *Id.* at 790.

   5.   *The Evolution of the Common Law from Unenforceable Agreements to Agree to Binding Preliminary Agreements.* As noted above, the Leval framework creating the binding preliminary agreement has quickly emerged, in the words of one court, as "the modern trend in contract law."[26] But what precisely are the factors that produce such innovations in contractual forms? In *Contract and Innovation: The Limited Role of Generalist Courts in the Evolution of Novel Contractual Forms*, 87 N.Y.U. L. Rev. ___ (forthcoming 2013), Professors Ronald Gilson, Charles Sabel, and Robert Scott argue that contractual innovation is the third step in a dynamic process. The first step is an exogenous change in the business environment — in this case the "information revolution" has greatly increased the level of uncertainty parties face. In an uncertain world the search for partners capable and willing to engage in incompletely specified agreement becomes an essential part of doing business. This change in the business environment then evokes a substantive innovation in business practices as parties adjust the existing structure of their agreements to the changed circumstances. Innovations in contract form such as reliance on enforceable preliminary agreements then arise to stabilize the new arrangements. Parties increasingly realize that the feasibility of many projects can only be determined by joint investment in the production of information to evaluate whether a project is profitable to pursue. It is only at this point that courts enter the picture, when they are asked to resolve disputes and standardize the workings of the contractual innovation. Their task is to adapt the contract law to the context presented by the contractual innovation by providing doctrine that facilitates the parties initial investments without imposing legal consequences on the outcome of the parties' collaborative activity.

C.   OUTPUT, REQUIREMENTS, AND EXCLUSIVE DEALINGS ARRANGEMENTS

In "one-shot" transactions, parties can usually negotiate a precise agreement on the quantity of goods (or services) to be provided under a contract. There is an obvious advantage to a contract term that specifies a determinate quantity. But in many relational contexts, especially those involving long-term contracts, the parties face real constraints that make such determinate agreements impractical. The

---

[26] *Burbach Broad. Co. v. Elkins Radio Corp.*, 278 F.3d 401, 409 (4th Cir. 2002).

future is often too uncertain and any estimate as to quantity that "averages" out the known future risks will invariably turn out to be wrong in the actual case. Parties, therefore, need flexibility in adjusting to changing circumstances over time. This usually means that one party (and perhaps both) needs some discretion over the quantity of goods that must be ordered by the buyer and the price that the buyer must pay. UCC § 2-306 offers bargainers a mechanism for adjusting the quantity of goods required to be exchanged in a contract where the quantity provision was left open at the time the contract was negotiated and signed. Note that two types of agreements are regulated by § 2-306: output or requirements contracts and exclusive dealing contracts. Each has its own basis for measuring the quantity which must be produced. "Good faith" is the touchstone for output and requirements contracts, while "best efforts" dictates quantity in exclusive dealings contracts. How are such broad, general concepts of any help in establishing the precise quantity of the goods to be exchanged? To what extent is discretion constrained by these terms? Consider the following cases, and the UCC provisions they refer to, as you attempt to answer that question.

[1]   Output and Requirements Contracts

EASTERN AIR LINES, INC. v. GULF OIL CORP.
United States District Court, Southern District of Florida
415 F. Supp. 429 (1975)

KING, J.

Eastern Air Lines, Inc., hereafter Eastern, and Gulf Oil Corporation, hereafter Gulf, have enjoyed a mutually advantageous business relationship involving the sale and purchase of aviation fuel for several decades.

This controversy involves the threatened disruption of that historic relationship and the attempt, by Eastern, to enforce the most recent contract between the parties. On March 8, 1974 the correspondence and telex communications between the corporate entities culminated in a demand by Gulf that Eastern must meet its demand for a price increase or Gulf would shut off Eastern's supply of jet fuel within fifteen days.

Eastern responded by filing its complaint with this court, alleging that Gulf had breached its contract and requesting preliminary and permanent mandatory injunctions requiring Gulf to perform the contract in accordance with its terms. By agreement of the parties, a preliminary injunction preserving the status quo was entered on March 20, 1974, requiring Gulf to perform its contract and directing Eastern to pay in accordance with the contract terms, pending final disposition of the case.

Gulf answered Eastern's complaint, alleging that the contract was not a binding requirements contract, was void for want of mutuality, and, furthermore, was "commercially impracticable" within the meaning of Uniform Commercial Code § 2-615.

The extraordinarily able advocacy by the experienced lawyers for both parties produced testimony at the trial from internationally respected experts who described in depth economic events that have, in recent months, profoundly affected the lives of every American.

On June 27, 1972, an agreement was signed by the parties, which, as amended, was to provide the basis upon which Gulf was to furnish jet fuel to Eastern at certain specific cities in the Eastern system. Said agreement supplemented an existing contract between Gulf and Eastern which, on June 27, 1972, had approximately one year remaining prior to its expiration.

The contract is Gulf's standard form aviation fuel contract and is identical in all material particulars with the first contract for jet fuel, dated 1959, between Eastern and Gulf and, indeed, with aviation fuel contracts antedating the jet age. It is similar to contracts in general use in the aviation fuel trade. The contract was drafted by Gulf after substantial arm's length negotiation between the parties. Gulf approached Eastern more than a year before the expiration of the then-existing contracts between Gulf and Eastern, seeking to preserve its historic relationship with Eastern. Following several months of negotiation, the contract, consolidating and extending the terms of several existing contracts, was executed by the parties in June, 1972, to expire January 31, 1977.

The parties agreed that this contract, as its predecessor, should provide a reference to reflect changes in the price of the raw material from which jet fuel is processed, i.e., crude oil, in direct proportion to the cost per gallon of jet fuel.

Both parties regarded the instant agreement as favorable, Eastern, in part, because it offered immediate savings in projected escalations under the existing agreement through reduced base prices at the contract cities; while Gulf found a long term outlet for a capacity of jet fuel coming on stream from a newly completed refinery, as well as a means to relate anticipated increased cost of raw material (crude oil) directly to the price of the refined product sold. The previous Eastern/Gulf contracts contained a price index clause which operated to pass on to Eastern only one-half of any increase in the price of crude oil. Both parties knew at the time of contract negotiations that increases in crude oil prices would be expected, were "a way of life," and intended that those increases be borne by Eastern in a direct proportional relationship of crude oil cost per barrel to jet fuel cost per gallon.

Accordingly, the parties selected an indicator (West Texas Sour), a crude which is bought and sold in large volume and was thus a reliable indicator of the market value of crude oil. From June 27, 1972 to the fall of 1973, there were in effect various forms of U.S. government imposed price controls which at once controlled the price of crude oil generally, West Texas Sour specifically, and hence the price of jet fuel. As the government authorized increased prices of crude those increases were in turn reflected in the cost of jet fuel. Eastern has paid a per gallon increase under the contract from 11 cents to 15 cents (or some 40%).

The indicator selected by the parties was "the average of the posted prices for West Texas sour crude, 30.0 — 30.9 gravity, of Gulf Oil Corporation, Shell Oil Company, and Pan American Petroleum Corporation." The posting of crude prices under the contract "shall be as listed for these companies in Platts Oilgram Service — Crude Oil Supplement. . . ."

"Posting" has long been a practice in the oil industry. It involves the physical placement at a public location of a price bulletin reflecting the current price at which an oil company will pay for a given barrel of a specific type of crude oil. Those posted price bulletins historically have, in addition to being displayed publicly, been mailed to those persons evincing interest therein, including sellers of crude oil, customers whose price of product may be based thereon, and, among others, Platts Oilgram, publishers of a periodical of interest to those related to the oil industry.

In recent years, the United States has become increasingly dependent upon foreign crude oil, particularly from the "OPEC" nations most of which are in the Middle East. OPEC was formed in 1970 for the avowed purpose of raising oil prices, and has become an increasingly cohesive and potent organization as its member nations have steadily enhanced their equity positions and their control over their oil production facilities. Nationalization of crude oil resources and shutdowns of production and distribution have become a way of life for oil companies operating in OPEC nations, particularly in the volatile Middle East. The closing of the Suez Canal and the concomitant interruption of the flow of Mid-East oil during the 1967 "Six-Day War," and Libya's nationalization of its oil industry during the same period, are only some of the more dramatic examples of a trend that began years ago. By 1969 "the handwriting was on the wall" in the words of Gulf's foreign oil expert witness, Mr. Blackledge.

During 1970 domestic United States oil production "peaked;" since then it has declined while the percentage of imported crude oil has been steadily increasing. Unlike domestic crude oil, which has been subject to price control since August 15, 1971, foreign crude oil has never been subject to price control by the United States Government. Foreign crude oil prices, uncontrolled by the Federal Government, were generally lower than domestic crude oil prices in 1971 and 1972; during 1973 foreign prices "crossed" domestic prices; by late 1973 foreign prices were generally several dollars per barrel higher than controlled domestic prices. It was during late 1973 that the Mid-East exploded in another war, accompanied by an embargo (at least officially) by the Arab oil-producing nations against the United States and certain of its allies. World prices for oil and oil products increased.

Mindful of that situation and for various other reasons concerning the nation's economy, the United States government began a series of controls affecting the oil industry culminating, in the fall of 1973, with the implementation of price controls known as "two-tier." In practice "two-tier" can be described as follows: taking as the bench mark the number of barrels produced from a given well in May of 1972, that number of barrels is deemed "old" oil. The price of "old" oil then is frozen by the government at a fixed level. To the extent that the productivity of a given well can be increased over the May, 1972, production, that increased production is deemed "new" oil. For each barrel of "new" oil produced, the government authorized the release from price controls of an equivalent number of barrels from those theretofore designated "old" oil. For example, from a well which in May of 1972, produced 100 barrels of oil; all of the production of that well would, since the imposition of "two-tier" in August of 1973, be "old" oil. Increased productivity to 150 barrels would result in 50 barrels of "new" oil and 50 barrels of "released" oil; with the result that 100 barrels of the 150 barrels produced from the well would be uncontrolled by the "two-tier" pricing system, while the 50 remaining barrels of "old" would remain government price controlled.

The implementation of "two-tier" was completely without precedent in the history of government price control action. Its impact, however, was nominal, until the imposition of an embargo upon the exportation of crude oil by certain Arab countries in October, 1973. Those countries deemed sympathetic to Israel were embargoed from receiving oil from the Arab oil producing countries. The United States was among the principal countries affected by that embargo, with the result that it experienced an immediate "energy crisis."

Following closely after the embargo, OPEC (Oil Producing Export Countries) unilaterally increased the price of their crude to the world market some 400/% between September, 1973, and January 15, 1974. Since the United States domestic production was at capacity, it was dependent upon foreign crude to meet its requirements. New and released oil (uncontrolled) soon reached parity with the price of foreign crude, moving from approximately $5 to $11 a barrel from September, 1974 [sic] to January 15, 1974.

Since imposition of "two-tier," the price of "old oil" has remained fixed by government action, with the oil companies resorting to postings reflecting prices they will pay for the new and released oil, not subject to government controls. Those prices, known as "premiums," are the subject of supplemental bulletins which are likewise posted by the oil companies and furnished to interested parties, including Platts Oilgram.

Platts, since the institution of "two-tier" has not published the posted prices of any of the premiums offered by the oil companies in the United States, including those of Gulf Oil Corporation, Shell Oil Company and Pan American Petroleum, the companies designated in the agreement. The information which has appeared in Platts since the implementation of "two-tier" with respect to the price of West Texas Sour crude oil has been the price of "old" oil subject to government control.

Under the court's restraining order, entered in this cause by agreement of the parties, Eastern has been paying for jet fuel from Gulf on the basis of the price of "old" West Texas Sour crude oil as fixed by government price control action, i.e., $5 a barrel. Approximately 40 gallons of finished jet fuel product can be refined from a barrel of crude.

Against this factual background we turn to a consideration of the legal issues.

Gulf has taken the position in this case that the contract between it and Eastern is not a valid document in that it lacks mutuality of obligation; it is vague and indefinite; and that it renders Gulf subject to Eastern's whims respecting the volume of jet fuel Gulf would be required to deliver to the purchaser Eastern. The contract talks in terms of fuel "requirements."[27] The parties have interpreted this provision to mean that any aviation fuel purchased by Eastern at one of the cities covered by the contract, must be bought from Gulf. Conversely, Gulf must make the necessary arrangements to supply Eastern's reasonable good faith demands at those same locations. This is the construction the parties themselves have placed on

---

[27] [4] "Gulf agrees to sell and deliver to Eastern, and Eastern agrees to purchase, receive and pay for their requirements of Gulf Jet A and Gulf Jet A-1 at the locations listed. . . ."

the contract and it has governed their conduct over many years and several contracts.

In early cases, requirements contracts were found invalid for want of the requisite definiteness, or on the grounds of lack of mutuality. Many such cases are collected and annotated at 14 A.L.R. 1300. As reflected in the foregoing annotation, there developed rather quickly in the law the view that a requirements contract could be binding where the purchaser had an operating business. The "lack of mutuality" and "indefiniteness" were resolved since the court could determine the volume of goods provided for under the contract by reference to objective evidence of the volume of goods required to operate the specified business. Therefore, well prior to the adoption of the Uniform Commercial Code, case law generally held requirements contracts binding.

The Uniform Commercial Code, adopted in Florida in 1965, specifically approves requirements contracts in U.C.C. § 2-306(1). The Uniform Commercial Code Official Comment interprets § 2-306(1) as follows:

> 2. Under this Article, a contract for output or requirements is not too indefinite since it is held to mean the actual good faith output or requirements of the particular party. Nor does such a contract lack mutuality of obligation since, under this section, the party who will determine quantity is required to operate his plant or conduct his business in good faith and according to commercial standards of fair dealing in the trade so that his output or requirements will approximate a reasonably foreseeable figure. Reasonable elasticity in the requirements is expressly envisaged by this section and good faith variations from prior requirements are permitted even when the variation may be such as to result in discontinuance. A shut-down by a requirements buyer for lack of orders might be permissible when a shut-down merely to curtail losses would not. The essential test is whether the party is acting in good faith. Similarly, a sudden expansion of the plant by which requirements are to be measured would not be included within the scope of the contract as made but normal expansion undertaken in good faith would be within the scope of this section. One of the factors in an expansion situation would be whether the market price has risen greatly in a case in which the requirements contract contained a fixed price. Reasonable variation of an extreme sort is exemplified in Southwest Natural Gas Co. v. Oklahoma Portland Cement Co., 102 F.2d 630 (C.C.A. 10, 1939).

Some of the prior Gulf-Eastern contracts have included the estimated fuel requirements for some cities covered by the contract while others have none. The particular contract contains an estimate for Gainesville, Florida requirement.

The parties have consistently over the years relied upon each other to act in good faith in the purchase and sale of the required quantities of aviation fuel specified in the contract. During the course of the contract, various estimates have been exchanged from time to time, and, since the advent of the petroleum allocations programs, discussions of estimated requirements have been on a monthly (or more frequent) basis.

The court concludes that the document is a binding and enforceable requirements contract. Gulf suggests that Eastern violated the contract between the parties by manipulating its requirements through a practice known as "fuel freighting" in the airline industry. Requirements can vary from city to city depending on whether or not it is economically profitable to freight fuel. This fuel freighting practice in accordance with price could affect lifting from Gulf stations by either raising such liftings or lowering them. If the price was higher at a Gulf station, the practice could have reduced liftings there by lifting fuel in excess of its actual operating requirements at a prior station, and thereby not loading fuel at the succeeding high price Gulf station. Similarly where the Gulf station was comparatively cheaper, an aircraft might load more heavily at the Gulf station and not load at other succeeding non-Gulf stations.

The court however, finds that Eastern's performance under the contract does not constitute a breach of its agreement with Gulf and is consistent with good faith and established commercial practices as required by U.C.C. § 2-306.

"Good Faith" means "honesty in fact in the conduct or transaction concerned" U.C.C. § 1-201(19). Between merchants, "good faith" means "honesty in fact and the observance of reasonable commercial standards of fair dealing in the trade;" U.C.C. § 2-103(1)(b) and Official Comment 2 of U.C.C. § 2-306. The relevant commercial practices are "courses of performance," "courses of dealing" and "usages of trade."[28]

Throughout the history of commercial aviation, including 30 years of dealing between Gulf and Eastern, airlines' liftings of fuel by nature have been subject to substantial daily, weekly, monthly and seasonal variations, as they are affected by weather, schedule changes, size of aircraft, aircraft load, local airport conditions, ground time, availability of fueling facilities, whether the flight is on time or late, passenger convenience, economy and efficiency of operation, fuel taxes, into-plane fuel service charges, fuel price, and, ultimately, the judgment of the flight captain as to how much fuel he wants to take.

All these factors are, and for years have been, known to oil companies, including Gulf, and taken into account by them in their fuel contracts. Gulf's witnesses at trial pointed to certain examples of numerically large "swings" in monthly liftings by Eastern at various Gulf stations. Gulf never complained of this practice and apparently accepted it as normal procedure.

---

[28] [6] U.C.C. § 2-208(1) defines "course of performance" as those "repeated occasions for performance by either party with knowledge of the nature of the performance and opportunity for objection to it by the other."

U.C.C. § 1-205(1) defines "course of dealing" as "a sequence of previous conduct between the parties to a particular transaction which is fairly to be regarded as establishing a common basis of understanding for interpreting their expressions and other conduct."

U.C.C. § 1-205(2) defines "usage of trade" as "any practice or method of dealing having such regularity of observance in a place, vocation or trade as to justify an expectation that it will be observed with respect to the transaction in question."

U.C.C. § 2-208(2) provides that "express terms shall control course of performance and course of performance shall control both course of dealings and usage of trade."

Some of the "swings" were explained by the fueling of a single aircraft for one flight, or by the addition of one schedule in mid-month. The evidence establishes that Eastern, on one occasion, requested 500,000 additional gallons for one month at one station, without protest from Gulf, and that Eastern increased its requirements at another station more than 50 percent year to year, from less than 2,000,000 to more than 3,000,000 gallons, again, without Gulf objection.

The court concludes that fuel freighting is an established industry practice, inherent in the nature of the business. The evidence clearly demonstrated that the practice has long been part of the established courses of performance and dealing between Eastern and Gulf. As the practice of "freighting" or "tankering" has gone on unchanged and unchallenged for many years accepted as a fact of life by Gulf without complaint, the court is reminded of Official Comment 1 to U.C.C. § 2-208:

> The parties themselves know best what they have meant by their words of agreement and their action under that agreement is the best indication of what that meaning was.

From a practical point of view, "freighting" opportunities are very few, according to the uncontradicted testimony, as the airline must perform its schedules in consideration of operating realities. There is no suggestion here that Eastern is operating at certain Gulf stations but taking no fuel at all. The very reason Eastern initially desired a fuel contract was because the airline planned to take on fuel, and had to have an assured source of supply.

If a customer's demands under a requirements contract become excessive, U.C.C. § 2-306 protects the seller and, in the appropriate case, would allow him to refuse to deliver unreasonable amounts demanded (but without eliminating his basic contract obligation); similarly, in an appropriate case, if a customer repeatedly had no requirements at all, the seller might be excused from performance if the buyer suddenly and without warning should descend upon him and demand his entire inventory, but the court is not called upon to decide those cases here.

Rather, the case here is one where the established courses of performance and dealing between the parties, the established usages of the trade, and the basic contract itself all show that the matters complained of for the first time by Gulf after commencement of this litigation are the fundamental given ingredients of the aviation fuel trade to which the parties have accommodated themselves successfully and without dispute over the years.

> The practical interpretation given to their contracts by the parties to them while they are engaged in their performance, and before any controversy has arisen concerning them, is one of the best indications of their true intent, and courts that adopt and enforce such a construction are not likely to commit serious error.

Manhattan Life Ins. Co. of New York v. Wright, 126 F. 82, 87 (8th Cir. 1903).

The court concludes that Eastern has not violated the contract. . . .[29]

---

[29] Another issue in the case is explored in Chapter 8. [Eds.]

EMPIRE GAS CORP. v. AMERICAN BAKERIES CO.
United States Court of Appeals, Seventh Circuit
840 F.2d 1333 (1988)

POSNER, J.

This appeal in a diversity contract case presents a fundamental question — surprisingly little discussed by either courts or commentators — in the law of requirements contracts. Is such a contract essentially a buyer's option, entitling him to purchase all he needs of the good in question on the terms set forth in the contract, but leaving him free to purchase none if he wishes provided that he does not purchase the good from anyone else and is not acting out of ill will toward the seller?

Empire Gas Corporation is a retail distributor of liquefied petroleum gas, better known as "propane." It also sells converters that enable gasoline-powered motor vehicles to operate on propane. The sharp rise in gasoline prices in 1979 and 1980 made American Bakeries Company, which operated a fleet of more than 3,000 motor vehicles to serve its processing plants and bakeries, interested in the possibility of converting its fleet to propane, which was now one-third to one-half less expensive than gasoline. Discussions between the companies resulted in an agreement in principle. Empire Gas sent American Bakeries a draft of its standard "Guaranteed Fuel Supply Contract," which would have required American Bakeries to install a minimum number of conversion units each month and to buy all the propane for the converted vehicles from Empire Gas for eight years. American Bakeries rejected the contract and Empire Gas prepared a new one, which was executed on April 17, 1980, and which was "for approximately three thousand (3,000) [conversion] units, more or less depending upon requirements of Buyer, consisting of Fuel Tank, Fuel Lock Off Switch, Converter & appropriate Carburetor & Small Parts Kit," at a price of $750 per unit. American Bakeries agreed "to purchase propane motor fuel solely from EMPIRE GAS CORPORATION at all locations where EMPIRE GAS has supplied carburetion and dispensing equipment as long as EMPIRE GAS CORPORATION remains in a reasonably competitive price posture with other major suppliers." The contract was to last for four years.

American Bakeries never ordered any equipment or propane from Empire Gas. Apparently within days after the signing of the contract American Bakeries decided not to convert its fleet to propane. No reason has been given for the decision.

Empire Gas brought suit against American Bakeries for breach of contract and won a jury verdict for $3,254,963, representing lost profits on 2,242 conversion units (the jury's estimate of American Bakeries' requirements) and on the propane fuel that the converted vehicles would have consumed during the contract period. . . .

The heart of this case is the instruction concerning American Bakeries' obligation under the contract. If there were no legal category of "requirements" contracts and no provision of the Uniform Commercial Code governing such contracts, a strong argument could be made that American Bakeries agreed to buy 3,000 conversion units or slightly more or slightly less, depending on its actual needs, and hence that it broke the contract by taking none. This is not only a semantically permissible reading of the contract but one supported by the discussions that the parties had before the contract was signed (and these discussions are admissible to explain though not to change the parties' undertakings), in which American Bakeries assured Empire Gas that it was planning to convert its entire fleet. American Bakeries insisted on adding the phrase "more or less depending upon requirements of Buyer" just in case its estimate of 3,000 was off, and this is quite different from supposing that the phrase was added so that American Bakeries would have no obligation to buy any units at all.

The parties agree, however, that despite the negotiating history and the inclusion in the contract of a specific estimate of quantity, the quoted phrase sorted the contract into the legal bin labeled "requirements contract" and thereby brought it under the governance of section 2-306(1) of the Uniform Commercial Code, which provides:

> A term which measures the quantity by the output of the seller or the requirements of the buyer means such actual output or requirements as may occur in good faith, except that no quantity unreasonably dispropor-tionate to any stated estimate or in the absence of a stated estimate to any normal or otherwise comparable prior output or requirements may be tendered or demanded.

Over American Bakeries' objection the judge decided to read the statute to the jury verbatim and without amplification, remarking to the lawyers,

> Now, I have nothing to do with the fact that there may be some ambiguity in 2-306. If there is ambiguity, well, that is too bad. This is the law that the legislature has adopted. With due respect to all these great judges that [American Bakeries' counsel] has cited and these great academic lawyers he has called to my attention, well, good, they have a lot of time to mull over these problems. But I have the problem of telling this jury what the law is, and the law is right here, right here in this statute, and I have a good deal of faith in this jury's ability to apply this statute to the facts of this case.

It is not true that the law is what a jury might make out of statutory language. The law is the statute as interpreted. The duty of interpretation is the judge's. Having interpreted the statute he must then convey the statute's meaning, as interpreted, in words the jury can understand. If section 2-306 means something different from what it seems to say, the instruction was erroneous.

The interpretive question involves the proviso dealing with "quantity unreason-ably disproportionate to any stated estimate." This limitation is fairly easy to understand when the disproportion takes the form of the buyer's demanding more than the amount estimated. If there were no ceiling, and if the price happened to be advantageous to the buyer, he might increase his "requirements" so that he could resell the good at a profit. . . . This would place him in competition with the seller — a result the parties would not have wanted when they signed the contract. So the "unreasonably disproportionate" proviso carries out the likely intent of the parties. The only problem is that the same result could easily be reached by interpretation of the words "good faith" in the preceding clause of section 2-306(1), thus making the proviso redundant. But redundancies designed to clarify or emphasize are common in legal drafting; and anyway the Uniform Commercial Code has its share of ambiguities.

The proviso does not distinguish between the buyer who demands more than the stated estimate and the buyer who demands less, and therefore if read literally it would forbid a buyer to take (much) less than the stated estimate. Since the judge did not attempt to interpret the statute, the jury may have read it literally, and if so the judge in effect directed a verdict for Empire Gas. The stated estimate was for 3,000 units; American Bakeries took none; if this was not unreasonably disproportionate to the stated estimate, what buyer shortfall could be?

So we must decide whether the proviso should be read literally when the buyer is demanding less rather than more than the stated estimate. There are no cases on the question in Illinois, and authority elsewhere is sparse, considering how often (one might think) the question must have arisen. But the clearly dominant approach is not to construe the proviso literally, but instead to treat the overdemanding and underdemanding cases differently. . . . We think this is right. We also note that it was the common law approach: "the seller assumes the risk of all good faith variations in the buyer's requirements even to the extent of a determination to liquidate or discontinue the business." HML Corp. v. General Foods Corp., 365 F.2d 77, 81 (3d Cir. 1966). . . .

Granted, there is language in the Official Comments (not official in Illinois, be it noted) which points to symmetrical treatment of the overdemanding and underdemanding cases: "the agreed estimate is to be regarded as a center around which the parties intend the variation to occur." UCC § 2-306, comment 3. But there is no elaboration; and the statement is in tension with the statement in comment 2 that "good faith variations from prior requirements are permitted even when the variation may be such as to result in discontinuance," for if that principle is sound in general, why should it cease to be sound just because the parties included an estimate of the buyer's requirements? A tiny verbal point against the symmetrical interpretation is the last word of the proviso — "demanded." The statement that "no quantity unreasonably disproportionate to any stated estimate . . . may be . . . demanded" is more naturally read as applying to the case where the buyer is demanding more than when he is reducing his demand below the usual or estimated level.

More important than this verbal skirmishing is the fact that the entire proviso is in a sense redundant given the words "good faith" in the main clause of the statute. The proviso thus seems to have been designed to explicate the term "good faith" rather than to establish an independent legal standard. And the aspect of good faith that required explication had only to do with disproportionately large demands. If the buyer saw an opportunity to increase his profits by reselling the seller's goods because the market price had risen above the contract price, the exploitation of that opportunity might not clearly spell bad faith; the proviso was added to close off the opportunity. There is no indication that the draftsmen were equally, if at all, concerned about the case where the buyer takes less than his estimated requirements, provided, of course, that he does not buy from anyone else. We conclude that the Illinois courts would allow a buyer to reduce his requirements to zero if he was acting in good faith, even though the contract contained an estimate of those requirements.

This conclusion would be greatly strengthened — too much so, as we shall see — if the only purpose of a requirements contract were to give the seller a reasonably assured market for his product by forbidding the buyer to satisfy any of his needs by buying from another supplier. (An output contract, also dealt with in section 2-306(1), gives the buyer a reasonably assured source of supply by forbidding the seller to sell any of his output to any other buyer.) The buyer's undertaking to deal exclusively with a particular seller gives the seller some, although far from complete, assurance of having a market for his goods; and of course he must compensate the buyer for giving up the opportunity to shop around for a better deal from competing sellers.

There was no breach of this obligation, or, at most, a trivial one. (American Bakeries did convert 229 of its vehicles to propane, using equipment bought from another company; but the record is silent on how many, if any, of these purchases occurred while the contract with Empire Gas was in force.) If the obligation were not just to refrain from buying a competitor's goods but to buy approximately the stated estimate (or, in the absence of any estimate, the buyer's "normal" requirements), the contract would be altogether more burdensome to the buyer. Instead of just committing himself not to buy from a competitor even if the competitor offered a better product or terms of sale, he would be committing himself to go through with whatever project generated the estimate of required quantity, no matter what happened over the life of the project save those exceptional events that would excuse performance under the related excuses of force majeure, impossibility, impracticability, or frustration. This would be a big commitment to infer from the inclusion in the contract of an estimated quantity, at least once the parties concede as they do here that their contract really is a requirements contract and not a contract for the estimate itself — not, in other words, a fixed-quantity contract.

Both extreme interpretations — that the buyer need only refrain from dealing with a competitor of the seller, and that the buyer cannot go significantly beneath the estimated quantity except in dire circumstances — must be rejected, as we shall see. Nevertheless the judge should not have read the "unreasonably disproportionate" proviso in section 2-306(1) to the jury. The proviso does not apply, though the requirement of good faith does, where the buyer takes less rather than more of the stated estimate in a requirements contract.

This error in instructions requires reversal and a new trial on liability unless it is clear either that American Bakeries acted in good faith or that it acted in bad faith, since the statute requires the buyer to take his "good faith" requirements from the seller, irrespective of proportionality. The Uniform Commercial Code does not contain a definition of "good faith" that seems applicable to the buyer under a requirements contract. Compare section 2-104(1) with section 2-103(1)(b). Nor has the term a settled meaning in law generally; it is a chameleon. . . . Clearly, American Bakeries was acting in bad faith if during the contract period it bought propane conversion units from anyone other than Empire Gas, or made its own units, or reduced its purchases because it wanted to hurt Empire Gas (for example because they were competitors in some other market). Equally clearly, it was not acting in bad faith if it had a business reason for deciding not to convert that was independent of the terms of the contract or any other aspect of its relationship with Empire Gas, such as a drop in the demand for its bakery products that led it to reduce or abandon its fleet of delivery trucks. A harder question is whether it was acting in bad faith if it changed its mind about conversion for no (disclosed) reason. There is no evidence in the record on why it changed its mind beyond vague references to "budget problems" that, so far as appears, may have been nothing more than a euphemism for a decision by American Bakeries not to allocate funds for conversion to propane.

If no reason at all need be given for scaling back one's requirements even to zero, then a requirements contract is from the buyer's standpoint just an option to purchase up to (or slightly beyond, i.e., within the limits of reasonable proportionality) the stated estimate on the terms specified in the contract, except that the buyer cannot refuse to exercise the option because someone offers him better terms. This is not an unreasonable position, but it is not the law. Among the less important reasons for this conclusion are that option contracts are dealt with elsewhere in the Code, see section 2-311, and that the Official Comments to section 306 state that "a shut-down by a requirements buyer for lack of orders might be permissible where a shut-down *merely to curtail losses* would not." UCC § 2-306, comment 2 (emphasis added). More compelling is the Illinois Code Comment to section 2-306, which states that "this section . . . is but a codification of prior Illinois decisional law," which had made clear that a requirements contract was more than a buyer's option. "By the original agreement, appellant was entitled to order all the coal which was required or needed in its business for the season named; by the modified contract, appellant was restricted to the privilege of ordering twelve thousand tons. It was not the intention here to contract for the mere option or privilege of buying coal at a future time, but simply to limit the quantity to be bought. . . . It was not intended to be an option contract." Minnesota Lumber Co. v. Whitebreast Coal Co., 160 Ill. 85, 96-97, 43 N.E. 774 (1896). "Requirements" are more than purely subjective "needs," which would be the equivalent of "wants." See National Furnace Co. v. Keystone Mfg. Co., 110 Ill. 427, 433-34 (1884). . . .

These cases are old, but nothing has happened to sap their strength. . . . The statement of an estimate invites the seller to begin making preparations to satisfy the contract, and although no reliance expense was incurred by the seller in this case, a seller is entitled to expect that the buyer will buy something like the estimated requirements unless it has a valid business reason for buying less. More important than the estimate (which was not a factor in the Illinois cases just cited) is the fact that ordinarily a requirements contract is terminated after performance has begun, rather than before as in the present case. Whether or not the seller can prove reliance damages, the sudden termination of the contract midway through performance is bound to disrupt his operations somewhat. The Illinois courts interpret a requirements contract as a sharing of risk between seller and buyer. The seller assumes the risk of a change in the buyer's business that makes continuation of the contract unduly costly, but the buyer assumes the risk of a less urgent change in his circumstances, perhaps illustrated by the facts of this case where so far as one can tell the buyer's change of mind reflected no more than a reassessment of the balance of advantages and disadvantages under the contract. American Bakeries did not agree to buy conversion units and propane for trucks that it got rid of, but neither did Empire Gas agree to forgo sales merely because new management at American Bakeries decided that its capital would be better employed in some other investment than conversion to propane.

The general distinction that we are trying to make is well illustrated by Southwest Natural Gas Co. v. Oklahoma Portland Cement Co., 102 F.2d 630 (10th Cir. 1939), which to the drafters of the Uniform Commercial Code exemplified "reasonable variation of an extreme sort" (at least in the absence of an estimate, but that is irrelevant, for reasons we have explained). UCC § 2-306, comment 2. A cement company agreed to buy all of its requirements of gas from the seller for 15 years. Seven years later, the cement company replaced its boiler, which had worn out, with more modern equipment; as a result its need for gas fell by 80 percent. The court deemed this a bona fide change in the cement company's requirements.

It would have been unreasonable to make the company replace its worn-out plant with an obsolete facility.

It is a nice question how exigent the buyer's change of circumstances must be to allow him to scale down his requirements from either the estimated level or, in the absence of estimate, the "normal" level. Obviously it need not be so great as to give him a defense under the doctrines of impossibility, impracticability, or frustration, or under a force majeure clause. Yet, although more than whim is required, see Tennessee Valley Authority v. Imperial Professional Coatings, 599 F. Supp. 436, 439 (E.D. Tenn. 1984), how much more is unclear. There is remarkably little authority on the question. This is a good sign; it suggests that, while we might think it unsatisfactory for the law to be unclear on so fundamental a question, the people affected by the law are able to live with the lack of certainty. The reason may be that parties linked in an ongoing relationship — the usual situation under a requirements contract — have a strong incentive to work out disagreements amicably rather than see the relationship destroyed by litigation.

The essential ingredient of good faith in the case of the buyer's reducing his estimated requirements is that he not merely have had second thoughts about the terms of the contract and want to get out of it. . . . Whether the buyer has any greater obligation is unclear, but need not be decided here. Once it is decided (as we have) that a buyer cannot arbitrarily declare his requirements to be zero, this becomes an easy case, because American Bakeries has never given any reason for its change of heart. It might seem that once the district judge decided to instruct the jury in the language of the statute, American Bakeries was foreclosed from arguing that it had scaled down its requirements in good faith; a reduction to zero could never be proportionate if, as the instruction implied, the proviso on disproportion applies to reductions as well as increases in the buyer's takings. But the judge did not make this decision until the instructions conference. Until then American Bakeries had every opportunity and incentive to introduce evidence of why it decided not to convert its fleet to propane. It introduced none, and even at the argument in this court its counsel could give no reason for the change of heart beyond a hint that it was due to a change in management, which would not be enough by itself to justify a change in the buyer's requirements.

Even though Empire Gas had the burden of proving breach of contract and therefore (we may assume) of proving that American Bakeries acted in bad faith in reducing its requirements from 3,000 conversion units to zero . . . no reasonable jury could have failed to find bad faith, and therefore the error in instructing the jury on proportionality was harmless. Empire Gas put in evidence, uncontested and incontestable, showing that American Bakeries had not got rid of its fleet of trucks and did have the financial wherewithal to go through with the conversion process. After this evidence came in, American Bakeries could avoid a directed verdict only by introducing some evidence concerning its reasons for reducing its requirements. It not only introduced no evidence, but as is plain from counsel's remarks at argument it has no evidence that it would care to put before the jury — no reasons that it would care to share with either the district court or this court. It disagrees with the standard of good faith, believing that so long as it did not buy conversion units elsewhere or want to hurt Empire Gas it was free to reduce its requirements as much as it pleased. It does not suggest that it has a case under the standard we have adopted, which requires at a minimum that the reduction of requirements not have been motivated solely by a reassessment of the balance of advantages and disadvantages under the contract to the buyer. . . .

The jury's finding of liability must stand; but was there error in the assessment of damages? American Bakeries objects violently to the assumption made by Empire Gas's expert witness that the vehicles converted by American Bakeries, had it honored what Empire Gas contends were its obligations under the contract, would have run 100 percent on propane. The conversion units would have been dual units, which permit the driver by a flick of a switch in the engine to run his vehicle on either gasoline or propane. But since the parties agree that the price of propane was lower than that of gasoline throughout the entire contract period, a driver would have switched his conversion unit to gasoline only when he was low on propane and too far away from a propane station to reach it before he ran out. This factor was not big enough to upset the expert witness's calculations significantly. The calculation of damages is estimation rather than measurement, and it is foolish to prolong a lawsuit in quest of delusive precision. . . .

The judgment is affirmed. . . .

[Judge Kanne's dissent is omitted.]

NOTES

1.   *Questions on* Eastern Air Lines *and* Empire Gas: *The Puzzling Problem of Reasonable Quantity Variations.* Deciding what is a reasonable quantity variation in requirements and output contracts is a recurring problem. How should a court decide this issue?

UCC § 2-306(1) provides some general guidelines. Quantities supplied or demanded cannot be "unreasonably disproportionate to any stated estimate or in the absence of a stated estimate to any normal or otherwise comparable prior output or requirements." This determination of "unreasonably disproportionate" quantities depends to a great extent on the specific facts of each case. But informing the decision is the requirement of "good faith" dealings. Judge Posner suggests in

Empire Gas that the "unreasonably disproportionate" test is not a separate condition that a requirements buyer must meet but rather only a specific elaboration of the obligation of good faith. Do you agree?

Revised Article 1 of the UCC defines good faith as "honesty in fact and the observance of reasonable commercial standards of fair dealing. § 1-201(19) (2001).[30] An examination of a buyer's motives for substantially reducing or increasing its requirements often is helpful in deciding if the transaction was conducted in good faith and is consistent with "reasonable commercial standards." In *Eastern Air Lines*, the court found that Eastern had acted in good faith and according to established industry practice in changing its fuel demands. Although the parties apparently exchanged estimates of fuel needs and supplies from time to time, Gulf never objected to the occasionally wild swings in fuel consumption by Eastern. Other firms have not been so fortunate when they deviated from estimated production or consumption of goods, however. Businesses often run into legal difficulties when they go from buying or selling a certain quantity of a product to no purchases or sales at all. A violation of the good faith requirement in § 2-306 is often cited as the reason for judicial intervention in such cases.

As a starting point for analyzing a particular case, you ought to consider the reason that the controversy arises. In *Eastern Air Lines*, the problem arose because the price of aviation fuel under the contract departed substantially from the market price of aviation fuel. Why didn't the parties contract to buy/sell the fuel at the price prevailing at time of sale? For Eastern, this contract replaced a more expensive current contract with one year to run. What did Gulf gain? The suggestion is that for Gulf the contract was a "means to relate anticipated increased cost of raw material (crude oil) directly to the price of the refined product sold." But could this not have been accomplished more straightforwardly through spot market sales? If the contract assured Gulf a customer for the output of a new refinery, are we to assume that the spot market might not have provided buyers for that output, however great it might have been?

Why did the parties not make the price equal to Gulf's costs plus a reasonable profit? Computational complexities and monitoring problems are probably the reason, and so the parties tried to peg the contract price to the market price of crude oil by using a proxy. Could the contract have been drafted to anticipate the possibility that the price index in the contract (the posted price of West Texas Sour crude oil) might fail to track actual market prices?[31]

Can you develop a line of argument for Gulf that permitting fuel freighting

---

[30] The original version of Article 1 defined good faith subjectively as "honesty in fact in the conduct or transaction concerned." § 1-201(19) (1989). Revised Article 1 adopts an objective as well as a subjective test of good faith by adding the test of "reasonable commercial standards of fair dealing." Note that as of 2011, 37 states have adopted the Revised Article 1 and its expanded definition of good faith. But the same standard would apply to cases such as *Empire Gas* and *Eastern Air Lines* in any event. The Article 2 definition of good faith between merchants in § 2-103(1)(b) is identical in substance to the definition in Revised Article 1.

[31] For an argument that delegating discretion to a court to select an alternative proxy ex post could have solved the problem in *Eastern Air Lines*, see Robert E. Scott & George G. Triantis, *Anticipating Litigation in Contract Design*, 115 YALE L.J. 814 (2006).

earlier in the contract should not foreclose its contention that fuel freighting later in the contract was a breach of good faith?

Suppose that, during the contract, technological developments allowed airplanes to fly on fuel substitutes, and Eastern outfitted its fleet to take advantage of such advances? What advice would you give Eastern as to whether they could reduce their requirements of fuel proportionately without being in breach of their contract with Gulf? Does Judge Posner's opinion in *Empire Gas* provide guidance? Do you agree with Posner that the "unreasonably disproportionate" test applies differently to the reduced demand case than to the excessive demand case? Suppose that because Eastern's costs are lower than its competitors' costs, it puts on more flights to the cities it ordinarily flies to, and begins to fly to new cities. Breach? Given the difficulty of these issues, some observers might conclude that the better result is for a court to declare the contract unenforceable because of indefiniteness, or to put it differently, § 2-306 is a bad idea.

2. *Is the Good Faith Standard too Vague?* Professor Charles Fried, in *Contract as Promise* (1981), argues that the words "good faith" stand for "a way of dealing with a contractual party: honestly, decently. It is an adverbial notion suggesting the avoidance of chicanery and sharp practice (bad faith) whether in coming to an agreement or in carrying out its terms." *Id.* at 74. On the other hand, Professor Victor Goldberg has criticized the application of the good faith standard in open quantity contracts. Goldberg argues that, rather than limiting a party's discretion, the "good faith" test of § 2-306(1) often involves supplanting the party's careful balancing of various concerns in the initial contract with a "wooden, uninformed reading of the agreement." Because courts have no theory of what constitutes good faith, Goldberg claims that they have required producers to behave in most peculiar ways: "for example, running a plant at below full capacity for the life of the contract."[32]

In this regard, consider bread crumbs. Assume that a bakery enters into a one-year contract with a bakery products wholesale distributor to sell the distributor all the bakery's output of bread crumbs. When a loaf of bread is over-baked, deformed in shape, or otherwise unusable, it can be processed into bread crumbs. The process involves the purchase of a toasting machine by the bakery. The bread crumbs thus are a waste product of the bakery. An estimate of the total poundage of crumbs is set out in the contract. When the contract is entered into, the bakery predicts that it will cost 75 cents per pound to make crumbs. The contract price is one dollar per pound. The distributor estimates that it can resell the bread crumbs at $1.50 per pound.

During the contract period, the cost to make bread crumbs turns out to be $1.06 per pound. At that price the bakery is unable to cover its variable costs. The bakery stops making crumbs, and the distributor claims the contract has been breached. Are any of the following facts (which Goldberg reports are true) relevant in answering the question of whether the bakery's decision to shut down was justified?

---

[32] Victor Goldberg, *Discretion in Long-Term Open Quantity Contracts: Reining in Good Faith*, 35 U.C. Davis L. Rev. 319, 320 (2002); *see also* Goldberg, Framing Contract Law: An Economic Perspective 117–19 (2007).

(1) The distributor had other suppliers of toasted bread crumbs which can be held in inventory for a longer period of time than baked loaves.

(2) This is not the only product of the bakery, and the company treasury will easily last the year.

(3) The bakery (not the distributor) purchased and operated the oven to toast the bread crumbs.

In *Feld v. Henry S. Levy & Sons, Inc.*, 37 N.Y.2d 466, 471–72, 373 N.Y.S.2d 102 (1975), the court held:

> The parties by their contract gave the right of cancellation to either by providing for a six months' notice to the other. . . . Short of such a cancellation, defendant was expected to continue to perform in good faith and could cease production of the bread crumbs, a single facet of its operation, only in good faith. Obviously, a bankruptcy or genuine imperiling of the very existence of its entire business caused by the production of the crumbs would warrant cessation of production of that item; the yield of less profit from its sale than expected would not.

In light of the economic structure of this contract, does the court's holding make sense?

3. *Unreasonably Disproportionate Demands.* *Empire Gas* involved the question of whether a company could opt to order substantially less than projected in a requirements contract. *Eastern Air Lines* involved a higher-than-projected demand due to a standard industry practice.

But under what other circumstances, and to what degree, can a buyer increase demand beyond the stated estimate?

Consider the case of *Orange & Rockland Utilities, Inc. v. Amerada Hess Corp.*, 59 A.D.2d 110, 397 N.Y.S.2d 814 (1977). Like *Eastern*, the case occurred against the backdrop of the 1970s oil crisis. Hess contracted to supply O&R's power plant with fuel oil for five years. The contract estimates anticipated that natural gas would be O & R's primary fuel used for power generation due to its lower cost. O & R expressly reserved its right to burn as much gas at it chose. In 1970, coincident with the increases in the cost of oil, O & R proceeded to notify Hess, on four separate dates, of increases in the fuel oil requirements estimates for the year. The final letter indicated a revised estimate of an increase of about 63%. In this letter, O & R attributed the vastly increased estimates to an inability to burn as much natural gas as had been planned and to the fact that O & R had been "required" to meet higher electrical demands on its "own system" and to furnish "more electricity to interconnected systems" than had been anticipated. Hess refused to supply the demanded amounts, but continued to deliver quantities approximately equal to the estimates stated in the subject contract.

The trial court found that as the price of oil rose throughout the lifetime of the contract, O & R greatly increased oil consumption due primarily to increases in sales of electricity to other utilities and a net shift from other fuels, primarily gas, to oil. Nonfirm sales from plaintiff's power plant increased nearly six fold in 1970. The significance of that increase in nonfirm sales lies in the fact that such sales did not enter into the budget calculations which formed the basis of the estimates included in the contract. On appeal, the court held that O & R's use of the requirements contract to dramatically propel itself into the position of a large seller of power to other utilities evidenced a lack of good faith dealing and found the demands were "unreasonably disproportionate" to the stated estimates.

In determining whether a party's demands in a requirements contract are "unreasonably disproportionate," the court suggested a set of criteria calculated to limit each party's risk in accordance with their reasonable expectations:

> It would be unwise to attempt to define the phrase "unreasonably disproportionate" in terms of rigid quantities. In order that the limitation contemplated by the section take effect, it is not enough that a demand for requirements be disproportionate to the stated estimate; it must be unreasonably so in view of the expectation of the parties. A number of factors should be taken into account in the event a buyer's requirements greatly exceed the contract estimate. These include the following: (1) the amount by which the requirements exceed the contract estimate; (2) whether the seller had any reasonable basis on which to forecast or anticipate the requested increase; (3) the amount, if any, by which the market price of the goods in question exceeded the contract price; (4) whether such an increase in market price was itself fortuitous; and (5) the reason for the increase in requirements.

If the focus of the "unreasonably disproportionate" inquiry shifts to the conduct of the parties and away from the permissible deviation from quantity estimates, as the analysis in *Orange & Rockland Utilities, Inc.* appears to do, then is the "unreasonably disproportionate" requirement of § 2-306 no more than a particular application of the obligation to deal in "good faith" as Judge Posner suggested?

4. *Output and Requirements Contracts: Explanation and Comparison.* In an output contract, the distributor/buyer agrees to take everything that is produced by the seller, usually on a per-item basis. The buyer is free to purchase comparable items from other sellers; the seller, however, can only sell the contract output to that particular buyer.

Since unforeseen events often occur throughout the life of the contract, and these contracts usually contain estimates rather than fixed quantities, there often will be some amount of variation in the quantity supplied. Both the market and the contract itself provide partial protections against supply fluctuations.

When the market price exceeds the contract price, there will be an under-supply of the desired good. Since the buyer is free to obtain similar items from other sellers, it can meet its needs on the open market. In doing so, however, the buyer will have to pay the greater market price. As a result, this "market check" provides only partial protection, as the buyer will have to pay more to obtain the same quantity of goods had the market price not increased.

In the event that the contract price exceeds the market price, the supplier will attempt to unload everything upon the buyer, as it can obtain a better price than would be available on the open market. This creates a problem with over-supply. The market cannot rectify the situation; instead, the parties will often create contractual devices to limit their vulnerability. Such devices take the form of either quantity controls or price controls. Price controls refer to some sort of external price index. The parties can control the expected quantity by putting in production estimates and requiring each party to act in good faith. Such good faith requirements are mirrored in § 2-306(1) of the UCC.

In a requirements contract, however, the quantity is determined not by the seller's production, but by the buyer's needs. Exclusivity is reversed; the seller is free to sell to multiple buyers, but the buyer cannot buy any of the contract-specified requirements from other sellers.

Once again, market checks and contractual devices protect the parties against price-driven changes in demand. If the contract price exceeds the market price, the buyer will seek to purchase fewer items than it would otherwise, thus creating an under-demand problem. The seller can partially protect itself by selling the goods to other buyers; since the market price is lower than the contract price, however, the market check only partially offsets the reduced demand.

The seller is also vulnerable in the event of a market price increase, as the buyer may opt to increase its demand for requirements. Contractual provisions can be used to protect the seller against excessive demand. For example, the parties might incorporate by reference external price indices, as in *Eastern Air Lines*. Conversely, they might agree upon contractual estimates as a target around which variations would be permissible subject to the good faith requirement of § 2-306(1).

5.   *Problem: Stanley Law Summaries.* Bill Stanley was a student at a leading law school. Like most first-year law students, Stanley took Contracts, and like most first-year law students he outlined his class notes at exam time. Stanley loaned his outline to a friend who was so impressed with its thoroughness that he touted the outline to others. By the time of second semester exams, Stanley had such a following that he was able to earn some money by renting his Contracts outline to other students.

Stanley realized, of course, the money to be made by selling outlines. He decided to publish and sell his Contracts outline and arranged a printing deal with the school's in-house copy center. Sales of the "Stanley Law Summary" were brisk both at Stanley's own law school and at other law schools in-state. Once Stanley graduated, however, he had less access to law schools and less credibility among students; sales of the summaries plummeted as students turned to a poorer, but widely advertised, commercial outline series.

After giving it some thought, Stanley decided that the endorsement of, and distribution and promotion of the summaries by, a well-respected Contracts professor would boost sales of his summaries. Stanley presented the idea to his former Contracts professor, Daniel Deacon, who agreed to serve as retail promoter and distributor of Stanley's Law Summaries.

Both Stanley and Deacon wanted latitude in their contractual relationship, especially during the first, uncertain year of selling the summaries. Stanley suggested that Deacon buy 3,000 Stanley Law Summaries the first year at a $10 wholesale price and then distribute them at the prevailing market retail price for commercial outlines. Deacon responded by proposing that Deacon promise "to buy from Stanley, at $10 per book, all Deacon's requirements of Stanley Law Summaries for distribution and sale during the upcoming academic year." Stanley comes to you for legal advice (it seems his expertise at contract law was short-lived). Assuming that the suggested contract language creates a legally enforceable requirements contract, is such a contract term appropriate for a distribution contract such as this? In particular, if the parties agree to a requirements contract will Stanley have trouble making sure his summaries are promoted to his satisfaction? What other constraints on the discretion of both Stanley and Deacon might be needed in order to achieve the parties objectives? (Hint: Might Deacon be reluctant to spend money in advertising and promotion of Stanley Summaries so long as Stanley had the right to license another distributor?) Suppose Deacon decides in February he no longer wants to market the summaries as he would rather spend the time writing an article requested by a law journal. Could Deacon order no summaries at all?

Essay: The Challenges of Designing Relational Contracts

Eastern Air Lines and *Empire Gas* are examples of what we have called "relational contracts." A contract is relational to the extent that the parties are unable (at reasonable cost) to reduce important terms of the arrangement to well-defined obligations. The parties may find it impractical to reach agreement on specific terms either because they are unable to identify all the possible uncertain conditions that might occur in the future or because they find they are incapable of working through all the complex adaptations that future events might require even where the contingencies can be identified in advance.[33] Which of these two factors — uncertainty or complexity — were the reasons for the parties use of requirements contracts rather than more definite quantity terms in *Eastern Air Lines* and *Empire Gas*? Certainly, in both instances the parties faced an uncertain future. But, in addition, even where they were able to anticipate the future contingencies (as in *Eastern Air Lines*), the complexity of working out acceptable quantity/price arrangements seemed daunting.

The concept of a relational contract is designed to give courts and scholars an alternative perspective from the presuppositions of classical contract doctrine. The classical "bargain" model of contract, you will remember, is premised implicitly on the idea of the "complete contingent contract." Parties in a bargaining context are presumed to be capable, at an acceptable cost, of allocating efficiently the risks of all (or at least most) future contingencies. But parties to relational contracts confront a vexing problem: The future is unknown and unknowable. As a result, when the level of uncertainty is high, it simply is not feasible for the parties to foresee and then describe appropriately the contractual outcomes for all (or even most) of the possible states of the world that might materialize. Under these circumstances, the ideal of the efficiently complete contingent contract — one that specifies the optimal pay offs for every relevant action and the corresponding sanctions for nonperformance — cannot be realized. Contracts will be incomplete in the sense that they will fail to discriminate between states of the world that optimally call for different obligations.

---

[33] *See* Charles J. Goetz & Robert E. Scott, *Principles of Relational Contracts*, 67 Va. L. Rev. 1089 (1981).

It is important to emphasize what is meant by efficient completeness. Parties can easily write an inefficient complete contract simply by specifying, for example, that no matter what circumstance may arise in the future, the buyer must always pay the seller the contract price. In such a contract the parties know at the time of contracting that in many of the realized states of the world, the contract will generate less surplus than their joint venture could have achieved. The challenge is to write an efficient complete contract, one that specifies the best outcome for both parties under all possible circumstances. This they cannot do.

In a relational contract, in which uncertainty and drafting costs are high, parties typically rely on a mix of enforcement strategies, both formal legal enforcement as well as informal or self-enforcement mechanisms ranging from reputational sanctions to the prospect of loss of future dealings to social norms of trust and reciprocity. The interaction between these formal and informal mechanisms is complex, however, and, as both *Eastern Air Lines* and *Empire Gas* illustrate, informal norms do not always forestall legal disputes. In any case, the fundamental question remains: how can (and do) parties cope with the uncertainties of relational contracting?

The Tension Between Commitment and Flexibility

Parties who enter into relational contracts typically face a conundrum. They want to write a contract that is optimal *ex ante*; that is, one that at the time of contracting encourages each party to invest in the contractual relationship so as to maximize the anticipated joint benefits from contracting. But they also want to write a contract that is optimal *ex post*, that is, one that still produces joint value to the parties after all future uncertainties have been resolved. There is, of course, an inherent tension between these two objectives. In order to motivate (and protect) investments in the enterprise, each investing party would like to ensure the commitment of the other to pay for that investment. But subsequent events may render inflexible commitments to pay for a specified performance inconsistent with the contractual objective of maximizing the joint surplus.

For example, suppose that, owing to future circumstances, the cost to the promisor of a particular performance will exceed the value the promisee expects to obtain from the contract. Anticipating this, the promisor would want the flexibility to be able to adjust his contract performance so as to increase the expected value of the contract. But if the contract is written to accommodate this desire to change its terms as future conditions warrant, the credibility of the promisor's commitment is undermined. This, in turn, may lead the promisee to decline to invest in performing her obligations under the contract for fear that the promisor will demand the right to adjust even when conditions do not warrant such a change. Thus, each party not only wants to preserve the flexibility to adjust to future uncertainties but also to insure that all commitments are credible. This tension between the need for credible commitments and the need for flexibility to adjust to future conditions influences the parties' decisions whether or not to contract and, if so, what kind of contract to write.

The Problems Caused by Private Information

One of the challenges parties to relational contracts seek to overcome is that, quite simply, prospective contracting partners do not know everything about each other. Rather, each party has private information about its preferences, and the way it chooses to perform its obligations that the other does not know. We can illustrate this point with a simple example. Assume Buyer wishes to purchase a new machine from Seller, but Buyer is unsure about the quality of the goods or services that are being offered. Seller knows the quality of the machine that he has contracted to sell but Buyer does not. To illustrate the problems that result from this asymmetry of information, assume that the sellers in this market fall into two groups: high-quality sellers and low-quality sellers. If quality varies among sellers, then buyers face a problem. Buyer does not know whether Seller's machine is of a high quality or a low quality. Unless the problem can be solved, Buyer has an incentive to offer only a blended price for the machine (a price less than the value of a high-quality machine but more than the value of one of low quality) reflecting the probability that Seller's goods are either high or low quality. Over time, this reluctance to pay full value will drive the high-quality sellers out of the market, because the blended price would not permit them to recover their higher costs. As a result, only low-quality sellers will remain in the market. This example illustrates the famous "lemons problem" caused by the adverse selection of low quality sellers.[34]

Parties can respond to this problem of hidden information in several ways. One familiar method is for the high-quality sellers to offer warranties to their buyers. Because high-quality goods perform better and last longer, a warranty of replacement or repair would cost the high-quality sellers less to provide, compared to their low-quality competitors. Warranties thus serve as valuable signals of quality to the extent that low-quality sellers cannot readily copy them. An effective signal creates a separating equilibrium in which both high- and low-quality sellers can exist in the same market.

But warranties are not a perfect signal because they are not self-executing. Rather, a Buyer must be able to prove to a court that the seller has breached its warranty of quality. To understand this problem, we need to distinguish between what Buyer can observe for herself and what she will be able to prove in court. To return to our example, absent a warranty, the quality of Seller's machine may remain completely private, in the sense that no prospective buyer will be able to observe the condition or quality of the goods prior to the sale. But once Buyer purchases the goods with a warranty, she will then be able to perceive whether the condition or quality of the machine matches the warranty, thus making the information observable. For the legal process to be effective, however, information must not only be observable, but verifiable, in the sense that Buyer can, at a reasonable cost, convince a court or other arbiter that her observation is valid.

In short, not all observable information is verifiable, and only verifiable conditions or qualities can be used to specify an obligation that a court can enforce. So, if Seller gives a warranty of quality and Buyer claims that the machine fails to meet

---

[34] *See* George A. Akerlof, *The Market for "Lemons": Quality Uncertainty and the Market Mechanism*, 84 Q. J. Econ. 488 (1970).

the warranty standard, Buyer then bears the burden of proving to a court that the machine does not conform to the agreed standard. Thus, even if Buyer can *observe* for herself that the goods fail to satisfy the warranty standard, she still must bear the additional burden of proving or *verifying* that fact to a court or other third party.

In addition to the problems caused by *hidden information regarding the attributes or characteristics* of a contract performance, the parties must also cope with the problems caused by the *hidden actions or behavior* of a contracting partner. Assume in our example that Seller warrants to use its best efforts to modify the contracted-for machine should Buyer encounter any problems in adapting it to Buyer's particular requirements. If Buyer is unable to monitor Seller's efforts to adapt the machine, then Seller's hidden actions create a problem of moral hazard. As the name implies, Buyer faces a risk that Seller will not fully exert its best efforts as promised, but rather will (immorally) chisel on or shirk a portion of its responsibility. And even if Buyer can observe Seller's actions, once again it faces the difficulty of verifying to a court that the efforts actually undertaken by Seller fall short of the standard of "best efforts."

Information asymmetries caused by hidden information and hidden action thus operate at two distinct levels. Between the parties, hidden information or action may prevent the uninformed party from observing a key fact or condition (in our example, the level of quality of the goods or the efforts undertaken by Seller). But even if the information known to one party is observable in the sense that her contracting partner can perceive it as well, it may not be verifiable in the sense that the observing party is unable at reasonable cost to establish the fact sufficiently to convince a neutral third party such as a court.

Alternative Responses to Information Deficits and High Uncertainty

Given the problems caused by private information and facing high uncertainty and high contracting costs, how should parties formulate the terms of their contracts? One option is to write a contract with precise rules, i.e., determinate outcomes that would apply across the board regardless of the state of the world that actually occurs. Returning to our earlier example, the parties could provide that Seller, who agrees to manufacture a customized machine for Buyer, will deliver the machine to Buyer at a fixed price regardless of any subsequent events that might increase Seller's costs or reduce the value of the machine to Buyer. The advantage of a contract with such "hard" terms is that it binds each party to their respective commitments, thus ensuring the credibility of their respective promises.

But a contract containing only "hard" terms will almost always turn out to be less than optimal once the future arrives. Under conditions of uncertainty, any outcome that is based on expected values (i.e., one that is optimal "on average") will always tend to be wrong in the particular situation that ultimately materializes. In short, once conditions change, a contract with hard terms will lead to outcomes that are less desirable than those the parties would have agreed to had they known the uncertainties in advance. Moreover, the prospect of incurring a loss *ex post* means that the parties will enjoy a smaller *ex ante* surplus. Each party will have an incentive to undertake costly precautions (purchasing insurance and the like) to guard against the risk of unfavorable future states. One solution to this problem, of course, is for the parties to renegotiate the contract once the future is known. But renegotiation raises the risk of a hold up. For example, if one of the parties has already made a sunk cost investment in the contract, she is vulnerable to a demand from the other that any renegotiation come at a higher price than was originally specified in the contract.

In the alternative, the parties might consider another option. They could draft a contract with vague standards, i.e., "soft" terms that invite subsequent adjustment to take account of new facts on the ground. Thus, for example, the parties might agree to adjust in good faith the terms in the contract if subsequent events imposed significant hardship on one of the parties. By agreeing to "good faith adjustment," the parties seek to ensure that their contract is efficient *ex post* and that the resulting surplus is shared in some manner between both of them.

Assume, for example, that future events cause the costs to Seller of manufacturing the contract machine to rise above the contract price. However, the Seller can produce a substitute machine at a lower cost that is of equivalent value to Buyer. If Buyer nonetheless insists on the original performance, the contract would yield a gain for Buyer but Seller would suffer a loss. Anticipating the prospect of a loss in certain states of the world will motivate Seller to take costly precautions. One solution, therefore, is for the contract to contain a standard of good faith adjustment by which Seller can provide the lower cost substitute, perhaps with a price reduction for Buyer. The prospect of a good faith adjustment would reduce, if not eliminate, the need for precautions against unfavorable conditions that do not materialize.

But a contract that uses such soft terms may raise the moral hazard problem that we identified earlier. Moral hazard results because a promisor who has the flexibility to adjust his performance in the future as conditions change will always choose the best alternative for him, even though it may not be best for both parties in terms of joint welfare. Assume, in our example above, that Seller, claiming changed circumstances, proposes to substitute an alternative machine at the original contract price because, as things turned out, his cost of producing the substitute machine is 10% less than the cost of producing the contract machine. Buyer values the substitute goods more than the contract price but 20% less than the contract goods. Buyer reluctantly acquiesces to the adjustment. But this adjustment comes at a cost. The effect of the "good faith" adjustment is that Seller can capture a larger share of a smaller surplus. Viewed *ex ante*, Seller's actions reduce joint welfare, because the reduction in the Buyer's share of the surplus under the adjusted contract is greater than Seller's gain.

Are There Any Solutions to the Problems of Relational Contracting?

Economic theorists have devised ways of surmounting the moral hazard and hold up problems that result from ex post adjustment or renegotiation. For example, they have imagined contractual mechanisms that induce parties to reveal their private information to a court. In theory, these mechanisms can eliminate the incentive to exploit a contracting partner's vulnerability while retaining the flexibility to adjust to new information during the course of contract performance. Other strategies include assigning bargaining power in any subsequent renegotiation to the party whose investments have left her the most vulnerable to exploitation. However, all these devices assume the existence of strong powers on the part of courts and other enforcement bodies to compel truthful testimony and/or to police the renegotiation process. In reality, of course, domestic courts do not have such power. So, what can lawyers do in the real world with the legal system as we know it?

Unfortunately, as we noted earlier, existing legal mechanisms cannot easily regulate either the renegotiation or the adjustment processes. Under these circumstances, parties to relational contracts can (and do) turn instead to informal means of enforcement based on trust, or the desire to maintain a good reputation in the relevant trade or community, or on the prospect of profitable future dealings. In many contexts, reputation, repeat dealings and norms of reciprocity provide the best available means of regulating the inevitable renegotiation and adjustment process so as to reduce the risk of exploitation of the parties' vulnerabilities. If parties to relational contracts are able to rely on these informal methods of enforcing promissory commitments, they can approximate in practice the theoretical goal of writing contracts that are credible enough to motivate efficient investments ex ante and flexible enough to ensure efficient trade ex post. In reading the cases in this chapter, therefore, it is important to keep in mind that these disputes only arise when the informal modes of enforcement have broken down. The cases, therefore, give us no clue of the power of reciprocity, reputation, and other informal mechanisms in enforcing the many agreements between parties to relational contracts that never reach litigation.

[2]   Exclusive Dealings Contracts

WOOD v. LUCY, LADY DUFF-GORDON
Court of Appeals of New York
222 N.Y. 88, 118 N.E. 214 (1917)

CARDOZO, J.

The defendant styles herself "a creator of fashions." Her favor helps a sale. Manufacturers of dresses, millinery and like articles are glad to pay for a certificate of her approval. The things which she designs, fabrics, parasols and what not, have a new value in the public mind when issued in her name. She employed the plaintiff to help her to turn this vogue into money. He was to have the exclusive right, subject always to her approval, to place her endorsements on the designs of others. He was also to have the exclusive right to place her own designs on sale, or to license others to market them. In return, she was to have one-half of "all profits and revenues" derived from any contracts he might make. The exclusive right was to last at least one year from April 1, 1915, and thereafter from year to year unless terminated by notice of ninety days. The plaintiff says that he kept the contract on his part, and that the defendant broke it. She placed her endorsement on fabrics, dresses and millinery without his knowledge, and withheld the profits. He sues her for the damages, and the case comes here on demurrer.

The agreement of employment is signed by both parties. It has a wealth of

[Margin notes, top left:]
Consideration §71
↳inducement.
Promise A is consideration
for promise B &
Promise B consideration
for promise A.

recitals. The defendant insists, however, that it lacks the elements of a contract. She says that the plaintiff does not bind himself to anything. It is true that he does not promise in so many words that he will use reasonable efforts to place the defendant's endorsements and market her designs.

[Margin note, left:]
* In every exclusive agreement, Wood (beneficiary) implicitly makes a promise to sell in good faith & use his best efforts (higher than good faith) b/c seller is vulnerable

We think, however, that such a promise is fairly to be implied. The law has outgrown its primitive stage of formalism when the precise word was the sovereign talisman, and every slip was fatal. It takes a broader view to-day. A promise may be lacking, and yet the whole writing may be "instinct with an obligation," imperfectly expressed (Scott, J., in McCall Co. v. Wright, 133 App. Div. 62). If that is so, there is a contract.

The implication of a promise here finds support in many circumstances. The defendant gave an exclusive privilege. She was to have no right for at least a year to place her own endorsements or market her own designs except through the agency of the plaintiff. The acceptance of the exclusive agency was an assumption of its duties. We are not to suppose that one party was to be placed at the mercy of the other. Many other terms of the agreement point the same way. We are told at the outset by way of recital that "the said Otis F. Wood possesses a business organization adapted to the placing of such endorsements as the said Lucy, Lady Duff-Gordon has approved." The implication is that the plaintiff's business organization will be used for the purpose for which it is adapted. But the terms of the defendant's compensation are even more significant. Her sole compensation for the grant of an exclusive agency is to be one-half of all the profits resulting from the plaintiff's efforts. Unless he gave his efforts, she could never get anything. Without an implied promise, the transaction cannot have such business "efficacy as both parties must have intended that at all events it should have" (Bowen, L.J., in The Moorcock, 14 P.D. 64, 68). But the contract does not stop there. The plaintiff goes on to promise that he will account monthly for all moneys received by him, and that he will take out all such patents and copyrights and trademarks as may in his judgment be necessary to protect the rights and articles affected by the agreement. It is true, of course, as the Appellate Division has said, that if he were under no duty to try to market designs or to place certificates of endorsement, his promise to account for profits or take out copyrights would be valueless. But in determining the intention of the parties, the promise has a value. It helps to enforce the conclusion that the plaintiff had some duties. His promise to pay the defendant one-half of the profits and revenues resulting from the exclusive agency and to render accounts monthly, was a promise to use reasonable efforts to bring profits and revenues into existence. For this conclusion, the authorities are ample. . . .

[Margin note, left:]
* Kraus. D should have sued w/ for breach of his implied duty to use best effort.

* Policy
best efforts means maximize gains for both parties

The judgment of the Appellate Division should be reversed, and the order of the Special Term affirmed, with costs in the Appellate Division and in this court.

Judgment reversed.

BLOOR v. FALSTAFF BREWING CORP.

United States Court of Appeals, Second Circuit

601 F.2d 609 (1979)

FRIENDLY, J.

This action, wherein federal jurisdiction is predicated on diversity of citizenship, 28 U.S.C. § 1332, was brought in the District Court for the Southern District of New York, by James Bloor, Reorganization Trustee of Balco Properties Corporation, formerly named P. Ballantine & Sons (Ballantine), a venerable and once successful brewery based in Newark, N. J. He sought to recover from Falstaff Brewing Corporation (Falstaff) for breach of a contract dated March 31, 1972, wherein Falstaff bought the Ballantine brewing labels, trademarks, accounts receivable, distribution systems and other property except the brewery. The price was $4,000,000 plus a royalty of fifty cents on each barrel of the Ballantine brands sold between April 1, 1972 and March 31, 1978. Although other issues were tried, the appeals concern only two provisions of the contract. These are:

> 8. Certain Other Covenants of Buyer. (a) After the Closing Date the [Buyer] will use its best efforts to promote and maintain a high volume of sales under the Proprietary Rights.

> 2(a)(v) [The Buyer will pay a royalty of $.50 per barrel for a period of 6 years], provided, however, that if during the Royalty Period the Buyer substantially discontinues the distribution of beer under the brand name "Ballantine" (except as the result of a restraining order in effect for 30 days issued by a court of competent jurisdiction at the request of a governmental authority), it will pay to the Seller a cash sum equal to the years and fraction thereof remaining in the Royalty Period times $1,100,000, payable in equal monthly installments on the first day of each month commencing with the first month following the month in which such discontinuation occurs. . . .

Bloor claimed that Falstaff had breached the best efforts clause, 8(a), and indeed that its default amounted to the substantial discontinuance that would trigger the liquidated damage clause, 2(a)(v). In an opinion that interestingly traces the history of beer back to Doomsday Book and beyond, Judge Brieant upheld the first claim and awarded damages but dismissed the second. Falstaff appeals from the former ruling, Bloor from the latter. Both sides also dispute the court's measurement of damages for breach of the best efforts clause.

We shall assume familiarity with Judge Brieant's excellent opinion, 454 F. Supp. 258 (S.D.N.Y. 1978), from which we have drawn heavily, and will state only the essentials. Ballantine had been a family owned business, producing low-priced beers primarily for the northeast market, particularly New York, New Jersey, Connecticut and Pennsylvania. Its sales began to decline in 1961, and it lost money from 1965 on. On June 1, 1969, Investors Funding Corporation (IFC), a real estate conglomerate with no experience in brewing, acquired substantially all the stock of Ballantine for $16,290,000. IFC increased advertising expenditures, leveling off in 1971 at $1 million a year. This and other promotional practices, some of dubious legality, led to steady growth in Ballantine's sales despite the increased activities in the northeast of the "nationals"[35] which have greatly augmented their market shares at the expense of smaller brewers. However, this was a profitless prosperity; there was no month in which Ballantine had earnings and the total loss was $15,500,000 for the 33 months of IFC ownership.

After its acquisition of Ballantine, Falstaff continued the $1 million a year advertising program, IFC's pricing policies, and also its policy of serving smaller accounts not solely through sales to independent distributors, the usual practice in the industry, but by use of its own warehouses and trucks — the only change being a shift of the retail distribution system from Newark to North Bergen, N.J., when brewing was concentrated at Falstaff's Rhode Island brewery. However, sales declined and Falstaff claims to have lost $22 million in its Ballantine brand operations from March 31, 1972 to June 1975. Its other activities were also performing indifferently, although with no such losses as were being incurred in the sale of Ballantine products, and it was facing inability to meet payrolls and other debts. In March and April 1975 control of Falstaff passed to Paul Kalmanovitz, a businessman with 40 years experience in the brewing industry. After having first advanced $3 million to enable Falstaff to meet its payrolls and other pressing debts, he later supplied an additional $10 million and made loan guarantees, in return for which he received convertible preferred shares in an amount that endowed him with 35% of the voting power and became the beneficiary of a voting trust that gave him control of the board of directors.

Mr. Kalmanovitz determined to concentrate on making beer and cutting sales costs. He decreased advertising, with the result that the Ballantine advertising budget shrank from $1 million to $115,000 a year.[36] In late 1975 he closed four of Falstaff's six retail distribution centers, including the North Bergen, N.J. depot, which was ultimately replaced by two distributors servicing substantially fewer accounts. He also discontinued various illegal practices that had been used in selling Ballantine products.[37] [In terms of sales volume,] with 1974 as a base, Ballantine declined 29.72% in 1975 and 45.81% in 1976 as compared with a 1975 gain of 2.24% and a 1976 loss of 13.08% for all brewers excluding the top 15. Other comparisons are similarly devastating, at least for 1976.[38] Despite the decline in the sale of its own labels as well as Ballantine's, Falstaff, however, made a substantial financial recovery. In 1976 it had net income of $8.7 million and its year-end working capital had increased from $8.6 million to $20.2 million and its cash and certificates of deposit from $2.2 million to $12.1 million.

---

[35] [1] Miller's, Schlitz, Anheuser-Busch, Coors and Pabst.

[36] [2] This was for cooperative advertising with purchasers.

[37] [3] There were two kinds of illegal practices, the testimony on both of which is, unsurprisingly, rather vague. Certain "national accounts," i.e. large draught beer buyers, were gotten or retained by "black bagging," the trade term for commercial bribery. On a smaller scale, sales to taverns were facilitated by the salesman's offering a free round for the house of Ballantine if it was available ("retention"), or the customer's choice ("solicitation"). Both practices seem to have been indulged in by many brewers, including Falstaff before Kalmanovitz took control.

[38] [5] Falstaff argues that a trend line projecting the declining volume of Ballantine's sales since 1966, before IFC's purchase, would show an even worse picture. We agree with plaintiff that the percentage figures since 1974 are more significant; at least the judge was entitled to think so.

Seizing upon remarks made by the judge during the trial that Falstaff's financial standing in 1975 and thereafter "is probably not relevant" and a footnote in the opinion, 454 F. Supp. at 267 n. 7,[39] appellate counsel for Falstaff contend that the judge read the best efforts clause as requiring Falstaff to maintain Ballantine's volume by any sales methods having a good prospect of increasing or maintaining sales or, at least, to continue lawful methods in use at the time of purchase, no matter what losses they would cause. Starting from this premise, counsel reason that the judge's conclusion was at odds with New York law, stipulated by the contract to be controlling, as last expressed by the Court of Appeals in Feld v. Henry S. Levy & Sons, Inc., 37 N.Y.2d 466, 373 N.Y.S.2d 102 (1975). The court was there dealing with a contract whereby defendant agreed to sell and plaintiff to purchase all bread crumbs produced by defendant at a certain factory. During the term of the agreement defendant ceased producing bread crumbs because production with existing facilities was "very uneconomical," and the plaintiff sued for breach. The case was governed by § 2-306 of the Uniform Commercial Code.

. . .

Affirming the denial of cross-motions for summary judgment, the court said that, absent a cancellation on six months' notice for which the contract provided:

> [D]efendant was expected to continue to perform in good faith and could cease production of the bread crumbs, a single facet of its operation, only in good faith. Obviously, a bankruptcy or genuine imperiling of the very existence of its entire business caused by the production of the crumbs would warrant cessation of production of that item; the yield of less profit from its sale than expected would not. Since bread crumbs were but a part of defendant's enterprise and since there was a contractual right of cancellation, good faith required continued production until cancellation, even if there be no profit. In circumstances such as these and without more, defendant would be justified, in good faith, in ceasing production of the single item prior to cancellation only if its losses from continuance would be more than trivial, which, overall, is a question of fact.

37 N.Y.2d 471-72, 373 N.Y.S.2d 106.[40] Falstaff argues from this that it was not bound

---

[39] [6] Even if Falstaff's financial position had been worse in mid-1975 than it actually was, and even if Falstaff had continued in that state of impecuniosity during the term of the contract, performance of the contract is not excused where the difficulty of performance arises from financial difficulty or economic hardship. As the New York Court of Appeals stated in 407 E. 61st St. Garage, Inc. v. Savoy Corp., 23 N.Y.2d 275, 281, 296 N.Y.S.2d 338, 344, 244 N.E.2d 37, 41 (1968):

> (W)here impossibility or difficulty of performance is occasioned only by financial difficulty or economic hardship, even to the extent of insolvency or bankruptcy, performance of a contract is not excused. (Citations omitted.)

[40] [7] The text of the Feld opinion did not refer to the case cited by Judge Brieant in the preceding footnote, 407 East 61st Garage, Inc. v. Savoy Fifth Avenue Corporation, 23 N.Y.2d 275, 296 N.Y.S.2d 338, 244 N.E.2d 37 (1968), which might suggest a more onerous obligation here. The Court of Appeals there reversed a summary judgment in favor of the defendant, which had discontinued operating the Savoy Hilton Hotel because of substantial financial losses, in alleged breach of a five-year contract with plaintiff wherein the defendant had agreed to use all reasonable efforts to provide the garage with exclusive opportunity for storage of the motor vehicles of hotel guests. Although the court did use the language quoted by Judge Brieant, the actual holding was simply that "an issue of fact is presented whether the

to do anything to market Ballantine products that would cause "more than trivial" losses.

We do not think the judge imposed on Falstaff a standard as demanding as its appellate counsel argues that he did. Despite his footnote 7, see note 6 *supra*, he did not in fact proceed on the basis that the best efforts clause required Falstaff to bankrupt itself in promoting Ballantine products or even to sell those products at a substantial loss. He relied rather on the fact that Falstaff's obligation to use its best efforts to promote and maintain a high volume of sales" of Ballantine products was not fulfilled by a policy summarized by Mr. Kalmanovitz as being: "We sell beer and you pay for it. . . . We sell beer, F.O.B. the brewery. You come and get it." — however sensible such a policy may have been with respect to Falstaff's other products. Once the peril of insolvency had been averted, the drastic percentage reductions in Ballantine sales as related to any possible basis of comparison, see fn. 5, required Falstaff at least to explore whether steps not involving substantial losses could have been taken to stop or at least lessen the rate of decline. The judge found that, instead of doing this, Falstaff had engaged in a number of misfeasances and nonfeasances which could have accounted in substantial measure for the cata-strophic drop in Ballantine sales. . . . These included the closing of the North Bergen depot which had serviced "Mom and Pop" stores and bars in the New York metropolitan area; Falstaff's choices of distributors for Ballantine products in the New Jersey and particularly the New York areas, where the chosen distributor was the owner of a competing brand; its failure to take advantage of a proffer from Guinness-Harp Corporation to distribute Ballantine products in New York City through its Metrobeer Division; Falstaff's incentive to put more effort into sales of its own brands which sold at higher prices despite identity of the ingredients and were free from the $.50 a barrel royalty burden; its failure to treat Ballantine products evenhandedly with Falstaff's; its discontinuing the practice of setting goals for salesmen; and the general Kalmanovitz policy of stressing profit at the expense of volume. In the court's judgment, these misfeasances and nonfeasances warranted a conclusion that, even taking account of Falstaff's right to give reasonable consideration to its own interests, Falstaff had breached its duty to use best efforts as stated in the *Van Valkenburgh* decision, *supra*, 30 N.Y.2d at 46, 330 N.Y.S.2d at 334, 281 N.E.2d at 145.

---

agreement did import an implied promise by Savoy to fulfill its obligations for an entire five-year period." 23 N.Y.2d at 281, 296 N.Y.S.2d at 343, 244 N.E.2d at 41.

Other cases suggest that under New York law a "best efforts" clause imposes an obligation to act with good faith in light of one's own capabilities. In Van Valkenburgh v. Hayden Publishing Co., 30 N.Y.2d 34, 330 N.Y.S.2d 329, 281 N.E.2d 142 (1972), the court held a publisher liable to an author when, in clear bad faith after a contract dispute, he hired another to produce a book very similar to plaintiff's and then promoted it to those who had been buying the latter. On the other hand, a defendant having the exclusive right to sell the plaintiff's product may sell a similar product if necessary to meet outside competition, so long as he accounts for any resulting losses the plaintiff can show in the sales of the licensed product. Parev Products Co. v. I. Rokeach & Sons, 124 F.2d 147 (2 Cir. 1941). A summary definition of the best efforts obligation, cited by Judge Brieant, 454 F. Supp. at 266, is given in Arnold Productions, Inc. v. Favorite Films Corp., 176 F. Supp. 862, 866 (SDNY 1959), aff'd 298 F.2d 540 (2d Cir. 1962), to wit, performing as well as "the average prudent comparable" brewer.

The net of all this is that the New York law is far from clear and it is unfortunate that a federal court must have to apply it.

Falstaff levels a barrage on these findings. The only attack which merits discussion is its criticism of the judge's conclusion that Falstaff did not treat its Ballantine brands evenhandedly with those under the Falstaff name. We agree that the subsidiary findings "that Falstaff but not Ballantine had been advertised extensively in Texas and Missouri" and that "[i]n these same areas Falstaff, although a 'premium' beer, was sold for extended periods below the price of Ballantine," while literally true, did not warrant the inference drawn from them. Texas was Falstaff territory and, with advertising on a cooperative basis, it was natural that advertising expenditures on Falstaff would exceed those on Ballantine. The lower price for Falstaff was a particular promotion of a bicentennial can in Texas, intended to meet a particular competitor.

However, we do not regard this error as undermining the judge's ultimate conclusion of breach of the best efforts clause. While that clause clearly required Falstaff to treat the Ballantine brands as well as its own, it does not follow that it required no more. With respect to its own brands, management was entirely free to exercise its business judgment as to how to maximize profit even if this meant serious loss in volume. Because of the obligation it had assumed under the sales contract, its situation with respect to the Ballantine brands was quite different. The royalty of $.50 a barrel on sales was an essential part of the purchase price. Even without the best efforts clause Falstaff would have been bound to make a good faith effort to see that substantial sales of Ballantine products were made, unless it discontinued under clause 2(a)(v) with consequent liability for liquidated damages. Cf. Wood v. Duff-Gordon, 222 N.Y. 88 (1917) (Cardozo, J.). Clause 8 imposed an added obligation to use "best efforts to promote and maintain a *high* volume of sales. . . ." (emphasis supplied). Although we agree that even this did not require Falstaff to spend itself into bankruptcy to promote the sales of Ballantine products, it did prevent the application to them of Kalmanovitz' philosophy of emphasizing profit uber alles without fair consideration of the effect on Ballantine volume. Plaintiff was not obliged to show just what steps Falstaff could reasonably have taken to maintain a high volume for Ballantine products. It was sufficient to show that Falstaff simply didn't care about Ballantine's volume and was content to allow this to plummet so long as that course was best for Falstaff's overall profit picture, an inference which the judge permissibly drew. The burden then shifted to Falstaff to prove there was nothing significant it could have done to promote Ballantine sales that would not have been financially disastrous.

Having correctly concluded that Falstaff had breached its best efforts covenant, the judge was faced with a difficult problem in computing what the royalties on the lost sales would have been. There is no need to rehearse the many decisions holding that, in a situation like this, certainty is not required; "[t]he plaintiff need only show a 'stable foundation for a reasonable estimate of royalties he would have earned had defendant not breached.' " Contemporary Mission, Inc. v. Famous Music Corp., 557 F.2d 918, 926 (2 Cir. 1977), quoting Freund v. Washington Square Press, Inc., 34 N.Y.2d 379, 383, 357 N.Y.S.2d 857, 861 (1974). After carefully considering other possible bases, the court arrived at the seemingly sensible conclusion that the most nearly accurate comparison was with the combined sales of Rheingold and Schaefer beers, both, like Ballantine, being "price" beers sold primarily in the northeast, and computed what Ballantine sales would have been if its brands had suffered only the same decline as a composite of Rheingold and Schaefer.

Falstaff's principal criticism of the method of comparison, in addition to that noted in fn. 5, supra, was that the judge erred in saying, 454 F. Supp. at 279, that inclusion of Rheingold made "the comparison a conservative one" since "[t]he brewery was closed in early 1974 and production halted for a time." Falstaff is right that the halt in Rheingold production works the other way since the lowered figure for the base year made the percentage decline in subsequent years appear to be less than it in fact was. Against this, however, is the fact that the Rheingold 1977 figures do not include sales for the end of 1977 after the sale of Rheingold to Schmidt's Brewery, which counterbalances this error in some degree. In any event the Rheingold sales were only 25.7% of the combined sales in 1974 and 16.8% in 1977. Another criticism is that the deduction from the initial computation of lost royalties of $29,193.50 for the period April 1976 to March 1978 as representing royalties lost through the cessation of illegal practices was insufficient; it may well have been but the judge used the best figures he had. A possible objection, namely, that Schaefer maintained its sales only by incurring large losses, a fact now possibly subject to judicial notice, see The F. & M. Schaefer Corporation v. C. Schmidt & Sons, Inc., 597 F.2d 814, 817 (2 Cir. 1979), was not advanced with sufficient specificity to have required consideration. It is true, more generally, that the award may overcompensate the plaintiff since Falstaff was not necessarily required to do whatever Rheingold and Schaefer did. But that is the kind of uncertainty which is permissible in favor of a plaintiff who has established liability in a case like this. As said in Wakeman v. Wheeler & Wilson Mfg. Co., 101 N.Y. 205, 209 (1886):

> [W]hen it is certain that damages have been caused by a breach of contract, and the only uncertainty is to their amount, there can rarely be good reason for refusing on account of such uncertainty, any damages whatever for the breach. A person violating his contract should not be permitted entirely to escape liability because the amount of damage which he caused is uncertain.

We also reject plaintiff's complaint on his cross-appeal that the court erred in not taking as its standard for comparison the grouping of all but the top 15 brewers, Ballantine having ranked 16th in 1971. The judge was entirely warranted in believing that the Rheingold-Schaefer combination afforded a better standard of comparison.

We can dispose quite briefly of the portion of the plaintiff's cross-appeal which claims error in the rejection of his contention that Falstaff's actions triggered the liquidated damage clause. One branch of this puts heavy weight on the word "distribution;" the claim is that the closing of the North Bergen center and Mr. Kalmanovitz' general come-and-get-it philosophy was, without more, a substantial discontinuance of "distribution." On this basis plaintiff would be entitled to invoke the liquidated damage clause even if Falstaff's new methods had succeeded in checking the decline in Ballantine sales. Another fallacy is that, country-wide, Falstaff substantially increased the number of distributors carrying Ballantine labels. Moreover the term "distribution," as used in the brewing industry, does not require distribution by the brewer's own trucks and employees. The norm rather is distribution through independent wholesalers. Falstaff's default under the best efforts clause was not in returning to that method simpliciter but in its failure to see to it that wholesale distribution approached in effectiveness what retail distribution had done.

Plaintiff contends more generally that permitting a decline of 63.12% in Ballantine sales from 1974 to 1977 was the equivalent of quitting the game.

However, as Judge Brieant correctly pointed out, a large part of this drop was attributable "to the general decline of the market share of the smaller brewers" as against the "nationals," 454 F. Supp. at 266, and even the 518,899 barrels sold in 1977 were not a negligible amount of beer.

The judgment is affirmed. Plaintiff may recover two-thirds of his costs.

Essay: Optimal Output in Relational Contracts

Bloor specified that "best efforts" were to be used in selling beer. Also, UCC § 2-306(2) establishes best efforts as the performance standard for exclusive dealing arrangements in addition to the general requirement of good faith. But what precisely constitutes "best efforts"? And how is that standard to be defined in any contract? Professors Charles Goetz and Robert Scott provide one answer in *Principles of Relational Contracts*, 67 VA. L. REV. 1089, 1111–26 (1981).[41] The following discussion describes their thesis.

Relational contracts may take a variety of forms, but in this context they share two characteristics: they are ongoing contracts for the supply of goods or services rather than agreements for a single discrete exchange, and, because these contracts concern what is actually a series of transactions over a period of time, the parties to them are incapable of reducing important features of their bargain to well-defined obligations. There are simply too many contingencies to account for in a cost-effective fashion. Complications can arise even in those relational contracts that appear simple.

Take, for example, the case of a homeowner wishing to hire someone to care for his garden while he is away in the summer. Such a contract on its face seems to be relatively straightforward to draft, but consider these possibilities and problems: when should the plants and lawn be watered? What should the gardener do if the area suffers unusually heavy rain or a drought? What actions should he take if there is an unpredicted invasion of insects? Should the homeowner spend the time and money to dicker out a specific arrangement for each potential problem? And, if he does not, how can he be assured that his garden will be adequately cared for?

One method of dealing with such problems is to set a performance standard in very broad terms. "Best efforts" clauses are the typical way of articulating performance standards in such relational contracts, particularly in cases like *Lady Duff-Gordon*, where the manufacturer relies exclusively on one distributor to get her product on the market. (Note, however, that the dispute in *Lady Duff-Gordon* did not arise from a breach of the exclusive arrangement by the distributor, but

---

[41] For another discussion of various possible approaches to defining "best efforts," see Rob Park, *Putting the "Best" in Best Efforts*, 73 U. CHI. L. REV. 705 (2006).

from a breach on the part of the "manufacturer" of the indorsements, the Lady herself.) But what precisely counts as "best efforts"? And how is that standard to be defined in a contract so that the parties will understand what is expected of them and be able to identify a breach if and when it occurs?

In its most fundamental sense, "best efforts" closely parallels the implicit requirement of good faith. Its purpose is to get the distributor to take into account the interests of the manufacturer as well as his own. In the homeowner-gardener hypothetical, for instance, it might mean that the gardener must apply common sense and diligence to the task of keeping the garden green and healthy without resorting to unnecessary expense and trouble (e.g., spraying for the insects that do arrive but not for those that don't). Any obligation of this kind is, of course, inherently difficult to monitor.

Goetz and Scott propose a definition of best efforts that is more expansive than the mere obligation to act in good faith. They argue that "best efforts" means an obligation to produce at a volume which maximizes the gains of both parties. This "optimal output" conception would require the distributor to take both parties' interests into account in marketing the product. One way to visualize this obligation is that it requires the distributor to market the same quantity of goods as could be expected if a single firm (with the manufacturing costs of the principal (the manufacturer) and the distribution costs of the agent (the distributor)) owned *both* the production and the marketing rights even though the rights are actually divided between the parties.

There is an alternative definition that might be advanced. One might argue that "best efforts" requires more than good faith but not necessarily an obligation to maximize the joint value of the contract for both parties. Rather, one could argue that best efforts requires the exercise of due diligence and ordinary business prudence. Under this conception, a breach of best efforts exists when a distributor's efforts do not meet the standard of diligent or reasonably prudent business conduct. Thus, best efforts clauses can also be seen as an explicit allocation of all risks created by potential blunders of the party promising his best efforts. Goetz and Scott refer to this view of best efforts as the "diligence insurance" definition. They argue that the diligence standard is subsumed within the optimal output definition, because the necessary amount of diligence is that amount which is cost-effective, i.e., an amount of diligence that maximizes the joint interests of the parties.

Despite the theoretical appeal of these arguments, however, it is difficult to find a definition of best efforts in the terms of traditional legal doctrine. Early common law courts were reluctant to sanction such ambiguous obligations. The majority of modern courts do enforce such contracts, yet they have not formulated a standard definition for the best efforts obligation. Perhaps the closest the law has come to articulating what it means by best efforts is § 2-306(2) of the UCC and its official comments.

In *Bloor*, the court showed an awareness of the diligence insurance concept, and the case illustrates that, courts are aware that "best efforts" in the standard distribution context requires more than the distributor's profit-maximizing volume. It is not so clear, however, that courts have adopted joint maximization (or optimal output) as the performance standard to apply in the absence of contrary agreement.

Most courts resolving best efforts disputes have not had to articulate in detail how the parties' interests are to be balanced, because most of the litigated cases involve obvious and substantial failures of performance. This may reflect the fact that the current legal ambiguity has created an onerous *de facto* burden for plaintiffs, which can only be overcome in cases of substantial breach.

For these reasons, among others, best efforts clauses are rife with problems of moral hazard. The best efforts promisor has an incentive to "chisel" on his obligation (the gardener, for instance, knowing that no one is around to watch him work, might elect to spend some of his "gardening time" at the beach). The best efforts promisee, on the other hand, will have to incur substantial costs to prove liability and damages, making a trip to court to enforce the bargain an unattractive option. But since this sort of arrangement also benefits both sides (the homeowner gets his garden cared for; the gardener earns money), both parties have an incentive *going into the deal* to shape a system of controls — or checks and balances — designed to make their arrangement work at an optimal level.

One kind of protective provision is a termination privilege, which gives the manufacturer-promisee the right to dismiss the distributor-promisor under certain conditions, sometimes after a specified period of time, sometimes for a specified cause. A right of termination is best seen as a means of bonding the distributor to the interests of the supplier. In a sense the distributor voluntarily assumes the risk of termination as an assurance of future efforts. The parties may include other provisions — a liquidated damages clause to guard against the difficulty of proving losses from lack of effort or perhaps a covenant not to compete, which protects the supplier from having the distributor set himself up in competition once he learns "the tricks of the trade." The parties should choose a combination of protective terms that minimize the costs of ensuring performance in their particular circumstances.

Now reconsider *Bloor* in terms of the foregoing analysis. At the time the contract was made, was the "best efforts" format the best solution to the needs of the parties? After all, this case is not a standard garden-variety distributorship arrangement. Falstaff was not purchasing the right to market Ballantine beer but rather was only purchasing the Ballantine brand name for a price. The problem was that the parties were uncertain as to what the brand was worth, hence the royalty agreement. Does that change your analysis of what "best efforts" requires in this case?

NOTES

1. ***Exclusive Dealings Contracts: Explanation and Analysis.*** Exclusive dealings contracts, such as those discussed in the above cases, feature a principal-agent relationship, where the principal agrees to operate only through the agent. Such exclusivity is necessary in order to prevent subsequent agents from enjoying a free ride at the expense of the initial agent. For instance, an author may agree to give a portion of revenues from her book to her publicist in exchange for setting up events such as a book tour and media appearances. Suppose that the publicist arranges for the author to be featured on programs such as "The Oprah Winfrey Show" and "Larry King Live." After making those appearances, the author should

not be able to sign on with another publicist, as many of the sales of the book will be generated by the initial efforts of the first publicist who helped her develop national prominence. By granting the agent exclusivity, the agent's incentive to under-invest is reduced.

Exclusive dealings contracts, unlike output or requirements contracts, often involve the provision of services rather than the supply of goods or materials. In addition, they typically are used in retail distribution contracts rather than wholesale supply contracts. They differ from requirements contracts in several significant ways. In a requirements contract, the parties are primarily interested in giving the buyer discretion over quantity decisions in the future. The seller/manufacturer also has flexibility as it can find other buyers if the first buyer's requirements are insufficient to sustain the optimal level of production. But in an exclusive dealings contract, the buyer/distributor is the sole agent who can distribute the seller's product. This exclusivity is designed to motivate the distributor to invest in promoting and marketing of the seller's product. Consequently, sellers are left more vulnerable under exclusive dealings contracts than under output or requirements contracts. The seller is dependent upon the actions of the buyer/distributor and has the potential to be harmed if the agent is lazy or incompetent. As a consequence, the parties must limit the distributor's discretion as well by contracting for best efforts or by building in other constraints that motivate the distributor to invest optimally.

An important question is whether the buyer/distributor can also handle the products of similarly-situated seller/manufacturers. In general, the courts hold that handling competing brands is not a per se violation of the best efforts obligation. As long as some other distributor on the market would similarly treat the competing product, the licensor cannot complain. Thus, for example, the publisher of this casebook, Lexis, also publishes and distributes competing casebooks authored by other Contracts professors. There is no violation of the publisher's best efforts obligation since if Lexis chose not to distribute those other casebooks, they would be marketed by another law book publishing company. A problem may arise, however, if the distributor does not treat each of the products evenhandedly. For instance, a company that imports, distributes, and promotes foreign beers may seek to limit the growth of one brand to encourage the sales of another. Thus, an importer who seeks to maximize the American sales of Molson is not acting with "best efforts" if he also seeks shelf space for Labatt's — which may be obtained only at Molson's expense.

2. *Restating the Facts in* **Lady Duff-Gordon.** Had the case been decided the other way, Professor Karl Llewellyn suggested how the facts of *Lady Duff-Gordon* might be put:

> The plaintiff in this action rests his case upon his own carefully prepared form agreement, which has as its first essence his own omission of any expression whatsoever of any obligation of any kind on the part of this same plaintiff. We thus have the familiar situation of a venture in which one party, here the defendant, has an asset, with what is, in advance, of purely speculative value. The other party, the present plaintiff, who drew the agreement, is a marketer eager for profit, but chary of risk. The legal

question presented is whether the plaintiff, while carefully avoiding all risk in the event of failure, can nevertheless claim full profit in the event that the market may prove favorable in its response. The law of consideration joins with the principles of business decency in giving the answer. And the answer is no.

Llewellyn, *A Lecture on Appellate Advocacy*, 29 U. CHI. L. REV. 627, 637–38 (1962). How would you respond to Llewellyn's argument that Wood was essentially trying to have it both ways?

3.   *The Context of* Lucy v. Lady Duff-Gordon. Professor Walter Pratt, in *American Contract Law at the Turn of the Century*, 39 S.C. L. REV. 415 (1988), gives additional background facts on *Wood v. Lucy, Lady Duff-Gordon.* Lucy was a successful British entrepreneur who, with little initial capital, became one of the world's most successful designers of women's clothing. For example, one of her singular accomplishments was designing different mourning dresses for one hundred women in Queen Victoria's funeral and then producing different designs for 200 women for the coronation of King Edward VII. As Lucy's reputation grew, she began to produce more than one dress of each design and hired others to design under her general supervision.

As Cardozo's opinion reveals, Lucy's strategy of marketing in the United States included selling her indorsements of women's clothing, a practice common today but less so in the early years of the twentieth century. Wood's background is not so well-developed in the literature, but it appears that he brought valuable United States business skills to the enterprise. The exclusive dealing contract with Lucy allowed Wood to market her indorsements without the worry that other agents would free-ride off his efforts.

The event that led to the friction, and ultimately the litigation, was Lucy's arrangement with Sears, Roebuck and Company to sell her dresses through its catalogues. A trade journal reported that the announcement of the agreement threw "a bomb into the camp of rival mail-order houses." Unfortunately, the arrangement with Sears was unsuccessful. Professor Victor Goldberg reports that Sears lost more than $26,000. Given that the dresses sold in the $20 to $45 price range and that per capita annual income at the time was $450, it is not surprising that the dresses were too expensive for the average farmer's wife. In any event, Sears dropped the "Lucile" line.[42]

4.   *Reinterpreting* Bloor. Courts and commentators have uniformly regarded *Bloor* as an exclusive dealings distribution contract and, thus, have agreed that Falstaff's lackluster efforts violated its best efforts obligation. But read the case once more and ask yourself, "is *Bloor* really a garden variety distributorship arrangement"? Professor Victor Goldberg believes that the answer to this question is no. In his article *In Search of Best Efforts: Reinterpreting* Bloor v. Falstaff, 44 ST. LOUIS. L.J. 1465 (2000), Goldberg argues that had the litigants (and the two federal judges) placed the contract in its proper business context, the outcome would have been different. Goldberg points out that Falstaff was not contracting to be a distributor for Ballantine Beer. Rather, the key to the contract was that Ballantine

---

[42] VICTOR GOLDBERG, FRAMING CONTRACT LAW: AN ECONOMIC PERSPECTIVE 57–58 (2007).

was leaving the beer business and was undertaking a one-time sale of some of its assets to Falstaff. The best efforts clause thus was part of a "contingent compensation" provision in which the amount of money that Falstaff agreed to pay for these assets would be based, in part, on the quality of the asset itself. The royalty arrangement, Goldberg argues, served as a meter of the quality of the asset based on Ballantine's gross sales. The best efforts clause, thus understood, was not designed to require Falstaff to actively promote the sales of Ballantine Beer but, rather, was designed to guard against any strategic behavior by which Falstaff sought to redirect revenues away from Ballantine's and toward other Falstaff brands. Since, under the facts, Falstaff clearly did not attempt to redirect revenues in that fashion, Goldberg argues that the case was wrongly decided.

After working through Goldberg's arguments are you persuaded that the best efforts clause in this contract was designed to function essentially as a guarantee of Falstaff's good faith? If Goldberg is right, shouldn't the attorneys who drafted the contract have used more careful language to prescribe Falstaff's obligations under the contract?

5. ***Impermissible Conduct in Exclusive Dealings Contracts.*** Contracting parties are obligated to refrain from conducting themselves in ways which would be wholly acceptable for nonparties or business rivals. Consider the case of *Van Valkenburgh, Nooger & Neville, Inc. v. Hayden Publishing Co.*, 30 N.Y.2d 34, 330 N.Y.S.2d 329, 281 N.E.2d 142 (1972). In this case, the plaintiff held a copyright on a series of books on basic electronics. Its contract with the publisher granted it a 15% royalty on each sale; the publisher, in turn, agreed to use its best efforts to promote the books. The publisher sought to reduce the royalty rate for future editions; the author refused to accept a lower rate. Shortly thereafter, the publisher contracted with another author to provide a series of electronics books which were remarkably similar in their content and organization. This author, however, received a mere 3% royalty. The publisher tried to sell these books to customers who had placed orders for the initial author's works. The court ruled that the publisher's actions had crossed the line "where that activity is so manifestly harmful to the author, and must have been seen by the publisher so to be harmful, as to justify the court in saying there was a breach of the covenant to promote the author's work."

Now, consider the following line of argument:

> In *Van Valkenburgh*, another publisher would have committed neither a tort, a copyright violation, nor a breach of contract had it published a book competing with plaintiff's, copied the format and style of plaintiff's book, given its author a royalty rate of 3% or less, and concealed the fact that it was doing these things. Therefore, isn't it clear that the defendant ought to be able to do those things also? If so, the only question properly considered by the court is whether the efforts made by defendant to market plaintiff's book were adequate under the contract without regard to the fact that defendant was also marketing a competing book.

What is wrong with this argument?

6. ***Problem: Stanley Law Summaries Revisited.*** Review the Problem on Stanley Law Summaries, *supra*. We return to the situation now, but it is several

years after the distributorship agreement was negotiated.

Professor Deacon has been quite successful in promoting and marketing the Stanley Law Summaries. No longer worried about the uncertainties of a new market, Deacon proposed to Stanley the following changes in the contract:

> Deacon shall have for a period of three years the exclusive license to market Stanley Law Summaries in the Mid-Atlantic region comprising the District of Columbia and the states of Maryland, Delaware, Virginia, West Virginia, and North Carolina. In exchange for the exclusive license to distribute Stanley Summaries in the region, Deacon will pay Stanley a $1 royalty per copy sold in addition to the per book wholesale price (currently at $10) which covers Stanley's costs in printing and production of the outlines.

Again Stanley, still rusty in contract law, approaches you for legal advice. Should Stanley accept the new terms of the contract? Does such a relationship offer any advantages to Stanley? If so, what are they? What difficulties will Stanley face in ensuring that his summaries are promoted satisfactorily in competition with other commercially available law outlines? Is there a better way to structure the relationship to ensure that the Stanley Summaries are adequately advertised and promoted? For example, would it be wise for Stanley to suggest a royalty payment of 50% of Deacon's net profits from distribution and sale of the summaries instead of the $1 per book royalty?[43]

Suppose Deacon adequately promotes the summaries for two years under the exclusive arrangement, but then decides to produce his own summaries. Can Stanley terminate the contract? What argument could Stanley make that would impose liability on Deacon if he failed to sell any summaries at all?

[3]   Reducing Conflicts of Interest by Contract

As we have seen, on-going contractual relations often involve costly conflicts of interest. Each party faces a temptation, after the contract is negotiated, to favor its own interest over the collective interests of the contracting parties. The deviation between individual and collective interests are often termed "agency" costs, reflecting the inherent conflict between each party as agent for the collective (the principal). One way to solve the problem of contractual conflicts is for the parties to form a firm — either a partnership or a corporation. This approach substitutes a hierarchical form of organization, and a centralized decision maker, for the individual decisions of each contracting party. But vertical integration of these functions into a firm carries offsetting costs including the complex network of internal controls on management and labor that characterize the firm.[44] An alternative approach is for the parties to agree on contractual provisions that are designed to reduce conflicts and preserve the relationship. If the parties can reduce these "agency costs" sufficiently, they will choose a relational contract over vertical

---

[43] For an explanation of the puzzling persistence of "net profit" arrangements in the entertainment industry, see Victor Goldberg, *The Net Profits Puzzle*, 97 COLUM. L. REV. 524 (1997). *See also* VICTOR GOLDBERG, FRAMING CONTRACT LAW: AN ECONOMIC PERSPECTIVE 13–36 (2007).

[44] *See* Alchian & Dempsetz, *Production, Information Costs, and Economic Organization*, 62 Am. Econ. Rev. 777, 777–83 (1972).

integration. One approach to reducing conflicts of interest is to specify in the contract an array of direct monitoring arrangements such as prescribed audits and pre-established performance standards, as well as "indirect" monitoring mechanisms, such as incentive systems.

Obviously, these monitoring arrangements are costly to both parties; such costs reduce the price that each party will agree to pay for the contract services of the other.[45] Each party — in its role as agent — has an incentive, therefore, to substitute reassurances of performance in the form of "bonding" provisions. Among the variety of possible bonding arrangements are capital contributions, covenants not to compete, self-imposed ethical standards, and termination clauses.

The extent to which these considerations are applicable to employment contracts, which account for more reported cases than any other area, is especially interesting.

[a] Termination Clauses

WAGENSELLER v. SCOTTSDALE MEMORIAL HOSP.
Supreme Court of Arizona
147 Ariz. 370, 710 P.2d 1025 (1985)

FELDMAN, J.

Catherine Sue Wagenseller petitioned this court to review a decision of the court of appeals affirming in part the trial court's judgment in favor of Scottsdale Memorial Hospital and certain Hospital employees (defendants). Catherine Wagenseller began her employment at Scottsdale Memorial Hospital as a staff nurse in March 1975, having been personally recruited by the manager of the emergency department, Kay Smith. Wagenseller was an "at-will" employee — one hired without specific contractual term. Smith was her supervisor. In August 1978, Wagenseller was assigned to the position of ambulance charge nurse, and approximately one year later was promoted to the position of paramedic coordinator, a newly approved management position in the emergency department. Three months later, on November 1, 1979, Wagenseller was terminated.

Most of the events surrounding Wagenseller's work at the Hospital and her subsequent termination are not disputed, although the parties differ in their interpretation of the inferences to be drawn from and the significance of these events. For more than four years, Smith and Wagenseller maintained a friendly, professional, working relationship. In May 1979, they joined a group consisting largely of personnel from other hospitals for an eight-day camping and rafting trip down the Colorado River. According to Wagenseller, "an uncomfortable feeling" developed between her and Smith as the trip progressed — a feeling that Wagenseller ascribed to "the behavior that Kay Smith was displaying." Wagenseller states that this included public urination, defecation and bathing, heavy drinking,

---

[45] *See* Jensen & Meckling, *Theory of the Firm: Managerial Behavior, Agency Costs and Ownership Structure*, 3 J. FIN. ECON. 305, 313–19 (1976).

and "grouping up" with other rafters. Wagenseller did not participate in any of these activities. She also refused to join in the group's staging of a parody of the song "Moon River," which allegedly concluded with members of the group "mooning" the audience. Smith and others allegedly performed the "Moon River" skit twice at the Hospital following the group's return from the river, but Wagenseller declined to participate there as well.

Wagenseller contends that her refusal to engage in these activities caused her relationship with Smith to deteriorate and was the proximate cause of her termination. She claims that following the river trip Smith began harassing her, using abusive language and embarrassing her in the company of other staff. Other emergency department staff reported a similar marked change in Smith's behavior toward Wagenseller after the trip, although Smith denied it.

Up to the time of the river trip, Wagenseller had received consistently favorable job performance evaluations. Two months before the trip, Smith completed an annual evaluation report in which she rated Wagenseller's performance as "exceed-[ing] results expected," the second highest of five possible ratings. In August and October 1979, Wagenseller met first with Smith and then with Smith's successor, Jeannie Steindorff, to discuss some problems regarding her duties as paramedic coordinator and her attitude toward the job. On November 1, 1979, following an exit interview at which Wagenseller was asked to resign and refused, she was terminated.

She appealed her dismissal in letters to her supervisor and to the Hospital administrative and personnel department, answering the Hospital's stated reasons for her termination, claiming violations of the disciplinary procedure contained in the Hospital's personnel policy manual, and requesting reinstatement and other remedies. When this appeal was denied, Wagenseller brought suit against the Hospital, its personnel administrators, and her supervisor, Kay Smith.

Wagenseller, an "at-will" employee, contends that she was fired for reasons which contravene public policy and without legitimate cause related to job performance. She claims that her termination was wrongful, and that damages are recoverable under both tort and contract theories. The Hospital argues that an "at-will" employee may be fired for cause, without cause, or for "bad" cause. We hold that in the absence of contractual provision such an employee may be fired for good cause or for no cause, but not for "bad" cause.

As early as 1562, the English common law presumed that an employment contract containing an annual salary provision or computation was for a one-year term. Originally designed for the protection of seasonal farm workers, the English rule expanded over the years to protect factory workers as well. Workers were well protected under this rule, for the one-year presumption was not easy to overcome. English courts held an employer liable for breaching the employment contract if he terminated an employee at any time during the year without "reasonable cause to do so." To uphold an employer's discharge of an employee without a showing of "good cause," the courts required a clear expression of a contrary intent as evidenced either on the face of the contract or by a clearly defined custom of the industry.

In the early nineteenth century, American courts borrowed the English rule. The legal rationale embodied in the rule was consistent with the nature of the predominant master-servant employment relationship at the time because it reflected the master's duty to make provision for the general well-being of his servants. In addition, the master was under a duty to employ the servant for a term, either a specified or implied time of service, and could not terminate him strictly at will. The late nineteenth century, however, brought the Industrial Revolution; with it came the decline of the master-servant relationship and the rise of the more impersonal employer-employee relationship. In apparent response to the economic changes sweeping the country, American courts abandoned the English rule and adopted the employment-at-will doctrine. This new doctrine gave the employer freedom to terminate an at-will employee for any reason, good or bad.

However unsound its foundation, [the] at-will doctrine was adopted by the New York courts and soon became the generally accepted American rule. In 1932, this court first adopted the rule for Arizona: "The general rule in regard to contracts for personal services, . . . where no time limit is provided, is that they are terminable at pleasure by either party, or at most upon reasonable notice." Thus, an employer was free to fire an employee hired for an indefinite term "for good cause, for no cause, or even for cause morally wrong, without being thereby guilty of legal wrong."

In recent years there has been apparent dissatisfaction with the absolutist formulation of the common law at-will rule. The Illinois Supreme Court is representative of courts that have acknowledged a need for a less mechanical application of the rule:

> With the rise of large corporations conducting specialized operations and employing relatively immobile workers who often have no other place to market their skills, recognition that the employer and employee do not stand on equal footing is realistic. In addition, unchecked employer power, like unchecked employee power, has been seen to present a distinct threat to the public policy carefully considered and adopted by society as a whole. As a result, it is now recognized that a proper balance must be maintained among the employer's interest in operating a business efficiently and profitably, the employee's interest in earning a livelihood, and society's interest in seeing its public policies carried out. Palmateer v. International Harvester Co., 85 Ill. 2d 124 (1981).

Today, courts in three-fifths of the states have recognized some form of a cause of action for wrongful discharge.

The trend has been to modify the at-will rule by creating exceptions to its operation. Three general exceptions have developed. The most widely accepted approach is the "public policy" exception, which permits recovery upon a finding that the employer's conduct undermined some important public policy. The second exception, based on contract, requires proof of an implied-in-fact promise of employment for a specific duration, as found in the circumstances surrounding the employment relationship, including assurances of job security in company personnel manuals or memoranda. Under the third approach, courts have found in the employment contract an implied-in-law covenant of "good faith and fair dealing" and have held employers liable in both contract and tort for breach of that covenant. Wagenseller raises all three doctrines.

The public policy exception to the at-will doctrine began with a narrow rule permitting employees to sue their employers when a statute expressly prohibited their discharge. This formulation was then expanded to include any discharge in violation of a statutory expression of public policy. *See Petermann v. Int'l Bhd. of Teamsters*, 174 Cal. App. 2d 184 (1959) (discharge for refusal to commit perjury). Courts later allowed a cause of action for violation of public policy, even in the absence of a specific statutory prohibition. *See Nees v. Hocks*, 272 Or. 210 (1975) (discharge for being absent from work to serve on jury duty). The New Hampshire Supreme Court announced perhaps the most expansive rule when it held an employer liable for discharging an employee who refused to go out with her foreman. The court concluded that termination "motivated by bad faith or malice or based on retaliation is not [in] the best interest of the economic system or the public good and constitutes a breach of the employment contract." *Monge v. Beebe Rubber Co.*, 114 N.H. 130, 133 (1974). Although no other court has gone this far, a majority of the states have now either recognized a cause of action based on the public policy exception or have indicated their willingness to consider it, given appropriate facts. The key to an employee's claim in all of these cases is the proper definition of a public policy that has been violated by the employer's actions.

[After extended discussion, the court found that Wagenseller had refused to participate in activities that arguably would have violated the Arizona indecent exposure statute.]

Thus, in an at-will hiring we continue to recognize the presumption or to imply the covenant of termination at the pleasure of either party, whether with or without cause. Firing for bad cause — one against public policy articulated by constitutional, statutory, or decisional law — is not a right inherent in the at-will contract, or in any other contract, even if expressly provided. Such a termination violates rights guaranteed to the employee by law and is tortious.

Although an employment contract for an indefinite term is presumed to be terminable at will, that presumption, like any other presumption, is rebuttable by contrary evidence. Thus, in addition to relying on the public policy analysis to restrict the operation of the terminable-at-will rule, courts have turned to the employment contract itself, finding in it implied terms that limit the employer's right of discharge. Two types of implied contract terms have been recognized by the courts: implied-in-law terms and implied-in-fact terms. An implied-in-law term arises from a duty imposed by law where the contract itself is silent; it is imposed even though the parties may not have intended it, and it binds the parties to a legally enforceable duty, just as if they had so contracted explicitly. The covenant of good faith and fair dealing is an implied-in-law contract term that has been recognized by a small number of courts in the employment-at-will context. An implied-in-fact contract term, on the other hand, is one that is inferred from the statements or conduct of the parties. It is not a promise defined by the law, but one made by the parties, though not expressly. Courts have found such terms in an employer's policy statements regarding such things as job security and employee disciplinary procedures, holding that by the conduct of the parties these statements may become part of the contract, supplementing the verbalized at-will agreement, and thus limiting the employer's absolute right to discharge an at-will employee. Arizona is among the jurisdictions that have recognized the implied-in-fact contract term as an exception to the at-will rule. In *Leikvold v. Valley View Community Hospital, supra*, this court held that a personnel manual can become part of an employment contract and remanded the cause for a jury determination as to whether the particular manual given to Leikvold had become part of her employment contract with Valley View.

The relevant facts in the case before us are not dissimilar to those in *Leikvold*. In October 1978, Scottsdale Memorial Hospital established a four-step disciplinary procedure to achieve the Hospital's stated policy of "provid[ing] fair and consistent discipline as required to assist with the improvement of employees' behavior or performance." Subject to 32 listed exceptions, prior to being terminated a Hospital employee must be given a verbal warning, a written performance warning, a letter of formal reprimand, and a notice of dismissal. The manual further qualifies the mandatory procedure by providing that the 32 exceptions "are not inclusive and are only guidelines." In appealing her dismissal, Wagenseller cited violations of this procedure, but the trial court ruled as a matter of law that the manual had not become part of the employment contract between Wagenseller and the Hospital. The court of appeals held that the Hospital's failure to follow the four-step disciplinary procedure did not violate Wagenseller's contract rights because she failed to prove her reliance on the procedure as a part of her employment contract. We disagree with both of these rulings.

[W]e held in *Leikvold* that entry of summary judgment was inappropriate "[b]ecause a material question — whether the policies manual was incorporated into and became part of the terms of the employment contract — remain[ed] in dispute." The court may determine as a matter of law the proper construction of contract terms which are "clear and unambiguous." Here, the court of appeals ruled, in effect, that the Hospital had adequately disclaimed any liability for failing to follow the procedure it had established. It found this disclaimer in the final item in the Hospital's list of exceptions to its disciplinary procedure: "20. These major and minor infractions are not inclusive and are only guidelines." The court concluded that the effect of this "clear" and "conspicuous" provision was "to create, by its terms, no rights at all."

We do not believe this document, read in its entirety, has the clarity that the court of appeals attributed to its individual portions. One reading the document might well infer that the Hospital had established a procedure that would generally apply in disciplinary actions taken against employees. Although such a person would also note the long list of exceptions, he might not conclude from reading the list that an exception would apply in every case so as to swallow the general rule completely. We do not believe that the provision for unarticulated exceptions destroys the entire articulated general policy as a matter of law. Not only does such a result defy common sense, it runs afoul of our reasoning in *Leikvold*, where we addressed this problem directly:

> Employers are certainly free to issue no personnel manual at all or to issue
> a personnel manual that clearly and conspicuously tells their employees

that the manual is not part of the employment contract and that their jobs are terminable at the will of the employer with or without reason. Such actions, either not issuing a personnel manual or issuing one with clear language of limitation, instill no reasonable expectations of job security and do not give employees any reason to rely on representations in the manual. However, if an employer does choose to issue a policy statement, in a manual or otherwise, and, by its language or by the employer's actions, encourages reliance thereon, the employer cannot be free to only selectively abide by it. Having announced a policy, the employer may not treat it as illusory.

We emphasize here that the rule set forth in *Leikvold* is merely a reiteration of employment law as it has existed for centuries, exemplified by the English common law one-year presumption and the at-will employment doctrine itself. The right of discharge without cause is an implied contractual term which is said to exist in an at-will relationship when there are no factual indications to the contrary. The intent to create a different relationship, as well as the parameters of that relationship, are to be discerned from the totality of the parties' statements and actions regarding the employment relationship.

The general rule is that the determination whether in a particular case a promise should be implied in fact is a question of fact. Where reasonable minds may draw different conclusions or inferences from undisputed evidentiary facts, a question of fact is presented. "[T]he very essence of [the jury's] function is to select from among conflicting inferences and conclusions that which it considers most reasonable." We believe that reasonable persons could differ in the inferences and conclusions they would draw from the Hospital's published manual regarding disciplinary policy and procedure. Thus, there are questions of fact as to whether this policy and procedure became a part of Wagenseller's employment contract. The trial court therefore erred in granting summary judgment on this issue.

We turn next to a consideration of implied-in-law contract terms which may limit an employer's right to discharge an at-will employee. Wagenseller claims that discharge without good cause breaches the implied-in-law covenant of good faith and fair dealing contained in every contract. In the context of this case, she argues that discharge without good cause violates the covenant of good faith and is, therefore, wrongful. The covenant requires that neither party do anything that will injure the right of the other to receive the benefits of their agreement. The duty not to act in bad faith or deal unfairly thus becomes a part of the contract, and, as with any other element of the contract, the remedy for its breach generally is on the contract itself. In certain circumstances, breach of contract, including breach of the covenant of good faith and fair dealing, may provide the basis for a tort claim.

The question whether a duty to terminate only for good cause should be implied into all employment-at-will contracts has received much attention in the case law and other literature. Courts have generally rejected the invitation to imply such a duty in employment contracts, voicing the concern that to do so would place undue restrictions on management and would infringe the employer's "legitimate exercise of management discretion." We think this concern is appropriate.

[W]e do not feel that we should treat employment contracts as a special type of agreement in which the law refuses to imply the covenant of good faith and fair dealing that it implies in all other contracts. As we noted above, the implied-in-law covenant of good faith and fair dealing protects the right of the parties to an agreement to receive the benefits of the agreement that they have entered into. The denial of a party's right to those benefits, whatever they are, will breach the duty of good faith implicit in the contract. Thus, the relevant inquiry always will focus on the contract itself, to determine what the parties did agree to. In the case of an employment-at-will contract, it may be said that the parties have agreed, for example, that the employee will do the work required by the employer and that the employer will provide the necessary working conditions and pay the employee for work done. What cannot be said is that one of the agreed benefits to the at-will employee is a guarantee of continued employment or tenure. The very nature of the at-will agreement precludes any claim for a prospective benefit. Either employer or employee may terminate the contract at any time.

We do, however, recognize an implied covenant of good faith and fair dealing in the employment-at-will contract, although that covenant does not create a duty for the employer to terminate the employee only for good cause. The covenant does not protect the employee from a "no cause" termination because tenure was never a benefit inherent in the at-will agreement. The covenant does protect an employee from a discharge based on an employer's desire to avoid the payment of benefits already earned by the employee, such as the sales commissions, but not the tenure required to earn the pension and retirement benefits. Thus, plaintiff here has a right to receive the benefits that were a part of her employment agreement with defendant Hospital. To the extent, however, that the benefits represent a claim for prospective employment, her claim must fail. The terminable-at-will contract between her and the Hospital made no promise of continued employment. To the contrary, it was, by its nature, subject to termination by either party at any time, subject only to the legal prohibition that she could not be fired for reasons which contravene public policy.

Thus, because we are concerned not to place undue restrictions on the employer's discretion in managing his workforce and because tenure is contrary to the bargain in an at-will contract, we reject the argument that a no cause termination breaches the implied covenant of good faith and fair dealing in an employment-at-will relationship.

[The court then discussed the personal liability of supervisor Smith to the plaintiff.]

CONSUMERS INT'L v. SYSCO CORP.
Court of Appeals of Arizona
191 Ariz. 32, 951 P.2d 897 (1997)

Voss, J.

Plaintiff-Appellant Consumers International, Inc. (CI) appeals from the trial court's judgment in favor of Defendant-Appellee Sysco Corporation (Sysco) on CI's claim of wrongful termination of the parties' business relationship. The sole issue on appeal is whether the implied covenant of good faith and fair dealing inherent in every contract requires that a termination-at-will clause in a distribution agreement be interpreted to require "good cause." Because we conclude that the contract contained no such requirement, and that the trial court correctly entered summary judgment on this basis, we affirm.

The parties entered into a written "Master Distribution Agreement" on October 1, 1993. The agreement provided that Sysco would serve as supplier of at least eighty percent of the enumerated food service products that CI distributed to its retail customers. The products included both national brands and Sysco brands.

The agreement provided as follows regarding its duration:

> The term of this Agreement will begin on October 1, 1993, and terminate two years from that date. This Agreement may be terminated prior to such date.
>
> (a)   By either party upon thirty (30) days written notice to the other party for failure of the other party to comply with any provision of this Agreement;
>
> (b)   By SYSCO upon written notice to Customer if Customer's financial position deteriorates materially, determined by SYSCO in its sole judgment; and
>
> (c)   By either party upon sixty (60) days prior written notice to the other party.

On December 13, 1993, Sysco sent the following termination letter to CI, indicating its sixty-day notice:

> This letter is to serve as notification to Consumers International that SYSCO Corporation, and its operating subsidiaries and divisions, is hereby terminating our Master Distribution Agreement with Consumers International. . . . The Master Distribution Agreement will therefore terminate sixty days hence, being February 12, 1994.

In August 1995, CI brought this action against SYSCO, alleging, among other things, wrongful termination of the contract based on Sysco's breach of the implied covenant of good faith and fair dealing. CI contended that the agreement implicitly contained an "implied covenant that the right of termination would only be exercised in good faith."

Sysco moved for summary judgment on this claim, asserting that it had the right to terminate the contract for any reason upon sixty days notice, under the explicit terms of the agreement. The trial court agreed and found:

THE COURT FINDS that the parties dealt at arms['] length.

THE COURT FURTHER FINDS that the parties had benefit of counsel when they entered into the contract.

THE COURT FURTHER FINDS that the parties were aware of paragraph 9(c) permitting termination of the contract without cause by the Defendant.

364 CONTRACTUAL RELATIONSHIPS AND CONDUCT CH. 4

THE COURT FURTHER FINDS no evidence of bad cause such as gender discrimination[,] racial discrimination or violation of public policies [as] in Wagenseller v. Scottsdale Memorial Hospital[,] 147 Ariz. 370, 710 P.2d 1025 (1985).

Based on these findings, the trial court granted Sysco summary judgment on the claim of wrongful termination of contract, and concluded that the agreement terminated on February 12, 1994. After the parties stipulated to the remaining issues, the court dismissed the action, and CI timely appealed from the final judgment.

On appeal, CI contends that the implied covenant of good faith and fair dealing inherent in every contract mandates that early termination of a distribution agreement be restricted to reasons constituting "good cause." Because Sysco has not given any "good cause" reason for early termination of this contract, CI contends that summary judgment was inappropriate on its wrongful termination claim.

As a preliminary matter, we note that CI asserts that its relationship with Sysco is "akin" to that of a franchisee. Much of the case law on which CI relies involves franchise relationships. We need not, however, determine whether this distribution agreement constituted a "franchise" to resolve this issue; even assuming, without deciding, that the business relationship at issue here was a franchise-type relationship, our conclusion would be the same.

CI contends that, because it is a small distributor and Sysco is a large supplier, the contractual relationship between them must be viewed as an unequal one, and that public policy therefore compels limiting enforcement of the broad termination clause to good cause. CI finds support for this argument in the common law of Arizona and other jurisdictions and in analogous Arizona statutory provisions relating to supplier/dealer relationships of oil companies and liquor suppliers.

We begin with the premise that, under general principles of contract law, absent statutory regulation, parties may freely contract for any lawful purposes, including franchise agreements for the distribution of products. Freedom to contract has long been considered a valuable right:

> If there is one thing which more than another public policy requires it is that [people] of full age and competent understanding shall have the utmost liberty of contracting, and that their contracts when entered into freely and voluntarily shall be held sacred and shall be enforced by Courts of justice. Therefore, you have this paramount public policy to consider — that you are not lightly to interfere with this freedom of contract.

This general rule has been modified by Arizona courts in some limited circumstances, however, when enforcement of contractual terms may be either unconscionable because of the unequal bargaining power of the parties, see Darner Motor Sales, Inc. v. Universal Underwriters Insurance Co., 140 Ariz. 383, 682 P.2d 388 (1984), or contravene public policy, see Wagenseller v. Scottsdale Memorial Hospital, 147 Ariz. 370, 710 P.2d 1025 (1985).

The Arizona Legislature has also statutorily modified the freedom to contract in certain limited types of franchise relationships. . . . Unlike many other states, however, our legislature has not statutorily regulated the termination of all franchise contracts . . .

We begin our analysis with an examination of the common law of other jurisdictions on the specific issue of franchise no-cause termination agreements, and then turn to existing general Arizona contract law to resolve this issue.

Many of the common law cases cited by CI in the area of "good-cause" termination developed in the 1970s during a shortage of oil supplies in the United States. During that economic crisis, many courts began to limit the enforcement of contractual termination rights between large oil companies and their smaller retail dealers by construing distribution contracts to include an inherent requirement that the contract not be terminated except for "good cause". . . . These courts based termination clause limitations on common law public policy concerns reflected in recent enactments of state legislation regulating either the petroleum industry specifically or franchise arrangements in general. For example, in [Shell Oil v. Marinello, 63 N.J. 402, 307 A.2d 598, 602 (N.J. 1973)], the court noted the New Jersey Legislature's recent enactment of the Franchise Practices Act, which "prohibits a franchisor from terminating, canceling or failing to renew a franchise without good cause which is defined as the failure by the franchisee to substantially comply with the requirements imposed on him by the franchise." 307 A.2d at 602.

Similarly, other courts have concluded that when parties to a "chain-style" franchise agreement do not expressly provide for termination without cause, the contract is interpreted to include a "good cause" termination requirement. Courts have also refused to enforce unilateral termination provisions based on the supplier's sole judgment that the dealer has impaired the supplier's good will. Additionally, courts have found implicit in a franchise contract for a term of years the "reasonable expectation," under "principles of good faith and commercial reasonableness," that the supplier will not arbitrarily or summarily terminate the franchise agreement. Atlantic Richfield v. Razumic, 480 Pa. 366, 390 A.2d 736, 742 (Pa. 1978).

As more states enacted laws regulating these business relationships, including franchises, such distribution agreements were frequently interpreted to include a "good cause" requirement for termination, basically requiring some act of default or wrongdoing on the part of the franchisee to enable the franchisor to assert its termination power. However, some courts were careful to limit the application of the "good cause" termination requirement to situations containing the following factors: (1) the existence of a true franchise-type relationship, regardless of the name placed on it, because of the concern of the unequal bargaining powers of the parties in such a relationship, and (2) the non-existence of an explicit provision allowing termination without cause. . . .

Not all jurisdictions followed this trend to imply a "good cause" termination requirement in a franchise contract. Some courts refused to equate "good cause" with "good faith," finding no breach of the covenant of good faith and fair dealing in a no-cause termination provided for by the explicit terms of the contract. . . . In [Witmer v. Exxon, 260 Pa. Super. 537, 394 A.2d 1276 (1978)], for example, the court reasoned that the existence of a no-cause termination clause in a contract was relevant to determine the . . . standards of good faith and commercial reasonableness to protect the "reasonable expectations" of the franchisee in maintaining his franchise:

> Where there is no explicit termination clause . . . , a franchisee indeed has a reasonable expectation that the relationship will not be terminated arbitrarily without cause. However, when the actions of the franchisor are within plain and explicit enabling clauses of the lease, we find it impossible to say that the reasonable expectations of the franchisee have been violated.

394 A.2d at 1285. Likewise, in Gianelli, the court concluded that the covenant of good faith and fair dealing did not require a good cause termination requirement be applied as a matter of law, for the following reasons:

> Cases carefully limit application of the covenant of good faith and fair dealing [to termination clauses] to situations in which there is a special relationship due to unequal bargaining power or a special element of reliance, whereas in an ordinary business contract where these special circumstances do not exist, we believe the covenant cannot be applied to specially protect one party by requiring cause for termination.

219 Cal. Rptr. at 209. Thus, the implied covenant of good faith and fair dealing "in and of itself" does not require "good cause" for termination of a franchise contract. Gianelli, 219 Cal. Rptr. at 209.

Other cases have refused to find franchise no-cause termination clauses either against public policy or unconscionable. . . .

A common thread in these cases is that an implied "good cause" requirement will not be imposed on a distribution agreement in situations where bargaining power exists for both parties, where the contract contains an explicit "no-cause" termination provision of which the parties were aware when entering the contract, or where no evidence of bad faith termination is otherwise established. As discussed below, all of those factors apply to the distribution agreement at issue in this case.

Arizona has not adopted a franchise regulation act analogous to those relied on in the decisions of many other jurisdictions to reflect the public policy of the state. Rather, our legislature has seen fit to regulate termination of such business relationships only in the areas of petroleum and liquor distribution and automobile dealers and wreckers. . . . We therefore need not engage in the "public policy" argument that other state courts have found compelling based on emerging legislation. We are also aware of the inherent dangers in declaring "public policy" in an area the legislature has not regulated. . . . We thus decline CI's invitation to find a "good cause" termination requirement in a franchise agreement as a matter of "public policy" based on the legislature's regulation in certain other industries. As the trial court aptly noted in this case, the legislature has regulated business relationships in the limited areas about which it was concerned; had it intended to include all franchise agreements within that statutory structure, it could have done so.

Instead, we look to Arizona common law as set forth in court decisions. In Wagenseller, our supreme court recognized a common law "public policy" exception to the termination at-will doctrine in an employment context, holding that an "at-will" employee may be fired for good cause or for no cause, "but not for bad cause — that which violates public policy." 147 Ariz. at 378, 710 P.2d at 1033. The court found Arizona's public policy "is articulated in our state's constitution and statutes, as embodiment of 'the public conscience of the people of this state,' " as well as in the decisions of our courts. Id. at 378, 379, 710 P.2d at 1033, 1034 (citation omitted). The court limited the public policy exception to apply only in "at-will" situations, where the parties have not made any express agreement regarding the duration of the relationship. Id. at 380-81, 710 P.2d at 1035-36.

The Wagenseller court rejected, however, the argument that the covenant of good faith and fair dealing that is implied in every contract prevents a "no cause" employment termination. Although "good faith" requires "that neither party do anything that will injure the rights of the other to receive the benefits of their agreement," it "does not create a duty for the employer to terminate the employee only for good cause," nor does it "protect the employee from a 'no-cause' termination." Id. at 383, 710 P.2d at 1038.

We reject CI's argument on appeal that Wagenseller compels us to equate "good cause" with "good faith." The lack of a "good cause" for termination of the distribution agreement is not any evidence that Sysco wrongfully terminated the contract. At the hearing on the motion for summary judgment, CI admitted that it had no other evidence of bad faith or "bad cause" for Sysco's termination:

> THE COURT: You can't show that they terminated for a bad reason such as, well, you have a certain race of people working for you that we don't like or a certain gender or —
>
> [COUNSEL FOR CI]: No.
>
> THE COURT: — some other type of criminal activity. You can't show any bad reason.
>
> [COUNSEL FOR CI]: No, no. All we can show is that Sysco has given us no reason and has given the court no reason why it[']s done this, that is correct. And I guess our position is that you just can't do that. . . .

Based on Wagenseller, as well as the reasoning of the jurisdictions in other states, and absent any evidence of bad faith or violation of public policy in enforcing the termination clause, we conclude that Sysco was entitled to summary judgment in its favor on the wrongful termination claim.

[The court then held that CI had no "reasonable expectation" based on circumstances surrounding the negotiation and drafting of the contract and the termination clause itself that the clause in question would not be enforced except for good cause].

We conclude that, in the absence of a contrary contract provision or statutory regulation, a franchisor's enforcement of a "no-cause" termination clause need not be for "good cause." Bad faith cannot be evidenced in a distribution agreement simply from a "no cause" termination in accordance with the explicit terms of the contract. CI has failed to establish any "reasonable expectation" of an implied requirement of a "good cause" termination under the circumstances of this case.

For the foregoing reason, the trial court properly entered summary judgment on the wrongful termination claim. . . .

AFFIRMED.

NOTES

1. ***Questions on* Consumers International v. Sysco.** What was the reason for the decision by Sysco to terminate the relationship with Consumers International? In a jurisdiction, such as Arizona, where courts will enforce a termination "without cause" but not a termination for a "bad cause," which party bears the burden of proof that the termination was in "bad faith" or for an otherwise impermissible cause? Assume that this contract was negotiated in a jurisdiction that implies a "good cause" limitation on termination provisions of the sort found in Sysco. Which party bears the burden of proof under those circumstances? Can you see why it is likely that the party with the burden of proof will generally lose? How easy is it for a contracting party to verify the facts necessary to either prove "good cause" or "bad cause"?

Sysco shows how termination provisions can be both useful ex ante and exploitative ex post. Ex ante, the willingness of Consumers International to agree to a termination without cause on 60 days notice is a useful means of providing a "performance bond" to Sysco that might be a key to obtaining the distribution contract in the first instance. But ex post, isn't it hard to know whether Sysco terminated the contract because of a disappointment over CI's performance or because of other external factors? When a distributor such as Consumers International agrees to such a termination provision, do they also agree to assume the risk of a change in business strategy by their supplier?

2. ***The Public Policy Aftermath of* Wagenseller.** In response to the court's decision in *Wagenseller*, the Arizona legislature codified much of the court's reasoning when it passed the Arizona Employment Protection Act (the "EPA") in 1996. *See* A.R.S. § 23-1501; *Cronin v. Sheldon*, 195 Ariz. 531, 991 P.2d 231 (1999). As often happens after a controversial case, the legislature considered the issue and enacted the law to supersede the common law developments:

> Under the EPA, an employee may only bring a claim for wrongful termination against the employer if: (a) the employer breaches a written contract that modified the at-will status of the relationship; (b) the employer violates a statute of the state in terminating the employee; (c) the employer terminates the relationship in retaliation for certain enumerated employee actions (e.g., "whistleblowing"); or (d) the employer violates the continued employment rights of a public employee. *Id.* The EPA is the exclusive remedy for terminations that violate public policy statutes, and a plaintiff is therefore limited to the remedies provided under statute.

Fallar v. Compuware Corp., 202 F. Supp. 2d 1067, 1076 (D. Ariz. 2002).

3. *Defending the At-Will Employment Rule.* How would you go about defending the at-will employment rule?[46] You would certainly cite the fact that in the 100 years that at-will has been the default rule, instances of individual, dickered contracts adopting a different standard have been rare. This is some evidence (powerful evidence, you would argue) that the parties — managers and workers — prefer the at-will rule.

Next, you would like to be able to tell a story about why the at-will rule is in the parties' best interest. The best story focuses on the expense of a good-cause-for-discharge rule. Under a good cause system, it is not enough for the employer to have a good faith belief for discharging, the employer must be able to satisfy a third party (judge or jury) of the grounds. This often demands expensive and cumbersome record keeping procedures and elaborate formalized warning systems. Even with such procedures, the third-party fact finder will make errors. The analogy will be to government employment and the difficulty of discharging an incompetent worker under a civil service system. Especially if the remedy is substantial, employers will tend to retain incompetent workers rather than risk liability.

The expense of such a system is widely borne. With the firm now being less profitable, there will be less money for wages. And workers who could formerly expect to move forward when incompetent or slacking senior workers were discharged or demoted will now remain in place.

The defects of a system of discharge for cause is only half the story. As usual, the question is "as compared to what"? Is there a limit on the abuses of an at-will system? You would argue that there are two important constraints on arbitrary discharges. The first is the profit motive of the employer. Arbitrary discharges are not in the interest of the firm. While the difficulty of monitoring managers allows some arbitrary discharges to escape, the profit motive is an effective limit. And market forces sharply reinforce the constraint. Second, firms that discharge workers arbitrarily cannot do so in secret. Either better workers will be reluctant to work for these firms, or the firms will be forced to pay wage premiums to attract workers. Neither is in the interest of the firm owners, and firms with these additional costs will not long survive in competitive markets.

4. *Attacking the At-Will Rule.* Suppose that you wanted to write a law review article attacking employment-at-will and arguing for judicial or legislative change. How would you proceed? First, you can find instances of litigated cases where the grounds for a discharge are stupid or immoral and yet the employee loses her case. Describe the worst of these cases. Second, you posit a reason that this regime is forced on the workers, for instance:

> It is a widely accepted proposition that large corporations now pose a threat to individual freedom comparable to that which would be posed if governmental power were unchecked. The proposition need not, however, be limited to the mammoth business corporation, for the freedom of the individual is threatened whenever he becomes dependent upon a private

---

[46] The best defense of the rule is Richard Epstein, *In Defense of the Contract at Will*, 51 U. Chi. L. Rev. 947 (1984).

entity possessing greater power than himself. Foremost among the relationships of which this generality is true is that of employer and employee.[47]

Third, present the details of your scheme for overturning the rule.[48]

The first tactic — parading some horrible cases — can be quite effective. Who wants to argue that your examples are not real, or has a heart cold enough to put the examples aside? Suppose you wanted to ban high school and college football on grounds that the sport is brutal to players. Horror stories ought not to be difficult to locate. But the football argument is incomplete and therefore flawed. The argument ignores the advantages of the current "rule" that sanctions football (the gains enjoyed by football players, and the pleasure felt by football fans) — taking the bitter with the sweet. This is not to say, returning to the issue presented in *Wagenseller*, that those arguing against the at-will rule are wrong, but rather that examples of bad discharges are not by themselves sufficient to make a convincing case.

The second strand of the argument for overturning the at-will employment rule rests on a contention that employment-at-will is the result of "unequal bargaining power." The problems with this contention were set out in the notes following *Williams v. Walker-Thomas Furniture Co. (II)* in Chapter 1.

One fact dramatically challenges the assertion that overwhelming experience shows that firms and workers prefer employment-at-will. It is that when workers unionize, one of their highest priorities is to secure a guaranty of just cause for discharge, enforced by grievance arbitration. This suggests either that there is something special about workers who unionize or the unionization process, or that the market mechanism that produces employment-at-will is flawed in some respect not described by the inequality of bargaining power claim. Which is it?[49]

Note that the arguments, pro and con, respecting at-will employment are applicable to franchise termination, except that franchisees are not allowed to unionize.

5. ***Redrafting the Hospital Manual.*** The Scottsdale hospital did not follow the procedures listed in its own manual. Draft language for the manual that would preclude an employee from suing successfully if these procedures are violated. Would the hospital be better off to remove the procedures from the manual altogether? The hospital might not want to do this; but if legal enforceability causes employers to remove these procedures, who is made better off by an enforceability rule?

6. ***Enforceability of Representations in Employee Handbooks.*** A promise in an employee handbook that claims that no employee would be fired except for just

---

[47] Lawrence E. Blades, *Employment at Will vs. Individual Freedom: On Limiting the Abusive Exercise of Employer Power*, 67 Colum. L. Rev. 1404 (1967) (footnotes omitted).

[48] For one of many articles adopting the strategy outlined in the Note, see Clyde W. Summers, *Individual Protection Against Unjust Dismissal: Time for a Statute*, 62 Va. L. Rev. 481 (1976).

[49] *See* J. Hoult Verkerke, *An Empirical Perspective on Indefinite Term Employment Contracts: Resolving the Just Cause Debate*, 1995 Wis. L. Rev. 838.

cause often is unenforceable — even to protect the employee who wrote the handbook. In *Lurton v. Muldon Motor Co.*, 523 So. 2d 706 (Fla. Dist. Ct. App. 1988), the Court of Appeals of Florida refused to enforce the contents of the handbook, holding that it "was nothing more than expression of firm policy, not an enforceable contract term." Since there was no additional consideration granted in exchange for waiving the at-will nature of the plaintiff's job, the court refused to award damages.

Other courts have required separate signed writings to enforce statements found in an employee handbook. In *Progress Printing Co. v. Nichols*, 244 Va. 337, 421 S.E.2d 428 (1992), the Supreme Court of Virginia ruled that the handbook, taken by itself, does not create an enforceable contract. An acknowledgment form signed by the employee, which contains provisions that run directly contrary to the contents of the handbook, provides greater evidence of what the parties assented to. Moreover, the conflicting testimony of the worker and the company is not sufficient to overcome the presumption of at-will employment.

Professor J. Hoult Verkerke notes in *An Empirical Perspective on Indefinite Term Employment Contracts: Resolving the Just Cause Debate*, 1995 WIS. L. REV. 837, that crafty employers may offer employees writings that do not require a signature, thus deceiving them into believing that they are protected from termination without just cause.

7.   *The Public Policy Exception.* Consider this problem. An unscrupulous research laboratory is buying dogs from a supplier without checking to see whether they are stolen. An employee of the laboratory phones the local newspaper with the information and a feature story is run. The laboratory discovers which worker gave the newspaper the story and fires her. She sues. You represent the laboratory in a state with no clear, modern precedent on a public-policy exception to the at-will doctrine. What will you argue? What will be argued against you? Would your case be weaker or stronger if a state statute imposed liability for using stolen animals in research?[50]

Should a public-policy exception to the traditional at-will employment rule be subject to countermanding by specific language in the employment contract? If the exception rests on the presumed intent of the parties, the answer is yes. Do you believe that typical workers and managers intend to further the public interest through private employment contracts? If the exception rests on a perceived need to supplement state law, there is no reason to permit parties to trump the exception.

---

[50] Varying state statutes protect whistleblowing employees who report illegal activities or, in some jurisdictions, threats to public interest. Additionally, federal employees may benefit from the Whistleblower Protection Act. *See* 5 U.S.C. § 1221(e).

[b]   Covenants Not to Compete

VALLEY MED. SPECIALISTS v. FARBER
Supreme Court of Arizona
982 P.2d 1277 (1999)

FELDMAN, J.

We granted review to determine whether the restrictive covenant between Dr. Steven Farber and Valley Medical Specialists is enforceable. We hold that it is not. Public policy concerns in this case outweigh Valley Medical's protectable interests in enforcing the agreement. We thus vacate the court of appeals' opinion, affirm the trial court's judgment, and remand to the court of appeals to resolve any remaining issues.

Facts and Procedural History

In 1985, Valley Medical Specialists (VMS), a professional corporation, hired Steven S. Farber, D.O., an internist and pulmonologist who, among other things, treated AIDS and HIV-positive patients and performed brachytherapy — a procedure that radiates the inside of the lung in lung cancer patients. Brachytherapy can only be performed at certain hospitals that have the necessary equipment. A few years after joining VMS, Dr. Farber became a shareholder and subsequently a minority officer and director. In 1991, the three directors, including Dr. Farber, entered into new stock and employment agreements. The employment agreement contained a restrictive covenant, the scope of which was amended over time.

In 1994, Dr. Farber left VMS and began practicing within the area defined by the restrictive covenant, which at that time read as follows:

The parties recognize that the duties to be rendered under the terms of this Agreement by the Employee are special, unique and of an extraordinary character. The Employee, in consideration of the compensation to be paid to him pursuant to the terms of this Agreement, expressly agrees to the following restrictive covenants:

(a)   The Employee shall not, directly or indirectly:

(i)   Request any present or future patients of the Employer to curtail or cancel their professional affiliation with the Employer;

(ii)   Either separately, jointly, or in association with others, establish, engage in, or become interested in, as an employee, owner, partner, shareholder or otherwise, or furnish any information to, work for, or assist in any manner, anyone competing with, or who may compete with the Employer in the practice of medicine.

(iii)   Disclose the identity of any past, present or future patients of the Employer to any other person, firm or corporation engaged in a medical practice the same as, similar to or in general competition with the medical services provided by the Employer.

    (iv)   Either separately, jointly or in association with others provide medical care or medical assistance for any person or persons who were patients or [sic] Employer during the period that Employee was in the hire of Employer.

        . . . .

  (d)   *The restrictive covenants set forth herein shall continue during the term of this Agreement and for a period of three (3) years after the date of termination, for any reason, of this Agreement. The restrictive covenants set forth herein shall be binding upon the Employee in that geographical area encompassed within the boundaries measured by a five (5) mile radius of any office maintained or utilized by Employer at the time of execution of the Agreement or at any time thereafter.*

  (e)   The Employee agrees that a violation on his part of any covenant set forth in this Paragraph will cause such damage to the Employer as will be irreparable and for that reason, that Employee further agrees that the Employer shall be entitled, as a matter of right . . . to an injunction from any court of competent jurisdiction, restraining any further violation of said covenants by Employee. . . . Such right to injunctive remedies shall be in addition to and cumulative with any other rights and remedies the Employer may have pursuant to this Agreement, including, specifically, the recovery of liquidated damages equal to forty percent (40%) of the gross receipts received for medical services provided by the Employee during the term of this Agreement and for a period of three (3) years after the date of termination, for any reason, of this Agreement. The Employee expressly acknowledges and agrees that the covenants and agreement contained in this Paragraph are reasonable in scope and are necessary to protect the legitimate interest of the Employer and its goodwill.

(Emphasis added.)

    VMS filed a complaint against Dr. Farber seeking (1) preliminary and permanent injunctions enjoining Dr. Farber from violating the restrictive covenant, (2) liquidated damages for breach of the employment agreement, and (3) damages for breach of fiduciary duty, conversion of patient files and confidential information, and intentional interference with contractual and/or business relations.

    Following six days of testimony and argument, the trial court denied VMS's request for a preliminary injunction, finding that the restrictive covenant was unenforceable because it was too broad. Specifically, the court found that: any covenant over six months would be unreasonable; the five-mile radius from each of the three VMS offices was unreasonable because it covered a total of 235 square miles; and the restriction was unreasonable because it did not provide an exception for emergency medical aid and was not limited to pulmonology.

The court of appeals reversed, concluding that a modified covenant was reasonable. The court noted that there were eight hospitals outside the restricted area where Dr. Farber could practice. Although the covenant made no exceptions for emergency medicine, the court held that the severability clause permitted the trial court to modify the covenant so Dr. Farber could provide emergency services within the restricted area. Moreover, VMS was allowed to stipulate that Dr. Farber could perform brachytherapy and treat AIDS and HIV patients within the restricted area, again even though the covenant contained no such exceptions.

The court of appeals found the restriction, when so modified, reasonable as to time and place. Although non-emergency patients might be required to travel further to see Dr. Farber, they could continue to see him if they were willing to drive that far. Three years was reasonable because the record contained testimony that it might take Dr. Farber's replacement three to five years to develop his pulmonary practice referral sources to the level they were when Dr. Farber resigned.

History of restrictive covenants

A brief reference to basic principles is appropriate. Historically, covenants not to compete were viewed as restraints of trade and were invalid at common law. See Harlan M. Blake, *Employee Agreements Not to Compete*, 73 Harv. L. Rev. 625 (1960). Eventually, ancillary restraints, such as those incident to employment or partnership agreements, were enforced under the rule of reason. *See* Restatement (Second) of Contracts § 188.. . . . To be enforced, the restriction must do more than simply prohibit fair competition by the employee. In other words, a covenant not to compete is invalid unless it protects some legitimate interest beyond the employer's desire to protect itself from competition. The legitimate purpose of post-employment restraints is "to prevent competitive use, for a time, of information or relationships which pertain peculiarly to the employer and which the employee acquired in the course of the employment." Blake, *supra*, at 647. Despite the freedom to contract, the law does not favor restrictive covenants. This disfavor is particularly strong concerning such covenants among physicians because the practice of medicine affects the public to a much greater extent.

We first address the level of scrutiny that should be afforded to this restrictive covenant. Dr. Farber argues that this contract is simply an employer-employee agreement and thus the restrictive covenant should be strictly construed against the employer. VMS contends that this is more akin to the sale of a business. . . . Although this agreement is between partners, it is more analogous to an employer-employee agreement than a sale of a business. *See* Restatement § 188 cmt. h ("A rule similar to that applicable to an employee or agent applies to a partner who makes a promise not to compete that is ancillary to the partnership agreement or to an agreement by which he disposes of his partnership interest."). Many of the concerns present in the sale of a business are not present or are reduced where, as here, a physician leaves a medical group, even when that physician is a partner. When a business is sold, the value of that business's goodwill usually figures significantly into the purchase price. The buyer therefore deserves some protection from competition from the former owner.

By restricting a physician's practice of medicine, this covenant involves strong public policy implications and must be closely scrutinized. Although stopping short of banning restrictive covenants between physicians, the American Medical Association "discourages" such covenants, finding they are not in the public interest. We therefore conclude that the doctor-patient relationship is special and entitled to unique protection. It cannot be easily or accurately compared to relationships in the commercial context. In light of the great public policy interest involved in covenants not to compete between physicians, each agreement will be strictly construed for reasonableness.

Reasonableness of covenant

Reasonableness is a fact-intensive inquiry that depends on the totality of the circumstances. A restriction is unreasonable and thus will not be enforced: (1) if the restraint is greater than necessary to protect the employer's legitimate interest; or (2) if that interest is outweighed by the hardship to the employee and the likely injury to the public. *See* Restatement § 188 cmt. a. Thus, in the present case, the reasonableness inquiry requires us to examine the interests of the employer, employee, patients, and public in general. Balancing these competing interests is no easy task and no exact formula can be used.

VMS's protectable interest

VMS contends, and the court of appeals agreed, that it has a protectable interest in its patients and referral sources. In the commercial context, it is clear that employers have a legitimate interest in retaining their customer base. "The employer's point of view is that the company's clientele is an asset of value which has been acquired by virtue of effort and expenditures over a period of time, and which should be protected as a form of property." Blake, *supra*, at 654. In the medical context, however, the personal relationship between doctor and patient, as well as the patient's freedom to see a particular doctor, affects the extent of the employer's interest.

Even in the commercial context, the employer's interest in its customer base is balanced with the employee's right to the customers. Where the employee took an active role and brought customers with him or her to the job, courts are more reluctant to enforce restrictive covenants. . . . Dr. Farber was a pulmonologist. He did not learn his skills from VMS. Restrictive covenants are designed to protect an employer's customer base by preventing "a skilled employee from leaving an employer and, based on his skill acquired from that employment, luring away the employer's clients or business while the employer is vulnerable — that is — before the employer has had a chance to replace the employee with someone qualified to do the job." We agree with VMS, however, that it has a protectable interest in its referral sources.

Scope of the restrictive covenant

The restriction cannot be greater than necessary to protect VMS's legitimate interests. A restraint's scope is defined by its duration and geographic area. The frequency of contact between doctors and their patients affects the permissible length of the restraint. The idea is to give the employer a reasonable amount of time to overcome the former employee's loss, usually by hiring a replacement and giving that replacement time to establish a working relationship. Even in the commercial context, "[w]hen the restraint is for the purpose of protecting customer relationships, its duration is reasonable only if it is no longer than necessary for the employer to put a new man on the job and for the new employee to have a reasonable opportunity to demonstrate his effectiveness to the customers." Blake, *supra*, at 677.

In this case, the trial judge found that the three-year period was an unreasonable duration because all of the experts agree that the practice of pulmonology entails treating patients with chronic conditions which require more hospital care than office care and which requires regular contact with the treating physician at least once within each six-month period so that any provision over six months is onerous and unnecessary to protect VMS's economic interests where virtually all of Dr. Farber's VMS patients had an opportunity by late 1994 or early 1995 (Farber left September 12, 1994) to decide which pulmonologist . . . they would consult for their ongoing treatment[.] On this record, we cannot say this factual finding was clearly erroneous. The three-year duration is unreasonable.

The activity prohibited by the restraint also defines the covenant's scope. The restraint must be limited to the particular specialty of the present employment. On its face, the restriction here is not limited to internal medicine or even pulmonology. It precludes any type of practice, even in fields that do not compete with VMS. Thus, we agree with the trial judge that this restriction is too broad.

Severance — the blue pencil rule

This contract contains a severance clause.[51] On its face, the covenant restriction forbids Dr. from providing "medical care or medical assistance for any person or persons who were patients of Employer during the period that Employee was in the hire of Employer." Arizona courts will "blue pencil" restrictive covenants, eliminating grammatically severable, unreasonable provisions. Here, however, the modifications go further than cutting grammatically severable portions. The court of appeals, in essence, rewrote the agreement in an attempt to make it enforceable. This goes too far. "Where the severability of the agreement is not evident from the contract itself, the court cannot create a new agreement for the parties to uphold the contract." *Olliver/Pilcher Ins.*, 148 Ariz. at 533, 715 P.2d at 1221.

Even the blue pencil rule has its critics. For every agreement that makes its way to court, many more do not. Thus, the words of the covenant have an *in terrorem*

---

51 [2] Since it is the agreement and desire of the parties hereto that the provisions of this Paragraph be enforced to the fullest extent possible under the laws and public policies applied in each jurisdiction in which enforcement is sought, should any particular provision of this Paragraph be deemed invalid or unenforceable, the same shall be deemed reformed and amended to delete that portion thus adjudicated invalid, and the deletion shall apply only with respect to the operation of said provision and, to the extent a provision of this Paragraph would be deemed unenforceable by virtue of its scope, but may be made unenforceable by limitation thereof, each party agrees that this Agreement shall be reformed and amended so that the same shall be enforceable to the fullest extent permissible under the laws and public policies applied in the jurisdiction in which enforcement is sought.

effect on departing employees. Employers may therefore create ominous covenants, knowing that if the words are challenged, courts will modify the agreement to make it enforceable. Although we will tolerate ignoring severable portions of a covenant to make it more reasonable, we will not permit courts to add terms or rewrite provisions.

Conclusion

We hold that the restrictive covenant between Dr. Farber and VMS cannot be enforced. Valley Medical Specialists' interest in enforcing the restriction is outweighed by the likely injury to patients and the public in general. *See* Restatement § 188. We stop short of holding that restrictive covenants between physicians will never be enforced, but caution that such restrictions will be strictly construed. The burden is on the party wishing to enforce the covenant to demonstrate that the restraint is no greater than necessary to protect the employer's legitimate interest, and that such interest is not outweighed by the hardship to the employee and the likely injury to the public. Here VMS has not met that burden. The restriction fails because its public policy implications outweigh the legitimate interests of VMS.

NOTES

1.   *Questions on* Valley Medical Services. Would the result in the case have been different if Farber had been an accountant rather than a physician? Why does a patient's need for medical services weigh more heavily in the calculus than the same individual's need for help in preparing his tax returns? The court in *Valley Medical Services* seemed to place emphasis on the fact that Dr. Farber was already a skilled pulmonologist when he joined the practice. The implication is that other than the client list there was little "on the job training" by the practice that represented a specific investment to be protected by the non-competition covenant. If you represented the practice could you argue that much more than a client list is involved in growing a successful medical practice, even for a physician who is already trained when he joins the firm?

2.   *Blue Lining versus Reformation*. The court in *Valley Medical Services* relied on Arizona's "blue line" rule by which courts can strike (but not add or change) portions of a non-compete clause so as to render it enforceable. But the court rejected language in earlier opinions that suggested it was prepared to adopt the modern "reasonableness" or "red line" rule by which a court can, in addition, reform the clause by, for example, limiting its scope and duration, or the precise nature of the prohibited activity. For an example of this modern view, see *Ferrofluidics Corp. v. Advanced Vacuum Components, Inc.*, 968 F. 2d 1463 (1st Cir. 1992) where the court found that a five-year covenant not to compete in an employment agreement was excessive but enforced a three-year restriction instead.

3.   *Covenants Not to Compete and At-Will Employment.* Is there a fundamental difference in philosophy between a court's recognition of an employer's right to discharge a worker for any reason and a court's strict construction of and policing of covenants not to compete? What arguments can you make using either the autonomy or the economic theories discussed in Chapter 1, to explain and reconcile these different approaches? In a portion of the opinion not reproduced here, the court in *Valley Medical Services* held that "unlike typical employer-employee agreements, Dr. Farber was not at a bargaining disadvantage. Thus, the case does not turn on any hardship to Dr. Farber." Assuming there are good reasons for parties to agree to a non-competition clause — for example, to encourage the employer to provide valuable specific investments in the form of on the job training — what accounts for the law's reluctance to enforce these restrictions so long as they are voluntary agreements between sophisticated parties?

4. ***Carrots Rather Than Sticks.*** Note that a recent trend in employment contracts has been to avoid absolute restrictions on workers' ability to join a competing enterprise. Instead, many employers rely on an incentive-based approach, tying the receipt of certain benefits (such as severance pay) to the employee's promise not to compete. If the worker chooses to join a competing enterprise upon leaving the company, he is not precluded per se, but the choice becomes less attractive due to the foregone benefits. Since this represents less of a restriction on workers' post-contractual liberty, courts have been more willing to support such incentive clauses.

As with most types of incentives, employers can also offer "carrots," which provide additional benefits if employees abide by the terms of the agreement. In *Marine Contractors Co. v. Hurley*, 365 Mass. 280, 310 N.E.2d 915 (1974), a five-year restrictive covenant was deemed permissible because, in exchange for the employees agreement not to compete, the company accelerated the payment of retirement benefits. The accelerated payments served as consideration for the promise not to compete; without it, the covenant may well have been deemed unduly restrictive.

Some jurisdictions have adopted the position that continued employment is sufficient consideration for a covenant not to compete. In *Leatherman v. Management Advisors, Inc.*, 448 N.E.2d 1048 (Ind. 1983), the court held that continued employment was adequate consideration for a covenant not to compete signed by an insurance agent. One justification for such a position is that an employer is free to terminate an at-will employee at any time for almost any cause, and so continued employment on new conditions is consideration. Furthermore, the employee can choose to leave if the new conditions are unacceptable.

5. ***Express and Implied Covenants in Employment Contracts.*** The courts protect employer rights in secret processes, formulas, and customer lists without explicit language in the employment contract.[52] On the other hand, a covenant not to compete will not be implied; it must exist in explicit contractual language — and even then, it is often strictly construed. Why the different treatment?

6. ***Relevance of the Occupation.*** An automobile mechanic signs an employment contract that specifies that the mechanic will not compete with the employer for six months in the county of his employment. If this covenant is found to be a reasonable and thus enforceable restriction would the result be different if the defendant was a lawyer joining an existing law firm who signed an agreement that if she left the firm, she would not practice law for six months in the county? While this provision might seem to fall within the standards of reasonableness, note that

---

[52] An example is *Morgan's Home Equipment Corp. v. Martucci*, 390 Pa. 618 (1957).

the American Bar Association Canons of Professional Responsibility contain a disciplinary rule that prohibits restrictive covenants between attorneys. *See* Model Rules of Professional Conduct, Rule 5.6. The rule that restrictive covenants between lawyers are per se unenforceable (with several exceptions) is based on the argument that there is a strong public interest in allowing clients to retain the lawyer of their choice. Are you persuaded that is the only reason for the ABA rule?

Certain positions require little specialized training or specific knowledge of a company's business practices. For instance, in *Brewer v. Tracy*, 198 Neb. 503, 253 N.W.2d 319 (1977), the Supreme Court of Nebraska invalidated a provision which prohibited a garbage man from engaging in the trash collection business within 15 miles of the company's headquarters in Hebron, Nebraska. The invalid covenant extended for five years. The court noted:

> . . . 5 years was an unreasonable limitation on the right of a working man to labor. We further hold that a contract to restrict a laborer from engaging in an occupation, if valid at all, must be restricted to the area in which the personal service was performed. Nothing appears in the record and no reason has been suggested to us that would justify a restriction on the defendant-employee engaging in the refuse and trash business in the other nine communities in Thayer County, Nebraska, in which neither the plaintiff-employer nor the employee ever served.

198 Neb. at 506.

Courts will look not only at the nature of the employment, but also the scope of a company's business activity in order to determine the validity of a covenant not to compete. In *Marcam Corporation v. Orchard*, 885 F. Supp. 294 (D. Mass. 1995), a software company's covenant restricting its Vice President of Development from joining a competing company anywhere in the United States was upheld. The court noted that although Marcam was headquartered in Massachusetts, "it maintains a customer base and does business throughout North America. Marcam has a national market for its products." Consequently, the employee was enjoined from joining a competing enterprise in New York, even though Marcam did not maintain an office there.

7. *Preserving Customer Relationships.* Courts are particularly likely to enforce covenants not to compete when they are based on personal relationships between the employee and the customer that were cultivated at the company's expense. For example, in *Maltby v. Harlow Meyer Savage, Inc.*, 633 N.Y.S.2d 926 (1995), the court ruled that stockbrokers had unique relationships with their customers, and as such, the brokerage was justified in requiring a covenant not to compete. The court noted:

> [P]laintiffs all have unique relationships with the customers with whom they have been dealing that have been developed while employed at HMS and, partially, at HMS expense. The testimony also showed that approximately six months is needed for a new employee to build such a relationship and bring business back to its normal level. The evidence adequately showed that a trader's absence from trading for six months does not render

him unemployable within the industry or substantially impair his ability to earn a living. The relationships previously developed with customers can be renewed after that time.

Accordingly, this court finds that the restrictive covenants at issue herein are reasonable on condition that plaintiffs continue to receive their salaries for six months while not employed by a competitor. The restrictive covenants are reasonable in that each protects the employer from severe economic injury while — at the same time — it protects the employee's livelihood, by requiring that he be paid his base salary. The duration of six months is reasonable because that is the amount of time HMS needs to recover from plaintiff's departure; it is not unduly long so as to cause permanent injury or loss of ability to earn a livelihood.

633 N.Y.S.2d at 930.

Why did the court require that the plaintiffs receive their base salaries for six months, even though they stopped working for the defendant?

8. ***The Strategic Value of Severence Restrictions.*** Although obtaining an injunction against a former employee based on a non-compete clause may be difficult, merely filing a complaint can often garner meaningful concessions from the former employee, the competitor, or both. A recent, high-profile case illustrates the benefits to the employer that may result from alleging violations of a severance agreement by a former employee who leaves for a competitor.[53] In August 2010, Mark Hurd left his job as CEO of technology giant Hewlett-Packard after the company's board grew concerned about his relationship with a marketing contractor that had raised sexual harassment concerns. By September 2010, Hurd had agreed to join another Silicon Valley technology firm, Oracle, as its president and a member of the board of directors. A day after Oracle announced Hurd's hiring, HP sued Hurd, claiming that by joining a rival technology firm, he would violate his severance agreement in which he promised to protect HP's secrets. For two weeks, executives from the two firms sparred publicly, posturing that the legal battle threatened the two companies' long-standing business relationship. However, HP and Hurd soon settled the legal dispute, with Hurd agreeing to protect HP's trade secrets. A subsequent SEC filing also noted that Hurd had agreed to forgo much of the compensation owed to him through his severance agreement.

D.   MODIFICATION OF EXISTING AGREEMENTS

This chapter on conduct within the contractual relationship ends by examining parties' attempts to modify or renegotiate an existing executory, or partially executed, contract. The common law governed contract modifications through the "pre-existing duty rule." See if you can discern the rule and its impact from the *Alaska Packers'* case reprinted below. In this instance, as in others we have seen, the UCC has substantially altered the common law rule by permitting "good faith" modification without a requirement of additional consideration. *See* UCC § 2-209,

---

[53] For more details, see Ashlee Vance & Verne G. Kopytoff, *H.P. Settles Lawsuit Against Hurd*, N.Y. TIMES, Sept. 20, 2010, at B1.

Comment 2. The Restatement follows the UCC in enforcing those modifications that are "fair and equitable" in the particular circumstance. *See* Restatement (Second) § 89. In reading the case that follows, try to formulate arguments in support of both the common law bright-line rule and the broader standards adopted by the UCC and the Restatement. Which rule would be easier to establish factually in litigation?

Which rule more accurately reflects the realities of bargaining in relational contracts?

ALASKA PACKERS' ASS'N v. DOMENICO
United States Court of Appeals, Ninth Circuit
117 F. 99 (1902)

Ross, J.

The libel in this case was based upon a contract alleged to have been entered into between the libelants and the appellant corporation on the 22d day of May, 1900, at Pyramid Harbor, Alaska, by which it is claimed the appellant promised to pay each of the libelants, among other things, the sum of $100 for services rendered and to be rendered. In its answer the respondent denied the execution, on its part, of the contract sued upon, averred that it was without consideration, and for a third defense alleged that the work performed by the libelants for it was performed under other and different contracts than that sued on, and that, prior to the filing of the libel, each of the libelants was paid by the respondent the full amount due him thereunder, in consideration of which each of them executed a full release of all his claims and demands against the respondent.

The evidence shows without conflict that on March 26, 1900, at the city and county of San Francisco, the libelants entered into a written contract with the appellant, whereby they agreed to go from San Francisco to Pyramid Harbor, Alaska, and return, on board such vessel as might be designated by the appellant, and to work for the appellant during the fishing season of 1900, at Pyramid Harbor, as sailors and fishermen, agreeing to do "regular ship's duty, both up and down, discharging and loading; and to do any other work whatsoever when requested to do so by the captain or agent of the Alaska Packers' Association." By the terms of this agreement, the appellant was to pay each of the libelants $50 for the season, and two cents for each red salmon in the catching of which he took part.

On the 15th day of April, 1900, 21 of the libelants signed shipping articles by which they shipped as seamen on the Two Brothers, a vessel chartered by the appellant for the voyage between San Francisco and Pyramid Harbor, and also bound themselves to perform the same work for the appellant provided for by the previous contract of March 26th; the appellant agreeing to pay them therefor the sum of $60 for the season, and two cents each for each red salmon in the catching of which they should respectively take part. Under these contracts, the libelants sailed on board the Two Brothers for Pyramid Harbor, where the appellant had about $150,000 invested in a salmon cannery. The libelants arrived there early in April of the year mentioned, and began to unload the vessel and fit up the cannery. A few days thereafter, to wit, May 19th, they stopped work in a body, and demanded of the company's superintendent there in charge $100 for services in operating the vessel to and from Pyramid Harbor, instead of the sums stipulated for in and by the contracts; stating that unless they were paid this additional wage they would stop work entirely, and return to San Francisco. The evidence showed, and the court below found, that it was impossible for the appellant to get other men to take the places of the libelants, the place being remote, the season short and just opening; so that, after endeavoring for several days without success to induce the libelants to proceed with their work in accordance with their contracts, the company's superintendent, on the 22d day of May, so far yielded to their demands as to instruct his clerk to copy the contracts executed in San Francisco, including the words "Alaska Packers' Association" at the end, substituting, for the $50 and $60 payments, respectively, of those contracts, the sum of $100, which document, so prepared, was signed by the libelants before a shipping commissioner whom they had requested to be brought from Northeast Point; the superintendent, however, testifying that he at the time told the libelants that he was without authority to enter into any such contract, or to in any way alter the contracts made between them and the company in San Francisco. Upon the return of the libelants to San Francisco at the close of the fishing season, they demanded pay in accordance with the terms of the alleged contract of May 22d, when the company denied its validity, and refused to pay other than as provided for by the contracts of March 26th and April 5th, respectively. Some of the libelants, at least, consulted counsel, and, after receiving his advice, those of them who had signed the shipping articles before the shipping commissioner at San Francisco went before that officer, and received the amount due them thereunder, executing in consideration thereof a release in full, and the others being paid at the office of the company, also receipting in full for their demands.

On the trial in the court below, the libelants undertook to show that the fishing nets provided by the respondent were defective, and that it was on that account that they demanded increased wages. On that point, the evidence was substantially conflicting, and the finding of the court was against the libelants, the court saying: "The contention of libelants that the nets provided them were rotten and unserviceable is not sustained by the evidence. The defedant's interest required that libelants should be provided with every facility necessary to their success as fisherman, for on such success depended the profits defendant would be able to realize that season from its packing plant, and the large capital invested therein. In view of this self-evident fact, it is highly improbable that the defendant gave libelants rotten and unserviceable nets with which to fish. It follows from this finding that libelants were not justified in refusing performance of their original contract." 112 Fed. 554. The evidence being sharply conflicting in respect to these facts, the conclusions of the court, who heard and saw the witnesses, will not be disturbed.

The real questions in the case as brought here are questions of law, and, in the view that we take of the case, it will be necessary to consider but one of those. Assuming that the appellant's superintendent at Pyramid Harbor was authorized to make the alleged contract of May 22d, and that he executed it on behalf of the appellant, was it supported by a sufficient consideration? From the foregoing statement of the case, it will have been seen that the libelants agreed in writing, for certain stated compensation, to render their services to the appellant in remote waters where the season for conducting fishing operations is extremely short, and in which enterprise the appellant had a large amount of money invested; and, after having entered upon the discharge of their contract, and at a time when it was impossible for the appellant to secure other men in their places, the libelants, without any valid cause, absolutely refused to continue the services they were under contract to perform unless the appellant would consent to pay them more money. Consent to such a demand, under such circumstances, if given, was, in our opinion, without consideration, for the reason that it was based solely upon the libelants' agreement to render the exact services, and none other, that they were already under contract to render. The case shows that they willfully and arbitrarily broke that obligation. As a matter of course, they were liable to the appellant in damages, and it is quite probable, as suggested by the court below in its opinion, that they may have been unable to respond in damages. But we are unable to agree with the conclusions there drawn, from these facts, in these words:

> Under such circumstances, it would be strange, indeed, if the law would not permit the defendant to waive the damages caused by the libelants' breach, and enter into the contract sued upon, — a contract mutually beneficial to all the parties thereto, in that it gave to the libelants reasonable compensation for their labor, and enabled the defendant to employ to advantage the large capital it had invested in its canning and fishing plant.

Certainly, it cannot be justly held, upon the record in this case, that there was any voluntary waiver on the part of the appellant of the breach of the original contract. The company itself knew nothing of such breach until the expedition returned to San Francisco, and the testimony is uncontradicted that its superintendent at Pyramid Harbor, who, it is claimed, made on its behalf the contract sued on, distinctly informed the libelants that he had no power to alter the original or to make a new contract; and it would, of course, follow that, if he had no power to change the original, he would have no authority to waive any rights thereunder. The circumstances of the present case bring it, we think, directly within the sound and just observations of the supreme court of Minnesota in the case of King v. Railway Co., 61 Minn. 482:

> No astute reasoning can change the plain fact that the party who refuses to perform, and thereby coerces a promise from the other party to the contract to pay him an increased compensation for doing that which he is legally bound to do, takes an unjustifiable advantage of the necessities of the other party. Surely it would be a travesty on justice to hold that the party so making the promise for extra pay was estopped from asserting that the promise was without consideration. A party cannot lay the foundation of an estoppel by his own wrong, where the promise is simply a repetition of a subsisting legal promise. There can be no consideration for the promise of the other party, and there is no warrant for inferring that the parties have voluntarily rescinded or modified their contract. The promise cannot be legally enforced, although the other party has completed his contract in reliance upon it.

In Lingenfelder v. Brewing Co., 103 Mo. 578, the court, in holding void a contract by which the owner of a building agreed to pay its architect an additional sum because of his refusal to otherwise proceed with the contract, said:

> It is urged upon us by respondents that this was a new contract. New in what? Jungenfeld was bound by his contract to design and supervise this building. Under the new promise, he was not to do anything more or anything different. What benefit was to accrue to Wainwright? He was to receive the same service from Jungenfeld under the new, that Jungenfeld was bound to tender under the original, contract. What loss, trouble, or inconvenience could result to Jungenfeld that he had not already assumed? No amount of metaphysical reasoning can change the plain fact that Jungenfeld took advantage of Wainwright's necessities, and extorted the promise of five per cent on the refrigerator plant as the condition of his complying with his contract already entered into. Nor had he even the flimsy pretext that Wainwright had violated any of the conditions of the contract on his part. Jungenfeld himself put it upon the simple proposition that "if he, as an architect, put up the brewery, and another company put up the refrigerating machinery, it would be a detriment to the Empire Refrigerating Company," of which Jungenfeld was president. To permit plaintiff to recover under such circumstances would be to offer a premium upon bad faith, and invite men to violate their most sacred contracts that they may profit by their own wrong. That a promise to pay a man for doing that which he is already under contract to do is without consideration is conceded by respondents. The rule has been so long imbedded in the common law and decisions of the highest courts of the various states that nothing but the most cogent reasons ought to shake it. [Citing a long list of authorities.] But it is "carrying coals to Newcastle" to add authorities on a proposition so universally accepted, and so inherently just and right in itself. The learned counsel for respondents do not controvert the general proposition. Their contention is, and the circuit court agreed with them, that, when Jungenfeld declined to go further on his contract, the defendant then had the right to sue for damages, and not having elected to sue Jungenfeld, but having acceded to his demand for the additional compensation, defendant cannot now be heard to say his promise is without consideration. While it is true Jungenfeld became liable in damages for the obvious breach of his contract, we do not think it follows that defendant is estopped from showing its promise was made without consideration. . . .

It results from the views above expressed that the judgment must be reversed, and the cause remanded, with directions to the court below to enter judgment for the respondent, with costs.

NOTES

1. *Avoiding the Pre-Existing Duty Rule.* There are two principal ways of avoiding the common law pre-existing duty rule.[54] The first is for the promisor to do or promise to do something in addition to her existing obligation. The second is to

---

[54] For a discussion of the enforceability of anti-modification clauses and other methods of discour-

rescind the first contract before entering into the second, revised contract.

Consider *Slattery v. Wells Fargo Armored Serv. Corp.*, 366 So. 2d 157 (Fla. Dist. Ct. App. 1979), where the Court of Appeals of Florida ruled that a polygraph operator was ineligible to collect an offered reward for providing information that led to the conviction of an armed bank robber. The court noted that the polygraph operator was under contract to the local police department to perform such services, and thus he was already being compensated for his efforts. He would be expected to conduct a polygraph examination on the subject regardless of the existence of the reward. Providing information to the police was something that he was already obligated to do as part of his job.

If you represented the polygraph operator, what advice would you give about strategies by which he might avoid the pre-existing duty rule and collect the reward?

A number of jurisdictions have abandoned the common law pre-existing duty rule in favor of case by case approach, using a broad standard of fairness, such as the one adopted by Restatement (Second) § 89. Consider, for example, *Winegardner v. Burns*, 361 So. 2d 1054 (Ala. 1978), where the Alabama Supreme Court ruled that "an executory agreement may be modified by the parties without any new considerations other than mutual assent." If both parties agree to the modification then why require additional consideration? What arguments can you make for potential benefits and vulnerabilities of such a rule?

2.   *Changed Circumstances.* Courts are more willing to enforce modifications to contracts in light of circumstances that were different or more burdensome than originally contemplated at the time of contract formation.[55] For example, in *Angel v. Murray*, 113 R.I. 482, 322 A.2d 630 (1974), the Supreme Court of Rhode Island enforced a modified contract that granted a trash-collection company an additional $10,000 per year in light of the city's increased population. At the time the contract was created, the city of Newport, Rhode Island had averaged an increase of between twenty and twenty-five homes per year; in the year after the contract was formed, the city experienced an unanticipated increase of 400 homes. The court ruled that the modification was fair and equitable under the circumstances. Rather than demanding more money for performing exactly what they were already obligated to do (like the fishermen in *Alaska Packers'*), the company had to do additional work in serving the new homes.

3.   *"No Modification" Clauses.* Suppose the parties to a contract agree that they cannot modify their agreement in the future even if they should subsequently agree to do so. Thus, they insert a clause in the contract that states "all subsequent modifications of this agreement shall be legally unenforceable." Why might the parties agree to such a clause? One possibility is that they might wish to tie their

---

aging contract modifications, see Kevin E. Davis, *The Demand for Immutable Contracts: Another Look at the Law and Economics of Contract Modifications*, 81 N.Y.U. L. Rev. 487 (2006).

[55] *See* Restatement (Second) of Contracts § 89. For a survey of judicial decisions as to whether and under what circumstances courts will uphold, as valid and enforceable, the voluntary promise of additional compensation because of unforeseen difficulties in the performance of an existing executory contract, see Annotation, *Enforceability of Voluntary Promise of Additional Compensation Because of Unforeseen Difficulties in Performance of Existing Contract*, 85 A.L.R. 3d 259 (1978).

hands initially so as to avoid just the sort of holdup problem that appeared to occur in *Alaska Packers'*.[56] Is this "no modification" clause legally enforceable? Although there are only a few cases, the answer appears to be no! *See, e.g.*, RESTATEMENT (SECOND) OF CONTRACTS § 311 cmt. A (1979); *Beatty v. Guggenheim Exploration Co.*, 122 N.E. 378, 381 (N.Y. 1919) ("Those who make a contract can unmake it. The clause that forbids a change can be changed like any other. Whenever two men contract, no limitation self-imposed can destroy their power to contract again." Cardozo, J). Why might the law treat the right to modify a contract as a mandatory rule rather than a default rule? Can you argue the ban on contract modifications is short-sighted? For discussion, see Alan Schwartz & Robert E. Scott, *Contract Theory and the Limits of Contract Law*, 113 YALE L.J. 541, 611–14 (2003).

4. *Modification Rules and Risk Allocation.* Recall the facts of *Stees v. Leonard*, Chapter 1, where the risk of unforeseen circumstances in a construction contract was borne by the contractor. Had the owner agreed to increase the contract price in order to compensate the contractor for the difficulties encountered in constructing the building on soft soil, would the modification have been enforceable under the pre-existing duty rule? If so, how does this affect the ex ante allocations of risk of the original agreement?

In *Brian Constr. & Development Co. v. Brighenti*, 176 Conn. 162, 405 A.2d 72 (1978), the Supreme Court of Connecticut upheld the modification of a contract when a subcontractor encountered unexpected debris below the surface of an old building. The parties later orally agreed that the subcontractor would be reimbursed for his costs in clearing the unforeseen rubble, plus an additional ten percent. The court noted that such actions clearly went above and beyond the scope of the original agreement, and as such, the modification created a separate enforceable contract.

5. *Evaluating the Pre-Existing Duty Rule.* Consider this problem. Brian Jordan was an all-pro safety for the Atlanta Falcons. For a number of years he had also been a very successful outfielder for the Atlanta Braves baseball team.[57] Assume that he is in the middle of a five-year contract at a salary of $3 million per year. It is the start of September, and the Braves are in the midst of a hotly-contested race for the division title. Jordan appears in the office of the general manager of the Braves with a football in his hand. The following conversation takes place.

Manager: What's with the football, Brian?

Jordan: I'm thinking of how much I loved my days in the NFL, and I was thinking I should give it another shot.

Manager: This wouldn't have anything to do with the big story in yesterday's paper about the rising salaries for NFL free agents?

---

[56] Professor Christine Jolls discusses other reasons why parties might wish to ban modifications in *Contracts as Bilateral Commitments: A New Perspective on Contract Modification*, 26 J. LEGAL STUD. 203 (1997).

[57] Brian Jordan has also played for the St. Louis Cardinals, the Los Angeles Dodgers and the Texas Rangers.

Jordan: Well, I noticed the story. Throw me some balls — I need to work on my interception technique.

Manager: Let me get hold of the owner about this. Maybe we can renegotiate your contract.

Jordan: Gosh, that sounds interesting. Why don't you get back to me this evening, right before the big game against the Mets?

The owner offered Jordan a new contract worth $5 million per year for the two-and one-half years that Jordan's contract had left to run, and he took the deal.

Alas, right before the playoffs began, Jordan was in an auto accident. A blow to his arm resulted in permanent shoulder damage, and he can no longer swing the bat. Both the old contract and the replacement contract stipulate that, in case of an injury, Jordan will be paid at 80% of the contract rate for the term of the contract. Is that contract rate $5 million per year or $3 million per year? If the rule is that the replacement contract is not binding, won't that mean that in future cases the Brian Jordans of the world will leave baseball and play football, even though it would be in their interests and in the interest of their teams to be able to renegotiate a binding contract? Or will professional sports teams simply later repudiate their modified agreements as the employer did in *Alaska Packers*?[58]

Indeed, in recent years, contract renegotiations have taken an added importance in the world of sports. Teams are careful to extend the contracts of their young, talented players so as to ensure that they will not lose them to free agency upon the expiration of their contracts. On the other side, players have withheld their services from their teams despite the existence of a binding contract — essentially, they have refused to play unless the team renegotiates their contract. Some players have been traded to a team that was willing to renegotiate with them; others have simply sat out for a significant portion — or in some cases, all — of the season notwithstanding their contract to play.

For an extreme example of this phenomenon, consider the case of Alexei Yashin, a center for the Ottawa Senators hockey team. Yashin had a brilliant 1998–99 season, and he was ultimately named one of three finalists for the Hart Trophy for the league's most valuable player. Even though one year remained on his contract (for $3.6 million dollars), Yashin demanded that the team extend his contract for several years, at nearly $10 million per year. When the team insisted that he honor his original deal, he sat out the entire season. Subsequently, the National Hockey League prevailed against Yashin in an arbitration proceeding, the arbitrator ruling that he still must play the remaining year that is on his contract.

6. *Alaskan Holidays.* Why did the *Alaska Packers'* workers demand more money after reaching Alaska? It is because they enjoyed a monopoly position (a.k.a., had the company over a barrel) once they reached Alaska, right?[59] Consider another

---

[58] The implications of this kind of opportunistic behavior by the promisee are analyzed in Subha Narasimhan, *Modification: The Self-Help Specific Performance Remedy*, 97 YALE L.J. 61 (1987). For another view, see Alan Schwartz, *Relational Contracts in the Courts: An Analysis of Incomplete Agreements and Judicial Strategies*, 21 J. LEGAL STUD. 271, 308–13 (1992).

[59] "[*Alaska Packers'*] seems a clear case where the motive for the modification was simply to exploit

possibility:

> There's a land where the mountains are nameless, And the rivers run God knows where. There are lives that are erring and aimless And death just hangs by a hair. I wanted the gold and I got it I scrabbled and mucked like a slave. Be it famine or scurvy I fought it I hurled my youth into a grave.

ROBERT SERVICE, THE SPELL OF THE YUKON (1907).

Watch your local sports channel and catch a story on fishing for salmon in Alaskan streams. Why are some of those who are fishing wearing nets over their faces? Do you think it is so the grizzly bears on the other side of the stream won't notice them?

Scholarship on the background of *Alaska Packers'* argues that the case may represent more than just the standard "holdup" story. In *A Fish Story:* Alaska Packers' Association v. Dominico, 2000 UTAH L. REV. 185, Professor Debora Threedy traces the history of salmon fishing in the region around the time of the *Alaska Packers'* litigation. Among her observations is the fact that the fishermen had alleged at trial that the reason for their demand to renegotiate was because the company had supplied them with substandard nets. Poor nets meant that much more effort would be required for the fishermen to catch a given amount of fish (from which they would earn $.02 per salmon caught). While the trial court rejected this allegation as not proved, *if* in fact the fishermen *believed* that the nets were substandard, would (should) that change the result? Given the way the contract was structured, would it be in the interests of the Alaska Packers' Company to supply its workers with substandard nets?

7. ***Termination is not Modification.*** What if the parties agree to cancel the contract or simply waive certain terms altogether? Is that action a modification that is subject to judicial scrutiny? In *El Paso Natural Gas Co. v. Minco Oil & Gas*, 8 S.W.3d 309 (Tex. 1999), the Supreme Court of Texas held that a contractual release should be considered a separate contract altogether, rather than a modification of the original agreement. Therefore, while § 2-209 requires the parties to exercise good faith in seeking modifications of the contract, no such good faith requirement exists for contract formation. The court noted:

> But this duty of good faith does not extend to the formation of a contract. And that includes releases because releases are contracts. Indeed, a final release is a contract by which the parties agree that there are no longer any duties to perform or enforce under the original contract. . . . Neither section 2.209 nor the comments refer to a duty of good faith in the formation of a contract. Rather, the express language of section 2.209(a) and the comments establish that this subsection's duty of good faith applies

---

a monopoly position conferred on the promisors by the circumstances of the contract. It might seem that the promisee would have been in worse shape if the men had quit as they threatened to do. However, since their only motive for threatening to quit was to extract a higher wage, there was probably little danger of their actually quitting. [Stupid for the company not to realize this. Eds.] The danger would have been truly negligible had they known that they could not extract an enforceable commitment to pay them a higher wage." Richard Posner, *Gratuitous Promises in Economics and Law*, 6 J. LEGAL STUD. 411 (1977).

only to contract "modifications." And, as discussed above, a release of liability is not an agreement to modify a contract, but is an agreement to completely relinquish the parties' performance obligations to each other.

Id. at 313–14.

8. *Pre-Existing Duty vs. UCC § 2-209: Revisiting the "Rules versus Standards" Debate.* Section 2-209 of the UCC essentially eliminates the pre-existing duty rule in sales contracts. However, the Comments state that contract modifications will not be legally enforced unless the parties have acted in good faith. Reconsider the facts of *Alaska Packers'* and the Jordan hypothetical in light of the good faith standard. Is that test preferable to the "bright-line" result dictated by the pre-existing duty rule? Under the pre-existing duty rule, the factual inquiry seems simple: Was there an existing contract? Was there a modification in that contract? Was it supported by independent consideration? Many more facts are relevant if the good faith test is applied. Reread Note 7 on rules versus standards, page 258, *supra*, and then consider these issues once again. That note discusses the features of precise or bright line rules and broadly framed or multi-factored standards in the context of UCC § 2-207. To summarize: Bright line or precise rules are easier to apply, thus process errors are reduced, but they may not mirror adequately the underlying legal principle. In the case of the pre-existing duty rule, for example, it is fairly simple to determine whether a party has given fresh consideration for a promise to modify an existing obligation. But if the underlying principle in *Alaska Packers'* is to deter extortionate or opportunistic demands to renegotiate, the rule is seriously under- and over-inclusive. One can imagine many good faith modifications that are captured by the rule and found unenforceable. Similarly, one can imagine a party making a strategic demand to renegotiate and then agreeing to undertake a modest addition to her prior contractual commitments so as to satisfy the literal requirements of the rule.

But is it clear that a multi-factored rule or the broad standard of UCC § 2-209 — enforcing those modifications that are made in "good faith" — are improvements? Clearly a broad standard of good faith aptly reflects the governing legal principle, but how easily and accurately can it be applied?[60] How is a fact finder to determine in any given case whether the request to modify is based on a legitimate claim or is only pretextual? How would you decide the Brian Jordan hypothetical in note 3 above? To the extent that "good faith" turns on facts that are neither observable nor verifiable to a court, the risk of process errors in applying the rule is very high. Process errors can occur in both directions — that is, bad faith modifications may be undetected while legitimate claims for renegotiation may be subject to sanction.

---

[60] In considering this question, consider the definition of "good faith" in UCC § 1-201(19) and § 2-103(1)(b). How would you go about showing to a jury that the other party in litigation was not "honest in fact"? What does it mean to "observe commercial standards of fair dealing in the trade"?

E. COLLABORATIVE CONTRACTING: THE BRAIDING OF FORMAL AND INFORMAL METHODS OF ENFORCEMENT

In the preceding Part, we discussed how parties can deal with the uncertainties of relational contracting by using flexible contract terms that permit the adjustment of quantity and price and effort as conditions warrant. These relational contracts employ a variety of well-known mechanisms for dealing with the moral hazard risk that one party will use the flexibility in the contract terms to either seek an unbargained-for advantage or shirk on a contractually assumed responsibility. Thus, output and requirements contracts can be used to reduce these risks by allocating discretion to the party least likely to be tempted to defect from the relationship. In turn, options to terminate offer further means of constraining the inherent conflicts that arise when burden and benefit are not shared equally. In all of these cases, the parties contract initially under conditions of uncertainty but they understand that when performance is due the uncertainties will have been clarified and thus their respective obligations can then be assessed and litigation pursued if one party has failed to comply with its responsibilities under the contract.

In this Part we turn to an even more complex contracting problem. What happens when the level of uncertainty is such that it not only exists at the outset of the relationship but is continuous throughout the relationship? How can that be? In *Contracting for Innovation: Vertical Disintegration and Interfirm Collaboration*, 109 COLUM. L. REV. 431 (2009), Professors Ronald Gilson, Charles Sabel and Robert Scott explain:

> In some markets and for some products, increases in the complexity of the technology and in the rate of change have made it difficult for a single firm to sustain state of the art capacity across all the technologies necessary for successful product development.. . . . What we see emerging are . . . explicit, formal contracts [between separate firms] that rely on collaboration and co-design to stimulate continuous improvement in product development and engineering. Because the collaborative process is continuous, the parties operate in an on-going state of uncertainty, one in which operational decisions must be continually updated and refined. This phenomenon of continuous uncertain change poses a unique challenge for contract design.

> In the new arrangements, innovation is the product of a joint effort by two or more [firms]; it is metaphorically situated between them and is dependent on both. The development of the Boeing 787 aircraft is a good example. Innovation in the design and manufacture of the wing, the province of one supplier (or group of suppliers), is dependent on the design and manufacture of the fuselage, the province of a different supplier (or group of suppliers), and vice versa. Innovation in one structure must mesh with innovation in the other in order for either to be successful. The wing must not only be compatible with the fuselage; the two must fit. Innovation is thus a collaborative and iterative process rather than a discrete product supplied by a party upstream in the supply chain according to specifications set by a downstream customer.

Precisely how have parties to these new collaborative relationships structured their contracts to deal with the unique problem of *continuous* uncertainty? And, are the resulting agreements legally enforceable? Study the following case and see if you can devise some tentative answers to both of these key contract design questions.

ELI LILLY & CO. v. EMISPHERE TECHS., INC.
United States District Court, Southern District of Indiana
408 F. Supp. 2d 668 (2006)

[Eli Lilly is a major pharmaceutical company with annual revenues of more than ten billion dollars. Emisphere is a relatively new and much smaller company whose principal assets are technology and know-how involving a family of chemical compounds that may offer a solution to a basic biological barrier to some forms of drug treatments. Emisphere believed that its compounds could be combined with therapeutic proteins to protect the proteins from the digestive mechanisms, so that the therapeutic proteins might pass intact into the bloodstream to provide effective therapy to the patient. This prospect was very interesting for Lilly: it is easier, cheaper, and more effective to deliver medicine orally than through injections or other methods that bypass the digestive system.

In 1997, Emisphere and Lilly entered into a Research Collaboration and Option Agreement in which both parties agreed to collaborate on a research and development program to research the use of Emisphere technology for oral delivery of selected therapeutic compounds. The research relationship required Lilly and Emisphere to share valuable information under an annual research plan approved by a joint research committee consisting of three members from each firm. The contract required open information exchange and provided that all decisions of the research committee had to be unanimous. If the committee could not reach unanimity on any matter, the issue would be referred to senior Vice Presidents for each firm. If they disagreed, then the decision-making process moved to the two CEOs. Only if the CEOs failed to resolve the differences could either party terminate the contract. Finally, the parties agreed that Emisphere would grant Lilly an option for an exclusive worldwide license to make and use the Emisphere carrier technology to develop oral products. Lilly could exercise that option by giving notice to Emisphere and by paying Emisphere a substantial sum of money.

The early results of the research were very promising such that Lilly paid Emisphere $4 million in April 1998 to exercise the option. But in early 2001, Dr. Amin Khan, the lead Lilly representative on the joint committee, began recruiting talent inside Lilly to form a new and secret team to study the mechanism of action of the Emisphere carriers, using other of Lilly's library of protein molecules. After receiving promising results from its secret research on Emisphere carriers, Lilly filed a patent application with the World Intellectual Property Organization for combinations of 56 different delivery agents, including Emisphere's proprietary carriers that had been used in the collaborative research. The application listed one inventor: Dr. Amin Khan.

In August 2004, two days before a scheduled settlement conference with the court, Novartis (a rival major pharmaceutical company) told Emisphere it was willing to go forward with commercial development of the Emisphere compounds if

Emisphere terminated the Lilly contracts. That same day, Emisphere sent a letter to Lilly terminating the collaborative research agreement and the License Agreement. The issue for the court was whether Lilly's violation of the agreement's protocols only gave rise to a suit for patent infringement by Emisphere, or whether it gave rise to an independent remedy for breach of contract and, if so, whether Emisphere could terminate the contract and thereby capture the fruits of a valuable, jointly created opportunity.]

HAMILTON, J.

Lilly's theory is that if Emisphere is unhappy about Lilly's secret research projects on Emisphere carriers, its legal remedies are limited to claims for patent infringement. . . . [But] Emisphere granted much more than a patent license. It agreed to a close and collaborative research relationship in which it would provide Lilly with a vast quantity of technical information, both public and confidential, only some of which might be protected by patent law. Emisphere delivered to Lilly "a package of valuable information." Under [this] reasoning, the court should find an implied covenant not to use that information outside the scope of the license-even without the statement that "Lilly shall have no rights to use" Emisphere's technology outside the PTH field. With that sentence, the conclusion in favor of Emisphere becomes even more secure.

In this respect, this case is comparable to *Medinol Ltd. v. Boston Scientific Corp.*, 346 F. Supp. 2d 575 (S.D.N.Y. 2004). In *Medinol*, the parties had entered into "a close and extensive contractual relationship" for research, development, manufacture, and distribution of stents for medical uses. *Id.* at 581. Medinol's primary role was to manufacture the stents. Boston Scientific was to sell them in the United States. Medinol granted a license for such sales of its patented stents.

Boston Scientific was concerned about the risk of supply disruptions with Medinol's production lines. The parties agreed that Medinol would establish a so-called "Alternative Line" for manufacturing stents, which Boston Scientific would be permitted to operate. Medinol granted Boston Scientific a license for the right to manufacture stents, but that license was limited to "the operation of the Alternative Line." Boston Scientific then set up a secret manufacturing operation outside the scope of the Alternative Line. Although there was no express covenant against such manufacture, the court found that the parties' close relationship and careful drafting showed that the unauthorized manufacturing amounted to a breach of contract, without limiting Medinol to a patent infringement suit. The court further found that Boston Scientific's stealth and secrecy showed it had acted in bad faith by setting up the unauthorized line. The court granted summary judgment for Medinol on liability for the breach, leaving only the issue of damages for trial.

Similarly here, the parties agreed to a cooperative venture, but with important limits. When Lilly ventured beyond those limits with its secret research projects, it did not risk only a claim of patent infringement. It also breached the contract that gave it the limited license in the first place.

Witnesses and documents from both parties recognized that the research collaboration between the parties requires a high degree of candor and trust in both directions. The court fully agrees. Emisphere understandably and justifiably feels it can no longer trust Lilly to protect the confidentiality of Emisphere's most valuable intellectual property and to work as part of a team. Lilly, in breach of its promises to Emisphere, actively concealed for several years the fact that the same people overseeing the collaborative effort for Lilly were also leading and aiding a parallel but secret project within Lilly that did not include Emisphere at all. That project was intended to bypass the need to work with Emisphere. There is no indication that Lilly could do anything to restore the needed level of trust.

By pursuing its secret and independent research projects with Emisphere's carriers, Lilly did not act in good faith and did not deal fairly with Emisphere. The breach of trust went to the root of the parties' agreement, and it is serious enough to support termination of the contracts.

Lilly contends that termination will harm it because it has spent tens of millions of dollars on the oral compounds, and because Lilly's existing injectable product will be vulnerable to competition if Lilly is not able to pursue oral delivery using the Emisphere carriers. The court has no doubt that termination will harm Lilly, but that harm is the direct consequence of Lilly's decision to pursue its own secret research on Emisphere's carriers in violation of the agreements with Emisphere

[F]or the reasons set forth above, the court finds that Lilly breached the [research collaboration agreement] and that the breach entitled Emisphere to terminate both agreements effective August 23, 2004.

NOTES

1. *Questions on* **Eli Lilly**. Lilly's argument in the case centered on the fact that the contract required the parties to collaborate but did not impose any further obligations on either party. There was no obligation for Lilly to go forward with the transaction after it exercised its option to license the Emisphere compounds. Lilly could have decided that the project was not commercially viable and abandoned it at any time. In essence, Lilly was arguing that there was a formal agreement to collaborate but that the balance of the relationship was informal — based on trust and cooperation. Therefore, Emisphere had no legal remedy under the contract and could only pursue Lilly for patent infringement if it could prove that case. Why didn't that argument succeed? What contract term did the court rely on to find that the agreement was legally enforceable at least to the extent of permitting Emisphere to terminate the license and walk away with the valuable scientific information that the collaboration had produced?

2. *Compare* **Eli Lilly** *to* **Medinol Lid v. Boston Scientific Corp.** A similar conflict over the violation of a collaborative contract occurred in *Medinol Ltd. v. Boston Sci. Corp.*, 346 F. Supp. 2d 575 (S.D.N.Y. 2004), the case discussed by the court in *Eli Lilly*. In *Medinol*, the parties agreed that Medinol would establish an "Alternative Line" for manufacturing stents, which Boston Scientific would be permitted to operate under license from Medinol. That license was limited to "the operation of the Alternative Line." Boston Scientific then set up a secret manufacturing operation outside the scope of the Alternative Line. Although there was no express covenant against such manufacture, the court found that the parties' close

collaborative relationship showed that the unauthorized manufacturing amounted to a breach of contract. The court further found that Boston Scientific's stealth and secrecy showed it had acted in bad faith by setting up the unauthorized line. The court granted summary judgment for Medinol on liability for the breach, leaving only the issue of damages for trial.

What damages, if any, would be appropriate for Medinol to recover in a second trial? Should Medinol be entitled to recover their expectancy based on the value of their contract rights had the agreement been pursued to a successful conclusion? *See Shaw v. E. I. Du Pont de Nemours & Co.*, 126 Vt. 206, 226 A.2d 903 (1967) (affirming a damage award for breach of an implied covenant not to use a patent beyond the scope of license).

3. *Collaborative Agreements as a "Braiding" of Formal and Informal Contracting*. In *Braiding: The Interaction of Formal and Informal Contracting in Theory, Practice, and Doctrine*, 110 COLUM. L. REV. 1377 (2010), Professors Ronald Gilson, Charles Sabel, and Robert Scott applaud the nuanced result reached by the court in both the *Elli Lilly* and *Medinol* cases. They argue that even though these collaborative agreements are "radically incomplete" the formal contract should be legally enforceable but only by the award of "low powered sanctions" such as reliance damages and not by granting the non breacher its expectancy. They explain:

> [At one level], *Lilly v. Emisphere* illustrates how courts can use formal enforcement to support a contractual relationship when informal mechanisms have failed. By only sanctioning "red-faced" violations of the collaborative agreement, such as the secret research group formed by Lilly outside the informal exchanges created by the agreement itself, the court did not attempt to regulate the nature or course of the collaborative interactions. Thus, the maintenance of the collaboration protocols established by the parties, and the resulting specific investments in information exchange, was left entirely within the province of the internally generated, informal enforcement mechanism. The formal enforcement only excluded a (secret) alternative process that undermined the trust that was in fact generated through braiding.

> Ideally, courts would respond to the challenge of searching for partners in uncertain environments by enforcing the chosen methods of mutual cooperation on terms consistent with the arrangements themselves; that is, by imposing low-powered sanctions designed to encourage compliance with the verifiable elements of the information exchange regime (and the informal relations it supports) while avoiding high-powered sanctions that that crowds out informality and destroys the braid. And, indeed, this is what we are beginning to see: Courts in leading cases are sanctioning shamelessly selfish abuse of information-exchange regimes and sometimes deploring the unwillingness of the abusing party to make use of the joint problem solving mechanism that it has co-sponsored. Because the sanction is tied only to verifiable breaches of the commitment to collaborate, damages for breach of the agreement in these instances are limited in principle to the reliance costs incurred in the collaboration. In this way, the

collaboration commitment can achieve its intended purpose of generating information and trust precisely because it never entails an obligation beyond nominally abiding by the commitment to collaborate during the period of joint exploration: formal enforcement is only low powered and thus the parties specific investments in information during the course of the collaboration are left entirely to informal mechanisms.

Id. at 1415, 1417–18.

4. *Informal Enforcement of Contractual Obligations and the Crowding Out Problem.* The court in *Eli Lilly* emphasized the value of trust and the development of norms of cooperation and reciprocity to the success of collaborative contracting. Indeed, informal methods of enforcement can be very powerful in all contractual relationships. They include the fear of losing expected future dealings with the counterparty, the threat of loss of reputation with the resulting reduction in future business with other potential counterparties in the relevant economic and social communities, or an individual taste for reciprocity that encourages performance and penalizes breach. A difficult question arises, however, when these informal sanctions are embedded in a formal contract that is subject to full legal enforcement as well. A rich experimental literature explicitly considers the interaction between the formal and informal methods of enforcement.[61] The central question is whether the introduction of formal contracting and legal enforcement "crowds out" or degrades the operation of informal contracting. For example, informal sanctions based on reputation may be displaced when the existence of a formal obligation turns a normative duty into a calculation of self-interest. In such a case, the two enforcement strategies are substitutes. Alternatively, the two strategies are complements when each reinforces the effectiveness of the other. This experimental literature tends to support the crowding out story. The most familiar example is the experiment of using formal sanctions to cause parents to be timely in picking up their children from day care. In an effort to improve punctuality, a fine was imposed to encourage compliance. But rather than increasing compliance, imposing a fine caused late pickups to increase. The formal fine "crowded out" the reputation-based norm by changing the parents' perception of their obligation from a commitment to the community to a price for additional day care.[62]

In their article on *Braiding* (see note 3 above), Professor Gilson, Sabel and Scott argue that crowding out can be avoided in cases such as *Eli Lilly* because the parties to these contracts have learned to avoid writing high-powered formal contracts that tie outcome variables to expectation damages. Rather, they write formal contracts to motivate low-powered incentives to collaborate. In this way, they braid formal and informal elements in ways that enhance the collaborative process.

---

[61] *See e.g.,* Ernst Fehr, Alexander Klein & Klaus M. Schmidt *Fairness and Contract Design,* 75 Econometrica 121 (2007); Ernst Fehr & Klaus M. Schmidt, *Adding a Stick to the Carrot? The Interaction of Bonuses and Fines,* 97 Am. Econ. Rev. 177 (2007).

[62] Uri Gneezy & Aldo Rustichini, *A Fine is a Price,* 29 J. Legal Stud. 1 (2000). An extensive literature in social psychology also considers the crowding out of intrinsic motivations. *See* Edward L. Deci, R. Koestner & Richard M. Ryan, *A Meta-Analytic Review of Experiments Examining the Effects of Extrinsic Rewards on Intrinsic Motivations,* 125 Psychol. Bull. 627 (1999).

Do you agree that the lesser sanctions imposed in *Eli Lilly* are the key to avoiding the crowding out problem?

F. BIBLIOGRAPHY AND SUGGESTED READING

Barry E. Adler, *The Questionable Ascent of* Hadley v. Baxendale, 51 STAN. L. REV. 1547 (1999).

Armen Alchian & Harold Dempsetz, *Production Information Costs and Economic Organization*, 62 AM. ECON. REV. 777, 777–83 (1972).

Aivazian, Trebilcock & Penny, *The Law of Contract Modifications: The Uncertain Quest for a Benchmark of Enforceability*, 22 OSGOODE HALL L.J. 173 (1984).

Ian Ayres & Robert Gertner, *Filling Gaps in Incomplete Contracts: An Economic Theory of Default Rules*, 99 YALE L.J. 87 (1989).

Ian Ayres & Robert Gertner, *Strategic Contractual Inefficiency and the Optimal Choice of Legal Rules*, 101 YALE L.J. 729 (1992).

Omri Ben-Shahar, *Mutual Assent Versus Gradual Ascent: The Debate over the Right to Retract*, 152 U. PA. L. REV. 1947 (2004).

Lawrence E. Blades, *Employment at Will vs. Individual Freedom: On Limiting the Abusive Exercise of Employer Power*, 67 COLUM. L. REV. 1404 (1967).

Richard Craswell, *Offer, Acceptance, and Efficient Reliance*, 48 STAN. L. REV. 481 (1996).

Richard Craswell, *Taking Information Seriously: Misrepresentation and Nondisclosure in Contract Law and Elsewhere*, 92 VA. L. REV. 565 (2006).

Kevin E. Davis, *The Demand for Immutable Contracts: Another Look at the Law and Economics of Contract Modifications*, 81 N.Y.U. L. REV. 487 (2006).

Gregory M. Duhl, Red Owl's *Legacy*, 87 MARQ. L. REV. 297 (2003).

Issac Ehrlich & Richard A. Posner, *An Economic Analysis of Legal Rulemaking*, 2 J. LEGAL STUD. 257 (1974).

Melvin Aron Eisenberg, *Contracts and Property Law: The Emergence of Dynamic Contract Law*, 2 THEORETICAL INQ. L 1 (2001).

Melvin Aron Eisenberg, *The Emergence of Dynamic Contract Law*, 88 CAL. L. REV. 1743 (2000).

Richard Epstein, *In Defense of the Contract at Will*, 51 U. CHI. L. REV. 947 (1984).

E. Allen Farnsworth, *Pre-Contractual Liability and Preliminary Agreements: Fair Dealing and Failed Negotiations*, 87 COLUM. L. REV. 217 (1987).

Jay Feinman, *Critical Approaches to Contract Law*, 30 UCLA L. REV. 829, 852–57 (1983).

CHARLES FRIED, CONTRACTS AS PROMISE (1981).

Earnest Gellhorn, *Limitations on Contract Termination Rights — Franchise*

Cancellations, 1967 DUKE L.J. 465.

Ronald Gilson, Charles Sabel & Robert Scott, *Contracting for Innovation*: *Vertical Disintegration and Interfirm Collaboration*, 109 COLUM. L. REV. 431 (2009).

Ronald Gilson, Charles Sabel & Robert Scott, *Braiding: The Interaction of Formal and Informal Contracting in Theory, Practice, and Doctrine*, 110 CCLUM. L. REV. 1377 (2010).

Ronald J. Gilson, Charles F. Sabel & Robert E. Scott, *Contract and Innovation: the Limited Role of Generalist Courts in the Evolution of Novel Contractual Forms* 87 N.Y.U. L. Rev. ___ (forthcoming 2013).

Charles J. Goetz & Robert E. Scott, *Principles of Relational Contracts*, 67 VA. L. REV. 1089 (1981).

Charles J. Goetz & Robert E. Scott, *The Mitigation Principle: Toward a General Theory of Contractual Obligation*, 69 VA. L. REV. 967 (1983).

Victor Goldberg, Brown v. Cara: *The Type II Preliminary Agreement and the Option to Unbundle* (conference paper presented at Conference on Contractual Innovation, NYU Law School, May 3–4, 2012).

Victor Goldberg, *Discretion in Long-Term Open Quantity Contracts: Reining in Good Faith*, 35 U.C. DAVIS L. REV. 319 (2002).

Victor Goldberg, *In Search of Best Efforts: Reinterpreting* Bloor v. Falstaff, 44 ST. LOUIS L.J. 1465 (2000).

Victor Goldberg, *The Net Profits Puzzle*, 97 COLUM. L. REV. 524 (1997).

Uri Gneezy & Aldo Rustichini, *A Fine is a Price*, 29 J. LEGAL STUD. 1 (2000).

Robert A. Hillman, *Policing Contract Modification Under the U.C.C.: Good Faith and the Doctrine of Economic Duress*, 64 IOWA L. REV. 849 (1979).

Robert Hillman, *Court Adjustment of Long-Term Contracts: An Analysis Under Modern Contract Law*, 1987 Duke L.J. 1.

Michael Jensen & William Meckling, *Theory of the Firm: Managerial Behavior, Agency Costs and Ownership Structure*, 3 J. FIN. ECON. 305, 313–19 (1976).

Jason Scott Johnston, *Communication and Courtship: Cheap Talk Economics and the Law of Contract Formation*, 85 VA. L. REV. 385 (1999).

Jason Scott Johnston, *Investment, Information, and Promissory Liability*, 152 U. PA. L. REV. 1923 (2004).

Jason Scott Johnston, *Strategic Bargaining and the Economic Theory of Contract Default Rules*, 100 YALE L.J. 615 (1990).

Christine Jolls, *Contracts as Bilateral Commitments: A New Perspective on Contract Modification*, 26 J. LEGAL STUD. 203 (1997).

Avery W. Katz, *Contractual Incompleteness: A Transactional Perspective*, 56 Case W. Res. 169 (2005).

Avery W. Katz, *When Should an Offer Stick? The Economics of Promissory Estoppel in Preliminary Negotiations*, 105 Yale L.J. 1249 (1996).

Charles Knapp, *Enforcing the Contract to Bargain*, 44 N.Y.U. L. REV. 673 (1969).

Juliet P. Kostritsky, *Bargaining with Uncertainty, Moral Hazard, and Sunk Costs: A Default Rule for Pre-Contractual Negotiations*, 44 HASTINGS L.J. 621 (1993).

Juliet P. Kostritsky, *Taxonomy for Justifying Judicial Intervention in an Imperfect World: What to Do When Parties Have Not Achieved Bargains or Have Drafted Incomplete Agreements*, 2004 WIS. L. REV. 323.

Saul Litvinoff, *Good Faith*, 71 TUL. L. REV. 1645 (1997).

Stewart Macaulay, *Non-Contractual Relations in Business*, 28 Am. Soc. Rev. 555 (1963).

IAN R. MACNEIL, CONTRACTS: EXCHANGE TRANSACTIONS AND RELATIONS (2d ed. 1978).

Ian R. Macneil, *Contracts: Adjustment of Long-Term Economic Relations Under the Classical, Neoclassical, and Relational Contract Law*, 72 NW. U. L. Rev. 854 (1978).

Ian R. Macneil, *The Many Faces of Contracts*, 47 S. CAL. L. REV. 691 (1974).

Subha Narasimhan, *Modification: The Self-Help Specific Performance Remedy*, 97 Yale L.J. 61 (1987).

Nadia E. Nedzel, *A Comparative Study of Good Faith, Fair Dealing, and Precontractual Liability*, 12 TUL. EUR. & CIV. L.F. 97 (1997).

Nicola W. Palmieri, *Good Faith Disclosures Required During Precontractual Negotiations*, 24 SETON HALL L. REV. 70 (1993).

Rob Park, *Putting the "Best" in Best Efforts*, 73 U. CHI. L. REV. 705 (2006).

Richard A. Posner, *Gratuitous Promises in Economics and Law*, 6 J. LEGAL STUD. 411 (1977).

Eric A. Posner, *A Theory of Contract Law Under Conditions of Radical Judicial Error*, 94 NW. U. L. REV. 749 (2000).

Walter Pratt, *American Contract Law at the Turn of the Century*, 39 S.C. L. REV. 415 (1988).

Gregory G. Sarno, Annotation, *Enforceability of Voluntary Promise of Additional Compensation Because of Unforeseen Difficulties in Performance of Existing Contract*, 85 A.L.R.3d 259 (1978).

Alan Schwartz, *Relational Contracts in the Courts: An Analysis of Incomplete Agreements and Judicial Strategies*, 21 J. LEGAL STUD. 271 (1992).

Alan Schwartz, *The Default Rule Paradigm and the Limits of Contract Law*, 3 S. CAL. INTERDISC. L.J. 389 (1994).

Alan Schwartz, *Incomplete Contracts*, 2 NEW PALGRAVE DICTIONARY OF ECONOMICS AND LAW 277 (1997).

Alan Schwartz & Robert E. Scott, *The Law and Economics of Preliminary Agreements*, 120 HARV. L. REV. 661(2007).

Robert E. Scott, Hoffman v. Red Owl Stores *and the Limits of the Legal Method*, 61 HASTINGS L.J. 859 (2010).

Robert E. Scott, *A Relational Theory of Default Rules for Commercial Contracts*, 19 J. LEGAL STUD. 597 (1990).

Robert E. Scott, *The Case for Formalism in Relational Contract*, 94 NW. U. L. REV. 849 (2000).

Robert E. & Scott, *A Theory of Self-Enforcing Indefinite Agreements*, 103 COLUM. L. REV. 1641 (2003).

G. Richard Shell, *Opportunism and Trust in the Negotiation of Commercial Contracts: Toward a New Cause of Action*, 44 VAND. L. REV. 221 (1991).

Richard E. Speidel, *Court-Imposed Price Adjustments Under Long-Term Supply Contracts*, 76 NW. U. L. REV. 369 (1981).

Richard E. Speidel, *The New Spirit of Contract*, 2 J.L. & COM. 193 (1982).

Clyde W. Summers, *Individual Protection Against Unjust Dismissal: Time for a Statute*, 62 VA. L. REV. 481 (1976).

Harvey L. Temkin, *When Does the Fat Lady Sing?: An Analysis of "Agreements in Principle" in Corporate Acquisitions*, 55 FORDHAM L. REV. 125 (1986).

J. Hoult Verkerke, *An Empirical Perspective on Indefinite Term Employment Contracts: Resolving the Just Cause Debate*, 1995 WIS. L. REV. 838.

William Whitford & Stewart Macaulay, Hoffman v. Red Owl Stores: *The Rest of the Story*, 61 HASTINGS L.J. 801 (2010).

William C. Whitford, *Relational Contracts and the New Formalism*, 2004 WIS. L. REV. 631.

Keith E. Witek, *Drafting a More Predictable Letter of Intent — Reducing Risk and Uncertainty in a Risky and Uncertain Transaction*, 9 TEX. INTELL. PROP. L.J. 185 (2001).

Chapter 5

négociation

REGULATING THE BARGAINING PROCESS

A. INTRODUCTION

There are two predominant approaches to justifying the enforcement of promises. The first justifies promissory liability on the ground that it promotes and respects individual autonomy. One aspect of autonomy is the ability to form, revise, and pursue a conception of the good — an individual's life plan — as one sees fit. Enforcing promises promotes this aspect of autonomy by increasing the reliability of the plans individuals make. The idea that individuals are autonomous also forms the basis for ascriptions of moral responsibility — because individuals are accorded the right to control their own lives, they are also held morally accountable for the effects of their behavior on others. The right of individuals to direct their own lives implies a correlative duty of each individual not to interfere with the equal rights of others. Thus, the idea of autonomy serves simultaneously as the foundation for both personal liberty and moral responsibility, both of which might be used as a justification for enforcing certain promises.

The second approach justifies the enforcement of promises as a means of promoting efficient reliance on promise-making. Promises enable parties to make a present, binding commitment to undertake a future exchange. The economic justification is thus premised on the assumption that the information provided by that commitment is valuable to the promisee. This, in turn, presupposes that the exchanges to which individuals commit by making promises are themselves value-enhancing. In economic parlance, value-enhancing exchanges are ones that maximize the joint gains (the "contractual surplus") from exchange transactions by transferring resources to higher-valued uses. The basic premise of the economic justification, therefore, is that contract law should facilitate the efforts of contracting parties to maximize joint gains because any system for allocating resources in society should strive to identify and facilitate exchanges that transfer resources to higher-valued uses. Any system that fails to do so wastes its resources.

Neither the autonomy nor economic justifications support the enforcement of all promises. Both would enforce only promises made voluntarily by informed, mentally competent adults (this is required to give meaning to the core concept of *choice*). The autonomy justification endorses these requirements because they are constitutive elements of autonomous choice. Only informed, mentally competent adults are fully autonomous moral agents, and the actions of such individuals are autonomous only if they are fully voluntary. Promises made without crucial information, by mentally impaired persons or minors, or under duress do not reflect the genuine or fully developed will of the promisor.

The economic justification also embraces these requirements as necessary to insure that contract law enforces only those promised exchanges likely to enhance welfare. If a mentally competent adult voluntarily makes a promise to undertake a future exchange, the return promise (and resulting exchange) is likely to make that person better off. But if a promise is made without crucial information, by a mentally impaired person or minor, or under duress, there is little reason to suppose the promised exchange will make the promisor better off. Under these conditions, the exchange mechanism is no longer a reliable signal of those transfers that enhance social welfare.

These justifications of contract law therefore provide different but compatible reasons for limiting enforcement of contracts to those made voluntarily by informed, mentally competent adults. This convergence between the autonomy and economic justifications of contract law can be captured in the notion of *expanded choice*; that is, for both reasons of autonomy and efficiency, more choice is better than less. By enforcing promises, the law enables individuals to make binding precommitments. Making commitments that enhance one's life plan promotes individual autonomy; such commitments also expand the possibilities for making welfare-enhancing exchanges. This coincidence between autonomy and economic justifications for the enforcement of promissory commitments should be unsurprising, since autonomous individuals are, on average, better able to look out for their own interests than any third party.

The challenge for contract law, then, is to define the requirements of voluntariness, information, mental competence, and majority. As is the case with any legal regime, two approaches are possible and can be found in both statutory and decisional law. The first is to draw bright-line *rules* that are easy to administer in particular cases. The advantages of this approach are relatively low costs of adjudication and relatively high transparency of the law to prospective contractors. The disadvantage is that rules are inevitably under- and over-inclusive; that is, the underlying justification of a particular rule argues against allowing some cases the rule permits and in favor of allowing some cases the rule prohibits. In short, rules by nature cannot be tailored on a case-by-case basis to conform to the underlying goals the rules are designed to advance. The second approach is to use broad, or vaguer *standards*. The advantage of this approach is that it potentially eliminates under- and over-inclusiveness by allowing for case-by-case tailoring. The disadvantages are its relatively higher costs of administration and its relatively lower degree of transparency to potential contractors. Adjudication costs will be higher because it will be more time-consuming and intellectually challenging for judges or juries to decide how to apply standards in individual cases. Transparency will be lower because the variance among outcomes of similar cases will be higher; it will be more difficult to predict how a judge or jury will decide particular cases. This not only increases the costs of transacting, but also increases the problem of unfairness due to unequal treatment among like cases.[1]

In this chapter, we begin by focusing on the doctrines designed specifically to prevent the enforcement of involuntary promises (the duress doctrine), promises induced by inaccurate or incomplete information attributable to the promisee's

---

[1] For a more extensive analysis of the rules-standards literature, see Note 7, page 258, *supra.*

wrongful conduct (the fraud doctrines), and promises made by infants and mentally impaired adults (the capacity doctrines). These doctrines constitute the backbone of the free market ideal underwritten by the autonomy and economic justifications of contract law. But even bargains that pass muster under these doctrines may nevertheless not be legally enforceable. The second part of this chapter covers the three broad doctrines that police the content of agreements and therefore circumscribe the free market conception of contract law. These are the doctrines of illegality, immorality, and unconscionability. Finally, the doctrine known as the statute of frauds prevents courts from enforcing certain agreements unless they are in writing. Our purpose throughout the chapter is the same: to identify and evaluate the objectives underlying each doctrine, the various means of achieving these objectives (e.g., rules versus standards), and the ways courts apply and shape these doctrines in individual cases. As you consider each of these doctrines, keep in mind that the key factor that distinguishes these rules from those we have studied thus far is that the rules policing the bargain are *mandatory*; they cannot be altered by a contrary agreement.

B.   DURESS

The voluntariness requirement for the enforcement of promises in contract is deceptively simple: courts will not enforce promises made under duress. But how should courts distinguish between voluntary promises and promises made under duress? We can begin with the clear cases. Everyone would concede that a promise demanded at gunpoint is involuntary and therefore subject to the defense of duress. And everyone equally agrees that a millionaire's promise to pay for a suit he agreed to purchase for retail price at Bloomingdale's is clearly voluntary and therefore not subject to the defense of duress. But in between these polar cases lies the grey area that preoccupies courts and scholars. As you read the following cases, ask yourself how the standards the courts invoke distinguish between so-called voluntary "hard bargains" and involuntary bargains subject to the defense of duress. If, for reasons unrelated to Bloomingdale's conduct, the millionaire would lose his fortune unless he purchased the suit from Bloomingdale's, should a court nonetheless enforce his promise even if Bloomingdale's used this opportunity to charge four times the usual price for the suit? What is the difference between the promise extracted at gunpoint and the millionaire's promise to pay for a suit extracted by exigent circumstances?

WOLF v. MARLTON CORP.

Superior Court of New Jersey, Appellate Division
57 N.J. Super. 278, 154 A.2d 625 (1959)

FREUND, J.

Plaintiffs, husband and wife, instituted this action in the Camden County Court to recover a deposit of $2,450 which they made under a contract to purchase a house to be built for them by the defendant, The Marlton Corporation. The sale was never consummated, and the defendant builder eventually sold to a third party the home which had been intended for the Wolfs. The theory of the action is that plaintiffs were at all times ready, willing, and able to comply with the building contract but that the builder unilaterally and unjustifiably terminated the contract without returning the down payment. The County Court judge, sitting without a jury, concluded in a written opinion that it was the defendant who refused to perform under the contract and that consequently a judgment in favor of plaintiffs was dictated. The Marlton Corporation (hereinafter "the builder") appeals. The agreement of sale, entered into by the parties on March 8, 1957, called for the construction of a dwelling in defendant's housing development in Haddon Township upon the following terms:

Cash at signing of this agreement (inclusive of any deposit) $2,450.00

An additional cash payment on or before house closed 2,450.00

Cash at final settlement 3,100.00

Bond and mortgage in the sum of 25 yr. conv. 512% 16,500.00

Total Purchase Price $24,500.00

"Should Buyer fail to make payment of any additional moneys as herein mentioned, or fail to make settlement as herein provided, the sum or sums paid on account may be retained by Seller either on account of the purchase price or as compensation for the charges and expenses which Seller has sustained, as Seller may elect, in which latter case this contract shall become null and void and all copies hereon shall be returned to the Seller for cancellation."

It is undisputed that the builder had completed the "closing in" of the house sometime in June 1957 and that plaintiffs did not make the second payment. . . .

The alternative ground briefed on behalf of the builder as basis for a reversal fixes upon a matter of far greater import. The point is captioned: "Buyers breached the agreement of sale by preventing its performance through threats to resell the house to an undesirable purchaser and to ruin defendants' building business if defendants carried out the contract."

The factual basis for the argument raised is not developed systematically in the briefs. As to those events which contributed to a mutual unwillingness to perform the contract, we are compelled to reconstruct them piecemeal from the briefs, the opinion of the trial judge, and such portions of the testimony the appellant has seen fit to submit. It appears that the eventual collapse of negotiations had its genesis in marital difficulties between the plaintiffs experienced in the summer of 1957. Apparently because of this, plaintiffs instructed their attorney that they would like to get out of the agreement of sale. The attorney in turn informed defendant's sales agent, Irving Gitomer, that there were "certain problems here," and that plaintiffs would like "to get the money back." Mr. Gitomer testified that he spoke with plaintiffs' attorney on at least three occasions during July and August of 1957. In one such conversation, the attorney told him the Wolfs were ready, willing and able to purchase the home, even if the terms were cash, but, as Mr. Gitomer testified:

[T]his conversation was coupled with the fact that they were reluctant to do it, but, if they had to do it, they would go through with the sale, and that a subsequent resale would be arranged to a purchaser who would be undesirable in our tract, and that we would not be happy with the results.

Martin Field had but one telephone conversation with plaintiffs' attorney, which was in the second week of September. The two discussed the possibility of a settlement, Field agreeing to honor the request for cancellation if defendant were allowed to retain $1,000 of the $2,450 deposit. Field testified as to what then ensued:

> [H]e reiterated in very strong and clear terms that if we did not accept his offer [of $450] it would be the sorriest move that I ever made in my building career. I accepted it as a threat, and I felt that at this point it was impossible to go ahead and continue with this thing. The threat was made in the terms that, "It's all right. If you are going to force us — you have got us over a barrel, and, if you are going to force us to make this settlement, we will make the settlement, but it will be the last settlement that you'll ever make, and it will be the last tract that you will ever build in New Jersey, and it will be the last house that you will sell in this tract," and he continued, he named a few of the attorneys who lived in the tract, and said, "Don't have the fellows who live in your tract tell me I shouldn't do it. It doesn't make any difference to me. I'm telling you what I'm going to do. I'm going to do it, and it will be the sorriest thing that you have ever done." At this point, although I had offered to refund $1,450.00, it became apparent that he was using this as leverage to drive us down to the $450.00 figure, and I told him no, that we wouldn't do it, and that's where the thing was left.

The first question asked of Field on cross-examination was:

> Despite this conversation of which you speak, Mr. Field, you never notified the people to come to a settlement or closing of this thing, did you?

He replied:

> I wasn't going to make a closing after someone threatened to ruin my building career.

Subsequently, by letter of December 30, 1957, the builder's counsel advised the attorney that by reason of plaintiffs' "material breach" of the contract, it had become "null and void" and that defendant would retain the down payment. The letter assigned as the cause of termination, "among other reasons," plaintiffs' failure to make the second payment. At the oral argument defense counsel, who had prepared this letter for the builder, stated that he had advisedly used the phrase "among other reasons" because he did not deem it discreet to make written reference to the threat that had actually been made and to which Field testified.

Based upon this letter, which plaintiffs maintain constituted the first breach of contract, suit was instituted for the recovery of the deposit.

We have already stated the basis upon which the County Court entered judgment in favor of the plaintiffs. But contrary to the assertion in plaintiffs' brief that the court found as a fact that the builder's refusal to consummate the sale was not justified by any threats, we do not read the opinion below as reaching any express determination on whether the threats, assuming they were made, justified the builder in declaring a breach and refusing further performance. The court cited what it called "the so called threat" — not in relation to whether there existed any justification for the builder's course of conduct, but rather to indicate that the builder was admittedly unwilling to perform under the contract and therefore would not be heard to contend plaintiffs should have made the second payment; the question of justification for the builder's action in rescinding seems not to have been adjudged. Moreover, even if the opinion is to be construed as containing an implied determination on the issue, we do not conceive that such would be a finding of fact, as distinguished from the determination of a legal issue. Whether duress exists in a particular transaction is generally a matter of fact, but what in given circumstances will constitute duress is a matter of law. Accordingly, the scope of appellate inquiry as to the correctness of the trial result is not so limited as plaintiffs suggest.

Duress doctrine

It is clear that where one party to a contract, by prevention or hindrance, makes it impossible for the other to carry out the terms thereof, the latter may regard the contract as breached and recover his damages thereunder from the first party. It is also clear that if the performance is prevented by physical threats, the threatened party may desist from performing, treat the contract as breached, and recover damages. He need not seek police protection or a judicial order to shield him in his performance of the contract. The builder directs our attention to [*Kroop v. Scala*, 5 N.J. Misc. 89 (Sup. Ct. 1927)] in particular. There a house owner had threatened a painting contractor that "if he went into the house to work he would cut his head off." 5 N.J. Misc. at page 90. The court held the contractor was entitled to terminate the contract and to recover his profits; he was not obliged to run the risk that the owner would carry out his threats. Defendant urges that, except for the degree of sophistication, there is no real difference between a threat to cut one's head off, there, and a threat to cut one's business head off, here. Plaintiffs contend, however, that threats to do bodily injury involve an obviously distinguishable form of coercion and that the present case is not one in which a party has physically prevented the other from carrying out the terms of a contract. We readily assent to the latter part of this argument; defendant was not physically prevented from enforcing the contract. But a distinction depending on the kind of pressure exerted carries little weight. "[D]uress is tested, not by the nature of the threats, but rather by the state of mind induced thereby in the victim." Rubenstein v. Rubenstein, 20 N.J. 359, 368 (1956). And in the present case, when plaintiffs' attorney threatened the builder that he would be ruined if the Wolfs were to be held to the bargain, the impress was the same as if physical pressure had been exerted. In the light of the *Rubenstein* case, it is significant, and perhaps crucially so, that defendant was as effectively prevented from forcing the Wolfs to comply with the contract as if a more immediate form of coercion had been employed.

Yet it was not indicated in the *Rubenstein* case that a party is to be relieved of the consequences of his action in all instances where the pressure used has had its designed effect, in all cases where he has been deprived of the exercise of his free will and constrained by the other to act contrary to his inclination and best interests. So much is evident from the court's qualification that "the pressure must be wrongful, and not all pressure is wrongful." 20 N.J. at page 367. It is also evident from the reference to 5 Williston, *Contracts* (Rev. ed. 1937), §§ 1606, 1607, pp. 4500, 4503. That authority, in language more nearly appropriate to the facts here, states:

Save under exceptional circumstances, the threatened act must be wrongful; it is not enough that the person obtaining the benefit threatened intentionally to injure the business, provided his threatened act was legal; and certainly there is no broad doctrine forbidding a person from taking advantage of the adversity of another to drive a hard bargain.

In this regard, plaintiffs assert that, once they bought the house, they had a legal right to sell to whomever they wished. They rely on the familiar general rule to the effect that a threat to do what one has a legal right to do does not constitute duress. That proposition, however, is not an entirely correct statement of the law of duress as it has developed in this jurisdiction. Under the modern view, acts or threats cannot constitute duress unless they are wrongful; but a threat may be wrongful even though the act threatened is lawful. We have come to deal, in terms of the business compulsion doctrine, with acts and threats that are wrongful, not necessarily in a legal, but in a moral or equitable sense. The leading case in this State on the subject of moral duress is Miller v. Eisele, 111 N.J.L. 268, 275-276 (E. & A. 1933), where the court quoted approvingly the definition of duress set forth in the Restatement, Contracts, § 492(g), p. 94:

> Acts or threats cannot constitute duress unless they are wrongful, even though they exert such pressure as to preclude the exercise of free judgment. But acts may be wrongful within the meaning of this rule though they are not criminal or tortious or in violation of a contractual duty. Just as acts contracted for may be against public policy and the contract vitiated for that reason, though the law imposes no penalty for doing them, so acts that involve abuse of legal remedies or that are wrongful in a moral sense, if made use of as a means of causing fear vitiate a transaction induced by that fear, though they may not in themselves be legal wrongs.

Further instructive is the decision in Hochman v. Zigler's, Inc., 139 N.J. Eq. 139, 143 (Ch. 1946). In that case, when the lease of a small businessman expired, the lessor refused to renew. The lessor said, however, that he would lease to a purchaser of the business if the tenant could find one. The tenant proceeded to find a buyer who agreed to pay $7,800, but the lessor refused to execute a lease with the buyer unless the tenant paid over to him $3,500 of the purchase price. The tenant, whose business was worth but a mere $500 if forced to liquidate, succumbed to the lessor's pressure. Notwithstanding that the defendant-lessor had the undoubted legal right to refuse to execute a lease, the court concluded that any defense on this ground was but a "mere legalism." The lessor was "compelled to disgorge," the court stating:

> Judgment whether the threatened action is wrongful or not is colored by the object of the threat. If the threat is made to induce the opposite party to do only what is reasonable, the court is apt to consider the threatened action not wrongful unless it is actionable in itself. But if the threat is made for an outrageous purpose, a more critical standard is applied to the threatened action.

The sale of a development home to an "undesirable purchaser" is, of course, a perfectly legal act regardless of any adverse effect it may have on the fortunes of the developer's enterprise. But where a party for purely malicious and unconscionable motives threatens to resell such a home to a purchaser, specially selected because he would be undesirable, for the sole purpose of injuring the builder's business, fundamental fairness requires the conclusion that his conduct in making this threat be deemed "wrongful," as the term is used in the law of duress. In our judgment, wrongful pressure was brought to bear on the defendant; he was thereby compelled to forego the right to hold plaintiffs to the contract they voluntarily signed.

As we noted above, if one party prevents another from performing a contract, the latter may treat the contract as breached, and recover damages. There is no reason why, in the application of this rule, economic or moral duress should not be treated as the equivalent of physical duress. We therefore hold that if the threats were in fact made and if the defendant actually believed that they would be carried out, and Field's will was thereby overborne, defendant was justified in treating the contract as breached and is entitled to recover whatever damages resulted therefrom.

We have decided that the interests of justice call for a remand of this case to the County Court. This disposition is made necessary by the circumstance that the record on appeal is somewhat obscure in several respects, now to be discussed. There is first the question as to whether the trial judge gave credence to the testimony of defendant's representatives concerning the making of the threats by plaintiffs' attorney. The opinion of the court makes reference to a "so called threat," but this terminology does not clearly make known what the actual findings of the trial judge were in this respect. This important factual issue should not be permitted to remain in doubt. Attention should also be directed to the question of whether or not the defendant's will was really overborne; that is, whether Field actually believed plaintiffs' attorney would carry out his threat and whether Field was actually fearful of the result.

The trial judge may also want to explore just what was meant by the use of the words "among other reasons" in the letter which the builder's counsel wrote plaintiffs' attorney on December 30, 1957 advising that there had been a "material breach" of the contract rendering it "null and void."

Moreover, should the trial judge decide in defendant's favor on the issue of actual duress, there remains for adjudication the actual amount by which defendant was damaged by reason of plaintiffs' breach. Although the agreement of sale provides for liquidated damages, such provision is operative only upon the contingency that the buyer failed to make additional payments or failed to make settlement, neither of which, as we have seen, is the gravamen of the defense. It will therefore be necessary for the court, upon remand, to determine, from the present record if it can, whatever damages defendant sustained as a result of plaintiffs' breach. In making these determinations, the trial judge may find useful the complete transcript of the testimony, which, as noted, has not been submitted on appeal; or he may depend upon his own recollection of the evidence, including the demeanor of the witnesses who testified. We leave to his discretion whether the taking of additional testimony is necessary.

The judgment is remanded for further proceedings not inconsistent with this opinion.

AUSTIN INSTRUMENT, INC. v. LORAL CORP.
Court of Appeals of New York
29 N.Y.2d 124, 324 N.Y.S.2d 22, 272 N.E.2d 533 (1971)

FULD, J.

The defendant, Loral Corporation, seeks to recover payment for goods delivered under a contract which it had with plaintiff Austin Instrument, Inc., on the ground that the evidence establishes, as a matter of law, that it was forced to agree to an increase in price on the items in question under circumstances amounting to economic duress.

In July of 1965, Loral was awarded a $6,000,000 contract by the Navy for the production of radar sets. The contract contained a schedule of deliveries, a liquidated damages clause applying to late deliveries and a cancellation clause in case of default by Loral. The latter thereupon solicited bids for some 40 precision gear components needed to produce the radar sets, and awarded Austin a subcontract to supply 23 such parts. That party commenced delivery in early 1966.

In May, 1966, Loral was awarded a second Navy contract for the production of more radar sets and again went about soliciting bids. Austin bid on all 40 gear components but, on July 15, a representative from Loral informed Austin's president, Mr. Krauss, that his company would be awarded the subcontract only for those items on which it was low bidder. The Austin officer refused to accept an order for less than all 40 of the gear parts and on the next day he told Loral that Austin would cease deliveries of the parts due under the existing subcontract unless Loral consented to substantial increases in the prices provided for by that agreement — both retroactively for parts already delivered and prospectively on those not yet shipped — and placed with Austin the order for all 40 parts needed under Loral's second Navy contract. Shortly thereafter, Austin did, indeed, stop delivery. After contacting 10 manufacturers of precision gears and finding none who could produce the parts in time to meet its commitments to the Navy,[2] Loral acceded to Austin's demands; in a letter dated July 22, Loral wrote to Austin that "We have feverishly surveyed other sources of supply and find that because of the prevailing military exigencies, were they to start from scratch as would have to be the case, they could not even remotely begin to deliver on time to meet the delivery requirements established by the Government. . . . Accordingly, we are left with no choice or alternative but to meet your conditions."

Loral thereupon consented to the price increases insisted upon by Austin under the first subcontract and the latter was awarded a second subcontract making it the supplier of all 40 gear parts for Loral's second contract with the Navy.[3] Although Austin was granted until September to resume deliveries, Loral did, in fact, receive parts in August and was able to produce the radar sets in time to meet its commitments to the Navy on both contracts. After Austin's last delivery under the

---

[2] [1] The best reply Loral received was from a vendor who stated he could commence deliveries sometime in October.

[3] [2] Loral makes no claim in this action on the second subcontract.

second subcontract in July, 1967, Loral notified it of its intention to seek recovery of the price increases.

On September 15, 1967, Austin instituted this action against Loral to recover an amount in excess of $17,750 which was still due on the second subcontract. On the same day, Loral commenced an action against Austin claiming damages of some $22,250 — the aggregate of the price increases under the first subcontract — on the ground of economic duress. The two actions were consolidated and, following a trial, Austin was awarded the sum it requested and Loral's complaint against Austin was dismissed on the ground that it was not shown that "it could not have obtained the items in question from other sources in time to meet its commitment to the Navy under the first contract." A closely divided Appellate Division affirmed (35 A.D.2d 387). There was no material disagreement concerning the facts; as Justice Steuer stated in the course of his dissent below, "[the] facts are virtually undisputed, nor is there any serious question of law. The difficulty lies in the application of the law to these facts."

The applicable law is clear and, indeed, is not disputed by the parties. A contract is voidable on the ground of duress when it is established that the party making the claim was forced to agree to it by means of a wrongful threat precluding the exercise of his free will. The existence of economic duress or business compulsion is demonstrated by proof that "immediate possession of needful goods is threatened" (Mercury Mach. Importing Corp. v. City of New York, 3 N.Y.2d 418, 425) or, more particularly, in cases such as the one before us, by proof that one party to a contract has threatened to breach the agreement by withholding goods unless the other party agrees to some further demand. However, a mere threat by one party to breach the contract by not delivering the required items, though wrongful, does not in itself constitute economic duress. It must also appear that the threatened party could not obtain the goods from another source of supply and that the ordinary remedy of an action for breach of contract would not be adequate. We find without any support in the record the conclusion reached by the courts below that Loral failed to establish that it was the victim of economic duress. On the contrary, the evidence makes out a classic case, as a matter of law, of such duress.

It is manifest that Austin's threat — to stop deliveries unless the prices were increased — deprived Loral of its free will. As bearing on this, Loral's relationship with the Government is most significant. As mentioned above, its contract called for staggered monthly deliveries of the radar sets, with clauses calling for liquidated damages and possible cancellation on default. Because of its production schedule, Loral was, in July, 1966, concerned with meeting its delivery requirements in September, October and November, and it was for the sets to be delivered in those months that the withheld gears were needed. Loral had to plan ahead, and the substantial liquidated damages for which it would be liable, plus the threat of default, were genuine possibilities. Moreover, Loral did a substantial portion of its business with the Government, and it feared that a failure to deliver as agreed upon would jeopardize its chances for future contracts. These genuine concerns do not merit the label "self-imposed, undisclosed and subjective" which the Appellate Division majority placed upon them. It was perfectly reasonable for Loral, or any other party similarly placed, to consider itself in an emergency, duress situation.

Austin, however, claims that the fact that Loral extended its time to resume deliveries until September negates its alleged dire need for the parts. A Loral official testified on this point that Austin's president told him he could deliver some parts in August and that the extension of deliveries was a formality. In any event, the parts necessary for production of the radar sets to be delivered in September were delivered to Loral on September 1, and the parts needed for the October schedule were delivered in late August and early September. Even so, Loral had to "work . . . around the clock" to meet its commitments. Considering that the best offer Loral received from the other vendors it contacted was commencement of delivery sometime in October, which, as the record shows, would have made it late in its deliveries to the Navy in both September and October, Loral's claim that it had no choice but to accede to Austin's demands is conclusively demonstrated.

We find unconvincing Austin's contention that Loral, in order to meet its burden, should have contacted the Government and asked for an extension of its delivery dates so as to enable it to purchase the parts from another vendor. Aside from the consideration that Loral was anxious to perform well in the Government's eyes, it could not be sure when it would obtain enough parts from a substitute vendor to meet its commitments. The only promise which it received from the companies it contacted was for commencement of deliveries, not full supply, and, with vendor delay common in this field, it would have been nearly impossible to know the length of the extension it should request. It must be remembered that Loral was producing a needed item of military hardware. Moreover, there is authority for Loral's position that nonperformance by a subcontractor is not an excuse for default in the main contract. In light of all this, Loral's claim should not be held insufficiently supported because it did not request an extension from the Government. Loral, as indicated above, also had the burden of demonstrating that it could not obtain the parts elsewhere within a reasonable time, and there can be no doubt that it met this burden. The 10 manufacturers whom Loral contacted comprised its entire list of "approved vendors" for precision gears, and none was able to commence delivery soon enough.[4] As Loral was producing a highly sophisticated item of military machinery requiring parts made to the strictest engineering standards, it would be unreasonable to hold that Loral should have gone to other vendors, with whom it was either unfamiliar or dissatisfied, to procure the needed parts. As Justice Steuer noted in his dissent, Loral "contacted all the manufacturers whom it believed capable of making these parts" (35 A.D.2d, at p. 393), and this was all the law requires.

It is hardly necessary to add that Loral's normal legal remedy of accepting Austin's breach of the contract and then suing for damages would have been inadequate under the circumstances, as Loral would still have had to obtain the gears elsewhere with all the concomitant consequences mentioned above. In other words, Loral actually had no choice, when the prices were raised by Austin, except to take the gears at the "coerced" prices and then sue to get the excess back.

Austin's final argument is that Loral, even if it did enter into the contract under duress, lost any rights it had to a refund of money by waiting until July, 1967, long

---

[4] [6] Loral, as do many manufacturers, maintains a list of "approved vendors," that is, vendors whose products, facilities, techniques and performance have been inspected and found satisfactory.

after the termination date of the contract, to disaffirm it. It is true that one who would recover moneys allegedly paid under duress must act promptly to make his claim known. In this case, Loral delayed making its demand for a refund until three days after Austin's last delivery on the second subcontract. Loral's reason — for waiting until that time — is that it feared another stoppage of deliveries which would again put it in an untenable situation. Considering Austin's conduct in the past, this was perfectly reasonable, as the possibility of an application by Austin of further business compulsion still existed until all of the parts were delivered.

In sum, the record before us demonstrates that Loral agreed to the price increases in consequence of the economic duress employed by Austin. Accordingly, the matter should be remanded to the trial court for a computation of its damages. The order appealed from should be modified, with costs, by reversing so much thereof as affirms the dismissal of defendant Loral Corporation's claim and, except as so modified, affirmed.

NOTES

1. ***Questions on* Wolf *and* Austin.** In *Wolf* and *Austin*, the promisees made explicit threats to induce specific promises. In *Wolf*, in order to induce Marlton to release them from their purchase agreement, the Wolfs threatened to resell their house to an "undesirable purchaser" and thereby ruin Marlton's business. In *Austin*, in order to induce Loral to increase the price it paid under its current contract and to award Austin its second contract, Austin threatened Loral with breach of their current contract.[5] Take both cases one element at a time.

First, were the threats improper? Neither threat appears to be illegal. As the *Wolf* court points out, it is perfectly legal for the Wolfs to sell their property to any buyer. In *Austin*, the breach threatened is not *illegal* — it simply triggers Loral's right to compensation. Or is it the promisee's motives for making the threat, rather than the threatened act itself, that makes the threat improper?

Consider the following hypothetical: Tower Records offers to purchase Plan 9 Records. If Plan 9 refuses to sell, Tower threatens to build one of its own stores directly adjacent to each of Plan 9's stores. What relevant differences, if any, do you see between the threats made by the Wolfs and Austin, and the threat made by Tower Records?

Second, did the threats induce the promises? In *Wolf*, Marlton does not claim its initial promise was induced by duress. Rather, we should ask whether Marlton's decision to treat the Wolfs as having breached their agreement was induced by the Wolfs' threat. What does the *Wolf* court believe? In *Austin*, the question is whether Loral's acquiescence to increase the price it paid under its first agreement with Austin and to award Austin its second contract was induced by Austin's threats. What does the *Austin* court believe and why?

Third, were Marlton's and Loral's decisions *reasonably* induced by the threats of their promisees? Should we use a subjective or objective standard to answer this

---

[5] For a detailed history of *Austin v. Loral*, see Meredith R. Miller, *Revisiting* Austin v. Loral: *A Study in Economic Duress, Contract Modification and Framing*, 2 HASTINGS BUS. L.J. 357 (2006).

question? On the subjective standard, do you believe that Marlton and Loral *in fact* believed their contracting partners would carry out their threats? On the objective standard, even if they actually believed the threats would be carried out, would a reasonable person have believed that as well? Do you see an analogy between Loral's plight and Alaska Packer's plight in *Alaska Packers' Ass'n v. Domenico,* Chapter 4? Does it make any difference that Loral was relying on Austin's performance to meet its obligations with the government to manufacture military equipment? Is there a benign story that you could tell to justify Austin's behavior?

Finally, consider the outcome in *Austin.* In essence, the remedy Loral received was specific performance, here by means of self-help. Do Austin's services satisfy the uniqueness standard set forth in UCC § 2-716 (see discussion in Chapter 1, *supra*)? Whether or not the outcome for Loral individually is viewed as fair, is self-help something courts should encourage in such circumstances? Are there contractual arrangements you can imagine that would allow for expedient resolutions of such disputes without resorting to self-help and a subsequent lawsuit? Consider, for example, the following argument: *Loral should not be allowed to recover from Austin by claiming duress since it could have taken reasonable steps prior to contracting that would have limited Austin's ability to extract the subsequent promise. One way to reduce the risk of a subsequent "holdup" is to multi-source; that is, to have several subcontractors available to respond to bids such as this. An alternative solution is to draft the contract with a "time is of the essence" clause that would make it clear that Austin would be subject to significant liquidated damages for breach or delay. In sum, undoing commercial contracts on the grounds of duress is generally a bad idea. When it is not too hard for the "victim" to have protected itself at the outset, we should be very reluctant to bail it out.* Do you agree?

2. *The Restatement on Threats and Duress.* The clearest factual predicate for the defense of duress is physical coercion that induces a promise. The Restatement (Second) § 174 defines this classic basis for the duress defense.

Wolf and *Loral*, however, each raise the question of when a *threat*, as opposed to actual physical coercion, grounds the duress defense. The Restatement (Second) also defines the conditions under which a threat renders a contract voidable and what constitutes an improper threat. Begin by studying §§ 175 and 176 and then consider the Restatement's comment:

> *Comment* to § 175:
>
> a. *Improper threat.* The essence of the type of duress dealt with in this Section is inducement by an improper threat. The threat may be expressed in words or it may be inferred from words or other conduct. Past events often import a threat. Thus, if one person strikes or imprisons another, the conduct may amount to duress because of the threat of further blows or continued imprisonment that is implied. Courts originally restricted duress to threats involving loss of life, mayhem or imprisonment, but these restrictions have been greatly relaxed and, in order to constitute duress, the threat need only be improper within the rule stated in § 176.

b. *No reasonable alternative.* A threat, even if improper, does not amount to duress if the victim has a reasonable alternative to succumbing and fails to take advantage of it. It is sometimes said that the threat must arouse such fear as precludes a party from exercising free will and judgment or that it must be such as would induce assent on the part of a brave man or a man of ordinary firmness. The rule stated in this Section omits any such requirement because of its vagueness and impracticability. It is enough if the threat actually induces assent on the part of one who has no reasonable alternative. The alternative may take the form of a legal remedy. For example, the threat of commencing an ordinary civil action to enforce a claim to money may be improper. However, it does not usually amount to duress because the victim can assert his rights in the threatened action, and this is ordinarily a reasonable alternative to succumbing to the threat, making the proposed contract, and then asserting his rights in a later civil action.

In a nutshell, the Restatement requires *an improper threat that reasonably induces assent.* In evaluating a duress defense, therefore, a court must confirm that three essential elements are present: (1) an "improper" threat made to the promisor, (2) inducement of the promise by that threat, and, if such inducement is found, (3) reasonable inducement. Thus, even if a promisor was induced to make a promise by an improper threat, the defense of duress will not lie unless the threat eliminated any reasonable alternatives to making the promise. But how should courts determine whether the victim of the threat was left with a reasonable alternative? Should they use a "reasonable person" standard, or should they take into account the particular characteristics of the victim?

3. ***Defining "Reasonable Person."*** The Louisiana Court of Appeals, First Division, faced this issue in *Lewis v. Lewis*, 387 So. 2d 1206 (La. Ct. App. 1980). In that case, Robert Lewis sought to divorce his wife, Edna Ann. The parties had signed a community property agreement shortly after separating, but at the divorce hearing Edna Ann sought to invalidate the agreement, claiming Robert had threatened "to take care of her" if she did not sign it. Two articles of the Louisiana Civil Code governed the situation. Articles 1850 and 1851 stated:

> Consent to a contract is void if it be produced by violence or threats, and the contract is invalid. . . . It is not every degree of violence or every kind of threat that will invalidate a contract; they must be such as would naturally operate on a person of ordinary firmness, and inspire a just fear of great injury to person, reputation or fortune. The age, sex, state of health, temper and disposition of the party, and other circumstances calculated to give greater or less effect to the violence or threats, must be taken into consideration.

The Court of Appeals quickly pointed out that the statute contained both an objective standard and a subjective standard. The court wrote:

> Despite the apparently inconsistent standards in Article 1851, our goal is to attempt to reconcile the standards without emasculating either one. The redactors of the code probably realized that applying an objective standard

to all situations could result in an injustice to those individuals who sincerely fear they will suffer great harm if they do not consent to an obligation, but whose fear would not be shared by a person of ordinary firmness. This may be the reason the redactors added the subjective qualities to the objective standard of Article 1851. On the other hand, the redactors probably felt that a defense based on threats or violence should not be taken lightly because of the relative ease with which a person can claim he or she has been forced into agreeing to a contract. This may have been the reason for giving Article 1851 its predominantly objective flavor. As a compromise, the redactors adopted both standards, and a proper interpretation of this Article must necessarily focus on objective and subjective characteristics. This can be done by first determining the subjective characteristics of the individual who claims he or she was forced by violence or threats into agreeing to a contract and then deciding whether other reasonable persons with the same subjective characteristics would have felt forced into signing the contract under the same type of threat or violence.

In the case at bar, the wife, whose age was not in the record, was separated from her husband on the grounds of cruel treatment. A meager amount of evidence indicated some physical cruelty was involved. At the time she signed the agreement, the wife was living in Shreveport many miles away from her husband. She admitted she was in fairly dire need of money. The wife and two witnesses testified that the husband threatened to "take care of" the wife if she failed to sign the community property settlement. But the same two witnesses admitted either that the threats were not made in connection with the community property settlement or that the threats were made during a normal husband-wife argument in the presence of other persons. And even the wife could not testify to any degree of certainty that she felt her husband would carry out his threats. At one point in her testimony, Mrs. Lewis claims that it was not necessarily the fear of violence but the lack of money which caused her to sign the documents. As noted previously, there is no evidence in the record to show that Mrs. Lewis was unfairly treated in the settlement agreements. We find that, under this set of circumstances, a reasonable person with the subjective characteristics of Mrs. Lewis would not have felt forced by violence of threats into signing the community property settlement upon which this suit is based. Mrs. Lewis has presented no evidence that the settlement was lesionary. In fact, she abandoned such a claim at trial. Her basic complaint, it seems, is that she signed the settlement because she was in need of money. The court in *Wilson*, under circumstances of duress which seem much more severe than those in this case, found that strong economic duress, by itself, was insufficient to vitiate the consent given to an otherwise valid contract. We feel the same rule must be applied in the case of the community property settlement between the husband and the wife.

Therefore, for the above and foregoing reasons, the decision of the trial court is reversed and the defendant-wife's claim is dismissed. The appellee will pay the costs of this appeal.

Id. at 1210.

The court purports to be applying a standard that attaches the subjective characteristics of Mrs. Lewis to the hypothetical reasonable person. To what extent is such an approach comprehensible? Consider whether you think it would be possible for a person with *all* of the subjective characteristics of Mrs. Lewis to behave differently than Mrs. Lewis?

4. *"Circumstantial" Economic Duress.* Suppose there is an unusually heavy snow in the New York City area. Two incidents are reported.

a. A local drug store charged $16.50 for a snow shovel that sold for $9.95 before the snow. A Columbia University professor bought one of the shovels and charged it to his VISA card. When he heard that the store had raised the price on account of the snow, he got mad and told the bank not to honor the charge.

b. Lester has a four-wheel drive Jeep with a plow on the front. He got a call from Jerry, who wanted Lester to use the Jeep to clear his quarter-mile long driveway. When Lester got to the house he found that Jerry's wife, Sandra, had just gone into labor and that a large pine tree, weakened by the weight of the snow, had taken down Jerry's phone line. Unless Lester dug him out, there was no way that Jerry could get either of their Porsche 928s out and thus get Sandra to the hospital. Lester, who doesn't have much money but knows an opportunity when it smacks him in the face, charged Jerry $300 to clear the drive. Ordinarily, he would have charged $50. Unfortunately, Jerry paid Lester by check, and he has now stopped payment on it.

Is either of these contracts voidable on account of duress? Consider *Chouinard v. Chouinard*, 568 F.2d 430 (5th Cir. 1978). In that case, Fred, the President and part owner of a security company, had through his own mismanagement placed the company in dire financial straits. In order to make payroll, Fred sought a loan from Heller, a commercial lender. Heller was aware of an ongoing ownership dispute between Fred and two co-owners, Ed and Al, and refused to grant the loan until the dispute was resolved. In order to get the loan, Fred bought out Ed's and Al's stakes in the company at a high price. The court said:

> A contract is voidable where undue or unjust advantage has been taken of a person's economic necessity or distress to coerce him into making the agreement. However, a duress claim of this nature must be based on the acts or conduct of the opposite party and not merely on the necessities of the purported victim. Thus, the mere fact that a person enters into a contract as a result of the pressure of business circumstances, financial embarrassment, or economic necessity is not sufficient. Unless wrongful or unlawful pressure is applied, there is no business compulsion or economic duress, and such a claim cannot be predicated on a demand which is lawful or on the insistence of a legal right.

> In the instant case, it is clear that the financial distress in which Fred found himself and his company was of his own making. He admitted that he had made "foolish" business judgments that had put the company in a bind regarding its cash flow. Moreover, at that point the banks with whom the company had been dealing withdrew their "line of credit" financing. Ed and

Al, who had nothing to do with the day-to-day operation of the company, obviously were not responsible for this sad state of affairs, and there is no contention that they ever discussed the situation with Heller.

While there is ample evidence of economic necessity and financial peril, neither the "threat of considerable financial loss" nor "impending bankruptcy" establish economic duress. Such economic stress must be attributable to the party against whom duress is alleged. "Mere hard bargaining positions, if lawful, and the press of financial circumstances, not caused by the [party against whom the contract is sought to be voided], will not be deemed duress." *Business Incentives Co. v. Sony Corp. of America*, 397 F. Supp. 63, 69 (S.D.N.Y. 1975). The only possible claim of duress is that Ed and Al, recognizing the weakened state of the company, seized that opportunity to settle the long-standing dispute regarding stock ownership. Because duress may not be implied merely from the making of a hard bargain, the question becomes whether the conduct of Ed and Al was wrongful. The law in Georgia and other jurisdictions makes clear that it was not, for the two men were merely asserting a legal right, i.e., their right to a certain share of the stock in the company. Fred admitted that Ed and Al were shareholders in the company, and the long-standing dispute was over the percentage of the company each owned. Thus, while there is no doubt that Fred was between the proverbial rock and a hard place, it is clear that his own actions put him there and that Ed and Al merely took advantage of the situation to insist upon settlement of the intra familial stock squabble.

We conclude, therefore, that there is simply no duress shown on this record, for one crucial element is missing: a wrongful act by the defendants to create and take advantage of an untenable situation. Ed and Al had nothing to do with the financial quagmire in which Fred found himself, and we cannot find duress simply because they refused to throw him a rope free of any "strings." Accordingly, we affirm the judgment in favor of the defendants.

Id. at 434–35. This seems to suggest that neither of the snowstorm contracts is voidable, but can the language be squared with *Austin*? Apparently not all courts agree with the test set forth in *Chouinard. See Wurtz v. Fleischman*, 89 Wis. 2d 291, 278 N.W.2d 266, 270–72 (Ct. App. 1979); *Rodziewicz v. Waffco Heavy Duty Towing*, 763 N.E. 2d 491, 493 (Ind. Ct. App. 2002). In *Rodziewicz*, the court stated that a contract for $4,070 for towing a truck that had broken down on the highway and for which the normal charge would be about $275 would not be enforceable on grounds of unconscionability. How would you distinguish a case like *Rodziewicz* from *Batsakis v. Demotsis* (*see* Chapter 2)?

5. *Admiralty Law's Solution to the Problem of "Circumstantial" Duress: Post v. Jones.* Perhaps the most celebrated duress case in American jurisprudence arose from the plight of a 19th century whaling ship, the *Richmond*. In *Post v. Jones*, 60 U.S. (19 How.) 150 (1857), the plaintiff's ship (the *Richmond*) ran aground in the Arctic Ocean towards the end of a three-year whaling voyage. Stranded on an island five thousand miles from the nearest port of safety and with the approaching Arctic winter certain to make the passage home unnavigable within weeks, the only hope of survival for the crew and cargo of the *Richmond* was rescue by another whaling ship. Within days, three whaling ships — the *Frith*, the *Panama*, and the *Junior* — spotted the wrecked ship, took the *Richmond's* crew on board, and agreed to salvage the *Richmond's* whale oil provided that it was put up for auction. At the auction (which took place on the ships), the masters of the three ships purchased as much oil as each needed at a price far below the prevailing price of whale oil at any port of safety (the *Frith* paid $1 per barrel and the other ships paid 75 cents per barrel). After returning to New England, the owners of the *Richmond* claimed that the sale was made under duress and sued to nullify the transaction. The Supreme Court agreed with the plaintiffs, holding that the defendant ship owners had taken advantage of their position to force an unreasonable bargain. According to the Court:

> The contrivance of an auction sale, under such circumstances, where the master of the *Richmond* was hopeless, helpless, and passive — where there was not market, no money, no competition — where one party had absolute power, and the other no choice but submission — where the vendor must take what is offered or get nothing — is a transaction which has no characteristic of a valid contract.

Id. at 159.

Instead of contract, the Court applied the admiralty law doctrine of salvage, under which any party who rescues or saves the cargo of another that is in peril is entitled to receive between one-third and one-half of the value of the cargo that is saved. The Court in *Post* employed "the most liberal allowance for salvage," to compensate the defendants for the loss they incurred by giving up the possible chance to take on a full cargo of their own oil.

Does the Court's decision adequately balance the dual concerns of encouraging the rescue of distressed cargo and preventing the extortion of parties in a weak bargaining position? While the owners of the *Frith*, the *Panama*, and the *Junior* acquired the *Richmond's* oil for a fraction of its value at a safe port, did the master of the *Richmond* receive any sort of threat? Was there any reasonable alternative available to him other than to accept the price each ship agreed to pay for the oil? If bargains such as the one in *Post* are not enforced, do you think that other ships will be as likely to salvage oil from ships in peril like the *Richmond*? Would the owner of the *Richmond* want the master of his ship to have the power to make a legally enforceable bargain for the sale of its whale oil?

6. ***Economic and Autonomy Approaches: The Potential Conflict Between Incentive Effects and Human Dignity.*** The economic justification of contract law typically focuses on the incentive effects of legal rules. In the case of duress, it asks what effect the duress doctrine will have on the future behavior of prospective promisees. If the duress doctrine allowed Sandra and Jerry (Note 4.b., *supra*) to escape their contract with Lester, and the owner of the *Richmond* to escape his contract with the ships that took on its cargo, how will people in the position of Lester and the ships behave in the future once they learn of the duress defense? That is, if everyone knows that so-called "hard bargains" will not be enforced in these circumstances (economists sometimes call such circumstances "situational monopolies"), will any bargains be made at all? Will Sandra and Jerry have no way

to get to the hospital? Will sailors and their oil be left in the islands? If you think no bargains at all will be struck in these circumstances, you might oppose the duress doctrine on that ground. After all, once the rule is announced, it would seem to make everyone worse off. At least a doctrine that leaves these agreements in force will provide individuals with the necessary incentives to avoid wasteful outcomes. Perhaps you think "soft" bargains will be struck in situational monopolies even if hard bargains are unenforceable under the duress doctrine. But is it clear, for example, that the *Frith* would have taken on the *Richmond's* oil if it had to pay significantly more per barrel?

On the other hand, an advocate of the autonomy approach might support application of the duress defense in situational monopolies even if it undermines incentives for some desirable contracts (and therefore produces social waste). On this view, allowing one person to take advantage of another's unfortunate situation, even where the former is not responsible for creating the latter's vulnerability, is inconsistent with the principle that all autonomous persons should be treated with equal dignity and respect. In the practice of indentured servitude, for example, wealthy individuals entered into agreements that bound poorer persons into their service for a specified period of years, often in return for passage from Europe to America. The abolition of these "slavery" contracts is thought to be a straightforward requirement of the principle of equal dignity and respect for autonomous persons, even though the servants entered into these agreements due to unfortunate circumstances for which their contracting partners bore no responsibility. Does this mean, however, that we should accept a duress doctrine that may leave Sandra and Jerry without transportation to the hospital, sailors stranded on an island, and whale oil wasted at sea?

7.   *Ex Ante and Ex Post Duress*

Is there a difference between situations in which duress is used to coerce a party into entering into a contract, as opposed to situations in which duress is used to coerce a party into modifying a contract? Professors Schwartz and Scott argue that courts should apply a different standard in each of these cases:

> The duress doctrine, however, is an enforcement rule that parties cannot create on their own. The law of duress applies in two contexts. Ex ante duress occurs when a party is wrongfully coerced to make a contract. Ex post duress occurs when a party is wrongfully coerced to modify an existing contract. Contract law applies the same legal standard in both cases: A contract or a modification is unenforceable if a party's consent thereto was obtained by an improper threat that left the party no reasonable alternative but to submit. Our focus here is on ex post duress, and we suggest that courts should ask a different question from those asked in ex ante duress cases. In an ex post duress case, the contact was fairly obtained and the parties could have provided for the situation that later arose had they thought about the issue. The court thus should ask whether parties with sufficient foresight would have wanted the later modification agreement to be enforceable.

Alan Schwartz & Robert E. Scott, *Contract Theory and the Limits of Contract Law,* 113 YALE L.J. 541, 566–67 (2003).

Professors Schwartz and Scott argue that parties will not want courts to enforce purely redistributional modifications, or those that create no new wealth and simply redistribute the contractual surplus among the contracting parties. On the other hand, parties will generally prefer to have courts enforce modifications that increase the contractual surplus. Are *Austin* and *Wolf* examples of ex ante or ex post duress? If either one is an example of ex post duress, how would it come out under this proposed test?

8. ***Settlement Agreements and Duress.*** Most lawsuits are settled out of court, an outcome that is generally preferable to both parties. While potentially advantageous to both parties, settlements can, in certain circumstances, be induced by duress, as the court found in *Totem Marine Tug & Barge v. Alyeska Pipeline Serv. Co.*, 584 P.2d 15 (Alaska 1978). Totem, a shipping company, settled its contract claims against Alyeska, then later sought to void the settlement agreement and recover further compensation. In ruling for Totem, the court wrote:

> Totem has alleged that Alyeska deliberately withheld payment of an acknowledged debt, knowing that Totem had no choice but to accept an inadequate sum in settlement of that debt; that Totem was faced with impending bankruptcy; that Totem was unable to meet its pressing debts other than by accepting the immediate cash payment offered by Alyeska; and that through necessity, Totem thus involuntarily accepted an inadequate settlement offer from Alyeska and executed a release of all claims under the contract. If the release was in fact executed under these circumstances, we think that under the legal principles discussed above this would constitute the type of wrongful conduct and lack of alternatives that would render the release voidable by Totem on the ground of economic duress.

Id. at 23–24.

How often are economic pressures at work in inducing settlement agreements? What effect does permitting duress claims for settlements have on such agreements?

C. FRAUD

Contract law enforces only voluntary promises made by informed, mentally competent adults. The preceding section examined the first of these elements — the duress doctrine, which selects for enforcement only those bargains not affected by improper coercion. In this section, we examine those doctrines designed to insure that only promises made by informed individuals are enforced. Contract law polices the bargain process so to increase the probability that the promises exchanged by contractual partners are reasonably informed. But instead of asking whether a promisor was fully apprised of all the relevant information bearing on her promise, the law seeks to insure that the bargaining process did not impair the promisor's ability to acquire the relevant information.

The law starts with the presumption that promisors can and will look out for their own interests — promisors are charged with the responsibility of informing themselves before making their promise. Ordinarily, therefore, a promisor's ignorance about the nature or consequences of her promise will not excuse her obligation to perform her promise. In this sense, contract law begins with the rule of "caveat emptor." But when a contracting party takes affirmative measures that she knew, or should have known, would lead the other to reach erroneous conclusions regarding material issues bearing on the transaction, the law will not enforce the promise. Indeed, contract law goes even farther than this. The contract doctrines we consider here range from prohibitions against intentional misrepresentation and intentional concealment to negligent misrepresentation and failure to disclose.

The rationale for prohibiting intentional misrepresentation and concealment appear to be obvious: Such behavior serves no socially productive purpose and only undermines the autonomy and efficiency of transactions. Yet the doctrines that have evolved to prevent such conduct are far from straightforward. For example, the law prohibits only intentional misrepresentations or concealment on which promisors reasonably rely. Harmless lying and lying that should not have been taken at face value do not excuse contractual liability. The negligent misrepresentation and failure to disclose doctrines raise problems of application and are more difficult to justify. Why should contract law require parties to warrant more than their sincere belief in the truth of the propositions they assert? And even if you think it reasonable for contract law to require individuals to take care that their affirmative representations are accurate, should it go further and require parties to take affirmative steps to inform their contracting partners of relevant information? As you consider these doctrines below, ask yourself what purpose they are designed to serve and how well they achieve that purpose.

We first examine willful and negligent misrepresentation. Perhaps not surprisingly, the contract rules closely parallel tort law in these areas. The elements of both willful and negligent misrepresentation are outlined in the following cases.

[1] Willful and Negligent Misrepresentation

SPIESS v. BRANDT
Supreme Court of Minnesota
230 Minn. 246, 41 N.W.2d 561 (1950)

MATSON, J.

Defendants appeal from an order denying a new trial in an action for the rescission, because of fraudulent representations, of a contract for the purchase of defendants' summer resort.

Defendants, father and son, in 1940 acquired Jameson's Wilderness Resort located 18 miles north of Hovland, Minnesota, on Lake McFarland. They continued to own and operate the resort until it was sold to plaintiffs by contract for deed December 17, 1947, for $95,000, with a down payment of $10,000 and with the principal balance of $85,000 payable as follows: $20,000 on or before February 15, 1948; $15,000 on or before April 15, 1948; $2,500 on or before July 15, 1948; $2,500 on or before October 1, 1948, and $2,500 on or before July 15 and October 1 of each year thereafter until paid in full. The contract provided that all sums paid prior to a default should be retained by the vendors as liquidated damages. Plaintiffs made the down payment of $10,000 and the $20,000 due February 15, 1948, but thereafter found themselves unable to pay the April 15 installment, with the exception of $6,000, which was not paid until May 28, 1948. The court found — and this finding is sustained by the evidence — that the $6,000 was paid after defendants had agreed that they would not then foreclose but would give plaintiffs a reasonable time to raise additional funds through the sale of an equity in a home owned by one of the plaintiffs. Ten days later, on June 7, 1948, defendants served on plaintiffs a notice of cancellation of the contract. Shortly thereafter plaintiffs, who had not at any time theretofore been represented by counsel, consulted an attorney at law. About June 19, 1948, plaintiffs brought an action to rescind the contract on the ground of fraud and misrepresentation and to restrain defendants pendente lite from further cancellation proceedings. In open court, plaintiffs made a tender of a deed and other instruments necessary for a retransfer of the real and personal property, which tender was refused by defendants. In addition to a finding that defendants had fraudulently concealed the fact that they had lost money each year, the trial court specifically found that during the negotiations and talks had between the parties prior to entering into the contract for deed defendants represented to plaintiffs:

(1)   That defendants were making good money out of the resort;

(2)   That plaintiffs could make good money out of it; and

(3)   That plaintiffs could make all future payments on the contract out of the profits.

There are further findings that said representations:

(1)   Were known by defendants to be untrue when they were made;

(2)   Were made by defendants for the purpose of deceiving and inducing plaintiffs to enter into the contract for the purchase of the property at a price clearly in excess of its real value;

(3)   Were relied upon by plaintiffs; and

(4)   Were material and were an inducing factor causing plaintiffs to enter into the contract.

The trial court also found that defendants at all times knew that plaintiffs were young and inexperienced; that they had no property; that they wished to acquire this property as a means of livelihood; and that, in order to make future payments on the contract, they would have to make them out of the profits from the resort business. Pursuant to its findings, the court ordered judgment for rescission of the contract and for a return to plaintiffs of the $36,000 which they had paid, with interest. Defendants then moved for amended findings or a new trial, and, upon denial thereof, we have this appeal.

We need consider only the first representation, namely, that defendants represented to plaintiffs that they were making good money out of the resort business. If the court's finding thereon is supported by the evidence, its order denying a new trial must be sustained, and it will be wholly unnecessary to consider the validity or factual basis of the other two representations or of the finding that defendants, when there was a duty to disclose, fraudulently concealed the material fact that they had lost money each year. It is well established that:

> A person is liable for fraud if he makes a false representation of a past or existing material fact susceptible of knowledge, knowing it to be false, or as of his own knowledge without knowing whether it is true or false, with intention to induce the person to whom it is made to act in reliance upon it, or under such circumstances that such person is justified in acting in reliance upon it, and such person is thereby deceived and induced to act in reliance upon it, to his pecuniary damage.

3 Dunnell, Dig. § 3818. A false representation as to past or present income and profits is a false representation of a past or existing material fact within the meaning of the above rule. This is particularly true where he who makes the representations knows them to be false.

There is ample evidence — although it is conflicting — to sustain the findings that defendants did misrepresent the past income and profits of the resort. We have testimony, which the court could accept as true, that plaintiff Lowell Spiess, when a price of $100,000 was asked, specifically inquired of one of the defendants how long it would take to pay off that amount out of resort profits, and he was told that it could be paid off in five operating seasons. This answer obviously involved something more than a prediction of possible future earnings, in that it would have relation to defendants' past earning experience. Reasonably, there could be no basis for the answer other than that of defendants' past experience. This is corroborated by more specific testimony when Lowell, in response to his direct inquiry, was told that defendants in 1946 "took in" $25,400 with expenses of $6,000. This would indicate net earnings of $19,400 for 1946, which on a five-year basis would practically amount to the asking price of $100,000. One of the defendants admitted that he had stated that the gross income for 1947 was around $19,000. The undisputed facts are that defendants had lost money every year of their operation, inclusive of the years 1946 and 1947, which were generally conceded to have been the most prosperous years in the history of Minnesota's resort business. Defendants also told Lowell Spiess that they were making "good money," and the making of "good money" does not in any man's language — when addressed to persons seriously considering the purchase of a business — square with an undisputed record of substantial loss year after year. We are not here dealing with the mere puff talk of an enthusiastic salesman, but with a statement of facts by one who is possessed of the facts to one to whom the facts are not readily available.[6]

Defendants' representations of making "good money" and of having taken in $25,400 in 1946 with expenses of $6,000 were made without qualification and were made as of the defendants' own knowledge. An unqualified affirmation amounts to an affirmation as of one's own knowledge. Whether the representations were made innocently or knowingly, they would equally operate as a fraud upon plaintiffs when

---

[6] [3] It has been held that, where the vendee after taking possession of a business at once experiences a business volume sharply below that represented to have been enjoyed by the vendor, an inference may be drawn that vendor's representation was false in that an established business will not at once seriously diminish without cause. Forman v. Hamilburg, 300 Mass. 138.

made unqualifiedly or as of defendants' own knowledge. A bad motive is not an essential element of fraud. In the instant case, aside from the unqualified representation by defendants of their own knowledge, we have the significant circumstances that on several occasions plaintiffs expressed a desire to see the books — although this is denied by defendants — and that they always received a reply that the books were being worked on and were not then available. In fact, the books were not made available until they were brought into court. The persistent withholding by vendors of the books of business operations, after the making of direct representations of expenses and profits to prospective purchasers who have expressed a desire to see the books, justifies an inference by the trier of fact that such vendors at all times knew their representations were false and that they were made with intent to conceal the truth.

The rule that "The recipient in a business transaction of a fraudulent misrepresentation is not justified in relying upon its truth if its falsity is obvious" (Restatement, Torts, § 541) has no application here. The facts as to past profits were not obvious. In fact, it is the well-established rule that in a business transaction the recipient of a fraudulent misrepresentation of a material fact is justified in relying upon its truth, although he might have ascertained its falsity had he made an investigation. Restatement, Torts, § 540. In the case at bar, we have the additional factors that defendants thwarted the efforts of plaintiffs to investigate, in that they withheld the books which were the only practical source of information for determining whether the resort had made money. Plaintiffs' attempt to make an investigation, and their subsequent conduct in proceeding with the transaction without having made it, was not a waiver of the right to rely upon defendants' representations.

Not only did plaintiffs have the right to rely upon the truth of defendants' representations, but they did so in fact. It was both natural and reasonable for them to do so. At the time of the transaction, plaintiffs, Lowell and Maurice, who were brothers, were of the respective ages of 21 and 26 years, and they had not had any experience in operating resorts, either large or small. Lowell, the young brother, had operated a motion picture theater under the friendly tutelage of his father. Plaintiffs' visits to the resort, with some insignificant exceptions, were primarily recreational and did not give them a knowledge of the business. Defendants, on the other hand, were mature men of considerable experience in the resort as well as other business. Although the element of disparity in business experience is not of itself a sufficient ground for relief, nevertheless, the law does not ignore such disparity, especially where, as here, the inexperience of youth is coupled with an added factor of special trust and confidence growing out of a reasonable assumption by plaintiffs that a genuine and close friendship existed between them and defendants. On various occasions when plaintiffs visited the resort to enjoy the out of doors, defendants had exhibited many manifestations of friendship. In youth, every manifestation of friendship seems genuine and deserving of special trust and confidence. Disparity may under some circumstance be a factor of considerable importance when we keep in mind that the question is not whether the representation would deceive the average man. In rescission actions for fraud, the question is whether the representations were of such a character and were made under such circumstances that they were reasonably calculated to deceive, not the average man, but a person of the capacity and experience of the particular individual who was the recipient of the representations. We have the further circumstance that defendants, by their long and personal operation of the resort, together with their exclusive possession of the books, were possessed of all the facts. We need not labor the point of plaintiffs' reasonable reliance on the representations made, because where representations are made by a party who is presumed to know their truth, reliance thereon will be presumed. We have repeatedly held that one who deceives another to his prejudice ought not to be heard to say in defense that the other party was negligent in taking him at his word.

The materiality of defendants' representations is so obvious from what has already been said that no discussion thereof is needed.

There was no unreasonable delay after the discovery of the fraud before commencing an action for rescission. Plaintiffs, who had been denied access to the books, were not in a position to learn the facts until they had a reasonable opportunity to observe the resort under operative conditions. They had no opportunity to commence operations until the spring of 1948. The evidence fully justifies a finding that plaintiffs discovered the fraudulent representations within a reasonable time after they had the opportunity to do so. We attach no significance to the fact that the action for rescission was not commenced until shortly after defendants — contrary to their agreement with plaintiffs, as found by the trial court — commenced cancellation proceedings. No doubt the unwarranted cancellation properly made them more vigilant in discovering the true nature of the transaction.

Defendants contend that the trial court's decision does not conform to either the pleadings or the proof, in that it is based primarily on the finding that defendants, in violation of a duty to disclose, had fraudulently concealed that they had regularly lost money. It is unnecessary to consider this contention, in that the trial court's decision is sustained upon a different and wholly independent finding, namely, that defendants fraudulently represented to plaintiffs that they were making "good money." Where a trial court has made two or more independent findings of fact, and one of these findings of fact — the making of which has manifestly not been influenced or controlled by an error of law — is wholly sufficient of and by itself to sustain the trial court's decision, no consideration need be given to the other findings, and any error with respect to them is immaterial. Where a decision is correct, it need not be sustained for the same reason or for all the reasons relied upon by the trial court. Much ado has been made about the finding that plaintiffs lost money on their operations of the resort in 1948. Although the evidence reasonably sustains the finding, it is of no material consequence, for two reasons. In the first place, we are not concerned in an action for rescission with a question of damages. In the second place, if the particular finding was used for any purpose other than that of throwing some light upon the rental value of the premises, as indicated by the subject of the paragraph in which it is embodied in the findings, such other purpose obviously must have been limited to the function of corroborating the finding that defendants fraudulently represented that plaintiffs could make "good money." Whether evidence of plaintiffs' failure to make money in 1948 should have been considered for such other purpose need not be determined, because, as already indicated, the trial court's decision is sustained solely on the ground that defendants fraudulently represented that they had made "good money," and not on the representation that plaintiffs could make good money. If it was error, it was error without prejudice. . . .

The rule requiring clear and convincing evidence to justify a rescission of a contract for fraud is merely a rule of caution against setting aside written instruments upon weak and inconclusive evidence. A fair preponderance of the evidence is sufficient.

The order of the trial court is affirmed.

PETERSON, J., dissenting.

While I concur in the views of the majority as to the rules of law stated in their opinion, I dissent upon the ground that, in any reasonable view of the facts, plaintiffs failed to prove a case of fraud.

The evidence conclusively shows that it became known that defendants were willing to sell the property in question for about $100,000. Plaintiffs were familiar with the property. They started negotiations to purchase it. Before defendants made any representations concerning the property, and consequently when plaintiffs were uninfluenced by any such representations, they made an offer to purchase for $90,000. After some negotiations, the parties agreed on $95,000 as the purchase price. The increase in the purchase price as a consequence of the negotiations was a little less than six percent of plaintiffs' offer before any representations had been made. A sale price increased, as a consequence of negotiations, such a slight amount above the buyers' offer, uninfluenced by any representations, cannot be said to be the result of fraud. As a practical proposition, the sale here was at plaintiffs' own price.

GALLAGHER, J., dissenting.

I concur in the dissent. The property was sold to plaintiffs for $95,000. There was substantial testimony, not seriously in dispute, that the reasonable value of the property was in excess of $100,000. In addition to the expert testimony on values submitted by the parties, the trial court, on its own initiative, called three neutral expert witnesses, owners and operators of similar resorts in the same general area, who were familiar with the property involved, to give their opinion as to its value. Their testimony thoroughly substantiated the opinions of defendants' experts as to value, and it clearly indicated that the property, if operated efficiently, was capable of producing a good net income. Under such circumstances, it would seem that was no substantial evidence to sustain the trial court's finding that the property had been sold for more than its worth.

The evidence submitted in support of plaintiffs' allegations as to misrepresentation relative to earnings would hardly seem to sustain a finding of fraud. The statements claimed to have been made by defendants relative thereto related to future prospects. Most of them were made prior to the time when either plaintiffs or defendants contemplated a sale of the property. The most that can be drawn therefrom was that defendants had at times stated that they were "making good money" or that they had a "darn good business."

Prior to the letter of September 26, 1947, in which plaintiff Maurice Spiess offered to purchase the property for $90,000 (some $5,000 less than the price finally agreed upon), he had had but one conversation with defendant William Brandt and no conversations whatever with defendant John Carlos Brandt. His talk with William Brandt was immediately after he and plaintiff Lowell Spiess had talked over the matter of a purchase. Nothing was said at that time by either of the Brandts as to earnings of the resort for the year 1946. The conversation reflected only the expectations of William Brandt as to future prospects, in the light of full resumption of auto transportation after the war.

A written instrument executed with due formality and known to be executed for the purpose of embodying the agreements of the parties should not be set aside on the ground of fraud unless the proof is clear and strong. First Nat'l Bank v. Schroeder, 175 Minn. 341; 3 Dunnell, Dig. & Supp. § 3839. Opinions expressed as to future prospects of a particular business cannot be used as a basis for fraud. Eurich v. Bartlett, 151 Minn. 86. Representations made after a decision to purchase cannot be regarded as inducements toward making the purchase agreement, since there could have been no reliance thereon.

With reference to the claim now made that defendants suppressed or withheld facts relating to their past experiences in the operation of the property, it may be said that this ground was never alleged by plaintiffs as a basis for recovery. Plaintiffs did request defendants' books covering past operations. These were not supplied, and at this point there was nothing to prevent plaintiffs from refusing to proceed with the transaction.

The court placed much reliance on the ages of plaintiffs, their lack of experience, and the fact that they had not operated properties of this type. John Carlos Brandt, one of the defendants, at the time he purchased the resort was not much older than plaintiff Lowell Spiess when he originally purchased it. Both plaintiffs had had experience in the operation of other properties. Lowell owned an interest in and operated a theater, while Maurice owned real state in Newport. Both of such properties were to be sold by plaintiffs so that the proceeds might be used as part of the purchase price herein. Their parents and older brother were interested in this transaction and counseled and advised them in connection therewith. The parties were at all times dealing at arm's length.

It is asserted that defendants sustained a loss during prior years. This may be largely explained by the extensive capital expenditures made by them in improving the resort. For example, in 1947, $14,231 was put back into the properties in improvements. This, in itself, would indicate that defendants were making "good money" in the business. Many of such improvements were not of a recurrent nature and could be depreciated over a number of years . . .

I cannot subscribe to the theory that this contract, made pursuant to an offer freely given, should be set aside on any of the grounds above outlined. If it may be thus rescinded, I fear that few contracts will withstand the onslaught of another business depression or the disappointment following an optimistic but inefficient purchaser's unsuccessful operation of property purchased.

DANANN REALTY CORP. v. HARRIS
Court of Appeals of New York
5 N.Y.2d 317, 157 N.E.2d 597 (1959)

BURKE, J.

The plaintiff in its complaint alleges that it was induced to enter into a contract of sale of a lease of a building held by defendants because of oral representations, falsely made by the defendants, as to the operating expenses of the building and as to the profits to be derived from the investment. Plaintiff, affirming the contract, seeks damages for fraud.

The Appellate Division unanimously reversed the order [of the Supreme Court] granting the dismissal of the complaint. Thereafter the Appellate Division granted leave to appeal, certifying the following question: "Does the first cause of action in the complaint state facts sufficient to constitute a cause of action?"

We must, of course, accept as true plaintiff's statements that during the course of negotiations defendants misrepresented the operating expenses and profits. Such misrepresentations are undoubtedly material. However, the provisions of the written contract which directly contradict the allegations of oral representations are of equal importance. The contract contains the following language: "The Purchaser has examined the premises agreed to be sold and is familiar with the physical condition thereof. The Seller has not made and does not make any representations as to the physical condition, rents, leases, *expenses, operation* or any other matter or thing affecting or related to the aforesaid premises, except as herein specifically set forth, and the Purchaser hereby *expressly acknowledges that no such representations have been made, and the Purchaser further acknowledges that it has inspected the premises and agrees to take the premises 'as is'.* . . . It is understood and agreed that all understandings and agreements heretofore had between the parties hereto are merged in this contract, which alone fully and completely expresses their agreement, *and that the same is entered into after full investigation, neither party relying upon any statement or representation*, not embodied in this contract, made by the other. The Purchaser has inspected the buildings standing on said premises and is thoroughly acquainted with their condition." (Emphasis supplied.)

Were we dealing solely with a general and vague merger clause, our task would be simple. A reiteration of the fundamental principle that a general merger clause is ineffective to exclude parol evidence to show fraud in inducing the contract would then be dispositive of the issue. To put it another way, where the complaint states a cause of action for fraud, the parol evidence rule is not a bar to showing the fraud — either in the inducement or in the execution — despite an omnibus statement that the written instrument embodies the whole agreement, or that no representations have been made.

Here, however, plaintiff has in the plainest language announced and stipulated that it is not relying on any representations as to the very matter as to which it now claims it was defrauded. Such a specific disclaimer destroys the allegations in plaintiff's complaint that the agreement was executed in reliance upon these contrary oral representations. The present case includes [such]a disclaimer as to specific representations.

This specific disclaimer is one of the material distinctions between this case and *Bridger v. Goldsmith (supra)* and *Crowell-Collier Pub. Co. v. Josefowitz (5 N Y 2d 998)*. In the *Bridger* case, the court considered the effect of a *general* disclaimer as to representations in a contract of sale, concluding that the insertion of such a clause at the insistence of the seller cannot be used as a shield to protect him from his fraud. Another material distinction is that nowhere in the contract in the *Bridger* case is there a denial of reliance on representations, as there is here. Similarly, in *Crowell-Collier Pub. Co. v. Josefowitz (supra)*, decided herewith, only a general merger clause was incorporated into the contract of sale. Moreover, the complaint there additionally alleged that further misrepresentations were made after the agreement had been signed, but while the contract was held in escrow and before it had been finally approved.

Consequently, this clause, which declares that the parties to the agreement do not rely on specific representations not embodied in the contract, excludes this case from the scope of the *Bridger* and *Crowell-Collier* cases (*supra*).

The complaint here contains no allegations that the contract was not read by the purchaser. We can fairly conclude that plaintiff's officers read and understood the contract, and that they were aware of the provision by which they aver that plaintiff did not rely on such extra-contractual representations. It is not alleged that this provision was not understood, or that the provision itself was procured by fraud. It would be unrealistic to ascribe to plaintiff's officers such incompetence that they did not understand what they read and signed. (Cf. *Ernst Iron Works v. Duralith Corp., 270 N. Y. 165, 171*.) Although this court in the *Ernst* case discounted the merger clause as ineffective to preclude proof of fraud, it gave effect to the specific disclaimer of representation clause, holding that such a clause limited the authority of the agent, and hence, plaintiff had notice of his lack of authority. But the larger implication of the *Ernst* case is that, where a person has read and understood the disclaimer of representation clause, he is bound by it. The court rejected, as a matter of law, the allegation of plaintiffs "that they relied upon an oral statement made to them in direct contradiction of this provision of the contract." The presence of such a disclaimer clause "is inconsistent with the contention that plaintiff relied upon the misrepresentation and was led thereby to make the contract."

The general rule was enunciated by this court over a half a century ago in *Schumaker v. Mather (133 N.Y. 590, 596)* that "if the facts represented are not matters peculiarly within the party's knowledge, and the other party has the means available to him of knowing, by the exercise of ordinary intelligence, the truth or the real quality of the subject of the representation, he must make use of those means, or he will not be heard to complain that he was induced to enter into the transaction by misrepresentations."

In this case, of course, the plaintiff made a representation in the contract that it was not relying on specific representations not embodied in the contract, while, it now asserts, it was in fact relying on such oral representations. Plaintiff admits then that it is guilty of deliberately misrepresenting to the seller its true intention. To condone this fraud would place the purchaser in a favored position. This is particularly so, where, as here, the purchaser confirms the contract, but seeks damages. If the plaintiff has made a bad bargain he cannot avoid it in this manner.

If the language here used is not sufficient to estop a party from claiming that he entered the contract because of fraudulent representations, then no language can accomplish that purpose. To hold otherwise would be to say that it is impossible for two businessmen dealing at arm's length to agree that the buyer is not buying in reliance on any representations of the seller as to a particular fact.

Accordingly, the order of the Appellate Division should be reversed and that of Special Term reinstated, without costs. The question certified should be answered in the negative.

FULD, J., dissenting.

If a party has actually induced another to enter into a contract by means of fraud — and so the complaint before us alleges — I conceive that language may not be devised to shield him from the consequences of such fraud. The law does not temporize with trickery or duplicity, and this court, after having weighed the advantages of certainty in contractual relations against the harm and injustice which result from fraud, long ago unequivocally declared that "a party who has perpetrated a fraud upon his neighbor may [not] . . . contract with him in the very instrument by means of which it was perpetrated, for immunity against its consequences, close his mouth from complaining of it and bind him never to seek redress." Public policy and morality are both ignored if such an agreement can be given effect in a court of justice. In the realm of fact it is entirely possible for a party knowingly to agree that no representations have been made to him, while at the same time believing and relying upon representations which in fact have been made and in fact are false but for which he would not have made the agreement. To deny this possibility is to ignore the frequent instances in everyday experience where parties accept . . . and act upon agreements containing . . . exculpatory clauses in one form or another, but where they do so, nevertheless, in reliance upon the honesty of supposed friends, the plausible and disarming statements of salesmen, or the customary course of business.

Although the clause in the contract before us may be differently worded from those in the agreements involved in the other cases decided by this court, it undoubtedly reflects the same thought and meaning, and the reasoning and the principles which the court deemed controlling in those cases are likewise controlling in this one. It is said, however, that the provision in this contract differs from those heretofore considered in that it embodies a specific and deliberate exclusion of a particular subject. The quick answer is that the clause now before us is not of such a sort. On the contrary, instead of being limited, it is all-embracing, encompassing every representation that a seller could possibly make about the property being sold and, instead of representing a special term of a bargain, is essentially "boiler plate." The more elaborate verbiage in the present contract cannot disguise the fact that the language which is said to immunize the defendants from their own fraud is no more specific than [a] general merger clause.

In any event, though, I cannot believe that the outcome of a case such as this, in which the defendant is charged with fraud, should turn on the particular language employed in the contract. As Judge Augustus Hand, writing for the Federal Court of Appeals, observed, "the ingenuity of draftsmen is sure to keep pace with the demands of wrongdoers, and if a deliberate fraud may be shielded by a clause in a contract that the writing contains every representation made by way of inducement, or that utterances shown to be untrue were not an inducement to the agreement," a fraudulent seller would have a simple method of obtaining immunity for his misconduct. (*Arnold v. National Aniline & Chem. Co., 20 F. 2d 364, 369.*)

The guiding rule — that fraud vitiates every agreement which it touches — has been well expressed not only by the courts of this state, but by courts throughout the country and by the House of Lords in England. And, in recognizing that the plaintiff may assert a cause of action in fraud, the courts have not differentiated between the type or form of exculpatory provision inserted in the contract. It matters not, the cases demonstrate, whether the clause simply recites that no representations have been made or more fully stipulates that the seller has not made any representations concerning certain enumerated subjects and that the purchaser has made his own investigation and has not relied upon any representation by the seller, not embodied in the writing. . . .

The cases cited — all upholding the sufficiency of a complaint based on fraud no matter how the exculpatory language in the contract is phrased — show how firmly established the rule is, and the passages quoted show how compelling are the reasons for the rule. Nor is their force or value weakened or impaired by the decisions upon which the court now appears to rely. . . .

Contrary to the intimation in the court's opinion, the nonreliance clause cannot possibly operate as an estoppel against the plaintiff. The statement that the representations in question were not made was, according to the complaint, false to the defendant's knowledge. Surely, the perpetrator of a fraud cannot close the lips of his victim and deny him the right to state the facts as they actually exist. Indeed, the contention that a person, such as the defendant herein, could urge an estoppel was considered and emphatically disposed of in *Bridger* v. *Goldsmith* with this statement: "The question now is whether [the no-representation noninducement clause] can be given the effect claimed for it by the learned counsel for the defendant, to preclude the plaintiff from alleging fraud in the sale and pursuing in the courts the remedies which the law gives in such cases. *It cannot operate by way of estoppel for the obvious reason that the statements were false to the defendant's knowledge.* He may, indeed, have relied upon its force and efficacy to protect him from the consequences of his own fraud, but he certainly could not have relied upon the truth of any statement in it. A mere device of the guilty party to a contract intended to shield himself from the results of his own fraud, practiced upon the other party, cannot well be elevated to the dignity and importance of an equitable estoppel" (*143 N. Y. 424, 427–428*).

The rule heretofore applied by this court presents no obstacle to honest business dealings, and dishonest transactions ought not to receive judicial protection. Whether the defendants made the statements attributed to them and, if they did, whether the plaintiff relied upon them, whether, in other words, the defendants were guilty of fraud, are questions of fact not capable of determination on the pleadings alone. The plaintiff is entitled to its day in court.

NOTES

1. *Questions on* Spiess.

a. The court in *Spiess* holds that the Spiess' did not waive their right to rely on the Brandts' representations even though they had unsuccessfully attempted to examine the books to verify those representations. If they intended to rely on the Brandts' representations, why would the Spiess' have sought to verify them? Suppose they had read the books and concluded that the representations were accurate, but subsequently learned that they had misread the books and the representations were inaccurate. Would the Brandts still be liable for misrepresentation? In *CBS, Inc. v. Ziff-Davis Pub. Co.*, 75 N.Y.2d 496 (1990), CBS made a bid to purchase a consumer magazine business from Ziff-Davis. CBS's offer was based on financial information supplied by Ziff-Davis. The parties signed a contract that included Ziff-Davis' express warranty that the financial information it provided to CBS was accurate. Before closing, CBS conducted its own investigation and made its own determination that Ziff-Davis' representations were not accurate. Nonetheless, CBS proceeded with the closing. The court poses the central question of that case: "Did the buyer's manifested lack of belief in and reliance on the truth of the warranted information prior to the closing relieve the seller of its obligations under the warranties?" *Id.* at 499. The court's answer is "no":

> The critical question is not whether the buyer believed in the truth of the warranted information, as Ziff-Davis would have it, but "whether [it] believed [it] was purchasing the [seller's] promise [as to its truth]." . . . This view of "reliance" — i.e., as requiring no more than reliance on the express warranty as being a part of the bargain between the parties — reflects the prevailing perception of an action for breach of express warranty as one that is no longer grounded in tort, but essentially in contract. . . . The express warranty is as much a part of the contract as any other term. Once the express warranty is shown to have been relied on as part of the contract, the right to be indemnified in damages for its breach does not depend on proof that the buyer thereafter believed that the assurances of fact made in the warranty would be fulfilled. The right to indemnification depends only on establishing that the warranty was breached.

Id. at 503.

b. The dissents: Justice Peterson's dissent points out that the Spiess' made their initial offer before the Brandts made any misrepresentation. Do you agree that this timing should be fatal to the Spiess' claim? Justice Gallagher's dissent argues that the property's past losses do not establish the inaccuracy of the Brandts' representation that they were making good money. If the records establish that the Brandts had consistently lost money on the property in the past, how can this be true? Is there a difference between so-called "accounting profits" and the real value of a property? How is the anticipated "resumption of auto transportation after the war" relevant to establishing the accuracy of the Brandts' representation?

c. What role, if any, should the age of the plaintiffs play in the Court's determination? As the majority notes, the Spiess' were aged 21 and 26 at the time of the sale. Ostensibly, the majority's ruling protects potentially vulnerable young investors from exploitation at the hands of more sophisticated parties. But consider the incentives the ruling creates. Will potential sellers be less likely to contract with young adults if they fear that the age of the buyers will expose them to misrepresentation claims? If so, does *Spiess* really serve the interests of young businesspeople?

2.   *Questions on* Danann Realty. Contracts for the sale of goods routinely assign either to buyer or seller the risk of loss of goods identified to the contract. (*See, e.g.*, UCC §§ 2-509, 2-510, 2-319, 2-320.) The central question raised in *Danann Realty* is whether contracts can be used to allocate the risk of fraudulent oral representations just as they allocate numerous other risks. According to the dissent, the risk of fraud always must be borne by the party perpetrating the fraud, even if the parties specifically agree that each will be held harmless for fraud. Is the objective of the disclaimer in *Danann Realty* to provide Danann (the seller) with an incentive to commit fraud? Why would Harris (the buyer) ever agree to bear the risk of Danann's fraudulent representations? Is there an argument that enforcement of the disclaimer benefits Harris?

When we later consider warranty disclaimers (*see* Chapter 7), you will learn that courts and statutes generally prohibit parties from both making and disclaiming a warranty in the same agreement. (*See, e.g.*, UCC § 2-316(1) cmt. 1.) Is the seller's conduct in *Danann Realty* equivalent to making and disclaiming a warranty in the same agreement? Would your view depend on whether the party forfeiting the right to sue for fraud is a commercially sophisticated party or an ordinary consumer? (Note the majority's statement: "We can fairly conclude that the plaintiff's officers read and understood the contract, and that they were aware of the provision by which they aver that plaintiff did not rely on such extra-contractual representations. . . . It would be unrealistic to ascribe to plaintiff's officers such incompetence that they did not understand what they read and signed."). The majority specifically would disapprove of enforcement of the same clause if that clause itself were allegedly procured by fraud. Does this answer one of the dissent's principal objections?

Suppose that, instead of stipulating that the buyer had not relied on seller's representations, the parties included the following clause in their written agreement: "Neither party warrants the truth of any statements made prior to this written agreement. Both parties agree that no misrepresentation, intentional or otherwise, shall provide the basis for liability under this agreement." Is this clause importantly different from the "no reliance" clause in *Danann Realty*? Should a court enforce this clause even if the buyer establishes that the seller intentionally made a material misrepresentation that induced the buyer to enter into the agreement?

The New York "rule of *Danann Realty*" was applied by the Second Circuit in *Grumman Allied Industries, Inc. v. Rohr Industries, Inc.*, 748 F.2d 729 (2d Cir. 1984). Grumman claimed that Rohr fraudulently misrepresented the testing done on two prototype buses, known as the Model 870. Rohr answered that the misrepresentation claim was barred by a specific disclaimer of any representations regarding the Model 870 together with a "non reliance" clause. The court held that

> where sophisticated businessmen engaged in major transactions enjoy access to critical information but fail to take advantage of that access, New York courts are particularly disinclined to entertain claims of justifiable reliance. . . . Grumman, the allegedly defrauded plaintiff, is a Fortune 500 company, renowned world-wide for its engineering expertise. The transaction is a $55 million corporate acquisition and at all stages Grumman was represented by a sophisticated group of counsel, executives and engineers.

Id. at 737–38.

3.   *The Rationale for No-Reliance Clauses*. While courts continue to debate the viability of no-reliance clauses, the persistence of their inclusion in commercial contracting indicates that they carry economic value for the contracting parties. *See* Kevin Davis, *Licensing Lies: Merger Clauses, the Parol Evidence Rule and Pre-Contractual Misrepresentations*, 33 Val. U. L. Rev. 485 (1999) ("Disclaimers of liability for pre-contractual misrepresentations are common features of all kinds of contracts, ranging from the complex agreements of purchase and sale used in connection with the acquisition of businesses, to contracts for the sale or the lease of consumer goods."). If such clauses open the door for fraud, why would a contracting party sign an agreement that contains one?

> First, a seller might want to include a no-reliance clause because, ex ante, it believes that there is a high risk that the buyer will try to hold the seller up by asserting, ex post, that the seller made fraudulent assertions. A no-reliance clause operates as a barrier to such a holdup problem. Sellers may be acutely concerned about the risk of a holdup in complex deals for at least two reasons: (1) in such deals, numerous different interactions between different buyer and seller agents on multiple facets of the deal may take place, potentially making the costs of verifying to a court that no fraud actually occurred particularly high; and (2) in such deals, the assertions being made may themselves be complex, thus increasing the risks that a court will erroneously conclude that an assertion was fraudulent when, in fact, it was merely negligent, inadvertent, or not factually incorrect at all.

> Second, a seller might want to include a no-reliance clause in situations where its agents are heavily involved in making pre-contractual and contractual representations, it is expensive for the seller to monitor its agents' conduct, and the buyer might be in a better position to monitor or observe the agents or protect itself against the agents' actions at a lower cost. Third, buyers or sellers might want to include a no-reliance clause in order to enhance precontractual information exchange, particularly in complex transactions where the functionality of a product or service may hinge, in part, on how that product or service interacts with the buyer's particular business. Inclusion of a no-reliance clause may, in such circumstances, facilitate a freer exchange of information by reducing the threat of postcontractual allegations of fraud. Finally, buyers might want to include

a no-reliance clause in order to protect their legitimate investments in private (as opposed to public) information about valuation.

Allen Blair, *A Matter of Trust: Should No-Reliance Clauses Bar Claims for Fraudulent Inducement of Contract?*, 92 Marq. L. Rev. 423, 467–68 (2009).

4. *The* Borat *Problem: No Reliance Clauses and Standard Form Contracts.* In the 2006 movie, *Borat: Cultural Learnings of America for Make Benefit Glorious Nation of Kazakhstan*, British comedian Sacha Baron Cohen played the role of a Kazakhstani TV reporter who uses his bizarre persona to elicit offensive statements and generally humiliate a number of Americans who clearly are not in on the joke. One of the victims of Cohen's efforts was etiquette expert Cindy Streit who hosted a dinner party for "Borat" at which he shocked her guests with racist and sexist comments, returned from the restroom with a bag of feces and ultimately invited a confederate posing as a prostitute to the dinner. Streit had been told that her dinner party would be "filmed for an educational documentary made for Belarus television." Shortly before the party, Streit signed a "Standard Consent Agreement" agreeing to appear in a "documentary-style . . . motion picture" . . . using "entertaining content and formats." The agreement also included a provision stating that the "participant is not relying upon any promises or statements made by anyone about the nature of the Film or the identity of any other persons involved in the Film." along with others who alleged being duped by Cohen, Streit filed suit in Federal District Court in New York alleging that she was fraudulently induced to enter the Agreement.

The court granted summary judgment for Cohen and Twentieth Century Fox, holding that the fraud claim was foreclosed "because Plaintiffs . . . waived his or her reliance on any promises or statements made by anyone about the nature of the film" (citing *Danann Realty Corp. v. Harris*). The court rejected the plaintiffs' claim that the non-reliance clause was too general or that defendants had a duty to disclose the nature of the film, and held that

> the Agreements are thus enforceable and the provisions contained therein waiving Plaintiffs respective rights to bring any and all claims against Defendants with respect to Borat prevent the instant actions.

Psenicska v. Twentieth Century Fox Film Corp., 2008 U.S. Dist. LEXIS 69214 (S.D.N.Y. Sept. 3, 2008.); *aff'd*, 409 Fed. Appx. 368 (2d Cir. 2009).

Can you think of compelling reasons why the *Danann Realty* rule might not be extended to reach transactions such as those in *Psenicska?* For a careful discussion of the trade offs involved in enforcing no-reliance clauses, see Russell Korobkin, *The* Borat *Problem in Contract Law: Fraud, Assent, and Standard Forms*, 101 Cal. L. Rev. 51 (2013).

4. *Liability for Fraud in Contract and Tort.* In the fraud setting, the law of contracts and the law of torts overlap. Often, a party has the option to bring a claim based on the same underlying fraudulent conduct in tort, contract, or both. The specific elements required to bring a claim in tort or contract vary by jurisdiction, but as a general principle, the elements required to bring a fraud claim in tort are stricter than the elements necessary to bring a fraud claim in contract. For example, Restatement (Second) § 164(1) provides that "if a party's manifestation of assent is induced by either a fraudulent or a material misrepresentation by the other party upon which the recipient is justified in relying, the contract is voidable by the recipient." Thus, under the Restatement, the misrepresentation may be either fraudulent *or* material. On the other hand, the Restatement (Second) of Torts § 538 provides that a misrepresentation must be both fraudulent *and* material. Because a nonfraudulent, material misrepresentation (i.e., a good faith misrepresentation) is potentially actionable in contract, a contract action based on an innocent misrepresentation could not be brought in tort but could be brought in contract.

Although the rules vary according to state law, tort actions typically have a higher burden of proof and a shorter statute of limitations than contract actions. (Some of these differences are moderated by the statute of frauds and parol evidence rule that apply to contractual enforcement and interpretation, respectively. These doctrines are discussed in Section H, *infra*, and Chapter 6.)

5. *Remedies for Fraud in Contract and Tort.* If a tort action for fraud implicates a higher burden of proof and shorter statute of limitations, why would a plaintiff bring the action in tort instead of contract? The answer is that tort law allows punitive damages, while contract law generally does not. The typical remedy for fraud in contract law is rescission. Recall that the plaintiffs in *Spiess* sought rescission of their contract — a return of each party to the *status quo ante* (the position each occupied before the contract was made). Courts have struggled over the question of whether to supplement a rescission award with additional money damages. Most courts will also allow restitutionary recovery if necessary to restore a party to the *status quo ante.* Compensatory damages are less common in contract claims. *See Classic Bowl, Inc. v. A M F Pinspotters, Inc.*, 403 F.2d 463 (7th Cir. 1968). But punitive damages are generally not available in contract. The case of *William B. Roberts, Inc. v. McDrilling Co.*, 579 S.W.2d 335, 340 (Tex. App. 1979), is representative. That court stated:

> In fraud cases, generally speaking, punitive damages may not be awarded unless the act complained of is of a malicious or wanton nature, and such an award cannot be supported if all that is shown by the record is that the act is merely wrongful. It is also the general rule that punitive damages in fraud cases may be awarded when the plaintiff has suffered actual damages as the result of fraud intentionally committed by the defendant for the purpose of injury to the plaintiff, which our Supreme Court classified as "willful and deliberate fraud." Punitive damages cannot be recovered in an action for breach of contract which is not accompanied by a tort, even though the breach is capricious and malicious.

Although some courts have entertained punitive damages in contract actions for fraud (*see, e.g., Robison v. Katz*, 94 N.M. 314, 610 P.2d 201 (Ct. App. 1980)), most courts do not. Why might courts think punitive damages should not be recoverable in a breach of contract action unless there is an accompanying tort? The justification offered by some courts is the promotion of efficient breaches, where the breaching party determines it will gain more from breaching and paying damages than fulfilling the contract. Would the prospect of punitive damages prevent some efficient breaches from taking place? Is there a danger that large damage awards will lead to strategic behavior? Does the holding in *Roberts* decrease the likelihood of such strategic behavior?

6.   *Ratification or Rescission.* Once the wronged party is on notice that a fraud has been perpetrated, she must decide whether to ratify or rescind the contract. If a party fails to seek rescission in a timely manner, or by some action explicitly or implicitly affirms the contract, she loses the option to void the contract. In *Spyder Enters. v. Ward*, 872 F. Supp. 8 (E.D.N.Y. 1994), the plaintiff purchased a vintage Lotus race car from the defendant. During negotiations, the defendant made an affirmative misrepresentation as to the engine's displacement. Thirty-one days after the purchase, the plaintiff realized the fraud and sought a refund. When the defendant refused to give a refund, the plaintiff attempted to sell the car to a third party (hoping to avoid the delay and expense of litigation). The negotiations to sell the car to the third party failed, and the plaintiff sought relief in court. The court found that the plaintiff had promptly attempted to rescind the contract and that the plaintiff's self-help attempt to sell did not constitute ratification. The court, however, noted that the right of rescission will be forfeited by acts constituting affirmation of the contract:

> [The plaintiff]'s conduct in discussing with a single individual the option of selling him the car simply does not evidence an intent to reaffirm the contract. Had the negotiations matured beyond infancy, had they flourished to the point of a meeting of the minds, then perhaps a case could be made that [the plaintiff] "accepted benefits flowing from the contract" by engaging in speculation, or that he acted in some other fashion inconsistent with the exercise of a right to rescind.

Id. at 14.

7.   *Fraud in the Inducement and Fraud in the Execution.* The law draws a distinction between fraud in the inducement and fraud in the execution (or "fraud in the factum"). All of the cases considered so far involve fraud in the inducement: a misrepresentation that induces the other party to agree to the terms of the bargain. In contrast, fraud in the execution consists of a misrepresentation as to the nature of the agreement itself, rather than a particular fact bearing on the agreement. For example, in *Curtis v. Curtis*, 248 P.2d 683 (N.M. 1952), a husband induced his wife to sign a separation agreement by representing to her that she was merely signing a tax-related document. The court voided the agreement on the ground of fraud in the execution. What other kinds of misrepresentations might qualify as fraud in the execution?

[2] Duty to Read

MERIT MUSIC SERVICE, INC. v. SONNEBORN
Court of Appeals of Maryland
245 Md. 213, 225 A.2d 470 (1967)

Finan, J.

Appellant, Merit Music Service, Inc., is a Maryland corporation engaged in the business of leasing coin-operated vending and amusement machines in various locations in and around Baltimore City. Appellees, Sidney Sonneborn and Jennie Sonneborn, his wife, own and operate a tavern located on South Monroe Street in Baltimore and trade as Jen's Park Inn, hereinafter referred to as Jen's, at that location. Prior to August 1962, appellees operated a similar business on Ridgely Street in Baltimore, which was closed during the latter part of July, 1962, due to urban renewal. For approximately five months appellees tried to find another location for their business and in November, 1962, the appellees were informed by a real estate agency that Jen's was for sale. In order to consummate the purchase of the new tavern, appellees approached the appellant for a loan of $1,500. Appellant had supplied amusement machines to appellees for a number of years at their former place of business and appellees owed appellant over $5,000 from their previous dealings.

Settlement for the purchase of the tavern took place on the evening of November 16, 1962, at Jen's. Present when settlement talks began were the seller, the appellees, Julius W. Lichter, appellees' attorney, and Lee Fine, a real estate agent for the seller. Shortly after settlement began Mr. Morris Silverberg, president of appellant, arrived. After discussions, which lasted almost half an hour, Silverberg agreed to loan appellees $1,500 provided that security was given for the loan; this much is not disputed. However the testimony is contradictory as regards the security discussed by the parties at the settlement. Mr. Lichter, appellees' attorney, testified that Silverberg requested that the appellees' prior indebtedness as well as the $1,500 loan be secured by the liquor license formerly located at appellees' previous place of business and that this was the only security agreement discussed or executed by the parties in his presence. Mr. Fine, the real estate agent and who is also an attorney, testified that in addition to the assignment of the liquor license Silverberg wanted additional security by way of a minimum guarantee from machines he was going to install in Jen's and that he believed appellees' attorney was present during this discussion. He further testified that he was not present when the contract embodying the minimum guarantee provision was signed. Mr. Silverberg, who is also a member of the Bar of Maryland but not a practicing attorney, corroborated the testimony of Fine and further testified that after he had given the Sonneborns his check for $1,500, he telephoned his son, David Silverberg, and told him to bring to Jen's a form contract relating to the leasing of amusement and vending machines from Merit to appellees. After his son arrived with the form agreement, Morris Silverberg testified that he inserted the minimum guarantee clauses[7] in the blank spaces, after explaining them to the appellees, after which the contract was executed by the Sonneborns. It was also Silverberg's testimony that the terms of this agreement were discussed with Mr. Lichter prior to its formal execution; however, from the preponderance of the evidence, it would appear that Mr. Lichter was not present when the contract was executed. According to the testimony of appellee Jennie Sonneborn, Mr. Silverberg left after he had given the appellees his check for $1,500 and received the assignment of the liquor license; that was the only security arrangement discussed before his departure. She further testified that Silverberg returned alone to Jen's about midnight and "asked us [Sidney Sonneborn et ux.] to sign a paper he had in his hand-writing in reference to the $1500. He said, 'Just sign this.' We thought it was a note that he had loaned us the $1500." The appellees signed the contract without reading it and alleged that no copy of the agreement was left by Silverberg with them.. . . .

According to the testimony of Jennie Sonneborn the appellees were first told in the early part of 1963 that they were going to be held to a minimum guarantee and they objected. It was not until after they refused to sign collection slips, reflecting a division of the proceeds according to the minimum guarantee clause, that they allegedly became aware of the leasing contract. Periodic collections continued on a regular basis until June of 1963, after which only intermittent collections were made because, according to Mr. Silverberg, of appellees' interference.

On August 21, 1964, by letter of their counsel, the appellees ordered the appellant to remove its equipment from their premises. Two subsequent letters dated February 16, and March 30, 1965, ordered removal of the machines and as a result of this correspondence, counsel for the parties reached an agreement for the removal of appellant's equipment and disposition of the proceeds from a final collection to be made without prejudicing the rights of either party.

On July 6, 1965, Merit filed a bill of complaint in the Circuit Court for Baltimore City alleging breach of paragraph g of the agreement of November 16, 1962, which reads as follows:

> During the terms of this lease, or of any renewal thereof, no other electrical, manual, or mechanical coin operated equipment, machines or phonographs of any kind, nature or description shall be permitted on the premises, and in accordance with such provision the Proprietor agrees to permit no other party, parties, firm, corporation or even the Proprietor himself to install and operate any such machine or machines on the said

---

[7] [1] 1. The Operator agrees:

  a. To install at his expense for the effective period of this lease as hereinafter stated in each space or spaces mutually agreed upon in the main room of the Proprietor's premises, the following machines:

    One Pinball Amusement Machine (at a minimum guarantee of $30.00 per week to operator) plus license taxes. One Music Machine (at a minimum guarantee to operator of $12.00 per week) plus license taxes, hereinafter known as "Equipment."

4. The Proprietor further agrees and guarantees that at no time shall the Operator's share be less than Forty Two Dollars (42.00) per week, each and every week, and in the event that the proceeds to the Operator falls below the aforesaid amount, the Operator shall have the right to terminate this agreement, and all monies due him shall become payable to him immediately."

premises during the term of this lease, or any renewal thereof. The Proprietor agrees for himself, his personal representatives, his heirs, successors and assigns, by reason of the forementioned consideration passing to him, that a decree may be passed by any Court of Equity in which suit is brought for such purpose, enjoining him, his personal representatives, [heirs], successors and assigns from violating this covenant.

The relief prayed was an injunction restraining appellees "from permitting any electrical, . . . coin-operated equipment, machines, or phonographs of any nature or description of any operator or operators than" appellant on appellees' premises; an accounting and a monetary decree for damages. Appellees' answer denied the existence of a valid, legal and enforceable contract between the parties and in the alternative pleaded that, assuming a valid contract, the appellant breached the agreement by its failure to properly service the equipment and account for the proceeds derived therefrom as provided for in the contract. The Chancellor dismissed the bill of complaint finding that the appellees never agreed to a minimum guarantee; that the alleged contract was without consideration; that the agreement would be unconscionable if the minimum guarantee were to be enforced and the minimum guarantee clause constituted a material addition to the agreement by the appellant. From the Chancellor's order dismissing the bill of complaint, appellant has taken this appeal.

The Chancellor, sitting as a judge of the law as well as of the facts, found that the contract between the appellant and the appellees on its face was valid despite the apparent harshness of its terms, citing Stamatiades v. Merit Music, 210 Md. 597 (1956), a case in which the present appellant was involved in litigation regarding a contract similar to that in the case at bar.

The question now before us is whether or not the Chancellor was clearly in error in his finding that the contract was materially altered by the appellant after its execution by the appellees. The Chancellor in his oral opinion stated: "I find as a fact that this contract was not the contract that the Sonneborns [appellees] agreed to; that the clause in dispute, namely the minimum guarantee clause, was not part of it [contract] at the time they signed it; that there has been a material addition made by the operator, [appellant]. . . ."

This Court is of the opinion that the evidence in this case does not support the finding of the lower court.

There was no question in the Chancellor's mind that the appellees executed a contract, the court stating:

> I have no doubt they both signed it. Mrs. Sonneborn identifies her signature and admits it to be her signature. Mr. Sonneborn is not so sure, but I believe this is his signature. I have no difficulty over that.

The persons who should have been in the best position to give testimony as to whether or not the contract had been altered after its execution were the appellees, but they foreclosed themselves from giving trustworthy testimony on this all important issue because, by their own admission, neither of them read the contract prior to signing it nor, according to their testimony, did they retain a copy in their possession. Mrs. Sonneborn, when asked by counsel what she thought she was signing, testified: "I imagined it was a note." Both appellees readily admitted that they did not read the written document prepared for their signature.

The date of execution of the contract was November 16, 1962. It was not until March of 1963, that their attorney obtained a photostatic copy of it. After he explained the contract to them, both appellees stated they would never have signed a contract with such harsh terms. Mrs. Sonneborn perhaps best summed it up when replying to a question from appellant's trial attorney regarding her reactions when the contract was explained to them, stating: "When he said it was a seven year contract I said I would never sign a seven year contract under those terms, I would be foolish to sign a contract for $30 a week on a pinball machine and $12 on a music box. I didn't know what those machines would take in a week." Again, later in her testimony, she said: "I never signed a seven year contract calling for a minimum." But the fact remains she did sign a contract and furthermore, she left herself in such a position that she cannot actually say what was, or was not, in the contract for the simple reason that she did not read it, and the same applies to Mr. Sonneborn.

In the case of Rossi v. Douglas, 203 Md. 190 (1953), wherein this Court reversed a decree of the Chancellor granting an injunction to restrain the appellant from using certain land reserved to them pursuant to a reservation in a lease agreement; Chief Judge Sobeloff, speaking for the Court, said:

> There is no claim here of fraud or duress or mutual mistake, and it is well established that in the absence of these features one having the capacity to understand a written document who reads it, or, without reading it or having it read to him, signs it, is bound by his signature. Indeed Williston says that even if an illiterate executes a deed under a mistake as to its contents, he is bound both at law and in equity if he did not require it to be read to him or its object explained. This is everywhere the rule. Williston, Contracts, sec. 1577.

There is a qualification to the above mentioned rule which this Court recognized in Binder v. Benson, 225 Md. 456 (1961). Judge Hammond (present Chief Judge), speaking for the Court, said:

> A qualification of the rule is that an apparent manifestation of assent will not operate to make a contract if the other party knows, or as a reasonable person should know, that the apparent acceptor does not intend what his words or other acts ostensibly indicate.

However, there is nothing in the facts of this case to justify the application of this exception.

In the case before us there is no evidence of fraud; unless we accept the gratuitous assumption that the appellant altered the lease after its execution and to arrive at such a conclusion, one must engage in unwarranted speculation.

The agreement in question was a form type of contract, part pre-typed and part left in blank, to be filled in to suit the specific terms of a given situation. It was these terms filled in by Morris Silverberg in ink, in his handwriting, that has caused the controversy between the parties.

If Silverberg filled in the blank spaces of the contract with the very material provisions covering the duration of the contract and the minimum guarantees, after he had obtained the appellees' signatures, then the contract was null and void because there was no *concursus ad idem* concerning essential provisions of the contract.

Conversely, if the material provisions had been inserted in the blank spaces prior to the execution of the contract by the appellees, it was a valid contract for the law presumes that a person knows the contents of a document that he executes and understands at least the literal meaning of its terms. As was said by Judge Boyd in Smith v. Humphreys, 104 Md. 285 (1906):

> Any person who comes into a Court of equity admitting that he can read, and showing that he has average intelligence, but asking the aid of the Court because he did not read a paper involved in the controversy, and was thereby imposed on, should be required to establish a very clear case before receiving the assistance of the Court in getting rid of such document. It is getting to be too common to have parties ask Courts to do what they could have done themselves, if they had exercised ordinary prudence, or, to state it in another way, to ask Courts to undo what they have done by reason of their own negligence or carelessness.

Morris Silverberg testified in effect that all insertions had been made at the time of the execution of the contract by the appellees and that a copy of the contract was left with them. . . . His testimony was corroborated by his son, David Silverberg. . . .

The parties to the contract in the case before us were not strangers to each other. Silverberg had loaned the Sonneborns money on other occasions. They had litigated against each other, they dealt at arms length and neither was prompted by altruism. Their association was sustained by business expediency — not by mutual respect; all the more compelling reasons why the appellees should have read the contract. Our sympathy, as did that of the lower court, runs with the appellees, yet we must not fall prey to the old maxim: "Hard cases make bad law." It is equally true that: "Hard cases must not be allowed to make bad equity any more than bad law." Moore v. Pierson, 71 Am. Dec. 409, 417 (Iowa 1858).

We are of the opinion that the Chancellor was clearly erroneous in his finding of fact . . . and accordingly, we reverse his order dismissing the bill of complaint. We further remand the case to the lower court for the granting of injunctive relief consistent with this opinion and for the assessment of damages.

Order reversed and remanded for injunctive relief and assessment of damages, appellees to pay the costs.

NOTES

1. ***Autonomy, Efficiency, and the Duty to Read.*** If a signatory to an agreement fails to read and understand the agreement before signing it, in what sense has she agreed to its terms? On the one hand, if she has neither read nor understood the writing, the terms of the agreement do not reflect her will. In this

sense, enforcing the agreement might seem inconsistent with respect for her autonomy. Similarly, the social welfare goal seems to argue against enforcement: There is no reason to believe the terms of the writing if enforced would be expected to make her better off. But is this analysis too quick? Wouldn't the norm of autonomy recommend holding individuals personally responsible for their free choices, including their choice to sign a writing they have not read, or to sign a writing they have read but not understood? The duty to read doctrine provides individuals with an incentive not to sign agreements unless they have read and understood them first. In this sense, it increases the likelihood that enforceable agreements will be informed and thus serves the value of autonomy. By increasing the likelihood that agreements are mutually informed, this rule would also increase the probability that agreements enhance social welfare. The duty to read doctrine, as applied in *Merit Music Service*, therefore appears to draw support from both dominant theories of contractual enforcement. Are there fairness concerns that would lead a pluralist judge to decline to follow the duty to read rule?

2. *Reconciling the Duty to Read with Ordinary Experience.* What implication does the duty to read have for the standard form lease you signed when you rented your apartment or for the sales agreement you signed when you bought your refrigerator? Did you actually assent to every term? Did you really read and understand each clause and its legal ramifications? Should the law treat the enforcement of unread contracts differently depending on the content, or reasonableness, of the terms? Should the sophistication of the parties matter? For one example of how courts treat both context and sophistication, consider *Birmingham Television Corp. v. Water Works*, 290 So. 2d 636 (Ala. 1974). The plaintiff, Birmingham Television, stored equipment with defendant-bailee which became damaged when a water main at defendant's warehouse burst. When Birmingham Television sued for damages, the defendant argued that terms on the back of the bailment receipt limited their liability. Birmingham Television claimed that the terms had not been brought to their attention and thus that they were not bound by them, despite the duty to read doctrine. The Alabama Supreme Court agreed:

> As applied to the case at bar, we think there existed for the jury's determination a genuine issue of fact as to whether the conditions of bailment set forth on the reverse side of the warehouse receipt were accepted by the appellant-bailor so as to become part of the bailment contract.
>
> The parties to a bailment may limit liability by special contract provided such diminishment of liability is not violative of law or public policy. Such special provision in a contract of bailment limiting bailee's liability, to be effective, must be known to, or brought to the notice of, the bailor, and be assented to by him. It is axiomatic that in bailments, as in other contracts, there must be a meeting of minds thereon and assent of both parties thereto; and a disclaimer of liability can only become effective if brought to the bailor's knowledge. More specifically, to the case at bar, the rule of modern authorities is that the bailor is not chargeable with notice of special provisions diminishing liability of the bailee which appear upon something not apparently related to the bailment contract itself or given to the bailor

ostensibly as a ticket of identification of the bailed property, unless called to his attention or known to him. . . .

Reviewing the facts in the instant case in light of the above stated principles, we find that a genuine issue of fact exists as to whether the terms on the reverse side of the warehouse receipt were accepted by the appellant-bailor and thereby became a part of the contract of bailment. Neither the motion for summary judgment nor appellees' pleas state whether the terms set forth on the reverse side of the warehouse receipt (which purport to materially modify both the common-law rights and obligations of bailor and bailee as well as the statutory provisions respecting limitation of actions) were called to the appellant's attention and were accepted by it.

Nor do we think that such knowledge on appellant's part can be presumed from the issuance of the warehouse receipt itself. The front of the warehouse receipt appears to be just that — a receipt identifying the bailed goods and listing charges — nothing more. No part of the contract appears on the face of the receipt. No notation appears on the face of the receipt advising the bailor to "see reverse side." Nothing on the face of the receipt in any way gives notice that the receipt is a contract of bailment which materially alters the rights of the parties.

Id. at 640–41.

3. *Lack of Understanding.* Courts generally are reluctant to rescind or void a contract simply because one party to the contract failed to understand the document or its implications. The most obvious example of this reluctance can be found where one party has signed a contract without reading it. Another frequent case occurs when both parties read a document but one fails to understand it. Absent misrepresentation, fraud, duress, mistake, or another mitigating circumstance, the contract will remain in force. In some cases, however, a party will be excused from the performance of a contract he failed to understand on the ground that enforcement would be unjust and inequitable. For example, the defendant in *St. John's Episcopal Hospital v. McAdoo*, 94 Misc. 2d 967, 405 N.Y.S.2d 935 (Civ. Ct. 1978), sought to avoid liability for his estranged wife's hospital bills even though he had signed a standard payment form at the hospital. At the time of signing, the defendant testified, he believed his wife would die without medical treatment and therefore felt he had no choice but to sign the form. He also testified that he believed the form entitled his wife to medical benefits under his insurance plan, but that he did not understand he would be personally liable for any charges not covered by that insurance. In releasing the defendant from liability under the contract, the court stated:

Of course, the principle that signed contracts are binding cannot be lightly disregarded. However, it is also unrealistic to continue insisting that in a society of mass marketing it is reasonable still to expect individuals, unrepresented by counsel, to read each clause of the many standardized contracts used by the various institutions with which we all deal. In certain instances it is certainly appropriate for courts to examine the circumstances under which a contract was signed in order to determine whether

1) there was a genuine opportunity for the signer to have read the clause in dispute; or 2) if he did not read it whether a reasonable person should have expected to find such a clause in the particular instrument he was signing. Where there are negative answers to these questions, a court can then address itself to the fairness of enforcing that clause. An analysis of the facts of this case convinces this Court that there is every reason to relax the rule here and to excuse defendant from performance under the contract. It is reasonable in this situation for defendant to have seen himself as powerless to do anything other than sign the form. A hospital emergency room is certainly not a place in which any but the strongest can be expected to exercise calm and dispassionate judgment. The law of contracts is not intended to use "superman" as its model. If the reasonable man standard is applied here, defendant's failure to read the document or to give it more than the most cursory attention is understandable.

It thus becomes vital that a document like the form involved here be clearly labeled and organized so that the signer is made aware of what it entails. Here, the paragraph signed by defendant bore a heading totally unrelated to the sentence on which plaintiff now relies to argue defendant's financial liability. Defendant would have been entirely justified in concluding from the heading that he was agreeing only to have his union insurance pay for his wife's hospital bills. This is a far cry from agreeing to assume personal liability.

Plaintiff hospital is surely no stranger to the trauma and anxiety experienced by those confronted with emergency medical crises. Armed with this knowledge it should have prepared the form it uses to impose liability so that the person being asked to sign it can readily grasp its meaning, even through a quick reading. Moreover, plaintiff should not be permitted to enforce a contractual obligation entered into under such tension-laden circumstances, as those defendant described. This is exactly the type of situation in which a flexible application of the doctrine of inviolability of contract is warranted to permit appropriate judicial compassion and understanding.

Id. at 969–71.

4.   *Contracting with Parties Who Do Not Speak English.* In some settings, contracts are negotiated either entirely or partially in a language other than English. Problems can be created when the transaction is memorialized in a writing in English that cannot be read and understood by the non-English speaking party to the contract. Should the non-English speaking party have a duty to have the written agreement translated? Should the party who supplies the contract have a duty to present a translation? There have been a number of federal and state legislative responses to these questions in industries with a history of abusive sales practices, such as the used car industry and door-to-door sales. If the contract negotiation is conducted in a language other than English, the statutory enactments provide that the contract must be written in the language of negotiation. Are these sensible remedies? Should they apply more broadly to include even those industries without a history of abusive practices against consumers? *See generally* Steven W.

Bender, *Consumer Protection for Latinos: Overcoming Language Fraud and English-Only in the Marketplace*, 45 Am. U. L. Rev. 1027 (1996).

5.   *"Illiteracy" and the Duty to Read.* The *Merit Music* court quoted Williston as stating that even parties who cannot read have the duty to inform themselves of the terms of a contract, presumably by having another party read and explain the contract provisions to them. Does Williston's rule make sense to you? Is it possible that a contrary rule might disadvantage those who cannot read?

The Supreme Court of Georgia initially followed Williston's lead in *West v. Carolina Housing & Mortgage Corp.*, 211 Ga. 789, 89 S.E.2d 188 (1955). In that case, the plaintiffs, a poor and illiterate couple, signed a mortgage with the defendant corporation late one night when there was no possibility of finding a disinterested party to read the document to them. In a two-paragraph opinion, the Georgia Supreme Court affirmed the trial court's decision that the mortgage was valid on the basis of the duty to read doctrine. *West* was effectively overruled seven years later in *Pirkle v. Gurr*, 218 Ga. 424, 128 S.E.2d 490 (1962). The plaintiff in *Pirkle* was an 85-year-old blind widow who transferred real estate to a church of which she was not a member, believing that she had merely put her property in trust for the church's use after her death. No one read the document to the plaintiff before she signed it. While not entirely abrogating the duty to read, the Georgia Supreme Court held that it was a jury question whether, under the circumstances, Mrs. Pirkle was negligent in failing to have the document read to her before she signed it. By allowing the question of whether the promisor who fails to read an agreement is negligent, courts can mitigate the otherwise harsh impact of the rule (as seen in *West*).

In *Literacy and Contract*, 13 Stan. L. & Pol'y Rev. 233 (2002), Alan White and Cathy Mansfield use recent studies in literacy and reading comprehension to question many courts' strict adherence to the duty to read doctrine. These studies suggest that the "degree of literacy required to comprehend the disclosure form and key contract terms simply is not within the reach of the majority of American adults." *Id.* at 239. If a standard sales agreement (i.e., a residential lease or home mortgage) contains clauses that a person of average intelligence and education cannot understand, what purpose is served by the duty to read doctrine?

7.   *Insurance Contracts and Restatement (Second) § 211.* Restatement (Second) § 211(3) carves out an exception to the duty to read doctrine: "Where the other party has reason to believe that the party manifesting such assent would not do so if he knew the writing contained a particular term, the term is not part of the agreement." This provision is often applied to insurance contracts. For example, in *Journal Co. v. General Acc. Fire & Life Assurance Corp.*, 205 N.W. 800, 803 (Wis. 1925), the court wrote: "The average individual accepts the [insurance] policy tendered relying upon the assurance on the part of the insurer, express or implied, that the policy affords him the coverage desired. In many instances a reading of the policy would not be enlightening to the assured. It is couched in technical terms and often complicated and involved." Should Restatement § 211(3) be applied more widely, or should it be limited to the insurance context?

8.   *Behavioral Psychology and the Failure to Read.* Given the risks of being bound to a contract that ill-serves one's purposes, why might parties nevertheless fail to read the contracts to which they have agreed? Do consumers actively consider the costs in terms of time and effort of reading lengthy standard form agreements? Some have argued that cognitive psychology can explain the failure of parties to fulfill their duty to read.

Studies have suggested that the failure to read contracts before signing them is widespread and occurs in a variety of situations:

> [A study] asked participants to sign a consent form to participate in research. The consent form was three pages long and it was opened to the third page for them to sign. Immediately above the line where they were asked to sign, three sentences read: "I have read the above information. I have all my questions answered. I consent to be in this study." Eighty-seven of the 91 participants in the study signed the form. Nearly all of those participants did not read the contract, and none of them read the form in its entirety. The form they signed committed them to participate in any future studies that the researchers might wish to conduct with or without credit in their undergraduate courses for doing so and with or without any compensation for their time. This was contrary to promises made to them when they first agreed to participate in the experiment and to what they were told immediately before they were given the consent form - that they would receive one credit for one hour's participation time. It also committed them to administer electric shocks to fellow participants, if instructed to do so (even if that participant screamed, cried, or asked for medical assistance) and to do push-ups if the experimenter instructed them to do so. Contrary to human-subject protection guidelines, the form required them to remain in the laboratory until and unless the experimenter allowed them to leave.

> We also investigated whether the finding that people fail to read contracts applies to important consumer transactions such as mortgage loan documents and home purchase agreements by surveying consumers about whether they read contracts. Twenty-seven percent of participants who had purchased a home admitted that they did not read the entire mortgage contract. Forty-three percent admitted that they did not read the entire home purchase agreement, 71% admitted that they did not read car rental contracts, and 95% admitted that they did not read end-user license agreements when they downloaded software from the Internet. Some of the psychological causes of failure to read contracts that we discussed in our 2009 work include: participants' assessment that the form was long and boring, their own attribution to themselves of laziness, information overload, social norms not to read contracts, and most importantly trust in what the researcher told them, as well as trust in DePaul University's Institutional Review Board. There is also a phenomenon called "reciprocity of trust," wherein signees may act as if they trust mortgage brokers and lenders, so that the mortgage broker or lender will trust them in return and loan them money).

Jessica M. Choplin, Deborah Progund Stark & Jasmine N. Ahmad, *A Psychological Investigation of Consumer Vulnerability to Fraud: Legal and Policy Implications*, 35 Law & Psychol. Rev. 61, 64 (2011).

What implications do these findings, if valid, have for the duty to read doctrine?

[3] Concealment and Disclosure

Although contract law begins with the premise of caveat emptor, the previous *[handwritten note: → Burden on buyers to reasonably examine property.]* section on intentional and negligent misrepresentation carves out a clear exception to this rule. But informational asymmetries also can be caused by conduct that falls short of intentional or negligent misrepresentation, yet is sometimes ethically dubious and/or economically undesirable. One defining characteristic of intentional and negligent misrepresentations is that they require the promisee (or a third party) to have affirmatively made a representation that he knew, or should have known, was false. The law of disclosure and concealment, however, covers cases in which the promisee (or a third party) does not make any affirmative representation at all. Instead, that party either takes affirmative steps to prevent the promisor from discovering a material fact, knowingly fails to disabuse the promisor of a mistaken belief about a material fact, or fails to apprise the promisor of a material fact of which he knows the promisor is ignorant.

In part, the distinction between the misrepresentation doctrines and the doctrines of disclosure and concealment turns on the act/omission distinction. The clearest contrast is between the promisee who knowingly misrepresents and the promisee who simply keeps material information to himself. In the first case, the promisee expends resources to produce an information asymmetry (without creating any new information). As we have said, such conduct is clearly inconsistent with the justifications for contractual enforcement. In the second case, both autonomy and economic theories provide reasons why we should not require individuals to share certain privately acquired information. For example, on certain conceptions of individual liberty, information is treated as private property and therefore subject to the exclusive control of the owner. Forcing individuals to share privately acquired information would be no less intrusive of personal autonomy than requiring them to share all their personal property with others. Similarly, the economic approach might protect individuals' property right in privately acquired information in order to ensure that individuals have incentives to discover such information, act on it in the marketplace, and thus effect welfare-enhancing transfers.

But in between these clear poles of impermissible acts and permissible omissions lies a spectrum of behaviors that are more difficult to characterize and evaluate. As you read the cases below, ask yourself how the courts draw the distinction between permissible and impermissible conduct. Does it help to distinguish between acts and omissions, permissible and impermissible motives, knowledge and speculation, fiduciary relationships and "arms length" transactions, consumer and commercial actors? Try to develop a theory of the circumstances under which a court would allow recovery for nondisclosure or concealment.

OBDE v. SCHLEMEYER
Supreme Court of Washington
56 Wash. 2d 449, 353 P.2d 672 (1960)

FINLEY, J.

Plaintiffs, Mr. and Mrs. Fred Obde, brought this action to recover damages for the alleged fraudulent concealment of termite infestation in an apartment house purchased by them from the defendants, Mr. and Mrs. Robert Schlemeyer. Plaintiffs assert that the building was infested at the time of the purchase; that defendants were well apprized of the termite condition, but fraudulently concealed it from the plaintiffs.

After a trial on the merits, the trial court entered findings of fact and conclusions of law sustaining the plaintiffs' claim, and awarded them a judgment for damages in the amount of $3,950. The defendants appealed. Their assignments of error may be compartmentalized, roughly, into two categories: (1) those going to the question of liability, and (2) those relating to the amount of damages to be awarded if liability is established.

First, as to the question of liability: The Schlemeyers concede that, shortly after they purchased the property from a Mr. Ayars on an installment contract in April 1954, they discovered substantial termite infestation in the premises. The Schlemeyers contend, however, that they immediately took steps to eradicate the termites, and that, at the time of the sale to the Obdes in November 1954, they had no reason to believe that these steps had not completely remedied the situation. We are not convinced of the merit of this contention.

The record reveals that when the Schlemeyers discovered the termite condition they engaged the services of a Mr. Senske, a specialist in pest control. He effected some measures to eradicate the termites, and made some repairs in the apartment house. Thereafter, there was no easily apparent or surface evidence of termite damage. However, portions of the findings of fact entered by the trial court read as follows:

> Senske had advised Schlemeyer that in order to obtain a complete job it would be necessary to drill the holes and pump the fluid into all parts of the basement floors as well as the basement walls. Part of the basement was used as a basement apartment. Senske informed Schlemeyer that the floors should be taken up in the apartment and the cement flooring under the wood floors should be treated in the same manner as the remainder of the basement. Schlemeyer did not care to go to the expense of tearing up the floors to do this and therefore this portion of the basement was not treated. Senske also told Schlemeyer even though the job were done completely, including treating the portion of the basement which was occupied by the apartment, to be sure of success, it would be necessary to make inspections regularly for a period of a year. Until these inspections were made for this period of time the success of the process could not be determined. Considering the job was not completed as mentioned, Senske would give Schlemeyer no assurance of success and advised him that he would make no

guarantee under the circumstances. No error has been assigned to the above findings of fact. Consequently, they will be considered as the established facts of the case. The pattern thus established is hardly compatible with the Schlemeyers' claim that they had no reason to believe that their efforts to remedy the termite condition were not completely successful.

The Schlemeyers urge that, in any event, as sellers, they had no duty to inform the Obdes of the termite condition. They emphasize that it is undisputed that the purchasers asked no questions respecting the possibility of termites. They rely on a Massachusetts case involving a substantially similar factual situation, Swinton v. Whitinsville Sav. Bank (1942), 311 Mass. 677. Applying the traditional doctrine of caveat emptor — namely, that, as between parties dealing at arms length (as vendor and purchaser), there is no duty to speak, in the absence of a request for information — the Massachusetts court held that a vendor of real property has no duty to disclose to a prospective purchaser the fact of a latent termite condition in the premises.

Without doubt, the parties in the instant case were dealing at arms length. Nevertheless, and notwithstanding the reasoning of the Massachusetts court above noted, we are convinced that the defendants had a duty to inform the plaintiffs of the termite condition. In Perkins v. Marsh (1934), 179 Wash.362, a case involving parties dealing at arms length as landlord and tenant, we held that,

> Where there are concealed defects in demised premises, dangerous to the property, health or life of the tenant, which defects are known to the landlord when the lease is made, but unknown to the tenant, and which a careful examination on his part would not disclose, it is the landlord's duty to disclose them to the tenant before leasing, and his failure to do so amounts to a fraud.

We deem this rule to be equally applicable to the vendor-purchaser relationship. See 15 Tex. Law Review (December 1936) 1, 14-16, Keeton: *Fraud — Concealment and Non-Disclosure.* In this article Professor Keeton also aptly summarized the modern judicial trend away from a strict application of caveat emptor by saying:

> It is of course apparent that the content of the maxim "caveat emptor," used in its broader meaning of imposing risks on both parties to a transaction, has been greatly limited since its origin. When Lord Cairns stated in Peek v. Gurney that there was no duty to disclose facts, however morally censurable their non-disclosure may be, he was stating the law as shaped by an individualistic philosophy based upon freedom of contract. It was not concerned with morals. In the present stage of the law, the decisions show a drawing away from this idea, and there can be seen an attempt by many courts to reach a just result in so far as possible, but yet maintaining the degree of certainty which the law must have. The statement may often be found that if either party to a contract of sale conceals or suppresses a material fact which he is in good faith bound to disclose then his silence is fraudulent.

↳ concealment !!!, not disclosure.

The attitude of the courts toward non-disclosure is undergoing a change and contrary to Lord Cairns' famous remark it would seem that the object of the law in these cases should be to impose on parties to the transaction a duty to speak whenever justice, equity, and fair dealing demand it. (page 31.)

A termite infestation of a frame building, such as that involved in the instant case, is manifestly a serious and dangerous condition. One of the Schlemeyers' own witnesses, Mr. Hoefer, who at the time was a building inspector for the city of Spokane, testified that ". . . if termites are not checked in their damage, they can cause a complete collapse of a building, . . . they would simply eat up the wood." Further, at the time of the sale of the premises, the condition was clearly latent — not readily observable upon reasonable inspection. As we have noted, all superficial or surface evidence of the condition had been removed by reason of the efforts of Senske, the pest control specialist. Under the circumstances, we are satisfied that "justice, equity, and fair dealing," to use Professor Keeton's language, demanded that the Schlemeyers speak — that they inform prospective purchasers, such as the Obdes, of the condition, regardless of the latter's failure to ask any questions relative to the possibility of termites.

Schlemeyers' final contentions, relating to the issue of liability, emphasize the Obdes' conduct after they discovered the termite condition. Under the purchase agreement with the Schlemeyers, the Obdes paid $5,000 in cash, and gave their promissory note for $2,250 to the Schlemeyers. In addition, they assumed the balance due on the installment contract, under which the Schlemeyers had previously acquired the property from Ayars. This amounted to $34,750. After they discovered the termites (some six weeks subsequent to taking possession of the premises in November 1954), the Obdes continued for a time to make payments on the Ayars contract. They then called in Senske to examine the condition — not knowing that he had previously worked on the premises at the instance of the Schlemeyers. From Senske the Obdes learned for the first time that the Schlemeyers had known of the termite infestation prior to the sale. Obdes then ceased performance of the Ayars contract, and allowed the property to revert to Ayars under a forfeiture provision in the installment contract.

The Schlemeyers contend that by continuing to make payments on the Ayars contract after they discovered the termites the Obdes waived any right to recovery for fraud. This argument might have some merit if the Obdes were seeking to rescind the purchase contract. However, this is not an action for rescission; it is a suit for damages, and thus is not barred by conduct constituting an affirmance of the contract.

Contrary to the Schlemeyers' final argument relative to the question of liability, the Obdes' ultimate default and forfeiture on the Ayars contract does not constitute a bar to the present action. The rule governing this issue is well stated in 24 Am. Jur. 39, *Fraud and Deceit*, § 212, as follows:

Since the action of fraud or deceit in inducing the entering into a contract or procuring its execution is not based upon the contract, but is independent thereof, although it is regarded as an affirmance of the contract, it is a general rule that a vendee is entitled to maintain an action against the vendor for fraud or deceit in the transaction even though he has not complied with all the duties imposed upon him by the contract. His default is not a bar to an action by him for fraud or deceit practiced by the vendor in regard to some matter relative to the contract. . . .

For the reasons hereinbefore set forth, we hold that the trial court committed no error in determining that the respondents (Obdes) were entitled to recover damages against the appellants (Schlemeyers) upon the theory of fraudulent concealment.

The judgment awarding damages of $3,950 is well within the limits of the testimony in the record relating to damages. The Obdes have not cross-appealed. The judgment of the trial court should be affirmed in all respects. It is so ordered.

REED v. KING
Court of Appeal of California
145 Cal. App. 3d 261 (1983)

BLEASE, J.

In the sale of a house, must the seller disclose it was the site of a multiple murder? Dorris Reed purchased a house from Robert King. Neither King nor his real estate agents (the other named defendants) told Reed that a woman and her four children were murdered there 10 years earlier. However, it seems "truth will come to light; murder cannot be hid long." (Shakespeare, Merchant of Venice, act II, scene II.) Reed learned of the gruesome episode from a neighbor after the sale. She sues seeking rescission and damages. King and the real estate agent defendants successfully demurred to her first amended complaint for failure to state a cause of action. Reed appeals the ensuing judgment of dismissal. We will reverse the judgment.

Facts

We take all issuable facts pled in Reed's complaint as true. King and his real estate agent knew about the murders and knew the event materially affected the market value of the house when they listed it for sale. They represented to Reed the premises were in good condition and fit for an "elderly lady" living alone. They did not disclose the fact of the murders. At some point King asked a neighbor not to inform Reed of that event. Nonetheless, after Reed moved in neighbors informed her no one was interested in purchasing the house because of the stigma. Reed paid $76,000, but the house is only worth $65,000 because of its past. The trial court sustained the demurrers to the complaint on the ground it did not state a cause of action. The court concluded a cause of action could only be stated "if the subject property, by reason of the prior circumstances, were *presently* the object of community notoriety. . . ." Reed declined the offer of leave to amend.

Discussion

Does Reed's pleading state a cause of action? Concealed within this question is the nettlesome problem of the duty of disclosure of blemishes on real property which are not physical defects or legal impairments to use. Reed seeks to state a cause of action sounding in contract, i.e. rescission, or in tort, i.e., deceit. In either event her allegations must reveal a fraud. "The elements of actual fraud, whether as the basis of the remedy in contract or tort, may be stated as follows: There must be (1) a *false representation* or concealment of a material fact (or, in some cases, an opinion) susceptible of knowledge, (2) made with *knowledge* of its falsity or without sufficient knowledge on the subject to warrant a representation, (3) with the *intent* to induce the person to whom it is made to act upon it; and such person must (4) act in *reliance* upon the representation (5) to his *damage*." (1 Witkin, Summary of Cal. Law (8th ed. 1973) Contracts, § 315.)

The trial court perceived the defect in Reed's complaint to be a failure to allege concealment of a material fact. "Concealment" and "material" are legal conclusions concerning the effect of the issuable facts pled. As appears, the analytic pathways to these conclusions are intertwined. Concealment is a term of art which includes mere nondisclosure when a party has a duty to disclose. Reed's complaint reveals only nondisclosure despite the allegation King asked a neighbor to hold his peace. There is no allegation the attempt at suppression was a cause in fact of Reed's ignorance.[8] Accordingly, the critical question is: does the seller have a duty to disclose here? Resolution of this question depends on the materiality of the fact of the murders.

In general, a seller of real property has a duty to disclose: "where the seller knows of facts *materially* affecting the value or desirability of the property which are known or accessible only to him and also knows that such facts are not known to, or within the reach of the diligent attention and observation of the buyer, the seller is under a duty to disclose them to the buyer." This broad statement of duty has led one commentator to conclude: "The ancient maxim *caveat emptor* ('let the buyer beware.') has little or no application to California real estate transactions." (1 Miller & Starr, Current Law of Cal. Real Estate (rev. ed. 1975) § 1:80.)

Whether information "is of sufficient materiality to affect the value or desirability of the property . . . depends on the facts of the particular case." (Lingsch, *supra*, 213 Cal. App. 2d at p. 737.) Materiality "is a question of law, and is part of the concept of right to rely or justifiable reliance." (3 Witkin, Cal. Procedure (2d ed. 1971) Pleading, § 578, p. 2217.) Accordingly, the term is essentially a label affixed to a normative conclusion. Three considerations bear on this legal conclusion: the gravity of the harm inflicted by nondisclosure; the fairness of imposing a duty of

---

[8] [2] Reed elsewhere in the complaint asserts defendants "actively concealed" the fact of the murders and this in part misled her. However, no connection is made or apparent between the legal conclusion of active concealment and any issuable fact pled by Reed. Accordingly, the assertion is insufficient. (See *Bacon v. Soule (1912) 19 Cal. App. 428, 438 [126 P. 384].*) Similarly we do not view the statement the house was fit for Reed to inhabit as transmuting her case from one of nondisclosure to one of false representation. To view the representation as patently false is to find "elderly ladies" uniformly susceptible to squeamishness. We decline to indulge this stereotypical assumption. To view the representation as misleading because it conflicts with a duty to disclose is to beg that question.

discovery on the buyer as an alternative to compelling disclosure, and the impact on the stability of contracts if rescission is permitted. Numerous cases have found nondisclosure of physical defects and legal impediments to use of real property are material.[9] However, to our knowledge, no prior real estate sale case has faced an issue of nondisclosure of the kind presented here. Should this variety of ill-repute be required to be disclosed? Is this a circumstance where "non-disclosure of the fact amounts to a failure to act in good faith and in accordance with reasonable standards of fair dealing[?]" (Rest. 2d Contracts, § 161, subd. (b).)

The paramount argument against an affirmative conclusion is it permits the camel's nose of unrestrained irrationality admission to the tent. If such an "irrational" consideration is permitted as a basis of rescission the stability of all conveyances will be seriously undermined. Any fact that might disquiet the enjoyment of some segment of the buying public may be seized upon by a disgruntled purchaser to void a bargain. In our view, keeping this genie in the bottle is not as difficult a task as these arguments assume. We do not view a decision allowing Reed to survive a demurrer in these unusual circumstances as endorsing the materiality of facts predicating peripheral, insubstantial, or fancied harms. The murder of innocents is highly unusual in its potential for so disturbing buyers they may be unable to reside in a home where it has occurred. This fact may foreseeably deprive a buyer of the intended use of the purchase. Murder is not such a common occurrence that *buyers* should be charged with anticipating and discovering this disquieting possibility. Accordingly, the fact is not one for which a duty of inquiry and discovery can sensibly be imposed upon the buyer.

Reed alleges the fact of the murders has a quantifiable effect on the market value of the premises. We cannot say this allegation is inherently wrong and, in the pleading posture of the case, we assume it to be true. [If information known or accessible only to the seller has a significant and measurable effect on market value and, as is alleged here, the seller is aware of this effect, we see no principled basis for making the duty to disclose turn upon the character of the information] Physical usefulness is not and never has been the sole criterion of valuation. Stamp collections and gold speculation would be insane activities if utilitarian considerations were the sole measure of value. Reputation and history can have a significant effect on the value of realty. "George Washington slept here" is worth something, however physically inconsequential that consideration may be. Ill-repute or "bad will" conversely may depress the value of property. Failure to disclose such a negative fact where it will have a foreseeably depressing effect on income expected to be generated by a business is tortious. (See Rest.2d Torts, § 551, illus. 11.) Some cases have held that *unreasonable* fears of the potential buying public that a gas or oil pipeline may rupture may depress the market value of land and entitle the owner to incremental compensation in eminent domain.

Whether Reed will be able to prove her allegation that the decade-old multiple

---

[9] [5] For example, the following have been held of sufficient materiality to require disclosure: the home sold was constructed on filled land; improvements were added without a building permit and in violation of zoning regulations or in violation of building codes; the structure was condemned; the structure was termite-infested; there was water infiltration in the soil; and the amount of net income a piece of property would yield was overstated.

murder has a significant effect on market value we cannot determine. If she is able to do so by competent evidence she is entitled to a favorable ruling on the issues of materiality and duty to disclose.[10] Her demonstration of objective tangible harm would still the concern that permitting her to go forward will open the floodgates to rescission on subjective and idiosyncratic grounds. A more troublesome question would arise if a buyer in similar circumstances were unable to plead or establish a significant and quantifiable effect on market value. However, this question is not presented in the posture of this case. Reed has not alleged the fact of the murders has rendered the premises useless to her as a residence. As currently pled, the gravamen of her case is pecuniary harm. We decline to speculate on the abstract alternative.

The judgment is reversed.

NOTES

1. *Questions on* Obde *and* Reed. Can you explain the results in *Obde* and *Reed*? In both cases, one party had special knowledge that would have significantly affected the other's assessment of the proposed deal. In each case, the court must choose whether to place a burden of disclosure on the seller or a burden of inquiry on the buyer. How do courts make this choice? In *Obde*, the sellers had taken affirmative steps (whether advertently or not) that made it more difficult for the buyers to notice and ask about the possibility of termite infestation. Should the act/omission distinction matter in drawing the line between impermissible conceal-ment and permissible non-disclosure? The court in *Reed* doesn't seem to think so, but then where should the line be drawn in California between the duty to disclose and permissible non-disclosure?

2. *Restatement on Non-disclosure.* The trend toward a limited duty to disclose is embodied in Restatement (Second) § 161. Read subsection 161(b) carefully. Assume a client asks whether she must affirmatively disclose the fact that the 10-year old used Jaguar X-J12 she is offering for sale had previously been in an accident that damaged the frame, which has subsequently been repaired, or whether she can simply sell the car "as is." The only lasting effect of the accident is that the tires on the Jaguar suffer from rapid wear. What would you advise in a state that follows the Restatement rule? What if your client is the buyer of such a car and asks whether he must disclose his knowledge that he has recently learned that a leading car magazine is about to name this model a "classic" and that experience shows such a distinction will significantly increase the resale value of cars of that vintage? Can you decline to disclose in the latter case on the grounds that the information he has acquired does not relate to a "basic assumption" of the contract, or that nondisclosure is not a "failure to act in good faith and in accordance

---

[10] [9] The ruling of the trial court requiring the additional element of notoriety, i.e. widespread public knowledge, is unpersuasive. Lack of notoriety may facilitate resale to yet another unsuspecting buyer at the "market price" of a house with no ill-repute. However, it appears the buyer will learn of the possibly unsettling history of the house soon after moving in. Those who suffer no discomfort from the specter of residing in such quarters per se, will nonetheless be discomforted by the prospect they have bought a house that may be difficult to sell to less hardy souls. Nondisclosure must be evaluated as fair or unfair regardless of the ease with which a buyer may escape this discomfort by foisting it upon another.

with reasonable standards of fair dealing" (Restatement (Second) § 161(b))?

In answering these questions, does the autonomy perspective argue in favor of disclosure in order to insure that the seller's choice is informed and thus truly expressive of her will? Or does it argue against disclosure in order to guarantee the buyer's right to private property, including private information? Does the economic perspective recommend for or against disclosure? Compare the incentives for buyers and sellers created by a disclosure and a non-disclosure rule. How will sellers and buyers behave in the future given that buyers have the burden of disclosing termites and past murders in houses? How will they behave given that buyers need not disclose the market speculations that inform their transactions?

3.   *Reasonableness and the Market Impact of Information.* *Reed* presents the question of whether sellers must disclose facts that affect the market value of property for purely psychological reasons. The court treats the fact that murders had occurred in the King's home as legally on a par with the fact that termites had infested the Schlemeyer's house. Are you satisfied that the duty to disclose should pertain equally to both kinds of facts?

Suppose that a house was widely reputed to be haunted by ghosts and seller fails to disclose this fact to buyer. Would the *Reed* court allow buyer to rescind because of seller's non-disclosure? Would rescission be allowed if the case were brought in a jurisdiction, unlike California, where house sales are clearly subject to the rule of caveat emptor? The court in *Stambovsky v. Ackley*, 572 N.Y.S.2d 672 (1991), answered this question in the affirmative:

> Plaintiff, to his horror, discovered that the house he had recently contracted to purchase was widely reputed to be possessed by poltergeists, reportedly seen by defendant seller and members of her family on numerous occasions over the last nine years. Plaintiff promptly commenced this action seeking rescission of the contract of sale. Supreme Court reluctantly dismissed the complaint, holding that plaintiff has no remedy at law in this jurisdiction.

> The unusual facts of this case, as disclosed by the record, clearly warrant a grant of equitable relief to the buyer who, as a resident of New York City, cannot be expected to have any familiarity with the folklore of the Village of Nyack. Not being a "local", plaintiff could not readily learn that the home he had contracted to purchase is haunted. Whether the source of the spectral apparitions seen by defendant seller are parapsychic or psycho-genic, having reported their presence in both a national publication (Readers' Digest) and the local press (in 1977 and 1982, respectively), defendant is estopped to deny their existence and, as a matter of law, the house is haunted. More to the point, however, no divination is required to conclude that it is defendant's promotional efforts in publicizing her close encounters with these spirits which fostered the home's reputation in the community. In 1989, the house was included in five-home walking tour of Nyack and described in a November 27th newspaper article as "a riverfront Victorian (with ghost)." The impact of the reputation thus created goes to the very essence of the bargain between the parties, greatly impairing both the value of the property and its potential for resale.

While I agree with Supreme Court that the real estate broker, as agent for the seller, is under no duty to disclose to a potential buyer the phantasmal reputation of the premises and that, in his pursuit of a legal remedy for fraudulent misrepresentation against the seller, plaintiff hasn't a ghost of a chance, I am nevertheless moved by the spirit of equity to allow the buyer to seek rescission of the contract of sale and recovery of his down payment. New York law fails to recognize any remedy for damages incurred as a result of the seller's mere silence, applying instead the strict rule of caveat emptor. Therefore, the theoretical basis for granting relief, even under the extraordinary facts of this case, is elusive if not ephemeral.

"Pity me not but lend thy serious hearing to what I shall unfold" (William Shakespeare, Hamlet, Act I, Scene V [Ghost]).

From the perspective of a person in the position of plaintiff herein, a very practical problem arises with respect to the discovery of a paranormal phenomenon: "Who you gonna' call?" as a title song to the movie "Ghostbusters" asks. Applying the strict rule of caveat emptor to a contract involving a house possessed by poltergeists conjures up visions of a psychic or medium routinely accompanying the structural engineer and Terminix man on an inspection of every home subject to a contract of sale. It portends that the prudent attorney will establish an escrow account lest the subject of the transaction come back to haunt him and his client — or pray that his malpractice insurance coverage extends to supernatural disasters. In the interest of avoiding such untenable consequences, the notion that a haunting is a condition which can and should be ascertained upon reasonable inspection of the premises is a hobgoblin which should be exorcised from the body of legal precedent and laid quietly to rest.

It has been suggested by a leading authority that the ancient rule which holds that mere nondisclosure does not constitute actionable misrepresentation "finds proper application in cases where the fact undisclosed is patent, or the plaintiff has equal opportunities for obtaining information which he may be expected to utilize, or the defendant has no reason to think that he is acting under any misapprehension" (PROSSER, TORTS § 106, at 696 [4th ed. 1971]). However, with respect to transactions in real estate, New York adheres to the doctrine of caveat emptor and imposes no duty upon the vendor to disclose any information concerning the premises . . . unless there is a confidential or fiduciary relationship between the parties . . . or some conduct on the part of the seller which constitutes "active concealment."

Caveat emptor is not so all-encompassing a doctrine of common law as to render every act of nondisclosure immune from redress, whether legal or equitable. . . . Common law is not moribund. *Ex facto jus oritur* (law arises out of facts). Where fairness and common sense dictate that an exception should be created, the evolution of the law should not be stifled by rigid application of a legal maxim.

The doctrine of caveat emptor requires that a buyer act prudently to assess the fitness and value of his purchase and operates to bar the purchaser who fails to exercise due care from seeking the equitable remedy of rescission. . . . For the purposes of the instant motion to dismiss the action . . . plaintiff is entitled to every favorable inference which may reasonably be drawn from the pleadings. . . . [S]pecifically, in this instance, that he met his obligation to conduct an inspection of the premises and a search of available public records with respect to title. It should be apparent, however, that the most meticulous inspection and the search would not reveal the presence of poltergeists at the premises or unearth the property's ghoulish reputation in the community. Therefore, there is no sound policy reason to deny plaintiff relief for failing to discover a state of affairs which the most prudent purchaser would not be expected to even contemplate. . . .

Where a condition which has been created by the seller materially impairs the value of the contract and is peculiarly within the knowledge of the seller or unlikely to be discovered by a prudent purchaser exercising due care with respect to the subject transaction, nondisclosure constitutes a basis for rescission as a matter of equity. Any other outcome places upon the buyer not merely the obligation to exercise care in his purchase but rather to be omniscient with respect to any fact which may affect the bargain. No practical purpose is served by imposing such a burden upon a purchaser. To the contrary, it encourages predatory business practice and offends the principle that equity will suffer no wrong to be without a remedy.

In the case at bar, defendant seller deliberately fostered the public belief that her home was possessed. Having undertaken to inform the public-at-large, to whom she has no legal relationship, about the supernatural occurrences on her property, she may be said to owe no less a duty to her contract vendee. It has been remarked that the occasional modern cases which permit a seller to take unfair advantage of a buyer's ignorance so long as he is not actively misled are "singularly unappetizing" (PROSSER, TORTS § 106, at 696 [4th ed. 1971]). Where, as here, the seller not only takes unfair advantage of the buyer's ignorance but has created and perpetuated a condition about which he is unlikely to even inquire, enforcement of the contract (in whole or in part) is offensive to the court's sense of equity. Application of the remedy of rescission, within the bounds of the narrow exception to the doctrine of caveat emptor set forth herein, is entirely appropriate to relieve the unwitting purchaser from the consequences of a most unnatural bargain.

Id. at 674–77. Would *Stambovsky* have come out differently if the seller had not been responsible for creating and perpetuating the reputation of her house as haunted? Should that matter? Given all the bad puns in the opinion, do you suppose it was ghost-written?

4. *Non-apparent virtues.* Suppose an agent approaches a landowner and makes the landowner an attractive offer to buy the property, prompting the landowner to sell to the agent. The agent makes no representations as to the intended use of the land, nor does the landowner ask. The landowner finds out later that the agent has been working to assemble land in the neighborhood on behalf of a third party, perhaps for a new university campus or even a new theme park. Those in the neighborhood that refused to sell quickly find out about the scheme and are now able to hold out for massive price concessions, well above what the first landowner sold for. Should this be considered a material misrepresentation? Should such concealment on behalf of buyers be treated the same or differently as the sellers in *Obde* and *Reed*?

Courts have consistently held that buyers bear no responsibility to reveal their purpose in purchasing property through such secret buying agents or for any other reason. *See, e.g., Kelo v. City of New London*, 545 U.S. 469, 490 n.24 (2005) ("private developers can use numerous techniques, including secret negotiations or precommitment strategies, to overcome holdout problems and assemble lands for genuinely profitable projects"); *Westgate Village Shopping Ctr. v. Lion Dry Goods Co.*, 21 F.3d 429 (6th Cir. 1994) (noting that using secret buying agents to develop shopping centers is "a common arms-length business practice that has to do with keeping real estate prices from escalating").

5. *Problems.*

a. Bob has been designated as the new plant manager at the Charlottesville General Electric plant, requiring (allowing, some would say) him to move his family to Charlottesville from Connecticut. In a quick trip to Charlottesville in July "just to canvass the market," Bob and his wife Andrea discover the "perfect house" for sale by its owner. It is in a very nice old neighborhood. Even though they don't have a real estate broker and seldom rush into anything, Bob and Andrea make a quick offer on the house. When they return to Charlottesville in early September and are ready to close on the deed, they discover to their horror that the beautiful, old house next door is a fraternity house. Andrea remembers talking to the sellers about how their children are gone and how they are looking forward to the peace and quiet of life in Charlottesville. They no longer want the house.

b. Mary enters John's Pipe Store. Mary's husband Bill died recently, and although Bill gave up smoking 20 years ago, Mary found some old pipes in the attic. John notices one early Dunhill pipe in the group and believes (correctly) that it is worth about $1,000. He offers Mary $25 for the entire group and Mary agrees. She later seeks to rescind and recover the pipes.

c. As Mark is looking through a bin of pipes at Smokers' Haven Pipe Store, he notices a Charatan Selected pipe. He believes (correctly) that it must have been put there by accident, for it sells for $275 and it is in the $25 bin. Mark buys it for $25. The owner of the store finds out about the sale later and seeks to rescind and recover the pipe or $250. The owner suspects that Mark may have stalled before buying the pipe until the owner went to lunch and a less experienced clerk was at the counter.

d. Bozkie buys 5,000 shares of XYZ stock from the Pipefitters' Pension Fund. Later the stock doubles in price, and it is discovered that Bozkie traded on insider information. The Fund sues Bozkie for the difference between the selling price and the subsequent market price.

e. Mary hires Francis to appraise her farm. Francis does so, but for a rather low value. Dealing through lawyers, Francis buys Mary's farm for the appraised price.

After Mary's death, her children seek to void the contract for sale, alleging that Francis and Mary had a relationship of trust breached by Francis. Francis contends that he performed his only obligation to Mary when he appraised the property. He claims that the purchase was a separate action at arms length. *See In re Estate of Evasew*, 526 Pa. 98 (1990).

   6.   *An Economic Theory of Disclosure.* In *Laidlaw v. Organ*, 15 U.S. (2 Wheat.) 178 (1817), the plaintiff, Organ, had begun negotiating with Francis Girault, a merchant with Laidlaw & Co., to buy a large quantity of tobacco from Girault. The day before the sale was to be consummated, news arrived that the War of 1812 had ended with the signing of the Treaty of Ghent, thus opening up the foreign tobacco market. The news was publicly announced in a handbill the morning of the tobacco sale, but Girault had not yet learned of the news at the time the contract was executed. Girault even asked Organ if there were any news that might enhance the price of tobacco, but Organ apparently refused or declined to answer the question. Girault went ahead with the contract anyway, and as a result sold his tobacco for 30 to 50% less than it was worth on the suddenly expanded market.

   The Supreme Court reversed and remanded a lower court ruling in favor of Girault, and held that Organ had no obligation to tell Girault of the changed "extrinsic circumstances," and that whether or not Organ had made an affirmative misrepresentation was a jury question. The court offered little reasoning or justification for its holding. Professor Anthony Kronman, however, discussed the *Laidlaw* decision in *Mistake, Disclosure, Information, and the Law of Contracts*, 7 J. LEGAL STUD. 1 (1978). Kronman proposed that the "morality of the market," or the risk that each party takes that his own assessment of the worth of goods may be erroneous, might justify the Supreme Court's decision in *Laidlaw.* Kronman then suggested a solution to the nondisclosure/disclosure problem. That solution is discussed in the following excerpt:

> One effective way of insuring that an individual will benefit from the possession of information (or anything else for that matter) is to assign him a property right in the information itself — a right or entitlement to invoke the coercive machinery of the state in order to exclude others from its use and enjoyment. The benefits of possession become secure only when the state transforms the possessor of information into an owner by investing him with a legally enforceable property right of some sort or other. The assignment of property rights in information is a familiar feature of our legal system. The legal protection accorded patented inventions and certain trade secrets rights are two obvious examples.

> One (seldom noticed) way in which the legal system can establish property rights in information is by permitting an informed party to enter — and enforce — contracts which his information suggests are profitable, without disclosing the information to the other party. Imposing a duty to disclose upon the knowledgeable party deprives him of a private advantage which the information would otherwise afford. A duty to disclose is tantamount to a requirement that the benefit of the information be publicly shared and is thus antithetical to the notion of a property right which — whatever else it may entail — always requires the legal protection of private appropriation.

Of course, different sorts of property rights may be better suited for protecting possessory interests in different sorts of information. It is unlikely, for example, that information of the kind involved in Laidlaw v. Organ could be effectively protected by a patent system. The only feasible way of assigning property rights in short-lived market information is to permit those with such information to contract freely without disclosing what they know.

It is unclear, from the report of the case, whether the buyer in *Laidlaw* casually acquired his information or made a deliberate investment in seeking it out (for example, by cultivating a network of valuable commercial "friendships"). If we assume the buyer casually acquired his knowledge of the treaty, requiring him to disclose the information to his seller (that is, denying him a property right in the information) will have no significant effect on his future behavior. Since one who casually acquires information makes no investment in its acquisition, subjecting him to a duty to disclose is not likely to reduce the amount of socially useful information which he actually generates. Of course, if the buyer in *Laidlaw* acquired his knowledge of the treaty as the result of a deliberate and costly search, a disclosure requirement will deprive him of any private benefit which he might otherwise realize from possession of the information and should discourage him from making similar investments in the future.

In addition, since it would enable the seller to appropriate the buyer's information without cost and would eliminate the danger of his being lured unwittingly into a losing contract by one possessing superior knowledge, a disclosure requirement will also reduce the seller's incentive to search. Denying the buyer a property right in deliberately acquired information will therefore discourage both buyers and sellers from investing in the development of expertise and in the actual search for information. The assignment of such a right will not only protect the investment of the party possessing the special knowledge, it will also impose an opportunity cost on the other party and thus give him an incentive to undertake a (cost-justified) search of his own.

If we assume that courts can easily discriminate between those who have acquired information casually and those who have acquired it deliberately, plausible economic considerations might well justify imposing a duty to disclose on a case-by-case basis (imposing it where the information has been casually acquired, refusing to impose it where the information is the fruit of a deliberate search). A party who has casually acquired information is, at the time of the transaction, likely to be a better (cheaper) mistake-preventer than the mistaken party with whom he deals — regardless of the fact that both parties initially had equal access to the information in question. One who has deliberately acquired information is also in a position to prevent the other party's error. But in determining the cost to the knowledgeable party of preventing the mistake (by disclosure), we must include whatever investment he has made in acquiring the information in the first place. This investment will represent a loss to him if the other party can avoid the contract on the grounds that the party with the information owes him a duty of disclosure.

If we take this cost into account, it is no longer clear that the party with knowledge is the cheaper mistake-preventer when his knowledge has been deliberately acquired. Indeed, the opposite conclusion seems more plausible. In this case, therefore, a rule permitting nondisclosure (which has the effect of imposing the risk of a mistake on the mistaken party) corresponds to the arrangement the parties themselves would have been likely to adopt if they had negotiated an explicit allocation of the risk at the time they entered the contract. The parties to a contract are always free to allocate this particular risk by including an appropriate disclaimer in the terms of their agreement. Where they have failed to do so, however, the object of the law of contracts should be (as it is elsewhere) to reduce transaction costs by providing a legal rule which approximates the arrangement the parties would have chosen for themselves if they had deliberately addressed the problem. This consideration, coupled with the reduction in the production of socially useful information which is likely to follow from subjecting him to a disclosure requirement, suggests that allocative efficiency is best served by permitting one who possesses deliberately acquired information to enter and enforce favorable bargains without disclosing what he knows.

A rule which calls for case-by-case application of a disclosure requirement is likely, however, to involve factual issues that will be difficult (and expensive) to resolve. *Laidlaw* itself illustrates this point nicely. On the facts of the case, as we have them, it is impossible to determine whether the buyer actually made a deliberate investment in acquiring information regarding the treaty. The cost of administering a disclosure requirement on a case-by-case basis is likely to be substantial.

As an alternative, one might uniformly apply a blanket rule (of disclosure or nondisclosure) across each class of cases involving the same sort of information (for example, information about market conditions or about defects in property held for sale). In determining the appropriate blanket rule for a particular class of cases, it would first be necessary to decide whether the kind of information involved is (on the whole) more likely to be generated by chance or by deliberate searching. The greater the likelihood that such information will be deliberately produced rather than casually discovered, the more plausible the assumption becomes that a blanket rule permitting nondisclosure will have benefits that outweigh its costs.

In *Laidlaw*, for example, the information involved concerned changing market conditions. The results in that case may be justified (from the more general perspective just described) on the grounds that information regarding the state of the market is typically (although not in every case) the product of a deliberate search. The large number of individuals who are actually engaged in the production of such information lends some empirical support to this proposition.[11]

---

[11] 7 J. Legal Stud. 1, 14–18 (1978).

How would Kronman's analysis apply to the second and third problem cases set out in Note 4, *supra*?[12] In footnote 27 of the article, Kronman writes:

> If Organ denied that he had heard any news of this sort [the treaty], he would have committed a fraud. It may even be, in light of Laidlaw's direct question, that silence on Organ's part was fraudulent. . . . In my discussion of the case, . . . I have put aside any question of fraud on Organ's part.

Yet it would seem that Kronman's analysis applies with equal force to this situation. If Kronman concedes a different result where Organ replies untruthfully, does this undercut the descriptive and normative persuasiveness of Kronman's analysis? For a more modern example of *Laidlaw*, see *L & N Grove, Inc. v. Chapman*, 291 So. 2d 217 (Fla. Dist. Ct. App. 1974). For a recent assessment of Kronman's analysis, see Jeffrey L. Harrison, *Rethinking Mistake and Nondisclosure in Contract Law*, 17 Geo. Mason L. Rev. 335 (2010).

6. ***Mandatory Disclosure.*** There are instances where Congress or an administrative agency decides that intervention to require disclosure is necessary. For example, in 1981 the Federal Trade Commission proposed extensive regulations governing the sale of used motor vehicles. 46 Fed. Reg. 41328 (1981) (codified at 16 C.F.R. § 455). One of the major purposes of the regulation was to require used car dealers to disclose certain information about possible defects in the vehicle to potential customers. One might ask in the face of this rule whether it is necessary for every consumer to be informed to ensure that contract terms reflect "true conditions." For example, assume that in a competitive market only some individuals shop for favorable terms, while others buy randomly without information. Could you still argue with some confidence that the sellers in such a market would compete for the comparison shoppers and thus the contract terms would reflect the available information even though many customers were "free riding" in ignorance on the efforts of the shoppers? If that argument is plausible, why doesn't it apply here? *See* Alan Schwartz & Louis Wilde, *Intervening in Markets on the Basis of Imperfect Information*, 127 U. Pa. L. Rev. 630 (1979).

Such mandated disclosure also raises the issue of governmental interference in private arrangements. We have studied contracts as agreements between private parties governed by a set of private law rules. But the unarticulated premise of this FTC rule is that although parties may fashion private agreements the aggregate effect of those agreements is a public policy matter. Perhaps the most vexing problem with mandated disclosure rules is the problem of what information to disclose. The importance and relevance of information will vary with the consumer of that information. Thus, selective disclosure of only that information that is commonly believed important or relevant to decisionmaking may be criticized on two grounds: 1) it may not disclose the information thought relevant to a particular consumer, and 2) by disclosing some and not all, it implies that no additional information exists. On the other hand, the full disclosure approach (as embodied in the FTC rule discussed above and other federal legislation) suffers from another

---

[12] A related article applies a similar analysis to the problem of nondisclosure in the stock and securities markets. *See* Saul Levmore, *Securities and Secrets: Insider Trading and the Law of Contracts*, 68 Va. L. Rev. 117 (1982).

problem. The sheer volume and complexity of disclosure may in a sense operate as "static" to reduce the effectiveness of any particular item of information that is revealed. This problem of "information overload" seems particularly acute when the information is technical and complex as with credit reporting and securities disclosure rules. Can you devise any way to avoid the disclosure dilemma? For more on this issue, see Landers & Rohner, *A Functional Analysis of Truth in Lending*, 26 UCLA L. REV. 711 (1979).[13]

Suppose in the hypothetical in Note 3d that a federal statute regulating insider trading makes no mention of voiding private transactions. As a matter of contract law policy, should Congressional inaction preclude a damage action by the Pension Fund?

7. *A New Perspective on Mandatory Disclosure in the Securities Context.* Securities and Exchange Commission rules compel the affirmative disclosure of information to investors about securities and their issuers. This disclosure requirement is normally justified on efficiency grounds. The traditional efficiency justification is that disclosing information to the public helps to insure that securities are properly valued by market participants based on all available information. In his article, *Mandatory Disclosure as a Solution to Agency Problems*, 62 U. CHI. L. REV. 1047 (1995), Dean Paul Mahoney terms this model the "accuracy enhancement model." According to that model, the free flow of information results in more accurately priced securities. As an alternative model of justification on efficiency grounds, Mahoney offers the "agency cost model." Under this model, mandatory disclosure serves to protect investors from abuse by corporate promoters (those creating corporations) and corporate managers. The agency cost model limits mandatory disclosure to information directly relevant to controlling promoter and manager abuse, while the accuracy enhancement model argues for full disclosure of all information relevant to the valuation of securities. Mahoney argues that the agency cost model is an historically more accurate justification for the original enactment of the securities laws. Moreover, he claims it presents the best model for the effective use of mandatory disclosure, one that contracting parties would bargain for if given the option. Do you see why it might make sense to require promoters and managers to disclose information about their *own* activities?

D. CAPACITY TO CONTRACT

We have so far considered the legal doctrines that limit contract law to the enforcement of voluntary, informed promises. But even if a promise is informed and voluntary, it may neither reflect the fully developed will of the promisor nor evidence a welfare enhancing transaction. Thus, both the autonomy and economic approaches to justifying contract law require doctrines that enforce bargains only

---

[13] There is some evidence that "information overload" does not seriously impair consumers' cognitive circuits. *See* Grether, Schwartz & Wilde, *The Irrelevance of Information Overload: An Analysis of Search and Disclosure*, 59 S. CAL. L. REV. 277 (1986). On the other hand, recent scholarship challenges the utility of mandatory disclosure as a means of overcoming information disparities. *See* Omri Ben-Shahar & Carl E. Schneider, *The Failure of Mandated Disclosure*, 159 U. PA. L. REV. 647 (2011) (arguing that mandatory disclosure "not only fails to achieve its stated goals but also leads to unintended consequences that often harm the very people it intends to serve.")

if the parties to them have the psychological and intellectual capacity to understand and evaluate the consequences of their agreements. The infancy and mental incapacity doctrines provide the two principal means of limiting contractual enforcement to persons with sufficient psychological and intellectual capacity. Although each raise unique problems, many of the same challenges confront both of them. As you consider each doctrine below, ask yourself whether the law does or should draw a bright-line distinction between persons with and without capacity, or does or should the law instead invoke vaguer standards that allow courts to customize their decisions on a case-by-case basis. Should one approach be used to regulate both the infancy and mental incapacity doctrines, or should each doctrine have a different approach?

[1]   Infancy

While courts are generally reluctant to tamper with otherwise voluntary and informed bargains on the basis of incapacity, one area where they readily intervene is contracts negotiated by minors. As it has been traditionally viewed, infancy is easily identified and almost always is statutorily designated as a particular age — typically under 18 years old. Everyone agrees that small children (e.g., a five-year old) lack the relevant capacity to enter into binding legal agreements possessed by a mentally capable 30-year old. But what precisely marks this distinction? Is there a gradual continuum between infancy and adulthood, or is there an age threshold beyond which we are confident that individuals have the relevant capacity? To what extent does the answer to this question depend on empirical facts about human physiological and psychological development? To what extent does it depend on social conventions or perceptions about age-appropriate behavior, such as drinking, engaging in sexual activity, marrying, fighting in wars, or running for public office? Should the age of legal majority be determined by science or sociology?

As you read the following case, think about what facts might be relevant, and the effects of alternative rules on minors, the parties with whom they contract, and society as a whole.

KIEFER v. FRED HOWE MOTORS, INC.
Wisconsin Supreme Court
39 Wis. 2d 20, 158 N.W.2d 288 (1968)

WILKIE, J.

Three issues are presented on this appeal. They are:

1. Should an emancipated minor over the age of eighteen be legally responsible for his contracts?

2. Was the contract effectively disaffirmed?

3. Is the plaintiff liable in tort for misrepresentation?

Legal Responsibility of Emancipated Minor

The law governing agreements made during infancy reaches back over many centuries. The general rule is that ". . . the contract of a minor, other than for necessaries, is either void or voidable at his option." The only other exceptions to the rule permitting disaffirmance are statutory or involve contracts which deal with duties imposed by law such as a contract of marriage or an agreement to support an illegitimate child. The general rule is not affected by the minor's status as emancipated or unemancipated.

Appellant does not advance any argument that would put this case within one of the exceptions to the general rule, but rather urges that this court, as a matter of public policy, adopt a rule that an emancipated minor over eighteen years of age be made legally responsible for his contracts.

The underpinnings of the general rule allowing the minor to disaffirm his contracts were undoubtedly the protection of the minor. It was thought that the minor was immature in both mind and experience and that, therefore, he should be protected from his own bad judgments as well as from adults who would take advantage of him. The doctrine of the voidability of minors' contracts often seems commendable and just. If the beans that the young naive Jack purchased from the crafty old man in the fairy tale "Jack and the Bean Stalk" had been worthless rather than magical, it would have been only fair to allow Jack to disaffirm the bargain and reclaim his cow. However, in today's modern and sophisticated society the "infancy doctrine" seems to lose some of its gloss.

Paradoxically, we declare the infant mature enough to shoulder arms in the military, but not mature enough to vote; mature enough to marry and be responsible for his torts and crimes, but not mature enough to assume the burden of his own contractual indiscretions. In Wisconsin, the infant is deemed mature enough to use a dangerous instrumentality — a motor vehicle — at sixteen, but not mature enough to purchase it without protection until he is twenty-one.

No one really questions that a line as to age must be drawn somewhere below which a legally defined minor must be able to disaffirm his contracts for nonnecessities. The law over the centuries has considered this age to be twenty-one. Legislatures in other states have lowered the age. We suggest that the appellant might better seek the change it proposes in the legislative halls rather than this court. A recent law review article in the Indiana Law Journal explores the problem of contractual disabilities of minors and points to three different legislative solutions leading to greater freedom to contract. The first approach is one gleaned from the statutes of California and New York, which would allow parties to submit a proposed contract to a court which would remove the infant's right of disaffirmance upon a finding that the particular contract is fair. This suggested approach appears to be extremely impractical in light of the expense and delay that would necessarily accompany the procedure. A second approach would be to establish a rebuttable presumption of incapacity to replace the strict rule. This alternative would be an open invitation to litigation. The third suggestion is a statutory procedure that would allow a minor to petition a court for the removal of disabilities. Under this procedure a minor would only have to go to court once, rather than once for each contract as in the first suggestion.

Undoubtedly, the infancy doctrine is an obstacle when a major purchase is involved. However, we believe that the reasons for allowing that obstacle to remain viable at this point outweigh those for casting it aside. Minors require some protection from the pitfalls of the marketplace. Reasonable minds will always differ on the extent of the protection that should be afforded. For this court to adopt a rule that the appellant suggests and remove the contractual disabilities from a minor simply because he becomes emancipated, which in most cases would be the result of marriage, would be to suggest that the married minor is somehow vested with more wisdom and maturity than his single counterpart. However, logic would not seem to dictate this result especially when today a youthful marriage is oftentimes indicative of a lack of wisdom and maturity.

Disaffirmance

The appellant questions whether there has been an effective disaffirmance of the contract in this case.

Williston, while discussing how a minor may disaffirm a contract, states:

> Any act which clearly shows an intent to disaffirm a contract or sale is sufficient for the purpose. Thus a notice by the infant of his purpose to disaffirm . . . a tender or even an offer to return the consideration or its proceeds to the vendor, . . . is sufficient.

The testimony of Steven Kiefer and the letter from his attorney to the dealer clearly establish that there was an effective disaffirmance of the contract.

Misrepresentation

Appellant's last argument is that the respondent should be held liable in tort for damages because he misrepresented his age. Appellant would use these damages as a set-off against the contract price sought to be reclaimed by respondent.

The 19th-century view was that a minor's lying about his age was inconsequential because a fraudulent representation of capacity was not the equivalent of actual capacity. This rule has been altered by time. There appear to be two possible methods that now can be employed to bind the defrauding minor: he may be estopped from denying his alleged majority, in which case the contract will be enforced or contract damages will be allowed; or he may be allowed to disaffirm his contract but be liable in tort for damages. Wisconsin follows the latter approach. In Wisconsin Loan & Finance Corp. v. Goodnough,[14] the defendant minor was a copartner in a business who had defaulted on a note given to the plaintiff in exchange for a loan. The defendant had secured the loan by fraudulently representing to the plaintiff that he was twenty-one years old. In adopting the tort theory and declining to adopt the estoppel theory, Mr. Chief Justice Rosenberry said:

> It is a matter of some importance, however, to determine whether an infant who secures benefits by misrepresenting his age to the person from whom

---

[14] [13] (1930), 201 Wis. 101.

he secured them is estopped to set up his infancy in order to defeat the contract or whether he becomes liable in an action for deceit for damages. In this case, if there is an estoppel which operates to prevent the defendant from repudiating the contract and he is liable upon it, the damages will be the full amount of the note plus interest and a reasonable attorney's fee. If he is held liable, on the other hand, in deceit, he will be liable only for the damages which the plaintiff sustained in this case, the amount of money the plaintiff parted with, which was $352 less the $25 repaid. There seems to be sound reason in the position of the English courts that to hold the contract enforceable by way of estoppel is to go contrary to the clearly declared policy of the law. But as was pointed out by the New Hampshire court, that objection lies no more for wrongs done by a minor by way of deceit than by way of slander or other torts. The contract is not enforced. He is held liable for deceit as he is for other torts such as slander, trover, and trespass.

It is considered that the sounder rule is that which holds an infant under such circumstances liable in tort for damages.

Having established that there is a remedy against the defrauding minor, the question becomes whether the requisites for a tort action in misrepresentation are present in this case.

The trial produced conflicting testimony regarding whether Steven Kiefer had been asked his age or had replied that he was "twenty-one." Steven and his wife, Jacqueline, said "No," and Frank McHalsky, appellant's salesman, said "Yes." Confronted with this conflict, the question of credibility was for the trial court to decide, which it did by holding that Steven did not orally represent that he was "twenty-one." This finding is not contrary to the great weight and clear preponderance of the evidence and must be affirmed.

Even accepting the trial court's conclusion that Steven Kiefer had not orally represented his age to be over twenty-one, the appellant argues that there was still a misrepresentation. The "motor vehicle purchase contract" signed by Steven Kiefer contained the following language just above the purchaser's signature:

I represent that I am 21 years of age or over and recognize that the dealer sells the above vehicle upon this representation.

Whether the inclusion of this sentence constitutes a misrepresentation depends on whether elements of the tort have been satisfied. They were not. In First Nat. Bank in Oshkosh v. Scieszinski[15] it is said:

A party alleging fraud has the burden of proving it by clear and convincing evidence. The elements of fraud are well established: "To be actionable the false representation must consist, first of a statement of fact which is untrue; second, that it was made with intent to defraud and for the purpose of inducing the other party to act upon it; third, that he did in fact rely on it and was induced thereby to act, to his injury or damage."

No evidence was adduced to show that the plaintiff had an intent to defraud the

---

[15] [15] (1964), 25 Wis. 2d 569.

dealer. To the contrary, it is at least arguable that the majority of minors are, as the plaintiff here might well have been, unaware of the legal consequences of their acts.

Without the element of scienter being satisfied, the plaintiff is not susceptible to an action in misrepresentation. Furthermore, the reliance mentioned in *Scieszinski* must be, as Prosser points out, "justifiable reliance." We fail to see how the dealer could be justified in the mere reliance on the fact that the plaintiff signed a contract containing a sentence that said he was twenty-one or over. The trial court observed that the plaintiff was sufficiently immature looking to arouse suspicion. The appellant never took any affirmative steps to determine whether the plaintiff was in fact over twenty-one. It never asked to see a draft card, identification card, or the most logical indicium of age under the circumstances, a driver's license. Therefore, because there was no intent to deceive, and no justifiable reliance, the appellant's action for misrepresentation must fail.

HALLOWS, J. (dissenting).

The majority opinion on the issue of whether an emancipated minor legally should be responsible for his contracts "doth protest too much." After giving very cogent reasons why the common-law rule should be abandoned, the opinion refrains from reshaping the rule to meet reality. Minors are emancipated by a valid marriage and also by entering military service. If they are mature enough to become parents and assume the responsibility of raising other minors and if they are mature enough to be drafted or volunteer to bear arms and sacrifice their life for their country, then they are mature enough to make binding contracts in the marketplace. The magical age limit of twenty-one years as an indication of contractual maturity no longer has a basis in fact or in public policy.

My second ground of the dissent is that an automobile to this respondent was a necessity and therefore the contract could not be disaffirmed. Here, we have a minor, aged twenty years and seven months, the father of a child, and working. While the record shows there is some public transportation to his present place of work, it also shows he borrowed his mother's car to go to and from work. Automobiles for parents under twenty-one years of age to go to and from work in our current society may well be a necessity and I think in this case the record shows it is. An automobile as a means of transportation to earn a living should not be considered a nonnecessity because the owner is five months too young. I would reverse.

NOTES

1. *Questions on* Kiefer.

a. In *Kiefer*, the minor signed a contract which contained a clause that said: "I represent that I am 21 years of age or over and recognize that the dealer sells the above vehicle upon this representation." That clause appeared just above the minor's signature. Why didn't the court give that clause effect in deciding the dispute? Why should the adult bargainer bear all risks in the contract, even that the other party is lying? Isn't this rule inconsistent with the comparative advantage criterion that we have used so frequently to justify the rules of contract law? If

Bailey had been a minor, would the result in *Bailey v. West, supra* p. 5, have been different? Is there any way a party who bargains with a minor can shift the risk of the minor lying about his age? Is such a rule consistent with the overall purpose of the infancy doctrine?

b. Despite the ineffectiveness of the "I am 21" clause in *Kiefer*, even that court recognized that a minor may be liable for some of the consequences of the contract if he intentionally misrepresents his age. The court in *Kiefer* pointed out two alternative results of such misrepresentation: (1) the infant would be estopped from denying his majority in later contract disaffirmance proceedings, or (2) the minor would be liable in tort for any damages sustained by the object of the contract, but still able to disaffirm the contract. Which rule did the court in *Kiefer* apply? Does it make sense to hold an infant liable for his torts when he cannot be responsible for his contracts? Can you justify these differing rules of tort and contract law?

3.   *Liability for Depreciation.* Another problem with disaffirming a contract, particularly for consumer goods such as a car, is determining which party bears the cost of product depreciation. Again, intentional misrepresentation of age plays a part in assigning liability. In *Halbman v. Lemke*, 99 Wis. 2d 241 (1980), James Halbman, a minor, entered into an agreement to buy Lemke's 1968 Oldsmobile for $1,250. At the time of the agreement, Halbman took possession of the car and paid Lemke $1,000, agreeing to pay Lemke $25 a week until the balance was paid off. A few weeks later, after Halbman had paid Lemke $1,100, a connecting rod in the engine broke. Halbman declined Lemke's offer to repair the car if Halbman supplied the parts, and instead took the car to a garage where it was repaired for $637.40. Halbman refused to pay the repair bill or pick up the car from the garage. Shortly afterward, in an attempt to avoid liability, Lemke endorsed title to the vehicle over to Halbman despite the fact that the full purchase price had not been paid. In response, Halbman returned the title to Lemke, disaffirmed the purchase contract and demanded Lemke return the $1,100 already paid. After six months, the garage removed the car's engine and transmission, and towed the car to the house of Halbman's father. While at the garage, the car had been repeatedly vandalized and had become unsalvageable. The trial court concluded that Halbman only had to return the property remaining in his possession and was not liable for use or depreciation. On appeal, the Wisconsin Supreme Court affirmed the judgment of the trial court, holding that: "absent misrepresentation or tortious damage to the property, a minor who disaffirms a contract for the purchase of an item which is not a necessity may recover his purchase price without liability for use, depreciation, damage or other diminution in value."

Does this rule make sense to you? Why is the law willing to put the minor in his status quo ante position, but not the vendor? Does this rule advance the purpose of the infancy doctrine?

In a case similar to *Halbman*, a 20-year-old minor lied about his age in order to purchase a new Ford. Several months later when he turned 21, he promptly disaffirmed the contract, returned the Ford, and demanded return of his car payments and the Pontiac given as a trade-in. The court held that the minor had committed a tort in misrepresenting his age and held him liable for depreciation of the Ford, though his absolute right to disaffirm the contract was unaffected. The minor, therefore, had to pay the difference between the reasonable value (not the contract value) of the Ford at time of delivery and its reasonable value at the time of disaffirmance. *Doenges-Long Motors, Inc. v. Gillen*, 138 Colo. 31, 328 P.2d 1077 (1958). For a contrary view, in which misrepresentation of age was held not to constitute a tortious act, see *Tyda v. Reiter-Schmidt, Inc.*, 16 Ill. App. 2d 370, 147 N.E.2d 690 (1958).

4. ***Purpose of the Infancy Doctrine.*** What is the purpose of the infancy doctrine according to cases such as *Kiefer* and *Halbman?* Does the common law rationale still hold given technological developments? In *Virtually Mature: Examining the Policy of Minor's Incapacity to Contract Through the Cyperscope*, 43 GONZ. L. REV. 239 (2008), Professor Juanda Lowder Daniel argues that the infancy doctrine does more harm than good given the rise of electronic commerce:

> Minors are online in astronomical numbers engaging in electronic commerce. The trend that young children are buying goods and services electronically exists. In fact, children comprise a significant segment of online consumers, a segment that is rapidly enlarging. While the legal community may not be adapted to the rampant involvement of children in electronic contracting, merchants have not missed it. Merchants recognize that children are consumers in their own right with strong purchasing power and in some cases depend on patronage by minors for their very existence. However, merchants are nevertheless forced to reckon with the minority incapacity doctrine, despite the level of sophistication demonstrated by minors in their interactions in cyberspace.

> Minors online are not only engaging in electronic commerce spurred by their initiation, but they are also engaging in sophisticated untoward behavior. Courts are increasingly facing matters involving sophisticated minors and their unauthorized computer-related activities. Recognizing the technological sophistication of minors, law enforcement agencies are taking proactive measures to alert parents of the potential that their children may be engaging in online criminal activity. In light of technological advancements and the sophistication of minors, it is befitting that the need for continued adherence to the long-standing minority incapacity doctrine be closely scrutinized against the backdrop of social science demonstrating the cognitive abilities and decision-making capacities of adolescents.

Id. at 255.

What reforms would you propose to the infancy doctrine to deal with these problems?

5. ***Necessity Alters the Rule.*** The court in *Kiefer* noted that the contract was not for necessities. When the subject of a contract is found to be a necessity, the minor's right to disaffirm the contract no longer exists, and the minor is considered an adult for purposes of contract liability. Some things traditionally considered to be necessities include "board, room, clothing, medical needs and education." *Valencia v. White*, 654 P.2d 287 (Ariz. Ct. App. 1982). Do you agree with the dissent in *Kiefer* that the car should have been considered a necessity?

Why should necessity change the infancy doctrine? If the rule is altered for purposes of necessities, why isn't it also altered when a minor entering a contract is emancipated? Should marriage change the infancy doctrine too? How about parenthood? What reasons did the *Kiefer* court offer for its refusal to hold emancipation and marriage sufficient to alter the infancy doctrine?

6. *The Timing of Disaffirmance and Ratification.* The infancy doctrine permits a minor to disaffirm his contract at any time while still a minor and within a reasonable time after reaching majority. How would you define a "reasonable" time? Do you suppose it is a fact-specific inquiry to be made in each post-majority disaffirmance case?

The court in *Bobby Floars Toyota, Inc. v. Smith*, 48 N.C. App. 580, 269 S.E.2d 320 (1980), considered the issue of a reasonable time for disaffirmance. In that case, Charles Smith purchased a new car from the Floars Toyota dealership five weeks before reaching majority, which was age 18 in North Carolina. Smith continued to make monthly payments on the car for ten months after his eighteenth birthday. When the eleventh month's payment fell due, Smith defaulted on the car and voluntarily returned it to Bobby Floars Toyota. The trial court found that Smith had disaffirmed the contract within a reasonable time. The North Carolina Court of Appeals overturned that holding on appeal, however. The higher court said that failure to disaffirm within a reasonable time would be taken as an acquiescence or affirmance of the contract. Further, the court noted that specific actions, rather than the unequivocal words "I affirm," could be interpreted as contract affirmation even before the reasonable time for disaffirmance had elapsed. In this case, the court held, ten months was an unreasonable time for disaffirmance and, further, that continued payments on the car effectively affirmed the contract. Smith, therefore, would not be able to disaffirm the contract or recover his money. Based on these facts, do you think the North Carolina court reached the correct result? When would it still have been reasonable for Smith to disaffirm his contract? How long after reaching majority could Kiefer and Halbman have disaffirmed their contracts?

What actions should be sufficient to constitute contract affirmation? Consider the case of *In re Score Bd., Inc. and Score Board Holding Corp.*, 238 B.R. 585 (Bankr. D.N.J. 1999). In that case, Kobe Bryant was a high school basketball star who had decided to forego college and enter the N.B.A. draft lottery. In anticipation of his future stardom and several months before reaching the majority age of eighteen, Kobe entered into an agreement with a sports memorabilia company. In exchange for compensation, Kobe agreed to a number of personal appearances, to sign a large number of autographs, and to license his image for various purposes, including trading cards. Approximately a year and a half after reaching majority, Kobe sought to disaffirm the contract. The court held that Kobe, by his actions, had ratified the contract and could not now disaffirm it. In finding that Kobe had ratified the contract, the court focused on two facts. The first was that three days after his eighteenth birthday, Kobe had deposited a check for his services. The second was that Kobe had performed some contractual obligations by signing autographs for a year and a half. The court stated, "it is clear that [Kobe] ratified the contract . . . because [he] consciously performed his contractual duties."

Would the result have been the same if Kobe had only deposited the check some three days after reaching majority? Probably. The court cited the principle that " '[a]ny conduct on the part of the former infant which evidences his decision that the transaction shall not be impeached is sufficient for [ratification].' "[16] Remember that the court in *Smith* held that Smith's continued payments constituted ratification of the agreement. Would merely driving the car not have been sufficient evidence of ratification? Would the court in *The Score Board* agree? Does it make sense to hold that performing contractual duties (i.e., making payments) constitutes ratification but enjoying the benefit of the bargain (i.e., driving the car) does not? What sort of behavior might this encourage?

7. *Distinguishing Between Infants and Adults.* Most states draw a bright line between infancy and adulthood for purposes of contracting: 18 years of age. But human psychological and physical development is gradual. In particular, the childhood/adulthood distinction fails to take into account the developmental stage of adolescence. Although contract law must consider the legal effects of contracts entered into on behalf of pre-adolescent children (consider child actors and models, for example), the question of legal capacity tends to arise once children reach adolescence. At this stage, they are more likely to attempt to enter into legally binding relationships and more likely to be perceived as legally competent actors by others. Are the reasons for prohibiting children and adolescents from entering into binding contracts the same? Should the law distinguish between children and adolescents, perhaps allowing greater latitude for adolescents to enter into contracts? Or do adolescents need protection even more precisely because they are more likely to enter into contracts yet no more psychologically able to take their own long-term interests into account? For an argument in favor of drawing a binary bright line between children and adults in civil contexts, but for taking adolescence into account in criminal contexts, see Elizabeth S. Scott, *The Legal Construction of Adolescence*, 29 Hofstra L. Rev. 547 (2000). For a contrary argument urging the adoption of a " 'factors' test" to determine if a minor lacked capacity to contract, see Larry DiMatteo, *Deconstructing the Myth of the "Infancy Law Doctrine": From Incapacity to Accountability*, 21 Ohio N.U. L. Rev. 481, 524 (1994).

[2] Mental Illness

The defense of mental incapacity raises the same central problems confronting the defense of infancy. Both defenses are relatively easy to adjudicate when the person who dealt with the infant or mentally ill party knew or had reason to know of the incapacity of their contracting partner. As a moral matter, the competent adult is prohibited from knowingly taking advantage of persons unable to look after their own interests, and, as a matter of efficiency, contracts entered into by infants or mentally impaired persons are not likely to enhance social welfare. In order to prevent these mistakes, contract law places the incentive on the party who is able at least cost to prevent such mistakes from happening. Obviously, the competent adult is ordinarily better able to prevent these contracts from being formed than are either infants or mentally impaired persons. But when the infant is reasonably believed to be an adult, or the person with a mental handicap appears

---

[16] *Notaro v. Notaro*, 38 N.J. Super. 311, 314 (1955).

normal, courts must choose between protecting vulnerable people from themselves and protecting the reasonable expectations of competent parties. Thus, "[a] contract made by a person who is mentally incompetent requires the reconciliation of two conflicting policies: the protection of justifiable expectations and of the security of transactions, and the protection of persons unable to protect themselves against imposition." Restatement (Second) § 15, comments. As a moral matter, whose interests should courts protect? As an economic matter, does it matter whose interests the law protects?

As we have seen in the previous section, courts have drawn a bright line between infancy and majority, despite the fact that contemporary psychology recognizes multiple stages of psychological development (including at least childhood, adolescence, and adulthood). Courts have had more difficulty drawing the line between capacity and incapacity as a result of mental illness.

In part, this is because defendants bear the burden of proving their mental incapacity and typically seek to carry this burden by introducing expert testimony from psychiatrists. Thus, courts are continually apprised of recent developments in our understanding of the nature of mental illnesses that defy simplistic binary models. As a result, courts have pressed beyond the traditional legal standard requiring that a mental incapacity sufficient to avoid contractual liability must be "of such a character that, at the time of execution, the person had no reasonable perception or understanding of the nature and terms of the contract." *Williamson v. Mathews*, 379 So. 2d 1245 (Ala. 1980). Yet once contract law allows parties who understand the nature and terms of their contracts to escape contractual liability, confidence in contracts may be eroded if the more flexible requirements for the mental incapacity defense are not drawn clearly and predictably. As you read the cases below, ask yourself whether the standards for incapacity drawn by the courts take into account both the complexities of mental illness and the need to preserve the predictability of contractual liability.

FABER v. SWEET STYLE MFG. CORP.
New York Supreme Court, Nassau County
40 Misc. 2d 212, 242 N.Y.S.2d 763 (1963)

MEYER, J.

The relationship of psychiatry to the criminal law has been the subject of study and recommendation by the Temporary Commission on Revision of the Penal Law and Criminal Code (Leg. Doc. [1963], No. 8, pp. 16-26). This court had reason to touch upon the relationship of psychiatry to matrimonial law in Anonymous v. Anonymous (37 Misc. 2d 773). The instant case presents yet a third aspect of the same basic problem: that involving the law of contract.

Plaintiff herein seeks rescission of a contract for the purchase of vacant land in Long Beach on the ground that he was not at the time the contract was entered into of sufficient mental competence. Defendant counterclaims for specific performance.

The evidence demonstrates that from April until July, 1961, plaintiff was in the depressed phase of a manic-depressive psychosis and that from August until the end of October he was in the manic stage. Though under care of Dr. Levine, a psychiatrist, beginning June 8 for his depression, he canceled his August 8 appointment and refused to see the doctor further. Previously frugal and cautious, he became more expansive beginning in August, began to drive at high speeds, to take his wife out to dinner, to be sexually more active and to discuss his prowess with others. In a short period of time, he purchased three expensive cars for himself, his son and his daughter, began to discuss converting his Long Beach bathhouse and garage property into a 12-story co-operative and put up a sign to that effect, and to discuss the purchase of land in Brentwood for the erection of houses. In September, against the advice of his lawyer, he contracted for land at White Lake in the Catskills costing $11,500 and gave a $500 deposit on acreage, the price of which was $41,000 and talked about erecting a 400-room hotel with marina and golf course on the land. On September 16, 1961, he discussed with Mr. Kass, defendant's president, the purchase of the property involved in this litigation for the erection of a discount drugstore and merchandise mart. During the following week Kass advised plaintiff that defendant would sell. On the morning of Saturday, September 23, plaintiff and Kass met at the office of defendant's real estate broker. Kass asked $55,000, plaintiff offered $50,000; when the broker agreed to take $1,500 commission, Kass offered to sell for $51,500 and plaintiff accepted. It was agreed the parties would meet for contract that afternoon. Kass obtained the services of attorney Nathan Suskin who drew the contract prior to the 2:00 P.M. conference. Plaintiff returned to that conference with his lawyer (who is also his brother-in-law) who approved the contract as to form but asked plaintiff how he would finance it and also demanded that the contract include as a condition that a nearby vacant property would be occupied by [a popular supermarket chain]. No mention was made of plaintiff's illness. When Suskin refused to consider such a condition, plaintiff's lawyer withdrew. The contract was signed in the absence of plaintiff's lawyer and the $5,150 deposit paid by check on plaintiff's checking account in a Rockaway bank.

On the following Monday morning, plaintiff transferred funds from his Long Beach bank account to cover the check. On the same day, he went to Jamaica and arranged with a title abstract company for the necessary search and policy, giving correct details concerning the property, price and his brother-in-law's address and phone number and asking that search be completed within one week. Between September 23 when the contract was signed and October 8 when plaintiff was sent to a mental institution, he persuaded Leonard Cohen, a former employee, to join in the building enterprise promising him a salary of $150 a week and a Lincoln Continental when the project was complete, caused a sign to be erected on the premises stating that "Faber Drug Company" and a "merchandise mart" were coming soon, hired an architect, initiated a mortgage application giving correct details as to price and property dimensions, hired laborers to begin digging (though title was not to close until Oct. 20), filed plans with city officials and when told by them that State Labor Department approval was required, insisted on driving to Albany with the architect and Leonard Cohen to obtain the necessary approval.

On September 25 plaintiff saw Dr. Levine as a result of plaintiff's complaint that his wife needed help, that she was stopping him from doing what he wanted to. He was seen again on September 26 and 28, October 2 and October 8, and hospitalized on October 8 after he had purchased a hunting gun. Dr. Levine, Dr. Sutton, who appeared for defendant, and the hospital all agree in a diagnosis of manic-depressive psychosis. Dr. Levine testified that on September 23 plaintiff was incapable of reasoned judgment; the hospital record shows that on October 9, Dr. Krinsky found plaintiff's knowledge good, his memory and comprehension fair, his insight lacking and his judgment defective. Dr. Sutton's opinion, based on the hospital record and testimony of plaintiff's wife and Dr. Levine, was that plaintiff was subject to mood swings, but that there was no abnormality in his thinking, that his judgment on September 23 was intact. The contract of a mental incompetent is voidable at the election of the incompetent, and if the other party can be restored to *status quo*, rescission will be decreed upon a showing of incompetence without more. If the status quo cannot be restored and the other party to the contract was ignorant of the incompetence and the transaction was fair and reasonable, rescission will, however, be denied notwithstanding incompetence. The burden of proving incompetence is upon the party alleging it, but once incompetence has been shown, the burden of proving lack of knowledge and fairness is upon the party asking that the transaction be enforced. In the instant case the contract concerns vacant land and is executory and though plaintiff caused some digging to be done on the premises, the proof shows that the land has been leveled again. Clearly, the status quo can be restored and plaintiff is, therefore, entitled to rescission if the condition described meets the legal test of incompetence.

The standards by which competence to contract is measured were, apparently, developed without relation to the effects of particular mental diseases or disorders and prior to recognition of manic-depressive psychosis as a distinct form of mental illness. Primarily they are concerned with capacity to understand: "so deprived of his mental faculties as to be wholly, absolutely and completely unable to understand or comprehend the nature of the transaction"; (Paine v. Aldrich, 133 N.Y. 544, 546) "such mental capacity at the time of the execution of the deed that he could collect in his mind without prompting, all the elements of the transaction and retain them for a sufficient length of time to perceive their obvious relations to each other, and to form a rational judgment in regard to them"; (Matter of Delinousha v. National Biscuit Co., 248 N.Y. 93, 95) "A contract may be avoided only if a party is so affected as to be unable to see things in their true relations and to form correct conclusions in regard thereto." If cognitive capacity is the sole criterion used, the manic must be held competent for manic-depressive psychosis affects motivation rather than ability to understand.

The law does, however, recognize stages of incompetence other than total lack of understanding. Thus it will invalidate a transaction when a contracting party is suffering from delusions if there is "some such connection between the insane delusions and the making of the deed as will compel the inference that the insanity induced the grantor to perform an act, the purport and effect of which he could not understand, and which he would not have performed if thoroughly sane" (Moritz v. Moritz, 153 App. Div. 147, 152, aff'd, 211 N.Y. 580). Moreover, it holds that understanding of the physical nature and consequences of an act of suicide does not render the suicide voluntary within the meaning of a life insurance contract if the insured "acted under the control of an insane impulse caused by disease, and derangement of his intellect, which deprived him of the capacity of governing his own conduct in accordance with reason." (Newton v. Mutual Benefit Life Ins. Co., 76 N.Y. 426, 429.) Finally, Paine v. Aldrich (*supra*) and the *Delinousha* case consider not only ability to understand but also capacity to form "a rational judgment" or "correct conclusions." Thus, capacity to understand is not, in fact, the sole criterion. Incompetence to contract also exists when a contract is entered into under the compulsion of a mental disease or disorder but for which the contract would not have been made. Whether under the latter test a manic will be held incompetent to enter into a particular contract will depend upon an evaluation of (1) testimony of the claimed incompetent, (2) testimony of psychiatrists, and (3) the behavior of the claimed incompetent as detailed in the testimony of others including whether by usual business standards the transaction is normal or fair. Testimony of the claimed incompetent often is not available, and in any event is subject to the weakness of his mental disorder, on the one hand, and of his self-interest on the other. The psychiatrist in presenting his opinion is, in final analysis, evaluating factual information rather than medical data, and is working largely with the same evidence presented to the court by the other witnesses in the action. Moreover, in the great majority of cases psychiatrists of equal qualification and experience will reach diametrically opposed conclusions on the same behavioral evidence. The courts have, therefore, tended to give less weight to expert testimony than to objective behavioral evidence.

In the instant case, plaintiff did not testify at the trial but his examination before trial was read into the record. It shows that he understood the transaction in which he was engaged, but throws no light on his motivation. Plaintiff introduced no evidence concerning the rationality or fairness of the transaction so the court has no basis for comparison in that respect. Plaintiff's evidence concerning the location of the property and the nature of the business he proposed to carry on there fell short of establishing irrationality, nor can it be said that the making of an all cash contract was abnormal, even if the two earlier White Lake dealings are considered, in view of the testimony of plaintiff and his wife that the Long Beach bathhouse property was worth $200,000 and that it was free and clear. But the rapidity with which plaintiff moved to obtain an architect and plans, hire laborers, begin digging on the property, and his journey to Albany to obtain building approval, all prior to title closing, are abnormal acts. Viewing those acts in the context of his actions, detailed above, with respect to the White Lake properties, his plans with respect to the Brentwood property and the conversion of his bathhouse premises, and his complaint to Dr. Levine on September 25 that his wife was in need of help because she was trying to hold him back, the court is convinced that the contract in question was entered into under the compulsion of plaintiff's psychosis. That conclusion is contrary to the opinion expressed by Dr. Sutton, but the court concludes that Doctors Levine and Krinsky as treating physicians had the better basis for the opinions they expressed. In any event their opinions are but confirmatory of the conclusion reached by the court on the basis of the evidence above detailed. Defendant argues, however, that the contract was ratified by the acts of plaintiff's attorney in forwarding a title objection sheet to defendant's attorney and in postponing the closing and by plaintiff himself. Ratification requires conscious action on the part of the party to be charged. Plaintiff was still in the mental hospital when the objection sheet was sent and the closing date postponed and these acts have not been shown to have been carried out with his knowledge or by his direction.

As for his own action it was merely to answer, in reply to an inquiry from defendant's president as to when he was going to take title, that he did not know, it was up to his attorney.

The contract with defendant had been signed on September 23, plaintiff had been sent to the hospital on October 8 and remained there until November 11, having a series of electro-shock treatments while there, and the complaint in this action was verified November 20. The conversation with defendant's president could not have occurred until after November 11 and must have occurred several days prior to November 20. An answer as equivocal in nature and made under the circumstances as the one under consideration cannot in any fair sense be characterized as an exercise of plaintiff's right of election to "hold on to the bargain if it is good and let it go if it is bad" (Blinn v. Schwarz, 177 N.Y. 252, 263).

Accordingly, defendant's motions at the end of plaintiff's case and of the whole case, on which decision was reserved, are now denied, and judgment will be entered declaring the contract rescinded and dismissing the counterclaim.

NOTES

1. **Questions on** Faber. In *Faber*, the contract in question was rescinded. Contrast that holding with *Uribe v. Olson*, 601 P.2d 818 (Or. 1979). In *Uribe*, the court heard evidence that Ruby Bonham, age 81, suffered from a heart blockage that caused seizures, blackouts and involutional psychosis resulting in depression. Friends and relatives all testified to a gradual deterioration of her mental acuity over several years prior to the transaction in question. This deterioration manifested itself in a number of ways, including periods of disorientation and depression, occasional paranoia, an increase in eccentric habits and delusions concerning people long dead and imagined friendships with Barry Goldwater and Frank Sinatra. Despite this evidence, the court declined to rescind her contract sell 80 acres of undeveloped land, finding that

> While there is ample evidence to establish that Mrs. Bonham's mental state on September 28, 1976, had deteriorated substantially from what it once had been, this does not resolve the matter. We are persuaded, largely by the circumstances of the sale, that Mrs. Bonham was competent to sell her land. Mrs. Bonham had definite ideas about how the property should be listed and accurately supplied all the necessary information. The purchase price was negotiated over several months and the offer that was ultimately accepted was made by Mrs. Bonham. . . . Before obtaining her signature, Mr. Martin read the important features of the earnest money agreement to Mrs. Bonham and had her read the document, a point of considerable significance. . . . In fact, defendant's primary dissatisfaction with the deal appears to be the price obtained, not the fact that the property was sold. In sum, the evidence indicates that Mrs. Bonham knew what she was doing and, though her reasons for selling may not have been altogether wise, she intended to sell and was cognizant of the consequences. . . .

Id. at 820.

Can you construct an underlying principle to justify and reconcile the different results? (Hint: Think about *Bailey v. West*, p. 5, *supra*, and the comparative advantage criterion.)

In *Faber*, the court noted that the law on mental incapacity had developed without regard to the causes and effects of various mental illnesses. Do you get a sense that the law has not kept pace with modern developments in psychology and psychiatry? Or is the attempt, at least in New York, to recognize different stages of incompetency premised on an unrealistic belief in the capacity of mental health professionals to accurately diagnose degrees of incompetency?

The court in *Uribe* placed great emphasis on the fact that Ruby Bonham read the contract and that the real estate agent, Mr. Martin, read important parts of the contract to her. Was it possible that Mrs. Bonham had the capacity to read and to listen to the contract, but not to understand the implications of the document? Was there evidence of such mental incapacity? Why, then, did the court uphold the contract? Would evidence of some other inequity, as in *Faber*, have helped Mrs. Bonham's claim?

2.   ***Fairness as a Factor.*** Unlike the clear, binary rule for infancy, the outcomes in the mental incompetency cases seem to vary depending on the courts' assessments of the "fairness" or "reasonableness" of the contract terms. If the contract is seen as fair, it is likely to be enforced despite evidence of mental illness, as in *Uribe*. On the other hand, contract terms that vary from the norm (at least as the court determines it) will be assumed to reflect exploitation of the disability and are likely to be nullified by the court, as in *Faber*. Such a fairness approach for contracts made by minors was proposed in New York and California, but was soundly rejected in Wisconsin in *Kiefer v. Fred Howe Motors, Inc.* Professor Milton Green referred to this unspoken fairness analysis as an "inarticulate standard." He wrote: "[M]any courts seem to approach the problem [of mental incompetency] in what may seem to be a reverse order; they appear to judge the transaction first; and only if it is queer, abnormal, or unfair do they proceed to the second stage and judge the author of the transaction." Milton Green, *Proof of Mental Incompetency and the Unexpressed Major Premise*, 53 YALE L.J. 271, 275 (1944). Do you see any problems with this approach to the incompetency issue? Can you reconcile the judicial effort to assess the fairness of contracts made by allegedly mentally disabled persons with the doctrine of adequacy of consideration? (*See Wolford v. Powers*, Chapter 2.)

Many cases where parties claim mental incapacity to contract are the result of extenuating circumstances such as divorce settlements, foreclosures on property, bankruptcy, or other settings that place enormous stress on the individuals involved and therefore might impair their judgment. After the crisis and subsequent reevaluation of their decisions, these parties sometimes attempt to rescind their agreements, arguing incapacity. If courts permitted these parties to rescind their agreements based solely on incapacity, what impact would there be on future parties in such circumstances? Why might courts require, in addition to incapacity, a showing of unfairness or injustice in such circumstances and in incapacity cases in general?

3.   ***Knowledge of Incompetency.*** Should it make a difference in the present law of mental incompetence whether the mentally capable party knows that the other

party is mentally ill? The plaintiff in *Uribe v. Olson* (*see* Note 1, *supra*) testified that while Mrs. Bonham appeared eccentric to him, he had no reason to believe she was mentally incompetent since she answered all his questions and gave him a thorough tour of the property. In the case of infants, the result is the same regardless of whether the contracting adult knew he was dealing with an infant or not. Given the other differences in the regulation of mental incompetency, do you think the result will remain the same regardless of the stable party's knowledge? Or should knowledge that the other party is mentally ill shift the burden of proof onto the mentally stable party? (In other words, the stable party would have to prove that the contract was fair and should not be voided. Presently, the law requires the mental incompetent to prove that the contract was unfair and should be rescinded.)

Louisiana requires that to annul a contract for mental incompetence, the party seeking annulment must prove that "he was incapacitated at the time of the contract and that it was generally known by those who saw and conversed with him or it was known to the person who contracted with him." *Fidelity Financial Services, Inc. v. McCoy*, 392 So. 2d 118, 119–20 (La. Ct. App. 1980). Do you approve of this rule? Does it embody what generally seems to be happening in courts anyway?

4. *The Elderly.* Should Mrs. Bonham have been given special protection because of her age? Senior citizens are common, and vulnerable, targets of those seeking unfair bargains. Yet unlike minors, seniors are not presumed to lack capacity. Should the law lower the standard of proof of incapacity after a certain age? Would such a rule be offensive or degrading? *See generally* Wendy Chung Rossiter, Comment, *No Protection for the Elderly: The Inadequacy of the Capacity Doctrine in Avoiding Unfair Contracts Involving Seniors*, 78 Or. L. Rev. 807 (1999).

E. PUBLIC POLICY LIMITATIONS

All elements of a valid contract may be present, yet a court will sometimes deem a fully voluntary, informed agreement between competent adults void as against public policy. At first blush, such limitations on freedom of contract appear to offend the autonomy and economic principles underlying the doctrines of contractual enforcement so far discussed. Both principles appear to support unfettered freedom of contract. Yet both principles in fact allow for significant limitations on freedom of contract if the effects of contractual enforcement are not confined to the contractual parties themselves.

In economic parlance, individuals who bear the total costs and benefits of their conduct are said to fully "internalize" the costs of their behavior. When individuals fully internalize the costs and benefits of their activity, their activity creates no costs or benefits other than those born by them. Thus, their private incentives lead them to engage in the socially optimal level of that behavior. When individuals do not fully internalize the costs and benefits of their behavior, however, the costs and benefits that are born by others are "externalities." When an individual's activity creates either negative or positive externalities, that individual no longer has the incentives to engage in that activity at the socially optimal level. If her activity creates positive externalities, she will perform less of the activity than would be socially optimal. But if her activity creates negative externalities, she will perform more of the activity than would be socially optimal. Thus, the economic approach recognizes that even fully voluntary and informed agreements between competent adults might nonetheless be socially undesirable because they might create negative externalities.

The autonomy approach likewise acknowledges that when contracts create third-party effects, the principle of autonomy will sometimes argue against their enforcement. In particular, the autonomy principle would reject enforcement of agreements that diminish the extent or value of the autonomy of third parties. More generally, moral theories predicated on the value of autonomy often support an array of equal individual rights that significantly circumscribe the principle of liberty of contract. On any plausible moral theory, individuals are prohibited from harming others. Contracts that create negative externalities therefore might be objected to as creating impermissible harm to others.

The sobering reality, however, is that virtually all conduct — including contractual behavior — creates both negative and positive externalities. If the conception of purely self-regarding behavior was ever an accurate description of any real life behavior, that day is long gone. Limiting freedom of contract to those agreements that do not create negative externalities would, in practice, eviscerate freedom of contract. The public policy exceptions to contractual enforcement cannot therefore be plausibly described as prohibitions on contracts creating negative externalities generally. Instead, they focus, in the first instance, on two particular kinds of negative externalities: illegal and immoral activities.

As you consider the illegality and immorality public policy exceptions below, ask yourself if these exceptions are based on perceived negative externalities, or whether they serve instead as alternative doctrines for reinforcing the duress, fraud, and capacity doctrines covered earlier. Even within these categories, how do the courts decide which activities are illegal and immoral? Do these doctrines serve the ends they purport to serve? Finally, do the means they employ justify those ends?

[1]   Illegality

WATTS v. MALATESTA
New York Court of Appeals
262 N.Y. 80, 186 N.E. 210 (1933)

CROUCH, J.

The action is under § 994 of the Penal Law to recover money paid by plaintiff to defendant upon the event of prohibited wagers or bets. Plaintiff proved conclusively that on divers dates and occasions from April 28, 1928, to April 17, 1930, he had paid defendant, a bookmaker, various sums of money aggregating $37,535 for wagers lost upon a series of horse races. The defendant adduced evidence which, it may be assumed, warranted a finding that during the same period defendant lost and paid to plaintiff like wagers aggregating a much larger sum. It was the contention of the defendant, under a pleaded counterclaim, that he was entitled to recover from the plaintiff a sum equal to the excess of the total amount lost and paid by him to the plaintiff over the total amount lost and paid by the plaintiff to him. That contention, accepted by the trial court, was rejected by the Appellate Division. Plaintiff was granted judgment for the entire amount of the wagers lost and paid by him to the defendant. As matter of law, the judgment was right.

Under the evidence and for the purpose of this case, plaintiff must be regarded as a casual, and the defendant as a professional gambler. "The statute against betting and gaming was enacted as a protection of the public morals. The intention of the legislature was to discourage and repress gambling in all its forms, and the law . . . is to be construed so as to accomplish, so far as possible, the suppression of the mischief against which it was directed." (Luetchford v. Lord, 132 N.Y. 465, 469.) But casual betting or gaming by individuals as distinguished from betting or gambling as a business or profession, is not a crime. The distinction between the two species has long "obtained in this state where ordinary betting has never been made a crime . . . while the keeping of a gambling house, selling lottery tickets and the profession of a common gambler have been subjected to severe punishment." Discouragement of casual betting has never gone beyond the point of making recovery by a winner impossible upon default by the loser (Penal Law, §§ 991 and 992); and of compelling return to the loser of voluntary payments made by him. (Penal Law, §§ 994 and 995.) Attack or defense in a civil action has been regarded as adequate — "as one of the best and surest means" for the suppression of that kind of betting. The evil which the law chiefly condemns and makes criminal is betting and gambling organized and carried on as a systematic business. The reason seems obvious. Curb the professional with his constant offer of temptation coupled with ready opportunity, and you have to a large extent controlled the evil. It is clear that in the eye of the law the professional gambler and his customer do not stand on the same plane. They are not *in pari delicto*.

To argue, therefore, that the Legislature, by using the phrase "any person" in § 994 of the Penal Law, intended to confer a right upon the professional to recover his losses from his customer, is unconvincing. Under such a construction, a criminal act would give rise to a cause of action. That cannot be the law. By no possibility could such a construction tend, as we have said it should, to "the suppression of the mischief against which it [the statute] is directed."

But it is urged that in any event the defendant, a professional specializing in the field of bookmaking, may offset his losses against the plaintiff's claim. How may that be, if he has no cause of action at all? To permit it would be to permit *pro tanto* what the law denies *in toto*. Nowhere in the statute is there any indication of an intent to afford a *locus poenitentiae* to the professional. Quite the contrary. Whatever his shape may be, he is an outlaw. Moreover it is to be remembered that the right of recovery given by statute to the casual gamester is not intended to benefit him, but to put teeth in the prohibition against all betting. . . .

The judgment should be affirmed, with costs.

CRANE, J. (dissenting).

The plaintiff and the defendant are two gamblers, the defendant being a bookmaker at the race tracks, and the plaintiff placing his bets on the races with the defendant through himself and his betting agent. These transactions covered the period between April 27, 1928, and May 28, 1929, during which time the plaintiff won nearly $250,000, and had lost about $150,000. His gains over losses were about $100,000. All the money he won was paid to him. He now brings this action under section 994 of the Penal Law to recover his losses but makes no offer to repay his winnings — these he wants to keep.

In his complaint he alleges that between the dates stated he paid to John B. Malatesta $37,773 as his wagers upon horse races at the Belmont track, the Jamaica race track and the Empire City race track; that having lost, he demanded back his money which the defendant failed to pay. Mind you, he sues to recover no single bet, nor does he even state or prove what the wagers were as made. He lumps his demands for a year's betting and asks for the total; he treats the transactions as a running account. The defendant in his answer admits that between the dates mentioned he and the plaintiff entered into a series of wagers upon horse races but denies that the plaintiff's losses have not been repaid. He further alleges, as a counterclaim, the fact that he paid the plaintiff $95,938, his winnings at the track over and above the losses, and demands judgment for its return.. . . . The result in my judgment is that both parties should have lost; that neither should have recovered from the other; that they were *in pari delicto* and that section 994 never intended that a person who makes a wager may sue for and recover the same, although he may at the same time keep all his own winnings made in the same course of transactions more than sufficient to meet his losses.

The plaintiff could not have recovered his winnings from the defendant. He would have no standing in court, for the law refuses to recognize gambling debts or afford the winner any relief. When, however, the plaintiff, under § 994, seeks to recover what he has lost, at the same time having in his possession and having received from the defendant more than sufficient to cover such losses, all coming out of the same course of transactions, the court should afford him no relief. Section 994 of the Penal Law was never intended to cover such a case. Instead of discouraging gambling and bookmaking, which is the purpose of the law, such a result would do the very reverse by encouraging people to wager on horse races with a bookmaker whose money they could legally take, and then recover all that they may have lost in the same afternoon. The very purpose of § 994 is thus nullified. . . . In interpreting our laws, we must have in mind as a fundamental principle the evils which they are sought to prevent and not so construe them as to create greater evils.

The remedy, under § 994 of the Penal Law, is not confined to those who bet with professional gamblers or with bookmakers at race tracks, but applies also to those who bet at poker or on the result of elections. The loser may always sue to recover back his lost wager. This he could not do at common law. Prior to these provisions of the Revised Statutes, followed by section 994 of the Penal Law, the loser could not maintain an action to recover his losses because, having participated in an illegal act, the courts would not aid him. It left the parties in the position in which it found them. . . . "*In pari delicto potior est conditio defendentis*," is the rule in such cases; but this is a rule which acknowledges no just or legal title in the defendant. It assumes, on the other hand, that the money or thing in his possession has been acquired in violation of the law, and it then denies a remedy to the other party because he has been an equal sharer in the same offense. Thus the parties are left where the law finds them, and the defendant prevails, not upon his own merits or title, but because the plaintiff is deemed unworthy to be heard in the particular case. The purpose of section 994 was merely to restore — to put the party back in the same position as if he had never parted with his property, to disregard the wager as an illegal act and to give the bettor that which he had lost, or, in the words of the decisions, that which the winner wrongfully kept. The statute, however, never intended to go further than this, or to permit one to profit out of his wrong, recover not only what he has lost, but also keep all that he has won. As above stated, to permit him to do this is to afford a rare opportunity for adventure or extortion, or betting on a "sure thing." . . .

I, therefore, am for reversal, the dismissal of the complaint and of the counterclaim, basing my opinion upon these two grounds: (1) Section 994 of the Penal Law was never intended to cover a case like this which would permit a bettor to recover all his losses without offsetting his winnings, and (2) for the reason that the winnings, growing out of the same course of transactions, amount to a repayment of the losses.

NOTES

1. ***Questions on* Watts.** Watts, the plaintiff, prevailed in his suit to recover over $37,000 in betting losses from the defendant, a professional bookmaker, even though he had netted over $100,000 in winnings during one year. Do you agree with this outcome? Why was Malatesta denied any relief on his counterclaim to have the plaintiff's winnings offset against his losses before a money award was granted? What distinction did the court draw between the two gamblers? Is that a realistic appraisal of the situation, given the amount of money involved?

The dissent in *Watts* wanted to deny relief to both parties. On what basis did Justice Crane arrive at that decision? What evil was Penal Law § 994 apparently trying to eliminate? How did the New York legislature change the common law by passing § 994? Why would the legislature want to effect such a change?

2. ***The End and Means of Deterrence.*** The *Watts* court stated, in its majority and dissenting opinions, that its decision was designed to deter illegal behavior. Did the court understand the incentive effects of its decision? The dissent argues that "No surer way can be devised to encourage the gambling instinct than to say to these semi-professional gamblers like the plaintiff, 'You can risk all your money on the horses and, if you lose, recover it back. If you win, you need never pay back.'" *Id.* at 90. The court is surely right that this rule would make gambling far more attractive for gamblers. But it takes two to tango. How would this rule affect the incentives of the bookie to take gambling debts? [footnote: For the argument that the majority in *Watts* got it right, *See* Juliet P. Kostritsky, *Illegal Contracts and Efficient Deterrence: A Study in Modern Contract Theory*, 74 Iowa L. Rev. 115, 143 (1988) (arguing that if "the courts consistently impose the loss on the professional wrongdoers, they will deter a party with incentive to engage in multiple illegal transactions.") Moreover, how important are the rules of contractual enforcement to parties engaged in illegal conduct? How often do you suppose gamblers or bookies would seek to enforce their agreements in court even if they were legally enforceable? If such contracts are legally unenforceable, does that mean they are

not enforced? (Can you think of any extra-legal sanctions that might ordinarily accompany such agreements?)

Suppose the court in *Watts* believed both parties were professional gamblers. Presumably it would treat them as *in pari delicto*. Would it leave both without legal remedy? Do the deterrence ends of the illegality doctrine justify treating litigants as mere means to the end of deterring future illegal conduct? Or should the court's decision take into account the rights or interests of either or both parties? What is the purpose served by the "clean hands" or *in pari delicto* doctrine? Another oft-used phrase is that courts decline to enforce illegal contracts so as not to "soil the judicial ermine." What does this mean?

3. *Who Determines Illegality?* What if two parties agree to a contract that provides for an alternative dispute resolution method such as arbitration and one of them later seeks rescission of the contract on grounds of illegality? The Supreme Court considered this issue in *Buckeye Check Cashing Inc. v. Cardegna.* There, the Cardegnas entered into several deferred-payment transactions with a check cashing service and signed an agreement each time requiring that any claims or disputes arising from the transaction be settled in arbitration. They later brought a putative class action alleging that the agreement violated state consumer protection and usury laws. Buckeye responded by moving to compel arbitration, arguing that the determination of illegality was subject to the arbitration clause. The Supreme Court agreed:

> First, as a matter of substantive federal arbitration law, an arbitration provision is severable from the remainder of the contract. Second, unless the challenge is to the arbitration clause itself, the issue of the contract's validity is considered by the arbitrator in the first instance. Third, this arbitration law applies in state as well as federal courts. The parties have not requested, and we do not undertake, reconsideration of those holdings. Applying them to this case, we conclude that because respondents challenge the Agreement, but not specifically its arbitration provisions, those provisions are enforceable apart from the remainder of the contract. The challenge should therefore be considered by an arbitrator, not a court.

Buckeye Check Cashing Inc. v. Cardegna, 546 U.S. 440, 445 (2006).

Would both parties tend to prefer arbitration ex ante, given the costs of litigation? If so, *Buckeye Check Cashing* could be justified on grounds of both autonomy and efficiency. On the other hand, is it troubling that parties can effectively insulate their agreements from judicial scrutiny? What role is left for courts in applying the public policy doctrine if sophisticated parties can contract out of judicial review?

4. *Illegal Performance.* In *Watts,* the majority found that the agreement itself was illegal and thus unenforceable. What about situations in which a contract is facially legal but executed in a manner contrary to public policy? The United States Court of Federal Claims grappled with this issue in *Transfair Int'l, Inc. v. United States,* 54 Fed. Cl. 78 (2002). There, Transfair entered into a contract with the United States to deliver humanitarian relief to Eritrea. Transfair had initially represented to the government that it would use a Ukrainian carrier to make the delivery, but the issue was not discussed in detail and the contract terms did not cover the nationality of the carrier. Shortly before the delivery, a bombing in Eritrea caused the Ukrainian government to prohibit any Ukrainian planes from landing near the delivery zone. Transfair was forced to switch to an Iranian carrier in violation of federal law. After the delivery, the United States refused to pay Transfair for its services on the ground that the performance of the contract was illegal, and therefore unenforceable. The Court rejected this argument:

> That leads us to defendant's second main proposition-that the illegal performance of this contract renders it per se unenforceable. This claim, too, appears defective. In support of this claim, defendant relies, inter alia, on the Restatement (Second) of Contracts, which deals with the unenforceability of bargains on the grounds of public policy, and cites, specifically, section 178 thereof. Perhaps, a highly selective reading of paragraph (1) of that section lends superficial credibility to defendant's position, as it provides that "[a] promise or other term of an agreement is unenforceable on grounds of public policy if legislation provides that it is unenforceable or the interest in its enforcement is clearly outweighed in the circumstances by a public policy against the enforcement of such terms." Yet, even this sentence, particularly, the "clearly outweighed" language, suggests anything but an absolute rule of unenforceability. This suspicion is immediately confirmed by the next two paragraphs of this section, which explicitly describe a balancing test for deciding whether not to enforce a contract term on grounds of public policy. . . .

> The accompanying commentary injects yet additional considerations into this balancing analysis. Thus, regarding the parties' justified expectations, comment e to section 178 provides that "[t]he promisee's ignorance or inadvertence, . . . is one factor in determining the weight to be attached to his expectations." *Id.* at cmt. e.; see also *id.* at § 180 (indicating that, in some circumstances, a promisee "excusably ignorant of the facts" that contravene the public policy may enforce the contract). . . . Rounding out this analysis, comment c indicates that "[a] disparity between a relatively modest criminal sanction provided by the legislature and a much larger forfeiture that will result if enforcement of the promise is refused may suggest that the policy is not substantial enough to justify the refusal." *Id.* at cmt. c.

> Far from supporting a strict prophylactic rule on illegality, then, the Restatement (Second) of Contracts categorically rejects such an approach in favor of a fact-driven inquiry-to wit, whether the enforcement of a contract term "is outweighed in the circumstances by a public policy harmed by enforcement of the agreement." Town of Newton, 480 U.S. at 392, 107 S. Ct. 1187. . . . Mindful of the reciprocal dangers of overdeterrence and underdeterrence, the Restatement, as well as the associated case law, thus require a balanced consideration of such things as: (i) the culpability of the promisee, including what it knew about the illegality; (ii) the corresponding culpability of the promisor, including whether it knew about the illegality prior to the completion of performance; (iii) whether effectuating a forfeiture, under the circumstances of a given case, would

serve the public purposes at issue, including deterring future violations of any statute or regulation involved; and (iv) finally, whether any forfeiture resulting from the nonenforcement of the contract terms is proportional to the illegality, considering, inter alia, how that penalty compares to the civil and criminal penalties directly imposed for the violation of the same statutes or regulations.9 Merely to identify these factors as being relevant is to refute defendant's contention that the contract is unenforceable irrespective of what Transfair knew, whether its overall actions were reasonable, and what the USAID officials knew as they supervised the loading of the planes bound for Eritrea.

Id. at 84.

[2] **Immorality**

IN RE BABY M
Supreme Court of New Jersey
109 N.J. 396, 537 A.2d 1227 (1988)

WILENTZ, J.

In February 1985, William Stern and Mary Beth Whitehead entered into a surrogacy contract. It recited that Stern's wife, Elizabeth, was infertile, that they wanted a child, and that Mrs. Whitehead was willing to provide that child as the mother with Mr. Stern as the father.

The contract provided that through artificial insemination using Mr. Stern's sperm, Mrs. Whitehead would become pregnant, carry the child to term, bear it, deliver it to the Sterns, and thereafter do whatever was necessary to terminate her maternal rights so that Mrs. Stern could thereafter adopt the child. Mrs. Whitehead's husband, Richard, was also a party to the contract; Mrs. Stern was not. Mr. Whitehead promised to do all acts necessary to rebut the presumption of paternity under the Parentage Act. Although Mrs. Stern was not a party to the surrogacy agreement, the contract gave her sole custody of the child in the event of Mr. Stern's death. Mrs. Stern's status as a nonparty to the surrogate parenting agreement presumably was to avoid the application of the baby-selling statute to this arrangement.

Mr. Stern, on his part, agreed to attempt the artificial insemination and to pay Mrs. Whitehead $10,000 after the child's birth, on its delivery to him. In a separate contract, Mr. Stern agreed to pay $7,500 to the Infertility Center of New York ("ICNY"). The Center's advertising campaigns solicit surrogate mothers and encourage infertile couples to consider surrogacy. ICNY arranged for the surrogacy contract by bringing the parties together, explaining the process to them, furnishing the contractual form, and providing legal counsel.

The history of the parties' involvement in this arrangement suggests their good faith. William and Elizabeth Stern were married in July 1974, having met at the University of Michigan, where both were Ph.D. candidates. Due to financial considerations and Mrs. Stern's pursuit of a medical degree and residency, they decided to defer starting a family until 1981. Before then, however, Mrs. Stern learned that she might have multiple sclerosis and that the disease in some cases renders pregnancy a serious health risk. Her anxiety appears to have exceeded the actual risk, which current medical authorities assess as minimal. Nonetheless that anxiety was evidently quite real, Mrs. Stern fearing that pregnancy might precipitate blindness, paraplegia, or other forms of debilitation. Based on the perceived risk, the Sterns decided to forego having their own children. The decision had special significance for Mr. Stern. Most of his family had been destroyed in the Holocaust. As the family's only survivor, he very much wanted to continue his bloodline.

Initially the Sterns considered adoption, but were discouraged by the substantial delay apparently involved and by the potential problem they saw arising from their age and their differing religious backgrounds. They were most eager for some other means to start a family.

The paths of Mrs. Whitehead and the Sterns to surrogacy were similar. Both responded to advertising by ICNY. The Sterns' response, following their inquiries into adoption, was the result of their long-standing decision to have a child. Mrs. Whitehead's response apparently resulted from her sympathy with family members and others who could have no children (she stated that she wanted to give another couple the "gift of life"); she also wanted the $10,000 to help her family.

Both parties, undoubtedly because of their own self-interest, were less sensitive to the implications of the transaction than they might otherwise have been. Mrs. Whitehead, for instance, appears not to have been concerned about whether the Sterns would make good parents for her child; the Sterns, on their part, while conscious of the obvious possibility that surrendering the child might cause grief to Mrs. Whitehead, overcame their qualms because of their desire for a child. At any rate, both the Sterns and Mrs. Whitehead were committed to the arrangement; both thought it right and constructive.

Mrs. Whitehead had reached her decision concerning surrogacy before the Sterns, and had actually been involved as a potential surrogate mother with another couple. After numerous unsuccessful artificial inseminations, that effort was abandoned. Thereafter, the Sterns learned of the Infertility Center, the possibilities of surrogacy, and of Mary Beth Whitehead. The two couples met to discuss the surrogacy arrangement and decided to go forward. On February 6, 1985, Mr. Stern and Mr. and Mrs. Whitehead executed the surrogate parenting agreement. After several artificial inseminations over a period of months, Mrs. Whitehead became pregnant. The pregnancy was uneventful and on March 27, 1986, Baby M was born.

Not wishing anyone at the hospital to be aware of the surrogacy arrangement, Mr. and Mrs. Whitehead appeared to all as the proud parents of a healthy female child. Her birth certificate indicated her name to be Sara Elizabeth Whitehead and her father to be Richard Whitehead. In accordance with Mrs. Whitehead's request, the Sterns visited the hospital unobtrusively to see the newborn child.

Mrs. Whitehead realized, almost from the moment of birth, that she could not part with this child. She had felt a bond with it even during pregnancy. Some indication of the attachment was conveyed to the Sterns at the hospital when they told Mrs. Whitehead what they were going to name the baby. She apparently broke into tears and indicated that she did not know if she could give up the child. She talked about how the baby looked like her other daughter, and made it clear that she was experiencing great difficulty with the decision.

Nonetheless, Mrs. Whitehead was, for the moment, true to her word. Despite powerful inclinations to the contrary, she turned her child over to the Sterns on March 30 at the Whiteheads' home.

The Sterns were thrilled with their new child. They had planned extensively for its arrival, far beyond the practical furnishing of a room for her. It was a time of joyful celebration — not just for them but for their friends as well. The Sterns looked forward to raising their daughter, whom they named Melissa. While aware by then that Mrs. Whitehead was undergoing an emotional crisis, they were as yet not cognizant of the depth of that crisis and its implications for their newly-enlarged family.

Later in the evening of March 30, Mrs. Whitehead became deeply disturbed, disconsolate, stricken with unbearable sadness. She had to have her child. She could not eat, sleep, or concentrate on anything other than her need for her baby. The next day she went to the Sterns' home and told them how much she was suffering.

The depth of Mrs. Whitehead's despair surprised and frightened the Sterns. She told them that she could not live without her baby, that she must have her, even if only for one week, that thereafter she would surrender her child. The Sterns, concerned that Mrs. Whitehead might indeed commit suicide, not wanting under any circumstances to risk that, and in any event believing that Mrs. Whitehead would keep her word, turned the child over to her. It was not until four months later, after a series of attempts to regain possession of the child, that Melissa was returned to the Sterns, having been forcibly removed from the home where she was then living with Mr. and Mrs. Whitehead, the home in Florida owned by Mary Beth Whitehead's parents.

The struggle over Baby M began when it became apparent that Mrs. Whitehead could not return the child to Mr. Stern. Due to Mrs. Whitehead's refusal to relinquish the baby, Mr. Stern filed a complaint seeking enforcement of the surrogacy contract. He alleged, accurately, that Mrs. Whitehead had not only refused to comply with the surrogacy contract but had threatened to flee from New Jersey with the child in order to avoid even the possibility of his obtaining custody. The court papers asserted that if Mrs. Whitehead were to be given notice of the application for an order requiring her to relinquish custody, she would, prior to the hearing, leave the state with the baby. And that is precisely what she did. After the order was entered, ex parte, the process server, aided by the police, in the presence of the Sterns, entered Mrs. Whitehead's home to execute the order. Mr. Whitehead fled with the child, who had been handed to him through a window while those who came to enforce the order were thrown off balance by a dispute over the child's current name.

The Whiteheads immediately fled to Florida with Baby M. They stayed initially with Mrs. Whitehead's parents, where one of Mrs. Whitehead's children had been living. For the next three months, the Whiteheads and Melissa lived at roughly twenty different hotels, motels, and homes in order to avoid apprehension. From time to time Mrs. Whitehead would call Mr. Stern to discuss the matter; the conversations, recorded by Mr. Stern on advice of counsel, show an escalating dispute about rights, morality, and power, accompanied by threats of Mrs. Whitehead to kill herself, to kill the child, and falsely to accuse Mr. Stern of sexually molesting Mrs. Whitehead's other daughter.

Eventually the Sterns discovered where the Whiteheads were staying, commenced supplementary proceedings in Florida, and obtained an order requiring the Whiteheads to turn over the child. Police in Florida enforced the order, forcibly removing the child from her grandparents' home. She was soon thereafter brought to New Jersey and turned over to the Sterns. The prior order of the court, issued ex parte, awarding custody of the child to the Sterns pendente lite, was reaffirmed by the trial court after consideration of the certified representations of the parties (both represented by counsel) concerning the unusual sequence of events that had unfolded. Pending final judgment, Mrs. Whitehead was awarded limited visitation with Baby M.

The Sterns' complaint, in addition to seeking possession and ultimately custody of the child, sought enforcement of the surrogacy contract. Pursuant to the contract, it asked that the child be permanently placed in their custody, that Mrs. Whitehead's parental rights be terminated, and that Mrs. Stern be allowed to adopt the child, i.e., that, for all purposes, Melissa become the Sterns' child. . . .

The trial court concluded that the various statutes governing this matter, including those concerning adoption, termination of parental rights, and payment of money in connection with adoptions, do not apply to surrogacy contracts. It reasoned that because the Legislature did not have surrogacy contracts in mind when it passed those laws, those laws were therefore irrelevant. Thus, assuming it was writing on a clean slate, the trial court analyzed the interests involved and the power of the court to accommodate them. It then held that surrogacy contracts are valid and should be enforced, and furthermore that Mr. Stern's rights under the surrogacy contract were constitutionally protected.

Mrs. Whitehead appealed. This Court granted direct certification. The briefs of the parties on appeal were joined by numerous briefs filed by amici expressing various interests and views on surrogacy and on this case. . . .

Invalidity and Unenforceability of Surrogacy Contract

We have concluded that this surrogacy contract is invalid. Our conclusion has two bases: direct conflict with existing statutes and conflict with the public policies of this State, as expressed in its statutory and decisional law. . . .

A. *Conflict With Statutory Provisions*

The surrogacy contract conflicts with: (1) laws prohibiting the use of money in connection with adoptions; [and] (2) laws requiring proof of parental unfitness or abandonment before termination of parental rights is ordered or an adoption is granted. . . .

Our law prohibits paying or accepting money in connection with any placement of a child for adoption. Violation is a high misdemeanor. Excepted are fees of an approved agency (which must be a non-profit entity) and certain expenses in connection with childbirth.

Considerable care was taken in this case to structure the surrogacy arrangement so as not to violate this prohibition. The arrangement was structured as follows: the adopting parent, Mrs. Stern, was not a party to the surrogacy contract; the money paid to Mrs. Whitehead was stated to be for her services — not for the adoption; the sole purpose of the contract was stated as being that "of giving a child to William Stern, its natural and biological father"; the money was purported to be "compensation for services and expenses and in no way . . . a fee for termination of parental rights or a payment in exchange for consent to surrender a child for adoption"; the fee to the Infertility Center ($7,500) was stated to be for legal representation, advice, administrative work, and other "services." Nevertheless, it seems clear that the money was paid and accepted in connection with an adoption.

The Infertility Center's major role was first as a "finder" of the surrogate mother whose child was to be adopted, and second as the arranger of all proceedings that led to the adoption. Its role as adoption finder is demonstrated by the provision requiring Mr. Stern to pay another $7,500 if he uses Mary Beth Whitehead again as a surrogate, and by ICNY's agreement to "coordinate arrangements for the adoption of the child by the wife." The surrogacy agreement requires Mrs. Whitehead to surrender Baby M for the purposes of adoption. The agreement notes that Mr. and Mrs. Stern wanted to have a child, and provides that the child be "placed" with Mrs. Stern in the event Mr. Stern dies before the child is born. The payment of the $10,000 occurs only on surrender of custody of the child and "completion of the duties and obligations" of Mrs. Whitehead, including termination of her parental rights to facilitate adoption by Mrs. Stern. As for the contention that the Sterns are paying only for services and not for an adoption, we need note only that they would pay nothing in the event the child died before the fourth month of pregnancy, and only $1,000 if the child were stillborn, even though the "services" had been fully rendered. Additionally, one of Mrs. Whitehead's estimated costs, to be assumed by Mr. Stern, was an "Adoption Fee," presumably for Mrs. Whitehead's incidental costs in connection with the adoption. . . .

The prohibition of our statute is strong. Violation constitutes a high misdemeanor, a third-degree crime, carrying a penalty of three to five years imprisonment. The evils inherent in baby-bartering are loathsome for a myriad of reasons. The child is sold without regard for whether the purchasers will be suitable parents. N. Baker, Baby Selling: The Scandal of Black Market Adoption 7 (1978). The natural mother does not receive the benefit of counseling and guidance to assist her in making a decision that may affect her for a lifetime. In fact, the monetary incentive to sell her child may, depending on her financial circumstances, make her decision less voluntary. *Id.* at 44. Furthermore, the adoptive parents may not be fully informed of the natural parents' medical history. . . .

The termination of Mrs. Whitehead's parental rights, called for by the surrogacy contract and actually ordered by the court, fails to comply with the stringent requirements of New Jersey law. Our law, recognizing the finality of any termination of parental rights, provides for such termination only where there has been a voluntary surrender of a child to an approved agency or to the Division of Youth and Family Services ("DYFS"), accompanied by a formal document acknowledging termination of parental rights, or where there has been a showing of parental abandonment or unfitness. A termination may ordinarily take one of three forms: an action by an approved agency, an action by DYFS, or an action in connection with a private placement adoption. The three are governed by separate statutes, but the standards for termination are substantially the same, except that whereas a written surrender is effective when made to an approved agency or to DYFS, there is no provision for it in the private placement context. . . .

In order to terminate parental rights under the private placement adoption statute, there must be a finding of "intentional abandonment or a very substantial neglect of parental duties without a reasonable expectation of a reversal of that conduct in the future." N.J.S.A. 9:3-48c(1). This requirement is similar to that of the prior law and to that of the law providing for termination through actions by approved agencies.. . . .

In this case a termination of parental rights was obtained not by proving the statutory prerequisites but by claiming the benefit of contractual provisions. From all that has been stated above, it is clear that a contractual agreement to abandon one's parental rights, or not to contest a termination action, will not be enforced in our courts. The Legislature would not have so carefully, so consistently, and so substantially restricted termination of parental rights if it had intended to allow termination to be achieved by one short sentence in a contract.

Since the termination was invalid, it follows, as noted above, that adoption of Melissa by Mrs. Stern could not properly be granted. . . .

B. *Public Policy Considerations*

The surrogacy contract's invalidity, resulting from its direct conflict with the above statutory provisions, is further underlined when its goals and means are measured against New Jersey's public policy. The contract's basic premise, that the natural parents can decide in advance of birth which one is to have custody of the child, bears no relationship to the settled law that the child's best interests shall determine custody. The fact that the trial court remedied that aspect of the contract through the "best interests" phase does not make the contractual provision any less offensive to the public policy of this State.

The surrogacy contract guarantees permanent separation of the child from one of its natural parents. Our policy, however, has long been that to the extent possible, children should remain with and be brought up by both of their natural parents. This is not simply some theoretical ideal that in practice has no meaning. The impact of failure to follow that policy is nowhere better shown than in the results of this surrogacy contract. A child, instead of starting off its life with as much peace and security as possible, finds itself immediately in a tug-of-war between contending mother and father.

The surrogacy contract violates the policy of this State that the rights of natural parents are equal concerning their child, the father's right no greater than the mother's. "The parent and child relationship extends equally to every child and to every parent, regardless of the marital status of the parents." N.J.S.A. 9:17-40. The whole purpose and effect of the surrogacy contract was to give the father the exclusive right to the child by destroying the rights of the mother.

The policies expressed in our comprehensive laws governing consent to the surrender of a child, stand in stark contrast to the surrogacy contract and what it implies. Here there is no counseling, independent or otherwise, of the natural mother, no evaluation, no warning.

The only legal advice Mary Beth Whitehead received regarding the surrogacy contract was provided in connection with the contract that she previously entered into with another couple. Mrs. Whitehead's lawyer was referred to her by the Infertility Center, with which he had an agreement to act as counsel for surrogate candidates. His services consisted of spending one hour going through the contract with the Whiteheads, section by section, and answering their questions. Mrs. Whitehead received no further legal advice prior to signing the contract with the Sterns.

Mrs. Whitehead was examined and psychologically evaluated, but if it was for her benefit, the record does not disclose that fact. The Sterns regarded the evaluation as important, particularly in connection with the question of whether she would change her mind. Yet they never asked to see it, and were content with the assumption that the Infertility Center had made an evaluation and had concluded that there was no danger that the surrogate mother would change her mind. From Mrs. Whitehead's point of view, all that she learned from the evaluation was that "she had passed." It is apparent that the profit motive got the better of the Infertility Center. Although the evaluation was made, it was not put to any use, and understandably so, for the psychologist warned that Mrs. Whitehead demonstrated certain traits that might make surrender of the child difficult and that there should be further inquiry into this issue in connection with her surrogacy. To inquire further, however, might have jeopardized the Infertility Center's fee. The record indicates that neither Mrs. Whitehead nor the Sterns were ever told of this fact, a fact that might have ended their surrogacy arrangement.

Under the contract, the natural mother is irrevocably committed before she knows the strength of her bond with her child. She never makes a totally voluntary, informed decision, for quite clearly any decision prior to the baby's birth is, in the most important sense, uninformed, and any decision after that, compelled by a pre-existing contractual commitment, the threat of a lawsuit, and the inducement of a $10,000 payment, is less than totally voluntary. Her interests are of little concern to those who controlled this transaction.

Although the interest of the natural father and adoptive mother is certainly the predominant interest, realistically the only interest served, even they are left with less than what public policy requires. They know little about the natural mother, her genetic makeup, and her psychological and medical history. Moreover, not even a superficial attempt is made to determine their awareness of their responsibilities as parents.

Worst of all, however, is the contract's total disregard of the best interests of the child. There is not the slightest suggestion that any inquiry will be made at any time to determine the fitness of the Sterns as custodial parents, of Mrs. Stern as an adoptive parent, their superiority to Mrs. Whitehead, or the effect on the child of not living with her natural mother.

This is the sale of a child, or, at the very least, the sale of a mother's right to her child, the only mitigating factor being that one of the purchasers is the father. Almost every evil that prompted the prohibition on the payment of money in connection with adoptions exists here.

The differences between an adoption and a surrogacy contract should be noted, since it is asserted that the use of money in connection with surrogacy does not pose the risks found where money buys an adoption. Katz, "Surrogate Motherhood and the Baby-Selling Laws," 20 Colum. J. L. & Soc. Probs. 1 (1986).

First, and perhaps most important, all parties concede that it is unlikely that surrogacy will survive without money. Despite the alleged selfless motivation of surrogate mothers, if there is no payment, there will be no surrogates, or very few. That conclusion contrasts with adoption; for obvious reasons, there remains a steady supply, albeit insufficient, despite the prohibitions against payment. The adoption itself, relieving the natural mother of the financial burden of supporting an infant, is in some sense the equivalent of payment.

Second, the use of money in adoptions does not produce the problem — conception occurs, and usually the birth itself, before illicit funds are offered. With surrogacy, the "problem," if one views it as such, consisting of the purchase of a woman's procreative capacity, at the risk of her life, is caused by and originates with the offer of money.

Third, with the law prohibiting the use of money in connection with adoptions, the built-in financial pressure of the unwanted pregnancy and the consequent support obligation do not lead the mother to the highest paying, ill-suited, adoptive parents. She is just as well-off surrendering the child to an approved agency. In surrogacy, the highest bidders will presumably become the adoptive parents regardless of suitability, so long as payment of money is permitted.

Fourth, the mother's consent to surrender her child in adoptions is revocable, even after surrender of the child, unless it be to an approved agency, where by regulation there are protections against an ill-advised surrender. In surrogacy, consent occurs so early that no amount of advice would satisfy the potential mother's need, yet the consent is irrevocable.

The main difference, that the unwanted pregnancy is unintended while the situation of the surrogate mother is voluntary and intended, is really not significant. Initially, it produces stronger reactions of sympathy for the mother whose pregnancy was unwanted than for the surrogate mother, who "went into this with her eyes wide open." On reflection, however, it appears that the essential evil is the same, taking advantage of a woman's circumstances (the unwanted pregnancy or the need for money) in order to take away her child, the difference being one of degree.

Intimated, but disputed, is the assertion that surrogacy will be used for the benefit of the rich at the expense of the poor. See, e.g., Radin, "Market Inalienability," 100 Harv. L. Rev. 1849, 1930 (1987). In response it is noted that the Sterns are not rich and the Whiteheads not poor. Nevertheless, it is clear to us that it is unlikely that surrogate mothers will be as proportionately numerous among those women in the top twenty percent income bracket as among those in the bottom twenty percent. Put differently, we doubt that infertile couples in the low-income bracket will find upper income surrogates.

The point is made that Mrs. Whitehead agreed to the surrogacy arrangement, supposedly fully understanding the consequences. Putting aside the issue of how compelling her need for money may have been, and how significant her understanding of the consequences, we suggest that her consent is irrelevant. There are, in a civilized society, some things that money cannot buy. In America, we decided long ago that merely because conduct purchased by money was "voluntary" did not mean that it was good or beyond regulation and prohibition. Employers can no longer buy labor at the lowest price they can bargain for, even though that labor is "voluntary," or buy women's labor for less money than paid to men for the same job, or purchase the agreement of children to perform oppressive labor, or purchase the agreement of workers to subject themselves to unsafe or unhealthful working conditions. There are, in short, values that society deems more important than granting to wealth whatever it can buy, be it labor, love, or life. Whether this principle recommends prohibition of surrogacy, which presumably sometimes results in great satisfaction to all of the parties, is not for us to say. We note here only that, under existing law, the fact that Mrs. Whitehead "agreed" to the arrangement is not dispositive. . . .

In sum, the harmful consequences of this surrogacy arrangement appear to us all too palpable. In New Jersey the surrogate mother's agreement to sell her child is void. Its irrevocability infects the entire contract, as does the money that purports to buy it. . . .

The judgment is affirmed in part, reversed in part, and remanded for further proceedings consistent with this opinion.

NOTES

1. ***The Grounds of Decision in* Baby M.** The court found the surrogacy contract in *Baby M* unenforceable on two different grounds: (1) illegality: the contract was found to violate specific provisions of the New Jersey statutes regulating adoption and the termination of parental rights; and (2) public policy: the contract was found violative of the policy of the State of New Jersey that custody decisions be made in accordance with the "best interests" of the child (and not, presumably, according to the terms of a contract).[17]

---

[17] The New Jersey legislature has codified the *Baby M* "best interests" standard:

In a contest between a person . . . objecting to the adoption and the prospective adoptive parent, the standard shall be the best interest of the child. The best interest of a child requires that a parent affirmatively assume the duties encompassed by the role of being a parent. In determining whether a parent has affirmatively assumed the duties of a parent, the court shall consider, but is not limited to consideration of, the fulfillment of financial obligations for the birth and care of the child, demonstration of continued interest in the child, demonstration of a genuine effort to maintain communication with the child, and demonstration of the

The question of whether the contract violated the private placement adoption statute is complicated by the fact that Mr. Stern was the natural father and not an adopting parent. Should this fact matter? Does it matter whether or not the New Jersey legislature had surrogacy contracts in mind when it enacted this statutory scheme?

The public policy argument is complicated as well. The trial court resolved the perceived conflict between the terms of the contract and the "best interests" standard for resolving custody disputes by making a preliminary determination that it was in Baby M's best interests that custody be awarded to the Sterns. Thereafter, the court decreed specific performance of the contract. Is this a satisfactory resolution to the problem? In any event, is the "best interests" standard relevant in a dispute between biological parents? In the case of divorcing parents, "best interests" is often used to resolve custody disputes, but in such a case the child will exist in either event. Here if surrogacy contracts are invalidated on "best interests" grounds, there will be no child. Can it be in Baby M's "best interests" not to have been born?

2. ***The Story and Aftermath of*** **Baby M.** Professor Elizabeth Scott describes the impact of *Baby M* on social perceptions of surrogacy and the legal landscape in *Surrogacy and the Politics of Commodification*, 72 LAW & CONTEMP. PROBS. 109 (2009):

> It would be hard to exaggerate the impact of Baby M on the legislative regulation of surrogacy arrangements in the late 1980s and early 1990s. When the case broke in 1987, no state had enacted a statute regulating surrogacy arrangements; those that began to consider the issue in the mid-1980s were inclined to regulate rather than to prohibit the contracts. But by December of 1987, even before the New Jersey Supreme Court decided Baby M, seventy bills concerning surrogacy had been introduced in twenty-seven legislatures, and by late 1988, six states had passed laws banning the agreements or declaring them void — often with little opposition. As Baby M played out, surrogacy opponents framed the transactions as baby-selling and exploitation of women, and legislatures responded to advocates' calls for restriction of the practice. Almost all the laws passed during the post-Baby M period either prohibited the agreements or discouraged them by disallowing payment to the surrogate or to intermediaries or by giving surrogates the right to rescind after the birth of the baby. In some states, lawmakers initiated the legislation, often with little apparent involvement by lobbying groups. In other states, such as New York, a coalition of religious groups, adoption and child-welfare advocates, and women's groups actively lobbied for laws that prohibited or discouraged the practice.

However:

> Contrary to predictions, surrogacy has flourished over the past decade and attitudes toward these arrangements have mellowed considerably in the

---

establishment and maintenance of a place of importance in the child's life.

N.J. STAT. ANN. § 9:3-46 (West).

political arena, despite restrictive laws in such key states as New York. Legislatures in several states have established procedures and requirements for enforcing surrogacy contracts, while in other states courts have upheld the agreements. A survey of these lawmaking activities and of recent media coverage suggests that surrogacy has assumed a new social meaning. Today the issue is seldom framed as baby selling and exploitation; instead, the discourse emphasizes the service provided by surrogates to couples who otherwise could not have genetically related children. Moreover, the legislative goal of discouraging and punishing a pernicious practice largely has been replaced by the pragmatic objective of providing certainty about parental status and protecting all participants, especially children.

Id. at 117-18, 120–21.

3. ***Autonomy and Externalities in* Baby M.** The court's discussion of the legal and public policy issues is infused with a number of autonomy-based grounds for voiding this agreement. First, the court argues that the statute prohibiting payment of money for adoptions is based on the premise that a mother's decision to put her baby up for adoption is "less than voluntary" if she is given a financial incentive to do so. Do we ordinarily believe that the voluntariness of a decision *decreases* as financial incentives increase? Second, in its discussion of that statute and in its public policy discussion, the court argues that any decision by a mother to put her baby up for adoption before the baby is born is necessarily involuntary. In both cases, the court finds that the absence of professional counseling of the natural mother vitiates consent. Would the court also require counseling for other momentous life decisions? The court also suggests that no amount of counseling could render pre-birth consent to adoption sufficiently informed. Do you agree? The court's claim is that no mother can know how her feelings will change once she holds her newborn baby. But might not some mothers know too well, and therefore seek to bind themselves *before* their child is born because they believe adoption will be in the baby's and their own best interest, notwithstanding the emotional attachment they will feel at birth? Indeed, isn't the pre-birth decision more dispassionate than a decision made after birth?

Despite these autonomy-based objections to the surrogacy agreement, the court's central public policy objection is that the agreement violates New Jersey's public policy (and statutory) requirement that adoptions be based exclusively on the best interests of the child. Agreements transferring parental rights are perhaps the clearest example of agreements that create externalities: They profoundly affect the interests of a third party — the child. Of course, as the note above points out, without surrogacy agreements the children affected by those agreements would not exist. The court's real concern seems to be that these agreements fail to insure that the children conceived will be placed with a suitable parent. But consider New Jersey's strong presumption in favor of the parental rights of natural parents. What safeguards does New Jersey have in place to insure children are born into suitable families? New Jersey (and every other state) allows individuals to become parents simply by deciding to have unprotected sex. To achieve parenthood by adopting pursuant to a surrogacy agreement, individuals' desire to become parents must be strong enough to overcome considerable financial, legal, medical, and logistical obstacles. Is there any reason to think parents who adopt pursuant to a surrogacy contract are less able to care for their children than the average non-adoptive parent?

4. ***Critics of the* Baby M *Decision.*** Professor Richard Epstein finds these anti-surrogacy arguments unpersuasive in *Surrogacy: The Case for Full Contractual Enforcement*, 81 VA. L. REV. 2305 (1995). He argues that surrogacy should not be treated differently than ordinary commercial transactions. Epstein rejects the claim that surrogacy agreements are likely to have negative effects on the children born pursuant to these agreements. Instead, "the people who have struggled so hard to conceive their own child are probably the best candidates to be good parents and not the worst." *Id.* at 2320. Moreover, because all parties to a surrogacy contract have strong incentives to vet their contracting partner, Epstein believes the market for surrogate mothers would be one of the most self-regulated markets in the country. In his view, the surrogacy market needs less regulation than other markets, not more. Any government regulation is likely to decrease the efficiency of the market without creating a corresponding increase in societal benefits.

One of the court's central arguments against surrogacy contracts is that they too closely resemble contracts for the outright purchase of babies. Is the selling of babies clearly beyond the pale, like contracts for indentured servitude? Or is there a respectable case to be made that creating a market for babies would be socially desirable? For just such an argument, see Elizabeth Landes & Richard Posner, *The Economics of the Baby Shortage*, 7 J. LEGAL STUD. 323 (1978). Landes and Posner argue that the long waiting lists for legal adoptions reflect the cost of government regulation, or prohibition, of legal baby-selling. High demand for children from infertile couples combines with the artificially high cost of obtaining a child through adoption agencies to produce an inefficient market, which in turn leads to a higher proportion of abandoned children being placed in foster care at public expense and a large level of dissatisfaction among potential adoptive parents. Landes and Posner posit that deregulating the market for babies, especially permitting adoption agencies to pay "fair market value" for abandoned babies, would foster greater efficiency while not resulting in the increased abuse or unacceptable commodification of adopted children feared by many regulators. Allowing adoption agencies to operate as profit-maximizing firms, they conclude, might lead to an overall increase in societal benefits. More recently, Judge Posner has applied this analysis specifically to the surrogacy market. *See* Richard Posner, *The Ethics and Economics of Enforcing Contracts of Surrogate Motherhood*, 5 J. CONTEMP. HEALTH L. & POL'Y 21 (1989).

5. ***Autonomy Considerations and Gestational Surrogacy Agreements.*** In *Johnson v. Calvert*, 851 P.2d 776 (Cal. 1993), the California Supreme Court enforced a surrogacy agreement on somewhat different facts than *Baby M*. Anna Johnson agreed to bear the child of the Calverts through a process of in vitro fertilization in exchange for $10,000 and a $200,000 life insurance policy. The relationship between the parties deteriorated during the pregnancy, and the Calverts sought a declaratory judgment that they were the unborn child's legal parents, while Johnson sought a judgment that the child was hers. In ruling for the Calverts, the court rejected the comparison between adoption and surrogacy agreements, and instead based its decision on the autonomy of women to enter into surrogacy agreements:

The argument that a woman cannot knowingly and intelligently agree to gestate and deliver a baby for intending parents carries overtones of the reasoning that for centuries prevented women from attaining equal economic rights and professional status under the law. To resurrect this view is both to foreclose a personal and economic choice on the part of the surrogate mother, and to deny intending parents what may be their only means of procreating a child of their own genetic stock. Certainly in the present case it cannot be seriously argued that Anna, a licensed vocational nurse who had done well in school and who had previously borne a child, lacked the intellectual wherewithal or life experience necessary to make an informed decision to enter into the surrogacy contract.

Id. at 784–85.

6. ***Morality as Law.*** The immorality doctrine raises one of the more controversial and hotly debated issues in American jurisprudence: the problem of judges determining what conduct is socially acceptable and what is undesirable conduct. In *Hewitt v. Hewitt*, 77 Ill. 2d 49 (1979), for example, the court treats as immoral a relationship that was merely lacking legal formality and did not stray from societal norms. The plaintiff and defendant, although never formally married, had held themselves out as having been married for 15 years, during which time they lived together and had children. Upon dissolution of the relationship, Mrs. Hewitt sought an equal share of defendant's assets. The court rejected her claim on the grounds that supporting her claim would undermine the state's interest in promoting marriage. The court identified this interest as dating back to a statute outlawing common law marriages and continuing in the recently-passed Illinois Marriage and Dissolution of Marriage Act. The court rejected the reasoning of *Marvin v. Marvin*, a widely publicized California case that held that common law principles of implied contract, equitable relief, and constructive trust govern the relations of parties in a pseudo-conventional family relationship in the absence of an express agreement. Allowing the plaintiff to recover as though she and the defendant had been married would create an alternative to marriage that was potentially more attractive than marriage. The court in *Hewitt* rejected the line of judicial decisions following *Marvin*, which reasoned that consideration for recovery could be found in the housekeeping and child-rearing services that the plaintiffs in these cases provided during the cohabitation.

The decision in *Hewitt* has not been followed by the majority of courts that have considered the issue in subsequent years. Indeed, an Indiana appellate court faced a case similar to *Hewitt* one year after the Illinois Supreme Court had handed down its decision. The Indiana court described the facts of *Glasgo v. Glasgo*, 410 N.E.2d 1325, 1325–26 (Ind. Ct. App. 1980), as follows:

Laurel and Jane were married from June 1956 until September 1967 during which time Jane worked outside, as well as within, their home to put Laurel through college and veterinarian school and during which time two sons were born to them. After the divorce Jane and the boys moved to Arkansas. In December 1972 Laurel sought a reconciliation with Jane, and in August 1973, after selling her home in Arkansas, Jane and the children moved back to Indiana to make their home with Laurel. They lived together as a family from August 1973 until August 1978 when Jane and the boys moved out of the home which they had helped the appellant construct on real estate owned by him. Financing for the construction of the home had come from the children's insurance policies and appellant's personal loan and earnings. . . . Jane brought the instant action seeking $25,000.00, which was one-half the value of what she believed the house to be worth, based upon their oral agreement that the assets which they were accumulating were owned equally.

Predictably, Jane based her claim upon *Marvin v. Marvin*. Laurel, on the other hand, defended with *Hewitt v. Hewitt*. In granting relief to Jane, the Indiana court had harsh words for the *Hewitt* decision:

Unlike the Illinois court, however, we are not convinced that the impact of the recognition of relationships such as the Hewitts' or the Glasgos' upon our society and the institution of marriage to be of greater importance than the rights of the immediate parties . . . We do not find that recognition of a claim for a declaration of property rights in specific property to be a claim which reinstates common law marriages. We remind ourselves, moreover, that we are not deciding all of the questions set out in *Hewitt*, or even all of those raised by the facts of *Hewitt* or *Marvin*, in this case. Here are we asking only one question based upon the Glasgos' unique circumstances: is there any set of facts contained in Jane's complaint against Laurel upon which a court could grant her relief? To that question we must answer "yes."

Implicit in this answer, of course, is the rejection of appellant's contention that to do so is against the public policy of this state. Rejection of common law marriages in Indiana was done ostensibly on the grounds that their recognition encouraged fraud and perjury, most notably in actions against decedent's estates and for social security or wrongful death benefits. Fundamental to the rationale of these cases, however, is the concurrent argument that such relationships are not only illegal, but also immoral and therefore against public policy. . . . We believe that it ill behooves courts to categorize either the Hewitts' or the Glasgos' relationships as "meretricious" or "illicit" in any sense of those terms. Here the specific facts which might give rise to a description of a meretricious relationship are conspicuously absent: the parties had been married formerly, they sought to rear their children in a family setting, they conducted themselves for a significant period of time as a conventional American family, the wife showed concern for her own and her children's future economic security. All the parties failed to do to conform to societal norms of marital behavior was to complete the legal formalities. To apply the traditional rationale denying recovery to one party in cases where contracts are held to be void simply because illegal sexual relations are posited as consideration for the bargain is unfair, unjust, and unduly harsh.

Id. at 1330.

F.   UNCONSCIONABILITY

Courts sometimes decline to enforce contracts because they find them to be unconscionable. Typically, courts use the label "unconscionable" to describe agreements whose process defects do not rise to the level of actionable fraud or duress. The roots of unconscionability can be traced to two sources in the law. The first is in the Roman doctrine of "just price," or *laesio enormis*; the second can be found in English equity courts and their refusal to enforce contracts that "shock the conscience." Unconscionability thus has evolved alongside the bargain principle and, at least in theory, has acted as an important counterweight to the principle of liberty of contract. Despite these historical roots, unconscionability is a term that has been defined only imprecisely, at best, and often not at all. Consider, for example, § 2-302 of the UCC.[18] Even the Official Comments to § 2-302 do not shed much light on the definition of unconscionability. Comment 1 contains the most illuminating statement: "The basic test is whether, in the light of the general commercial background and the commercial needs of the particular trade or case, the clauses involved are so one-sided as to be unconscionable under the circumstances existing at the time of the making of the contract."

WILLIAMS v. WALKER-THOMAS FURNITURE CO. I
District of Columbia Court of Appeals
198 A.2d 914 (1964)

See p. 53, *supra.*

WILLIAMS v. WALKER-THOMAS FURNITURE CO. II
United States Court of Appeals, District of Columbia Circuit
350 F.2d 445 (1965)

See p. 55, *supra.*

SEABROOK v. COMMUTER HOUSING CO.
Civil Court of the City of New York, State of New York
72 Misc. 2d 6, 338 N.Y.S.2d 67 (1972)

KASSOFF, J.

This action was brought by plaintiff for the return of one month's rent and a security deposit totaling $464. Plaintiff entered into a written lease agreement with the defendant on or about November 30, 1971 for an apartment in defendant's building. The lease and occupancy were to commence on March 1, 1972. The building in which the apartment was located was under construction when the parties executed the lease. Defendant's printed form lease contained a clause which

---

[18] For the classic analysis of the lack of content in UCC § 2-302 and its historical antecedents, see Arthur Leff, *Unconscionability and the Code — The Emperor's New Clause*, 115 U. PA. L. REV. 485 (1967).

provided that if the building was not completed on the date occupancy was to commence, occupancy would begin on the day the building was completed and the three-year period of the lease would commence with occupancy. On or about June 29, 1972 defendant notified plaintiff that the apartment would be ready for occupancy on July 1, 1972, four months after the lease was to commence. On May 12, 1972, plaintiff notified defendant that because of the landlord's delay in construction she was forced to vacate her premises and seek shelter elsewhere. Plaintiff requested that the lease be canceled. Defendant refused to cancel the lease and refused to return the rent and security deposit. At the trial, plaintiff testified that neither the landlord nor his renting agent explained the construction clause to her before she executed the lease. She also testified that she was not represented by an attorney.

The lessees in situations such as this one are usually occasional customers, not acquainted with the carefully drafted legal terms set forth in such printed form leases. The landlord and his agents, assisted by expert legal counsel, carefully draft the lease in language designed solely for the landlord's protection. When the landlord presents the lease to the lessee for acceptance and execution he is usually fully cognizant of the fact that the other party has not read or bargained for many of the incidental terms of the contract. The terms of the printed contract are usually nonnegotiable. In most cases the tenant is not represented by counsel. The landlord's position is superior.

He not only possesses superior knowledge, but offers a scarce commodity. The lessee is often under an existing lease which usually expires at or about the time the new lease is to become effective.

The landlord is a merchant in a sellers' market place. The word "merchant" as used by this court has the same definition as used in § 2-104 of the Uniform Commercial Code. The Code defines merchant as "a person who deals in goods of the kind or otherwise by his occupation holds himself out as having knowledge or skill peculiar to the practices or goods involved in the transaction or to whom such knowledge or skill may be attributed by his employment of an agent or broker or other intermediary who by his occupation holds himself out as having such knowledge or skill." If one is a merchant, he has a special skill or a particular knowledge; and for this reason he is held by the court to a completely different set of rules which are generally more strict than the rules that apply to nonmerchants. As a result, one who contracts with a merchant will generally find himself in a more favorable position with the court and protected to a greater extent than if he had contracted with a nonmerchant. A merchant is to be held to a higher standard of conduct by the court.

The lessee that has no choice but to sign an unconscionable lease agreement or not take the premises must be protected against the bad bargain he enters into. The lease in such cases is the equivalent of a consumer contract. The concept of laissez faire, that is if the purchaser does not agree to lease of the seller he can go elsewhere, has no place in our enlightened society where lessor and lessee do not deal on equal terms and where lessee for all practical purposes does not have the option of shopping around for available renting accommodations of his choice. The Uniform Commercial Code by its definition applies only to the sale of goods.

However, § 2-302 of the code does not mention the sale of goods. The official comment to § 2-302 of the code states that the purpose of the section is to prevent suppression and unfair surprise by avoiding enforcement of unconscionable contracts made by parties who lacked equal bargaining power. It is this court's view that the code's prohibition represents a crystallization of the law's view toward all such contracts, whether for the sale of goods or otherwise. Although the lease agreement in this case does not come within the scope of § 2-302 of the code, it presents a business pattern closely akin to what the drafters of § 2-302 sought to prohibit, and may be related to the code by analogy. . . .

A consideration of applicable case law and of economic reason leads this court to conclude that the principles set forth in § 2-302 of the Uniform Commercial Code should be extended to govern the lease before the court.

The doctrine of unconscionability is used by the courts to protect those who are unable to protect themselves and to prevent injustice, both in consumer and nonconsumer areas.

The plaintiff was presented with a long complex lease, printed in small, practically illegible print. The court finds the lease to contain fifty-four clauses. The lease is four pages long and contains approximately 10,000 words. If typed on 11 by 8 1/2 paper, the lease would contain approximately 50 pages of highly technical legal terms, terms not commonly used or understood by the occasional lessee. How can a consumer be expected to fully comprehend or intelligently execute a lease of this length?

Clause number 33 entitled "New Building" states:

> The building being erected on the premises by the Landlord is presently in the course of construction and, notwithstanding anything herein contained to the contrary as to either the commencement and termination of this lease or the provisions of paragraph No. 19 hereof, or any other provisions of this lease, it is agreed that if the building should be completed on a date other than the date set for the commencement of the term hereunder, this lease shall continue in full force and effect, except that the term shall not commence until notice is given by the landlord to the tenant that the apartment is ready for occupancy by the tenant and the termination date of this lease shall be the last calendar day of the thirty-sixth month from the commencement date set by the landlord in said notice.

Paragraph number 19 entitled "Failure to Give Possession" reads in part:

> If landlord shall be unable to give possession of the demised premises on the date of the commencement of the term hereof by reason of the fact that the premises are located in a building being constructed and which has not been sufficiently completed to make the premises ready for occupancy or by reason of the fact that a certificate of occupancy has not been procured or for any other reason, landlord shall not be subject to any liability for the failure to give possession, on said date. Under such circumstances the rent reserved or covenanted to be paid herein shall not commence until the possession of demised premises is given or the premises are available for occupancy by tenant, and no such failure to give possession on the date of

commencement of the term shall in any wise affect the validity of this lease or the obligations of tenant hereunder, nor shall same be construed in any wise to extend the term of this lease. The issuance to landlord of a temporary certificate of occupancy shall be deemed conclusive evidence, as against tenant, that the premises are available for occupancy by the tenant.

These two clauses alone contain 340 words and are separated by some 13 complex legal clauses containing approximately 2,000 words. In Williams v. Walker-Thomas Furniture Co. (350 F.2d 445) the court found that unequal bargaining powers and the absence of a meaningful choice on the part of one of the parties, together with contract terms which unreasonably favor the other party, may spell out unconscionability. Both clauses are constructed by the landlord for the purpose of guaranteeing full occupancy. Once the consumer enters the merchant's trap and executes the lease, he is caught in a web from which there is no escape. The two clauses fail to set forth a reasonable period for extension of the time of commencement of the lease and fail to give the tenant the option of canceling the lease agreement if the premises are not ready for occupancy within a reasonable time after the lease was to commence. The court realizes that by not setting forth a time for extending the commencement of lease implies that a reasonable time will apply. However, it is the court's opinion that the landlord was under an affirmative duty and obligation to set forth a reasonable time limit and thereby relieve lessee of the burden and risk of determining what period of time is reasonable. The landlord merchant was also under an affirmative duty to bring clauses 19 and 33 to the attention of the lessee and to explain their meaning before asking the lessee to execute the lease. Hiding these clauses in a maze of legal terms will not shield the landlord from his obligations to the lessee.

The court finds these two clauses to be unconscionable and will not enforce them. In doing this, the court in no way seeks to abridge the parties' right to contract, but merely holds that an expert cannot hide behind legal clauses of this kind when dealing with an occasional lessee that has neither a knowledge of real estate law nor the advice of legal counsel.

Accordingly, the court orders that one month's rent and one month's security, totaling $464 be returned to the plaintiff, with interest from May 12, 1972.

HENNINGSEN v. BLOOMFIELD MOTORS, INC.
Supreme Court of New Jersey
32 N.J. 358, 161 A.2d 69 (1960)

[Plaintiffs Claus and Helen Henningsen bought a Plymouth from the defendant, Bloomfield Motors. When ordering the car (as a gift for his wife on Mother's Day), Mr. Henningsen signed a pre-printed purchase order form, with 12 and 6 point type on both front and back. On the back of the form eight and one-half inches of fine type set out the rights and liabilities of each party to the contract. One of these provisions was a clause limiting the warranties extended by both the manufacturer Chrysler, and the dealer, Bloomfield Motors. Liability was limited to a 90-day warranty on "each new motor vehicle . . . , chassis or parts manufactured by it to be free from defects in material or workmanship under normal use and service."

Any other warranties, express or implied, made by any party, were expressly disavowed.

[Ten days and 468 miles after purchasing the car, the steering mechanism failed, and Mrs. Henningsen, who was driving the car at the time, crashed into a brick wall, totaling the car and seriously injuring herself. The Henningsens subsequently filed suit against Bloomfield Motors and Chrysler Corp., alleging a breach of express and implied warranties, and negligence. The defendants relied on the signed purchase order which limited liability in responding to the allegations. There was a jury verdict in favor of the plaintiffs.]

Francis, J. . . .

In the light of these matters, what effect should be given to the express warranty in question which seeks to limit the manufacturer's liability to replacement of defective parts, and which disclaims all other warranties, express or implied? In assessing its significance we must keep in mind the general principle that, in the absence of fraud, one who does not choose to read a contract before signing it, cannot later relieve himself of its burdens. And in applying that principle, the basic tenet of freedom of competent parties to contract is a factor of importance. But in the framework of modern commercial life and business practices, such rules cannot be applied on a strict, doctrinal basis. . . .

It is apparent that the public has an interest not only in the safe manufacture of automobiles, but also, as shown by the Sales Act, in protecting the rights and remedies of purchasers, so far as it can be accomplished consistently with our system of free enterprise. In a society such as ours, where the automobile is a common and necessary adjunct of daily life, and where its use is so fraught with danger to the driver, passengers and the public, the manufacturer is under a special obligation in connection with the construction, promotion and sale of his cars. Consequently, the courts must examine purchase agreements closely to see if consumer and public interests are treated fairly.

What influence should these circumstances have on the restrictive effect of Chrysler's express warranty in the framework of the purchase contract? As we have said, warranties originated in the law to safeguard the buyer and not to limit the liability of the seller or manufacturer. It seems obvious in this instance that the motive was to avoid the warranty obligations which are normally incidental to such sales. The language gave little and withdrew much. In return for the delusive remedy of replacement of defective parts at the factory, the buyer is said to have accepted the exclusion of the maker's liability for personal injuries arising from the breach of the warranty, and to have agreed to the elimination of any other express or implied warranty. An instinctively felt sense of justice cries out against such a sharp bargain. But does the doctrine that a person is bound by his signed agreement, in the absence of fraud, stand in the way of any relief?

The traditional contract is the result of free bargaining of parties who are brought together by the play of the market, and who meet each other on a footing of approximate economic equality. In such a society there is no danger that freedom of contract will be a threat to the social order as a whole. But in present-day commercial life the standardized mass contract has appeared. It is used primarily by enterprises with strong bargaining power and position. "The weaker party, in need of the goods or services, is frequently not in a position to shop around for better terms, either because the author of the standard contract has a monopoly (natural or artificial) or because all competitors use the same clauses. His contractual intention is but a subjection more or less voluntary to terms dictated by the stronger party, terms whose consequences are often understood in a vague way, if at all." Kessler, *Contracts of Adhesion — Some Thoughts About Freedom of Contract*, 43 Colum. L. Rev. 629, 632 (1943). . . .

The warranty before us is a standardized form designed for mass use. It is imposed upon the automobile consumer. He takes it or leaves it, and he must take it to buy an automobile. No bargaining is engaged in with respect to it. In fact, the dealer through whom it comes to the buyer is without authority to alter it; his function is ministerial — simply to deliver it. The form warranty is not only standard with Chrysler but, as mentioned above, it is the uniform warranty of the Automobile Manufacturers Association. Of these companies, the "Big Three" (General Motors, Ford, and Chrysler) represented 93.5/% of the passenger-car production for 1958 and the independents 6.5/%. . . .

The gross inequality of bargaining position occupied by the consumer in the automobile industry is thus apparent. There is no competition among the car makers in the area of the express warranty. Where can the buyer go to negotiate for better protection? Such control and limitation of his remedies are inimical to the public welfare and, at the very least, call for great care by the courts to avoid injustice through application of strict common-law principles of freedom of contract. Because there is no competition among the motor vehicle manufacturers with respect to the scope of protection guaranteed to the buyer, there is no incentive on their part to stimulate good will in that field of public relations. Thus, there is lacking a factor existing in more competitive fields, one which tends to guarantee the safe construction of the article sold. Since all competitors operate in the same way, the urge to be careful is not so pressing. . . .

In the context of this warranty, only the abandonment of all sense of justice would permit us to hold that, as a matter of law, the phrase "its obligation under this warranty being limited to making good at its factory any part or parts thereof" signifies to an ordinary reasonable person that he is relinquishing any personal injury claim that might flow from the use of a defective automobile. Such claims are nowhere mentioned. The draftsmanship is reflective of the care and skill of the Automobile Manufacturers Association in undertaking to avoid warranty obligations without drawing too much attention to its effort in that regard. No one can doubt that if the will to do so were present, the ability to inform the buying public of the intention to disclaim liability for injury claims arising from breach of warranty would present no problem. . . .

The task of the judiciary is to administer the spirit as well as the letter of the law. On issues such as the present one, part of that burden is to protect the ordinary man against the loss of important rights through what, in effect, is the unilateral act of the manufacturer. The status of the automobile industry is unique. Manufacturers are few in number and strong in bargaining position. In the matter of warranties on the sale of their products, the Automotive Manufacturers Association has enabled them to present a united front. From the standpoint of the purchaser, there can be no arms length negotiating on the subject. Because his capacity for bargaining is so grossly unequal, the inexorable conclusion which follows is that he is not permitted to bargain at all. He must take or leave the automobile on the warranty terms dictated by the maker. He cannot turn to a competitor for better security.

Public policy at a given time finds expression in the Constitution, the statutory law and in judicial decisions. In the area of sale of goods, the legislative will has imposed an implied warranty of merchantability as a general incident of sale of an automobile by description. The warranty does not depend upon the affirmative intention of the parties. It is a child of the law; it annexes itself to the contract because of the very nature of the transaction. The judicial process has recognized a right to recover damages for personal injuries arising from a breach of that warranty. The disclaimer of the implied warranty and exclusion of all obligations except those specifically assumed by the express warranty signify a studied effort to frustrate that protection. True, the Sales Act authorizes agreements between buyer and seller qualifying the warranty obligations. But quite obviously the Legislature contemplated lawful stipulations (which are determined by the circumstances of a particular case) arrived at freely by parties of relatively equal bargaining strength. The lawmakers did not authorize the automobile manufacturer to use its grossly disproportionate bargaining power to relieve itself from liability and to impose on the ordinary buyer, who in effect has no real freedom of choice, the grave danger of injury to himself and others that attends the sale of such a dangerous instrumentality as a defectively made automobile. In the framework of this case, illuminated as it is by the facts and the many decisions noted, we are of the opinion that Chrysler's attempted disclaimer of an implied warranty of merchantability and of the obligations arising therefrom is so inimical to the public good as to compel an adjudication of its invalidity.

NOTES

1. *Procedural vs. Substantive Unconscionability.* Courts and commentators often distinguish between two kinds of unconscionability. An agreement is procedurally unconscionable when the bargaining process that produced it is defective. As we have seen, contract law enforces only voluntary, informed agreements between mentally competent adults. Of course, the duress, fraud, and incapacity doctrines we previously considered provide the standard avenues for voiding defective bargains. Thus, if the promise is induced at gunpoint, induced by a misrepresentation, or made by an infant or mentally incompetent person, these doctrines will render it unenforceable. However, when the duress, fraud, or incapacity is less direct or clear, procedural unconscionability provides a more flexible judicial tool for voiding a contract on these same grounds. The substantive unconscionability doctrine, however, can be invoked to void an agreement based solely on its content. When courts find a contract to be substantively unconscionable, they often state that its terms are inherently unfair or oppressive. In principle, procedural and substantive unconscionability are independent doctrines: a procedurally unconscionable bargain need not contain unfair or oppressive terms, and a substantively unconscionable bargain need not have been produced by a defective bargaining process. But in practice, the relatively few cases in which courts have struck down bargains as unconscionable have been premised on both procedural and substantive unconscionability. (For the claim that an agreement can be substantively but not procedurally unconscionable, see *Gillman v. Chase Manhattan Bank*, N. A., 534 N.E.2d 824, 829 (N.Y. 1988) and Restatement (Second) § 208 cmt. c. For the claim that procedural unconscionability cannot void a contract that is not also substantively unconscionable, see *Communications Maintenance, Inc. v. Motorola, Inc.*, 761 F.2d 1202 (7th Cir. 1985).) Thus, whereas the doctrines of duress, fraud, and incapacity can be valid defenses even to bargains with fair terms, unconscionability generally will apply only to bargains held substantively unfair. Can you determine whether *Seabrook* and *Henningsen* were decided on procedural and/or substantive unconscionability grounds? Could the cases have been decided on duress, fraud, or incapacity grounds?

2. ***Autonomy, Efficiency, and Procedural Unconscionability in*** Seabrook. Just as autonomy and economic principles support the duress, fraud, and incapacity limitations to unfettered freedom of contract, for the same reasons they likewise would appear to support invalidating procedurally unconscionable contracts. As was the case in *Seabrook*, such agreements are not expressive of the individual's will, conducive to advancing an individual's life plan, nor likely to effect welfare enhancing transfers. But is the agreement struck down in *Seabrook* involuntary, under-informed, or made by non-fully autonomous persons? Note that there is no allegation that the lessee was under-age or mentally incompetent. Instead, the court invalidates the extension of the commencement clause on grounds that the lessor, (1) who possessed superior legal knowledge and (2) a scarce commodity that lessee needed, (3) knew the lessee had not read or understood, nor (4) received legal counsel regarding (5) the legally technical terms in (6) the fine print of the lessor's (7) lengthy contract. All of these factors except (2) suggest the court's view that the promisor was insufficiently informed for his promise to be enforceable. Yet the court does not strike down the clause on the ground of fraud. Why not? Isn't the court implying that the use of technical terms and fine print in a lengthy contract amounts to fraudulent concealment? What is the difference between this conduct and a seller's conduct in taking steps to conceal evidence of a prior termite infestation from his buyers? (Recall the Schlemeyers' conduct in *Obde, supra*. Is the lessee's failure to consult legal counsel equivalent to Obde's failure to hire a termite inspector?) But if there was no fraud, isn't it incumbent on the lessee to read and understand the agreement before signing it (remember the duty to read doctrine, *supra*)? The court holds instead that these factors combine to transform the promisor's ordinary burden of reading and understanding contract terms into the promisee's duty to inform the promisor of the terms of his promise. The court's argument is that the lessor knowingly exacerbated, and then took unfair advantage of, the lessee's legal ignorance. If the lessor's contractual practices have no purpose other than to exacerbate the lessee's legal ignorance, both the autonomy and economic justifications would support the court's finding that they are procedurally unconscionable. Do you think each of the enumerated factors serve only this purpose? What is the significance of factor (2)? Is the court suggesting that sellers of scarce commodities bear a higher burden of insuring that their buyers fully understand the terms of their sales? Is the court implying that the terms of the agreement, even if fully understood by the lessee, are substantively unconscionable?

What does the court mean when it says that it "in no way seeks to abridge the parties' right to contract"?

3. **Henningsen *and the Relationship Between Procedural and Substantive Unconscionability.*** While *Seabrook* illustrates how procedural unconscionability provides an alternative venue for claims that fail to rise to the level of duress, fraud, and incapacity, *Henningsen* might be viewed as illustrating how substantive unconscionability provides an alternative venue for claims that might otherwise be brought under the public policy exceptions. To what extent does *Henningsen* rely on procedural instead of substantive unconscionability? What is the significance of the court's claim that Bloomfield Motors has "gross inequality of bargaining position" and that "there is no competition among the motor vehicle manufacturers with respect to the scope of protection guaranteed to the buyer"? Does the court invalidate the warranty disclaimer because it is inherently unfair, oppressive, or unjust, or because it resulted from a deficient bargaining procedure? The court in *Seabrook* left room for the possibility that the commencement extension clauses in the lease might have been enforceable if the lessee had read and understood it. Does the *Henningsen* court leave room for the possibility of enforcing the warranty disclaimer clauses if the bargaining process had not been defective? Is there any condition under which a mentally competent, informed adult would voluntarily agree to the disclaimer? Is the term so obviously undesirable that the court would be justified in presuming the bargaining process was unfair, or is the bargaining process so obviously unfair that the court would be justified in presuming the contract is one-sided?

4. ***Unequal Bargaining Power Revisited.*** We explored in Chapter 1 the concept of unequal bargaining power. See the notes following *Williams v. Walker Thomas Furniture*, p. 57, *supra.* Perhaps because that concept is amorphous, the drafters of both the UCC and the Restatement (Second) of Contracts sought to limit its use as a device to correct bad bargains. Comment 1 to UCC § 2-302 states: "The principle is one of the prevention of oppression and unfair surprise . . . and not of disturbance of allocation of risks because of superior bargaining power." Similarly, Comment d of § 208 of the Restatement (Second) reads:

> d. *Weakness in the bargaining process.* A bargain is not unconscionable merely because the parties to it are unequal in bargaining position, nor even because the inequality results in an allocation of risks to the weaker party. But gross inequality of bargaining power, together with terms unreasonably favorable to the stronger party, may confirm indications that the transaction involved elements of deception or compulsion, or may show that the weaker party had no meaningful choice, no real alternative, or did not in fact assent or appear to assent to the unfair terms. Factors which may contribute to a finding of unconscionability in the bargaining process include the following: belief by the stronger party that there is no reasonable probability that the weaker party will fully perform the contract; knowledge of the stronger party that the weaker party will be unable to receive substantial benefits from the contract; knowledge of the stronger party that the weaker party is unable reasonably to protect his interest by reason of physical or mental infirmities, ignorance, illiteracy or inability to understand the language of the agreement, or similar factors.

This Comment lists a number of factors that would justify a finding of unconscionability. Why would these same factors not provide the basis for rescission on the grounds of fraudulent concealment or nondisclosure? One answer is that the superior party's informational advantage does not relate to the product or service that is being sold but to superior knowledge of the needs or desires of the consumer buyer. The argument, then, is grounded in paternalism: the seller knows better than the buyer what the buyer wants. In theory, this argument has much to commend it if you accept the premise of superior knowledge. But how would you determine this fact in specific cases? More importantly, how would you advise sellers who must distinguish "competent" from "incompetent" consumers in advance?

5. ***Autonomy and Economic Perspectives on Substantive Unconscionability.*** If substantive unconscionability serves to prevent enforcement of contracts creating negative externalities, the economic approach would support it. For example, even if contracts for indentured servitude were constitutionally and statutorily permissible, courts would likely strike them down as substantively unconscionable, no matter how pristine the bargaining process that led to them. One economic justification for such a decision is that allowing individuals to be even temporarily enslaved to another has "spill over" effects on how people perceive and treat other human beings in society generally. Thus, by sanctioning such contracts, courts would allow a practice of temporary human ownership that leads some to devalue and therefore disrespect the rights of others. One autonomy justification for such a decision is that it allows persons to be treated as mere means to the ends of others and is therefore inconsistent with the inherent dignity of persons. On this view, autonomy is an inalienable right. (Perhaps paradoxically, an unqualified commitment to allowing individuals to make their own choices is thought to entail a prohibition on their right to choose entirely to relinquish their autonomy.) But when these spill over effects and the inherent dignity of persons are not implicated by contractual arrangements, both approaches often reject substantive unconscionability on the ground that it interferes with the principle of freedom of contract. The autonomy approach rejects it as inconsistent with every individual's right to form, revise, and pursue his conception of the good (even if a court disapproves of that conception.) The economic approach rejects it as an attempt to redistribute wealth by interfering with transactions that increase social welfare. Economists generally argue that redistribution should take place through tax transfers, rather than through contract regulation.[19]

6. ***Challenging the Received Economic Wisdom on Substantive Unconscionability.*** Professor Eric Posner has argued that, contrary to the prevailing view, the economic approach should support many instances of substantive contractual regulation, such as usury laws which restrict the rate of interest lenders may charge or reasonableness limitations on price terms in contracts. Posner's claim is that the existence of a welfare system prevents individuals from fully internalizing the risks of their contracts. Because the welfare system provides a social safety net, it is rational for poor people (who are most likely to benefit from welfare if a risk materializes) to enter into risky transactions. In effect, a poorer person can use welfare to insure against the downside risk of volatile contracts with a high potential

---

[19] *See* Louis Kaplow & Steven Shavell, *Fairness Versus Welfare*, 114 HARV. L. REV. 961 (2001).

reward offset by an equally high potential loss. If the upside risk materializes, the poor person will retain all the benefits. If the downside risk materializes, the poor person can do no worse than the welfare system guarantees him. (Welfare also provides wealthy people with the same insurance, but that insurance does not protect them from losing the far greater wealth they have already accumulated.) Posner thus argues that substantive regulation of contract terms can be justified to prevent individuals from using welfare to insure themselves against risks they would not take in the absence of the welfare system. *See* Eric A. Posner, *Contract Law in the Welfare State: A Defense of the Unconscionability Doctrine, Usury Laws, and Related Limitations on the Freedom to Contract*, 24 J. LEGAL. STUD. 283 (1995). Would the autonomy approach similarly support such regulation on the ground that the welfare system distorts individuals' will?

  7. *Contracts Limiting Negligence Liability.* Many contracts contain clauses designed to release promisors from tort liability due to their negligence in fulfilling contractual obligations. In general, courts will enforce these provisions unless they find the bargaining process was procedurally unconscionable or the terms violated public policy. For example, in *Mutual Marine Office, Inc. v. Atwell, Vogel & Sterling, Inc.*, 485 F. Supp. 351, 354 (S.D.N.Y. 1980), an insurance company hired a firm to inspect properties it had agreed to insure. An inspector for the firm sent the insurance company a report that failed to mention the possibility of flooding from the Susquehanna River (apparently a good faith omission), located only a few 100 feet from the property. When the property flooded, the insurance company paid on its policy and sued the inspection firm for negligence in failing to report the existence and close proximity of the river. The inspection firm had included in its report the following disclaimer of any liability for negligence in the inspection:

> This report made from observation and interview, and concerns such conditions and practices as were observed and considered at time of call; it is not intended to indicate that there are no other exposures. . . . We do not assume any legal liability due to misinformation given our inspector, nor for inaccuracies, human error, etc. . . . [O]ur inspections . . . are made at a very moderate fee, and we cannot accept any legal liability for error or omission.

Id. at 353. The court enforced the liability disclaimer:

> Where, as here, the language and intent of the disclaimer is clear and unequivocal, the parties were on notice of the disclaimer prior to entering the transaction, the disclaimer was not forced on one party to the bargain by the other, and the disclaimer was common in the type of transaction under consideration and was to be expected by ordinary custom, there is no reason to reject the disclaimer.

Id. at 354.

  The *Mutual Marine* court also held that the disclaimer in that case would not release the defendant from liability for gross negligence, a position shared by most courts. Though the inspection firm expressly stated in the report to their insurer that the possibility of flooding was not a concern, the court concluded that this did not amount to gross negligence because the plaintiff-insurer could have inspected the property itself. Do you agree with the court's conclusion? Would the court enforce a clause expressly disclaiming liability for gross negligence?

Mutual Marine dealt with a dispute between two large corporations. However, courts have held similarly when the dispute involves a consumer and a corporation, despite judicial concern regarding unequal bargaining power mentioned in *Mutual Marine*. In *Ciofalo v. Vic Tanney Gyms, Inc.*, 10 N.Y.2d 294, 220 N.Y.S.2d 962, 177 N.E.2d 925 (1961), the plaintiff, a member of a gym, was injured in a pool-side fall on slippery ground. The membership agreement for the gym contained a disclaimer of liability by the defendant, which the plaintiff asserted was in violation of public policy. The court concluded otherwise:

> Here there is no special legal relationship and no overriding public interest which demand that this contract provision, voluntarily entered into by competent parties, should be rendered ineffectual. Defendant, a private corporation, was under no obligation or legal duty to accept plaintiff as a "member" or patron. Having consented to do so, it had the right to insist upon such terms as it deemed appropriate. Plaintiff, on the other hand, was not required to assent to unacceptable terms, or to give up a valuable legal right, as a condition precedent to obtaining employment or being able to make use of the services rendered by a public carrier or utility. She voluntarily applied for membership in a private organization, and agreed to the terms upon which this membership was bestowed. She may not repudiate them now.

Id. at 297–98. Do you think it would make a difference to the court if plaintiff had demonstrated that every gym in her area required members to sign a similar disclaimer? Should it? In ruling against the plaintiff, the court points out that she entered into this agreement voluntarily. UCC § 2-719(3) holds that "[l]imitation of consequential damages for injury to the person in the case of consumer goods is prima facie unconscionable." Does UCC § 2-719(3) contravene the premise that all voluntary agreements are enforceable? Though still widely cited, note that *Ciofalo* apparently has been superseded by statute in New York. *See Lagos v. Krollage*, 78 N.Y.2d 95, 100 (1991).

8. ***Bounded Rationality and Unconscionability.*** Economic theory assumes that parties are rational decisionmakers who consider all the benefits and costs of their transactions. The prominence of standard form contracts poses certain difficulties for this assumption. In *Bounded Rationality, Standard Form Contracts, and Unconscionability*, 70 U. CHI. L. REV. 1203 (2003), Professor Russell Korobkin suggests that consumers more often exercise "bounded rationality": they consider certain contractual terms, such as price, which he calls "salient" terms, while disregarding all other contract terms, or "non-salient" terms. Sellers will provide efficient salient terms, but "[a]ssuming that price is always a salient product attribute for buyers, market competition actually will force sellers to provide low-quality non-salient attributes in order to save costs that will be passed along to buyers in the form of lower prices." *Id.* at 1206. Korobkin argues that market checks will not protect buyers from inefficient non-salient terms. He therefore concludes that courts and legislatures should do so. Professor Korobkin argues that:

(1) "procedural unconscionability" analysis should be motivated by an inquiry into a term's salience, (2) "substantive unconscionability" determinations should depend on whether terms are more costly to buyers than they are beneficial to sellers ex ante, (3) courts should require buyers to meet an exacting burden of proof before finding a term unconscionable under this criterion, and (4) courts should liberally refuse to enforce terms found unconscionable under this standard, and even refuse to enforce entire contracts on some occasions, in order to provide an incentive to sellers to draft efficient form contract terms ex ante when the market fails to provide such an incentive.

Id. at 1208.

Do you agree with the Professor Korobkin's "bounded rationality" assessment of most consumers? Is his claim that market competition will not eliminate inefficient non-salient terms compelling? How would the above unconscionability analysis have been applied in *Seabrook* and *Henningsen*?

9. ***Arbitration Clauses and Unconscionability.*** The Supreme Court has recently addressed the issue of whether the threshold determination of unconscionability can be delegated to an arbiter or is reserved exclusively for the judiciary. In *Rent-A-Center, W., Inc. v. Jackson*, 130 S. Ct. 2772 (2010), defendant Rent-A-Center moved to compel arbitration after Jackson, a former employee, filed an employment discrimination claim against them in federal court. Jackson argued that the agreement as a whole was unconscionable, rendering the arbitration clause unenforceable. The Supreme Court disagreed. The Court distinguished Jackson's challenge to the contract as a whole from claims that challenged only the validity of the arbitration clause itself. The Court held that claims that challenged the entirety of the contract were subject to its arbitration provision, and that the determination of unconscionability had thus been delegated to an arbiter:

> Here, the "written provision . . . to settle by arbitration a controversy," that Rent–A–Center asks us to enforce is the delegation provision — the provision that gave the arbitrator "exclusive authority to resolve any dispute relating to the . . . enforceability . . . of this Agreement," The "remainder of the contract," is the rest of the agreement to arbitrate claims arising out of Jackson's employment with Rent–A–Center. To be sure this case differs from Prima Paint, Buckeye, and Preston, in that the arbitration provisions sought to be enforced in those cases were contained in contracts unrelated to arbitration — contracts for consulting services, see Prima Paint, supra, at 397, 87 S. Ct. 1801, check-cashing services, see Buckeye, supra, at 442, 126 S. Ct. 1204, and "personal management" or "talent agent" services, see Preston, supra, at 352, 128 S. Ct. 978. In this case, the underlying contract is itself an arbitration agreement. But that makes no difference. Application of the severability rule does not depend on the substance of the remainder of the contract. Section 2 operates on the specific "written provision" to "settle by arbitration a controversy" that the party seeks to enforce. Accordingly, unless Jackson challenged the delegation provision specifically, we must treat it as valid under § 2, and must

enforce it under §§ 3 and 4, leaving any challenge to the validity of the Agreement as a whole for the arbitrator.

Id. at 2779.

Justice Stevens, writing for the dissent, disagreed:

In my view, a general revocation challenge to a standalone arbitration agreement is, invariably, a challenge to the "'making'" of the arbitration agreement itself, Prima Paint, 388 U.S., at 403, 87 S. Ct. 1801, and therefore, under Prima Paint, must be decided by the court. A claim of procedural unconscionability aims to undermine the formation of the arbitration agreement, much like a claim of unconscionability aims to undermine the clear-and-unmistakable-intent requirement necessary for a valid delegation of a "discrete" challenge to the validity of the arbitration agreement itself, Preston, 552 U.S., at 354, 128 S. Ct. 978. Moreover, because we are dealing in this case with a challenge to an independently executed arbitration agreement — rather than a clause contained in a contract related to another subject matter — any challenge to the contract itself is also, necessarily, a challenge to the arbitration agreement. They are one and the same.

Id. at 2787.

G. STATUTE OF FRAUDS

The statute of frauds doctrine is the final way in which the law purports to regulate the bargaining process. The Statute of Frauds was first enacted by Parliament in 1677 to prohibit fraud and perjury in disputes over the enforceability of oral contracts. The relevant parts of the original Statute, called an Act for Prevention of Frauds and Perjuries, are sections four and seventeen. Section four provided:

And be it further enacted by the authority aforesaid, that from and after the said four and twentieth day of June no action shall be brought (1) whereby to charge any executor or administrator upon any special promise, to answer damages out of his own estate, (2) or whereby to charge the defendant upon any special promise to answer for the debt, default or miscarriages of another person; (3) or to charge any person upon any agreement made upon consideration of marriage; (4) or upon any contract or sale of lands, tenements, or hereditaments, or any interest in or concerning them; (5) or upon any agreement that is not to be performed within the space of one year from the making thereof; (6) unless the agreement upon which such action shall be brought, or some memorandum or note thereof, shall be in writing, and signed by the party to be charged therewith, or some other person thereunto by him lawfully authorized.

Section seventeen added:

And be it further enacted by the authority aforesaid, That from and after the said four and twentieth day of June no contract for the sale of any goods, wares and merchandizes, for the price of ten pounds sterling or upwards, shall be allowed to be good, except the buyer shall accept part of the goods so sold, and actually receive the same, or give something in earnest to bind the bargain, or in part payment, or that some note or memorandum in writing of the said bargain be made and signed by the parties to be charged by such contract, or their agents thereto lawfully authorized.

The intent of the Statute was to limit the enforceability of certain kinds of oral contracts, especially contracts for the sale of land and goods, suretyship contracts, and those obligations whose performance requires more than one year. Requiring the parties to make a written note of their agreement was intended to coerce promise makers into memorializing their contracts, thereby creating reliable evidence and reducing the possibility of enforcing fraudulent contracts proved by perjured testimony.

State legislatures in the United States have generally enacted statutes tracking section four of the original Statute, and the Uniform Sales Act paralleled the provisions of Section Seventeen. Although England repealed its statute of frauds requirements for the sale of goods in 1954, the United States has preserved the 300-year-old Statute in § 2-201 of the UCC. But despite the fortified position the statute of frauds occupies as a part of the UCC, it is still under assault. Critics charge that the statute of frauds' requirement of a writing operates as a trap for the unwary by inappropriately providing a defense to a party who regrets an unfavorable oral contract. Thus, the statute of frauds may sometimes operate to nullify the bargained-for allocation of risks in an otherwise valid agreement.

As you read the following cases, ask yourself how the various forms of the statute of frauds evolved, what purposes the doctrine ostensibly serves, and whether courts have chosen rules or standards to implement it.

McINTOSH v. MURPHY
Supreme Court of Hawaii
52 Haw. 29, 469 P.2d 177 (1970)

LEVINSON, J.

This case involves an oral employment contract which allegedly violates the provision of the Statute of Frauds requiring "any agreement that is not to be performed within one year from the making thereof" to be in writing in order to be enforceable. In this action the plaintiff-employee Dick McIntosh seeks to recover damages from his employer, George Murphy and Murphy Motors, Ltd., for the breach of an alleged one-year oral employment contract.

While the facts are in sharp conflict, it appears that defendant George Murphy was in southern California during March, 1964 interviewing prospective management personnel for his Chevrolet-Oldsmobile dealerships in Hawaii. He interviewed the plaintiff twice during that time. The position of sales manager for one of the dealerships was fully discussed but no contract was entered into. In April, 1964 the plaintiff received a call from the general manager of Murphy Motors informing him of possible employment within thirty days if he was still available. The plaintiff indicated his continued interest and informed the manager that he would be available. Later in April, the plaintiff sent Murphy a telegram to the effect that he would arrive in Honolulu on Sunday, April 26, 1964. Murphy then telephoned McIntosh on Saturday, April 25, 1964 to notify him that the job of assistant sales manager was open and work would begin on the following Monday, April 27, 1964. At that time McIntosh expressed surprise at the change in job title from sales manager to assistant sales manager but reconfirmed the fact that he was arriving in Honolulu the next day, Sunday. McIntosh arrived on Sunday, April 26, 1964 and began work on the following day, Monday, April 27, 1964.

As a consequence of his decision to work for Murphy, McIntosh moved some of his belongings from the mainland to Hawaii, sold other possessions, leased an apartment in Honolulu and obviously forwent any other employment opportunities. In short, the plaintiff did all those things which were incidental to changing one's residence permanently from Los Angeles to Honolulu, a distance of approximately 2200 miles. McIntosh continued working for Murphy until July 16, 1964, approximately two and one-half months, at which time he was discharged on the grounds that he was unable to close deals with prospective customers and could not train the salesmen.

At the conclusion of the trial, the defense moved for a directed verdict arguing that the oral employment agreement was in violation of the Statute of Frauds, there being no written memorandum or note thereof. The trial court ruled that as a matter of law the contract did not come within the Statute, reasoning that Murphy bargained for acceptance by the actual commencement of performance by McIntosh, so that McIntosh was not bound by a contract until he came to work on Monday, April 27, 1964. Therefore, assuming that the contract was for a year's employment, it was performable within a year exactly to the day and no writing was required for it to be enforceable. Alternatively, the court ruled that if the agreement was made final by the telephone call between the parties on Saturday, April 25, 1964, then that part of the weekend which remained would not be counted in calculating the year, thus taking the contract out of the Statute of Frauds. With commendable candor the trial judge gave as the motivating force for the decision his desire to avoid a mechanical and unjust application of the Statute.[20]

The case went to the jury on the following questions: (1) whether the contract was for a year's duration or was performable on a trial basis, thus making it terminable at the will of either party; (2) whether the plaintiff was discharged for just cause; and (3) if he was not discharged for just cause, what damages were due the plaintiff. The jury returned a verdict for the plaintiff in the sum of $12,103.40. The defendants appeal to this court on four principal grounds, three of which we find to be without merit. The remaining ground of appeal is whether the plaintiff can maintain an action on the alleged oral employment contract in light of the

---

[20] [1] THE COURT: You make the law look ridiculous, because one day is Sunday and the man does not work on Sunday; the other day is Saturday; he is up in Fresno. He can't work down there. And he is down here Sunday night and shows up for work on Monday. To me that is a contract within a year. I don't want to make the law look ridiculous, Mr. Clause, because it is one day after, one day too much, and that one day is a Sunday, and a non-working day.

prohibition of the Statute of Frauds making unenforceable an oral contract that is not to be performed within one year.

I. Time of Acceptance of the Employment Agreement

The defendants contend that the trial court erred in refusing to give an instruction to the jury that if the employment agreement was made more than one day before the plaintiff began performance, there could be no recovery by the plaintiff. The reason given was that a contract not to be performed within one year from its making is unenforceable if not in writing.

The defendants are correct in their argument that the time of acceptance of an offer is a question of fact for the jury to decide. But the trial court alternatively decided that even if the offer was accepted on the Saturday prior to the commencement of performance, the intervening Sunday and part of Saturday would not be counted in computing the year for the purposes of the Statute of Frauds. The judge stated that Sunday was a non-working day and only a fraction of Saturday was left which he would not count. In any event, there is no need to discuss the relative merits of either ruling since we base our decision in this case on the doctrine of equitable estoppel which was properly briefed and argued by both parties before this court, although not presented to the trial court.

II. Enforcement by Virtue of Action in Reliance on the Oral Contract

In determining whether a rule of law can be fashioned and applied to a situation where an oral contract admittedly violates a strict interpretation of the Statute of Frauds, it is necessary to review the Statute itself together with its historical and modern functions. The Statute of Frauds, which requires that certain contracts be in writing in order to be legally enforceable, had its inception in the days of Charles II of England. Hawaii's version of the Statute is found in HRS § 656-1 and is substantially the same as the original English Statute of Frauds.

The first English Statute was enacted almost 300 years ago to prevent "many fraudulent practices, which are commonly endeavored to be upheld by perjury and subornation of perjury." 29 Car. 2, c. 3 (1677). Certainly, there were compelling reasons in those days for such a law. At the time of enactment in England, the jury system was quite unreliable, rules of evidence were few, and the complaining party was disqualified as a witness so he could neither testify on direct-examination nor, more importantly, be cross-examined. The aforementioned structural and evidentiary limitations on our system of justice no longer exist.

Retention of the Statute today has nevertheless been justified on at least three grounds: (1) the Statute still serves an evidentiary function thereby lessening the danger of perjured testimony (the original rationale); (2) the requirement of a writing has a cautionary effect which causes reflection by the parties on the importance of the agreement; and (3) the writing is an easy way to distinguish enforceable contracts from those which are not, thus channeling certain transactions into written form.

In spite of whatever utility the Statute of Frauds may still have, its applicability has been drastically limited by judicial construction over the years in order to mitigate the harshness of a mechanical application.[21] Furthermore, learned writers continue to disparage the Statute, regarding it as "a statute for promoting fraud" and a "legal anachronism."

Another method of judicial circumvention of the Statute of Frauds has grown out of the exercise of the equity powers of the courts. Such judicially imposed limitations or exceptions involved the traditional dispensing power of the equity courts to mitigate the "harsh" rule of law. When courts have enforced an oral contract in spite of the Statute, they have utilized the legal labels of "part performance" or "equitable estoppel" in granting relief. Both doctrines are said to be based on the concept of estoppel, which operates to avoid unconscionable injury

Part performance has long been recognized in Hawaii as an equitable doctrine justifying the enforcement of an oral agreement for the conveyance of an interest in land where there has been substantial reliance by the party seeking to enforce the contract. Other courts have enforced oral contracts (including employment contracts) which failed to satisfy the section of the Statute making unenforceable an agreement not to be performed within a year of its making. This has occurred where the conduct of the parties gave rise to an estoppel to assert the Statute

[It is appropriate for modern courts to cast aside the raiments of conceptualism which cloak the true policies underlying the reasoning behind the many decisions enforcing contracts that violate the Statute of Frauds.] There is certainly no need to resort to legal rubrics or meticulous legal formulas when better explanations are available. The policy behind enforcing an oral agreement which violated the Statute of Frauds, as a policy of avoiding unconscionable injury, was well set out by the California Supreme Court. In Monarco v. Lo Greco, 220 P.2d 737, 739 (1950), a case which involved an action to enforce an oral contract for the conveyance of land on the grounds of 20 years performance by the promisee, the court said:

> The doctrine of estoppel to assert the statute of frauds has been consistently applied by the courts of this state to prevent fraud that would result from refusal to enforce oral contracts in certain circumstances. Such fraud may inhere in the unconscionable injury that would result from denying enforcement of the contract after one party has been induced by the other seriously to change his position in reliance on the contract.

In seeking to frame a workable test which is flexible enough to cover diverse factual situations and also provide some reviewable standards, we find very persuasive section 217A of the Second Restatement of Contracts. That section specifically covers those situations where there has been reliance on an oral contract which falls

---

[21] [3] Thus a promise to pay the debt of another has been construed to encompass only promises made to a creditor which do not benefit the promisor (Restatement of Contracts § 184 (1932); 3 Williston, *Contracts* § 452 (Jaeger ed. 1960)); a promise in consideration of marriage has been interpreted to exclude mutual promises to marry (Restatement, *supra* § 192; 3 Williston, *supra* § 485); a promise not to be performed within one year means a promise not performable within one year (Restatement, *supra* § 198; 3 Williston, *supra*, § 495); a promise not to be performed within one year may be removed from the Statute of Frauds if one party has fully performed (Restatement, *supra* § 198; 3 Williston, *supra* § 504); and the Statute will not be applied where all promises involved are fully performed (Restatement, *supra* § 219; 3 Williston, *supra* § 528).

within the Statute of Frauds. Section 217A states:

> (1) A promise which the promisor should reasonably expect to induce action or forbearance on the part of the promisee or a third person and which does induce the action or forbearance is enforceable notwithstanding the Statute of Frauds if injustice can be avoided only by enforcement of the promise. The remedy granted for breach is to be limited as justice requires. (2) In determining whether injustice can be avoided only by enforcement of the promise, the following circumstances are significant: (a) the availability and adequacy of other remedies, particularly cancellation and restitution; (b) the definite and substantial character of the action or forbearance in relation to the remedy sought; (c) the extent to which the action or forbearance corroborates evidence of the making and terms of the promise, or the making and terms are otherwise established by clear and convincing evidence; (d) the reasonableness of the action or forbearance; (e) the extent to which the action or forbearance was foreseeable by the promisor.

We think that the approach taken in the Restatement is the proper method of giving the trial court the necessary latitude to relieve a party of the hardships of the Statute of Frauds. Other courts have used similar approaches in dealing with oral employment contracts upon which an employee had seriously relied. This is to be preferred over having the trial court bend over backwards to take the contract out of the Statute of Frauds. In the present case the trial court admitted just this inclination and forthrightly followed it.

There is no dispute that the action of the plaintiff in moving 2200 miles from Los Angeles to Hawaii was foreseeable by the defendant. In fact, it was required to perform his duties. Injustice can only be avoided by the enforcement of the contract and the granting of money damages. No other remedy is adequate. The plaintiff found himself residing in Hawaii without a job.

It is also clear that a contract of some kind did exist. The plaintiff performed the contract for two and one-half months receiving $3,484.60 for his services. The exact length of the contract, whether terminable at will as urged by the defendant, or for a year from the time when the plaintiff started working, was up to the jury to decide.

In sum, the trial court might have found that enforcement of the contract was warranted by virtue of the plaintiff's reliance on the defendant's promise. Naturally, each case turns on its own facts. Certainly there is considerable discretion for a court to implement the true policy behind the Statute of Frauds, which is to prevent fraud or any other type of unconscionable injury. We therefore affirm the judgment of the trial court on the ground that the plaintiff's reliance was such that injustice could only be avoided by enforcement of the contract.

ABE, J., dissenting.

. . . [T]his court holds that though the alleged one-year employment contract came within the Statute of Frauds, nevertheless the judgment of the trial court is affirmed "on the ground that the plaintiff's reliance was such that injustice could only be avoided by enforcement of the contract."

I believe this court is begging the issue by its holding because to reach that conclusion, this court is ruling that the defendant agreed to hire the plaintiff under a one-year employment contract. The defendant has denied that the plaintiff was hired for a period of one year and has introduced into evidence testimony of witnesses that all hiring by the defendant in the past has been on a trial basis. The defendant also testified that he had hired the plaintiff on a trial basis.

Here on one hand the plaintiff claimed that he had a one-year employment contract; on the other hand, the defendant claimed that the plaintiff had not been hired for one year but on a trial basis for so long as his services were satisfactory. I believe the Statute of Frauds was enacted to avoid the consequences this court is forcing upon the defendant. In my opinion, the legislature enacted the Statute of Frauds to negate claims such as has [sic] been made by the plaintiff in this case. But this court holds that because the plaintiff in reliance of the one-year employment contract (alleged to have been entered into by the plaintiff, but denied by the defendant) has changed his position, "injustice could only be avoided by enforcement of the contract." Where is the sense of justice?

Now assuming that the defendant had agreed to hire the plaintiff under a one-year employment contract and the contract came within the Statute of Frauds, I cannot agree, as intimated by this court, that we should circumvent the Statute of Frauds by the exercise of the equity powers of courts. As to statutory law, the sole function of the judiciary is to interpret the statute and the judiciary should not usurp legislative power and enter into the legislative field. Thus, if the Statute of Frauds is too harsh as intimated by this court, and it brings about undue hardship, it for the legislature to amend or repeal the statute and not for this court to legislate.

NOTES

1. *Questions on* **McIntosh**. The statute of frauds doctrines applied in *McIntosh* has origins in both law and equity. The legal doctrine tends to take the form of a rule, and equitable exceptions take the form of a standard. Is the regulation resulting from the combination of the two approaches in one jurisdiction effective? Do you think the two approaches are in a "stable equilibrium," or do you think there will be an on-going ebb and flow from law to equity and back to law again? If you think the two approaches make the regulation less clear and predictable, why do you suppose both approaches co-exist in the same jurisdictions?[22]

This tension between law and equity illustrated in *McIntosh* is exemplified by the extremely technical analysis courts employ together with the considerable flexibility courts have in construing the one-year period. This should not obscure the peculiarity of the one-year criterion. Professor Allen Farnsworth wrote in his treatise, CONTRACTS:

---

[22] For a discussion of the continuing tension between the formal rules of law and the flexible standards of equity, see Jody S. Kraus & Robert E. Scott, *Contract Design and the Structure of Contractual Intent*, 84 N.Y.U. L. REV. 1023 (2009).

If the one-year provision is based on the tendency of memory to fail and of evidence to go stale with the passage of time, it is ill-conceived, because the one-year period does not run from the making of the contract to the proof of the making, but from the making of the contract to the completion of performance. If an oral contract that cannot be performed within a year is broken the day after its making, the provision applied though the terms of the contract are fresh in the minds of the parties. But if an oral contract that can be performed within a year is broken and suit is not brought until nearly six years (the usual statute of limitations for contract actions) after the breach, the provision does not apply, even though the terms of the contract are no longer fresh in the minds of the parties.

If the one-year provision is an attempt to separate significant contracts of long duration, for which writings should be required, from less significant contracts of short duration, for which writings are unnecessary, it is equally ill-contrived because the one-year period does not run from the commencement of performance to the completion of performance, but from the making of the contract to the completion of performance. If an oral contract to work for one day, 13 months from now, is broken, the provision applies, even though the duration of performance is only one day. But if an oral contract to work for a year beginning today is broken, the provision does not apply, even though the duration of performance is a full year.

Id. at 39.

Given Farnsworth's arguments, what possible justification remains for the one-year rule in its current form?

2. *Part Performance of an Oral Contract.* Recall the language in *McIntosh* listing three common policy justifications for the statute of frauds ["evidentiary," "cautionary," and "channeling"]. As a general rule, part performance of an oral contract not to be performed within a year will not take the contract out of the statute unless, in some jurisdictions, the part performance is reliable evidence of the agreement. Similarly, part performance of an oral contract to sell land will take the contract out of the statute of frauds only if the acts of partial performance are

> unequivocally referable to that contract. The sufficiency of acts to constitute such part performance can be decided as a matter of law. Such acts as obtaining financing and making studies of the real property have been held insufficient part performance to preclude the defense of the statute of frauds.

Schwedes v. Romain, 587 P. 2d 388 (Mont. 1978).

In *Schwedes,* the court held that the acts of part performance relied on by the plaintiffs — securing financing and offering to pay the full purchase price to respondents' attorney — were merely actions undertaken in contemplation of performance and did not constitute a part performance of the oral contract. *Id.* at 391.

On the other hand, part performance of oral contracts to provide suretyship apparently will not take those contracts out of the statute regardless of its value as evidence of an agreement. In light of the policy justifications, what explains this difference in treatment?

Even in those instances where part performance will not take a contract in the "one-year" category out of the statute, full performance will generally remove the bar of the statute. Can you explain the different treatment of part performance and full performance?

3. ***Promissory Estoppel.*** The use of promissory estoppel to avoid the statute of frauds is a relatively recent and quite controversial development. Some jurisdictions have refused to allow parties to evade the requirements of the statute of frauds via promissory estoppel. In *Olympic Holding Co., L.L.C. v. ACE Ltd.*, 909 N.E.2d 93 (Ohio 2009), appellant ACE Ltd. had breached an oral promise to sign a bargained-for agreement to create a title insurance joint venture. Appellee Olympic Holding Co. sued for breach of contract and sought specific performance of the contract and punitive damages. Both the trial court and the court of appeals held that ACE Ltd. should be equitably estopped from raising the affirmative defense of the statute of frauds given Olympic Holding's detrimental reliance on the promise. The Ohio Supreme Court disagreed:

> We begin by examining whether breaching a promise to execute an agreement equitably removes the agreement from the statute of frauds. We recognize that numerous jurisdictions have held that under various circumstances, promissory estoppel may be used to remove an agreement from having to comply with the statute of frauds. However, we decline to adopt that exception under the circumstances of this case because it is both unnecessary and damaging to the protections afforded by the statute of frauds.

> R.C. 1335.05, Ohio's codification of the statute of frauds, provides:

>> "No action shall be brought whereby to charge * * * a person upon an agreement * * * that is not to be performed within one year from the making thereof; unless the agreement upon which such action is brought, or some memorandum or note thereof, is in *writing* and *signed* by the party to be charged therewith * * *." (Emphasis added.))

> Agreements that do not comply with the statute of frauds are unenforceable. The purpose of the statute of frauds is to prevent "frauds and perjuries." The statute does so by informing the public and judges of what is needed to form a contract and by encouraging parties to follow these requirements by nullifying those agreements that do not comply. "[T]he statute of frauds is supposed both to make people take notice of the legal consequences of a writing and to reduce the occasions on which judges enforce non-existent contracts because of perjured evidence." Kennedy, Form and Substance in Private Law Adjudication, 89 HARV. L. REV. 1685, 1691 (1976). "In every case, the formality means that unless the parties adopt the prescribed mode of manifesting their wishes, they will be ignored. The reason for ignoring them, for applying the sanction of nullity,

is to force them to be self conscious and to express themselves clearly." *Id.* at 1692.

Courts have long recognized that a signed contract constitutes a party's final expression of its agreement. Thus, the statute of frauds is necessary because a "signed writing provides greater assurance that the parties and the public can reliably know when such a transaction occurs." *Seale v. Citizens Sav. & Loan Asso.*, 806 F.2d 99, 104 (6th Cir. 1986).

If promissory estoppel is used as a bar to the writing requirements imposed by the statute of frauds, based on a party's oral promise to execute the agreement, the predictability that the statute of frauds brings to contract formation would be eroded. Parties negotiating a contract would no longer know what signifies a final agreement. Promissory estoppel used this way would open contract negotiations to fraud, the very evil that the statute of frauds seeks to prevent. Thus, "[t]o allow [a] plaintiff to recover on a theory of promissory estoppel where the oral contract is precluded by the Statute of Frauds, ' "would abrogate the purpose and intent of the legislature in enacting the statute of frauds and would nullify its fundamental requirements." ' " Essco Geometric, Inc. v. Harvard Industries, Inc. (Sept. 30, 1993), E.D.Mo. No. 90–1354C(6), 1993 WL 766952, We decline to recognize an exception to the statute of frauds even when the promise to execute an agreement is fraudulent or misleading. If a party establishes that a promise to execute an agreement is misleading or fraudulent, promissory estoppel is an equitable remedy available to recover reliance damages.

As recognized by the Supreme Court of Utah, "[i]n most instances of negotiations for transactions included within the Statute [of Frauds], a reduction of the contract to writing is contemplated and, in all probability, the parties will discuss who will draw the instrument and when and where it will be signed." Easton v. Wycoff, 4 Utah 2d 386, 388–89, 295 P.2d 332 (1956). However, until parties execute the agreement, "'[r]eliance on a statement of future intent made prior to the conclusion of negotiations in a complex business transaction is unreasonable as a matter of law. * * * Such a rule is particularly appropriate when two sophisticated business entities are involved in negotiations. "Until the documents are signed and delivered the game is not over. Businessmen would be undesirably inhibited in their dealings if expressions of intent and the exchange of drafts were taken as legally binding agreements."

Accordingly, we hold that a party may not use promissory estoppel to bar the opposing party from asserting the affirmative defense of the statute of frauds, which requires that an enforceable contract be in writing and signed by the party to be charged, but may pursue promissory estoppel as a separate remedy for damages . . .

O'DONNELL, J., dissenting.

In my view, today's holding leads to an unjust result and will adversely affect business in Ohio, much of which involves complex transactions that must of necessity be taken on a step-by-step and handshake basis. This court should instead join the majority position among jurisdictions that have considered this issue, embrace the view espoused by legal scholars, and hold that the equitable doctrine of promissory estoppel may preclude assertion of a statute-of-frauds defense. . . .

The facts in the instant case demonstrate the injustice of permitting ACE to assert that the agreement it had with Olympic is unenforceable for lack of a writing pursuant to the statute of frauds. The record here demonstrates that executives for Olympic and ACE reached a mutual understanding on the essential terms of their joint business venture. Richard Reese, the chief operating officer of ACE, assured Olympic that ACE would sign the agreement as soon as Olympic closed on its acquisition of the local title insurance companies. The record further reveals that Reese told Olympic that their agreement was "just awaiting signature" by ACE's board of directors, implying not only that the agreement had been, or would be, reduced to writing, but also that the term sheets exchanged by the parties substantially reflected their mutual understanding.

Id. at 104, 106.

Which side has the better argument? Would allowing sophisticated commercial parties to avoid the requirements of the statute of frauds when they have reasonably relied on a promise hinder commercial transactions by exposing parties to unexpected liability, or would it facilitate negotiations by enhancing the credibility of promises?

Note that the majority would allow reliance damages for a separate promissory estoppel claim based on breach of an oral promise. Does this also run the risk of opening contract negotiations to fraud, as the majority fears, since parties may not be able to determine when they will be held liable for their promises? Might parties have an incentive to over-rely on or over-invest in an oral promise if they can recover reliance damages when the promise is breached?

4. ***The Autonomy and Economic Justifications of the Statute of Frauds.*** The statute of frauds is designed to insure that contractual liability is not imposed on a party who did not make a legally enforceable promise. Both the autonomy and economic perspectives would therefore support the doctrine if it is generally effective in achieving that objective. But why would the law need to require individuals to provide evidence of their agreement? Isn't it in the parties own interest to provide whatever evidence they think advisable to enable them to prove the contract exists in the event of a subsequent dispute? Economic theory would predict that individuals will devote time and resources to creating evidence of their agreements until the marginal costs equal the marginal expected benefits of doing so. On that theory, why not leave the parties to their own (evidentiary) devices? Why should the law compel them to provide any particular kind or extent of evidence if they see fit to proceed without it? After all, won't they alone have to live with the risk that they will be unable to prevail in a subsequent dispute? Don't contracting parties fully internalize the costs of adjudicating their disputes? Or do they?

McIntosh applies the common law statute of frauds. Contracts for the sale of goods are governed by UCC § 2-201. Before reading the following case, read carefully UCC § 2-201 and compare it to the common law statute of frauds. To what extent do they overlap or conflict?

MONETTI, S.P.A. v. ANCHOR HOCKING CORP.
United States Court of Appeals, Seventh Circuit
931 F.2d 1178 (1991)

POSNER, CIRCUIT JUDGE

[The plaintiff, Monetti, alleged that it had an agreement with the defendant, Anchor Hocking, for Anchor Hocking to be the sole U.S. distributor of Monetti's food service products for a ten year term. During the negotiations, plaintiff had prepared and sent to defendant a proposed draft agreement. Subsequently, the parties met and, as plaintiff alleged, reached an understanding based on the draft agreement but no one from Anchor Hocking signed this or any other draft of the agreement. Subsequently, as provided in the draft agreement, Monetti turned over to Anchor all tangible and intangible assets of Melform, a wholly owned subsidiary of Monetti, which had until then been the distributor of its products. There were two writings related to this agreement. The first was a memo incorporating the terms of the proposed draft agreement that had been dictated by defendant's agent, Steve Schneider, before the negotiations over the final agreement. This memo was evidenced by his typed initials "SS and it contained all of the plaintiff's proposed terms plus two more suggested by Schneider. The second writing was a draft of the agreement that was included in an internal memo written by Raymond Davis, the defendant's marketing director, on Anchor Hocking letterhead. It contained all of the terms of the earlier draft except one, and was referred to by Davis as representing the "summary agreement" with Monetti. Shortly after the second memo was written, the parties' relationship began to deteriorate and Monetti sued for breach of contract. Anchor Hocking raised the statute of frauds as a defense.]

Illinois' general statute of frauds forbids a suit upon an agreement that is not to be performed within a year "unless the promise or agreement upon which such action shall be brought, or some memorandum or note thereof, shall be in writing, and signed by the party to be charged therewith, or some other person thereunto by him lawfully authorized." The statute of frauds in Article 2 of the Uniform Commercial Code makes a contract for the sale of goods worth at least $500 unenforceable "unless there is some writing sufficient to indicate that a contract for sale has been made between the parties and signed by the party against whom enforcement is sought or by his authorized agent or broker." The differences between these formulations are subtle but important. The Illinois statute requires that the writing "express the substance of the contract with reasonable certainty." *Frazer v. Howe*, 106 Ill. 564, 574 (1883). The UCC statute of frauds does not require that the writing contain the terms of the contract. Comment 1 to UCC § 2-201. In fact it requires no more than written corroboration of the alleged oral contract. Even if there is no such signed document, the contract may still be valid "with respect to goods . . . which have been received and accepted." § 2-201(3)(c). This provision may appear to narrow the statute of frauds still further, but if anything it curtails a traditional exception, and one applicable to Illinois' general statute: the exception for partial performance. . . . The Uniform Commercial Code does not treat partial delivery by the party seeking to enforce an oral contract as a partial performance of the *entire* contract, allowing him to enforce the contract with respect to the undelivered goods.

Let us postpone the question of partial performance for a moment and focus on whether there was a signed document of the sort that the statutes of frauds require. The judge, over Monetti's objection, refused to admit oral evidence on this question. He was right to refuse. The use of oral evidence to get round the requirement of a writing would be bootstrapping, would sap the statute of frauds of most of its force, and is therefore forbidden. . . .

We have two documents (really, two pairs of documents) to consider. The first is Steve Schneider's "Topics for Discussion" memo with its "Attachment #1." Since "signed" in statute-of-frauds land is a term of art, meaning executed or adopted by the defendant, UCC § 1-201(39) and Ill. Code Comment thereto, Schneider's typed initials are sufficient. The larger objection is that the memo was written before the contract — any contract — was made. The memo indicates that Schneider (an authorized representative of the defendant) agrees to the principal provisions in the draft agreement prepared by Monetti, but not to all the provisions; further negotiations are envisaged. There was no contract when the memo was prepared and signed, though it is fair to infer from the memo that a contract much like the draft attached to it would be agreed upon — if Monetti agreed to Anchor Hocking's demand for Canada, as Monetti concedes (and the Davis memo states) it did.

Can a memo that precedes the actual formation of the contract ever constitute the writing required by the statute of frauds? Under the Uniform Commercial Code, why not? Its statute of frauds does not require that any contracts "be in writing." All that is required is a document that provides solid evidence of the existence of a contract; the contract itself can be oral. Three cases should be distinguished. In the first, the precontractual writing is merely one party's offer. We have held, interpreting Illinois' version of the Uniform Commercial Code, that an offer won't do. *R.S. Bennett & Co. v. Economy Mechanical Industries, Inc., supra,* 606 F.2d at 186. Otherwise there would be an acute danger that a party whose offer had been rejected would nevertheless try to use it as the basis for a suit. The second case is that of notes made in preparation for a negotiating session, and this is another plausible case for holding the statute unsatisfied, lest a breakdown of contract negotiations become the launching pad for a suit on an alleged oral contract. Third is the case — arguably this case — where the precontractual writing — the Schneider memo and the attachment to it — indicates the promisor's (Anchor Hocking's) acceptance of the promisee's (Monetti's) offer; the case, in other words, where all the essential terms are stated in the writing and the only problem is that the writing was prepared before the contract became final. The only difficulty with holding that such a writing satisfies the statute of frauds is the use of the perfect tense by the draftsmen of the Uniform Commercial Code: the writing must be sufficient to demonstrate that "a contract for sale *has been made.* . . . The 'futuristic' nature of the writing disqualifies it." *Micromedia v. Automated Broadcast Controls,* 799 F.2d 230, 234 (5th Cir. 1986) (emphasis in original). Yet under a general statute of frauds, "it is well settled that a memorandum satisfying the Statute may be made before the contract is concluded." *Farrow v. Cahill,* 663 F.2d

201, 209, 214 U.S. App. D.C. 24 (D.C. Cir. 1980) (footnote omitted). And while merely because the UCC's draftsmen relaxed one requirement of the statute of frauds — that there be a writing containing all the essential terms of the contract — doesn't exclude the possibility that they wanted to stiffen another, by excluding writings made before the contract itself was made, the choice of tenses is weak evidence. No doubt they had in mind, as the typical case to be governed by section 2-201, a deal made over the phone and evidenced by a confirmation slip. They may not have foreseen a case like the present, or provided for it. The distinction between what is assumed and what is prescribed is critical in interpretation generally. . . .

We agree with Professor Farnsworth that in appropriate circumstances a memorandum made before the contract is formed can satisfy the statute of frauds, 2 *Farnsworth on Contracts, supra,* § 6.7, at p. 132 and n. 16, including the UCC statute of frauds. This case illustrates why a rule of strict temporal priority is unnecessary to secure the purposes of the statute of frauds.

Nor need we decide whether the first memo (Schneider's) can be linked with the second (Davis's) — probably not, since they don't refer to each other — to constitute a post-contract writing and eliminate the issue just discussed. For, shortly after the Schneider memo was prepared, Monetti gave dramatic evidence of the existence of a contract by turning over its entire distribution operation in the United States to Anchor Hocking. (In fact it had started to do this even earlier.) Monetti was hardly likely to do that without a contract — without in fact a contract requiring Anchor Hocking to purchase a minimum of $27 million worth of Monetti's products over the next ten years, for that was a provision to which Schneider in the memo had indicated agreement, and it is the only form of compensation to Monetti for abandoning its distribution business that the various drafts make reference to and apparently the only one the parties ever discussed.

This partial performance took the contract out of the general Illinois statute of frauds. Unilateral performance is pretty solid evidence that there really was a contract — for why else would the party have performed unilaterally? Almost the whole purpose of contracts is to protect the party who performs first from being taken advantage of by the other party, so if a party performs first there is some basis for inferring that he had a contract. The inference of contract from partial performance is especially powerful in a case such as this, since while the nonenforcement of an oral contract leaves the parties free to pursue their noncontractual remedies, such as a suit for quantum meruit (a form of restitution), once Monetti turned over its trade secrets and other intangible assets to Anchor Hocking it had no way of recovering these things. (Of course, Monetti may just have been foolish.) The partial-performance exception to the statute of frauds is often explained (and its boundaries fixed accordingly) as necessary to protect the reliance of the performing party, so that if he can be made whole by restitution the oral contract will not be enforced. It supports enforcement of the oral contract in this case.

This discussion assumes, however, that the contract is governed by the general Illinois statute of frauds rather than, as the district judge believed, by the UCC's statute of frauds (or in addition to it — for both might apply, as we shall see), with its arguably narrower exception for partial performance. The UCC statute of frauds at issue in this case appears in Article 2, the sale of goods article of the Code, and, naturally therefore, is expressly limited to contracts for the sale of goods. That is a type of transaction in which a partial-performance exception to a writing requirement would make no sense if the seller were seeking payment for more than the goods he had actually delivered. Suppose A delivers 1,000 widgets to B, and later sues B for breach of an alleged oral contract for 100,000 widgets and argues that the statute of frauds is not a bar because he performed his part of the contract in part. In such a case partial performance just is not indicative of the existence of an oral contract for any quantity greater than that already delivered, so it is no surprise that the statute of frauds provides that an oral contract cannot be enforced in a quantity greater than that received and accepted by the buyer. § 2-201(3)(c); cf. § 2-201(1). The present case is different. The partial performance here consisted not of a delivery of goods alleged to be part of a larger order but the turning over of an entire business. *That* kind of partial performance *is* evidence of an oral contract and also shows that this is not the pure sale of goods to which the UCC's statute of frauds was intended to apply.

This is not to say that the *contract* is outside the Uniform Commercial Code. It is a contract for the sale of goods plus a contract for the sale of distribution rights and of the assets associated with those rights. Courts forced to classify a mixed contract of this sort ask, somewhat unhelpfully perhaps, what the predominant purpose of the contract is. *Yorke v. B.F. Goodrich Co.*, 130 Ill. App. 3d 220, 223, 85 Ill. Dec. 606, 474 N.E.2d 20, 22 (1985), and cases cited there. And, no doubt, they would classify this contract as one for the sale of goods, therefore governed by the UCC, because the $27 million in sales contemplated by the contract (if there was a contract, as we are assuming) swamped the goodwill and other intangibles associated with Melform's very new, very small operation. Distributorship agreements, such as this one was in part, and even sales of businesses as going concerns, are frequently though not always classified as UCC contracts under the predominant-purpose test.

We may assume that the UCC applies to this contract; but must *all* of the UCC apply? We have difficulty seeing why. Because of the contract's mixed character, the UCC statute of frauds doesn't make a nice fit; it's designed for a pure sale of goods. The general statute works better. The fact that Article 2, which we have been loosely referring to as the sale of goods article, in fact applies not to the sale of goods as such but rather to "transactions in goods," § 2-102, while its statute of frauds is limited to "contract[s] for the sale of goods," § 2-201(1), could be thought to imply that the statute of frauds does not cover every transaction that is otherwise within the scope of Article 2.2 *Farnsworth on Contracts, supra*, § 6.6, at p. 126 and n. 5. Perhaps the contract in this case is better described as a transaction in goods than as a contract for the sale of goods, since so much more than a mere sale of goods was contemplated.

Another possibility is to interpret the UCC statute of frauds flexibly in consideration of the special circumstances of the class of cases represented by this case, so that it does make a smooth fit. . . . *This* case, at all events, presents no dangers of the sort the provision in question was designed to eliminate. The semantic lever for the interpretation we are proposing is that the UCC does not abolish the partial-performance exception. It merely limits the use of partial delivery as a ground for insisting on the full delivery allegedly required by the oral contract. That is not what Monetti is trying to do.

We need not pursue these interesting questions about the applicability and scope of the UCC statute of frauds any further in this case, because our result would be unchanged no matter how they were answered. For we have said nothing yet about the second writing in the case, the Davis memorandum of June 12. It was a writing on Anchor Hocking's letterhead, so satisfied the writing and signature requirements of the UCC statute of frauds, and it was a writing sufficient to evidence the existence of the contract upon which Anchor Hocking is being sued. It is true that "Exhibit A" does not contain all the terms of the contract; it makes no reference to the handing over of Melform's assets. But, especially taken together with the Davis memo itself (and we are permitted to connect them provided that the connections are "apparent from a comparison of the writings themselves," *Western Metals Co. v. Hartman Co., supra,* 303 Ill. at 483, 135 N.E. at 746, and they are, since the Davis memo refers explicitly to Exhibit A), Exhibit A is powerful evidence that there was a contract and that its terms were as Monetti represents. Remember that the UCC's statute of frauds does not require that the contract be in writing, but only that there be a sufficient memorandum to indicate that there really was a contract. The Davis memorandum fits this requirement to a t. So even if the partial-performance doctrine is not available to Monetti, the UCC's statute of frauds was satisfied. And since the general Illinois statute was satisfied as well, we need not decide whether, since the contract in this case both was (we are assuming) within the UCC *and* could not be performed within one year, it had to satisfy both statutes of frauds. 2 *Farnsworth on Contracts, supra,* § 6.2, at pp. 90-91.

Our conclusion that Monetti's suit for breach of contract is not barred by the statute(s) of frauds makes the district judge's second ruling, refusing to allow Monetti to add a claim for promissory estoppel, academic. The only reason Monetti wanted to add the claim was as a backstop should it lose on the statute of frauds. In light of our decision today, he does not need a backstop.

. . .

Reversed and remanded.

NOTES

1. *Deciding Which Law to Apply: The Predominant Purpose Test.* In *Monetti,* Judge Posner ultimately decides for the plaintiff under both the common law statute of frauds and under UCC § 2-201, the statute of frauds governing sales of goods. But his discussion (which is *dicta* in this case) provides a useful lens for understanding how courts have developed rules for deciding which contract regime to apply when two or more conflicting regimes arguably apply to the same transaction. Referring to the agreement between Monetti and Anchor Hocking Corporation, Judge Posner notes that "[d]istributor agreements, such as this one was in part, and even sales of businesses as going concerns, are frequently though not always classified as UCC contracts under the predominant-purpose test." The predominant purpose test applies the UCC to transactions if their predominant purpose is to sell goods, but applies the common law of contracts if their predominant purpose is to sell services.

But as Judge Posner argues, problems arise when a statute designed to apply pure contracts for the sale of goods is applied to a mixed goods and services contract. For example, the partial performance exception to the common law statute of frauds allows an individual to enforce an oral contract otherwise unenforceable without a writing if one individual has partially performed the agreement. UCC § 2-201 allows that an oral agreement otherwise unenforceable without a writing is enforceable if one party performs, but only "with respect to goods for which payment has been made and accepted or which have been received and accepted." As Posner explains, this partial performance exception limits the enforceability of an oral sales agreement to the quantity of goods actually paid for or accepted, rather than an allegedly greater amount, because the partial performance provides credible evidence of the existence of an agreement for the amount of goods paid for or accepted only — not the alleged greater amount. But in *Monetti*, Monetti had partially performed by turning over its trade secrets and other intangible assets, not by paying for or accepting goods. This is precisely the kind of partial performance that would render the contract enforceable under the common law, but which falls outside of the typical goods-oriented partial performance exception contemplated by UCC § 2-201(3)(c).

How should courts determine which law to apply when transactions arguably fall within the jurisdiction of conflicting contract regimes? Should the underlying purposes of the regimes govern, or should predictability and consistency take precedence? As Posner notes, some courts apply different rules to different parts of the transaction. Do you think that UCC Article 2 should or could govern contracts for the sale of electricity? *See* Jason B. Myers, *The Sale of Electricity in a Deregulated Industry: Should Article 2 of the Uniform Commercial Code Govern?*, 54 SMU L. REV. 1051 (2001). In Kentucky, a contract to install a swimming pool "is primarily one [for the sale] of goods and the services are necessary to insure that those goods are merchantable." Thus, UCC Article 2 applies. *Riffe v. Black*, 548 S.W.2d 175, 177 (Ky. Ct. App. 1977). But in Connecticut, the same transaction is construed as a services contract, so Article 2 does not apply. *Gulash v. Stylarama, Inc.*, 33 Conn. Supp. 108, 364 A.2d 1221 (1975).

2.   *Oral Evidence and the Statute of Frauds.* Monetti argued in the district court that it should be allowed to offer oral evidence on the question of whether certain vague documents meet the requirements of the statute of frauds. The district court disallowed the oral evidence, and Posner upheld the denial: "The use of oral evidence to get round the requirement of a writing would be bootstrapping, would sap the statute of frauds of most of its force, and is therefore forbidden." *Monetti* at 1181. Posner distinguishes *Monetti* from *Impossible Electronics Techniques, Inc. v. Wackenhut Protective Systems, Inc.*, 669 F.2d 1026, 1034 (5th Cir. 1982), in which the court allowed oral evidence to the establish the identity of one of the parties, but only after the writing was first held to satisfy the statute of frauds. Do you think this distinction is tenable? Why would admitting oral evidence to establish whether a writing satisfies the statute of frauds defeat the purpose of the statute of frauds, while admitting oral evidence to establish who is a party to the contract would not?

3. *Writing Preceding the Agreement as Evidence of the Agreement.* One of the questions raised in *Monetti* is whether a memo that precedes the actual formation of the alleged contract can constitute the writing required by the statute of frauds. The court distinguishes between precontractual writings that are "merely one party's offer," "notes made in preparation for a negotiating session," and a memo indicating a promisor's acceptance of the promisee's offer before the agreement becomes finalized. In the first two cases, the court holds the writing is insufficient to satisfy the statute of frauds because the disappointed offeror and negotiator might try to use the writing to prove a contract that never existed. But in the third case, the court appears to argue that the writing can satisfy the statute of frauds even though it preceded the final agreement. Isn't there an equal risk of a false allegation of a final agreement based on written evidence of acceptance of an offer before the agreement was finalized?

4. *The Signature Requirement.* Under UCC § 2-201, a contract for $500 or more is not enforceable without "some writing sufficient to indicate that a contract for sale has been made between the parties and signed by the party against whom enforcement is sought or by his authorized agent or broker." UCC § 1-201(39) defines "signed" as including "any symbol executed or adopted by a party with a present intention to authenticate a writing." Thus, in addition to a traditional signature, a writing might be "signed" by a preprinted or stamped authentication. Even a baldhead or letterhead without more might qualify as a signature. *See* UCC § 1-201 cmt. Could a typed letter on a blank sheet of paper qualify as a "signed" writing under UCC § 1-201?

5. *Problem on UCC § 2-201.* On July 1, Safety, a manufacturer of children's toys, and Bonnie Butler, a law professor at a leading law school, agreed to a contract under which Safety promised to manufacture and deliver 100 model train sets to Butler at a unit price of $95 per set. Butler ordered the trains as part of a long-planned venture into the retail toy trade. On July 14, Safety sent Butler the following note:

> SAFETY, INC.
>
> Just a note to confirm that we will provide you with the 50 special train sets for $95 each as we agreed to on July 1.

On July 18, Butler discovered that she could purchase a comparable set from Toys for Tots, Inc. for $80 each. On July 20, Butler replied to Safety as follows:

> I thought we agreed on 75 trains, but no matter, because I've decided that I no longer want them. Hope to do business in the future.
>
> /s/ Bonnie Butler

Safety brings an action against Butler for breach of contract. May Butler rely on the statute of frauds as a defense?

6. *The Statute of Frauds and Business Norms.* Many commentators have asserted that the writing requirement of the statute of frauds fails to reflect modern commercial practices, which often employ general, oral understandings rather than specific, written instruments. Professor Jason Johnston disagrees with this assessment of the statute, and argues that enforcement of the statute of frauds' writing requirement has adapted to meet the needs of modern transactional relationships, while avoiding the frustration of business feared by so many contracts scholars.

Using game theory, Professor Johnston first hypothesized that parties to a commercial transaction would dispense with written instruments most often when the parties possessed a history of prior dealings. A history of prior dealings encourages extra-legal sanctions, and thus decreases the parties' expectation that the transaction would result in litigation. On the other hand, the parties would retain the writing requirement when their transaction involved an unfamiliar partner, or when the transaction encompassed a complex set of rights and obligations requiring written clarification. Johnston then conducted an empirical survey of an admittedly small number of cases (25) from the UCC Reporting Service, analyzing each litigated case according to this set of variables designed to reflect modern commercial practice regarding the use of written instruments.

Johnston's study confirmed his predictions for the sampling of cases reviewed. Parties with a history of prior dealings frequently dispensed with the writing requirement, unless the particular transaction was unusually complex. "Strangers," however, tended to rely more heavily on written documentation of agreements, presumably due to the increased potential for litigation between two unfamiliar parties. Most interesting, Johnston's small survey revealed that courts generally recognize these subtle relationships and their effect on adherence to the statute of frauds. In litigation between two parties with a long relationship, courts were more likely to dismiss the statute of frauds claim for various reasons, while often upholding a statute of frauds action when the parties were relative strangers. *See* Jason Johnston, *The Statute of Frauds and Business Norms: A Testable Game-Theoretic Model*, 144 U. Pa. L. Rev. 1859 (1996).

7. *The New Economy.* As technology has changed, the way in which business is conducted has also changed. Today, parties contract by phone, fax, e-mail, and the internet. To many, the statute of frauds' requirements is out of step with modern business practices, as mentioned above. Consider, for example, Professor Raj Bhala's discussion of the interaction between the practices of the global currency bazaar, the world's largest financial market, and the statute of frauds' writing requirement:

> There is an uneasy tension between the technology and business practices of the foreign exchange market on the one hand, and the demands of contract enforceability rules in sales law on the other hand. The technology is telephonic. It expands the ways in which market participants negotiate and execute currency trades. Communications between [currency traders] are not face-to-face meetings in which written draft contracts are exchanged and marked up by lawyers representing the parties during endless rounds of coffee and take-out sandwiches. The trading floors of [currency traders] are entirely different from the conventional lawyers' conference room; traders often communicate by telephone. In sum, the deals made in the currency bazaar are oral and are concluded rapidly and informally.

> The statute of frauds must adapt to this telephonic technology. Foreign exchange market participants might not reduce their agreements to

writing for good reason. Because bid-ask spreads are thin for trading in liquid currencies, profits are made through a high volume of trading. To maximize profits, market participants seek to conclude as many transactions as cheaply and quickly as possible. Outdated legal formalities like the statute of frauds requirements lead to higher transaction costs and delay the completion of transactions. Not surprisingly, many market participants prefer tape recordings of conversations among traders instead of written agreements.

The law also must account for the culture of the currency bazaar. Trust among participants in the foreign exchange market is high. Perhaps this aspect of business culture also distinguishes the trading floor from the conference room. The participants repeatedly deal with one another. To engage in fraudulent or deceptive practices is to invite ostracism: a trader's unctuous behavior quickly becomes widely known and other traders decide it is risky and imprudent to deal with the rogue trader.

Raj Bhala, *A Pragmatic Strategy for the Scope of Sales Law, the Statute of Frauds, and the Global Currency Bazaar*, 72 Denv. U. L. Rev. 1, 27–28 (1994). Note the similarity between Professor Bhala's discussion of the culture of the currency bazaar and Professor Johnston's analysis of the use of extra-legal sanctions by repeat players. Does a more context-specific statute of frauds that takes into account a given business community's norms of behavior seem sensible? For a similar discussion of the statute of frauds and electronic contracting over the internet, see Shawn Pompian, Note, *Is the Statute of Frauds Ready for Electronic Contracting?*, 85 Va. L. Rev 1447 (1999).

H.   BIBLIOGRAPHY AND SUGGESTED READING

Kenneth S. Abraham, Distributing Risk (1986).

George J. Alexander & Szasz, *From Contract to Status Via Psychiatry*, 13 Santa Clara L. Rev. 537 (1973).

Raj Bhala, *A Pragmatic Strategy in the Scope of Sales Law, the Statute of Frauds, and the Global Currency Bazaar*, 72 Denv. U. L. Rev. 1 (1994).

Omri Ben-Shahar & Carl E. Schneider, *The Failure of Mandated Disclosure*, 159 U. Pa. L. Rev. 647 (2011).

Allen Blair, *A Matter of Trust: Should No-Reliance Clauses Bar Claims for Fraudulent Inducement of Contract?*, 92 Marq. L. Rev. 423 (2009).

John D. Calamari, *Duty to Read — A Changing Concept*, 43 Fordham L. Rev. 341 (1974).

Jessica M. Choplin, Deborah Progund Stark, Jasmine N. Ahmad, *A Psychological Investigation of Consumer Vulnerability to Fraud: Legal and Policy Implications*, 35 Law & Psychol. Rev. 61, 64 (2011).

Jeffrey Davis, *Protecting Consumers from Overdisclosure and Gobbledygook*, 63 Va. L. Rev. 841 (1977).

Kevin Davis, *Licensing Lies: Merger Clauses, the Parol Evidence Rule and Pre-Contractual Misrepresentations*, 33 VAL. U. L. REV. 485 (1999).

Robert Edge, *Voidability of Minors' Contracts: A Feudal Doctrine in Modern Economy*, 1 GA. L. REV. 205 (1967).

Carolyn M. Edwards, *The Statute of Frauds of the Uniform Commercial Code and the Doctrine of Estoppel*, 62 MARQ. L. REV. 205 (1978).

Melvin A. Eisenberg, *The Bargaining Principle and Its Limits*, 95 HARV. L. REV. 741 (1982).

Richard Epstein, *Surrogacy: The Case for Full Contractual Enforcement*, 81 VA. L. REV. 2305 (1995).

Beth A. Eisler, *Oral Modification of Sales Contracts Under the Uniform Commercial Code: The Statute of Frauds*, 58 WASH. U. L.Q. 277 (1980).

Daniel A. Farber, *Contract Law and Modern Economic Theory*, 78 Nw. U. L. REV. 303 (1983).

Green, *Public Policies Underlying the Law of Mental Incompetency*, 38 MICH. L. REV. 1189 (1940).

Robert Hale, *Bargaining, Duress, and Economic Liberty*, 43 COLUM. L. REV. 603 (1943).

Jeffrey L. Harrison, *Rethinking Mistake and Nondisclosure in Contract Law*, 17 GEO. MASON L. REV. 335 (2010).

Robert A. Hillman, *Debunking Some Myths About Unconscionability: A New Framework for U.C.C Section 2-302*, 67 CORNELL L.REV. 1 (1981).

Jason Johnston, *The Statute of Frauds and Business Norms*, 144 U. PA. L. REV. 1859 (1996).

Ellen Jordan, *Unconscionability at the Gas Station*, 62 MINN. L. REV. 813 (1978).

Louis Kaplow & Steven Shavell, *Fairness Versus Welfare*, 114 HARV. L. REV. 961 (2001).

Jody S. Kraus & Robert E. Scott, *Contract Design and the Structure of Contractual Intent*, 84 N.Y.U. L. REV. 1023 (2009).

Duncan M. Kennedy, *Distributive and Paternalist Motives in Contract and Tort Law, With Special Reference to Compulsory Terms and Unequal Bargaining Power*, 41 MD. L. REV. 563 (1982).

Russell Korobkin, *Bounded Rationality, Standard Form Contracts, and Unconscionability*, 70 U. CHI. L. REV. 1203 (2003).

Juliet P. Kostritsky, *Illegal Contracts and Efficient Deterrence: A Study in Modern Contract Theory*, 74 IOWA L. REV. 115, 143 (1988).

Frederich Kessler, *Contracts of Adhesion — Some Thoughts About Freedom of Contract*, 43 COLUM. L. REV. 629 (1943).

Anthony Kronman, *Paternalism and the Law of Contracts*, 92 YALE L.J. 763

(1983).

Jonathan Landers & Rohner, *A Functional Analysis of Truth in Lending*, 26 UCLA L. REV. 711 (1979).

Arthur A. Leff, *Injury, Ignorance, and Spite — The Dynamics of Coercive Collection*, 80 YALE L.J. 1 (1970).

Arthur A. Leff, *Unconscionability and the Code — The Emperor's New Clause*, 115 U. PA. L. REV. 485 (1967).

Juanda Lowder, *Virtually Mature: Examining the Policy of Minor's Incapacity to Contract Through the Cyperscope*, 43 GONZ. L. REV. 239 (2008).

Mellinkoff, *How to Make Contracts Illegible*, 5 STAN. L. REV. 418 (1953).

Meredith R. Miller, *Revisiting Austin v. Loral: A Study in Economic Duress, Contract Modification and Framing*, 2 HASTINGS BUS. L.J. 357 (2006).

Jane B. Myers, *The Sale of Electricity in a Deregulated Industry: Should Article 2 of the Uniform Commercial Code Govern?*, 54 SMU L. REV. 1051 (2001).

Subha Narasimhan, *Modification: The Self-Help Specific Performance Remedy*, 97 YALE L.J. 61 (1987).

Walter D. Navin, Jr., *The Contracts of Minors Viewed From the Perspective of Fair Exchange*, 50 N.C. L. REV. 517 (1972).

Ralph Newman, *The Renaissance of Good Faith in Contracting in Anglo-American Law*, 54 CORNELL L. REV. 553 (1969).

Edwin Patterson, *Compulsory Contracts in the Crystal Ball*, 43 COLUM. L. REV. 731 (1943).

Eric Posner, *Contract Law in the Welfare State: A Defense of the Unconscionability Doctrine*, 24 J. LEGAL STUD. 283 (1995).

Richard Posner, *The Ethics and Economics of Enforcing Contracts of Surrogate Motherhood*, 5 J. CONTEMP. HEALTH L. & POL'Y 21 (1989).

OTTO PRAUSNITZ, THE STANDARDIZATION OF COMMERCIAL CONTRACTS IN ENGLISH AND CONTINENTAL LAW 145 (1937).

Alan Schwartz & Robert E. Scott, *Contract Theory and the Limits of Contract Law*, 113 YALE L.J. 541 (2003).

Alan Schwartz, *Seller Unequal Bargaining Power and the Judicial Process*, 49 IND. L.J. 367 (1974).

Alan Schwartz, *A Reexamination of Non-Substantive Unconscionability*, 63 VA. L. REV. 1053 (1977).

Alan Schwartz & Louis Wilde, *Imperfect Information in Markets for Contract Terms: The Examples of Warranties and Security Interests*, 69 VA. L. REV. 1387 (1983).

Elizabeth Scott, *Surrogacy and the Politics of Commodification*, 72 LAW & CONTEMP. PROBS. 109 (2009).

Robert E. Scott & William J. Stuntz, *Plea Bargaining as Contract*, 101 YALE L.J. 1909 (1992).

Patrick W. Semegen, *Plain Language Legislation*, 85 CASE & COMMENT 42 (1980).

Robert H. Skilton & Orrin L. Helstad, *Protection of the Installment Buyer of Goods Under the UCC*, 65 MICH. L. REV. 1465 (1967).

David Slawson, *Standard Form Contracts and Democratic Control of Lawmaking Power*, 84 HARV. L. REV. 529 (1971).

George Stigler, *Information in the Labor Market*, 70 J. POL. ECON. 94 (1962).

George Stigler, *The Economics of Information*, 69 J. POL. ECON. 213 (1961).

Henry Weihofen, *Mental Incompetency to Contract or Convey*, 39 S. CAL. L. REV. 211 (1966).

Zipporah Wiseman, *The Limits of Vision: Karl Llewellyn and the Merchant Rules*, 100 HARV. L. REV. 465 (1987).

Chapter 6

IDENTIFYING AND INTERPRETING THE TERMS OF AN AGREEMENT

A. INTRODUCTION

Contract law enforces agreements. Once a court has determined that an agreement has been reached, it must determine the content of that agreement. To do so, the court must first identify and then interpret the meaning of the various terms that together constitute the promises the parties have made to each other. In order to identify the terms of an agreement, the court looks to the words or conduct of the parties. But here the court faces a basic problem: what words and conduct were intended by the parties to form the agreement and what were intended to be discarded or excluded? This problem is addressed by the parol evidence rule. The premise of the parol evidence rule is that parties to an agreement may wish to reduce the risk that a court will subsequently misinterpret their agreement or that they will misunderstand their own commitments. The parol evidence rule enables the parties to reduce this risk by committing some or all of the terms of their agreement to a writing, and then agreeing that neither of them will be permitted to introduce evidence in court other than that writing if they subsequently dispute the terms of their agreement. This strategy not only narrows the range of possible misinterpretation but also allows the parties to engage in prior oral and written negotiations without fear that statements they make in the course of the negotiations will be used to influence a court's subsequent identification of the terms of their written agreement. By banning the use of evidence other than their writing — so-called "extrinsic evidence" — the parties can negotiate without fear that statements and proposals made during negotiations will later be used to expand or contract the parties' written obligations. This reduces their costs of negotiating and increases the predictability, and thus the reliability, (and perhaps also reduces the cost) of the judicial enforcement of their agreement.

While the goals underlying the parol evidence rule are relatively straightforward, the rule itself (both in traditional common law and modern formulations) and the accompanying principles of interpretation are complex and difficult. Before you read any of the cases in this chapter, therefore, we have set out for you in the introduction that follows (as clearly and concisely as we can) the key doctrinal points and how they fit together. As with any introduction to new material, the analysis may seem hard to understand in the absence of the context that follows. We recommend, therefore, that you treat the introductory essay as a framework to evaluate the cases that follow. Thereafter, you should return to our analysis and evaluate it critically in light of what you have learned for yourselves.

[1]   Identifying the Terms of an Agreement: The Common Law and the Code

The first challenge courts face is to determine whether the parties committed any or all the terms of their agreement to a final writing. If they did not, then their agreement is not "integrated" (that is, it is not embodied in the writing) and the parol evidence rule does not apply. In this case, if a dispute subsequently arises, the parties are free to introduce any kind of evidence ordinarily admissible in order to prove that their agreement either does or does not contain any particular term. But if the parties did commit either some or all of their agreement to a final writing, the parol evidence rule applies. If the parties committed *some but not all of the terms* of the agreement to a final writing, their agreement is said to be "partially integrated." In that event, the parties are allowed to introduce evidence of *additional* terms of their agreement provided those terms do not *contradict* the terms in the final writing. If the parties have included *all of the terms* of their agreement in a final writing, the agreement is "fully integrated." In that event, the parties are not allowed to introduce extrinsic evidence of any additional terms whether or not these terms would be consistent with the terms in the writing.

Whether an agreement is unintegrated, partially integrated, or fully integrated is determined by the parties' intent. A writing constitutes the final expression of some or all of the parties' terms only if the parties so intended at the time of the writing. In determining whether the writing was intended to be complete and exclusive, the common law courts apply the "natural omission" doctrine: evidence of additional terms of the agreement is admissible only if a court finds that the parties *would naturally have omitted those terms* in the writing. If the court concludes that the extrinsic evidence consists of terms that parties would naturally have omitted from their writing (perhaps, for example, because the evidence appears to be of a separate or unrelated agreement), the court can infer the parties' intent not to fully integrate their agreement with respect to the disputed terms. But it can be difficult in any particular case for courts to determine the parties' intent to have "naturally omitted" certain terms. To aid courts in making this judgment, the common law developed the "four corners" presumption: If the writing appears on its face to be a complete and exclusive statement of all the terms of the agreement, then the agreement is presumptively fully integrated and the court must exclude all evidence of terms other than those in the writing itself. Under the four corners presumption, therefore, courts determine intent by looking first to the character of the writing. If the writing looks complete from an examination of its "four corners," the contesting party bears a heavy burden in overcoming the presumption of integration. Parties can overcome some of the difficulty courts may have in trying to reconstruct their intent ex post by signaling their intent more clearly in the writing itself. Thus, parties can by-pass the "natural omission" and "four corners" inquiry by including in the agreement a "merger" or "integration" clause announcing that both parties regard the writing as the final and exclusive statement of the terms of their agreement. Common law courts treat the merger clause as presumptively conclusive evidence of a full integration.

The four corners presumption and the preclusive effect of merger clauses have been heavily criticized by some courts and scholars on the ground that a writing cannot prove its own finality or exclusivity. These critics argue that a rule that limits the evidence of the parties' intent to the writing itself is arbitrary and unjustified: There is no reason to suppose that the writing is the only probative evidence of whether the parties intended to integrate their agreement. Thus, even though the majority of common law courts continue to apply a "hard" parol evidence rule that often excludes extrinsic evidence, a number of courts (supported by the Second Restatement) favor of a "soft" rule that admits extrinsic evidence notwithstanding an unambiguous merger clause declaring the contract to be an integrated writing, or, absent such a clause, notwithstanding the fact that the writing appears final and complete on its face.[1] These courts regard the merger clause as merely creating a rebuttable presumption of integration, one that can be overridden by extrinsic evidence that the parties lacked any such intent.

For contracts governing the sale of goods, the common law parol evidence rule has been supplanted by UCC § 2-202. Section 2-202 adopts a "soft" version of the parol evidence rule that differs from the common law parol evidence rule primarily in the test for integration. In addition to rejecting the common law's four corners presumption, the comments to § 2-202 provide that, if there is a written agreement, evidence of terms not included in that writing are only inadmissible "[i]f the additional terms are such that, if agreed upon, *they would certainly have been included* in the document in the view of the court."[2] The principle difference between this "certain inclusion" test and the common law "natural omission" test is that under the Code the court must find that the parties "certainly," rather than merely "naturally," would have included the terms in their writing in order to hold the writing is integrated. Thus, the Code rule raises the hurdle, relative to the common law, for proving an agreement is integrated.

[2] Interpreting the Terms of an Agreement: The Common Law and the Code

The common law parol evidence rule only determines the admissibility of evidence for purposes of identifying the *terms* of a contract. But even after it identifies these terms, a court must still interpret their *meaning.* Although this is a separate question, the common law's approach to questions of meaning is closely associated with its parol evidence rule, and is designed to promote the goal underlying the rule: to respect the parties' efforts to create a reliable agreement by insulating it as much as possible from disputes over its terms. The common law thus presumes that it is possible to determine the "plain meaning" of the terms in a writing by examining the contract as a whole in isolation from its extrinsic context. In the absence of obvious ambiguity, therefore, the court will presume that

---

[1] A recent state-by-state survey showed that 38 states follow the traditional approach to determining whether or not an agreement is fully integrated. Nine states, joined by the Uniform Commercial Code for sales cases and the Restatement (Second) of Contracts, have adopted a contextualist or "anti-formalist" interpretive regime. The rules in the remaining states are indeterminate. *See* Alan Schwartz & Robert E. Scott, *Contract Interpretation Redux,* 119 YALE L. J. 926 (2010).

[2] UCC § 2-202, cmt. 1a, 3.

the parties intended to give a standard, dictionary or "objective" meaning to any disputed terms.

In sum, the plain meaning rule addresses the question of what legal meaning should be attributed to the contract terms that the parol evidence rule has identified. Contests over the meaning of contract terms thus follow a predictable pattern: one party claims that the words in a disputed term should be given their "plain" or standard dictionary meaning as read in light of the contract as a whole and the pleadings. The counterparty argues either that the contract term in question is ambiguous and extrinsic evidence will resolve the ambiguity, or that extrinsic evidence will show that the parties intended the words to be given a specialized or idiosyncratic meaning that varies from the meaning in the standard language. As with the division over hard and soft parol evidence rules, courts have divided on the question whether express contract terms should be given a contextual or a plain meaning interpretation. Under the latter practice, followed by the majority of common law courts, when words or phrases in a writing appear to be clear and unambiguous, extrinsic evidence of a possible contrary meaning is inadmissible.

To be sure, some terms will lack a plain meaning because they have more than one objective meaning and are therefore *ambiguous*. Under these circumstances, *all* courts will consider extrinsic evidence in an effort to resolve the ambiguity. For example, if a seller agrees to sell "one Ming vase" to a buyer, but the seller owns four Ming vases, the term "one Ming vase" is ambiguous as between the seller's four Ming vases. Other terms will lack a plain meaning because they are imprecise and therefore *vague*. For example, if a seller agrees to sell "ten hard, dark red MacIntosh apples," the terms "hard" and "dark red" are vague because they do not precisely determine what constitutes a conforming apple — how hard and how dark red must the apples be? In both cases, the common law directs courts to consider context when interpreting the meaning of terms that have no plain meaning.[3]

The idea that words in a contract can have plain meanings has been severely criticized by some courts and scholars. Proponents of a more liberal approach to interpretation have argued that meaning is necessarily contextual. In an often-quoted case, Justice Holmes argued against the plain meaning rule and in favor of a contextual approach to interpretation, maintaining that "[a] word is not a crystal, transparent and unchanged; it is the skin of a living thought and may vary greatly in color and content according to the circumstances and the time in which it is used."[4] The debate between the common law plain meaning rule and its critics raises deep philosophical questions about the nature and knowledge of meaning.

---

[3] The ambiguity requirement applies both to terms that have multiple objective meanings (literally ambiguous) and terms that are vague (not literally ambiguous) because in both cases the terms cannot not be assigned a plain meaning. In order to determine whether a term is ambiguous, the traditional common law approach limits courts to the "four corners" of the writing. Just as the four corners test for integration requires courts to base their determination of whether a writing is partially or fully integrated on an examination of the writing alone, the four corners test for ambiguity requires courts to base their determination of whether a written term is ambiguous on an examination of the writing alone.

[4] *Towne v. Eisner*, 245 U.S. 418, 425 (1918).

But in contract law, the pressing question is not this deep philosophical one, Even if terms do not strictly speaking have a unique, plain meaning, the meanings they can be given range along a continuum from purely subjective to largely objective. For example, suppose a party to an agreement used the term "dog" to mean cat. Clearly, there are objective grounds for asserting that the term "dog" ordinarily does not mean cat, even if some context is required to determine precisely what "dog" does mean. The most plausible candidate for the objective meaning of the word "dog" is the meaning that most people who use the term assign to it. Although parties might attach purely subjective meanings to ordinary words, this surely does not demonstrate that the same terms do not admit of relatively more objective meanings. Thus, the central question is whether contract law should seek to determine the relatively objective meaning of the parties words as viewed ex ante at the time of contracting or the relatively subjective meaning as viewed ex post during litigation.

There are a number of distinct standards that courts might use to interpret the meaning of contract terms. While the First Restatement of Contracts largely followed the common law's objective standards,[5] the Second Restatement endorses a relatively subjective, context-sensitive interpretive standard.[6] The Second Restatement thus rejects the plain meaning rule and the ambiguity requirement for extrinsic evidence.[7] Although a number of courts follow the Second Restatement, as noted above the majority of common law courts continue to apply the traditional plain meaning rule.

Section 2-202 of the UCC adopts a more systematic statement of the liberal, context-sensitive approach taken by the Second Restatement. In addition to clearly rejecting the common law's plain meaning rule,[8] the Code substitutes in its place a robust scheme for interpreting the meaning of a contract's terms in light of the relevant layers of commercial context in which the agreement was made. The Code's interpretive approach argues that in order to ascertain "the true understanding of the parties," their written agreement must "be read on the assumption that the course of prior dealings between the parties and the usages of trade were taken for granted when the document was phrased. Similarly, the course of actual performance by the parties is considered the best indication of what they intended the writing to mean."[9] In other words, according to the Code, because all meaning is necessarily contextual, all interpretation must take context into account.

---

[5] The First Restatement of Contracts identifies six conceivable standards of interpretation, four of which are objective and two of which are subjective. *See* RESTATEMENT § 227, cmt. a; *see also* Murray on Contracts § 87 (2001).

[6] RESTATEMENT (SECOND) § 212.

[7] *Id.* cmt. b ("It is sometimes said that extrinsic evidence cannot change the plain meaning of a writing, but meaning can almost never be plain except in a context. Accordingly, the rule stated in Subsection (1) is not limited to cases where it is determined that the language used is ambiguous. Any determination of meaning or ambiguity should only be made in the light of the relevant evidence of the situation and relations of the parties, the subject matter of the transaction, preliminary negotiations and statements made therein, usages of trade, and the course of dealing between the parties.").

[8] UCC § 2-202 cmt. 1(b), (c).

[9] *Id.* cmt. 2.

To make sense of this area of law, we suggest you hew as closely as possible to the distinction between (a) the rules governing the identification of the terms in a contract (hard or soft parol evidence), and (b) the rules that determine how those terms are to be interpreted (plain or contextual meaning).[10] In addition, also keep in mind the difference between (a) contracts for the sale of services, land and intellectual property rights that continue to be governed by the common law (and where there remains a considerable variation in interpretive approaches), and (b) contracts for the sale of goods which are governed by the UCC, a statute that displaces the common law. Even if the courts run them together, try in your analysis of the cases you read to pull them apart. We believe this approach will advance both your understanding and evaluation of the doctrines.

B. IDENTIFYING THE TERMS OF AGREEMENT

[1] The Common Law Parol Evidence Rule

Section 1 of this Part begins with an introduction to the classic common law debate over parol evidence and the four corners presumption. Section 2 then turns to the merger doctrine: How is the debate over parol evidence changed if a writing contains a clear merger clause stating that the writing embodied the complete and exclusive statement of all the terms of their agreement? Section 3 introduces the Uniform Commercial Code's parol evidence rule.

Consider first the following two cases, both exemplars of the division among common law courts between "hard" and "soft' versions of the parol evidence rule.

MITCHILL v. LATH

Court of Appeals of New York

247 N.Y. 377, 160 N.E. 646 (1928)

ANDREWS, J.

In the fall of 1923 the Laths owned a farm. This they wished to sell. Across the road, on land belonging to Lieutenant Governor Lunn, they had an icehouse which they might remove. Mrs. Mitchill looked over the land with a view to its purchase. She found the icehouse objectionable. Thereupon "the defendants orally promised and agreed, for and in consideration of the purchase of their farm by the plaintiff, to remove the said icehouse in the spring of 1924." Relying upon this promise, she made a written contract to buy the property for $8,400, for cash and mortgage and containing various provisions usual in such papers. Later receiving a deed, she entered into possession, and has spent considerable sums in improving the property for use as a summer residence. The defendants have not fulfilled their promise as to the icehouse, and do not intend to do so. We are not dealing, however, with their

---

[10] For an excellent analysis of the distinction between contract interpretation (determining questions of meaning) and the parol evidence rule (determining the terms of the contract), see Margaret N. Kniffin, *Conflating and Confusing Contract Interpretation and the Parol Evidence Rule: Is the Emperor Wearing Someone Else's Clothes?*, 62 Rutgers L. Rev. 75 (2009).

moral delinquencies. The question before us is whether their oral agreement may be enforced in a court of equity.

This requires a discussion of the parol evidence rule — a rule of law which defines the limits of the contract to be construed. It is more than a rule of evidence, and oral testimony, even if admitted, will not control the written contract, unless admitted without objection. It applies, however, to attempts to modify such a contract by parol. It does not affect a parol collateral contract distinct from and independent of the written agreement. It is, at times, troublesome to draw the line. Williston, in his work on *Contracts* (§ 637) points out the difficulty. "Two entirely distinct contracts," he says, "each for a separate consideration, may be made at the same time, and will be distinct legally. Where, however, one agreement is entered into wholly or partly in consideration of the simultaneous agreement to enter into another, the transactions are necessarily bound together. . . . Then if one of the agreements is oral and the other in writing, the problem arises whether the bond is sufficiently close to prevent proof of the oral agreement." That is the situation here. It is claimed that the defendants are called upon to do more than is required by their written contract in connection with the sale as to which it deals.

The principle may be clear, but it can be given effect by no mechanical rule. As so often happens it is a matter of degree, for, as Prof. Williston also says, where a contract contains several promises on each side it is not difficult to put any one of them in the form of a collateral agreement. If this were enough, written contracts might always be modified by parol. Not form, but substance, is the test.

In applying this test, the policy of our courts is to be considered. We have believed that the purpose behind the rule was a wise one, not easily to be abandoned. Notwithstanding injustice here and there, on the whole it works for good. Old precedents and principles are not to be lightly cast aside, unless it is certain that they are an obstruction under present conditions. New York has been less open to arguments that would modify this particular rule, than some jurisdictions elsewhere. Thus in Eighmie v. Taylor, 98 N.Y. 288, it was held that a parol warranty might not be shown, although no warranties were contained in the writing.

Under our decisions before such an oral agreement as the present is received to vary the written contract, at least three conditions must exist: (1) The agreement must in form be a collateral one; (2) it must not contradict express or implied provisions of the written contract; (3) it must be one that parties would not ordinarily be expected to embody in the writing, or, put in another way, an inspection of the written contract, read in the light of surrounding circumstances, must not indicate that the writing appears "to contain the engagements of the parties, and to define the object and measure the extent of such engagement." Or, again, it must not be so clearly connected with the principal transaction as to be part and parcel of it.

The respondent does not satisfy the third of these requirements. It may be, not the second. We have a written contract for the purchase and sale of land. The buyer is to pay $8,400 in the way described. She is also to pay her portion of any rents, interest on mortgages, insurance premiums, and water meter charges. She may have a survey made of the premises. On their part, the sellers are to give a full covenant deed of the premises as described, or as they may be described by the surveyor, if the survey is had, executed, and acknowledged at their own expense; they sell the personal property on the farm and represent they own it; they agree that all amounts paid them on the contract and the expense of examining the title shall be a lien on the property; they assume the risk of loss or damage by fire until the deed is delivered; and they agree to pay the broker his commissions. Are they to do more? Or is such a claim inconsistent with these precise provisions? It could not be shown that the plaintiff was to pay $500 additional. Is it also implied that the defendants are not to do anything unexpressed in the writing?

That we need not decide. At least, however, an inspection of this contract shows a full and complete agreement, setting forth in detail the obligations of each party. On reading it, one would conclude that the reciprocal obligations of the parties were fully detailed. Nor would his opinion alter if he knew the surrounding circumstances. The presence of the icehouse, even the knowledge that Mrs. Mitchill thought it objectionable, would not lead to the belief that a separate agreement existed with regard to it. Were such an agreement made it would seem most natural that the inquirer should find it in the contract. Collateral in form it is found to be, but it is closely related to the subject dealt with in the written agreement — so closely that we hold it may not be proved. Where the line between the competent and the incompetent is narrow the citation of authorities is of slight use. Each represents the judgment of the court on the precise facts before it. How closely bound to the contract is the supposed collateral agreement is the decisive factor in each case. . . .

Our conclusion is that the judgment of the Appellate Division and that of the Special Term should be reversed and the complaint dismissed, with costs in all courts.

LEHMAN, J. (dissenting).

I accept the general rule as formulated by Judge Andrews. I differ with him only as to its application to the facts shown in the record. . . .

Judge Andrews has formulated a standard to measure the closeness of the bond. Three conditions, at least, must exist before an oral agreement may be proven to increase the obligation imposed by the written agreement. I think we agree that the first condition that the agreement "must in form be a collateral one" is met by the evidence. I concede that this condition is met in most cases where the courts have nevertheless excluded evidence of the collateral oral agreement. The difficulty here, as in most cases, arises in connection with the two other conditions.

The second condition is that the "parol agreement must not contradict express or implied provisions of the written contract." Judge Andrews voices doubt whether this condition is satisfied. The written contract has been carried out. The purchase price has been paid; conveyance has been made; title has passed in accordance with the terms of the written contract. The mutual obligations expressed in the written contract are left unchanged by the alleged oral contract. When performance was required of the written contract, the obligations of the parties were measured solely by its terms. By the oral agreement the plaintiff seeks to hold the defendants to other obligations to be performed by them thereafter upon land which was not conveyed to the plaintiff. The assertion of such further obligation is not inconsistent with the written contract, unless the written contract contains a provision, express or implied, that the defendants are not to do anything not expressed in the writing. Concededly there is no such express provision in the contract, and such a provision may be implied, if at all, only if the asserted additional obligation is "so clearly connected with the principal transaction as to be part and parcel of it," and is not "one that the parties would not ordinarily be expected to embody in the writing." The hypothesis so formulated for a conclusion that the asserted additional obligation is inconsistent with an implied term of the contract is that the alleged oral agreement does not comply with the third condition as formulated by Judge Andrews. In this case, therefore, the problem reduces itself to the one question whether or not the oral agreement meets the third condition. I have conceded that upon inspection the contract is complete. "It appears to contain the engagements of the parties, and to define the object and measure the extent of such engagement"; it constitutes the contract between them, and is presumed to contain the whole of that contract. Eighmie v. Taylor, 98 N.Y. 288. That engagement was on the one side to convey land; on the other to pay the price. The plaintiff asserts further agreement based on the same consideration to be performed by the defendants after the conveyance was complete, and directly affecting only other land. It is true, as Judge Andrews points out, that "the presence of the icehouse, even the knowledge that Mrs. Mitchill thought it objectionable, would not lead to the belief that a separate agreement existed with regard to it"; but the question we must decide is whether or not, assuming an agreement was made for the removal of an unsightly icehouse from one parcel of land as an inducement for the purchase of another parcel, the parties would ordinarily or naturally be expected to embody the agreement for the removal of the icehouse from one parcel in the written agreement to convey the other parcel. Exclusion of proof of the oral agreement on the ground that it varies the contract embodied in the writing may be based only upon a finding or presumption that the written contract was intended to cover the oral negotiations for the removal of the icehouse which lead up to the contract of purchase and sale. To determine what the writing was intended to cover, "the document alone will not suffice. What it was intended to cover cannot be known till we know what there was to cover. The question being whether certain subjects of negotiation were intended to be covered, we must compare the writing and the negotiations before we can determine whether they were in fact covered." Wigmore on Evidence (2d Ed.) § 2430.

The subject-matter of the written contract was the conveyance of land. The contract was so complete on its face that the conclusion is inevitable that the parties intended to embody in the writing all the negotiations covering at least the conveyance. The promise by the defendants to remove the icehouse from other land was not connected with their obligation to convey except that one agreement would not have been made unless the other was also made. The plaintiff's assertion of a parol agreement by the defendants to remove the icehouse was completely established by the great weight of evidence. It must prevail unless that agreement was part of the agreement to convey and the entire agreement was embodied in the writing. . . .

The rule of integration undoubtedly frequently prevents the assertion of fraudulent claims. Parties who take the precaution of embodying their oral agreements in a writing should be protected against the assertion that other terms of the same agreement were not integrated in the writing. The limits of the integration are determined by the writing, read in the light of the surrounding circumstances. A written contract, however complete, yet covers only a limited field. I do not think that in the written contract for the conveyance of land here under consideration we can find an intention to cover a field so broad as to include prior agreements, if any such were made, to do other acts on other property after the stipulated conveyance was made. In each case where such a problem is presented, varying factors enter into its solution. Citation of authority in this or other jurisdictions is useless, at least without minute analysis of the facts. The analysis I have made of the decisions in this state leads me to the view that the decision of the courts below is in accordance with our own authorities and should be affirmed.

MASTERSON v. SINE
Supreme Court of California
68 Cal. 2d 222, 436 P.2d 561 (1968)

TRAYNOR, J.

Dallas Masterson and his wife Rebecca owned a ranch as tenants in common. On February 25, 1958, they conveyed it to Medora and Lu Sine by a grant deed "Reserving unto the Grantors herein an option to purchase the above described property on or before February 25, 1968" for the "same consideration as being paid heretofore plus their depreciation value of any improvements Grantees may add to the property from and after two and a half years from this date." Medora is Dallas' sister and Lu's wife. Since the conveyance Dallas has been adjudged bankrupt. His trustee in bankruptcy and Rebecca brought this declaratory relief action to establish their right to enforce the option.

The case was tried without a jury. . . . The court . . . determined that the parol evidence rule precluded admission of extrinsic evidence offered by defendants to show that the parties wanted the property kept in the Masterson family and that the option was therefore personal to the grantors and could not be exercised by the trustee in bankruptcy. The court entered judgment for plaintiffs, declaring their right to exercise the option, specifying in some detail how it could be exercised, and reserving jurisdiction to supervise the manner of its exercise and to determine the amount that plaintiffs will be required to pay defendants for their capital expenditures if plaintiffs decide to exercise the option.

Defendants appeal. They contend that the option provision is too uncertain to be enforced and that extrinsic evidence as to its meaning should not have been admitted. The trial court properly refused to frustrate the obviously declared intention of the grantors to reserve an option to repurchase by an overly meticulous insistence on completeness and clarity of written expression. It properly admitted extrinsic evidence to explain the language of the deed to the end that the consideration for the option would appear with sufficient certainty to permit specific enforcement. The trial court erred, however, in excluding the extrinsic evidence that the option was personal to the grantors and therefore nonassignable.

When the parties to a written contract have agreed to it as an "integration" — a complete and final embodiment of the terms of an agreement — parol evidence cannot be used to add to or vary its terms. When only part of the agreement is integrated, the same rule applies to that part, but parol evidence may be used to prove elements of the agreement not reduced to writing. The crucial issue in determining whether there has been an integration is whether the parties intended their writing to serve as the exclusive embodiment of their agreement. The instrument itself may help to resolve that issue. It may state, for example, that "there are no previous understandings or agreements not contained in the writing," and thus express the parties' "intention to nullify antecedent understandings or agreements." (See 3 Corbin, *Contracts* (1960) § 578, p. 411.) Any such collateral agreement itself must be examined, however, to determine whether the parties intended the subjects of negotiation it deals with to be included in, excluded from, or otherwise affected by the writing. Circumstances at the time of the writing may also aid in the determination of such integration.

California cases have stated that whether there was an integration is to be determined solely from the face of the instrument and that the question for the court is whether it "appears to be a complete . . . agreement. . . ." Neither of these strict formulations of the rule, however, has been consistently applied. The requirement that the writing must appear incomplete on its face has been repudiated in many cases where parol evidence was admitted "to prove the existence of a separate oral agreement as to any matter on which the document is silent and which is not inconsistent with its terms" — even though the instrument appeared to state a complete agreement. Even under the rule that the writing alone is to be consulted, it was found necessary to examine the alleged collateral agreement before concluding that proof of it was precluded by the writing alone. (See 3 Corbin, *Contracts* (1960) § 582, pp. 444-446.) It is therefore evident that "The conception of a writing as wholly and intrinsically self-determinative of the parties' intent to make it a sole memorial of one or seven or twenty-seven subjects of negotiation is an impossible one." (9 Wigmore, *Evidence* (3d ed. 1940) § 2431, p. 103.) For example, a promissory note given by a debtor to his creditor may integrate all their present contractual rights and obligations, or it may be only a minor part of an underlying executory contract that would never be discovered by examining the face of the note.

In formulating the rule governing parol evidence, several policies must be accommodated. One policy is based on the assumption that written evidence is more accurate than human memory. This policy, however, can be adequately served by excluding parol evidence of agreements that directly contradict the writing. Another policy is based on the fear that fraud or unintentional invention by witnesses interested in the outcome of the litigation will mislead the finder of facts. McCormick has suggested that the party urging the spoken as against the written word is most often the economic underdog, threatened by severe hardship if the writing is enforced. In his view the parol evidence rule arose to allow the court to control the tendency of the jury to find through sympathy and without a dispassionate assessment of the probability of fraud or faulty memory that the parties made an oral agreement collateral to the written contract, or that preliminary tentative agreements were not abandoned when omitted from the writing. (See McCormick, *Evidence* (1954) § 210.) He recognizes, however, that if this theory were adopted in disregard of all other considerations, it would lead to the exclusion of testimony concerning oral agreements whenever there is a writing and thereby often defeat the true intent of the parties. (See McCormick, *op. cit. supra*, § 216, p. 441.)

Evidence of oral collateral agreements should be excluded only when the fact finder is likely to be misled. The rule must therefore be based on the credibility of the evidence. One such standard, adopted by section 240(1)(b) of the Restatement of Contracts, permits proof of a collateral agreement if it "is such an agreement as might *naturally* be made as a separate agreement by parties situated as were the parties to the written contract." The draftsmen of the Uniform Commercial Code would exclude the evidence in still fewer instances: "If the additional terms are such that, if agreed upon, they would *certainly* have been included in the document in the view of the court, then evidence of their alleged making must be kept from the trier of fact." (Com. 3, § 2-202, italics added.)[11]

The option clause in the deed in the present case does not explicitly provide that it contains the complete agreement, and the deed is silent on the question of assignability. Moreover, the difficulty of accommodating the formalized structure of a deed to the insertion of collateral agreements makes it less likely that all the terms of such an agreement were included. The statement of the reservation of the option might well have been placed in the recorded deed solely to preserve the grantors' rights against any possible future purchasers and this function could well be served without any mention of the parties' agreement that the option was personal. There is nothing in the record to indicate that the parties to this family transaction, through experience in land transactions or otherwise, had any warning of the disadvantages of failing to put the whole agreement in the deed. This case is one, therefore, in which it can be said that a collateral agreement such as that alleged "might naturally be made as a separate agreement." *A fortiori*, the case is not one in which the parties "would certainly" have included the collateral agreement in the deed.

It is contended, however, that an option agreement is ordinarily presumed to be assignable if it contains no provisions forbidding its transfer or indicating that its performance involves elements personal to the parties. The fact that there is a written memorandum, however, does not necessarily preclude parol evidence rebutting a term that the law would otherwise presume. . . .

In the present case defendants offered evidence that the parties agreed that the option was not assignable in order to keep the property in the Masterson family. The trial court erred in excluding that evidence. The judgment is reversed.

---

[11] [1] Corbin suggests that, even in situations where the court concludes that it would not have been natural for the parties to make the alleged collateral oral agreement, parol evidence of such an agreement should nevertheless be permitted if the court is convinced that the unnatural actually happened in the case being adjudicated. (3 Corbin, *Contracts*, § 485, pp. 478, 480; cf. Murray, *The Parol Evidence Rule: A Clarification*, (1966) 4 Duquesne L. R. 337, 341-342.) This suggestion may be based on a belief that judges are not likely to be misled by their sympathies. If the court believes that the parties intended a collateral agreement to be effective, there is no reason to keep the evidence from the jury.

Burke, J.

I dissent. The majority opinion: (1) Undermines the parol evidence rule as we have known it in this state since at least 1872 by declaring that parol evidence should have been admitted by the trial court to show that a written option, absolute and unrestricted in form, was intended to be limited and nonassignable; (2) Renders suspect instruments of conveyance absolute on their face; (3) Materially lessens the reliance which may be placed upon written instruments affecting the title to real estate; and (4) Opens the door, albeit unintentionally, to a new technique for the defrauding of creditors.

The opinion permits defendants to establish by parol testimony that their grant[12] to their brother (and brother-in-law) of a written option, absolute in terms, was nevertheless agreed to be nonassignable by the grantee (now a bankrupt), and that therefore the right to exercise it did not pass, by operation of the bankruptcy laws, to the trustee for the benefit of the grantee's creditors.

And how was this to be shown? By the proffered testimony of the bankrupt optionee himself! Thereby one of his assets (the option to purchase defendants' California ranch) would be withheld from the trustee in bankruptcy and from the bankrupt's creditors. Understandably the trial court, as required by the parol evidence rule, did not allow the bankrupt by parol to so contradict the unqualified language of the written option. [T]here was nothing ambiguous about the *granting* language of the option and not the slightest suggestion in the document that the option was to be nonassignable. Thus, to permit such words of limitation to be added by parol is to *contradict* the absolute nature of the grant, and to directly violate the parol evidence rule.

Just as it is unnecessary to state in a deed to "lot X" that the house located thereon goes with the land, it is likewise unnecessary to add to "I grant an option to Jones" the words *"and his assigns"* for the option to be assignable. As hereinafter emphasized in more detail, California statutes expressly declare that it is assignable, and only if I add language in writing showing my intent to withhold or restrict the right of assignment may the grant be so limited. Thus, to seek to restrict the grant by parol is to *contradict* the written document in violation of the parol evidence rule.

The majority opinion arrives at its holding via a series of false premises which are not supported either in the record of this case or in such California authorities as are offered. The parol evidence rule is set forth in clear and definite language in the statutes of this state. (Civ. Code, § 1625; Code Civ. Proc., § 1856.) It "is not a rule of evidence but is one of substantive law. . . . The rule as applied to contracts is simply that as a matter of substantive law, a certain act, the act of embodying the complete terms of an agreement in a writing (the 'integration'), *becomes the contract of the parties."* (Hale v. Bohannon (1952) 38 Cal. 2d 458, 465. The rule is based upon the sound principle that the parties to a written instrument, after committing their agreement to or evidencing it by the writing, are not permitted to add to, vary or *contradict* the terms of the writing by parol evidence.

---

[12] [2] The option was in the form of a reservation in a deed; however, in legal effect it is the same as if it had been contained in a separate document.

At the outset the majority in the present case reiterate that the rule against contradicting or varying the terms of a writing remains applicable when only part of the agreement is contained in the writing, and parol evidence is used to prove elements of the agreement not reduced to writing. But having restated this established rule, the majority opinion inexplicably proceeds to subvert it. . . .

Options are property, and are widely used in the sale and purchase of real and personal property. One of the basic incidents of property ownership is the right of the owner to sell or transfer it. The author of the present majority opinion, speaking for the court in Farmland Irr. Co. v. Dopplmaier (1957), 48 Cal.2d 208, 222, put it this way: "The statutes in this state clearly manifest a policy in favor of the free transferability of all types of property, including rights under contracts."[13] (Citing Civ. Code, §§ 954, 1044, 1458).[14] These rights of the owner of property to transfer it, confirmed by the cited code sections, are elementary rules of substantive law and not the mere disputable presumptions which the majority opinion in the present case would make of them. Moreover, the right of transferability applies to an option to purchase, unless there are words of limitation in the option forbidding its assignment or showing that it was given because of a peculiar trust or confidence reposed in the optionee. . . .

The right of an optionee to transfer his option to purchase property is accordingly one of the basic rights which accompanies the option unless limited under the language of the option itself. To allow an optionor to resort to parol evidence to support his assertion that the written option is not transferable is to authorize him to limit the option by attempting to restrict and reclaim rights with which he has already parted. A clearer violation of two substantive and basic rules of law — the parol evidence rule and the right of free transferability of property — would be difficult to conceive.

NOTES

1. ***Andrews vs. Lehman in*** Mitchill: ***Understanding the Common Law Rules.*** Since the question in *Mitchill* is whether Mrs. Mitchill should be permitted to introduce oral evidence of a term not included in the writing, the court must first decide whether the parol evidence rule applies. Both Justices Andrews and Lehman agree that the writing constitutes a "complete agreement" as to the terms of the conveyance. At a minimum, then, they agree that the writing is at least partially integrated and the parol evidence rule therefore applies. If it is only partially integrated (that is, it is "final" as to its terms but not necessarily exclusive of all other terms), then the oral evidence of an additional term of the agreement is

---

[13] [4] The opinion continues: "The terms and purpose of a contract may show, however, that it was intended to be nonassignable." With this qualification of the general rule I am in accord, but here it is inapplicable as language indicating any intention whatever to restrict assignability is completely nonexistent.

[14] [5] Section 1044: "Property of any kind may be transferred, except as otherwise provided by this article." The *only* property the article provides cannot be transferred is "A mere possibility, not coupled with an interest." (§ 1045.)

Section 1458: "A right arising out of an obligation is the property of the person to whom it is due, and may be transferred as such."

admissible unless it contradicts the terms in the writing. Alternatively, if it is fully integrated (i.e., both final and exclusive), then such evidence must be excluded even if it does not contradict the terms in the writing. But Justices Andrews and Lehman do not discuss integration by name. Instead, they debate whether the oral agreement satisfies the "collateral agreement exception." This means that they believe the ice-house agreement is admissible only if the ice house agreement is collateral (i.e., separate from) the written land contract, does not contradict provisions of the written contract, and the written land agreement is only partially integrated.

The disagreement between Justices Andrews and Lehman, therefore, amounts to a disagreement over whether the written agreement is partially or fully integrated. Both employ the "natural omission" test for answering this question. Where then do they disagree? As in all contracts cases, the dispute here boils down to a factual question of intent: Did the parties intend the writing to extinguish the prior oral agreement, or did they presume the writing would have no effect on the prior oral agreement? Did the parties intend the writing to constitute all of their obligations to one another in connection with the sale of the house, or merely to provide all of the details of the sale transaction exclusive of other related obligations? Does your answer depend on whether or not the "four corners" presumption applies? Should the courts answer these questions by attempting to discern the parties' actual intent, or should they strive to base their decision as much as possible on the objective meaning of their writing viewed as of the time of contracting?

2.   *Traynor vs. Burke in* Masterson. The central question in *Masterson* is whether the court should admit oral evidence that the written option term (in fact a reservation in the conveyed deed) was non-assignable. Justice Traynor's opinion is relatively straightforward. The oral evidence is admissible unless (a) the agreement is partially integrated and the non-assignability term contradicts the terms of the writing or (b) the agreement is fully integrated and thus excludes all extrinsic evidence. Since the writing does not contain a merger clause, he must turn to some other test for full integration. Significantly, he rejects the four corners test, thus eliminating any presumption that if the writing appears complete on its face the parties must have intended to include all terms relevant to the transaction. Then he applies the "natural omission" test for integration. He asks whether the parties might naturally have omitted the non-assignability term from the written deed. What is the argument that the parties might well have omitted the non-assignability clause from the deed? Are you persuaded?

How does Justice Burke argue that the evidence should be excluded under the parol evidence rule? If we assume, with Burke, that the agreement is only partially integrated, his argument must be that the non-assignability term contradicts the option term in the deed. Is that persuasive? Even if California presumes an option to be assignable, would evidence that the parties orally agreed to make the option non-assignable contradict the written agreement? Or would it only demonstrate that the parties opted-out of the state-supplied default rule? If we assume, as Burke at one point seems to, that the agreement is fully integrated, does it follow that the oral evidence must be excluded? Must we construe that as evidence of an additional term, or could we construe it instead as evidence of the meaning of the option term?

3. ***Dispute Resolution vs. Prospective Regulation: The Problem of Fairness to the Parties.*** In *Mitchill*, Judge Andrews says of New York's narrow construction of the parol evidence rule: "Notwithstanding injustice here and there, on the whole it works for good." Judge Andrews illustrates his point by summarizing *Eighmie v. Taylor*, 98 N.Y. 288 (1885), in which the court refused to admit evidence that an oral warranty was made even though the written agreement contained no warranty. His point appears to be that even though the parol evidence rule may in some cases deprive a party of a benefit he was promised, it is nonetheless justified. Assuming the rule sometimes does have this effect, what is its justification? Is there a greater purpose to serve than that of doing justice between the parties? If there is a goal advanced by the parol evidence rule in such cases, can that purpose ever justify depriving one party of the benefit of his bargain? Justice Traynor in *Masterson* cites with approval the statement that "the party urging the spoken as against the written word is most often the economic underdog, threatened by severe hardship if the writing is enforced." Should the status of the parties matter in determining how to apply the parol evidence rule? Do you think this means that a court should reach a different result if the agreement in question has been negotiated between two large commercial entities, both ably represented by counsel?

4. ***A Major League Example.*** After Frank McCourt purchased the Los Angeles Dodgers in 2006, he and his wife, Jamie, signed a post-nuptial agreement that stated the Dodgers were solely his property. But the agreement wasn't as clear as Frank McCourt thought, which came back to haunt him when the couple divorced a few years later:

> The McCourts' lawyer, Larry Silverstein, had the couple sign six copies of the post-nup. Frank signed three at their home in Boston and another three in Los Angeles two weeks later, because Silverstein felt that it would be safer to have some copies of the agreement signed in California. . . . When Jamie's lawyers began looking through Silverstein's files, they found the mother of all snafus. Silverstein, it seemed, had inadvertently allowed the McCourts to sign three of the six documents with an error in the exhibit: instead of saying that Frank was the sole owner of all their property "inclusive" of the Dodgers, the L.A. copies said that he was the owner of all property "exclusive" of the Dodgers. Silverstein eventually caught the mistake, which he claims was a simple drafting error, but instead of having the McCourts sign corrected documents, he simply switched out the exhibits for ones with the correct language. It was a decision made for efficiency's sake — but it cost Frank the case against Jamie, at least in part. The post-nup was thrown out in December 2010.

See Vanessa Grigoriadis, *A Major-League Divorce*, VANITY FAIR, Aug. 2011. Should extrinsic evidence of Frank McCourt's intent been admissible to rectify the drafting error?

[2] Merger Clauses

UAW-GM HUMAN RESOURCE CTR. v. KSL REC. CORP.
Michigan Court of Appeals
228 Mich. App. 486, 579 N.W.2d 411 (1998)

MARKMAN, J.

Defendants appeal as of right a trial court order granting summary disposition to plaintiff on its claims of breach of contract, conversion, and fraud. Defendants also appeal as of right the trial court's denial of their motion for summary disposition. We reverse and remand for determination of damages pursuant to the liquidated damages formula set forth in the contract.

In December 1993, plaintiff entered into a contract with Carol Management Corporation (CMC) for the use of its property, Doral Resort and Country Club, for a convention scheduled in October 1994. The "letter of agreement" included a merger clause that stated that such agreement constituted "a merger of all proposals, negotiations and representations with reference to the subject matter and provisions." The letter of agreement did not contain any provision requiring that Doral Resort employees be union-represented. However, plaintiff contends in its appellate brief that it signed the letter of agreement in reliance on an "independent, collateral promise to provide [plaintiff] with a union-represented hotel." Plaintiff provided the affidavits of Herschel Nix, plaintiff's agent, and Barbara Roush, CMC's agent, who negotiated the contract. In his affidavit, Nix states that during the contract negotiation he and Roush discussed plaintiff's requirement that the hotel employees be union-represented and that Roush agreed to this requirement. In her affidavit, Roush states that "prior to and at the time" the contract at issue was negotiated she "was well aware" of plaintiff's requirement that the hotel employees be union-represented and that "that there is no doubt that I agreed on behalf of the Doral Resort to provide a union hotel."

Later in December 1993, the hotel was sold to defendants, who subsequently replaced the resort's union employees with a nonunionized work force.[15] In June 1994, when plaintiff learned that the hotel no longer had union employees, it canceled the contract and demanded a refund of its down payment. Defendants refused to refund the down payment, retaining it as a portion of the liquidated damages allegedly owed to them pursuant to the contract. Plaintiff filed suit for return of the down payment and asserted claims of breach of contract, conversion of the deposit, and fraud. Defendants filed a counterclaim and moved for summary disposition and enforcement of the liquidated damages clause. Plaintiff filed a cross-motion for summary disposition. The trial court granted plaintiff's motion for summary disposition regarding the breach of contract count on the basis of its determination that there was a separate agreement requiring that the hotel

---

[15] [2] Federal labor law recognizes the right of a successor employer to avoid its predecessor's obligations under a collective bargaining agreement by choosing not to retain the predecessor's work force, *NLRB v. Burns Int'l Security Services*, 406 U.S. 272, 288-291; 92 S. Ct. 1571; 32 L. Ed. 2d 61 (1972), provided that hiring decisions are not a product of union affiliation, *Id.* at 280, n 5.

employees be union-represented. It also granted plaintiff's motion for summary disposition on the conversion and fraud counts.

This Court reviews decisions on motions for summary disposition de novo to determine if the moving party was entitled to judgment as a matter of law.

Merger Clause

Defendants claim that the trial court erred in granting plaintiff's motion for summary disposition and in denying defendants' motion for summary disposition. Regarding the breach of contract count, they specifically contend that parol evidence of a separate agreement providing that the hotel would have union employees at the time of the convention was inadmissible because the letter of agreement included an express merger clause. . . .

The parol evidence rule may be summarized as follows: "parol evidence of contract negotiations, or of prior or contemporaneous agreements that contradict or vary the written contract, is not admissible to vary the terms of a contract which is clear and unambiguous." *Schmude Oil Co v. Omar Operating Co.*, 184 Mich. App. 574, 580; 458 N.W.2d 659 (1990). "The practical justification for the rule lies in the stability that it gives to written contracts; for otherwise either party might avoid his obligation by testifying that a contemporaneous oral agreement released him from the duties that he had simultaneously assumed in writing." 4 Williston, Contracts, § 631. In other words, the parol evidence rule addresses the fact that "disappointed parties will have a great incentive to describe circumstances in ways that escape the explicit terms of their contracts." Fried, *Contract as Promise* (Cambridge: Harvard University Press, 1981) at 60. . . .

The first issue before us is whether parol evidence is admissible with regard to the threshold question of integration even when the written agreement includes an explicit merger or integration clause. While this issue is one of first impression, its answer turns on well-established principles of contract law. 4 Williston, Contracts, § 633, p 1014 states in pertinent part:

> Since it is only the intention of the parties to adopt a writing as a memorial which makes that writing an integration of the contract, and makes the parol evidence rule applicable, any expression of their intention in the writing in regard to the matter will be given effect. If they provide in terms that the writing shall be a complete integration of their agreement . . . the expressed intention will be effectuated.

3 Corbin, Contracts, § 578, pp 402-411 states in pertinent part:

> If a written document, mutually assented to, declares in express terms that it contains the entire agreement of the parties . . . this declaration is conclusive as long as it has itself not been set aside by a court on grounds of fraud or mistake, or on some ground that is sufficient for setting aside other contracts. . . . It is just like a general release of all antecedent claims.
>
> . . . [B]y limiting the contract to the provisions that are in writing, the parties are definitely expressing an intention to nullify antecedent under-

standings or agreements. They are making the document a complete integration. Therefore, even if there had in fact been an antecedent warranty or other provision, it is discharged by the written agreement.

Thus, both Corbin and Williston indicate that an explicit integration clause is conclusive and that parol evidence is not admissible to determine whether a contract is integrated when a written contract contains such a clause. The conclusion that parol evidence is not admissible to show that a written agreement is not integrated when the agreement itself includes an integration clause is consistent with the general contract principles of honoring parties' agreements as expressed in their written contracts and not creating ambiguities where none exist.[16] This conclusion accords respect to the rules that the parties themselves have set forth to resolve controversies arising under the contract. The parties are bound by the contract because they have chosen to be so bound.

The conclusion that parol evidence is not admissible regarding this "threshold issue" when there is an explicit integration clause honors the parties' decision to include such a clause in their written agreement. It gives effect to their decision to establish a written agreement as the exclusive basis for determining their intentions concerning the subject matter of the contract.

This rule is especially compelling in cases such as the present one, where defendants, successor corporations, assumed performance of another corporation's obligations under a letter of agreement. Because defendants were not parties to the negotiations resulting in the letter of agreement, they would obviously be unaware of any oral representations made by CMC's agent to plaintiff's agent in the course of those negotiations. Defendants assumed CMC's obligations under the letter of agreement, which included an explicit merger clause. Defendants could not reasonably have been expected to discuss with every party to every contract with CMC whether any parol agreements existed that would place further burdens upon defendants in the context of a contract with an explicit merger clause. Under these circumstances, it would be fundamentally unfair to hold defendants to oral representations allegedly made by CMC's agent. . . . We believe that defendants acted reasonably in their reliance and that the contract should be interpreted in accordance with its express provisions.

For these reasons, we hold that when the parties include an integration clause in their written contract, it is conclusive and parol evidence is not admissible to show that the agreement is not integrated except in cases of fraud that invalidate the integration clause. . . .

---

[16] [4] This is the only rule that treats the parties to the contract as consenting adults who are able to establish their own rules for the resolution of future controversies between themselves. The dissenting opinion fails to respect the parties' clearly expressed intent to be bound only by the terms of the letter of agreement. While the dissenting opinion attempts to minimize the import of the merger clause, the merger clause is an explicit term of the parties' contract and therefore an expression of their intent to which this Court is obligated to give meaning.

Fraud

Because plaintiff made fraud allegations here, we will consider the effect of such allegations on a contract with a merger clause. Parol evidence is generally admissible to demonstrate fraud. However, in the context of an integration clause, which releases all antecedent claims, only certain types of fraud would vitiate the contract. . . . In other words, while parol evidence is generally admissible to prove fraud, fraud that relates solely to an oral agreement that was nullified by a valid merger clause would have no effect on the validity of the contract. Thus, when a contract contains a valid merger clause, the only fraud that could vitiate the contract is fraud that would invalidate the merger clause itself, i.e., fraud relating to the merger clause or fraud that invalidates the entire contract including the merger clause.

Here, defendants contended that the contract was fully integrated and presented the letter of agreement with its express and unambiguous merger clause as evidence. Plaintiff presented the affidavits of Nix and Roush in support of its argument that the letter of agreement was not fully integrated because the alleged agreement providing that the hotel would have union employees at the time of the convention was not reduced to writing. In its fraud count, plaintiff contends that Roush's representations that the hotel would have union employees and her failure to inform plaintiff of the impending sale of the hotel constituted fraud. These fraud claims turn on an alleged agreement that the hotel employees would be union-represented. However, the merger clause would nullify any such agreement not included in the letter of agreement. The various species of fraud alleged here all require reliance on a misrepresentation. Here, the merger clause made it unreasonable for plaintiff's agent to rely on any representations not included in the letter of agreement. Any injury suffered by plaintiff appears to have resulted from its agent's failure to include a requirement that hotel employees be union-represented in the integrated letter of agreement rather than from reliance on any misrepresentations by Roush. Thus, the allegations in plaintiff's fraud count are not the type of fraud claims that could invalidate a contract with a valid merger clause.

Plaintiff made no allegations of fraud that would invalidate the contract or the merger clause itself. The written agreement is detailed and complete on its face and its words are unambiguous. There is no indication that the integration clause itself is void for any reason. Accordingly, as a matter of law, parol evidence was not admissible here to contradict the explicit integration clause. Therefore, we hold that the trial court erred in granting plaintiff's motion for summary disposition and equally erred in denying defendants' motion for summary disposition.[17]

Reversed and remanded for proceedings consistent with this opinion.

---

[17] [14] An integration clause is not merely an additional "factor" to be weighed in light of the affidavits and other extrinsic evidence to determine the parties' understandings, nor is it merely one more piece of evidence to be used to determine whether there is a "genuine issue of material fact" to be evaluated at trial. Rather, an integration clause, if construed as precluding summary disposition for plaintiff, does so because it establishes an internal rule of construction for the contract explicitly agreed to by the parties to the contract. The parties' choice to include such an internal rule of construction precludes consideration of any prior or contemporaneous agreements and compels summary disposition here for defendants.

HOLBROOK, JR., J., (dissenting).

I respectfully dissent.

The contract's merger clause — "a merger of all proposals, negotiations and representations with reference to the subject matter and provisions" — appears plain and unambiguous. While it is often stated that courts may not create an ambiguity in a contract where none exists, and that parol evidence is generally not admissible to vary or contradict the terms of a written contract . . . strict adherence to these rules can be problematic. . . .The trouble is that the court's assumption or decision as to the completeness and accuracy of the integration may be quite erroneous. *The writing cannot prove its own completeness and accuracy. Even though it contains an express statement to that effect, the assent of the parties thereto must still be proved. Proof of its completeness and accuracy, discharging all antecedent agreements, must be made in large part by the oral testimony of parties and other witnesses.* The very testimony that the "parol evidence rule" is supposed to exclude is frequently, if not always, necessary before the court can determine that the parties have agreed upon the writing as a complete and accurate statement of terms. The evidence that the rule seems to exclude must sometimes be heard and weighed before it can be excluded by the rule. This is one reason why the working of this rule has been so inconsistent and unsatisfactory. This is why so many exceptions and limitations to the supposed rule of evidence have been recognized by various courts.

There is ample judicial authority showing that, in determining the issue of completeness of the integration in writing, evidence extrinsic to the writing itself is admissible. *The oral admissions of the plaintiff that the agreement included matters not contained in the writing may be proved to show that it was not assented to as a complete integration, however complete it may look on its face. . . .* Accord Restatement Contracts, 2d, § 216, comment e, p 140 (observing that a merger "clause does not control the question of whether the writing was assented to as an integrated agreement").

The fact that plaintiff's representative read and signed the contract does not obviate the applicability of the principles outlined [above]. Indeed, Professor Corbin illustrates the principles of the section by analyzing the case of *Int'l Milling Co. v. Hachmeister, Inc.*, 380 Pa. 407; 110 A.2d 186 (1955), in which the parties entered into a contract for the sale and purchase of flour. During negotiations, buyer insisted that each shipment of flour meet certain established specifications and that such a provision be included in the contract. Seller refused to put the provision in the contract, but agreed to write a confirmation letter to buyer tying in the required specifications. Buyer placed a written order, indicating that the flour must meet the required specifications. Seller sent to buyer a printed contract form, which contained none of the specifications, but did contain an express integration clause. Seller also sent a separate letter assuring delivery in accordance with the required specifications. Buyer signed the written contract form. When a subsequent shipment of flour failed to meet the specifications, buyer rejected it and canceled all other orders. The Pennsylvania Supreme Court held that extrinsic evidence of the parties' negotiations and antecedent agreements was admissible with regard to the issue whether buyer had assented to the printed contract form as a complete and accurate integration of the contract, *notwithstanding its express provision to the contrary.* Corbin, *supra* at 458.[18]

Thus, examination of the written document alone is insufficient to determine its completeness; extrinsic evidence that is neither flimsy nor implausible is admissible to establish whether the writing was in fact intended by the parties as a completely integrated contract. *Franklin v. White*, 493 N.E.2d 161, 166 (Ind. 1986) ("An integration clause is only some evidence of the parties' intentions. The trial court should consider an integration clause along with all other relevant evidence on the question of integration."); *Sutton v. Stacey's Fuel Mart, Inc.*, 431 A.2d 1319, 1322, n 3 (Me. 1981) (citing Restatement Contracts, 2d for the proposition that a "merger clause does not control the question of whether a writing was intended to be a completely integrated agreement"); Restatement Contracts, 2d, § 209, comment b, p 115 ("Written contracts may include an explicit declaration that there are no other agreements between the parties, but such a declaration may not be conclusive.").

"The cardinal rule in the interpretation of contracts is to ascertain the intention of the parties. To this rule all others are subordinate." *McIntosh v. Groomes*, 227 Mich. 215, 218; 198 N.W. 954 (1924). It is undisputed in this case that plaintiff's decision to hold its convention at the resort was predicated on the understanding of the representatives for both defendants' predecessor and plaintiff that the resort employed a unionized staff. Had plaintiff been made aware that the resort was for sale or that a sale was pending, I believe it is reasonable to assume that plaintiff's representative would have insisted that such a clause be incorporated into the agreement. Courts should not require that contracting parties include provisions in their agreement contemplating every conceivable, but highly improbable, manner of breach. In my opinion, the circumstances surrounding execution of the contract, as well as the material change in circumstance that occurred when the resort was sold and the union staff fired, establishes as a matter of law that plaintiff did not assent to a completely integrated agreement.

Accordingly, I would affirm the trial court's order granting summary disposition in favor of plaintiff.

DANANN REALTY CORP. v. HARRIS
Court of Appeals of New York
5 N.Y.2d 317, 157 N.E.2d 597 (1959)

See p. 428, supra.

NOTES

1. *Questions on* **UAW-GM Human Resource Center.** The majority opinion in UAW-GM represents the predominant view of those courts that retain the "hard" version of the parol evidence rule: unless claims of duress, fraud or scrivener's error

---

[18] [2] "The presence of an integration clause cannot invest a writing with any greater sanctity than the writing merits where, as here, it assuredly does not fully express the essential elements of the parties' undertakings." *Hachmeister, supra* at 417.

are proven, the court will give presumptively conclusive effect to merger or integration clauses. The dissent, on the other hand, articulates the view of courts that have adopted a "soft" version of parol evidence: Here the test for integration admits extrinsic evidence notwithstanding an unambiguous merger clause declaring the contract to be an integrated writing. These courts regard the merger clause as merely creating a rebuttable presumption of integration that can be overridden by extrinsic evidence that the parties lacked any such intent. What different outcomes result from these two differing interpretive styles? The majority granted the defendants' motion for summary judgment, while the dissent would have ordered the case set for trial to consider the extrinsic evidence. Why might it matter to parties at the time of contracting that a future interpretive dispute would be resolved on summary judgment rather than after a full evidentiary trial?

All courts would agree that the existence of a written merger clause creates, at a minimum, a strong evidentiary presumption that an agreement is fully integrated. There are several ways to overcome this burden. One is to demonstrate that one of the parties agreed to the clause under duress. Another is to show that the clause was a mutual mistake due to a scrivener's error — the writing failed to reflect the parties' agreement because of a mechanical mistake in its drafting. Finally, a party could also argue that he was induced to agree to the merger clause by the other party's intentional or material misrepresentation, or by outright fraud. The majority in *UAW-GM* concedes these defenses but then dismisses plaintiff's claim of fraud without hearing any evidence. Why? What kinds of allegations of fraud, if any, would have persuaded the majority to order an evidentiary trial? Do you agree with plaintiff's contention that "there is no effective means by which parties to a contract can preclude courts from looking beyond the four corners of a contract in interpreting such contract"?

2.   *Putting UAW-GM in context.* The court mentions in passing that in December of 1993, the hotel was sold to KSL Recreation Corp. At the time, KSL was a subsidiary of the major private equity firm, KKR. We can assume, therefore, that KSL was represented by sophisticated counsel and undertook due diligence to understand the types of agreements to which the hotel was a party. From this perspective, it becomes clearer why extrinsic evidence such as the discussion between the plaintiff's agent and CMC's agent would make doing business more difficult and costly. If, in addition to normal due diligence, the acquirer of a business were obligated to look for evidence beyond that which is memorialized in writing before it could proceed with an acquisition, the costs and risks of such M&A activity would increase substantially. At the same time, KKR and other private equity firms that have a practice of preferring non-union labor may have some familiarity with disputes of this sort. Given this fact, should they nonetheless be expected to research extrinsic contractual evidence?

3.   *Williston and Corbin on Merger Clauses.* The debate over interpretive styles began with the titans of contract, Samuel Williston and Arthur Corbin, and, as we have suggested, it continues to the present. That debate was reflected in their different views on the effect to be given to merger clauses. Professor Williston adopted the position that if the parties "provide in terms that the writing shall be a complete integration of their agreement . . . the expressed intent will be effectuated." 4 S. Williston, *Contracts* § 633, at 1014 (3d ed. 1961). Professor Corbin might not have agreed:

> The writing cannot prove its own completeness and accuracy. *Even though it contains an express statement to that effect*, the assent of the parties thereto must still be proved.

3 A. Corbin, Contracts § 582, at 448-49 (2d ed. 1960) (emphasis added). Yet Corbin also claims:

> If a written document, mutually assented to, declares in express terms that it contains the entire agreement of the parties, and that there are no antecedent or extrinsic representations, warranties, or collateral provisions that are not intended to be discharged and nullified, this declaration is conclusive as long as it has itself not been set aside by a court on grounds of fraud or mistake, or on some ground that is sufficient for setting aside other contracts.

Id. § 578, at 402-03. Corbin's position seems inconsistent. Can you reconcile his two statements?

4. ***Merger Clauses and the Preferences of Sophisticated Commercial Parties***. Merger clauses are ubiquitous in commercial contracts that are negotiated between sophisticated parties represented by counsel. This raises the question why such parties seem always to include these clauses in their contracts. As we have seen, a party disappointed by the apparent meaning of the words in a contract will likely be precluded by a merger clause from introducing extrinsic evidence at trial. Why don't sophisticated parties choose to preserve their option to litigate contractual disputes to the fullest extent? In *Contract Interpretation Redux*, 119 YALE L.J. 926 (2010), Professors Alan Schwartz and Robert Scott argue that

> [A]lthough accurate judicial interpretations are desirable, accurate interpretations are costly for parties and courts to obtain. If contract writing were free, parties could minimize interpretive error by exhaustively detailing their intentions. And if adjudication were free, courts could minimize interpretive error by hearing all relevant and material evidence. Contract writing and litigation are costly, however. Since no interpretive theory can justify devoting infinite resources to achieving interpretive accuracy, any socially desirable interpretive rule would trade accuracy off against contract writing and adjudication cost. Such a rule, we argue, tells courts in some cases to exclude relevant evidence.

Given, the high cost of evidentiary trials versus summary judgment, Schwartz & Scott conclude

> [T]he state should defer to party preferences regarding interpretation, just as it defers today to party preferences over a contract's substantive terms, and that any rules the state adopts should be defaults. We argue, therefore, that the state should choose interpretive rules that conform to majoritarian party preferences, and courts should obey party instructions to depart from those rules in particular cases. . . . Thus, we do not argue that the state should enact mandatory rules that require courts to make formalist

interpretations. Rather, we argue that the state should create interpretative rules that instantiate party preferences; it is the business parties that commonly prefer formalist interpretations.

5. *Procedural Unconscionability and Merger Clauses*. In *Seibel v. Layne & Bowler, Inc.*, 56 Or. App. 387, 641 P.2d 668 (1982), the Seibels sued the defendant-corporation for damages due to a malfunctioning water pump purchased from defendants in 1977. The pump failed to work properly from installation, prompting plaintiffs to declare breach and seek recovery from the corporation in 1978. Plaintiffs alleged that defendant made various express oral warranties prior to the purchase of the water pump, and that these warranties were violated by the pump's subsequent failure. These oral warranties were not included in the written contract. In response, defendant presented the written agreement, signed by both parties, which included a merger clause indicating that the written agreement was intended to be the parties' complete and exclusive expression of their agreement. Thus, defendants argued, any prior oral warranties were unenforceable under the clear terms of the agreement.

The court disagreed, finding the form merger clause too inconspicuous to be enforced against the plaintiffs. Describing the merger text placed on the back of the contract, the court wrote, "[t]he type is smaller than that used for footnotes in this court's permanent reports and the lines are longer and more closely spaced . . . There is neither indentation nor extra spacing between paragraphs. The print is generally difficult to read. The exculpatory provisions themselves are set out no differently than the other terms." 56 Or. App. at 391. The court concluded by asserting

> that it would be unconscionable to permit an inconspicuous merger clause to exclude evidence of an express oral warranty . . . That is, a disclaimer of the implied warranties of fitness and merchantability must be conspicuous to prevent surprise. We think a merger clause which would deny effect to an express warranty must be conspicuous to prevent an even greater surprise.

Id. at 392.

Do you think the Seibels would likely have understood the legal significance of the merger clause even if they were asked to sign it separately? Is the court's true objective to prevent sellers from hiding terms adverse to their customers? If the Seibels read the merger clause but failed to realize that it invalidated the seller's previous oral promises, could the court invalidate the merger clause, or the entire contract, on other grounds?

[3] The UCC Parol Evidence Rule

Section 2-202 of the UCC contains the Code's parol evidence rule. The section sets out rules designed to assist courts in identifying the *terms* of an agreement. Recall that the common law parol evidence rule uses the merger doctrine, the four corners presumption, or the "natural omission" test to determine integration. The

Code also implicitly endorses a version of the merger doctrine.[19] But in the Code's comments elaborating on the procedure courts should use to test for full integration (whether an agreement constitutes the "complete and exclusive" statement of all the terms of the agreement under UCC 2-202(b)), the Code's drafters endorse a more liberal version of the "natural omission" test: "If the additional terms are such that, if agreed upon, they would *certainly have been included* in the document in the view of the court, then evidence of their alleged making must be kept from the trier of fact." UCC 2-202, comment 3. This "certain inclusion" test differs from the "natural omission" test because it excludes extrinsic evidence of consistent additional terms only if the parties *certainly*, rather than merely "naturally," would have included them in their written agreement.[20]

As you consider the Code's parol evidence rule in *Hunt Foods & Industries v. Doliner*, ask yourself how a court should go about determining whether the parties intended their agreement as the "complete and exclusive" statement of the terms of their agreement. Does the Code make it more or less difficult to prove an agreement is fully integrated?

HUNT FOODS & INDUSTRIES, INC. v. DOLINER
Supreme Court of New York, Appellate Division
26 A.D.2d 41, *aff'd*, 272 N.Y.S.2d 686 (1966)

STEUER, J.

In February, 1965 plaintiff corporation undertook negotiations to acquire the assets of Eastern Can Company. The stock of the latter is owned by defendant George M. Doliner and his family to the extent of 73%. The balance is owned by independent interests. At a fairly early stage of the negotiations agreement was reached as to the price to be paid by plaintiff ($5,922,500 if in cash, or $5,730,000 in Hunt stock), but several important items, including the form of the acquisition, were not agreed upon. At this point it was found necessary to recess the negotiations for several weeks. The Hunt negotiators expressed concern over any adjournment and stated that they feared that Doliner would use their offer as a basis for soliciting a higher bid from a third party. To protect themselves they demanded an option to purchase the Doliner stock. Such an option was prepared and signed by George Doliner and the members of his family and at least one other person associated with him who were stockholders. It provides that Hunt has the option to buy all of the Doliner stock at $5.50 per share. The option is to be exercised by giving notice on

---

[19] UCC 2-202(b) prohibits courts from considering evidence of even consistent additional terms if "the court finds the writing to have been intended also as a complete and exclusive statement of the terms of the agreement." The presence of a merger clause in a written agreement would thus provide courts with significant evidence that the parties intended their writing to serve as the complete and exclusive statement of their agreement, although whether the merger clause would be regarded as presumptively conclusive is an open question.

[20] Here, we follow the convention of treating the "natural omission" test, which holds that a written agreement *is not* integrated if the parties naturally would have omitted the proffered nonwritten terms from their writing, as equivalent to the "natural inclusion" test, which holds that a written agreement is integrated if the parties naturally would have included the proffered nonwritten terms in their writing.

B.   IDENTIFYING THE TERMS OF AGREEMENT   563

or before June 1, 1965, and if notice is not given the option is void. If given, Hunt is to pay the price and the Doliners to deliver their stock within seven days thereafter. The agreement calls for Hunt to pay $1,000 for the option, which was paid. To this point there is substantial accord as to what took place.

Defendant claims that when his counsel called attention to the fact that the option was unconditional in its terms, he obtained an understanding that it was only to be used in the event that he solicited an outside offer; and that plaintiff insisted that unless the option was signed in unconditional form negotiations would terminate. Plaintiff contends there was no condition. Concededly, on resumption of negotiations the parties failed to reach agreement and the option was exercised. Defendants declined the tender and refused to deliver the stock.

Plaintiff moved for summary judgment for specific performance. We do not believe that summary judgment lies. Plaintiff's position is that the condition claimed could not be proved under the parol evidence rule and, eliminating that, there is no defense to the action.

The parol evidence rule, at least as that term refers to contracts of sale, is now contained in Section 2-202 of the Uniform Commercial Code, which reads:[21]

> Terms with respect to which the confirmatory memoranda of the parties agree or which are otherwise set forth in a writing intended by the parties as a final expression of their agreement with respect to such terms as are included therein may not be contradicted by evidence of any prior agreement or of a contemporaneous oral agreement but may be explained or supplemented . . .
>
> (b) by evidence of consistent additional terms unless the court finds the writing to have been intended also as a complete and exclusive statement of the terms of the agreement.

The term (that the option was not to be exercised unless Doliner sought outside bids), admittedly discussed but whose operative effect is disputed, not being set out in the writing, is clearly "additional" to what is in the writing. So the first question presented is whether that term is "consistent" with the instrument. In a sense any oral provision which would prevent the ripening of the obligations of a writing is inconsistent with the writing. But that obviously is not the sense in which the word is used (Hicks v. Bush, 10 N.Y.2d 488, 491, 225 N.Y.S.2d 34). To be inconsistent the term must contradict or negate a term of the writing. A term or condition which has a lesser effect is provable.

The Official Comment prepared by the drafters of the Code contains this statement:

> If the additional terms are such that, if agreed upon, they would certainly have been included in the document in the view of the court, then evidence of their alleged making must be kept from the trier of fact.

---

[21] [*] While article 2 of the Uniform Commercial Code which contains this section does not deal with the sale of securities, this section applies to article 8, dealing with securities. *Cf.* Agar v. Orda, 264 N.Y. 248, 190 N.E. 479, 90 A.L.R. 269; Official Comment, McKinney's Uniform Commercial Code, Part 1, pp. 96-97; Note, 65 Col. L. Rev. 880, 890-1. All parties and Special Term so regarded it.

Special Term interpreted this language as not only calling for an adjudication by the court in all instances where proof of an "additional oral term" is offered, but making that determination exclusively the function of the court. We believe the proffered evidence to be inadmissible only where the writing contradicts the existence of the claimed additional term. The conversations in this case, some of which are not disputed, and the expectation of all the parties for further negotiations, suggest that the alleged oral condition precedent cannot be precluded as a matter of law or as factually impossible. It is not sufficient that the existence of the condition is implausible. It must be impossible.

The order should be reversed on the law and the motion for summary judgment denied with costs and disbursements to abide the event.

NOTES

1. ***Questions on* Hunt Foods.** In *Hunt Foods*, the question presented is whether the courts should admit oral evidence that a written term granting an option was conditional. The court treats the question as exclusively one of the admissibility of evidence under the parol evidence rule. The court states that "[t]he term (that the option was not to be exercised unless Doliner sought outside bids), . . . not being set out in the writing, is clearly 'additional' to what is in the writing." The dissent in *Masterson, supra*, might argue that the question instead is whether the written option has a plain meaning according to which it is unconditional absent express (written?) agreement otherwise. If so, oral evidence of a condition would contradict the plain meaning of an unambiguous agreement. Is this approach to the question equally plausible?

The court in *Hunt Foods* states that "the first question presented is whether the [term restricting the option] is 'consistent' with the instrument." The court argues that every additional term based on extrinsic evidence is, in a broad sense, inconsistent with any writing because it would alter the terms of the writing. But the court interprets the Code as requiring inconsistency with a particular term of the writing: "To be inconsistent the term must contradict or negate a term of the writing." The court then holds that "a term or condition which has a lesser effect is provable." Thus, because the oral term would not eliminate the option granted, but instead merely reduces its effect, it is consistent with the option term. Do you agree with this criterion for assessing consistency with a writing? Suppose the written term in a writing provides that seller promises to deliver two dozen horses, and seller later argues that the parties made a prior oral agreement that seller's obligation was to deliver only one dozen horses. Would you say that the oral evidence is consistent with the written quantity term of the agreement? Doesn't it "have a lesser effect" than absolute negation of the written quantity term?

The court then applies the "certain inclusion" test for integration and finds the agreement is not integrated with respect to the proffered term limiting the option: "It is not sufficient that the existence of the condition is implausible. It must be impossible." The court seems to be reading the word "certainly" in the Code's "certain inclusion" test to require that it be impossible to believe that the parties would have agreed to the proffered term and nonetheless have decided to exclude it in their written agreement. On this reading, is there any evidence a court could exclude? Can you think of any term in any contract that the parties would never intentionally omit from the writing?

For a critique of the court's reasoning in *Hunt Foods*, see Jody S. Kraus & Robert E. Scott, *Contract Design and the Structure of Contractual Intent*, 84 N.Y.U. L. Rev 1023, 1046–57 (2009).

2. *The Meaning of "Inconsistent."* The court in *Snyder v. Herbert Greenbaum & Associates, Inc.*, 38 Md. App. 144, 380 A.2d 618 (1977), explicitly rejected the reasoning of *Hunt Foods*. In that case, Herbert Greenbaum & Associates, Inc. contracted with Twin Lakes Partnership to supply and install carpeting and the underlying carpet pads for 228 garden apartments which Twin Lakes was about to construct. During negotiations for the contract, Greenbaum estimated that approximately 19,000 to 20,000 yards of carpeting would be required for the job. Between April 4, 1972, the date the contract was signed, and September 1973, Greenbaum purchased large amounts of carpet from carpet wholesalers to be used on the Twin Lakes job. However, Twin Lakes, through Alvin Snyder, canceled the contract in September 1973 when it became apparent that 19,000 to 20,000 yards of carpet was an overestimate (the actual amount needed was between 17,000 and 17,500 yards). At trial, Greenbaum successfully recovered $19,407.20 from Twin Lakes Partnership for breach of contract.

On appeal, the court addressed the parol evidence issue. At trial, Snyder offered five documents purporting to be prior contracts between the parties, each of which had been rescinded or canceled. Snyder claimed that these documents established a prior course of dealing or oral agreement between the parties that enabled either party unilaterally to modify or cancel any contract between them. The court of appeals, on two grounds, upheld the trial court's refusal to admit the documents and rejected Snyder's course of dealing analysis.

First, the court held that, while a course of dealing could serve as an interpretive device to give meaning to the words and terms of a contract, the documents Snyder sought to introduce comprised an agreement that added to the terms of the written contract, and thus should be analyzed under § 2-202(b). The court decided that unconditional, unilateral rescission was a term the parties "certainly" would have included in the final written agreement, and concluded that the contract was intended to be a complete and exclusive statement of the contract terms.

Alternatively, the court went further and rejected the analysis offered in *Hunt Foods*:

> At any rate, for much the same reason, we hold that the additional terms offered by appellants are inconsistent with the contract itself. In so doing we reject the narrow view of inconsistency espoused in Hunt Foods v. Doliner, 26 A.D.2d 41, 270 N.Y.S.2d 937 (1966), and Schiavone and Sons v. Securalloy Co., 312 F. Supp. 801 (D. Conn. 1970). Those cases hold that to be inconsistent the "additional terms" must negate or contradict express terms of the agreement.

> This interpretation of "inconsistent" is itself inconsistent with a reading of the whole of § 2-202. Direct contradiction of express terms is forbidden in

the initial paragraph of § 2-202. The *Hunt Foods* interpretation renders that passage a nullity, a result which is to be avoided. Gillespie v. R & J Constr. Co., 275 Md. 454 (1975).

Rather we believe "inconsistency" as used in § 2-202(b) means the absence of reasonable harmony in terms of the language and respective obligations of the parties. § 1-205(4); see Southern Concrete Services v. Mableton Contractors, 407 F. Supp. 581 (N.D. Ga. 1975). In terms of the obligations of the appellee, which required appellee to make extensive preparations in order to perform, unqualified unilateral cancellation by appellants is not reasonably harmonious. Therefore, evidence of the additional terms was properly excluded by the trial judge, and we find no error.

Id. at 152.

3. *A Deliberate Omission?* Comment 3 to UCC § 2-202 indicates that additional terms should be kept from the trier of fact only if the additional terms are such that, if agreed upon, they would certainly have been included in the document. In *Hunt Foods*, can you think of a good explanation for why the parties intentionally would have left such an important term (that the option was not to be exercised unless Doliner sought outside bids) out of the written document?

4. *Opting Out of the Code: An Empirical Analysis of the Parol Evidence Rule and Choice of Law.* What influence, if any, does the method of interpretation adopted in a given jurisdiction have on commercial parties' choice of a jurisdiction (and its rules of interpretation) to resolve disputes under their contracts? A recent empirical study supports the view that sophisticated parties prefer "hard" parol evidence rules and formal modes of interpretation. *See generally* Theodore Eisenberg & Geoffrey P. Miller, *The Flight to New York: An Empirical Study of Choice of Law and Choice of Forum Clauses in Publicly-Held Companies' Contracts*, 30 CARDOZO L. REV. 1475 (2009). By examining forum selection clauses in nearly 3,000 merger contracts (publicly available because of federal disclosure rules), Professors Eisenberg and Miller found that parties chose New York law, with its relatively strict parol evidence rule, in 46% of the contracts. In contrast, parties only chose California, with its more flexible parol evidence rule, in less than 8% of the contracts even though its commercial activity was second only to New York. The study illustrates the apparent preferences of commercial parties for the formal contract law of New York in lieu of the frequent exercise of equitable overrides by courts in California.

The Miller and Eisenberg study raises the question of whether sophisticated commercial parties to sales contracts that fall under the UCC would be permitted to opt out of the soft parol evidence rule of § 2-202 in favor of having their contracts governed by the hard parol evidence rule that applies to other contracts in states, like New York, that continue to follow the traditional approach to interpretation. Your editors know of no case that has authorized this option but Professor Fred Miller, the former Executive Director (and current President) of NCCUSL, argues that parties should be free to opt out of the Code in *Writing Your Own Rules: Contracting Out of (and Into) the Uniform Commercial Code; Intrastate Choice of Law*, 40 LOY. L.A. L. REV. 217 (2006).

5. *Avoiding the Operation of the Parol Evidence Rule.* It is generally agreed that the parol evidence rule is limited to prior agreements or contemporaneous oral agreements, and thus does not apply to an agreement made subsequent to the writing. Thus, the parol evidence rule cannot bar evidence of a subsequent modification of the contract. Also, "[t]he parol evidence rule is predicated upon the assumption that the parties have entered into a valid agreement; a party is always permitted to show that no valid agreement was made." Sweet, *Contract Making and Parol Evidence: Diagnosis and Treatment of a Sick Rule*, 53 CORNELL L. REV. 1036, 1039 (1968). Hence, the rule does not bar the admission of evidence of illegality, fraud, duress, mistake, or any other invalidating cause that proves a breakdown in the bargaining process. *See* Restatement (Second) § 214(d); 3 A. Corbin § 580 (2d ed. 1960) (cases cited therein). This is true even if the case is governed by UCC § 2-202, which makes no express provision for the admission of such evidence.

Finally, the parol evidence rule does not bar the admission of evidence to prove that the performance of a contract was subject to an oral condition precedent. *See* 3 A. Corbin § 589 (2d ed. 1960); Restatement (Second) § 217. Comment b to § 217 indicates that the condition may be shown even though it contradicts the writing, under the theory that the writing is not an integrated agreement or that the writing is only partially integrated until the condition occurs. The UCC makes no express provision for oral conditions precedent, and cases have held that evidence of such conditions is admissible even if the contract contains an integration or "merger clause." *See, e.g., Luther Williams, Jr., Inc. v. Johnson*, 229 A.2d 163 (D.C. 1967).[22]

6. *Contemporary Deal Protection Measures.* Other than locking in a favorable price, why might Hunt Foods have negotiated a purchase option with the Doliners? Parties may pursue deal protection measures such as the purchase option in *Hunt Foods* for several reasons:

> The accepted rationale for deal protection measures is to protect a beneficial business transaction from attack by an interloper and, where the primary purpose is unsuccessful, to compensate the unsuccessful party for lost economic and opportunity costs. There are several reasons why potential merger partners would desire the inclusion of deal protection measures. As an initial matter, no company wants to be a stalking horse. There is simply no benefit or utility to an acquirer simply to become the initial bidder, incur significant costs in terms of money and time, and then not be able to consummate the contemplated transaction. In addition to

---

[22] In *Luther Williams*, the company attempted to recover from Mr. Johnson $670.00 as liquidated damages under a contract for home improvements. The contract contained the following clause:

> This contract embodies the entire understanding between the parties, and there are no verbal agreements or representations in connection therewith.

Mr. Johnson claimed that performance of the contract was conditioned on his ability to obtain financing from his bank, and that it was both parties' understanding that Mr. Johnson would not become obligated under the contract until he had procured the funds. The Appeals Court affirmed the lower court's decision to admit the evidence. Since there was nothing in the writing regarding the financing, the evidence did not contradict the terms of the writing and was held admissible.

For an analysis of UCC § 2-202 and the common law exceptions to the parol evidence rule, see Broude, *The Consumer and the Parol Evidence Rule: § 2-202 of the Uniform Commercial Code*, 1970 DUKE L.J. 881, 890–902.

direct costs incurred in this process, there also may be indirect costs. Such indirect costs could include opportunity costs arising from focusing on the potential merger at hand and the costs and risks associated with the public announcement of the proposed merger.

Deal protection measures can aid the consummation of the negotiated transaction in several ways. First, the existence of such measures could discourage other potential business partners from coming forward with a proposal of their own. Second, assuming another party did come forward, such protective measures could make it more difficult procedurally for such bidder to pursue its alternative proposal. Third, these protective measures could also make it more difficult economically for a subsequent offer to succeed.

Gregory V. Varallo & Srinivas M. Raju, *A Process Based Model for Analyzing Deal Protection Measures*, 55 BUS. LAW. 1609, 1611, 1612 (2000).

Today, parties often use measures other than the purchase option in *Hunt Foods* to protect their deals. For example, sophisticated parties may agree to pay termination, or "break-up," fees when a certain condition occurs, such as a party walking away from the bargaining table. This occurred in 2011, when AT&T paid a record $4 billion in break-up fees after negotiations to acquire competitor T-Mobile collapsed. *See* Jenna Wortham, *AT&T in $6.7 Billion Loss on Failure of T-Mobile Deal*, N.Y. TIMES, Jan. 26, 2011, at B2. Another method parties may use to protect their deals is a "no-shop" provision. These clauses typically prevent parties from soliciting offers from third parties, but often allow them to exchange information regarding the deal if third parties approach them first.

C. INTERPRETATION OF THE TERMS OF AN AGREEMENT

We now turn from the problem of identifying the terms of an agreement to the problem of determining the meaning of those terms. To be sure, both the common law and Code parol evidence rules identify the terms of an agreement by determining whether an agreement is integrated and all the tests for integration require courts first to engage in some interpretation.[23] We set out the problem of interpretation separately, however, because it is conceptually distinct from the problem of identifying the terms of the agreement. We first explore the debate between the plain meaning rule and the more liberal contextualism embraced by the Second Restatement. We then examine how this same debate has resurfaced in the cases applying UCC § 2-202. Section 1 begins by presenting three cases applying and debating the common law's interpretive regimes.

---

[23] For example, before a court can determine whether an agreement is integrated, under the "natural omission" test, it must interpret the terms of the writing and the proffered terms to assess whether the parties would have included the proffered terms in the writing. Likewise, it must interpret the terms of the express terms of a writing to determine whether the writing contains an express merger clause.

[1] Plain Meaning and Contextual Meaning in Common Law Interpretation

Consider the following three cases that together frame the debate between textualist and contextualist theories of meaning in contract interpretation.

W.W.W. ASSOCS. v. GIANCONTIERI
Court of Appeals of New York
566 N.E.2d 639 (1990)

Kaye, J.

In this action for specific performance of a contract to sell real property, the issue is whether an unambiguous reciprocal cancellation provision should be read in light of extrinsic evidence, as a contingency clause for the sole benefit of plaintiff purchaser, subject to its unilateral waiver. Applying the principle that clear, complete writings should generally be enforced according to their terms, we reject plaintiff's reading of the contract and dismiss its complaint.

Defendants, owners of a two-acre parcel in Suffolk County, on October 16, 1986 contracted for the sale of the property to plaintiff, a real estate investor and developer. The purchase price was fixed at $750,000–$25,000 payable on contract execution, $225,000 to be paid in cash on closing (to take place "on or about December 1, 1986"), and the $500,000 balance secured by a purchase-money mortgage payable two years later.

The parties signed a printed form Contract of Sale, supplemented by several of their own paragraphs. Two provisions of the contract have particular relevance to the present dispute — a reciprocal cancellation provision (para. 31) and a merger clause (para. 19). Paragraph 31, one of the provisions the parties added to the contract form, reads: "The parties acknowledge that Sellers have been served with process instituting an action concerned with the real property which is the subject of this agreement. In the event the closing of title is delayed by reason of such litigation it is agreed that closing of title will in a like manner be adjourned until after the conclusion of such litigation provided, *in the event such litigation is not concluded, by or before 6–1–87 either party shall have the right to cancel this contract whereupon the down payment shall be returned and there shall be no further rights hereunder.*" (Emphasis supplied.) Paragraph 19 is the form merger provision, reading: "All prior understandings and agreements between *seller* and *purchaser* are merged in this contract [and it] completely expresses their full agreement. It has been entered into after full investigation, neither party relying upon any statements made by anyone else that are not set forth in this contract."

The Contract of Sale, in other paragraphs the parties added to the printed form, provided that the purchaser alone had the unconditional right to cancel the contract within 10 days of signing (para. 32), and that the purchaser alone had the option to cancel if, at closing, the seller was unable to deliver building permits for 50 senior citizen housing units (para. 29).

The contract in fact did not close on December 1, 1986, as originally contemplated. As June 1, 1987 neared, with the litigation still unresolved, plaintiff on May 13 wrote defendants that it was prepared to close and would appear for closing on May 28; plaintiff also instituted the present action for specific performance. On June 2, 1987, defendants canceled the contract and returned the down payment, which plaintiff refused. Defendants thereafter sought summary judgment dismissing the specific performance action, on the ground that the contract gave them the absolute right to cancel.

Plaintiff's claim to specific performance rests upon its recitation of how paragraph 31 originated. Those facts are set forth in the affidavit of plaintiff's vice-president, submitted in opposition to defendants' summary judgment motion.

As plaintiff explains, during contract negotiations it learned that, as a result of unrelated litigation against defendants, a lis pendens had been filed against the property. Although assured by defendants that the suit was meritless, plaintiff anticipated difficulty obtaining a construction loan (including title insurance for the loan) needed to implement its plans to build senior citizen housing units. According to the affidavit, it was therefore agreed that paragraph 31 would be added for plaintiff's sole benefit, as contract vendee. As it developed, plaintiff's fears proved groundless — the lis pendens did not impede its ability to secure construction financing. However, around March 1987, plaintiff claims it learned from the broker on the transaction that one of the defendants had told him they were doing nothing to defend the litigation, awaiting June 2, 1987 to cancel the contract and suggesting the broker might get a higher price.

Defendants made no response to these factual assertions. Rather, its summary judgment motion rested entirely on the language of the Contract of Sale, which it argued was, under the law, determinative of its right to cancel.

The trial court granted defendants' motion and dismissed the complaint, holding that the agreement unambiguously conferred the right to cancel on defendants as well as plaintiff. The Appellate Division, however, reversed and, after searching the record and adopting the facts alleged by plaintiff in its affidavit, granted summary judgment to plaintiff directing specific performance of the contract. We now reverse and dismiss the complaint.

Critical to the success of plaintiff's position is consideration of the extrinsic evidence that paragraph 31 was added to the contract solely for its benefit. The Appellate Division made clear that this evidence was at the heart of its decision: "review of the record reveals that under the circumstances of this case the language of clause 31 was intended to protect the plaintiff from having to purchase the property burdened by a notice of pendency filed as a result of the underlying action which could prevent the plaintiff from obtaining clear title and would impair its ability to obtain subsequent construction financing." 548 N.Y.S.2d 580.) In that a party for whose sole benefit a condition is included in a contract may waive the condition prior to expiration of the time period set forth in the contract and accept the subject property "as is", *Satterly v. Plaisted*, 384 N.Y.S.2d 334, 366 N.E.2d 1362, plaintiff's undisputed factual assertions — if material — would defeat defendants' summary judgment motion.

We conclude, however, that the extrinsic evidence tendered by plaintiff is not material. In its reliance on extrinsic evidence to bring itself within the "party benefited" cases, plaintiff ignores a vital first step in the analysis: before looking to evidence of what was in the parties' minds, a court must give due weight to what was in their contract.

A familiar and eminently sensible proposition of law is that, when parties set down their agreement in a clear, complete document, their writing should as a rule be enforced according to its terms. Evidence outside the four corners of the document as to what was really intended but unstated or misstated is generally inadmissible to add to or vary the writing. That rule imparts "stability to commercial transactions by safeguarding against fraudulent claims, perjury, death of witnesses * * * infirmity of memory * * * [and] the fear that the jury will improperly evaluate the extrinsic evidence." (Fisch, New York Evidence § 42, at 22 [2d ed.].) Such considerations are all the more compelling in the context of real property transactions, where commercial certainty is a paramount concern.

Whether or not a writing is ambiguous is a question of law to be resolved by the courts. In the present case, the contract, read as a whole to determine its purpose and intent plainly manifests the intention that defendants, as well as plaintiff, should have the right to cancel after June 1, 1987 if the litigation had not concluded by that date; and it further plainly manifests the intention that all prior under-standings be merged into the contract, which expresses the parties' full agreement. Moreover, the face of the contract reveals a "logical reason" for the explicit provision that the cancellation right contained in paragraph 31 should run to the seller as well as the purchaser. A seller taking back a purchase-money mortgage for two thirds of the purchase price might well wish to reserve its option to sell the property for cash on an "as is" basis if third-party litigation affecting the property remained unresolved past a certain date.

Thus, we conclude there is no ambiguity as to the cancellation clause in issue, read in the context of the entire agreement, and that it confers a reciprocal right on both parties to the contract.

The question next raised is whether extrinsic evidence should be considered in order to *create* an ambiguity in the agreement. That question must be answered in the negative. It is well settled that "extrinsic and parol evidence is not admissible to create an ambiguity in a written agreement which is complete and clear and unambiguous upon its face." (Intercontinental Planning v. Daystrom, Inc., 24 N.Y.2d 372, 379.)

Plaintiff's rejoinder — that defendants indeed had the specified absolute right to cancel the contract, but it was subject to plaintiff's absolute prior right of waiver — suffers from a logical inconsistency that is evidence in a mere statement of the argument. But there is an even greater problem. Here, sophisticated businessmen reduced their negotiations to a clear, complete writing. In the paragraphs imme-diately surrounding paragraph 31, they expressly bestowed certain options on the purchaser alone, but in paragraph 31 they chose otherwise, explicitly allowing both buyer and seller to cancel in the event the litigation was unresolved by June 1, 1987. By ignoring the plain language of the contract, plaintiff effectively rewrites the bargain that was struck. An analysis that begins with consideration of extrinsic evidence of what the parties meant, instead of looking first to what they said and reaching extrinsic evidence only when required to do so because of some identified ambiguity, unnecessarily denigrates the contract and unsettles the law.

Finally, plaintiff's conclusory assertion of bad faith is supported only by its vice-president's statement that one of the defendants told the broker on the transaction, who then told him, that defendants were doing nothing to defend the action, waiting for June 2 to cancel, and suggesting that the broker might resell the property at a higher price. Where the moving party "has demonstrated its entitlement to summary judgment, the party opposing the motion must demonstrate by admissible evidence the existence of a factual issue requiring a trial of the action or tender an acceptable excuse for his failure so to do." (*Zuckerman v. City of New York*, 49 N.Y.2d 557, 560) Even viewing the burden of a summary judgment opponent more generously than that of the summary judgment proponent, plaintiff fails to raise a triable issue of fact.

Accordingly, the Appellate Division order should be reversed, with costs, defendants' motion for summary judgment granted, and the complaint dismissed.

NOTES

1. ***Plain Meaning and Ambiguity: The "Peerless" Exception.*** In *W.W.W. Associates*, the New York Court of Appeals reaffirmed its long-standing commitment to textualist interpretation in general and to the plain meaning rule in particular. But the court did acknowledge an exception where it found the contract or some of its terms to be ambiguous. But what does it mean to say that the contract is ambiguous? How should courts choose among the alternative meanings of an ambiguous term? The "Peerless" case, *Raffles v. Wichelhaus*, 2 H & C 906, 159 Eng. Rep. 375 (1864), is perhaps the most well-known example of the problem of ambiguity. In that case, the defendant agreed to buy from plaintiff 125 bales of cotton which would arrive from Bombay on a ship named "Peerless." Unfortunately, there were two different ships named "Peerless" that left Bombay carrying cotton. Defendants claimed that the parties had different ships in mind when they entered into the contract. The court agreed, and held that because there was no meeting of the minds, no contract had been formed.

The resolution in *Raffles* is consistent with both a contextualist and a textualist approach to interpretation. The contextualist approach takes as its starting point the assumption that the purpose of interpretation is to determine what the parties collectively and subjectively intended at the time of the contract. Once the court finds that the parties lacked the same subjective intent about the meaning of a term in their agreement, there is no agreement for the court to enforce. An objectivist approach analysis begins with the rule that terms will be given their plain meaning. But here, the term "Peerless" refers to two different ships. The textualist's method of assigning terms in a writing their plain meaning provides no guidance for deciding the ship to which the term refers. Even under the plain meaning rule, then, if a court finds a term of an agreement is ambiguous, it is permitted to admit contextual evidence to resolve the ambiguity. In *Raffles*, the contextual evidence revealed that each party understood the term to refer to a different ship. Hence, in cases of ambiguity, there is often little or no difference in interpretive result under either interpretive regime.

2.   *When Plain Meaning is Clearly Wrong: In re Soper's Estate.* What should a plain meaning court do if it must interpret a term that has an unambiguous plain meaning but which the court believes is at variance with the meaning the parties clearly intended the term to have? Such a case might test the convictions of even the most hard-boiled, dyed-in-the-wool textualists. In *In re Estate of Soper*, 264 N.W. 427 (Minn. 1935), the court confronted just this situation. Ira Soper married Adeline Westphal in 1911 and lived with her until August 1921 when he disappeared. His wife never heard from him again during his remaining years. Ira Soper moved to Minneapolis and assumed the name John W. Young, which he kept until his actual death by suicide in 1932. While in Minneapolis he married Gertrude, with whom he lived until his death. In Minneapolis, Young (Soper) and one Karstens formed the Young Fuel Company. This business invested in a stock and life insurance plan which provided that upon the death of either partner, the Minneapolis Trust Company was to pay the proceeds of the life insurance policy to the deceased's wife. Upon Young's (Soper's) death the Trust Company paid the proceeds to Gertrude as his "wife." Several months later, Mrs. Soper appeared and sued to recover the insurance money.

The court held that, notwithstanding the plain meaning of "wife" as referring to Young's only legal spouse, Mrs. Soper, the proceeds should go to Gertrude:

> The real question presented is whether under the escrow agreement designating the "wife" of depositor Young as the beneficiary parol proof is admissible that Gertrude was so intended and not Mrs. Soper, the true wife. Plaintiffs claim that the written instrument is free from ambiguity, latent or otherwise. They strenuously assert that the agreement is not subject to construction, that it is perfectly plain in its language, and that the only thing for the court to determine is whether Mrs. Soper was the lawful wife of the deceased husband, or if Gertrude was such.

> From the facts and circumstances hereinbefore related, the conclusion seems inescapable that Gertrude was intended. She was the only one known or considered by the contracting parties. . . .All friends and acquaintances knew and recognized her as his wife. There was nothing in Minneapolis or in this state indicating otherwise. Were we to award the insurance fund to plaintiff Adeline, it is obvious that we would thereby be doing violence to the contract entered into by the decedent Young with his associate Mr. Karstens. That agreement points to no one else than Gertrude as Young's "wife." To hold otherwise is to give the word "wife" "a fixed symbol," as "something inherent and objective, not subjective and personal." . . . The question is not just what words mean literally but how they are intended to operate practically on the subject matter. Thus, seemingly plain language becomes susceptible of construction, and frequently requires it, if ambiguity appears when attempt is made to operate the contract. . . . That is the situation here.

In dissent, Justice Olsen wrote: "The contract in this case designates the 'wife' as the one to whom the money was to be paid. I am unable to construe this word to mean anyone else than the only wife of Soper then living." On the one hand, Justice Olsen presents a powerful plain meaning critique of the majority's contextualist approach. After all, the term "wife" seems to have about as clear and unambiguous a plain meaning as any term. Among professional philosophers of language, the paradigm example of a term with a clear and unambiguous plain meaning is "bachelor." No one, it is routinely asserted, can deny that "bachelor" means an unmarried man. If it is possible, the meaning of "wife" seems even less assailable than the meaning of "bachelor." The term "wife" is defined by the laws of marriage and is therefore immune from confusion or informal change. Like the term "bachelor," its meaning can be discovered easily by examining any English dictionary.

On the other hand, the majority's opinion presents perhaps the most powerful challenge to a plain meaning regime. Although the plain meaning of the term "wife" is clear and unambiguous, it is equally clear that Mr. Soper and Mr. Karstens actually intended the term "wife" in their escrow agreement to refer to Gertrude Young, not Mr. Soper's wife, Adeline. As the majority argues, if the goal of contractual interpretation is "to ascertain the intention of the parties themselves," then indeed, "[it] would sacrifice rationalism to that 'primitive formalism which views the document as a self-contained and self-operative formula,' rather than an instrument the whole of which is in relation to extrinsic matter."

Is there a coherent rationale for ignoring the parties' clear intent when they use terms with a meaning at variance with their unambiguous plain meaning? Could you argue that by vindicating the actual intent of the parties, the majority diminishes the autonomy of all contractors who subsequently use the term "wife" to refer to the woman to whom they are legally married?

2. *Public Policy and Interpretation.* In light of the strong public policy arguments for strengthening the institution of marriage, and against adultery and spousal abandonment, could you argue that the court in *In re Soper's Estate* should have given the term "wife" its plain meaning? Wouldn't such a ruling simultaneously protect Adeline Soper's financial interests and thwart Ira Soper's efforts to preserve his fraudulent marriage to Gertrude? Or should the principles of contractual interpretation be insulated from the objectives of other substantive public policies?

PACIFIC GAS & ELECTRIC CO. v. G.W. THOMAS DRAYAGE & RIGGING CO.
Supreme Court of California
69 Cal. 2d 33, 69 Cal. Rptr. 561, 442 P.2d 641 (1968)

TRAYNOR, J.

Defendant appeals from a judgment for plaintiff in an action for damages for injury to property under an indemnity clause of a contract.

In 1960 defendant entered into a contract with plaintiff to furnish the labor and equipment necessary to remove and replace the upper metal cover of plaintiff's steam turbine. Defendant agreed to perform the work "at (its) own risk and expense" and to "indemnify" plaintiff "against all loss, damage, expense and liability resulting from . . . injury to property, arising out of or in any way connected with the performance of this contract." Defendant also agreed to procure not less than

$50,000 insurance to cover liability for injury to property. Plaintiff was to be an additional named insured, but the policy was to contain a cross-liability clause extending the coverage to plaintiff's property.

During the work the cover fell and injured the exposed rotor of the turbine. Plaintiff brought this action to recover $25,144.51, the amount it subsequently spent on repairs. During the trial it dismissed a count based on negligence and thereafter secured judgment on the theory that the indemnity provision covered injury to all property regardless of ownership.

Defendant offered to prove by admissions of plaintiff's agents, by defendant's conduct under similar contracts entered into with plaintiff, and by other proof that in the indemnity clause the parties meant to cover injury to property of third parties only and not to plaintiff's property. Although the trial court observed that the language used was "the classic language for a third party indemnity provision" and that "one could very easily conclude that . . . its whole intendment is to indemnify third parties," it nevertheless held that the "plain language" of the agreement also required defendant to indemnify plaintiff for injuries to plaintiff's property. Having determined that the contract had a plain meaning, the court refused to admit any extrinsic evidence that would contradict its interpretation.

When a court interprets a contract on this basis, it determines the meaning of the instrument in accordance with the ". . . extrinsic evidence of the judge's own linguistic education and experience." (3 *Corbin on Contracts* (1960 ed.) (1964 Supp. § 579, p. 225, fn. 56).) The exclusion of testimony that might contradict the linguistic background of the judge reflects a judicial belief in the possibility of perfect verbal expression. This belief is a remnant of a primitive faith in the inherent potency and inherent meaning of words.

The test of admissibility of extrinsic evidence to explain the meaning of a written instrument is not whether it appears to the court to be plain and unambiguous on its face, but whether the offered evidence is relevant to prove a meaning to which the language of the instrument is reasonably susceptible.

A rule that would limit the determination of the meaning of a written instrument to its four-corners merely because it seems to the court to be clear and unambiguous, would either deny the relevance of the intention of the parties or presuppose a degree of verbal precision and stability our language has not attained.

Some courts have expressed the opinion that contractual obligations are created by the mere use of certain words, whether or not there was any intention to incur such obligations.[24] Under this view, contractual obligations flow, not from the intention of the parties but from the fact that they used certain magic words. Evidence of the parties' intention therefore becomes irrelevant.

In this state, however, the intention of the parties as expressed in the contract is the source of contractual rights and duties. A court must ascertain and give effect to this intention by determining what the parties meant by the words they used.

---

[24] [4] "A contract has, strictly speaking, nothing to do with the personal, or individual, intent of the parties. A contract is an obligation attached by the mere force of law to certain acts of the parties, usually words, which ordinarily accompany and represent a known intent."

Accordingly, the exclusion of relevant, extrinsic evidence to explain the meaning of a written instrument could be justified only if it were feasible to determine the meaning the parties gave to the words from the instrument alone.

If words had absolute and constant referents, it might be possible to discover contractual intention in the words themselves and in the manner in which they were arranged. Words, however, do not have absolute and constant referents. "A word is a symbol of thought but has no arbitrary and fixed meaning like a symbol of algebra or chemistry. . . ." (Pearson v. State Social Welfare Board (1960) 54 Cal. 2d 184, 195). The meaning of particular words or groups of words varies with the ". . . verbal context and surrounding circumstances and purposes in view of the linguistic education and experience of their users and their hearers or readers (not excluding judges). . . . A word has no meaning apart from these factors; much less does it have an objective meaning, one true meaning." (Corbin, The Interpretation of Words and the Parol Evidence Rule (1965) 50 Cornell L.Q. 161, 187.) Accordingly, the meaning of a writing ". . . can only be found by interpretation in the light of all the circumstances that reveal the sense in which the writer used the words. The exclusion of parol evidence regarding such circumstances merely because the words do not appear ambiguous to the reader can easily lead to the attribution to a written instrument of a meaning that was never intended.

Although extrinsic evidence is not admissible to add to, detract from, or vary the terms of a written contract, these terms must first be determined before it can be decided whether or not extrinsic evidence is being offered for a prohibited purpose. The fact that the terms of an instrument appear clear to a judge does not preclude the possibility that the parties chose the language of the instrument to express different terms. That possibility is not limited to contracts whose terms have acquired a particular meaning by trade usage,[25] but exists whenever the parties' understanding of the words used may have differed from the judge's understanding.

Accordingly, rational interpretation requires at least a preliminary consideration of all credible evidence offered to prove the intention of the parties.[26] Such evidence includes testimony as to the "circumstances surrounding the making of the agreement . . . including the object, nature and subject matter of the writing . . ."

---

[25] [6] Extrinsic evidence of trade usage or custom has been admitted to show that the term "United Kingdom" in a motion picture distribution contract included Ireland (Ermolieff v. R.K.O. Radio Pictures (1942) 19 Cal. 2d 543, 549-552, 122 P.2d 3); that the word "ton" in a lease meant a long ton or 2,240 pounds and not the statutory ton of 2,000 pounds (Higgins v. Cal. Petroleum, etc., Co. (1898) 120 Cal. 629, 630-632, 52 P. 1080); that the word "stubble" in a lease included not only stumps left in the ground but everything "left on the ground after the harvest time" (Callahan v. Stanley (1881) 57 Cal. 476, 477-479); that the term "north" in a contract dividing mining claims indicated a boundary line running along the "magnetic and not the true meridian" (Jenny Lind Co. v. Bower & Co. (1858) 11 Cal. 194, 197-199) and that a form contract for purchase and sale was actually an agency contract (Body-Steffner Co. v. Flotill Products (1944) 63 Cal. App. 2d 555, 558-562, 147 P.2d 84).

[26] [7] When objection is made to any particular item of evidence offered to prove the intention of the parties, the trial court may not yet be in a position to determine whether in the light of all of the offered evidence, the item objected to will turn out to be admissible as tending to prove a meaning of which the language of the instrument is reasonably susceptible or inadmissible as tending to prove a meaning of which the language is not reasonably susceptible. In such case the court may admit the evidence conditionally by either reserving its ruling on the objection or by admitting the evidence subject to a motion to strike. (See Evid. Code, § 403.)

so that the court can "place itself in the same situation in which the parties found themselves at the time of contracting." If the court decides, after considering this evidence, that the language of a contract, in the light of all the circumstances, is "fairly susceptible of either one of the two interpretations contended for . . ." extrinsic evidence relevant to prove either of such meanings is admissible.[27]

In the present case the court erroneously refused to consider extrinsic evidence offered to show that the indemnity clause in the contract was not intended to cover injuries to plaintiff's property. Although that evidence was not necessary to show that the indemnity clause was reasonably susceptible of the meaning contended for by defendant, it was nevertheless relevant and admissible on that issue. Moreover, since that clause was reasonably susceptible of that meaning, the offered evidence was also admissible to prove that the clause had that meaning and did not cover injuries to plaintiff's property.[28]

Accordingly, the judgment must be reversed.

TRIDENT CTR. v. CONNECTICUT GEN. LIFE INS. CO.
United States Court of Appeals, Ninth Circuit
847 F.2d 564 (1988)

KOZINSKI, J.

The parties to this transaction are, by any standard, highly sophisticated business people: Plaintiff is a partnership consisting of an insurance company and two of Los Angeles' largest and most prestigious law firms; defendant is another

---

[27] [8] Extrinsic evidence has often been admitted in such cases on the stated ground that the contract was ambiguous. This statement of the rule is harmless if it is kept in mind that the ambiguity may be exposed by extrinsic evidence that reveals more than one possible meaning.

[28] [9] The court's exclusion of extrinsic evidence in this case would be error even under a rule that excluded such evidence when the instrument appeared to the court to be clear and unambiguous on its face. The controversy centers on the meaning of the word "indemnify" and the phrase "all loss, damage, expense and liability." The trial court's recognition of the language as typical of a third party indemnity clause and the double sense in which the word "indemnify" is used in statutes and defined in dictionaries demonstrate the existence of an ambiguity. (Compare Civ. Code, § 2772, "Indemnity is a contract by which one engages to save another from a legal consequence of the conduct of one of the parties, or of some other person," with Civ. Code, § 2527, "Insurance is a contract whereby one undertakes to indemnify another against loss, damage, or liability, arising from an unknown or contingent event.")

Plaintiff's assertion that the use of the word "all" to modify "loss, damage, expense and liability" dictates an all inclusive interpretation is not persuasive. If the word "indemnify" encompasses only third-party claims, the word "all" simply refers to all such claims. The use of the words "loss," "damage," and "expense" in addition to the word "liability" is likewise inconclusive. These words do not imply an agreement to reimburse for injury to an indemnitee's property since they are commonly inserted in third-party indemnity clauses, to enable an indemnitee who settles a claim to recover from his indemnitor without proving his liability. The provision that defendant perform the work "at his own risk and expense" and the provisions relating to insurance are equally inconclusive. By agreeing to work at its own risk defendant may have released plaintiff from liability for any injuries to defendant's property arising out of the contract's performance, but this provision did not necessarily make defendant an insurer against injuries to plaintiff's property. Defendant's agreement to procure liability insurance to cover damages to plaintiff's property does not indicate whether the insurance was to cover all injuries or only injuries caused by defendant's negligence.

insurance company. Dealing at arm's length and from positions of roughly equal bargaining strength, they negotiated a commercial loan amounting to more than $56 million. The contract documents are lengthy and detailed; they squarely address the precise issue that is the subject of this dispute; to all who read English, they appear to resolve the issue fully and conclusively.

Plaintiff nevertheless argues here, as it did below, that it is entitled to introduce extrinsic evidence that the contract means something other than what it says. This case therefore presents the question whether parties in California can ever draft a contract that is proof to parol evidence. Somewhat surprisingly, the answer is no.

The facts are rather simple. Sometime in 1983 Security First Life Insurance Company and the law firms of Mitchell, Silberberg & Knupp and Manatt, Phelps, Rothenberg & Tunney formed a limited partnership for the purpose of constructing an office building complex on Olympic Boulevard in West Los Angeles. The partnership, Trident Center, the plaintiff herein, sought and obtained financing for the project from defendant, Connecticut General Life Insurance Company. The loan documents provide for a loan of $56,500,000 at 1214 percent interest for a term of 15 years, secured by a deed of trust on the project. The promissory note provides that "[m]aker shall not have the right to prepay the principal amount hereof in whole or in part" for the first 12 years. In years 13-15, the loan may be prepaid, subject to a sliding prepayment fee. The note also provides that in case of a default during years 1-12, Connecticut General has the option of accelerating the note and adding a 10 percent prepayment fee.

Everything was copacetic for a few years until interest rates began to drop. The 1214 percent rate that had seemed reasonable in 1983 compared unfavorably with 1987 market rates and Trident started looking for ways of refinancing the loan to take advantage of the lower rates. Connecticut General was unwilling to oblige, insisting that the loan could not be prepaid for the first 12 years of its life, that is, until January 1996.

Trident then brought suit in state court seeking a declaration that it was entitled to prepay the loan now, subject only to a 10 percent prepayment fee. Connecticut General promptly removed to federal court and brought a motion to dismiss, claiming that the loan documents clearly and unambiguously precluded prepayment during the first 12 years. The district court agreed and dismissed Trident's complaint. The court also "*sua sponte*, sanction[ed] the plaintiff for the filing of a frivolous lawsuit."

Trident makes two arguments as to why the district court's ruling is wrong. First, it contends that the language of the contract is ambiguous and proffers a construction that it believes supports its position. Second, Trident argues that, under California law, even seemingly unambiguous contracts are subject to modification by parol or extrinsic evidence. Trident faults the district court for denying it the opportunity to present evidence that the contract language did not accurately reflect the parties' intentions.

As noted earlier, the promissory note provides that Trident "shall not have the right to prepay the principal amount hereof in whole or in part before January 1996." It is difficult to imagine language that more clearly or unambiguously expresses the idea that Trident may not unilaterally prepay the loan during its first 12 years. Trident, however, argues that there is an ambiguity because another clause of the note provides that "[i]n the event of a prepayment resulting from a default hereunder or the Deed of Trust prior to January 10, 1996 the prepayment fee will be ten percent (10%)." Trident interprets this clause as giving it the option of prepaying the loan if only it is willing to incur the prepayment fee.

We reject Trident's argument out of hand. In the first place, its proffered interpretation would result in a contradiction between two clauses of the contract; the default clause would swallow up the clause prohibiting Trident from prepaying during the first 12 years of the contract. The normal rule of construction, of course, is that courts must interpret contracts, if possible, so as to avoid internal conflict.

In any event, the clause on which Trident relies is not on its face reasonably susceptible to Trident's proffered interpretation. Whether to accelerate repayment of the loan in the event of default is entirely Connecticut General's decision. The contract makes this clear at several points: "in each such event [of default], the entire principal indebtedness, or so much thereof as may remain unpaid at the time, shall, *at the option of Holder*, become due and payable immediately" (emphasis added); "[i]n the event Holder exercises its *option to accelerate* the maturity hereof . . ." (emphasis added); "in each such event [of default], beneficiary *may* declare all sums secured hereby immediately due and payable. . . ." Even if Connecticut General decides to declare a default and accelerate, it "may rescind any notice of breach or default."

Finally, Connecticut General has the option of doing nothing at all: "Beneficiary reserves the right at its sole option to waive noncompliance by Trustor with any of the conditions or covenants to be performed by Trustor hereunder."

Once again, it is difficult to imagine language that could more clearly assign to Connecticut General the exclusive right to decide whether to declare a default, whether and when to accelerate, and whether, having chosen to take advantage of any of its remedies, to rescind the process before its completion. . . .

Trident argues in the alternative that, even if the language of the contract appears to be unambiguous, the deal the parties actually struck is in fact quite different. It wishes to offer extrinsic evidence that the parties had agreed Trident could prepay at any time within the first 12 years by tendering the full amount plus a 10 percent prepayment fee. As discussed above, this is an interpretation to which the contract, as written, is not reasonably susceptible. Under traditional contract principles, extrinsic evidence is inadmissible to interpret, vary or add to the terms of an unambiguous integrated written instrument.

Trident points out, however, that California does not follow the traditional rule. Two decades ago the California Supreme Court in Pacific Gas & Electric Co. v. G.W. Thomas Drayage & Rigging Co., 69 Cal. 2d 33, 69 Cal. Rptr. 561, 442 P.2d 641 (1968), turned its back on the notion that a contract can ever have a plain meaning discernible by a court without resort to extrinsic evidence. The court reasoned that contractual obligations flow not from the words of the contract, but from the intention of the parties. . . .

Under *Pacific Gas*, it matters not how clearly a contract is written, nor how completely it is integrated, nor how carefully it is negotiated, nor how squarely it addresses the issue before the court: the contract cannot be rendered impervious to attack by parol evidence. If one side is willing to claim that the parties intended one thing but the agreement provides for another, the court must consider extrinsic evidence of possible ambiguity. If that evidence raises the specter of ambiguity where there was none before, the contract language is displaced and the intention of the parties must be divined from self-serving testimony offered by partisan witnesses whose recollection is hazy from passage of time and colored by their conflicting interests. We question whether this approach is more likely to divulge the original intention of the parties than reliance on the seemingly clear words they agreed upon at the time.

Pacific Gas casts a long shadow of uncertainty over all transactions negotiated and executed under the law of California. As this case illustrates, even when the transaction is very sizeable, even if it involves only sophisticated parties, even if it was negotiated with the aid of counsel, even if it results in contract language that is devoid of ambiguity, costly and protracted litigation cannot be avoided if one party has a strong enough motive for challenging the contract. While this rule creates much business for lawyers and an occasional windfall to some clients, it leads only to frustration and delay for most litigants and clogs already overburdened courts.

It also chips away at the foundation of our legal system. By giving credence to the idea that words are inadequate to express concepts, *Pacific Gas* undermines the basic principle that language provides a meaningful constraint on public and private conduct. If we are unwilling to say that parties, dealing face to face, can come up with language that binds them, how can we send anyone to jail for violating statutes consisting of mere words lacking "absolute and constant referents"? How can courts ever enforce decrees, not written in language understandable to all, but encoded in a dialect reflecting only the "linguistic background of the judge"? Can lower courts ever be faulted for failing to carry out the mandate of higher courts when "perfect verbal expression" is impossible? Are all attempts to develop the law in a reasoned and principled fashion doomed to failure as "remnant[s] of a primitive faith in the inherent potency and inherent meaning of words"?

Be that as it may. While we have our doubts about the wisdom of *Pacific Gas*, we have no difficulty understanding its meaning, even without extrinsic evidence to guide us. As we read the rule in California, we must reverse and remand to the district court in order to give plaintiff an opportunity to present extrinsic evidence as to the intention of the parties in drafting the contract. It may not be a wise rule we are applying, but it is a rule that binds us. Erie R.R. Co. v. Tompkins, 304 U.S. 64, 78 (1938).

NOTES

1. ***Questions on* Pacific Gas & Electric.** For purposes of interpreting the parties' agreement in *Pacific Gas & Electric*, does it matter whether their agreement is integrated? Justice Traynor appears to presuppose that it is integrated, but argues that integration has no implication for interpretation: "Although extrinsic evidence is not admissible to add to, detract from, or vary the terms of a

written contract, these terms must first be determined before it can be decided whether or not extrinsic evidence is being offered for a prohibited purpose." If integration identifies the terms of an agreement, but provides no constraints on the interpretation of the meaning of those terms, what purpose does it serve?

Justice Traynor also states that the "test for admissibility of extrinsic evidence to explain the meaning of a written instrument is not whether it appears to the court to be plain and unambiguous on its face, but whether the offered evidence is relevant to prove a meaning to which the language of the instrument is reasonably susceptible." Justice Traynor thus believes judges should be prohibited from relying on their own view of whether a term's meaning is plain and unambiguous on its face. Yet he would require courts to determine whether a particular term is "reasonably susceptible" to an alleged meaning. What basis could a court use to judge whether a term is reasonably susceptible to a given meaning other than whether that meaning would be inconsistent with court's view of the plain and unambiguous meaning of the term? How is a court supposed to tell the difference between those meanings to which a term is reasonably susceptible and those to which it is not?

2.   *Questions on* Trident Center. The parties' agreement in *Trident Center* stated that "in the event of a prepayment resulting from a default . . . the prepayment fee will be ten percent (10%)." Trident argued that this clause gave it the right to prepay the principal if it paid a 10 percent prepayment fee. Judge Kozinski argues that Trident's interpretation of that clause contradicts the plain meaning of the clause providing that "maker shall not have the right to prepay the principal amount hereof in whole or in part." Couldn't the point be put the other way around? Doesn't the clause apparently barring prepayment contradict the plain meaning of the clause specifying that Trident must pay a ten percent prepayment fee if it prepays the principal? Judge Kozinski buttresses his argument by examining other clauses in the writing that grant Connecticut General the right to decide whether and when to declare a default, to accelerate the loan, and to reverse its decision to declare a default or accelerate the loan. These clauses, he argues, confirm his view that Trident's interpretation is inconsistent with the plain meaning of the clause denying Trident the right to prepay. Although Judge Kozinksi's argument is based on evidence within "the four corners" of the writing, his interpretation of the clause denying Trident the right to prepay takes into account the context of the writing as a whole. If the meaning of one clause in a writing cannot be made plain without taking into account the context of the remaining clauses in the writing, isn't it possible that the meaning of the whole writing can't be properly interpreted without taking into account the whole context in which the writing was made?

Why did Judge Kozinski dispute the validity of Trident's claim and criticize *Pacific Gas and Electric* at length, only to hold that *Pacific Gas and Electric* bound him to rule in Trident's favor? What are the legitimate purposes judges can pursue in the course of writing their opinions?

4.   *"New Textualism" and Statutory Interpretation.* As the new textualist or formalist approach to contract interpretation grew in the 2000s, a similar movement gained momentum among legal scholars focused on statutory interpretation. New textualism, whose foremost advocate is Justice Antonin Scalia, requires the reviewing court to reject statutory interpretation based on parol evidence, such as legislative history, pushing instead a "four-corners" approach to understanding the purpose and meaning of a statute. New textualists argue that permitting the judiciary to employ extrinsic evidence, including committee hearings and legislative reports, will allow an unhealthy degree of judicial discretion, and facilitate decisions based on the judge's own policy preferences.

Consider the response of Professors Stephen F. Ross & Daniel Tranen, *The Modern Parol Evidence Rule and Its Implications for New Textualist Statutory Interpretation*, 87 GEO. L.J. 195, 217–20 (1998):

> The most obvious problem with the New Textualist approach to statutory construction is that in many cases textual context provides insufficient insight to enable the legal community to reach a consensus on the proper interpretation of a statute. Language is almost always open to interpretation. This is particularly true in Supreme Court cases, because challenges to statutes with a widely agreed upon meaning are usually resolved before they reach that level. As a result, reliance upon the dictionary definition of words (many of which have multiple and often very different meanings) or interpretive canons is an inadequate substitute for the type of context that can be provided by outside sources. . . .

> Most significantly, while New Textualists claim that reliance on legislative history allows judges to engage in policymaking, the use of "judicial common sense" in determining plain meaning also allows considerable judicial subjectivity. While New Textualists complain that legislative history contains so much information that judges can willfully select those portions that support the result they otherwise prefer, the textual quiver also contains a plethora of sources to choose from. When left only with the text, without benefit of the legislative history to provide context, judges are forced to supply their own context instead.

How do the arguments above apply to the textualist approach to contract interpretation Does the preceding analysis actually support the argument advanced by the new textualist contract scholars that the rules of contract interpretation should not be mandatory but rather should be defaults? Under this view, the state would choose interpretive rules that conform to majoritarian party preferences and permit individual parties to opt out. Would it be wise, therefore, to have different interpretive rules for sophisticated parties and for contracts with consumers? In answering this question, does it matter that textualist interpretation of commercial contracts serves the function of permitting sophisticated parties to limit the expected costs of litigation by having their interpretation disputes resolved by summary judgment, while consumer protection doesn't have the same cost concerns?

5. *A Reply to Judge Kozinski.* In *Trident*, Judge Kozinski asserted that California had abandoned the parol evidence rule, which he felt was a dangerous and irrational decision. In *Yes, Judge Kozinski, There Is a Parol Evidence Rule in California — The Lessons of a Pyrrhic Victory*, 25 SW. U. L. REV. 1 (1995), Professor Susan Martin-Davidson questions both of these propositions. She examined a number of California cases that raised the issue of admissibility of extrinsic

evidence between 1983 and 1993. Her case study indicated that California courts continued to use the parol evidence rule to reject extrinsic evidence, though disagreement over the proper test and circumstances for rejecting proffered evidence caused these cases to suffer a disproportionate number of reversals on appeal. In fact, Martin-Davidson's analysis demonstrated that parol evidence jurisprudence in California represented one of the most confused and incoherent areas of law in the state:

> The cases in the study did not confirm the accusation that California has abandoned the parol evidence rule. On the other hand, neither did they suggest that the rule is alive and well. Instead, they supported a different accusation: that the parol evidence rule persists in California like a neomort maintained on permanent life-support as a ready source of transplant organs. The many standard but incompatible formulations of the parol evidence rule are ready as needed in this ongoing and inconclusive battle. One faction is fighting in defense of the written word while its many enemies insist that a written agreement is not "all they wrote."

Id. at 9.

Second, Martin-Davidson questioned Kozinski's assertion that abandonment of the parol evidence rule could wreak havoc with contract jurisprudence. She concluded that California's compromise on the rule was responsible for the confused nature of extrinsic evidence litigation, and that the state should completely reject the rule on the grounds that the rule was unnecessary and ineffective as a means of guarding against fraud and perjury. Do you agree with Professor Martin-Davidson's critique of the parol evidence rule? Does the parol evidence rule presume that one party is likely to be more honest than the other? Are there other reasons for preferring written agreements to oral evidence?

6.   *Value-Maximizing in the Choice Between a "Hard" or "Soft" Parol Evidence Rule.* In *The Parol Evidence Rule, the Plain Meaning Rule, and the Principles of Contractual Interpretation*, 146 U. PA. L. REV. 533 (1998), Professor Eric Posner argues that the optimal approach to contractual interpretation would direct courts to adopt a relatively conservative approach in some cases, and a more liberal approach in others. Professor Posner distinguishes two polar positions from the numerous and varied formulations of the parol evidence rule (PER). Under "hard-PER," "the court generally excludes extrinsic evidence and relies entirely on the writing. Under the 'soft-PER,' the court gives weight both to the writing and to the extrinsic evidence." *Id.* at 534. Posner then describes a value-maximizing approach for courts that he believes should be used by courts when attempting to choose between hard or soft-PER.

First, Posner contends that courts, when faced with an omitted or ambiguous contractual term, should attempt to deduce two factors when deciding whether to use hard- or soft-PER. The first factor is the transaction cost of either including the additional term or describing with specificity the ambiguous term. If the transaction cost for the parties of conducting additional negotiations over this addition or specification was high, then the parties could reasonably have neglected to conduct the additional negotiations though they might still want that extrinsic term or meaning enforced; therefore, soft-PER should be used by the court. However, if the transaction cost to the parties was low, then their failure to include the additional term, or elaborate on the ambiguous term, signals to the court that the parties decided not to make that extrinsic term or meaning enforceable; otherwise, the parties would have included it in their written agreement. In these situations, hard-PER should be used by the court.

The second factor for courts to consider when deciding on a hard- or soft-PER is the parties' estimation of possible judicial error when litigating the contract. If the parties believed when negotiating the contract that judicial error was likely in litigation, then courts should employ a hard-PER since the parties probably attempted to spell out as many terms as possible in the written agreement and would be afraid of mistake should the court consider extrinsic evidence. However, if the parties thought error was unlikely in adjudication, then courts should employ a soft-PER because negotiating parties would be less likely to specify every essential term in a written document.

Posner continues by positing certain characteristics that would help a court assess whether the contract before it entailed high transaction costs and whether the parties at bar would have foreseen a high probability of judicial error. He writes that:

> transaction costs . . . are likely to be high when the parties are unsophisticated or the contract is complex. Unsophisticated parties face high transaction costs because they cannot draw upon experience in order to allocate terms among writings and because they may not know the law. Parties to complex contracts face high transaction costs because they must remember to put a large number of terms into a writing. [T]he probability of judicial error . . . is likely to be high when the contract is unconventional, because courts do a better job of enforcing terms they have seen before than terms they have not.

Id. at 553.

Thus, Posner sets up a relatively simple methodology for courts to employ when deciding whether to use a hard- or soft-PER in disputes over the admissibility of extrinsic evidence. If the parties to a contract are unsophisticated, or if their contract is complex, then soft-PER should be used since it was reasonable for the parties not to have included additional terms but still expect them to be enforced. If the contract is unconventional, the court should employ hard-PER since the probability of judicial error increases when the contract at bar is unusual. Do you think that this categorization is a workable solution to the tension between contextualist and formalist interpretations?

[2]   Interpreting Ambiguous Contracts; The Importance of the Burden of Proof

FRIGALIMENT IMPORTING CO. v. B. N. S. INTERNATIONAL SALES CORP.

United States District Court, Southern District of New York
190 F. Supp. 116 (1960)

[The plaintiff contracted to purchase 100,000 pounds of fresh frozen chicken from the defendant. The contract called for : US Fresh Frozen Chicken, Grade A, Government Inspected, Eviscerated 2 1/2-3 lbs. and 1 1/2-2 lbs. each all chicken individually wrapped in cryovac, packed in secured fiber cartons or wooden boxes, suitable for export

75,000 lbs. 2 1/2-3 lbs . . . . @$33.00

25,000 lbs. 1 1/2-2 lbs . . . . @$36.50

When the shipment arrived, the plaintiff found that the birds were not the higher grade young chickens suitable for broiling or frying, as it had expected, but rather lower grade stewing chicken or "fowl." The plaintiff sued the defendant for breach on the ground that "chicken" meant "broiler chicken" under widely accepted trade usage. The defendant argued that the term "chicken" as it appeared in the contract included all types of chicken.]

FRIENDLY, J.

The issue is, what is chicken? Plaintiff says "chicken" means a young chicken, suitable for broiling and frying. Defendant says "chicken" means any bird of that genus that meets contract specifications on weight and quality, including what it calls "stewing chicken" and plaintiff pejoratively terms "fowl." Dictionaries give both meanings, as well as some others not relevant here. To support its, plaintiff sends a number of volleys over the net; defendant essays to return them and adds a few serves of its own. Assuming that both parties were acting in good faith, the case nicely illustrates Holmes' remark "that the making of a contract depends not on the agreement of two minds in one intention, but on the agreement of two sets of external signs- not on the parties' having meant the same thing but on their having said the same thing." The Path of the Law, in Collected Legal Papers, p. 178. I have concluded that plaintiff has not sustained its burden of persuasion that the contract used "chicken" in the narrower sense.

. . . .

Since the word "chicken" standing alone is ambiguous, I turn first to see whether the contract itself offers any aid to its interpretation. Plaintiff says the 1 1/2-2 lbs. birds necessarily had to be young chicken since the older birds do not come in that size, hence the 2 1/2-3 lbs. birds must likewise be young. This is unpersuasive- a contract for 'apples' of two different sizes could be filled with different kinds of apples even though only one species came in both sizes. Defendant notes that the contract called not simply for chicken but for "US Fresh Frozen Chicken, Grade A,

Government Inspected." It says the contract thereby incorporated by reference the Department of Agriculture's regulations, which favor its interpretation; I shall return to this after reviewing plaintiff's other contentions.

The first hinges on an exchange of cablegrams which preceded execution of the formal contracts. The negotiations leading up to the contracts were conducted in New York between defendant's secretary, Ernest R. Bauer, and a Mr. Stovicek, who was in New York for the Czechoslovak government at the World Trade Fair. A few days after meeting Bauer at the fair, Stovicek telephoned and inquired whether defendant would be interested in exporting poultry to Switzerland. Bauer then met with Stovicek, who showed him a cable from plaintiff dated April 26, 1957, announcing that they 'are buyer' of 25,000 lbs. of chicken 2 1/2-3 lbs. weight, Cryovac packed, grade A Government inspected, at a price up to 33¢ per pound, for shipment on May 10, to be confirmed by the following morning, and were interested in further offerings. After testing the market for price, Bauer accepted, and Stovicek sent a confirmation that evening. Plaintiff stresses that, although these and subsequent cables between plaintiff and defendant, which laid the basis for the additional quantities under the first and for all of the second contract, were predominantly in German, they used the English word "chicken"; it claims this was done because it understood "chicken" meant young chicken whereas the German word, "Huhn," included both "Brathuhn" (broilers) and "Suppenhuhn" (stewing chicken), and that defendant, whose officers were thoroughly conversant with German, should have realized this. Whatever force this argument might otherwise have is largely drained away by Bauer's testimony that he asked Stovicek what kind of chickens were wanted, received the answer "any kind of chickens," and then, in German, asked whether the cable meant "Huhn" and received an affirmative response. . . .

Plaintiff's next contention is that there was a definite trade usage that "chicken" meant "young chicken." Defendant showed that it was only beginning in the poultry trade in 1957, thereby bringing itself within the principle that "when one of the parties is not a member of the trade or other circle, his acceptance of the standard must be made to appear" by proving either that he had actual knowledge of the usage or that the usage is 'so generally known in the community that his actual individual knowledge of it may be inferred.' 9 Wigmore, Evidence (3d ed. § 1940) 2464. Here there was no proof of actual knowledge of the alleged usage; indeed, it is quite plain that defendant's belief was to the contrary. In order to meet the alternative requirement, the law of New York demands a showing that "the usage is of so long continuance, so well established, so notorious, so universal and so reasonable in itself, as that the presumption is violent that the parties contracted with reference to it, and made it a part of their agreement." Walls v. Bailey, 1872, 49 N.Y. 464, 472-473.

Plaintiff endeavored to establish such a usage by the testimony of three witnesses and certain other evidence.. . . . In addition to this opinion testimony, plaintiff relied on the fact that the Urner-Barry service, the Journal of Commerce, and Weinberg Bros. & Co. of Chicago, a large supplier of poultry, published quotations in a manner which, in one way or another, distinguish between "chicken," comprising broilers, fryers and certain other categories, and "fowl," which, Bauer acknowledged, included stewing chickens. This material would be impressive if there were nothing to the contrary. However, there was, as will now be seen.

Defendant's witness Weininger, who operates a chicken eviscerating plant in New Jersey, testified "Chicken is everything except a goose, a duck, and a turkey. Everything is a chicken, but then you have to say, you have to specify which category you want or that you are talking about." Its witness Fox said that in the trade "chicken" would encompass all the various classifications. Sadina, who conducts a food inspection service, testified that he would consider any bird coming within the classes of "chicken" in the Department of Agriculture's regulations to be a chicken. The specifications approved by the General Services Administration include fowl as well as broilers and fryers under the classification "chickens." Statistics of the Institute of American Poultry Industries use the phrases "Young chickens" and "Mature chickens," under the general heading "Total chickens." and the Department of Agriculture's daily and weekly price reports avoid use of the word "chicken" without specification.

Defendant advances several other points which it claims affirmatively support its construction. Primary among these is the regulation of the Department of Agriculture, 7 C.F.R. § 70.300-70.370, entitled, "Grading and Inspection of Poultry and Edible Products Thereof." and in particular 70.301 which recited: 'Chickens. The following are the various classes of chickens: (a) Broiler or fryer. ., (b) Roaster . . . , (c) Capon . . . , d) Stag . . . , (e) Hen or stewing chicken or fowl . . . , f) Cock or old rooster. . . . Defendant argues, as previously noted, that the contract incorporated these regulations by reference. Plaintiff answers that the contract provision related simply to grade and Government inspection and did not incorporate the Government definition of "chicken," and also that the definition in the Regulations is ignored in the trade. However, the latter contention was contradicted by Weininger and Sadina; and there is force in defendant's argument that the contract made the regulations a dictionary . . .

Defendant makes a further argument based on the impossibility of its obtaining broilers and fryers at the 33¢ price offered by plaintiff for the 2 1/2-3 lbs. birds. There is no substantial dispute that, in late April, 1957, the price for 2 1/2-3 lbs. broilers was between 35 and 37¢ per pound, and that when defendant entered into the contracts, it was well aware of this and intended to fill them by supplying fowl in these weights. It claims that plaintiff must likewise have known the market. . . . It is scarcely an answer to say, as plaintiff does in its brief, that the 33¢ price offered by the 2 1/2-3 lbs. "chickens" was closer to the prevailing 35¢ price for broilers than to the 30¢ at which defendant procured fowl. Plaintiff must have expected defendant to make some profit- certainly it could not have expected defendant deliberately to incur a loss.

. . . .

When all the evidence is reviewed, it is clear that defendant believed it could comply with the contracts by delivering stewing chicken in the 2 1/2-3 lbs. size. Defendant's subjective intent would not be significant if this did not coincide with an objective meaning of "chicken." Here it did coincide with one of the dictionary meanings, with the definition in the Department of Agriculture Regulations to which the contract made at least oblique reference, with at least some usage in the trade, with the realities of the market, and with what plaintiff's spokesman had said. Plaintiff asserts it to be equally plain that plaintiff's own subjective intent was to obtain broilers and fryers; the only evidence against this is the material as to market prices and this may not have been sufficiently brought home. In any event it is unnecessary to determine that issue. For plaintiff has the burden of showing that "chicken" was used in the narrower rather than in the broader sense, and this it has not sustained.

This opinion constitutes the Court's findings of fact and conclusions of law. Judgment shall be entered dismissing the complaint with costs.

NOTES

1. ***Chicken in Context.*** Judge Friendly seems to believe that the word "chicken" in the chicken industry has both a general and a specialized meaning. If both meanings are equally plausible, should the court decide which meaning to apply by asking whether the moving party has carried its burden of proof? If the buyer had refused delivery, and the seller was forced to sue the buyer for breach, would *Frigaliment* have been decided differently? Does Judge Friendly believe that, all else equal, the general usage is more common than the specialized? Based on Judge Traynor's opinion in *Pacific Gas* regarding the scope of a court's authority to interpret language, do you think he would have admitted extrinsic evidence in *Frigaliment*? How would Judge Kozinski have ruled?

2. ***Corbin's Analysis: A Farmer's View.***

> [In *Frigaliment,*] the court was not interpreting the word chicken, standing alone; but rather in a context of other words in the integration, in the broader context of relevant communications, and the still broader context of the linguistic usages of other men. Dictionary usage could not be decisive, for "Dictionaries give both meanings, as well as some others not relevant here." Moreover, no dictionary interprets the word chicken in its present context. . . . The 50 or more words of the integration itself did not make the interpretation plain and unambiguous to the judge. It might have seemed otherwise to the present writer if he had been the judge. In his own linguistic experience and education, he had heard of broilers and fryers, and also of fowl, but to him the word chickens included them all. For 10 years on a Kansas farm it had been a regular job to feed the chickens, with no suggestion that the old hens and roosters were to be excluded. In the campaign of 1928, the country was informed that one of the issues was "a chicken in every pot," obviously a bird for stewing. But in spite of his limited knowledge of other people's usages, he would have admitted extrinsic evidence, as the court did in this case.

Arthur Corbin, *The Interpretation of Words and the Parol Evidence Rule*, 50 CORNELL L.Q. 161, 167–68 (1965).

Essay: The Goals of Contractual Interpretation

At the outset of this book, we began by distinguishing the subjective and objective theories of intent. At first blush, both autonomy and economic justifications for contract law seem to require that contractual obligations derive from the parties' actual, subjective intent. If contract law construes parties' contractual obligations according to the objective meaning of their conduct or words, then they might be held accountable for obligations they never intentionally undertook. Doesn't this undermine both of the justifications for contract law?

The key to solving this puzzle lies in distinguishing between the effects of legal rules on the parties in the case at bar and the effects of legal rules on all individuals in the future. The significance of a system of precedent, nowhere more evident than in the common law, is that courts must simultaneously consider the ex post and the ex ante perspective in adjudication: The ex post perspective requires them to resolve the disputes before them by attempting to "do justice" between the parties; the ex ante perspective requires them to ensure that their decision's prospective regulatory effect as precedent is justified as well. Thus, courts cannot focus exclusively on doing justice between the parties in the case at bar. To do so would be to abdicate their responsibility to consider the important prospective regulatory effects of their decisions.

A contractual regime that predicates liability on the reasonable belief of the promisee, rather than the actual intent of the promisor, allows individuals to rely on commitments based on apparent intent, whether or not the promisor has the actual intent to promise. Although such a regime imposes contractual liability despite the lack of actual intent in some cases, it nonetheless provides a superior means of promoting autonomous and mutually beneficial exchanges in the long run. A party may be held liable even though his commitment did not reflect his will and was not beneficial for him, but the rule that holds him liable according to his objective intent increases the reliability of reasonable perceptions for all individuals who wish to undertake or receive commitments in the future.

Yet this perspective treats the litigants in the case at bar as mere means to a greater institutional end — namely, promoting the autonomy and efficiency of transactions for others in the future. Some might argue that the principle of autonomy itself bars courts from sacrificing the autonomy of the parties in the case at bar in order to promote the greater good of others, even if that greater good enhances respect for the autonomy of others. There is, therefore, an inherent tension in adjudication between the rights of the parties in the case at bar (the ex post perspective) and the effect of their dispute's resolution on the rights of others in the future (the ex ante perspective). By predicating contractual liability on objective intent, contract law seems clearly to take the ex ante perspective. But the same instincts that have led some courts to resist the objective intent doctrine have a continuing and significant effect on the common law's and Code's approaches to interpreting the meaning of contractual terms.

The common law's plain meaning and parol evidence rules side squarely with the ex ante perspective. As we have seen, the traditional plain meaning rule bars courts from admitting extrinsic evidence of the meaning of an express term if it has an unambiguous plain meaning. Similarly, the common law parol evidence rule treats the parties ex ante, objective manifestations in an apparently complete writing as presumptively conclusive evidence of the terms of their agreement. In contrast, contextualists argue that terms should be interpreted in light of all the relevant circumstances. Contextualist courts, such as California, carry this view to its logical limit and reject the notion that words in a contract can have a plain or unambiguous — context free — meaning at all. By the same logic they favor a soft parol evidence rule. These courts also regard the merger clause as merely creating a rebuttable presumption of integration that can be overridden by extrinsic evidence that the parties lacked any such intent. The resulting debate between contextualism and textualism is intense precisely because there is a normative justification for each approach.

1. *The Justification for Contextualism.* Under autonomy theories of contract, the parties' agreement has normative force because the parties actually agreed to it. Thus, the law's task is to enforce the parties' will the better to permit parties to realize their goals. These theories of contract require courts to find out, as far as is possible, what the parties actually did mean by the words they used. A contextualist approach to interpretation appears to follow logically from this freedom of contract premise: it invites courts first to learn about the commercial context and then to interpret express contract terms in light of that context.[29] Implicit in a contextual approach are two key assumptions: 1) that courts have the capability of learning about the commercial context, and 2) that the parties could have and would have completed the contract as the court has done had they been able to do so.

These two contextualist assumptions derive from quite separate concerns about textualist rules of interpretation. The assumption that courts can accurately recover the context undergirds the "incorporation" approach to commercial sales contracts championed by Karl Llewellyn and enshrined in Article 2 of the UCC. A separate concern about the risk of fraud and exploitation in consumer transactions animates the second contextualist assumption. Contextualist interpretations are often justified as necessary to prevent the exploitation of unsophisticated individuals who enter into written contracts with sophisticated parties who supply written contract terms that alter previously settled understandings. By examining the context ex post, courts presumably are able to monitor the process by which certain terms were reduced to writing, thereby protecting unsophisticated parties from difficult-to-detect forms of exploitation.

In sum, the contextualist approach focuses on contracts between parties to mass-market, standardized transactions (the consumer context) or contracts embedded in customary norms and terms of trade (the sales context). Both of these transactional prototypes undermine our assumptions about the capacity of parties to accurately and reliably reduce their "true" agreements to the terms of a formal writing. Rather, the contextualist regime rests on the powerful intuition that fair and efficient contracting takes place in a social setting, and that parties (and society) would prefer courts to take advantage of hindsight in bringing that context into view in a way that supports the realization of their (legitimate) contractual objectives.

Despite the fact that common law courts traditionally have followed a textualist approach, the UCC and the Second Restatement continue to encourage courts to be

---

[29] For a sampling of contextualist analyses, *see* James W. Bowers, *Murphy's Law and the Elementary Theory of Contract Interpretation: A Response to Schwartz and Scott*, 57 RUTGERS L. REV. 587 (2005), and Juliet P. Kostritsky, *Plain Meaning vs. Broad Interpretation: How the Risk of Opportunism Defeats a Unitary Default Rule for Interpretation*, 96 KY. L.J. 43 (2007).

contextual. Conventional scholarly wisdom has long held that the Code's interpretive approach represents a significant improvement over the formalism of the common law. This is because contextualism is assumed to ascertain the parties' intentions more accurately. More evidence usually is better than less. Particular parties may have intended apparently clear language to be read in a nonstandard way, or acted under the contract in ways neither explicitly directed nor prohibited given the contractual language. Excluding evidence of these parties' prior negotiations or subsequent practices risks interpreting their contracts in opposition to the parties' actual intentions.[30]

2. *The Justification for Textualism.* As compelling as it seems, however, the contextualist justification of a two-stage regime of contract interpretation rests on an unsupported premise: that parties want a court to reinterpret the formal terms of their contract in light of the surrounding context of the transaction so as to better achieve their shared contractual purposes. But there is good reason to doubt that commercially sophisticated parties typically, let alone always, prefer this method of interpreting their contracts. Rather than a rule that always subordinates formal contract terms to ex post judicial revision, both theory and available evidence suggests that sophisticated parties would prefer a regime that follows the parties' instructions specifying when to enforce formal contract terms strictly and when to delegate authority to a court to consider surrounding context evidence.

Textualist arguments accordingly focus on the importance of customized contract design and the insight that for sophisticated parties, context is endogenous; the parties can embed as much or as little context into an agreement as they wish and they can do so in many different ways. By eliminating the risk that courts will erroneously infer the parties' preference for any particular contextual interpretation, such a regime reduces the costs of contract enforcement and enhances the parties' control over the content of their contract. That control, in turn, permits sophisticated commercial parties to implement the most efficient design strategies available to them.

Textualists offer several justifications to support their claims. First, as noted above, a valuable state function is to create standard vocabularies for the conduct of commercial transactions.[31] When a phrase has a set, easily discoverable meaning, parties who use it will know what the phrase requires of them and what courts will say the phrase requires. By insulating the standard meaning of terms from deviant interpretations, this strategy preserves a valuable collective good, namely a set of terms with clear, unambiguous meaning that is already understood by the vast majority of commercial parties.

---

[30] Of course, the reverse could be true. The Code directs courts to construe express terms and extrinsic evidence from practices or usages as consistent with each other. But sometimes the parties may actually have intended that their clear language should be read in the standard (plain meaning) way despite the fact that the language itself conflicts with the prior practices and negotiations of the parties. In such a case, a court that relies too heavily on context risks misinterpreting the parties' actual intentions.

[31] See Robert E. Scott, *The Case for Formalism in Relational Contract*, 94 Nw. U. L. Rev. 847, 853–56 (2000); Alan Schwartz, *Contract Theory and Theories of Contract Regulation*, 92 Revue D'Economie Industrielle 101 (2000).

Second, a textualist theory of interpretation also creates an incentive to draft carefully. Under a contextualist theory, a party for whom a deal has turned out badly has an incentive to claim that the parties meant their contract to have a different meaning than the obvious or standard one. Such a party can often find in the parties' negotiations, in their past practices and in trade customs enough evidence to ground a full, costly trial, and thus to force a settlement on terms more favorable than those that the contract, as facially interpreted, would direct. If a party can impeach careful contract drafting with evidence of this type, the rewards to careful contract drafting will fall relative to the costs of such efforts. In consequence, parties will write precise, directive contracts less frequently and the expected costs of litigation initiated by the party disfavored by the ultimate outcome of the contract will rise, encouraged by the chance that the court will make a mistake.

Finally, textualist interpretation permits sophisticated commercial parties to economize on contracting costs by shifting costs from the back end of the contracting process (the enforcement function) to the front end of the contracting process (the negotiating and drafting function).[32] Parties can do this by drafting a merger clause that integrates their entire understanding, including relevant context, into the written contract and then having the court apply a plain meaning interpretation to those contract terms that are facially unambiguous. When parties fully integrate the agreement and use a merger clause, an interpretation dispute over contract terms may be resolved on summary judgment. If a court decides to consider additional context evidence, it must necessarily deny a motion for summary judgment and set the case for full trial on the merits. Thus, if litigation cost is considered, there is a strong argument that in cases where uncertainty is low and risks can be allocated in advance, many commercial parties prefer textualist interpretation so that disputes can be resolved without the punishing costs of a full trial. Such parties will rationally invest in sufficient drafting costs to ensure that a court interpreting the written document together with the pleadings and briefs will be able to arrive at the "correct interpretation" more often than not.[33]

This description of the two approaches and their key assumptions exposes a deep puzzle: Since the two competing approaches to interpretation are grounded on different assumptions about the contracting environment, why do they engage in debate at all, much less struggle for supremacy? The answer lies in their shared belief in the unitary and mandatory nature of the law of contract interpretation. For both sides in the interpretation debate, when a court (or legislature) chooses either a textualist or a contextualist approach to interpretation, that choice applies to all transactional prototypes, and particular parties cannot choose ex ante to have their contract interpreted according to the disfavored approach. Thus, the on-going interpretation debate is binary — either text or context — and in any particular

---

[32] For a discussion of how contracting parties can economize on total contracting costs by shifting costs between the drafting or front end of the contracting process and the adjudication or back end of the process, *see* Robert E. Scott & George G. Triantis, *Anticipating Litigation in Contract Design*, 115 YALE L.J. 814 (2006).

[33] *See* Alan Schwartz & Robert E. Scott, *Contract Interpretation Redux*, 119 YALE L.J. 926 (2010); Alan Schwartz & Robert E. Scott, *Contract Theory and the Limits of Contract Law*, 113 YALE L.J. 541 (2003).

"jurisdiction" victory is total for one approach or the other.[34]

[3]   Interpretation in the UCC

UCC § 2-202 codifies the liberal, contextualist approach to interpretation set out in the Restatement (Second). As we have seen, the Code rejects the common law's plain meaning rule,[35] and states that even a fully integrated agreement may be "explained or supplemented" by usage of trade, course of dealing, and course of performance evidence that is consistent with the terms in the final writing.[36] The Code substitutes in its place a robust scheme for interpreting the meaning of a contract's terms in light of the relevant layers of the contract's commercial context. The Code's interpretive approach argues that in order to ascertain "the true understanding of the parties," their written agreement must "be read on the assumption that the course of prior dealings between the parties and the usages of trade were taken for granted when the document was phrased. Similarly, the course of actual performance by the parties is considered the best indication of what they intended the writing to mean."[37]

If we assume that terms can have an unambiguous plain meaning, there is little question that the Code's interpretive regime will create a greater risk of judicial misinterpretation than that created by a plain meaning regime. Each term has many possible meanings under the Code's regime, but many terms have only one possible meaning under a plain meaning regime. Judicial interpretive error is more likely under the Code's regime because the Code requires courts to choose among so many more meanings for each term than courts would have to choose among under a plain meaning regime.

But the Code's use of extrinsic evidence increases the likelihood of interpretive error for a different reason as well. The Code directs courts to interpret the meaning of terms in light of relevant usage of trade, course of dealing, or course of performance. For example, if wholesale buyers of yarn routinely accept deliveries as much as three days after the delivery date specified in their agreements, the Code would direct courts to interpret the delivery date term of agreements in the yarn industry in light of this usage of trade. If a buyer sued a seller for breaching his agreement by delivering yarn one day after the September 1 delivery date, a court might hold that the term, "for delivery on September 1," in the yarn industry

---

[34] *See also* James W. Bowers, *Murphy's Law and the Elementary Theory of Contract Interpretation: A Response to Schwartz and Scott,* 57 Rutgers L. Rev. 587 (2005); Juliet P. Kostritsky, *Plain Meaning vs. Broad Interpretation: How the Risk of Opportunism Defeats a Unitary Default Rule for Interpretation,* 96 Ky. L.J. 43 (2007); *see also* Jeffrey M. Lipshaw, *The Bewitchment of Intelligence: Language and Ex Post Illusions of Intention,* 78 Temp. L. Rev. 99 (2005); Jeffrey M. Lipshaw, *Models and Games: The Difference Between Explanation and Understanding for Lawyers and Ethicists,* 56 Clev. St. L. Rev. 613 (2008).

[35] UCC § 2-202 cmt. 1(b), (c).

[36] A usage of trade is industry-wide custom, a course of dealing is a custom between the parties established by prior dealings with each other, and a course of performance is conduct by the parties in performing the contract in dispute. See Section A, Note 21, *supra,* for the Code's formal definitions of these terms.

[37] UCC § 2-202 cmt. 2.

means "delivery no later than September 4." It is possible, however, that the widespread practice of allowing delivery three days following the express delivery date does not demonstrate that the parties mean "delivery no later than September 4" when they write "delivery by September 1." The practice of accepting deliveries up to three days after the stated delivery date might instead reflect a series of *optional, one-time waivers*. Even though the parties might understand that the buyer can insist on its legal right to delivery on the date specified in its contract, the seller and buyer might both expect that the buyer routinely will waive its right in order to accommodate the needs of its seller. By doing so, both parties benefit by cultivating a long-term, cooperative relationship. But by providing for the legally enforceable, specific delivery date, buyer protects itself against seller's strategic behavior when cooperation breaks down. For example, if unforeseen financial difficulties prevent seller from making timely delivery at a time when buyer will face severe losses from late delivery, buyer can stand on its right to delivery on the date stated in the contract and sue for damages in the event of seller's breach.

Thus, transacting partners might wish to provide a two-tiered structure to their relationship. The first tier consists of the formal legal terms of their agreement. The second consists of the informal norms that govern the enforcement of those terms and the parties' expectations for a cooperative relationship. When the latter break down, the former protects the parties' interests. The integrity of this two-tiered regulatory framework for commercial transactions depends on the ability of courts to distinguish between a regular practice of waiver, which has no bearing on the meaning of the terms of agreement, and a regular practice which does in fact indicate how the parties interpreted the terms of their agreement. Thus, courts applying the Code's interpretive regime might misinterpret contracts by failing accurately to determine when usage of trade, course of dealing, and course of performance evidences only informal norms and therefore should have no effect on the interpretation of the meaning of terms in the parties' contract when those norms no longer apply (say because the dispute involves much larger stakes).[38]

What then is the justification for the Code's liberal interpretive regime? Arguably the chief advantage of the Code's regime is that it reduces the parties' costs of specifying all of the terms of their agreement along with definitions of their associated meaning. By interpreting terms in light of context, the Code in theory allows parties to use the terminology that has evolved to suit transactions in their particular trade. The context-specific meaning of such terms incorporates the

---

[38] *See* Jody S. Kraus & Robert E. Scott, *Contract Design and the Structure of Contractual Intent*, 84 N.Y.U. L. Rᴇᴠ. 1023 (2009); Robert E. Scott, *A Relational Theory of Default Rules in Commercial Contracts*, 19 J. Lᴇɢᴀʟ Sᴛᴜᴅ. 597 (1990). For an argument against the Codes' interpretive regime based on an analysis of how this dual structure exacerbates the risk of judicial misinterpretation, *see* Lisa Bernstein, *Merchant Law in a Merchant Court: Rethinking the Code's Search for Immanent Business Norms*, 144 U. Pᴀ. L. Rᴇᴠ. 1765 (1996). For a defense of the Code's interpretive regime, and a critique of Bernstein's and other arguments against the Code's regime, *see* Jody S. Kraus & Steven D. Walt, *In Defense of the Incorporation Strategy, in* Tʜᴇ Jᴜʀɪsᴘʀᴜᴅᴇɴᴄᴇ ᴏꜰ Cᴏʀᴘᴏʀᴀᴛᴇ ᴀɴᴅ Cᴏᴍᴍᴇʀᴄɪᴀʟ Lᴀᴡ (Jody S. Kraus & Steven D. Walt, eds., 2000). For an empirical defense of the superiority of the common law plain meaning regime over the Code's contextualist interpretive regime, *see* Robert E. Scott, *The Uniformity Norm in Commercial Law: A Comparative Analysis of Common Law and Code Methodologies, in* Tʜᴇ Jᴜʀɪsᴘʀᴜᴅᴇɴᴄᴇ ᴏꜰ Cᴏʀᴘᴏʀᴀᴛᴇ ᴀɴᴅ Cᴏᴍᴍᴇʀᴄɪᴀʟ Lᴀᴡ (Jody S. Kraus & Steven D. Walt eds., 2000).

evolved wisdom of decades or more of transactional practice in specific trades. And, by incorporating commercial practice into the very meaning of the terms parties use, the Code allows courts to avoid imposing upon the terms of an agreement a meaning clearly not intended by the parties. While this argument has theoretical appeal, it is less convincing in practice: it is based on the assumption that generalist courts can (and do) recover the contextual meaning embedded in trade usages and other context evidence. While empirical studies are incomplete, the evidence suggests that in this respect courts have often failed in their attempt to incorporate trade usage. The reasons for this are varied: usages as such do not often emerge as clearly defined practices and, as a consequence, most such litigation consists of interested party testimony rather than a careful evaluation by experts of the trading environment.[39]

As you read *Columbia Nitrogen* and *Southern Concrete*, decide whether the proffered evidence in each case can be fairly interpreted as an indication of what the parties meant by the terms of their agreements, or instead reflects an informal practice that has no bearing on the meaning of the formal terms of their written agreements. Did the parties contract with the expectation that extrinsic evidence would inform the interpretation of their written contracts? Is the source of the extrinsic evidence a neutral expert or an interested party? How you would differently draft an agreement in a jurisdiction governed by *Columbia Nitrogen* and one governed by *Southern Concrete*?

COLUMBIA NITROGEN CORP. v. ROYSTER CO.
United States Court of Appeals, Fourth Circuit
451 F.2d 3 (1971)

BUTZNER, J.

Columbia Nitrogen Corp. appeals a judgment in the amount of $750,000 in favor of F. S. Royster Guano Co. for breach of a contract for the sale of phosphate to Columbia by Royster. Columbia defended on the grounds that the contract, construed in light of the usage of the trade and course of dealing, imposed no duty to accept at the quoted prices the minimum quantities stated in the contract. It also asserted a counterclaim based on Royster's alleged reciprocal trade practices. The district court excluded the evidence about course of dealing and usage of the trade. It refused to submit [to the jury]the theory of non-coercive reciprocity. The jury found for Royster on the contract claim. . . . We hold that Columbia's proffered evidence was improperly excluded and Columbia is entitled to a new trial on the contractual issues.

---

[39] *See* Richard Craswell, *Do Trade Customs Exist?*, in The Jurisprudential Foundations of Corporate and Commercial Law 118 (2000); Lisa Bernstein, Trade Usage in the Courts: The Flawed Evidentiary Basis of Article 2's Incorporation Strategy (mimeo 2012).

I

Royster manufactures and markets mixed fertilizers, the principal components of which are nitrogen, phosphate and potash. Columbia is primarily a producer of nitrogen, although it manufactures some mixed fertilizer. For several years Royster had been a major purchaser of Columbia's products, but Columbia had never been a significant customer of Royster. In the fall of 1966, Royster constructed a facility which enabled it to produce more phosphate than it needed in its own operations. After extensive negotiations, the companies executed a contract for Royster's sale of a minimum of 31,000 tons of phosphate each year for three years to Columbia, with an option to extend the term. The contract stated the price per ton, subject to an escalation clause dependent on production costs.[40] Phosphate prices soon plunged precipitously. Unable to resell the phosphate at a competitive price, Columbia ordered only part of the scheduled tonnage.

At Columbia's request, Royster lowered its price for diammonium phosphate on shipments for three months in 1967, but specified that subsequent shipments would

---

[40] [2] In pertinent part, the contract provides: "Contract made as of this 8th day of May between COLUMBIA NITROGEN CORPORATION, a Delaware corporation, (hereinafter called the Buyer) hereby agrees to purchase and accept from F.S. ROYSTER GUANO COMPANY, a Virginia corporation (hereinafter called the Seller) agrees to furnish quantities of Diammonium Phosphate 18-46-0, Granular Triple Superphosphate 0-46-0, and Run-of-Pile Triple Superphosphate 0-46-0 on the following terms and conditions.

"Period Covered by Contract — This contract to begin July 1, 1967, and continue through June 30, 1970, with renewal privileges for an additional three year period based upon notification by Buyer and acceptance by Seller on or before June 30, 1969. Failure of notification by either party on or before June 30, 1969, constitutes an automatic renewal for an additional one-year period beyond June 30, 1970, and on a year-to-year basis thereafter unless notification of cancellation is given by either party 90 days prior to June 30 of each year.

"Products Supplied Under Contract

Minimum Tonnage Per Year

"Diammonium Phosphate 18-46-0 15,000 Granular Triple Superphosphate 0-46-0 15,000 Run-of-Pile Triple Superphosphate 0-46-0 1,000 "Seller agrees to provide additional quantities beyond the minimum specified tonnage for products listed above provided Seller has the capacity and ability to provide such additional quantities. . . .

"Price — In Bulk F.O.B. Cars, Royster, Florida.

"Diammonium Phosphate 18-46-0 $61.25 Per Ton.

"Granular Triple Superphosphate 0-46-0 $40.90 Per Ton.

"Run-of-Pile Triple Superphosphate 0-46-0 $0.86 Per Unit. . . .

"Default — If Buyer fails to pay for any delivery under this contract within 30 days after Seller's invoice to Buyer and then if such invoice is not paid within an additional 30 days after the Seller notifies the Buyer of such default, then after that time the Seller may at his option defer further deliveries hereunder or take such action as in their judgment they may decide including cancellation of this contract. Any balances carried beyond 30 days will carry a service fee of 3/4 of 1% per month. . . .

"Escalation — The escalation factor up or down shall be based upon the effects of changing raw material cost of sulphur, rock phosphate, and labor as follows. These escalations up or down to become effective against shipments of products covered by this contract 30 days after notification by Seller to Buyer. . . .

"No verbal understanding will be recognized by either party hereto; this contract expresses all the terms and conditions of the agreement, shall be signed in duplicate and shall not become operative until approved in writing by the Seller."

be at the original contract price. Even with this concession, Royster's price was still substantially above the market. As a result, Columbia ordered less than a tenth of the phosphate Royster was to ship in the first contract year. When pressed by Royster, Columbia offered to take the phosphate at the current market price and resell it without brokerage fee. Royster, however, insisted on the contract price. When Columbia refused delivery, Royster sold the unaccepted phosphate for Columbia's account at a price substantially below the contract price.

II

Columbia assigns error to the pretrial ruling of the district court excluding all evidence on usage of the trade and course of dealing between the parties. It offered the testimony of witnesses with long experience in the trade that because of uncertain crop and weather conditions, farming practices, and government agricultural programs, express price and quantity terms in contracts for materials in the mixed fertilizer industry are mere projections to be adjusted according to market forces.

Columbia also offered proof of its business dealings with Royster over the six-year period preceding the phosphate contract. Since Columbia had not been a significant purchaser of Royster's products, these dealings were almost exclusively nitrogen sales to Royster or exchanges of stock carried in inventory. The pattern which emerges, Columbia claimed, is one of repeated and substantial deviation from the stated amount or price, including four instances where Royster took none of the goods for which it had contracted. Columbia offered proof that the total variance amounted to more than $500,000 in reduced sales. This experience, a Columbia officer offered to testify, formed the basis of an understanding on which he depended in conducting negotiations with Royster.

The district court held that the evidence should be excluded. It ruled that "custom and usage or course of dealing are not admissible to contradict the express, plain, unambiguous language of a valid written contract, which by virtue of its detail negates the proposition that the contract is open to variances in its terms. . . ."

A number of Virginia cases have held that extrinsic evidence may not be received to explain or supplement a written contract unless the court finds the writing is ambiguous. This rule, however, has been changed by the Uniform Commercial Code which Virginia has adopted. The Code expressly states that it "shall be liberally construed and applied to promote its underlying purposes and policies," which include "the continued expansion of commercial practices through custom, usage and agreement of the parties. . . ." [§ 1-103(2)]. The importance of usage of trade and course of dealing between the parties is shown by § .2-202, which authorizes their use to explain or supplement a contract. The official comment states this section rejects the old rule that evidence of course of dealing or usage of trade can be introduced only when the contract is ambiguous. And the Virginia commentators, noting that "[t]his section reflects a more liberal approach to the introduction of parol evidence . . . than has been followed in Virginia," express the opinion that [the earlier] Virginia cases no longer should be followed. § .2-202, Va. Comment. We hold, therefore, that a finding of ambiguity is not necessary for the admission of extrinsic evidence about the usage of the trade and the parties' course of dealing.

We turn next to Royster's claim that Columbia's evidence was properly excluded because it was inconsistent with the express terms of their agreement. There can be no doubt that the Uniform Commercial Code restates the well established rule that evidence of usage of trade and course of dealing should be excluded whenever it cannot be reasonably construed as consistent with the terms of the contract. Royster argues that the evidence should be excluded as inconsistent because the contract contains detailed provisions regarding the base price, escalation, minimum tonnage, and delivery schedules. The argument is based on the premise that because a contract appears on its face to be complete, evidence of course of dealing and usage of trade should be excluded. We believe, however, that neither the language nor the policy of the Code supports such a broad exclusionary rule. Section.2-202 expressly allows evidence of course of dealing or usage of trade to explain or supplement terms intended by the parties as a final expression of their agreement. When this section is read in light of [UCC. § 1-303 (e)] it is clear that the test of admissibility is not whether the contract appears on its face to be complete in every detail, but whether the proffered evidence of course of dealing and trade usage reasonably can be construed as consistent with the express terms of the agreement.

The proffered testimony sought to establish that because of changing weather conditions, farming practices, and government agricultural programs, dealers adjusted prices, quantities, and delivery schedules to reflect declining market conditions. For the following reasons it is reasonable to construe this evidence as consistent with the express terms of the contract.

The contract does not expressly state that course of dealing and usage of trade cannot be used to explain or supplement the written contract.

The contract is silent about adjusting prices and quantities to reflect a declining market. It neither permits nor prohibits adjustment, and this neutrality provides a fitting occasion for recourse to usage of trade and prior dealing to supplement the contract and explain its terms.

Minimum tonnages and additional quantities are expressed in terms of "Products Supplied Under Contract." Significantly, they are not expressed as just "Products" or as "Products Purchased Under Contract." The description used by the parties is consistent with the proffered testimony.

Finally, the default clause of the contract refers only to the failure of the buyer to pay for delivered phosphate. During the contract negotiations, Columbia rejected a Royster proposal for liquidated damages of $10 for each ton Columbia declined to accept. On the other hand, Royster rejected a

Columbia proposal for a clause that tied the price to the market by obligating Royster to conform its price to offers Columbia received from other phosphate producers. The parties, having rejected both proposals, failed to state any consequences of Columbia's refusal to take delivery — the kind of default Royster alleges in this case. Royster insists that we span this hiatus by applying the general law of contracts permitting recovery of damages upon the buyer's refusal to take delivery according to the written provisions of the contract. This solution is not what the Uniform Commercial Code prescribes.

Before allowing damages, a court must first determine whether the buyer has in fact defaulted. It must do this by supplementing and explaining the agreement with evidence of trade usage and course of dealing that is consistent with the contract's express terms. [UCC §§ .1-303(e), .2-202]. Faithful adherence to this mandate reflects the reality of the marketplace and avoids the overly legalistic interpretations which the Code seeks to abolish.

Royster also contends that Columbia's proffered testimony was properly rejected because it dealt with mutual willingness of buyer and seller to adjust contract terms to the market. Columbia, Royster protests, seeks unilateral adjustment. This argument misses the point. What Columbia seeks to show is a practice of mutual adjustments so prevalent in the industry and in prior dealings between the parties that it formed a part of the agreement governing this transaction. It is not insisting on a unilateral right to modify the contract.

Nor can we accept Royster's contention that the testimony should be excluded under the contract clause:

> No verbal understanding will be recognized by either party hereto; this contract expresses all the terms and conditions of the agreement, shall be signed in duplicate, and shall not become operative until approved in writing by the Seller.

Course of dealing and trade usage are not synonymous with verbal understandings, terms and conditions. Section 2-202 draws a distinction between supplementing a written contract by consistent additional terms and supplementing it by course of dealing or usage of trade. Evidence of additional terms must be excluded when "the court finds the writing to have been intended also as a complete and exclusive statement of the terms of the agreement." Significantly, no similar limitation is placed on the introduction of evidence of course of dealing or usage of trade. Indeed the official comment notes that course of dealing and usage of trade, unless carefully negated, are admissible to supplement the terms of any writing, and that contracts are to be read on the assumption that these elements were taken for granted when the document was phrased. Since the Code assigns course of dealing and trade usage unique and important roles, they should not be conclusively rejected by reading them into stereotyped language that makes no specific reference to them. Indeed, the Code's official commentators urge that overly simplistic and overly legalistic interpretation of a contract should be shunned. . . .

We conclude, therefore, that Columbia's evidence about course of dealing and usage of trade should have been admitted. Its exclusion requires that the judgment against Columbia must be set aside and the case retried.

SOUTHERN CONCRETE SERVICES, INC. v. MABLETON CONTRACTORS, INC.

United States District Court, Northern District of Georgia
407 F. Supp. 581 (1975)

EDENFIELD, C. J.

This is a diversity action in which plaintiff seller seeks to recover lost profits and out-of-pocket expenses from defendant buyer for buyer's alleged breach of contract. The case is currently before the court on plaintiff's motion for a ruling on the admissibility of certain evidence.

In September 1972 the parties entered into a contract for the sale of concrete for use in the construction of the building foundation of a power plant near Carrollton, Georgia. The contract stipulated that plaintiff was to supply "approximately 70,000 cubic yards" of concrete from September 1, 1972 to June 15, 1973. The price to be paid for such concrete was $19.60 per cubic yard. The contract further stipulated that "No conditions which are not incorporated in this contract will be recognized." During the time period involved defendant ordered only 12,542 cubic yards of concrete, that being the total amount needed by the defendant for its construction work. The plaintiff has brought this action to recover the profits lost by defendant's alleged breach and the costs plaintiff incurred in purchasing and delivering over $20,000 in raw materials to the jobsite.

The defendant claims that the written contract must be interpreted both in light of the custom of the trade and in light of additional terms allegedly intended by the parties. Defendant contends that under such custom and additional terms, it was understood that the quantity stipulated in the contract was not mandatory upon either of the parties and that both quantity and price were understood to be subject to renegotiation. It is this evidence of custom in the trade and of additional conditions allegedly agreed to by the parties that defendant seeks to introduce at trial.

In support of its position, defendant relies upon UCC § 2-202 which provides that a written contract may be explained or supplemented "by a course of dealing or usage of trade" and by evidence of "consistent additional terms."[41] This section was meant to liberalize the common law parol evidence rule to allow evidence of

---

[41] [1] "Terms with respect to which the confirmatory memoranda of the parties agree or which are otherwise set forth in a writing intended by the parties as a final expression of their agreement with respect to such terms as are included therein may not be contradicted by evidence of any prior agreement or of a contemporaneous oral agreement but may be explained or supplemented

(a) by course of dealing or usage of trade or by course of performance [1-303]; and

(b) by evidence of consistent additional terms unless the court finds the writing to have been intended also as complete and exclusive statement of the terms of the agreement.

[UCC § 1-303(c)], in turn, reads:

. . . (2) A usage of trade is any practice or method of dealing having such regularity of observance in a place, vocation or trade as to justify an expectation that it will be observed with respect to the transaction in question. The existence and scope of such a usage are to be proved as facts. If it is established that such a usage is embodied in a written trade code or similar writing the interpretation of the writing is for the court.

agreements outside the contract, without a prerequisite finding that the contract was ambiguous. In addition, the section requires contracts to be interpreted in light of the commercial context in which they were written and not by the rules of legal construction.

The question then becomes what is meant by the term "explained or supplemented"; does defendant's evidence "explain" the contract or does it attempt to "contradict" it? The court will examine this question with regard to the trade usage issue first, and then deal with the "additional terms" question.

I

In the official comment to UCC § 2-202, the draftsmen emphasize that contracts are to be interpreted with the assumption that the usages of trade "were taken for granted when the document was phrased. Unless carefully negated they have become an element of the meaning of the words used," Comment No. 2. In Columbia Nitrogen Corp. v. Royster Co., 451 F.2d 3 (4th Cir. 1971), the court was faced with a contract similar to the one in the instant case. The contract provided for the sale of at least 31,000 tons of phosphate each year for three years at a stated price, subject to an escalation clause dependent on production costs. The buyer bought less than one-tenth the minimum amount contracted for in the first year and the seller brought suit. The defendant offered to introduce evidence showing that contracts of the type involved were meant to be mere projections of price and quantity due to the rapid fluctuation in demand in the fertilizer industry. The defendant buyer also sought to introduce evidence of prior dealings between the parties in which the plaintiff, as buyer, often failed to purchase the entire amount contracted for from defendant. Since the contract was silent on the subject of adjusting prices and quantities to reflect a declining market, and since it did "not expressly state that course of dealing and usage of trade cannot be used to explain or supplement the written contract," the court allowed the evidence to be admitted. 451 F.2d at 9, 10.

There are, however, certain important differences between *Royster* and the case at hand. In *Royster*, the court noted that the contract default clause dealt only with the buyer's failure to pay for delivered phosphate, thus raising the possibility that the contract was not meant to require the buyer to accept the entire contract amount. In addition, the court was faced with a situation where the equities were strongly in favor of the defendant. In previous dealings between the parties, the defendant had apparently never insisted on purchase of the entire contract amount by plaintiff. Now that plaintiff was the seller it was insisting on strict compliance with the literal terms of the contract. The plaintiff also enjoyed the protection of an escalation clause in the contract which allowed it to raise prices to compensate for increased production costs, while plaintiff refused to allow the defendant to renegotiate for a lower price to reflect market conditions. Thus the court in *Royster* faced a situation in which one party may have been trying to take unfair advantage of a long-standing customer.

Such a situation is not present in this case, however, and this court has grave doubts about applying the reasoning of *Royster* to different fact situations. Here, no prior dealings are alleged by either party; the contract by its terms does not intimate that the buyer would only be liable for concrete actually delivered, and the contract does not contain provisions granting one party special repricing rights. Instead, the contract sets out fairly specific quantity, price, and time specifications.[42] To allow such specific contracts to be challenged by extrinsic evidence might jeopardize the certainty of the contractual duties which parties have a right to rely on. Certainly customs of the trade should be relevant to the interpretation of certain terms of a contract, and should be considered in determining what variation in specifications is considered acceptable, see Modine Manufacturing Co. v. Northeast Ind. School District, 503 S.W.2d 833 (Texas Ct. of Civ. App. 1973) (where the court allowed a 6% deviation in cooling capacity of an air-conditioning system since such deviation was acceptable in the trade), but this court does not believe that section 2-202 was meant to invite a frontal assault on the essential terms of a clear and explicit contract.

The type of evidence which the *Royster* decision might allow and which the defendant here undoubtedly wishes to introduce would probably show that very few contracts specifying quantity and price in a particular industry have been strictly enforced. While in some industries it may be virtually impossible to predict future needs under a contract, in other industries, such contracts may not be strictly adhered to for entirely different reasons. Lawsuits are costly and they do not facilitate good business relations with customers. A party to a contract may very much prefer to work out a renegotiation of a contract rather than rest on its strict legal rights. Yet, the supplier or purchaser knows that he may resort to those enforceable contract rights if necessary. If the courts were to conclude that this reluctance to enforce legal rights resulted in an industry-wide waiver of such rights, then contracts would lose their utility as a means of assigning the risks of the market. The defendant here may be correct in its assertion that contracts for the sale of concrete are often subject to renegotiation, but that fact alone does not convince the court that the parties here did not contemplate placing on the buyer the risk of variation in quantity needs.

The court recognizes that all ambiguity as to the applicability of trade usage could be eliminated by a blanket condition that the express terms of the contract are in no way to be modified by custom, usage, or prior dealings. Indeed, the *Royster* court found the absence of such a clause to be a determinative factor in allowing in extrinsic evidence. This court, however, is reluctant to encourage the use of yet another standard boilerplate provision in commercial contracts. If such a clause is necessary to preserve the very essence of a contract, then the purposes of the Code will be quickly frustrated. Consideration of commercial custom is an important aid in the interpretation of the terms of a contract, but parties will have no choice but to foreclose the use of such an aid if the inevitable result of such consideration is to have explicit contracts negated by an evidentiary free-for-all.

Although the official comments suggest that parties which do not want trade usage to apply should so stipulate in the contract (Comment 2 to § 2-202), that provision could not have been meant to allow the full-scale attack on the contract

---

[42] [2] The court is not concerned about the use of the term "approximately 70,000 cubic yards." Obviously the parties anticipated some slight variation in the final amount, but defendant cannot claim that by use of the term "approximately" the parties contemplated acceptance of only 12,000 cubic yards.

suggested here. The more reasonable approach is to assume that specifications as to quantity and price are intended to be observed by the parties and that the unilateral right to make a major departure from such specifications must be expressly agreed to in the written contract. That way, the courts will still be free to apply custom and trade usage in interpreting terms of the contract without raising apprehension in the commercial world as to the continued reliability of those contracts. Such an approach is consistent with the underlying purposes of the Uniform Commercial Code, which dictates that the express terms of a contract and trade usage shall be construed as consistent with each other only when such construction is reasonable.[43] A construction which negates the express terms of the contract by allowing unilateral abandonment of its specifications is patently unreasonable.

II

The defendant also claims that section 2-202 allows the introduction of evidence of additional terms of the agreement between the parties. Those terms presumably called for price renegotiation and contained an understanding that the quantity quoted in the contract was intended only as an estimate. The court suspects, however, that the defendant is attempting to use section 2-202(b) as merely an alternative vehicle to get in evidence as to trade usage. The defendant does not specify in its brief the terms of the alleged extrinsic agreement and does not indicate whether it was oral or written, prior or contemporaneous. Rather, the defendant merely tags its 202(b) request on its trade usage claim as an apparent afterthought. But even if this court assumes that defendant will attempt to show additional terms of the contract, such evidence would be inadmissible. Section 2-202 requires that written contracts "not be contradicted" by evidence of agreements outside of the written contract, but that they may be explained or supplemented by evidence of "consistent additional terms" if the court finds the contract was not meant to be the complete statement of the agreement.

Whether or not the contract in issue was meant to be complete in itself, it is clear that the additional terms sought to be proved are not consistent with it. The type of evidence which may be admitted under subsection (b) deals with agreements covering matters not dealt with in the written contract. To admit evidence of an agreement which would contradict the express terms of the contract would clearly eviscerate the purpose of § 2-202.

The court is aware that at least one court has favored a broader construction of § 2-202, holding that evidence of a contemporaneous oral agreement to provide up to 500 tons of steel was consistent with a written provision in the contract stipulating delivery of 500 tons. Schiavone & Sons, Inc. v. Securalloy Co., Inc., 312 F. Supp. 801 (D. Conn. 1970). That court explained:

---

[43] [3] [UCC § 1-303(e)] provides: "The express terms of an agreement and an applicable course of dealing or usage of trade shall be construed wherever reasonable as consistent with each other; but when such construction is unreasonable express terms control both course of dealing and usage of trade and course of dealing controls usage of trade."

In making this determination, it must be borne in mind that to be inconsistent the terms must contradict or negate a term of the written agreement; and a term which has a lesser effect is deemed to be a consistent term.

312 F. Supp. 804.

This court respectfully disagrees with the above reasoning; for the buyer who wished to obtain all 500 tons, and who had to cover his requirements elsewhere, the term "up to 500" tons was clearly inconsistent with the contract. Similarly, a hypothetical agreement between the instant parties that quantity and price terms were to be mere estimates is inconsistent with the written contract.

Finally, the contract at issue specified that conditions not incorporated in the contract would not be recognized. In contrast, in *Schiavone, supra,* the court noted the absence of such a clause in finding the parol evidence admissible. The presence of such a clause here further convinces the court that the writing was intended to be the "complete and exclusive statement" of the terms of the agreement, UCC § 2-202(b).

The court therefore concludes that the evidence sought to be introduced by the defendant is inadmissible at trial.

NOTES

1. *Questions on* **Columbia Nitrogen** *and* **Southern Concrete.** The court in *Southern Concrete* held that "the more reasonable approach" is to assume that quantity and price terms carry a "plain meaning" and are always meant to be strictly observed. Do you agree? In the absence of clear guidance from the express agreement, what assumptions would you make about the parties' intention to incorporate trade usage into their agreement? What empirical data would you like to have in answering this question?

On the other hand, exactly what was the agreement Columbia Nitrogen was trying to establish by introducing extrinsic evidence? In this connection consider the following evaluation of the case from Professor Victor Goldberg in Framing Contract Law: An Economic Perspective (2007):

> If we try to write down the contract that the Court of Appeals has recognized, what do we get? Columbia Nitrogen agrees to take a fixed amount of fertilizer at a fixed price for three years. If, however, the market price falls by enough, CNC can ask Royster to modify the price and/or quantity term. If Royster refuses, then. . . . To paraphrase Gertrude Stein, there is no "then" there. This is too vague to be an enforceable contract. The court has managed to transform a perfectly reasonable contract into an unenforceable gentleman's agreement. Well, maybe it would be enforceable if we hold that Royster must bargain in good faith. The fact question for the jury, then, would be the adequacy of the process: Did Royster try hard enough to work something out? This seems like a pretty dubious path. Even CNC, in its throw-everything-against-the-wall approach, didn't dare suggest that Royster had breached their agreement.

Id. at 183. Goldberg concludes that the decision in *Columbia* Nitrogen represents "the court's ratification of a cynical attempt by CNC's counsel to undo, by whatever means necessary, what had turned out to be a bad bargain. In the process it converted a straightforward agreement into an incoherent mess." Do you agree?

2.   *Opting Out of the Code's Regime.* In *Columbia Nitrogen*, the court suggests that evidence of course of dealing and trade usage may not be introduced to explain or interpret the written contract, if expressly excluded by the writing. Consider the following merger clause:

> This document represents the final agreement on all terms, and may not be explained, supplemented, or modified by additional terms, usage of trade, or course of dealing.

Would this language serve to exclude evidence of the various usages offered in the principal cases? Is this the sort of careful negation alluded to in § 2-202 Comment 2 or is it just a new kind of boilerplate, subject to all the criticisms that we have already considered? Faced with such a clause, must a court interpret a disputed term according to the "plain meaning" of the words used? If the language has no plain meaning to a lay reader, is the court precluded from applying the meaning generally understood by persons in the trade? Such clauses are becoming more common in UCC form books. *See, e.g., McKinney's Forms, Uniform Commercial Code* § 1-303, Form 1 (2010); R. Anderson, UNIFORM COMMERCIAL CODE LEGAL FORMS § 87 (1974). Does this indicate that commercial actors generally prefer plain meaning regimes to contextual regimes such as the Code's?

3.   *The Danger of Course of Dealing and Performance Evidence.* The court in *Columbia Nitrogen* held that evidence of the course of dealings between the parties over a six year period was relevant to understanding the meaning of the minimum quantity term in the contract. In *Contract Theory and The Limits of Contract Law*, 113 YALE L.J. 541 (2003), Alan Schwartz and Robert Scott suggest that supplementing contracts with course-of-performance evidence would frequently be a mistake. They suggest that evidence of course of dealing or course of performance differs from evidence in the other evidential categories because it can be offered not only to show what the parties originally meant, but also to prove that the parties' meaning had changed:

> [E]vidence that a buyer has accepted shipments at quality levels below those specified in the contract may show that the parties modified the contract's quality requirement. Thus, admitting course of performance evidence to prove a change in meaning is consistent with the traditional contract law rule that the parties' agreement may be inferred from acts or silence. Nevertheless, courts should be reluctant to admit act or acquiescence evidence to show a change in the meaning of a written contract.

> To see why, suppose that [parties contract for the seller to deliver goods of a specified quality to the buyer at a] contract price of $2000 per lot delivered and that the contract contained a "no oral modification" clause in addition to the quality specification. The parties expect that deviations from the specified contract quality will sometimes occur. For the buyer, the expected loss from the *average* deviation is $100. Thus, sometimes a deviation will

create a cost that approaches zero (perhaps the buyer has forgiving customers or the quality shortfall can be quickly corrected). At other times, a deviation can impose a loss whose expected value equals or exceeds $500 (say the buyer has a new, potentially large customer for whom quality is important, or the particular deviation would be slow to correct in a high demand period). The parties also know that it would not be cost justified to litigate against the average quality shortfall (the litigation cost, say, would be $150 per deviation).

The contract in this example . . . support[s] two conclusions with respect to the interpretive relevance of course-of-performance evidence. First, the parties do not expect to litigate the average quality deviation. Rather, the buyer will accept nonconforming deliveries that cause average losses, with the cost to it of these deviations reflected in a lower fixed price. The inclusion of the no oral modification clause is meant to tell the seller that it cannot infer from a series of acceptances of goods whose defects cause the buyer to incur losses in the neighborhood of the average (or less) that the buyer also will accept a nonconforming delivery that would cause it to incur a large loss. The second conclusion that the example supports, therefore, is that high cost deviations in product quality are prohibited. This example captures an important feature of contracting behavior. When business parties incur costs to cast obligations in written form, they do so partly to permit a party to stand on its rights under the written contract when standing on its rights matters. Course-of-performance evidence therefore commonly will be irrelevant to show what the contract originally meant or what it currently means. The parties' amicable behavior after the contract likely evidences only their view regarding how the average case should be treated. Courts, however, see the unusual case that the contract was written to govern.

Id. at 592–94. Schwartz and Scott conclude that courts should recognize that parties sometimes have multiple intentions. They argue that parties' actions under the contract will evidence their intentions for typical cases, but ordinarily will not evidence their intentions for the atypical case. Thus, a court is likely to make a mistake when it infers the parties' preferences regarding how a litigated case should be treated from an evidentiary base comprised in large part of the parties' behavior in non-litigated cases. Do you agree?

4. ***Knowledge of Trade Usage.*** Should a party's ignorance of a usage of trade preclude a court from assuming that such usage is part of the contract? In *Heggblade-Marguleas-Tenneco, Inc. v. Sunshine Biscuit, Inc.*, 59 Cal. App. 3d 948, 131 Cal. Rptr. 183 (1976), HMT agreed to sell 100,000 sacks of potatoes to defendant's wholly-owned subsidiary, Bell Brand. The court responded to HMT's contention that its officer, Thomas, in his negotiations with defendant buyer's representative, Smith, had not understood that the quantity term was regarded in the trade only as an estimate:

[T]he testimony that Thomas refused to reduce the quantity as Smith had requested does not negate the applicability of the custom as a matter of law. The Thomas-Smith negotiations give rise to conflicting inferences: either that Smith agreed to Thomas' assertion that the quantity was fixed and not subject to later adjustment, or that regardless of Thomas' protestations, Smith intended, and Thomas understood quantity was an estimate only. Smith had told Thomas earlier that the 100,000-sack figure was too high, thereby giving Thomas notice that Bell Brand might not be able to process that amount of potatoes the following spring. Yet, when the formal contracts were executed on October 17, 1970, nothing was inserted in the contracts suggesting that the quantity was "fixed" or "firm." From this omission, a reasonable inference arises that when Smith signed the contracts on behalf of Bell Brand he intended the 100,000 figure to be an estimate and that Thomas understood this to be so.

Appellant's argument that the evidence of custom should not have been considered by the jury in interpreting the contracts because the officers of HMT were inexperienced in the marketing of processing potatoes and lacked knowledge of the custom is similarly without merit. Mr. Hoffman, [an employee of HMT who had signed the contract with Bell Brand] was knowledgeable in the potato processing business and was aware of the trade custom. Since appellant pleaded that the contracts had been entered into on October 15, 1970, his knowledge was imputed to HMT.

Moreover, persons carrying on a particular trade are deemed to be aware of prominent trade customs applicable to their industry. The knowledge may be actual or constructive, and it is constructive if the custom is of such general and universal application that the party must be presumed to know of it. . . .

Because potatoes are a perishable commodity and their demand is dependent upon a fluctuating market, and because the marketing contracts are signed eight or nine months in advance of the harvest season, common sense dictates that the quantity would be estimated by both the grower and the processor. Thus, it cannot be said as a matter of law that HMT was ignorant of the trade custom.

We conclude that the trial court properly admitted the evidence of usage and custom to explain the meaning of the quantity figures in the contracts.

59 Cal. App. 3d at 955–57.

The court charged HMT with constructive knowledge of the usage based on its participation in the potato processing business. Is trade usage properly used to explain or supplement a disputed term where the contracting parties are completely ignorant of the business that is the subject of their agreement? (See the language of § 1-303(c): A trade usage must be sufficiently common "as to justify an expectation that it will be observed with respect to the transaction in question.") How should a court react when a failure to discuss or exclude a trade usage indicates that the parties attached materially different meanings to their mutual representations? If your answer is that no contract was formed, how do you deal with the problem of losses sustained by both parties in reliance on the existence of a valid contract? What effect would such a solution have on the behavior of future contracting parties? How does the UCC resolve this question? *See generally* § 2-204.

   5.   ***Contextual Evidence Under the UCC.*** Under the UCC, should a court ever permit introduction of evidence of a course of dealing or usage of trade tending to contradict the plain meaning of the express terms of a written agreement? The court in *Modine Mfg. Co. v. North East Independent School Dist.*, 503 S.W.2d 833 (Tex. Civ. App. 1973), held that evidence of a trade custom permitting "reasonable variations in cooling capacity" of air conditioners could be introduced for the purpose of explaining a written agreement, notwithstanding a provision that "capacities shall not be less than indicated." The court cited *Columbia Nitrogen* in noting that "[t]he contract does not expressly state that course of dealing and usage of trade cannot be used to explain or supplement the written contract," and holding that trade customs "should not be conclusively rejected by reading them into stereotyped language that makes no specific reference to them." The court also cited *Michael Schiavone & Sons, Inc. v. Securalloy Co.*, 312 F. Supp. 801 (D. Conn. 1970) (disapproved in *Southern Concrete*), for the proposition that "to be inconsistent the terms must contradict or negate a term of the written agreement; and a term which has a lesser effect is deemed to be a consistent term." The *Modine* court held: "So tested, there is no inconsistency, as defined in [§ 2-202]." Do you agree that this is the proper construction of that section?

   On the other hand, in *Doppelt v. Wander & Co.*, 19 U.C.C. Rep. Serv. (Callaghan) 503 (N.Y. Civ. Ct. 1976), a diamond was entrusted by one dealer to another under the terms of a "memorandum" providing, inter alia, that: "A sale of this merchandise can only be effected and title will pass only if, as and when we the said owner shall agree to such sale and a bill of sale rendered therefore." The owner sought to recover the diamond from a third-party "purchaser," who contended that trade custom was to disregard the strict terms of such memoranda, and that the dealer to whom a diamond was entrusted could sell the stone to a third party, after which the original owner would immediately render to the dealer a bill of sale. The court held that such evidence could not be introduced, for it would contradict the plain meaning of the writing. Are you satisfied that this is the correct interpretation of §§ 2-202 and 1-303(e)? Is there a possible middle ground between these two decisions?

   > Determining the intent of the parties requires that the court attempt to construe the written term consistently with the commercial practice, if that is reasonable. If consistent construction is unreasonable, the Code directs that the written term be taken as expressing the parties' intent. Before concluding that a jury could not reasonably find a consistent construction, the judge must understand the commercial background of the dispute. Because the stock printed forms cannot always reflect the changing methods of business, members of the trade may do business with a standard clause in the forms that they ignore in practice. [Why?] If the trade consistently ignores obsolete clauses at variance with actual trade practices, a litigant can maintain that it is reasonable that the courts also ignore the clauses. Similarly, members of a trade may handle a particular subset of commercial transactions in a manner inconsistent with written terms because the writing cannot provide for all variations and contingen-

cies. Thus, if the trade regards an express term and a trade usage as consistent because the usage is not a complete contradiction but only an occasional but definite exception to a written term, the courts should interpret the contract according to the usage.

Roger W. Kirst, *Usage of Trade and Course of Dealing: Subversion of the UCC Theory*, 1977 U. ILL. L. F. 811, 824.

D.   BIBLIOGRAPHY AND SUGGESTED READING

Layman Allen, *Symbolic Logic: A Razor Edged Tool for Drafting and Interpreting Legal Documents*, 66 YALE L.J. 833 (1957).

James W. Bowers, *Murphy's Law and the Elementary Theory of Contract Interpretation: A Response to Schwartz and Scott*, 57 RUTGERS L. REV. 587 (2005).

Lisa Bernstein, *Merchant Law in a Merchant Court: Rethinking the Code's Search for Immanent Business Norms*, 144 U. PA. L. REV. 1765 (1996).

Richard F. Broude, *The Consumer and the Parole Evidence Rule: § 2-202 of the Uniform Commercial Code*, 1970 DUKE L.J. 881.

David Charny, *Hypothetical Bargains: The Normative Structure of Contract Interpretation*, 89 MICH. L. REV. 1815, 1827 (1991).

Arthur Corbin, *The Interpretation of Words and the Parol Evidence Rule*, 50 CORNELL L.Q. 161 (1965).

Theodore Eisenberg & Geoffrey P. Miller, *The Flight to New York: An Empirical Study of Choice of Law and Choice of Forum Clauses in Publicly-Held Companies' Contracts*, 30 CARDOZO L. REV. 1475 (2009).

E. Allan Farnsworth, *Your Loss or My Gain? The Dilemma of the Disgorgement Principle in Breach of Contract*, 94 YALE L.J. 1339 (1985).

Charles J. Goetz & Robert E. Scott, *The Limits of Expanded Choice: An Analysis of the Interactions Between Express and Implied Contract Terms*, 73 CAL. L. REV. 261 (1985).

Victor Goldberg, *Emotional Distress Damages and Breach of Contract: A New Approach*, 20 U.C. DAVIS L. REV. 57 (1986).

Victor Goldberg, Framing Contract Law: An Economic Perspective (2007).

Robert A. Hillman, *The "New Conservatism" in Contract Law and the Process of Legal Change*, 40 B.C. L. REV. 879 (1999).

Oliver Wendell Holmes, Jr., *The Theory of Legal Interpretation*, 12 HARV. L. REV. 417 (1899).

Roger W. Kirst, *Usage of Trade and Course of Dealing: Subversion of the UCC Theory*, 1977 U. ILL. L. F. 811.

Juliet P. Kostritsky, *Plain Meaning vs. Broad Interpretation: How the Risk of*

Opportunism Defeats a Unitary Default Rule for Interpretation, 96 Ky. L.J. 43 (2007)

Jody S. Kraus & Robert E. Scott, *Contract Design and the Structure of Contractual Intent*, 84 N.Y.U. L. Rev 1023, 1046–1057 (2009).

Jody Kraus & Steven D. Walt, *In Defense of the Incorporation Strategy, in* The Jurisprudence of Corporate and Commercial Law (J. Kraus & S. Walt eds., 2000).

Levie, *Trade Usage and Custom*, 40 N.Y.U. L. Rev. 1101 (1965).

Jeffrey M. Lipshaw, *The Bewitchment of Intelligence: Language and Ex Post Illusions of Intention*, 78 Temp. L. Rev. 99 (2005).

Jeffrey M. Lipshaw, *Models and Games: The Difference Between Explanation and Understanding for Lawyers and Ethicists*, 56 Clev. St. L. Rev. 613 (2008).

Stephen L. Lubben, *Chief Justice Traynor's Contract Jurisprudence and the Free Law Dilemma: Nazism, the Judiciary, and California's Contract Law*, 7 S. Cal. Interdisc. L.J. 81 (1998).

Susan Martin-Davidson, *Yes, Judge Kozinski, There Is a Parol Evidence Rule in California — The Lessons of a Pyrrhic Victory*, 25 Sw. U. L. Rev. 1 (1995).

Charles T. McCormick, *The Parol Evidence Rule as a Procedural Device for Control of the Jury*, 41 Yale L.J. 365 (1932).

Ralph Mooney, *The New Conceptualism in Contract Law*, 74 Or. L. Rev. 1131 (1995).

John Murray, *The Parol Evidence Process and Standardized Agreements Under the Restatement, Second, Contracts*, 123 U. Pa. L. Rev. 1342 (1975).

Edwin Patterson, *The Apportionment of Business Risks Through Legal Devices*, 24 Colum. L. Rev. 335 (1924).

Edwin Patterson, *The Interpretation and Construction of Contracts*, 64 Colum. L. Rev. 833 (1964).

Joseph Perillo, *The Origins of the Objective Theory of Contract Formation and Interpretation*, 69 Fordham L. Rev. 427 (2000).

Eric Posner, *The Parol Evidence Rule, the Plain Meaning Rule, and the Principles of Contractual Interpretation*, 146 U. Pa. L. Rev. 533 (1998).

Stephen Ross & Daniel Tranen, *The Modern Parol Evidence Rule and its Implications for New Textualist Statutory Interpretation*, 87 Geo. L.J. 195 (1998).

Alan Schwartz, *Contract Theory and Theories of Contract Regulation*, 92 Revue D'Economie Industrielle 101 (2000).

Alan Schwartz & Robert E. Scott, *Contract Interpretation Redux*, 119 Yale L.J. 926 (2010).

Alan Schwartz & Robert E. Scott, *Contract Theory and the Limits of Contract*

Law, 113 YALE L.J. 541 (2003).

Robert E. Scott & George G. Triantis, *Anticipating Litigation in Contract Design*, 115 YALE L.J. 814 (2006).

Robert E. Scott, *The Case for Formalism in Relational Contract*, 94 Nw. U. L. REV. 847 (2000).

Robert E. Scott, *The Uniformity Norm in Commercial Law: A Comparative Analysis of the Common Law and Code Methodologies, in* THE JURISPRUDENCE OF CORPORATE AND COMMERCIAL LAW (J. Kraus & S. Walt eds., 2000).

Robert E. Scott & Charles J. Goetz, *The Limits of Expanded Choice*, 73 CAL. L. REV. 261 (1985).

Justin Sweet, *Promissory Fraud and the Parol Evidence Rule*, 49 CAL. L. REV. 877 (1961).

Justin Sweet, *The Lawyer's Role in Contract Drafting*, 43 CAL. ST. B.J. 362 (1968).

Gregory V. Varallo & Srinivas M. Raju, *A Process Based Model for Analyzing Deal Protection Measures*, 55 BUS. LAW. 1609 (2000).

Chapter 7

DEFINING THE TERMS OF PERFORMANCE

A. INTRODUCTION

We begin this chapter with an examination of those contract default rules that define the performance obligations of the respective parties. At the outset, two points need to be emphasized. First, the performance of every contract will have both a "procedural" and a "substantive" aspect. Procedural default rules define the sequence of performances: when, where, and to what extent must each party perform (and, most importantly, what is the relationship between one party's obligation to perform and the other party's reciprocal obligation)? Substantive default rules then provide the quality standard against which any particular performance must be assessed.

Second, it is important to recall that these various default terms — although they carry different doctrinal labels (implied conditions, covenants, and warranties.) — are responses to a common problem. Between the time of contracting and the time of performance various contingencies may materialize and cause one of the contracting parties to regret having made the agreement. The default terms of the contract assign the risk of these contingencies to one party or the other. They accomplish this task in several ways: First, a number of default rules specify the obligations of both parties regarding the performance of their respective promises. Second, additional default rules specify when and under what circumstances those obligations may be excused or modified. This chapter takes up the set of rules that specify performance obligations. We then consider the question of excuse in Chapter 8.

It is important for the drafting attorney to remember that these contract doctrines are only defaults. If the basic risk allocation provided by the state's default rules fails to suit the purposes of particular parties, they are free *ex ante* to design an alternative allocation of risks. Most commonly, this is accomplished by parties making express promises (express covenants and warranties) regarding their performance and/or by expressly conditioning their own obligation to perform. In any case, whatever the doctrinal label, our initial inquiry should be the same: What principle justifies or explains why the law imposes the default risk on one party rather than the other? Why aren't the consequences shared as in any common disaster? In answering these questions you might begin by returning to the familiar benchmark employed throughout this course: How would the broadest number of contracting parties allocate these risks if they were required to bargain over the specific question in advance?

B. CONDITIONS

[1] Implied Conditions

Before any express terms governing performance of a contract (quality specifications, the sequence of tender of delivery and payment, and conditions on performance) can be negotiated, the drafting attorney faces an initial choice. Should she "accept" the implied (or default) terms that define the performance obligations of the parties as provided by the law, or should she design specially tailored alternatives? Obviously, the answer to this key question of contract design depends, in large part, on how the risks that attend the obligation to perform are allocated by the default terms the law initially provides. Thus, at the outset the drafting lawyer needs to answer two related questions: Which party bears the risks associated with any contractual performance? And, what are the legal doctrines that implement the default risk assignments in specific contexts?

[a] Allocating the Risks of Performance

You will recall from Chapter 1 that, in general, the risks associated with the performance of an executory promise are allocated to the promisor — the party whose performance is thereby affected. This "performer's risk" principle is one of the central default rules of contract law. The rule seems to be based on the notion that the performing party, who has some control over her performance and thus can take cost-justified precautions, enjoys a comparative advantage in reducing the risk that her performance will be more onerous or difficult than originally anticipated. But, even so, recall that our test of the efficacy of such a default is whether we can imagine that most bargainers would voluntarily so agree if required to allocate the risk explicitly in advance. Why would any promisor voluntarily agree at the time of contracting to assume this sort of responsibility?[1] In theory, the answer is straightforward: The promisor will be "paid" to bear the risks associated with her promise as a part of the contract price. One way to visualize how this basic default rule works is to imagine that the two parties to an executory contract are engaged in the process of exchanging insurance policies with each other. As with any insurer, the performing party (the "insurer") will assume a risk for a price whenever she can bear it at a lower cost than can her contracting partner (the "insured"). As a result, the risks associated with the future performance of the executory contract are reduced and both parties presumably share the resulting gains with each other as part of the contractual surplus.

---

[1] For further discussion of this question, see Robert E. Scott & George G. Triantis, *Anticipating Litigation in Contract Design*, 115 YALE L.J. 814 (2006).

STEES v. LEONARD
Supreme Court of Minnesota
20 Minn. 494 (1874)

See p. 74, *supra.*

[b]   Implied or Constructive Conditions of Exchange

The "performer's risk" principle imposes an obligation on the promisor to perform her promise notwithstanding the occurrence of contingencies that make performance more difficult or onerous. But the obligation to perform is not absolute. Rather, it is subject to certain implied or "constructive" conditions that must first be satisfied before the promisee is entitled to demand performance. The doctrines defining these implied conditions can be confusing at first, but keep in mind that these are simply supplementary default rules that spell out the basic principle that each party should be responsible only for her own performance and not for that of the other party. As a party to a bilateral exchange, I am both a promisor and a promisee, and I need to know to what extent my performance is linked to your performance.

One straightforward implied condition of my performance, therefore, is that your return performance will be forthcoming as well. For example, assume that on Monday I agree to sell you my dog, Lucy, for $400, delivery on Thursday. On Thursday, I bring Lucy, but you say that you will give me the $400 on Saturday. I refuse to deliver Lucy. The courts will provide two default rules to resolve this dispute. Although the contract did not specify when you were to pay the $400, a court will say that it is payable at the time of delivery. Thus, you are in breach of contract. Second, although the contract did not specify whether I had a duty to deliver Lucy if you did not pay, a court will say that your delivery of the $400 was a condition precedent to my duty to deliver Lucy. Thus, I am not in breach of contract. In the terms traditionally used, therefore, the tender of payment of $400 and the tender of delivery of Lucy are implied concurrent conditions.

Suppose instead that you and I agree (in writing) that in exchange for $1,000 you will train Lucy to be an obedient dog. The training will take one month. After training Lucy for one week, you ask for $250. I refuse to pay until the training is complete, and you refuse to continue with the training. I remove Lucy from your care and take her to another trainer, at a higher price. A court will hold that, although the contract says nothing about when payment is due, the default rule is that I have no duty to pay until the training is substantially complete, and I do not owe you periodic payments. Thus, your refusal to continue with the training was a failure to substantially perform your part of the contract, and your substantial performance was an implied condition precedent to my duty to perform the contract. You are in breach and I am not.

Do you have an explanation for the difference in outcomes in these two hypothetical cases? Do the outcomes match what the parties would most likely have stipulated had they considered the possibility of these events at the time of contracting?

BELL v. ELDER

Court of Appeals of Utah

782 P.2d 545, 121 Utah Adv. Rep. 16 (1989)

BULLOCK, J.

Plaintiffs Bell appeal from a judgment dismissing their claims for rescission of a contract to buy real property and for restitution of the amounts paid thereunder. We affirm.

The Bells . . . contracted in 1977 to purchase ten acres of undeveloped land from a partnership comprised of the defendants (Elders) for a total of $25,000. Part of the price was paid at closing, with the remainder to be paid later. The Elders were to convey legal title on receipt of payment in full.

The land sold was zoned for agricultural use at the time of the contract, with no more than one residence per ten-acre parcel permitted. The parties had hopes of developing the area more extensively than the zoning then permitted, but their hopes did not prove feasible. Property values in the area have generally declined since the contract was made.

The contract was reduced to writing by filling in a pre-printed form entitled "Uniform Real Estate Contract," into which the following typewritten words were inserted:

> The Seller [Elders] hereby agrees and warrantys [sic] to furnish water and electrical power [and] roads to this Property by July, 1978. If Buyer is unable to obtain [a] building permit by July, 1978, the seller agrees to endemnify [sic] and repay this contract within 6 months.

This insertion in the original contract was the subject of a "Supplemental [sic] Agreement" dated November 3, 1978, which read as follows:

> Because of unforeseen circumstances that have arisen with regard to furnishing utilities to the [subject] property, the following Supplimental [sic] Agreement is added. . . . It is now understood and agreed that the Sellers ([Elders]) at their expense will furnish to each of [2 5-acre] plots, the culinary water, electrical power, and roads. That Buyer is to pay $1,000 hook-up and installation fee for culinary water. The fee to be paid at the time of home construction and no fees payable for electrical power or roads, to property fade lines.
>
> If Buyers should sell any lots from their 5[-]acre plots, then and in this event a $4,000 utilities improvement fee is payable to Sellers at the time of sale for each and every lot sold. This pays for the utilities, roads, electrical power and culinary water. Buyers of these lots would pay in addition $1,000 culinary water hook-up and installation fee.
>
> Sellers ([Elders]) hereby agrees to furnish at their cost, sewer facilities to each of these 5[-]acre plots. . . .

It is further understood and agreed that if the Sellers are unable to furnish these utilities on or before October 15, 1980 the Sellers agree to endemnify [sic] and repay this contract within six months.

The provisions of this Supplemental Agreement shall not alter or reduce in any way the conditions, terms, and provisions of the original contract.

At the time of trial, Elders had not furnished water to the property, but the court found that they were "ready, willing, and able at all times" to supply the required water. Bells, however, had not obtained, or applied for, a building permit, and had not paid the $1,000 hook-up and installation fee. The trial court found that the Bells had "decided not to build on the [property] because they were going to live elsewhere."

The Bells sued to rescind the contract and recover the amounts they had paid thereunder, arguing in essence that the Elders had breached it by failing to supply culinary water to the property as the contract required. However, the trial court saw no purpose in requiring installation of culinary water facilities to serve rather remote property not intended for residential use, and held that the Elders were required by the contract to be merely able to furnish water to the subject property by October 15, 1980, and that they were required to actually furnish the water to the property only if the Bells had obtained a building permit and were about to construct a house, so that the water would be put to "beneficial use." The Bells appeal, challenging the findings (1) that the Elders were able to supply culinary water and (2) that the culinary water would have no value until the defendants would be able to use it. Bells also argue that residential use of the property was not a condition precedent to the Elders' obligation to furnish culinary water. . . .

As noted above, the trial court interpreted the contract as requiring that the Elders merely be able to furnish water to the subject property by October 15, 1980, and not that water actually be furnished, observing that there was as yet no house on the property, nor was construction of a house imminent. In thus interpreting the contract as requiring only that the Elders be able to furnish water by October 15, 1980, the trial court relied extensively on parol evidence to augment the tersely worded operative provisions of the written contract. The propriety of admitting parol evidence to facilitate the contract's interpretation has not been challenged. Accordingly, the court's interpretation is reviewed on appeal under the standard applied to findings of fact. That standard, as noted above, permits us to reverse only if the appellant marshals all evidence relevant to the finding in question and thereby shows it to be clearly erroneous. The Bells have failed both to thoroughly marshall the evidence and to demonstrate that the trial court's fact-based interpretation of this term of the contract is clearly erroneous. We therefore affirm the holding that the Elders were contractually required to be able to furnish culinary water to the property by October 15, 1980. Since they were thus able at all material times, it follows that the Elders did not breach their obligation to be able to furnish water.

We recognize that interpreting the contract to require that the Elders merely be able to furnish water falls short of requiring them to actually furnish water, and that the Bells did not contract only for the Elders' mere, inchoate ability to furnish water. Both the original agreement and the supplemental agreement contain express promises by the Elders to actually supply water to the Bells. However, although the contract contains a promise by the Elders to supply water, as well as a related promise by the Bells to obtain a building permit for the construction of a house to receive the water, no time is specified for performing either promise. The sequence in which those promises were to be performed is nevertheless the very essence of the present controversy. The situation at trial consisted of the Bells, on the one hand, seeking to rescind the contract on the grounds that the Elders had breached an obligation to actually furnish water to the property, and, on the other hand, the Elders insisting that they would supply the required water when the Bells demanded it and performed their obligations. The question thus presented boils down to the order in which these parties must perform their related obligations.

In determining the order of performance of exchanged promises, we look first to the contract itself, and, if no order of performance is therein specified, we apply the common law of constructive contractual conditions. This contract is silent on the time or times for actually furnishing water and for obtaining a building permit. In such a case, where there is no express indication of the intended order for performance, the law implies a covenant and condition that the related obligations be performed concurrently. . . . Since performance of these obligations was due concurrently, neither party could claim a breach by the other until the party claiming the breach tendered performance of its concurrent obligation. The rule requiring such a tender has been explained in a case in which a real estate purchaser and seller each demanded and awaited performance by the other of their respective obligations to pay the price and deliver the property. The Supreme Court's words in that case apply here as well:

> This is precisely the sort of deadlock meant to be resolved by the requirement of tender . . . During the executory period of a contract whose time of performance is uncertain but which contemplates simultaneous performance by both parties . . . neither party can be said to be in default . . . until the other party has tendered his own performance. In other words, the party who desires to use legal process to exercise his legal remedies under such a contract must make a tender of his own agreed performance in order to put the other party in default. Century 21 All Western Real Estate and Inv. Inc. v. Webb, 645 P.2d 52, 55-56 (Utah 1982).

This case demonstrates that the rule requiring tender before claiming breach of a concurrent promise is not a mere formality or trap for the unwary. Here, the claimant's tender would demonstrate the continued practical vitality and purposefulness of the promise owed the claimant. Public policy and common sense oppose the waste of installing a culinary water line to serve land which, for all that appears, will remain unused. The rule requiring tender thus serves, among other purposes, to prevent a claimant from insisting upon a purposeless performance, or from avoiding his own obligations on pretext.

Inasmuch as the material findings do not appear to be clearly erroneous and the failure of the plaintiffs to perform their own obligations precludes recovery on their claims, the judgment is affirmed.

NOTES

1. *The "Work Before Pay" Rule*: Stewart v. Newbury. In an important category of disputes, one party asserts the right to periodic payments as the promised performance progresses, while the other party refuses to pay until the performance is substantially complete. A typical example is the building contractor who demands progress payments from the owner under a construction contract. If the parties have not expressly made periodic payments a condition of the contractor's duty to continue with the job, the law implies a condition of substantial performance before payment is due.[2] Hence the default rule is "work before pay."

Consider *Stewart v. Newbury*, 220 N.Y. 379 (Ct. App. 1917), in which the plaintiff agreed to erect a concrete mill building for the defendants, partners of Newbury Manufacturing Company, at Monroe, NY. Nothing was said in writing about the time or manner of payment. The plaintiff claimed the custom was to pay 85% every 30 days or at the end of each month, 15% being retained till the work was completed. In July, 1911 the plaintiff commenced work and continued until September 29th, progressing with the construction as far as the first floor. He then sent a bill to the defendants for the work done up to that date for $896.35. The defendants refused to pay the bill and work was discontinued. The contractor brought suit to recover the amount of the bill presented. At trial, the court instructed the jury by saying, "[I]f there was no agreement between the parties respecting the payments, the defendants' obligation was to make payments at reasonable times." *Id.* at 384.

The Court of Appeals disagreed:

> This is not the law. Counsel for the plaintiff omits to call our attention to any authority sustaining such a proposition and our search reveals none. In fact the law is very well settled to the contrary. This was an entire contract. Where a contract is made to perform work and no agreement is made as to payment, the work must be substantially performed before payment can be demanded.

Id. at 384–85.

2. *The Restatement on Order of Performances*. The Restatement (Second) § 234 deals with the order of performance. Comment a to that section justifies the "presumption" of subsection (1) on the grounds that "it offers both parties maximum security against disappointment of their expectations of a subsequent exchange of performance by allowing each to defer until he has been assured that the other will perform." Comment a provides a second justification: that this result "avoids placing on either party the burden of financing the other before the latter has performed."

Such a burden cannot be avoided entirely in the situation described in subsection (2), which covers cases like *Stewart v. Newbury*, but the burden could be reduced by an implied term calling for periodic payments. Why do you suppose that employees "finance" their employers between paychecks? Why do students pay tuition in

---

[2] *See Jacob & Youngs v. Kent*, Chapter 1.

advance of their school's performance? Is the court's rule in *Stewart v. Newbury* one you would expect most building contractors to follow?

3. ***Implied Conditions in Other Contexts.*** Implied conditions resolve performance issues in many different contractual contexts. Consider *Ethyl Corp. v. United Steelworkers of America, etc.*, 768 F.2d 180 (7th Cir. 1985). In *Ethyl*, the collective bargaining agreement between the company and the union contained a provision guaranteeing paid vacations to workers who worked a specified number of hours at a plant in a particular year. In late 1981, the company decided to close the plant, but ultimately reopened it 18 months later. The company sought to withhold 1982 vacation pay from the employees, because they did not meet the mandatory hours requirement for that year due to the temporary closing of the plant. The arbitrator ruled that even though the employees were laid off, they were all entitled to vacation pay. The Seventh Circuit affirmed the arbitrator's award. Judge Posner held that "the authority of an arbitrator to interpret a collective bargaining contract includes the power to discover [implied] terms." In this case, the employees' duty to work a prescribed number of hours before earning paid vacations was subject to the implied condition that the company not have prevented them from satisfying the work requirements.

4. ***Anticipatory Repudiation.*** In *Bell*, the Court of Appeals states that "[t]he trial court found that the Bells had "decided not to build on the [property] because they were going to live elsewhere." If the Elders learned that the Bells had made this decision, a court might find that it constituted an implied anticipatory repudiation of the agreement. In those common law jurisdictions that recognize a right to demand adequate assurances of performance, the Bells' decision would likely constitute "reasonable grounds for insecurity" triggering the Elders' right to demand assurances of performance. These doctrines are covered in detail in Chapter 9.

[c] Divisibility

JOHN v. UNITED ADVERTISING, INC.
Supreme Court of Colorado
165 Colo. 193, 439 P.2d 53 (1968)

McWILLIAMS, J.

This is a contract case. The central issue is whether the contract in question is "entire" or "severable" in nature.

Dwight John, who will hereinafter be referred to as the plaintiff, as the owner and operator of two motels located on South Broadway street in Englewood, Colorado, entered into a written contract with United Advertising, Inc., a corporation which will hereinafter be referred to as the defendant. Under the terms and provisions of this contract the defendant agreed to construct, install and then maintain at its own expense for a period of three years seven outdoor display signs advertising the two motels owned and operated by the plaintiff, in return for which the plaintiff promised to pay the defendant the sum of $95 per month for three years.

In view of the trial court's ultimate disposition of this controversy, two other provisions of the contract between the parties should now be mentioned. The contract "broke down" the aggregate monthly rental of $95 and provided that the rental on one of the seven signs, which was to be 10'x30' in size, would be $35 per month and that the rental on each of the remaining six signs, which were each to be 4'x8' in size, would be $10 per month. As concerns possible termination or modification of the agreement, there was a provision that the termination or modification "of any item of this agreement constitutes that part of the agreement only and does not affect any other item or part of the agreement."

The present writ of error stems from the plaintiff's claim against the defendant for damages for an alleged breach of contract. In his complaint the plaintiff alleged that the defendant failed to erect and maintain the advertising signs as it had agreed to do and averred that as a result thereof plaintiff suffered damages in the total sum of $10,655. Of this amount, according to the plaintiff, $10,000 represented a so-called loss of business profits, and the remaining $655 represented monies paid the defendant under the contract.

By answer the defendant alleged that each of the seven signs had been properly erected and maintained, except for one small sign, which will be referred to as sign No. 4. The defendant asserted no counterclaim for the reason that shortly before the institution of the present action, the defendant assigned its claim against the plaintiff for unpaid monthly rentals to a collection agency.

Trial of this matter was to the court, at the conclusion of which the trial court made very detailed findings of fact and conclusions of law. Specifically, the trial court found that five signs which were referred to as signs No. 1, 2, 3, 6 and 7 were erected in substantial compliance with the terms of the contract. However, the trial court found that sign No. 4 was never erected and that sign No. 5, though erected, was not erected in the particular location called for by the contract. In short, then, the trial court found that the defendant had in fact breached the contract in these two particulars.

It was in this particular setting, that the trial court then found that the contract in question was "divisible" and that the failure of the defendant to properly erect and maintain signs No. 4 and 5 constituted only a "severable breach." However, the trial court then went on to find that even though the plaintiff had established two so-called severable breaches, he nonetheless had failed to establish by "satisfactory evidence" that he sustained any damage by reason of the failure of the defendant to properly install signs No. 4 and 5. The trial court accordingly entered judgment dismissing the plaintiff's claim for relief, and by writ of error plaintiff now seeks reversal of the judgment thus entered.

As above indicated, probably the basic issue is whether the contract between the parties is entire or severable. In other words, whether the seven signs in question were, or were not, erected in substantial compliance with the terms and provisions of the contract is basically a question of fact. Our review of the record convinces us that there is evidence to support the trial court's determination that signs No. 1, 2, 3, 6 and 7 were installed substantially in accord with the contract, but that on the contrary the defendant did in fact breach the contract as concerns signs No. 4 and 5. These findings then cannot be disturbed, as there is evidence to support them.

Digressing for a moment from a consideration of the contract itself, our perusal of the record convinces us that the trial court's finding that the plaintiff failed to establish any so-called loss of business by reason of defendant's aforementioned breach of contract must also be sustained. Granted that it was perhaps difficult for the plaintiff to establish, for example, the number of customers he lost because of the defendant's failure to properly erect signs No. 4 and 5, still the burden to prove such an item of damage is his. Under all the circumstances we are therefore disinclined to disturb the finding of the trial court that in this particular, at least, the plaintiff failed to sustain his burden of proof. . . .

However, there is one remaining item of damage which must be considered, and that is the money paid by plaintiff to defendant under the contract. The contract itself called for plaintiff to pay the defendant the last four months rent on all seven signs. This the plaintiff did, paying defendant the total sum of $380 upon the signing of the contract, or within a very short time thereafter. Then, while the defendant was in the process of erecting the various signs, plaintiff also paid defendant additional sums totaling $300. In other words, the evidence showed that the plaintiff paid defendant the total sum of $680 under the contract, and this was the eventual finding of the trial court. However, the trial court apparently did not consider this to be an item of damage, and in this particular it did err.

Of the total sum given defendant by the plaintiff, namely $680, our study of the findings made by the trial court indicates that $120 represented money paid for the two signs (signs No. 4 and 5) which defendant failed to properly install. So, if the contract be severable or divisible, then the plaintiff is only entitled to recover those monies paid defendant for signs No. 4 and 5, which sum is $120. But if the contract be deemed entire in nature, the plaintiff would be entitled to recover all of the monies paid by him to the defendant, which would be the sum of $680. It is in this setting that it then becomes necessary to determine the correctness of the trial court's determination that the contract is severable, and not entire.

Whether a contract is entire or severable is a matter which cannot be determined with mathematical precision, as it has been said that there is no set formula which furnishes a foolproof method for determining in a given case just which contracts are severable and which are entire. The primary objective is to ascertain the intent of the contracting parties, as such intent is manifested by not only the several terms and provisions of the contract itself, but also as such are viewed in the light of all the surrounding circumstances, including the conduct of the parties before any dispute has arisen. And the singleness or apportionability of the consideration is said to be an important factor to be considered. See Swinney v. Continental Building Co. 102 S.W.2d 11. x

. . . [W]hether a number of promises constitute one contract, or more than one, is to be determined by inquiring "whether the parties assented to all the promises as a whole, so that there would have been no bargain whatever, if any promise or set of promises were struck out." U.S. v. Bethlehem Steel Corp., 315 U.S. 289. Plaintiff's position on this point is that it was intended that this be a "package deal," that at least four of the signs were to be so situated as to "lead" tourists to the very doorstep of his motel, and that he received no benefit under the contract unless all seven signs were properly erected and in place. Therefore, it is argued, the contract is entire in nature.

The defendant, on the contrary, urges that it was the intent of the parties that the contract be severable. In support thereof defendant points to the fact that the money due it from the plaintiff was not a lump sum for the seven signs, but was apportioned as so much, per individual sign. Also, the defendant argues that the termination and modification clause, referred to at the outset of this opinion, certainly looks toward severability. Finally, defendant notes that the several billings were on a "so much per sign basis," and each sign is said to be complete within itself, with no one sign by any language printed thereon being "tied in" to any other sign.

The foregoing recital indicates that the testimony bearing on this particular matter is in at least a degree of conflict. Certainly reasonable persons could well differ as to the proper inferences to be drawn from the testimony and documentary evidence which was before the trial court. In such circumstance we are not at liberty to overturn the trial court's determination that the contract in the instant case was a severable one. There being evidence, then, to support this finding of the trial court, its determination must therefore be upheld. Accordingly, the judgment of the trial court dismissing plaintiff's claim is reversed and the cause remanded with direction that judgment be entered in favor of plaintiff and against defendant in the sum of $120, which is the rental paid on signs No. 4 and 5.

NOTES

1. *Determining Divisibility.* The general rules of divisibility are found in §§ 237 and 240 of the Restatement (Second). Whether a contract is divisible is not always a straightforward question.[3] For example, in *Buffalo Seminary v. Tomaselli*, 107 Misc. 2d 536, 435 N.Y.S.2d 507 (1981), the plaintiff, a private school, suspended one of its students in May of the 1980 school year, then attempted to collect tuition and fees on a *pro rata* basis for its performance during the school year. After noting that the school had fallen short of substantial performance, the court disallowed collection of the tuition fees, deeming them "indivisibility is based upon the integral nature of the academic year." *Id.* at 538, 435 N.Y.S.2d at 509. Nonetheless the court allowed the plaintiff to recover a claim for the value of meals and other items of personal property which were consumed or otherwise retained by the student. Is this result internally consistent?

Similarly, in *First S&L Ass'n v. Am. Home Assur. Co.*, 29 N.Y.2d 297 (1971), the plaintiff, a bank holding the mortgage of a homeowner, asserted a claim to the proceeds of the homeowner's insurance contract with the defendant-insurance company. The homeowner had initially purchased home insurance coverage of $7,000. Subsequently, he increased his insurance to $15,000 for an additional premium. However, he neglected to pay the additional premium, after which the insurance company canceled the entire policy. When the home burned down, the mortgagee sued, claiming that the contract was divisible into amounts of $7,000 and

---

[3] For a discussion of the conditions required to sever contract clauses, see Mark L. Movsesian, *Severability in Statutes and Contracts*, 30 GA. L. REV. 41, 43–57 (1995).

$8,000, and that the notice of cancellation applied only to the increased coverage. The court held that the contract was not severable and affirmed summary judgment for the defendant. Do you agree with this decision?

2. *Divisibility Under the UCC.* Read the UCC's divisibility rule found in § 2-307 and the UCC rule on installment contracts found in § 2-612. Why should a contract for the sale of goods, as compared to other types of contracts, call for a more (or less) restrictive rule of divisibility?

3. *Restitution to a Defaulting Plaintiff.* Assume you represent a party to a contract who has performed part but not all (or even substantially all) of her contractual obligation. If the contract is not divisible, your client is barred by the concurrent condition default rule from seeking recovery of the other party's return performance. Is there any way you can recover at least something on behalf of your client? One way of avoiding (at least in part) the strictures of an implied condition is for the contract breacher to seek to recover the reasonable value of his partial performance in quantum meruit even though he has not substantially performed on the contract. This issue is considered in depth in Chapter 10.

[2] Express Conditions

[a] Promises and Conditions

Imagine that you are retained to draft a complex contract for a commercial client. From your studies in contract law, you know that "the contract" will include both the written terms of the agreement together with many implied terms as well. You also know from the rules of interpretation we studied in Chapter 6 that courts may have difficulty determining the meaning of contracts that combine express and implied terms.[4] This raises a further question: In designing express contract terms that vary from the basic default rules, should the drafting lawyer frame the respective rights and obligations of the parties as precise (or bright line) "rules" or should the respective rights and obligations be framed as broad, general "standards"? Drafting express terms as precise "rules" reduces the risk that a court (or jury) may subsequently misunderstand the parties' agreement, say by modifying a performance obligation that the parties had intended to be unqualified. On the other hand, drafting express terms as broad standards has the advantage of delegating more discretion to a court which, after all, has the benefit of hind-sight.[5] You should consider the advantages and disadvantages of each of these approaches in the materials that follow.

Whether framed as "rules" or as "standards," the attorney has a major responsibility to design and draft the contract so that the parties' ex ante intentions are realized. The default terms supplied by the law of contracts provide the starting point for this drafting exercise. Thereafter, the drafting attorney must both trump

---

[4] For a discussion of the tensions between express and implied terms, see Charles J. Goetz & Robert E. Scott, *The Limits of Expanded Choice: An Analysis of the Interactions Between Express and Implied Terms*, 73 Cal. L. Rev. 261 (1985).

[5] For further discussion of this question, *see* Robert E. Scott & George G. Triantis, *Anticipating Litigation in Contract Design*, 115 Yale L.J. 814 (2006).

any ill-fitting default terms and supplement those that remain with additional express terms. A number of particular requirements must be specified in the contract if each party's contractual expectations are to be met. In translating these requirements into contract language, the first challenge is to decide whether the requirements important to your client should be framed as express promises made by the other party or as express conditions to your client's duty to perform her reciprocal obligation, or both. Consider, for example, the following case.

HOWARD v. FEDERAL CROP INS. CORP.
United States Court of Appeals, Fourth Circuit
540 F.2d 695 (1976)

WIDENER, CIRCUIT JUDGE:

Plaintiff-appellants sued to recover for losses to their 1973 tobacco crop due to alleged rain damage. The crops were insured by defendant-appellee, Federal Crop Insurance Corporation (FCIC). Suits were brought in a state court in North Carolina and removed to the United States District Court. The three suits are not distinguishable factually so far as we are concerned here and involve identical questions of law. They were combined for disposition in the district court and for appeal. The district court granted summary judgment for the defendant and dismissed all three actions. We remand for further proceedings. Since we find for the plaintiffs as to the construction of the policy, we express no opinion on the procedural questions.

Federal Crop Insurance Corporation, an agency of the United States, in 1973, issued three policies to the Howards, insuring their tobacco crops, to be grown on six farms, against weather damage and other hazards.

The Howards (plaintiffs) established production of tobacco on their acreage, and have alleged that their 1973 crop was extensively damaged by heavy rains, resulting in a gross loss to the three plaintiffs in excess of $35,000. The plaintiffs harvested and sold the depleted crop and timely filed notice and proof of loss with FCIC, but, prior to inspection by the adjuster for FCIC, the Howards had either plowed or disked under the tobacco fields in question to prepare the same for sowing a cover crop of rye to preserve the soil. When the FCIC adjuster later inspected the fields, he found the stalks had been largely obscured or obliterated by plowing or disking and denied the claims, apparently on the ground that the plaintiffs had violated a portion of the policy which provides that the stalks on any acreage with respect to which a loss is claimed shall not be destroyed until the corporation makes an inspection.

The holding of the district court is best capsuled in its own words:

> The inquiry here is whether compliance by the insureds with this provision of the policy was a condition precedent to the recovery. The court concludes that it was and that the failure of the insureds to comply worked a forfeiture of benefits for the alleged loss.

There is no question but that apparently after notice of loss was given to defendant, but before inspection by the adjuster, plaintiffs plowed under the tobacco stalks and sowed some of the land with a cover crop, rye. The question is whether, under paragraph 5(f) of the tobacco endorsement to the policy of insurance, the act of plowing under the tobacco stalks forfeits the coverage of the policy. Paragraph 5 of the tobacco endorsement is entitled Claims. Pertinent to this case are subparagraphs 5(b) and 5(f), which are as follows:

> 5(b) *It shall be a condition precedent* to the payment of any loss that the insured establish the production of the insured crop on a unit and that such loss has been directly caused by one or more of the hazards insured against during the insurance period for the crop year for which the loss is claimed, and furnish any other information regarding the manner and extent of loss as may be required by the Corporation. (Emphasis added.)

> 5(f) The tobacco stalks on any acreage of tobacco of types 11a, 11b, 12, 13, or 14 with respect to which a loss is claimed *shall not be destroyed until the Corporation makes an inspection.* (Emphasis added.)

The arguments of both parties are predicated upon the same two assumptions. First, if subparagraph 5(f) creates a condition precedent, its violation caused a forfeiture of plaintiffs' coverage. Second, if subparagraph 5(f) creates an obligation (variously called a promise or covenant) upon plaintiffs not to plow under the tobacco stalks, defendant may recover from plaintiffs (either in an original action, or, in this case, by a counterclaim, or as a matter of defense) for whatever damage it sustained because of the elimination of the stalks. However, a violation of subparagraph 5(f) would not, under the second premise, standing alone, cause a forfeiture of the policy.

Generally accepted law provides us with guidelines here. There is a general legal policy opposed to forfeitures. Insurance policies are generally construed most strongly against the insurer. When it is doubtful whether words create a promise or a condition precedent, they will be construed as creating a promise. The provisions of a contract will not be construed as conditions precedent in the absence of language plainly requiring such construction. . . .

Plaintiffs rely most strongly upon the fact that the term "condition precedent" is included in subparagraph 5(b) but not in subparagraph 5(f). It is true that whether a contract provision is construed as a condition or an obligation does not depend entirely upon whether the word "condition" is expressly used. . . . However, the persuasive force of plaintiffs' argument in this case is found in the use of the term "condition precedent" in subparagraph 5(b) but not in subparagraph 5(f). Thus, it is argued that the ancient maxim to be applied is that the expression of one thing is the exclusion of another. . . .

The Restatement of the Law of Contracts states:

§ 261. INTERPRETATION OF DOUBTFUL WORDS AS PROMISE OR CONDITION.

Where it is doubtful whether words create a promise or an express condition, they are interpreted as creating a promise; but the same words may sometimes mean that one party promises a performance and that the other party's promise is conditional on that performance.

Two illustrations (one involving a promise, the other a condition) are used in the Restatement:

2. A, an insurance company, issues to B a policy of insurance containing promises by A that are in terms conditional on the happening of certain events. The policy contains this clause: 'provided, in case differences shall arise touching any loss, *the matter shall be submitted to impartial arbitrators*, whose award shall be binding on the parties.' This is a promise to arbitrate and does not make an award a condition precedent of the insurer's duty to pay.

3. A, an insurance company, issues to B an insurance policy in usual form containing this clause: 'In the event of disagreement as to the amount of loss it shall be ascertained by two appraisers and an umpire. The loss shall *not be payable until 60 days after the award of the appraisers when such an appraisal is required*' This provision is not merely a promise to arbitrate differences but makes an award a condition of the insurer's duty to pay in case of disagreement. (Emphasis added)

We believe that subparagraph 5(f) in the policy here under consideration fits illustration 2 rather than illustration 3. Illustration 2 specifies something to be done, whereas subparagraph 5(f) specifies something not to be done. Unlike illustration 3, subparagraph 5(f) does not state any conditions under which the insurance shall "not be payable," or use any words of like import. We hold that the district court erroneously held, on the motion for summary judgment, that subparagraph 5(f) established a condition precedent to plaintiffs' recovery which forfeited the coverage.

From our holding that defendant's motion for summary judgment was improperly allowed, it does not follow the plaintiffs' motion for summary judgment should have been granted, for if subparagraph 5(f) be not construed as a condition precedent, there are other questions of fact to be determined. At this point, we merely hold that the district court erred in holding, on the motion for summary judgment, that subparagraph 5(f) constituted a condition precedent with resulting forfeiture.

The explanation defendant makes for including subparagraph 5(f) in the tobacco endorsement is that it is necessary that the stalks remain standing in order for the Corporation to evaluate the extent of loss and to determine whether loss resulted from some cause not covered by the policy. However, was subparagraph 5(f) inserted because without it the Corporation's opportunities for proof would be more difficult, or because they would be impossible? Plaintiffs point out that the Tobacco Endorsement, with subparagraph 5(f), was adopted in 1970, and crop insurance goes back long before that date. Nothing is shown as to the Corporation's prior 1970 practice of evaluating losses. Such a showing might have a bearing upon establishing defendant's intention in including 5(f). Plaintiffs state, and defendant does not deny, that another division of the Department of Agriculture, or the North Carolina Department, urged that tobacco stalks be cut as soon as possible after harvesting as a means of pest control. Such an explanation might refute the idea that plaintiffs plowed under the stalks for any fraudulent purpose. Could these conflicting directives affect the reasonableness of plaintiffs' interpretation of defendant's prohibition upon plowing under the stalks prior to adjustment?

We express no opinion on these questions because they were not before the district court and are mentioned to us largely by way of argument rather than from the record. . . . Nothing we say here should preclude FCIC from asserting as a defense that the plowing or disking under of the stalks caused damage to FCIC if, for example, the amount of the loss was thereby made more difficult or impossible to ascertain whether the plowing or disking under was done with bad purpose or innocently. To repeat, our narrow holding is that merely plowing or disking under the stalks does not of itself operate to forfeit coverage under the policy.

The case is remanded for further proceedings not inconsistent with this opinion.

VACATED AND REMANDED.

NOTES

1. *Analyzing "Conditional" Clauses.* Read the definition of "condition" in Restatement (Second) § 224. As *Howard v. Federal Crop Insurance Co.* demonstrates, contractual language can be interpreted so as to create either a condition or a promise. In *In re Carter*, 390 Pa. 365, 134 A.2d 908 (1957), the contract for the sale of a business contained the statement that the firm's closing financial condition shall be no less favorable than the firm's condition on June 30, 1954. If this statement is a promise, then a damage action lies against the seller for its breach. If the statement is a condition, then the buyer can walk away from the sale if the firm's financial condition upon closing is less favorable, but there is no breach by the seller. Alternatively, the statement could be both a condition and a promise. Why might the buyer in this case prefer to walk away from the deal rather than have a damage remedy? Why doesn't a buyer in this context always negotiate both a promise and a condition? What is the seller's view of this choice?[6]

The common law traditionally prefers to construe ambiguous contractual statements as promises, rather than as conditions, because the latter interpretation may result in a forfeiture of accrued contract rights. Comment b to section 227 of the Restatement (Second) states:

> The policy favoring freedom of contract requires that, within broad limits . . . , the agreement of the parties should be honored even though forfeiture results. When, however, it is doubtful whether or not the agreement makes an event a condition of an obligor's duty, an interpretation is preferred that will reduce the risk of forfeiture.

2. *The Schizophrenic Law of Conditions. The Pluralist Challenge to the Economic Approach.* Since parties incur duties in contracts by making promises, a party who makes an event an express condition of its promise is under a duty to

---

[6] For discussion, see Robert A. Hillman, *An Analysis of the Cessation of Contractual Relations*, 68 CORNELL L. REV. 617 (1983).

perform that promise only if the event occurs. As exemplified by *Howard v. FCIC*, common examples of express conditions are found in many insurance contracts: a typical condition to the duty to pay requires the insured to bring his claim within a specified time period after the insured suffers a covered loss. Here, the insurer's duty to pay arises when the insured suffers a covered loss, but that duty is discharged if the insured fails to bring the claim within the specified time period. The law of conditions explicitly endorses the principle of freedom of contract by committing to the strict enforcement of all express conditions. *See, e.g., Renovest Co. v. Hodges Dev. Corp.*, 600 A.2d 448, 452–53 (N.H. 1991) ("[W]hen the parties expressly condition their performance upon the occurrence or non-occurrence of an event, rather than simply including the event as one of the general terms of the contract, the parties' bargained-for expectation of strict compliance should be given effect."). Yet the law of conditions also embraces the equitable maxim that the law abhors a forfeiture. *See, e.g., Naftalin v. John Wood Co.*, 116 N.W.2d 91, 100 (Minn. 1962) ("[It is a] well-recognized principle that forfeitures are not favored either in law or equity. . . . One claiming forfeiture carries a heavy burden of establishing his right thereto by clear and unmistakable proof."). The anti-forfeiture norm envelops the law of conditions, thus producing a schizophrenic result: On the one hand, the law insists on the sanctity of strict construction and enforcement of conditions in spite of forfeiture, while, on the other hand, it admonishes courts, whenever interpretation allows, to avoid the enforcement of a condition that would raise the specter of forfeiture.

This tension is best seen as a further example of the divide between ex ante and ex post perspectives. The ex post perspective — urging courts to avoid a forfeiture — is one that is likely embraced by pluralist scholars who support the courts' duty to impose "fair" outcomes ex post even if that undermines the parties ex ante commitments. Such a view was advocated by Professor Robert Childres in *Conditions in the Law of Contracts*, 45 N.Y.U. L. Rev. 33 (1970). In his view, the traditional law of conditions has been subordinated to a policy which promotes good faith conduct — "fundamental honesty, fair play, and right dealing" — in contract performance. In this process, various theories have been developed to nullify the old law of conditions: "Waiver, estoppel, substantial performance and abhorrence of forfeitures are among the doctrines which have allowed the law of conditions to survive by making it inoperative." The widespread use of these equitable doctrines to undermine the law of express conditions has been criticized by economic theorists. Professors Jody Kraus and Robert Scott argue in *Contract Design and the Structure of Contractual Intent*, 84 N.Y.U. L. Rev. 1023 (2009), that

> the law of conditions explicitly stacks the deck heavily against the finding and enforcement of conditions on the ground that the law abhors a forfeiture. . . . We have argued that considerations of contract design often favor the selection of precise terms that create rule-like obligations that are easy for the parties to observe and to enforce in court. Express conditions serve just this purpose: they afford a promisor protection from certain risks, in lieu of having to prove losses that are difficult to verify in a suit for damages. When sophisticated commercial parties clearly agree to express conditions, there is no systematic reason to doubt that the promisee

understood the risk of forfeiture and bargained for compensating contractual benefits from the promisor.

Id. at 1084.

As you examine the various doctrines of conditions and substantial performance, ask yourself if materiality or "fairness" is central to understanding the cases, or if some other guiding policy is present.

3. *Pay-if-Paid Clauses.* As we have seen, courts are often reluctant to interpret contractual language so as to impose conditions on a return performance, especially in cases where one party performs and then does not receive its expected consideration.[7] A recent example of this interpretive bias against express conditions is *Main Elec., Ltd. v. Printz Servs. Corp.*, 980 P.2d 522 (Colo. 1999). In this case, the contract stated that the subcontractor would be paid when the owner paid the general contractor. The contract was silent on the question of whether the subcontractor would be paid in the event that the owner defaulted.

The Supreme Court of Colorado ruled that the provision was sufficiently ambiguous that it should be construed as a promise, rather than a condition which would allow the general contractor to escape payment. The court noted:

> We construe the relevant payment phrase in this contract, that the subcontractor would be paid "provided like payment shall have been made by owner to contractor," to be insufficient to constitute a condition precedent that results in shifting the risk of the owner's nonpayment from the general contractor to the subcontractor. We hold that in order to create a condition precedent, the language of the parties' agreement must clearly express their intent that the subcontractor is to be paid only if the owner first pays the general contractor. Thus, we hold that the payment clause in this contract constitutes a pay-when-paid clause — that is, an unconditional promise by the general contractor to pay its subcontractor even if the owner becomes insolvent.

Id. at 523–24.

The court refused to infer a condition precedent, claiming that such constructions are "not favored and will not be given effect unless established by clear and unequivocal language." As discussed in the preceding note, the court noted a long-standing policy to avoid forfeitures whenever possible. In deciding that the pay-if-paid clause did not constitute a condition precedent, the court noted the traditional structure of construction contracts, namely, that subcontractors typically look to the general contractor rather than the owner for payment, and thus the subcontractor need not account for the possibility of the owner's default. Due to the ambiguous phrasing of the clause and the court's policy against enforcing forfeiture provisions, the court ruled that the pay-if-paid clause created a promise, rather than a condition for the subcontractor's recovery.

3. *Strategic Invocations of Conditions.* Consider the following hypothetical

---

[7] For discussion, *see* John W. Cooley, *"Show Me the Money!": A Comment on the Enforceability of "Pay-if-Paid" Clauses in Contracts for Professional Services*, 33 U.S.F. L. Rev. 99 (1998).

situation: An importer agrees over the summer to buy a specified amount of rice, and the contract requires the buyer to provide two weeks notice to receive a shipment. The contract provides for payment via a letter of credit from a bank. The bank is authorized to pay for delivery only during December. Thus, December 17 is the last day on which the buyer can provide sufficient notice for a December shipment. The buyer fails to provide shipping instructions by December 17. In the meantime, the price of rice has increased substantially. Is the shipper justified in rescinding the remainder of the order on December 18?

How might the parties have viewed the matter of whether the giving of notice ought to be a condition or a promise if they considered the issue before the events occurred? How did the seller view his options after the instructions were late?[8]

Courts frown on parties who opportunistically seek to justify their nonperformance due to the nonoccurrence of a condition.[9] This principle was amply demonstrated in *Rohde v. Massachusetts Mut. Life Ins. Co.*, 632 F.2d 667 (6th Cir. 1980), where an applicant for a life insurance policy suffered a fatal heart attack the day that he sent his application to the insurance company. The contract provided that he would be covered from the day that he sent in the form, as long as he received clearance from the insurer that he was an "acceptable risk." In light of his death, the insurer decided that he would not be an acceptable risk, although objective statistical and actuarial evidence indicated that he would have been accepted had he survived, suggesting that the insurer acted in bad faith in rejecting his application. Based on this evidence, the court held that the insurer was liable to his widow for the full value of the policy.

4. *Conditions and Public Policy:* Inman v. Clyde Hall Drilling Co. Consider *Inman v. Clyde Hall Drilling Co.*, 369 P.2d 498 (Alaska 1962), where Inman sued Clyde Hall Drilling Co., his employer, for breach of his employment contract when he was allegedly discharged from his job as a derrickman in Alaska without justification. The company denied that it had breached the contract, and asserted that Inman had been paid in full the wages that were owed to him and was entitled to no damages. Subsequently, the company moved for summary judgment on the ground that Inman's failure to give written notice of his claim to the company, as required by the contract, was a bar to his action based on the contract. The contract provided that compliance with its requirement as to giving written notice of a claim within 30 days from the time it arose and prior to bringing suit "shall be a condition precedent to any recovery." Inman argued that this provision was void as against public policy. The court was not persuaded, stating that the public policy grounds for judicial interference with private contract terms must be clear:

> It is conceivable, of course, that a thirty-day notice of claim requirement could be used to the disadvantage of a workman by an unscrupulous employer. If this danger is great, the legislature may act to make such a

---

[8] For a full discussion of this situation, see *Internatio-Rotterdam, Inc. v. River Brand Rice Mills, Inc.*, 259 F.2d 137 (2d Cir. 1958).

[9] For a discussion concerning the role of the court where the parties fail to make any provision for an obligation or contingency, see Ian Ayres, *Preliminary Thoughts on Optimal Tailoring of Contractual Rules*, 3 S. Cal. Interdisc. L.J. 1 (1993); Robert A. Hillman, *Court Adjustment of Long-Term Contracts: An Analysis Under Modern Contract Law*, 1987 Duke L.J. 1.

provision unenforceable. But we may not speculate on what in the future may be a matter of public policy in this state. It is our function to act only where an existent public policy is clearly revealed from the facts and we find that it has been violated. That is not the case here.

Id. at 501.

Inman also argued that since he had served a complaint on the company within 30 days of his claim, he had substantially complied with the contractual requirement. The court again disagreed, holding that while the complaint probably gave the company actual knowledge of the claim, it did not give the kind of written notice called for by the contract. The agreement stated that no suit would be instituted "prior to six (6) months *after the filing of the written notice of claim.*" *Id.*

The filing and service of the law suit would seem to satisfy the 30-day notice required by the contract. The more important question, left unaddressed by the court, is whether the undertaking to wait six months after notice before filing suit is also a condition precedent, and if so, whether it is void as against public policy. Arguably, the purpose of the waiting period is to bar recourse to the courts in the hope that the plaintiff will return to the "lower forty-eight." Maintaining suit from there would be too costly. Thus, with the one hand the contract gives a promise for employment for a set term; with the other hand it renders the promise unenforceable, as a practical matter.

If an argument to this effect had been made by Inman's lawyer, how would you respond if you represented the company?

5.   *Conditions and Timing Clauses.* Suppose that I agree to deed over my 2008 Jeep to you, and you agree to pay me $10,000 when your trustee sends you the money from your trust fund. In fact, your trustee has fled to the Cayman Islands with the money. Do I get my $10,000? Do you get to keep the Jeep without paying me (on the argument that the transfer from the trust was a condition precedent to your duty to pay)? Is this similar to a pay-if-paid clause of the kind discussed above? How is it different?

A court might hold that the transfer of money from the trust was not a condition, but was a term that merely fixed a convenient timing for paying the debt — and that the debt was still owing. When the parties do not specify, the court has to decide whether a term was meant to be a condition or a timing term. How should it approach that question in the hypothetical case?

[b]   Conditions Precedent and Conditions Subsequent

Understanding the difference between promises and conditions is only the first step in formulating the express terms of an agreement. Thereafter, you must consider two vexing questions: When would it be in *both* parties' interests to agree on an express condition, and does it matter whether the condition is designated as precedent or subsequent?

GRAY v. GARDNER

Supreme Judicial Court of Massachusetts

17 Mass. 188 (1821)

Assumpsit on a written promise to pay the plaintiff 5198 dollars 87 cents, with the following condition annexed, *viz.*

> [O]n the condition that if a greater quantity of sperm oil should arrive in whaling vessels at *Nantucket* and *New Bedford*, on or between the first day of April and the first day of October of the present year, both inclusive, than arrived at said places, in whaling vessels, on or within the same term of time the last year, then this obligation to be void. — Dated April 14, 1819.

The consideration of the promise was a quantity of oil, sold by the plaintiff to the defendants. On the same day another note unconditional had been given by the defendants, for the value of the oil estimated at sixty cents per gallon; and the note in suit was given to secure the residue of the price estimated at eighty five cents, to depend on the contingency mentioned in the said condition.

At the trial before the Chief Justice, the case depended upon the question, whether a certain vessel, called the *Lady Adams*, with a cargo of oil, arrived at Nantucket on the first day of October 1819, about which fact the evidence was contradictory. The judge ruled that the burden of proving the arrival within the time was on the defendants: and further that, although the vessel might have, within the time, gotten within the space which might be called Nantucket Roads, yet it was necessary that she should have come to anchor, or have been moored, somewhere within that space before the hour of twelve following the first day of October, in order to have arrived, within the meaning of the contract.

The opinion of the Chief Justice on both these points was objected to by the defendants, and the questions were saved. If it was wrong on either point, a new trial was to be had: otherwise judgment was to be rendered on the verdict, which was found for the plaintiff.

Whitman, for the defendants. As the evidence at the trial was contradictory, the question on whom the burden of proof rested became important. We hold that it was on the plaintiff. This was a condition precedent. Until it should happen, the promise did not take effect. On the occurrence of a certain contingent event, the promise was to be binding, and not otherwise. To entitle himself to enforce the promise, the plaintiff must show that the contingent event has actually occurred.

PARKER, C. J.

The very words of the contract show that there was a promise to pay, which was to be defeated by the happening of an event, *viz.* the arrival of a certain quantity of oil, at the specified places in a given time. It is like a bond with a condition; if the obligor would avoid the bond, he must show performance of this condition. The defendants in this case promise to pay a certain sum of money, on condition that the promise shall be void on the happening of an event. It is plain that the burden of proof is upon them; and if they fail to show that the event has happened, the promise remains good.

The other point is equally clear for the plaintiff. Oil is to arrive at a given place before twelve o'clock at night. A vessel with oil heaves in sight, but she does not come to anchor, before the hour is gone. In no sense, can the oil be said to have arrived. The vessel is coming until she drops anchor or is moored. She may sink, or take fire, and never arrive, however near she may be to her port. It is so in contracts of insurance; and the same reason applies to a case of this sort. Both parties put themselves upon a nice point in this contract: it was a kind of wager as to the quantity of oil, which should arrive at the ports mentioned, before a certain period. They must be held strictly to their contract, there being no equity to interfere with the terms of it.

Judgment on the verdict.

NOTES

1.   *Conditions Precedent and Subsequent.* Restatement (First) of Contracts § 250 distinguishes between a condition precedent and a condition subsequent: a condition precedent "must occur or exist before a duty of immediate performance arises," while a condition subsequent "will extinguish a duty to make compensation for breach of contract after the breach has occurred."

Suppose that you are to pay me $50 on the condition that John comes to school on Tuesday. Draft this term as a condition precedent and then as a condition subsequent. Is the difference one of the timing of the condition? It could be that if it is drafted as a condition precedent, then you don't pay until the event occurs; but if it is a condition subsequent, you pay but I have to give the money back if the event does not occur.

In *Gray*, the parties arranged for the buyer to share the risk of scarcity of oil with the seller. If oil was scarce (and therefore did not arrive in Nantucket by October 1, 1819), then the defendant-buyer was obligated to pay a premium price for the delivery. The court did not treat the matter as one of the timing of the condition. Rather, it held that if the contract contains a condition precedent, the plaintiff-seller bears the burden of proving that the ship failed to arrive on time. As you can tell, the question of "arrival" was a very close one and the allocation of the burden of proof of paramount importance; since the exact time of arrival could not be shown, whichever party bore that burden would lose. The court, however, decided that the parties meant that if the oil arrived by October 1, then the obligation to pay the premium price was extinguished. Under that reading, the clause is a condition subsequent, and the defendant-buyer bears the burden of proof. Thus the plaintiff-seller wins. The distinction between winning and losing in this case seems to turn largely on semantics — whether the condition is characterized as precedent or subsequent as a matter of form. Do you find such a rule of decision satisfactory?

The reporters of the Second Restatement decided to abandon the distinction between precedent and subsequent conditions and to deal with conditions subsequent (as defined in the First Restatement) in § 230, which covers the discharge of obligations. The reporters also provided that:

> Occasionally, although the language of an agreement says that if an event does not occur a duty is "extinguished," "discharged," or "terminated," it

can be seen from the circumstances that the event must ordinarily occur before performance of the duty can be expected. When a court concludes that for this reason, performance is not to become due unless the event occurs, the event is, in spite of the language, a condition of the duty.

Restatement (Second) of Contracts § 224 cmt. e.

2. *Attorney Approval Clauses.* People who buy residential property are often legally unsophisticated, and many people purchase homes without the assistance of a lawyer. In order to ensure that they are sufficiently protected, parties to the sale of a home frequently use attorney approval clauses, which allow lawyers to review the document within a predetermined period after the contract has been signed. If the attorney objects to certain clauses, the parties are not bound by the agreement, rather they may seek to renegotiate the deal in accordance with the attorney's recommendations.

Courts are unclear as to how to classify such arrangements. Some courts have determined that such clauses are conditional acceptances; others have analyzed them under the condition precedent/condition subsequent rubric.[10]

Professor Alice Noble-Allgire has argued that the conditional acceptance interpretation of such clauses is generally misguided, because both parties have agreed to the provision. She observes, "most courts, however, have characterized attorney approval clauses as a 'condition subsequent,' stating that a valid contract is formed when both parties agree to the sale, but the rights and duties are conditioned upon the attorney's approval."[11]

An interesting twist on attorney approval clauses occurred in *Gaglia v. Kirchner*, 721 A.2d 1028 (N.J. 1999). The buyer's attorney (Mr. Winget) proposed changes following the initial signing of the agreement, and the sellers continued to show their house during the period in which the parties were reworking the agreement. Ultimately, the sellers (the Kirchners) received a better offer as a result of this re-showing, and they instructed their attorney to send a formal notice that they were terminating all negotiations with the buyer (Mr. Gaglia). The court held that the sellers, even if they acted in bad faith, were not liable to the would-be buyer. The court noted:

> When Mr. Gaglia and Mr. and Ms. Kirchner signed the purchase agreement, they had a binding contract that would not have been subject to unilateral modification by either party in any manner if it had not included an attorney review provision.. . . .
>
> After Mr. Binder's receipt of Mr. Winget's disapproval letter, they did not have a binding contract and would not have one unless and until the prospective buyer and sellers all agreed in writing to identical terms. . . . Showing their house to other prospective buyers after June 10 was

---

[10] For discussion, *see* Alice M. Noble-Allgire, *Attorney Approval Clauses in Residential Real Estate Contracts-Is Half a Loaf Better Than None?*, 48 Kan. L. Rev. 339 (2000).

[11] Noble-Allgire, *supra* n.10, at 361.

therefore not inconsistent with the assurances the Kirchners had given . . . that they had no significant objections to the terms of the revised contract which Mr. Winget proposed.

Id. at 1031–32.

[c] Modification, Waiver, Election, and Estoppel of Conditions

This part has focused thus far on determining precisely what performance obligations are required under particular circumstances. It closes by examining parties' attempts to modify or to waive particular provisions of the agreement once performance has begun. You will recall from Chapter 4 that the common law governed attempted modifications with the "pre-existing duty rule."[12] Modification and waiver are related, yet distinct, concepts. A waiver is often defined as the intentional relinquishment of a known right. A rough rule of thumb for keeping a waiver distinct from a modification is to remember that *promises are modified and conditions are waived.* As you read the following cases, note the key differences between the two concepts. Note as well the contrast between the UCC approach to the question of waiver and modification and that of the common law.

CLARK v. WEST
Court of Appeals of New York
193 N.Y. 349, 86 N.E. 1 (1908)

[On February 12, 1900, the plaintiff and the defendant entered into a contract whereby the plaintiff was to write a series of law books for the defendant. In return, the defendant agreed to pay the plaintiff, "$2 per page, . . . on each book prepared by [plaintiff] under this contract and if [plaintiff] abstains from intoxicating liquor . . . he shall be paid an additional $4 per page in manner hereinbefore stated." After having completed a three-volume work entitled "Clark and Marshall on Corporations," the plaintiff sued to recover the additional $4 per page, which the defendant had denied him. The plaintiff alleged that he had fully performed his obligations under the contract, except that he had not totally abstained from the use of intoxicating liquor. However, he also alleged that the defendant knew of this non-abstinence, did not object to it, continued to require the plaintiff's performance of other stipulations and to accept the work as offered, and at no time intimated that he would require strict compliance with the clause at the risk of plaintiff's forfeiting the royalty. Rather, the plaintiff alleged, the defendant promised the plaintiff that he would receive the royalty notwithstanding his indulgence. On these grounds, the plaintiff alleged a waiver of the abstinence provision.]

WERNER, J.

. . . [B]riefly stated, the defendant's position is that the stipulation as to plaintiff's total abstinence is the consideration for the payment of the difference between $2 and $6 per page and therefore could not be waived except by a new

---

[12] *See Alaska Packers'*, Chapter 4.

agreement to that effect based upon a good consideration; that the so-called waiver alleged by the plaintiff is not a waiver but a modification of the contract in respect of its consideration. The plaintiff on the other hand argues that the stipulation for his total abstinence was merely a condition precedent intended to work a forfeiture of the additional compensation in case of a breach and that it could be waived without any formal agreement to that effect based upon a new consideration.

The subject-matter of the contract was the writing of books by the plaintiff for the defendant. The duration of the contract was the time necessary to complete them all. The work was to be done to the satisfaction of the defendant, and the plaintiff was not to write any other books except those covered by the contract unless requested so to do by the defendant, in which latter event he was to be paid for that particular work by the year. The compensation for the work specified in the contract was to be $6 per page, unless the plaintiff failed to totally abstain from the use of intoxicating liquors during the continuance of the contract, in which event he was to receive only $2 per page. That is the obvious import of the contract construed in the light of the purpose for which it was made, and in accordance with the ordinary meaning of plain language. It is not a contract to write books in order that the plaintiff shall keep sober, but a contract containing a stipulation that he shall keep sober so that he may write satisfactory books. When we view the contract from this standpoint it will readily be perceived that the particular stipulation is not the consideration for the contract, but simply one of its conditions which fits in with those relating to time and method of delivery of manuscript, revision of proof, citation of cases, assignment of copyrights, keeping track of new cases and citations for new editions, and other details which might be waived by the defendant, if he saw fit to do so. This is made clear, it seems to us, by the provision that, "In consideration of the above promises," the defendant agrees to pay the plaintiff $2 per page on each book prepared by him, and if he "abstains from the use of intoxicating liquor and otherwise fulfills his agreements as hereinbefore set forth, he shall be paid an additional $4 per page in manner hereinbefore stated.". . . . It is obvious that the parties thought that the plaintiff's normal work was worth $6 per page. That was the sum to be paid for the work done by the plaintiff and not for total abstinence. . . .

This, we think, is the fair interpretation of the contract, and it follows that the stipulation as to the plaintiff's total abstinence was nothing more nor less than a condition precedent. If that conclusion is well founded there can be no escape from the corollary that this condition could be waived; and if it was waived the defendant is clearly not in a position to insist upon the forfeiture which his waiver was intended to annihilate. The forfeiture must stand or fall with the condition. If the latter was waived, the former is no longer a part of the contract. Defendant still has the right to counterclaim for any damages which he may have sustained in consequence of the plaintiff's breach, but he cannot insist upon strict performance. . . .

The [defendant's] theory . . . is that even if he has represented to the plaintiff that he would not insist upon the condition that the latter should observe total abstinence from intoxicants, he can still refuse to pay the full contract price for his work. The inequity of this position becomes apparent when we consider that this contract was to run for a period of years, during a large portion of which the plaintiff was to be entitled only to the advance payment of $2 per page, the balance being contingent, among other things, upon publication of the books and returns from sales. Upon this theory the defendant might have waived the condition while the first book was in process of production, and yet when the whole work was completed, he would still be in a position to insist upon the forfeiture because there had not been strict performance. Such a situation is possible in a case where the subject of the waiver is the very consideration of a contract . . . [But here], the waiver is not of the consideration or subject-matter, but of an incident to the method of performance.

The cases which present the most familiar phases of the doctrine of waiver are those which have arisen out of litigation over insurance policies where the defendants have claimed a forfeiture because of the breach of some condition in the contract but it is a doctrine of general application which is confined to no particular class of cases. A "waiver" has been defined to be the intentional relinquishment of a known right. It is voluntary and implies an election to dispense with something of value, or forego some advantage which the party waiving it might at its option have demanded or insisted upon, and this definition is supported by many cases in this and other states. As said by my brother Vann in the *Kiernan* Case (150 N.Y. 190): "[T] the doctrine of waiver is to relieve against forfeiture; it requires no consideration for a waiver, nor any prejudice or injury to the other party."

It remains to be determined whether the plaintiff has alleged facts which, if proven, will be sufficient to establish his claim of an express waiver by the defendant of the plaintiff's breach of the condition to observe total abstinence. In the 12th paragraph of the complaint, the plaintiff alleges facts and circumstances which we think, if established, would prove defendant's waiver of plaintiff's performance of that contract stipulation. These facts and circumstances are that long before the plaintiff had completed the manuscript of the first book undertaken under the contract, the defendant had full knowledge of the plaintiff's non-observance of that stipulation, and that with such knowledge he not only accepted the completed manuscript without objection, but "repeatedly avowed and represented to the plaintiff that he was entitled to and would receive said royalty payments (i.e., the additional $4 per page), and plaintiff believed and relied upon such representations . . . and at all times during the writing of said treatise on corporations, and after as well as before publication thereof as aforesaid, it was mutually understood, agreed and intended by the parties hereto that notwithstanding plaintiff's said use of intoxicating liquors, he was nevertheless entitled to receive and would receive said royalty as the same accrued under said contract." . . .

[The court then summarized its holding, noting that on these facts the complaint did state a cause of action, that the plaintiff's total abstinence represented a condition precedent rather than consideration for the defendant's offer of payment, and that the complaint alleged facts which sufficiently raised the question of a valid waiver of the condition precedent. The defendant was given 20 days after payment of court costs to answer the complaint.]

―――――――――

Clark v. West provides a good example of the common law approach to waiver and modification. Note that the common law doctrine of waiver is comprised of two main strands: waiver by election and waiver by estoppel. The former addresses the situation where the waiver occurs after the time for occurrence of the condition. The latter is for situations where the waiver occurs before the time for occurrence of the condition. For example, suppose Jack and Jill have a contract where Jack sells apples to Jill on the condition that all deliveries are made by noon on Monday. If Jack fails to deliver until Tuesday morning, Jill can elect to waive the condition instead of insisting on perfect compliance. Alternatively, if on the Friday before delivery Jill tells Jack that it is okay if he does not make the delivery by the time stated in the contract, she may be estopped from insisting on compliance with the condition in the future. While both forms of waiver have the same operative effect, it is important to note that only waiver by election is binding immediately. Waiver by estoppel, however, requires reliance by the recipient (in our example, Jack) before the waiver becomes binding and irrevocable. With this common law backdrop, we now turn to waiver and modification under the Code's § 2-209. Consider how two highly esteemed jurists grapple with attempting to determine how the Code seeks to accept and modify the common law doctrines.

WISCONSIN KNIFE WORKS v. NATIONAL METAL CRAFTERS
United States Court of Appeals, Seventh Circuit
781 F.2d 1280 (1986)

POSNER, J.

. . . [W]isconsin Knife Works, having some unused manufacturing capacity, decided to try to manufacture spade bits for sale to its parent, Black & Decker, a large producer of tools, including drills. A spade bit is made out of a chunk of metal called a spade bit blank; and Wisconsin Knife Works had to find a source of supply for these blanks. National Metal Crafters was eager to be that source. After some negotiating, Wisconsin Knife Works sent National Metal Crafters a series of purchase orders on the back of each of which was printed, "Acceptance of this Order, either by acknowledgment or performance, constitutes an unqualified agreement to the following." A list of "Conditions of Purchase" follows, of which the first is, "No modification of this contract, shall be binding upon Buyer [Wisconsin Knife Works] unless made in writing and signed by Buyer's authorized representative. Buyer shall have the right to make changes in the Order by a notice, in writing, to Seller." There were six purchase orders in all, each with the identical conditions. National Metal Crafters acknowledged the first two orders (which had been placed on August 21, 1981) by letters that said, "Please accept this as our acknowledgment covering the above subject order," followed by a list of delivery dates. The purchase orders had left those dates blank. Wisconsin Knife Works filled them in, after receiving the acknowledgments, with the dates that National Metal Crafters had supplied in the acknowledgments. There were no written acknowledgments of the last four orders (placed several weeks later, on September 10, 1981). Wisconsin Knife Works wrote in the delivery dates that National Metal Crafters orally supplied after receiving purchase orders in which the space for the date of delivery had again been left blank.

Delivery was due in October and November 1981. National Metal Crafters missed the deadlines. But Wisconsin Knife Works did not immediately declare a breach, cancel the contract, or seek damages for late delivery. Indeed, on July 1, 1982, it issued a new batch of purchase orders (later rescinded). By December 1982 National Metal Crafters was producing spade bit blanks for Wisconsin Knife Works under the original set of purchase orders in adequate quantities, though this was more than a year after the delivery dates in the orders. But, in January 13, 1983, Wisconsin Knife Works notified National Metal Crafters that the contract was terminated. By that date only 144,000 of the more than 281,000 spade bit blanks that Wisconsin Knife Works had ordered in the six purchase orders had been delivered.

Wisconsin Knife Works brought this breach of contract suit, charging that National Metal Crafters had violated the terms of delivery in the contract that was formed by the acceptance of the six purchase orders. National Metal Crafters replied that the delivery dates had not been intended as firm dates. It also counterclaimed for damages for (among other things) the breach of an alleged oral agreement by Wisconsin Knife Works to pay the expenses of maintaining machinery used by National Metal Crafters to fulfill the contract. The parties later stipulated that the amount of these damages was $30,000.

The judge ruled that there had been a contract but left to the jury to decide whether the contract had been modified and, if so, whether the modified contract had been broken. The jury found that the contract had been modified and not broken. Judgment was entered dismissing Wisconsin Knife Works' suit and awarding National Metal Crafters $30,000 on its counterclaim. Wisconsin Knife Works has appealed from the dismissal of its suit. The appeal papers do not discuss the counterclaim, and the effect on it of our remanding the case for further proceedings on Wisconsin Knife Works' claim will have to be resolved on remand.

The principal issue is the effect of the provision in the purchase orders that forbids the contract to be modified other than by a writing signed by an authorized representative of the buyer. The theory on which the judge sent the issue of modification to the jury was that the contract could be modified orally or by conduct as well as by a signed writing. National Metal Crafters had presented evidence that Wisconsin Knife Works had accepted late delivery of the spade bit blanks and had canceled the contract not because of the delays in delivery but because it could not produce spade bits at a price acceptable to Black & Decker.

Section 2-209(2) of the Uniform Commercial Code provides that "a signed agreement which excludes modification or rescission except by a signed writing cannot be otherwise modified or rescinded, but except as between merchants such a requirement on a form supplied by the merchant must be separately signed by the other party." . . . The meaning of this provision and its proviso is not crystalline and there is little pertinent case law. One might think that an agreement to exclude modification except by a signed writing must be signed in any event by the party against whom the requirement is sought to be enforced, that is, by National Metal Crafters, rather than by the party imposing the requirement. But if so the force of the proviso ("but except as between merchants . . .") becomes unclear, for it contemplates that between merchants no separate signature by the party sought to be bound by the requirement is necessary. A possible reconciliation, though not one we need embrace in order to decide this case, is to read the statute to require a separate signing or initialing of the clause forbidding oral modifications, as well as of the contract in which the clause appears. There was no such signature here; but it doesn't matter; this was a contract "between merchants." Although in ordinary language a manufacturer is not a merchant, "between merchants" is a term of art in the Uniform Commercial Code. It means between commercially sophisticated parties (see UCC § 2-104(1);, which these were.

Of course there must still be a "signed agreement" containing the clause forbidding modification other than by a signed writing, but there was that (see definition of "agreement" and of "signed" in UCC § 1-201(3), (39)). National Metal Crafters' signed acknowledgments of the first two purchase orders signified its assent to the printed conditions and naturally and reasonably led Wisconsin Knife Works to believe that National Metal Crafters meant also to assent to the same conditions should they appear in any subsequent purchase orders that it accepted. Those subsequent orders were accepted, forming new contracts on the same conditions as the old, by performance — that is, by National Metal Crafters' beginning the manufacture of the spade bit blanks called for by the orders. See UCC § 2-207(3). So there was an agreement, signed by National Metal Crafters, covering all the purchase orders. The fact that the delivery dates were not on the purchase orders when received by National Metal Crafters is nothing of which it may complain; it was given carte blanche to set those dates.

We conclude that the clause forbidding modifications other than in writing was valid and applicable and that the jury should not have been allowed to consider whether the contract had been modified in some other way. This may, however, have been a harmless error. Section 2-209(4) of the Uniform Commercial Code provides that an "attempt at modification" which does not satisfy a contractual requirement that modifications be in writing nevertheless "can operate as a waiver." Although in instructing the jury on modification the judge did not use the word "waiver," maybe he gave the substance of a waiver instruction and maybe therefore the jury found waiver but called it modification. Here is the relevant instruction:

> Did the parties modify the contract? The defendant bears the burden of proof on this one. You shall answer this question yes only if you are convinced to a reasonable certainty that the parties modified the contract.

> If you determine that the defendant had performed in a manner different from the strict obligations imposed on it by the contract, and the plaintiff by conduct or other means of expression induced a reasonable belief by the defendant that strict enforcement was not insisted upon, but that the modified performance was satisfactory and acceptable as equivalent, then you may conclude that the parties have assented to a modification of the original terms of the contract and that the parties have agreed that the different mode of performance will satisfy the obligations imposed on the parties by the contract.

To determine whether this was in substance an instruction on waiver we shall have to consider the background of section 2-209, the Code provision on modification and waiver.

[T]he most important thing which the law does is to facilitate exchanges that are not simultaneous by preventing either party from taking advantage of the vulner-abilities to which sequential performance may give rise. If A contracts to build a highly idiosyncratic gazebo for B, payment due on completion, and when A completes the gazebo B refuses to pay, A may be in a bind — since the resale value of the gazebo may be much less than A's cost — except for his right to sue B for the price. Even then, a right to sue for breach of contract, being costly to enforce, is not a completely adequate remedy. B might therefore go to A and say, "If you don't reduce your price I'll refuse to pay and put you to the expense of suit"; and A might knuckle under. If such modifications are allowed, people in B's position will find it harder to make such contracts in the future, and everyone will be worse off.

The common law dealt with this problem by refusing to enforce modifications unsupported by fresh consideration. See, e.g., Alaska Packers' Ass'n v. Domenico, 117 F. 99 (9th Cir. 1902). Thus in the hypothetical case just put B could not have enforced A's promise to accept a lower price. But this solution is at once overinclusive and underinclusive — the former because most modifications are not coercive and should be enforceable whether or not there is fresh consideration, the latter because, since common law courts inquire only into the existence and not the adequacy of consideration, a requirement of fresh consideration has little bite. B might give A a peppercorn, a kitten, or a robe in exchange for A's agreeing to reduce the contract price, and then the modification would be enforceable and A could no longer sue for the original price.

The draftsmen of the Uniform Commercial Code took a fresh approach, by making modifications enforceable even if not supported by consideration (see section 2-209(1)) and looking to the doctrines of duress and bad faith for the main protection against exploitive or opportunistic attempts at modification, as in our hypothetical case. See UCC § 2-209, official comment 2. But they did another thing as well. In section 2-209(2) they allowed the parties to exclude oral modifications. National Metal Crafters argues that two subsections later they took back this grant of power by allowing an unwritten modification to operate as a waiver.

The common law did not enforce agreements such as section 2-209(2) authorizes. The "reasoning" was that the parties were always free to agree orally to cancel their contract and the clause forbidding modifications not in writing would disappear with the rest of the contract when it was cancelled. This is not reasoning; it is a conclusion disguised as a metaphor. It may have reflected a fear that such clauses, buried in the fine print of form contracts, were traps for the unwary . . . But the framers of the Uniform Commercial Code, as part and parcel of rejecting the requirement of consideration for modifications, must have rejected the traditional view; must have believed that the protection which the doctrines of duress and bad faith give against extortionate modifications might need reinforcement . . . from a grant of power to include a clause requiring modifications to be in writing and signed.

If section 2-209(4), which as we said provides that an attempted modification which does not comply with subsection (2) can nevertheless operate as a "waiver," is interpreted so broadly that any oral modification is effective as a waiver notwithstanding section 2-209(2), both provisions become superfluous and we are back in the common law — only with not even a requirement of consideration to reduce the likelihood of fabricated or unintended oral modifications.

The path of reconciliation with subsection (4) is found by attending to its precise wording. It does not say that an attempted modification "is" a waiver; it says that "it can operate as a waiver." It does not say in what circumstances it can operate as a waiver; but if an attempted modification is effective as a waiver only if there is reliance, then both sections 2-209(2) and 2-209(4) can be given effect. Reliance, if reasonably induced and reasonable in extent, is a common substitute for consideration in making a promise legally enforceable, in part because it adds something in the way of credibility to the mere say-so of one party. The main purpose of forbidding oral modifications is to prevent the promisor from fabricating a modification that will let him escape his obligations under the contract; and the danger of successful fabrication is less if the promisor has actually incurred a cost, has relied. There is of course a danger of bootstrapping — of incurring a cost in order to make the case for a modification. But it is a risky course and is therefore less likely to be attempted than merely testifying to a conversation; it makes one put one's money where one's mouth is. . . .

Our approach is not inconsistent with section 2-209(5), which allows a waiver to be withdrawn while the contract is executory, provided there is no "material change of position in reliance on the waiver." [T]he section has a different domain from section 2-209(4). It is not limited to attempted modifications invalid under subsections (2) or (3); it applies, for example, to an express written and signed waiver, provided only that the contract is still executory. Suppose that while the contract is still executory the buyer writes the seller a signed letter waiving some term in the contract and then, the next day, before the seller has relied, retracts it in writing; we have no reason to think that such a retraction would not satisfy section 2-209(5), though this is not an issue we need definitively resolve today. In any event we are not suggesting that "waiver" means different things in (4) and (5); it means the same thing; but the effect of an attempted modification as a waiver under (4) depends in part on (2), which (4) (but not (5)) qualifies.. . . .

We know that the draftsmen of section 2-209 wanted to make it possible for parties to exclude oral modifications. They did not just want to give "modification" another name — "waiver." Our interpretation gives effect to this purpose.

Missing from the jury instruction on "modification" in this case is any reference to reliance, that is, to the incurring of costs by National Metal Crafters in reasonable reliance on assurances by Wisconsin Knife Works that late delivery would be acceptable. And although there is evidence of such reliance, it naturally was not a focus of the case, since the issue was cast as one of completed (not attempted) modification, which does not require reliance to be enforceable. The question of reliance cannot be considered so open and shut as to justify our concluding that the judge would have had to direct a verdict for National Metal Crafters, the party with the burden of proof on the issue. Nor, indeed, does National Metal Crafters argue that reliance was shown as a matter of law. . . .

Obviously National Metal Crafters has a strong case both that it relied on the waiver of the delivery deadlines and that there was no causal relationship between its late deliveries and the cancellation of the contract. We just are not prepared to say on the record before us that it is such a strong case as not to require submission to a jury.

Reversed and remanded.

EASTERBROOK, J. (dissenting).

The majority demonstrates that the clause of the contract requiring all modifications to be in writing is enforceable against National Metal Crafters. There was no modification by a "signed writing." Yet § 2-209(4) of the Uniform Commercial Code, which Wisconsin has adopted, provides that "an attempt at modification" that is ineffective because of a modification-only-in-writing clause "can operate as a waiver." The majority holds that no "attempt at modification" may be a "waiver" within the meaning of § 2-209(4) unless the party seeking to enforce the waiver has relied to its detriment. I do not think that detrimental reliance is an essential element of waiver under § 2-209(4).

"Waiver" is not a term the UCC defines. At common law "waiver" means an intentional relinquishment of a known right. A person may relinquish a right by engaging in conduct inconsistent with the right or by a verbal or written declaration. I do not know of any branch of the law — common, statutory, or constitutional — in which a renunciation of a legal entitlement is effective only if the other party relies to his detriment. True, the law of "consideration" imposed something like a reliance rule; payment of a pine nut (the peppercorn of nouvelle cuisine) is a tiny bit of detriment, and often the law of consideration is expressed in terms of detriment. But § 2-209(1) of the UCC provides that consideration is unnecessary to make a modification effective. The introduction of a reliance requirement into a body of law from which the doctrine of consideration has been excised is novel. . . .

Not all novel things are wrong, although legal novelties, like biological mutations, usually die out quickly. This novelty encounters an obstacle within § 2-209. Section 2-209(5) states that a person who "has made a waiver affecting an executory portion of the contract may retract the waiver" on reasonable notice "unless the retraction would be unjust in view of a material change of position in reliance on the waiver." Section 2-209 therefore treats "waiver" and "reliance" as different. Under § 2-209(4) a waiver may be effective; under § 2-209(5) a waiver may be effective prospectively only if there was also detrimental reliance.

The majority tries to reconcile the two subsections by stating that they have different domains. Section 2-209(4) deals with oral waivers, while § 2-209(5) "is not limited to attempted modifications invalid under subsections (2) or (3); it applies, for example, to express written waivers, provided only that the contract is executory." This distinction implies that subsection (4) applies to a subset of the subjects of subsection (5). Things are the other way around. Subsection (4) says that an attempt at modification may be a "waiver," and subsection (5) qualifies the effectiveness of "waivers" in the absence of reliance. See comment 4 to § 2-209. The two have the same domain — all attempts at modification, be they oral, written, or implied from conduct, that do not satisfy the Statute of Frauds, § 2-209(3), or a "signed writing" requirement of a clause permitted under § 2-209(2). The majority suggests that

§ 2-209(5) also applies to signed waivers, but this gets things backward. A "signed writing" is binding as a modification under § 2-209(2) without the need for "waiver." § 2-209(1) lifts the requirement of consideration, so a signed pledge not to enforce a term of a contract may not be revoked under § 2-209(5) unless the pledge reserves the power of revocation. Because "waiver" is some subset of failed effort to modify, it cannot be right to treat a successful effort to modify (a signed writing) as a "waiver" governed by subsection (5).

"Waiver" therefore ought to mean the same in subsections (4) and (5). Unsuccessful attempts at modification may be waivers under § 2-209(4). Then § 2-209(5) deals with a subset of these "waivers," the subset that affects the executory portion of the contract. Waivers affecting executory provisions are enforceable or not depending on reliance. We know from the language and structure of § 2-209 that there is a difference between waivers that affect the executory portions of contracts and waivers that do not. Under the majority's reading, however, there is no difference. No waiver is effective without detrimental reliance. It is as if the majority has eliminated § 2-209(4) from the UCC and rewritten § 2-209(5) to begin: "A party who has made [an ineffectual attempt at modification] affecting [any] portion of the contract may retract. . . ."

The subsections read well together if waiver means "intentional relinquishment of a known right" in both. Section 2-209(4) says that a failed attempt at modification may be a waiver and so relinquish a legal entitlement (such as the entitlement to timely delivery); § 2-209(5) adds that a waiver cannot affect the executory portion of the contract (the time of future deliveries, for example) if the waiving party retracts, unless there is also detrimental reliance. But for § 2-209(2) the oral waiver could affect the executory portion of the contract even without reliance. It is not necessary to vary the meaning of the word to make sense of each portion of the statute.

The majority makes reliance an ingredient of waiver not because the structure of the UCC demands the reading, but because it believes that otherwise the UCC would not deal adequately with the threat of opportunistic conduct. The drafters of the UCC chose to deal with opportunism not through a strict reading of waiver, however, but through a statutory requirement of commercial good faith. See § 2-103 and comment 2 to § 2-209. The modification-only-in-writing clause has nothing to do with opportunism. A person who has his contracting partner over a barrel, and therefore is able to obtain a concession, can get the concession in writing. The writing will be the least of his worries. In almost all of the famous cases of modification the parties reduced the new agreement to writing.

A modification-only-in-writing clause may permit the parties to strengthen the requirement of commercial good faith against the careless opportunist, but its principal function is to make it easier for businesses to protect their agreement against casual subsequent remarks and manufactured assertions of alteration. It strengthens the Statute of Frauds. Even so, the Code does not allow the clause to be airtight. Comment 4 to § 2-209 states: "Subsection (4) is intended, despite the provisions of subsections (2) and (3), to prevent contractual provisions excluding modification except by a signed writing from limiting in other respects the legal effect of the parties' actual later conduct. The effect of such conduct as a waiver is further regulated in subsection (5)." In other words, the UCC made modification-only-in-writing clauses effective for the first time, but the drafters meant to leave loopholes. The majority's observation that waiver under § 2-209(4) could nullify some benefits of clauses permitted under § 2-209(2) is true, but it is not a reason for adding novel elements to "waiver." It might be sensible to treat claims of oral waiver with suspicion and insist on waiver by course of performance — for example, accepting belated deliveries without protest, or issuing new orders (or changing the specifications of old orders) while existing ones are in default. Waiver implied from performance is less prone to manipulation. This method of protecting modification-only-in-writing clauses gives waiver the same meaning throughout the statute, but it does not help Wisconsin Knife, for the claim of waiver here is largely based on the course of performance.

NOTES

1. *Questions on UCC § 2-209.* Read carefully UCC § 2-209 and comments. How would you clarify the language of subsections (4) and (5) so as to resolve the debate that separates Judge Posner and Judge Easterbrook in *Wisconsin Knife*? For a contemporary application of § 2-209 and the principles laid down in *Wisconsin Knife*, see *American Suzuki Motor Corp. v. Bill Kummer, Inc.*, 65 F.3d 1381 (7th Cir. 1995). Kummer had a dealership which sold Suzuki motorcycles. Suzuki sent notice indicating that it intended to terminate the agreement in 60 days; Kummer, as a result, ceased to order any more Suzuki products. Kummer also filed a complaint which created a mandatory stay period during which their initial agreement would remain in effect. Again, during this extended period (which lasted nearly four years), Kummer refused to stock Suzuki products. The Office of the Commissioner of Transportation of Wisconsin, which adjudicated the initial complaint, ruled that Suzuki improperly terminated the initial agreement. But in light of Kummer's nonperformance during the mandatory stay period, Suzuki sought once again to terminate the agreement. Both parties accused the other of breaching the dealership agreement.

The trial court found that the parties' actions constituted a mutual abandonment or modification of the agreement. Suzuki appealed the finding that such a modification occurred. The Seventh Circuit Court of Appeals concluded that actions under § 2-209(4), which would constitute "an attempt at modification" that "can operate as a waiver," must be unequivocal and unambiguous in their nature. The court found that the parties' conduct did not indicate that Suzuki and Kummer agreed that Kummer did not have to perform. Instead, actions such as Suzuki's sending written notices of model allocations and shipment of technical manuals indicated that they sought continued performance from Kummer. As a result, the actions were not sufficiently unequivocal under § 2-209(4) to support a finding that the contract was waived.

2. *Waiver and the Preexisting Duty Rule.* At this point it would be helpful to recall the preexisting duty rule and the *Alaska Packers'* case. The common law places "waiver" cases in a category separate from cases involving contract modification. Is this a valid categorization? For example, did Professor Clark give fresh consideration in exchange for his release from the total abstinence clause? If the plaintiff in *Wisconsin Knife* can be found to have waived the requirement that all

modifications of the contract must be in writing to be binding, what independent purpose do the rules governing modification serve? Is the "voluntary relinquishment" of the right the key variable that separates the categories? These waiver cases frequently arise, and the parties claiming waiver often are successful. What explains the apparent contradiction between "easy" waiver and the rigid rules governing modification at common law? Does the answer lie in the distinction between a promise and a condition? Is there a reason why express conditions are strictly construed ("the law abhors a forfeiture") and thus found quite readily to have been "waived"?[13]

3.   *Types of Waiver Redux.* Now that you have studied both *Clark v. West* and *Wisconsin Knife*, consider again the differences in the two types of waiver that together describe the situation where one party claims that his contractual partner has excused some aspect of performance without formal contractual modification.

(a) Plaintiff-insured has not satisfied a timely notice requirement in an insurance contract, and defendant-insurer, with knowledge of the nonfulfillment of the condition, initially elects to settle but later refuses to do so, asserting the unfulfilled condition. *Lee v. Casualty Co. of Am.*, 90 Conn. 202, 96 A. 952 (1916), is usually cited as the paradigmatic example of "election" waiver. This type of waiver by election was present in *Clark v. West.*

(b) Plaintiff-insured is told by defendant-insurer immediately after an accident that fulfillment of a timely notice requirement is not necessary. Plaintiff-insured relies on this information, filing notice after the time period has run. Defendant-insurer then refuses to settle, citing the notice requirement. This is known as "estoppel" waiver. A variation of estoppel waiver is at issue in *Wisconsin Knife.*

4.   *The Paradox of the Idiosyncratic Bargainer.* As we noted earlier, construing a clause as a promise instead of a condition, or finding a condition waived or estopped, are all ways for courts to allow parties to escape (at least in part) their contract obligations. Why does the law permit this? What has compelled the development of these various doctrines? It seems safe to presume that, absent other factors, contracting parties would want a clear definition of their rights and duties. The use of specific conditions allows them to structure performance obligations as they wish. Courts, however, sometimes refuse to enforce the conditions the parties have made. Why?

Specially designed contract provisions, such as express conditions, protect atypical parties who wish to guard against exploitation of their special needs. Express conditions thus permit parties — such as the Kents in *Jacob & Youngs v. Kent*, Chapter 1, Section D — to withhold their own performance whenever specified contingencies materialize (or fail to materialize). In the absence of such express conditions, the standard default rules governing implied conditions would govern. For example, a return performance would be owed if the other party's performance was judged to be "substantial" even though the deviation was a serious omission from the perspective of the atypical or idiosyncratic party. At first glance, therefore, express conditions seem to favor parties with peculiar requirements

---

[13] For discussion of these questions, see David V. Snyder, *Public and Private Attempts to Regulate Modification, Waiver, and Estoppel*, 1999 Wis. L. Rev. 607.

(such as the Kents who insisted on replacing Cohoes pipe with Reading pipe even though both brands were of equal quality) and disadvantage those who are relying on market assessments of the value of any performance (such as the construction firm of Jacob & Youngs). But viewed *ex ante*, the express condition must be "paid for" by the party with peculiar or special requirements. If the idiosyncratic bargainer qualifies her promise expressly (thus narrowing her responsibility for performance) it will be worth less to the other party, who presumably will reduce the "value" of his return promise. Thus, the parties can be expected to bargain against the backdrop of any express conditions.

This discussion provides a clue to understanding (if not endorsing) the law's reluctance to enforce express conditions "as written." This response is another illustration of the paradox of the idiosyncratic bargainer. As we saw in Chapter 6, the law invites contracting parties to design their own contractual terms and promises to enforce them as the parties objectively intended. But keeping this promise requires an interpretive exercise. The courts, who after all are the authors of the standard default rules, are asked to imagine that these particular litigants prefer an entirely different arrangement than the sensible and intuitive allocation of risks reflected in the majoritiarian defaults. Since, viewed from the lens of a typical transaction, the express condition appears unusual, it is treated with suspicion. A metaphor such as how "the law abhors a forfeiture" is simply a reflection of the presumption that ordinary people do not expressly condition their obligations in this way. Similarly, the doctrines of waiver reflect the assumption that the atypical allocation was not what the parties ultimately desired.

The judicial hostility to such arrangements might be explained as varying with the presence or absence of a competitive market for the goods or services being exchanged. For example, assume that a seller tenders contract goods that are suitable for all practical purposes, but deviate from the contract description in a minor detail. It is tempting to be concerned that the buyer may "reject" this tender merely to escape the deal or to extort a discount price reduction in exchange for his agreement to accept the "defective" tender. But if this exchange takes place in a well-developed market, we need no longer fear the possibility that the buyer's behavior will be opportunistic. If the buyer rejects the goods for strategic reasons, the seller can simply take back the goods and resell the original goods in the same market. If the buyer's objection was idiosyncratic or opportunistic, the market price for the "defective" goods will reflect this — the market price for the "defective" goods will equal the market price for the replacement goods.

Thus, ordinarily, the market checks opportunistic behavior. In our example, the buyer cannot exploit the seller because the seller can test the buyer's claim on the market. However, specialized or "specific" investments in performing a contract may remove the parties from the discipline of a competitive market.[14] In the case of a contract where one party makes an investment that is specific to the relationship — such as the construction of a specially designed building — express conditions may instead invite strategic behavior. Here, for example, if the buyer rejects the building because of the failure of a condition that is apparently

---

[14] An investment is "specific" to a particular contract to the extent that it cannot be redeployed elsewhere.

insignificant, the contractor is vulnerable to a hold-up since he has sunk costs in the project and, except at great cost, he cannot remove his materials and then reassemble them in order to sell the house to someone else. Thus, the buyer (who otherwise no longer values the house at its contract price) can use the threat of the express condition to renegotiate the price of the construction project. In this environment, therefore, a presumption against interpreting contractual obligations as express conditions may be justifiable if the law prefers to discourage strategic behavior even at the risk of limiting the freedom of the atypical bargainer.[15]

C. PERFORMANCE STANDARDS

[1] Warranties

In drafting a contract, the most important substantive concern is to define the quality and character of the performance obligation of each party. Where the performance calls for a discrete exchange, the respective obligations often can be clearly specified. Thus, for example, seller can agree to deliver to buyer a single unit of a standardized product "off the shelf" at a stipulated price. On the other hand, as we have seen, in relational contexts the parties must often rely on broad, general standards of performance such as the obligation to use "best efforts" to achieve a particular performance objective. In most cases, however, the contractual performance to be described will fall somewhere between these two extremes. In this case, the parties typically use combinations of bright-line or precise terms together with broad standards to define the contract performance. Courts then use various maxims of interpretation to guide them in interpreting both the broad standard as well as the accompanying precise terms.[16] To see how the law

---

[15] *See* Charles J. Goetz & Robert E. Scott, *The Mitigation Principle: Toward a General Theory of Contractual Obligation*, 69 Vᴀ. L. Rᴇᴠ. 967, 1000–01 (1983). For an argument that concerns about strategic behavior are often mitigated by informal sanctions — such as reputation, repeated dealings and norms of reciprocity — and thus sophisticated parties should be entitled to enforce express conditions "as written," see Jody Kraus & Robert E. Scott, *Contract Design and the Structure of Contractual Intent*, 84 N.Y.U. L. Rᴇᴠ. 1023 (2009).

[16] Three well-known maxims are particularly relevant: *ejusdem generis, noscitur a sociis*, and *expressio unius est exclusio alterius*. If a contract uses only precise terms to describe a contract obligation, the *expressio unius* maxim cautions the court against considering other possible terms at the time of trial. Under *expressio unius*, the expression in the contract of one or more things of a class implies exclusion of all that is not expressed. Thus, when a contract provides that a thing should be done in a certain way, it is presumed to be exclusive. Where the parties combine standards and rules that relate to the same subject matter, the *ejusdem generis* canon applies. The meaning of the general language is then limited to matters similar in kind or classification to the enumerated specific terms. Contracting parties can avoid a restrictive interpretation under the *ejusdem* rule by providing that the general language includes but is not limited to the specific enumerated items that either precede or follow it. Under *noscitur a sociis*, which means "it is known by its associates," the court determines the meaning of vague phrases by reference to their relationship with other associated words and phrases. Under this maxim, the coupling of words or phrases indicates that they should be understood in the same general sense. For example, where the parties provide for specific terms but no standard, *expressio unius* might prevent the court from reading a general purpose. But when a broad standard is added to a listing of specific terms, it communicates the underlying objective and helps the court interpret the specific terms in light of the general purpose. The *noscitur a sociis* maxim requires that the general and the specific words must be considered together in determining the contract's meaning, so as to give effect

facilitates the parties' efforts to combine precise specifications with broad standards of performance, consider the case of sales warranties under the UCC.

[a] Express Warranties

An express warranty arises only if the seller of goods makes some explicit representation about the goods. Not all seller statements will create express warranties, however. The question, then, is when do sellers' utterances become part of the contractual obligation?

SESSA v. RIEGLE
United States District Court, Eastern District Pennsylvania
427 F. Supp. 760 (1977)

HANNUM, J.

This civil action was instituted by the buyer of a standardbred race horse against the seller, to recover for breach of express warranties, an implied warranty of merchantability and an implied warranty of fitness for particular purpose. . . . Plaintiff, Joseph Sessa, Jr. (Sessa) is . . . employed as a beer distributor in Philadelphia, and as an avocation owns and races standardbred horses. In connection with his avocation, Sessa has bought, sold, valued, selected and generally dealt in standardbreds at various locations in the Eastern United States.

Riegle buys, sells, owns, trains, drives and deals in and with standardbred horses and engages in racing competition at various harness tracks in Ohio, Illinois and other parts of the country.

Sessa became interested in purchasing a standardbred race horse named Tarport Conaway owned by defendants, Mrs. Gene Riegle and Mrs. John A. Frantz after hearing about the horse and his record in February and March of 1973 from one Robert J. Maloney. Maloney had seen the horse at Riegle's farm in Greenville, Ohio. At all times herein relevant, Riegle acted for himself and as agent for Mrs. Riegle and Mrs. Frantz in connection with the sale of Tarport Conaway.

Based on what Robert J. Maloney had told him, on March 9, 1973, Sessa sent Maloney to Riegle's place of business in Greenville, Ohio as his agent to effect the purchase of Tarport Conaway. Maloney carried Sessa's check for the $25,000 purchase price to be delivered to Riegle if the sale was consummated . . . . . . Sessa was relying chiefly on Maloney's judgment and evaluation in purchasing Tarport Conaway.

Maloney arrived in Ohio on Friday, March 9, 1973. On Saturday, March 10, 1973 he examined and jogged Tarport Conaway. His examination was not restricted in any way. Maloney then telephoned Sessa from Riegle's house. He reported that he had jogged Tarport Conaway and "liked him." Maloney then gave the telephone to Riegle who spoke to Sessa. In a short conversation he told Sessa that Sessa would

---

to both the particular and the general words. For discussion, see Robert E. Scott & George G. Triantis, *Anticipating Litigation in Contract Design*, 115 YALE L.J. 814, 848–56 (2006).

like the horse, that he was a good one and that he was sound. They also discussed arrangements for transportation of the horse and the manner in which he could best be driven. Sessa indicated that he would send a van for transportation. Riegle then gave the phone back to Maloney. After a brief conversation, the telephone call ended.

At some point just prior to or after the telephone call, Maloney delivered Sessa's check for the $25,000 purchase price to Riegle. . . . Tarport Conaway remained in Riegle's custody until March 23, 1973. During this interval he received proper care. On March 23, 1973, Riegle placed the horse in the hands of an ICC approved carrier for shipment to plaintiff at Freehold Raceway in Freehold, New Jersey. At 4:30 A.M., on March 24, 1973 Tarport Conaway arrived at Freehold Raceway. At 8:00 A.M., that morning, Tarport Conaway was examined by Dr. S. P. Dey, D.V.M., and was found to have tendinitis (swelling of the tendons) in both front legs. The cause of the tendinitis was not determined, however, it could have been caused by incidents during shipping. . . . By March 26, 1973, Tarport Conaway had recovered from tendinitis. When jogged by Richard Sessa for Riegle and Maloney, the horse jogged normally. Subsequently, on March 29, 1973, Tarport Conaway went lame in his hind legs while being jogged on the track at Freehold Raceway. This lameness resulted from "intermittent claudication," a condition created by the stoppage of the flow of blood through the arteries. . . . None of the medical experts who testified was able to identify the cause of the thrombosis in Tarport Conaway.

Tarport Conaway was put back into training in March of 1975. Between June 6, 1975 and December 29, 1975, the date of trial, Tarport Conaway raced 13 times, winning 3 races and earning a total of $1306.00. Between March 24, 1973, the date of Tarport Conaway's arrival at Freehold, through December 29, 1975, the date of trial, Sessa incurred necessary expenses for the horse's transportation, maintenance, training and veterinary care in the amount of $9073.00.

Discussion

As previously stated, this is an action to recover damages for breach of warranties on the sale of a three year old standardbred race horse. Plaintiff buyer contends that the defendant seller breached express warranties, an implied warranty to merchantability and an implied warranty of fitness for particular purpose.

This case involved a sale of livestock to which Article 2 of the Uniform Commercial Code applies. . . .

On March 10, 1973, the day of the sale of Tarport Conaway, Sessa and Riegle had a telephone conversation during which the horse was discussed in general terms. Arrangements were made for transportation, and Riegle gave Sessa some instructions for driving Tarport Conaway based on Riegle's experience with him. Sessa contends that certain statements made by Riegle during that conversation constitute express warranties on which Riegle is liable in this action. The most important of these is Riegle's alleged statement that, "the horse is sound," or words to that effect.[17]

In deciding whether statements by a seller constitute express warranties, the Court must look to UCC § 2-313 which presents three fundamental issues. First, the Court must determine whether the seller's statement constitutes an "affirmation of fact or promise" or "description of the goods" under § 2-313(1)(a) or (b) or whether it is rather "merely the seller's opinion or commendation of the goods" under § 2-313(2). Second, assuming the Court finds the language used susceptible to creation of a warranty, it must then be determined whether the statement was "part of the basis of the bargain." If it was, an express warranty exists and, as the third issue, the Court must determine whether the warranty was breached.

With respect to the first issue, the Court finds that in the circumstances of this case, words to the effect that "The horse is sound" spoken during the telephone conversation between Sessa and Riegle constitute an opinion or commendation rather than express warranty. This determination is a question for the trier of fact. There is nothing talismanic or thaumaturgic about the use of the word "sound." Whether use of that language constitutes warranty, or mere opinion or commendation depends on the circumstances of the sale and the type of goods sold. While § 2-313 makes it clear that no specific words need be used and no specific intent need be present, not every statement by a seller is an express warranty.

Several older Pennsylvania cases dealing with horse sales show that similar statements as to soundness are not always similarly treated under warranty law. In Wilkinson v. Stettler, 46 Pa. Super. 407 (1911), the statement that a horse "was solid and sound and would work any place" was held not to constitute an express warranty. . . . However, in Flood v. Yeager, 52 Pa. Super. 637 (1912) an express warranty was found where the plaintiff informed the defendant that, "he did not know anything at all about a horse and that he did not want . . . the defendant to make a mean deal with him; whereupon the defendant said that the horse was solid and sound; that he would guarantee him to be solid and sound."

The results in these cases are consistent with custom among horse traders as alluded to by Gene Riegle. He testified that it is "not a common thing" to guarantee a horse, that he has never guaranteed a horse unless he had an "understanding" with the buyer and that he did not guarantee Tarport Conaway. In other words, because horses are fragile creatures, susceptible to myriad maladies, detectable and undetectable, only where there is an "understanding" that an ignorant buyer, is relying totally on a knowledgeable seller not "to make a mean deal," are statements as to soundness taken to be anything more than the seller's opinion or commendation.

The facts suggest no special "understanding" between Sessa and Riegle. Sessa was a knowledgeable buyer, having been involved with standardbreds for some

---

[17] [1] Sessa also cites the statement,

> Tarport Conaway can leap like a deer, take a forward position, and if you brush him from the head of the stretch home, he would just jog home in preferred company every week.

as an express warranty. However, this statement is instruction on driving based on Riegle's experience and constitutes merely an opinion, not an express warranty. Sessa cites other statements as express warranties. However, the credible evidence does not establish that these statements were in fact made.

years. Also, Sessa sent Maloney, an even more knowledgeable horseman, as his agent to inspect the horse.

Also militating against the finding of express warranty is the nature of the conversation between Sessa and Riegle. It seemed largely collateral to the sale rather than an essential part of it. Although Sessa testified that Riegle's "personal guarantee" given during the conversation was the quintessence of the sale, the credible evidence suggests otherwise. While on the telephone, Riegle made statements to the effect that "the horse is a good one" and "you will like him." These bland statements are obviously opinion or commendation, and the statement, "The horse is sound," falling within their penumbra takes on their character as such.

Under all the facts and circumstances of this case, it is clear to the Court that Riegle's statements were not of such a character as to give rise to express warranties under § 2-313(1) but were opinion or commendation under § 2-313(2).

Even assuming that Riegle's statements could be express warranties, it is not clear that they were "part of the basis of the bargain," the second requisite of § 2-313. This is essentially a reliance requirement and is inextricably intertwined with the initial determination as to whether given language may constitute an express warranty since affirmations, promises and descriptions tend to become part of the basis of the bargain. It was the intention of the drafters of the UCC not to require a strong showing of reliance. In fact, they envisioned that all statements of the seller became part of the basis of the bargain unless clear affirmative proof is shown to the contrary. See Official Comments 3 and 8 to UCC § 2-313.

It is Sessa's contention that his conversation with Riegle was the principal factor inducing him to enter the bargain. He would have the Court believe that Maloney was merely a messenger to deliver the check. The evidence shows, however, that Sessa was relying primarily on Maloney to advise him in connection with the sale. Maloney testified that he had talked to Sessa about the horse on several occasions and expressed the opinion that he was convinced "beyond the shadow of a doubt" that he was a good buy. With respect to his authority to buy the horse he testified

> Well, Mr. Sessa said he had enough confidence and faith in me and my integrity and honesty that I, what I did say about the horse, I was representing the horse as he is or as he was, and that if the horse, in my estimation, was that type of a horse and at that given price, the fixed price of $25,000 he would buy the horse.

When, at the airport, Maloney protested that he did not want to accept full responsibility to go to Ohio alone, Sessa told him ". . . I take your word. I trust your judgment and I trust your honesty, that if this horse is right, everything will be all right." In Ohio, Maloney examined the horse, jogged him and reported to Sessa over the telephone that he "liked him."

The Court believes that Maloney's opinion was the principal, if not the only, factor which motivated Sessa to purchase the horse. The conversation with Riegle played a negligible role in his decision.

[The court also denied the plaintiff's claims of breach of an implied warranty under § 2-314 of the Code and breach of an implied warranty of fitness for a particular purpose under § 2-314. Judgment was entered for defendants.]

NOTES

1. *Affirmation of Fact or Opinion? Sessa* should be compared with two other cases involving statements regarding the condition of animals being offered for sale. In *Frederickson v. Hackney*, 159 Minn. 234, 198 N.W. 806 (1924), the plaintiff-buyer, a breeder of thoroughbred Holstein "Freisan" cattle, purchased a male calf that turned out to be sterile. The defendant-seller had advised the plaintiff to buy the calf for breeding, claiming that it would help build the plaintiff's herd. The court held this claim to be "trade talk of the conventional type . . . and it cannot be expanded into a warranty simply because the expectations of both parties were disappointed" and denied recovery. However, in *McNeir v. Greer-Hale Chinchilla Ranch*, 194 Va. 623, 74 S.E.2d 165 (1953), statements to inexperienced buyers asserting that pairs of chinchillas were "proven breeders" were held sufficient to enable the buyers to get to the jury on the express warranty issue. Note the *Sessa* court's observation regarding the disparate Pennsylvania results in the *Wilkinson, Walker,* and *Flood* cases:"[T]hey do show that statements of the same tenor receive varying treatment depending on the surrounding circumstances." *Sessa*, 427 F. Supp. at 766. Can you isolate the key circumstance that harmonizes the outcomes? If so, why should that variable be determinative?

When encouraging prospective buyers to purchase their merchandise, sellers often make a variety of descriptive statements about the goods. Some are statements of past performance, others describe future expectations about how the product is expected to perform, and others draw primarily upon subjective criteria. How should courts analyze such statements?

In *Royal Business Machines, Inc. v. Lorraine Corp.*, 633 F.2d 34 (7th Cir. 1980), the court analyzed a variety of claims made by a manufacturer of copy machines:

> The decisive test for whether a given representation is a warranty or merely an expression of the seller's opinion is whether the seller asserts a fact of which the buyer is ignorant or merely states an opinion or judgment on a matter of which the seller has no special knowledge and on which the buyer may be expected also to have an opinion and to exercise his judgment. . . . General statements to the effect that goods are "the best,", or are "of good quality,", or will "last a lifetime" and be "in perfect condition,", are generally regarded as expressions of the seller's opinion or "the puffing of his wares" and do not create an express warranty.

> No express warranty was created by Royal's affirmation that both RBC machine models and their component parts were of high quality. This was a statement of the seller's opinion, the kind of "puffing" to be expected in any sales transaction, rather than a positive averment of fact describing a product's capabilities to which an express warranty could attach.

> Similarly, the representations by Royal that experience and testing had shown that the frequency of repair was "very low" and would remain so lack the specificity of an affirmation of fact upon which a warranty could be predicated. These representations were statements of the seller's opinion.

It was also erroneous to find that an express warranty was created by Royal's assurances to Booher that purchase of the RBC machines would bring him substantial profits. Such a representation does not describe the goods within the meaning of UCC 2-313(1)(b), nor is the representation an affirmation of fact relating to the goods under UCC 2-313(1)(a). It is merely sales talk and the expression of the seller's opinion.

On the other hand, the assertion that the machines could not cause fires is an assertion of fact relating to the goods, and substantial evidence in the record supports the trial judge's findings that the assertion was made by Royal to Booher. The same may be said for the assertion that the machines were tested and ready to be marketed. Substantial evidence in the record supports the finding that Royal made the assertion to Booher that maintenance cost for the machine would run 12 cent per copy and that this assertion was not an estimate but an assertion of a fact of performance capability.

Id. at 41–44.

2. *A Theory of Express Warranty.* A seller's statement must satisfy two requirements in order to become an express warranty under UCC § 2-313: (a) it must "become a basis of the bargain," and (b) it must not be "a statement purporting to be merely the seller's opinion or commendation."[18] Unfortunately, the Code's language is conclusory, and it does not help in determining when a particular statement will be a basis of the bargain (as opposed to a mere opinion). In many respects, then, express warranty problems are much like the questions raised in interpreting express conditions. If the contracting parties clearly indicate that a particular provision is an express condition rather than a promise, the law will give effect to that understanding. On the other hand, where the parties do not clearly specify the nature of the provision, the law provides a baseline assumption (i.e., the preference for promises over conditions). A similar issue is raised in categorizing seller's statements as to quality. If the seller in *Sessa* had "guaranteed" the condition of the horse, the statement would most likely have constituted an express warranty under § 2-313. The question, however, is how to characterize a seller's affirmation about the product that does not explicitly purport to accept the risk that the product will fail to perform in the agreed fashion.

When a buyer claims that a seller made an express warranty, the issue thus is

---

[18] Courts and commentators disagree as to whether a buyer's reliance upon a seller's affirmation of fact is necessary to create an express warranty under UCC § 2-313. The Uniform Sales Act, the precursor to the UCC, required that the seller's affirmation of fact "induced the buyer to purchase the goods and if the buyer purchased the goods relying thereon." USA § 12. In contrast, UCC § 2-313 makes no express reference to "reliance." However, UCC § 2-313 Comment 3 provides guidance: "In actual practice affirmations of fact made by the seller about the goods during a bargain are regarded as part of the description of those goods; hence no particular reliance on such statements need be shown in order to weave them into the fabric of the agreement." Thus, the Code assumes that all affirmations of fact are part of the basis of the bargain, and the buyer must have relied upon them during the exchange. For further discussion, see Thomas J. Holdych & Bruce D. Mann, *A Market and Economic Based Analysis of Express Warranties — Getting What You Pay for and Paying for What You Get*, 45 DePaul L. Rev. 781 (1996); Sidney Kwestel, *Freedom from Reliance: A Contract Approach to Express Warranty*, 26 Suffolk U. L. Rev. 959 (1992).

whether a seller's agreement to bear the risk of nonperformance can reasonably be inferred from the affirmations or representations the seller made, considered in the light of the surrounding circumstances. If such an agreement can be inferred, the seller's statement would have become "part of the basis of the bargain." If such an agreement cannot be inferred from what the seller said, the seller's affirmation is not part of the bargain and should be classified as an "opinion or commendation." *Sessa* suggests that the relative expertise of buyer and seller are relevant factors in determining who has implicitly agreed to bear the risk of nonperformance. Why should that matter? Are any other factors relevant?[19]

3. ***Description of Components.*** Express warranties cover the performance of a product and its component parts; they do not necessarily protect general descriptions of the nature of such parts. In *Zappanti v. Berge Serv. Ctr.*, 26 Ariz. App. 398, 549 P.2d 178 (1976), the court held that the buyers of a 1969 reconstructed Volkswagen Dunebuggy could not claim that the express warranty of description was breached when it was discovered that some of the parts came from the 1967 model year. Reconstructed vehicles are not assigned model years by the manufacturer; rather, some states simply mandate that the model year reflect the year that the vehicle was assembled. The court found that no express statements existed relating to the model year of the vehicle's components.

4. ***Specificity.*** How specific must a statement be to constitute an affirmation of fact rather than "mere puffery"? Consider *Searls v. Glasser*, 64 F.3d 1061 (7th Cir. 1995), where the plaintiff-shareholders alleged misrepresentations against the defendant-corporation which repeatedly characterized itself as "recession-resistant," despite the fact that it was negatively affected by a subsequent economic recession. In examining the statement's specificity, the court said:

> First, the phrase "recession-resistant" is simply too vague to constitute a material statement of fact. Plaintiffs apparently interpret the phrase to mean "recession-proof." But it could be just as easily used to describe a company that although not impervious to the effects of a recession will nevertheless survive it better than others. It is a promotional phrase used to champion the company but is devoid of any substantive information. Just as indefinite predictions of "growth" are better described as puffery rather than as material statements of fact, describing a company as "recession-resistant" lacks the requisite specificity to be considered anything but optimistic rhetoric. Its lack of specificity precludes it from being deemed material; it contains no useful information upon which a reasonable investor would base a decision to invest.

Id. at 1066.

Compare the result in *Searls* to *Keith v. Buchanan*, 173 Cal. App. 3d 13, 22 (1985), where the court held that sales brochures describing a cruise ship as "a picture of sure-footed seaworthiness" and "a carefully well-equipped and very seaworthy vessel," were specific enough to be an affirmation of fact. Likewise, in *Downie v. Abex Corp.*, 741 F.2d 1235 (10th Cir. 1984), the court held that declaring

---

[19] For an economic approach to risk allocation in the sale of horses, *see* Robert S. Miller, *The Sale of Horses and Horse Interests: A Transactional Approach*, 78 Ky. L.J. 517 (1990).

a feature on an airline jetway to be "fail-safe" was sufficiently specific to constitute and express warranty.

Are these cases reconcilable? Is it enough to say that a statement is an affirmation of fact if it passes a "reasonable person" test? Or must the statement also contain information that is objectively measurable, as the court in *Searls v. Glasser* suggests? Compare these two statements: (1) "This is a good car" and (2) "This car is in good condition." Which statement can bargainers objectively measure with some external reference point?

[b]   Implied Warranties

Frequently, disputes arise between contracting parties concerning the quality of the promisor's performance where the promisor has not made any statement that might give rise to an express warranty. In such cases, the law is forced to resolve a few vexing questions: (1) What is the standard of performance against which the promisor's tender is to be measured? (2) If the performance is defective, who bears the risk of quality defects that could not have been reasonably avoided? If the performance is defective and the risk is assigned by default to the promisor, then we say that an implied warranty exists with respect to that transaction. Much of the law of implied warranty has evolved from the law of sales. In reading the following case, you should ask yourself why sellers of goods are deemed to give implied warranties against quality defects while providers of services, such as construction contractors and sellers of real estate, do not traditionally assume these risks.

FLIPPO v. MODE O'DAY FROCK SHOPS
Supreme Court of Arkansas
248 Ark. 1, 449 S.W.2d 692 (1970)

HARRIS, J.

This litigation is occasioned by a spider bite. Gladys Flippo, appellant herein, went into a ladies clothing store in Batesville, operated by Rosie Goforth, and known as Mode O'Day Frock Shops of Hollywood. Mrs. Flippo tried on two pairs of pants, or slacks, which were shown to her by Mrs. Goforth. The first pair proved to be too small, and according to appellant's evidence, when Mrs. Flippo put on the second pair, she suddenly felt a burning sensation on her thigh; she immediately removed the pants, shook them, and a spider fell to the floor which was then stepped upon. An examination of her thigh revealed a reddened area, which progressively grew worse. Mrs. Flippo was subsequently hospitalized for approximately 30 days. According to her physician, the injury was caused by the bite of a brown recluse spider. Suit for damages was instituted against Mode O'Day Frock Shops and Rosie Goforth, the complaint asserting three grounds for recovery, first that a pair of slacks in a defective condition (by reason of the presence of a poisonous spider), and unreasonably dangerous was sold to appellant; second, that both appellees were guilty of several acts of negligence, and third, that there was an implied warranty that the slacks were fit for the purpose for which they were purchased, though actually not fit, because of the poisonous spider concealed therein. On trial, the court refused requested instructions offered by appellant on theories of implied warranty, and strict tort liability, and instructed the jury only on the issue of appellees' alleged negligence as the proximate cause of the injury. The jury returned a verdict for both appellees, and judgment was entered accordingly. From the judgment so entered, appellant brings this appeal, not however, appealing from the finding of no negligence; instead, the appeal is based entirely upon the court's refusal to submit the case upon implied warranty and strict tort liability theories. Accordingly, for reversal, it first urged that "there was sufficient evidence to justify a finding that Mrs. Flippo was injured by goods unfit for their intended use, supplied by a merchant with respect to goods of that kind, and therefore the trial court erred in refusing to instruct upon the law of implied warranty of merchantability."

It might be said at the outset that appellant has filed a very thorough and comprehensive brief in support of the positions taken; however, we are unable to agree with the views presented under the circumstances of this case. As pointed out by appellant, there was ample evidence to support a finding that Mrs. Flippo suffered a bite by a brown recluse spider concealed on the slacks furnished her by Mrs. Goforth (it is not conceded by appellees that the bite occurred in this manner). Appellant says:

> . . . If that be true, then appellant submits that such an article of clothing is not reasonably fit for use as an article of clothing and is thus not merchantable.

It is contended that appellees were bound by the implied warranty of merchantability imposed by UCC 2-314, this statute providing that, in order to be merchantable, the goods must, inter alia, be fit for the ordinary purposes for which such goods are used. Appellant argues that an article of clothing which conceals a venomous creature is certainly unfit for use, and therefore at the time the slacks were handed to Mrs. Flippo, the garment was unfit for the use for which it was intended, and there was accordingly a breach of the implied warranty of merchantability under either the statute or common law.

We cannot agree that the law of implied warranty of merchantability is applicable to a case of this nature. The pair of pants itself was fit for the ordinary purposes for which stretch pants are used; there was nothing wrong from a manufacturing standpoint. In fact, the evidence reflects that Mrs. Flippo bought this particular pair after being bitten, and she has worn and laundered them since the accident. There is absolutely no evidence that the goods were defective in any manner. It is, of course, readily apparent that the spider was not a part of the product, and there is no evidence that either the manufacturer or retailer had any control of the spider, or caused it to be in the pants. Mrs. Goforth said she receives the shipments once a week in pasteboard cartons sealed with tape, and that upon receiving the cartons, she immediately opens them, places the garments on plastic hangers, and hangs them out. The cartons are delivered by truck line, and the witness stated that the slacks in question had been in the store for some time in excess of 20 days.

Irrespective of whether the spider attached itself to the garment in Kansas City, or in Batesville, it was not a part of the garment. The three cases cited by appellant as authority for the common law implied warranty of merchantability, all deal with a defective product, which is not the situation in the present litigation. Perhaps our position can best be made clear by simply stating that the spider was not a part of the manufactured article, and the injury to Mrs. Flippo was caused by the spider — and not the product. We find no cause of action under either the statute or the common law.

Nor can we agree that the trial court erred in refusing to instruct the jury upon the principles of strict tort liability. It is at once obvious that the product sold in the instant case was a pair of slacks, and the slacks were not in a defective condition; nor were they unreasonably dangerous; in fact, they were not dangerous at all; still further, the slacks did not cause any physical harm to Mrs. Flippo.

Were we inclined to a more liberal view of the theory of strict tort liability, it would not be applied in this case, for we have no hesitancy in stating that the facts in the instant litigation do not support the submission of the case on that theory. This case was properly submitted upon the issue of negligence, and it would have been improper for the court to have given the instructions sought by appellant.

Affirmed.

NOTES

1. ***Analyzing Implied Warranty of Merchantability Problems.*** It may help to approach implied warranty of merchantability problems systematically so as to separate the issues more clearly. At the outset, note a basic point: the UCC's implied warranty of merchantability, § 2-314, applies only to merchants. Consider the possibility that a buyer purchased food from a seller on the seller's first day in the restaurant business. Applying the test of § 2-104(1), can this seller be said to deal in goods of the kind such that he is a merchant for purposes of § 2-314? Might there be other ways of certifying that the seller is a merchant?[20]

In addition to determining that the seller was a merchant and thus that a warranty of merchantability was implied in the sale, the buyer must prevail on two additional issues:

(a) Was the warranty breached?;[21] and,

(b) Did the breach proximately cause the damage to the buyer?[22]

Which question is involved in *Flippo*?

2. ***Expected Impurities.*** Certain products — particularly food products — contain "natural imperfections," some of which may lead to injury. Examples of such naturally-occurring impurities are fish bones, crystallized corn grains, and un-shelled nuts. Courts tend to side with the manufacturer/seller in such cases, as long as the imperfection is not a foreign substance.

An example of such a case is *Coffer v. Standard Brands, Inc.*, 30 N.C. App. 134,

---

[20] *See* comment 2 to UCC § 2-104; for further discussion, see Franklin E. Crawford, *Fit for Its Ordinary Purpose? Tobacco, Fast Food, and the Implied Warranty of Merchantability*, 63 Ohio St. L.J. 1165 (2002).

[21] *See* UCC § 2-314(2).

[22] *See* UCC § 2-314 cmt. 13.

226 S.E.2d 534 (1976), where a consumer who purchased a canister of mixed nuts was injured after biting an unshelled filbert nut. The court noted that the North Carolina Board of Agriculture "permitted between 1% and 2.5% of peanuts to be unshelled," and thus concluded that there was a basic recognition within the nut industry that some impurities would occur. As a result, the court concluded that the presence of one unshelled nut did not render the batch of mixed nuts unfit for their ordinary use, noting that "the presence of natural impurities is no basis for liability."

Presumably, the "ordinary use" of the mixed nuts contemplated by this buyer was consumption. The defendant introduced minimum government standards to bolster its case, claiming that the existence of an unshelled filbert in this lot of nuts was not unnatural. Does it strike you that these data miss the point? Do they tell the court anything about the edibility of these nuts? Do they tell the court what the ordinary buyer should expect to find in his jar? If you were Coffer's lawyer, what type of evidence would you marshal in his favor? Might you ignore industry data altogether and instead present the issue as one of safety to the consumer rather than edibility?

Indeed, the court's comparison to a batch of peanuts is flawed in two ways. First, the defective nut in question was a filbert, which, if unshelled, may pose a greater threat to unknowing consumers. More significantly, however, the contents of a can of peanuts are nearly indistinguishable; an unshelled nut would certainly stand out among the others. A container of mixed nuts, however, by definition contains nuts of many types, so a defective nut would not stand out as vividly as in a container with highly uniform contents.

Courts do not always look to governmentally established impurity levels. Sometimes their analysis simply focuses on the nature of the food and the consumer's expectations. In *Webster v. Blue Ship Tea Room, Inc.*, 198 N.E.2d 309 (Mass. 1964), the court rejected the claim of a woman who encountered a bone in a bowl of fish chowder, noting:

> A person sitting down in New England to consume a good New England fish chowder embarks on a gustatory adventure that may entail the removal of some fish bones from his bowl as he proceeds. . . . We should be prepared to cope with the hazards of fish bones, the occasional presence of which in chowders is, it seems to us, to be anticipated, and which, in the light of a hallowed tradition, do not impair their fitness or merchantability.

3. *Intersection with Torts.* Many of the cases discussed above represent instances where the law of warranty intersects with the law of torts. Indeed, William Prosser described warranty as "a freak hybrid born of the illicit intercourse of tort and contract."[23] Consequently, many such cases invoke not only analysis of the standards for merchantability, but also use concepts of tort law such as negligence and strict liability.

There are key differences between tort and contract, however, even in the context of warranty claims. One important difference is between the default rules of contract and the mandatory rules in tort. As we will see in Section C[1][c], *infra*, the

---

[23] Prosser, *The Fall of the Citadel*, 50 Minn. L. Rev. 791, 800 (1966).

implied warranties under the UCC are default rules and, even though opting out is carefully regulated by the law governing disclaimers of warranty,[24] at least in theory the seller can disclaim any liability for breach of implied warranty but cannot similarly avoid liability in tort.

4. *The Implied Warranty of Workmanlike Performance.* Contract law and tort law become particularly intermingled with respect to implied warranties of workmanlike performance. This type of implied warranty is unique to construction and service contracts. Courts often approach the warranty of workmanlike performance "not as a default rule or gap-filler, but as a duty which is independent of the parties' agreement and supports the imposition of tort liability." Timothy Davis, *The Illusive Warranty of Workmanlike Performance: Constructing a Conceptual Framework*, 72 NEB. L. REV. 981, 983 (1993). While, in theory, parties could contract around the warranty of workmanlike performance, rare is the individual who would hire someone to build his home who would refuse to commit to doing a good job.

When courts examine workmanlike performance, they evaluate the performance as it goes on, whereas more traditional warranty inquiries focus on the end product. Professor Davis notes:

> Commentators and scholars agree that the warranty of workmanlike performance is not an end result warranty such as the warranty of merchantability under Article Two of the Uniform Commercial Code. Indeed, unlike the warranty of merchantability and the warranty of habitability, the implied warranty of workmanlike performance is an "in process" concept. "In process" refers to those situations in which the liability of the service provider hinges on the nature of the conduct he or she provides when rendering services. Therefore, "in process" is to be contrasted with a "true warranty" in that the former focuses on conduct, while the latter focuses on the end result. Accordingly, conformance by the service provider with the governing standard of care will more than likely relieve it of liability for defects resulting from its performance.

Id. at 1012–13.

Thus, the inquiry for such warranties often corresponds to the negligence standard of tort law. This mode of inquiry is the key difference between a warranty of workmanlike performance and a warranty of habitability, which applies uniquely to construction contracts. Because they are service-oriented in nature, warranties of habitability also have no UCC equivalent.

The extension of each of these warranties represents a move away from the doctrine of caveat emptor. In validating the implied warranty of workmanlike performance, the Court of Appeals of Kentucky noted in *Crawley v. Terhune*, 437 S.W.2d 743, 745 (Ky. Ct. App. 1969):

> Because the caveat emptor rule is completely unrealistic and inequitable as applied in the case of the ordinarily inexperienced buyer of a new house from the professional builder-seller, and because a contract by the builder to sell a new house is not much distinguishable from a contract to build a

---

[24] *See* UCC § 2-316.

new house for another, we are disposed to adopt the minority view to the extent of holding that in the sale of a new dwelling by the builder, there is an implied warranty that in its major structural features the dwelling was constructed in a workmanlike manner and using suitable materials.

Unlike the implied warranty of habitability, however, implied warranties of workmanlike performance are not limited to construction contracts.[25] Additionally, workmanlike performance warranties are a prominent feature in many admiralty cases.

5. *The Implied Warranty of Fitness for a Particular Purpose.* Read UCC § 2-315 and Comments. Compare the implied warranty of fitness for a particular purpose with the implied warranty of merchantability. UCC § 2-314 imposes on merchant sellers the risk that goods will not conform to "the ordinary purposes for which such goods are used." Section 2-315, on the other hand, provides that a seller may also bear the risk that his goods will not suit a "particular purpose" of the buyer if the seller has reason to know of the purpose and of the buyer's reliance on his skill in selecting conforming goods. What is the purpose of the Code's distinction between ordinary and particular purposes? Why should the seller bear the risk of the buyer's noncustomary or idiosyncratic expectations?

Note that the warranty of fitness for a particular purpose does not apply if a buyer does not rely on the seller's judgment in selecting an appropriate item. This principle is exemplified by *Lewis & Sims v. Key Indus.*, 16 Wash. App. 619, 557 P.2d 1318 (1976). There, Lewis and Sims were awarded a subcontract to install water and sewer lines in North Pole, Alaska. In ordering the pipe necessary to complete the job, they specified that the pipe had to be coal-tar enamel lined, as well as indicating other specific requirements for the pipe. Ultimately, the enamel lining cracked due to the extreme cold; Lewis and Sims ordered the same type of pipe from another supplier and sued to recover the cost of replacement. The court ruled that the warranty of fitness for a particular purpose did not apply under these circumstances, holding:

> [W]e find ample evidence to conclude that Lewis and Sims ordered a specific size and type of pipe and that any deviation from the coal-tar enamel lined pipe that was manufactured would not have been accepted by Lewis and Sims. In short, neither Liberty nor Northwest was asked for its recommendations, nor did either select the pipe or lining to be used. Liberty merely filled a specific purchase order for pipe — a job it held itself out to do. Moreover, Mr. Sims testified that he knew exactly what he was ordering from Liberty and that it would not have been within Liberty's province to substitute another type of pipe. . . .

---

[25] For extensions of this warranty in other contexts, see *Davis v. New England Pest Control Co.*, 576 A.2d 1240 (R.I. 1990) (contract for termite inspector contains implied warranty of workmanlike performance); *Leonard & Harral Packing Co. v. Ward*, 971 S.W.2d 671 (Tex. App. 1998) (implied warranty of workmanlike performance extends to cattle transporter); *Zenda Grain & Supply Co. v. Farmland Indus.*, 20 Kan. App. 2d 728, 894 P.2d 881 (1995) (contract for management services for grain seller has implied warranty of workmanlike performance).

> The warranty for fitness for a particular purpose was not meant to be applied in a situation such as we face today. The central tenet — reliance upon the skill, judgment, or experience of the seller — is not manifested. What is apparent is the fact that both parties to this action knew what was desired, and that desire was fulfilled. It is also important to note that the pipe itself was not negligently manufactured; rather the lining was susceptible to cracking upon exposure to extreme cold.

16 Wash. App. at 624–26.

6. *Problem: The Scope of Warranty Liability.* Mr. and Mrs. Gulash entered into a contract with Stylarama, Inc. for the sale and installation of a Stylarama "Wavecrest" above-ground swimming pool, for the price of $3,690. The pool was installed in May of 1997. Soon thereafter, the Gulashes discovered: (i) that the vinyl liner was improperly installed and was "wrinkled and folded in many places"; (ii) there was inadequate support under the plywood deck, resulting in the deck being uneven, unsteady and dangerous to persons using the pool; (iii) there were multiple surface bubbles on the plywood decking; (iv) the sides of the pool were bowing out, and the 2 x 4 wooden supports were rotted, twisted and misaligned; and (v) the entire swimming pool was not level. Stylarama, Inc. had made no representations to the Gulashes other than their promise to install a "Wavecrest" pool.

> (a) Assuming the Gulashes can prove these facts, but cannot prove Stylarama failed to exercise ordinary care, can they recover damages from Stylarama? What arguments would you anticipate the defendant making?[26]

> (b) Would your analysis change if the Gulashes had rented the property from Stylarama with the pool already installed? What if they had purchased the home and pool from Stylarama?

If your answer to question (b) is different from (a) above, what explains the distinction in assessing liability? What principle, if any, justifies assigning the risk of "unavoidable" quality defects to one party or the other when neither party has explicitly assumed any responsibility?[27]

[c] Warranty Disclaimers

The Code permits sellers to make no warranties at all. A seller reluctant to make an express warranty may, of course, say nothing about the quality or characteristics of his goods, and § 2-316(2) and (3) authorize sellers to disclaim the implied warranties of fitness and merchantability. Disclaimers at first blush seem no different from (and thus should be enforced in the same way as) other contract clauses in which parties seek to opt out of the standard default rules. To be sure, § 2-314 reflects a belief that merchant sellers have a comparative advantage over buyers in reducing or insuring against risks of nonconformity, but this advantage will not always exist. Buyers may sometimes be able to bear such risks more

---

[26] *See* UCC §§ 2-313, 2-314, 2-102, 2-105; *Gulash v. Stylarama, Inc.*, 364 A.2d 1221 (Conn. Super. Ct. 1975).

[27] For further discussion of these questions, *see* Jean Braucher, *An Informal Resolution Model of Consumer Product Warranty Law*, 1985 Wis. L. Rev. 1405.

cheaply than their sellers. Nonetheless, courts are often reluctant to enforce warranty disclaimers, and, at a minimum, may insist on clear and conspicuous language.[28] By using specific contractual language, however, the seller can usually make it clear that the contract contains no implied warranties.

PELC v. SIMMONS
Appellate Court of Illinois
249 Ill. App. 3d 852, 620 N.E.2d 12 (1993)

WELCH, J.

The defendant, Mark Simmons, appeals from a judgment of $1,200; the judgment stated that if defendant paid plaintiff $1,400 defendant could take possession of the automobile. The judgment was entered by the circuit court sitting without a jury on plaintiff's small claims complaint. On appeal, defendant only contends that the judgment is against the manifest weight of the evidence.

The small claims complaint alleged that "on 7-11, 1992 Defendant orally alleged the 1978 Sunbird sold to Plaintiff was in above-average condition. However, [the] vehicle fails to run at all, causing Plaintiff to lose employment, money for college and personal and emotional distress."

Defendant's automobile was placed on Wayne Dressel's used car lot for exposure. When plaintiff expressed an interest in the car, she was referred to defendant, who sold her the automobile. Donald Henson testified that he is plaintiff's uncle. Henson went to Dressel's used car lot, started defendant's automobile, a 1978 Pontiac Sunbird, listened to it run, checked the oil, and looked at the engine. Henson noticed that the engine had been repainted and asked Dressel what he knew about the car. Dressel replied that defendant or defendant's father had told him that the engine had been rebuilt; to what extent Dressel did not know. When Henson telephoned defendant, defendant stated that he had rebuilt the engine because the timing chain "went out." Defendant stated that he wanted $2,200 for the car, and Henson responded they wanted to spend approximately $1,500. Approximately 90 minutes later, defendant telephoned Henson and stated that he would sell it for $1,500. In response to Henson's statement that the engine had been rebuilt or repainted, defendant responded that he had personally rebuilt the engine. He further stated, "The only thing that's wrong with it [the automobile] is the air conditioning," which needed the compressor charged. The next day, plaintiff purchased defendant's vehicle.

Henson further testified that several days later, in response to plaintiff's call for assistance, he was able to start the car after the first attempt failed. Because smoke was coming out "real bad," Henson pulled all four spark plugs and observed that they were caked with oil. Henson ran a compression check, and each cylinder would

---

[28] For a discussion of the tension between courts' restrictive view of warranty disclaimers and the need for sellers to fully disclose terms after purchase with the advent of "rolling" contracts, see Gregory J. Krabacher, *Revocation of Tripartite Rolling Contracts: Finding a Remedy in the Twenty- First Century Usage of Trade*, 66 OHIO ST. L.J. 397 (2005); Stephen E. Friedman, *Text and Circumstance: Warranty Disclaimers in a World of Rolling Contracts*, 46 ARIZ. L. REV. 677 (2004).

hold only approximately 60 pounds of pressure rather than the 95 to 98 pounds of pressure that a properly functioning cylinder should hold. Air was blowing out of the tray case, coming through the carburetor, and coming out the intake. Henson could turn the crank by hand. He opined that in its present condition the vehicle is worth $200 for parts. The vehicle is drivable, but it would have to be refilled with four quarts of oil daily. Henson had previously rebuilt an automobile engine. Henson conceded that he checked the oil and drove the automobile on the used car lot. Dressel would not allow him to drive it off the lot because it was not insured. Henson explained that he could not tell if the automobile was smoking, because the used car lot "was chat [sic] and dusty."

Plaintiff, age 22, testified that she purchased the Sunbird on July 10, 1992. She had previously gone with her uncle to Dressel's used car lot to look at the vehicle, and Dressel stated that it was a good car. On the Sunbird was a sign: "sold as is." Her uncle repeated to her the representations concerning the vehicle that defendant made to Henson. On July 14, she heard the engine knocking. She drove five miles home and put oil in the car. Plaintiff had to replace the car's battery on July 15 and fill the engine with oil. Between July 11 and July 15 she drove 103 miles. On July 19, she had the oil changed and drove from Valley Park, Missouri, to O'Fallon, Illinois, and back to Valley Park, approximately 60 miles round trip. On July 20, there was no oil in the automobile. On July 21, she took the Sunbird to a mechanic, and after conferring with the mechanic, plaintiff telephoned defendant in an effort to get her money back. Defendant stated that the automobile would stop using oil once the rings became seated; in approximately 500 to 2,000 miles. She then asked, "so after I put two thousand miles on this car, the rings will be seated?" Defendant said, "No, that's not what I said." Defendant explained that he was talking about a normal car, which confused plaintiff. When she next tried to start the automobile, the starter would not work. She did not have the money to repair the car. She paid $1,600 for the Sunbird and operated it for two weeks during which time she checked the oil daily, because Simmons told Henson the engine had been rebuilt and to check the oil. She did not remember how many times she added oil. Between the time she bought the car and July 15 when she added oil, she had driven the Sunbird 103 miles.

Diane Marie Henson, wife of Donald Henson, testified that when she went to pick up the Sunbird, defendant and Dressel were on the lot. Mrs. Henson asked defendant, "Will this [the Sunbird] make it back and forth to school and get her [plaintiff] to and from her work or whatever?" Defendant responded, "Oh, yes, it was a good little car." Defendant advised that the oil needed to be checked every couple hundred miles for the first 1,000 miles and then every 2,000 or 3,000 miles.

In awarding judgment for the plaintiff, the court found:

> "The evidence is persuasive that there was a verbal representation made relative to the condition of this vehicle and that in fact — and also that the instructions given relative to what is to be done with making sure the vehicle didn't burn up because of lack of oil were not sufficient. Mr. Simmons' testimony is that he told the folks — the buyers to check it often.
>
> The testimnoy in evidence which is uncontradicted was it was to be checked at least four days and then another days [sic] afterward if it wasn't checked

every day. I just can't buy the fact that this car has to be checked on a daily basis, that running approximately two hundred fifty miles or three hundred fifty miles is sufficient to burn up that engine.

I believe that the evidence is sufficient to persuade me that the representations were improper, that the warranties were breached, and that the damage that was done to the engine was not caused by any misuse of the vehicle by the plaintiff.

I'm not suggesting, by the way, in this comment that the defendant did — the defendant did anything purposely wrong or negligent. That's not the issue in this case. The issue in this case is a breach of a contract and a warranty. And therefore, I believe that the — therefore, I find in favor of the plaintiff."

Defendant initially contends that no warranties were made by defendant to plaintiff. Plaintiff testified that a sign on the Sunbird stated "sold as is." The term "as is" is generally understood to mean that the buyer is purchasing goods in its present condition with whatever faults it may possess. The term is similar to terms such as "with all faults" or "in its present condition" and implies that the seller is relieved of any further obligation to reimburse for loss or damage because of the condition of the goods.

Section 2-316(3)(a) of the Uniform Commercial Code (UCC) states:

(a) unless the circumstances indicate otherwise, all implied warranties are excluded by expressions like 'as is,' 'with all faults' or other language which in common understanding calls the buyer's attention to the exclusion of warranties and makes plain that there is no implied warranty.

In the case at bar, the vehicle had a sticker which stated that it was "sold as is." Defendant's statement that he had rebuilt the engine did not create an express warranty for the engine. If we were to accept the argument that defendant had made an express warranty of the engine by merely stating that he had rebuilt it, then anyone who stated that he had made a specific repair of a vehicle would be expressly warranting that repair. Further, plaintiff presented no evidence as to what caused the engine to use excessive amounts of oil. With no such evidence before the court, we are unable to determine the cause of the failure.

Words do have meaning. "Sold as is" when posted on a used car means just that; to rule otherwise would make it meaningless and create a new body of law as to what words need be published and what words need to be said or not said in order to sell something without a warranty.

For the foregoing reasons, the judgment of the circuit court is reversed.

Reversed

NOTES

1. ***The Seller's Obligations.*** Declaring that a used car is to be sold "as is" does not automatically protect the seller. The seller still must be careful to follow other duties and obligations relating to the formation of contracts. For instance, in *Morris*

v. Mack's Used Cars, 824 S.W.2d 538 (Tenn. 1992), a used car dealer was held liable for knowingly concealing the fact that a 1979 pickup truck was reconstructed; this, in turn, reduced the market value of the vehicle by 30-50%.

The court was unconvinced by the defendant's argument that the car was sold "as is," noting that the parties nonetheless had a duty to execute the contract in good faith and non fraudulently, and that obligation could not be waived by any sort of contractual disclaimer. The court noted:

> Although the Uniform Commercial Code does expressly permit disclaimers in the sale of goods between merchants, § 2-316 refers specifically to disclaimers of implied warranties, suggesting to us that it was intended only to permit a seller to limit or modify the contractual bases of liability which the Code would otherwise impose on the transaction.

> The section does not appear to preclude claims based on fraud or other deceptive conduct.

Id.

Likewise, sellers may run the risk of creating express warranties with their statements and declarations, notwithstanding an "as is" disclaimer of *implied* warranties under UCC § 2-316.[29] For example, several courts have held that the terms "good condition,"[30] "good running condition,"[31] and "good mechanical condition"[32] created express warranties. In *Jones v. Kellner*, 5 Ohio App. 3d 242 (1982),the buyer test drove the car and the seller orally represented the car was in "A-1" condition mechanically. The buyer agreed to purchase the car for $600. On the way home, the car stalled and had to be towed. From that time on the car was mechanically inoperable. When the buyer sought to return the automobile, the seller refused to take it back and return the purchase price. The court found that the seller's description of the car's "A-1" mechanical condition, combined with the buyer's reliance on this representation, created an express warranty.

Re-read UCC § 2-316 carefully. Why do you suppose the defendant's statements in *Pelc v. Simmons* hadn't created an express warranty? Recall the discussion of affirmations of fact versus opinion and puffery in Section C[1][a], *supra*. The seller in *Pelc* stated that the vehicle was a "good car" and a "good little car." What terms distinguish affirmations of fact and opinions?

---

[29] For discussion, see Charles Pierson, *Does "Puff" Create an Express Warranty of Merchantability? Where the Hornbooks Go Wrong*, 36 Duq. L. Rev. 887 (1998).

[30] *Pake v. Byrd*, 286 S.E.2d 588 (N.C. Ct. App. 1982).

[31] *Melotz v. Scheckla*, 801 P.2d 593 (Mont. 1990).

[32] *Valley Datsun v. Martinez*, 578 S.W.2d 485 (Tex. App. 1979).

2. *A Question of Context.* Purchasers of used cars often expect that their new vehicle may not necessarily run flawlessly. Purchasers in other contexts, however, expect to receive exactly what they have contracted for, and demand that it function properly. Consequently, if a seller chooses to waive or disclaim any warranties that apply to the product, it must do so in a clear and conspicuous manner, so that erstwhile buyers can properly account for the disclaimed warranties in their decision to buy or not.

Such disclaimers became the point of contention in *Weisz v. Parke-Bernet Galleries, Inc.*, 67 Misc. 2d 1077, 325 N.Y.S.2d 576 (1971). This case involved two paintings, ostensibly the work of French artist Raoul Dufy, which were purchased at an auction and later discovered to be forgeries. The gallery attempted to disclaim any warranties relating to the genuineness or authenticity of the artwork by providing a 15-paragraph list of "Conditions of Sale" several pages into an 80-page catalogue which described the artwork featured in each auction. The disclaimer was in smaller type than the rest of the catalogue. At each auction, the auctioneer announced that any purchases were subject to the conditions of sale, without directly alluding to the disclaimer. Furthermore, the rest of the catalogue was designed to impress upon buyers the idea that the artwork was genuine, noting for each painting that it was signed by the artist.

The court ruled that the disclaimer was insufficient given the circumstances, paying particular attention to the relative expertise of the parties. The court held:

> Where one party in a contractual relationship occupies a position of superior knowledge and experience, and where that superior knowledge is relied upon and intended to be relied upon by the other, surely more is required for an effective disclaimer than appears here. . . . The language used, the understated manner of its presentation, the failure to refer to it explicitly in the preliminary oral announcement at the auction all lead to the conclusion that Parke-Bernet did not expect the bidders to take the disclaimer too seriously or be too concerned about it. I am convinced that the average reader of this provision would view it as some kind of technicality that should in no way derogate from the certainty that he was buying genuine artistic works, and that this was precisely the impression intended to be conveyed.

What mistakes were made by the lawyers for Parke-Bernet in drafting (or reviewing) the firm's advertising material? Was Parke-Bernet trying to "pull a fast one" on the art-buying public? As counsel for Parke-Bernet, how would you draft a clause that meets the concerns of this court?

3. *Disclaimers Under the Code.* Section 2-316 governs disclaimers of implied warranties in sales cases. Note the two different standards governing disclaimers in §§ 2-316(2) and 2-316(3). Can these two provisions be reconciled? Would you reach a different result in *Pelc v. Simmons* by following the guidelines of § 2-316(2)?

A number of commentators criticize § 2-316 for not requiring contracts to communicate adequately that they contain clauses imposing on buyers certain risks of nonconformity. Thus, for instance, the word "merchantability," which is required for disclaimers to satisfy § 2-316(2), may not be informative to many buyers.

Assuming that this is so, is there nonetheless an argument for requiring disclaimers to be phrased in standardized language? One justification for standardization is that it permits a buyer who invests resources to fully understand a disclaimer in one transaction to reuse his knowledge to understand subsequent disclaimers cast in the same language. Furthermore, if all sellers who use disclaimers must use the same language, buyers can conveniently compare the warranty terms of different firms. This analysis suggests that even if a buyer fully understands a disclaimer improper in form, it should not be enforceable. Otherwise, sellers would have less incentive to use the prescribed standard form. Do you agree? Does this analysis explain the distinctions drawn in § 2-316(2) between the implied warranty of merchantability and the implied warranty of fitness for a particular purpose? In thinking about these questions, consider the 2003 Amendments to § 2-316(2). Is the additional language required to disclaim the merchantability warranty in the case of a consumer contract an improvement on the existing statute?

[2]   Measuring Compliance

The preceding analysis underscores the central importance of implied warranties of quality, and thereby also serves to emphasize the central importance of the implied default terms in contract formation. By implying terms that specify the standards of quality that will govern contractual performance, the law supplies basic, standardized risk assignments. As we have seen, these broad standards are often supplemented by specific affirmations and descriptions that further define the parties obligations.

These quality standards purport to answer a fundamental question: What are the criteria by which the promisor's performance is to be measured?

In this part, we turn to a related question. Assume that the parties have stipulated (either expressly or by default) the standards by which the promisor's performance is to be judged. We now ask: how much deviation from those standards will be permitted before we conclude that the performance has not been rendered? As we learned in Chapter 1, the answer to this question turns in large part on whether the promisor's performance is governed by a standard of "perfect tender" or one of "substantial performance." As you study the following cases try to isolate the variables that might lead parties (and therefore the courts) to prefer a substantial performance rule in some cases and a perfect tender rule in others.

[a]   Substantial Performance

JACOB & YOUNGS v. KENT
Court of Appeals of New York
230 N.Y. 239, 129 N.E. 889 (1921)

See p. 66, *supra*.

O.W. GRUN ROOFING & CONSTRUCTION CO. v. COPE
Court of Civil Appeals of Texas
529 S.W.2d 258 (1975)

CADENA, J.

Plaintiff, Mrs. Fred M. Cope, sued defendant, O.W. Grun Roofing & Construction Co., for damages in the sum of $1,500.00 suffered by plaintiff as a result of the alleged failure of defendant to perform a contract calling for the installation of a new roof on plaintiff's home. Defendant, in addition to a general denial, filed a cross-claim for $648.00, the amount which plaintiff agreed to pay defendant for installing the roof.

Following trial to a jury, the court below entered judgment awarding plaintiff $122.60 as damages for defendant's failure to perform the contract; and denying defendant recovery on its cross-claim. It is from this judgment that defendant appeals.

The jury found (1) defendant failed to perform his contract in a good and workmanlike manner; (2) defendant did not substantially perform the contract; (3) plaintiff received no benefits from the labor performed and the materials furnished by defendant; the reasonable cost of performing the contract in a good and workmanlike manner would be $777.60. Although the verdict shows the cost of proper performance to be $777.60, the judgment describes this finding as being in the amount of $770.60, and the award of $122.60 to plaintiff is based on the difference between $770.60 and the contract price of $648.00. . . .

The written contract required defendant to install a new roof on plaintiff's home for $648.00. The contract describes the color of the shingles to be used as "russet glow," which defendant defined as a "brown varied color." Defendant acknowledges that it was his obligation to install a roof of uniform color.

After defendant had installed the new roof, plaintiff noticed that it had streaks which she described as yellow, due to a difference in color or shade of some of the shingles. Defendant agreed to remedy the situation and he removed the nonconforming shingles. However, the replacement shingles do not match the remainder, and photographs introduced in evidence clearly show that the roof is not of a uniform color. Plaintiff testified that her roof has the appearance of having been patched, rather than having been completely replaced. According to plaintiff's testimony, the yellow streaks appeared on the northern, eastern and southern sides of the roof, and defendant only replaced the non-matching shingles on the northern and eastern sides, leaving the southern side with the yellow streaks still apparent. The result is that only the western portion of the roof is of uniform color.

When defendant originally installed the complete new roof, it used 24 "squares" of shingles. In an effort to achieve a roof of uniform color, five squares were ripped off and replaced. There is no testimony as to the number of squares which would have to be replaced on the southern, or rear, side of the house in order to eliminate the original yellow streaks. Although there is expert testimony to the effect that the disparity in color would not be noticeable after the shingles have been on the roof for about a year, there is testimony to the effect that, although some nine or ten months have elapsed since defendant attempted to achieve a uniform coloration, the roof is still "streaky" on three sides. One of defendant's experts testified that if the shingles are properly applied the result will be a "blended" roof rather than a streaked roof.

In view of the fact that the disparity in color has not disappeared in nine or ten months, and in view of the fact that there is testimony to the effect that it would be impossible to secure matching shingles to replace the nonconforming ones, it can reasonably be inferred that a roof of uniform coloration can be achieved only by installing a completely new roof.

The evidence is undisputed that the roof is a substantial roof and will give plaintiff protection against the elements.

The principle which allows recovery for part performance in cases involving dependent promises may be expressed by saying that a material breach or a breach which goes to the root of the matter or essence of the contract defeats the promisor's claim despite his part performance, or it may be expressed by saying that a promisor who has substantially performed is entitled to recover, although he has failed in some particular to comply with his agreement. The latter mode of expressing the rule is generally referred to as the doctrine of substantial performance and is especially common in cases involving building contracts, although its application is not restricted to such contracts.

It is difficult to formulate a definitive rule for determining whether the contractor's performance, less than complete, amounts to "substantial performance," since the question is one of fact and of degree, and the answer depends on the particular facts of each case. But, although the decisions furnish no rule of thumb, they are helpful in suggesting guidelines. One of the most obvious factors to be considered is the extent of the nonperformance. The deficiency will not be tolerated if it is so pervasive as to frustrate the purpose of the contract in any real or substantial sense. The doctrine does not bestow on a contractor a license to install whatever is, in his judgment, "just as good." The answer is arrived at by weighing the purpose to be served, the desire to be gratified, the excuse for deviating from the letter of the contract and the cruelty of enforcing strict adherence or of compelling the promisee to receive something less than for which he bargained. Also influential in many cases is the ratio of money value of the tendered performance and of the promised performance. In most cases the contract itself at least is an indication of the value of the promised performance, and courts should have little difficulty in determining the cost of curing the deficiency. But the rule cannot be expressed in terms of a fraction, since complete reliance on a mathematical formula would result in ignoring other important factors, such as the purpose which the promised performance was intended to serve and the extent to which the nonperformance would defeat such purpose, or would defeat it if not corrected.

Although definitions of "substantial performance" are not always couched in the same terminology and, because of the facts involved in a particular case, sometimes vary in the recital of the factors to be considered, the following definition by the Commission of Appeals in Atkinson v. Jackson Bros., 270 S.W. 848, 851 (Tex. Comm. App. 1925), is a typical recital of the constituent elements of the doctrine:

> To constitute substantial compliance the contractor must have in good faith intended to comply with the contract, and shall have substantially done so in the sense that the defects are not pervasive, do not constitute a deviation from the general plan contemplated for the work, and are not so essential that the object of the parties in making the contract and its purpose cannot, without difficulty, be accomplished by remedying them. Such performance permits only such omissions or deviations from the contract as are inadvertent and unintentional, are not due to bad faith, do not impair the structure as a whole, and are remediable without doing material damage to other parts of the building in tearing down and reconstructing.

What was the general plan contemplated for the work in this case? What was the object and purpose of the parties? It is clear that, despite the frequency with which the courts speak of defects that are not "pervasive," which do not constitute a "deviation from the general plan," and which are "not so essential that the object of the parties in making the contract and its purpose cannot, without difficulty, be accomplished by remedying them," when an attempt is made to apply the general principles to a particular case difficulties are encountered at the outset. Was the general plan to install a substantial roof which would serve the purpose which roofs are designed to serve? Or, rather, was the general plan to install a substantial roof of uniform color? Was the object and purpose of the contract merely to furnish such a roof, or was it to furnish such a roof which would be of a uniform color? It should not come as a shock to anyone to adopt a rule to the effect that a person has, particularly with respect to his home, to choose for himself and to contract for something which exactly satisfies that choice, and not to be compelled to accept something else. In the matter of homes and their decoration, as much as, if not more than, in many other fields, mere taste or preference, almost approaching whimsy, may be controlling with the homeowner, so that variations which might, under other circumstances, be considered trifling, may be inconsistent with that "substantial performance" on which liability to pay must be predicated. Of mere incompleteness or deviations which may be easily supplied or remedied after the contractor has finished his work, and the cost of which to the owner is not excessive and readily ascertainable, present less cause for hesitation in concluding that the performance tendered constitutes substantial performance, since in such cases the owner can obtain complete satisfaction by merely spending some money and deducting the amount of such expenditure from the contract price.

In the case before us there is evidence to support the conclusion that plaintiff can secure a roof of uniform coloring only by installing a completely new roof. We cannot say, as a matter of law, that the evidence establishes that in this case that a roof which so lacks uniformity in color as to give the appearance of a patch job serves essentially the same purpose as a roof of uniform color which has the appearance of being a new roof. We are not prepared to hold that a contractor who tenders a performance so deficient that it can be remedied only by completely redoing and work for which the contract called has established, as a matter of law, that he has substantially performed his contractual obligation.

The judgment of the trial court is affirmed.

HAYMORE v. LEVINSON
Supreme Court of Utah
8 Utah 2d 66, 328 P.2d 307 (1958)

CROCKETT, J.

Plaintiffs Haymore recovered judgment for $2,739 for money payable under a contract by which they sold defendants Levinson a house. The essence of Levinsons' defense below and contention for reversal here is that there had been no "satisfactory completion" of the house as required by the contract.

The question involved is what the term "satisfactory completion" comprehends.

Plaintiff Arnold Haymore, a contractor and builder, was constructing the house in question at Holladay in Salt Lake County. In November of 1955, when it was well along toward completion, defendants contracted to purchase it for $36,000 on terms described therein. The provision pertinent here was that $3,000 of the purchase price was to be placed in escrow to be held until "satisfactory completion of the work" which referred to a list of items attached to the contract.

The Levinsons moved in and Haymore proceeded with the work, and when he finished, requested the release of the $3,000. The Levinsons stated that they were not "satisfied" with certain of the items and refused to release the money. After some discussion, Haymore agreed to take care of another list of items which the Levinsons insisted must be completed. When he and his workman came to do this work, the Levinsons indicated dissatisfaction with this second list they had agreed upon and demanded still further work, to which Haymore would not agree. The Levinsons thereupon told him that unless he would agree to and do all the work they then requested and in a manner they required, he could do none; and when he refused, ordering him off the property, taking the position that they would not release the money until he fully satisfied their demands.

The defendants' position is in essence that the words "satisfactory completion of the work" are to be given a subjective meaning: i. e., that it is a matter of their choice and unless they are satisfied and so declare, the money is not payable; whereas the plaintiffs assert that it means only that the work must meet a standard reasonable under the circumstances.

The adjudicated cases recognize that contracts wherein one party agrees to perform to the satisfaction of the other fall into two general classes: the first is where the undertaking is to do something of such a nature that pleasing the personal taste, fancy or sensibility of the other, which cannot be readily determined by objective standards, must reasonably be considered an element of predominant importance in the performance. In such cases the covenant that something will be done to the satisfaction of the favored party ordinarily makes him the sole judge thereof and he may give or withhold his approval as he desires.

The other class of cases involves satisfaction as to such things as operative fitness, mechanical utility or structural completion in which the personal sensibilities just mentioned would not reasonably be deemed of such predominant importance to the performance. As to such contracts the better considered view, and the one we adhere to, is that an objective standard should be applied: that is, that the party favored by such a provision has no arbitrary privilege of declining to acknowledge satisfaction and that he cannot withhold approval unless there is apparent some reasonable justification for doing so.

Building contracts, such as the one in question generally fall within the second class of contracts above discussed. In regard to them it is plain to be seen that giving the word "satisfactory" an entirely subjective meaning, might produce unconscionable results. The favored party could, upon any whim or caprice, and without reason, refuse to acknowledge satisfaction and thereby escape his obligations under the contract. The ends of justice are obviously better served by the application of the objective standard which only requires the work to be completed in a reasonably skillful and workmanlike manner in accordance with the accepted standards in the locality. If, in the light of such standards, it would meet the approval of reasonable and prudent persons, that should be sufficient.

The above view is consonant with our recent holding that a clause in a contract for the furnishing of heat was to be within the lessor's "sole judgment," could not be arbitrarily applied to justify the furnishing of entirely inadequate heat, but was subject to a sensible interpretation in relation to the reasonable needs of the lessees under the circumstances.

The trial court correctly adopted and applied the standard to which we give our approval herein. In doing so it found that the plaintiff had completed the original list of items attached to the contract in a satisfactory manner, (except some minor deficiencies of a total value of $261 for which an offset in favor of defendants was allowed) and that there were no structural defects.

Affirmed. Costs to respondents.

NOTES

1. *Noteworthy Doctrinal Elements.* Section 241 of the Restatement (Second) lists the factors for determining when a failure to perform is material (i.e., when a contract cannot be said to have been substantially performed).[33]

Some additional doctrinal points should also be noted. First, a willful or

---

[33] For a critique and proposed modification to the material breach doctrine, see Amy B. Cohen, *Reviving* Jacob and Youngs, Inc. v. Kent: *Material Breach Doctrine Reconsidered*, 42 VILL. L. REV. 65 (1997).

intentional deviation from the contract is a per se material failure to perform; a defendant may not, at his own discretion, substitute whatever he believes is "just as good." *Material Movers, Inc. v. Hill*, 316 N.W.2d 13 (Minn. 1982). This "good faith" obligation is said to discourage attempts to unilaterally restructure the contract. On the other hand, if the substituted performance really is "just as good," then the contract can be performed at less cost, which seems to be a benefit for both parties. Under the "willful breach" rule, any savings from a substituted performance will require the assent of the promisee. If the goal is to enhance the contract surplus, is this rule desirable? If the promisor has to share the gains from a substituted performance won't he reduce his efforts in searching for substitutions? And, if he is unable to exploit fully future opportunities to reduce his costs of performance (at no reduction in the quality of that performance), won't he adjust upward the "price" he requires for that performance in the initial contract? Perhaps the answer is that whether a particular substituted performance is "just as good" is itself controversial, and a rule permitting deliberate substitute performance may inadequately deter strategic behavior.

Second, as Justice Cardozo noted in *Jacob & Youngs*, "intention not otherwise revealed may be presumed to hold in contemplation the reasonable and probable." 129 N.E. at 891. The negative implication of this statement is that a party may contract out of the default rule by explicitly requiring a performance that satisfies his idiosyncratic preferences. But as the decision in *Haymore v. Levinson* shows, opting out of substantial performance in favor of a contract provision calling for "satisfactory completion of the work" does not guarantee that the homeowner will be entitled to their subjective assessments of the performance. Instead, an objective gloss is added by courts to those performances that do not involve artistic judgment or matters of personal taste. Is there anything that a drafting attorney who represented the Levinsons could do to guarantee that their idiosyncratic preferences could be protected? How can the party with special needs communicate them to her counterparty?

Finally, you should note that the party asserting substantial performance in an attempt to gain a set-off or recoupment against damages for nonperformance bears the burden of proof on that issue. *Hopkins Constr. Co. v. Reliance Ins. Co.*, 475 P.2d 223 (Alaska 1970).

2. *More on Contracting Out of the Rule.* The court in *O.W. Grun Roofing* stated:

> It should not come as a shock to anyone to adopt a rule to the effect that a person has, particularly with respect to his home, to choose for himself and to contract for something which exactly satisfies that choice, and not to be compelled to accept something else. In the matter of homes and their decoration, as much as, if not more than, in many other fields, mere taste or preference almost approaching whimsy, may be controlling with a homeowner, so that variations which might, under other circumstances, be considered trifling, may be inconsistent with that "substantial performance" on which liability may be predicated.

529 S.W.2d at 262.

And yet, in *Jacob & Youngs*, the contract specifically noted that all pipe was to be of Reading manufacture, but the court refused to yield to the defendant's "whimsy" concerning the pipe. Can these two cases be reconciled? (Hint: Would a typical owner be expected to care more about the color of his roof than about the brand of his water pipes?) If so, why is that fact relevant?

3. ***Substantial Performance and Valuation.*** The case of *Plante v. Jacobs*, 10 Wis. 2d 567, 103 N.W.2d 296 (1960), illustrates the two possible methods of valuing a party's loss due to the failure of the other party to fully perform. In *Plante*, a homebuilder misplaced a wall between the living room and the kitchen of a new house. The cost of tearing down the wall and replacing it would have been approximately one-fourth of the entire contract price. The court discussed applying either the "diminished value" rule or the "cost of repair" rule, before ultimately determining that, in this particular case, the "diminished value" was preferable because it avoided economic waste.

The economic waste rationale for distinguishing between diminished value and replacement cost has been widely accepted by a number of courts as an exception to the general rule that the homeowner (or other buyer) can recover the full cost of completion when the contractor/seller fails to substantially perform the contract. But sometimes, as in *Jacob & Youngs v. Kent*, the cost of completion greatly exceeds the gain in the market value of the buyer's property that the contractor/seller's performance would have produced. Awarding cost of completion damages in these cases has been thought to subsidize economic waste: The buyer could use the damages to purchase a performance whose cost much exceeds its value. The economic waste rationale is unsatisfactory, however, because a rational buyer will not use the cost of completion damage award to purchase a performance that is worth less to him than its price. The buyer will spend the legal award, but he will not waste it. Modern courts realize that the economic waste rationale is flawed. But courts continue to restrict the buyer to diminution in value damages whenever the cost of completion would be much greater in order to avoid giving the buyer a "windfall."

The consequences of denying cost of completion damages in these contexts have been poorly understood. In *Market Damages, Efficient Contracting, and The Economic Waste Fallacy*, 108 COLUM. L. REV. 1610 (2008), Professors Alan Schwartz and Robert Scott argue that the desirability of awarding cost of completion damages *whenever* the buyer can purchase a substitute performance on the market becomes clear only when those consequences are exposed. Schwartz and Scott argue first that the seller's windfall loss is smaller than is generally realized in the common case where the buyer prepays for the contract service. A buyer who has prepaid is entitled *both* to restitution of that portion of the purchase price that represents the builder's promise to repair and to market damages for the breach. Cost of completion damages incorporate this restitutionary component. Courts and most commentators have overlooked this implication because they have not recognized that buyers prepay for the repair services that commonly appear in the cases. This omission probably occurs because the services are bundled together and are not separately priced. As an example, the cost of constructing a building seldom is disaggregated into separate prices for the promise to install the plumbing and the promise to correct defective work. But to deny that the buyer in such cases has prepaid is to assert, implausibly, that the contractor did not charge for the service of correcting nonconforming plumbing. This analysis leads to the second claim: restricting homeowners and other buyers to the diminution in value creates a moral hazard. Builders and other sellers sometimes can reduce the cost of performing the contract service by taking reliance actions *in the interim* between the time of contract and the time when the builder is to complete the entire performance. But the incentive to invest efficiently in cost reduction is materially reduced if her damage exposure for failing to invest is capped by the diminution in value caused by the breach. Cost of completion damages, they argue, thus are an efficient deterrent against this moral hazard.

4.   *Substantial Performance in Another Context.* In *Bruner v. Hines*, 295 Ala. 111, 324 So. 2d 265 (1975), the plaintiff-buyer sued for specific performance of a contract for the sale of a "15 acre" plot of land. The contract provided that the buyer would take the land in exchange for his agreement to pay $15,000, produce an accurate survey of the land by a registered civil engineer, and install a fence around the property. The latter two obligations were to be completed within 60 days. Numerous difficulties regarding the land survey arose. Ultimately, the buyer provided a survey of 15.1 acres and offered to pay $500 for the extra one-tenth of an acre. The defendant refused to sell, claiming that the survey did not comply with the contract and that a conforming survey constituted a condition precedent to his duty to convey.

The court first decided that the survey was nonconforming and that the buyer had partially breached the contract, but refused to release the seller from his duty to convey the land. The court based this decision on the doctrine of substantial performance, noting that it arose "to mitigate the harsh results that could flow from constructive conditions of exchange in those contracts which require one party to render performance before the other party's reciprocal promise is enforceable." *Id.* at 115. The court then reviewed the classic building construction scenario, deciding that, due to the difficulty of producing a perfect land survey, the doctrine of substantial performance was appropriate in this context. The court remanded the case for an evaluation of the substantiality of the performance and, if necessary, an alteration of the agreed purchase price "which may be necessary to compensate either party for deviations from 15.0 acres." *Id.* at 117. Is this a proper substantial performance case? What do you think of the court's proposed remedy?

5.   *Market Theory and Substantial Performance.* As we have seen, courts imply a substantial performance standard to service and construction contracts. The substantial performance rule discourages promisees from exploiting inadvertent breaches. Do you see the advantage of such a rule in construction contracts, where both parties make specific investments in the contract, and where renegotiation would, therefore, be very costly? Once construction is well underway, the parties' other opportunities become inferior to the existing relationship. Once the parties make a specific investment in the contract, they incur sunk costs and the market for alternative contracts with third parties no longer restrains strategic behavior. The owner-promisee would have an incentive to exploit this situation — threatening to reject the entire project due to a minor defect in construction — were it not for the substantial performance rule. Yet a minor deviation does not significantly increase the risk that a contractor-promisor can evade its responsibility because objective damages will correct any such deficiencies. Viewed ex ante, the parties themselves would prefer the less draconian substantial performance rule in these settings in order to reduce opportunistic behavior. Otherwise, the contractor would have to increase the contract price to insure against the risk of an opportunistic refusal to renegotiate over a minor deviation.[34] Does this analysis aid in reconciling *Jacobs & Young* and *O.W. Grun*?[35]

6. ***The Boundaries of Substantial Performance.*** The cases we have read thus far that have invoked the doctrine of substantial performance have all involved a major construction contract where the choice of that default rule has been relatively uncontroversial. Sometimes, however, the subject matter of the contract raises the question of whether substantial performance or perfect tender is the appropriate default rule. Such was the case in *Chlan v. KDI Sylvan Pools, Inc.*, 53 Md. App. 236, 452 A.2d 1259 (1982), where the substantial performance rule was applied to a contract for the construction of an outdoor swimming pool. The court noted the circumstances under which that doctrine, rather than the UCC's perfect tender rule, was applicable:

> [Article] 2 of the MUCC applies solely to "transactions in goods." § 2-102. Goods are those things movable at the time of identification to the contract. § 2-105 (1). Inasmuch as the swimming pool was a future good — it did not exist when the contract was signed — existence and identification to the contract are synonymous in this case. This pool made of concrete would be immobile once constructed. Thus, this in-ground swimming pool is not a "good" covered by [the] . . . MUCC as goods are simultaneously movable and existing. *Helvey v. Wabash County REMC*, 278 N.E.2d 608 (1972). Hence, appellant is not entitled to demand "perfect tender" under § 2-601.

53 Md. App. at 240.

[b]   Perfect Tender and Cure

Section 2-601 of the UCC incorporates the perfect tender rule for measuring the seller's performance. If the goods or the tender fail to conform to the contract in any respect, the buyer has an absolute right to reject them. Section 2-106, in turn, specifies that the goods are "conforming" when they comply with the obligations under the contract.

One obvious advantage of a perfect tender rule is its clarity. Unlike a broad standard (such as substantial performance), a clear, bright line rule (such as perfect tender) is easier to apply because it requires fewer facts to be verified by a court. Consequently, evasion of contractual obligations should be easier to detect and to police. But there are corresponding disadvantages as well. A precise rule may be overinclusive, thus inviting strategic behavior by the buyer-promisee. Not surprisingly, the drafters of the UCC sought to ameliorate this concern by providing the seller the right to "cure" his defective performance in certain circumstances.

---

[34] *See* Charles J. Goetz & Robert E. Scott, *The Mitigation Principle*, 69 Va. L. Rev. 967, 1009–11 (1983).

[35] For an interesting perspective on these issues, see Steve Thel & Peter Siegelman, *You Do Have to Keep Your Promises: A Disgorgement Theory of Contract Remedies*, 52 Wm. & Mary L. Rev. 1181 (2011).

Consider, for example, the following case.

RAMIREZ v. AUTOSPORT
Supreme Court of New Jersey
88 N.J. 277, 440 A.2d 1345 (1982)

POLLOCK, J.

This case raises several issues under the Uniform Commercial Code concerning whether a buyer may reject a tender of goods with minor defects and whether a seller may cure the defects. We consider also the remedies available to the buyer, including cancellation of the contract. The main issue is whether plaintiffs, Mr. and Mrs. Ramirez, could reject the tender by defendant, Autosport, of a camper van with minor defects and cancel the contract for the purchase of the van.

The trial court ruled that Mr. and Mrs. Ramirez rightfully rejected the van and awarded them the fair market value of their trade-in van. The Appellate Division affirmed in a brief per curiam decision which, like the trial court opinion, was unreported. We affirm the judgment of the Appellate Division.

Following a mobile home show at the Meadowlands Sports Complex, Mr. and Mrs. Ramirez visited Autosport's showroom in Somerville. On July 20, 1978 the Ramirez's and Donald Graff, a salesman for Autosport, agreed on the sale of a new camper and the trade-in of the van owned by Mr. and Mrs. Ramirez. Autosport and the Ramirez's signed a simple contract reflecting a $14,100 purchase price for the new van with a $4,700 trade-in allowance for the Ramirez van, which Mr. and Mrs. Ramirez left with Autosport. After further allowance for taxes, title and documentary fees, the net price was $9,902. Because Autosport needed two weeks to prepare the new van, the contract provided for delivery on or about August 3, 1978.

On that date, Mr. and Mrs. Ramirez returned with their checks to Autosport to pick up the new van. Graff was not there so Mr. White, another salesman, met them. Inspection disclosed several defects in the van. The paint was scratched, both the electric and sewer hookups were missing, and the hubcaps were not installed. White advised the Ramirez's not to accept the camper because it was not ready.

Mr. and Mrs. Ramirez wanted the van for a summer vacation and called Graff several times. Each time Graff told them it was not ready for delivery. Finally, Graff called to notify them that the camper was ready. On August 14 Mr. and Mrs. Ramirez went to Autosport to accept delivery, but workers were still touching up the outside paint. Also, the camper windows were open, and the dining area cushions were soaking wet. Mr. and Mrs. Ramirez could not use the camper in that condition, but Mr. Leis, Autosport's manager, suggested that they take the van and that Autosport would replace the cushions later. Mrs. Ramirez counteroffered to accept the van if they could withhold $2,000, but Leis agreed to no more than $250, which she refused. Leis then agreed to replace the cushions and to call them when the van was ready.

Between August 15 and September 1, 1978 Mrs. Ramirez called Graff several times urging him to complete the preparation of the van, but Graff constantly advised her that the van was not ready. He finally informed her that they could pick it up on September 1.

When Mr. and Mrs. Ramirez went to the showroom on September 1, Graff asked them to wait. And wait they did — for one and a half hours. No one from Autosport came forward to talk with them, and the Ramirez's left in disgust.

On October 5, 1978 Mr. and Mrs. Ramirez went to Autosport with an attorney friend. Although the parties disagreed on what occurred, the general topic was whether they should proceed with the deal or Autosport should return to the Ramirez's their trade-in van. Mrs. Ramirez claimed they rejected the new van and requested the return of their trade-in. Mr. Lustig, the owner of Autosport, thought, however, that the deal could be salvaged if the parties could agree on the dollar amount of a credit for the Ramirez's. Mr. and Mrs. Ramirez never took possession of the new van and repeated their request for the return of their trade-in. Later in October, however, Autosport sold the trade-in to an innocent third party for $4,995.

On November 20, 1978 the Ramirez's sued Autosport seeking, among other things, rescission of the contract. Autosport counterclaimed for breach of contract.

Our initial inquiry is whether a consumer may reject defective goods that do not conform to the contract of sale. The basic issue is whether under the UCC a seller has the duty to deliver goods that conform precisely to the contract. We conclude that the seller is under such a duty to make a "perfect tender" and that a buyer has the right to reject goods that do not conform to the contract. That conclusion, however, does not resolve the entire dispute between buyer and seller. A more complete answer requires a brief statement of the history of the mutual obligations of buyers and sellers of commercial goods.

In the nineteenth century, sellers were required to deliver goods that complied exactly with the sales agreement. That rule, known as the "perfect tender" rule, remained part of the law of sales well into the twentieth century.

By the 1920's the doctrine was so entrenched in the law that Judge Learned Hand declared "[t]here is no room in commercial contracts for the doctrine of substantial performance." Mitsubishi Goshi Kaisha v. J. Aron & Co., Inc., 16 F. 2d 185, 186 (2 Cir. 1926).

The harshness of the rule led courts to seek to ameliorate its effect and to bring the law of sales in closer harmony with the law of contracts, which allows rescission only for material breaches. Nevertheless, a variation of the perfect tender rule appeared in the Uniform Sales Act. The chief objection to the continuation of the perfect tender rule was that buyers in a declining market would reject goods for minor nonconformities and force the loss on surprised sellers. . . .

To the extent that a buyer can reject goods for any nonconformity, the UCC retains the perfect tender rule. Section 2-106 states that goods conform to a contract "when they are in accordance with the obligations under the contract." Section 2-601 authorizes a buyer to reject goods if they "or the tender of delivery fail in any respect to conform to the contract." The Code, however, mitigates the harshness of the perfect tender rule and balances the interests of buyer and seller. See Restatement (Second), Contracts, 241 comment (b) (1981). The Code achieves that result through its provisions for revocation of acceptance and cure. UCC §§ 2-608, 2-508.

Initially, the rights of the parties vary depending on whether the rejection occurs before or after acceptance of the goods. Before acceptance, the buyer may reject goods for any nonconformity. UCC § 2-601. Because of the seller's right to cure, however, the buyer's rejection does not necessarily discharge the contract. UCC § 2-508. Within the time set for performance in the contract, the seller's right to cure is unconditional. . . . The rights of the parties vary if rejection occurs after the time set for performance. After expiration of that time, the seller has a further reasonable time to cure if he believed reasonably that the goods would be acceptable with or without a money allowance. UCC § 2-508(2). The determination of what constitutes a further reasonable time depends on the surrounding circumstances, which include the change of position by and the amount of inconvenience to the buyer. UCC § 2-508, Official Comment 3. Those circumstances also include the length of time needed by the seller to correct the nonconformity and his ability to salvage the goods by resale to others. Thus, the Code balances the buyer's right to reject nonconforming goods with a "second chance" for the seller to conform the goods to the contract under certain limited circumstances.

After acceptance, the Code strikes a different balance: the buyer may revoke acceptance only if the nonconformity substantially impairs the value of the goods to him. UCC § 2-608. . . . This provision protects the seller from revocation for trivial defects. It also prevents the buyer from taking undue advantage of the seller by allowing goods to depreciate and then returning them because of asserted minor defects. Because this case involves rejection of goods, we need not decide whether a seller has a right to cure substantial defects that justify revocation of acceptance. . . .

A further problem, however, is identifying the remedy available to a buyer who rejects goods with insubstantial defects that the seller fails to cure within a reasonable time. The Code provides expressly that when "the buyer rightfully rejects, then with respect to the goods involved, the buyer may cancel." UCC § 2-711. "Cancellation" occurs when either party puts an end to the contract for breach by the other. UCC § 2-106(4). Nonetheless, some confusion exists whether the equitable remedy of rescission survives under the Code. . . .

Although the complaint requested rescission of the contract, plaintiffs actually sought not only the end of their contractual obligations, but also restoration to their pre-contractual position. That request incorporated the equitable doctrine of restitution, the purpose of which is to restore plaintiff to as good a position as he occupied before the contract. In UCC parlance, plaintiffs' request was for the cancellation of the contract and recovery of the price paid. UCC §§ 2-106(4), 2-711.

Although the Code permits cancellation by rejection for minor defects, it permits revocation of acceptance only for substantial impairments. That distinction is consistent with other Code provisions that depend on whether the buyer has accepted the goods. Acceptance creates liability in the buyer for the price, and precludes rejection. UCC § 2-607(2). Also, once a buyer accepts goods, he has the burden to prove any defect. UCC § 2-607(4). By contrast, where goods are rejected for not conforming to the contract, the burden is on the seller to prove that the nonconformity was corrected. Miron v. Yonkers Raceway, Inc., 400 F.2d 112, 119 (2 Cir. 1968).

Underlying the Code provisions is the recognition of the revolutionary change in business practices in this century. The purchase of goods is no longer a simple transaction in which a buyer purchases individually-made goods from a seller in a face-to-face transaction. Our economy depends on a complex system for the manufacture, distribution, and sale of goods, a system in which manufacturers and consumers rarely meet. Faceless manufacturers mass-produce goods for unknown consumers who purchase those goods from merchants exercising little or no control over the quality of their production. In an age of assembly lines, we are accustomed to cars with scratches, television sets without knobs and other products with all kinds of defects. Buyers no longer expect a "perfect tender." If a merchant sells defective goods, the reasonable expectation of the parties is that the buyer will return those goods and that the seller will repair or replace them.

Recognizing this commercial reality, the Code permits a seller to cure imperfect tenders. Should the seller fail to cure the defects, whether substantial or not, the balance shifts again in favor of the buyer, who has the right to cancel or seek damages. In general, economic considerations would induce sellers to cure minor defects. . . . Assuming the seller does not cure, however, the buyer should be permitted to exercise his remedies under UCC § 2-711. The Code remedies for consumers are to be liberally construed, and the buyer should have the option of canceling if the seller does not provide conforming goods.

To summarize, the UCC preserves the perfect tender rule to the extent of permitting a buyer to reject goods for any nonconformity. Nonetheless, that rejection does not automatically terminate the contract. A seller may still effect a cure and preclude unfair rejection and cancellation by the buyer.

The trial court found that Mr. and Mrs. Ramirez had rejected the van within a reasonable time under UCC § 2-602. The court found that on August 3, 1978 Autosport's salesman advised the Ramirez's not to accept the van and that on August 14, they rejected delivery and Autosport agreed to replace the cushions. Those findings are supported by substantial credible evidence, and we sustain them. Although the trial court did not find whether Autosport cured the defects within a reasonable time, we find that Autosport did not effect a cure. Clearly the van was not ready for delivery during August, 1978 when Mr. and Mrs. Ramirez rejected it, and Autosport had the burden of proving that it had corrected the defects. Although the Ramirez's gave Autosport ample time to correct the defects, Autosport did not demonstrate that the van conformed to the contract on September 1. In fact, on that date, when Mr. and Mrs. Ramirez returned at Autosport's invitation, all they received was discourtesy.

Because Autosport had sold the trade-in to an innocent third party, the trial court determined that the Ramirez's were entitled not to the return of the trade-in, but to its fair market value, which the court set at the contract price of $4,700. A buyer who rightfully rejects goods and cancels the contract may, among other possible remedies, recover so much of the purchase price as has been paid. The Code, however, does not define "pay" and does not require payment to be made in cash.

A common method of partial payment for vans, cars, boats and other items of personal property is by a "trade-in." When concerned with used vans and the like, the trade-in market is an acceptable, and perhaps the most appropriate, market in which to measure damages. It is the market in which the parties dealt; by their voluntary act they have established the value of the traded-in article. The ultimate issue is determining the fair market value of the trade-in. . . . Although the value of the trade-in van as set forth in the sales contract was not the only possible standard, it is an appropriate measure of fair market value.

For the preceding reasons, we affirm the judgment of the Appellate Division.

NOTES

1. ***The Perfect Tender Rule and the Right to "Cure."*** Under the common law's perfect tender rule, the buyer has no duty to accept the seller's tender of nonconforming goods. The rule gives the buyer a choice: Accept the defective tender and recover the reduction in value as damages, or reject the performance and recover the contract price/market price differential. To the extent it requires perfect tender, the law reduces the incentive for the buyer to mitigate damages by accepting a substantial performance together with a discount. Conversely, to the extent the law deviates from the clear rule of perfect tender by allowing substantial performance, it increases the moral hazard risk that a seller may evade her contractual obligation by claiming that the tendered goods are "just as good." The law's choice between perfect tender or substantial performance as a default rule may thus turn on whether it is more concerned with reducing moral hazard by sellers or encouraging buyers to mitigate the consequences of an inadvertent breach.

This suggests that a perfect tender rule may be appropriate in those instances where there is less need to encourage buyers to mitigate. One such instance is a contract to sell goods that are traded in a well-developed market: The law can require perfect tender in market situations because there is every likelihood a buyer will still cooperate by mitigating the loss caused by the seller's breach. This is because the market provides a check on the buyer's claim that the product does not measure up to the contract. If the buyer refuses to accept the goods (together with an appropriate accommodation), the seller can offer the same goods on the open market at the competitive price. The existence of many opportunities for salvaging the contract by reselling the goods on the market thus reduces the risk of strategic claims.[36]

Suppose, however, that intervening contingencies impair the value of performance for both the buyer and the seller. For instance, suppose a temporary shortage of the blue widgets that seller contracted to supply for a fixed price causes the wholesale price to triple. Seller therefore offers red widgets (only slightly inferior) plus a price discount. Meanwhile, assume that demand for the finished product for which widgets are a key component has fallen. Thus, the buyer has decided he doesn't want widgets after all. In such a "double lightning bolt" situation,

---

[36] *See* Charles J. Goetz & Robert E. Scott, *The Mitigation Principle: Toward a General Theory of Contractual Obligation*, 69 VA. L. REV. 967, 995–1000 (1983).

the seller cannot provide the contract performance except at a substantial loss but the buyer has another, different reason to avoid the contract. Viewed ex ante, the seller would have an expectation that the buyer would accept this substitute tender (with a money allowance). The buyer, however, wishing to escape the contract, rejects the "nonconforming" tender, citing § 2-601. The drafters of the UCC doubted that, in such a case, the perfect tender rule would produce the best result, fearing the incidence of "surprise rejections" and the imposition of unnecessary costs on the breaching party. This concern led to the adoption of the right to "cure" the defect in UCC § 2-508(2).[37]

2. *When Should a Seller Be Surprised by a Nonconforming Tender?* The right to cure provided in § 2-508(2) has generated considerable controversy among legal commentators. In trying to divine the true § 2-508(2) case, one major distinction that commentators have made is between a seller who fully expected his product to conform (and is therefore surprised by rejection) and the seller who knew the product was nonconforming but expected that the buyer would accept it anyway perhaps with a price adjustment (and is therefore surprised when the buyer rejects). The issue might be phrased in this manner: To come under the aegis of § 2-508(2), must the seller have reasonable grounds to believe the tender will be acceptable, or reasonable grounds to believe the *nonconforming* tender will be acceptable? Professors White and Summers, citing the well-known case of *Wilson v. Scampoli*, 228 A.2d 848 (D.C. 1967), argue that the seller should be entitled to cure in either case:

> When a retailer receives goods from a wholesaler or a manufacturer and simply sells them off the shelf, he too has a reasonable cause to believe that the goods will be acceptable and so is entitled to further reasonable time in which to cure. . . . Such reasonable cause will arise from the retailer's past dealings with the manufacturer.

JAMES J. WHITE & ROBERT S. SUMMERS, UNIFORM COMMERCIAL CODE § 8-5 at 323 (4th ed. 1995).

3. *Does § 2-508(2) Encompass Cure by Repair?* Section 2-508 does not explicitly allow cure by repair rather than replacement, but no court has yet invalidated such a cure, apparently because of the belief that limiting sellers to replacement would effectively negate the right to cure, especially in cases involving complex mechanical products. Note, however, that courts have been reluctant to impose cure by repair on buyers if the defect involves a vital mechanical part.

In *Zabriskie Chevrolet v. Smith*, 99 N.J. Super. 441, 240 A.2d 195 (1968), the transmission in the buyer's new car failed less than two and one-half miles from the seller's showroom. The court ruled that the seller could not cure by installing "a substituted transmission, not from the factory and of unknown lineage from another vehicle in the dealer's showroom":

---

[37] For a discussion of the intersection of the right to cure and good faith in a falling market, see Jeffrey M. Dressler, Note, *Good Faith Rejection of Goods in a Falling Market*, 42 CONN. L. REV. 611 (2009).

It was not the intention of the Legislature that the right to "cure" is a limitless one to be controlled only by the will of the seller. A "cure" which endeavors by substitution to tender a chattel not within the agreement or contemplation of the parties is invalid.

For the majority of people the purchase of a new car is a major investment, rationalized by the peace of mind that flows from its dependability and safety. Once their faith is shaken, the vehicle loses not only its real value in their eyes, but becomes an instrument whose integrity is substantially impaired and whose operation is fraught with apprehension. The attempted cure in the present case was ineffective.

99 N.J. Super. at 458.

Should the reasonable buyer be expected to accept repaired goods when he has originally purchased new goods? Should he perhaps be forced to accept repair but be allowed a court-determined discount on the goods at the same time? How does the market react to repaired goods? Is it possible that even if goods are perfectly repaired, the market will discount their value? Should the seller pay the buyer this market discount? What result in the situation where the buyer values the goods more than the market does?[38]

4. *Cure Following Acceptance of Nonconforming Goods.* If the buyer has accepted nonconforming goods and seeks not to revoke his acceptance but rather to recover damages for breach of warranty, it has been held that the Code imposes no duty upon the buyer to accept an offer of cure by the seller. *Bonebrake v. Cox*, 499 F.2d 951 (8th Cir. 1974) (contract for the sale and installation of used pin spotters in a bowling alley); *Boies v. Norton*, 526 S.W.2d 651 (Tex. App. 1975) (contract for the sale and installation of a mobile home damaged during delivery).[39]

Essay: Substantial Performance Versus Perfect Tender — The Dilemma of Contractual Performance[40]

In most of the cases studied in Chapter 7, we have encountered a similar problem: Commercial parties have sought to supplement the default rules supplied by the law of contracts with express understandings that were (apparently) designed to allocate risks in a manner that maximized the *ex ante* value of the contract to both parties. Yet in each case the parties' efforts to resolve anticipated problems in advance by carefully drafting express contract terms failed to avoid subsequent costly litigation. It is tempting to suggest that these parties were simply

---

[38] For a thorough analysis of the adverse consequences to the buyer of cure by repair, *see* Alan Schwartz, *Cure and Revocation for Quality Defects: The Utility of Bargains*, 16 B.C. Indus. & Com. L. Rev. 543 (1975). On the other hand, Professor Priest has argued that courts apply the repair and cure rules of the Code so as to minimize the risk of such strategic behavior. George Priest, *Breach and Remedy for the Tender of Nonconforming Goods Under the UCC*, 91 Harv. L. Rev. 960 (1978).

[39] For a comparison of cure under the UCC with the treatment of it in the Second Restatement, *see* William Lawrence, *Cure After Breach of Contract Under the Restatement (Second) of Contracts: An Analytical Comparison with the Uniform Commercial Code*, 70 Minn. L. Rev. 713 (1986).

[40] This Essay draws on the discussion in Alan Schwartz & Robert E. Scott, Sales Law and The Contracting Process 230–32 (1991).

poorly represented by counsel. But, in fact, the cases suggest a deeper problem: There is an inevitable and often unavoidable tension that exists in connection with the rules that govern the performance of contracts.

To introduce that tension, begin by recalling that, at the time of contract, each party wants to choose terms that will maximize the expected value of the contract. In the usual case, where markets exist, commercial parties will have alternatives to the contract under negotiation. Thus, the deal that is eventually made is commonly the best deal that the parties can reach. This is another way of saying that each negotiated contract is optimal ex ante — it generates more expected surplus for the parties to divide up in some fashion than other feasible alternatives. But after a deal is made, the parties sometimes receive new information about the state of the world in which performance is to occur. In light of this new information, the parties on occasion see that their contract will not maximize the surplus that the parties could share. Thus, while the contract was optimal ex ante, it is no longer optimal ex post — it maximized *expected* surplus but not *actual* surplus. In this circumstance the parties have an incentive to bargain to a new arrangement. But an effort to renegotiate the contract after the new information about the state of the world is known raises the problem of hold up that we have seen before. If the party whose performance is due has already made sunk cost investments in the contract, there is a risk that the counterparty will behave strategically and only agree to renegotiate on condition that the performing party substantially reduce the contract price. On the other hand, if the contract gives the performing party the unilateral right to adjust his performance without the other's consent, there is a moral hazard risk: the performing party may demand the right to adjust even where the ex post conditions do not justify it. The tension mentioned above exists, therefore, because the effort to achieve an ex post adjustment (either by renegotiation or unilateral adjustment) may sacrifice ex ante value.

This difficulty can be illustrated by an example. Suppose that a contract requires a seller at a fixed price to deliver a machine that meets certain specifications. After the contract is made, the seller learns that its actual costs are higher than it expected. With these costs, the seller's actual profit would be reduced. The seller, however, could deviate from the contract specifications and produce a machine that is almost as good for the original cost. This machine would generate lower revenues for the buyer. The buyer's value from the modified machine would thus be less, and its actual net gain would be reduced. Suppose that the loss to the seller from having to satisfy the original contractual specifications would be greater than the loss to the buyer if the seller delivered the modified machine. In this case, the optimal ex post adjustment would permit the seller to deliver the modified machine with a price concession. In legal terms, the best rule ex post would require the seller to provide substantial performance rather than make a perfect tender (or, alternatively, require the buyer to accept the seller's offer to cure).

But there is a problem with this solution. The best ex post adjustment may compromise the parties efforts to reach the best deal ex ante. Assume, for example, that sellers anticipate that the law will permit them to tender a substantial performance just because their costs might rise. Now sellers have less incentive to confine cost increases or to perform as they said that they would. In addition, the imprecise substantial performance rule itself creates a disincentive to perform.

Because it is more difficult for the buyer to prove deviations from substantial performance than from perfect tender, the seller may deviate very substantially from the contract specifications. For these reasons, buyers may often prefer ex ante a contract that requires a seller to make a perfect tender. But, as we have seen, a perfect tender rule may also generate costs ex post (when the seller's costs actually have risen and the buyer renegotiates strategically).

There is no easy resolution of this tension between ex post and ex ante perspectives in contractual performance. The tension discussed here may be rephrased in a way that captures more vividly an important aspect of the parties' problem. If the law requires substantial performance in the example above, the buyer is thereby encouraged to work with the seller to see just what product modification comes closest to meeting its needs at least cost to the seller. Were the law to require perfect tender, this incentive to make the best ex post adjustment is reduced — the buyer may just demand the performance that the contract requires unless the seller renegotiates the contract terms. Thus, the tension that performance rules create may be put as the question whether the legal rules should be flexible, so as to encourage cooperative adjustment, or inflexible, which encourages a renegotiation that could produce conflict. This way of putting the question only captures part of the truth, however. While cooperation is desirable ex post, rules that encourage too much cooperation, as we have seen, may provoke strategic behavior and thus generate excessive costs in ex ante precautions at the time of contract negotiation.[41]

D.   BIBLIOGRAPHY AND SUGGESTED READING

[1]   Conditions

Ian Ayres, *Preliminary Thoughts on Optimal Tailoring of Contractual Rules*, 3 S. CAL. INTERDISC. L.J. 1 (1993).

Robert Childres, *Conditions in the Law of Contracts*, 45 N.Y.U. L. REV. 33 (1970).

John W. Cooley, *"Show Me the Money!": A Comment on the Enforceability of "Pay-if-Paid" Clauses in Contracts for Professional Services*, 33 U.S.F. L. REV. 99 (1998).

Charles J. Goetz & Robert E. Scott, *The Limits of Expanded Choice: An Analysis of the Interactions Between Express and Implied Terms*, 73 CAL. L. REV. 261 (1985).

Charles J. Goetz & Robert E. Scott, *The Mitigation Principle: Toward a General Theory of Contractual Obligation*, 69 VA. L. REV. 967 (1983).

Robert A. Hillman, *Court Adjustment of Long-Term Contracts: An Analysis Under Modern Contract Law*, 1987 DUKE L.J. 1.

---

[41] These issues are discussed in Robert E. Scott, *Conflict and Cooperation in Long-Term Contracts*, 75 CAL. L. REV. 2005, 2019–30 (1987) and in Alan Schwartz & Robert E. Scott, *Contract Theory and the Limits of Contract Law*, 113 YALE L.J. 541, 565–68 (2003).

Jody S. Kraus & Robert E. Scott, *Contract Design and the Structure of Contractual Intent*, 84 N.Y.U. L. REV. 1023 (2009).

William McGovern, *Dependent Promises in the History of Leases and Other Contracts*, 52 TUL. L. REV. 659 (1978).

Mark L. Movsesian, *Severability in Statutes and Contracts*, 30 GA. L. REV. 41 (1995).

Subha Narasimhan, *Modification: The Self-Help Specific Performance Remedy*, 97 YALE L.J. 61 (1987).

Alice Noble-Allgire, *Attorney Approval Clauses in Residential Real Estate Contracts: Is Half a Loaf Better Than None?*, 48 KAN. L. REV. 339 (2000).

Keith A. Rowley, *A Brief History of Anticipatory Repudiation in American Contract Law*, 69 U. CIN. L. REV. 565 (2001).

Alan Schwartz, *Relational Contracts in the Courts: An Analysis of Incomplete Agreements and Judicial Strategies*, 21 J. LEGAL STUD. 271 (1992).

Robert E. Scott & George G. Triantis, *Anticipating Litigation in Contract Design*, 115 YALE L.J. 814 (2006).

David V. Snyder, *Public and Private Attempts to Regulate Modification, Waiver, and Estoppel*, 1999 WIS. L. REV. 607.

[2] Performance Standards

Jean Braucher, *An Informal Resolution Model of Consumer Product Warranty Law*, 1985 WIS. L. REV. 1405.

Amy B. Cohen, *Reviving* Jacob and Youngs, Inc. v. Kent: *Material Breach Doctrine Reconsidered*, 42 VILL. L. REV. 65 (1997).

George Cohen, *The Negligence-Opportunism Tradeoff in Contract Law*, 20 HOFSTRA L. REV. 941 (1992).

Comment, *Article Two Warranties in Commercial Transactions*, 64 CORNELL L. REV. 30 (1978).

Richard Craswell, *Performance, Reliance and One-Sided Information*, 18 J. LEGAL STUD. 365 (1989).

Franklin E. Crawford, *Fit for Its Ordinary Purpose? Tobacco, Fast Food, and the Implied Warranty of Merchantability*, 63 OHIO ST. L.J. 1165 (2002).

Timothy Davis, *The Illusive Warranty of Workmanlike Performance: Constructing a Conceptual Framework*, 72 NEB. L. REV. 981, 983 (1993).

John Eddy, *On the "Essential" Purposes of Limited Remedies: The Metaphysics of UCC Section 2-719(2)*, 65 CAL. L. REV. 28 (1977).

Stephen E. Friedman, *Text and Circumstance: Warranty Disclaimers in a World of Rolling Contracts*, 46 ARIZ. L. REV. 677 (2004).

Charles J. Goetz & Robert E. Scott, *The Mitigation Principle: Toward a General*

Theory of Contractual Obligation, 69 Va. L. Rev. 967 (1983).

Thomas J. Holdych & Bruce D. Mann, *A Market and Economic Based Analysis of Express Warranties — Getting What You Pay For and Paying for What You Get*, 45 DePaul L. Rev. 781 (1996).

Sidney Kwestel, *Freedom from Reliance: A Contract Approach to Express Warranty*, 26 Suffolk U. L. Rev. 959 (1992).

Gregory J. Krabacher, *Revocation of Tripartite Rolling Contracts: Finding a Remedy in the Twenty- First Century Usage of Trade*, 66 Ohio St. L.J. 397 (2005).

William Lawrence, *Cure After Breach of Contract Under the Restatement (Second) of Contracts: An Analytical Comparison With the Uniform Commercial Code*, 70 Minn. L. Rev. 713 (1986).

Robert S. Miller, *The Sale of Horses and Horse Interests: A Transactional Approach*, 78 Ky. L.J. 517 (1990).

Charles Pierson, *Does "Puff" Create an Express Warranty of Merchantability? Where the Hornbooks Go Wrong*, 36 Duq. L. Rev. 887 (1998).

George Priest, *Breach and Remedy for the Tender of Nonconforming Goods Under the UCC*, 91 Harv. L. Rev. 960 (1978).

George Priest, *A Theory of the Consumer Product Warranty*, 90 Yale L.J. 1352 (1981).

William Prosser, *The Fall of the Citadel*, 50 Minn. L. Rev. 791, 800 (1966).

Alan Schwartz, *Cure and Revocation for Quality Defects: The Utility of Bargains*, 16 B.C. Indus. & Com. L. Rev. 543 (1975).

Alan Schwartz & Robert E. Scott, *Contract Theory and the Limits of Contract Law*, 113 Yale L.J. 541 (2003).

Alan Schwartz & Robert E. Scott, *Market Damages, Efficient Contracting, and the Economic Waste Fallacy*, 108 Colum. L. Rev. 1610 (2008).

Robert E. Scott, *Conflict and Cooperation in Long-Term Contracts*, 75 Cal. L. Rev. 2005 (1987).

Steve Thel & Peter Siegelman, *You Do Have to Keep Your Promises: A Disgorgement Theory of Contract Remedies*, 52 Wm. & Mary L. Rev. 1181 (2011).

James J. White, *Retail Sellers and the Enforcement of Manufacturer Warranties: An Application of the Uniform Commercial Code to Consumer Product Distribution Systems*, 32 Wayne L. Rev. 1045 (1986).

Chapter 8

MISTAKE AND EXCUSE

A. INTRODUCTION

The law of mistake and excuse are doctrines that appear to allow parties to avoid liability they contractually agreed to bear. The doctrine of mistake is said to excuse performance when an "endogenous" risk materializes — that is, when one or both parties are mistaken about a material fact that exists at the time of their agreement. Excuse doctrines are said to discharge performance when an "exogenous" risk materializes — that is, when an unanticipated future event not contemplated by the agreement renders performance impossible, impracticable, or pointless. Thus, under the law of mistake, if a seller agrees to sell his cow to a buyer, and both believe that the cow is barren at the time of their agreement, the seller is allowed to avoid the sale if the parties later discover the cow was fertile at the time of agreement. Similarly, under the excuse of impossibility, if an owner agrees to permit a performer to use his concert hall for a fee, neither party is bound by their agreement if the concert hall burns down before the agreed dates of use.

Upon examination, however, these doctrines actually do not allow parties to avoid liability they have contractually incurred. Instead, they are merely rules for allocating risks not expressly allocated by the parties. As we have seen in previous chapters, absent incapacity, force, fraud, or public policy objections, courts generally will enforce the express terms of contracts. But when disputes arise over matters not governed by express terms, courts must determine whether the parties implicitly agreed on a resolution of those matters or failed to come to any such agreement. Parties might fail to agree on how a particular matter should be resolved either because they considered the matter but were unwilling or unable to come to an agreement, or because they never considered it. In either case, their contract will contain a gap. Courts and legislatures have therefore developed default rules that fill the gaps in such agreements. Absent the parties' agreement to the contrary, these terms will be included in all contracts. The law of mistake and excuse thus provides interpretive rules for deciding whether, in fact, the parties agreed (either expressly or implicitly) to allocate the risk in question, and if not, what default terms should be implied in their agreement to resolve the question.

Indeed, the law of mistake and excuse can be understood as more general applications of the same interpretive doctrines governing the law of conditions, which we examined in Chapter 7. There the question arose whether one party's duty to perform was subject to an implied or constructive condition (imputed by default). This question is structurally the same one that arises here. Are either of the parties' performance duties subject to an implied or constructive condition that (1) they are not mistaken about a material fact, or (2) a (typically unanticipated) subsequent event will not render their performance impossible, impracticable, or pointless. Properly understood, therefore, when a party successfully invokes the law of mistake or excuse, that party demonstrates that his performance duty was subject to a condition that was not satisfied. Hence, the law of mistake and excuse directs courts to respect the conditions parties place on the duties they voluntarily undertake (either in their agreement or by default).

Once we conceive of mistake and excuse as interpretive rules, we can apply familiar criteria to better understand and evaluate these doctrines. The law of mistake should excuse a party's performance only if most people similarly situated would so condition their duty to perform. The justification for this rule is two-fold. First, if the parties did consider whether their agreement should be subject to an excuse based on such a mistake, a majoritarian default rule is likely to reconstruct the parties' actual, implied agreement better than a non-majoritarian default rule. Second, this majoritarian default rule saves the majority of parties the expense of including an explicit term in their agreement excusing performance based on mistake. Only the minority of contractors will have to opt out of the default rule and thereby incur the costs of specifying their desired excuse term.

This same analysis applies to the law of excuse based on a subsequent event making performance impracticable, impossible, or pointless.

The law of excuse provides a default rule for interpreting the parties' allocation of the risk of subsequent events that adversely affect one of the parties to a contract. Economic analysis recommends that contracts be interpreted as allocating the risk of such events as most similarly situated parties would allocate them.

The analysis of the law of mistake and excuse, so described, seems unremarkable. It treats the risk of mistakes and subsequent events just as it treats all risks not expressly allocated in an agreement. However, both courts and commentators often argue that the risks to be allocated by the law of mistake and excuse cannot be explained or justified by standard default rule analysis because, unlike other contractual risks, these are risks that never occurred to the parties, and would not be likely to occur to parties in the future. If so, then the rules allocating those risks hold out little prospect of reducing contracting costs for future parties. Contrast, for example, the default rule for allocating the risk of defective goods with the default rule governing whether performance should be excused if the goods are destroyed by a meteor. The latter risk is so remote that it likely would not occur to any contracting parties, even if it had materialized in a past case. Thus, it is claimed, this excuse default rule cannot be understood as an effort to save contracting costs for future parties. On this view, the excuse default rule serves solely as an ex post device for allocating loss between two parties who never agreed on how to allocate such a loss. Therefore, criteria such as fairness and loss sharing are more likely to explain the law of mistake and excuse than any principles of cost saving offered by economic analysis.[1]

---

[1] The same argument can be applied to the risks that excuse performance under the law of mistake. If the risk of mistake about a particular material fact is so remote that virtually all parties will fail to consider it, the default rule for allocating that risk cannot be justified on the ground that it will save parties the costs of specifying their most preferred allocation of that risk. Consider, for example, the risk that a delivery date specified in a contract refers to the arrival of a particular ship, but in fact there are

The law of mistake and excuse, therefore, provides an ideal context to evaluate the limits of economic analysis. If there are no prospective effects at stake in the law of mistake and excuse, economic analysis would seem to be irrelevant. But are you convinced that default rules allocating remote risks have no prospective effects? Even if parties do not, or cannot, anticipate in particular that the goods might be destroyed by a meteor, can they anticipate the possibility that their goods will be destroyed by causes they might not anticipate? If so, majoritarian default rule analysis might provide guidance in specifying the appropriate omnibus mistake and excuse term (i.e., one that allocates the risk of unanticipated or remote risks, whatever they turn out to be)?

An autonomy analysis of mistake and excuse doctrine addresses many of the same questions. If the parties explicitly or implicitly allocated the risks of material mistakes or subsequent events, autonomy theory recommends enforcing those terms. If an agreement contains no express allocation of these risks, autonomy theory, like economic theory, supports a majoritarian default rule in order to maximize the probability of reconstructing the parties' actual, but implied, agreement (absent idiosyncratic evidence to the contrary, the parties are most likely to have agreed to those terms to which most parties would have agreed). If the parties failed even to consider these risks, then their agreement contains a genuine gap. Versions of autonomy theory that rely exclusively on the parties' actual agreement to justify legal rules would be unable to explain a rule for allocating these risks. Other versions of autonomy theory view contract law as an instrumental means for increasing opportunities for autonomous action. These theories join economic theories in recommending majoritarian default rules for filling genuine gaps in order to decrease the future costs of contracting.

In contrast, pluralists identify these doctrines as paradigm cases where courts must rely on their judgment to apply a mix of relevant values to resolve a case. In particular, when ex ante considerations run out, ex post considerations of fairness might be controlling. If there is no good reason for one party rather than the other to bear the loss resulting from an unforeseen and unforeseeable contingency, then perhaps fairness dictates that the parties share the loss equally. However, pluralists might also recognize additional values, or different understandings of ex post fairness, that take into account a broad array of considerations, such as the moral desert of each party (e.g., how each party has treated the other throughout their contractual relationship), the public perception of the fairness of the adjudication, the relative age and experience of the parties, and the like.

As you consider these broader theoretical questions, ask yourself in each of the cases that follow whether you believe the parties either explicitly or implicitly allocated the risk that has materialized, or whether their agreement contains a genuine gap. Then ask yourself whether the case should come out differently than the court decided it. Are the stakes in the case limited to allocating a loss between the parties to the dispute, or is the decision likely to have significant prospective effects as well?

---

two ships with that same name, each leaving the same port and arriving at the same destination but on different dates. This example is drawn from the "Peerless" case, Section B, *infra*. This type of risk is arguably so remote that it will never occur to future contracting parties to allocate it.

B. MISTAKEN BELIEFS ABOUT FACTS THAT EXIST AT THE TIME OF AGREEMENT

In one of the celebrated cases of contract law, *Raffles v. Wichelhaus*, 2 H & C 906, 159 Eng. Rep. 375 (1864), defendants agreed to buy 125 bales of Surat cotton from plaintiff, that cotton to arrive from Bombay on a ship named "Peerless." Plaintiffs tendered cotton that arrived in Liverpool on a ship named "Peerless" that had departed Bombay in December. Defendants refused to accept and pay for that cotton, contending that they had agreed to buy cotton arriving in Liverpool on a ship named "Peerless" that departed Bombay in October. In fact, there was one ship named "Peerless" sailing from Bombay to Liverpool in October, and another ship also named "Peerless" sailing from Bombay to Liverpool in December. The court held that "the defendant meant one 'Peerless' and the plaintiff another. That being so, there was no consensus ad idem, and therefore no binding contract." The *Peerless* case illustrates one problem that occurs when parties are formulating and expressing the terms of a bargain: When the terms of a contract hold a different meaning for each party, who bears the cost of the mistake? Section 20 of the Restatement (Second) explains how courts generally allocate the risk of unilateral or mutual misunderstanding of the meaning or reference of contract terms.

In this section, however, we explore the question of how courts do and should allocate the risks that one or both parties will enter into an agreement based on a mistaken belief not about the meaning of contract terms, but about material facts that exist at the time of agreement. Sections 151 through 155 of the Restatement (Second) set out the framework for allocating such risks.

[1] Excuse Based on Mistake (Herein of "Unilateral" and "Mutual" Mistake)

SHERWOOD v. WALKER
Supreme Court of Michigan
66 Mich. 568, 33 N.W. 919 (1887)

Morse, J.

Replevin for a cow. Suit commenced in justice's court. Judgment for plaintiff. Appealed to circuit court. The defendants bring error, and set out 25 assignments of the same.

The main controversy depends upon the construction of a contract for the sale of the cow. The plaintiff claims that the title passed, and bases his action upon such claim. The defendants contend that the contract was executory, and by its terms no title to the animal was acquired by plaintiff.

The defendants reside at Detroit, but are in business at Walkerville, Ontario, and have a farm at Greenfield, in Wayne County, upon which were some blooded cattle supposed to be barren as breeders. The Walkers are importers and breeders of polled hornless² Angus cattle.

The plaintiff is a banker living at Plymouth, in Wayne County. He called upon the defendants at Walkerville for the purchase of some of their stock, but found none there that suited him. Meeting one of the defendants afterwards, he was informed that they had a few head upon their Greenfield farm. He was asked to go out and look at them, with the statement at the time that they were probably barren, and would not breed. May 5, 1886, plaintiff went out to Greenfield and saw the cattle. A few days thereafter, he called upon one of the defendants with the view of purchasing a cow, known as "Rose 2d of Aberlone." After considerable talk, it was agreed that defendants would telephone Sherwood at his home in Plymouth in reference to the price. The second morning after this talk he was called up by telephone, and the terms of the sale were finally agreed upon. He was to pay five and one-half cents per pound, live weight, fifty pounds shrinkage. He was asked how he intended to take the cow home, and replied that he might ship her from King's cattle-yard. He requested defendants to confirm the sale in writing, which they did by sending him the following letter:

Walkerville, May 15, 1886

T. C. Sherwood,

President, etc. —

Dear Sir: We confirm sale to you of the cow Rose 2d of Aberlone, lot 56 of our catalogue, at five and a half cents per pound, less fifty pounds shrink. We inclose herewith order on Mr. Graham for the cow. You might leave check with him, or mail to us here, as you prefer.

Yours truly,

Hiram Walker & Sons.

The order upon Graham inclosed in the letter read as follows:

Walkerville, May 15, 1886

George Graham: You will please deliver at King's cattle-yard to Mr. T. C. Sherwood, Plymouth, the cow Rose 2d of Aberlone, lot 56 of our catalogue. Send halter with cow, and have her weighed.

Yours truly,

Hiram Walker & Sons.

On the twenty-first of the same month the plaintiff went to defendants' farm at Greenfield, and presented the order and letter to Graham, who informed him that the defendants had instructed him not to deliver the cow. Soon after, the plaintiff tendered to Hiram Walker, one of the defendants, $80, and demanded the cow. Walker refused to take the money or deliver the cow. The plaintiff then instituted this suit. After he had secured possession of the cow under the writ of replevin, the

---

² "Polled" means hornless. [Eds.]

plaintiff caused her to be weighed by the constable who served the writ, at a place other than King's cattle-yard. She weighed 1,420 pounds . . . .The defendants introduced evidence tending to show that at the time of the alleged sale it was believed by both the plaintiff and themselves that the cow was barren and would not breed; that she cost [them] $850, and if not barren would be worth from $750 to $1,000 . . . .

It appears from the record that both parties supposed this cow was barren and would not breed, and she was sold by the pound for an insignificant sum as compared with her real value if a breeder. She was evidently sold and purchased on the relation of her value for beef, unless the plaintiff had learned of her true condition, and concealed such knowledge from the defendants. Before the plaintiff secured possession of the animal, the defendants learned that she was with calf, and therefore of great value, and undertook to rescind the sale by refusing to deliver her. The question arises whether they had a right to do so. The circuit judge ruled that this fact did not avoid the sale, and it made no difference whether she was barren or not. I am of the opinion that the court erred in this holding. I know that this is a close question, and the dividing line between the adjudicated cases is not easily discerned. But it must be considered as well settled that a party who has given an apparent consent to a contract of sale may refuse to execute it, or he may avoid it after it has been completed, if the assent was founded, or the contract made, upon the mistake of a material fact, — such as the subject-matter of the sale, the price, or some collateral fact materially inducing the agreement, and this can be done when the mistake is mutual . . . .

If there is a difference or misapprehension as to the substance of the thing bargained for, if the thing actually delivered or received is different in substance from the thing bargained for and intended to be sold, then there is no contract; but if it be only a difference in some quality or accident, even though the mistake may have been the actuating motive to the purchaser or seller, or both of them, yet the contract remains binding. The difficulty in every case is to determine whether the mistake or misapprehension is as to the substance of the whole contract, going, as it were, to the root of the matter, or only to some point, even though a material point, an error as to which does not affect the substance of the whole consideration. Kennedy v. Panama, etc., Mail Co. L.R. 2 Q-B 580, 588. It has been held, in accordance with the principles above stated, that where a horse is bought under the belief that he is sound, and both vendor and vendee honestly believe him to be sound, the purchaser must stand by his bargain, and pay the full price, unless there was a warranty.

It seems to me, however, in the case made by this record, that the mistake or misapprehension of the parties went to the whole substance of the agreement. If the cow was a breeder, she was worth at least $750; if barren, she was worth not over $80. The parties would not have made the contract of sale except upon the understanding and belief that she was incapable of breeding, and of no use as a cow. It is true she is now the identical animal that they thought her to be when the contract was made; there is no mistake as to the identity of the creature. Yet the mistake was not of the mere quality of the animal, but went to the very nature of the thing. A barren cow is substantially a different creature than a breeding one. There is as much difference between them for all purposes of use as there is between an ox and a cow that is capable of breeding and giving milk. If the mutual mistake had simply related to the fact whether she was with calf or not for one season, then it might have been a good sale; but the mistake affected the character of the animal for all time, and for her present and ultimate use. She was not in fact the animal, or the kind of animal, the defendants intended to sell or the plaintiff to buy. She was not a barren cow, and, if this fact had been known, there would have been no contract. The mistake affected the substance of the whole consideration, and it must be considered that there was not contract to sell or sale of the cow as she actually was. The thing sold and bought had in fact no existence. She was sold as a beef creature would be sold; she is in fact a breeding cow, and a valuable one.

The court should have instructed the jury that if they found that the cow was sold, or contracted to be sold, upon the understanding of both parties that she was barren, and useless for the purpose of breeding, and that in fact she was not barren, but capable of breeding, then the defendants had a right to rescind, and to refuse to deliver, and the verdict should be in their favor.

The judgment of the court below must be reversed, and a new trial granted, with costs of this Court to defendants.

SHERWOOD, J. (dissenting).

I do not concur in the opinion given by my brethren in this case. I think the judgments before the justice and at the circuit were right.

I agree with my Brother Morse that the contract made was not within the statute of frauds, and that payment for the property was not a condition precedent to the passing of the title from the defendants to the plaintiff. And I further agree with him that the plaintiff was entitled to a delivery of the property to him when the suit was brought, unless there was a mistake made which would invalidate the contract; and I can find no such mistake. There is no pretense that there was any fraud or concealment in the case, and an intimation or insinuation that such a thing might have existed on the part of either of the parties would undoubtedly be a greater surprise to them than anything else that has occurred in their dealings or in the case.

As has already been stated by my brethren, the record shows that the plaintiff is a banker, and farmer as well, carrying on a farm, and raising the best breeds of stock, and lived in Plymouth, in the county of Wayne, 23 miles from Detroit; that the defendants lived in Detroit and were also dealers in stock of the higher grades; that they had a farm at Walkerville, in Canada, and also one in Greenfield, in said county of Wayne, and upon these farms the defendants kept their stock. The Greenfield farm was about 15 miles from the plaintiffs . . . .

There is no question but that the defendants sold the cow representing her of the breed and quality they believed the cow to be, and that the purchaser so understood it. And the buyer purchased her believing her to be of the breed represented by the sellers, and possessing all the qualities stated, and even more. He believed she would breed. There is no pretense that the plaintiff bought the cow for beef, and there is nothing in the record indicating that he would have bought her at all only that he thought she might be made to breed. Under the foregoing facts — and these are all that are contained in the record material to the contract — it is held that because it turned out that the plaintiff was more correct in his judgment as to one quality of the cow than the defendants, and a quality, too, which could not by any possibility be positively known at the time by either party to exist, the contract may be annulled by the defendants at their pleasure. I know of no law, and have not been referred to any, which will justify any such holding, and I think the circuit judge was right in his construction of the contract between the parties.

It is claimed that a mutual mistake of a material fact was made by the parties when the contract of sale was made. There was no warranty in the case of the quality of the animal. When a mistaken fact is relied upon as ground for rescinding, such fact must not only exist at the time the contract is made, but must have been known to one or both of the parties. When there is no warranty, there can be no mistake of fact when no such fact exists, or, if in existence, neither party knew of it, or could know of it; and that is precisely this case. If the owner of a Hambletonian horse had speeded him, and was only able to make him go a mile in three minutes, and should sell him to another, believing that was his greatest speed, for $300, when the purchaser believed he could go much faster, and made the purchase for that sum, and a few days thereafter, under more favorable circumstances, the horse was driven a mile in 2 min. 16 sec., and was found to be worth $20,000, I hardly think it would be held, either at law or in equity, by any one, that the seller in such case could rescind the contract. The same legal principles apply in each case.

In this case neither party knew the actual quality and condition of this cow at the time of the sale. The defendants say, or rather said to the plaintiff, "they had a few head left on their farm in Greenfield, and asked plaintiff to go and see them, stating to plaintiff that in all probability they were sterile and would not breed." Plaintiff did go as requested, and found there three cows, including the one purchased, with a bull. The cow had been exposed, but neither knew she was with calf or whether she would breed. The defendants thought she would not, but the plaintiff says that he thought she could be made to breed, but believed she was not with calf. The defendants sold the cow for what they believed her to be, and the plaintiff bought her as he believed she was, after the statements made by the defendants. No conditions whatever were attached to the terms of sale by either party. It was in fact as absolute as it could well be made, and I know of no precedent as authority by which this Court can alter the contract thus made by these parties in writing, and interpolate in it a condition by which, if the defendants should be mistaken in their belief that the cow was barren, she should be returned to them, and their contract should be annulled. It is not the duty of courts to destroy contracts when called upon to enforce them, after they have been legally made. There was no mistake of any such material fact by either of the parties in the case as would license the vendors to rescind. There was no difference between the parties, nor misapprehension, as to the substance of the thing bargained for, which was a cow supposed to be barren by one party, and believed not to be by the other. As to the quality of the animal, subsequently developed, both parties were equally ignorant, and as to this each party took his chances. If this were not the law, there would be no safety in purchasing this kind of stock . . . . In this case, if either party had superior knowledge as to the qualities of this animal to the other, certainly the defendants had such advantage.

I understand the law to be well settled that there is no breach of any implied confidence that one party will not profit by his superior knowledge as to facts and circumstances equally within the knowledge of both, because neither party reposes in any such confidence unless it be specially tendered or required, and that a general sale does not imply warranty of any quality, or the absence of any; and if the seller represents to the purchaser what he himself believes as to the qualities of an animal, and the purchaser buys relying upon his own judgment as to such qualities, there is no warranty in the case, and neither has a cause of action against the other if he finds himself to have been mistaken in judgment . . . . The judgment should be affirmed.

ANDERSON BROS. CORP. v. O'MEARA
United States Court of Appeals, Fifth Circuit
306 F.2d 672 (1962)

JONES, J.

The appellant, Anderson Brothers Corporation, a Texas corporation engaged in the business of constructing pipelines, sold a barge dredge to the appellee, Robert W. O'Meara, a resident of Illinois who is an oil well driller doing business in several states and Canada. The appellee brought this suit seeking rescission of the sale or, in the alternative, damages. After trial without a jury, the appellee's prayer for rescission was denied, but damages were awarded. The court denied the appellant's counterclaim for the unpaid purchase price of the dredge. Both parties have appealed.[3] Appellant contends that no relief should have been given to the appellee, and the appellee contends that the damages awarded to him were insufficient.

The dredge which the appellant sold to the appellee was specially designed to perform the submarine trenching necessary for burying a pipeline under water. In particular it was designed to cut a relatively narrow trench in areas where submerged rocks, stumps and logs might be encountered. The dredge could be disassembled into its larger component parts, moved over land by truck, and reassembled at the job site. The appellant built the dredge from new and used parts in its own shop. The design was copied from a dredge which appellant had leased and successfully used in laying a pipeline across the Mississippi River. The appellant began fabrication of the dredge in early 1955, intending to use it in performing a contract for laying a pipeline across the Missouri River. A naval architect testified that the appellant was following customary practice in pipeline operations by designing a dredge for a specific use. Dredges so designed can be modified, if necessary, to meet particular situations. For some reason construction of the dredge was not completed in time for its use on the job for which it was intended, and the dredge was never used by the appellant. After it was completed, the dredge was advertised for sale in a magazine. This advertisement came to the appellee's attention in early December, 1955. The appellee wanted to acquire a dredge capable of digging canals fifty to seventy-five or eighty feet wide and six to twelve feet deep to provide access to off-shore oil well sites in southern Louisiana.

---

[3] [1] Anderson Brothers Corporation will be referred to as the appellant and O'Meara as the appellee.

On December 8, 1955, the appellee or someone employed by him contacted the appellant's Houston, Texas, office by telephone and learned that the price of the dredge was $45,000. Terms of sale were discussed, and later that day the appellant sent a telegram to the appellee who was then in Chicago, saying it accepted the appellee's offer of $35,000 for the dredge to be delivered in Houston. The appellee's offer was made subject to an inspection. The next day Kennedy, one of the appellee's employees, went to Houston from New Orleans and inspected the dredge. Kennedy, it appears, knew nothing about dredges but was familiar with engines. After inspecting the engines of the dredge, Kennedy reported his findings to the appellee by telephone and then signed an agreement with the appellant on behalf of the appellee. In the agreement, the appellant acknowledged receipt of $17,500. The agreement made provision for payment of the remaining $17,500 over a period of seventeen months. The dredge was delivered to the appellee at Houston on December 11, 1955, and from there transported by the appellee to his warehouse in southern Louisiana. The barge was transported by water, and the ladder, that part of the dredge which extends from the barge to the stream bed and to which the cutting devices are attached, was moved by truck. After the dredge arrived at his warehouse the appellee executed a chattel mortgage in favor of the appellant and a promissory note payable to the order of the appellant. A bill of sale dated December 17, 1955, was given the appellee in which the appellant warranted only title and freedom from encumbrances. Both the chattel mortgage and the bill of sale described the dredge and its component parts in detail.

The record contains much testimony concerning the design and capabilities of the dredge including that of a naval architect who, after surveying the dredge, reported "I found that the subject dredge . . . had been designed for the purpose of dredging a straight trench over a river, lake or other body of water." The testimony shows that a dredge designed to perform sweep dredging, the term used to describe the dredging of a wide channel, must be different in several respects from one used only for trenching operations. The naval architect's report listed at least five major items to be replaced, modified, or added before the dredge would be suited to the appellee's intended use. It is clear that the appellee bought a dredge which, because of its design, was incapable, without modification, of performing sweep dredging.

On July 10, 1956, about seven months after the sale and after the appellee had made seven monthly payments pursuant to the agreement between the parties, the appellee's counsel wrote the appellant stating in part that "Mr. O'Meara has not been able to put this dredge in service and it is doubtful that it will ever be usable in its present condition." After quoting at length from the naval architect's report, which was dated January 28, 1956, the letter suggested that the differences between the parties could be settled amicably by the appellant's contributing $10,000 toward the estimated $12,000 to $15,000 cost of converting the trenching dredge into a sweep dredge. The appellant rejected this offer and on July 23, 1956, the appellee's counsel wrote the appellant tendering return of the dredge and demanding full restitution of the purchase price. This suit followed the appellant's rejection of the tender and demand.

In his complaint the appellee alleged breaches of expressed and implied warranty and fraudulent representations as to the capabilities of the dredge. By an amendment he alleged as an alternative to the fraud count that the parties had been mistaken in their belief as to the operations of which the dredge was capable, and thus there was a mutual mistake which prevented the formation of a contract. The appellee sought damages of over $29,000, representing the total of principal and interest paid the appellant and expenses incurred in attempting to operate the dredge. In the alternative, the appellee asked for rescission and restitution of all moneys expended by him in reliance on the contract. The appellant answered denying the claims of the appellee and counterclaiming for the unpaid balance.

The district court found that:

> At the time the dredge was sold by the defendant to the plaintiff, the dredge was not capable of performing sweep dredging operations in shallow water, unless it was modified extensively. Defendant had built the dredge and knew the purpose for which it was designed and adapted. None of the defendant's officers or employees knew that plaintiff intended to use the dredge for shallow sweep dredging operations. Gier [an employee of the appellant who talked with the appellee or one of his employees by telephone] mistakenly assumed that O'Meara intended to use the dredge within its designed capabilities.

> At the time the plaintiff purchased this dredge he mistakenly believed that the dredge was capable without modification of performing sweep dredging operations in shallow water.

The court further found that the market value of the dredge on the date of sale was $24,500, and that the unpaid balance on the note given for part of the purchase price was $10,500. Upon its findings the court concluded that:

> The mistake that existed on the part of both plaintiff and defendant with respect to the capabilities of the subject dredge is sufficient to and does constitute mutual mistake, and the plaintiff is entitled to recover the damages he has suffered as a result thereof.

These damages were found to be "equal to the balance due on the purchase price" plus interest, and were assessed by cancellation of the note and chattel mortgage and vesting title to the barge in the appellee free from any encumbrance in favor of the appellant. The court also concluded that the appellee was "not entitled to rescission of this contract." Further findings and conclusions, which are not challenged in this Court, eliminate any considerations of fraud or breach of expressed or implied warranties. The judgment for damages rests entirely upon the conclusion of mutual mistake.[4]

The district court's conclusion that the parties were mutually mistaken "with respect to the capabilities of the subject dredge" is not supported by its findings. "A mutual mistake is one common to both parties to the contract, each laboring under the same misconception." St. Paul Fire & Marine Insurance Co. v. Culwell, Tex. Com. App., 62 S.W.2d 100. The appellee's mistake in believing that the dredge was

---

[4] [2] The disposition of this appeal does not require a review of the district court's action in awarding damages as a remedy for mutual mistake rather than granting rescission and attempting restoration of the status quo ante.

capable, without modification, of performing sweep dredging was not a mistake shared by the appellant, who had designed and built the dredge for use in trenching operations and knew its capabilities. The mistake on the part of the appellant's employee in assuming that the appellee intended to use the dredge within its designed capabilities was certainly not one shared by the appellee, who acquired the dredge for use in sweep dredging operations. The appellee alone was mistaken in assuming that the dredge was adapted, without modification, to the use he had in mind.

The appellee insists that even if the findings do not support a conclusion of mutual mistake, he is entitled to relief under the well-established doctrine that knowledge by one party to a contract that the other is laboring under a mistake concerning the subject matter of the contract renders it voidable by the mistaken party. See 3 Corbin, *Contracts* 692, § 610. As a predicate to this contention, the appellee urges that the trial court erred in finding that "None of defendant's officers or employees knew that plaintiff intended to use the dredge for shallow sweep dredging operations." Moreover, the appellee contends that the appellant's knowledge of his intended use of the dredge was conclusively established by the testimony of two of the appellant's employees, because, on the authority of Griffin v. Superior Insurance Co., 161 Tex. 195, this testimony constitutes admissions, conclusive against the appellant. In the *Griffin* case, it was held that a party's testimony must be "deliberate, clear and unequivocal" before it is conclusive against him. The testimony on which the appellee relies falls short of being "clear and unequivocal." If the statement of one witness were taken as conclusive, it would not establish that he knew the appellee intended to use the dredge as a sweep dredge,

The testimony is not conclusive and is only one factor to be considered by the finder of facts.

There is a conflict in the evidence on the question of the appellant's knowledge of the appellee's intended use, and it cannot be held that the district court's finding is clearly erroneous. It is to be noted that the trial court before whom the appellee testified, did not credit his testimony that he had made a telephone call in which, he said, he personally informed an employee of the appellant of his plans for the use of the dredge.

The appellee makes a further contention that when he purchased the dredge he was laboring under a mistake so grave that allowing the sale to stand would be unconscionable. The ground urged is one which has apparently been recognized in some circumstances. However, the Texas courts have held that when unilateral mistake is asserted as a ground for relief, the care which the mistaken complainant exercised or failed to exercise in connection with the transaction sought to be avoided is a factor for consideration. American Maid Flour Mills v. Lucia, Tex. Civ. App., 285 S.W. 641. It has been stated that "though a court of equity will relieve against mistake, it will not assist a man whose condition is attributable to the want of due diligence which may be fairly expected from a reasonable person." American Maid Flour Mills v. Lucia, *supra.* This is consistent with the general rule of equity that when a person does not avail himself of an opportunity to gain knowledge of the facts, he will not be relieved of the consequences of acting upon supposition. Whether the mistaken party's negligence will preclude relief depends to a great extent upon the circumstances in each instance.

The appellee saw fit to purchase the dredge subject to inspection, yet he sent an employee to inspect it who he knew had no experience with or knowledge of dredging equipment. It was found that someone familiar with such equipment could have seen that the dredge was then incapable of performing channel type dredging. Although, according to his own testimony, the appellee was conscious of his own lack of knowledge concerning dredges, he took no steps, prior to purchase, to learn if the dredge which he saw pictured and described in some detail in the advertisement, was suited to his purpose. Admittedly he did not even inquire as to the use the appellant had made or intended to make of the dredge, and the district court found that he did not disclose to the appellant the use he intended to make of the dredge. The finding is supported by evidence. The appellee did not attempt to obtain any sort of warranty as to the dredge's capabilities. The only conclusion possible is that the appellee exercised no diligence, prior to the purchase, in determining the uses to which the dredge might be put. Had he sent a qualified person, such as the naval architect whom he later employed, to inspect the dredge he would have learned that it was not what he wanted, or had even made inquiry, he would have been informed as to the truth or have had a cause of action for misrepresentation if he had been given misinformation and relied upon it. The appellee chose to act on assumption rather than upon inquiry or information obtained by investigation, and, having learned his assumption was wrong, he asks to be released from the resulting consequences on the ground that, because of his mistaken assumption, it would be unconscionable to allow the sale to stand. The appellee seeks this, although the court has found that the appellant was not guilty of any misrepresentation or fault in connection with the transaction.

The appellant is in the same position as the party seeking relief on the grounds of mistake in Wheeler v. Holloway, *supra*, and the same result must follow. In the *Wheeler* case it was held that relief should be denied where the mistaken party exercised "no diligence whatever" in ascertaining the readily accessible facts before he entered into a contract.

The appellee should have taken nothing on his claim; therefore, it is unnecessary to consider the question raised by the cross-appeal. The other questions raised by the appellant need not be considered. The case must be reversed and remanded for further proceeding consistent with what we have here held.

Reversed and remanded.

NOTES

1. *Questions on* Sherwood *and* Anderson Brothers. Can you reconcile the differing outcomes in *Sherwood* and *Anderson Brothers*? In *Sherwood*, the majority opinion stated that the fertility of Rose 2d went to the essence of the bargain, and because both parties had been mistaken about the cow, there was no binding contract. Why didn't the ability of the dredge to cut channels go to the essence of the bargain between O'Meara and Anderson Brothers? The district court had essentially held that the essence of the bargain was affected and awarded damages to O'Meara. On what basis did the court of appeals reverse that holding?

The dissenting opinion in *Sherwood* would reach a result closer to *Anderson Brothers*. On what premise does the dissent differ with the majority?

The court in *Anderson Brothers* said that the corporation had no knowledge of the purpose for which O'Meara intended to use the dredge. Would it have made a difference in *Sherwood* if the owner of the cow had known the purpose for which the buyer was going to use the cow? What is the dissent's position on this question?

The *Anderson Brothers* court also emphasized O'Meara's failure to have the dredge inspected by someone with knowledge about dredges. But Anderson Brothers knew the kind of dredge it was selling. Couldn't the court have held that Anderson Brothers had the duty to tell O'Meara precisely what the dredge was designed to do? Could the case have been decided under the disclosure doctrine discussed in Chapter 5, Section C(3), or under the doctrine of implied warranty of fitness for particular purpose, discussed in Chapter 7, Section C(1)(b)? Which party was best able to avoid the risk of a mistake? Is this analysis helpful in *Sherwood*?[5]

2. *Mistake, According to the Restatement.* As *Sherwood v. Walker* suggests, the starting point in the legal analysis of who bears the cost of mistake is to first classify the mistake as "unilateral" or "mutual." Based on this distinction the Restatement (Second) proposes an elaborate formulation for resolving mistake issues. Section 151 defines mistake as "a belief that is not in accord with the facts." Read §§ 153 and 154, which indicate who bears liability when one party has made a contract mistake.

These sections indicate that a party bears the liability of a unilateral mistake when he commits the error. That liability shifts only when the other party knew or should have known that a mistake was being made. Why do you suppose the Restatement allocates liability this way?

Section 152(1) of the Restatement (Second) addresses the problem of mistake committed by both parties. Where the mistake is "mutual" the contract is voidable by the adversely affected party unless the risk is assigned to him by § 154. Obviously, it will be advantageous to the adversely affected party if he can classify the mistake as mutual so as to come under the more forgiving provisions of § 152.

Comment h notes that:

> The rule stated in this section applies only where both parties are mistaken as to the same basic assumption. Their mistakes need not be, and often they will not be, identical. If, however, the parties are mistaken as to different assumptions, the rule stated in § 153, rather than that stated in this Section, applies.

According to the Restatement (Second), the burden of proving that a mutual mistake should be grounds for voiding a contract rests with the party who wants the contract voided. Generally, and naturally enough, it is the party adversely affected by enforcement of the contract who argues for avoidance. If the adversely affected

---

[5] For an argument that the default non-disclosure rule should be changed to minimize the risk of mistakes, see Jeffrey Harrison, *Rethinking Mistake and Nondisclosure in Contract Law*, 17 Geo. Mason L. Rev. 335 (2010).

party fails to carry her burden of proof, the court will refuse to intervene, the contract will be enforced, and the loss will lie where it fell originally as a result of the mistake.

3. *The Baseball Card Case, Unilateral Mistake, and Disclosure. Irmen v. Wrzesinski*, No. 90 SC 5362 (Ill. Cir. Ct. 1990) (the "Baseball Card Case"), concerned the purchase by a 12 year-old baseball card collector of a Nolan Ryan rookie card. The card's price was marked as "1200/." The store clerk interpreted this to mean $12.00 (rather than the correct $1200.00) and sold it for that price. When the proprietor of the store realized the clerk's error, he asked the young collector to return the card. The young collector refused and the parties went to court. Moments before the judge was to issue her decision, the parties settled by agreeing to auction the card and donate the proceeds to charity.

In *Unilateral Mistake: The Baseball Card Case*, 70 Wash. U. L.Q. 57 (1992), Andrew Kull demonstrates how the Baseball Card Case provides a good example of the interaction between the contract law doctrines of unilateral mistake and disclosure. Traditionally, a party with superior information has no duty to disclose their superior information. As we saw in Chapter 5, many scholars continue to argue for this result because a rule requiring disclosure would lessen the incentive to acquire information in the first place. On the other hand, the approach to unilateral mistake recognized in Restatement (Second) §§ 153 and 154 allows contracts to be rescinded where one party knew that the other party was operating under a mistaken belief. As Kull explains.

> The baseball card case makes a splendid example of "unilateral mistake" in contract formation because it illustrates two rules at once. If the buyer knew the card was not in fact being offered at the price accepted by the clerk, there could be no contract of sale. On the other hand, if the buyer realized that the card was actually being offered at a price equal to one percent of its value, he was, by the traditional rule [of non-disclosure], entirely free to take advantage of the seller's mistake. The explanation of these contrasting results depends on a "subjective" theory of contract; though its only subjective feature, in this application, is to insist that one party cannot enforce a contract to which he knows the other party did not in fact agree. While a manifest failure of mutual assent necessarily prevents contract formation, standard doctrine sees no objection to a party's freely negotiating a bad bargain, whether as a result of ill luck or inferior information. It is for this reason that a unilateral mistake as to value, whether or not known to the other party, will not, by traditional standards, constitute grounds for rescission.

Id. at 83–84.

Kull concludes:

> Courts faced with new claims of "unilateral mistake" must decide whether it is worth countenancing some unequal exchanges in order to preserve an area of economic affairs in which the law leaves competent persons to look after themselves. Economists might ask not only whether rules mandating

disclosure can be administratively efficient, but whether the freedom to acquire information in pursuit of private advantage is not in itself a significant source of utility.

Id. at 84.

For an interesting argument that courts, for the most part, leave losses associated with mistaken contracts on whom they fall and that they are right to do so, see Andrew Kull, *Mistake, Frustration, and the Windfall Principle of Contract Remedies*, 43 HASTINGS L.J. 1 (1991).

4. ***Mistake and the Use of "As Is" Clauses.*** "As is" clauses are commonly employed in contracts for the sale of real property as well as the sale of goods. *See, e.g.*, UCC § 2-316(3)(a). An "as is" clause ordinarily waives any implied warranties associated with the sale. By waiving implied warranties against latent defects, the risk of any latent defect is effectively imposed on the purchaser (the party who receives the property "as is"). If both the seller and buyer in an "as is" sale are unaware of a latent defect, can the aggrieved buyer avoid the sale by invoking the mistake doctrine, notwithstanding the "as is" clause in the agreement?

In *Lenawee County Bd. of Health v. Messerly*, 417 Mich. 17, 331 N.W.2d 203 (1982), the Messerlys sold a 600 square foot piece of property with a three-apartment complex to the Pickles, who intended to continue to use the property for rental purposes. The contract for sale included an "as is" provision. After the purchase, the Pickles discovered that an owner prior to the Messerlys had illegally installed a malfunctioning septic system. The Board of Health condemned the property, and its small size prevented the repair or replacement of the defective septic system. The Pickles sought rescission of the contract based on mutual mistake. In considering whether the doctrine of mutual mistake should apply, the court reexamined its holding in *Sherwood*:

> [Sherwood] arguably distinguishes mistakes affecting the essence of the consideration from those which go to its quality or value [collateral mistakes], affording relief on a per se basis for the former but not the latter . . . . However, the distinctions which may be drawn from *Sherwood* . . . do not provide a satisfactory analysis of the nature of a mistake sufficient to invalidate a contract. Often, a mistake relates to an underlying factual assumption which, when discovered, directly affects value, but simultaneously and materially affects the essence of the contractual consideration. It is disingenuous to label such a mistake collateral . . . . [The Messerlys and the Pickles] both mistakenly believed that the property which was the subject of their land contract would generate income as rental property. The fact that it could not be used for human habitation deprived the property of its income earning potential and rendered it less valuable. However, this mistake, while directly and dramatically affecting the property's value, cannot accurately be characterized as collateral because it affects the very essence of the consideration . . . . We find that the inexact and confusing distinction between contractual mistakes running to value and those touching the substance of the consideration serves only as an impediment to a clear and helpful analysis for the equitable resolution of

cases in which mistake is alleged and proven. Accordingly, the [holding of *Sherwood* is limited to the facts of that case.]

417 Mich. at 28–29. The court found the agreement was subject to a mutual mistake, applying the principles of Restatement (Second) § 152. Was the court correct to reject the distinction between mistakes that go to the essence of a bargain and those that are merely collateral?

The court next looked to Restatement (Second) § 154 for guidance in choosing a remedy. The court stated:

> In cases of mistake by two equally blameless parties, we are required, in the exercise of our equitable powers, to determine which blameless party should assume the loss resulting from the misapprehension they shared. Normally that can only be done by drawing upon our 'own notions of what is reasonable and just under all the surrounding circumstances . . . .' Equity suggests that, in this case, the risk should be allocated to the purchasers. We are guided to that conclusion, in part, by the standards announced in § 154 of the Restatement of Contracts, [Second], for determining when a party bears the risk of mistake . . . . Section 154(a) suggests that the court should look first to whether the parties have agreed to the allocation of the risk between themselves. While there is no express assumption in the contract by either party of the risk of the property becoming uninhabitable, there was indeed some agreed allocation of the risk to the vendees by the incorporation of an "as is" clause into the contract . . . . [The incorporation] of this clause is a persuasive indication that, as between them, such risk as related to the 'present condition' of the property should lie with the purchaser. If the 'as is' clause is to have any meaning at all, it must be interpreted to refer to those defects which were unknown at the time that contract was executed.

Id. at 31–32.

Thus, although the doctrine of mutual mistake applied, the "as is" clause in the contract allocated the risk of this contingency to the purchasers, the Pickles. Do you agree with the court's reasoning? Recall the discussion in the introductory essay to this chapter concerning parties' inability to anticipate particular, unlikely contingencies, and parties' ability to contract to assign unanticipated risks in general.

5. *The Duty to Investigate.* In *Anderson Brothers*, the court found that the buyer had failed in his duty to properly investigate the nature of the dredge he was purchasing. The court was concerned that the buyer did not disclose his intended use of the dredge, inquire as to the seller's understanding of the proper use of the dredge, request any sort of warranty, or send a qualified person to inspect the dredge. The court approvingly cited the principle that "relief should be denied where the mistaken party exercised 'no diligence whatever' in ascertaining the readily accessible facts before he entered into a contract." To what extent must a party exercise diligence in investigation? Did the buyer really exercise "no diligence whatever"? (He sent *someone* to look at the dredge after all.) If the buyer had done just one of the things cited by the court but nonetheless was mistaken would he have performed a sufficient investigation according to the court?

In *Gartner v. Eikill*, 319 N.W.2d 397 (1982), the Supreme Court of Minnesota considered the degree of investigation required of a purchaser of real property. In that case, a purchaser of real property sought rescission of a sale when he realized that a zoning limitation had been placed on the development of the property years before the sale, effectively rendering the property valueless. The seller also did not know of the restriction. Though the restriction was in the records at the local city hall, the buyer simply relied on the erroneous statements of the seller's agent concerning the property's zoning when making the contract. The court rescinded the contract based on mutual mistake. The court held that the buyer had behaved reasonably in relying on the seller's agent's statements and "had [no] duty to inquire further." *Id.* at 398–99. The court found it important that the buyer had engaged in many similar contracts previously and had never felt the need to check the records at city hall.

Do you agree with this result? If the parties had recognized the risk before contracting, on whom do you think the parties would have placed the risk? Would either party be better able to prevent the mistake? Will future parties look to the local records after this result?

6. *Clerical Errors.* It is not uncommon for a buyer or seller to make a clerical error when negotiating or drafting a contract. If a party accidentally miscalculates a numerical term of a contract, for example, how should the mistake doctrine apply? Generally, courts apply the same basic test for mistake in this context that they would apply in any other context. In *S.T.S. Transport Service, Inc. v. Volvo White Truck Corp.*, 766 F.2d 1089, 1093 (7th Cir. 1985), the Seventh Circuit applying Illinois law listed three conditions: "(1) the mistake must relate to a material feature of the contract; (2) it must have occurred despite the exercise of reasonable care; and (3) the other party must be placed in the position it was in before the contract was made."

One of the operative questions is thus whether the miscalculation is sufficiently material to justify rescission. In *Elsinore Union Elementary School Dist. v. Kastorff*, 54 Cal. 2d 380, 353 P.2d 713 (1960), the California Supreme Court rescinded a contract based on mistake where a winning bidder on a construction contract had bid thousands of dollars less than the next closest bid due to a miscalculation. Determination of whether any particular numerical error is sufficiently large to be material is, of course, a question of fact that will vary under the circumstances of any particular case.

Another consideration is whether the mistake occurred despite the exercise of reasonable care by the mistaken party. The court in *S.T.S. Transport Service, Inc., supra*, discussed this requirement:

> Although reasonable care is as difficult to be precise about in [clerical error cases] as it is [in other types of cases], there are some fairly clear groupings of mistake cases that can serve as guideposts. Most helpful is the knowledge that Illinois courts will generally grant relief for errors "which are clerical or mathematical . . . ." The reason for the special treatment for such errors, of course, is that they are difficult to prevent, and that no useful social purpose is served by enforcing the mistaken term. No incentives exist to make such mistakes; all the existing incentives work, in

fact, in the opposite direction. There is every reason for a contractor to use ordinary care, and, if errors of this sort — clerical or mathematical — slip through anyway, the courts will generally find it more useful to allow the contract to be changed or rescinded than to enforce it as it is. Naturally there are cases of extreme negligence to which this presumption should not apply . . . .

Id. at 1093.

In addition to these considerations, consider an efficiency analysis of the clerical error cases. For example, in *Elsinore, supra,* the court rescinded a contract involving a contractor who submitted a bid thousands of dollars less than the second-lowest bidder. Contractors already have extra-legal incentives to avoid errors and submit accurate bids. Absent a legal rule allowing rescission, however, owners merely have an incentive to accept the lowest bid — even if it is obvious, when compared to competing bids, that the submission was based on a mistake. How will the court's decision affect the behavior of future contracting parties?

7. *Mistake in Transmission.* One final problem concerns the question of who bears liability when a mistake is made in transmitting an offer or acceptance.

Generally, this problem arises when offers and acceptances are transmitted by telegraph or telegram. For example, suppose an offeror wants to notify an offeree that he will sell the offeree 100 bushels of wheat for $10 a bushel. Western Union transmits the offer via telegraph, but mistakenly indicates that 1000 bushels of wheat are for sale. The offeree telegraphs back his acceptance of the offer. The offeror, naturally, will deny that any contract ever was made. But the common law rule holds that the party who selects and uses the method of communication bears the cost of a mistake. If this rule applied, the offeror would be bound to a contract for 1000 bushels of wheat.

As in other types of mistakes, however, liability will shift when the party receiving the message knows or should know that a mistake was made in the communication. Again, the analysis of the least-cost risk bearer is useful in justifying a rule of law. For an example of this "method of communication" rule, see *Ayer v. Western Union Tel. Co.,* 79 Me. 493 (1887).

8. *Problems.* Apply the Restatement rules of mistake to the following problems:

a. Plaintiffs, cattle breeders, bought a 16-day-old bull calf at auction for $5000. They intended to use the calf for breeding purposes. The calf would have been worth only $30 at the time of the sale had the parties known it was sterile; however, the minimum age at which the fertility of a bull can be determined is about 12 months. When the calf was 18 months old, tests by experts proved conclusively that the calf had been born incurably sterile. Plaintiffs seek rescission of the contract. What result? *See Backus v. MacLaury,* 278 A.D. 504, 106 N.Y.S.2d 401 (1951).

b. Park Trust Co. held the mortgages on several lots in a new subdivision. The realty company that was developing the lots instructed its contractors to build houses on lots 158, 159, 160, and 161. By mistake, construction was begun on lots 157, 158, 159, and 160. Although officials of the realty and trust companies visited the building sites several times with a plan of the lots in hand, they never consulted the plot maps to see that construction was commencing according to plan. When the houses were complete, a sale was held and Jeselsohn bought Lot 161 for $4250. He soon discovered that no house had been built on Lot 161, and that his investment was worth only about $400. Jeselsohn wants to recover his money. Will he prevail? *See Jeselsohn v. Park Trust Co.*, 241 Mass. 388 (1922).

[2]   Mutual Mistake and Reformation

ALUMINUM CO. OF AMERICA v. ESSEX GROUP, INC.
United States District Court, Western District of Pennsylvania
499 F. Supp. 53 (1980)

TEITELBAUM, J.

Plaintiff, Aluminum Company of America (ALCOA), brought the instant action against defendant, Essex Group, Inc. (Essex), in three counts. The first count requests the Court to reform or equitably adjust an agreement entitled the Molten Metal Agreement entered into between ALCOA and Essex.

Count One

ALCOA's first count seeks an equitable modification of the contract price for its services. The pleadings, arguments and briefs frame the issue in several forms. ALCOA seeks reformation or modification of the price on the basis of mutual mistake of fact, unilateral mistake of fact, unconscionability, frustration of purpose, and commercial impracticability.

A

The facts pertinent to count one are few and simple. In 1967 ALCOA and Essex entered into a written contract in which ALCOA promised to convert specified amounts of alumina supplied by Essex into aluminum for Essex. The service is to be performed at the ALCOA works at Warrick, Indiana. The contract is to run until the end of 1983. Essex has the option to extend it until the end of 1988. The price for each pound of aluminum converted is calculated by a complex formula which includes three variable components based on specific indices. The initial contract price was set at fifteen cents per pound, computed as follows: chart

A. Demand Charge	$0.05/lb.
B. Production Charge	
(i) Fixed component	.04/lb
(ii) Non-labor production cost component	.03/lb.
(iii) Labor production cost component	.03/lb.
Total Initial Charge	$0.15/lb.

The demand charge is to vary from its initial base in direct proportion to periodic changes in the Engineering News Record Construction Cost-20 Cities Average Index published in the Engineering News Record. The Non-labor Production Cost Component is to vary from its initial base in direct proportion to periodic changes in the Wholesale Price Index-Industrial Commodities (WPI-IC) published by the Bureau of Labor Statistics of the United States Department of Labor. The Labor Production Cost Component is to vary from its initial base in direct proportion to periodic changes in ALCOA's average hourly labor cost at the Warrick, Indiana works. The adjusted price is subject to an over-all "cap" price of 65% of the price of a specified type of aluminum sold on specified terms, as published in a trade journal, American Metal Market.

The indexing system was evolved by ALCOA with the aid of the eminent economist Alan Greenspan. ALCOA examined the non-labor production cost component to assure that the WPI-IC had not tended to deviate markedly from their non-labor cost experience in the years before the contract was executed. Essex agreed to the contract including the index provisions after an examination of the past record of the indices revealed an acceptable pattern of stability.

ALCOA sought, by the indexed price agreement, to achieve a stable net income of about 4 cents per pound of aluminum converted. This net income represented ALCOA's return (i) on its substantial capital investment devoted to the performance of the contracted services, (ii) on its management, and (iii) on the risks of short-falls or losses it undertook over an extended period. The fact that the non-labor production cost component of ALCOA's costs was priced according to a surrogate, objective index opened the door to a foreseeable fluctuation of ALCOA's return due to deviations between ALCOA's costs and the performance of the WPI-IC. The range of foreseeable deviation was roughly three cents per pound. That is to say that in some years ALCOA's return might foreseeably (and did, in fact) rise to seven cents per pound, while in other years it might foreseeably (and did, in fact) fall to about one cent per pound. See Table I.

Essex sought to assure itself of a long term supply of aluminum at a favorable price. Essex intended to and did manufacture a new line of aluminum wire products. The long term supply of aluminum was important to assure Essex of the steady use of its expensive machinery. A steady production stream was vital to preserve the market position it sought to establish. The favorable price was important to allow Essex to compete with firms like ALCOA which produced the aluminum and manufactured aluminum wire products in an efficient, integrated operation.

In the early years of the contract, the price formula yielded prices related, within the foreseeable range of deviation, to ALCOA's cost figures. Beginning in 1973, OPEC actions to increase oil prices and unanticipated pollution control costs greatly increased ALCOA's electricity costs. Electric power is the principal non-labor cost factor in aluminum conversion, and the electric power rates rose much more rapidly than did the WPI-IC. As a result, ALCOA's production costs rose greatly and unforeseeably beyond the indexed increase in the contract price. Table I illustrates the relation between the WPI-IC and ALCOA's costs over the years of the contract, and the resulting consequences for ALCOA:

TABLE I

YEAR	BASE WPI–IC[1]	WARRICK NON-LABOR PRODUCTION COSTS[2] PER POUND		PROFIT/LOSS PER LB.	POUNDS DELIVERED	PROFIT/LOSS
		¢	%			
1968	102.5	4.371	110.5	5.799	25,300,000	$1,467,147
1969	106.0	4.010	101.4	7.097	54,694,317	3,881,656
1970	110.0	4.397	111.1	6.517	84,370,265	5,498,410
1971	114.1	5.215	131.8	5.367	65,522,280	3,516,581
1972	117.9	5.309	134.2	5.721	83,128,209	4,755,765
1973	125.9	5.819	147.1	4.535	82,201,940	3,727,857
1974	153.8	9.009	227.1	2.070	86,234,310	1,785,050
1975	171.5	11.450	289.4	.189	76,688,530	144,941
1976	182.4	13.948	352.6	(.301)[3]	83,363,502	250,924
1977	195.1	17.806	450.1	(4.725)[3]	72,289,722	(3,415,689)
1978	209.4	22.717	574.2	(10.484)[3]	82,235,337	(8,620,504)

[1] The contract calls for a recomputation of the WPI-IC, so that the "Base Wholesale Price Index" = 100 in 1967.

[2] Warrick Non-Labor Production Costs 1967 — 100%.

[3] The profit (loss) shown in years 1976 through 1978 was affected by a temporary surcharge agreement. Without the temporary surcharge the loss in cents per pound would have been as follows: 1976 (1.699); 1977 (6.725); 1978 (10.984). The loss each year would have been as follows: 1976 ($1,416,346); 1977 ($4,861,484); 1978 ($9,031,631).

During the most recent years, the market price of aluminum has increased even faster than the production costs. At the trial ALCOA introduced the deposition of Mr. Wilfred Jones, an Essex employee whose duties included the sale of surplus metal. Mr. Jones stated that Essex had resold some millions of pounds of aluminum which ALCOA had refined. The cost of the aluminum to Essex (including the purchase price of the alumina and its transportation) was 36.35 cents per pound around June of 1979. Mr. Jones further stated that the resale price in June 1979 at one cent per pound under the market, was 73.313 cents per pound, yielding Essex a gross profit of 37.043 cents per pound. This margin of profit shows the tremendous advantage Essex enjoys under the contract as it is written and as both parties have performed it. A significant fraction of Essex's advantage is directly attributable to the corresponding out of pocket losses ALCOA suffers. ALCOA has sufficiently shown that without judicial relief or economic changes which are not presently foreseeable, it stands to lose in excess of $75,000,000 out of pocket, during the remaining term of the contract . . . .

C

ALCOA initially argues that it is entitled to relief on the theory of mutual mistake. ALCOA contends that both parties were mistaken in their estimate of the suitability of the WPI-IC as an objective index of ALCOA's non-labor production costs, and that their mistake is legally sufficient to warrant modification or avoidance of ALCOA's promise. Essex appropriately raised several defenses to these claims. Essex first argues that the asserted mistake is legally insufficient because it is essentially a mistake as to future economic events rather than a mistake of fact. Essex next argues that ALCOA assumed or bore the risk of the mistake. Essex finally argues that the requested remedy of reformation is not available under Indiana law.

The present case involves a claimed mistake in the price indexing formula. This is clearly a mistake concerning a factor affecting the value of the agreed exchange. Of such mistakes Corbin concluded that the law must consider the character of the risks assumed by the parties. *Corbin on Contracts* at § 605.

He further concluded:

> In these cases, the decision involves a judgment as to the materiality of the alleged factor, and as to whether the parties made a definite assumption that it existed and made their agreement in the belief that there was no risk with respect to it. Opinions are almost sure to differ on both of these matters, so that decisions must be, or appear to be, conflicting. The court's judgment on each of them is a judgment on a matter of fact, not a judgment as to law. No rule of thumb should be constructed for cases of this kind. 3 *Corbin on Contracts* § 605 at p. 643 (1960).

The new Restatement 2d of Contracts § [152] follows a similar approach.

Both Professor Corbin and the Restatement emphasize the limited place of the doctrine of mistake in the law of contracts. They, along with most modern commentators, emphasize the importance of contracts as devices to allocate the risks of life's uncertainties, particularly economic uncertainties. Where parties to a contract deliberately and expressly undertake to allocate the risk of loss attendant on those uncertainties between themselves or where they enter a contract of a customary kind which by common understanding, sense, and legal doctrine has the [effect] of allocating such risks, the commentators and the opinions are agreed that there is little room for judicial relief from resulting losses. *Corbin on Contracts* § 598 and authorities there cited. The new Restatement agrees, § [154]. This is, in part, the function of the doctrine of assumption of the risk as a limitation of the doctrine of mistake. Whether ALCOA assumed the risk it seeks relief from is at issue in this case. The doctrine of assumption of the risk is therefore considered below. The important point to note here is that the doctrine of assumption of the risk is not the only risk allocating limitation on the doctrine of mistake. Other important risk allocating limitations are inherent in the doctrine of mistake itself. They find expression in the cases and treatises in declarations that there has been no mistake, or no legally cognizable mistake, or a mistake of the wrong sort.

ALCOA claims that there was a mutual mistake about the suitability of the WPI-IC as an index to accomplish the purposes of the parties. Essex replies that the mistake, if any, was not a mistake of fact, but it was rather a mistake in predicting future economic conditions. Essex asserts that such a mistake does not justify legal relief for ALCOA. The conflicting claims require the Court to resolve three questions: (1) Was the mistake one of "fact" as the cases and commentators use that word? (2) If so, was it of the sort of fact for which relief could be granted? (3) If the mistake was not one of "fact," is relief necessarily foreclosed? . . .

The Court finds the parties' mistake in this case to be one of fact rather than one of simple prediction of future events. Plainly the mistake is not wholly isolated from predictions of the future or from the searching illuminations of painful hindsight. But this is not the legal test. At the time the contract was made both parties were aware that the future was unknown, and their agreed contract was intended to bind them for many years to come. Both knew that Essex sought an objective pricing formula and that ALCOA sought a formula which would cover its out of pocket costs over the years and which would yield it a return of around four cents a pound. Both parties to the contract carefully examined the past performance of the WPI-IC before agreeing to its use. The testimony was clear that each assumed the Index was adequate to fulfill its purpose. This mistaken assumption was essentially a present actuarial error.

The parties took pains to avoid the full risk of future economic changes when they embarked on a twenty-one year contract involving services worth hundreds of millions of dollars. To this end they employed a customary business risk limiting device — price indexing — with more than customary sophistication and care. They chose not a single index formula but a complex one with three separate indices. Their care to limit the risk of the future distinguishes this case from cases like Leasco Corporation v. Taussig, 473 F.2d 777 (2nd Cir. 1972). In Leasco the plaintiff corporation contracted to sell to Taussig a subsidiary which engaged in civil engineering and consulting. Taussig was, at the time, the vice-president of the subsidiary. The parties fixed the sales price by capitalizing the anticipated $200,000 earnings of the subsidiary in the year of the sale. Both parties knew that the subsidiary's earnings were volatile. "The civil engineering business is personalized, highly technical, and extremely risky." Id. at 781. But the parties made no provision to limit their risk. In fact the projected $200,000 earnings turned into a $12,000 loss due to a design error in a construction project. The court held that this loss did not make the contract voidable: "[W]e hold that there was no mutual mistake. Both Taussig and Leasco may have hoped, but surely could not have been certain, that [the subsidiary] would earn $200,000 in fiscal 1971 . . . . Neither party could safely assume the projected earnings would be realized." Id. The "fact" which led to the dispute was a prediction. The court characterized the situation as one where the parties realized there was doubt about an important fact and assumed, or more accurately placed on the purchaser, the risk of its existence. See Restatement of Contracts § 502, comment f.

The Taussig decision rested on two legs: the absence of a mistake of "fact" and the assumption of the risk of future uncertainties. The decision was plainly correct. The parties bottomed their agreement on a naked prediction without the protection of conditions or limitations. The only protection for the parties lay in practical matters. Both were well familiar with the business. And the contract was a short term one for the outright sale of the business. In the short term the parties might think they could sensibly risk uncertainties without specific contractual limits. Having made no attempt to limit future uncertainties, the disappointed purchaser could point to no fact which existed when the contract was made which would justify an award of judicial relief.

The contrast between *Taussig* and the present case is striking. Here the practical necessities of the very long term service contract demanded an agreed risk limiting device. Both parties understood this and adopted one. The capacity of their selected device to achieve the known purposes of the parties was not simply a matter of acknowledged uncertainty like the *Taussig* prediction. It was more in the nature of an actuarial prediction of the outside limits of variation in the relation between two variable figures — the WPI-IC and the non-labor production costs of ALCOA. Its capacity to work as the parties expected it to work was a matter of fact, existing at the time they made the contract.

This crucial fact was not known, and was scarcely knowable when the contract was made.[6] But this does not alter its status as an existing fact. The law of mistake has not distinguished between facts which are unknown but presently knowable, e.g., Raffles v. Wichelhaus, 2 H. & C. 906 (1864), and facts which presently exist but are unknowable, e.g., Sherwood v. Walker, 66 Mich. 568 (1887). Relief has been granted for mistakes of both kinds.

To conclude that the parties contracted upon a mistake of fact does not, by itself, justify an award of judicial relief to ALCOA. Relief can only follow if the mistake was mutual, if it related to a basic assumption underlying the contract, and if it caused a severe imbalance in the agreed exchange.

The doctrine of mistake has long distinguished claims of mutual mistake from claims of unilateral mistake. *Corbin on Contracts* § 608. The standards for judicial relief are higher where the proven mistake is unilateral than where it is mutual. Compare, e.g., Restatement 2d of Contracts § [153] with § [152].

Essex asserts that ALCOA's mistake was unilateral. Mr. O'Malley, Chairman of the Board of Essex Corporation, testified at trial that he had no particular concern for ALCOA's well-being and that in the negotiations of the contract he sought only Essex's best interests. Essex claims this testimony tends to rebut any possible mutual mistake of fact between the parties. The Court disagrees.

The cases clearly establish that mutual mistake lies in error concerning mutually understood material facts. The law of mutual mistake is not addressed primarily to motivation or to desire to have a good bargain, such as that credibly testified to by Mr. O'Malley. As Mr. O'Malley struck the bargain for Essex, he understood the function of the Wholesale Price Index, as part of the pricing formula, to be the protection of ALCOA from foreseeable economic fluctuations. He further had every reason to believe that the formula was selected on the factual prediction that it would, within tolerable limits, serve its purpose. While he did not share the motive

---

[6] [5] Clear hindsight suggests the flaw might have been anticipated and cured by a "floor" resembling the 65% "cap" that Essex wrote into the price formula. To the extent this possibility might be thought material to the case, the Court specifically finds that when the contract was made, even people of exceptional prudence and foresight would not have anticipated a need for this additional limitation to achieve the purpose of the parties.

to protect ALCOA, he understood the functional purposes of the agreement. He therefore shared this mistake of fact. And his mistake was Essex's. The Court recognizes that Mr. O'Malley and Essex would cheerfully live with the benefit of their mistake, but the law provides otherwise. As a matter of law Mr. O'Malley's testimony of Essex's indifference concerning ALCOA's motivation for the use of the Wholesale Price Index as a gauge for tracking non-labor costs is immaterial.

Is it enough that one party is indifferent to avoid a mutual mistake? The Court thinks not. This situation resembles that in Sherwood v. Walker, *supra*, the celebrated case of Rose of Aberlone. There the owner of a prize breeding cow sold her for slaughter at the going rate for good slaughter cattle. The owner had unsuccessfully tried to breed her and had erroneously concluded she was sterile. In fact she was pregnant at the time of the sale and she was much more valuable for breeding than for slaughter. There as here, the buyer was indifferent to the unknown fact; he would have been pleased to keep the unexpected profit. But he understood the bargain rested on a presumed state of facts. The court let the seller avoid the contract because of mutual mistake of fact.

In *Sherwood*, the buyer didn't know the highly pedigreed Rose was with calf. He probably could not have discovered it at the time of the sale with due diligence. Here the parties could not possibly have known of the sudden inability of the Wholesale Price Index to reflect ALCOA's non-labor costs. If, over the previous twenty years, the Wholesale Price Index had tracked, within a 5% variation, pertinent costs to ALCOA, a 500% variation of costs to Index must be deemed to be unforeseeable, within any meaningful sense of the word.

Essex has not seriously argued that the mistake does not relate to an assumption which is basic to the contract. The relation is clear. The assumed capacity of the price formula in a long term service contract to protect against vast windfall profits to one party and vast windfall losses to the other is so clearly basic to the agreement as to repel dispute. While the cases often assert that a mistake as to price or as to future market conditions will not justify relief, this is not because price assumptions are not basic to the contracts. Instead, relief is denied because the parties allocated the risk of present price uncertainties or of uncertain future market values by their contract. Where a "price mistake" derives from a mistake about the nature or quantity of an object sold, the courts have allowed a remedy; they have found no contractual allocation of that sort of risk of price error. Indiana cases hold that where land is sold as a tract for a set price, and it later appears that there was a material error in the parties' estimate of the quantity of land conveyed, the court will correct the error by adjusting the price, McMahan v. Terkhorn, 67 Ind. App. 501 (1917), or by allowing rescission, Earl v. VaNatta, 29 Ind. App. 532 (1902). See *Corbin on Contracts* §§ 604-05. Similarly many cases allow relief from unilateral price errors by construction contractors. An Indiana decision reached this result. Board of School Comm'rs v. Bender, 36 Ind. App. 164 (1904). See *Corbin on Contracts* § 609. Restatement 2d of Contracts § [153], comment b. These cases demonstrate that price assumptions may be basic to the contract.

Essex concedes that the result of the mistake has a material effect on the contract and that it has produced a severe imbalance in the bargain. See Restatement 2d of Contracts § [152], comment c. The most that Essex argues is this: ALCOA has not proved that enforcement of the contract would be unconscionable. Essex correctly points out that at the time of the trial ALCOA had shown a net profit of $9 million on the contract. Essex further argues that ALCOA has failed to prove that it ever will lose money on the contract, and that such proof would require expert testimony concerning future economic values and costs. These arguments are insufficient.

The evidence shows that during the last three years ALCOA has suffered increasingly large out of pocket losses.[7] If the contract were to expire today that net profit of $9 million would raise doubts concerning the materiality of the parties' mistake. But even on that supposition, the court would find the mistake to be material because it would leave ALCOA dramatically short of the minimum return of one cent per pound which the parties had contemplated.

But the contract will not expire today. Essex has the power to keep it in force until 1988. The Court rejects Essex's objection to the absence of expert testimony concerning future costs and prices. The objection is essentially based on the traditional refusal of courts to award speculative damages. But Essex presses the argument too far. The law often requires courts to make awards to redress anticipated losses. The reports are filled with tort and contract cases where such awards are made without the benefit of expert testimony concerning future economic trends. Awards are commonly denied because they are too speculative where there is a claim for lost future profits and there is insufficient evidence of present profits to form a basis for protecting future profits.

Similarly the courts often decline to speculate concerning future economic trends in calculating awards for lost future earnings. Many states refuse to consider any possibility of future inflation in calculating such awards despite the presence of expert testimony and the teachings of common experience. This demonstrates the law's healthy skepticism concerning the reliability of expert predictions of economic trends. Where future predictions are necessary, the law commonly accepts and applies a prediction that the future economy will be much like the present (except that inflation will cease). Since some prediction of the future is inescapable in this case, that commonly accepted one will necessarily apply.[8] On that prediction, ALCOA has proved that over the entire life of the contract it will lose, out of pocket, in excess of $60 million, and the whole of this loss will be matched by an equal windfall profit to Essex.[9] This proof clearly establishes that the mistake had the required material effect on the agreed exchange. Indeed, if this case required a

---

[7] [6] The Court recognizes that ALCOA has suffered even larger losses of potential profits which it might have earned, but for the contract, in the strong aluminum market in recent years. Essex, rather than ALCOA, has enjoyed those profits. But their existence is immaterial to the questions.

[8] [7] Since the effect of this decision is to modify the contract but to keep it in force, both parties may be adequately protected against severe and surprising economic developments. Each continues to have recourse to the courts.

[9] [8] The equivalence of ALCOA's loss and Essex's gain may distinguish this case from the concededly more difficult "Suez cases." In those cases an unexpected closing of the canal materially increased the cost of performing the contract leaving the courts to determine the allocation of a loss not balanced by an equal profit. Those cases might also be distinguished in that they involved the doctrine of frustration of purpose rather than the doctrine of mistake. However, the similarity of these doctrines renders this distinction doubtful.

determination of the conscionability of enforcing this contract in the current circumstances, the Court would not hesitate to hold it unconscionable.

Essex next argues that ALCOA may not be relieved of the consequences of the mistake because it assumed or bore the risk of the market. Essex relies on both Restatements and on a variety of cases fairly typified by Leasco Corp. v. Taussig, *supra;* McNamara Const. of Manitoba Ltd. v. United States, 509 F.2d 1166 (Ct. Cl. 1963), and Flippin Materials Co. v. United States, 312 F.2d 408 (Ct. Cl. 1963) . . . .

The Restatements and these cases reveal four facets of risk assumption and risk allocation under the law of mistake. First, a party to a contract may expressly assume a risk. If a contractor agrees to purchase and to remove 114,000 cubic yards of fill from a designated tract for the landowner at a set price "regardless of subsurface soil and water conditions" the contractor assumes the risk that subsurface water may make the removal unexpectedly expensive.

Customary dealing in a trade or common understanding may lead a court to impose a risk on a party where the contract is silent. Often the result corresponds to the expectation of both parties, but this will not always be true. See Berman, *Excuse for Nonperformance in the Light of Contract Practices in International Trade,* 63 Colum. L. Rev. 1413, 1420-24 (1963). At times legal rules may form the basis for the inferred common understanding. Equity traditionally put the risk of casualty losses on the purchaser of land while the purchase contract remained executory. This allocation was derived from the doctrine of equitable conversion. "Equity regards as done that which ought to be done." The rule could always be modified by express agreement. It survives today — where it does survive — largely by reason of its acceptance as part of the common expectations of real estate traders and their advisors.

Third, where neither express words nor some particular common understanding or trade usage dictate a result, the court must allocate the risk in some reasoned way. Two examples from the Restatement 2d of Contracts § [154] illustrate the principle. A farmer who contracts to sell land may not escape the obligation if minerals are discovered which make the land more valuable. And in the case of the sale of fill stated above, if there is no express assumption of the risk of adverse conditions by the contractor, he may still bear the risk of losing his expected profits and suffering some out of pocket losses if some of the fill lies beneath the water table. These cases rest on policies of high generality. Contracts are — generally — to be enforced. Land sales are — generally — to be treated as final.

Fourth, where parties enter a contract in a state of conscious ignorance of the facts, they are deemed to risk the burden of having the facts turn out to be adverse, within very broad limits. Each party takes a calculated gamble in such a contract. Because information is often troublesome or costly to obtain, the law does not seek to discourage such contracts. Thus if parties agree to sell and purchase a stone which both know may be glass or diamond at a price which in some way reflects their uncertainty, the contract is enforceable whether the stone is in fact glass or diamond. If, by contrast, the parties both mistakenly believe it to be glass, the case is said not to be one of conscious ignorance but one of mutual mistake. Consequently the vendor may void the contract.

In this case Essex raises two arguments. First, it asserts that ALCOA expressly or by fair implication assumed the risk that the WPI-IC would not keep up with ALCOA's non-labor production costs. Second, it asserts that the parties made a calculated gamble with full awareness that the future was uncertain, so the contract should be enforced despite the mutual mistake. Both arguments are correct within limits, and within those limits they affect the relief ALCOA may receive. Both arguments fail as complete defenses to ALCOA's claim.

Essex first asserts that ALCOA expressly or implicitly assumed the risk that the WPI-IC would not track ALCOA's non-labor production costs. Essex asserts that ALCOA drafted the index provision; that it did so on the basis of its superior knowledge of its cost experience at the Warrick Works; and that ALCOA's officials knew of the inherent risk that the index would not reflect cost changes. Essex emphasizes that, during the negotiation of the contract, it insisted on the inclusion of a protective "ceiling" on the indexed price of ALCOA's services at 65% of a specified published market price. Essex implies that ALCOA could have sought a corresponding "floor" provision to limit its risks.

Essex's arguments rely on two ancient and powerful principles of interpretation. The first is reflected in the maxim "expressio unius est exclusio alterius." The second is the principle that a contract is to be construed against its drafter. To agree to an indexed price term subject to a ceiling but without a floor is to make a deliberate choice, Essex argues. It is to choose one principle and to reject another. The argument is plausible but not sufficient. The maxim rules no farther than its reason, and its reason is simply this: often an expression of a rule couched in one form reflects with high probability the rejection of a contradictory rule. Less often it reflects a probable rejection of a supplementary rule. To know if this is true of a particular case requires a scrupulous examination of the thing expressed, the thing not expressed, and the context of the expression. The question here is precisely this: By omitting a floor provision did ALCOA accept the risk of any and every deviation of the selected index from its costs, no matter how great or how highly improbable? The course of dealing between the parties repels the idea. Essex and ALCOA are huge industrial enterprises. The management of each is highly trained and highly responsible. The corporate officers have access to and use professional personnel including lawyers, accountants, economists and engineers. The contract was drafted by sophisticated, responsible businessmen who were intensely conscious of the risks inherent in long term contracts and who plainly sought to limit the risks of their undertaking. The parties' laudable attention to risk limitation appears in many ways: in the complex price formula, in the 65% ceiling, in the "most favored customer" clause which Essex wrote into the contract, and in the elaborate "force majeure" clause favoring ALCOA. It appears as well in the care and in the expense of the negotiations and drafting process. Essex negotiated with several aluminum producers, seeking a long term assured supply, before agreeing to the ALCOA contract. Its search for an assured long term supply for its aluminum product plants itself bespeaks a motive of limiting risks. Essex settled on ALCOA's offer rather than a proffered joint venture on the basis of many considerations including the required capital, engineering and management demands of the joint venture, the cost, and the comparative risks and burdens of the two arrangements. When ALCOA proposed the price formula which appears in the contract, Essex's management examined the past behavior of the indices for stability to assure they would not cause their final aluminum cost to deviate unacceptably from the going market rate. ALCOA's management was equally attentive to risk limitation. They went so far as to retain the noted economist Dr. Alan Greenspan as a consultant to advise them on the drafting of an objective pricing formula. They selected the WPI-IC as a pricing element for this long term contract only after they assured themselves that it had closely tracked ALCOA's non-labor production costs for many years in the past and was highly likely to continue to do so in the future. In the context of the formation of the contract, it is untenable to argue that ALCOA implicitly or expressly assumed a limitless, if highly improbable, risk. On this record, the absence of an express floor limitation can only be understood to imply that the parties deemed the risk too remote and their meaning too clear to trifle with additional negotiation and drafting.

The principle that a writing is to be construed against its maker will not aid Essex here. That principle once sounded as a clarion call to retrograde courts to pervert agreements if they could. Today it is happily domesticated as a rule with diverse uses. In cases involving issues of conscience or of strong policy, such as forfeiture cases, the principle complements the familiar doctrine of strict construction to favor lenient results. In other cases it serves as an aid in resolving otherwise intractable ambiguities. This case presents neither of these problems. The question of defining the risks ALCOA assumed is one of interpretation. It implicates no strong public policy. Neither does it present an intractable ambiguity.

Neither is this a case of "conscious ignorance" as Essex argues. Essex cites many cases which establish the general rule that mistaken assumptions about the future are not the sort of mistaken assumptions which lead to relief from contractual duties. Leasco Corp. v. Taussig, *supra*, is typical of these cases. The general rule is in fact as Essex states it. But that rule has limited application. The new Restatement notes that the rule does not apply where both parties are unconscious of their ignorance — that is, where both mistakenly believe they know the vital facts. See § [154] comment c.

This distinction is sufficient to settle many cases but it is framed too crudely for sensible application to cases like the present one. The distinction posits two polar positions: certain belief that a vital fact is true and certain recognition that a vital fact is unknown. Such certainties are seldom encountered in human affairs. They are particularly rare in the understanding of sophisticated businessmen. In *Taussig* the parties anticipated the subsidiary would earn $200,000 in the year of the sale. Had anyone asked them whether they were certain of that prediction, they would surely have answered that such predictions are always made with the recognition of a range of uncertainty. The prediction indicates that the parties believe there is a good chance that the earnings will lie between $175,000 and $225,000 and a very high probability that they will lie between $100,000 and $300,000. If pressed, the parties might agree that there could be a new loss for the year. But they would regard a loss as very highly unlikely. Of course predictions of future earnings must be viewed skeptically because the people who make them are often vitally interested in their contents and in their uses . . . .

Once courts recognize that supposed specific values lie, and are commonly understood to lie, within a penumbra of uncertainty, and that the range of probability is subject to estimation, the principle of conscious uncertainty requires reformulation. The proper question is not simply whether the parties to a contract were conscious of uncertainty with respect to a vital fact, but whether they believed that uncertainty was effectively limited within a designated range so that they would deem outcomes beyond that range to be highly unlikely. In this case the answer is clear. Both parties knew that the use of an objective price index injected a limited range of uncertainty into their projected return on the contract. Both had every reason to predict that the likely range of variation would not exceed three cents per pound. That is to say both would have deemed deviations yielding ALCOA less of a return on its investment, work and risk of less than one cent a pound or of more than seven cents a pound to be highly unlikely. Both consciously undertook a closely calculated risk rather than a limitless one. Their mistake concerning its calculation is thus fundamentally unlike the limitless conscious undertaking of an unknown risk which Essex now posits.

What has been said to this point suffices to establish that ALCOA is entitled to some form of relief due to mutual mistake of fact . . . .

E

[In determining the appropriate remedy, the court first rejects rescission of the contract as that would serve to grant ALCOA a windfall gain and deprive Essex of the long-term supply of aluminum for which it had legitimately contracted. The court holds instead that in cases such as this one an appropriate remedy is one that modifies the contract's price term to take into account the unforeseen circumstances which disrupted the parties' intended price formula. In granting reformation because of mutual mistake, the court modified the price term to require Essex to pay ALCOA the ceiling price term specified in the contract. The court recognizes, however, that a price fixed at the contract ceiling may turn out to favor ALCOA if circumstances in the aluminum market changed dramatically during the contract period. Therefore, the court adopted as the contract price term the lesser of Price A (the ceiling price as specified in the contract) or Price B (calculated as the greater of 1) the price specified in the contract, or 2) that price which yields ALCOA a profit of one cent per pound of aluminum converted). The design of this reformation, according to the court, is to grant Essex the benefit of its favorable bargain while at the same time reducing ALCOA's disappointment to the limit of the risk contemplated by the parties in making the contract.]

Conclusion

[In its conclusion, the court argues that the fiduciary duty of corporate managers and the established practice of risk limitation in long term contracts are strong indicators that the parties to this commercial contract intended to limit their risks, and judicial remedies should be framed to protect that purpose. In determining the appropriate legal response to long term contracts, such as this one, in which inflation has disturbed the basic equivalence of the agreement, the court suggests four factors that ought to be considered in determining whether to modify these contracts: "(1) the parties' prevision of the problems which eventually upset the balance of the agreements and their allocation of associated risks; (2) the parties' attempts at risk limitation; (3) the existence of severe out of pocket losses and (4) the customs and expectations of the particular business community."

The court concludes that an indexed price term in a contract, such as the index in this case, is evidence of a general purpose to limit the risks of a long term contract rather than a prevision for the specific problem facing the parties. Even if an index fails to account for the specific effects of inflation, it still serves as an indication of the parties' intention to limit the risks of a long term contract, and courts should modify the contract's price terms if the deviation between the index and the pertinent costs was a risk the parties intended to allocate in the contract. Finally, the court concludes that judicial relief should be limited to those cases where the parties show a desire to limit their risks and one party suffers severe out of pocket losses which were not adequately foreseen and provided for by the parties in formulating their contract.]

NOTES

1. *Questions on* Alcoa.

a. Alcoa *versus* Eastern Air Lines. The court in *Alcoa* holds that the price escalator clause did not function as the parties intended because the WPI-IC did not accurately reflect the rise in Alcoa's non-labor costs. Recall that in *Eastern Air Lines v. Gulf Oil*, Chapter 4, and Section D, *infra*, Gulf argued that the parties' price escalator clause did not function as the parties intended when Platts Oilgram, to which the escalator clause was indexed, failed to report the price of "new oil" which was deregulated following the OPEC oil embargo. Is the case for reformation based on mutual mistake stronger or weaker in *Alcoa* than in *Eastern Air Lines*? Why didn't the court consider the mutual mistake doctrine in *Eastern Air Lines*? Even if the price terms did not function as the parties had intended, does it follow that the parties intended, at the time of their agreement, for an adversely affected party to be excused on that basis, or for a court to rewrite their agreement so that the price term functions as they had hoped? Note that the court remarks that Alan Greenspan, then an eminent economist and subsequently the Chairman of the Federal Reserve, was hired by Alcoa to design the price escalator clause. Is this fact relevant to how the court should decide *Alcoa*?

b. *Goldberg on* Alcoa. A critical factor in the court's decision was the finding that the escalator clause had been designed by Alan Greenspan and had historically tracked non-labor costs within a margin that granted Alcoa a profit ranging from one cent to seven cents per pound. Was that finding, in fact, true? Victor Goldberg says no:

> [M]ost of the *Alcoa* commentary takes as correct the judge's claim that the WPI-IC had closely tracked Alcoa's nonlabor production costs in the past. Even if it were correct, I don't think the subsequent failure would warrant excusing Alcoa. But it was not correct . . . . Greenspan's involvement can usually be counted on for a good laugh in classroom discussions. Did it happen? Essex, in its brief, said not. "Contrary to the trial court's finding,

[Alcoa's key negotiator] testified that Alan Greenspan . . . was not consulted by Alcoa in connection with the Contract." (p. 16)

The court gave a numerical illustration: "If over the previous twenty years, the Wholesale Price Index had tracked within a 5% variation, pertinent costs to ALCOA, a 500% variation of costs to Index must be deemed unforeseeable, within any meaningful sense of the word." It is not clear whether this was meant to be a rhetorical flourish or an accurate rendition of the facts. If the latter, it missed. The Warrick plant was only seven years old at the time of the contract. As it expanded and took advantage of economies of scale, nonlabor costs fell by 60% while the WPIIC was rising by 5%. If Alcoa was drawing on its cost history, it was on the cost performance of its eight other plants, which used different sources of power for electricity. So, the implicit assumption would have been that Alcoa's experience with plants located elsewhere and using a different power source would be an adequate predictor of the future course of this component of Alcoa's costs. That is a bigger leap than suggested by the court's description . . . . So, if the purpose of the index was to track the nonlabor costs of the Warrick plant, the parties were indeed mistaken, but the mistake was one of bad judgment. There was no track record at Warrick, the implication of the court notwithstanding. Nor was there a historical basis for presuming that the costs of hydro and coal power would be closely correlated over a twenty-year period.[10]

c. *Fairness in* Alcoa. In an appendix to the *Alcoa* decision, Judge Teitelbaum noted the following:

> Although the facts in this case do not require us to address the problem, the Court has studied various remedies utilized by courts in foreign countries, when beset with contracts that are no longer deemed "fair" in light of changed circumstances: that is, when it is determined that fairness requires a change in a contract because events occurring subsequent to the execution of the contract have made its performance unfair. These approaches 1) try to establish the original economic position and intent of the parties; 2) try to distribute the consequences of the unforeseen burden equally between the parties; 3) try to determine what the parties would have agreed to had they been aware of what was going to happen, and 4) order termination unless the party against whom relief is sought makes an equitable offer to modify the contract.

499 F. Supp. at 93. Does the notion of "fairness" have clear implication in *Alcoa*? As to number (3), if parties had been aware of what was going to happen, wouldn't there have been no need for an escalator clause? If the parties designed their contract to allocate risks in the face of their unavoidable uncertainty about the future at the time of contracting, how would it help to ask what the parties would have done at the time of contracting if they had known facts that they could not have known at that time? Isn't the real question how the parties intended to handle the risks caused by their uncertainty about future events, not how they would have

---

[10] Victor Goldberg, Framing Contract Law: An Economic Perspective 361-62 (2007).

written their contract if they were certain about future events?

2. *Remedy for Relief from Mistake.* Parties arguing for relief from mistake have some choice of requested remedy. A party can argue for enforcement of the contract (assuming, of course, that the mistake works to his benefit). Where a mistake was made in the formulation of the contract, a party can argue for rescission and be placed in the position he occupied before the contract was made. In that event, the contract is voided and, if possible, both parties are returned, through the payment of damages, to the positions they occupied before the contract was made.

Where a mistake was made in the expression of the contract — as in the case of a scrivener's error, where a written contract does not match earlier oral agreements between the parties — the party can argue for reformation. Reformation allows the written document to be altered to reflect earlier agreements.

In *Atlas Corp. v. United States*, 895 F.2d 745 (Fed. Cir. 1990), the court considered whether the mutual mistake doctrine can be invoked to support reformation rather than rescission. The plaintiffs in that case entered into contracts with the U.S. government for the production of uranium and thorium in the 1950s. According to the court's opinion, "[t]he contracts contained pricing provisions designed so that the private companies could recover their costs, plus a reasonable profit." In the process of milling uranium and thorium ore, a radioactive residue called "tailings" was created and collected in large tailings piles. Although at the time of contract formation there was a general awareness that these residual tailings emitted low levels of radiation, it was not until the 1970's that the long-term health effects associated with these tailings became fully understood. As a result of the potential health hazards posed by uranium mill tailings, Congress enacted the Uranium Mill Tailings Radiation Control Act which required the plaintiff companies to undertake costly measures to stabilize and decontaminate the tailing piles. The plaintiffs sued the government for reformation of these contracts, claiming that the parties were mutually mistaken that the tailings piles did not pose a significant health risk and would not require costly decontamination procedures.

The court rejected the plaintiffs' claim for reformation under the doctrine of mutual mistake on the grounds that they failed to allege that the parties to the contract were mistaken in their belief regarding a fact. The court described the rule as follows:

> A "mistake" that can support reformation is a belief that is not in accord with the facts . . . To satisfy this element of a reformation claim, a plaintiff must allege that he held an erroneous belief as to an existing fact. If the *existence* of a fact is not known to the contracting parties, they cannot have a belief concerning that fact; therefore, there can be no "mistake."

Id. at 750.

The court cited a number of cases in which courts permitted the reformation of contracts on the basis that "the parties held an erroneous belief concerning a fact whose existence the parties recognized and about which they could reach agree-ment." The plaintiffs cited *Alcoa* for the proposition that the mutual mistake doctrine does not distinguish between unknown facts which are presently knowable, and presently existing facts which are unknowable. In response, the court stressed the distinction between the *existence* of a fact being unknown and the *outcome* of a fact being unknown:

> It is true that even though the outcome of a fact is unknowable, the parties can make a mistake concerning that fact. But where the existence of a fact is unknowable, the parties cannot have a belief concerning that fact, and they cannot make a mistake about it. Thus, in the famous case of *Sherwood v. Walker*, 66 Mich. 568, 33 N.W. 919 (1887), the contract for the sale of was held to be voidable where the cow was assumed to be barren but later was discovered to be pregnant. The *existence* of the fact as to whether the cow was barren or fertile was known to the parties even if the *outcome* of that fact was unknown.
>
> In this case, the plaintiffs' allegations of their "mistake" do not show that they held an erroneous belief concerning a fact whose existence the parties could recognize and about which they could negotiate an agreement. The statements the plaintiffs make in their complaints and briefs demonstrate that the parties could not have contemplated the potential tailings hazard when they entered into the contracts. Therefore, they could not have reached an agreement on the now-required tailings stabilization, and they could not have held a mutually mistaken belief concerning the abatement of the tailings hazard.

Id. at 751–52.

Do you find the court's reasoning persuasive? While it is true that the parties did not have mistaken beliefs about who would bear the tailings clean-up costs, isn't this because both parties implicitly but incorrectly believed there would not be any tailings costs? The court views reformation as inappropriate in *Atlas* because the parties had no belief at all about whether the tailings were hazardous. Is this convincing? Didn't the parties have an implicit yet mistaken belief (didn't both parties implicitly believe that there would be no costs associated with the tailings)?

3. **Determining the *Parties' Intention: The Distinction between Intended Means and Intended Ends.*** What did the parties in *Alcoa* intend? The court essentially finds that both parties believed they were agreeing to a cost-plus contract, and interprets the agreement accordingly. But if is this is the case, why would Alcoa and Essex incur the costs of negotiating a sophisticated pricing formula when they could have simply drafted a cost-plus contract? Professors Scott and Kraus argue that by conflating the *contractual means* of the contract with its *contractual ends*, the court in *Alcoa* undermines the true intent of both parties:

> Viewed ex post, the decision in *Alcoa* may seem justifiable. Indeed, Victor Goldberg, who sharply criticizes the transactional lawyers who wrote the Alcoa-Essex contract and the litigators who argued the case, nonetheless concludes that "the judge imposed a cost-plus gloss on the contract which was not explicit in the contract but most likely comported with the parties' intentions." But this understanding of the parties' intentions mistakenly equates contractual intent with the parties' intended contractual ends. While the court may well have correctly recognized the parties' contractual

ends, it failed to take account of the contractual mechanisms that serve as essential means of achieving those ends . . . .

The evidence reflects that the parties intended to create a pricing mechanism that tracked Alcoa's costs (and thus implicitly tracked the market price for the smelting services subject to a built-in price discount). One alternative would have been to agree to a cost-plus contract, one in which Alcoa could recover its costs of performance plus an agreed profit. Cost-plus contracts have many problems, however. They reduce the seller's incentives to economize on costs, they are hard to monitor, and they require revelation and verification of confidential information. So the parties may have been motivated instead to create a verifiable proxy for a cost-plus contract that avoided these difficulties. From that perspective, the agreed-upon price index was intended to allow Alcoa to recover its capital costs in the Warrick plant plus a return on its investment and to permit Essex to obtain a favorable price for the smelting services over the life of the contract. These were the parties' intended contractual ends. But the question before the court concerned the parties' intended contractual means: What instruments did the parties select in order to achieve their goal of having the contract price track the market price of smelting services? . . .

By choosing a precisely defined price index, sophisticated parties implicitly allocate to the seller the risk that the index might malfunction and increase too slowly, and allocate to the buyer the risk that the index might malfunction and increase too rapidly. The court claimed to be maintaining fidelity to the parties' contractual intent by reforming the price index when it did not function as the parties anticipated it would. Ironically, however, the court's decision undermines commercial parties' ability to design their contracts optimally. Even if the court correctly interpreted the parties' intended *ends* in this case, the prospect of judicial intervention under these circumstances nonetheless impairs the ability of future commercial parties to choose the contractual *means* that best achieve their contractual ends.

Jody S. Kraus & Robert E. Scott, *Contract Design and the Structure of Contractual Intent*, 84 N.Y.U.L. REV. 1023, 1069–73 (2009).

4. ***Majoritarian Default Rules and Efficient Risk Allocation.*** If we suppose that contracting parties will take into account the default rule for allocating the risk of mistake (i.e., despite the remoteness of the risk, they consider the risk and the default rule for allocating it), then both economic and autonomy theories seem to support a majoritarian rule that would impute into their agreement the allocation of this risk to which most parties would agree if they considered and allocated the risk. According to economic analysis, that term would allocate the risk to the party best able to bear it. In some cases that will be the party adversely affected by the mistake; in others, it will be the party who benefits from the mistake. By placing liability initially on the party better able to avoid the mistake in the first place, future bargainers will have an incentive to take cost-effective precautions to guard against foreseeable risks. The problem becomes more complex, however, when one recognizes that errors are endemic to life — a certain irreducible number of

mistakes will occur notwithstanding the imposition of legal liability. The social cost of any risk (a mistake is the materialization of a risk) is the product of two factors — the probability (P) times its impact (I). Thus $R = P \times I$. Allocating liability initially to the party with the comparative advantage in mistake prevention will encourage reduction in P. But once a mistake is made it is equally important to reduce I as well. This can be accomplished by a "compound liability" rule that encourages cost-effective precautions by *both parties*. Thus, the law might allocate liability initially to the party in the best position to avoid the mistake, but shift liability to the other whenever she was better able to reduce its impact (i.e., she knew or should have known that a mistake was made). The most common compound liability rules are found, of course, in the rules of negligence, contributory negligence, and last clear chance in the law of torts. But examples in contracts can be found as well. Perhaps the clearest illustration is the law of unilateral mistake. For the argument that the fault principle plays a significant role in contract law, see Melvin A. Eisenberg, *The Role of Fault in Contract Law: Unconscionability, Unexpected Circumstances, Interpretation, Mistake, and Nonperformance*, 107 MICH. L. REV. 1413 (2009).

Suppose that a court cannot identify any reason why either the buyer or the seller would have the comparative advantage in identifying probability or impact. A possible result is to "let the loss lie where it falls." There is an ambiguity in this concept, however. Suppose that *Sherwood v. Walker* is such a case. The concept could mean that the court will refuse (to intervene) to enforce the contract, or it could mean that the court will enforce the contract as it would have done absent the mistake defense. Or the result of the case could be different if Rose had been delivered to the buyer or was still on the seller's farm. Suppose "title" to Rose had passed. Should that fact make a difference as to who bears the risk of mistake? For more, see Ian Ayres & Eric Rasmusen, *Mutual and Unilateral Mistake in Contract Law*, 22 J. LEGAL STUD. 309 (1993).

C. IMPOSSIBILITY AND COMMERCIAL IMPRACTICABILITY

As we said above, the excuse doctrines can usefully be viewed as a particular application of the principles of implied or constructive conditions examined previously in Chapter 7. If the risk of a particular contingency is expressly allocated by agreement, then courts ordinarily will not excuse the performance of the party to whom that risk is allocated when that risk materializes.

However, when the parties' agreement does not expressly anticipate a contingency that materializes after their agreement is made, courts must decide whether the agreement implicitly allocated that risk or instead failed to allocate the risk at all. On this analysis, the threshold question presented by a claim of excuse is whether unconditional language creates an unconditional obligation. Two historic excuse cases illustrate how the doctrine of impossibility originated as an application of contractual interpretation. A brief discussion of them should help avoid two common "false starts" in the analysis of excuse doctrine. The first is the view that express obligations undertaken without express conditions are inevitably unconditional. The second is that contract law has no choice but to excuse parties when their performance becomes impossible.

In *Paradine v. Jane* (Aleyn 26, 82 Eng. Rep. 897 (K.B. 1647)), the court stated that "when the party by his own contract creates a duty or charge upon himself, he is bound to make it good, *if he may*, notwithstanding any accident by inevitable necessity, because he might have provided against it by his contract. (emphasis added)" *Id.* at 27–28, 82 Eng. Rep. at 897–98. Thus, if Bob agrees to paint Jody's barn, then Bob's obligation to Jody is unconditional because of Bob's failure to expressly condition his obligation. There is, however, a fundamental flaw in this reasoning. Bob's obligation to paint Jody's barn is neither expressly conditional nor expressly unconditional. To be expressly unconditional, the agreement would have to state that "Bob *unconditionally* agrees to paint Jody's barn." However, even though Bob's obligation is not expressly conditional, it might be *implicitly* conditional. As we have seen, many contractual duties are subject to implied conditions or terms. The rule laid out in *Paradine* adopts the interpretive rule that all conditions to performance must be express. But contract law allows for all manner of implied conditions and terms of agreements. Indeed, the *Paradine* court conceded as much when it stated that the promisor is bound to discharge his obligation only "if he may." By this phrase, the court acknowledged that, notwithstanding his failure to expressly condition his obligation, the promisor will be excused from his obligation if performance becomes impossible. *Stees v. Leonard*, 20 Minn. 494 (1874), Chapter 1, confirms the rule that "[h]e that agrees to do an act should do it, *unless absolutely impossible.*" Thus, the law of excuse in contract originates with the impossibility doctrine, which itself presupposes that obligations not subject to express conditions can nevertheless be subject to an implied condition that excuses performance.

The *Paradine* and *Stees* courts appear to limit the law of excuse to the doctrine of impossibility. On this view, all contractual duties that become impossible to perform *must* be excused because there is no alternative. How can a court (or the obligee) require performance by the promisor if performance is literally impossible? The flaw in this reasoning is equally clear, however. The impossibility of performance only eliminates the possibility of imposing the equitable remedy of specific performance. But impossibility of performance does not affect the availability of the standard legal remedies for breach of contract. Thus, courts can hold promisors liable for breach of an obligation that has become impossible by requiring them to pay damages for their failure to perform. Indeed, it has always been clear that contract law does not excuse a buyer from performing when the buyer can demonstrate that it is impossible for him to pay because he lacks sufficient (access to) funds.[11] In such cases, for example, courts can order that future earnings be garnered to pay off the debt with interest. Similarly, if a seller's duty becomes impossible to perform, he can be held liable under his contract and ordered to pay the buyer damages for breach. The law of excuse is driven, therefore, not by any inherent limitations on the parties' ability to perform, but by the challenge of interpreting parties' agreements.

---

[11] However, state and federal bankruptcy laws, rather than contract law, sometimes excuse buyers based on inability to pay.

The fundamental question in excuse law is not whether performance is actually impossible, but whether the parties (explicitly or implicitly) allocated the risk of the contingency that has materialized. In discussing the history of the impossibility defense, Judge Posner explains that:

> It was recognized that physical impossibility was irrelevant, or at least inconclusive; a promisor might want his promise to be unconditional, not because he thought he had superhuman powers but because he could insure against the risk of nonperformance better than the promisee . . . Thus the proper question in an "impossibility" case is not whether the promisor could not have performed his undertaking but whether his nonperformance should be excused because the parties, if they had thought about the matter, would have wanted to assign the risk of the contingency that made performance impossible or uneconomical to the promisor or to the promisee; if to the latter, the promisor is excused.

Northern Indiana Public Service Co. v. Carbon County Coal Co., 799 F.2d 265, 276 (7th Cir. 1986).

We begin this section with a set of cases presenting particular paradigms within the impossibility doctrine. The first two cases involve contracts for the sale of particular goods or the provision of services that are either dependent on particular individuals or to be provided on particular pieces of property. When the particular property or goods subject to a contract are destroyed, or the particular individual who was to provide the service dies or becomes unable to perform, courts are generally inclined to excuse performance based on impossibility. *See generally* Restatement (Second) §§ 262 and 263.

[1]   The Traditional Impossibility Doctrine: Agreements Concerning Particular Property, Goods, or Services

TAYLOR v. CALDWELL
King's Bench
3 B. & S. 826, 122 Eng. Rep. 309 (1863)

See p. 85, *supra.*

HOWELL v. COUPLAND
Court of Appeals, Queen's Bench Division
1 Q.B.D. 258 (1876)

[Plaintiff, a potato merchant, contracted with the defendant, a farmer, to purchase 200 tons of potatoes grown on land belonging to the defendant. After a disease attacked the defendant's potato crop and caused it to fail, the plaintiff sued to recover damages for nondelivery. The Queen's Bench ruled that the defendant was excused from performance due to impossibility, and the plaintiff appealed.]

LORD COLERIDGE, J.

I am of opinion that the judgment ought to be affirmed. The Court of Queen's Bench held that, under these circumstances, the principle of Taylor v. Caldwell and Appleby v. Myers applied, and the defendant was excused from the performance of his contract. The true ground, as it seems to me, on which the contract should be interpreted, and which is the ground on which, I believe, the Court of Queen's Bench proceeded, is that by the simple and obvious construction of the agreement both parties understood and agreed, that there should be a condition implied that before the time for the performance of the contract the potatoes should be, or should have been, in existence, and should still be existing when the time came for the performance. They had been in existence, and had been destroyed by causes over which the defendant, the contractor, had no control, and it became impossible for him to perform his contract; and, according to the condition which the parties had understood should be in the contract, he was excused from the performance. It was not an absolute contract of delivery under all circumstances, but a contract to deliver so many potatoes, of a particular kind, grown on a specific place, if deliverable from that place. On the facts the condition did arise and the performance was excused. I am, therefore, of opinion that the judgment of the Queen's Bench should be affirmed.

SEITZ v. MARK-O-LITE SIGN CONTRACTORS, INC.
Superior Court of New Jersey
210 N.J. Super. 646, 510 A.2d 319 (1986)

OPINION:

MILBERG, A.J.S.C.

This is an action for breach of contract in which plaintiff, George Seitz, seeks damages from defendant, Mark-O-Lite Sign Contractors, Inc., in the amount of $7,200.

At trial, counsel for the parties agreed to submit the dispute to the court's determination based on the following stipulated facts:

1. Prior to December 1983, plaintiff submitted a bid to the Ocean County Center for the Arts on a contract involving renovations to the Strand Theater in Lakewood, New Jersey.

2. A portion of the Strand Theater project involved the restoration and replacement of a neon sign marquee.

3. Plaintiff was the low bidder on the Strand project.

4. Plaintiff first spoke with a representative of defendant in December 1983, and received a verbal estimate of from $10,000 to $12,000 for the sign work required in connection with the Strand project.

5. No written estimate was rendered by defendant and no contract was executed by plaintiff and defendant as of the end of 1983.

6. Plaintiff signed a contract for the Strand Theater renovation with the Ocean County Center for the Arts on December 26, 1983.

7. Items 1, 2, 3 and 4 of the contract pertain to the sign work and totaled $19,500 of the total contract price for the Strand Theater project of $51,200.

8. Plaintiff obtained quotations from other sign companies in early 1984, including one from Garden State Sign Company dated January 20, 1984, in the amount of $20,228.

9. Plaintiff had further discussions with defendant and on April 18, 1984, a contract was executed between the parties in the total amount of $12,800 for the sign work. On that date plaintiff gave defendant a deposit check in the amount of $3,200.

10. The contract between the parties contained a provision in paragraph (2) which reads as follows: "The Company shall not be liable for any failure in the performance of its obligation under this agreement which may result from strikes or acts of labor union, fires, floods, earthquakes, or acts of God, or other conditions or contingencies beyond its control."

11. Within a few days of the execution of the contract, defendant discovered that its expert sheet metal worker, Al Jorgenson, a diabetic, was required to enter the hospital and would be unable to work for an unknown period of time. Jorgenson was the only employee of defendant capable of performing the expert and detailed sheet metal work required.

12. Defendant advised plaintiff of the situation with its employee by telephone and on May 3, 1984, sent a letter to plaintiff returning the uncashed deposit check offering to complete any portion of the work which defendant was able to perform.

13. Defendant also contacted other sign companies and was advised that the cost of the work would be $18,000 to $20,000 and, therefore, it would have been economically infeasible for defendant to retain the services of another sign company.

14. Plaintiff entered into an agreement with City Sign Service, Inc. to perform the necessary work for the total sum of $20,000. It is to be noted that the items listed for additional rail, additional neon, and a neon border were extra items added to the project and were not encompassed within the specifications which defendant had originally agreed to perform.

15. The total damages claimed by plaintiff are in the amount of $7,200, representing the difference between the City Sign Service price of $20,000 and the price of $12,800 stated in the contract between the parties.

Defendant asserts the defense of impossibility of performance due to the disability of its sheet metal worker, Jorgenson. Specifically, defendant urges that the illness of Jorgenson discharged its obligation of performance pursuant to paragraph 2 of the contract. Paragraph 2, commonly known as a force *majeure* clause, reads:

The Company shall not be liable for any failure in the performance of its obligations under this agreement which may result from strikes or acts of

Labor Union, fires, floods, earthquakes, or acts of God, War *or other conditions or contingencies beyond its control.* [Emphasis supplied]

Defendant contends that Jorgenson's disability was a "condition or contingency beyond its control," that its obligation of performance was therefore excused under the above-quoted, exculpatory language.

In construing broad, exculpatory language of this type, however, the courts of this State and the majority of jurisdictions invoke the rule of *ejusdem generis.* Under this principle, the catch-all language of the force *majeure* clause relied upon by defendant is not to be construed to its widest extent; rather, such language is to be narrowly interpreted as contemplating only events or things of the same general nature or class as those specifically enumerated.

Jorgenson's disability does not fall into the same class as that of labor strikes, fires, floods, earthquakes or war. Nor can it be termed an "act of God." Jorgenson's condition was not the consequence of a stroke or a heart attack, either of because of its suddenness. Jorgenson is a diabetic. His disability — a partial amputation of his foot — was the result of the *progressive* aggravation of an infection, which aggravation was apparently rooted in his diabetes. Jorgenson's affliction was not sudden; indeed, his disability was a reasonably foreseeable consequence of his unfortunate malady. Hence, Jorgenson's incapacitation cannot be classed an "act of God" by any logical stretch of the term. Defendant's force *majeure* clause does not apply.

It does not necessarily follow, however, that defendant is bereft of the defense of impossibility of performance; thus far, it has merely been determined that the force *majeure* clause is unavailing.

There is very little, if any, recent New Jersey case law pertinent to the impossibility defense asserted herein; yet the general principles are well settled and relatively unchanged. The traditional rule with respect to impossibility by virtue of the death or illness of a particular person is set forth in the *Restatement, Contracts,* § 459 (1932):

A duty that requires for its performance action that can be rendered only by the promisor or some other particular person is discharged by his death or by such illness as makes the necessary action by him impossible or seriously injurious to his health, unless the contract indicates a contrary intention or there is contributing fault on the part of the person subject to the duty.

A more modern formulation of the doctrine is found in §§ 261 and 262 of the *Restatement, Contracts* 2d (1981), which speak in terms of "impracticability" rather than "impossibility":

§ 261. Discharge by Supervening Impracticability

Where, after a contract is made, a party's performance is made impracticable without his fault by the occurrence of an event the non-occurrence of which was a basic assumption on which the contract was made, his duty to render that performance is discharged, unless the language or the circumstances indicate the contrary.

§ 262. Death or Incapacity of Persons Necessary for Performance

If the existence of a particular person is necessary for the performance of a duty, his death or such incapacity as makes performance impracticable is an event the non-occurrence of which was a basic assumption on which the contract was made.

Section 262 states a specific instance for the application of the rule stated in § 261 and, thus, is subject to the qualifications stated in that preceding section. *See* Comment a to § 262, *supra.*

Regardless of which *Restatement* is adopted with respect to impossibility, however, the success of the defense in the particular mode asserted herein turns on a determination that the duty in question, as understood by the parties, can be performed only by a particular person. *Restatement, Contracts* 2d, § 459, Comment c, § 262, Comment b. Such has long been the governing standard in this State.

Thus, it is clear from the foregoing that the primary application of the impossibility defense in the form asserted by defendant is in the area of personal service contracts, that is, contracts which contemplate the peculiar skill or discretion of a particular person. *Restatement, Contracts* 2d, *supra,* § 262 Comment b. Where, as here, the agreement is silent as to whether a particular person is or is not necessary for performance, all the circumstances will be considered to determine whether the duty, as understood by the parties, sufficiently involves elements of personal service or discretion as to require performance by a particular individual. *Restatement, Contracts* 2d, § 262, Comment b.

The real question, therefore, is whether the duty of performance can be delegated to another: If the act to be performed is delegable, then the illness of the promisor or of a third person who is expected to perform the act does not excuse performance. *See Restatement, Contracts* 2d, § 262, Comment b ("If an obligor can discharge his duty by the performance of another, his own disability will not discharge him."); *Restatement, Contracts* 2d, § 459, Comment c ("If a contractor without violation of duty can go abroad and perform by means of another, his death or illness will not make subsequent performance of his contract impossible."). The preceding is merely a corollary of the general rule that, for impossibility to operate as an excuse, it must be objective ("the thing cannot be done") rather than subjective ("I cannot do it"). *Calamari & Perillo, supra* § 13-12 at 497; *see Restatement, Contracts* 2d, § 261, Comment e.

It is readily apparent from an application of the foregoing principles that defendant cannot prevail on its claim of impossibility of performance. Nothing in the language of the contract contemplates performance only by Jorgenson; nor do the circumstances demonstrate that the performance to be rendered by Jorgenson was so personal in nature, calling for a peculiar skill or special exercise of discretion, as to make it nondelegable. To be sure, the conduct of defendant — and that of plaintiff — following the advent of Jorgenson's incapacitation belies any claim of special need for his services. Defendant contacted a number of outside shops in an attempt to engage someone else to perform the sheet metal work. Defendant admitted that the sheet metal work could still be performed, albeit through someone other than Jorgenson. *Cf.* 13 *Am. Jur.* 2d, *Building and Construction Contracts,* § 63 (A contract to build a house does not involve such a personal relation that it may not be performed by persons other than the contracting parties thereto and, therefore, is not terminated by the death of one of the parties).

At best, defendant's claim is that of subjective impossibility which, as was previously stated, is no excuse for nonperformance.

Any claim by defendant that its obligation of performance should be excused, because to assume the higher cost of subcontracting the sheet metal work would have resulted in a marginal profit or even a loss, must fail. "Where one agrees to do, for a fixed sum, a thing possible to be performed, he will not be excused or become entitled to additional compensation because unforeseen difficulties are encountered." *United States v. Spearin, 248 U.S. 132, 136, 39 S.Ct. 59, 61, 63 L.Ed. 166 (1918),* quoted in *Hartford Fire Ins. Co. v. Riefolo Constr. Co., 81 N.J. 514, 524 (1980).*

An anticipatory breach is a definite and unconditional declaration by a party to an executory contract — through word or conduct — that he will not or cannot render the agreed upon performance. If the breach is material — that is, if it "goes to the essence of the contract" — the nonbreaching party may treat the contract as terminated and commence suit forthwith.

Here, defendant's letter of May 3, 1984, and the simultaneous return of plaintiff's deposit constituted a clear and unequivocal declaration that the agreed upon performance would not be forthcoming. Defendant's expression of inability to perform the sheet metal work, without legal excuse, was a repudiation going to the "essence of the contract" and, thus, justified plaintiff in considering the contract at an end and reaching out to another subcontractor. Particularly in view of the admitted time constraints which plaintiff was burdened with under his contract with the Ocean County Center for the Arts, it cannot be said that he acted wrongfully, or unreasonably, in subcontracting the entire sign project to another company.

Plaintiff expected to disburse $12,800 toward the completion of the sign project under his contract with defendant; in the end, he paid $20,000 for the contemplated work as a consequence of defendant's breach. His damages are equal to the difference or $7,200. Judgment will be entered in that amount in favor of plaintiff and against defendant.

Plaintiff is hereby directed to submit an appropriate form of judgment.

NOTES

1. ***Questions on*** **Howell** ***and Section 2-613.*** Read UCC § 2-613. Presumably *Howell* would be decided the same way today under this Code section. In *Howell*, would you like to know the market price of potatoes as compared to the contract price on the day specified by the contract for delivery? Are we to understand that the *buyer* in *Howell* could have refused to accept potatoes grown on any other plot of ground? Would the buyer be likely to know where the potatoes were grown?

Assume that Jack Sherman is a hog farmer in Iowa. A litter of eight pigs has just been born and thinking to protect himself against a drop in hog prices, Sherman contracts to sell eight pigs, delivery in six months. Alas, Sherman's pigs all die from a disease over which Sherman had no control. Can Sherman get out of the contract under § 2-615? (Why is § 2-613 unavailable on these facts?)

2. ***Questions on*** **Seitz.** The *Seitz* court distinguishes between objective impossibility ("The thing cannot be done.") and subjective impossibility ("I cannot do it."). Only objective impossibility grounds excuse. But when a promised performance is particularized to specific persons or goods, subjective impossibility is equivalent to objective impossibility: "The thing cannot be done because I can't do it, and the thing to be done is an act by me." How can courts tell the difference between particularized and non-particularized agreements? Does it matter whether courts look to the promisee's or the promisor's expectations in determining whether the performance is objectively impossible? Should Mark-O-Lite's expectation that it would use Jorgenson to make the neon marquee be relevant, or should Seitz's expectations control?

3. ***Impossibility and Recovery for Partial Performance.*** In the typical impossibility case, one party seeks to be excused from its performance duty on the ground that performance had become impossible. However, the impossibility defense can also be invoked as grounds for recovering for partial performance. In *Carroll v. Bowersock*, 100 Kan. 270 (1917), the plaintiff contracted with the owner of a warehouse to construct a concrete floor in the warehouse. After part of the work had been completed, the warehouse was destroyed by fire through no fault of either party. The defendant had insured the building in its pre-improvement condition. After collecting on that insurance, the defendant refused to build again, rendering further performance by the plaintiff impossible. Treating the impossibility doctrine on analogy with the mutual mistake doctrine, the court held that the parties' agreement was valid only under the basic assumption that the warehouse continued to exist throughout the duration of the performance period. Because the parties never contemplated the destruction of the warehouse, the allocation of that risk was not specified in the agreement, and therefore, cannot be settled by contract doctrine. The court then turned to the law of unjust enrichment and restitution. In the absence of a contract, the court stated:

> It takes something more to make the owner liable for what the contractor has done toward performance. The owner must be benefited. He should not be enriched at the expense of the contractor. That would be unjust, and to the extent that the owner has been benefited the law may properly consider him as resting under a duty to pay. The benefit which the owner has received may or may not be equivalent to the detriment which the contractor has suffered. The only basis on which the law can raise an obligation on the part of the owner is the consideration he has received by way of benefit, advantage, or value to him.

Id. at 274–75.

The court determined that the plaintiff was entitled to recover for work done in removing the old floor and the completed concrete footings, but not for material furnished or labor performed in the construction of any temporary devices that were not themselves wrought into the warehouse. In reaching this conclusion, the court stated: "The test is whether or not the work would have inured to his [defendant's] benefit as contemplated by the contract if the fire had not occurred." *Id.* at 277.

In Carroll, the contractor *was* excused from full performance since it had become impossible. But even if impossibility excuses the contractor from full performance, does it follow that he should be compensated for partial performance? Is the court's theory that the contract remains in effect to the extent of the partial performance?

According to the *Carroll* court, it is settled law that "If a contractor should engage to furnish all labor and material and build a house, and the house should burn before completion, the loss falls on him. If a contractor should engage to refloor two rooms of a house already in existence, and should complete one room before the house burned, he ought to be paid something." *Id.* at 274. Why should it matter whether the house already exists? Suppose an owner owns the land on which a contractor subsequently half-completes a new house when the house burns down. Is the builder entitled to the difference between the value of the land before the half-completed house was built and after the half-completed house was built? For a variation on this factual scenario, see *Olson v. Moore*, 590 N.E.2d 160 (1992), in which prospective purchasers of a house received the sellers' approval to renovate the home while their negotiations continued. The house burned down before the parties concluded their agreement but after many of the renovations had been completed. The court held in favor of the prospective purchasers and awarded them the costs of their improvements. Would the *Carroll* court approve of this remedy? Is it consistent with the *Carroll* court's theory of liability?

4. *Allocating Risk in Contracts with Middlemen*. As is the case with contracts for services that require the continued existence of a structure or the services of a particular individual, when faced with contracts for particular goods, courts must decide whether the parties allocated the risk that the performance might become impossible or whether the parties' obligation was implicitly conditioned on performance remaining possible throughout the performance period. *Canadian Industrial Alcohol Co. v. Dunbar Molasses Co.*, 258 N.Y. 194 (1932), is an example of how a court may determine that the risk of impossibility was allocated by the parties. In that case, the defendant, acting as a middleman, agreed to supply the plaintiff with 1,500,000 gallons of molasses from the usual run of a particular refinery. The run of that refinery was insufficient for the defendant to meet its obligations, and it only delivered approximately 350,000 gallons. The court, in an opinion by Judge Cardozo, rejected defendant's impossibility defense based on the unusually low production by the specified refinery. The court argued:

> We may assume, in the defendant's favor, that there would have been a discharge of its duty to deliver if the refinery had been destroyed, or if the output had been curtailed by the failure of the sugar crop, or the ravages of war, or conceivably in some circumstances by unavoidable strikes . . . The inquiry is merely this, whether the continuance of a special group of circumstances appears from the terms of the contract, interpreted in the setting of the occasion, to have been a tacit or implied presupposition in the minds of the contracting parties, conditioning their belief in a continued obligation.

. . . The defendant asks us to assume that a manufacturer, having made a contract with a middleman for a stock of molasses to be procured from a particular refinery, would expect the contract to lapse whenever the refiner chose to diminish his production, and this in the face of the middleman's omission to do anything to charge the refiner with a duty to continue.

Id. at 198–99.

According to Justice Cardozo, a buyer that contracts for a particular good with a middleman, rather than directly with the refinery, does not intend to assume the risk of non-delivery due to underproduction. Rather, the court held that the very purpose of the buyer's contract was to transfer this risk to the middleman. Clearly, Dunbar Molasses could have made the contract expressly contingent on the refinery's production, but then so too could Canadian Industrial Alcohol have expressly allocated to Dunbar Molasses the risk of the refinery's underproduction. Since the contract is silent on this question, how does the court determine how the parties would have allocated the risk? Does the court treat this as a gap case or as an implied agreement? Does this distinction matter here?

5. *The "Better Risk Bearer" Rationale in Excuse Cases.* The same economic analysis that applies to mistake cases can be applied to excuse cases. When potatoes are blighted or molasses factories fail to produce as expected, contractual expectations may be disappointed. Allowing an excuse defense to discharge contractual obligations does not produce the potatoes or increase molasses production. Someone is going to lose something in these cases. We suggested in Chapter 1, that if the parties had thought about the risk in advance, they would place the risk on the party with the comparative advantages in anticipating the risk, and taking appropriate precautions and/or acquiring insurance. The reasoning is that at the time of contracting the parties have a mutual interest in reducing the costs associated with the contract as much as possible. In these cases, the comparative advantages would all seem to be with the seller, and, indeed, that is where the loss ordinarily falls — excuse is a defense that is available only in exceptional cases. Does this reasoning presuppose that the parties will consciously consider these risks at the time of contracting? If so, is this a plausible assumption?

6. *Death of a Guarantor.* The death of an important party is a risk in many business deals. For example, in *Ft. M Development Corp. v. Inland Credit Corp.*, 54 A.D.2d 862, 388 N.Y.S.2d 603 (1976), the parties executed a mortgage agreement to finance the plaintiff's apartment complex project. The agreement stipulated that, as a condition precedent to obtaining the mortgage, five personal guaranties would have to be provided. The agreement also required the plaintiff to pay $9,600 in order to hold the financing open for a twelve month period. Within that period, Fort M requested that Inland honor the commitment. Inland learned that one of the personal guarantors had died in the interim, and Inland refused to proceed with the deal. Fort M sued, demanding return of the commitment fee, and asking either for damages (presumably for the increased cost of financing necessitated by Inland's action) or for specific performance of the deal. On appeal, the court held that since Inland had kept the loan commitment open for the specified time it was entitled to the $9,600 fee. At the same time it excused Inland's performance due to the nonoccurrence of a condition precedent (the continued life of all guarantors). As a result, Inland kept the fee but did not finance the project. The dissent vigorously attacked the majority's reasoning, questioning the court's ability to affirm the validity of the commitment fee while at the same time excusing the defendant's performance. Are the holdings in the case inconsistent?

7. *Problems.*

a. In 1989, Murray bids on a contract to provide 1,200 school bus chassis (transmissions and engines) to the North Carolina Department of Administration by 1990. He bases his bid on engines and transmissions available at General Motors, which is his sole source for these items. After his bid is accepted, the EPA issues new regulations for bus emissions, effective 1991, with which the currently available GM motors do not comply. In addition, GM informs Murray that the transmissions he will need for his chassis would not be available until 1991. Thus, the unavailability of the transmissions prevents Murray from delivering the chassis in 1990, and the new emissions standards prevent him from delivering them in 1991 or later. North Carolina sues Murray for breach, and Murray defends by claiming his performance is excused because of GM's delay in delivering the transmissions and the EPA's issuance of the new regulations. What facts would you need to know to apply *Dunbar Molasses* to this case? Who should win? *See Alamance County Bd. of Educ. v. Bobby Murray Chevrolet, Inc.*, 121 N.C. App. 222 (1996).

b. In July 2001, Cantor Fitzgerald Securities leased office space in the World Trade Center from One World Trade Center LLC. Cantor agreed to a front-loaded rent agreement — a lease in which initial rental payments are higher than those near the end of the lease period — in anticipation of maintaining its office for several years. The parties included a standard *force majeure* clause in their lease. In September 2001, the office was destroyed during the September 11 terrorist attacks. Cantor conceded that the attacks fell within the scope of the *force majeure* clause, but contended that it should be allowed to recover the increased rent it paid during the initial months of the lease. Does Cantor have a valid claim? *See One World Trade Ctr. LLC v. Cantor Fitzgerald Sec.*, 789 N.Y.S.2d 652 (Sup. Ct. 2004). For a general discussion of the impact of terrorism on the doctrine of excuse, see Mark B. Baker, *"A Hard Rain's A-Gonna Fall" — Terrorism and Excused Contractual Performance in a Post September 11th World*, 17 Transnat'l Law. 1 (2004).

[2] The Modern Excuse of Commercial Impracticability

The second set of cases in this section explores the evolution of the traditional impossibility doctrine into the modern doctrine of commercial impracticability. Although the commercial impracticability doctrine is in principle more flexible because it allows excuse when performance becomes merely difficult or excessively costly, but not necessarily impossible, courts rarely grant excuse on this basis. On its surface, the doctrine often places emphasis on whether the contingency that has materialized was foreseeable.[12] Courts are less likely to grant excuse on the basis

---

[12] Section 261 of the Restatement (Second) excuses on the basis of commercial impracticability if the non-occurrence of an event was "a basic assumption on which the contract was made." The introductory note to Chapter 11 of the Restatement (Second) states that "Determining whether the non-occurrence

of foreseeable rather than unforeseeable contingencies. As you read the following cases, ask yourself whether the parties' agreement expressly or implicitly allocates the risk of the contingency that has materialized. Does it matter whether the risk was foreseeable? In this connection, it may be helpful to ask how the parties *would have* allocated the risk if they had considered it.

TRANSATLANTIC FINANCING CORP. v. UNITED STATES
United States Court of Appeals, District of Columbia Circuit
363 F.2d 312 (1966)

WRIGHT, J.

[The United States contracted with Transatlantic to carry a cargo of wheat from a United States Gulf port to Iran, but the contract did not specify the route to be taken. Shortly before the contract was executed, Egypt had nationalized the Suez Canal Company and taken over operation of the canal. After the contract was executed, Israel invaded Egypt, and Great Britain and France invaded the Suez Canal Zone. Egypt responded by closing the Suez Canal. This resulted in Transatlantic's voyage being substantially more expensive than anticipated. After routing the voyage around the Cape of Good Hope, they sued *in quantum meruit* to recover the added costs of the voyage.]

Transatlantic's claim is based on the following train of argument. The charter was a contract for a voyage from a Gulf port to Iran. Admiralty principles and practices, especially stemming from the doctrine of deviation, require us to imply into the contract the term that the voyage was to be performed by the "usual and customary" route. The usual and customary route from Texas to Iran was, at the time of contract, via Suez, so the contract was for a voyage from Texas to Iran via Suez. When Suez was closed this contract became impossible to perform. Consequently, appellant's argument continues, when Transatlantic delivered the cargo by going around the Cape of Good Hope, in compliance with the Government's demand under claim of right, it conferred a benefit upon the United States for which it should be paid in *quantum meruit.*

The doctrine of impossibility of performance has gradually been freed from the earlier fictional and unrealistic strictures of such tests as the "implied term" and the parties' "contemplation." Page, *The Development of the Doctrine of Impossibility of Performance,* 18 Mich. L. Rev. 589, 596 (1920). See generally 6 Corbin, *Contracts* 1320-1372 (rev. ed. 1962); 6 Williston, *Contracts* 1931-1979 (rev. ed. 1938). It is now recognized that "A thing is impossible in legal contemplation when it is not practicable; and a thing is impracticable when it can only be done at an excessive and unreasonable cost." Mineral Park Land Co. v. Howard, 172 Cal. 289, 293 (1916). The doctrine ultimately represents the ever-shifting line, drawn by courts hopefully responsive to commercial practices and mores, at which the community's interest in

---

of a particular event was or was not a basic assumption involves a judgment as to which party assumed the risk of its occurrence . . . . The fact that the event was unforeseeable is significant as suggesting that its non-occurrence was a basic assumption. However, the fact that it was foreseeable, or even foreseen, does not, of itself, argue for a contrary conclusion, since the parties may not have thought it sufficiently important a risk to have made it a subject of their bargaining."

having contracts enforced according to their terms is outweighed by the commercial senselessness of requiring performance. When the issue is raised, the court is asked to construct a condition of performance based on the changed circumstances, a process which involves at least three reasonably definable steps. First, a contingency — something unexpected — must have occurred. Second, the risk of the unexpected occurrence must not have been allocated either by agreement or by custom. Finally, occurrence of the contingency must have rendered performance commercially impracticable. Unless the court finds these three requirements satisfied, the plea of impossibility must fail.

The first requirement was met here. It seems reasonable, where no route is mentioned in a contract, to assume the parties expected performance by the usual and customary route at the time of contract. Since the usual and customary route from Texas to Iran at the time of contract was through Suez, closure of the Canal made impossible the expected method of performance. But this unexpected development raises rather than resolves the impossibility issue, which turns additionally on whether the risk of the contingency's occurrence had been allocated and, if not, whether performance by alternative routes was rendered impracticable.

Proof that the risk of a contingency's occurrence has been allocated may be expressed in or implied from the agreement. Such proof may also be found in the surrounding circumstances, including custom and usages of the trade. The contract in this case does not expressly condition performance upon availability of the Suez route. Nor does it specify "via Suez" or, on the other hand, "via Suez or Cape of Good Hope." Nor are there provisions in the contract from which we may properly imply that the continued availability of Suez was a condition of performance. Nor is there anything in custom or trade usage, or in the surrounding circumstances generally, which would support our constructing a condition of performance. The numerous cases requiring performance around the Cape when Suez was closed, see e.g., Ocean Tramp Tankers Corp. v. V/O Sovfracht (The Eugenia), (1964) 2 Q.B. 226, and cases cited therein, indicate that the Cape route is generally regarded as an alternative means of performance. So the implied expectation that the route would be via Suez is hardly adequate proof of an allocation to the promisee of the risk of closure. In some cases, even an express expectation may not amount to a condition of performance. The doctrine of deviation supports our assumption that parties normally expect performance by the usual and customary route, but it adds nothing beyond this that is probative of an allocation of the risk.

If anything, the circumstances surrounding this contract indicate that the risk of the Canal's closure may be deemed to have been allocated to Transatlantic. We know or may safely assume that the parties were aware, as were most commercial men with interests affected by the Suez situation, see *The Eugenia, supra,* that the Canal might become a dangerous area. No doubt the tension affected freight rates, and it is arguable that the risk of closure became part of the dickered terms. U.C.C. § 2-615, comment 8. We do not deem the risk of closure so allocated, however. Foreseeability or even recognition of a risk does not necessarily prove its allocation. Compare U.C.C. § 2-615, Comment 1; Restatement, Contracts 457 (1932). Parties to a contract are not always able to provide for all the possibilities of which they are aware, sometimes because they cannot agree, often simply because they are too busy. Moreover, that some abnormal risk was contemplated is probative but does not necessarily establish an allocation of the risk of the contingency which actually occurs. In this case, for example, nationalization by Egypt of the Canal Corporation and formation of the Suez Users Group did not necessarily indicate that the Canal would be blocked even if a confrontation resulted. The surrounding circumstances do indicate, however, a willingness by Transatlantic to assume abnormal risks, and this fact should legitimately cause us to judge the impracticability of performance by an alternative route in stricter terms than we would were the contingency unforeseen.

We turn then to the question whether occurrence of the contingency rendered performance commercially impracticable under the circumstances of this case. The goods shipped were not subject to harm from the longer, less temperate Southern route. The vessel and crew were fit to proceed around the Cape.[13] Transatlantic was no less able than the United States to purchase insurance to cover the contingency's occurrence. If anything, it is more reasonable to expect owner-operators of vessels to insure against the hazards of war. They are in the best position to calculate the cost of performance by alternative routes (and therefore to estimate the amount of insurance required), and are undoubtedly sensitive to international troubles which uniquely affect the demand for and cost of their services. The only factor operating here in appellant's favor is the added expense, allegedly $43,972.00 above and beyond the contract price of $305,842.92, of extending a 10,000 mile voyage by approximately 3,000 miles. While it may be an overstatement to say that increased cost and difficulty of performance never constitute impracticability, to justify relief there must be more of a variation between expected cost and the cost of performing by an available alternative than is present in this case, where the promisor can legitimately be presumed to have accepted some degree of abnormal risk, and where impracticability is urged on the basis of added expense alone.

We conclude, therefore, as have most other courts considering related issues arising out of the Suez closure, that performance of this contract was not rendered legally impossible. Even if we agreed with appellant, its theory of relief seems untenable. When performance of a contract is deemed impossible it is a nullity. In the case of a charter party involving carriage of goods, the carrier may return to an appropriate port and unload its cargo, The Malcolm Baxter, Jr., 277 U.S. 323 (1928), subject of course to required steps to minimize damages. If the performance rendered has value, recovery in quantum meruit for the entire performance is proper. But here Transatlantic has collected its contract price, and now seeks *quantum meruit* relief for the additional expense of the trip around the Cape. If the contract is a nullity, Transatlantic's theory of relief should have been *quantum meruit* for the entire trip, rather than only for the extra expense. Transatlantic attempts to take its profit on the contract, and then force the Government to absorb the cost of the additional voyage. When impracticability without fault occurs, the law seeks an equitable solution, see 6 Corbin, *supra*, 1321, and *quantum meruit* is

---

[13] [13] The issue of impracticability should no doubt be "an objective determination of whether the promise can reasonably be performed rather than a subjective inquiry into the promisor's capability of performing as agreed." Symposium, *The Uniform Commercial Code and Contract Law: Some Selected Problems*, 105 U. Pa. L. Rev. 836, 880, 887 (1957). Dealers should not be excused because of less than normal capabilities. But if both parties are aware of a dealer's limited capabilities, no objective determination would be complete without taking into account this fact.

one of its potent devices to achieve this end. There is no interest in casting the entire burden of commercial disaster on one party in order to preserve the other's profit. Apparently the contract price in this case was advantageous enough to deter appellant from taking a stance on damages consistent with its theory of liability. In any event, there is no basis for relief.

Affirmed.

NOTES

1. ***Foreseeability vs. Risk-Bearing Advantage.*** *Transatlantic Financing* reveals how difficult it is to apply the foreseeability test in a meaningful way. Can you explain the result in the case on the rationale that the contingency was foreseeable? If these events were foreseeable, then what kinds of events would justify excuse? Richard Posner and Andrew Rosenfield suggest altering the traditional foreseeability inquiry to avoid the complexities inherent in questions of foreseeability and causation. They believe that rather than attempting to determine whether the party pleading excuse *actually foresaw* the events or not (or, as a reasonable commercial party, should have foreseen the events), the court should ask which party could more cheaply have avoided or insured against the events.[14] The question, then, becomes one of comparative advantage in risk bearing rather than a speculative issue of whether the parties could have actually foreseen the events at the time of contract. Posner & Rosenfield, *Impossibility and Related Doctrines in Contract Law: An Economic Analysis*, 6 J. Legal Stud. 83 (1977). In *Transatlantic Financing*, the court holds that such a risk allocation is implicit. Recall the *Bowersock* case (Note 3, p. 735, *supra*), which excused the promisor from complete performance because the occurrence of an unforeseen contingency rendered completion impossible. Can that decision be justified using the Posner and Rosenfield analysis? Is the suggested analysis persuasive or do you perhaps believe that, in targeting a surrogate for foreseeability, the analysis focuses on the periphery of the issue rather than on the issue itself? What justification is there for asking which party was better able to bear a risk if the risk was reasonably unforeseeable? What effects, if any, would such a rule be likely to have on the behavior of future contracting parties? For a critique of Posner & Rosenfield's view, see John Elofson, *The Dilemma of Changed Circumstances in Contract Law: An Economic Analysis of the Foreseeability and Superior Risk Bearer Tests*, 30 Colum. J.L. & Soc. Probs. 1 (1996). For an argument for expanding the domain of the excuse doctrines based on the presumed inability of private actors to anticipate remote risks, see Melvin A. Eisenberg, *Impossibility, Impracticability, and Frustration*, 1 J. of Legal Analysis 207 (2009). For a critique of Eisenberg's analysis,

---

[14] "Posner and Rosenfield consider which party is the most efficient bearer of the risk of supervening events, that is, which party is best at foreseeing such events and which party can most cheaply insure against them. They then argue that courts should assign the risk to the most efficient risk bearer because this is the result the parties would usually reach on their own. Because the ability to predict and to insure often go hand in hand, the Posner-Rosenfield approach frequently will yield the same outcome as that yielded by asking the prediction question alone." Alan Schwartz & Robert E. Scott, Commercial Transactions: Principles and Policies 457 (2d ed. 1991).

see Victor Goldberg, *The Eisenberg Uncertainty Principle*, 2 J. LEGAL ANALYSIS 359 (2010).

2. *Pluralist Analyses of Commercial Impracticability.* We have already noted that efficiency analysis provides no guidance on how to implement the doctrine of commercial impracticability if future parties rationally ignore both remote risks and the legal rules courts use to allocate remote risks not expressly allocated by the parties to a contract. As we have seen, pluralist scholars argue that principles of fairness must therefore guide the doctrine. In Daniel T. Ostas & Frank P. Darr, *Understanding Commercial Impracticability: Tempering Efficiency with Community Fairness Norms*, 27 RUTGERS L.J. 343 (1996), the authors argue that both economic efficiency criteria and community fairness norms must be combined in a hybrid view of commercial impracticability that "tempers efficiency with fairness."

In a similar vein, Robert Hillman argues for a pluralist approach to commercial impracticability that takes fairness norms into account. In *An Analysis of the Cessation of Contractual Relations*, 68 CORNELL L. REV. 617 (1983), Hillman identifies four "fairness norms" that guide courts' determinations of whether one party to an agreement is entitled to cease performance under the doctrines of impossibility, impracticability, and frustration. In *Court Adjustment of Long-Term Contracts: An Analysis Under Modern Contract Law*, 1987 DUKE L.J. 1, Hillman argues that parties are:

> entitled to some form of relief in at least some situations, that these situations can be identified with sufficient precision, that courts have adequate tools to shape appropriate relief, and that court adjustment is good policy in limited, but distinct, circumstances . . . . I identify two situations in which court adjustment is appropriate. The first situation calling for adjustment, the "agreement model," occurs when the supplier reasonably expects the buyer to adjust in case of a serious disruption. The buyer's failure to adjust is a breach of contract. The agreement model accounts for the "relational" realities of many contract settings through a theory of the parties' implicit risk allocation. The second situation calling for adjustment, the "gap model," occurs when the supplier has no reasonable expectation of adjustment, but the parties simply fail to allocate the risk of some calamitous event. The supplier will suffer substantial harm from continued performance, but the buyer has materially relied on that performance. The gap model is based primarily on the fairness principle that the parties should agree to share unallocated losses.

Id. at 3.

Mary Jo Frug offered a feminist analysis of the scholarly debate on the impossibility doctrine in *Rescuing Impossibility Doctrine: A Postmodern Feminist Analysis of Contract Law*, 140 U. PA. L. REV. 1029 (1992). Because Posner and Rosenfeld focus on the singular objective of allocating the risk of impossibility to the superior risk-bearer, Frug argued that "the rhetoric and analytical characteristics of the Posner/Rosenfield position on impossibility doctrine are helpfully understood as stereotypically masculine, both in their strengths and in their weaknesses." *Id.* at 1032. She contrasted their view on the impossibility doctrine with Hillman's views. Frug claimed that because Hillman's theoretical approach to the impossibility doctrine "is characterized by a concern for multiple objectives, by an appreciation of contextualized relationships, and by a desire to achieve flexibility and sharing in the administration of contract remedies, his proposal neatly fits the popular interpretation of Carol Gilligan's depiction of the virtuous feminine attitudes toward justice." *Id.* at 1029, 1036.

Do you agree that the dispute between the singular analysis of Posner and Rosenfeld and Hillman's multi-factored analysis boils down to a contest between differently gendered perspectives, or is it possible to argue on objective grounds that one view is more defensible than the other? What would such "objective" grounds be?

3. ***Commercial Impracticability and Time for Performance: An Analogy with UCC § 2-315?*** In *Williamette Crushing Co. v. State by & Through DOT*, 932 P.2d 1350 (Ariz. Ct. App. 1997), a contractor agreed to complete a construction project for the state within the deadline set by the state in its request for bids. In order to complete the project on time, the contractor spent an additional $2.9 million. The contractor then sued the state to be reimbursed on the ground that performance by the deadline the state had set for the project was commercially impracticable. The contractor argued that he relied on the state's implicit claim that the job could be done using ordinary means within the deadline it had set. The court ruled against the contractor on the ground that the contractor knew of the deadline at the time he submitted his bid. Recall that under UCC § 2-315, the seller warrants that goods are fit for the seller's particular purpose if the buyer relies on the seller's skill and judgment in making the purchase. But the seller does not make this warranty if the buyer supplies the plans or designs for the goods (Chapter 7, Section C(1)(b), Note 6). Could you argue that the state should be treated like the buyer who submits plans to an expert seller? A buyer cannot claim a warranty of fitness for a particular purpose, even when the seller is an expert and aware of the buyer's particular purpose, if the buyer asks the seller to manufacture goods according to the buyer's specifications. Could you argue that, likewise, the state cannot claim it allocated the risk of extraordinary expenses for meeting the contractual deadline if it determined what a reasonable deadline would be, rather than asking the contractor to make that calculation?

4. ***Bankruptcy and Excuse.*** Although courts are reluctant to excuse performance under common law contract principles, federal bankruptcy law routinely excuses performance when one party is unable to perform due to insolvency. Bankruptcy law, then, is a mandatory implied term in every contract. Should courts be less inclined to excuse performance because the reliability of performance is already diminished by the existence of bankruptcy law? Or if bankruptcy law is a good idea, does that mean courts should be more favorably disposed to finding an excuse in contracts cases? For a discussion of the relationship between bankruptcy and excuse doctrine, see Robert A. Hillman, *Contract Excuse and Bankruptcy Discharge*, 43 STAN. L. REV. 99 (1990).

Is there an argument for excuse if enforcing a contract will cause a party to file for bankruptcy? In *Hoosier Energy Rural Elec. Co-op., Inc. v. John Hancock Life Ins. Co.*, 582 F.3d 721 (7th Cir. 2009), Judge Easterbrook rejected the argument that a party should be excused from performing its promise because enforcement would bankrupt the promisor:

> [T]he "impossibility" doctrine never justifies failure to make a payment, because financial distress differs from impossibility. See *Restatement (Second) of Contracts* § 261 & comment d . . . .

> The uranium case illustrates these propositions. Westinghouse sold uranium on long-term requirements contracts at fixed prices, thus assuming the risk that market prices would rise (and it would lose money). Westinghouse anticipated that market prices would fall; its customers thought they would rise, or at least wanted protection against higher prices. And rise they did, partly as a result of a cartel. Westinghouse had neglected to protect its position in futures markets or through long-term forward contracts. Faced with large losses if it had to buy uranium on the spot market and resell to customers at lower prices, Westinghouse contended that the unanticipated spike in uranium prices made its performance impossible. The argument failed; the court observed that Westinghouse and its customers had negotiated over the risk of higher prices for uranium, and that the occurrence of the risk did not excuse one side's performance. Even if the losses drove Westinghouse into bankruptcy, that would not make performance "impossible"; it would just assure that all of Westinghouse's creditors received equal treatment. See *In re Westinghouse Electric Corp. Uranium Contracts Litigation*, 563 F.2d 992 (10th Cir. 1977).

> Much the same can be said about Hoosier Energy. If keeping its promise to Ambac drives it into bankruptcy, this ensures equal treatment of its creditors. It is hard to see why Hoosier Energy should be able to stiff John Hancock or Ambac, while paying 100¢ on the dollar to all of its other trading partners, just because the very risk specified in the contracts between Hoosier Energy and John Hancock has occurred. Hoosier Energy did not expect an economic downturn, but Westinghouse did not expect an international uranium cartel. Downturns and cartels are types of things that happen, and against which contracts can be designed. When they do happen, the contractual risk allocation must be enforced rather than set aside. The district court called the credit crunch of 2008 a "once-in-a-century" event. That's an overstatement (the Great Depression occurred within the last 100 years, and the 20th Century also saw financial crunches in 1973 and 1987), and also irrelevant. An insurer that sells hurricane or flood insurance against a "once in a century" catastrophe, or earthquake insurance in a city that rarely experiences tremblors, can't refuse to pay on the ground that, when a natural event devastates a city, its very improbability makes the contract unenforceable.

Id. at 728.

6. *Military Contracts and Commercial Impracticability*. The United States often contracts with private military companies to perform a range of security services during conflicts. Clearly, war presents foreseeable risks that both parties can anticipate during contracting. But what if a risk materializes that neither contracting party anticipated, such as the loss of a key supply route due to geopolitical developments? What if the parties contract to use a supply route they believe to be secure, but a convoy delivering supplies is attacked and destroyed before it can make a delivery? Does the fact that the parties might have contemplated unforeseen developments in the conflict preclude an excuse of commercial impracticability under UCC § 2-615? Should it? On one hand, the government requires military supplies during conflicts and, in order to encourage necessary precautions, might prefer a strict interpretation of UCC §2-615 that prevents contractors from using an impracticability excuse. On the other hand, if contractors are held liable for unanticipated events, they may be less willing to contract with the government in the first place given the inevitability of unforeseen developments. For a discussion of this problem, see Jennifer S. Martin, *Adapting U.C.C. § 2-615 Excuse for Civilian-Military Contractors in Wartime*, 61 FLA. L. REV. 99 (2009).

7. *Problems.*

a. Paul has designed a very attractive toy airplane. To complete the plane, he needs to add a small and inexpensive computer to the plane and to the control module by which the plane is controlled from the ground. Paul has no computer experience, so he contacts Larry and explains to him precisely what the computer has to be able to do. Larry has designed and manufactured several small computers in the past. Larry contracts with Paul to deliver 7500 computers for $231,800. If the plane sells as Paul hopes, he expects to order a lot more computers.

Paul takes his prototype plane to a leading retail toy distributor. The toy distributor agrees to purchase 7000 planes at a price that will yield Paul a profit of $45 per plane over his costs. Delivery is to be at Thanksgiving, in time for the Christmas holiday buying season.

Reducing the computer to a size that will fit in the plane and yet not be destroyed during every landing has proved to be a problem for Larry. Larry writes to Paul: "I cannot perform as per the contract. There are basic engineering difficulties, and it would take between one and two years and cost a million to a million and a half dollars to overcome them, with success likely but not certain."

Has Larry breached the contract? *See United States v. Wegematic Corp.*, 360 F.2d 674 (2d Cir. 1966).

b. The plaintiff Mishara Construction Co. (Mishara) was the general contractor under contract with the Pittsfield Housing Authority for the construction of Rose Manor, a housing project for the elderly. In September 1966, the plaintiff negotiated with the defendant Transit-Mixed Concrete Corp. (Transit) for the supplying of ready-mixed concrete to be used on the project. An agreement was reached that Transit would supply all the concrete needed on the project at a price of $13.25 a cubic yard, with deliveries to be made at the times and in the amounts as ordered by Mishara. This agreement was evidenced by a purchase order signed by the parties on September 21, 1966. That purchase order identified the Rose Manor project and indicated that delivery was to be made "[a]s required by Mishara Construction Company." Performance under this contract was satisfactory to both parties until April, 1967. In that month a labor dispute disrupted work on the job site. Although work resumed on June 15, 1967, a picket line was maintained on the site until the completion of the project in 1969. Throughout this period, with very few exceptions, no deliveries of concrete were made by Transit notwithstanding frequent requests by Mishara. After notifying Transit of its intention, Mishara purchased the balance of its concrete requirements elsewhere. Mishara sought in damages the additional cost of concrete incurred by virtue of the higher price of the replacement product, as well as the expenses of locating an alternative source. Does the labor dispute excuse performance or are more facts needed to make this determination? *See Mishara Constr. Co. v. Transit-Mixed Concrete Corp.*, 365 Mass. 122, 310 N.E.2d 363 (1974).

EASTERN AIR LINES, INC. v. GULF OIL CORP.
United States District Court, Southern District of Florida
415 F. Supp. 429 (1975)

KING, J.

[Eastern Air Lines entered into a requirements contract for the purchase of fuel from Gulf Oil Corporation. When conditions changed such that the pricing formula the parties had agreed to no longer yielded a profit for Gulf Oil, they threatened to cut off Eastern's supply of fuel unless Eastern agreed to a price increase. Eastern filed a complaint, alleging breach of contract and requesting specific performance. Gulf replied, alleging that the contract was not a binding requirements contract and, furthermore performance was "commercially impracticable" within the meaning of UCC § 2-615. The court reviewed the contract, described in Chapter 4, Section B, and held that the requirements contract was enforceable, and that Eastern had not breached it. The court then addressed the § 2-615 issue.]

In short, for U.C.C. § 2-615 to apply there must be a failure of a pre-supposed condition, which was an underlying assumption of the contract, which failure was unforeseeable, and the risk of which was not specifically allocated to the complaining party. The burden of proving each element of claimed commercial impracticability is on the party claiming excuse. Ocean Air Tradeways, Inc. v. Arkay Realty Corp., 480 F.2d 1112, 1117 (9th Cir. 1973).

The modern U.C.C. § 2-615 doctrine of commercial impracticability has its roots in the common law doctrine of frustration or impossibility and finds its most recognized illustrations in the so-called "Suez Cases," arising out of the various closings of the Suez Canal and the consequent increases in shipping costs around the Cape of Good Hope. Those cases offered little encouragement to those who would wield the sword of commercial impracticability. As a leading British case arising out of the 1957 Suez closure declared, the unforeseen cost increase that would excuse performance "must be more than merely onerous or expensive. It must be positively unjust to hold the parties bound." Ocean Tramp Tankers v. V/O Sovfracht (The Eugenia), 2 Q.B. 226, 239 (1964) . . . .

Other recent American cases similarly strictly construe the doctrine of commercial impracticability. For example, one case found no U.C.C. defense, even though costs had doubled over the contract price, the court stating, "It may have been unprofitable for defendant to have supplied the pickers, but the evidence does not establish that it was impossible. A mere showing of unprofitability, without more, will not excuse the performance of a contract." Schafer v. Sunset Packing Co., 256 Or. 539 (1970).

Recently, the Seventh Circuit has stated: "The fact that performance has become economically burdensome or unattractive is not sufficient for performance to be excused. We will not allow a party to a contract to escape a bad bargain merely because it is burdensome." "(T)he buyer has a right to rely on the party to the contract to supply him with goods regardless of what happens to the market price. That is the purpose for which such contracts are made," Neal-Cooper Grain C. v. Texas Gulf Sulfur Co., 508 F.2d 283, 293, 294 (7th Cir. 1974).

Gulf's argument on commercial impracticability has two strings to its bow. First, Gulf contends that the escalator indicator does not work as intended by the parties by reason of the advent of so-called "two-tier" pricing under Phase IV government price controls. Second, Gulf alleges that crude oil prices have risen substantially without a concomitant rise in the escalation indicator, and, as a result, that performance of the contract has become commercially impracticable.

[The court held that Gulf had not satisfied the hardship requirement for excuse.]

But even if Gulf had established great hardship under U.C.C. § 2-615, which it has not, Gulf would not prevail because the events associated with the so-called energy crises were reasonably foreseeable at the time the contract was executed. If a contingency is foreseeable, it and its consequences are taken outside the scope of U.C.C. § 2-615, because the party disadvantaged by fruition of the contingency might have protected himself in his contract, Ellwood v. Nutex Oil Co., 148 S.W.2d 862 (Tex. Civ. App. 1941).

The record is replete with evidence as to the volatility of the Middle East situation, the arbitrary power of host governments to control the foreign oil market, and repeated interruptions and interference with the normal commercial trade in crude oil. Even without the extensive evidence present in the record, the court would be justified in taking judicial notice of the fact that oil has been used as a political weapon with increasing success by the oil-producing nations for many years, and Gulf was well aware of and assumed the risk that the OPEC nations would do exactly what they have done.

With respect to Gulf's argument that "two-tier" was not "foreseeable," the record shows that domestic crude oil prices were controlled at all material times, that Gulf foresaw that they might be de-controlled, and that Gulf was constantly urging to the Federal Government that they should be de-controlled. Government price regulations were confused, constantly changing, and uncertain during the period of the negotiation and execution of the contract. During that time frame, high ranking Gulf executives, including some of its trial witnesses, were in constant repeated contact with officials and agencies of the Federal Government regarding petroleum policies and were well able to protect themselves from any contingencies.

Even those outside the oil industry were aware of the possibilities. Eastern's principal contract negotiator advised his superior in recommending this contract to him:

While Gulf is apparently counting on crude price increases, such increases are a fact of life for the future, except as the government may inhibit by price controls, therefore all suppliers have such anticipation.

1975 is the year during which the full effect of energy shortages will be felt in the United States according to most estimates.

Knowing all the factors, Gulf drafted the contract and tied the escalation to certain specified domestic postings in Platt's. The court is of the view that it is bound thereby.

IV. *Remedy*

Having found and concluded that the contract is a valid one, should be enforced, and that no defenses have been established against it, there remains for consideration the proper remedy.

The Uniform Commercial Code provides that in an appropriate case specific performance may be decreed. This case is a particularly appropriate one for specific performance. The parties have been operating for more than a year pursuant to a preliminary injunction requiring specific performance of the contract and Gulf has stipulated that it is able to perform. Gulf presently supplies Eastern with 100,000,000 gallons of fuel annually or 10 percent of Eastern's total requirements. If Gulf ceases to supply this fuel, the result will be chaos and irreparable damage.

Under the U.C.C. a more liberal test in determining entitlement to specific performance has been established than the test one must meet for classic equitable relief. U.C.C. § 2-716(1); Kaiser Trading Co. v. Associated Metals & Minerals Corp., 321 F. Supp. 923, 932 (N.D. Cal. 1970), *appeal dismissed per curiam*, 443 F.2d 1364 (9th Cir. 1971).

It has previously been found and concluded that Eastern is entitled to Gulf's fuel at the prices agreed upon in the contract. In the circumstances, a decree of specific performance becomes the ordinary and natural relief rather than the extraordinary one. The parties are before the court, the issues are squarely framed, they have been clearly resolved in Eastern's favor, and it would be a vain, useless and potentially harmful exercise to declare that Eastern has a valid contract, but leave the parties to their own devices. Accordingly, the preliminary injunction heretofore entered is made a permanent injunction and the order of this court herein.

ALUMINUM CO. OF AMERICA v. ESSEX GROUP, INC.
United States District Court, W.D. Pennsylvania
499 F. Supp. 53 (1980)

[*See also* p. 710, *supra*.]

TEITELBAUM, J.

Plaintiff, Aluminum Company of America (ALCOA), brought the instant action against defendant, Essex Group, Inc. (Essex), in three counts. The first count requests the Court to reform or equitably adjust an agreement entitled the Molten Metal Agreement entered into between ALCOA and Essex.

ALCOA's first count seeks an equitable modification of the contract price for its services. The pleadings, arguments and briefs frame the issue in several forms. ALCOA seeks reformation or modification of the price on the basis of mutual mistake of fact, unilateral mistake of fact, unconscionability, frustration of purpose, and commercial impracticability.

A

[The facts of the case as reported by Judge Teitlebaum are provided with that portion of the opinion dealing with mutual mistake and reformation, see Section B[2], *supra*].

D

ALCOA argues that it is entitled to relief on the grounds of impracticability and frustration of purpose. The Court agrees.

The court must still consider those aspects of doctrines of frustration and impracticability which differ from the doctrine of mistake. In the Foreword to Tentative Draft No. 10 of the New Restatement, Professor Wechsler wrote, "Cases involving impracticability or frustration . . . involve mistake but to the extent that the focus is on hardships to the adversely affected party (they receive separate treatment)."

The focus of the doctrines of impracticability and of frustration is distinctly on hardship. Section [261] declares a party is discharged from performing a contract where a supervening event renders his performance impracticable. Comment d discusses the meaning of "impracticability." The comment states the word is taken from Uniform Commercial Code § 2-615(a). It declares that the word denotes an impediment to performance lying between "impossibility" and "impracticability."

Performance may be impracticable because *extreme and unreasonable difficulty, expense, injury, or loss to one of the parties will be involved* . . . .

A mere change in the degree of difficulty or expense due to such causes as increased wages, prices of raw materials, or costs of construction, unless well beyond the normal range, does not amount to impracticability since it is this sort of risk that a fixed-price contract is intended to cover. Restatement 2nd Contracts § [261] com. (d).

Similarly, § [265] declares a party is discharged from performing his contract where his principal purpose is *substantially* frustrated by the occurrence of a supervening event. The extent of the necessary frustration is further described in comment a: "(T)he frustration must be substantial. It is not enough that the transaction has become less profitable for the affected party or even that he will sustain a loss. The frustration must be so severe that it is not fairly to be regarded as within the risks that he assumed under the contract."

Professor Corbin explained this requirement of a severe disappointment by relating this doctrine to the broad public policies that parties should generally be required to perform their contracts.

> Variations in the value of a promised performance, caused by the constantly varying factors that affect the bargaining appetites of men, are the rule rather than the exception. Bargainers know this and swallow their losses and disappointments, meantime keeping their promises. Such being the business mores, court decisions that are not in harmony with them will not make for satisfaction or prosperity. Relief from duty, outside of the bankruptcy court, can safely be granted on the ground of frustration of purpose by the rise or fall of values, only when the variation in value is very great and is caused by a supervening event that was not in fact contemplated by the parties and the risk of which was not allocated by them. *Corbin on Contracts* § 1355.

This strict standard of severe disappointment is clearly met in the present case. ALCOA has sufficiently proved that it will lose well over $60 million dollars out of pocket over the life of the contract due to the extreme deviation of the WPI-IC from ALCOA's actual costs.[15]

Is this, then, a case of impracticability, of frustration, or both? The doctrine of impracticability and of frustration focus on different kinds of disappointment of a contracting party. Impracticability focuses on occurrences which greatly increase the costs, difficulty, or risk of the party's performance. Restatement 2d of Contracts § [261].

The doctrine of frustration, on the other hand, focuses on a party's severe disappointment which is caused by circumstances which frustrate his principal purpose for entering the contract. Restatement 2d of Contracts § [265]. The doctrine of frustration often applies to relieve a party of a contract which could be performed without impediment; relief is allowed because the performance would be of little value to the frustrated party . . . .

In the present case ALCOA has satisfied the requirements of both doctrines. The impracticability of its performance is clear. The increase in its cost of performance is severe enough to warrant relief, and the other elements necessary for the granting of relief have been proven. Essex argues that the causes of ALCOA's losses are due to market price increases to which the doctrine of impracticability does not apply. The doctrine of impracticability of the new Restatement is one of recent evolution in the law. The first Restatement used the term as part of the definition of "impossibility." The interesting legal evolution from the strict standards of impossibility, evident at least by dictum in Parradine v. Jane, Aleyn, 26 (1647, K.B.), to modern standards of impracticability is traced in Professor Gilmore's *The Death*

---

[15] [15] The Court recognizes the additional requirement that the frustration or impracticability must not be the fault of the party who seeks relief. Restatement 2d of Contracts §§ [261, 265]. Essex has not claimed or shown that ALCOA's dealings during the contract caused or contributed to ALCOA's losses. The record sufficiently proves that the great cost increases of some of the non-labor cost components (power, electrolytes, carbon) were beyond ALCOA's control. This distinguishes the present case from Iowa Elec. Light & Power Co. v. Atlas Corp., 467 F. Supp. 129 (N.D. Iowa 1978) where the court concluded that it was not clear that Atlas, an uranium supplier, could not have protected itself contractually from some of the risk which caused its loss.

of Contract 35-90 (1974). The drafters of the Uniform Commercial Code adopted this line of development, particularly in § 2-615. The new Restatement expressly draws upon § 2-615 in defining the scope of the doctrine. § [261] comments reporter's notes. The official comment to § 2-615 lends strength to Essex's claim.

> 1. This section excuses a seller from timely delivery of goods contracted for, where his performance has become commercially impracticable because of unforeseen supervening circumstances not within the contemplation of the parties at the time of contracting.

However,

> 4. Increased cost alone does not excuse performance unless the rise in cost is due to some unforeseen contingency which alters the essential nature of the performance. Neither is a rise or a collapse in the market in itself a justification, for that is exactly the type of business risk which business contracts made at fixed prices are intended to cover. But a severe shortage of raw materials or of supplies due to a contingency such as war, embargo, local crop failure, unforeseen shutdown of major sources of supply or the like, which either causes a marked increase in cost or altogether prevents the seller from securing supplies necessary to his performance is within the contemplation of this section.

Several of the cases cited by Essex rely on comment 4 in denying claims for relief. Each is distinguishable from the present case in the absolute extent of the loss and in the proportion of loss involved . . . .

If it were important to the decision of this case, the Court would hold that the foreseeability of a variation between the WPI-IC and ALCOA's costs would not preclude relief under the doctrine of impracticability. But the need for such a holding is not clear, for the Court has found that the risk of a wide variation between these values was unforeseeable in a commercial sense and was not allocated to ALCOA in the contract.

The Court holds that ALCOA is entitled to relief under the doctrine of impracticability. The cases Essex relies on and the other cases discovered by the Court are all distinguishable with respect to the gravity of harm which the aggrieved contracting party was liable to suffer. Except for Transatlantic Financing, they are also distinguishable with respect to the question of allocation of the risk, inferred from the circumstances known to the parties at the time of the contract and from the contract terms . . . .

[The court found actionable Alcoa's frustration of purpose claim. It then addressed the problem of fashioning an appropriate remedy. The part of the opinion discussing the remedy is included in the portion of the *Alcoa* opinion reprinted in Part B, section 2 of this chapter on Mutual Mistake and Reformation]

NOTES

1. **Eastern Air Lines and *Force Majeure*.** The contract in the *Eastern Air Lines* case contained a broad exculpatory or "force majeure" clause. Such clauses, as the court noted, are becoming increasingly common. The effect of a force

majeure clause is to shift risks that would ordinarily fall on the party whose performance is adversely affected in circumstances where the event is beyond the performers' effective control. Since most people believe that an important objective of commercial law is to give statutory form to clauses which are in common use (and thereby to reduce transaction costs to the parties), perhaps other states should follow the lead of the Mississippi legislature and adopt the following as § 2-617:

> Force Majeure. Deliveries may be suspended by either party in case of Act of God, war, riots, fire, explosion, flood, strike, lockout, injunction, inability to obtain fuel, power, raw materials, labor, containers, or transportation facilities, accident, breakage of machinery or apparatus, national defense requirements, or any cause beyond the control of such party, preventing the manufacture, shipment, acceptance, or consumption of a shipment of the goods or of a material upon which the manufacture of the goods is dependent. If, because of any such circumstance, seller is unable to supply the total demand for the goods, seller may allocate its available supply among itself and all of its customers, including those not under contract, in an equitable manner. Such deliveries so suspended shall be canceled without liability, but the contract shall otherwise remain unaffected.

Miss. Code Ann. § 75-2-617 (1972).

2. Alcoa *and Impracticability*. In holding that impracticability requires a dramatic adverse effect on the party seeking relief, the court in *Alcoa* quotes Corbin: "A party is excused on the basis of impracticability 'only when the variation in value is very great and is caused by a supervening event that was not in fact contemplated by the parties and the risk of which was not allocated by them.'" Corbin's statement implicitly acknowledges that the risk of some unforeseeable, supervening events might nonetheless be allocated by the parties. How could this be so? Just as the Restatement insists that the non-occurrence of an event can be a basic assumption of the parties' agreement even though the parties never consciously considered the assumption, could the parties have allocated this risk to one of the parties as a basic assumption of their agreement, even if they had never consciously considered the risk?

3. *"Gross Inequity" Clauses: Opting into a Duty to Adjust*. Suppose that an electric utility company and a coal company enter into a 15-year coal supply contract which contains the following "gross inequity clause":

> It is the intent of the parties hereto that this Agreement, as a whole and in all of its parts, shall be equitable to both parties throughout its term. The parties recognize that omissions or defects in this Agreement beyond the control of the parties or not apparent at the time of its execution may create inequities or hardship during the term of the Agreement, and further, that supervening conditions, circumstances or events beyond the reasonable and practicable control of the parties may from time to time give rise to inequities which impose economic or other hardships upon one or both of the parties.

> In the event an inequitable condition occurs which adversely affects one party, it shall be the joint and equal responsibility of both parties to act

promptly to determine the action required to cure the inequity and effectively to implement such action. Upon written claim of inequity served by one party upon the other, the parties shall act jointly to reach an agreement concerning the claimed inequity within sixty (60) days of the date of such written claim. The party claiming inequity shall include in its claim such information and data as may be reasonably necessary to substantiate the claim and shall freely and without delay furnish such other information and data as the other party reasonably may deem relevant and necessary.

In addition, the parties set a "base price" of $20 per ton for all coal delivered under the agreement that is to be adjusted under an "adjustment clause" that indexes the price to changes in variables specified in the United States Department of Labor statistical indices, royalty rates, labor costs, and taxes.

Suppose that half way through the term of the agreement, the price adjustment formula raises the contract price to $34 per ton even though the average market price for coal at that time remains at the contract base price of $20 per ton. Does the "gross inequity clause" entitle the electric utility company to demand that the price be significantly lowered? On these facts, the court in *Beaver Creek Coal Co. v. Nevada Power Co.*, 1992 U.S. App. LEXIS 13505 (10th Cir. May 27, 1992), answered in the negative:

Our reading of the contract as a whole convinces us that the parties did not intend for [the gross inequity clause] to address claims of inequity resulting merely from a disparity between market and contract price such as developed here . . . . We reach this decision in part on the basis of the base price adjustment provisions . . . . The contract language indicates that the parties intended to tie the price to variables other than the market price. We agree . . . that the contract does not indicate that the parties intended the contract price to approximate the market price or to track its production costs. Some other mechanism designed to determine the actual market price of coal and to track Beaver Creek's production costs could have been fashioned to do that. Furthermore, the contract contained no price-reopener provision. We would effectively rewrite the price formula in the contract if we interpreted the language to mean that one party was free to reopen price negotiations through the [gross inequity] clause because the contract price did not track the market price.

Id. at *9–*10.

Do you find the court's analysis persuasive? If the parties had omitted the price adjustment term, would the court have applied the gross inequity clause to adjust the price? Does the plain meaning of the clause argue in favor or against adjustment? How could you have better drafted the gross inequity clause if your client intended it to provide grounds for adjusting the price? Is this case consistent with *Alcoa*? The court distinguished *Alcoa* on the ground that it was based on mutual mistake, and then rejected the reasoning of *Alcoa*, echoing the concern of other courts that under the logic of *Alcoa*, "there would be no predictability or certainty for contracting parties who selected a future variable to measure their contract liability." *Id.* at *14 (quoting *Printing Industries Asso. v. International*

Printing & Graphic Communications Union, Local No. 56, 584 F. Supp. 990, 998 (N.D. Ohio 1984) (quoting *Wabash, Inc. v. Avnet, Inc.*, 516 F. Supp. 995, 999 n.6 (N.D. Ill. 1981)).

4. ***Uranium Markets and the*** **Westinghouse** ***Cases.*** Assume you represent one of the parties in settlement negotiations in the following case (most of the cases from which this summary was taken were eventually settled). How would you argue your case? What information would you like to have to buttress your theory of causation?

Uranium markets were sufficiently unstable in the early 1970s to produce a large group of excuse cases known collectively as the *Westinghouse* cases. Westinghouse and General Electric were in the business of designing, building, and licensing the 31 nuclear reactors that came on-line in the mid 1970s. To get ahead of the competition, Westinghouse also served as a buying agent for the power companies, signing long-term supply contracts for "yellowcake," the processed uranium products. It became apparent in 1975 that Westinghouse had come up short in its obligations; that is, Westinghouse had contracted to supply more yellowcake than it had purchased from mining companies or mined from its own supplies. As it turned out, Westinghouse was significantly short: 40,000 tons for the period 1975–1978, while the world's capacity for producing yellowcake stood at only 13,000 tons per year. The problem was perhaps exacerbated by the fact that Westinghouse had, in some sense, cornered the market, so that smaller buying agents had keyed their prices and supply projections to those of Westinghouse. In a short time, the price of yellowcake rose precipitously, from $8–10 per pound in early 1974 to $35 per pound in December 1975, when Westinghouse announced its short position. The price rise would have subjected Westinghouse to a loss of approximately $2 billion if all its contracts were enforced. The Westinghouse announcement came in the form of a legalistic memorandum to its obligees, claiming excuse under UCC § 2-615 due to the significant, "unforeseen" increase in all energy prices precipitated by the oil price shock of 1973. In addition to the above explanation of the "incredible" price rise, a number of alternative rationales have been offered:

(a) The OPEC cartel caused oil prices to rise radically. Since oil is a substitute for uranium, the rise in oil prices could have induced users of energy to switch to uranium, which in turn could have forced up uranium prices.

(b) It takes almost 10 years to build a nuclear reactor. Since the uranium price rise occurred in much less time than that, any major increase in demand must have come from an expansion in the output of existing plants.

(c) The Atomic Energy Commission ("AEC"), in late 1972, required uranium for use in nuclear power plants to be richer than it previously had been. This requirement increased demand for uranium ore because it requires more ore to produce the higher grade final product. In addition, increases in the cost of reprocessing used fuel, together with increased objections to current reprocessing techniques from environmental groups, caused the availability of reprocessed uranium as fuel to decline. This too increased demand for uranium ore. Nevertheless, expected nuclear generating capacity had declined since 1970 as the result of a lessened expected demand for electricity, increased costs of nuclear construction, construction delays, and financing difficulties. In fact, the AEC's projections of expected United States uranium requirements in the 1970s and 1980s have been reduced since the first successful exercise of OPEC power.

(d) The demand projections for uranium made in 1972–1973 for 1979–1980 assumed a future commitment by the suppliers of uranium to expand output. This inconsistency between projected supply and demand was noted by some observers in the industry in early 1973. Such an inconsistency can be expected to cause higher prices, at least until output expands.

(e) Prices were forced up by domestic and foreign cartels among the suppliers. (No direct proof of a domestic cartel exists as yet, but there is evidence that some cartelization by foreign producers were assisted by their governments — e.g., Canada.) The top eight firms in the industry control 78.5 % of the market, a figure higher than that of industries regarded as vigorously competitive but lower than that of industries regarded as tightly oligopolistic. Between 1969–1975 many major suppliers suffered losses.[16]

5. *Impracticability and Relational Contracts. Eastern Air Lines* and *Alcoa* involved contracts that were regretted by one party largely because of a sharp rise in oil prices due to a major oil embargo. Both involved long-term contracts governing business relationships spanning several decades. In *Eastern Air Lines*, the court was unwilling to imply an excuse of impracticability because "the events associated with the so-called energy crises were reasonably foreseeable at the time the contract was executed." The *Alcoa* court, however, excused performance because the same events caused an extreme increase in the cost of performance "severe enough to warrant relief." Do you see a way easily to determine what costs are "severe enough" to be considered impracticable? After these decisions, will contracting parties worry about court intervention in their contracts whenever unforeseen events occur? If so, what effect will this rule have on ex ante risk allocation? Will such uncertainty in the legal outcome result in an increase in opportunistic behavior during the contract's performance?

This problem becomes especially significant when dealing with long-term contracts, where circumstances have the opportunity to change dramatically over the life of the contract. Why then do parties make relational contracts, knowing that in a long-term relationship there will be unforeseen contingencies that may cause them to regret the contract and even induce opportunistic behavior by the other party? Why do parties choose to do business with long-term contracts as opposed to a series of one-time agreements, a joint venture, or vertical integration?

Donald Smythe, in *Bounded Rationality, the Doctrine of Impracticability, and the Governance of Relational Contracts*, 13 S. CAL. INTERDISC. L.J. 227 (2004), notes that companies form relational contracts when the governing cost of transacting through a long-term contract will be less than by any other means. He argues that:

---

[16] *See* Paul Joskow, *Commercial Impossibility, the Uranium Market and the* Westinghouse *Case*, 6 J. LEGAL STUD. 119 (1977).

[E]conomic agents are inevitably characterized by both bounded rationality and opportunism. Because they are boundedly rational, the parties must leave larger gaps in a relational contract as the environment becomes more uncertain. This places a greater onus on subsequent adaptations of the agreement. The likelihood that one of the parties will behave opportunistically, however, and refuse to cooperate in adapting the agreement will rise as the degree of uncertainty rises. Thus, a cloud hangs over the transaction, growing larger as the environment becomes more uncertain. At some point, one of the parties will prefer to organize the transaction internally, so as to eliminate the risk of disruptions and other inefficiencies caused by the possibility of the other's opportunism.

. . . One can infer that as the degree of uncertainty and discount rates rise, the governance costs of a relational contract also rise. This should make the alternatives to relational contracting, particularly the integration of the transaction within an administrative hierarchy, relatively more attractive.

Most importantly, the analysis also suggests an important linkage to the law of contracts. It implies that any legal doctrine that helps to reduce the uncertainties surrounding a transaction may also help to reduce the governance costs of a relational contract. Thus, legal doctrines may have important consequences for the manner in which transactions are organized more generally. A transaction will normally only be conducted through a relational contract if there is no other mode of organization with lower governance costs. If legal doctrines help to lower the governance costs of relational contracts, firms will be less likely to organize transactions internally. At the margin, the volume of transactions conducted through relational contracts will be greater, and the volume conducted through internal organization will be smaller. The legal environment may thus have subtle, though important and pervasive, consequences for the way in which an economy is organized overall.

Id. at 242–49. If Smythe's argument is correct, how would you structure a rule for excusing performance based on impracticability? Would your rule differ according to the type of transaction or contract involved?

Essay: Unforeseeability and the Limits of Economic Analysis

Unforeseeability, commercial impracticability, and excuse have received considerable academic attention in recent years for three reasons. First, the unpredictable price fluctuations of the 1970s significantly increased the frequency with which claims of commercial impracticability were pressed. The excuse doctrine has been invoked much more often than other grounds for relief because of market fluctuations that were historically without precedent and therefore caught contracting parties by surprise. As inflation appears to be endemic in modern economies, academics and contracting parties have sought to create contractual methods to deal with the problems brought on by inflation. Second, the cases in which such claims were made often involved large transactions in expensive raw materials; thus the claims were of a "high stakes" variety. Third, the very nature of unforeseeable contingencies has raised the possibility of legal remedies, such as cost-splitting between parties, not often employed in contract law.[17] Truly unforeseeable problems may be a unique area of contract law. One might argue that since courts are unable to create incentives for future parties to minimize unforeseeable losses, courts should be free to consider a "fair" allocation of the loss.[18]

The principal theoretical basis for the law of excuse, then, is that some risks are unforeseeable and therefore cannot be allocated by the parties at the time of formation. Given this premise, some scholars have argued that "loss sharing" is the proper resolution when the contingencies that materialize are unforeseeable. These theorists argue that this remedy is warranted here because of the peculiar nature of unforeseeable events. If the event at issue was, as a practical matter, unforeseeable when the contract was made, the argument goes, then the parties could not have made contingency plans no matter what degree of prescience they exercised. And in future similar contracting situations, the parties would again not make contingency plans for the event. Excuse would be appropriate, on this view, only if a risk that materializes is unforeseeable at the time of contract. If it was unforeseeable, then neither party could have been paid to bear it. Therefore, neither party should be made to bear it alone. Thus, according to this analysis, once an appropriate case for excuse is identified, a focus on behavioral incentives becomes irrelevant, and fairness between the parties becomes the paramount concern. The key issue then becomes how the losses should be divided. For example, should the costs be split 50-50, or can the court instead devise some ratio that reflects the parties' relative responsibilities in bearing materialized risks, particularly if multiple causes are involved?

The questions in dividing losses are formidable, and it would be preferable if the parties could be induced to agree to a redistribution themselves. At least one author has urged courts to force the parties to reach an after-the-fact agreement on their own. Richard E. Speidel, *Excusable Nonperformance in Sales Contracts: Some Thoughts About Risk Management*, 32 S.C. L. Rev. 241 (1980). As the *Alcoa* court itself noted, there are considerable historical and institutional barriers to the judicial imposition of wide-ranging contractual solutions. Interestingly, Alcoa and Essex mutually agreed to modify the agreement after they saw the remedy devised by the court. What incentive would both parties have in coming to an agreement after the decision has been handed down? Perhaps courts ought to devise solutions that are unappealing to both parties in order to force them to reach an agreement on their own.

There are several problems, however, with judicially imposed adjustments of long-term contracts. In the first place, the prospect of being able to persuade a court to adjust terms *ex post* offers an unfortunate temptation to parties who have

---

[17] By "cost-splitting" we are referring to the type of solution derived in *Alcoa, e.g.*, a judicially imposed reallocation of the contractual pie in the event of an unforeseen price change of great magnitude. For example, a court might, as the *Alcoa* court did, specify that if a price rise of X occurs in a fixed-price contract, the seller is to recoup the amount $12X$ (or $13X$ or $14X$ depending on how the court wishes to allocate the cost) from the buyer. In this manner, the court splits the seller's costs (or, looked at from the other perspective, splits the buyer's gains).

[18] For a discussion of the division of gains and losses on the basis of a model of "just desserts," see Alan Schwartz, *Sales Law and Inflation*, 50 S. Cal. L. Rev. 1 (1976).

come to regret the *ex ante* allocation of risks. Thus, parties may exploit the uncertainty of the excuse and adjustment rules and opportunistically renegotiate their deals. In addition, there is good reason to believe that the parties to long-term contracts develop *informal* patterns of cooperative adjustment on their own, without recourse to legal rules. These actions are enforced by a norm of conditional cooperation (or tit-for-tat). Maintaining this cooperative "equilibrium" requires each party to "punish" the other for defecting from the cooperative norm, but then to resume the cooperative behavior thereafter. If self-enforcement based on reciprocity does, in fact, emerge over time, the effect of judicially implied adjustment may be to unwittingly upset the delicate balance between the parties and "crowd out" the cooperative behavior. For an elaboration of this argument, see Robert E. Scott, *Conflict and Cooperation in Long-Term Contracts*, 75 CAL. L. REV. 2005 (1987); and Robert E. Scott, *A Theory of Self-Enforcing Indefinite Agreements*, 103 COLUM. L. REV. 1641 (2003).

A more fundamental objection to the current law of excuse, however, rejects the basic premise that parties cannot allocate unforeseeable risks. In *Contractual Allocations of Unknown Risks: A Critique of the Doctrine of Commercial Impracticability*, 42 U. Toronto L. J. 450 (1992), George G. Triantis "challenges the assumption that contracting parties are unable rationally to manage and allocate risks of unanticipated events":

> While an unknown risk cannot be priced and allocated specifically, it can be priced and allocated as part of the package of a more broadly framed risk. For example, consider a party who agrees to transport a shipment of goods for a fixed fee. The risk of a nuclear accident in the Middle East that causes a dramatic decrease in the production of oil and a consequent increase in its price might not be foreseen. As a result, this risk cannot be allocated explicitly in the contract. However, the broader risk of a large increase in the price of oil for any reason can be. Therefore, there is no gap to be filled by the doctrine of impracticability: the risk of nuclear accident, though unforeseen, is allocated implicitly. Instead, the doctrine alters the contractual allocation of the risk and its proponents must advance a rationale for the reallocation.

Id. at 452.

Even though parties can in principle allocate all remote risks, however, it may not be cost-effective for them to do so. In such cases, Triantis would allow courts to allocate these risks *ex post*, provided they do so in a predictable manner. *See* GEORGE G. TRIANTIS, *Unforeseen Contingencies, Risk Allocation in Contracts, in* THE ENCYCLOPEDIA OF LAW AND ECONOMICS 4500 (1998).

D. FRUSTRATION OF PURPOSE

As we have seen, the doctrine of commercial impracticability works to excuse the duties of a party who is obligated to perform specified acts under a contract (e.g., to manufacture and deliver custom goods or to perform stipulated services). But changed circumstances can also disappoint the contractual expectations of the party whose only obligation under the contract is to pay for the performance in question.

Thus, for example, the buyer of specially manufactured electronic parts will be reluctant to complete the deal if, before the seller's performance, a technological advance makes the finished product obsolete. Ordinarily, we would assume that the buyer (who, after all, enjoys the comparative advantage) would bear the risks of his disappointed expectations. Sometimes, however, purchasers of goods or services are able to plead excuse successfully on the grounds of commercial frustration. This raises questions of the following sort: Do the same variables that lead courts to excuse performance on the grounds of impossibility operate in frustration cases as well? If so, will there be similar problems in sorting legitimate claims of excuse from strategic ones? Consider, for example, the following cases.

KRELL v. HENRY
Court of Appeal
2 K.B. 740 (1903)

Appeal from a decision of DARLING J.

The plaintiff, Paul Krell, sued the defendant, C. S. Henry, for 50£, being the balance of a sum of 75£, for which the defendant had agreed to hire a flat at 56A, Pall Mall on the days of June 26 and 27, for the purpose of viewing the processions to be held in connection with the coronation of His Majesty. The defendant denied his liability, and counter-claimed for the return of the sum of 25£, which had been paid as a deposit, on the ground that, the processions not having taken place owing to the serious illness of the King, there had been a total failure of consideration for the contract entered into by him . . . .

Darling J., on August 11, 1902, held, upon the authority of Taylor v. Caldwell and *The Moorcock*, that there was an implied condition in the contract that the procession should take place, and gave judgment for the defendant on the claim and counter-claim.

The plaintiff appealed . . . .

Aug. 11. Vaughan William L. J. read the following written judgment: The real question in this case is the extent of the application in English law of the principle of the Roman law which has been adopted and acted on in many English decisions, and notably in the case of Taylor v. Caldwell . . . . That case at least makes it clear that "where, from the nature of the contract, it appears that the parties must from the beginning have known that it could not be fulfilled unless, when the time for the fulfillment of the contract arrived, some particular specified thing continued to exist, so that when entering into the contract they must have contemplated such continued existence as the foundation of what was to be done; there, in the absence of any express or implied warranty that the thing shall exist, the contract is not to be considered a positive contract, but as subject to an implied condition that the parties shall be excused in case, before breach, performance becomes impossible from the perishing of the thing without default of the contractor."

Thus far it is clear that the principle of the Roman law has been introduced into the English law. The doubt in the present case arises as to how far this principle extends. The Roman law dealt with *obligationes de certo corpore*. Whatever may have been the limits of the Roman law, the case of Nickoll v. Ashton makes it plain that the English law applies the principle not only to cases where the performance of the contract becomes impossible by the cessation of existence of the thing which is the subject-matter of the contract, but also to cases where the event which renders the contract incapable of performance is the cessation or non-existence of an express condition or state of things, going to the root of the contract, and essential to its performance. It is said, on the one side, that the specified thing, state of things, or condition the continued existence of which is necessary for the fulfillment of the contract, so that the parties entering into the contract must have contemplated the continued existence of that thing, condition, or state of things as the foundation of what was to be done under the contract, is limited to things which are either the subject-matter of the contract or a condition or state of things, present or anticipated, which is expressly mentioned in the contract. But, on the other side, it is said that the condition or state of things need not be expressly specified, but that it is sufficient if that condition or state of things clearly appears by extrinsic evidence to have been assumed by the parties to be the foundation or basis of the contract, and the event which causes the impossibility is of such a character that it cannot reasonably be supposed to have been in the contemplation of the contracting parties when the contract was made. In such a case the contracting parties will not be held bound by the general words which, though large enough to include, were not used with reference to a possibility of a particular event rendering performance of the contract impossible.

I do not think that the principle of the civil law as introduced into the English law is limited to cases in which the event causing the impossibility of performance is the destruction or non-existence of some thing which is the subject-matter of the contract or of some condition or state of things expressly specified as a condition of it. I think that you first have to ascertain, not necessarily from the terms of the contract, but, if required, from necessary inferences, drawn from surrounding circumstances recognized by both contracting parties, what is the substance of the contract, and then to ask the question whether that substantial contract needs for its foundation the assumption of the existence of a particular state of things. If it does, this will limit the operation of the general words, and in such case, if the contract becomes impossible of performance by reason of the non-existence of the state of things assumed by both contracting parties as the foundation of the contract, there will be no breach of the contract thus limited.

Now what are the facts of the present case? The contract is contained in two letters of June 20 which passed between the defendant and the plaintiff's agent, Mr. Cecil Bisgood. These letters do not mention the coronation, but speak merely of the taking of Mr. Krell's chambers, or, rather, of the use of them, in the daytime of June 26 and 27, for the sum of 75£, 25£, then paid, balance 50£ to be paid on the 24th. But the affidavits, which by agreement between the parties are to be taken as stating the facts of the case, shew that the plaintiff exhibited on his premises, third floor, 56A, Pall Mall, an announcement to the effect that windows to view the Royal coronation procession were to be let, and that the defendant was induced by that announcement to apply to the housekeeper on the premises, who said that the owner was willing to let the suite of rooms for the purpose of seeing the Royal procession for both days, but not nights, of June 26 and 27.

In my judgment the use of the rooms was let and taken for the purpose of seeing the Royal procession. It was not a demise of the rooms, or even an agreement to let and take the rooms. It is a license to use rooms for a particular purpose and none other. And in my judgment the taking place of those processions on the days proclaimed along the proclaimed route, which passed 56A, Pall Mall, was regarded by both contracting parties as the foundation of the contract; and I think that it cannot reasonably be supposed to have been in the contemplation of the contracting parties, when the contract was made, that the coronation would not be held on the proclaimed days, or the processions not take place on those days along the proclaimed route; and I think that the words imposing on the defendant the obligation to accept and pay for the use of the rooms for the named days, although general and unconditional, were not used with reference to the possibility of the particular contingency which afterwards occurred . . . .

Each case must be judged by its own circumstances. In each case one must ask oneself, first, what, having regard to all the circumstances, was the foundation of the contract? Secondly, was the performance of the contract prevented? Thirdly, was the event which prevented the performance of the contract of such a character that it cannot reasonably be said to have been in the contemplation of the parties at the date of the contract? (as I think they should be in this case), I think both parties are discharged from further performance of the contract. I think that the coronation procession was the foundation of this contract, and that the non-happening of it prevented the performance of the contract; and, secondly, I think that the non-happening of the procession, to use the words of Sir James Hannen in Baily v. De Crespigny, was an event "of such a character that it cannot reasonably be supposed to have been in the contemplation of the contracting parties when the contract was made, and that they are not to be held bound by general words which, though large enough to include, were not used with reference to the possibility of the particular contingency which afterwards happened."

The test seems to be whether the event which causes the impossibility was or might have been anticipated and guarded against. It seems difficult to say, in a case where both parties anticipate the happening of an event, which anticipation is the foundation of the contract, that either party must be taken to have anticipated, and ought to have guarded against, the event which prevented the performance of the contract . . . .

I wish to observe that cases of this sort are very different from cases where a contract or warranty or representation is implied, such as was implied in *The Moorcock*, and refused to be implied in Hamlyn v. Wood. But *The Moorcock* is of importance in the present case as shewing that whatever is the suggested implication — be it condition, as in this case, or warranty or representation — one must, in judging whether the implication ought to be made, look not only at the words of the contract, but also at the surrounding facts and the knowledge of the parties of those facts. There seems to me to be ample authority for this proposition. Thus in Jackson v. Union Marine Insurance Co., in the Common Pleas, the question whether the object of the voyage had been frustrated by the delay of the ship was left as a question of fact to the jury, although there was nothing in the charter party defining the time within which the charterers were to supply the cargo of iron rails for San Francisco, and nothing on the face of the charterparty to indicate the importance of time in the venture; and that was a case in which, as Bramwell B. points out in his judgment at p. 148, Taylor v. Caldwell was a strong authority to support the conclusion arrived at in the judgment — that the ship not arriving in time for the voyage contemplated, but at such time as to frustrate the commercial venture, was not only a breach of the contract but discharged the charterer, though he had such an excuse that no action would lie . . . .

I myself am clearly of opinion that in this case, where we have to ask ourselves whether the object of the contract was frustrated by the non-happening of the coronation and its procession on the days proclaimed, parol evidence is admissible to shew that the subject of the contract was rooms to view the coronation procession, and was so to the knowledge of both parties. When once this is established, I see no difficulty whatever in the case. It is not essential to the application of the principle of Taylor v. Caldwell that the direct subject of the contract should perish or fail to be in existence at the date of performance of the contract. It is sufficient if a state of things or condition expressed in the contract and essential to its performance perishes or fails to be in existence at that time. In the present case the condition which fails and prevents the achievement of that which was, in the contemplation of both parties, the foundation of the contract, is not expressly mentioned either as a condition of the contract or the purpose of it; but I think for the reasons which I have given that the principle of Taylor v. Caldwell ought to be applied. This disposes of the plaintiff's claim for 50£ unpaid balance of the price agreed to be paid for the use of the rooms.

The defendant at one time set up a cross-claim for the return of the 25£ he paid at the date of the contract. As that claim is now withdrawn it is unnecessary to say anything about it. I have only to add that the facts of this case do not bring it within the principle laid down in Stubbs v. Holywell Ry. Co.; that in the case of contracts falling directly within the rule of Taylor v. Caldwell the subsequent impossibility does not affect rights already acquired, because the defendant had the whole of June 24 to pay the balance, and the public announcement that the coronation and processions would not take place on the proclaimed days was made early on the morning of the 24th, and no cause of action could accrue till the end of that day. I think this appeal ought to be dismissed . . . .

LLOYD v. MURPHY
Supreme Court of California
25 Cal. 2d 48, 153 P.2d 47 (1944)

TRAYNOR, J.

On August 4, 1941 plaintiffs leased to defendant for a five-year term beginning September 15, 1941, certain premises located at the corner of Almont Drive and Wilshire Boulevard in the city of Beverly Hills, Los Angeles County, "for the sole purpose of conducting thereon the business of displaying and selling new automobiles (including the servicing and repairing thereof and of selling the petroleum products of a major oil company) and for no other purpose whatsoever without the written consent of the lessor" except "to make an occasional sale of a used automobile." Defendant agreed not to sublease or assign without plaintiffs' written consent.

On January 1, 1942 the federal government ordered that the sale of new automobiles be discontinued. It modified this order on January 8, 1942 to permit sales to those engaged in military activities, and on January 20, 1942, it established a system of priorities restricting sales to persons having preferential ratings of A-1-j or higher. On March 10, 1942, defendant explained the effect of these restrictions on his business to one of the plaintiffs authorized to act for the others, who orally waived the restrictions in the lease as to use and subleasing and offered to reduce the rent if defendant should be unable to operate profitably. Nevertheless defendant vacated the premises on March 15, 1942, giving oral notice of repudiation of the lease to plaintiffs, which was followed by a written notice on March 24, 1942. Plaintiffs affirmed in writing on March 26th their oral waiver and, failing to persuade defendant to perform his obligations, they rented the property to other tenants pursuant to their powers under the lease in order to mitigate damages.

On May 11, 1942, plaintiffs brought this action praying for declaratory relief to determine their rights under the lease, and for judgment for unpaid rent. Following a trial on the merits, the court found that the leased premises were located on one of the main traffic arteries of Los Angeles County; that they were equipped with gasoline pumps and in general adapted for the maintenance of an automobile service station; that they contained a one-story storeroom adapted to many commercial purposes; that plaintiffs had waived the restrictions in the lease and granted defendant the right to use the premises for any legitimate purpose and to sublease to any responsible party; that defendant continues to carry on the business of selling and servicing automobiles at two other places. Defendant testified that at one of these locations he sold new automobiles exclusively and when asked if he were aware that many new automobile dealers were continuing in business replied: "Sure. It is just the location that I couldn't make a go, though, of automobiles."

Although there was no finding to that effect, defendant estimated in response to inquiry by his counsel, that 90 per cent of his gross volume of business was new car sales and 10 per cent gasoline sales. The trial court held that war conditions had not terminated defendant's obligations under the lease and gave judgment for plaintiffs, declaring the lease as modified by plaintiffs' waiver to be in full force and effect, and ordered defendant to pay the unpaid rent with interest, less amounts received by plaintiffs from re-renting. Defendant brought this appeal, contending that the purpose for which the premises were leased was frustrated by the restrictions placed on the sale of new automobiles by the federal government, thereby terminating his duties under the lease.

Although commercial frustration was first recognized as an excuse for nonper-formance of a contractual duty by the courts of England (Krell v. Henry, C.A., 1903, 2 K.B. 740; Blakely v. Muller, K.B., 19 T.L.R. 186; see McElroy and Williams, *The Coronation Cases*, 4 Mod. L. Rev. 241) its soundness has been questioned by those courts (see Maritime National Fish, Ltd. v. Ocean Trawlers, Ltd., (1935) A.C. 524, 528-29; 56 L.Q. Rev. 324, arguing that Krell v. Henry, *supra*, was a misapplication of Taylor v. Caldwell, 1863, 3 B. & S. 826, the leading case on impossibility as an excuse for nonperformance), and they have refused to apply the doctrine to leases on the ground that an estate is conveyed to the lessee, which carries with it all risks. Many courts, therefore, in the United States have held that the tenant bears all risks as owner of the estate, but the modern cases have recognized that the defense may be available in a proper case, even in a lease. As the author declares in 6 Williston, *Contracts* (Rev. Ed. 1938), § 1955, pp. 5485-5487,

> The fact that lease is a conveyance and not simply a continuing contract and the numerous authorities enforcing liability to pay rent in spite of destruction of leased premises however, have made it difficult to give relief. That the tenant has been relieved, nevertheless, in several cases indicates the gravitation of the law toward a recognition of the principle that fortuitous destruction of the value of performance wholly outside the contemplation of the parties may excuse a promisor even in a lease . . . .

> Even more clearly with respect to leases than in regard to ordinary contracts the applicability of the doctrine of frustration depends on the total or nearly total destruction of the purpose for which, in the contemplation of both parties, the transaction was entered into.

The principles of frustration have been repeatedly applied to leases by the courts of this state and the question is whether the excuse for nonperformance is applicable under the facts of the present case.

Although the doctrine of frustration is akin to the doctrine of impossibility of performance since both have developed from the commercial necessity of excusing performance in cases of extreme hardship, frustration is not a form of impossibility even under the modern definition of that term, which includes not only cases of physical impossibility but also cases of extreme impracticability of performance. Performance remains possible but the expected value of performance to the party seeking to be excused has been destroyed by a fortuitous event, which supervenes to cause an actual but not literal failure of consideration.

The question in cases involving frustration is whether the equities of the case, considered in the light of sound public policy, require placing the risk of a disruption or complete destruction of the contract equilibrium on defendant or plaintiff under the circumstances of a given case, and the answer depends on whether an unanticipated circumstance, the risk of which should not be fairly thrown on the promisor, has made performance vitally different from what was reasonably to be expected (6 Williston, *supra*, § 1963, p. 5511; Restatement, Contracts, § 454). The purpose of a contract is to place the risks of performance upon the promisor, and the relation of the parties, terms of the contract, and circumstances surrounding its formation must be examined to determine whether it can be fairly inferred that the risk of the event that has supervened to cause the alleged frustration was not reasonably foreseeable. If it was foreseeable there should have been provision for it in the contract, and the absence of such a provision gives rise to the inference that the risk was assumed.

The doctrine of frustration has been limited to cases of extreme hardship so that businessmen, who must make their arrangements in advance, can rely with certainty on their contracts. The courts have required a promisor seeking to excuse himself from performance of his obligations to prove that the risk of the frustrating event was not reasonably foreseeable and that the value of counterperformance is totally or nearly totally destroyed, for frustration is no defense if it was foreseeable or controllable by the promisor, or if counterperformance remains valuable.

Thus laws or other governmental acts that make performance unprofitable or more difficult or expensive do not excuse the duty to perform a contractual obligation. It is settled that if parties have contracted with reference to a state of war or have contemplated the risks arising from it, they may not invoke the doctrine of frustration to escape their obligations.

At the time the lease in the present case was executed the National Defense Act, approved June 28, 1940, authorizing the President to allocate materials and mobilize industry for national defense, had been law for more than a year. The automotive industry was in the process of conversion to supply the needs of our growing mechanized army and to meet lend-lease commitments. Iceland and Greenland had been occupied by the army. Automobile sales were soaring because the public anticipated that production would soon be restricted. These facts were commonly known and it cannot be said that the risk of war and its consequences necessitating restriction of the production and sale of automobiles was so remote a contingency that its risk could not be foreseen by defendant, an experienced automobile dealer. Indeed, the conditions prevailing at the time the lease was executed, and the absence of any provision in the lease contracting against the effect of war, gives rise to the inference that the risk was assumed. Defendant has therefore failed to prove that the possibility of war and its consequences on the production and sale of new automobiles was an unanticipated circumstance wholly outside the contemplation of the parties.

Nor has defendant sustained the burden of proving that the value of the lease has been destroyed. The sale of automobiles was not made impossible or illegal but merely restricted and if governmental regulation does not entirely prohibit the business to be carried on in the leased premises but only limits or restricts it, thereby making it less profitable and more difficult to continue, the lease is not terminated or the lessee excused from further performance. Defendant may use the premises for the purpose for which they were leased. New automobiles and gasoline continue to be sold. Indeed, defendant testified that he continued to sell new automobiles exclusively at another location in the same county.

Defendant contends that the lease is restrictive and that the government orders therefore destroyed its value and frustrated its purpose. Provisions that prohibit subleasing or other uses than those specified affect the value of a lease and are to be considered in determining whether its purpose has been frustrated or its value destroyed. See Owens, *The Effect of the War Upon the Rights and Liabilities of Parties to a Contract*, 19 California State Bar Journal 132, 143. It must not be forgotten, however, that "The landlord has not covenanted that the tenant shall have the right to carry on the contemplated business or that the business to which the premises are by their nature or by the terms of the lease restricted shall be profitable enough to enable the tenant to pay the rent but has imposed a condition for his own benefit; and, certainly, unless and until he chooses to take advantage of it, the tenant is not deprived of the use of the premises." 6 Williston, *Contracts, supra*, § 1955, p. 5485. In the present lease plaintiffs reserved the rights that defendant should not use the premises for other purposes than those specified in the lease or sublease without plaintiffs' written consent. Far from preventing other uses or subleasing they waived these rights, enabling defendant to use the premises for any legitimate purpose and to sublease them to any responsible tenant. This waiver is significant in view of the location of the premises on a main traffic artery in Los Angeles County and their adaptability for many commercial purposes. The value of these rights is attested by the fact that the premises were rented soon after defendants vacated them. It is therefore clear that the governmental restrictions on the sale of new cars have not destroyed the value of the lease. Furthermore, plaintiffs offered to lower the rent if defendant should be unable to operate profitably, and their conduct was at all times fair and cooperative.

The consequences of applying the doctrine of frustration to a leasehold involving less than a total or nearly total destruction of the value of the leased premises would be undesirable. Confusion would result from different decisions purporting to define "substantial" frustration. Litigation would be encouraged by the repudiation of leases when lessees found their businesses less profitable because of the regulations attendant upon a national emergency. Many leases have been affected in varying degrees by the widespread governmental regulations necessitated by war conditions.

The cases that defendant relies upon are consistent with the conclusion reached herein. In Industrial Development & Land Co. v. Goldschmidt, [56 Cal. App. 2d 507, 206 p. 134], the lease provided that the premises should not be used other than as a saloon. When national prohibition made the sale of alcoholic beverages illegal, the court excused the tenant from further performance on the theory of illegality or impossibility by a change in domestic law. The doctrine of frustration might have been applied, since the purpose for which the property was leased was totally destroyed and there was nothing to show that the value of the lease was not thereby totally destroyed. In the present case the purpose was not destroyed but only restricted, and plaintiffs proved that the lease was valuable to defendant. In Grace v. Croninger, 12 Cal. App. 2d 603, the lease was for the purpose of conducting a "saloon and cigar store, and for no other purpose" with provision for subleasing a portion of the premises for bootblack purposes. The monthly rental was $650. It was clear that prohibition destroyed the main purpose of the lease, but since the premises could be used for bootblack and cigar store purposes, the lessee was not excused from his duty to pay the rent. In the present case new automobiles and gasoline may be sold under the lease as executed and any legitimate business may be conducted or the premises may be subleased under the lease as modified by plaintiff's waiver . . . . No case has been cited by defendant or disclosed by research in which an appellate court has excused a lessee from performance of his duty to pay rent when the purpose of the lease has not been totally destroyed or its accomplishment rendered extremely impracticable or where it has been shown that the lease remains valuable to the lessee.

The judgment is affirmed.

NOTES

1. ***The Doctrinal Definition.*** Restatement (Second) § 265, states:

Where, after a contract is made, a party's principal purpose is substantially frustrated without his fault by the occurrence of an event the non-occurrence of which was a basic assumption on which the contract was made, his remaining duties to render performance are discharged, unless the language or the circumstances indicate the contrary.

According to the Restatement, how should the following case, which deals with claims of impossibility and frustration of purpose arising out of unanticipated governmental action, be decided? In *West Los Angeles Institute for Cancer Research v. Mayer*, 366 F.2d 220 (9th Cir. 1966), the plaintiffs contracted to sell their business to the defendant-cancer institute. The parties constructed the deal so that the plaintiffs might avail themselves of certain tax advantages then offered for such sale and leaseback arrangements by the Internal Revenue Service. The IRS, however, later altered its rulings regarding these arrangements. As a result, the deal became considerably less profitable to the plaintiffs and they sued for a return of the property.

Would a careful parsing of the Restatement tell you how this case ought to be decided? The court granted the relief requested. Compare *Consumers Power Co. v. Nuclear Fuel Services*, 509 F. Supp. 201 (W.D.N.Y. 1981), where an excuse claim arising out of changing governmental nuclear waste disposal policy was denied as a matter of law. What happens when the government subsequently *eliminates*, rather than adds, a regulation affecting the value of the transaction?

Consider *Washington State Hop Producers, Inc. Liquidation Trust v. Goschie Farms, Inc.*, 112 Wash. 2d 694 (1989), in which the Washington State Hop Producers Liquidation Trust had formed to consolidate and sell allotments that were required, by federal regulatory order, for any vender to sell hops. After a number of growers purchased allotments, the federal government terminated the regulatory order thereby making the purchased allotments unnecessary and valueless. The growers refused to pay for the allotments and claimed excuse based on frustration of purpose. As part of its analysis under Restatement § 265, the court accepted the growers' excuse of frustration, arguing that the enormous price decline in the hop allotments following the termination order, and the unforeseeability of the termination order, demonstrated that "the continued need to own or control hop base in order to sell hops was an assumption central to the subject matter of the contract." *Id.* at 706. The court concluded that "the irrelevance of control of hop base . . . supplies the frustration justifying rescision." *Id.* at 705.

2. ***The Story of* Krell: *Was Cancellation Foreseeable?*** The court in *Krell* finds that "it cannot reasonably be supposed to have been in the contemplation of the contracting parties, when the contract was made, that the coronation would not be held on the proclaimed days." Professor Victor Goldberg disagrees:

> The risk of postponement looks less remote if we tell the story differently. Although this particular contract was entered into only six days before the event, the planning horizon for the event was roughly six months, the date and route being announced in December 1901. The likelihood that a sixty-year-old, grossly overweight, heavy smoker, who had been the target of at least one assassination attempt might be unavailable was not trivial. Moreover, the procession was to be in a city renowned for its miserable

weather. That someone might have thought about a possible postponement or cancellation no longer seems so far-fetched.

And, in fact, they did. Less than a week before the coronation Lloyds was quoting odds of 300 to 1 against cancellation. "Many thousands of pounds sterling were underwritten on this basis. This shows to what extent public nervousness has grown in certain circles" (*New York Times*, June 22, 1902). In an article the day after the postponement was announced, the *New York Times* provided an indication of the extensive insurance coverage.

> The loss of the British insurance companies, particularly those of London, which accepted risks on the coronation, will, it is estimated, run into the millions. . . . [T]housands of insurance policies have been issued during the past year to tradesmen and others who depended for their livelihood for some time to come upon the ability of the King to pass through the coronation ceremonies. The business took a great boom when active preparations were begun for the coronation, and nearly all classes of tradesmen who were directly or indirectly dependent upon the successful termination of the great event bought policies.

(*New York Times*, June 25, 1902).

Victor Goldberg, *Excuse Doctrine: The Eisenberg Uncertainty Principle*, 2 J. LEGAL ANALYSIS 359, 363, 366 (2010).[19]

3. ***When is a Purpose Frustrated?*** It is not always a simple matter to determine when a subsequent event frustrates the buyer's purpose. In *Arabian Score v. Lasma Arabian, Ltd.*, 814 F.2d 529 (8th Cir. 1987), the buyer (Arabian) purchased a horse ("Score") from Lasma Arabian Limited. In addition to the fee for the horse, Arabian paid Lasma $250,000 in return for Lasma's agreement to provide "various services in the promotion of Score" for five years following the sale. Score died less than one year after the purchase, at which time Lasma had spent approximately $53,000 promoting Score. Arabian refused to pay Lasma the balance of approximately $197,000, arguing that the purpose for which that payment was intended (to promote Score) was frustrated by the horse's death. The court denied Arabian's frustration defense on the grounds that Score's death was foreseeable and thus constituted an assumed risk, and that the unrebutted evidence established Lasma "regularly promoted deceased horses. This is done to enhance the owning entity's reputation and to increase the value of the stallion's progeny." *Id.* at 532. The court was mindful that this outcome might not be intuitive to the lay person:

---

[19] Professor Goldberg's analysis of *Krell* is part of a larger debate with Professor Melvin Eisenberg over whether the ex post or ex ante perspective should be used to evaluate the excuse doctrines. For the article that started the debate, and to which Professor Goldberg is responding, see Melvin A. Eisenberg, *Impossibility, Impracticability, and Frustration*, 1 J. LEGAL ANALYSIS 207 (2009). For Professor Eisenberg's response to Professor Goldberg's critique, see Melvin A. Eisenberg, *Impossibility, Impracticability, and Frustration — Professor Goldberg Constructs an Imaginary Article, Attributes it to Me, and Then Critiques It*, 2 J. LEGAL ANALYSIS 383 (2010). For Professor Goldberg's rejoinder, see Victor Goldberg, *After Frustration: Three Cheers for* Chandler v. Webster, 68 WASH. & LEE L. REV. 1133 (2011).

It is with some reluctance that we affirm the district court's grant of summary judgment. That reluctance stems from the thought that spending $197,108.86 to promote a dead horse borders on the bizarre. The parties to this agreement were sophisticated and, we assume, well-heeled business persons, however, and that which we find to be somewhat unusual may be commonplace to those who inhabit the wealthy world of the horsey set.

Id.

Compare Arabian Score, with Ryan v. Estate of Sheppard (In Re Estate of Shepphard), 789 N.W.2d 616 (2010). In that case, a flight instructor brought a claim against the estate of a deceased flight student based on a personal services contract. The student had agreed to pay the instructor $35,000 per year for flight lessons but passed away before they could begin. The court rejected the instructor's claim:

While Sheppard's promise in the agreement was only to pay, his purpose in making the contract is clear: to obtain personal flight instruction and pilot services, as evidenced by Ryan's obligations. In a personal service contract such as this one, a basic assumption is that both parties will be alive. See Restatement (Second) of Contracts §§ 262, 265 cmt. a. Sheppard's death, then, frustrated the contract's purpose-it made personal flight instruction unfeasible. When there is nothing an obligor can do to fulfill his or her contractual duties, the obligee's duty to compensate is excused.

Id. at 620.

Can these two cases be reconciled?

4. ***The Substantiality Requirement.*** In *Haas v. Pittsburgh Nat'l Bank*, 495 F. Supp. 815 (W.D. Pa. 1980), the plaintiffs filed a class action suit challenging the defendant's use of certain interest and accounting procedures regarding Bank Americard and Mastercharge accounts. The suit was settled, and the parties agreed that the defendants would pay interest on the settlement amount ($2.76 million) at an amount equal to the prevailing passbook savings rate. However, the matter was prolonged by a dispute over legal fees for the plaintiffs' counsel. In the meantime, the money remained in the defendant's control, earning interest at a rate considerably above the passbook savings rate due to a general rise in the inflation and interest rates. In fact, in May 1980, the interest rate surpassed the passbook savings rate by 13.25%. The plaintiffs sued to reform the settlement agreement, hoping to have the court allot to them the added "windfall" that the bank had reaped as a result of the settlement delay. Among the plaintiffs' claims was a contention that the plaintiffs' purpose in negotiating for the passbook savings clause (e.g., to keep pace with inflation) had been frustrated by the rise in the prime rate of interest. The court denied this claim, citing comment a to § 265 of the Second Restatement for a requirement that the frustration be "substantial":

It is not enough that the transaction has become less profitable . . . or even that [the promisor] will sustain a loss. The frustration must be so severe that it is not fairly to be regarded as within the risks that he assumed under the contract.

Justice Traynor warned that confusion would result from different decisions purporting to define "substantial" frustration. What purpose does the substantiality requirement serve?

5. *Whose Purpose Must Be Frustrated?* An important element of the frustration doctrine was stated in *Edwards v. Leopoldi*, 20 N.J. Super. 43, 55, 89 A.2d 264, 271 (1952):

> To sustain a defense under the doctrine of frustration it does not appear to be sufficient to disclose that the "purpose" or "desired object" of but one of the contracting parties has been frustrated. It is their common object that has to be frustrated, not merely the individual advantage which one party or the other might have achieved from the contract.

Is this statement helpful? In this connection, consider *Power Eng'g & Mfg., Ltd. v. Krug Int'l*, 501 N.W.2d 490 (Iowa 1993). In this case, Power Engineering agreed to manufacture a gearbox for Krug, which Krug intended to incorporate into a "human centrifuge" for training airline pilots. Unbeknownst to Power, Krug had agreed to sell the centrifuge to Iraqi Airways, in Iraq. When the Gulf War began in August of 1990, the United Nations immediately implemented an embargo against all shipment of any materials to Iraq. The embargo prevented Krug from selling the centrifuge to Iraqi Airways. Krug directed Power to cease manufacture of the gearbox but Power had already completed it. When Power insisted on payment, Krug invoked a force majeure in the contract, as well as the defense of commercial impracticability under UCC § 2-615. The court ruled against Krug, holding that:

> Krug's performance cannot truly be said to be commercially impracticable . . . . The embargo does not prevent Krug from fulfilling its contractual obligations with Power Engineering. Although the embargo prevents products from being shipped to Iraq, it does not prohibit a domestic purchaser from buying, from a domestic manufacturer, a machinery component part intended for shipment there . . . . Although Krug may have made assumptions regarding such unforeseen contingencies, Power Engineering was not privy to Krug's planned use of the gear box. Under the circumstances Krug must be found to have assumed the risk that its purchaser would not, or could not, perform.

Id. at 495.

Are you persuaded by the court's reasoning? The court's holding implies that the outcome of this case might have been different if Krug had informed Power as to its intended purpose for purchasing the gearbox. Why should this matter? Even if Power was aware of Krug's intended use of the product after purchasing it, does this knowledge create a common objective between the parties? In other words, upon being made aware of Krug's planned use of the gearbox, do you think Power's objective would change?

6. *Problem.* Jethro Pugh and Rayfield Wright, two veteran members of the Dallas Cowboys football team, signed in 1974 to play with the Alabama club of the new World Football League. Each player signed for the years 1977, 1978, and 1979 and was given a $75,000 signing bonus. The contracts provided for total payment to be made in five stages: (1) the aforementioned bonus, (2) an additional bonus upon reporting to Alabama's training camp in 1977, and (3), (4) and (5), yearly salary payments. The league, however, collapsed before the players ever made it to their first Alabama camp. Alabama Football, Inc. sued for return of its original bonus payment, claiming frustration of purpose and impossibility. How should Wright and Pugh have responded? What result do you predict? *See Alabama Football, Inc. v. Wright*, 452 F. Supp. 182 (N.D. Tex. 1977).

E.   BIBLIOGRAPHY AND SUGGESTED READING

Ian Ayres & Eric Rasmusen, *Mutual and Unilateral Mistake in Contract Law*, 22 J. LEGAL STUD. 309 (1993).

Mark B. Baker, *"A Hard Rain's A-Gonna Fall" — Terrorism and Excused Contractual Performance in a Post September 11th World*, 17 TRANSNAT'L LAW. 1 (2004).

W. Buckland, *Casus and Frustration in Roman and Common Law*, 46 HARV. L. REV. 1281 (1933).

John Dawson, *Judicial Revision of Frustrated Contracts: The United States*, 64 B.U. L. REV. 1, 26 (1984).

Melvin A. Eisenberg, *Impossibility, Impracticability, and Frustration*, 1 J. LEGAL ANALYSIS 207 (2009).

Melvin A. Eisenberg, *Impossibility, Impracticability, and Frustration — Professor Goldberg Constructs an Imaginary Article, Attributes it to Me, and Then Critiques It*, 2 J. LEGAL ANALYSIS 383 (2010).

Melvin A. Eisenberg, *The Role of Fault in Contract Law: Unconscionability, Unexpected Circumstances, Interpretation, Mistake, and Nonperformance*, 107 MICH. L. REV. 1413 (2009).

M.P. Ellinghaus, *In Defense of Unconscionability*, 78 YALE L.J. 757 (1969).

John Elofson, *The Dilemma of Changed Circumstances in Contract Law: An Economic Analysis of the Forseeability and Superior Risk Bearer Tests*, 30 COLUM. J.L. & SOC. PROBS. 1 (1996).

Mary Joe Frug, *Rescuing Impossibility Doctrine: A Postmodern Feminist Analysis of Contract Law*, 140 U. PA. L. REV. 1029 (1992).

Clayton P. Gillette, *Commercial Rationality and the Duty to Adjust Long-Term Contracts*, 69 MINN. L. REV. 521 (1985).

Victor Goldberg, *Excuse Doctrine: The Eisenberg Uncertainty Principle*, 2 J. LEGAL ANALYSIS 359 (2010).

VICTOR GOLDBERG, FRAMING CONTRACT LAW: AN ECONOMIC PERSPECTIVE (2007).

Victor Goldberg, *After Frustration: Three Cheers for Chandler v. Webster*, 68 WASH. & LEE L. REV. 1133 (2011).

Sheldon W. Halpern, *Application of the Doctrine of Commercial Impracticability: Searching for "The Wisdom of Solomon,"* 135 U. PA. L. REV. 1123 (1987).

Jeffrey Harrison, *Rethinking Mistake and Nondisclosure in Contract Law*, 17 GEO. MASON L. REV. 335 (2010).

Robert A. Hillman, *An Analysis of the Cessation of Contractual Relations*, 68 CORNELL L. REV. 617 (1983).

Robert A. Hillman, *Court Adjustment of Long-Term Contracts: An Analysis Under Modern Contract Law*, 1987 DUKE L.J. 1.

Robert A. Hillman, *Contract Excuse and Bankruptcy Discharge*, 43 STAN. L. REV. 99 (1990).

Paul Joskow, *Commercial Impossibility, The Uranium Market and the Westinghouse Case*, 6 J. LEGAL STUD. 119 (1977).

Andrew Kull, *Mistake, Frustration, and the Windfall Principle of Contract Remedies*, 43 HASTINGS L.J. 1 (1991).

Andrew Kull, *Unilateral Mistake: The Baseball Card Case*, 70 WASH. U. L.Q. 57 (1992).

Jody S. Kraus & Robert E. Scott, *Contract Design and the Structure of Contractual Intent*, 84 N.Y.U.L. REV. 1023 (2009).

Jennifer S. Martin, *Adapting U.C.C. § 2-615 Excuse for Civilian-Military Contractors in Wartime*, 61 FLA. L. REV. 99 (2009).

John E. Murray, *A Postscript: Ruminations and Presentations About Impracticability and Mistake*, 1 J.L. & COM. 60 (1981).

Subha Narasimhan, *Relationship or Boundary? Handling Successive Contracts*, 77 Cal. L. Rev. 1077 (1989).

Daniel T. Ostas & Frank P. Darr, *Understanding Commercial Impracticability: Tempering Efficiency with Community Fairness Norms*, 27 RUTGERS L.J. 343 (1996).

Richard A. Posner & Andrew Rosenfield, *Impossibility and Related Doctrines in Contract Law: An Economic Analysis*, 6 J. LEGAL STUD. 83 (1977).

John Henry Schlegel, *Of Nuts, and Ships, and Sealing Wax, Suez, and Frustrating Things — The Doctrine of Impossibility of Performance*, 23 RUTGERS L. REV. 419 (1969).

ALAN SCHWARTZ & ROBERT E. SCOTT, COMMERCIAL TRANSACTIONS: PRINCIPLES AND POLICIES (1991).

Alan Schwartz, *Sales Law and Inflations*, 50 S. CAL. L. REV. 1 (1976).

Robert E. Scott, *Conflict and Cooperation in Long-Term Contracts*, 75 CAL. L. REV. 1005 (1987).

Robert E. Scott, *A Theory of Self-Enforcing Indefinite Agreements*, 103 Colum. L. Rev. 1641 (2003).

Hans Smit, *Frustration of Contract: A Comparative Attempt at Consolidation*, 58 COLUM. L. REV. 287 (1958).

Donald Smythe, *Bounded Rationality, the Doctrine of Impracticability, and the Governance of Relational Contracts*, 13 S. CAL. INTERDISC. L.J. 227 (2004).

John Spanogle, *Analyzing Unconscionability Problems*, 117 U. PA. L. REV. 931 (1969).

Richard E. Speidel, *The New Spirit of Contract*, 2 J.L. & COM. 193 (1983).

Stroh, *The Failure of the Doctrine of Impracticability*, 5 CORP. L. REV. 195 (1982).

Alan Sykes, *The Doctrine of Commercial Impracticability in a Second-Best World*, 19 J. LEGAL STUD. 43 (1990).

Leon Trakman, *Winner Take Some: Loss Sharing and Commercial Impracticability*, 69 MINN. L. REV. 471 (1985).

George G. Triantis, *Contractual Allocation of Unknown Risks: The Search for Justifications for the Doctrine of Commercial Impracticability*, 42 U. TORONTO L.J. 377 (1992).

GEORGE G. TRIANTIS, *Unforeseen Contingencies, Risk Allocation in Contracts, in* THE ENCYCLOPEDIA OF LAW AND ECONOMICS 4500 (1998).

Steven D. Walt, *Expectancy, Loss Distribution and Commercial Impracticability*, 24 IND. L.J. 65 (1990).

Michelle White, *Contract Breach and Contract Discharge Due to Impossibility: A Unified Theory*, 17 J. LEGAL STUD. 353 (1988).

John D. Wladis, *Common Law and Uncommon Events: The Development of the Doctrine of Impossibility of Performance in English Contract Law*, 75 GEO. L.J. 1575 (1987).

William F. Young, *Half Measures*, 81 COLUM. L. REV. 19 (1981).

Chapter 9

CONDUCT CONSTITUTING BREACH

A. INTRODUCTION[1]

In Chapter 8, we saw that when contingencies materialize that cause a party to regret a contractual commitment, that party may seek to evade his performance duties by insisting that he agreed to perform only if these contingencies did not materialize. The law of mistake and excuse set out interpretive rules for determining whether a contract assigned the risk of a given contingency to the promisor, or instead conditioned the promisor's performance obligation on the non-occurrence of the contingency. But the parties have an incentive not merely to assign these risks in their contract, but also to reduce the expected costs of the contingencies that do materialize. It is true that once the contract is formed, and these risks have been assigned, each party may have little reason to care about the other party's costs of bearing these risks.[2] But before these risks are assigned, each party has a strong incentive to care about the costs of bearing them: The higher the costs, the lower the value of the contract. As these costs increase, the total expected gains from contracting decrease, thereby decreasing the maximum expected gain for each party.[3] This means that the ideal contract would be structured so that the costs of bearing risks are minimized.

[1] The Ideal Allocation of Risk

When a future contingency is identified at the time of contracting, the cost of bearing the risk of that event's occurrence is minimized by assigning it to the party who can better take cost-effective measures to reduce both the probability that the

---

[1] This essay draws in part on Charles J. Goetz & Robert E. Scott, *The Mitigation Principle: Toward a General Theory of Contractual Obligation*, 69 Va. L. Rev. 967 (1983).

[2] Parties still have *some* reason to care about the other party's costs of bearing risks. First, because bankruptcy law (more or less) protects persons against claims that exceed their ability to pay, if the losses caused by a subsequent event exceed the assets of the party bearing the risk of the occurrence of that event, then that party will not be required to reimburse the losses sustained by the other party due to the occurrence of that event. Thus, for example, a buyer might help his seller reduce the costs of a materialized risk in order to reduce the probability that the seller will be released by bankruptcy law from his duty to compensate the buyer for her losses. Second, since parties may contemplate future business with their contractual partners, or with others who will be affected by their business reputation, parties have reason to help reduce their contractual partner's costs of bearing contractual risks, even after they have been assigned. Third, some contractual partners may simply care about each other's welfare.

[3] Put differently, the costs of these risks are "impounded" in the price that each party charges the other for his contractual promise: The higher the costs of bearing these risks, the less the party bearing them will agree to pay for the other party's promise.

event will occur and the contractual losses the event would cause. Parties could choose to allocate the liability for the costs of such an event to one party, but assign the duty to take these cost-effective measures to the other party. For example, a buyer might agree to pay the costs of a fire at the seller's manufacturing plant, even though the seller agrees to take cost-effective precautions to prevent and reduce the impact of such a fire. Unfortunately, since the buyer bears the costs of the fire, the seller may attempt to save money by shirking his obligation to reduce the probability and impact of a fire. Unless the buyer can verify the seller's failure to a court, the seller may be able to use the buyer's agreement to pay as insurance against the risk of fire without having to bear the costs of guarding against fire. Dividing the liability for a loss and the duty to take cost-effective precautions creates what economists call a "moral hazard" problem. A moral hazard problem exists when an individual lacks the incentive to behave efficiently because he does not fully "internalize" both the costs and the benefits of his behavior. In this example, the seller suffers no loss by failing to take efficient precautions, nor secures any gain by taking such precautions. One solution is to assign the risk of losses caused by a fire to the seller, the party who has the comparative advantage in reducing the probability and/or impact of its occurrence. In such a case, the seller fully internalizes the costs and benefits of precautions.

As we have seen, however, it is difficult to identify all possible contingencies at the time of contract formation. Moreover, it is equally difficult to predict which party will be in the best position to respond to a contingency that materializes. Indeed, sometimes the most efficient response to a given event is for *both* parties to take cost-effective measures. For these reasons, it is not possible for parties, at the time of formation, to specify a complete set of contractual duties that lead them to engage in efficient behavior throughout the course of their contract.

One theoretical alternative would be for the parties to agree to a general obligation to undertake all cost-effective measures warranted by subsequent events. For example, suppose an air conditioning manufacturer contracts to deliver in six months an air-conditioning unit to buyer for $250,000. The buyer plans to install the air conditioning unit in a building that will be under construction at the time of delivery. Four months after formation, an explosion at the seller's plant delays the seller's manufacturing schedule by two months. Under the contract, there is no question that the seller is liable for any losses caused by his inability to perform. The cost of purchasing an air conditioning unit of the same quality and design for delivery in two months is $300,000. But suppose that for $30,000 the buyer could alter its construction plans to delay installation of the air conditioning unit for two months past the original contract delivery date. In this example, it is clear that if both parties had considered this possible scenario, the buyer and seller would have agreed that the buyer would be required to make the $30,000 adjustment and that the seller would be required to pay for it. The alternative requires the seller to spend $50,000 more to purchase a substitute air conditioning unit when the buyer would be equally well off if the seller paid the $30,000 adjustment cost to delay delivery. The contract would therefore have a higher expected cost to the seller if the buyer did not agree to make cost-effective adjustments, and this higher cost would be reflected in a higher initial contract price that the buyer would be required to pay. In principle, then, the value of every contract would be increased (for both parties) if the duty to make cost-effective adjustments to future events is assigned to the party who can do so at the least cost.

[2] Obstacles to Ideal Risk Allocation: Evasion and Opportunism

There are good reasons, however, for parties not to include a general term in their agreement requiring mutual adjustment to future contingencies. First, it will be difficult for both parties to know, let alone prove to a court, which of them can best make cost-effective adjustments to future contingencies. As a result, a rule requiring the party who can adjust to subsequent events at least cost to do so invites the bad faith, strategic options of *evasion* and *opportunism* by either party. Each party can use this general adjustment obligation to *evade* his own contractual obligations by maintaining that the other party failed to adjust to a given contingency, or can *opportunistically* exploit the other by deliberately overestimating its own costs of adjustment.

Returning to our example above, the seller might seek to evade his obligation to deliver the air conditioning unit as required by the contract by alleging that the buyer could adjust to the plant explosion by accepting a delayed delivery *at no additional expense.* If the buyer refuses to accept a delay without the seller's payment of $30,000, the seller might then declare the buyer in breach in the hope of avoiding the contract entirely. The success of this gambit would turn on the extent to which the buyer's adjustment costs are observable to both parties, and more important, verifiable to a court. Likewise, the buyer could exploit his ability to adjust to the loss more cheaply by opportunistically refusing to adjust until the seller agrees to share some (or all) of the benefits the seller anticipates from the buyer's adjustment.

To see how, consider that by extending the delivery date the buyer saves the seller the cost of buying a substitute air conditioning unit ($50,000 above the contract price). The buyer's actual costs of the extension is $30,000. Thus, because the seller values the buyer's adjustment at $20,000 more than the buyer's cost of adjustment, the buyer can attempt to bargain for the additional $20,000 value of his adjustment. He might, for example, misrepresent that his costs of delay are $48,000. The success of this gambit turns on the extent to which buyer's adjustment costs are observable by seller, and the extent to which the parties engage in costly strategic behavior, such as "holding out" and playing "chicken" to intimidate their partner into accepting a one-sided bargain. Thus, by obscuring the parties' performance duties, a generalized contractual duty to adjust creates incentives for the parties to engage in evasion and opportunism, both of which increase the expected costs of performance for each party.

The prospect of evasion and opportunism helps justify the historic reluctance of the common law of contracts to impute into every contract a generalized duty to adjust to post-formation events. Historically, the default rule in contracts is that neither party has a duty to make any post-contract adjustments unless and until the other party breaches. In the above example, absent agreement to the contrary, the buyer would not be under a duty to adjust to the seller's plant explosion by accepting $30,000 from the seller to delay delivery by two months. Instead, the seller has no power to compel the buyer to make post-contract adjustments, even at the seller's expense, unless the seller breaches. By breaching, the seller triggers the buyer's duty to mitigate damages.[4] At that point, the buyer's right to compensation is limited by the mitigation doctrine to losses he could not reasonably have avoided following breach.

But since the duty to mitigate only arises upon breach, it falls far short of the theoretical ideal that would require both contractual partners to make cost-effective adjustments throughout the life of their contract. Breach not only requires the breacher to compensate the nonbreacher, but also compels him to forfeit his right to the nonbreacher's performance. This makes breach an extremely costly, and therefore limited, tool for forcing a contractual partner to adjust to contingencies. For instance, in the above example, if required first to breach, the seller would be unable to require the buyer to adjust by delaying the seller's delivery date by two months. By breaching, the seller reneges on his promise to perform and so forfeits the right to the buyer's performance in the future. Ideally, the seller should be able to compel the buyer's adjustment without also breaching and thereby forfeiting the right to the buyer's performance. But the "breach first" rule is justified by the increased prospect of evasion and opportunism attending a generalized duty to adjust. The effect of this rule is that the party who bears the risk of a subsequent event will require the other to adjust to that event only if the costs saved by that adjustment exceed the value of the right to the other party's performance.[5]

[3] Defining the Conduct Constituting Breach

Given that the duty to mitigate is triggered by breach (and not before), the question of what conduct constitutes a breach of contract assumes substantial importance. Obviously, one way to breach is to fail to perform when performance is due. But parties concerned about the need to adjust to unexpected contingencies will engage in behaviors that call into question *in advance of performance* either their willingness or their ability to perform when the time for performance arrives. These behaviors may be in the nature of a request (or demand) that the other party adjust to subsequent events or it may simply be "foot-dragging" or other manifestations of a reluctance to suffer an anticipated loss under the contract. In any event, the law must develop rules by which parties can accurately and predictably interpret these behaviors. The doctrine of anticipatory repudiation (and its companion, the "right to assurances of performance") embody default rules that define the conduct constituting breach and specify its consequences.

---

[4] To be more precise, mitigation is not strictly speaking an affirmative duty of the nonbreacher, but rather is an affirmative defense allowing the breacher to deduct avoidable losses from the nonbreacher's damage award in an action for breach. For convenience, we will nonetheless refer to the nonbreacher's "duty" to mitigate.

[5] For an economic analysis of the effects of the anticipatory repudiation doctrine on efficient post-formation investment decisions, see Jody S. Kraus & George G. Triantis, *Anticipatory Repudiation Reconsidered*, 6 Va. J. 54 (2003).

This chapter begins by considering how the doctrine of anticipatory repudiation emerged at common law and then evolved into its current forms. As always, your first objective should be to discern the contours of the doctrine. But doctrinal mastery should be just your first step on the way to synthesizing and evaluating the legal rules governing the question of breach. What should the law's objectives be? How well do these doctrines achieve these objectives?

B.   ANTICIPATORY BREACH

In this section, we consider two cases presenting the basic contours of the doctrine of anticipatory repudiation. In the first, a common law court struggles to find conceptual room for anticipatory repudiation, given that the classic contract model only allows breach after the time of performance has expired. The second case considers what conduct constitutes an anticipatory repudiation.

HOCHSTER v. DE LA TOUR
Queen's Bench
2 E. & B. 678, 118 Eng. Rep. 922 (1853)

. . . On the trial, before Erle, J., at the London sittings in last Easter Term, it appeared that plaintiff was a courier, who, in April, 1852, was engaged by defendant to accompany him on a tour, to commence on June 1st, 1852, on the terms mentioned in the declaration. On May 11th, 1852, defendant wrote to plaintiff that he had changed his mind, and declined his services. He refused to make him any compensation. The action was commenced on May 22d. The plaintiff, between the commencement of the action and June 1st, obtained an engagement with Lord Ashburton, on equally good terms, but not commencing till July 4th. The defendant's counsel objected that there could be no breach of the contract before June 1st. The learned judge was of a contrary opinion, but reserved leave to enter a non-suit on this objection. The other questions were left to the jury, who found for plaintiff . . . .

LORD CAMPBELL, C.J.

On this motion in arrest of judgment, the question arises, whether if there be an agreement between A and B whereby B engages to employ A on and from a future day for a given period of time, to travel with him into a foreign country as a courier, and to start with him in that capacity on that day, A being to receive a monthly salary during the continuance of such service, B may, before the day, refuse to perform the agreement and break and renounce it, so as to entitle A before the day to commence an action against B to recover damages for breach of the agreement; A having been ready and willing to perform it, till it was broken and renounced by B. The defendant's counsel very powerfully contended that, if the plaintiff was not contented to dissolve the contract, and to abandon all remedy upon it, he was bound to remain ready and willing to perform it till the day when the actual employment as courier in the service of the defendant was to begin; and that there could be no breach of the agreement, before that day, to give a right of action.

But it cannot be laid down as a universal rule that, where by agreement an act is to be done on a future day, no action can be brought for a breach of the agreement till the day for doing the act has arrived. If a man promises to marry a woman on a future day, and before that day marries another woman, he is instantly liable to an action for breach of promise of marriage; Short v. Stone, 8 Q.B. 358. If man contracts to execute a lease on and from a future day for a certain term, and, before that day, executes a lease to another for the same term, he may be immediately sued for breaking the contract. Ford v. Tiley, 6 B. & C. 325. So, if a man contracts to sell and deliver specific goods on a future day, and before the day he sells and delivers them to another, he is immediately liable to an action at the suit of the person with whom he first contracted to sell and deliver them. Bowdell v. Parsons, 10 East, 359. One reason alleged in support of such an action is, that the defendant has, before the day, rendered it impossible for him to perform the contract at the day: but this does not necessarily follow; for, prior to the day fixed for doing the act, the first wife may have died, a surrender of the lease executed might be obtained, and the defendant might have repurchased the goods so as to be in a situation to sell and deliver them to the plaintiff. Another reason may be that, where there is a contract to do an act on a future day, there is a relation constituted between the parties in the meantime by the contract, and that they impliedly promise that in the meantime neither will do anything to the prejudice of the other inconsistent with that relation. As an example, a man and woman engaged to marry are affianced to one another during the period between the time of the engagement and the celebration of the marriage.

In this very case, of traveller and courier, from the day of the hiring till the day when the employment was to begin, they were engaged to each other; and it seems to be a breach of an implied contract if either of them renounces the engagement. This reasoning seems in accordance with the unanimous decisions of the Exchequer Chamber in Elderton v. Emmens, 6 C.B. 160, which we have followed in subsequent cases in this court. The declaration in the present case, in alleging a breach, states a great deal more than a passing intention on the part of the defendant which he may repent of, and could only be proved by evidence that he had utterly renounced the contract, or done some act which rendered it impossible for him to perform it. If the plaintiff has no remedy for breach of contract unless he treats the contract as in force, and acts upon it down to the 1st June, 1852, it follows that, till then, he must enter into no employment which will interfere with his promise "to start with the defendant on such travels on the day and year," and that he must then be properly equipped in all respects as a courier for a three months' tour on the continent of Europe.

But it is surely much more rational, and more for the benefit of both parties, that, after the renunciation of the agreement by the defendant, the plaintiff should be at liberty to consider himself absolved from any future performance of it, retaining his right to sue for any damage he has suffered from the breach of it. Thus, instead of remaining idle and laying out money in preparations which must be useless, he is at liberty to seek service under another employer, which would go in mitigation of the damages to which he would otherwise be entitled for a breach of the contract. It seems strange that the defendant, after renouncing the contract, and absolutely declaring that he will never act under it, should be permitted to object that faith is given to his assertion, and that an opportunity is not left to him of changing his mind. If the plaintiff is barred of any remedy by entering into an engagement inconsistent with starting as a courier with the defendant on the 1st June, he is prejudiced by putting faith in the defendant's assertion: and it would be more consistent with principle, if the defendant were precluded from saying that he had not broken the contract when he declared that he entirely renounced it. Suppose that the defendant, at the time of his renunciation, had embarked on a voyage to Australia, so as to render it physically impossible for him to employ the plaintiff as a courier on the continent of Europe in the months of June, July and August 1852: according to decided cases, the action might have been brought before the 1st June; but the renunciation may have been founded on other facts, to be given in evidence, which would equally have rendered the defendant's performance of the contract impossible. The man who wrongfully renounces a contract into which he has deliberately entered cannot justly complain if he is immediately sued for a compensation in damages by the man whom he has injured: and it seems reasonable to allow an option to the injured party, either to sue immediately, or to wait till the time when the act was to be done, still holding it as prospectively binding for the exercise of this option, which may be advantageous to the innocent party, and cannot be prejudicial to the wrongdoer.

An argument against the action before the 1st of June is urged from the difficulty of calculating the damages: but this argument is equally strong against an action before the 1st of September, when the three months would expire. In either case, the jury in assessing the damages would be justified in looking to all that had happened, or was likely to happen, to increase or mitigate the loss of the plaintiff down to the day of trial. We do not find any decision contrary to the view we are taking of this case . . . .

If it should be held that, upon a contract to do an act on a future day, a renunciation of the contract by one party dispenses with a condition to be performed in the meantime by the other, there seems no reason for requiring that other to wait till the day arrives before seeking his remedy by action: and the only ground on which the condition can be dispensed with seems to be, that the renunciation may be treated as a breach of the contract.

Upon the whole, we think that the declaration in this case is sufficient. It gives us great satisfaction to reflect that, the question being on the record, our opinion may be reviewed in a Court of Error. In the meantime we must give judgment for the plaintiff.

Judgment for plaintiff.

TRUMAN L. FLATT & SONS CO. v. SCHUPF
Appellate Court of Illinois
271 Ill. App. 3d 983, 649 N.E.2d 990 (1995)

KNECHT, J.

Plaintiff Truman L. Flatt & Sons Co., Inc., filed a complaint seeking specific performance of a real estate contract made with defendants Sara Lee Schupf, Ray H. Neiswander, Jr., and American National Bank and Trust Company of Chicago

(American), as trustee under trust No. 23257. Defendants filed a motion for summary judgment, which the trial court granted. Plaintiff now appeals from the trial court's grant of the motion for summary judgment. We reverse and remand.

In March 1993, plaintiff and defendants entered a contract in which defendants agreed to sell plaintiff a parcel of land located in Springfield, Illinois. The contract stated the purchase price was to be $160,000. The contract also contained the following provisions:

> "1. This transaction shall be closed on or before June 30, 1993, or upon approval of the relief requested from the Zoning Code of the City of Springfield, Illinois, whichever first occurs ('Closing Date'). The closing is subject to contingency set forth in paragraph 14.

> 14. This Contract to Purchase Real Estate is contingent upon the Buyer obtaining, within one hundred twenty (120) days after the date hereof, amendment of, or other sufficient relief of, the Zoning Code of the City of Springfield to permit the construction and operation of an asphalt plant. In the event the City Council of the City of Springfield denies the request for such use of the property, then this contract shall be voidable at Buyer's option and if Buyer elects to void this contract Buyer shall receive a refund of the earnest money paid."

On May 21, plaintiff's attorney sent a letter to defendants' attorney informing him of substantial public opposition plaintiff encountered at a public meeting concerning its request for rezoning. The letter concluded:

> "The day after the meeting all of the same representatives of the buyer assembled and discussed our chances for successfully pursuing the re-zoning request. Everyone who was there was in agreement that our chances were zero to none for success. As a result, we decided to withdraw the request for rezoning, rather than face almost certain defeat.

> The bottom line is that we are still interested in the property, but the property is not worth as much to us as a 35-acre parcel zoned I-1, as it would be if it were zoned I-2. At this juncture, I think it is virtually impossible for anyone to get that property re-zoned I-2, especially to accommodate the operation of an asphalt plant. In an effort to keep this thing moving, my clients have authorized me to offer your clients the sum of $142,500.00 for the property, which they believe fairly represents its value with its present zoning classification. Please check with your clients and advise whether or not that revision in the contract is acceptable. If it is, I believe we can accelerate the closing and bring this matter to a speedy conclusion. Your prompt attention will be appreciated. Thanks."

Defendants' attorney responded in a letter dated June 9, the body of which stated, in its entirety:

> "In reply to your May 21 letter, be advised that the owners of the property in question are not interested in selling the property for $142,500 and, accordingly, the offer is not accepted.

> I regret that the zoning reclassification was not approved."

Plaintiff's attorney replied back in a letter dated June 14, the body of which stated, in its entirety:

> "My clients received your letter of June 9, 1993[,] with some regret, however upon some consideration they have elected to proceed with the purchase of the property as provided in the contract. At your convenience please give me a call so that we can set up a closing date."

After this correspondence, plaintiff's attorney sent two more brief letters to defendants' attorney, dated June 23 and July 6, each requesting information concerning the status of defendants' preparation for fulfillment of the contract. Defendants' attorney replied in a letter dated July 8. The letter declared it was the defendants' position plaintiff's failure to waive the rezoning requirement and elect to proceed under the contract at the time the rezoning was denied, coupled with the new offer to buy the property at less than the contract price, effectively voided the contract. Plaintiff apparently sent one more letter in an attempt to convince defendants to honor the contract, but defendants declined. Defendants then arranged to have plaintiff's earnest money returned.

Plaintiff filed a complaint for specific performance and other relief against defendants and American, asking the court to direct defendants to comply with the terms of the contract. Defendants responded by filing a, motion for summary judgment . . . on the basis [that] plaintiff [had] repudiated the contract.

Prior to the hearing on the motions, plaintiff filed interrogatories requesting, among other things, information concerning the current status of the property. Defendants' answers to the interrogatories stated defendants had no knowledge of any third party's involvement in a potential sale of the property, defendants had not made any offer to sell the property to anyone, no one had made an offer to purchase the property or discussed the possibility of purchasing the property, and defendants had not sold the property to, received any offer from, or discussed a sale of the property with, any other trust member.

After a hearing on the motions, the trial court granted the defendants' motion for summary judgment without explaining the basis for its ruling. Plaintiff filed a post-trial motion to vacate the judgment. The trial court denied the post-trial motion, declaring defendants' motion for summary judgment was granted because plaintiff had repudiated the contract. Plaintiff now appeals the trial court's grant of summary judgment, arguing the trial court erred because (1) it did not repudiate the contract, and (2) even if it did repudiate the contract, it timely retracted that repudiation.

Here, there are no facts in dispute. Thus, the question is whether the trial court erred in declaring defendant was entitled to judgment as a matter of law based on those facts.

Plaintiff first argues summary judgment was improper because the trial court erred in finding plaintiff had repudiated the contract.

"The doctrine of anticipatory repudiation requires a clear manifestation of an intent not to perform the contract on the date of performance. . . . That intention must be a definite and unequivocal manifestation that he will not render the promised performance when the time fixed for it in the contract arrives. [Citation.] Doubtful and indefinite statements that performance may or may not take place are not enough to constitute anticipatory repudiation." (*In re Marriage of Olsen* (1988) 528 N.E.2d 684, 686.)

These requirements exist because "anticipatory breach is not a remedy to be taken lightly." (*Olsen*, 528 N.E.2d at 687.) The Restatement (Second) of Contracts adopts the view of the Uniform Commercial Code (UCC) and states "language that under a fair reading 'amounts to a statement of intention not to perform except on conditions which go beyond the contract' constitutes a repudiation. Comment 2 to Uniform Commercial Code § 2-610." (Restatement (Second) of Contracts § 250 Comment, b, at 273 (1981).) Whether an anticipatory repudiation occurred is a question of fact and the judgment of the trial court thereon will not be disturbed unless it is against the manifest weight of evidence.

As can be seen, whether a repudiation occurred is determined on a case-by-case basis, depending on the particular language used. According to the commentators, a suggestion for modification of the contract does not amount to a repudiation. (J. Calamari & J. Perillo, Contracts § 12-4, at 524 n.74 (3d ed. 1987) (hereinafter Calamari). Plaintiff also cites cases in other jurisdictions holding a request for a change in the price term of a contract does not constitute a repudiation. Defendants attempt to distinguish these cases by arguing here, under the totality of the language in the letter and the circumstances surrounding the letter, the request by plaintiff for a decrease in price clearly implied a threat of nonperformance if the price term was not modified. We disagree.

The language in the May 21 letter did not constitute a clearly implied threat of nonperformance. First, although the language in the May 21 letter perhaps could be read as implying plaintiff would refuse to perform under the contract unless the price was modified, given the totality of the language in the letter, such an inference is weak. More important, even if such an inference were possible, Illinois law requires a repudiation be manifested clearly and unequivocally. Plaintiff's May 21 letter at most created an ambiguous implication whether performance would occur. Indeed, during oral argument defense counsel conceded the May 21 letter was "ambiguous" on whether a repudiation had occurred. This is insufficient to constitute a repudiation under well-settled Illinois law. Therefore, the trial court erred in declaring the May 21 letter anticipatorily repudiated the real estate contract as a matter of law.

Moreover, even if plaintiff had repudiated the contract, the trial court erred in granting summary judgment on this basis because plaintiff timely retracted its repudiation . . . . The Restatement (Second) of Contracts states:

> "The effect of a statement as constituting a repudiation under § 250 or the basis for a repudiation under § 251 is nullified by a retraction of the statement if notification of the retraction comes to the attention of the injured party before he materially changes his position in reliance on the repudiation or indicates to the other party that he considers the repudiation to be final." (Emphasis added.) (Restatement (Second) of Contracts § 256(1), at 293 (1981).)

The UCC adopts the same position:

> "Retraction of Anticipatory Repudiation. (1) Until the repudiating party's next performance is due he can retract his repudiation unless the aggrieved party has since the repudiation cancelled or materially changed his position or otherwise indicated that he considers the repudiation final." (§ 2-611(1) (West 1992).)

Professors Calamari and Perillo declare section 2-611 of the UCC:

> ". . . is in general accord with the common law rule that an anticipatory repudiation may be retracted until the other party has commenced an action thereon or has otherwise changed his position. The Code is explicit that no other act of reliance is necessary where the aggrieved party indicates 'that he considers the repudiation final.'" (Calamari § 12.7, at 528.)

"The majority of the common law cases appear to be in accord with this position." (Calamari § 12.7, at 528 n.93.) Other commentators are universally in accord. Professor Farnsworth states: "The repudiating party can prevent the injured party from treating the contract as terminated by retracting before the injured party has acted in response to it." (2 E. Farnsworth, Contracts § 8.22, at 482 (1990).) Professor Corbin declares one who has anticipatorily repudiated his contract has the power of retraction until the aggrieved party has materially changed his position in reliance on the repudiation. Corbin goes on to say the assent of the aggrieved party is necessary for retraction only when the repudiation is no longer merely anticipatory, but has become an actual breach at the time performance is due. (4 Corbin § 980, at 935.) Williston states an anticipatory repudiation can be retracted by the repudiating party "unless the other party has, before the withdrawal, manifested an election to rescind the contract, or changed his position in reliance on the repudiation." 11 W. Jaeger, Williston on Contracts § 1335, at 180 (3d ed. 1968).

Defendants then cite authorities [that] stand for the proposition that after an anticipatory repudiation, the aggrieved party is entitled to choose to treat the contract as rescinded or terminated, to treat the anticipatory repudiation as a breach by bringing suit or otherwise changing its position, or to await the time for performance. The UCC adopts substantially the same position. (UCC § 2-610) Defendants here assert they chose to treat the contract as rescinded, as they had a right to do under well-settled principles of law.

Plaintiff admits the law stated by defendants is well settled, and admits if the May 21 letter was an anticipatory breach, then defendants had the right to treat the contract as being terminated or rescinded. However, plaintiff points out defendants' assertions ignore the great weight of authority, discussed earlier, which provides a right of the repudiating party to retract the repudiation before the aggrieved party has chosen one of its options allowed under the common law. Plaintiff argues defendants' letter of June 9 failed to treat the contract as rescinded, and absent notice or other manifestation defendants were pursuing one of their options, plaintiff was free to retract its repudiation. Plaintiff is correct.

Defendants' [argue that]

an aggrieved party may treat the contract as terminated or rescinded without notice or other indication being given to the repudiating party, and once such a decision is made by the aggrieved party, the repudiating party no longer has the right of retraction. It is true no notice is required to be given to the repudiating party if the aggrieved party materially changes its position as a result of the repudiation. Here, however, the defendants admitted in their answers to plaintiff's interrogatories they had not entered another agreement to sell the property, nor even discussed or considered the matter with another party. Defendants had not changed their position at all, nor do defendants make any attempt to so argue. As can be seen from the language of the Restatement, the UCC, and the commentators, shown earlier, they are in accord that where the aggrieved party has not otherwise undergone a material change in position, the aggrieved party must indicate to the other party it is electing to treat the contract as rescinded. This can be accomplished either by bringing suit, by notifying the repudiating party, or by in some other way manifesting an election to treat the contract as rescinded. Prior to such indication, the repudiating party is free to retract its repudiation.

This rule makes sense as well. If an aggrieved party could treat the contract as rescinded or terminated without notice or other indication to the repudiating party, the rule allowing retraction of an anticipatory repudiation would be eviscerated. No repudiating party ever would be able to retract a repudiation, because after receiving a retraction, the aggrieved party could, if it wished, simply declare it had already decided to treat the repudiation as a rescission or termination of the contract. Defendants' theory would effectively rewrite the common-law rule regarding retraction of anticipatory repudiation so that the repudiating party may retract an anticipatory repudiation only upon assent from the aggrieved party. This is not the common-law rule, and we decline to adopt defendants' proposed revision of it.

Applying the actual common-law rule to the facts here, plaintiff sent defendants a letter dated June 14, which clearly and unambiguously indicated plaintiff intended to perform under the contract. However, defendants did not notify plaintiff, either expressly or impliedly, of an intent to treat the contract as rescinded until July 8. Nor is there anything in the record demonstrating any indication to plaintiff, prior to July 8, of an intent by defendants to treat the contract as rescinded or terminated. Thus, assuming plaintiff's May 21 request for a lower purchase price constituted an anticipatory repudiation of the contract, plaintiff successfully retracted that repudiation in the letter dated June 14 because defendants had not yet materially changed their position or indicated to plaintiff an intent to treat the contract as rescinded. Therefore, because plaintiff had timely retracted any alleged repudiation of the contract, the trial court erred in granting summary judgment for defendants on the basis plaintiff repudiated the contract. Defendants were not entitled to judgment as a matter of law.

The trial court's grant of summary judgment for defendants is reversed, and the cause is remanded.

Reversed and remanded.

NOTES

1. *The Reasoning in* **Hochster.** In *Hochster*, Lord Campbell held that the plaintiff could bring an immediate action upon the renunciation of the contract rather than having to wait until the time for performance.

Consider this commentary:

> De la Tour's counsel argued that the suit was brought prematurely, since there could be no breach of contract before June 1, when performance was to begin. To the sensible premise that Hochster should be "at liberty to consider himself absolved from any future performance," Lord Campbell added the non sequitur: "If the plaintiff has no remedy for breach of the contract unless he treats the contract as in force, and acts upon it down to the 1st June 1852, it follows that, till then, he must enter into no employment which will interfere with his promise . . . ." On this reasoning he concluded that Hochster's action was not premature. This doctrine of anticipatory repudiation soon became the center of controversy.
>
> Critics of the doctrine were quick to point out the flaw in Lord Campbell's argument. The court could have decided that, although De la Tour's repudiation freed Hochster to take other employment, he had no cause of action for performance until the breach came. Although it was important to Hochster to know whether he was free to take other jobs, he was not helped in this by being allowed to sue before the time for performance. For this purpose it would have sufficed to regard the repudiation as the nonoccurrence of a condition of Hochster's remaining duties, which discharged these duties but did not act as a breach. Critics of the doctrine also objected that mere words could not amount to a breach of duty the performance of which was not yet due.

E.A. FARNSWORTH, CONTRACTS 628–29 (1982).

Do you agree with this reasoning or does the plaintiff, by mitigating and waiting until the date of performance to bring suit, risk the possibility that the defendant may decide to perform? Alternatively, the court may hold that the defendant's words or conduct neither amounted to a "nonoccurrence of a condition" nor signaled a breach.

Critics of the anticipatory repudiation doctrine also argue that it is illogical to find a present breach of contract, prior to the performance date. By awarding damages early, the court in effect renders performance due prior to the contractually agreed-upon date. This results in the plaintiff receiving additional benefits not bargained for under the contract. Further, it is argued that it is too speculative to measure damages in advance. Do you agree with these arguments?

Despite such criticism, recent cases and statutes continue to allow the plaintiff to bring suit for total breach of the contract before the time for performance (*i.e.*, UCC § 2-610(b), which allows the aggrieved party to "resort to any remedy for breach"). If the plaintiff waits until the performance date to bring suit, however, he is still excused from all contractual obligations and, contrary to Lord Campbell's reasoning, need not stand ready to perform if the defendant later decides to fulfill his obligation. By waiting and not changing his position, however, the plaintiff leaves the defendant the option to retract his repudiation (*see* UCC § 2-611).

Evaluate the following argument:

> The *Hochster* state of affairs enures to the unjustified advantage of the "non-breacher." The non-breacher may "speculate" in the market during the time between notice of anticipatory repudiation and date of contract performance, with the risk of speculation falling entirely upon the breacher. For example, assume that on June 1 Buyer agrees to purchase from Seller 10,000 bushels of corn at $1.25 per bushel. The agreed date of performance is September 1. On July 15 Seller notifies Buyer of his inability to perform. If the *Hochster* result governs, Buyer now has the option of covering on the market at any time between July 15 and September 1. Thus, in a rising market, Buyer's incentive will be to "speculate" without risk — to purchase substitute goods "on the side" and then wait as long as possible to declare breach and recover contract/market damages. If the market falls, Buyer will declare breach at an early date. Thus, Seller's losses depend entirely upon Buyer's decision as to when to declare a breach.

Do you see a flaw in this reasoning? (Hint: If you *knew* that the corn market was going to rise, or fall, in the next few months, how much money could you make?) Could the Buyer speculate on Seller's checkbook by buying corn at the time of repudiation *and* at the time of performance, and then characterizing as "cover" the one that yielded him the greater damages award from Seller?

2. ***Conduct Constituting Repudiation: The "Unequivocal" Requirement.*** The doctrine of anticipatory repudiation relies on vague concepts, such as "repudiation" and "retraction" that require further elaboration to apply to real-world settings. Common law courts have attempted to provide that elaboration through their interpretation of those concepts in individual cases.

In *Taylor v. Johnston*, 15 Cal. 3d 130 (1975), the plaintiff contracted to breed two of his mares with defendant's stallion, Fleet Nasrullah, for a fee of $3,500 per mare. The contract, executed in 1965, specified that the breeding was to take place the following summer in 1966. It also guaranteed a live foal, and stipulated that if no live foal was produced, the plaintiff was entitled to return the following season, in 1967, for breeding at no additional charge. After the contract was formed but prior to the time that breeding was to take place, the defendant sold the stallion to a Dr. Pessin, who then syndicated the sire by selling shares. Each share entitled its holder to breed one mare each season with the stallion.

Immediately after this sale, the defendant notified the plaintiff of the sale and informed him that "you are, therefore, released from your reservations made to the stallion." When the plaintiff objected and threatened suit, defendant arranged for plaintiff's mares to be bred with the same stallion at the new owner's farm. The plaintiff arranged to board the mares at Elmhurst Farm, which was near the farm boarding Fleet Nasrullah. Clinton Frazier, of Elmhurst Farm, contacted Dr. Pessin, who agreed to make the necessary arrangements to breed the mares to Fleet Nasrullah. Frazier then repeatedly attempted to arrange breeding for one of the mares with the Fleet Nasrullah but was repeatedly turned away on the grounds that a shareholder had a reservation at each of the times that the mare was in heat.

After over a year of fruitless efforts, Frazier eventually arranged for plaintiff's mares to be bred with a Kentucky Derby winner for a fee of $10,000. Both breedings resulted in unsuccessful pregnancies that had to be aborted. Plaintiff sued for anticipatory breach of the contract. The appellate court reversed the trial court, holding instead that there was no anticipatory or actual breach because the time for performance, either the end of the calendar year or the end of the breeding season, had not expired when the mares were bred with the Derby winner.

The court described the two possible avenues of repudiation, express and implied, which result in anticipatory breach. According to the court, "An express repudiation is a clear, positive, unequivocal refusal to perform; an implied repudiation results from conduct where the promisor puts it out of his power to perform so as to make substantial performance of his promise impossible." In response to a repudiation, the court explained, the injured party may *either* treat the repudiation as an anticipatory breach, which terminates the contractual relation between the parties, *or* he can wait until the time for performance has passed and seek remedies for an actual breach, if the other party fails to perform. However, if the injured party disregards the repudiation, and the repudiation is retracted prior to the time of performance, then the repudiation is nullified.

The court then considered two separate actions the defendant had taken that might constitute repudiation. First, defendant clearly repudiated when he sold the stallion and "released" plaintiff from his "reservations." However, plaintiff did not want to be released from these reservations and insisted on performance and threatened to sue. Accordingly, defendant arranged for alternative performance of the contract by arranging for a breeding with the sire at his new home in Kentucky. The court characterized this conduct as constituting a retraction of the repudiation. Second, the court disagreed with the conclusion of the trial court that because the defendant had given the plaintiff "the runaround, . . . [he] had no intention of performing the contract in the manner required by its terms." The appellate court held instead that an implied repudiation requires "conduct equivalent to an unequivocal refusal to perform [which requires] the promisor to put it out of his power to perform." Because the defendants had the power to perform the contract at any time after the mares arrived in Kentucky, an implied repudiation could not have occurred. The defendant's conduct fell short of an implied repudiation because its delays had not yet made performance impossible.

The facts in *Taylor* illustrate how difficult it can be accurately to predict how courts will operationalize the requirements for repudiation and retraction. In *Taylor*, the court held that there was no express or implied repudiation once the initial repudiation had been retracted. The defendant's actions neither made performance impossible nor did they signal an unequivocal refusal to perform the obligation. In *Truman Flatt & Sons*, the buyer's letter seemed to suggest the buyer would not perform absent a modification (doesn't the buyer's description of his proposed modification as "an effort to keep this thing moving" strongly imply that absent the modification he will not proceed with the deal?). Nonetheless, the court held that the buyer's letter "at most created an ambiguous implication whether the performance would occur," and thus fell short of an express or implied repudiation.

The decision in these cases therefore follows the common law rule that requires an anticipatory repudiation to be "a positive, unconditional, and unequivocal declaration of fixed purpose not to perform the contract in any event or at any time." *Dingley v. Oler*, 117 U.S. 490, 502 (1886).

3. *Relaxing the "Unequivocal" Requirement.* A number of courts, however, have declined to apply the strict repudiation rule. Consider *Wholesale Sand & Gravel v. Decker*, 630 A.2d 710 (Me. 1993). In that case, a homeowner, James Decker, contracted with Wholesale Sand and Gravel, Inc. to install a gravel driveway on his property. The contract contained no provision specifying a time for completion. Wholesale began work, but soon experienced difficulty installing the driveway due to the wetness of the ground. Apparently deciding to wait for the ground to dry out before proceeding further, Wholesale removed their equipment from the site. Concerned about the lack of equipment and activity at the site, Decker repeatedly contacted Wholesale. Each time Decker contacted Wholesale, Wholesale promised to "get right on it." Wholesale never did "get right on it," however. Some 45 days after the signing of the contract, Decker decided to terminate the agreement and hired another earth moving company to complete the work. Wholesale then sued Decker for breach of contract. Decker counterclaimed that Wholesale's conduct constituted an anticipatory repudiation of their agreement. The court granted judgment for Decker, explaining that "[o]n this record it was reasonable for Decker to conclude that Wholesale would never complete its performance under the contract." *Id.* at 711. Do you agree that Wholesale's conduct was sufficient to constitute an anticipatory repudiation of the agreement? Recall that there was no provision in the contract specifying a time for completion. Consider this language from the dissent:

> The record is devoid of any words or conduct on the part of the plaintiff that distinctly, unequivocally, and absolutely evidence a refusal or inability to perform . . . . There was a disagreement between the parties as to how much time was allowed for performance, but it is clear that [Wholesale] expected to perform the contract as soon as circumstances permitted.

Id. at 712.

On the other hand, is the dissent expecting too much? On the record, Wholesale never explained its concerns regarding the wetness of the ground. Would a reasonable person not be justified in believing that Wholesale had no intention of completing the project barring a contrary explanation?

This trend toward liberalizing the rule has crystalized in the UCC. Consider *Bonebrake v. Cox*, 499 F.2d 951 (8th Cir. 1974). The buyers of bowling alley equipment learned that the seller, who ran a one-man operation, had died unexpectedly. They checked the seller's warehouse, called his suppliers, and spoke with his sister, all in an unsuccessful effort to locate the missing equipment. Due to time pressure, the buyers ordered equipment from another source. In an action brought by the seller's estate, the court refused to find that the buyer had breached the contract, noting that the requirements of anticipatory repudiation "were clearly present":

The statutory requirement for anticipatory repudiation is not that performance be literally or utterly impossible. The Code was framed with the day to day requirements and customs of businessmen in mind, not the legalisms of counsel. The Code does not require the certainty of the physicist or the utter frustration of literal impossibility . . . . Viewed in the light of the situation confronting the buyers at the time, . . . there was, beyond doubt, a reasonable indication of a rejection of the continuing obligation.

Id. at 961.

When a party facing failure of performance by the other has clearly taken reasonable action in good faith to minimize losses from the breach, the courts have been understandably reluctant to impose additional losses upon him, even though the breaching party has not unequivocally declared his intention not to perform. *Bonebrake* is a good example. Further delays would only have compounded the buyers' losses, and their belief that seller would not perform seems perfectly reasonable under the circumstances. Yet the cost of flexibility is always the loss of certainty.

4.   *Conduct Constituting Repudiation: Good Faith Interpretive Errors.* The agreement in *Truman Flatt & Sons* made it clear that the buyer's obligation to purchase was conditional on it receiving approval to build its asphalt plant on the property. Sometimes, however, contracts fail to make risk allocations clear. Suppose, for example, that one party refuses to perform on the ground that a condition precedent to his obligation was not satisfied, but the other party disagrees that the contract contains such a condition. If a court subsequently rules that the contract does not contain the condition, does that mean the party who refused to perform has anticipatorily repudiated (even though he believed in good faith that he did not have the obligation to perform)?

In *Lak, Inc. v. Deer Creek Enterprises*, 976 F.2d 328 (7th Cir. 1992), a real estate contract for the sale of a condominium specified that "532 units shall be available to the property in accordance with an appropriate site plan." After the contract had been negotiated, new local zoning regulations limited the number of possible units at the site to 508. Following discovery of the new regulation, the seller sent a letter to the buyer offering to close the property "as is." Under the seller's interpretation of the contract, the burden of securing zoning approval was on the buyer, so that the new zoning regulations did not release the buyer from its obligations under the contract. The buyer, however, interpreted the contract as placing the burden of securing the zoning approval on the seller and therefore proposed to the seller that the contract price be reduced to account for the changed circumstances. When the seller rejected the buyer's interpretation, the buyer sought relief, claiming that the seller had anticipatorily breached by insisting on closing "as is." The court found that the contract was ambiguous as to which party was required to secure zoning approval. To determine whether the seller had anticipatorily repudiated, the court conducted a two-pronged inquiry. Under the first prong, a party ordinarily will not be held to have repudiated if its actions are based on a reasonable interpretation of the contract, even if a court subsequently rejects that interpretation. Since the seller's interpretation of the ambiguity was reasonable in this case, its proposal to modify the terms of the contract accordingly did not by itself constitute an anticipatory repudiation. Under the second prong, a party that acts on a reasonable interpretation subsequently rejected by a court can nonetheless be held to have repudiated if it unequivocally insists on its interpretation of the contract. Because the seller in this case left open the possibility of future negotiation regarding the ambiguous part of the contract, the court held it had not anticipatorily repudiated the agreement.

The *Lak* court's approach has had mixed success in other jurisdictions. One court considered and rejected the view that there is a good faith exception to the doctrine of anticipatory repudiation (the first prong of the *Lak* court's analysis). In *Record Club of America, Inc. v. United Artists Records, Inc.*, 643 F. Supp. 925 (S.D.N.Y. 1986), RCOA anticipatorily repudiated the contract because it erroneously believed that UAR had already breached the agreement. RCOA sought to avoid UAR's recovery for RCOA's anticipatory breach because of its alleged good faith belief that UAR had earlier breached the agreement. The court declined to accept the principle that there was a good faith exception to the doctrine of anticipatory breach:

> [A]ssuming that UAR was acting in good faith, that would not excuse its repudiation. The test for an anticipatory repudiation is an objective one and good faith is immaterial. [Citations omitted.] An anticipatory repudiation may be based upon an erroneous contract interpretation just as it may be based on a refusal to perform for any other reason. Whatever the breaching party's state of mind, the impact on the innocent party is the same — he faces total loss of the repudiator's performance, to which the contract entitled him. This principle is in accord with the Restatement of Contracts which provides that "a party acts at his peril if, insisting on what he mistakenly believes to be his rights, he refuses to perform his duty." *Restatement (Second)* § 250 comment d, at 274-5 (1981).

Id. at 939.

On the other hand, in *Chamberlin v. Puckett Constr.*, 277 Mont. 198, 921 P.2d 1237 (1996), the Supreme Court of Montana accepted the view that proposals for modification do not constitute repudiations unless they are demanded (the second prong of the *Lak* court's analysis). The court held that only where a party offers terms in accordance with its interpretation of the agreement "accompanied by an unequivocal statement that [he will] not perform unless the additional term is met, [will the party's actions constitute] an anticipatory breach of the contract excusing performance by the other party."

5. *The Right to Retract an Anticipatory Repudiation.* In *Taylor v. Johnston*, Note 2, *supra*, the court held the defendants retracted their repudiation by agreeing to breed the plaintiff's two mares to Fleet Nasrullah in Kentucky. Similarly, in *Truman Flatt & Sons*, the court held that even if the buyer had repudiated the agreement, it effectively retracted the repudiation when plaintiffs sent the June 14th letter indicating they were still interested in purchasing the property at the original contract price. Neither party made an explicit retraction. Instead, both parties implicitly retracted by making it clear that they intended to fulfill their performance obligations despite their earlier repudiation. Retractions therefore can arise from conduct indicating that the repudiating party is still willing to be bound by the contract. Consider *Gibbs, Nathaniel (Canada), Ltd. v.*

International Multifoods Corp., 804 F.2d 450 (8th Cir. 1986), which concerned a peanut purchasing agreement. Under the contract, the buyer had the ability to reject unsatisfactory peanuts, but the seller had the right to "recondition" them for subsequent approval by the buyer. When the seller delivered insect-infested peanuts, the buyer rejected the delivery and cancelled the agreement, telling the seller that he would not accept reconditioned peanuts. During later discussions with the seller, however, the buyer agreed to permit the reconditioning of the insect-infested peanuts. When the seller's second delivery, post-reconditioning, also proved to be insect-infested, the buyer again cancelled the agreement. The seller claimed that the buyer's attempt to cancel the agreement after the initial delivery amounted to a repudiation of the agreement. The court agreed, but held that the later agreement between the buyer and seller providing for the reconditioning of the peanuts amounted to "a retraction of any repudiation [the buyer] may have made." *Id.* at 452.

In both *Taylor v. Johnson* and *Truman Flatt & Sons*, the courts acknowledge that the repudiating party exercised its right of retraction. Does UCC § 2-611(1) change the common law rule? Does the rule permitting retraction impose unjustifiable breach costs on an innocent party? Is the retraction notice requirement discussed in *Truman Flatt & Sons* sufficient to protect the nonbreacher? Would it help to eliminate these costs by providing the nonrepudiator with the option of accepting or denying a retraction, rather than allowing the repudiater to retract unilaterally?

6. *Insolvency as Implied Repudiation.* The common law refused to excuse a party who repudiates when his contractual partner becomes insolvent after entering into the contract. In *Keppelon v. W.M. Ritter Flooring Corp.*, 97 N.J.L. 200 (1922), for example, the defendant, having contracted with plaintiff to build an apartment house, refused to commence construction when the performance date arrived. Responding to the plaintiff's request for performance, the defendant repudiated, refusing to perform at any time. The defendant answered plaintiff's complaint, claiming that his repudiation of the contract was justified by the status of the plaintiff's credit. The court held that:

> the mere insolvency of a party to a building contract (to whom by the terms of the contract labor and materials are to be furnished) does not terminate the contract, in the absence of provisions to that effect therein, nor does it justify the other party in refusing altogether to perform, for it does not follow therefrom that the insolvent party could not and would not perform his part even though insolvent. . . . It might well be that the insolvent party might find it advantageous and possible to carry out his part of the contract, since insolvency does not necessarily mean a total lack of assets. To hold that mere insolvency of a party puts an end to a contract, and excuses the solvent party from the obligation altogether, would be intolerable. If the mere fact of insolvency terminates a contract every insolvent contractor would automatically be shorn of all property rights and beneficial interests in contracts. Of course, this cannot be.

Id. at 204–05. If the *Keppelon* case involved a sale of goods, how would UCC § 2-609 bear on the controversy? Note UCC § 2-702.

7. *Repudiation After Partial Performance.* In *Hochster*, the breach was truly anticipatory in that it occurred before the commencement of the contracted for activity was to begin. What if the alleged repudiation had occurred after the performance commenced but before it has been completed? The Supreme Court of Virginia addressed this issue in *Bennett v. Sage Payment Solutions, Inc.*, 710 S.E.2d 736 (Va. 2011). In that case, Bennett entered into a one-year contract in February 2008 to serve as the president of Sage Payment Solutions, Inc. The contract included a severance package that guaranteed Bennett a year's salary as well as bonuses and other benefits unless Bennett resigned without "good reason," as defined by the agreement, or unless Sage terminated Bennett with "good cause." After Bennett began his employment, the parties continued without success to negotiate the terms of his compensation, and on June 7, 2008 Bennett wrote an email to Sage stating that he would require increased compensation to the $1 million range, "or we agree to my transition out of the company." Bennett's employment was ultimately terminated on September 30, 2008.

In response, Bennett filed a claim against Sage seeking severance payments. Sage responded by asserting repudiation as a defense. Bennett argued that he could not have repudiated a contract that he had partially performed. The Supreme Court of Virginia disagreed:

> The question presented now becomes whether the court erred by allowing Sage to assert repudiation as a defense to Bennett's breach of contract claim based on Bennett's demand for increased compensation or his "transition out of the company," after he had already begun performance under the Agreement. While we acknowledge the line of Virginia cases that characterizes repudiation before performance is due under a contract as an anticipatory breach, we hold that repudiation may also apply to a contract that has been partially performed, when future obligations under the contract are repudiated . . . .

> The Restatement (Second) of Contracts also supports the view that a party may repudiate his or her contractual duties after performance has commenced. [T]he Restatement's definition [of repudiation in Section 250] does not provide that repudiation must occur prior to the commencement of any performance under the contract. When a contract requires performance continuously for some period of time, a party's renunciation of his or her contractual obligation may constitute a repudiation. Arthur L. Corbin, 9 Corbin on Contracts § 954, at 738 (interim ed.2002). In such cases, the repudiation of the contractual obligation is "anticipatory with respect to the performances that are not yet due." Id.

> In sum, we hold that a party's renunciation or abandonment of his or her contractual duties, after performance has commenced under a contract requiring continuous performance, constitutes a repudiation, which may be treated by the party to whom the duty is owed as an anticipatory breach of the contract.

Id. at 740, 741.

Essay: Anticipatory Repudiation and the Mitigation Principle

At early common law, the requirement that a party must breach to trigger the other party's duty to mitigate meant that neither party could be required to adjust to post-formation events until after the time for performance. This was because, on the classical common law view, a party could not be in breach of a duty until that party's duty matured and he failed to discharge it. In *Hochster*, however, the common law made an exception to this rule. A promisor could effectively declare a breach before the time for performance by anticipatorily repudiating his contract. Likewise, if an event occurring prior to the time for performance rendered it *impossible* for a promisor to perform by that deadline, the promisee could use the doctrine of anticipatory repudiation to declare the promisor presently in breach of the agreement.

In principle, therefore, anticipatory repudiation allows the promisor to trigger the promisee's duty to mitigate before the time of performance has expired. As a consequence, the parties are able to avoid costs of nonperformance that would be incurred if they were required (or allowed) to delay mitigation until the time of performance. To see this, return to our earlier example in which Seller on July 1 agrees to deliver an air conditioning unit to Buyer on December 1 at a cost of $250,000, and subsequently suffers an explosion in its plant that will delay delivery by two months. Suppose in the above example, that when the seller informs the buyer on September 1 that it will not be able to meet the delivery deadline, the buyer could, at an expense of $10,000, redesign the building under construction to accommodate an equivalent quality but differently designed air conditioning unit that can be purchased for a December 1 delivery at $260,000. Thus, the buyer's total losses due to the seller's nonperformance would be $20,000 — the additional price for the substitute air conditioner plus the additional costs of redesigning the buyer's building [($260,000 – $250,000) = $10,000 + $10,000 = $20,000]. If the seller had to wait until the time of performance to breach, it could not trigger the buyer's duty to mitigate at the time of the plant explosion. The seller therefore would be forced to choose between two alternatives. First, it could purchase an equivalent air conditioning unit for $300,000, and thereby incur a certain loss of $50,000. Second, it could wait until the time for performance to breach and compensate the buyer for the difference between the contract price and the market price at that time. Since the September 1 price of $300,000 for a December 1 delivery reflects the market's best guess at the December 1 price, the seller's expected loss from taking this option would be $50,000.[6] As against these options, the seller would prefer limiting its maximum loss to $20,000 by having the buyer adjust by redesigning its building. By anticipatorily repudiating at the time of its plant explosion, the seller might be able to force the buyer to mitigate its damages.[7] If the buyer refuses to adjust and instead purchases the $300,000 unit, the seller might not be liable for the additional

---

[6] The September 1 price for a December 1 delivery reflects the market's best guess at the December 1 price. It therefore reflects an implicit assignment of probabilities over possible price points on December 1 according to which the $300,000 price is the most likely price, based on the information available to market participants on September 1.

[7] We say seller "might" be able to force buyer to mitigate because some jurisdictions allow the nonbreacher the option of waiting until the time for performance before mitigating in response to an

$30,000 the buyer could have avoided by redesigning and purchasing the less expensive unit instead.

The doctrine of anticipatory repudiation, then, might serve to extend the duty of mitigation to a period before the time for performance has expired. Because it potentially enables the parties to avoid wasteful actions taken in reliance on performance when subsequent events lead one or both parties to believe performance has become unlikely or impossible, it brings actual contracts closer to the ideal contract, which would require parties to make all cost-effective adjustments to events occurring after formation. Two problems, however, potentially undermine the positive effects of the anticipatory repudiation doctrine.

First, to the extent that an anticipatory repudiation might be held effective even if ambiguous, it is subject to two kinds of "strategic," or bad faith, manipulation. In the first kind of manipulation, a promisor who wishes to avoid the contract seeks to provoke the promisee into declaring the contract terminated, thereafter claiming that the promisee has breached the contract and the promisor is justified in rescinding. To use this ploy, a promisor who wishes to evade performance sends a communication that leads the promisee to believe the promisor may not be able to perform, but that deliberately falls short of expressly repudiating the agreement. If the promisee is sufficiently insecure, he may believe the promisor has repudiated the contract and thus attempt to secure a substitute performance. The promisor can then deny that it repudiated and sue the promisee for breach. To illustrate, suppose that instead of experiencing a plant explosion, the seller's production costs have increased above the contract price. In an attempt to escape the contract, the seller sends a letter to the buyer stating: "Please be advised we are having production difficulties and now wonder if December 1 delivery is realistic. We'll do all we can." This communication causes the buyer to make a cover contract for $300,000. The seller now denies that it has repudiated and argues that the buyer's cover constituted breach, thereby releasing the seller from its duty to perform. Whether the gambit works depends on whether or not a court would hold that the seller's communication constitutes a repudiation. But the ambiguity of the communication itself makes the outcome of adjudication uncertain, and therefore paves the way for a settlement in which the seller reduces its original liability under the agreement.

In the second kind of manipulation, a promisor again sends a communication suggesting that she may not be able to perform. Then the promisor waits until the time of performance to see if the contract is beneficial for her. If it is, she performs and denies that her earlier communication constituted a repudiation. If not, she claims that her earlier communication constituted a repudiation and refuses to reimburse the promisee for the increase in damages between the time of the (alleged) repudiation and the time of performance. To illustrate, return to our earlier hypothetical in which a plant explosion on September 1 renders the seller unable to manufacture and deliver the air conditioning unit to the buyer by the contract delivery deadline. Although the seller could cover on September 1 for $300,000 and suffer a $50,000 loss, if it waits until the time for performance it is possible that the price of substitute units will fall below $300,000. Unfortunately, it

---

anticipatory repudiation. We discuss this variation of the mitigation rule for anticipatory repudiation below.

is equally likely that the price will increase above $300,000. The seller can use the anticipatory repudiation doctrine in an attempt to have its cake and eat it too. In this gambit, on September 1 the seller sends the buyer the same letter as above. If the market price of air conditioners increases above $300,000 by the time of performance, the seller will insist that it repudiated the agreement in September when it sent the letter to the buyer, and therefore is responsible only for the difference between the contract price and the market price at the time of repudiation ($50,000), rather than the larger difference between the contract price and the higher market price at the time of performance. If the market price at the time of performance is less than $300,000, however, the seller will insist it did not repudiate the agreement in September, and instead will purchase the air conditioner from another seller and tender it to the buyer on December 1. This strategy in effect allows the seller to speculate at the buyer's expense, forcing the buyer to subsidize the seller against the downside of the risk of waiting until performance (i.e., the chance that the price will increase from September 1 to December 1) while enjoying the upside of the risk of waiting until performance (i.e., the chance that the price will decrease from September 1 to December 1).

Both kinds of strategic manipulation are possible only if there is a significant prospect that courts will hold that an ambiguous communication constitutes an anticipatory repudiation. Therefore, one way to reduce the risk of these kinds of strategic abuses is to adopt a strict rule that anticipatory repudiations must be unambiguous. Most common law jurisdictions in fact have adopted this rule. Parties are still free to communicate information bearing on the probability of performance. But because such communications will not trigger a duty to mitigate, a promisee is free to ignore this information. The promisee therefore may over-rely: It might take actions in reliance that are not justified given the probability of the promisor's breach based on the new information the promisee received. The promisee may over-rely because the promisor will be liable to compensate the promisee for its reliance expenditures.

On the other hand, the promisee may wish to avoid overreliance if he doesn't expect to be fully compensated for all losses due to breach. In the American legal system, nonbreachers are subject to systematic undercompensation because breachers are not required to compensate them for their attorney's fees or, typically, to pay them pre-judgment interest at a competitive market rate. Thus, once a promisee learns that a promisor's performance is less likely, he may wish to reduce his reliance expenditures to mitigate any uncompensated losses resulting from promisor's breach. In any event, absent a clear repudiation from the promisor, a promisee must be careful lest the actions he takes to reduce his reliance on the promisor's performance (such as entering into a cover transaction) are subsequently construed as a breach.[8]

---

[8] In order to enhance a promisee's ability to protect itself against an increased risk of the promisor's breach, some common law jurisdictions have followed UCC § 2-609 in adopting an "insecurity" default rule called *the right to demand adequate assurances* (*See* Section D, *infra*). This doctrine entitles a party with reasonable grounds for insecurity to demand adequate assurances from the party causing the insecurity. If adequate assurances are not forthcoming, the insecure party is entitled to treat the contract as anticipatorily repudiated.

C.   MEASURING DAMAGES FOR ANTICIPATORY REPUDIATION

In the preceding section, we suggested that the doctrine of anticipatory repudiation might serve the purpose of allowing the promisor to trigger the duty to mitigate before the time for performance elapses. But to protect the promisee from undercompensation and strategic manipulation, courts have sometimes been hesitant to require mitigation at the time of repudiation. As a result, promisees may exacerbate their damages by waiting until the time for performance to mitigate. The rule that allows the promisee to wait until the time of performance to mitigate its damages might be justified nonetheless because the opposite rule subjects the promisee to the additional risk that it will be held to have improperly mitigated its damages, or that it's ostensible mitigation constituted instead an affirmative breach. In addition, allowing the nonbreacher to wait until performance to mitigate its damages reduces its exposure to the bad faith, strategic behavior discussed above. By allowing the promisee to wait until the time of performance, the law insulates the promisee from conduct that a bad faith promisor might use as a factual predicate for avoiding the contract.

Notwithstanding these legitimate concerns, the rule providing the promisee with the option to wait until the time of performance before responding to an anticipatory repudiation undermines, rather than enhances, the goal of facilitating mutually beneficial post-contract adjustments. For this reason, some scholars and commentators favor the competing rule that requires promisees to mitigate within a reasonable time following an anticipatory repudiation.

As you read *Cosden Oil*, pay careful attention to the split in the statutory authority on the question of when the aggrieved party must mitigate following repudiation. Given that authority exists for both the time of repudiation and time of performance views, what theoretical concerns would lead you to choose one over the other in *Cosden Oil*, and in contracts in general?

COSDEN OIL & CHEMICAL CO. v. KARL O. HELM AKTIENGESELLSCHAFT
United States Court of Appeals, Fifth Circuit
736 F.2d 1064 (1984)

REAVLEY, J.

We must address one of the most difficult interpretive problems of the Uniform Commercial Code — the appropriate time to measure buyer's damages where the seller anticipatorily repudiates a contract and the buyer does not cover. The district court applied the Texas version of Article 2 and measured buyer's damages at a commercially reasonable time after seller's repudiation. We affirm, but remand for modification of damages on another point.

This contractual dispute arose out of events and transactions occurring in the first three months of 1979, when the market in polystyrene, a petroleum derivative used to make molded products, was steadily rising. During this time Iran, a major petroleum producer, was undergoing political turmoil. Karl O. Helm Aktiengesell-schaft (Helm or Helm Hamburg), an international trading company based in Hamburg, West Germany, anticipated a tightening in the world petrochemical supply and decided to purchase a large amount of polystyrene. Acting on orders from Helm Hamburg, Helm Houston, a wholly-owned subsidiary, initiated negotiations with Cosden Oil & Chemical Company (Cosden), a Texas-based producer of chemical products, including polystyrene.

Rudi Scholtyssek, general manager of Helm Houston, contacted Ken Smith, Cosden's national sales coordinator, to inquire about the possibility of purchasing quantities of polystyrene. Negotiating over the telephone and by telex, the parties agreed to the purchase and sale of 1250 metric tons of high impact polystyrene at $.2825 per pound and 250 metric tons of general purpose polystyrene at $.265 per pound. The parties also discussed options on each polystyrene type. On January 18, 1979, Scholtyssek met with Smith in Dallas, leaving behind two purchase confirmations. Purchase confirmation 04 contained the terms for high impact and 05 contained the terms for general purpose. Both confirmations contained the price and quantity terms listed above, and specified the same delivery and payment terms. The polystyrene was to be delivered during January and February in one or more lots, to be called for at Helm's instance. Confirmation 04 specified that Helm had an option for an additional 1000 metric tons of high impact, and confirmation 05 expressed a similar option for 500 metric tons of general purpose. The option amounts were subject to the same terms, except that delivery was to be during February and March. The options were to be declared, at the latest, by January 31, 1979.

On January 22, Helm called for the first shipment of high impact under order 04, to be delivered FAS at a New Jersey port to make a January 29 shipping date for a trans-Atlantic voyage. On January 23, Helm telexed Cosden to declare the options on purchase orders 04 and 05, designating the high impact option quantity as order 06 and the general purpose option quantity as order 07. After exercising the options, Helm sent purchase confirmations 06 and 07, which Cosden received on January 29. That same day Helm Houston received confirmations 04 and 05, which Smith had signed.

Cosden shipped 90,000 pounds of high impact polystyrene to Helm on or about January 26. Cosden then sent an invoice for that quantity to Helm Houston on or about January 31. The front of the invoice stated, "This order is subject to the terms and conditions shown on the reverse hereof." Among the "Conditions of Sale" listed on the back of the invoice was a force majeure provision.[9] Helm paid for the first shipment in accordance with the agreement.

As Helm had expected, polystyrene prices began to rise in late January, and continued upward during February and March. Cosden also experienced problems

---

[9] [3] "No liability hereunder shall result to either party from delay in performance or nonperformance caused by circumstances beyond the control of the party affected including, but not limited to: Acts of God, fire, flood, war, governmental regulation, direction or request, accident, strike, labor trouble, shortage of or inability to obtain material, equipment or transportation. The affected party may omit purchases or deliveries during the period of continuance of such circumstances and the contract quantities shall be reduced by the quantities so omitted."

at two of its plants in late January. Normally, Cosden supplied its Calumet City, Illinois, production plant with styrene monomer, the "feed stock" or main ingredient of polystyrene, by barges that traveled from Louisiana up the Mississippi and Illinois Rivers to a canal that extended to Cosden's plant. Due to the extremely cold winter of 1978-79, however, the Illinois River and the canal froze, suspending barge traffic for a few weeks. A different problem beset Cosden's Windsor, New Jersey, production plant. A new reactor, used in the polystyrene manufacturing process, had recently been installed at the Windsor plant. A manufacturing defect soon became apparent, however, and Cosden returned the reactor to the manufacturer for repair, which took several weeks. At the time of the reactor breakdown, Cosden was manufacturing only general purpose at the Windsor plant. Cosden had planned on supplying Helm's high impact orders from the Calumet City plant.

Late in January Cosden notified Helm that it was experiencing problems at its production facilities and that the delivery under 04 might be delayed. On February 6, Smith telephoned Scholtyssek and informed him that Cosden was cancelling orders 05, 06, and 07 because two plants were "down" and it did not have sufficient product to fill the orders. Cosden, however, would continue to honor order 04. Smith confirmed the cancellation in a letter dated February 8, which Scholtyssek received on or about February 12. After Helm Hamburg learned of Cosden's cancellation, Wolfgang Gordian, a member of Helm's executive board, sent an internal memorandum to Helm Houston outlining a strategy. Helm would urge that Cosden continue to perform under 04 and, after receiving the high impact polystyrene, would offset amounts owing under 04 against Helm's damages for nondelivery of the balance of polystyrene. Gordian also instructed Helm Houston to send a telex to Cosden. Following instructions, Scholtyssek then requested from Cosden "the relevant force majeure certificate" to pass on to Helm Hamburg. Helm also urged Cosden to deliver immediately several hundred metric tons of high impact to meet two February shipping dates for which Helm had booked shipping space.

In mid-February Cosden shipped approximately 1,260,000 pounds of high impact to Helm under order 04. This shipment's invoice, which also included the force majeure provision on the reverse side, specified that Helm owed $355,950, due by March 15 or 16. After this delivery Helm requested that Cosden deliver the balance under order 04 for shipment on a vessel departing March 16. Cosden informed Helm that a March 16 delivery was not possible. On March 15, citing production problems with the 04 balance, Cosden offered to sell 1000 metric tons of styrene monomer at $.41 per pound. Although Cosden later lowered the price on the styrene monomer, Helm refused the offer, insisting on delivery of the balance of 04 polystyrene by March 31 at the latest. Around the end of March, Cosden informed Scholtyssek by telephone that it was cancelling the balance of order 04.

Cosden sued Helm, seeking damages for Helm's failure to pay for delivered polystyrene. Helm counterclaimed for Cosden's failure to deliver polystyrene as agreed. The jury found on special verdict that Cosden had agreed to sell polystyrene to Helm under all four orders. The jury also found that Cosden anticipatorily repudiated orders 05, 06, and 07 and that Cosden canceled order 04 before Helm's failure to pay for the second 04 delivery constituted a repudiation. The jury fixed the per pound market prices for polystyrene under each of the four orders at three different times: when Helm learned of the cancellation, at a commercially reasonable time thereafter, and at the time for delivery.

The district court, viewing the four orders as representing one agreement, determined that Helm was entitled to recover $628,676 in damages representing the difference between the contract price and the market price at a commercially reasonable time after Cosden repudiated its polystyrene delivery obligations and that Cosden was entitled to an offset of $355,950 against those damages for polystyrene delivered, but not paid for, under order 04.

II.
Time for Measuring Buyer's Damages

Both parties find fault with the time at which the district court measured Helm's damages for orders 05, 06, and 07.[10] Cosden argues that damages should be measured when Helm learned of the repudiation. Helm contends that market price as of the last day for delivery — or the time of performance — should be used to compute its damages under the contract-market differential. We reject both views, and hold that the district court correctly measured damages at a commercially reasonable point after Cosden informed Helm that it was cancelling the three orders.

Article 2 of the Code has generally been hailed as a success for its comprehensiveness, its deference to mercantile reality, and its clarity. Nevertheless, certain aspects of the Code's overall scheme have proved troublesome in application. The interplay among §§ 2-610, 2-711, 2-712, 2-713, and 2-723, represents one of those areas, and has been described as "an impossible legal thicket." J. White & R. Summers, *Uniform Commercial Code* § 6-7 at 242 (2d ed. 1980). The aggrieved buyer seeking damages for seller's anticipatory repudiation presents the most difficult interpretive problem. Section 2-713 describes the buyer's damages remedy.

> (a) Subject to the provisions of this chapter with respect to proof of market price (Section 2-723), the measure of damages for non-delivery or repudiation by the seller is the difference between the market price *at the time when the buyer learned of the breach* and the contract price together with any incidental and consequential damages provided in this chapter (Section 2-715), but less expenses saved in consequence of the seller's breach.

Courts and commentators have identified three possible interpretations of the phrase "learned of the breach." If seller anticipatorily repudiates, buyer learns of the breach: (1) When he learns of the repudiation; (2) When he learns of the repudiation plus a commercially reasonable time; or (3) When performance is due under the contract.

We would not be free to decide the question if there were a Texas case on point, bound as we are by *Erie* to follow state law in diversity cases. We find, however, that no Texas case has addressed the Code question of buyer's damages in an

---

[10] [5] The damages measurement problem does not apply to Cosden's breach of order 04, which was not anticipatorily repudiated. The time Helm learned of Cosden's intent to deliver no more polystyrene under 04 was the same time as the last date of performance, which had been extended to the end of March.

anticipatory repudiation context. Texas, alone in this circuit, does not allow us to certify questions of state law for resolution by its courts.

Fredonia Broadcasting Corp. v. RCA Corp., 481 F.2d 781 (5th Cir. 1973) (*Fredonia I*), contains dicta on this question. The court merely quoted the language of the section and noted that the time for measuring market price — when buyer learns of the breach — was the only difference from pre-Code Texas law. We have found no Texas case quoting or citing *Fredonia I* for its dicta on damages under § 2-713. Although *Fredonia I* correctly stated the statutory language, it simply did not address or recognize the interpretive problems peculiar to seller's anticipatory repudiation.

Since *Fredonia I*, four Texas courts have applied § 2-713 to measure buyer's damages at the time he learned of the breach. In all of these cases the aggrieved buyer learned of the breach at or after the time of performance . . . .

We do not doubt, and Texas law is clear, that market price at the time buyer learns of the breach is the appropriate measure of § 2-713 damages in cases where buyer learns of the breach at or after the time for performance. This will be the common case, for which § 2-713 was designed. In the relatively rare case where seller anticipatorily repudiates and buyer does not cover, the specific provision for anticipatory repudiation cases, § 2-610, authorizes the aggrieved party to await performance for a commercially reasonable time before resorting to his remedies of cover or damages.

In the anticipatory repudiation context, the buyer's specific right to wait for a commercially reasonable time before choosing his remedy must be read together with the general damages provision of § 2-713 to extend the time for measurement beyond when buyer learns of the breach. Comment 1 to § 2-610 states that if an aggrieved party "awaits performance beyond a commercially reasonable time he cannot recover resulting damages which he should have avoided." This suggests that an aggrieved buyer can recover damages where the market rises during the commercially reasonable time he awaits performance. To interpret 2-713's "learned of the breach" language to mean the time at which seller first communicates his anticipatory repudiation would undercut the time that 2-610 gives the aggrieved buyer to await performance.

The buyer's option to wait a commercially reasonable time also interacts with § 2-611, which allows the seller an opportunity to retract his repudiation. Thus, an aggrieved buyer "learns of the breach" a commercially reasonable time after he learns of the seller's anticipatory repudiation. The weight of scholarly commentary supports this interpretation.

Typically, our question will arise where parties to an executory contract are in the midst of a rising market. To the extent that market decisions are influenced by a damages rule, measuring market price at the time of seller's repudiation gives seller the ability to fix buyer's damages and may induce seller to repudiate, rather than abide by the contract. By contrast, measuring buyer's damages at the time of performance will tend to dissuade the buyer from covering, in hopes that market price will continue upward until performance time.

Allowing the aggrieved buyer a commercially reasonable time, however, provides him with an opportunity to investigate his cover possibilities in a rising market without fear that, if he is unsuccessful in obtaining cover, he will be relegated to a market-contract damage remedy measured at the time of repudiation. The Code supports this view. While cover is the preferred remedy, the Code clearly provides the option to seek damages. See § 2-712(c) & comment 3. If "[t]he buyer is always free to choose between cover and damages for non-delivery," and if § 2-712 "is not intended to limit the time necessary for [buyer] to look around and decide as to how he may best effect cover," it would be anomalous, if the buyer chooses to seek damages, to fix his damages at a time before he investigated cover possibilities and before he elected his remedy. See *id.* comment 2 & 3. Moreover, comment 1 to § 2-713 states, "The general baseline adopted in this section uses as a yardstick the market in which the buyer would have obtained cover had he sought that relief." See § 2-610 comment 1. When a buyer chooses not to cover, but to seek damages, the market is measured at the time he could have covered — a reasonable time after repudiation. See §§ 2-711 & 2-713.

Persuasive arguments exist for interpreting "learned of the breach" to mean "time of performance," consistent with the pre-Code rule. If this was the intention of the Code's drafters, however, phrases in §§ 2-610 and 2-712 lose their meaning. If buyer is entitled to market-contract damages measured at the time of performance, it is difficult to explain why the anticipatory repudiation section limits him to a commercially reasonable time to await performance. See § 2-610 comment 1. Similarly, in a rising market, no reason would exist for requiring the buyer to act "without unreasonable delay" when he seeks to cover following an anticipatory repudiation. See § 2-712(a).

The interplay among the relevant Code sections does not permit, in this context, an interpretation that harmonizes all and leaves no loose ends. We therefore acknowledge that our interpretation fails to explain the language of § 2-723(a) insofar as it relates to aggrieved buyers. We note, however, that the section has limited applicability — cases that come to trial before the time of performance will be rare. Moreover, the comment to § 2-723 states that the "section is not intended to exclude the use of any other reasonable method of determining market price or of measuring damages . . . ." In light of the Code's persistent theme of commercial reasonableness, the prominence of cover as a remedy, and the time given an aggrieved buyer to await performance and to investigate cover before selecting his remedy, we agree with the district court that "learned of the breach" incorporates § 2-610's commercially reasonable time.[11]

---

[11]   [11] We note that two circuits arrived at a similar conclusion by different routes. In Cargill, Inc. v. Stafford, 553 F.2d 1222 (10th Cir. 1977), the court began its discussion of damages by embracing the "time of performances" interpretation urged by Professors White and Summers. *Id.* Nevertheless, the court

> conclude[d] that under § 4-2-713 a buyer may urge continued performance for a reasonable time. At the end of a reasonable period he should cover if substitute goods are readily available. If substitution is readily available and buyer does not cover within a reasonable time, damages should be based on the price at the end of that reasonable time rather than on the price when performance is due.

Id. at 1227. The *Cargill* court would employ the time of performances measure only if buyer had a valid reason for not covering.

The cause is remanded to the district court to modify Helm's damages under orders 05 and 07 and to decide the matter of appellate attorneys' fees.

NOTES

1. ***Justifying an Additional Waiting Period.*** Ultimately, the *Cosden Oil* court allows the aggrieved party to wait a commercially reasonable period of time before mitigating damages because it "provides him with an opportunity to investigate his cover possibilities in a rising market without fear that, if he is unsuccessful in obtaining cover, he will be relegated to a market-contract damage remedy measured at the time of repudiation." If there is a competitive market (rising or not), doesn't that mean the aggrieved party *can* cover? Exactly what investigation does the aggrieved buyer require in a competitive market? Why allow any delay at all? If the seller repudiates, isn't it clear that he would be better off if the buyer covered at the time of repudiation? If so, why not require the aggrieved party to cover at that time or receive damages equivalent to the cost of cover at that time (the difference between the price of the original forward contract and the market price for the same forward contract at the time of repudiation)? If, however, the market of equivalent forward contracts is thin, then cover may be difficult to obtain. But no special rule is required to allow the seller a reasonable time to cover under such circumstances. The standard mitigation doctrine requires only that the non-aggrieved party take reasonable measures to reduce its damages, which would allow for reasonable delay of cover in a thin market. What, then, is the rationale for allowing aggrieved parties an additional period of time to mitigate their damages following a repudiation?

2. ***A Rising Market?*** The court in *Cosden Oil* makes two statements about how the damage formula for anticipatory repudiation will affect the buyer's and seller's incentives. The court claims that "[t]ypically, our question will arise where parties to an executory contract are in the midst of a rising market. To the extent that market decisions are influenced by a damages rule, measuring market price at the time of seller's repudiation gives seller the ability to fix buyer's damages and may

---

In First Nat'l Bank of Chicago v. Jefferson Mortgage Co., 576 F.2d 479 (3d Cir. 1978), the court initially quoted with approval legislative history that supports a literal or "plain meaning" interpretation of New Jersey's section 2-713. Nevertheless, the court hedged by interpreting that section "to measure damages within a commercially reasonable time after learning of the repudiation". *Id.* at 492. In light of the unequivocal repudiation and because cover was "easily and immediately . . . available . . . in the well-organized and easily accessible market," *id.* at 493 (quoting Olofffson v. Coomer, 11 Ill. App. 3d 918, 296 N.E.2d 871 (1973)), a commercially reasonable time did not extend beyond the date of repudiation.

We agree with the *First National* court that "the circumstances of the particular market involved should determine the duration of a 'commercially reasonable time.'" 576 F.2d at 492; *see* Tax. Bus. & Com. Code § 1.204(b). In this case, however, there was no showing that cover was easily and immediately available in an organized and accessible market and that a commercially reasonable time expired on the day of Cosden's cancellation. We recognize that § 2.610's "commercially reasonable time" and § 2.712's "without unreasonable delay" are distinct concepts. Often, however, the two time periods will overlap, since the buyer can investigate cover possibilities while he waits performance. *See* Sebert, *supra*, at 876-77 & n. 80.

Although the jury in the present case did not fix the exact duration of a commercially reasonable time, we assume that the jury determined market price at a time commercially reasonable under all the circumstances, in light of the absence of objection to the form of the special issue.

induce seller to repudiate, rather than abide by the contract. By contrast, measuring buyer's damages at the time of performance will tend to dissuade the buyer from covering, in hopes that market price continues upward until performance time."

Consider both of these claims. When the court imagines an anticipatory repudiation occurring in the midst of a rising market, is it supposing the parties *know* that the market is rising, or is it supposing that *it turns out* the market was rising even though the parties could not have known it? Which is more plausible? If only *you* knew that the market price for oranges was going to double next week, what would you do right now (that is, right before you retire to the several Caribbean islands you would soon be able to buy)? If you and everyone else knew that the market price for oranges was going to double next week, what would happen to the price of oranges today and the price of forward contracts for oranges next week? Given what would happen to these prices, what advantage would seller have in repudiating, even if damages are measured at the time of repudiation?

Now suppose, more realistically, that neither party knows whether the market is going to rise or fall between the time of repudiation and the time of performance, but instead can merely assign probabilities to both eventualities. The court claims that "measuring buyer's damages at the time of repudiation gives the seller the ability to fix the buyer's damages and may induce the seller to repudiate rather than abide by the contract." Is failure to "abide by the contract" necessarily a bad thing? Assuming the seller does not know whether the market will rise or fall, does his benefiting from repudiating, even if damages are measured at the time of repudiation, turn on whether or not the seller is risk-averse? (Hint: Under what circumstances would the seller benefit by not repudiating and waiting until time for performance?) The court also states: "measuring buyer's damages at the time of performance will tend to dissuade the buyer from covering, in hopes that market price will continue upward until performance time." Clearly the court here is imagining that the buyer (and presumably everyone else) does not know that the market is rising. If the seller repudiates, and the price rises between the time of repudiation and the time of performance, why would the buyer benefit by waiting until the time of performance to cover? It is true that his damages will be higher, but so will his costs of covering. Wouldn't a buyer be indifferent between covering at the lower market price at the time of repudiation and covering at the higher market price at the time of performance, given that he is reimbursed for the difference between the contract price and the cover price either way? In what situation would the buyer prefer waiting until the time of performance? (Hint: How could he arrange his affairs so as to take advantage of the difference between the contract and market price at the time of performance?)

3. *Reasonable Certainty and Anticipatory Repudiation.* Contract law limits damages to those that can be proven with a reasonable certainty. *See* Chapter 10, *infra.* This rule can create problems when applied to long-term contracts that one party anticipatorily repudiates. Can you see why? The Second Circuit grappled with this issue in *Tractebel Energy Mktg. v. AEP Power Mktg.*, 487 F.3d 89 (2d Cir. 2007). In that case, TEMI, the buyer, contracted to purchase electricity from AEP over 20 years. After the contract had been signed but before AEP commenced performance, the energy market collapsed and TEMI sought to extricate itself from the agreement. The district court determined that the contract was enforceable, but refused to award AEP damages for lost profits stemming from TEMI's repudiation on the grounds that they could not be proven with a reasonable degree of certainty.

The Second Circuit rejected this argument out of fear it might imperil all long-term contracts:

> Not a single product or service exists for which a company's profit margin, over time, is unaffected by fluctuating supply and demand, changes in operating costs, increased competition from alternatives, alterations to the relevant regulatory regime, population increases or decreases in the targeted market, or technological advances. The variables identified by the district court exist in every long-term contract. It is not the case that all such contracts may be breached with impunity because of the difficulty of accurately calculating damages.

Id. at 112.

Can you square the Second Circuit's holding with the certainty principle? One commentator has argued that this tension is likely to arise in disputes over long-term contracts in thin markets — those in which few buyers and sellers exist, making prices volatile and thus harder to estimate — and that a different standard for measuring damages should be applied to these cases. Can you think of a standard that might produce more efficient results in cases like these? For suggestions, see Matthew Milikowsky, Note, *A Not Intractable Problem: Reasonable Certainty, Tractebel, and the Problem of Damages for Anticipatory Breach of a Long-Term Contract in a Thin Market*, 108 COLUM. L. REV. 452 (2008).

   3. ***Damages for Anticipatory Repudiation of Option Contracts.*** In a typical option contract, the owner of the option is free to exercise the option as he chooses. In most cases, the time period during which the option may be exercised is limited by the contract. If the option owner does not exercise the option before the period elapses, the option is extinguished. If, on the other hand, the option owner does exercise the option before the period elapses, the obligor must perform on the contract. A difficult issue is presented in the case where an obligor repudiates an option before the option has been exercised, but also before its time for exercise has elapsed. In such a scenario, the obligor has clearly breached the agreement by withdrawing the option before the exercise period elapsed. But at what point should the option owner's damages be measured?

   This measurement question was raised in *Lucente v. IBM*, 146 F. Supp. 2d 298 (S.D.N.Y. 2001). That case concerned a stock option agreement. Under the terms of the agreement, Lucente, an IBM employee, had a number of options to purchase IBM stock at different times in the future at pre-determined prices. Each option had a different time period in which it could be exercised. Failure to exercise the option during that time period would extinguish the option. Because of massive growth by IBM, the pre-determined prices turned out to be significantly lower than the market prices for IBM stock at the times the options were exercisable. By exercising the options during their exercise periods, Lucente would have made significant gains. However, Lucente left IBM and IBM repudiated the options agreements before any of the options reached their exercise period. Lucente initially sought settlement from IBM for their repudiation of the agreement. During the settlement negotiation, Lucente did not attempt to exercise the repudiated options as their respective exercise periods begun. When the settlement negotiations ultimately failed, Lucente brought suit for unlawful repudiation. By this time, however, all but one of the option exercise periods had elapsed. When he filed suit, Lucente attempted to exercise the one option with an unexpired exercise period.

The court held that IBM's repudiation of the agreement was unlawful. The difficult issue was how to measure Lucente's damages. Because of the large growth in the value of IBM stock following the cancellation, Lucente preferred to measure his damages at a date much later than IBM's repudiation. One possibility was to treat the date of cancellation as the date of breach and to award Lucente the value of the options on that date. None of the options were "in the money" at that time, nor had any of the option exercise periods commenced. A damage award based on the value of the options at that time would have yielded a modest award for Lucente, based on the value of the stock options at that time (i.e., even though they were not in the money then, they had a measurable market value based on their chance of being in the money when their exercise periods commenced later).

Another possibility was to treat the cancellation of the options as an anticipatory breach that would allow Lucente to wait for each option to become exercisable and then to attempt to exercise it if he so desired. However, Lucente had failed to attempt to exercise all but one of his options on the ground that IBM's repudiation had made such attempts at exercise futile. Thus, this damage measure would provide no recovery for Lucente on all the options he failed to exercise.

Lucente urged the court to allow a jury to make a finding of fact of whether and when he would have exercised the options had IBM not repudiated the agreement. The court declined. "To ask a jury to speculate as to whether and when an option would have been exercised is impermissible — especially where, as here, such speculation could resurrect options that long ago expired." *Id.* at 312. The court thus gave Lucente two choices. He could elect to treat the entire contract as breached on the date of the repudiation, and therefore recover the modest market value of the options had they been sold (not exercised) on that date. Or he could elect to view his prior failure to attempt to exercise the options as a refusal to accept IBM's repudiation. On this theory, Lucente could have exercised each option during its exercise period, but by failing to attempt to do so he allowed each to expire when the exercise period ended. He would therefore be viewed as forfeiting his right to exercise these expired options. However, on this approach, Lucente still retained and exercised his last option during its exercise period. He would therefore be entitled to recover damages for IBM's failure to deliver the stock to which he was entitled upon exercising his final stock option. The exercise price for this remaining option was 25% of the market price of IBM stock, yielding a profit to Lucente of nearly $6 million.

Do you agree that Lucente's failure to attempt to exercise his options should prevent him from recovering anything but their market value at the time of repudiation? Lucente chose not to attempt to exercise the options in part because of his on-going settlement negotiations with IBM. Does this fact make you more or less sympathetic with the requirement that Lucente attempt to exercise the options during their exercise period on pain of forfeiture?

Essay: Measuring Damages for Anticipatory Breach

Section 2-713 of the UCC provides that the buyer's damages for nondelivery or repudiation are computed by subtracting the contract price from the market price at the time when the buyer "learned of the breach." "Learned of the breach" is not defined in the Code. Does the buyer learn of the breach only at the time for performance? Or does he learn of the breach earlier when the seller "unequivocally" repudiates? Using §§ 2-610, 2-713, and 2-723, construct an argument for the buyer and then one for the seller. Which argument is more persuasive?

Consider this hypothetical. On January 2, Seller agrees to sell to Buyer 100 Intel Pentium 4, 2.2GHz computer chips at $400 a chip, delivery to be on December 2. On April 2, when the market price for computer chips to be delivered on December 2 — the forward contract price — is $500, Seller unequivocally repudiates and Buyer cancels the contract in response. What ought the legal rule require Buyer to do?[12]

First, consider what positions the parties would have been in had there been no anticipatory repudiation — what their expectations were *ex ante*. If the price of chips on December 2 is $300, the Buyer is unhappy because she guessed wrong. She is paying $100 per chip more than she would have had she not contracted. The Seller is delighted, he guessed correctly. If the price of chips is $500 on December 2, the fortunes are reversed: Seller would have done $100 better had he not contracted, and Buyer is $100 better off because she did contract.

Now, consider the situation on April 2, the date that Seller repudiates. Assume that Seller will fully compensate Buyer's damages. Would Buyer prefer damages to be measured at the time of repudiation or the time of performance? How Buyer reasons depends on her motive for entering into the forward contract in the first place. One possibility is that Buyer may have entered into the contract purely as a speculative undertaking and thus plans to resell rather than use the chips. But if so, it is hard to explain why Buyer would not simply purchase a call option on the futures market rather than undertaking the more cumbersome process of contracting for the chips themselves.[13]

---

[12] This hypothetical is drawn from Thomas H. Jackson, *"Anticipatory Repudiation" and the Temporal Element of Contract Law: An Economic Inquiry into Contract Damages in Cases of Prospective Nonperformance*, 31 Stan. L. Rev. 69 (1978).

[13] To understand a call option, assume that Buyer in our example wishes to "cash in" the contract with Seller on April 2 when the Seller repudiates the contract to deliver 400 computer chips on December 2 at a price of $4,00 per chip. Recall that on April 2, the forward price for December 2 delivery of the chips is $500. Buyer could cash out of her original contract on April 2 by simply selling to another buyer the right to purchase 100 chips from Buyer at $400 per chip on December 2. Such a contract is called a "call option" (it grants the buyer the right to "call" on the Seller to deliver the chips at the agreed price). Since that right is worth $500 on April 2, Buyer would be paid $100 per chip for that contract. Even though Buyer's interest in her original contract will be measured on December 2, any potential gain beyond the April 2 $100 per chip gain on that contract (i.e., any gain that Buyer otherwise would realize if the December price of chips is greater than $500 per chip) will be cancelled out by a counterbalancing loss on the call option contract. The effect of this contract would be to leave Buyer with a net gain of the $100 per chip it received as the price for the call option it sells on April 2.

Assume, therefore, that Buyer must purchase chips on December 2 to use as parts in computers she is committed to manufacturing. Under these more realistic conditions, her motivation on January 2 is to *reduce the risk* that she will have to pay more than $400 for each chip on December 2. The January 2 forward price of $400 is the market's best guess of the December 2 price; it is the price that buyers and sellers in this market on January 2 think will prevail on December 2. When Seller repudiates on April 2, Buyer presumably still wishes to eliminate the risk that she will have to pay more than $400 per chip on December 2. If she is allowed to choose whether mitigate at the time of repudiation or wait until the time of performance, she can do either and still eliminate the risk of paying more than $400 per chip on December 2. If she "covers" on April 2, the new forward contract will cost her $100 more per chip, and Seller will have to compensate her in that amount (100 x $100). She will then be in precisely the same position she was before Seller's repudiation (i.e., she will have a guaranteed out-of-pocket expense of $400 per chip on December 2). If she waits to cover by purchasing chips at the time of performance, Seller will be required to compensate her for the difference between the "spot" market price of chips on December 2 and the $400 contract price. Again, Buyer will be in the same position she was before Seller breached (i.e., $400 per chip out-of-pocket expense on December 2).

On the other hand, Buyer's cancellation of the contract following Seller's repudiation bars Seller from enforcing the $400 contract price at the time of performance. Therefore, if the market price is below $400 per chip on December 2, Buyer will be free to purchase chips at the lower market price. For this reason, it appears that Buyer should always prefer to wait until the time of performance. She has nothing to lose: If the market price is higher than $400 per chip, Seller will reimburse her for the difference; if the market price is lower than $400 per chip, Buyer does better than she would have under her contract with Seller — she pays *less than* $400 per chip.[14] On this analysis, Buyer will prefer her damages to be measured at the time of performance because it allows her, in effect, to speculate at Seller's expense — a right she did not have before Seller repudiated.

Now consider how two judges might approach this issue. They are trying to decide whether to measure damages as of the time of repudiation (April 2) or as of the time of performance (December 2). The first judge:

> My dissenting colleague and I agree on two matters at the outset. Our goal is to come as close as possible to reaching the result that we believe the parties would have contracted for had they anticipated this situation in advance. I am forced to guess what might motivate a seller in this situation to announce to his buyer that he intends to breach. Since our rule will apply

---

[14] As we have seen, the repudiating seller retains the right of retraction absent the buyer's acceptance of the repudiation and cancellation of the contract. If the buyer does not cancel, then the buyer gains no advantage by waiting until the time of performance to measure its damages. If the price falls below $400 per chip on December 2, Seller would surely retract his repudiation (he can always purchase the chips on the spot market and sell them to Buyer for a profit). Thus, absent Buyer's acceptance of the repudiation, Seller's right of retraction offsets the advantage to Buyer of waiting until the time of performance to cover. By repudiating, however, Seller takes the chance that Buyer will rely on Seller's repudiation (e.g., by covering before the time of performance) and thereby extinguish Seller's right of retraction.

to future buyers and sellers, I am interested in what motivated Seller in this case only insofar as it gives me a glimpse into the motivation of repudiators generally. Seller seems to be acting against his self-interest. On April 2, there was a sense in which he had already suffered a loss — if he tried to "cash out" at that date, by making a market purchase of 100 chips for December delivery, he would lose $100/chip. If Buyer is allowed to sit on the repudiation and measure damages at the time of performance, Seller has the same potential to suffer a loss that he had when he entered into the contract. But unless he retracts his repudiation before the market falls below the contract price, by repudiating he has given up any potential to make a gain. It is therefore difficult to understand why Seller would intentionally exacerbate his potential losses by repudiating.

In my view, the best explanation of Seller's behavior is that by repudiating the contract Seller was, in effect, saying to the Buyer that he (Seller) wanted to take his $100 per chip loss and get out of the gamble. He wanted to avoid the risk that the market would go even higher and visit more of a loss on him. The only reason that I can see for Seller repudiating rather than buying a substitute contract (for $500) is that Buyer could find a substitute contract more cheaply than Seller could. This is plausible because buyers have more experience in finding sellers than sellers have in finding sellers.

It does not affect this analysis at all whether Buyer "covers" or sues for market damages on April 2 or not. The Buyer can take her sure gain of $100 if she wants to, or she can continue to gamble on the market by buying a substitute December 2 contract. I hold that damages are to be fixed as of the time of the repudiation. This allows Seller to use repudiation as a device to enlist Buyer's assistance in purchasing a cover contract at a presumably lower cost than Seller could have done himself. Allowing buyers to wait until the time of performance to measure damages will therefore undermine the sole rationale for the doctrine of anticipatory repudiation.

The second judge, dissenting:

I agree with much of my colleague's reasoning, but I have a different explanation of why the Seller may have repudiated. It is true that on April 2 the Seller is worse off for having contracted. He may well want to get out of the contract entirely if he can do so at no cost. There are a host of reasons why the Buyer may never sue. Prosecuting a lawsuit is costly and time-consuming, and these costs are not chargeable to the breacher as a part of the damages bill. Anticipatory repudiation cases in sales law most commonly occur when prices fluctuate substantially during short time periods. These fluctuations generally occur in markets for commodities or raw materials, such as corn, soybeans, or, as in this case, computer chips. Well-developed futures markets often exist for such goods. Seller in this case could probably purchase a December futures contract with a phone call to an appropriate broker. In addition, a buyer's greater expertise in purchasing generally entails a superior ability to evaluate product quality and seller reliability; in markets where anticipatory repudiations occur, however, the goods generally are homogeneous — all Intel Pentium 4, 2.2 Ghz chips are alike — eliminating the need to make quality comparisons. Moreover, seller reliability is less important with homogeneous goods than it is with machines — breakdown and repair are rarely an issue. I conclude that sellers are often able to cover just as cheaply as their buyers. Therefore, the likely reason for Seller's repudiation (in a thick market like the market for computer chips) is to use the threat of under compensating Buyer to extort a settlement or modification that allows him to evade part of his liability under their agreement.

In my view, had these parties foreseen these problems in advance they would have agreed to make the contract more secure; that is, insulated from the breacher's strategic behavior. This is to the *ex ante* benefit of both parties. Thus, in thick market contexts, I would permit the Buyer to measure damages at the time of performance. In thick markets, there simply is no legitimate need for the doctrine of anticipatory repudiation. However, in thin markets buyers are likely to have a comparative advantage in securing cover contracts. Thus, in thin markets, sellers should be allowed to use anticipatory repudiation to enlist their buyer's assistance in securing a cover contract. This purpose is served by measuring damages at the time of repudiation.

With which judge would you cast your vote?

D.   INSECURITY AND THE RIGHT TO DEMAND ASSURANCES

Assume that Seller contracts with Buyer to supply complex electronic parts in three installments on 30 days' credit. Before manufacture, Seller learns that Buyer is experiencing cash flow problems and his credit rating has dipped. What are Seller's options in responding to this disturbing news? Under the common law rule, Seller would face a difficult choice: He must perform unless Buyer has unequivocally repudiated. Otherwise, if Seller suspends performance to wait and see what happens, he may be found to be in breach. In other words, unless the parties explicitly agreed otherwise, Seller would bear the risk of his own insecurity. The drafters of the UCC believed that the common law rule was inconsistent with commercial understandings. In the terms we have used in this book, they guessed that most parties would bargain to shift the risk of insecurity to the party causing the concern — the potential breacher. Section 2-609 purports to provide such a risk allocation as a default rule. Recall that the common law rule requiring that anticipatory repudiations be unequivocal helps reduce the opportunity to use ambiguous repudiation signals for strategic reasons, such as evasion and opportunism. As you read the following cases, ask yourself whether § 2-609 recreates the opportunity for strategic behavior that the common law clear-repudiation rule was designed to eliminate. If so, are those costs out-weighed by the benefits it provides to insecure parties? For one scholar's view on these questions, see Richard Craswell, *Insecurity, Repudiation, and Cure*, 19 J. LEGAL STUD. 399 (1990).

NATIONAL FARMERS ORGANIZATION v. BARTLETT & CO., GRAIN
United States Court of Appeals, Eighth Circuit
560 F.2d 1350 (1977)

Van Oosterhout, J.

This is a diversity action brought by the National Farmers Organization (hereinafter Seller) against Bartlett and Company, Grain (hereinafter Buyer) to recover an alleged balance due, in the stipulated amount of $18,441.62, on the price of grain sold and delivered under four of a series of fourteen contracts between the parties. The Buyer admits that the $18,441.62 was withheld from the total payment otherwise due but claims by way of setoff that the stated sum was properly withheld as damages due it by virtue of the Seller's alleged breach or anticipatory repudiation of all fourteen contracts. The pertinent facts were largely stipulated, and the cause was tried to the district court sitting without a jury. The court, agreeing with the Buyer that the Seller had breached or anticipatorily repudiated all fourteen contracts, rendered judgment for the Buyer. We affirm.

I

Prior to January 30, 1973, the parties had entered into forty-five contracts for the sale of grain. Of these contracts, thirty-one were performed in full by both parties and are not in issue. The remaining fourteen, which are the subject of this lawsuit, are summarized in the following table.

Table 1.

Contract Number	Date of Execution (all 1972)	Quantity (bushels)	Price (per bu.)	Delivery Dates
22868	Aug. 5	40,000	$1.80	Dec. 1972
996	Aug. 7	5,000	1.68	Aug. 7-Sept. 22, 1972
1338	Sept. 6	3,400	1.97	Feb.-Mar., 1973
1366	Sept. 11	10,000	1.96	Jan. 15-Mar. 15, 1973
1371	Sept. 11	12,000	1.96	Jan. 15-Mar. 15, 1973
1380	Sept. 11	5,400	1.99	Jan. 15-Mar. 15, 1973
1389	Sept. 12	20,000	1.98	Dec. 1972
1400	Sept. 13	750	2.035	Jan. 15-Mar. 15, 1973
1425	Sept. 16	5,500	1.86	June-Aug., 1973
1575	Oct. 12	10,000	1.87	June-Aug., 1973
7415	Oct. 17	30,000	1.155	Oct.-Dec., 1972
1729	Nov. 13	15,000	1.87	June-Aug., 1973
1824	Nov. 29	13,000	2.26	Dec. 1972
1845	Dec. 4	2,700	2.34	Jan. 1973

Contract No. 7415 was for the sale of corn; each of the others was for the sale of wheat.

The controversy over the above contracts began in December 1972. As of December 1, the only contract on which the delivery date had passed was No. 996; although the September 22 last delivery date had long since expired, 1672 of the 5,000 bushels called for under the contract remained undelivered. Deliveries were due in December on Nos. 22868, 1389, 7415 and 1824. At the end of the month, none of the 40,000 bushels had been delivered on No. 22868, 16,480 of the 20,000 bushels had been delivered on No. 1389, 19,364 of the 30,000 bushels had been delivered on No. 7415, and 8,125 of the 13,000 bushels had been delivered on No. 1824. Additional deliveries on these four contracts, although late, were tendered and accepted in January 1973; by the end of January, 31,725 of 40,000 bushels remained undelivered on No. 22868, 397 of 20,000 bushels remained undelivered on No. 1389, 8,049 of 30,000 bushels remained undelivered on No. 7415, and 648 of 13,000 bushels remained undelivered on No. 1824. In addition, none of the 2,700 bushels due in January under No. 1845 were delivered. The eight contracts not mentioned above in this paragraph had last delivery dates subsequent to January 31, 1973. No deliveries were ever made on any of these contracts, except that 3,943 of 12,000 bushels due no later than March 15 under No. 1371 were delivered in January. On several occasions during the month of January, prior to January 26, the Buyer had given notice to the Seller that the Seller had not completed delivery on certain contracts by the delivery dates designated in the contracts.

Beginning early in December 1972 and continuing throughout January 1973 the Buyer "was retaining some of the purchase price of grain actually delivered as protection against realized or potential loss caused by failure on the [Seller's] part to perform all contracts not yet fully performed." On several occasions during December and January the Seller made verbal demands for the purchase price of grain already delivered.

On or about January 26, 1973, the Seller notified the Buyer that the Seller "was not going to deliver any grain to [Buyer] on any of the 14 outstanding contracts between the parties unless and until [Buyer] paid [Seller] a substantial amount of money due on deliveries already made as of that date on contracts Nos. 22868, 1371, 1389 and 1824." The Seller did in fact suspend performance on all fourteen contracts as of January 27. Thereafter, no grain was ever tendered under any of the contracts.

It is the above communication which the Buyer elected to treat as an anticipatory repudiation of the contracts not yet due. On January 30, the Buyer sent the Seller the following telegram (punctuation supplied in part):

> AS OF TODAY'S MARKET CLOSE WE ARE BRINGING ALL OUTSTANDING CONTRACTS WE HAVE WITH YOUR OFFICE TO CURRENT MARKET PRICE, NAMELY, OUR CONTRACTS 996, 1338, 1366, 1371, 1380, 1425, 1575, 1729, AND 22868. SETTLEMENT WILL BE FORTHCOMING.

On or about January 30-31, the Buyer mailed a debit memo and two credit memos to the Seller. The numerical accuracy of the figures used and calculations made in these memos is stipulated. These memos reflect a balance due the Seller for deliveries made under contracts Nos. 22868, 1371, 1389, and 1824 of $72,894.89 and a balance due the Seller for deliveries made under contract No. 7415 of $1,919.50, for a total balance due of $74,814.39.

The same credit and debit memos claimed setoffs on thirteen of the fourteen contracts, in each case by virtue of the Seller's past breach or alleged anticipatory repudiation of the particular contract. The claimed setoffs were as follows:

Table 2.

Contract No.	Undelivered Quantity (bushels)	Difference in Market and Contract Prices (see note 3, supra)	Claimed Setoff
22868	31,732	$.785	$ 24,909.62
996	1,673	.67	1,154.37
1338	3,400	.40	1,360.00
1366	10,000	.41	4,100.00
1371	8,057	.41	3,303.37
1380	5,400	.38	2,052.00
1389	405	.39	157.95
1400	750	.335	251.25
1425	5,500	.25	1,375.00
1575	10,000	.24	2,400.00
7415	8,770	.125	1,096.25
1729	15,000	.24	3,600.00
1845	2,700	.03	81.00
		Total	$45,840.81

The Buyer, deducting the claimed setoff of $45,840.81 from the net balance due of $74,814.39, sent the Seller a check dated February 9 for the $28,973.58 difference. The check was subsequently paid.

The Seller, one day after receiving the January 30 telegram, informed the Buyer that, while it consented to cancellation of contracts Nos. 22868 and 996, it did not recognize and would not agree to cancellation of contracts for future delivery. It is now stipulated that the claimed setoffs shown in Table 2 were proper as to all contracts with last delivery dates of January 31 or earlier, viz., Nos. 22868, 996, 1389, 1845 and 7415. Accordingly, at issue herein is the propriety of claimed setoffs, totaling $18,441.62, on those contracts having last delivery dates subsequent to January 31, viz., Nos. 1338, 1366, 1371, 1380, 1400, 1425, 1575 and 1729. The resolution of this issue turns on the question whether the Seller's January 26 communication constituted an anticipatory repudiation of these contracts.

Before turning to the legal issue presented, we mention one additional fact not expressly stipulated or expressly found by the district court. It is quite clear from the stipulations that as of January 26 a very substantial sum, over and above the amount of damages by then sustained by the Buyer as a consequence of the Seller's past defaults, was due the Seller for deliveries already made under contracts Nos. 22868, 1371, 1389 and 1824, and a very substantial portion of that sum was not only due but past due.[15]

---

[15] [8] The four contracts had payment terms as follows: No. 22868 "each Tuesday and Friday;" No. 1371 "Cash on Delivery;" No. 1389 "Defer Payments until January 2, 1973;" No. 1824 "Daily upon delivery by noon of the following business day." Deliveries on No. 1389 subsequent to January 2 would

II

The question tendered to us for decision whether the Seller's communication of January 26 constituted an anticipatory repudiation of the contracts on which performance was not yet due is a difficult and close one. Ultimately, its resolution is governed by § 2-610 of the Uniform Commercial Code and the common law. However, as the parties readily concede, neither the Code language nor the case law of any jurisdiction provides a definitive answer. Before examining the tendered question directly, we find it useful for the purpose of comparison to consider what the Seller clearly could have done on January 26 under Uniform Commercial Code § 2-609 and what it clearly could not have done on January 26 under Uniform Commercial Code § 2-612.

Uniform Commercial Code § 2-609(1) provides in part: "When reasonable grounds for insecurity arise with respect to the performance of either party the other may in writing demand adequate assurance of due performance and until he receives such assurance may if commercially reasonable suspend any performance for which he has not already received the agreed return." Comment 3 to this section states in part:

> Under commercial standards and in accord with commercial practice, a ground for insecurity need not arise from or be directly related to the contract in question . . . .

Thus a buyer who falls behind in "his account" with the seller, even though the items involved have to do with separate and legally distinct contracts, impairs the seller's expectation of due performance.

The example just cited conforms precisely to the facts before us. Plainly, the seller could have availed itself of a § 2-609 remedy on January 26. Equally plainly, however, it did not do so.[16]

Uniform Commercial Code § 2-612(3) provides in part: "Whenever nonconformity or default with respect to one or more installments substantially impairs the value of the whole contract there is a breach of the whole." Comment 6 to this section states in part:

> Whether the non-conformity in any given installment justifies cancellation as to the future depends [on] . . . whether the non-conformity substantially impairs the value of the whole contract. If only the seller's security in regard to future installments is impaired, he has the right to demand

---

be governed by Uniform Commercial Code § 2-310, providing that unless otherwise agreed payment is due on delivery. Thus, in each case prompt payment was part of the contract. The Seller concedes that payment within five days was acceptable to it. Even if we assume ten days, payment for all deliveries prior to January 16 would be past due on January 26. Slightly more than $5000 worth of grain was delivered on the four contracts between January 16 and 26. All other sums due on the four contracts on January 26 were past due.

[16] [9] The Seller so concedes. For two reasons, the concession is a proper one. First, the communication of January 26 was not in writing. Second, the communication did not seek assurance of performance on the future contracts; it sought actual part performance on the contracts on which payment was past due.

The Buyer, we note, has also conceded that it never pursued a remedy under § 2-609.

adequate assurances of proper future performance but has not an immediate right to cancel the entire contract.

Although the Buyer was on January 26 substantially behind on payment on some of the contracts, in none of the contracts was time of the essence, and there is no indication that the Buyer's ability to pay was impaired. With respect to those contracts on which payments had not been withheld, at least, the value of each such contract was plainly not substantially impaired as a whole on January 26, and the Seller plainly could not have cancelled those contracts on that date. Equally plainly, however, the Seller did not purport to cancel any of the contracts.[17]

With the above comments in mind, we turn to the controlling issue under Uniform Commercial Code § 2-610. The district court, acknowledging that the issue was a close one, concluded that the Seller anticipatorily repudiated the contracts with last delivery dates subsequent to January 31 when on January 26 it notified the Buyer that no grain would be delivered under any of the contracts unless and until the Buyer made a substantial payment for deliveries already made under contracts Nos. 22868, 1371, 1389 and 1824. The court reasoned:

> Plaintiff's imposition on January 26 of a condition precedent that defendant perform under various independent contracts clearly amounted to a statement of intention not to perform except on conditions which went beyond each of (the contracts not yet due) . . . . A party to a contract may not refuse performance simply because the other party has breached a separate contract between them.

Uniform Commercial Code § 2-610 provides in part: "When either party repudiates the contract with respect to a performance not yet due the loss of which will substantially impair the value of the contract to the other, the aggrieved party may . . . (b) resort to any remedy for breach . . . ." The Code does not articulate what constitutes an anticipatory repudiation. Comment 2 to § 2-610, however, offers the following guidance:

> It is not necessary for repudiation that performance be made literally and utterly impossible. Repudiation can result from action which reasonably indicates a rejection of the continuing obligation . . . . Under the language of this section, a demand by one or both parties for more than the contract

---

[17] [11] The communication of January 26 was to the effect that deliveries would be withheld or suspended until the Seller received a substantial payment for past deliveries. Ignoring for the moment the complicating and ultimately decisive factor that the present case involves not one but a number of installment contracts, we point out that the distinction between renouncing a contract altogether and suspending performance until past-due counter-performance is received is a well-recognized one:

> Generally, but not quite always, the seller will be privileged to suspend the succeeding delivery until the previous installment has been paid for . . . . A buyer is not justified in refusing to pay an installment for the mere reason that he fears that the seller will fail to make future deliveries. Such a refusal, with accompanying factors, will justify the refusal to make further deliveries. It has been held in such a case, however, that the seller was not justified in renouncing the contract. Such a decision is correct if the actual risk of non-payment is not increased and if further performance by the seller is not thereby made more difficult. Note also, that a seller may be justified in holding up further deliveries until paid, without being justified in renouncing the contract.

3A A. Corbin, *Contracts* § 690 at 254 & 256 (1960) (footnotes omitted).

calls for in the way of counter-performance is not in itself a repudiation nor does it invalidate a plain expression of desire for future performance. However, when under a fair reading it amounts to a statement of intention not to perform except on conditions which go beyond the contract, it becomes a repudiation.

The general rule is not subject to variance when the stated condition derives from a separate contract or contracts regardless of the validity of the repudiator's claim under the separate contract or contracts. It is well established that the breach of one contract does not justify the aggrieved party in refusing to perform another separate and distinct contract. 3A Corbin, *Contracts* § 696 (1960).

The decision cited by the district court, Northwest Lumber Sales, Inc. v. Continental Forest Products, Inc., 261 Or. 480 (1972), illustrates the separate contracts rule perhaps as well as any. In that case the plaintiff seller had separately contracted for a delivery of pine lumber and a delivery of 2 x 4 studs to the defendant buyer. After the pine lumber had been delivered and allegedly after payment therefor had become thirty days past due, the seller informed the buyer that it would not deliver the studs. The Supreme Court of Oregon, assuming that payment for the pine lumber had been wrongfully withheld, held: "[n]either the Uniform Commercial Code nor general contract law gives either party to a contract the right to refuse performance because the other has breached a separate contract between them." Judgment was accordingly rendered for the buyer on its claimed setoff.

On the basis of the authorities cited above, we believe that the *Northwest Lumber Sales* decision was correct and that the Missouri Supreme Court, if confronted with the issue, would agree with the Oregon Supreme Court. Moreover, although the facts before us do present a closer question, we think the Missouri Supreme Court would apply the same principle here.

We may concede to the Seller that the general rule could occasionally dictate a result which for commercial reasons would be unacceptable. Perhaps in such a case the Missouri Supreme Court would decline to apply the rule. The Seller makes an argument of some merit in that regard. Two facts stand out. First, . . . the Buyer was withholding payment on some contracts to cover losses on other contracts. Under Uniform Commercial Code § 2-717, it was not privileged to do so. Second, the Seller's communication of January 26, unlike the communication in *Northwest Lumber Sales*, did not purport to be an outright cancellation or renouncement of any obligation under any of the contracts. These two facts lend some credence to the Seller's contention that the January 26 communication was a justified one under the circumstances.

On the other hand, as noted previously, time was not of the essence under the contracts, and there is no indication that the Buyer's ability to pay was impaired. Measures short of suspending delivery on all contracts could have preserved the Seller's contractual right to payment. Moreover, as we have concluded above, a § 2-609 remedy was specifically available but not used. Despite the Buyer's wrongful withholding of payment on contracts not in default, the separate identities of the various contracts were unquestionably preserved, as all deliveries and payments were separately accounted for throughout the pertinent time period. In addition the

Seller, having failed to deliver 1672 bushels of wheat on contract No. 996 by the September 22 last delivery date, was the first breaching party on any of the contracts. Finally, no grain was in fact tendered under any of the contracts after January 27, even though a substantial payment was received and accepted shortly after February 9. Taking all of the above-mentioned facts into account, we agree with the view of the district court that the Supreme Court of Missouri would find an anticipatory repudiation here. At the very least, the district court's conclusion on this question of state law in a diversity case is entitled to great deference and should be sustained.

The judgment appealed from is affirmed.

NORCON POWER PARTNERS, L.P. v. NIAGARA MOHAWK POWER CORP.
Court of Appeals of New York
92 N.Y.2d 458, 705 N.E.2d 656 (1998)

BELLACOSA, J.

The doctrine, known as demand for adequate assurance of future performance, is at the heart of a Federal lawsuit that stems from a 1989 contract between Norcon Power Partners, L.P., an independent power producer, and Niagara Mohawk Power Corporation, a public utility provider. Niagara Mohawk undertook to purchase electricity generated at Norcon's Pennsylvania facility. The contract was for 25 years, but the differences emerged during the early years of the arrangement.

The case arrives on this Court's docket by certification of the substantive law question from the United States Court of Appeals for the Second Circuit. Our Court is presented with an open issue that should be settled within the framework of New York's common-law development. We accepted the responsibility to address this question involving New York contract law:

> "Does a party have the right to demand adequate assurance of future performance when reasonable grounds arise to believe that the other party will commit a breach by non-performance of a contract governed by New York law, where the other party is solvent and the contract is not governed by the UCC?"

As framed by the particular dispute, we answer the law question in the affirmative with an appreciation of this Court's traditional common-law developmental method, and as proportioned to the precedential sweep of our rulings.

I.

The Second Circuit Court of Appeals describes the three pricing periods, structure and details as follows:

> In the first period, Niagara Mohawk pays Norcon six cents per kilowatt-hour for electricity. In the second and third periods, the price paid by Niagara Mohawk is based on its "avoided cost." The avoided cost reflects

the cost that Niagara Mohawk would incur to generate electricity itself or purchase it from other sources. In the second period, if the avoided cost falls below a certain floor price (calculated according to a formula), Niagara Mohawk is obligated to pay the floor price. By the same token, if the avoided cost rises above a certain amount (calculated according to a formula), Niagara Mohawk's payments are capped by a ceiling price. An "adjustment account" tracks the difference between payments actually made by Niagara Mohawk in the second period and what those payments would have been if based solely on Niagara Mohawk's avoided cost.

In the third period, the price paid by Niagara Mohawk is based on its avoided cost without any ceiling or floor price. Payments made by Niagara Mohawk in the third period are adjusted to account for any balance existing in the adjustment account that operated in the second period. If the adjustment account contains a balance in favor of Niagara Mohawk — that is, the payments actually made by Niagara Mohawk in the second period exceeded what those payments would have been if based solely on Niagara Mohawk's avoided cost — then the rate paid by Niagara Mohawk will be reduced to reflect the credit. If the adjustment account contains a balance in favor of Norcon, Niagara Mohawk must make increased payments to Norcon. If a balance exists in the adjustment account at the end of the third period, the party owing the balance must pay the balance in full within thirty days of the termination of the third period (*Norcon Power Partners v. Niagara Mohawk Power Corp.*, 110 F.3d 6, 7, *supra*).

In February 1994, Niagara Mohawk presented Norcon with a letter stating its belief, based on revised avoided cost estimates, that substantial credits in Niagara Mohawk's favor would accrue in the adjustment account during the second pricing period. "[A]nalysis shows that the Cumulative Avoided Cost Account . . . will reach over $610 million by the end of the second period." Anticipating that Norcon would not be able to satisfy the daily escalating credits in the third period, Niagara Mohawk demanded that "Norcon provide adequate assurance to Niagara Mohawk that Norcon will duly perform all of its future repayment obligations."

Norcon promptly sued Niagara Mohawk in the United States District Court, Southern District of New York. It sought a declaration that Niagara Mohawk had no contractual right under New York State law to demand adequate assurance, beyond security provisions negotiated and expressed in the agreement. Norcon also sought a permanent injunction to stop Niagara Mohawk from anticipatorily terminating the contract based on the reasons described in the demand letter. Niagara Mohawk counterclaimed. It sought a counter declaration that it properly invoked a right to demand adequate assurance of Norcon's future payment performance of the contract.

The District Court granted Norcon's motion for summary judgment. It reasoned that New York common law recognizes the exceptional doctrine of demand for adequate assurance only when a promisor becomes insolvent, and also when the statutory sale of goods provision under UCC § 2-609, is involved. Thus, the District Court ruled in Norcon's favor because neither exception applied, in fact or by analogy to the particular dispute.

The Second Circuit Court of Appeals preliminarily agrees with the District Court that, except in the case of insolvency, no common-law or statutory right to demand adequate assurance exists under New York law which would affect non-UCC contracts, like the instant one. Because of the uncertainty concerning this substantive law question the Second Circuit certified the question to our Court as an aid to its correct application of New York law, and with an eye toward settlement of the important precedential impact on existing and future non-UCC commercial law matters and disputes.

II.

Our analysis should reference a brief review of the evolution of the doctrine of demands for adequate assurance. Its roots spring from the doctrine of anticipatory repudiation (*see*, Garvin, *Adequate Assurance of Performance: Of Risk, Duress, and Cognition*, 69 U Colo. L. Rev. 71, 77 [1998]). Under that familiar precept, when a party repudiates contractual duties "prior to the time designated for performance and before" all of the consideration has been fulfilled, the "repudiation entitles the nonrepudiating party to claim damages for total breach" (*Long Is. R.R. Co. v. Northville Indus. Corp.*, 41 N.Y.2d 455, 463.

That switch in performance expectation and burden is readily available, applied and justified when a breaching party's words or deeds are unequivocal. Such a discernible line in the sand clears the way for the nonbreaching party to broach some responsive action. When, however, the apparently breaching party's actions are equivocal or less certain, then the nonbreaching party who senses an approaching storm cloud, affecting the contractual performance, is presented with a dilemma, and must weigh hard choices and serious consequences. One commentator has described the forecast options in this way:

> "If the promisee regards the apparent repudiation as an anticipatory repudiation, terminates his or her own performance and sues for breach, the promisee is placed in jeopardy of being found to have breached if the court determines that the apparent repudiation was not sufficiently clear and unequivocal to constitute an anticipatory repudiation justifying nonperformance. If, on the other hand, the promisee continues to perform after perceiving an apparent repudiation, and it is subsequently determined that an anticipatory repudiation took place, the promisee may be denied recovery for post-repudiation expenditures because of his or her failure to avoid those expenses as part of a reasonable effort to mitigate damages after the repudiation" (Crespi, *The Adequate Assurances Doctrine after UCC § 2-609: A Test of the Efficiency of the Common Law*, 38 Vill L Rev 179, 183 [1993]).

III.

The Uniform Commercial Code settled on a mechanism for relieving some of this uncertainty. It allows a party to a contract for the sale of goods to demand assurance of future performance from the other party when reasonable grounds for insecurity exist. When adequate assurance is not forthcoming, repudiation is deemed confirmed, and the nonbreaching party is allowed to take reasonable actions as though a repudiation had occurred.

In theory, this UCC relief valve recognizes that "the essential purpose of a contract between commercial [parties] is actual performance . . . and that a continuing sense of reliance and security that the promised performance will be forthcoming when due, is an important feature of the bargain" (UCC 2-609, Comment 1). In application, section 2-609 successfully implements the laudatory objectives of quieting the doubt a party fearing repudiation may have, mitigating the dilemma flowing from that doubt, and offering the nonbreaching party the opportunity to interpose timely action to deal with the unusual development.

Indeed, UCC 2-609 has been considered so effective in bridging the doctrinal, exceptional and operational gap related to the doctrine of anticipatory breach that some states have imported the complementary regimen of demand for adequate assurance to common-law categories of contract law, using UCC 2-609 as the synapse (see, e.g., Lo Re v. Tel-Air Communications, 200 N.J. Super. 59, 490 A.2d 344.

Commentators have helped nudge this development along. They have noted that the problems redressed by UCC 2-609 are not unique to contracts for sale of goods, regulated under a purely statutory regime. Thus, they have cogently identified the need for the doctrine to be available in exceptional and qualifying common-law contractual settings and disputes because of similar practical, theoretical and salutary objectives (e.g., predictability, definiteness, and stability in commercial dealings and expectations) (see generally, White, Eight Cases and Section 251, 67 Cornell L. Rev. 841 [1982]).

The American Law Institute through its Restatement (Second) of Contracts has also recognized and collected the authorities supporting this modern development:

> (1) Where reasonable grounds arise to believe that the obligor will commit a breach by non-performance that would of itself give the obligee a claim for damages for total breach under § 243, the obligee may demand adequate assurance of due performance and may, if reasonable, suspend any performance for which he has not already received the agreed exchange until he receives such assurance.

> (2) The obligee may treat as a repudiation the obligor's failure to provide within a reasonable time such assurance of due performance as is adequate in the circumstances of the particular case (Restatement [Second] of Contracts § 251).

Modeled on UCC 2-609, Restatement § 251 tracks "the principle that the parties to a contract look to actual performance 'and that a continuing sense of reliance and security that the promised performance will be forthcoming when due, is an important feature of the bargain'" (Restatement [Second] of Contracts § 251, comment a, quoting UCC 2-609, Comment 1). The duty of good faith and fair dealing in the performance of the contract is also reflected in section 251 (see, Restatement [Second] of Contracts § 251, comment a).

Some States have adopted Restatement § 251 as their common law of contracts, in varying degrees and classifications (*see, e.g., Carfield & Sons v. Cowling,* 616 P.2d 1008 [Colo.] [construction contract]; *Spitzer Co. v. Barron,* 581 P.2d 213 [Alaska] [construction contract]; *Drinkwater v. Patten Realty Corp.,* 563 A.2d 772 [Me.] [sale of real estate]; *Jonnet Dev. Corp. v. Dietrich Indus.,* 463 A.2d 1026 [real estate lease]; *but see, Mollohan v. Black Rock Contr.,* 160 W. Va. 446, 235 S.E.2d 813 [declining to adopt section 251, except to the extent that failure to give adequate assurance on demand may be some evidence of repudiation]).

IV.

New York, up to now, has refrained from expanding the right to demand adequate assurance of performance beyond the Uniform Commercial Code. The only other recognized exception is the insolvency setting (*see, Hanna v. Florence Iron Co.,* 222 N.Y. 290; *Pardee v. Kanady,* 100 N.Y. 121). Hence, the need for this certified question emerged so this Court could provide guidance towards a correct resolution of the Federal lawsuit by settling New York law with a modern pronouncement governing this kind of contract and dispute.

Niagara Mohawk, before our Court through the certified question from the Federal court, urges a comprehensive adaptation of the exceptional demand tool. This wholesale approach has also been advocated by the commentators. Indeed, it is even reflected in the breadth of the wording of the certified question.

This Court's jurisprudence, however, usually evolves by deciding cases and settling the law more modestly. The twin purposes and functions of this Court's work require significant professional discipline and judicious circumspection.

We conclude, therefore, that it is unnecessary, while fulfilling the important and useful certification role, to promulgate so sweeping a change and proposition in contract law, as has been sought, in one dramatic promulgation . . . .

This Court is now persuaded that the policies underlying the UCC 2-609 counterpart should apply with similar cogency for the resolution of this kind of controversy. A useful analogy can be drawn between the contract at issue and a contract for the sale of goods. If the contract here was in all respects the same, except that it was for the sale of oil or some other tangible commodity instead of the sale of electricity, the parties would unquestionably be governed by the demand for adequate assurance of performance factors in UCC 2-609. We are convinced to take this prudent step because it puts commercial parties in these kinds of disputes at relatively arm's length equilibrium in terms of reliability and uniformity of governing legal rubrics. The availability of the doctrine may even provide an incentive and tool for parties to resolve their own differences, perhaps without the necessity of judicial intervention. Open, serious renegotiation of dramatic developments and changes in unusual contractual expectations and qualifying circumstances would occur because of and with an eye to the doctrine's application.

The various authorities, factors and concerns, in sum, prompt the prudence and awareness of the usefulness of recognizing the extension of the doctrine of demand for adequate assurance, as a common-law analogue. It should apply to the type of long-term commercial contract between corporate entities entered into by Norcon and Niagara Mohawk here, which is complex and not reasonably susceptible of all security features being anticipated, bargained for and incorporated in the original contract. Norcon's performance, in terms of reimbursing Niagara Mohawk for credits, is still years away. In the meantime, potential quantifiable damages are accumulating and Niagara Mohawk must weigh the hard choices and serious consequences that the doctrine of demand for adequate assurance is designed to mitigate. This Court needs to go no further in its promulgation of the legal standard as this suffices to declare a dispositive and proportioned answer to the certified question.

Accordingly, the certified question should be answered in the affirmative. Chief Judge Kaye and Judges Smith, Levine, Ciparick and Wesley concur.

NOTES

1. ***The Purpose of Section 2-609.*** Before attempting to rationalize the decisions in *Bartlett* and *Norcon*, it may be helpful to consider the commercial purpose that the drafters intended for § 2-609. Study Comments 1 and 2 to that section.

As you see, Comment 2 outlines three protective mechanisms that the insecure party may employ. He may (1) suspend his performance until the situation has been clarified; (2) require adequate assurance that the other party's performance will be duly forthcoming; or (3) treat the contract as broken if his reasonable grounds for insecurity still remain after a reasonable time.

For example, the *Bartlett* court seemed very concerned that the plaintiff-seller did not avail himself of § 2-609 when grounds for insecurity arose. In fact, one might even read the court as punishing the plaintiff for this failure in that the court "[takes] into account" the fact that a § 2-609 remedy was specifically available but not used. Why not? Note that the communication of January 26th was not in writing contrary to the explicit requirements of UCC § 2-609. Is § 2-609 in any way intended to be mandatory? Compare the use of the section in *Kunian v. Development Corp. of America*, 165 Conn. 300, 334 A.2d 427 (1973) (liberally reading § 2-609(1) to allow a verbal demand to have effect); *Tennell v. Esteve Cotton Co.*, 546 S.W.2d 346, 354 n.4 (Tex. App. 1976) (holding that seller could not suspend performance despite buyer's anticipatory repudiation until adequate assurances were demanded); and *Indussa Corp. v. Reliable Stainless Steel Supply Co.*, 369 F. Supp. 976, 979 (E.D. Pa. 1974) (holding "the right to demand assurance conferred by § 2-609 is stated as permissive, not mandatory").

If the proper interpretation is that use of the section is not mandatory when insecurity arises, then what purpose does it serve? Why is the court less concerned with defendant-Bartlett's failure to use § 2-609?

2. ***Questions on* Bartlett.** As Note 1 indicates, one of the court's grounds for ruling in favor of the buyer appears to be that the seller failed to invoke its right to demand adequate assurances before suspending its performance. Among the other grounds the court provides are (1) time was not of the essence under the contracts, (2) measures short of suspending delivery on all contracts could have preserved the seller's contractual right to payment, (3) despite buyer's wrongful withholding of payment on contracts not in default, the separate identities of the various contracts were preserved (by accounting practices), (4) the seller was the first to breach, and

(5) seller tendered no grain even after it received a substantial payment after January 27. Are each of these factors relevant to determining whether seller's January 26th communication constituted a repudiation?

Consider (1), (4), and (5). Wasn't seller's concern that it would not be paid for future shipments? How is this concern reduced when time is not of the essence (all that means is that buyer's interests won't necessarily be prejudiced by delay)? How does seller's status as a prior breacher (because of delayed delivery) affect the interpretation of its January 26th communication as a repudiation? Finally, using factor (5), the court would determine whether the January 26th communication constituted a repudiation by looking to seller's behavior more than two weeks later, following a subsequent payment made by the buyer. If conduct after the communication is relevant to determining whether it constituted a repudiation, how could the buyer decide whether the seller's communication constituted a repudiation at the time the buyer receives it?

3. *Reasonable Grounds for Insecurity.*

a. *The Case Law.* In *Pittsburgh-Des Moines Steel Co. v. Brookhaven Manor Water Co.*, 532 F.2d 572 (7th Cir. 1976), the plaintiff offered to erect a one-million gallon water tank for $170,000, at the outset of contract negotiations, on the following terms: sixty percent payment upon receipt of materials in Pittsburgh-Des Moines Steel Co.'s (PDM) plant, thirty percent upon completion of the erection and the balance within 30 days after the tank was made ready for testing. Brookhaven refused these terms and the parties eventually agreed that Brookhaven would pay the full price after the tank had been accepted and tested. Later PDM's credit department became wary of the deal when it learned that Brookhaven was attempting to secure a loan to pay for the tank. PDM notified Brookhaven that it would hold the order in abeyance until either Brookhaven deposited the full purchase price in escrow or until Brookhaven's president personally agreed to be a surety for the payment. In holding that PDM had not established reasonable grounds for insecurity, the court emphasized that Brookhaven's financial situation had not changed since the contract was signed, and that PDM could not claim that it had reasonable grounds for insecurity when it was willing to accept the risk of later payment at the time the contract was negotiated:

> Section 2-609 is a protective device when reasonable grounds for insecurity arise; it is not a pen for rewriting a contract in the absence of those reasonable grounds having arisen, particularly when the proposed rewriting involves the very factors which had been waived by the one now attempting to wield the pen.

Id. at 582.

Note the unpleasant result for PDM. Since PDM was without reasonable grounds for insecurity, the court looked to Comment 2 of § 2-610 and decided that PDM's actions amounted to a statement of intention not to perform except on conditions that went beyond the original contract and therefore constituted anticipatory repudiation. If PDM were found to have had reasonable grounds for insecurity (the concurring judge argued that it did), Brookhaven's refusal to respond would be treated as a repudiation under § 2-609(4), giving PDM a right to remedy for breach under § 2-610. However, since PDM's demand was treated as a repudiation, it lost the bargain and also had to pay a judgment for damages.

In *Hornell Brewing Co. v. Spry*, 664 N.Y.S.2d 698 (1997), Hornell, the maker of Arizona Iced Tea, had entered into an agreement with Spry, an apparently reputable dealer, to market and sell Arizona Iced Tea in Canada. Problems quickly developed between the parties when Spry failed to promptly remit payment for shipments. The court held that Hornell did have reasonable grounds for insecurity because of Spry's failure to make payment according to the contract's terms. The court reached this decision despite the fact that Hornell had made no investigation of Spry's financial situation prior to entering into the agreement. The court stated that "[r]easonable grounds for insecurity can arise from the sole fact that a buyer has fallen behind in his account with the seller, even where the items involved have to do with separate and legally distinct contracts [that is, payments for separate shipments], because this 'impairs the seller's expectation of due performance.' " *Id.* at 703. Unlike the seller in *Bartlett*, Hornell used Spry's failure to make contractually required payments as grounds to assert his right to seek adequate assurances, rather than suspending his agreement with Spry.

Reasonable grounds for insecurity based on a party's failure to properly perform under a contract need not involve a failure to make payments. Tendering an inadequate product might be enough. This was the case in *AMF v. McDonald's Corp.*, 536 F.2d 1167 (7th Cir. 1976). AMF entered into an agreement with McDonald's to provide computerized cash registers. AMF initially provided a test model to McDonald's for evaluation purposes. The test model performed very poorly, requiring frequent service calls. During this time, McDonald's also discovered that AMF was having difficulty at its plant meeting the production requirements for future delivery under the agreement. The court held that McDonald's had reasonable grounds for insecurity, and even waived the requirement under UCC § 2-609(1) that demand for adequate assurances be made in writing.

b. *The Code and Theory.* The Code itself provides no objective guidelines for determining reasonable grounds for insecurity. Section 2-609(2) provides that between merchants reasonable grounds are to be determined by "commercial standards." Apparently then, reasonable grounds are to be established by a contextual inquiry rather than by a more precise rule.

What standards or criteria could be used to measure the "reasonableness" of specific claims of insecurity? In the introduction to this chapter, we suggested that future performance is jeopardized whenever a contingency occurs that causes one party to regret the contract. In such a situation, the promisor may either (1) bear the loss of performing an obligation he now regrets, or (2) breach and incur a corresponding sanction. The compensation principle of contract damages implies the existence of remedies that should make the *promisee* indifferent between receiving the contracted-for performance and accepting the promisor's breach plus damages. In either case, the promisee's expectations are protected. Numerous factors however, can thwart this objective. First, the nonbreacher will be required to "lend" the amount of any damage recovery to the breacher until judgment is satisfied. Second, since the recovery of prejudgment interest is restricted, the "loan" may be repaid at less than current market rates. Additionally, litigation costs

— particularly attorneys' fees — may not be recouped following breach. These factors encourage the promisor to use the prospect of uncompensated breach costs to induce a renegotiation of contract risks. One element in this strategy is to make the promisee insecure by creating uncertainty as to whether performance will occur. Based on this analysis, one might conclude that a party is "reasonably insecure" when (1) the occurrence of contingencies has caused the promisor to regret the agreed-upon allocation of risks; (2) the choice between performance or damages increases the risk of opportunistic behavior by the promisor; and (3) there is at least some ambiguity as to whether the promisor will perform.

4. *The Requirement of a Written Demand.* Section 2-609 could be read as requiring that a demand for assurance be in writing to be effective, yet at least two courts have waived this requirement. In *AMF*, Note 3(a), *supra*, the court refused to take "a formalistic approach" to § 2-609 and held that McDonald's failure to make a written demand was excusable because other evidence showed that AMF clearly understood that McDonald's would suspend performance until it received adequate assurances of performance. The result was that AMF's failure to respond justified McDonald's in treating the contract as repudiated under § 2-609(4) and allowed McDonald's its options for anticipatory repudiation under § 2-610.[18]

5. *Assurances as Enforceable Promises.* Section 2-609 allows insecure parties to demand assurances. Sometimes these can appear to take the form of new promises. In *Hornell*, (discussed in Note 3, supra), after Spry fell behind on his payments, Hornell expressed concern and negotiated a new, more rigorous financing agreement whereby they would extend Spry a $300,000 line of credit provided that payments were made on a net 14 day basis. *Hornell*, at 700. The court found that this constituted a reasonable demand for assurance. As one scholar has noted, this has potentially far-reaching implications:

> Yet there is another question lurking in this case, a question that courts have yet to address. When Hornell initially found that Spry was delinquent in its payments, it demanded that Spry agree to new credit terms in order to assuage its insecurity. In giving these assurances, Spry made a promise. The question that neither the Hornell court, nor any other court, seems to have explicitly confronted is, how long should this new arrangement endure? Is it to last the lifetime of the contract? Should it persist only until Spry establishes a record of timely payment? Or should Spry be required to comply with the promise of the assurances until Hornell has been made whole? The first option suggests that the assurances amount to a modification of the contract. The second, which is probably what the Hornell court would have chosen, would more closely tie the assurance to the insecurity — when the promisee is no longer insecure, the assurance is no longer

---

[18] At least one court has declined to follow *AMF*, finding that its "holdings are contrary to the language of the statute which requires evidence of a written demand for assurance of performance." *Scotts Co. v. Cent. Garden & Pet Co.*, 2002 WL 1578781, *4 (S.D. Ohio, Apr. 22, 2002). This does not, however, reflect the majority rule. *See Koch Materials Co. v. Shore Slurry Seal, Inc.*, 205 F. Supp. 2d 324, 332 (D.N.J. 2002) ("courts have routinely accepted as sufficient under § [2-]609 requests for assurances of a far less formal nature.").

needed. The last option would indicate that the assurance represents an independent promise in the nature of a separate contract.

Michael J. Borden, *The Promissory Character of Adequate Assurances of Performance*, 76 BROOK. L. REV. 167, 181 (2010).

6.   *The Information-Forcing Aspect of Section 2-609.* Section 2-609 performs a very useful information-forcing function. It allows an insecure promisee to ask a promisor who is sending ambiguous signals whether the promisor intends to breach. Presumably, the answer allows the promisee to be secure in the prospect of the promisor's performance or, alternatively, alerts him to the possibility of nonperformance and allows him to make alternative plans. The idea certainly seems useful despite the generality of § 2-609 and the resultant difficulty in deciding whether or not the promisor's response actually entitles the promisee to procure performance elsewhere.

Given the theoretical soundness of the concept, should it be expanded to enable a promisor weighing the choice between performance and breach plus damages to ask the promisee what the cost of the breach and payment option will be, without risking designation as a breacher? Analytically, the breach and pay option is tantamount to saying to the promisee, "Rather than performing myself, I would prefer that you arrange for a substitute performance (since you can do it more cheaply) and send me the damage bill."

Or is there reason to worry that the information forced by a demand for adequate assurances will have unintended negative consequences? In *The Secrecy Interest in Contract Law*, 109 YALE L.J. 1885 (2000), Professors Omri Ben-Shahar and Lisa Bernstein criticize the UCC's adequate assurances doctrine on the ground that it undermines the secrecy interest in contract law. They broadly define the secrecy interest as that value a party places on information it would prefer to keep private. The secrecy interest figures most prominently in breach of contract actions. Because an injured party may value maintaining the secrecy of its financial condition, it may be willing to forego contract damages to which it would be entitled were it willing to make public the proof of its losses. Bernstein and Ben-Shahar argue that a right to demand adequate assurances would increase the costs of revealing private financial information in the course of seeking compensatory damages. Once such information is revealed, it might provide other parties (to unrelated contracts with the plaintiff) with grounds for insecurity that would justify a demand for adequate assurances. In addition, the right to demand adequate assurances by itself provides a promisee with a conditional right to information from its contractual partner following formation, and thereby increases the costs of contracting by exposing parties to the risk that they might have to reveal information they would prefer to keep secret.

Could this problem be resolved by allowing parties to opt out of the adequate assurances doctrine? If not, do the expected benefits to insecure promisees outweigh the expected costs to promisors?

7.   *The Right to Adequate Assurances as a Corrective for Cognitive Error.* In *Adequate Assurance of Performance: Of Risk, Duress, and Cognition*, 69 U. COLO. L. REV. 71 (1998), Professor Larry Garvin considers and rejects the claim that the doctrine of adequate assurances unduly modifies the parties' *ex ante* risk allocation by providing promisees with a means of *ex post* risk adjustment. The argument Garvin considers holds that:

> [i]f the parties to the agreement have allowed for the risk of the promisor's non-performance . . . then the promisee has already been paid for the risk. It can insure against the risk, whether by purchasing insurance or by self-insuring. Whichever it chooses, it has been paid for the risk; accordingly, it should not be allowed to demand a modification when the risk comes about.

Id. at 74.

Garvin claims, however, that the doctrine can be justified as a corrective for parties' systematic underestimation of the probability of their partner's breach. Using findings in cognitive psychology, Garvin argues that contracting parties will systematically underestimate remote risks. In such cases, the promisee will "underprice the risk, charging less than the proper risk premium, and so the promisee will not be able to insure fully against the risk [ex ante]." The adequate assurances doctrine compensates for the promisee's biased *ex ante* risk assessment by allowing him to update overly optimistic initial risk assessments in light of new information.

According to the logic of Garvin's argument, should the right to adequate assurance be a mandatory, rather than a default, term in every contract? Would the same logic compel an expansion of current excuse and mistake doctrine as well? How would such an expansion affect the commercial reliability of contracts?

8. ***Repudiation, Retraction, and Adequate Assurance in the Employment Context.*** *Ticali v. Roman Catholic Diocese*, 41 F. Supp. 2d 249 (E.D.N.Y. 1999), is an interesting modern example of the interaction between the doctrines of anticipatory repudiation, retraction, and the right to demand adequate assurance. Ticali was a first grade teacher in a Catholic private school. Her employment contract, subject to certain easily-satisfied conditions, was automatically renewed yearly. Before Ticali was to begin work for a new term under her contract, however, the school terminated her, allegedly in order to replace her with an Hispanic teacher. Ticali, who was white, complained to the school that she believed this constituted racial discrimination. Fearing liability, the school instead transferred Ticali to what it considered to be an equivalent position, teaching pre-kindergarten classes. Ticali was unsatisfied with her change in position, believing that falling enrollments in the pre-kindergarten classes threatened the cancellation of the classes and that the transfer itself (to what she believed to be a substantially different position) violated her contract and amounted to a constructive discharge.

Ticali brought suit under Title VII of the Civil Rights Act for employment discrimination and also brought a claim for simple breach of contract. The court found no evidence of discrimination and dismissed her Title VII claim. The court also dismissed her contract claim. The court held that the initial termination did constitute an anticipatory repudiation of her renewed contract for employment. However, the court found that the school timely retracted the repudiation (following her complaints) and that the doctrine of anticipatory breach was thus inapplicable.

The court also found that her new position as a pre-kindergarten teacher was sufficiently equivalent so as not to amount to a constructive discharge that violated the terms of her contract. Moreover, the court noted that "[if] Ticali had doubts about the School's ability or intent to perform [because they transferred her to a new position], she could have demanded an assurance of performance." *Id.* at 258. In this context, what sort of assurance would have been adequate? If declining enrollments really were threatening the financial health of the pre-kindergarten classes, would the school be required to assure Ticali that it would not cancel the classes regardless of financial considerations? Note that there was no danger of the first grade classes being cancelled.

E.   INSTALLMENT CONTRACTS

Recall that the court in *Bartlett*, Section D, *supra*, considered each of the National Farmer's Organization's agreements with Bartlett to be installment contracts. Frequently, an alleged anticipatory repudiation will occur in the course of performance of an installment contract. For instance, the seller in *Bartlett* contracted to deliver grain to the buyer in a number of installments during the term of each of 14 separate contracts. When the buyer failed to pay for prior installments, the seller refused to deliver additional installments. When such disputes occur, the key question is whether a repudiation with respect to a particular installment is a breach of the entire contract as well.[19] As you read these next two cases, consider the following question: When is it appropriate to treat a sale of goods transaction as an installment contract? Read and analyze UCC § 2-612, which governs installment sales of goods. Pay careful attention to the conflict between the courts' holdings and the provisions of the Code. What, if anything, is the unifying rationale underlying the various rules governing installment contracts?

PAKAS v. HOLLINGSHEAD
Court of Appeals of New York
184 N.Y. 211, 77 N.E. 40 (1906)

O'BRIEN, J.

On the 30th of August, 1898, the defendants, by an executory contract in writing, agreed to sell and deliver to the plaintiff 50,000 pairs of bicycle pedals, the goods to be delivered and paid for in installments, as specified in the contract. It has been found by the trial court that the defendants delivered 2,608 pairs of pedals under the contract, and refused to make further deliveries. When the fact is established that the seller of goods to be delivered and paid for in installments, as in this case, refuses to deliver the goods, that amounts to a repudiation of the contract and a breach of it, for which the buyer may recover damages. So we start in this case with a breach of a contract on the part of the defendants by their refusal to be bound by its obligations.

---

[19] For a discussion of the strategic problems of successor contracts, see Subha Narasimhan, *Relationship or Boundary? Handling Successive Contracts*, 77 CAL. L. REV. 1077 (1989).

It is found that on the 15th of March, 1899, the plaintiff commenced an action against the defendants in the City Court of New York for breach of this contract, in that they failed to deliver to the plaintiff the pedals which, by the terms of the agreement, the defendants were bound to deliver up to the 1st of March, 1899 to wit, 19,000 pair, of which the defendants had delivered only the 2,608 pairs, and had failed to deliver 16,892 pairs, which were to be delivered up to the 1st of March, 1899. This action was put at issue, and after a trial the plaintiff recovered judgment against the defendants for the full amount claimed in the complaint in the action as damages for the breach of the contract, which judgment has been paid by the defendants in full.

Subsequently, and in February, 1900, the plaintiff commenced the present action to recover damages for a failure to deliver the balance of the goods, and both parties have pleaded the former suit and judgment. The plaintiff claims that it is conclusive evidence in his favor with respect to the existence, validity, terms and breach of the contract, while the defendants interpose it as a bar to the present action. This situation presents the question of law involved in the case. Judgment was given at the trial court in favor of the defendants and this judgment was affirmed on appeal. The question of law arising upon these facts is whether the former judgment concludes the plaintiff and is a bar to a second action to recover damages on the same contract. There can be no doubt that the contract was entire. It could not be performed on the part of the defendants without delivery of the property stipulated in the contract and the whole of it. As was said by Judge Bradley in Brock v. Knower, 37 Hun, 609, the fact that the property was deliverable and the purchase money payable at different times in the future did not necessarily deprive the contract of the character of entirety or make it other than a single one in respect to all the goods embraced in its terms. The learned counsel for the plaintiff contends that the former judgment did not constitute a bar to the present action, but that the plaintiff had the right to elect to waive or disregard the breach, keep the contract in force and maintain successive actions for damages from time to time as the installments of goods were to be delivered, however numerous these actions might be. It is said that this contention is supported in reason and justice, and has the sanction of authority at least in other jurisdictions.

We do not think that the contention can be maintained. There is not, as it seems to us, any judicial authority in this state that gives it any substantial support. On the contrary, we think that the cases, so far as I have been able to examine them, are all the other way, and are to the effect that inasmuch as there was a total breach of the contract by the defendants' refusal to deliver, the plaintiff cannot split up his demand and maintain successive actions, but must either recover all his damages in the first suit or wait until the contract matured or the time for the delivery of all the goods had arrived. In other words, there can be but one action for damages for a total breach of an entire contract to deliver goods, and the fact that they were to be delivered in installments from time to time does not change the general rule.

It was held in the case of Bendernagle v. Cocks, 19 Wend. 207, that where a party had several demands or existing causes of action growing out of the same contract or resting in matter of account which may be joined and sued for in the same action they must be joined; and if the demands or causes of action be split up and a suit brought for part only and subsequently a second suit for the residue is brought, the first action may be pleaded in abatement or in bar of the second action. That it seems to us, is what has been decided in this case. The case referred to was elaborately discussed by Judge Cowen, and the English authorities on the subject cited and distinguished.

The English cases point to but two alternative remedies open to the buyer upon a breach of contract for the sale of goods to be delivered in installments. One is to sue upon repudiation for a total breach before the time for performance has arrived and the other is to await the time for full performance and then sue for the damages. No suggestion is to be found in any of the cases that I have observed, to the effect that the buyer had an option to bring successive actions as the time for the delivery of each installment matures. It is said in many of the cases that the injured party had an option, but that option was not to bring several successive actions, but to elect whether, upon a breach, he shall proceed to recover all his damages or to await the time for full performance. The cases in the English courts on this question are very numerous, but they were all reviewed and the rule approved and followed in the case of Roehm v. Horst, 178 U.S. 1, where it was held that the English rule was reasonable and just . . . .

The cases bearing upon this question have been very fully collated in 2 Black on Judgments (§ 734), where the rule is stated in these words:

> When a demand or right of action is in its nature entire and indivisible it cannot be split up into several causes of action and made the basis of as many separate suits, but a recovery for one part will bar a subsequent action for the whole, the residue or another part . . . . If it appears that the first judgment involved the whole claim or extended to the whole subject-matter and settled the entire defense to the whole series of notes or claims, and adjudicated the whole subject-matter of a defense equally relevant to and conclusive of the controversy between the parties, as well in respect of the claim or defense in judgment as in respect to other claims and defenses thereto, pertaining to the same transaction or subject-matter, then the first judgment operates as an estoppel as to the whole.

Id. § 751; Bouchaud v. Dias, 3 Denio, 238.

It was admitted upon the argument of this case, and is admitted upon the brief of plaintiff's counsel, that the plaintiff could have recovered all his damages for a breach of the whole contract in the first action. The only contention is that he was not obliged to do so, but could maintain as many other actions as there were deliveries provided for in the contract in case of default. It does not seem to us that this proposition can be supported in reason or upon authority. The plaintiff claims in this action that the former judgment was conclusive as to him; that is, that it cuts off the defendants from any defense which they might originally have made, and thus it is sought to make this case an exception to the general rule that estoppels must be mutual; that is, that in general if the judgment is binding on one party it is equally binding in its effect upon the other. I think it would not be wise to engraft such a distinction upon the law of this state as was said in the case of Sykes v. Gerber, 98 Pa. 179: "The law does not tolerate a second judgment for the same thing between the same parties, whether the claim is upon a contract or tort . . . ."

We think the judgment below was right, and should be affirmed, with costs.

CULLEN, J. (dissenting).

I dissent from the decision about to be made. I concede to the fullest extent the principle that the plaintiff cannot split up a single cause of action, and that if he does a recovery on any part of the cause of action bars a suit for the remainder. I also concede the principle that in an executory contract for the sale of a number of articles or of a quantity of material, to be delivered in installments, and payment made therefor as delivered, in the case of a breach by either party as to one of the installments the other party may elect to treat the default as a complete breach of the contract, and maintain a suit for all his damages. I further concede that where there have been several breaches of a single contract the plaintiff must include in his action all breaches which have occurred prior to the commencement of the action. But I insist that none of these principles controls the question before us, which is not whether the plaintiff upon the default in the delivery of the first installment of pedals could rescind the contract as having been abrogated by the act of the defendant, reserving his right to recover damages, but whether he was obliged to adopt that course. Had he not as the aggrieved party the option to treat the contract as still continuing in force and, therefore, assert his right to recover damages for each default as it might occur? There can be no question that there may be a continuous agreement or covenant for every breach of which a new cause of action arises . . . .

Where the obligation is for the payment of money in installments the obligee has not, on default in the payment of one installment, even a right to elect to treat the contract as entirely broken, but must sue for the installments as they become due, unless the contract gives him the right of election. Where such an election is given by the contract, as is now quite common in the case of bonds and mortgages, the obligee is not bound to exercise it, but may do as he pleases. Therefore, to hold that the aggrieved party to a contract of the character of the one before us is not bound to accept a single breach of the contract as a total repudiation of its obligations, but can sue for each breach as it occurs, creates no anomaly in the law, and I can find no case where it has directly been held that he cannot. As I read them, in none of the cases cited by my Brother O'Brien, except those relating to contracts of employment, was the question before us involved. They all present the question as to the right of an aggrieved party on a single breach to recover as for a total abrogation of the contract, not the question whether he is obliged so to do. In fact, in most of the cases it is said that the aggrieved party may elect to treat the contract as abrogated. An election necessarily imports a right of choice. The question not being settled by authority should be determined on principle. Why should it be within the power of a party to a contract which may last over a long term of years, and the items or obligations of which are easily severable, to transmute by his own wrong his contract obligations into an unliquidated claim of damages against him, damages which as far as the future obligations of his contract are concerned are necessarily speculative. A person being about to contract for the construction of some work the execution of which will require a long period of time needs, to carry out the contract, brick, stone, or steel, and to secure himself against subsequent fluctuations in the market price of these articles, which he may believe will be greatly enhanced in price in the future, contracts with a materialman for their delivery in installments. It is by no means improbable that he has paid more than the present market price solely by reason of the uncertainty of the market price in the future. Under the decision about to be made he must either sue at the time of the first breach, when his damages will necessarily be speculative, a speculation it was the very object of the contract to avoid, or perhaps wait till the time for the last delivery has passed, when it may be that under the doctrine now declared his cause of action would be barred by the statute of limitations . . . .

It does not lie in the mouth of the defaulting party to say that the contract is still in force; but how about the aggrieved party? May he not say the contract is still in force? Of course, where a party sues for damages for only a single breach of a contract, he elects to continue it in force. Therefore, he must live up to the future obligations of the contract and cannot justify a subsequent breach on his part by the previous breach on the part of the other party. But whether the contract shall be continued in force or shall be rescinded seems to me should be entirely within the election of the aggrieved party . . . .

The judgment appealed from should be reversed, and a new trial granted; costs to abide the event.

CHERWELL-RALLI, INC. v. RYTMAN GRAIN CO.
Supreme Court of Connecticut
180 Conn. 714, 433 A.2d 984 (1980)

PETERS, J.

This case involves a dispute about which of the parties to an oral installment contract was the first to be in breach. The plaintiff, Cherwell-Ralli, Inc., sued the defendant, Rytman Grain Co., Inc., for the nonpayment of moneys due and owing for accepted deliveries of products known as Cherco Meal and C-R-T Meal. The defendant, conceding its indebtedness, counterclaimed for damages arising out of the plaintiff's refusal to deliver remaining installments under the contract. The trial court, Bordon, J., trial referee, having found all issues for the plaintiff, rendered judgment accordingly, and the defendant appealed.

The trial court's unchallenged finding of fact establishes the following: The parties, on July 26, 1974, entered into an instalment contract for the sale of Cherco Meal and C-R-T Meal on the basis of a memorandum executed by the Getkin Brokerage House. As modified, the contract called for shipments according to weekly instructions from the buyer, with payments to be made within ten days after delivery. Almost immediately the buyer was behind in its payments, and these arrearages were often quite substantial. The seller repeatedly called these arrearages to the buyer's attention but continued to make all shipments as requested by the buyer from July 29, 1974 to April 23, 1975.

By April 15, 1975, the buyer had become concerned that the seller might not complete performance of the contract, because the seller's plant might close and because the market price of the goods had come significantly to exceed the contract price. In a telephonic conversation between the buyer's president and the seller's president on that day, the buyer was assured by the seller that deliveries would continue if the buyer would make the payments for which it was obligated. Thereupon, the buyer sent the seller a check in the amount of $9825.60 to cover shipments through March 31, 1975.

Several days later, on April 23, 1975, the buyer stopped payment on this check because he was told by a truck driver, not employed by the seller, that this shipment would be his last load. The trial court found that this was not a valid reason for stoppage of payment. Upon inquiry by the seller, the buyer restated his earlier concerns about future deliveries. Two letters, both dated April 28, 1975, describe the impasse between the parties: the seller again demanded payment, and the buyer, for the first time in writing, demanded adequate assurance of further deliveries. The buyer's demand for assurance was reiterated in its direct reply to the seller's demand for payment. The buyer, however, made no further payments, either to replace the stopped check or otherwise to pay for the nineteen accepted shipments for which balances were outstanding. The seller made no further deliveries after April 23, 1975, when it heard about the stopped check; the buyer never made specific requests for shipments after that date. Inability to deliver the goods forced the seller to close its plant, on May 2, 1975, because of stockpiling of excess material.

The trial court concluded, on the basis of these facts, that the party in breach was the buyer and not the seller. The court concluded that the seller was entitled to recover the final balance of $21,013.60, which both parties agreed to be due and owing. It concluded that the buyer could not prevail on its counterclaim because it had no reasonable grounds to doubt performance from the seller and had in fact received reasonable assurances. Further, the buyer had presented no reasonably accurate evidence to establish the damages it might have sustained because of the seller's failure to deliver.

The buyer on this appeal challenges first the conclusion that the buyer's failure to pay "substantially impair[ed] the value of the whole contract," so as to constitute "a breach of the whole contract," as is required by the applicable law governing instalment contracts. § 2-612(3). What constitutes impairment of the value of the whole contract is a question of fact. The record below amply sustains the trial court's conclusion in this regard, particularly in light of the undenied and uncured stoppage of a check given to comply with the buyer's promise to reduce significantly the amount of its outstanding arrearages.

The buyer argues that the seller in an instalment contract may never terminate a contract, despite repeated default in payment by the buyer, without first invoking the insecurity methodology of § 2-609. That is not the law. If there is reasonable doubt about whether the buyer's default is substantial, the seller may be well advised to temporize by suspending further performance until it can ascertain whether the buyer is able to offer adequate assurance of future payments. But if the buyer's conduct is sufficiently egregious, such conduct will, in and of itself, constitute substantial impairment of the value of the whole contract and a present breach of the contract as a whole. An aggrieved seller is expressly permitted, by § 2-703(f), upon breach of a contract as a whole, to cancel the remainder of the contract "with respect to the whole undelivered balance." Nor is the seller's remedy to cancel waived, as the buyer argues, by a law suit seeking recovery for payments due. While § 2-612(3) states that a contract is reinstated if the seller "brings an action with respect only to past installments," it is clear in this case that the seller intended, as the buyer well knew, to bring this contract to an end because of the buyer's breach.

The buyer's attack on the court's conclusions with respect to its counterclaim is equally unavailing. The buyer's principal argument is that the seller was obligated, on pain of default, to provide assurance of its further performance. The right to such assurance is premised on reasonable grounds for insecurity. Whether a buyer has reasonable grounds to be insecure is a question of fact. AMF, Inc. v. McDonald's Corporation, 536 F.2d 1167, 1170 (7th Cir. 1976). The trial court concluded that in this case the buyer's insecurity was not reasonable and we agree. A party to a sales contract may not suspend performance of its own for which it has "already received the agreed return." At all times, the buyer had received all of the goods which it had ordered. The buyer could not rely on its own nonpayments as a basis for its own insecurity. The presidents of the parties had exchanged adequate verbal assurances only eight days before the buyer itself again delayed its own performance on the basis of information that was facially unreliable. Contrary to the buyer's argument, subsequent events proved the buyer's fears to be incorrect, since the seller's plant closed due to a surplus rather than due to a shortage of materials. Finally, it is fatal to the buyer's appeal that neither its oral argument nor its brief addressed its failure to substantiate, with probative evidence, the damages it alleged to be attributable to the seller's nondeliveries.

There is no error.

NOTES

1. ***Installment Contracts: Key Variables.*** Chief Justice Cullen noted in his *Pakas* dissent that the employment contract cases establish that the discharged employee must sue in one action for both his discharge and all contract payments due him or lose his right of action on all related claims. The majority used that principle to find that the plaintiff, by suing earlier for nondelivery of the pedals, had exhausted his right of action for later nondelivery. *Cherwell-Ralli* shows that § 2-612(3) allowed the promisee to sue on the earlier installments yet maintain an action on later installments. Is there a variable that harmonizes *Pakas, Cherwell-Ralli*, and the employment contract cases? If you were the plaintiff's lawyer in *Pakas*, how would you distinguish the employment contract cases from your client's situation?

2. ***The Buyer's Right to Cancel.*** *Cherwell-Ralli* considers whether the seller has a right to cancel because of a breach by the buyer. To what extent would the same analysis apply to a case involving a breach by a seller? Read and evaluate § 2-612, cmt. 6.

Comment 6 indicates that the policy is to put "the rule as to buyer's default on the same footing as that in regard to seller's default." But couldn't you argue that a different rule should apply where the seller's breach as to one or more installments raises severe doubts as to the seller's ability or intent to perform future obligations? What argument would support a rule giving buyers a more liberal right to cancel?

The buyer's right to cancel was first considered in *Graulich Caterer, Inc. v. Hans Holterbosch, Inc.*, 101 N.J. Super. 61, 243 A.2d 253 (1968). Holterbosch, the buyer, was granted the franchise to operate the Lowenbrau Pavilion at the 1964 New York World's Fair. He subsequently contracted with Graulich for the latter to provide frozen platters of German food to be heated in microwave ovens and served to patrons of the Pavilion. Graulich submitted satisfactory samples of its food to Holterbosch during their negotiations. The contract provided that Graulich would make daily deliveries to the Pavilion, as ordered by Holterbosch, for the duration of the Fair. Unhappily, the first delivery of food on April 23, 1964, was completely unacceptable. The food was " 'bland,' unpresentable, tasteless, and 'just [not] the type of food that we could sell.' " *Id.* at 66, 243 A.2d at 256. Holterbosch rejected this installment but continued to work with Graulich in order to improve the quality of the food. The second delivery, on April 25, was no better than the first. In response, Holterbosch ceased talking with Graulich, and instead converted its microwave cooking area into a conventional kitchen to prepare food needed for the Fair. The court offered this analysis of "substantial impairment":

> What amounts to substantial impairment presents a question of fact. Analyzing this factual question, the New Jersey commentators counsel that the test as to whether the nonconformity in any given installment justifies canceling the entire contract depends on whether the nonconformity substantially impairs the value of the whole contract, and not on whether it indicates an intent or likelihood that the future deliveries also will be defective. Continuing, the Comment relates the intent underlying a breach to insecurity and those sections of the Code providing buyer with adequate assurance of performance, § 2-609, and anticipatory repudiation, § 2-610. More practical in its treatment of "substantial impairment," the official Comment states that "substantial impairment of the value of an installment can turn not only on the quality of the goods but also on such factors as time, quantity, assortment and the like. It must be judged in terms of the normal or specifically known purposes of the contract." Comment to § 2-612, par. 4 . . . .

> At the Lowenbrau Pavilion on April 23, 1964 plaintiff Graulich, timely noticed [sic] of the nonconforming initial tender, gave assurance that future tenders would be cured to match the original samples. Unequivocally committed to the microwave kitchen method, defendant lent plaintiff three members from its staff in aid of this adjustment. Since plaintiff was given the opportunity to cure, there is no need to touch upon the substantiality of the initial nonconforming installment.

> The second installment tender was as unsatisfactory as the first. The meat was dry, the gravy "gooey" and the complaints abundant. After the nonconforming second delivery it became apparent that eleventh-hour efforts attempting to rework and adjust the platters failed. Translating this into legal parlance, there was a nonconforming tender of the initial installment on a contract for the sale of goods; upon tender the buyer

Holterbosch notified the seller Graulich of the nonconformity and unacceptable nature of the platters tendered; the failure of the cure assured by plaintiff, seller, was evidenced by a subsequently defective nonconforming delivery. The second unacceptable delivery and the failure of plaintiff's additional curative efforts left defendant in a position for one week without food. Time was critical. Plaintiff knew that platters of maximum quality were required on a daily installment basis. Because of defendant's immediate need for quality food and plaintiff's failure to cure, we find that the nonconforming of the second delivery, projected upon the circumstances of this case, "substantially impair[ed] the value of the whole contract [and resulted in] a breach of the whole." 2-612(3). If the breach goes to the whole contract, the buyer may cancel the whole contract. 2-711(1). Accordingly, we find that Holterbosch was justified in canceling the installment agreement signed on April 1, 1964.

Id. at 75–77, 243 A.2d at 262.

3. *Installment Contract Breaches and Lump-Sum Future Damages.* Consider a promisor who has performed his obligation under an agreement in exchange for installment payments in the future. If the party obligated by the promisor's past performance defaults on a *single* installment payment, should the promisor recover not only the failed present payment, but also all future payments due under the installment contract? Courts have responded differently to the problem of lump-sum damages in breached installment contracts.

In *First State Bank v. Jubie*, 86 F.3d 755 (8th Cir. 1996), the Eighth Circuit decided the question in the negative. Jubie, former owner of the First State Bank, had resigned from the Bank's board of directors in exchange for a life pension of $1,500 per month. The Bank was subsequently sold amid rumors that Jubie had approved illicit loans and otherwise "cooked the books" of the Bank. The Purchasers of the Bank promptly defaulted on Jubie's pension payments, arguing that Jubie's mismanagement of the Bank permitted them to void the retirement agreement. Jubie sued for recovery of present payments not received, *and* for a lump-sum payment of future installment obligations as calculated by the court.

Though the federal district court granted Jubie this lump-sum award, the Eighth Circuit reversed despite agreeing with the trial court that the

Purchaser's suspension of the installment contract was wrong. The Eighth Circuit concluded that:

> The Bank is not disabled from meeting its future Retirement Agreement obligations. [R]eplacing fixed monthly future obligations with a large lump-sum judgment will adversely impact a struggling financial institution and seems entirely contrary to the original purposes of the Retirement Agreement.

Id. at 761.

The court went on to identify the Retirement Agreement's lack of an acceleration clause as support for their decision. The presence of an acceleration clause, which would cause the entire amount owed to come due in the case of default by the

Purchasers, would have signaled the parties' intention to include all future payments in any contract damages awarded in case of breach. Failure to include an acceleration clause thus further demonstrates the parties' *ex ante* preference against lump-sum damages. The court then granted Jubie damages for currently-breached installment payments, and reaffirmed the Purchaser's obligation to pay future installments of the Retirement Agreement. *But see Barnett v. Oliver*, 858 P.2d 1228 (1993) (despite absence of an acceleration clause, trial court can accelerate the entire balance due under an installment contract should payors default on initial installments).

4. ***Anticipatory Repudiation, Installment Contracts, and Statutes of Limitation.*** Generally, a statute of limitation begins to run from the moment of contract breach. Should the injured party fail to assert his claim under the agreement before the statute of limitations has run, his recovery on the breach is forfeited. Though this principle appears simple enough, courts over the years have found difficulty in applying it to installment contracts. The primary problem involves whether default on a single payment should be considered an anticipatory repudiation of future payments. If a single default *is* an anticipatory repudiation of future payments, then the statute of limitations begins to run for the *entire* installment contract the moment of that first default.[20] If the single default *is not* considered an anticipatory repudiation, but is instead termed an independent breach of that particular installment payment, then each subsequent installment payment on which a payor defaults initiates a new and independent statute of limitations.

Consider *Keefe Co. v. Americable Int'l, Inc.*, 755 A.2d 469 (D.C. 2000), in which Keefe agreed to provide lobbying services to Americable in exchange for, among other things, monthly installment payments that would continue despite termination of the contract. Around 1988, Americable terminated the agreement. In addition, and in violation of the contract, Americable suspended the monthly installment payments. Keefe failed to assert its claim to the installment payments until 1994. The jurisdiction of decision was the District of Columbia, which has a statute of limitations for contract damages of three years. Americable argued that Keefe's complaint should be rejected since its termination and suspension of payment in 1988 amounted to an anticipatory repudiation of the *entire* installment contract and thus the statute of limitations for both present *and future* payments had begun to run in 1988.

The *Keefe* court rejected Americable's claim here, asserting that the "installment obligation rule" makes "clear that nonpayment of one installment triggers no requirement to sue on the totality of the debt[.]" *Id.* at 477. The court stated further that "the very principle of anticipatory repudiation is in doubt" when applied to installment contracts. *Id.* Accordingly, there existed no single statute of limitations for the entirety of the contract, but rather separate statutes of limitation were initiated with each Americable monthly default beginning in 1988. The court thus entered judgment for plaintiff Keefe in the amount of all installment payments owed by Americable from the years 1991 through 1994 (in other words, those installment payments whose independent statutes of limitation had not run when Keefe filed the claim in 1994).

---

[20] for an example of this, see *Miller v. Fortis Benefits Ins. Co.*, 475 F.3d 516 (3d Cir. 2007).

Do you agree with the court's holding? Didn't the court in *Bartlett*, Section D, *supra*, find that an installment contract was anticipatorily repudiated by the seller?

F. BIBLIOGRAPHY AND SUGGESTED READING

Omri Ben-Shahar & Lisa Bernstein, *The Secrecy Interest in Contract Law*, 109 YALE L.J. 1885 (2000).

Michael J. Borden, *The Promissory Character of Adequate Assurances of Performance*, 76 BROOK. L. REV. 167 (2010).

Richard Craswell, *Insecurity, Repudiation, and Cure*, 19 J. LEGAL STUD. 399 (1990).

Larry Garvin, *Adequate Assurance of Performance: Of Risk, Duress, and Cognition*, 69 U. COLO. L. REV. 71 (1998).

Charles J. Goetz & Robert E. Scott, *The Mitigation Principle: Toward a General Theory of Contractual Obligation*, 69 VA. L. REV. 967 (1983).

Thomas H. Jackson, *Anticipatory Repudiation of the Temporal Element of Contract Law: An Economic Inquiry into Contract Damages in Cases of Prospective Nonperformance*, 31 STAN. L. REV. 69 (1978).

Jody S. Kraus & George G. Triantis, *Anticipatory Repudiation Reconsidered*, 6 VA. J. 54 (2003).

Matthew Milikowsky, Note, *A Not Intractable Problem: Reasonable Certainty, Tractebel, and the Problem of Damages for Anticipatory Breach of a Long-Term Contract in a Thin Market*, 108 COLUM. L. REV. 452 (2008).

Subha Narasimhan, *Relationship or Boundary? Handling Successive Contracts*, 77 CAL. L. REV. 1077 (1989).

Madlyn Gleich Primoff & Erica G. Weinberger, *E-Commerce and Dot-Com Bankruptcies: Assumption, Assignment and Rejection of Executory Contracts, Including Intellectual Property Agreements, and Related Issues Under Sections 365(c), 365(e) and 365(n) of the Bankruptcy Code*, 8 AM. BANKR. INST. L. REV. 307 (2000).

Arthur Rosett, *Partial, Qualified and Equivocal Repudiation of Contract*, 81 COLUM. L. REV. 93 (1981).

Robert H. Skilton & Orrin Helstad, *Protection of the Installment Buyer of Goods Under the UCC*, 65 MICH. L. REV. 1465 (1967).

Lauriz Vold, *Withdrawal of Repudiation After Anticipatory Breach of Contract*, 5 TEX. L. REV. 9 (1926).

George I. Wallach, *Anticipatory Repudiation and the UCC*, 13 UCC L.J. 48 (1980).

Chapter 10

REMEDIES

A. THE BASIC STANDARDS

In Chapter 1, we introduced the topic of remedies for breach of contract and considered, as a matter of theory, what remedial options would best serve the goals of contract law. The legal rules providing particular remedies for breach of contract are (at least in one respect) no different from the many other "rules" that govern contractual performance. The various damages rules and other remedial options offer parties a set of default contract terms to cover the contingency that one or the other may breach.

Remedies for breach of contract thus allocate risks between the parties in much the same way as the rules governing, say, conditions and excuse. Similarly, individual parties remain free to opt out and (within certain limits) custom design their own "liquidated" damages rules. Not surprisingly, the issues (and questions) remain the same. In evaluating which damages rules are "best," it is useful to ask the now familiar question: How would most parties be expected to agree if required to bargain out a remedial scheme explicitly in advance? We begin the analysis in this section by reviewing in detail the various remedial options that are available to an aggrieved promisee who is asserting the right to compensation for breach of contract by the promisor. The key issue in each case is to determine the appropriate default term governing remedies where the contract itself is silent on the question. This basic issue involves a number of subsidiary questions: 1) If the promisee is, as a general proposition, entitled to be put in the same position as if the contract had been performed, how is that full performance position to be determined? 2) When is that full performance position to be measured by expectation damages and when by a decree of specific performance? 3) What options are available to the promisee to seek alternative damages measures — such as reliance and restitution — in lieu of expectation damages?

[1] Expectation Damages as a Substitute for Performance

Our analysis of the default rules governing remedies for breach begins, logically, with the foundational principle that if promises are to be sufficiently reliable, remedies for breach of contract must substitute for the performance that was originally promised under the contract. As we learned in Chapter 1, the basic assumption is that the promisor must either perform her promise or, if the promise is breached, put the promisee in the same position she would have occupied had the promise been performed. On the other hand, the promisee has no interest in the promise being *more reliable* than it is worth, so the promisee is not entitled to a recovery that places her in a *better* position than performance would have done. Contract disputes rarely involve a disagreement about this substitution principle per se, but rather what is required to properly implement the principle in particular cases.

In Chapter 1, we considered the concept of efficient breach. Part of that analysis hypothesizes a promisor who makes a rational, cost-efficient choice when confronted with a contractual obligation that he would prefer not to perform.[1] The choice is between performing the contract despite his regret (and thus incurring any associated losses) and electing to breach and pay the promisee damages sufficient to "make her whole." The concept of compensatory damages — making the promisee whole — thus assumes critical conceptual importance.

We also noted the existence of two alternative damage measures (ignoring for the time being the restitution of out-of-pocket losses) that can be used to satisfy the compensation principle. Reliance damages are measured by the amount of actual detrimental reliance suffered by the disappointed promisee. She is made whole by a payment equaling her true loss, the monetary equivalent of her disappointment. Essentially, the promisee is put back in the position she occupied before entering into the contract. Expectancy damages represent the amount the promisee expected to realize as a result of full performance, the difference between the promisee's current position and the position she would have been in had the contract been fully performed.

Although reliance and expectancy are alternative measures of the "value" of performance, expectancy is the standard default measure. Why is expectancy preferred over reliance? One way to evaluate the choice between reliance and expectancy damages is to ask which measure better achieves the principal goals of the contracting parties. While a number of such objectives might be identified, none is more important than to promote the reliability of the promises that each makes to the other.

If the only goal of contract law were to protect the reliability of those promises that are already made, we might well adopt a rule of punitive damages for breach. For instance, if the rule were that breachers paid damages of 10 times actual losses, few, if any, breaches would occur, and promises would have maximum reliability. However, the paradox of legal enforcement is that efforts to increase the reliability of promises already made also serve to reduce, to some extent, the number of future promises. If potential promisors are aware that they will have to pay 10 times actual losses should they be unable to perform their promises, on the margin they will be more cautious about making promises in the first place, and we would expect fewer total promises to be made (this is what economists call "an activity level" effect). Since promises carry beneficial information about the future, this result might be counterproductive. Thus, if the goal is to maximize the total social benefits from promise-making activity, the damages for breach need to be more carefully calibrated.

---

[1] For an argument that this choice is not properly characterized as a choice whether to breach efficiently but rather should be understood as a choice between alternative ways to perform the contract, see Daniel Markovits & Alan Schwartz, *The Myth of Efficient Breach: New Defenses of the Expectation Interest*, 97 VA. L. REV. 1939 (2011).

There is an argument that reliance is, at least in theory, the damage measure that best implements the goal of increasing the reliability of promises already made without deterring future promise making activity. A true reliance measure would guarantee a promisee that if the promise is breached she would be awarded damages equal to her next best alternative to the promise.

Since often (or surely at least sometimes) the promise will be performed, and since the promisee under a reliance rule can never do worse than the next best alternative, the promisee will, under these conditions, always choose to rely on the promise made by the promisor (do you see why?).

The theoretical attraction of reliance dissipates, however, once the difficulty and costs of verifying "true" reliance losses are considered. This is because:

> [T]rue reliance damages, which include the value of opportunities foregone as well as the costs of actions taken, are extraordinarily difficult to measure accurately. . . . The administrative and error costs of attempting to apply a theoretically optimal reliance standard suggest that it may be worthwhile to adopt a surrogate measure that is easier to apply. . . . A clear rule, such as expectation damages, yields benefits of reduced litigation costs. . . . The apparent tension between reliance and expectation simply reflects the failure to discriminate between ideal and pragmatic objectives. . . . Introducing the complexities of measurement and proof indicates that the traditional choice between reliance and expectancy damages should be recast as an attempt to select from potential contract rules the best achievable approximation of the optimal enforcement standard.

Charles J. Goetz & Robert E. Scott, *Enforcing Promises: An Examination of the Basis of Contract*, 89 YALE L.J. 1261, 1286–88, 1290–91 (1980).

The debate over whether reliance or expectancy is the better method of measuring damages for breach of contract may never be completely resolved. Moreover, both expectancy and reliance may be less than ideal in that both measures create an incentive for the promisee to over-rely on promises by failing to take steps to avoid losses from breach. Since the breaching promisor will be paying the bill, there is a moral hazard risk that a promisee who is guaranteed his full reliance or expectation damages will over invest in the contract and fail to adjust to the risk of non-performance by the promisor. While the mitigation principle moderates this problem to some extent, the duty to mitigate is not triggered until the promisor actually breaches the contract. The absence of any obligation to mitigate prior to breach thus may cause excessive reliance by the promisee. On this account, a liquidated damages clause will induce better reliance behavior by the promisee, since under that measure the value of the contract to the promisee is fixed at the time of contract.

In any case, you should remember that the issue of "ideal" damages is far less important when the question concerns damages for breach of a bargained for promise. There are two reasons why this is so. First, in the case of bargained for promises, a plausible, empirical generalization is that the promisee's acceptance of one promise frequently requires her to forego a potential substitute promise. In a well-organized market, alternative promises will be close, if not perfect, substitutes.

In that case, detrimental reliance is equal to the full performance expectancy of the breached promise since the foregone value of the best substitute promise available — the opportunity cost — is the same as the value of the promised performance.

Second, in the case of a bargained-for promise, the principal objective of a promisor is to obtain consideration in the form of a return promise (one must give to get). Thus, the bargaining process has a feedback mechanism whereby the parties can reallocate the risks of regretted promises by buying or selling "insurance" protection through the terms of their agreement. Thus, the parties can always bargain out from the damage rule, for instance by a stipulated damages agreement. Although the existence of transaction costs renders bargaining over damages rules costly in practice, the feedback adjustment of the return promise markedly reduces the potentially inefficient effects of any particular damages default rule.

The preceding argument suggests that the standard expectation damages rule is no different from other contract default rules. Expectation damages are an "off the rack" allocation of the risk of breach that, presumably, many (if not most) contracting parties would affirmatively select in order to cope with the contingency that one or the other may breach the contract.

To see how expectation damages default rules may be useful in "typical" settings, consider the following example:

> *Seller, a Los Angeles manufacturer of electronic parts, contracts on June 1 with Buyer, a New York wholesaler, to deliver specially manufactured electronic components on September 1. The contract price is $100,000 f.o.b. Los Angeles. Unfortunately, after the contract is concluded, but before delivery of the components, an unexpected technological breakthrough renders these electronic parts obsolete. Buyer now expects to be unable to make any use whatsoever of the contract goods. Because of the contract, Buyer bears the risk that the goods will no longer have a market value that is equal to or greater than the contract price and must now evaluate its options. What actions can (should) Buyer take?*

Basically, Buyer has three choices.

First, Buyer can perform the contract as agreed, accept delivery on September 1, pay Seller $100,000 and then attempt to salvage its loss on the contract by reselling the components to another buyer (presumably at a greatly reduced price). Under this option, Buyer will simply absorb its losses internally.

Second, Buyer can repudiate the contract and pay Seller whatever damages are assessed. Since there is no contract term specifying the damages upon breach, the contract law default rule governing damages for breach of such a contract will apply.

Finally, Buyer can attempt to renegotiate the contract with Seller in light of these events. Obviously, the cost of the first two options must first be known before Buyer can determine its bargaining position in any subsequent renegotiation.

In order to decide what course of action to take, therefore, Buyer must determine both the net losses it will likely incur if it were to choose the "perform and resell" option as well as the expected damages it will be required to pay Seller if it should choose the "breach and pay damages" option. Since a rational buyer would select the cheaper of these alternatives, it is obvious that the particular damage measure that contract law supplies as a default will influence Buyer's decision-making.

If the parties were to consider these possibilities during the initial bargaining process, what kind of damages rule would they choose? We have suggested that their shared goal at the time of contracting is to minimize the joint or collective losses that can be anticipated from the occurrence of a contingency that causes either party to regret making the agreement. In order to minimize the costs of unanticipated events, the parties need a damages rule that encourages the potential breacher (Buyer, in our example) to select the least cost option once the contingency arises and, in turn, encourages the promisee (Seller, in our example) to cooperate in mitigating the breacher's losses. In this case, any damages rule less than expectation (or full performance) damages would motivate Buyer to breach in the above example *whether or not Buyer were better able to salvage the broken contract by reselling the goods itself.* (Do you see why?)

On the other hand, any amount of damages greater than Seller's expectation losses would motivate Buyer to always select the "perform and resell" option even in instances where Seller actually is better positioned to find another buyer for the components at the best available price (and thus where the option of "breach and pay damages" would yield the smallest losses under the contract). Only an expectancy measure will produce the basic equivalency between performance and breach. With that equivalency, so long as Buyer is not acting strategically, it will be motivated to select between the first and second options above ("perform and resell" or "breach and pay damages") based upon its best guess as to which party — Seller or Buyer — can resell the components to another buyer at the highest price and least cost, thereby minimizing Buyer's ultimate losses on the contract.

In sum, minimizing the costs of contingencies that cause a party to regret the contract requires the parties: 1) to take precautions against such risks before they occur and 2) to adjust cooperatively once they do. Unfortunately, as we shall see, there is an inherent tension between these two objectives. This tension is best seen in the choice between ways of measuring expectancy losses. Thus, for example, a clear, bright-line rule governing breach, such as specific performance, will reduce the risk that the promisor might evade its contractual responsibilities and thus will encourage maximum *ex ante* precautions by the promisor. But then, under such a rule, the promisee will have no incentive to cooperate *ex post* since the promisee will know that a court will order the promisor to perform in all events. On the other hand, a more flexible expectancy damages rule such as the market-based contract/market differential in sales contracts gives the promisor more choices once a regret contingency has occurred. This rule encourages mitigation and cooperation after the contingency has materialized since it permits the promisor (through the election to breach) to require the promisee to find an alternative salvage contract. But, unless damages are perfectly measured, this remedy may also create a moral hazard; that is, it may invite the promisor to shirk his duty to satisfy the promisee's expectancy in full (for example, by challenging the promisee's actions as violating her duty to reasonably mitigate the breacher's losses). In studying the cases that follow in this section, you should consider whether the default rules provided by contract law are successful in accommodating this tension, and, if they are not, whether any superior alternatives are available.

[2]   Measuring Expectancy: Cost of Completion or Diminution in Value

In order to measure expectation damages accurately, two economic positions (or states of the world) must be determined. First, we must know what position the promisee currently occupies following the breach of contract. That seems straightforward enough as it turns on known facts that can be verified to the court. But then we must also know what position the promisee *would have occupied* had the promise been performed. In the case of a sale of goods traded in a regular market, that, too, is readily established by proof of what the market price of the goods in question were at the time performance was due. But in many cases, such as where the contract involves services performed on land owned by the promisee, the issue of what performance, precisely, was owed to the injured promisee is less clear. Consider, for example, the following case.

PEEVYHOUSE v. GARLAND COAL & MINING CO.
Supreme Court of Oklahoma
382 P.2d 109 (1962)

Jackson, J.

In the trial court, plaintiffs Willie and Lucille Peevyhouse sued the defendant, Garland Coal and Mining Company, for damages for breach of contract. Judgment was for plaintiffs in an amount considerably less than was sued for. Plaintiffs appeal and defendant cross-appeals.

In the briefs on appeal, the parties present their argument and contentions under several propositions; however, they all stem from the basic question of whether the trial court properly instructed the jury on the measure of damages.

Briefly stated, the facts are as follows: plaintiffs owned a farm containing coal deposits, and in November, 1954, leased the premises to defendant for a period of five years for coal mining purposes. A "stripmining" operation was contemplated in which the coal would be taken from pits on the surface of the ground, instead of from underground mine shafts. In addition to the usual covenants found in a coal mining lease, defendant specifically agreed to perform certain restorative and remedial work at the end of the lease period. It is unnecessary to set out the details of the work to be done, other than to say that it would involve the moving of many thousands of cubic yards of dirt, at a cost estimated by expert witnesses at about $29,000.00. However, plaintiffs sued for only $25,000.00.

During the trial, it was stipulated that all covenants and agreements in the lease contract had been fully carried out by both parties, except the remedial work mentioned above; defendant conceded that this work had not been done.

Plaintiffs introduced expert testimony as to the amount and nature of the work to be done, and its estimated cost. Over plaintiffs' objections, defendant thereafter introduced expert testimony as to the "diminution in value" of plaintiffs' farm resulting from the failure of defendant to render performance as agreed in the contract — that is, the difference between the present value of the farm, and what its value would have been if defendant had done what it agreed to do.

At the conclusion of the trial, the court instructed the jury that it must return a verdict for plaintiffs, and left the amount of damages for jury determination. On the measure of damages, the court instructed the jury that it might consider the cost of performance of the work defendant agreed to do, "together with all of the evidence offered on behalf of either party."

It thus appears that the jury was at liberty to consider the "diminution in value" of plaintiffs' farm as well as the cost of "repair work" in determining the amount of damages.

It returned a verdict for plaintiffs for $5000.00 — only a fraction of the "cost of performance," but more than the total value of the farm even after the remedial work is done.

On appeal, the issue is sharply drawn. Plaintiffs contend that the true measure of damages in this case is what it will cost plaintiffs to obtain performance of the work that was not done because of defendant's default. Defendant argues that the measure of damages is the cost of performance "limited, however, to the total difference in the market value before and after the work was performed." [. . .]

In the case before us, it is argued by defendant with some force that the performance of the remedial work defendant agreed to do will add at the most only a few hundred dollars to the value of plaintiffs' farm, and that the damages should be limited to that amount because that is all plaintiffs have lost.

Plaintiffs rely on Groves v. John Wunder Co., 205 Minn. 163. In that case, the Minnesota court, in a substantially similar situation, adopted the "cost of performance" rule as — opposed to the "value" rule. The result was to authorize a jury to give plaintiff damages in the amount of $60,000, where the real estate concerned would have been worth only $12,160, even if the work contracted for had been done.

It may be observed that Groves v. John Wunder Co., *supra*, is the only case which has come to our attention in which the cost of performance rule has been followed under circumstances where the cost of performance greatly exceeded the diminution in value resulting from the breach of contract. Incidentally, it appears that this case was decided by a plurality rather than a majority of the members of the court.

Defendant relies principally upon Sandy Valley & E. R. Co. v. Hughes, 175 Ky. 320; Bigham v. Wabash-Pittsburg Terminal Ry. Co., 223 Pa. 106; and Sweeney v. Lewis Const. Co., 66 Wash. 490. These were all cases in which, under similar circumstances, the appellate courts followed the "value" rule instead of the "cost of performance" rule. Plaintiff points out that in the earliest of these cases (*Bigham*) the court cites as authority on the measure of damages an earlier Pennsylvania tort case, and that the other two cases follow the first, with no explanation as to why a measure of damages ordinarily followed in cases sounding in tort should be used in contract cases. Nevertheless, it is of some significance that three out of four appellate courts have followed the diminution in value rule under circumstances where, as here, the cost of performance greatly exceeds the diminution in value.

The explanation may be found in the fact that the situations presented are artificial ones. It is highly unlikely that the ordinary property owner would agree to pay $29,000 (or its equivalent) for the construction of "improvements" upon his property that would increase its value only about ($300) three hundred dollars. The result is that we are called upon to apply principles of law theoretically based upon reason and reality to a situation which is basically unreasonable and unrealistic.

In Groves v. John Wunder Co., *supra*, in arriving at its conclusions, the Minnesota court apparently considered the contract involved to be analogous to a building and construction contract, and cited authority for the proposition that the cost of performance or completion of the building as contracted is ordinarily the measure of damages in actions for damages for the breach of such a contract.

In an annotation following the Minnesota case beginning at 123 A.L.R. 515, the annotator places the three cases relied on by defendant (*Sandy Valley, Bigham* and *Sweeney*) under the classification of cases involving "grading and excavation contracts."

We do not think either analogy is strictly applicable to the case now before us. The primary purpose of the lease contract between plaintiffs and defendant was neither "building and construction" nor "grading and excavation." It was merely to accomplish the economical recovery and marketing of coal from the premises, to the profit of all parties. The special provisions of the lease contract pertaining to remedial work were incidental to the main object involved.

Even in the case of contracts that are unquestionably building and construction contracts, the authorities are not in agreement as to the factors to be considered in determining whether the cost of performance rule or the value rule should be applied. The American Law Institute's Restatement of the Law, Contracts, Volume 1, Sections 346(1)(a)(i) and (ii) submits the proposition that the cost of performance is the proper measure of damages "if this is possible and does not involve *unreasonable economic waste*"; and that the diminution in value caused by the breach is the proper measure "if construction and completion in accordance with the contract would involve *unreasonable economic waste.*" (Emphasis supplied.) In an explanatory comment immediately following the text, the Restatement makes it clear that the "economic waste" referred to consists of the destruction of a substantially completed building or other structure. Of course no such destruction is involved in the case now before us.

On the other hand, in McCormick, *Damages*, § 168, it is said with regard to building and construction contracts that ". . . in cases where the defect is one that can be repaired or cured *without undue expense*" the cost of performance is the proper measure of damages, but where ". . . the defect in material or construction is one that cannot be remedied without *an expenditure for reconstruction dispro-portionate to the end to be attained*" (emphasis supplied) the value rule should be followed. The same idea was expressed in Jacob & Youngs, Inc. v. Kent as follows:

> The owner is entitled to the money which will permit him to complete, unless the cost of completion is grossly and unfairly out of proportion to the

good to be attained. When that is true, the measure is the difference in value.

It thus appears that the prime consideration in the Restatement was "economic waste;" and that the prime consideration in McCormick, *Damages*, and in Jacob & Youngs, Inc. v. Kent, *supra*, was the relationship between the expense involved and the "end to be attained" — in other words, the "relative economic benefit."

In view of the unrealistic fact situation in the instant case, and certain Oklahoma statutes to be hereinafter noted, we are of the opinion that the "relative economic benefit" is a proper consideration here. This is in accord with the recent case of Mann v. Clowser, 190 Va. 887, where, in applying the cost rule, the Virginia court specifically noted that ". . . the defects are remediable from a practical standpoint and the costs *are not grossly disproportionate to the results to be obtained*" (emphasis supplied).

23 O.S. 1961 §§ 96 and 97 provide as follows:

> § 96. . . . Notwithstanding the provisions of this chapter, no person can recover a greater amount in damages for the breach of an obligation, than he would have gained by the full performance thereof on both sides. . . .

> § 97. . . . Damages must, in all cases, be reasonable, and where an obligation of any kind appears to create a right to unconscionable and grossly oppressive damages, contrary to substantial justice no more than reasonable damages can be recovered.

Although it is true that the above sections of the statute are applied most often in tort cases, they are by their own terms, and the decisions of this court, also applicable in actions for damages for breach of contract. It would seem that they are peculiarly applicable here where, under the "cost of performance" rule, plaintiffs might recover an amount about nine times the total value of their farm. Such would seem to be "unconscionable and grossly oppressive damages, contrary to substantial justice" within the meaning of the statute. Also, it can hardly be denied that if plaintiffs here are permitted to recover under the "cost of performance" rule, they will receive a greater benefit from the breach than could be gained from full performance, contrary to the provisions of Sec. 96.

An analogy may be drawn between the cited sections, and the provisions of 15 O.S. 1961 §§ 214 and 215. These sections tend to render void any provisions of a contract which attempt to fix the amount of stipulated damages to be paid in case of a breach, except where it is impracticable or extremely difficult to determine the actual damages. This results in spite of the agreement of the parties, and the obvious and well known rationale is that insofar as they exceed the actual damages suffered, the stipulated damages amount to a penalty or forfeiture which the law does not favor.

23 O.S. 1961 §§ 96 and 97 have the same effect in the case now before us. In spite of the agreement of the parties, these sections limit the damages recoverable to a reasonable amount not "contrary to substantial justice;" they prevent plaintiffs from recovering a "greater amount in damages for the breach of an obligation" than they would have "gained by the full performance thereof."

We therefore hold that where, in a coal mining lease, lessee agrees to perform certain remedial work on the premises concerned at the end of the lease period, and thereafter the contract is fully performed by both parties except that the remedial work is not done, the measure of damages in an action by lessor against lessee for damages for breach of contract is ordinarily the reasonable cost of performance of the work; however, where the contract provision breached was merely incidental to the main purpose in view, and where the economic benefit which would result to lessor by full performance of the work is grossly disproportionate to the cost of performance, the damages which lessor may recover are limited to the diminution in value resulting to the premises because of the non-performance.

We believe the above holding is in conformity with the intention of the Legislature as expressed in the statutes mentioned, and in harmony with the better-reasoned cases from the other jurisdictions where analogous fact situations have been considered. It should be noted that the rule as stated does not interfere with the property owner's right to "do what he will with his own" (Chamberlain v. Parker, 45 N.Y. 569), or his right, if he chooses, to contract for "improvements" which will actually have the effect of reducing his property's value. Where such result is in fact contemplated by the parties, and is a main or principal purpose of those contracting, it would seem that the measure of damages for breach would ordinarily be the cost of performance.

The above holding disposes of all of the arguments raised by the parties on appeal.

Under the most liberal view of the evidence herein, the diminution in value resulting to the premises because of non-performance of the remedial work was $300.00. After a careful search of the record, we have found no evidence of a higher figure, and plaintiffs do not argue in their briefs that a greater diminution in value was sustained. It thus appears that the judgment was clearly excessive, and that the amount for which judgment should have been rendered is definitely and satisfactorily shown by the record. . . .

We are of the opinion that the judgment of the trial court for plaintiffs should be, and it is hereby, modified and reduced to the sum of $300.00, and as so modified it is affirmed.

IRWIN, J. (dissenting).

[. . .] Defendant admits that it failed to perform its obligations that it agreed and contracted to perform under the lease contract and there is nothing in the record which indicates that defendant could not perform its obligations. Therefore, in my opinion defendant's breach of the contract was willful and not in good faith.

Although the contract speaks for itself, there were several negotiations between the plaintiffs and defendant before the contract was executed. Defendant admitted in the trial of the action, that plaintiffs insisted that the [remedial and restoration] provisions be included in the contract and that they would not agree to the coal mining lease unless the [those] provisions were included.

In consideration for the lease contract, plaintiffs were to receive a certain amount as royalty for the coal produced and marketed and in addition thereto their land was to be restored as provided in the contract.

Defendant received as consideration for the contract, its proportionate share of the coal produced and marketed and in addition thereto, the *right to use* plaintiffs' land in the furtherance of its mining operations.

The cost for performing the contract in question could have been reasonably approximated when the contract was negotiated and executed and there are no conditions now existing which could not have been reasonably anticipated by the parties. Therefore, defendant had knowledge, when it prevailed upon the plaintiffs to execute the lease, that the cost of performance might be disproportionate to the value or benefits received by plaintiff for the performance.

Defendant has received its benefits under the contract and now urges, in substance, that plaintiffs' measure of damages for its failure to perform should be the economic value of performance to the plaintiffs and not the cost of performance.

If a peculiar set of facts should exist where the above rule should be applied as the proper measure of damages (and in my judgment those facts do not exist in the instant case) before such rule should be applied, consideration should be given to the benefits received or contracted for by the party who asserts the application of the rule.

Defendant did not have the right to mine plaintiffs' coal or to use plaintiffs' property for its mining operations without the consent of plaintiffs. Defendant had knowledge of the benefits that it would receive under the contract and the approximate cost of performing the contract. With this knowledge, it must be presumed that defendant thought that it would be to its economic advantage to enter into the contract with plaintiffs and that it would reap benefits from the contract, or it would have not entered into the contract.

Therefore, if the value of the performance of a contract should be considered in determining the measure of damages for breach of a contract, the value of the benefits received under the contract by a party who breaches a contract should also be considered. However, in my judgment, to give consideration to either in the instant action, completely rescinds and holds for naught the solemnity of the contract before us and makes an entirely new contract for the parties. . . .

In the instant action defendant has made no attempt to even substantially perform. The contract in question is not immoral, is not tainted with fraud, and was not entered into through mistake or accident and is not contrary to public policy. It is clear and unambiguous and the parties understood the terms thereof, and the approximate cost of fulfilling the obligations could have been approximately ascertained. There are no conditions existing now which could not have been reasonably anticipated when the contract was negotiated and executed. The defendant could have performed the contract if it desired. It has accepted and reaped the benefits of its contract and now urges that plaintiffs' benefits under the contract be denied. If plaintiffs' benefits are denied, such benefits would inure to the direct benefit of the defendant.

Therefore, in my opinion, the plaintiffs were entitled to specific performance of the contract and since defendant has failed to perform, the proper measure of damages should be the cost of performance. Any other measure of damage would be holding for naught the express provisions of the contract; would be taking from the plaintiffs the benefits of the contract and placing those benefits in defendant which has failed to perform its obligations; would be granting benefits to defendant without a resulting obligation; and would be completely rescinding the solemn obligation of the contract for the benefit of the defendant to the detriment of the plaintiffs by making an entirely new contract for the parties.

I therefore respectfully dissent to the opinion promulgated by a majority of my associates.

NOTES

1. ***Measuring Expectancy: The Choice Between Cost of Completion and Diminution in Value****.* Courts are split on whether to award damages equal to the cost of completion or the diminution in value in cases similar to *Peevyhouse.* For an example of a court choosing the cost of completion measure despite the concern about "economic waste," consider *American Standard, Inc. v. Schectman*, 439 N.Y.S.2d 529 (1981). Until 1972, American Standard operated a pig iron manufacturing plant. The company then wished to sell the land. It entered into a contract with Schectman, in which American Standard agreed to convey the buildings and most of the equipment on the land to Schectman in exchange for $275,000 and his promise to remove the equipment, demolish any structures remaining on the land, and grade the property according to the contract's specifications. The purpose of this grading was "to provide a reasonably attractive vacant plot for resale." *Id.*

Schectman did not grade the land to the level specified in the contract. To do so would have cost him approximately $110,000, and the increase in land value was minimal. In fact, American Standard had already sold the land, ungraded, at a price only $3,000 less than full market value. Nevertheless, the court awarded American Standard cost of completion damages:

> Defendant's completed performance would not have involved undoing what in good faith was done improperly but only doing what was promised and left undone. That the burdens of performance were heavier than anticipated and the cost of completion disproportionate to the end to be obtained does not, without more, alter the rule that the measure of plaintiffs' damage is the cost of completion. Disparity in relative economic benefits is not the equivalent of 'economic waste' which will invoke the rule in *Jacob & Youngs v. Kent* [see *infra* p. 65]. Moreover, faced with the jury's finding that the reasonable cost of removing the large concrete and stone walls and other structures extending above grade was $90,000, defendant can hardly assert that he has rendered substantial performance of the contract or that what he left unfinished was 'of trivial or inappreciable importance.' Finally, defendant, instead of attempting in good faith to complete the removal of the underground structures, contended that he was not obliged by the contract to do so and, thus, cannot claim to be a 'transgressor whose default is unintentional and trivial [and who] may hope for mercy if he will offer

atonement for his wrong.' We conclude, therefore, that the proof pertaining to the value of plaintiffs' property was properly rejected. . . .

Id.

In both *American Standard* and *Peevyhouse*, the court purported to be applying the expectation damages default rule. Yet the results in each case are significantly different. These cases show that often the issue is not whether to use the expectation measure per se, but rather how best to measure the promisee's expectancy. In each of these cases the issue is the same: What is the position the promisee expected to occupy upon performance of the contract? There are two possibilities. The promisee may have bargained (and paid) for *graded-value land*. If that is so, then diminution in market value should be the best measure of the lost expectancy. Alternatively, the promisee may have bargained (and paid) for *graded land, regardless of the market value of the grading*. In that case, only cost of completion damages will provide the promisee her lost expectancy. What did the plaintiff bargain for in each case? Is it clear from the facts what contractual expectation each promisee was entitled to rely upon (i.e., what did each plaintiff pay for)? Is the *ex ante* expected cost of grading (a cost that presumably was reflected in the contract price paid to the promisor) the same as the actual cost of grading *ex post*? Isn't the expected cost that was presumably paid for by the promisee likely to be greater than the ex post diminution in market value but less than the ex post cost of completion? If so, which damage default should the court award?

2. *Should Subjective (or Idiosyncratic) Value be Protected?* In an excellent historical analysis, Professor Judith Maute notes that the *Peevyhouse* court ignored the parties' ex ante intentions, as discussed in Justice Irwin's dissent. The Oklahoma Supreme Court dismissed the Peevyhouses' subjective valuation of their property, even though there were signals of this value in the agreement with Garland Mining. Consider the following:

> From the Peevyhouses' perspective, obtaining the promised remedial work was essential. Having observed the effects of strip-mining under the standard arrangement, they agreed to forego immediate payment of $3000 in consideration for Garland's promises of basic reclamation. The leased acreage was part of their homestead estate and connected to the land on which they lived but refused to lease. When placed against this backdrop, it is clear that the Peevyhouses highly valued the future utility of the leased land. These fundamental facts relate to their main purpose, as evidence of the express bargained-for-exchange, with payment of separate valuable consideration for the remedial provisions. . . .

> Willie and Lucille still live on the land located outside Stigler. The land they leased to Garland has changed little from when the mining stopped more than thirty-five years ago. About half of the leased acreage remains unusable.

Judith Maute, Peevyhouse v. Garland Coal & Mining Co. *Revisited: The Ballad of Willie and Lucille*, 89 Nw. U. L. Rev. 1341, 1413, 1404 (1995). Professor Peter Linzer has agreed with this view:

When people enter into contracts, they also may be motivated by non-monetary considerations. The end to be achieved by performance may be desired in and of itself, not as a means to an increase in wealth measured by conventional methods of valuation. Consider the well-known case of *Peevyhouse v. Garland Coal & Mining Co.* . . . If the land was important to them as a home as well as a source of income, the loss caused them by breach could not be measured solely by a reduction in market value. Any economic analysis that assigns no value to their love of home or treats the promise to restore the land as merely instrumental to protecting its market value is incapable of measuring the true costs and benefits of breach.

Peter Linzer, *On the Amorality of Contract Remedies — Efficiency, Equity, and the Second Restatement*, 81 COLUM. L. REV. 111, 117 (1981).

Now consider the *American Standard* case discussed in Note 1, *supra*. In an attempt to avoid the oft-criticized conclusion of *Peevyhouse*, the court granted American Standard cost of completion damages totaling $90,000 even though the property subsequently sold for only $3,000 less than its full fair market value. Given the context in *American Standard*, does this make sense? Arguably no. The contract in *Schectman* required defendant to restore the land such that it is a *"reasonably attractive vacant lot for resale."* 80 A.D.2d at 320 (emphasis added). After defendant failed to complete the agreed-upon remedial work, plaintiff still sold the land for only $3,000 less than the full market price. It is unlikely that the promisee would have agreed *ex ante* to pay $90,000 to increase the expected market value of the property by only $3,000. Thus, unless the value of the land fell dramatically *ex post*, it is likely that the expected cost of grading (which the plaintiff presumably paid for) was substantially less than $90,000. Since the parties' *ex ante* intentions for the property (resale) were clear, the best inference is that the promisee only "paid" for damages sufficient to cover the difference in market value.

Was the damage assessment of $90,000 a windfall for a corporation with no subjective valuation of the land? Professor Timothy Muris probably would answer yes. He argues that courts should differentiate between businesses and consumers when calculating damages in a *Peevyhouse* or *Schectman* situation:

> On the other hand, nonpecuniary elements, such as sentimental value, often play a prominent part in consumers' decisions. Businesses often purchase for resale, making value to the buyer presumably a function of the item's market price. Consumers typically buy, not for resale, but for use; only at the margin will a consumer's subjective value equal the market value. Of course, a business may purchase for use as well, but any claim that the business values the item differently from the market should still be evaluated in terms of its effect on the business's profits.

Timothy Muris, *Cost of Completion or Diminution in Market Value: The Relevance of Subjective Value*, 12 J. LEGAL STUD. 379, 382–83 (1983).

3. ***Who Gets the Windfall?*** Even though cost of completion is the standard default rule in the case of a breached contract to perform a service, many courts continue to limit the buyer who has contracted for the service to diminution in value damages whenever the ex post cost of completion greatly exceeds the economic

benefit to the disappointed buyer. (Recall, for example, Justice Cardozo's decision in *Jacob & Youngs v. Kent, supra* Chapter 1). Modern courts realize that buyers will not use the money to undertake repairs that require substantial and inefficient demolition or that have little economic benefit, but they continue to reject damages measured by the ex post cost of performance. Since the cost of completion award is meant to enable the buyer to purchase a substitute, and since the buyer will purchase something else, the contemporary rationale holds that cost of completion damages would only redistribute wealth from sellers to buyers. Courts thus restrict buyers to the diminution in market value to avoid giving them a "windfall."

But in cases such as *Peevyhouse* and *Jacob & Youngs* (*supra*), if the buyer is restricted to only recovering the diminution in market value then the windfall goes to the breaching seller. This is because, as in *Peevyhouse*, the buyer has already "paid" for the restoration service as part of the initial contract price. Thus, the breaching party is permitted to keep the value of the promise to restore the land without having to undertake any restoration services. Given that either damage rule will give a windfall to one of the parties, then courts must choose between two unpalatable options. As Alan Schwartz and Robert Scott explain in in *Market Damages, Efficient Contracting, and the Economic Waste Fallacy*, 108 COLUM. L. REV. 1610 (2008):

> A buyer who has prepaid is entitled *both* to restitution of the price and to market damages. Cost of completion damages incorporate this restitutionary component. The cost of completion is the ex post market price for the contract service: this price, in turn, is the sum of (a) the ex ante market price and (b) the difference, if any, between the ex post market price and the ex ante market price. Hence, if the initial contract and the replacement contract were both made at current market prices, awarding the buyer the cost of completion satisfies his restitutionary claim to recover back the price and his expectation interest claim for market damages. . . .
>
> Courts and most commentators have overlooked this implication because they have not recognized that buyers prepay for the services that commonly appear in the cases. This omission probably occurs because the services are bundled together and are not separately priced. As an example, the royalty on a mineral lease is smaller if the lessee agrees to restore the land after mining, but there seldom is an explicit "sub-price" for restoration. The cost of constructing a building seldom is disaggregated into separate prices for the promise to install the plumbing and the promise to correct defective work. But to deny that the buyer in such cases has prepaid is to assert, implausibly, that the mining lessee had agreed to restore for nothing or that the contractor did not charge for the service of correcting nonconforming plumbing.
>
> The bundling problem would sometimes make it infeasible for a court to retain the economic waste rule but apply it only when the [diminution in market value] is well below the market damages component. This version of the economic waste rule is hard to implement in the prepayment case because the court must disaggregate a cost of completion award into its constituent elements — restitution (i.e., the ex ante contract price of the

service) and market damages. If the contract has one price for a bundled set of tasks (i.e., mining plus restoration), identifying which portion of the price is for the service at issue can be difficult. A court's realistic choices will often reduce either to continuing current practice [of comparing cost of completion to the diminution in value] or awarding cost of completion damages in all cases.

Id. at 1617–19.

4. **Peevyhouse's *Subsequent Case History.*** The *Peevyhouse* decision has been strongly criticized by both the Oklahoma legal community and by numerous commentators. In *Rock Island Improv. Co. v. Helmerich & Payne*, 698 F.2d 1075 (10th Cir. 1983), the United States Tenth Circuit Court of Appeals stated that they were "convinced that the Oklahoma Supreme Court would no longer apply the rule it established in *Peevyhouse* in 1963 if it had the instant dispute before it. . . . Although we are bound by decisions of a state supreme court in diversity cases, we need not adhere to a decision if we think it no longer would be followed." *Id.* at 1078.

But the case continues to have vitality notwithstanding these views. In *Schneberger v. Apache Corp.*, 890 P.2d 847 (Okla. 1994), the Oklahoma Supreme Court reaffirmed the *Peevyhouse* holding in a case with facts substantially identical to *Peevyhouse* and *Rock Island.* The court stated that the Tenth Circuit had "misinterpreted" Oklahoma law in *Rock Island* and asserted that the "essence of the *Peevyhouse* holding — to award diminution in value rather than cost of performance — has been consistently adhered to in cases giving rise to temporary and permanent injuries to property." *Id.* 851.

5. ***Expectation Damages and the Reliance Decision.*** At the beginning of this section, we suggested that a consensus has emerged among scholars that the expectation remedy provided parties with incentives to make efficient decisions regarding whether to breach or perform. Recall, however, that there are other stages of the contracting process that are also affected by the damages measure selected by the parties. In particular, once the contract is made, the parties must then choose the level of investment in the deal that is best for them (the reliance decision). With respect to this decision, expectation damages (as well as reliance damages) are not necessarily optimal. In particular, expectation damages encourage parties to over invest in reliance. This is because the expectancy remedy insures the promisee against breach: the promisee receives its expected net gain either when the promisor performs or pays damages. Thus, the promisee does not need to discount its reliance investment to reflect the possibility that later events may make performance of the contract more costly than breach.[2]

---

[2] *See* George G. Triantis & Alexander J. Triantis, *Timing Problems in Contract Breach Decisions*, 41 J.L. & ECON. 163 (1998); Richard Craswell, *Contract Remedies, Renegotiation, and the Theory of Efficient Breach*, 61 S. CAL. L. REV. 629 (1988); Richard Craswell, *Performance, Reliance, and One-Sided Information*, 18 J. LEGAL STUD. 365 (1989). *But see* Melvin A. Eisenberg & Brett H. McDonnell, *Expectation Damages and the Theory of Overreliance*, 54 HASTINGS L.J. 1335 (2003).

[3]   Specific Performance

SEDMAK v. CHARLIE'S CHEVROLET, INC.
Missouri Court of Appeals
622 S.W.2d 694 (1981)

SATZ, J.

This is an appeal from a decree of specific performance. We affirm.

. . . [T]he record reflects the Sedmaks to be automobile enthusiasts, who, at the time of trial, owned six Corvettes. In July, 1977, "Vette Vues," a Corvette fancier's magazine to which Dr. Sedmak subscribed, published an article announcing Chevrolet's tentative plans to manufacture a limited edition of the Corvette. The limited edition of approximately 6,000 automobiles was to commemorate the selection of the Corvette as the Indianapolis 500 Pace Car. The Sedmaks were interested in acquiring one of these Pace Cars to add to their Corvette collection. In November, 1977, the Sedmaks asked Tom Kells, sales manager at Charlie's Chevrolet, about the availability of the Pace Car. Mr. Kells said he did not have any information on the car but would find out about it. Kells also said if Charlie's were to receive a Pace Car, the Sedmaks could purchase it.

On January 9, 1978, Dr. Sedmak telephoned Kells to ask him if a Pace Car could be ordered. Kells indicated that he would require a deposit on the car, so Mrs. Sedmak went to Charlie's and gave Kells a check for $500.00. She was given a receipt for that amount bearing the names of Kells and Charlie's Chevrolet, Inc. At that time, Kells had a pre-order form listing both standard equipment and options available on the Pace Car. Prior to tendering the deposit, Mrs. Sedmak asked Kells if she and Dr. Sedmak were "definitely going to be the owners." Kells replied, "yes." After the deposit had been paid, Mrs. Sedmak stated if the car was going to be theirs, her husband wanted some changes made to the stock model. She asked Kells to order the car equipped with an L82 engine, four speed standard transmission and AM/FM radio with tape deck. Kells said that he would try to arrange with the manufacturer for these changes. Kells was able to make the changes, and, when the car arrived, it was equipped as the Sedmaks had requested.

Kells informed Mrs. Sedmak that the price of the Pace Car would be the manufacturer's retail price, approximately $15,000.00. The dollar figure could not be quoted more precisely because Kells was not sure what the ordered changes would cost, nor was he sure what the "appearance package" — decals, a special paint job — would cost. Kells also told Mrs. Sedmak that, after the changes had been made, a "contract" — a retail dealer's order form — would be mailed to them. However, no form or written contract was mailed to the Sedmaks by Charlie's.

On January 25, 1978, the Sedmaks visited Charlie's to take delivery on another Corvette. At that time, the Sedmaks asked Kells whether he knew anything further about the arrival date of the Pace Car. Kells replied he had no further information but he would let the Sedmaks know when the car arrived. Kells also requested that Charlie's be allowed to keep the car in their showroom for promotional purposes until after the Indianapolis 500 Race. The Sedmaks agreed to this arrangement.

On April 3, 1978, the Sedmaks were notified by Kells that the Pace Car had arrived. Kells told the Sedmaks they could not purchase the car for the manufacturer's retail price because demand for the car had inflated its value beyond the suggested price. Kells also told the Sedmaks they could bid on the car. The Sedmaks did not submit a bid. They filed this suit for specific performance.

[The court first rejected defendant's contention that the suit must fail because the contract price was indefinite. The court held that the parties agreed the selling price would be the price suggested by the manufacturer. The court held that the contract was valid under the Statute of Frauds because receipt of the deposit was part performance. The court then turned to the specific performance issue.]

Finally, Charlie's contends the Sedmaks failed to show they were entitled to specific performance of the contract. We disagree. Although it has been stated that the determination whether to order specific performance lies within the discretion of the trial court, this discretion is, in fact, quite narrow. When the relevant equitable principles have been met and the contract is fair and plain, "'specific performance goes as a matter of right.'" Miller v. Coffeen, 280 S.W.2d 100, 102 (Mo. 1955). Here, the trial court ordered specific performance because it concluded the Sedmaks "have no adequate remedy at law for the reason that they cannot go upon the open market and purchase an automobile of this kind with the same mileage, condition, ownership and appearance as the automobile involved in this case, except, if at all, with considerable expense, trouble, loss, great delay and inconvenience." Contrary to defendant's complaint, this is a correct expression of the relevant law and it is supported by the evidence.

Under the Code, the court may decree specific performance as a buyer's remedy for breach of contract to sell goods "where the goods are unique or in other proper circumstances." § 2-716(1). The general term "in other proper circumstances" expresses the drafters' intent to "further a more liberal attitude than some courts have shown in connection with the specific performance of contracts of sale." § 2-716, Comment 1. This Comment was not directed to the courts of this state, for long before the Code, we, in Missouri, took a practical approach in determining whether specific performance would lie for the breach of contract for the sale of goods and did not limit this relief only to the sale of "unique" goods. Boeving v. Vandover, 240 Mo. App. 117, 218 S.W.2d 175 (1945). In *Boeving*, plaintiff contracted to buy a car from defendant. When the car arrived, defendant refused to sell. The car was not unique in the traditional legal sense but, at that time, all cars were difficult to obtain because of war-time shortages. The court held specific performance was the proper remedy for plaintiff because a new car "could not be obtained elsewhere except at considerable expense, trouble or loss, which cannot be estimated in advance and under such circumstances (plaintiff) did not have an adequate remedy at law." Thus, *Boeving* presaged the broad and liberalized language of § 2-716(1) and exemplifies one of the "other proper circumstances" contemplated by this subsection for ordering specific performance. § 2-716, Comment 1. The present facts track those in *Boeving*.

The Pace Car, like the car in *Boeving*, was not unique in the traditional legal sense. It was not an heirloom or, arguably, not one of a kind. However, its "mileage, condition, ownership and appearance" did make it difficult, if not impossible, to obtain its replication without considerable expense, delay and inconvenience. Admittedly, 6,000 Pace Cars were produced by Chevrolet. However, as the record reflects, this is limited production. In addition, only one of these cars was available to each dealer, and only a limited number of these were equipped with the specific options ordered by plaintiffs. Charlie's had not received a car like the Pace Car in the previous two years. The sticker price for the car was $14,284.21. Yet Charlie's received offers from individuals in Hawaii and Florida to buy the Pace Car for $24,000.00 and $28,000.00 respectively. As sensibly inferred by the trial court, the location and size of these offers demonstrated this limited edition was in short supply and great demand. We agree with the trial court. This case was a "proper circumstance" for ordering specific performance.

Judgment affirmed.

NOTES

1. ***The Choice Between Specific Performance and Damages: What are "Other Proper Circumstances"?*** As exemplified by *Sedmak v. Charlie's Chevrolet*, there is no magic threshold for the quantity of substitute goods that must be available before a court will award specific performance rather than damages. Since goods are rarely "unique" in the plain language sense of that word, the litigation centers on what constitutes "other proper circumstances" under UCC § 2-716. This, in turn, depends on the nature of the market for substitute goods. Why should it matter whether or not there are sufficient substitutes for the contract goods on the market? One answer, of course, is that the buyer faces an enhanced risk of strategic behavior by the seller if the buyer is unable at reasonable cost to make a "cover" contract for substitute goods on the market. The difficult issue is how to determine precisely when the market is so "thin" that specific performance should properly be awarded. Courts examine the nature of the particular good, as well as factors such as the opportunity and likelihood of resale or replacement. Because it is difficult for courts to assess the relative "thickness" of a market in the abstract, specific performance cases, viewed in the aggregate, often appear unprincipled, as individual cases turn on a variety of fact-specific considerations.

Though specific performance is traditionally used with respect to contracts for tangible assets that lack ready substitutes, such as land or goods traded in thin markets, courts have also been willing to award specific performance for certain "intangible" assets. This is particularly true in situations where there are substantial valuation problems or where no true replacement exists. Consider *Triple-A Baseball Club Associates v. Northeastern Baseball, Inc.*, 832 F.2d 214 (1st Cir. 1987). Here, a specific performance decree requiring the sale of an AAA minor league baseball team was upheld, even though the injured buyer had the opportunity to cover the breach by purchasing an AA minor league team. In doing so, the court noted the differences between an AAA team — the highest level of minor league baseball — and an AA team, as well as the concomitant differences in locations and facilities.

2. ***Monetary Specific Performance.*** Specific performance allows a court to order a breaching seller to transfer a particular, "unique" good to the buyer. If, however, the breaching seller already has sold the good to a third party, courts also

have the power to order monetary specific performance, where the defaulting seller must transfer the proceeds from the third-party sale of goods with a fluctuating price to the original, injured buyer. Monetary specific performance thus enables the injured buyer to recover a value sometimes much greater than any estimate of the contract/market damages resulting from the breach.

Bander v. Grossman, 161 Misc. 2d 119, 611 N.Y.S.2d 985 (1994), illustrates how cautiously courts employ the monetary specific performance doctrine. In this case, the defendant-dealer failed to deliver to the plaintiff-buyer a rare Aston Martin automobile when he was unable to clear the title. In December 1987, the plaintiff declared that the $40,000 sales contract had been breached. At that time, the car's approximate market value had appreciated to $60,000 and continued to rise thereafter. Prior to the commencement of the case, the defendant sold the car for $225,000. By July 1989, the car's value was estimated at $335,000. Subsequently, the market for collectible automobiles crashed, and, by the time of trial, the car's market value was estimated at $80,000. The plaintiff asked the court to award him the $225,000 defendant had realized from the subsequent sale as monetary specific performance, an amount 10 times greater than the contract price.

The trial court rejected this plea and awarded damages of $20,000, based on the market price that the buyer would have had to pay at the time of breach in December 1987. The appellate court affirmed the award and refused to impose a constructive trust on the proceeds from the subsequent sale. In doing so, the court emphasized that specific performance is a time-sensitive remedy:

> With the passage of time, specific performance becomes disfavored. For example, because goods are subject to a rapid change in condition, or the cost of maintenance of the goods is important, time may be found to have been of the essence, and even a month's delay may defeat specific performance. . . .

> Turning to the facts in the instant case, the plaintiff did not sue in December of 1987, when it is likely a request for specific performance would have been granted. At that point, the defendant had disclaimed the contract and plaintiff was aware of his rights. The plaintiff was not protected by a continued firm assurance that defendant definitely would perfect the car's title. . . . The court does not accept plaintiff's protest that he believed the commercial relationship was intact; the parties had already had a heated discussion and were communicating through attorneys. A more likely explanation of plaintiff's inaction is that he proceeded to complete the purchase in April of 1988 of a Ferrari Testarrosa for $128,000 and a Lamborghini for $40,000 in 1989.

Id. at 990.

The court noted that, although there were very few similar Aston Martins in existence, they were traded with sufficient frequency that the buyer, had he surfaced in December 1987 with $60,000, undoubtedly would have had the opportunity to purchase one.

3. *Specific Performance and Personal Service Contracts.* Generally speaking, courts are reluctant to specifically enforce a contract to perform personal services. A party that performs only when compelled by a court order often will not expend best efforts to perform in a satisfactory manner. Moreover, such an order may spark claims of constitutionally-prohibited involuntary servitude. [Add footnote: A recent article has argued that such fears are overstated. *See* Nathan B. Oman, *Specific Performance and the Thirteenth Amendment*, 93 MINN. L. REV. 2020 (2009).] An example of the traditional attitude of courts with respect to specific performance in service contracts is *Beverly Glen Music, Inc. v. Warner Communications, Inc.*, 178 Cal. App. 3d 1142 (1986). Here, singer Anita Baker breached her contract with Beverly Glen Music and signed with Beverly's competitor, Warner Communications. Beverly Glen at first sought to specifically enforce Ms. Baker's contract, but the court ruled this a violation of the Constitution's prohibition of involuntary servitude. They then asked for an injunction from the court prohibiting Ms. Baker from working for other music companies, which was also rejected by the court. Finally, Beverly Glen requested an injunction preventing Warner from hiring her. Consider the court's response:

> Whether plaintiff proceeds against Ms. Baker directly or against those who might employ her, the intent is the same; to deprive Ms. Baker of her livelihood and thereby pressure her to return to plaintiff's employ. Plaintiff contends that this is not an action against Ms. Baker, but merely an equitable claim against Warner to deprive it of the wrongful benefits it gained when it "stole" Ms. Baker away. Thus, plaintiff contends, the equities lie not between the plaintiff and Ms. Baker, but between plaintiff and the predatory Warner Communications company. Yet if Warner's behavior has actually been predatory, plaintiff has an adequate remedy by way of damages. An injunction adds nothing to plaintiff's recovery from Warner except to coerce Ms. Baker to honor her contract. Denying someone his livelihood is a harsh remedy. . . . To expand this remedy so that it could be used in virtually all breaches of a personal service contract is to ignore over 100 years of common law on this issue.

Id. at 1145.

Occasionally, however, courts will specifically enforce contracts for services, particularly if the contract contains a geographic component or other aspects that render the contract non-personal in nature. A prime example occurred in *Mellon v. Cessna Aircraft Co.*, 64 F. Supp. 2d 1061 (D. Kan. 1999), where the court upheld a decree of specific performance with respect to an agreement to provide maintenance to an airplane. In doing so, the court noted:

> The court rejects Cessna's argument that the contract between the parties was for personal services and, therefore, not subject to specific performance. Cessna's mechanics are licensed by the FAA and trained to service and repair Cessna aircraft. Cessna service is available throughout the country at a number of authorized Cessna service centers. Cessna presumably would not disagree that its own service centers provide better service for Cessna aircraft than non-Cessna service centers. The very availability of Cessna-authorized service at multiple locations distinguishes Cessna's obligation under this contract from a personal services contract between, for example, a performer with a unique style and a promoter or theatre.

Id. at 1064.

4. *Specific Performance and Marketing Contracts.* In *American Brands, Inc. v. Playgirl, Inc.*, 498 F.2d 947 (2d Cir. 1974), the Court of Appeals rejected a request by the plaintiff that the court require Playgirl Magazine to run plaintiff's tobacco advertisements on its back cover as per their contractual agreement. The plaintiff claimed that "back cover advertising is not fungible, and that Playgirl alone and uniquely provides an advertising audience composed of young, malleable, and affluent females." The court dismissed this argument, noting that the record contained no evidence that Playgirl's readership was as unique as plaintiff claimed it to be.

The Appellate Court of Illinois drew a sharp contrast with *Playgirl* in *Gold v. Ziff Communications Co.*, 553 N.E.2d 404 (Ill. App. Ct. 1989). Here, the defendant magazine publisher decided to unilaterally eliminate a discount on advertising that it gave to the plaintiff's mail-order computer company, PC Brand. In granting a preliminary injunction, the court differentiated *American Brands v. Playgirl*, noting:

> However, American Brands is clearly distinguishable from this case. PC Brand is a much smaller company than American Brands, Inc., a tobacco company, and its target market is more limited. PC Brand is a mail order computer company, whose only clients come from its magazine advertisements, which include mail and telephone order forms. In contrast, American Brands, Inc.'s advertising targets are much more diverse. Moreover, the tobacco company was not structured around an advertising and discount scheme as was PC Brand, and it would not have suffered irreparable injury nor been put out of business due to the absence of one advertising vehicle.

Id. at 410.

Can you reconcile these two cases? Which court's approach do you believe is preferable?

Essay: The Case for Specific Performance

The paradigmatic case for specific performance is a contract for the sale of "unique" goods (or land, see *Lucy v. Zehmer*, Chapter 1). *Sedmak* appears to fit that paradigm; the court notes, for example, that "the Sedmaks have no adequate remedy at law for the reason that they cannot go upon the open market and purchase an automobile of this kind. . . ." Thus the court determines that specific performance is the proper remedy.

Even if we think that a Corvette might have been available from another dealer, clearly specific performance is the remedy that most accurately measures the disappointed promisee's loss. Why, then, is it not used more often? In answering that question, consider the following excerpt from Alan Schwartz, *The Case for Specific Performance*, 89 YALE L.J. 271 (1979).

> Specific performance is the most accurate method of achieving the compensation goal of contract remedies because it gives the promisee the

precise performance that he purchased. The natural question, then, is why specific performance is not routinely available. Three explanations of the law's restrictions on specific performance are possible. First, the law's commitment to the compensation goal may be less than complete; restricting specific performance may reflect an inarticulate reluctance to pursue the compensation goal fully. Second, damages may generally be fully compensatory. In that event, expanding the availability of specific performance would create opportunities for promisees to exploit promisors by threatening to compel, or actually compelling, performance, without furthering the compensation goal. The third explanation is that concerns of efficiency or liberty may justify restricting specific performance, despite its greater accuracy; specific performance might generate higher transaction costs than the damage remedy, or interfere more with the liberty interests of promisors. The first justification is beyond the scope of the analysis here. The second and third explanations will be examined in detail.

With respect to the second justification, current doctrine authorizes specific performance when courts cannot calculate compensatory damages with even a rough degree of accuracy. If the class of cases in which there are difficulties in computing damages corresponds closely to the class of cases in which specific performance is now granted, expanding the availability of specific performance is obviously unnecessary. Further, such an expansion would create opportunities for promisees to exploit promisors. The class of cases in which damage awards fail to compensate promisees adequately is, however, broader than the class of cases in which specific performance is now granted. Thus the compensation goal supports removing rather than retaining present restrictions on the availability of specific performance.

It is useful to begin by examining the paradigm case for granting specific performance under current law, the case of unique goods. When a promisor breaches and the promisee can make a transaction that substitutes for the performance the promisor failed to render, the promisee will be fully compensated if he receives the additional amount necessary to purchase the substitute plus the costs of making a second transaction. In some cases, however, such as those involving works of art, courts cannot identify which transactions the promisee would regard as substitutes because that information often is in the exclusive possession of the promisee. Moreover, it is difficult for a court to assess the accuracy of a promisee's claim. For example, if the promisor breaches a contract to sell a rare emerald, the promisee may claim that only the Hope Diamond would give him equal satisfaction, and thus may sue for the price difference between the emerald and the diamond. It would be difficult for a court to know whether this claim is true. If the court seeks to award money damages, it has three choices: granting the price differential, which may overcompensate the promisee; granting the dollar value of the promisee's foregone satisfaction as estimated by the court, which may overcompensate or undercompensate; or granting restitution of any sums paid, which undercompensates the promisee. The promisee is fully compensated without risk of overcompensation or undercompensation if the remedy of specific performance is available to him and its use encouraged by the doctrine that damages must be foreseeable and certain.

If specific performance is the appropriate remedy in such cases, there are three reasons why it should be routinely available. The first reason is that in many cases damages actually are undercompensatory. Although promisees are entitled to incidental damages, such damages are difficult to monetize. They consist primarily of the costs of finding and making a second deal, which generally involve the expenditure of time rather than cash; attaching a dollar value to such opportunity costs is quite difficult. Breach can also cause frustration and anger, especially in a consumer context, but these costs also are not recoverable.

Substitution damages, the court's estimate of the amount the promisee needs to purchase an adequate substitute, also may be inaccurate in many cases less dramatic than the emerald hypothetical discussed above. This is largely because of product differentiation and early obsolescence. As product differentiation becomes more common, the supply of products that will substitute precisely for the promisor's performance is reduced. For example, even during the period when there is an abundant supply of new Datsuns for sale, two-door, two-tone Datsuns with mag wheels, stereo, and air conditioning may be scarce in some local markets. Moreover, early obsolescence gives the promisee a short time in which to make a substitute purchase. If the promisor breaches late in a model year, for example, it may be difficult for the promisee to buy the exact model he wanted. For these reasons, a damage award meant to enable a promisee to purchase "another car" could be undercompensatory.

In addition, problems of prediction often make it difficult to put a promisee in the position where he would have been had his promisor performed. If a breach by a contractor would significantly delay or prevent completion of a construction project and the project differs in important respects from other projects — for example, a department store in a different location than previous stores — courts may be reluctant to award "speculative" lost profits attributable to the breach.

Second, promisees have economic incentives to sue for damages when damages are likely to be fully compensatory. A breaching promisor is reluctant to perform and may be hostile. This makes specific performance an unattractive remedy in cases in which the promisor's performance is complex, because the promisor is more likely to render a defective performance when that performance is coerced, and the defectiveness of complex performances is sometimes difficult to establish in court. Further, when the promisor's performance must be rendered over time, as in construction or requirements contracts, it is costly for the promisee to monitor a reluctant promisor's conduct. If the damage remedy is compensatory, the promisee would prefer it to incurring these monitoring costs. Finally, given the time necessary to resolve lawsuits, promisees would commonly prefer to make substitute transactions promptly and sue later for damages rather than hold their affairs in suspension while awaiting equitable relief. The very fact that a promisee requests specific performance thus implies that damages are an inadequate remedy.

The third reason why courts should permit promisees to elect routinely the remedy of specific performance is that promisees possess better information than courts as to both the adequacy of damages and the difficulties of coercing performance. Promisees know better than courts whether the damages a court is likely to award would be adequate because promisees are more familiar with the costs that breach imposes on them. In addition, promisees generally know more about their promisors than do courts; thus they are in a better position to predict whether specific performance decrees would induce their promisors to render satisfactory performances.

In sum, restrictions on the availability of specific performance cannot be justified on the basis that damage awards are usually compensatory. On the contrary, the compensation goal implies that specific performance should be routinely available. This is because damage awards actually are undercompensatory in more cases than is commonly supposed; the fact of a specific performance request is itself good evidence that damages would be inadequate; and courts should delegate to promisees the decision of which remedy best satisfies the compensation goal. Further, expanding the availability of specific performance would not result in greater exploitation of promisors. Promisees would seldom abuse the power to determine when specific performance should be awarded because of the strong incentives that promisees face to seek damages when these would be even approximately compensatory.

Id. at 274–78.[3]

[4]   Reliance Damages

In their groundbreaking article, Lon Fuller and William R. Perdue discussed the role of the reliance interest in contract damages:

[T]he plaintiff has in reliance on the promise of the defendant changed his position. For example, the buyer under a contract for the sale of land has incurred expense at the investigation of the seller's title, or has neglected the opportunity to enter other contracts. We may award damages to the plaintiff for the purpose of undoing the harm which his reliance on the defendant's promise has caused him. Our object is to put him in as good a position as he was in before the promise was made. The interest protected in this case may be called the reliance interest.

Lon Fuller & William R. Perdue, *The Reliance Interest in Contract Damages*, 46 Yale L.J. 52, 54 (1936).

---

[3] For further discussion, see Robert E. Scott & George G. Triantis, *Embedded Options and the Case Against Compensation In Contract Law*, 104 Colum. L. Rev. 1428 (2004). *But see* Edward Yorio, *In Defense of Money Damages for Breach of Contract*, 82 Colum. L. Rev. 1365 (1982).

We know that reliance damages purport to put the promisee in the same position she would have occupied had the promise never been made, and that expectation damages aim to put the promisee in the position she would have occupied had the promise been performed. Assuming contracts are generally advantageous to the promisee (otherwise why would she enter into them), it follows that she would generally prefer expectation damages to reliance damages. Do you see why? If that is so, the questions for this part are: When will the promisee be *required* to use reliance damages (rather than expectancy) as the appropriate default term? And, when, if ever, will the promisee *prefer* to, and be entitled to, use reliance damages in lieu of expectation damages as the measure of her losses from breach?

SULLIVAN v. O'CONNOR
Supreme Judicial Court of Massachusetts
363 Mass. 579, 296 N.E.2d 183 (1973)

KAPLAN, J.

The plaintiff patient secured a jury verdict of $13,500 against the defendant surgeon for breach of contract in respect to an operation upon the plaintiff's nose. The substituted consolidated bill of exceptions presents questions about the correctness of the judge's instructions on the issue of damages.

The declaration was in two counts. In the first count, the plaintiff alleged that she, as patient, entered into a contract with the defendant, a surgeon, wherein the defendant promised to perform plastic surgery on her nose and thereby to enhance her beauty and improve her appearance; that he performed the surgery but failed to achieve the promised result; rather the result of the surgery was to disfigure and deform her nose, to cause her pain in body and mind, and to subject her to other damage and expense. The second count, based on the same transaction, was in the conventional form for malpractice, charging that the defendant had been guilty of negligence in performing the surgery. Answering, the defendant entered a general denial.

On the plaintiff's demand, the case was tried by jury. At the close of the evidence, the judge put to the jury, as special questions, the issues of liability under the two counts, and instructed them accordingly. The jury returned a verdict for the plaintiff on the contract count, and for the defendant on the negligence count. The judge then instructed the jury on the issue of damages.

As background to the instructions and the parties' exceptions, we mention certain facts as the jury could find them. The plaintiff was a professional entertainer, and this was known to the defendant. The agreement was as alleged in the declaration. More particularly, judging from exhibits, the plaintiff's nose had been straight, but long and prominent; the defendant undertook by two operations to reduce its prominence and somewhat to shorten it, thus making it more pleasing in relation to the plaintiff's other features. Actually the plaintiff was obliged to undergo three operations, and her appearance was worsened. Her nose now had a concave line to about the midpoint, at which it became bulbous; viewed frontally, the nose from bridge to midpoint was flattened and broadened, and the two sides of the tip had lost symmetry. This configuration evidently could not be improved by further surgery. The plaintiff did not demonstrate, however, that her change of appearance had resulted in loss of employment. Payments by the plaintiff covering the defendant's fee and hospital expenses were stipulated at $622.65.

The judge instructed the jury, first, that the plaintiff was entitled to recover her out-of-pocket expenses incident to the operations. Second, she could recover the damages flowing directly, naturally, proximately, and foreseeable from the defendant's breach of promise. These would comprehend damages for any disfigurement of the plaintiff's nose — that is, any change of appearance for the worse — including the effects of the consciousness of such disfigurement on the plaintiff's mind, and in this connection the jury should consider the nature of the plaintiff's profession. Also consequent upon the defendant's breach, and compensable, were the pain and suffering involved in the third operation, but not in the first two. As there was no proof that any loss of earnings by the plaintiff resulted from the breach, that element should not enter into the calculation of damages.

By his exceptions the defendant contends that the judge erred in allowing the jury to take into account anything but the plaintiff's out-of-pocket expenses (presumably at the stipulated amount). The defendant excepted to the judge's refusal of his request for a general charge to that effect, and, more specifically, to the judge's refusal of a charge that the plaintiff could not recover for pain and suffering connected with the third operation or for impairment of the plaintiff's appearance and associated mental distress.

The plaintiff on her part excepted to the judge's refusal of a request to charge that the plaintiff could recover the difference in value between the nose as promised and the nose as it appeared after the operations. However, the plaintiff in her brief expressly waives this exception and others made by her in case this court overrules the defendant's exceptions; thus she would be content to hold the jury's verdict in her favor.

We conclude that the defendant's exceptions should be overruled.

It has been suggested on occasion that agreements between patients and physicians by which the physician undertakes to effect a cure or to bring about a given result should be declared unenforceable on grounds of public policy. But there are many decisions recognizing and enforcing such contracts, and the law of Massachusetts has treated them as valid, although we have had no decision meeting head on the contention that they should be denied legal sanction. These causes of action are, however, considered a little suspect, and thus we find courts straining sometimes to read the pleadings as sounding only in tort for negligence, and not in contract for breach of promise, despite sedulous efforts by the pleaders to pursue the latter theory.

It is not hard to see why the courts should be unenthusiastic or skeptical about the contract theory. Considering the uncertainties of medical science and the variations in the physical and psychological conditions of individual patients, doctors can seldom in good faith promise specific results. Therefore it is unlikely that physicians of even average integrity will in fact make such promises. Statements of opinion by the physician with some optimistic coloring are a different thing, and may indeed have therapeutic value. But patients may transform such statements into firm promises in their own minds, especially when they have been disappointed in the event, and testify in that sense to sympathetic juries.[4] If actions for breach of promise can be readily maintained, doctors, so it is said, will be frightened into practicing "defensive medicine." On the other hand, if these actions were outlawed, leaving only the possibility of suits for malpractice, there is fear that the public might be exposed to the enticements of charlatans, and confidence in the profession might ultimately be shaken. The law has taken the middle of the road position of allowing actions based on alleged contract, but insisting on clear proof. Instructions to the jury may well stress this requirement and point to tests of truth, such as the complexity or difficulty of an operation as bearing on the probability that a given result was promised.

If an action on the basis of contract is allowed, we have next the question of the measure of damages to be applied where liability is found. Some cases have taken the simple view that the promise by the physician is to be treated like an ordinary commercial promise, and accordingly that the successful plaintiff is entitled to a standard measure of recovery for breach of contract — "compensatory" ("expectancy") damages, an amount intended to put the plaintiff in the position he would be in if the contract had been performed, or, presumably, at the plaintiff's election, "restitution" damages, an amount corresponding to any benefit conferred by the plaintiff upon the defendant in the performance of the contract disrupted by the defendant's breach. See Restatement: Contracts § 329 and comment a, §§ 347, 384(1). Thus in Hawkins v. McGee, 84 N.H. 114, the defendant doctor was taken to have promised the plaintiff to convert his damaged hand by means of an operation into a good or perfect hand, but the doctor so operated as to damage the hand still further. The court, following the usual expectancy formula, would have asked the jury to estimate and award to the plaintiff the difference between the value of a good or perfect hand, as promised, and the value of the hand after the operation. (The same formula would apply, although the dollar result would be less, if the operation had neither worsened nor improved the condition of the hand.) If the plaintiff had not yet paid the doctor his fee, that amount would be deducted from the recovery. There could be no recovery for the pain and suffering of the operation, since that detriment would have been incurred even if the operation had been successful; one can say that this detriment was not "caused" by the breach. But where the plaintiff by reason of the operation was put to more pain than he would have had to endure, had the doctor performed as promised, he should be compensated for that difference as a proper part of his expectancy recovery. It may be noted that on an alternative count for malpractice the plaintiff in the *Hawkins* case had been nonsuited; but on ordinary principles this could not affect the contract claim, for it is hardly a defense to a breach of contract that the promisor acted innocently and without negligence. The New Hampshire court further refined the *Hawkins* analysis in McQuaid v. Michou, 85 N.H. 299, all in the direction of treating the

---

4 [2] Judicial skepticism about whether a promise was in fact made derives also from the possibility that the truth has been tortured to give the plaintiff the advantage of the longer period of limitations sometimes available for actions on contract as distinguished from those in tort or for malpractice. *See* Richard B. Lillich, *The Malpractice Statute of Limitations in New York and Other Jurisdictions*, 47 Cornell L.Q. 339 (1962); Annotation, 80 A.L.R.2d 368.

patient-physician cases on the ordinary footing of expectancy.

Other cases, including a number in New York, without distinctly repudiating the *Hawkins* type of analysis, have indicated that a different and generally more lenient measure of damages is to be applied in patient-physician actions based on breach of alleged special agreements to effect a cure, attain a stated result, or employ a given medical method. This measure is expressed in somewhat variant ways, but the substance is that the plaintiff is to recover any expenditures made by him and for other detriment (usually not specifically described in the opinions) following proximately and foreseeable upon the defendant's failure to carry out his promise. This, be it noted, is not a "restitution" measure, for it is not limited to restoration of the benefit conferred on the defendant (the fee paid) but includes other expenditures, for example, amounts paid for medicine and nurses; so also it would seem according to its logic to take in damages for any worsening of the plaintiff's condition due to the breach. Nor is it an "expectancy" measure, for it does not appear to contemplate recovery of the whole difference in value between the condition as promised and the condition actually resulting from the treatment. Rather the tendency of the formulation is to put the plaintiff back in the position he occupied just before the parties entered upon the agreement, to compensate him for the detriments he suffered in reliance upon the agreement. This kind of intermediate pattern of recovery for breach of contract is discussed in the suggestive article by Fuller and Perdue, *The Reliance Interest in Contract Damages*, 46 Yale L.J. 52, 373 (1936), where the authors show that, although not attaining the currency of the standard measures, a "reliance" measure has for special reasons been applied by the courts in a variety of settings, including noncommercial settings. See 46 Yale L.J. at 396-401.[5]

For breach of the patient-physician agreements under consideration, a recovery limited to restitution seems plainly too meager, if the agreements are to be enforced at all. On the other hand, an expectancy recovery may well be excessive. The factors, already mentioned, which have made the cause of action somewhat suspect, also suggest moderation as to the breadth of the recovery that should be permitted. Where, as in the case at bar and in a number of the reported cases, the doctor has been absolved of negligence by the trier, an expectancy measure may be thought harsh. We should recall here that the fee paid by the patient to the doctor for the alleged promise would usually be quite disproportionate to the putative expectancy recovery. To attempt, moreover, to put a value on the condition that would or might have resulted, had the treatment succeeded as promised, may sometimes put an exceptional strain on the imagination of the fact finder. As a general consideration, Fuller and Perdue argue that the reasons for granting damages for broken promises to the extent of the expectancy are at their strongest when the promises are made in a business context, when they have to do with the production or distribution of goods or the allocation of functions in the market place; they become weaker as the context shifts from a commercial to a noncommercial field. 46 Yale L.J. at 60-63.

---

[5] [4] Some of the exceptional situations mentioned where reliance may be preferred to expectancy are those in which the latter measure would be hard to apply or would impose too great a burden; performance was interfered with by external circumstances; the contract was indefinite. *See* 46 Yale L.J. at 373-386; 394-396.

There is much to be said, then, for applying a reliance measure to the present facts, and we have only to add that our cases are not unreceptive to the use of that formula in special situations. We have, however, had no previous occasion to apply it to patient-physician cases.

The question of recovery on a reliance basis for pain and suffering or mental distress requires further attention. We find expressions in the decisions that pain and suffering (or the like) are simply not compensable in actions for breach of contract. The defendant seemingly espouses this proposition in the present case. True, if the buyer under a contract for the purchase of a lot of merchandise, in suing for the seller's breach, should claim damages for mental anguish caused by his disappointment in the transaction, he would not succeed; he would be told, perhaps, that the asserted psychological injury was not fairly foreseeable by the defendant as a probable consequence of the breach of such a business contract. See Restatement: Contracts, § 341, and comment a. But there is no general rule barring such items of damage in actions for breach of contract. It is all a question of the subject matter and background of the contract, and when the contract calls for an operation on the person of the plaintiff, psychological as well as physical injury may be expected to figure somewhere in the recovery, depending on the particular circumstances. Again, it is said in a few of the New York cases, concerned with the classification of actions for statute of limitations purposes, that the absence of allegations demanding recovery for pain and suffering is characteristic of a contract claim by a patient against a physician, that such allegations rather belong in a claim for malpractice. These remarks seem unduly sweeping. Suffering or distress resulting from the breach going beyond that which was envisaged by the treatment as agreed, should be compensable on the same ground as the worsening of the patient's condition because of the breach. Indeed it can be argued that the very suffering or distress "contracted for" — that which would have been incurred if the treatment achieved the promised result — should also be compensable on the theory underlying the New York cases. For that suffering is "wasted" if the treatment fails. Otherwise stated, compensation for this waste is arguably required in order to complete the restoration of the *status quo ante*.[6]

In the light of the foregoing discussion, all the defendant's exceptions fail: the plaintiff was not confined to the recovery of her out-of-pocket expenditures; she was entitled to recover also for the worsening of her condition,[7] and for the pain and

---

[6] [6] Recovery on a reliance basis for breach of the physician's promise tends to equate with the usual recovery for malpractice, since the latter also looks in general to restoration of the condition before the injury. But this is not paradoxical, especially when it is noted that the origins of contract lie in tort. *See* E. Allan Farnsworth, *The Past of Promise: An Historical Introduction to Contract*, 69 Col. L. Rev. 576, 594-596 (1969); Breitel, J. in Stella Flour & Feed Corp. v. National City Bank, 285 App. Div. 182, 189, 136 N.Y.S.2d 139 (dissenting opinion). A few cases have considered possible recovery for breach by a physician of a promise to sterilize a patient, resulting in birth of a child to the patient and spouse. If such an action is held maintainable, the reliance and expectancy measures would, we think, tend to equate, because the promised condition was preservation of the family status quo. It would, however, be a mistake to think in terms of strict "formulas." For example, a jurisdiction which would apply a reliance measure to the present facts might impose a more severe damage sanction for the willful use by the physician of a method of operation that he undertook not to employ.

[7] [7] That condition involves a mental element and appraisal of it properly called for consideration of the fact that the plaintiff was an entertainer. *Cf.* McQuaid v. Michou, 85 N.H. 299, 303-304, 157 A. 881

suffering and mental distress involved in the third operation. These items were compensable on either an expectancy or a reliance view. We might have been required to elect between the two views if the pain and suffering connected with the first two operations contemplated by the agreement, or the whole difference in value between the present and the promised conditions, were being claimed as elements of damage. But the plaintiff waives her possible claim to the former element, and to so much of the latter as represents the difference in value between the promised condition and the condition before the operations.

Plaintiff's exceptions waived.

Defendant's exceptions overruled.

NOTES

1.   *Questions on* Sullivan. What was the promise that the jury found that Dr. O'Connor made to the plaintiff? Does Justice Kaplan think it is the kind of promise that doctors ordinarily make to their patients? If not, arguably the plaintiff ought to have a higher burden of proof in this case than she would if the promise were of a more ordinary sort. Does changing from an expectation measure to a smaller reliance measure, assuming that it is smaller, accomplish the same objectives?

2.   *The Damage Measure in* Sullivan. Suppose in *Sullivan* that Ms. Sullivan expected to pay the equivalent of $1,622 for a more attractive nose. This amount consists of the fees involved and the costs to her of the pain and suffering expected, converted into dollars. (Ignore, for convenience, the fact that her nose worsened and that she suffered unanticipated pain and suffering.) What award is necessary to satisfy her expectancy interest? Don't you need to know what value she put on the improvement in the attractiveness of her nose? This might have been far greater than $1,622. Why don't we have the same problem when Buyer purchases wheat from Seller? Is it easier to measure Ms. Sullivan's reliance interest? Had she not contracted with Dr. O'Connor, shouldn't we conclude that she would have entered into the same contract with another doctor?

KIZAS v. WEBSTER
United States District Court, District of Columbia
532 F. Supp. 1331 (1982)

OBERDORFER, J.

This case is currently before the Court on plaintiffs' Motion for Summary Judgment on damages. The Court previously granted the plaintiff's Motion for Summary Judgment on liability, holding that defendants' termination of a program whereby clerical employees of the Federal Bureau of Investigation received preferential consideration for jobs as special agents with the FBI was a taking of private property without just compensation, in violation of the Fifth Amendment. That memorandum requested further submissions on the measure of damages,

---

(discussion of continuing condition resulting from physician's breach).

noting that "it may well be impossible to compensate plaintiffs precisely; money damages awarded on the basis of 'rough justice' are in order." Kizas v. Webster, 492 F. Supp. 1135, 1150 (D.D.C.1980). The plaintiffs' motion is supported by voluminous affidavits from individual plaintiffs and from several economic experts. At oral argument defendant conceded the accuracy of the amounts but disputed the recoverability of all of the elements of damages plaintiffs have claimed on legal grounds.

Consequently, a determination by this Court of the elements of damages that are legally recoverable should be dispositive of the issue of damages in this case.

While plaintiffs present two theories of damages in their moving papers, the theory which they urge most strongly is denominated "Theory B." Essentially, this theory seeks to place plaintiffs in as good a position as they would have occupied had the wrongfully terminated clerk-to-agent program never existed. This is contrasted with "Theory A," which would attempt to compensate plaintiffs for termination of the program by placing them in as good a position as they would have occupied had the clerk-to-agent program not been terminated. As such, the distinction corresponds rather closely with the distinction in contract law between reliance damages (Theory B) and expectancy damages (Theory A). See generally Fuller & Perdue, The Reliance Interest in Contract Damages, (Parts I & II), 46 Yale L.J. 52, 373 (1963-37); J. Calamari & J. Perillo, Contracts § 14-9 (2d ed. 1977).

By analogy to contract law, plaintiffs argue that here the benefit of the bargain, which is the preferential path to special agent status, is too difficult to value, and plaintiffs' damages should accordingly be measured by what the plaintiffs gave up in reliance on the existence of the preference. This is particularly true, plaintiffs claim, where the reliance theory will fully compensate plaintiffs at a lesser cost to defendants than would an expectancy theory. It is clear from the record that the value of the preference is difficult to quantify, since among other things the percentage of clerks who actually became special agents under the program is unknown. The defendant does not really dispute the appropriateness of this theory itself. Accordingly, the Court concludes that in the context of this case, where the value of the expectancy is admittedly speculative, the reliance measure of damages is the appropriate measure of damages. . . .

The chief argument which defendants make is that, had the contract been fully performed, the value of the performance would have been zero, and that reliance damages must not exceed the value of the contract had it been fully performed. L. Albert & Son v. Armstrong Rubber Co., 178 F.2d 182 (2d Cir. 1949). In support of this defendants cite a number of cases involving employment contracts, in which courts have held that where employment is terminable at will there is no breach of contract, and therefore no damages. This issue has, however, already been resolved against the defendants. Thus, it is irrelevant that, for example, a teacher with a one-year contract who is wrongfully terminated is entitled to only salary for the remainder of that year. In such a case, the only wrong suffered is the loss of pay for the remainder of the year. This is not a case in which a wrongful dismissal from a job as a special agent is alleged. Rather, the wrong of which plaintiffs complain is the termination of the opportunity for preferential consideration for the position of special agent, an opportunity which had value even though it was not guaranteed that any particular plaintiff would become a special agent or that he would not be fired if he did become one. Each plaintiff had some chance of becoming such an agent and some chance of remaining in that position. For that chance plaintiffs incurred losses, and these losses are legally compensable where, as here, plaintiffs have been deprived of that opportunity by defendants. . . .

It is of course true, as defendants argue, that if plaintiff has entered into a losing bargain he is not entitled to better his position at the expense of defendant. However, the burden of proof is upon defendant on this issue, and defendant has offered no evidence that plaintiffs here entered into a losing contract. Rather, for most of the plaintiffs the contract is likely to have been a very beneficial one had it been performed. The defendants' contention that the value of becoming a special agent should be set at zero because special agents can be fired at will overlooks the fact that most special agents are not so fired; the average agent maintains that position 26.77 years. Here, therefore, where there is no showing or attempt to show that plaintiffs would have in fact suffered a loss had the contract been fully performed, plaintiffs are entitled to recover at least the loss they suffered in reliance on the clerk-to-agent program. . . .

The Court thus concludes that plaintiffs are entitled to recover their reliance losses and reliance expenditures. There remains the necessity of deciding what these losses and expenditures include. The plaintiffs claim as the loss element the difference between what a plaintiff would have earned if he or she had not relied upon the opportunity offered by the FBI and what a plaintiff did earn as a FBI clerk. Plaintiffs use as the amount which a plaintiff would have earned the average earnings of a person of the plaintiff's age, education, sex and race as determined by the Bureau of the Census. There is no dispute over the accuracy of the census figures proffered by plaintiffs or over the appropriateness of use of this data in estimating what each plaintiff would have earned absent the clerk-to-agent program. Plaintiffs then claim as each plaintiff's loss the amount determined by subtracting from the census-derived figure the amount actually earned by that plaintiff during the relevant time period. The loss calculation method proposed by plaintiffs is unexceptional and is approved for purposes of this case.

Plaintiffs claim that the relevant time period runs from when each plaintiff began work at the FBI until that plaintiff left or should have left that employment. The date on which plaintiffs assert that a duty to mitigate damages arose is April 4, 1978, the date on which plaintiffs were notified that they could seek alternative employment and still receive credit for their clerical experience in applying for future special agent vacancies. This date is almost one year after the termination of the clerk-to-agent program was announced. As such, it represents a reasonable compromise date, since it would be clearly unreasonable to expect plaintiffs to obtain alternative employment immediately after termination of the clerk-to-agent program. Defendants have not disputed the validity of this date, and the Court thus adopts it as a reasonable date after which any reduced pay suffered by remaining at the FBI will be deemed to be a result of the plaintiff's own choice to remain there. Thus, plaintiffs are entitled to basic damages in the amount of the difference between the amount they earned at the FBI between (a) the time they began and (b) the earlier of their actual departure dates or April 4, 1978 and the average amounts, that persons of their age, sex, race and education earned.

Plaintiffs also claim the right to compensation for their reduced earning capacity beyond this date as a result of their having worked at the FBI during the relevant time period. This argument must be rejected. These damages are too speculative to be awarded. Some plaintiffs may have actually been benefited by their FBI employment; others may have been harmed. The degree of this harm and the rate at which it will diminish in the future is extremely uncertain. As stated previously, it is impossible to calculate these damages with too much precision; a "rough justice" is all that can be expected. This is best achieved by giving the plaintiffs the aforementioned period of slightly less than one year in which to obtain other employment, and to terminate the period of damages after that date.

To this figure there should be added those expenses incurred by plaintiffs in traveling to their place of employment with the FBI. Defendant claims that these expenses are not recoverable because they are made in preparation for performance but such preparatory expenses are of course recoverable under the reliance approach, since they are clearly foreseeable costs of entering into the contract. See Restatement (Second) of Contracts, supra, § 363. However, costs of moving to new jobs obtained by plaintiffs after leaving the FBI are not so recoverable, since they would have in all probability been incurred even had there been no clerk-to-agent program. For example, if a plaintiff moved from Pittsburgh to Washington to join the clerk-to-agent program his expenses of so moving are a consequence of reliance on the program and properly recoverable. However, if the same plaintiff moved to New York after leaving the FBI the expenses of such a move would not be recoverable, since plaintiff would have had to move to New York to obtain that job even had the program never existed.

Plaintiffs also claim a right to recover for amounts spent on educational expenses incurred as a result of the program. However, it is completely speculative whether or not individual plaintiffs would have chosen to obtain a college degree, for example, had the clerk-to-agent program not existed. In addition, the plaintiffs who incurred educational expenses of course obtained the offsetting benefit of the value of the education received. The amount of any difference between what plaintiffs paid for these benefits and what they were worth to plaintiffs is speculative; such expenses may not be recovered here.

Finally, five plaintiffs claim that their spouses suffered unemployment or reduced wages as a result of their decision to join the clerk-to-agent program. Again, such damages are not recoverable here. It is impossible to tell which plaintiffs' spouses would have been unemployed had they taken employment with someone other than the FBI. In addition, there is no evidence that the defendants could have anticipated that such consequences were likely to flow from the program, and any damages from spousal unemployment would thus appear to be barred by the rule requiring that damages from a breach of contract be reasonably foreseeable. See Hadley v. Baxendale, 156 Eng. Rep. 145 (1854).

Finally, defendant claims that a reduction in the damages awarded should be made to reflect the possibility that some of the plaintiffs might have been unemployed had the clerk-to-agent program not existed. However, this factor is more than compensated for by the fact that the Department of Commerce Current Population Reports, from which the plaintiffs have calculated their amounts for average wages of workers in the plaintiffs respective age, education, race and sex groups tend to understate income by approximately ten percent. . . . Defendants have not contested this fact. This discount effect more than compensates for the possibility that some of the plaintiffs may have been unemployed in the absence of the program. Even if this were not true, the other items of plaintiff's damages which have been disallowed here as speculative would more than adequately compensate for this speculative possibility.

The Court thus concludes that plaintiffs are entitled to recover the amounts claimed under Phase I of their Theory B for lost wages, as well as any expenses of moving to their jobs at the FBI, less any tax savings enjoyed with respect to moving expenses.

Plaintiffs' remaining elements of damages are disallowed. The parties have represented that the amount are not in dispute.

Accordingly, plaintiffs shall, on or before February 22, 1982, submit a form of judgment with the relevant amounts to which each plaintiff is entitled, which order shall have been seen by defendants. Defendants may on or before February 26, 1982, file an objection to these amounts. Upon receipt of these papers, the Court will enter the appropriate summary judgment order.

NOTES

1. _Appellate History of_ Kizas. The district court awarded Kizas and the 69 other employees joining his class action lawsuit a total of $490,603 (roughly $7,000 per employee). On cross-appeals to the circuit court, the district court's decision was reversed. _See Kizas v. Webster_, 707 F.2d 524 (D.C. Cir. 1983). The circuit panel held that the employees had no vested right in the special preference for promotion formerly given to FBI employees. Consequently, they could not receive compensation for the loss of the preference. Though the district court's opinion is of no use to Mr. Kizas and the other plaintiffs, it provides law students a clear example of how a court calculates reliance damages. Consider the various losses that Kizas asked the court to consider as reliance costs. In determining reliance damages, what factors did the court consider relevant?

2. _Losing Contracts and Reliance Damages._ In _Kizas_, the court notes that the defendant is allowed to show that the employees would have been worse off had full performance actually occurred (i.e., the continued existence of the program), but that, absent such proof, the employees are entitled to recoup their reliance losses. As a practical matter, reconstructing what "would have happened had full performance occurred" is often problematic, and proving that it would have been detrimental to the promisee buyer is likely to be even more difficult. Let us assume, then, that most promisors will not sustain this burden of proof and consequently they will be required to reimburse the promisee for his reliance loss.

Does this result "[impose] the risk of the promisee's contract upon the promisor"? Assume, for instance, that the employee made a bad business decision to enter the F.B.I.'s labor market at a time when Congress cut the Bureau's budget and froze all hiring of new agents. In this case, the promisee's decision actually causes the reliance loss rather than the promisor's failure to perform. Of course, the court will allow the promisor to prove these facts, but we have already noted the difficulty of that task. The burden of proof then becomes a paramount issue.

The court decided that since the defendant breached, it bears that burden of proof. Alternatively, burdens of proof can be assigned according to the relative probabilities of certain outcomes. Would an analysis along "relative probability" lines mandate a different result? If so, which method of assigning the burden of proof is better?

3. *Reliance Losses That Exceed Expectancy Damages.* Contract theory assumes that normally expectancy damages will exceed reliance losses. That is because reliance damages return the injured party to the position she was in before she contracted, while expectancy damages place the injured party in the position she expected to be in after performance of the contract. The injured party expected to be made better off by contracting, and since she did not breach, we have no reason to believe that her calculation was incorrect.

L. Albert & Son v. Armstrong Rubber Co., 178 F.2d 182 (2d Cir. 1949), however, does not fit this paradigm. During World War II, when new rubber was scarce and thus demand for reconditioned rubber was high, Armstrong Rubber ordered four "refiners" for reconditioning old rubber. By the time of delivery, however, the war was winding down, and Armstrong recognized that the demand for reconditioned rubber would decline, rendering their contract with Albert a losing deal. When Albert failed to timely deliver two of the refiners, Armstrong seized the opportunity to declare breach and sued Albert for damages sustained due to Armstrong's reliance on the contract, which eventually boiled down to foundations laid in anticipation of the "refiners." In a decision by Learned Hand, the court permitted Armstrong to recover these reliance damages, but also allowed Albert to offset those damages by proving the amount saved by Armstrong due to non-delivery of the "refiners."

Professor Richard Craswell, in *Against Fuller and Perdue*, 67 U. CHI. L. REV. 99 (2000), contends that the fluctuation of reliance damages, varying from awards over and under the expectation interest, is one of many reasons to restructure the categories of potential damage awards. Suggesting that Fuller and Perdue's rigid three-interest system (expectancy, reliance, and restitution) has outlived its usefulness, Craswell believes a more fluid categorization reflecting the tendency of damage awards to be greater than expectancy, less than expectancy, or approximating expectancy better defines both doctrine and practice in contract remedies. Rather than the three traditional categories introduced by Fuller and Perdue, Craswell proposes a laundry list of possible remedies, including the traditional three but also adding with relatively equal emphasis such recoveries as specific performance, liquidated damages, and punitive damages, and arranging all these possible remedies along a spectrum with the expectancy interest at the center and irrespective of whether the recovery would traditionally be termed reliance, expectancy, or restitution.[8]

----

[8] *See also* David W. Barnes & Deborah Zalesne, *A Unifying Theory of Contract Damage Rules*, 55 SYRACUSE L. REV. 495 (2005); David W. Barnes & Deborah Zalesne, *The Shadow Code*, 56 S.C. L. REV. 93 (2004).

4. *Foreseeability and Reliance.* The conduct that induces reliance by the promisee must be related to the reliance expenses incurred. This principle was exemplified in *Wartzman v. Hightower Productions, Ltd.*, 456 A.2d 82 (Md. Ct. Spec. App. 1983). In this colorful case, promoters formed a corporation (Hightower) that sponsored "Woody Hightower," an entertainer who tried to break the world record for flagpole sitting. The corporation, however, was improperly structured, which prevented the promoters from selling shares in the corporation until the legal problems were addressed. The promoters sued their law firm for malpractice, and the court ruled against the lawyers. The court rejected the defendant's arguments that the promotional expenses incurred by Hightower were not made in reliance upon the lawyer's performance, holding:

> In the present case the appellants knew, or should have known, that the success of the venture rested upon the ability of Hightower to sell stock and secure advertising as public interest in the adventure accelerated. Appellants' contention that their failure to properly incorporate Hightower was collateral and lacked the necessary nexus to permit consideration of reliance damages is not persuasive. The very life blood of the project depended on the corporation's ability to sell stock to fund the promotion. This is the reason for the employment of the appellants. In reliance thereon, Hightower sold stock and incurred substantial obligations. When it could no longer sell its stock, the entire project failed. No greater nexus need be established.

Id. at 86–87.

5. *Problem.* Anglia planned to produce a play for television. Anglia arranged a place where the play was to be filmed, hired a director, a stage manager, and so forth. Selection of a leading man for the play was critical. The company contracted with actor Robert Reed to play the part. Due to an error on the part of Reed's agent, Reed was already under contract to perform somewhere else, and Reed repudiated the contract. Anglia tried hard to find a substitute for Reed, but they were unable to do so, and they had to abandon the film. They had to pay the director, etc. Anglia could not show whether the film would have earned a profit, and so they sued Reed for their expenses. Reed contended that Anglia could recover only those expenses incurred *after* Anglia contracted with him. What result?[9]

[5] Restitution

The "restitution interest," involving a combination of unjust impoverishment with unjust gain, presents the strongest case for relief. If, following Aristotle, we regard the purpose of justice as the maintenance of an equilibrium of goods among members of society, the restitution interest presents twice as strong a claim to judicial intervention as the reliance interest, since if A not only causes B to lose one unit but appropriates that unit to himself, the resulting discrepancy between A and B is not one unit but two.

---

[9] *See Anglia Television, Ltd. v. Reed*, 9 All Eng. Rep. 690 (C.A. 1971).

Lon L. Fuller & William R. Perdue, *The Reliance Interest in Contract Damages*, 46 YALE L.J. 52, 56 (1936).

Despite the strong justification for restitution damages offered by Fuller and Perdue in the excerpt quoted above, a plaintiff's right to restitution is often the subject of extensive litigation. One reason for this is the frequency of claims by the breaching party that, notwithstanding the breach, she is entitled to restitution of benefits conferred on the promisee prior to the breach. Another source of contention concerns the appropriate method of measuring a claim for restitution even in those cases where some recovery is, in theory, warranted. For examples of these and related issues involving claims for restitution consider the following cases.

UNITED STATES USE OF SUSI CONTRACTING CO. v. ZARA CONTRACTING CO.
Circuit Court of Appeals, Second Circuit
146 F.2d 606 (1944)

CLARK, J.

Plaintiffs, Susi Contracting Co., Inc., and D'Agostino & Cuccio, Inc., brought this action under the provisions of the Miller Act, 40 U.S.C.A. 270a et seq., in the name of the United States against Zara Contracting Co., Inc., and American Bonding Company of Baltimore, the surety on its bond, to recover for work performed for and equipment supplied Zara in the performance of its contract with the United States, dated March 4, 1941, for the extension of Tri-Cities Airport, Endicott, New York. On April 2, 1941, Zara entered into a subcontract with plaintiffs, wherein plaintiffs agreed, except for one $100 item, to perform the entire work called for by the main contract with the United States. This work involved the excavation of material and placing, manipulating, rolling, and compacting it as a base and surface course for landing strips or runways. During the course of the excavation plaintiffs encountered unexpected soil conditions, mostly due to the presence of a great deal of clay material, which made progress of their work extremely difficult, caused the breakdown of their tools, and, according to their allegations, generally required the performance of work not called for by the contract. Consequently on several occasions they made demands on Zara for extra money; and eventually the dispute arose which led to mutual claims of breach of contract and, by easy stages, to the opposing claims for monetary solace of this action. At any rate, defendant Zara took over the completion of the contract about July 12, 1941, or two months after plaintiffs had begun work. It also took possession of and for some three months utilized the equipment furnished by plaintiffs at the contract site.

In this action plaintiffs alleged that Zara wrongfully terminated the subcontract, and sought recovery for the reasonable cost and value of the actual work performed, and the fair and reasonable rental value of the equipment for the period of its retention and use.

The District Court found generally for the plaintiffs, holding that Zara had wrongfully terminated the contract and that there was due them $39,107.10 for work done at the contract rate, $18,600 for increased cost of excavation due to the soil conditions encountered, and $5,157.75 as rental allowance for plaintiffs' equipment, less $43,345.20, the amount advanced by Zara during the course of the work, or a net of $19,519.65, together with interest from the date of the filing of the suit. All parties have appealed, plaintiffs because the rental allowance was too small, and both defendants because of the holding that Zara was the one who breached the contract and because of the allowance for increased cost of excavation. [The court affirmed the ruling below that Zara had breached the contract.]

This, of course disposes of Zara's claim for damages and leaves for consideration the amount of recovery due the plaintiffs. In their complaint originally plaintiffs had a second count claiming an accounting of profits; but this they abandoned, and they have made no claim for damages for breach of contract. Their only claim, therefore, is for the value of the work performed and of the rental of equipment retained by Zara on the job. Taking up, first, the value of the work performed, three theories are suggested to justify the additional award made below — in addition to that made at the regular contract rate — of $18,600 for the increased cost of excavating the clay material. The first, apparently most favored by the plaintiffs, is that this excavating (as well as the separate mixing of materials to form the airport runways made necessary by the soil condition) was extra work, not covered by the contract figures, and hence was separately compensable. Apparently their complaint was drawn on this theory; but the allegations are of a general nature, and, of course, after trial the judgment must grant the relief to which plaintiffs' case as presented entitled them. The second, relied on by the trial court, is that, since the subcontract made the provisions of the main contract determinative and applicable to the subparties, except where otherwise provided, the plaintiffs should have the advantage of the provisions of the main contract under which Zara successfully sought additional compensation against the United States. And the third is that, in view of Zara's default, they may waive the contract entirely and sue in quantum meruit for the reasonable value of the work performed.

Defendants contend, however, that under the terms of the subcontract plaintiffs were not entitled to any allowance for extra costs over and above the contract price, even though entailed in consequence of the misrepresentations as to the subsoil conditions. They rely principally on Article 5 of the subcontract, wherein plaintiffs agreed that no representations as to subsurface conditions have been made, nor have they been induced to enter into the contract in reliance upon the drawings or plans, and they promised to make no claim for damages for unknown conditions. In support of their contention they cite such cases as T. J. W. Corporation v. Board of Higher Education of City of New York, 251 App. Div. 405, 296 N.Y.S. 693, and Niewenhous Co. v. State, 248 App. Div. 658, 288 N.Y.S. 224. But these cases are limited to claims for extra work, where the contract has not been wrongfully terminated by the employer. The situation is quite otherwise where, as here, defendants have breached the agreement. We agree that the definite commitment which the plaintiffs have made in Article 5 is one they must stand by so long as they must rely upon their contract; and hence we find it difficult to see why the first two theories presented above, that particularly pressed by the plaintiffs and that relied on by the trial court, do not conflict directly with this agreement, which seems to contemplate the very situation to which it would then be held inapplicable. No such infirmity attaches to the third theory, however.

For it is an accepted principle of contract law, often applied in the case of construction contracts, that the promisee upon breach has the option to forego any suit on the contract and claim only the reasonable value of his performance. This is well settled in the New York cases. [. . .]

[The] authorities make it quite clear that under the better rule the contract price or the unit price per cubic yard of a construction or excavation contract does not limit recovery. This, too, is the rule in New York. This doctrine is particularly applicable to unit prices in construction contracts;, a plaintiff may well have completed the hardest part of a job for which an average cost had been set. But it seems settled now in New York that with the breach fall all the other parts of the contract. Hence it is clear that plaintiffs are not limited to the contract prices in the situation disclosed here.

As we have noted, the trial court granted recovery for $39,107.10 for the work done at the contract price, together with an additional sum of $18,600 for the extra cost of excavation of the clay, computed as 62,000 cubic yards at the additional expense of 30 cents per cubic yard. . . . As to the monetary amounts, these are based on the cost of the work to Zara, as well as expert testimony for plaintiffs, and are not seriously disputed. Indeed, in fixing the additional allowance at 30 cents per cubic yard, the judge relied particularly on Zara's claim to the United States wherein it stated that its records showed an actual cost to it of the extra work, amounting to 28.7 cents per cubic yard for placing the excavated material in the runways. Professor Williston points out that the measure of recovery by way of restitution, though often confused with recovery on the contract, should not be measured or limited thereby; but he does point out that the contract may be important evidence of the value of the performance to the defendant, as may also the cost of the labor and materials. It is therefore appropriate here, particularly in default of any challenging evidence, to base recovery on proper expenditures in performance, or for extra work, and to make use of the contract as fixing the basic price.

It is to be noted that, since it is the defendant who is in default, and plaintiffs' performance here is "part of the very performance" for which the defendant had bargained, "it is to be valued, not by the extent to which the defendant's total wealth has been increased thereby, but by the amount for which such services and materials as constituted the part performance could have been purchased from one in the plaintiff's position at the time they were rendered." Restatement, Contracts, § 347, comment c. It is to be noted that in fact defendant Zara did receive benefits most substantial from plaintiffs' performance. Plaintiffs had actually excavated 211,390 cubic yards, for which Zara's profit, as determined by the spread between the main and the subcontract of 512 cents per cubic yard as a minimum, with higher amounts for a part, would be around $12,000; it had already collected $17,115.79 from the United States for the additional cost of removing the "cohesive silt," of which most was done by plaintiffs, and it had pending a claim against the United States for $18,840.10 more; and what is perhaps most important, it had received a performance which it needed to make to ensure recovery of these profits and sums from the United States and avoid the danger of being in default, and which it would have had to do itself or purchase in the market. Hence the allowance made by the

District Court is justified on the evidence and the law, and we find no error, therefore, in this item of recovery.

[The judgment was affirmed with a modification of damages for the fair rental value of some furnished equipment.]

BRITTON v. TURNER
Supreme Court of New Hampshire
6 N.H. 481 (1834)

Assumpsit for work and labor, performed by the plaintiff, in the service of the defendant, from March 9th, 1831 to December 27, 1831. The declaration contained the common counts, and among them a count in quantum meruit, for the labor, averring it to be worth one hundred dollars. At the trial in the C.C. Pleas, the plaintiff proved the performance of the labor as set forth in the declaration.

The defense was that it was performed under a special contract — that the plaintiff agreed to work one year, from some time in March, 1831, to March, 1832, and that the defendant was to pay him for said year's labor the sum of one hundred and twenty dollars; and the defendant offered evidence tending to show that such was the contract under which the work was done. Evidence was also offered to show that the plaintiff left the defendant's service without his consent, and it was contended by the defendant that the plaintiff had no good cause for not continuing in his employment. There was no evidence offered of any damage arising from the plaintiff's departure, farther than was to be inferred from his non-fulfillment of the entire contract.

The court instructed the jury, that if they were satisfied from the evidence that the labor was performed, under a contract to labor a year, for the sum of one hundred and twenty dollars, and if they were satisfied that the plaintiff labored only the time specified in the declaration, and then left the defendant's service, against his consent, and without any good cause, yet the plaintiff was entitled to recover, under his quantum meruit count, as much as the labor he performed was reasonably worth, and under this direction the jury gave a verdict for the plaintiff for the sum of $95.

The defendant excepted to the instruction thus given to the jury. . . .

Parker, J.

It may be assumed, that the labor performed by the plaintiff, and for which he seeks to recover a compensation in this action, was commenced under a special contract to labor for the defendant the term of one year for the sum of one hundred and twenty dollars, and that the plaintiff has labored but a portion of that time, and has voluntarily failed to complete the entire contract. It is clear, then, that he is not entitled to recover upon the contract itself, because the service, which was to entitle him to the sum agreed upon, has never been performed. But the question arises, can the plaintiff, under these circumstances, recover a reasonable sum for the service he has actually performed, under the count in quantum meruit. Upon this, and questions of a similar nature, the decisions to be found in the books are not easily reconciled.

It has been held, upon contracts of this kind for labor to be performed at a specified price, that the party who voluntarily fails to fulfill the contract by performing the whole labor contracted for, is not entitled to recover any thing for the labor actually performed, however much he may have done towards the performance, and this has been considered the settled rule of law upon this subject. . . . That such rule in its operation may be very unequal, not to say unjust, is apparent. A party who contracts to perform certain specified labor, and who breaks his contract in the first instance, without any attempt to perform it, can only be made liable to pay the damages which the other party has sustained by reason of such nonperformance, which in many instances may be trifling — whereas a party who in good faith has entered upon the performance of his contract, and nearly completed it, and then abandoned the further performance — although the other party has had the full benefit of all that has been done, and has perhaps sustained no actual damage — is in fact subjected to a loss of all which has been performed, in the nature of damages for the non-fulfillment of the remainder, upon the technical rule, that the contract must be fully performed in order to [obtain] a recovery of any part of the compensation.

By the operation of this rule, then, the party who attempts performance may be placed in a much worse situation than he who wholly disregards his contract, and the other party may receive much more, by the breach of the contract, than the injury which he has sustained by such breach, and more than he could be entitled to were he seeking to recover damages by an action.

The case before us presents an illustration. Had the plaintiff in this case never entered upon the performance of his contract, the damage could not probably have been greater than some small expense and trouble incurred in procuring another to do the labor which he had contracted to perform. But having entered upon the performance, and labored nine and a half months, the value of which labor to the defendant as found by the jury is $95, if the defendant can succeed in this defense, he in fact receives nearly five sixths of the value of a whole year's labor, by reason of the breach of contract by the plaintiff a sum not only utterly disproportionate to any probable, not to say possible damage which could have resulted from the neglect of the plaintiff to continue the remaining two and a half months, but altogether beyond any damage which could have been recovered by the defendant, had the plaintiff done nothing towards the fulfillment of his contract.

[The court discussed cases where the breaching party was not allowed to recover in quantum meruit for partial performance.] There are other cases, however, in which principles have been adopted leading to a different result. It is said, that where a party contracts to perform certain work, and to furnish materials, as, for instance, to build a house, and the work is done, but with some variations from the mode prescribed by the contract, yet if the other party has the benefit of the labor and materials he should be bound to pay so much as they are reasonably worth. . . .

Those cases are not to be distinguished, in principle, from the present, unless it be in the circumstance, that where the party has contracted to furnish materials, and do certain labor, as to build a house in a specified manner, if it is not done according to the contract, the party for whom it is built may refuse to receive it — elect to take no benefit from what has been performed — and therefore if he does receive, he shall be bound to pay the value — whereas in a contract for labor, merely, from day to day, the party is continually receiving the benefit of the contract under an expectation that it will be fulfilled, and cannot, upon the breach of it, have an election to refuse to receive what has been done, and thus discharge himself from payment. But we think this difference in the nature of the contracts does not justify the application of a different rule in relation to them.

The party who contracts for labor merely, for a certain period, does so with full knowledge that he must, from the nature of the case, be accepting part performance from day to day, if the other party commences the performance, and with knowledge also that the other may eventually fail of completing the entire term. If under such circumstances he actually receives a benefit from the labor performed, over and above the damage occasioned by the failure to complete, there is as much reason why he should pay the reasonable worth of what has thus been done for this benefit, as there is when he enters and occupies the house which has been built for him, but not according to the stipulation of the contract, and which he perhaps enters, not because he is satisfied with what has been done, but because circumstances compel him to accept it, such as it is, that he should pay for the value of the house. [. . .]

In fact we think the technical reasoning, that the performance of the whole labor is a condition precedent, and the right to recover any thing dependent upon it — that the contract being entire there can be no apportionment — and that there being an express contract no other can be implied, even upon the subsequent performance of service — is not properly applicable to this species of contract, where a beneficial service has been actually performed; for we have abundant reason to believe, that the general understanding of the community is, that the hired laborer shall be entitled to compensation for the service actually performed, though he did not continue the entire term contracted for, and such contracts must be presumed to be made with reference to that understanding, unless an express stipulation shows the contrary. . . .

It is easy, if parties so choose, to provide by an express agreement that nothing shall be earned, if the laborer leaves his employer without having performed the whole service contemplated, and then there can be no pretense for a recovery if he voluntarily deserts the service before the expiration of the time. The amount, however, for which the employer ought to be charged, where the laborer abandons his contract, is only the reasonable worth, or the amount of advantage he receives upon the whole transaction . . . and, in estimating the value of the labor, the contract price for the service cannot be exceeded. . . .

The benefit and advantage which the party takes by the labor, therefore, is the amount of value which he receives, if any, after deducting the amount of damage. . . . This rule, by binding the employer to pay the value of the service he actually receives, and the laborer to answer in damages where he does not complete the entire contract, will leave no temptation to the former to drive the laborer from his service, near the close of his term, by ill treatment, in order to escape from payment; nor to the latter to desert his service before the stipulated time, without a sufficient reason; and it will in most instances settle the whole controversy in one action, and prevent a multiplicity of suits and cross actions. . . .

The defendant sets up a mere breach of the contract in defense of the action, but this cannot avail him. He does not appear to have offered evidence to show that he was damnified by such breach, or to have asked that a deduction should be made upon that account. The direction to the jury was therefore correct, that the plaintiff was entitled to recover as much as the labor performed was reasonably worth, and the jury appear to have allowed a pro rata compensation, for the time which the plaintiff labored in the defendant's service. [. . .]

Judgment on the verdict.

NOTES

1. ***Restitution for Breachers and for Nonbreachers.*** For years before the decision in *Britton* (and for years after in some jurisdictions), defaulting plaintiffs could not seek restitution damages. The remedy of *quantum meruit* was reserved for non-breaching parties such as the plaintiffs in *Zara*. Though the remedy is now available to breachers and non-breachers alike, does the law still retain a preference for non-breachers? *Zara* holds that recovery in quantum meruit is not limited by what the promisee would have gained had there been no breach. Consider also the following:

> The impact of quantum meruit is to allow a promisee to recover the value of services he gave to the defendant irrespective of whether he would have lost money on the contract and been unable to recover in a suit on the contract. The measure of recovery for *quantum meruit* is the reasonable value of the performance; and recovery is undiminished by any loss which would have been incurred by complete performance. While the contract price may be evidence of reasonable value of the services, it does not measure the value of the performance or limit recovery. Rather, the standard for measuring the reasonable value of the services rendered is the amount for which such services could have been purchased from one in the plaintiff's position at the time and place the services were rendered.

United States v. Algernon Blair, Inc., 479 F.2d 638, 641 (4th Cir. 1973).

Is this the position of the drafters of the Restatement (Second) of Contracts? Consult §§ 371 and 373(2). Is this an attempt to punish someone for breaching a contract?

Compare *Zara* and *Algernon Blair* to *United States use of Palmer Constr., Inc. v. Cal State Electric, Inc.*, 940 F.2d 1260 (9th.Cir. 1991). In *Palmer*, a breaching subcontractor sued the prime contractor for restitution based on services rendered before the breach. The Court found that the prime contractor owed the breaching subcontractor $90,086.28 in *quantum meruit*, but that the subcontractor could not recover because a breaching party's restitution was limited by the original contract price. Since the promisee, the prime contractor, had to pay $6,295.54 *over* the contract price to finish the job after the breach, the subcontractor was not entitled to restitution damages.

> When the party performing the work breaches the contract, it may nevertheless recover all or a portion of the value of the services it has actually rendered, but only under certain circumstances. The breaching party may not recover any amount which, when added to the amount previously paid to the breaching party, and the amount paid or owing to any party whose services are used to complete the job, would cause the contract price to be exceeded . . . the contract price represents a ceiling on the amount the non-breaching party may be required to pay — *in toto.* Similarly, regardless of the value of the work performed by the breaching party, if the amount the non-breaching party must pay to a third party to finish the job, when added to the amount it has already paid to the breaching party, exceeds the contract price, the non-breaching party may recover the excess amount from the breaching party as damages.

Id. at 1265 (1991) (Reinhardt, J., concurring). Does the distinction between breaching and non-breaching parties make sense?

2. *Quantum Meruit and Quasi-Contract.* Under what circumstances is restitution an alternative remedy for breach of contract? Consider the following:

> In the case of a breach by non-performance, . . . the injured party's alternative remedy by way of restitution depends upon the extent of the non-performance by the defendant. The defendant's breach may be nothing but a failure to perform some minor part of his contractual duty. Such a minor non-performance is a breach of contract and an action for damages can be maintained. The injured party, however, can not maintain an action for restitution of what he has given the defendant unless the defendant's non-performance is so material that it is held to go to the "essence". . . . A minor breach by one party does not discharge the contractual duty of the other party; and the latter being still bound to perform as agreed can not be entitled to the restitution of payments already made by him or to the value of other part performances rendered.

Farash v. Sykes Datatronics, Inc., 59 N.Y.2d 500, 507 (1983).

The Eighth Circuit went even further in *Ventura v. Titan Sports, Inc.,* 65 F.3d 725 (8th Cir. 1995). Jesse "The Body" Ventura, a professional wrestler,[10] sued Titan in *quantum meruit* to recover royalties from the sale of videotapes featuring his color commentary. Titan claimed that revenues from the sale of those videotapes were part of an earlier express contract between Ventura and the company, thus excluding restitutionary recovery. The court agreed, holding that if subsequent videotape sales were even contemplated during the bargaining process, an action in *quantum meruit* was not available to Ventura. However, the court found no evidence that videotape royalties were discussed or considered during the bargaining for the express contract, and "The Body" could recover restitutionary damages.

3. *Using Restitution to Encourage Precautions.* In *Leebov v. United States*

---

[10] Jesse Ventura was subsequently elected the 38th Governor of Minnesota, and served from January 4, 1999, to January 6, 2003, without seeking a second term. Titan Sports owned the World Wrestling Federation, known as the WWF.

Fidelity and Guaranty Co., 165 A.2d 82 (1960), a contractor sacrificed his trucks and other equipment to stabilize a hillside on which he was excavating, thereby preventing a landslide that would have destroyed neighboring homes. The contractor's insurer refused to accept liability for the loss of the contractor's vehicles, deeming the acts here intentional and thus not covered by the contractor's policy. The Supreme Court of Pennsylvania, however, found for the plaintiff-contractor under a restitution theory because it recognized the inefficiency of a contrary result. Reasoning that the contractor conferred a benefit upon the insurer by preventing widespread "accidental" damages for which the insurer might have been liable, the Court stated:

> If the plaintiff had not taken immediate and substantial measures to remedy the perilous situation, disastrous consequences might have befallen the adjoining and nearby properties. If that had happened, the defendant would have been required to pay considerably more than is involved in the present lawsuit. It would be a strange kind of justice which would hold that the defendant would be compelled to pay out, let us say, the sum of $100,000 if the plaintiff had not prevented what would have been inevitable, and yet not be called upon to pay the smaller sum which the plaintiff actually expended to avoid a foreseeable disaster.

Id. at 84.[11]

4.   *Measuring the Restitution Value.* One variable in the restitution cases is that it may be either the breacher or the nonbreacher who is suing to recover in restitution. Another variable is the way to measure the value of the benefit conferred. The benefit could be measured by its value in the hands of the recipient, or by the cost of conferring the benefit, or by the cost that a third party would have incurred in conferring the benefit, or, finally, the price that a third party would pay for the benefit. The latter two measures are, in some sense, a "market measure." Finally, there is the question of whether the benefit has been "accepted." How ought the courts to handle these variables? For an in-depth discussion of the difficulties in calculating restitutionary recovery, see Saul Levmore, *Explaining Restitution*, 71 Va. L. Rev. 65, 69–73 (1985).

5.   *Problem.* Dickey Moore, a former child movie star fallen on hard times, contracted for $50,000 to do a low-budget movie: a musical remake of "The African Queen." As part of the contract, Dickey agreed to go on "talk shows" on national television to promote the film. After the film was over, the movie studio demanded that Dickey appear on Good Morning America. Dickey, who had Oprah in mind, decided that 5 a.m. was too early to get up to appear on television, and he flatly refused. Nevertheless, the film was a surprise hit and has earned millions for its producers. Dickey has not been paid anything, so he has sued for $1,000,000, the reasonable value of his services. What recovery, if any, and on what theory? If Moore's breach was not "willful," how would you characterize it?

---

[11]   Professor Saul Levmore has argued that courts and lawyers should pursue restitutionary remedies more aggressively to promote this sort of efficiency. *See* Saul Levmore, *Obligation or Restitution for Best Efforts*, 67 S. Cal. L. Rev. 1411 (1994).

[6]   Punitive Damages

We have seen many courts articulate the basic principle that contract damages are a substitution for a promised performance and not a deterrent against breach per se. Given the salience of the compensation principle, under what circumstances, if any, should courts ever entertain a claim that, in addition to providing full compensation, a breaching promisor should also be assessed punitive damages? Before you read the materials in this section, formulate an hypothesis based on what you now know about contract law and contract remedies as to the availability of punitive damages for breach of contract. Test your hypothesis against the following case and accompanying notes.

MILLER BREWING CO. v. BEST BEERS OF BLOOMINGTON, INC.
Supreme Court of Indiana
608 N.E.2d 975 (1993)

[Miller Brewing Co., a Wisconsin corporation that brews a variety of beers, had been in a contractual relationship with Best Beers, an Indiana beer distributor, for decades. In the mid-1980s, the relationship between Miller and Best Beers began to sour. In October of 1986, Miller sent Best Beers a preliminary notice of termination of their distribution contract. After a period where Best Beers attempted to cure alleged deficiencies in their distributorship, Miller terminated the contract. Soon after, Miller entered into a distributing contract with another company. Evidence showed that Miller's complaints about Best Beers may have been partially fabricated in order to provide Miller reason to terminate the contract. Best Beers brought an action against Miller, alleging that Miller had wrongfully terminated the contract in violation of an Indiana statute. The jury awarded Best Beers compensatory damages of $397,620 and punitive damages of $1,989,260. On appeal, Miller sought judgment in its favor on the punitive damages claim.]

KRAHULIK, J.

*   *   *

Punitive Damages

Miller next attacks Best Beer's entitlement to punitive damages. We reverse the grant of a new trial on punitive damages because Best Beers failed to meet its burden of proof for punitive damages in this breach of contract case.

Opinions of this Court have consistently stated the general rule that punitive damages are not allowed in a breach of contract action. [. . .] Such statements suggest that there are exceptions to this rule, but upon close examination of the opinions of this Court, we find that no exceptions have ever been applied. Today we hold that, in fact, no exception exists.

The notion that in some instances punitive damages are available for a breach of contract appears to have begun in *Vernon Fire & Casualty v. Sharp*, 264 Ind. 599,

349 N.E.2d 173. In that case, plaintiff sued his insurer for breach of an insurance contract, and the jury awarded compensatory damages for the breach. Plaintiff also alleged tortious conduct on part of the insurer for refusing to pay policy proceeds admittedly due, and was awarded punitive damages. In addressing whether punitive damages were available when a breach of contract was proven, this Court noted the general rule that such damages are not recoverable because a plaintiff is "not entitled to mulct the promisor in punitive damages" for a breach of contract. 264 Ind. at 608, 349 N.E.2d at 180. The Court reasoned that such damages were not legally appropriate because (1) "the well-defined parameters of compensatory and consequential damages which may be assessed against a promisor who decides for whatever reason not to live up to his bargain lend a needed measure of stability and predictability to the free enterprise system," and (2) the promisee will be compensated for all damages proximately resulting from the promisor's breach. 264 Ind. at 607, 349 N.E.2d at 180. The Court acknowledged, however, the widely-recognized principle that where the conduct of the breaching party independently establishes the elements of a common law tort, and where the proven tort is of the kind for which punitive damages are allowed, then punitive damages may be awarded. *Id.* In such a case, however, the punitive damages are awarded for the tort, and not for the breach of contract. The majority then found that the *Vernon Fire* plaintiff had established the elements of the common law tort of fraud and affirmed the award of punitive damages. 264 Ind. at 617.

In spite of its conclusion that the plaintiff had established the elements of fraud as an independent tort, the majority proceeded to opine that the requirement of an independent tort was not very compelling "when it appears from the evidence as a whole that a serious wrong, tortious in nature, has been committed, but the wrong does not conveniently fit the confines of a pre- determined tort" and where "the public interest will be served by the deterrent effect punitive damages will have upon future conduct of the wrongdoer and parties similarly situated." 264 Ind. at 608, 349 N.E.2d at 180 (emphasis omitted). Such language has been cited in subsequent Indiana cases addressing the availability of punitive damages in a breach of contract action. We do not find this authority persuasive. . . .

Although the notion that punitive damages are available in contract actions where there is "tort-like" conduct has been cited in all cases of this Court which address the issue of punitive damages since *Vernon Fire* was decided, in fact, such an exception has never been applied by this Court. Instead, where punitive damages were affirmed in a breach of contract case, this Court has found evidence of an independent tort. [. . .] In *Hibschman Pontiac, Inc. v. Batchelor* (1977), 266 Ind. 310, 316, a majority of this Court found there was "cogent proof to establish malice, fraud, gross negligence and oppressive conduct" on the part of a car dealership whose employees failed to repair an automobile despite the purchaser's repeated requests. By contrast, in *Travelers Indem. Co. v. Armstrong* (1982), Ind., 442 N.E.2d 349, 364, a majority of this Court reversed an award of punitive damages in an insurance contract dispute because of insufficient evidence. Similarly, in *Lawyers Title Ins. Corp. v. Pokraka*, 595 N.E.2d 244, 250, this Court concluded that because the plaintiff "did not succeed in establishing the existence of an independent tort which would support the imposition of punitive damages," that portion of the judgment was reversed.

After further consideration of *Vernon Fire* and the results in subsequent cases, we conclude that the language in *Vernon Fire* was *dicta* when it suggested that punitive damages are available in contract actions even if the plaintiff does not also establish each element of a recognized tort for which Indiana law would permit the recovery of punitive damages. Moreover, such a notion rests on an unwise policy.

The reasons for this are several. First, we have stated that there is no right to punitive damages, which are in the nature of a criminal penalty. Punitive damages are "designed to punish the wrongdoer and to dissuade him and others from similar conduct in the future." *Orkin Exterminating Co., Inc. v. Traina* (1986), Ind., 486 N.E.2d 1019, 1021. . . .

A rule that requires establishment of an independent tort furthers the public interest in recognizing the existence of *bona fide* business disputes and separating them from breaches of contract achieved in a tortious manner. As we stated in *Travelers*, breaches of contract "will almost invariably be regarded by the complaining party as oppressive if not outright fraudulent." 442 N.E.2d at 363. "The public interest cannot be served by any policy that deters resort to the courts for the determination of bona fide business disputes," *Travelers*, 442 N.E.2d at 363, or prohibits one party to a contract from exercising his common law rights to breach a contract and pay a rightful amount of compensatory damages. Unlike torts, where the duty is owed to all and a broad measure of damages is available, contract obligations are owed only to the parties to the contract and damages are limited to those reasonably within the expectations of the parties when the contract is made. Finally, as stated earlier, the *dicta* in *Vernon Fire* has never, in fact, been applied by this Court. [. . .]

We hold that in order to recover punitive damages in a lawsuit founded upon a breach of contract, the plaintiff must plead and prove the existence of an independent tort of the kind for which Indiana law recognizes that punitive damages may be awarded.

Having stated the proper legal standard for punitive damages in contract cases, we now address the parties' contentions as to whether the evidence presented in this case was sufficient. Best Beers claims the following evidence supports the imposition of punitive damages: 1) Miller employees made false statements (to their superiors) about Best Beers' sales efforts. 2) Miller employees made false statements (to their superiors) about the conduct of Best Beers' employees. 3) Miller made accusations in its termination letter which weren't supported by its own employees' reports. 4) Miller tolerated overage beer in the market after terminating Best Beers ostensibly because Best Beers had permitted overage beer to remain in the market. 5) A Miller employee said she would not rate Best Beers' performance as satisfactory no matter how well they did. 6) Miller solicited unfavorable comments about Best Beers in writing from selected retailers.

Best Beers does not seriously contend that there was sufficient evidence of an independent tort upon which punitive damages could have been awarded, but merely asserts that the above evidence is clear and convincing evidence of a "serious wrong tortious in nature." As discussed above, such evidence is insufficient to support an award of punitive damages in a breach of contract case. At best, such evidence establishes that Miller wrongfully terminated the contract, for which Best

Beers was awarded compensatory damages. Under elementary contract principles, those compensatory damages fully compensate

Best Beers to the extent allowed by law for all losses suffered by it as a result of the breach of contract. We discern nothing, based on the evidence presented at trial, compelling the conclusion that Best Beers is entitled to punitive damages. [. . .]

Accordingly, we grant transfer, vacate the opinion of the Court of Appeals, affirm the award of compensatory damages, and vacate the award of punitive damages.

DICKSON, J. dissenting.

In *Vernon Fire & Casualty Ins. Co. v. Sharp* (1976), 264 Ind. 599, this Court recognized two exceptions to the general rule that punitive damages are not recoverable in a contract action. The first arises when conduct of the breaching party not only constitutes breach of contract but also independently establishes the elements of a common law tort. *Id.* at 608. The second occurs when the evidence reveals that a serious wrong, tortious in nature, has been committed, although the wrong "does not conveniently fit the confines of a pre-determined tort." *Id.*

Judicial response to the *Vernon* exceptions has been both positive and widespread. Not only have Indiana courts consistently endorsed the opinion, but other jurisdictions have also cited *Vernon* while recognizing recovery of punitive damages within the context of a contractual relationship. . . .

This Court is unanimous in its recognition of the continued viability of the first *Vernon* exception based upon the establishment of an independent tort. Today, however, the majority abruptly seeks to modify *Vernon* and its progeny by relegating to *dicta* the exception permitting punitive damages where a contract breach attended by egregiously culpable conduct falls short of an independently actionable tort. However attractive it may be to limit an award of punitive damages to such bright-line situations, reprehensible behavior often defies strict tort categorization and should not go undeterred merely because it fails to completely conform to the precise contours of pre-existing tort classifications.

The majority speculates that recovery of punitive damages under the second *Vernon* exception would "reopen" the floodgates of punitive damages in contract cases. I disagree. . . . Ind. Code § 34-4-34-2 likewise emphasizes that facts supporting punitive damages must be established by "clear and convincing evidence." It is not surprising that, notwithstanding *Vernon*, there has been no flood of punitive damages judgments in Indiana courts.

Vernon's flexible and responsive application of the law to category-resistant dimensions of human behavior represents an enlightened approach to the infinite variations that elude rigid doctrinal formulations. Experience has shown this approach to be wise, effective, balanced, and just. It should not now be discarded.

NOTES

1. ***The Backlash Against Punitive Damages for Breach of Contract.*** In the 1970s and 1980s, a number of states became more willing to award punitive damages for contractual breaches, Indiana included. Sixteen years before *Miller Brewing*, the Indiana Supreme Court awarded punitive damages after a car dealership breached its contract with a customer, even though there was no finding that the dealership's conduct independently established a common law tort. *See Hibschman Pontiac, Inc. v. Batchelor*, 362 N.E.2d 845, 847 (Ind. 1977). The court held that "whenever the elements of fraud, malice, gross negligence or oppression *mingle* in the controversy," punitive damages could be awarded. Though expressly denying that it overturns *Hibschman, Miller Brewing* only allows for punitive damages if there is a finding of an independent tort. What part of the *Hibschman* holding remains good law, then?

Like the Indiana Supreme Court in *Miller Brewing*, many courts have either backed away from awarding punitive damages in contract cases or have reasserted their opposition to this remedy in recent years. A survey in 1999 revealed that 39 American jurisdictions do not permit punitive damages for breach of contract unless the plaintiff proves the existence of an independent tort, the rule announced in *Miller Brewing.* Twelve states permit punitive damages in limited circumstances for breach of contract.[12] This trend reflects an attempt to more clearly differentiate contract and tort remedies, which many have argued was becoming dangerously blurred. Consider the following:

> Nowhere but in the Cloud Cuckooland of modern tort theory could a case like this have been concocted. One large corporation is complaining that another obstinately refused to acknowledge they had a contract. For this shocking misconduct it is demanding millions of dollars in punitive damages. I suppose we will next be seeing lawsuits seeking punitive damages for maliciously refusing to return telephone calls or adopting a condescending tone in interoffice memos. Not every slight, nor even every wrong, ought to have a tort remedy. The intrusion of courts into every aspect of life, and particularly into every type of business relationship, generates serious costs and uncertainties, trivializes the law, and denies individuals and businesses the autonomy of adjusting mutual rights and responsibilities through voluntary contractual agreement.

> This tortification of contract law — the tendency of contract disputes to metastasize into torts — gives rise to a new form of entrepreneurship: investment in tort causes of action. "If Pennzoil won $11 billion from Texaco, why not me?" That thought must cross the minds of many enterprising lawyers and businessmen. . . . The potential rewards are large, the rules nebulous, and the parties unconstrained by such annoying technicalities as the language of the contract to which they once agreed. Here, for example, the contract was largely beside the point. Microtech instead relied on statements in Oki's pleadings, rumors racing through the Oki grapevine, and a letter in which Oki's president offers his interpretation

---

[12] *See* William S. Dodge, *The Case for Punitive Damages in Contracts*, 48 DUKE L.J. 629 (1999).

of the contract. On the basis of these minutiae, Microtech stakes its claim to $600,000 of compensatory damages and $2.5 million in punitive damages. And why not? Even a one in ten chance of winning would justify an investment of over $300,000 in attorney's fees.

Perhaps most troubling, the willingness of courts to subordinate voluntary contractual arrangements to their own sense of public policy and proper business decorum deprives individuals of an important measure of freedom. The right to enter into contracts — to adjust one's legal relationships by mutual agreement with other free individuals — was unknown through much of history and is unknown even today in many parts of the world. Like other aspects of personal autonomy, it is too easily smothered by government officials eager to tell us what's best for us. The recent tendency of judges to insinuate tort causes of action into relationships traditionally governed by contract is just such overreaching. It must be viewed with no less suspicion because the government officials in question happen to wear robes.

Oki America, Inc. v. Microtech Int'l, Inc., 872 F.2d 312, 315–16 (9th Cir. 1988) (Kozinski, J., concurring).

Are Judge Kozinski's fears overblown? Some have suggested so. See Anthony J. Sebok, *Punitive Damages: From Myth to Theory*, 92 Iowa L. Rev. 957 (2007) and Stephen Daniels & Joanne Martin, *Myth and Reality in Punitive Damages*, 75 Minn. L. Rev. 1 (1990), who contend that the fear of punitive damage awards is exaggerated and provide detailed empirical studies demonstrating that awards are relatively infrequent and recoveries generally reasonable.

2.   *The Exploding Pinto Case.* *Grimshaw v. Ford Motor Co.*, 119 Cal. App. 3d 757, 174 Cal. Rptr. 348 (1981), involved litigation of the claim of a 13-year-old boy, irreparably deformed by burns suffered in a car accident in which the Ford Pinto he was traveling in was hit from behind and exploded.

The evidence showed that in 1968 Ford decided to move quickly to produce an inexpensive subcompact car. Since this was a "rush project," "styling preceded engineering and dictated engineering design to a greater degree than usual." 119 Cal. App. 3d at 774. Due to engineering deficiencies, the car failed Ford's "fuel integrity" tests, designed to ensure compliance with a proposed federal regulation requiring all cars manufactured in 1972 "to be able to withstand a 20-mile-per-hour fixed barrier impact without significant fuel spillage." However, these tests were not mandated by law at the time they were administered by Ford.

Ford did not respond to these design deficiencies although "the standard of care for engineers in the industry [upon failure of such a test] was to redesign and retest" the prototype. Moreover, there were a number of inexpensive (i.e., between $2 and $16 per car) measures that would have "enhanced the integrity of the fuel tank system" that were not taken. Instead, the entire Ford corporate structure approved the car, and it entered the market despite Ford's knowledge of the defects.

The jury awarded the plaintiff-child $2,516,000 compensatory damages and $125 million punitive damages. The plaintiff-driver of the car received $559,680 compensatory damages. As a condition of a denial of Ford's motion for a retrial, the child was required to remit all but $3.5 million of his punitive award.

A number of interesting issues are raised by these facts. For example, what if the test Ford conducted was federally mandated rather than permissive and Ford and its executives were then amenable to federal prosecution? If Ford had made considerable efforts to disclaim any claims of safety regarding the car, would Ford's disclaimer be effective? Finally, how does one calculate punitive damages? What factors are relevant (human suffering, corporate indifference, economic modeling suggesting the mistake was a benign miscalculation rather than a deliberate disregard of established facts)? Can the trial judge's reduction of the jury's $125 million punitive damage award, as a condition of denying a retrial, be justified?

3. *Punitive Damages in Legal and Economic Theory.* Many courts base their opposition to punitive damages for breach of contract on an economic analysis.[13] In *Thyssen, Inc. v. S.S. Fortune Star*, 777 F.2d 57, 62 (2d Cir. 1985), the court explained its rejection of punitive damages for a breach of contract:

> A[n] explanation, offered by economists, is the notion that breaches of contract that are in fact efficient and wealth-enhancing should be encouraged, and that such "efficient breaches" occur when the breaching party will still profit after compensating the other party for its "expectation interest." The addition of punitive damages to traditional contract remedies would prevent many such beneficial actions from being taken.

Many law and economics scholars have debated this position.[14] Consider Professor Cooter's conclusion in *Economic Analysis of Punitive Damages*, 56 S. Cal. L. Rev. 79, 79–80 (1982):

> For most potential injurers, it is far cheaper to comply with the law than risk liability, so noncompliance will usually be unintentional. If fault is unintentional, then imposing punitive damages in addition to compensatory damages is both unnecessary for deterrence and undeserved as punishment. However, there may be a small group of unusual persons who derive illicit pleasure from noncompliance or incur exceptional costs from compliance. Such people may cross the threshold of fault intentionally and, once crossed, it usually pays them to cross it a long way. The situation is analogous to the historical conflict between France and Germany in which armies did not cross the Rhine merely to occupy the far bank. This fact provides a behavioral test for intentionality: Intentional fault is usually aggravated and constitutes gross negligence, willful and wanton disregard for others, and the like. Three policy conclusions follow from this analysis: (1) punitive damages should be restricted to intentional faults; (2) a

---

[13] For discussion of the merits of punitive damages based on corrective justice theory, see Curtis Bridgeman, *Corrective Justice in Contract Law: Is There a Case for Punitive Damages?*, 56 Vand. L. Rev. 237 (2003); Ernest J. Weinrib, *Punishment and Disgorgement as Contract Remedies*, 78 Chi.-Kent L. Rev. 55 (2003).

[14] For a review of the economic arguments and an efficiency analysis of damages set above, below, and equal to expectancy, see Aaron S. Edlin & Alan Schwartz, *Optimal Penalties in Contracts*, 78 Chi.-Kent L. Rev. 33 (2003).

criterion for identifying intentional fault is that it is gross or repeated; and (3) punitive damages should be computed to offset the injurer's illicit pleasure from noncompliance or exceptional cost of compliance.

Professor Dodge, on the other hand, believes that punitive damages for contract breaches would be the most efficient default rule:

> Efficiency, however, supports a very different rule from the one most courts employ — a rule allowing punitive damages for any willful breach of contract. At a minimum, courts concerned with efficiency should permit the recovery of punitive damages on a showing that the breach was opportunistic. Opportunistic breaches by definition do not increase societal wealth. They have "no economic justification and ought simply to be deterred."
>
> Efficiency also supports extending liability for punitive damages beyond opportunistic breaches to those that are, in theory, "efficient." This Article argue[s] that the threat of punitive damages will not require inefficient performance but will simply require the promisor to negotiate with the promisee for a release from her contractual obligations. Whether such negotiations are more efficient than allowing the promisor to breach and pay damages turns on a comparison of the costs of negotiation and the costs of litigation. This Article has shown that the transaction costs of negotiation, while not negligible, are generally lower than the assessment costs of litigation. Litigation . . . involves other costs that need not be incurred in negotiations, such as the cost of hiring lawyers, the costs of informing the court, and the error costs of misdetermining damages.
>
> Nor will punitive damages increase the amount of litigation or undermine the stability of contractual relations as many have feared. Such arguments ignore the fact that the threat of punitive damages for willful breach will decrease the number of breaches. Fewer breaches should mean less litigation as well as greater stability and predictability in contracts. Allowing punitive damages for willful breaches of contract is the best way to encourage negotiations by the parties and to reduce the number of occasions on which damages of any sort need be awarded.

William Dodge, *The Case for Punitive Damages*, 48 DUKE L.J. 629, 698 (1999).

Professor Dodge appears to argue for punitive damages any time the breach is deliberate or "advertent." How would he deal with a breach that was motivated by the promisor's "cry for help" — requesting the promisee's assistance in salvaging a broken contract so as to minimize losses? Does he consider the "activity level" effect of a punitive damages award on a promisor's willingness to make the promise in the first place? What about the moral hazard risk that a promisee will be tempted to induce breach so as to capture the monetary award of punitive damages?

4. *Are Punitive Damages Unconstitutional?* Some defendants, facing large punitive damage awards for tortious breach of contract, have claimed that such punitive awards violate the due process clause of the Constitution. Though the Supreme Court has held that judges must be able to review punitive awards for violations of due process, see *Honda Motor Co. v. Oberg*, 512 U.S. 415 (1994), a due process limitation on the amount of punitive recoveries remains unclear. For instance, in *TXO Prod. Corp. v. Alliance Res. Corp.*, 509 U.S. 443 (1993), the Court ruled that a punitive award 526 times as large as actual damages was constitutional. The Court concluded by acknowledging that "[t]he punitive damages award in this case is certainly large, but in light of the amount of money potentially at stake, the bad faith of petitioner, the fact that the scheme employed in this case was part of a larger pattern of fraud, trickery and deceit, and petitioner's wealth, we are not persuaded that the award was so 'grossly excessive' as to be beyond the power of the State to allow." *Id.* at 462 (footnotes omitted).

Compare *TXO Production Corp* to *State Farm Mut. Auto. Ins. Co. v. Campbell*, 538 U.S. 408 (2003), where the plaintiff sued State Farm Insurance for misrepresenting his liability from an automobile accident and was subsequently awarded $1 million in compensatory damages and $145 million in punitive damages by a jury. The Supreme Court reversed and remanded citing three guideposts: (1) the degree of reprehensibility of the defendant's misconduct, (2) the disparity between the actual or potential harm suffered by the plaintiff and the punitive damages award, and (3) the difference between the punitive damages awarded by the jury and the civil penalties authorized or imposed in comparable cases.

Since *State Farm*, the Court has done little to clear the muddy waters surrounding the constitutionality of punitive damages. In *Phillip Morris USA v. Williams*, 549 U.S. 346 (2007), Williams — the widow of a heavy cigarette smoker who died of lung cancer — brought a state lawsuit against the cigarette manufacturer for negligence and deceit. After a jury awarded Williams $75 million in punitive damages, the Oregon Supreme Court reduced the award to $32 million. A divided Supreme Court vacated the award. The Court held that the award was based on harm done to people that were not parties to the litigation, and that awarding punitive damages on this basis was a due process violation. Still, the Court explained that harm done to nonparties could be a factor in determining the reprehensibility of a defendant's misconduct. Dissenting, Justice Thomas found scant comfort in the distinction. "Today's opinion proves once again that this Court's punitive damages jurisprudence is 'insusceptible of principled application.'" *Id.* at 361 (internal citations omitted).

B.   SPECIAL PROBLEMS IN MEASURING EXPECTANCY

The preceding section has confirmed the centrality of the basic compensation principle of contract damages. As we have seen, the general default is to measure compensation by awarding expectation damages rather than specific performance. Recall from Chapter 1 the foundational contract law principle that in order for promises to be sufficiently reliable the promisor must either perform her promise or, if the promise is breached, put the promisee in the same position she would have occupied had the promise been performed — i.e., the expectancy measure. In measuring expectation damages, a court must know what position the promisee occupies following the breach of contract *and* what position the promise would have occupied had the promise been performed. In contracts for the sale of goods, the parties' expectations are often objectively verifiable, established by proof of market prices at the time performance was due. In this section we analyze fact patterns in the sale of goods where determining the full performance position has been particularly problematic. In the cases that follow, information necessary for measuring a party's expectancy may be internal to the promisee, and thus may not be verifiable to a court through evidence of an external objective standard such as market values. As you consider these cases, ask what costs and problems of proof each party faces when seeking to verify its expectancy to a court.

[1] Lost Volume Sellers

In the ordinary situation, market-based damages, whether resale under UCC § 2-706 or the contract/market price differential under UCC § 2-708(1), should provide a seller of market-traded goods with an accurate measure of the lost expectancy caused by a buyer's breach (together, of course, with any incidental expenses and costs associated with the breach as provided in UCC § 2-710). But, what if a seller wishes to argue that, while it resold the contract goods to a second buyer, it had the *capacity* to satisfy both contracts — that is, to have supplied both the breaching buyer and the resale buyer with the contract goods. Thus, argues Seller, "the contract/market differential does not make me whole in this case as I could have earned two profits on two sales and, owing the breach, I was only able to earn one profit (on the sale to the second buyer)." In order to be made whole in this "lost volume" situation, Seller claims the right to recover the "lost" profit on the breached contract with Buyer. Not only is this argument plausible on its face, but, if you read UCC § 2-708(2), the Code appears to endorse just such a recovery by Seller. But, in point of fact, determining the market conditions under which a lost profits claim is properly available to a seller has proven vexing to both courts and commentators. Consider, for example, the following cases and commentary.

R.E. DAVIS CHEMICAL CORP. v. DIASONICS, INC.
United States Court of Appeals, Seventh Circuit
826 F.2d 678 (1987)

CUDAHY, J.

Diasonics, Inc. appeals from the orders of the district court denying its motion for summary judgment and granting R.E. Davis Chemical Corp.'s summary judgment motion. Diasonics also appeals from the order dismissing its third- party complaint against Dr. Glen D. Dobbin and Dr. Galdino Valvassori. We affirm the dismissal of the third-party complaint, reverse the grant of summary judgment in favor of Davis and remand for further proceedings.

I.

Diasonics is a California corporation engaged in the business of manufacturing and selling medical diagnostic equipment. Davis is an Illinois corporation that contracted to purchase a piece of medical diagnostic equipment from Diasonics. On or about February 23, 1984, Davis and Diasonics entered into a written contract under which Davis agreed to purchase the equipment. Pursuant to this agreement, Davis paid Diasonics a $300,000 deposit on February 29, 1984. Prior to entering into its agreement with Diasonics, Davis had contracted with Dobbin and Valvassori to establish a medical facility where the equipment was to be used. Dobbin and Valvassori subsequently breached their contract with Davis. Davis then breached its contract with Diasonics; it refused to take delivery of the equipment or to pay the balance due under the agreement. Diasonics later resold the equipment to a third party for the same price at which it was to be sold to Davis.

Davis sued Diasonics, asking for restitution of its $300,000 down payment under section 2-718(2) of the Uniform Commercial Code (the "UCC" or the "Code"). Diasonics counterclaimed. Diasonics did not deny that Davis was entitled to recover its $300,000 deposit less $500 as provided in section 2-718(2)(b). However, Diasonics claimed that it was entitled to an offset under section 2-718(3). Diasonics alleged that it was a "lost volume seller," and, as such, it lost the profit from one sale when Davis breached its contract. Diasonics' position was that, in order to be put in as good a position as it would have been in had Davis performed, it was entitled to recover its lost profit on its contract with Davis under section 2-708(2) of the UCC.

[The court holds that UCC § 2-708 is the proper section to be applied.]

Concluding that Diasonics is entitled to seek damages under 2-708, however, does not automatically result in Diasonics being awarded its lost profit. Two different measures of damages are provided in 2-708. [footnote omitted]. Subsection 2-708(1) provides for a measure of damages calculated by subtracting the market price at the time and place for tender from the contract price. [footnote omitted]. The profit measure of damages, for which Diasonics is asking, is contained in 2-708(2). However, one applies 2-708(2) only if "the measure of damages provided in subsection (1) is inadequate to put the seller in as good a position as performance would have done. . . ." 2-708(2) (1985). Diasonics claims that 2-708(1) does not provide an adequate measure of damages when the seller is a lost volume seller. To understand Diasonics' argument, we need to define the concept of the lost volume seller. Those cases that have addressed this issue have defined a lost volume seller as one that has a predictable and finite number of customers and that has the capacity either to sell to all new buyers r to make the one additional sale represented by the resale after the breach. According to a number of courts and commentators, if the seller would have made the sale represented by the resale whether or not the breach occurred, damages measured by the difference between the contract price and market price cannot put the lost volume seller in as good a position as it would have been in had the buyer performed. The breach effectively cost the seller a "profit," and the seller can only be made whole by awarding it damages in the amount of its "lost profit" under 2-708(2).

We agree with Diasonics' position that, under some circumstances, the measure of damages provided under 2-708(1) will not put a reselling seller in as good a position as it would have been in had the buyer performed because the breach resulted in the seller losing sales volume. However, we disagree with the definition of "lost volume seller" adopted by other courts. Courts awarding lost profits to a lost volume seller have focused on whether the seller had the capacity to supply the breached units in addition to what it actually sold. In reality, however, the relevant questions include, not only whether the seller could have produced the breached units in addition to its actual volume, but also whether it would have been profitable for the seller to produce both units. Charles J. Goetz & Robert E. Scott, *Measuring*

Sellers' Damages: The Lost- Profits Puzzle, 31 Stan. L. Rev. 323, 332-33, 346-47 (1979). As one commentator has noted, under "the economic law of diminishing returns or increasing marginal costs[,] . . . as a seller's volume increases, then a point will inevitably be reached where the cost of selling each additional item diminishes the incremental return to the seller and eventually makes it entirely unprofitable to conclude the next sale." Shanker, *supra* p. 7 n. 6, at 705. Thus, under some conditions, awarding a lost volume seller its presumed lost profit will result in overcompensating the seller, and 2-708(2) would not take effect because the damage formula provided in 2-708(1) does place the seller in as good a position as if the buyer had performed. Therefore, on remand, Diasonics must establish, not only that it had the capacity to produce the breached unit in addition to the unit resold, but also that it would have been profitable for it to have produced and sold both. Diasonics carries the burden of establishing these facts because the burden of proof is generally on the party claiming injury to establish the amount of its damages; especially in a case such as this, the plaintiff has easiest access to the relevant data. *Finance America Commercial Corp. v. Econo Coach, Inc.*, 454 N.E.2d 1127, 1131 (2d Dist.1983) ("A party seeking to recover has the burden not only to establish that he sustained damages but also to establish a reasonable basis for computation of those damages."); *see also Snyder*, 38 Md.App. at 158-59 & n. 7, 380 A.2d at 627 & n. 7.[15]

One final problem with awarding a lost volume seller its lost profits was raised by the district court. This problem stems from the formulation of the measure of damages provided under 2-708(2) which is "the profit (including reasonable overhead) which the seller would have made from full performance by the buyer, together with any incidental damages provided in this Article (Section 2-710), due allowance for costs reasonably incurred and due credit for payments or *proceeds of resale*." UCC 2-708(2) (1985) (emphasis added). The literal language of 2-708(2) requires that the proceeds from resale be credited against the amount of damages awarded which, in most cases, would result in the seller recovering nominal damages. In those cases in which the lost volume seller was awarded its lost profit as damages, the courts have circumvented this problem by concluding that this language only applies to proceeds realized from the resale of uncompleted goods for scrap. . . . Although neither the text of 2-708(2) nor the official comments limit its application to resale of goods for scrap, there is evidence that the drafters of 2-708 seemed to have had this more limited application in mind when they proposed amending 2-708 to include the phrase "due credit for payments or proceeds of resale." We conclude that the Illinois Supreme Court would adopt this more restrictive interpretation of this phrase rendering it inapplicable to this case.

We therefore reverse the grant of summary judgment in favor of Davis and remand with instructions that the district court calculate Diasonics' damages under 2-708(2) if Diasonics can establish, not only that it had the capacity to make the sale to Davis as well as the sale to the resale buyer, but also that it would have been profitable for it to make both sales. Of course, Diasonics, in addition, must show that

---

[15] [14] As some commentators have pointed out, the cost of calculating a loss of profit may be very high. Charles J. Goetz & Robert E. Scott, *supra*, at 353 ("the complexity of the lost-volume problem suggests that the information costs of exposing an overcompensatory rule are relatively high").

it probably would have made the second sale absent the breach. [. . .]

Accordingly, we affirm the district court's dismissal of the third-party complaint, reverse the grant of summary judgment in favor of Davis and remand for further proceedings consistent with this opinion.

RODRIGUEZ v. LEARJET, INC.
Court of Appeals of Kansas
24 Kan. App. 2d 461, 946 P.2d 1010 (1997)

MARQUARDT, J.:

Miguel A. Diaz Rodriguez (Diaz) appeals from the district court's decision that a liquidated damages clause in his contract with Learjet, Inc., (Learjet) was reasonable and enforceable.

On August 21, 1992, Diaz executed a contract with Learjet to purchase a model 60 jet aircraft. The contract called for a $250,000 deposit to be made upon execution of the contract; a $750,000 payment to be made on September 18, 1992; a $1,000,000 payment to be made 180 days before the delivery date of July 30, 1993; and the balance of the purchase price to be paid upon delivery.

Diaz paid Learjet $250,000 on the day that he executed the contract, but made no other payment.

At the time of the purchase, Diaz worked for Televisa. Diaz was purchasing the aircraft at the request of Alejandro Burillo, his supervisor at Televisa. Near the end of September 1992, Burillo told Diaz that he no longer wanted the aircraft. Diaz testified that he called Alberto Castaneda at Learjet and told him that he was not going to buy the aircraft and that he wanted Learjet to return his $250,000 deposit.

On September 30, 1992, Castaneda sent Diaz a fax, requesting payment. On October 6, 1992, Castaneda wrote Diaz a letter, which stated, in part: "Unless we receive payment from you or your company by October 9, 1992, [Learjet, Inc.,] will consider this agreement terminated and will retain all payments as liquidation damages in accordance with Paragraph C . . . of Section VII . . . of said agreement." By letter dated October 20, 1992, Learjet informed Diaz that it considered their contract terminated and that the $250,000 deposit was being retained as liquidated damages.

The contract provides, in part:

> "Learjet may terminate this Agreement as a result of the Buyer's . . . failure to make any progress payment when due. . . . If this Agreement is terminated by Learjet for any reason stipulated in the previous sentence Learjet shall retain all payments theretofore made by the Buyer as liquidated damages and not as a penalty and the parties shall thenceforth be released from all further obligations hereunder. Such damages include, but are not limited to, loss of profit on this sale, direct and indirect costs incurred as a result of disruption in production, training expense advance and selling expenses in effecting resale of the Airplane."

After Diaz had breached the parties' contract, Circus Circus Enterprises, Inc., (Circus) contracted with Learjet to buy the aircraft. Circus requested that changes be made to the aircraft, which cost $1,326. Learjet realized a $1,887,464 profit on the sale of the aircraft to Circus, which was a larger profit than Learjet had originally budgeted.

Diaz filed suit against Learjet, seeking to recover the $250,000 deposit. Diaz' petition alleged, in part, that the actual amount of Learjet's liquidated damages was not $250,000 and that Learjet's retention of the $250,000 deposit was unreasonable and an unenforceable penalty. . . .

Following the presentation of evidence, the district court found that Learjet was a lost volume seller and that its actual damages included lost profits. The district court held that $250,000 in liquidated damages was reasonable and upheld the liquidated damages clause.

Diaz argues that the district court erred in holding that the liquidated damages clause was reasonable and enforceable. Diaz reasons that the liquidated damages clause was unreasonably large and, therefore, void as a penalty.

This court [has] paraphrased the three criteria for measuring the reasonableness of a liquidated damages clause provided in UCC 2-718: "(1) anticipated or actual harm caused by breach; (2) difficulty of proving loss; and (3) difficulty of obtaining an adequate remedy."

A liquidated damages clause that "fixes damages in an amount grossly dispro-portionate to the harm actually sustained or likely to be sustained" is considered a penalty and will not be enforced by the courts. . . . If a liquidated damages clause is invalidated as a penalty, then the nonbreaching party may recover actual damages instead. The burden of proving that a liquidated damages clause is unenforceable rests with the party challenging its enforcement.

Diaz' challenge to the reasonableness of the liquidated damages clause focuses on the first factor of UCC 2-718- the anticipated or actual harm caused by the breach. The question of whether a seller qualifies as a lost volume seller is relevant when evaluating whether a liquidated damages clause is reasonable in light of the anticipated or actual harm caused by the breach.

Diaz argues that the district court erred in concluding that Learjet qualifies as a lost volume seller. As a lost volume seller, Learjet's actual damages would include lost profits, notwithstanding that Circus purchased the aircraft which Diaz had contracted to buy and that Learjet made a profit on the Circus sale. The two contracts contained identical base prices, and both contracts had escalation clauses. The evidence indicates that the lost profit from the Diaz contract would have been approximately $1.8 million.

Courts have "unanimously" held that a lost volume seller can recover lost profits under § 2-708(2) of the Uniform Commercial Code.. . . . In *Jetz Serv. Co. v. Salina Properties*, 19 Kan. App. 2d at 148, this court explained:

"The 'lost volume seller' measure of damages 'refers to the lost volume of business the non-breaching seller incurs on buyer's breach. When the seller resells the entity he expected to sell to the original buyer, he usually deprives himself of something of value — the sale to a new buyer of another similar entity.' (*Snyder v. Herbert Greenbaum & Assoc.*, 38 Md. App. 144, 154 n. 3, 380 A.2d 618 (1977))."

Similarly, Restatement (Second) of Contracts § 350, Comment d (1979) notes that if a seller would have entered into both transactions but for the breach, then the seller has lost volume as a result of the breach. Thus, lost profits are awarded to a lost volume seller, notwithstanding that the seller resells the item that a buyer contracted to buy, based on the principle that the seller was deprived of an additional sale and the corresponding profit by the buyer's breach.

Awarding lost profits to a lost volume seller serves the general principle that the purpose of awarding damages is to make a party whole by restoring the nonbreaching party to the position that party occupied prior to the breach- to place a seller in as good a position as if a buyer had performed. UCC 1-106.

The *Jetz* court held that lost volume status is available to businesses providing services and identified the following evidence as sufficient to affirm the trial court's finding that the plaintiff was a lost volume lessor:

> "[J]etz Service is in the business of supplying coin-operated laundry equipment; it has several warehouses in which it has available for lease about 1,500 used washers and dryers; it continually looks for new locations in which to install laundry equipment; it would have been able to fulfill the Kansas City lease without using the machines from Salina Properties; and it is uncontroverted Jetz Service would have been able to enter into both transactions irrespective of the breach by Salina Properties." 19 Kan. App. 2d at 152,.

In *Diasonics*, 826 F.2d at 685, the court held that in order to qualify as a lost volume seller and recover for lost profits, a seller must establish three factors: (1) that it possessed the capacity to make an additional sale, (2) that it would have been profitable for it to make an additional sale, and (3) that it probably would have made an additional sale absent the buyer's breach.

Applying the more specific criteria established in *Diasonics*, 826 F.2d at 684-85, there is adequate evidence to support the district court's finding. The master scheduler for Learjet testified that Learjet was operating at 60 percent capacity during the relevant time period and that Learjet was able to accelerate its production schedule to produce more of the model 60 planes in any given year. Learjet also presented testimony about its accounting system which indicated that an additional sale would have been profitable to Learjet. Learjet's profit from the Circus transaction and the similarity between the Diaz contract price and the Circus contract price also indicate that the additional sale would have been profitable.

We agree with the district court that Learjet qualifies as a lost volume seller and that the $250,000 in liquidated damages was reasonable in light of the anticipated or actual harm caused by the breach. See 2-718(2).

Affirmed.

NOTES

1. *Questions on* **Rodriguez v. Learjet.** Learjet argued that it was a lost volume seller in order to defend its retention of the $250,000 progress payment against Diaz's argument that the payment was void as a penalty. But recall that Learjet resold the plane to another customer for a "profit" of $1,887,464. Wouldn't it have been a better strategy for Learjet to concede that the liquidated damages clauses was unenforceable and instead sue for $1,887,464 lost volume damages under § 2-708(2)? Professor Goldberg suggests that Learjet was being farsighted: it was "more concerned about establishing the legality of its standard system of progress payments than about making a one time killing"[16] Do you find that explanation more plausible than the alternative: bad lawyering?

2. *Replacement Sales and Market Assumptions.* Many recent lost volume decisions under UCC § 2-708(2) have assumed that the resale was not a replacement for the breached contract because the seller had an ability to supply the contract goods to any potential buyer. This assumption is flawed, however, because mere ability to supply additional volume in no way implies that such volume could have been supplied profitably. Even where the seller's ability to expand output seemed virtually unbounded, a combination of cost and revenue constraints would necessarily limit this ability. Therefore, in order to make a valid lost volume claim the seller must show not only that he *could* have made the subsequent sale absent the buyer's breach, but that he *would* have done so profitably. If sales to other buyers were unaffected by the breach, a lost volume claim might be justified so long as profitable volume declined by the full amount of the breach. Conversely, the seller would have lost no volume if the breach altered its cost and demand conditions so that supplying other buyers suddenly became profitable.

In any particular case, therefore, the extent to which the resale contract does or does not replace the breached contract presents a difficult empirical question. Courts are often left to make assumptions one way or the other without access to the key economic information. It is puzzling, however, that courts (and Code commentators) who are often sensitive to consumer interests would assume (based only on evidence that a merchant has the capacity to make both sales) that there is no replacement and thus a merchant seller is entitled to an entire lost profit. Isn't it equally plausible in the absence of evidence to assume that both sales would not have been made and thus the breaching consumer should be permitted to "cancel" and only pay contract/market damages (plus any incidental expenses associated with the costs of reselling the goods). Cancellation rights seem common in certain settings. Rarely do clothing retailers object to a return of an unwanted shirt or tie or dress. What accounts for the different outcomes in retail sales of expensive consumer products such as cars and boats?[17]

---

[16] VICTOR GOLDBERG, FRAMING CONTRACT LAW: AN ECONOMIC PERSPECTIVE 241–42 (2007).

[17] For more detailed analyses of the lost volume problem arguing that lost profits awards are too readily granted by courts, see Robert E. Scott, *The Case for Market Damages: Revisiting the Lost Profits Puzzle*, 57 U. CHI. L. REV. 1155 (1990), and Charles J. Goetz & Robert E. Scott, *Measuring Sellers' Damages: The Lost-Profits Puzzle*, 31 STAN. L. REV. 323 (1979). For other economic-based arguments evaluating the award of lost profits for lost volume sellers, see Alan Schwartz, *Price Discrimination with Contract Terms: The Lost-Volume Problem*, 12 AM. L. & ECON. REV. 394 (2010);

3. *Personal Service Contracts and Lost Volume Sellers.* Can a wrongfully terminated employee accept a new and comparable position, and then claim status as a lost volume seller to recover "lost profits" from her first job? Generally, courts hold that an employee operating under a personal services contract cannot be classified as a lost volume seller. For an interesting example, consider *In re WorldCom, Inc.*, 361 B.R. 675 (Bankr. S.D.N.Y. 2007). In 1995, basketball star Michael Jordan entered into an endorsement agreement with WorldCom. The agreement granted WorldCom the non-exclusive right to use Jordan's likeness for ten years to promote their telecommunications products. In 2002, however, World-Com declared bankruptcy. Seeking a larger damages award, Jordan argued that he was a "lost volume seller." According to Jordan, since he could have entered other endorsement agreements along with WorldCom's, any additional endorsement would not have acted as a replacement to the WorldCom deal. The bankruptcy court rejected his argument:

> In his arguments, Jordan focuses primarily on his *capacity* to enter subsequent agreements, arguing that the loss of MCI's sixteen-hour annual time commitment hardly affected his ability to perform additional endorsement services. On this prong alone, Jordan likely would be considered a lost volume seller of endorsement services because he had sufficient time to do multiple endorsements. Although he does not have the "infinite capacity" that some cases discuss, a services provider does not need unlimited capacity but must have the requisite capacity and intent to perform under multiple contracts at the same time. . . .
>
> Contrary to Jordan's analysis, courts do not focus solely on the seller's capacity. The seller claiming lost volume status must also demonstrate that it *would* have entered into subsequent transactions. . . . Jordan has not shown he could and *would have* entered into a subsequent agreement. Rather, the evidence shows that Jordan did not have the "subjective intent" to take on additional endorsements. *See Ullman–Briggs*, 754 F. Supp. at 1008. The testimony from Jordan's representatives establishes that although Jordan's popularity enabled him to obtain additional product endorsements in 2003, Jordan desired to scale back his level of endorsements. . . . Jordan had implemented a strategy of not accepting new endorsements because of a belief that new deals would jeopardize his ability to achieve his primary goal of National Basketball Association ("NBA") franchise ownership."

Id. at 687.

4. *Lost Volume Sellers and the Duty to Mitigate.* Another unusual case involving the theory of "lost volume sales" in the context of a dispute about mitigation of damages is *In re 375 Park Ave. Assocs.*, 182 B.R. 690 (Bankr. S.D.N.Y. 1995). 375 Park Avenue had committed to donating $3 million dollars to construct the National Holocaust Museum in Washington, D.C., in exchange for which they were to receive a highly prized donor recognition in the museum. 375 Park Avenue

---

Victor Goldberg, *An Economic Analysis of the Lost-Volume Retail Seller*, 57 S. Cal. L. Rev. 283 (1984); and Robert Cooter & Melvin A. Eisenberg, *Damages for Breach of Contract*, 73 Cal. L. Rev. 1432 (1985).

subsequently went broke and defaulted on their promise to the museum organizers, who sued them in bankruptcy court and requested summary judgment from the court. In its defense, 375 Park Avenue claimed any damages resulting from their breach should be reduced by the museum's failure to mitigate, since, they contended, finding another $3 million donor would have been relatively simple. The museum organizers responded with a rather original defense to 375's claim that they had failed to mitigate:

> [T]he Council argues that it could not effectively mitigate the loss of [375's] $3 million contribution because had the Council found another donor, it could have accepted both pledges. In this way, the Council likens itself to a lost volume seller, a well settled exception to the duty to mitigate. Under the lost volume seller doctrine, even though the seller sold the goods that the breaching buyer was entitled to purchase, the seller is entitled to the benefit of the both [sic] bargains because it would have made both sales had the buyer not breached. . . . In support of its lost volume seller argument, the Council states that "anyone who would contribute $3 million for that particular honor [the naming of the Archives] would have made a comparable payment for another honorarium at the Museum. The Council has more honorariums than it has contributors."

Id. at 697.

The bankruptcy court decided not to issue a final ruling on the matter in this initial action, rejecting the museum's summary judgment motion. The court called for further evidence at trial on the question of the museum's possible status as a lost volume seller and their duty to mitigate damages. Do you think the Holocaust Museum's unlimited supply of "naming opportunities" and other forms of donor recognition should qualify it as a lost volume seller? Is this a potential misapplication of the theory, or a justified expansion?

Essay: Trying to Justify the Lost-Profits Remedy

In theory, the remedies of market damages and lost profits are simply alternative ways of measuring the same economic loss: both attempt to give the seller its lost profit from the breached contract. Suppose, for example, that following the buyer's breach a seller resells the contract goods on the market. Market damages award the seller the difference between the contract and resale prices plus the incidental costs of making the resale. When added to the revenue the seller received from the resale (i.e., the resale price), market damages provide the seller with the same net revenue it would have had if the buyer had not breached. Thus, the seller will end up with the same profit it would have made had the buyer not breached (resale price plus market damages minus the seller's costs of supplying the good and minus the savings from not concluding the sale to the breaching buyer). Alternatively, the seller might seek a lost profits award to recover the same amount. Here instead of reselling the good, or estimating its resale value, the seller attempts to prove the amount of profit it would have made on the contract that the buyer breached. This requires the seller to prove the total costs it would have incurred had buyer not breached. The seller will then be entitled to the difference between the contract price and those costs (i.e., its lost profit).

Although both market damages and lost profits attempt to give the seller its lost profit (i.e., its expectation interest), contract law does not ordinarily allow the seller to recover its lost profits directly because profits are more difficult to measure accurately than market damages. Unlike a lost profits award, market damages do not require the seller to prove any of its costs other than its incidental expenses from reselling the good. If the seller resells the good, market damages can be measured simply by subtracting the actual resale price from the contract price and adding incidental damages. Thus, the principal source of undercompensation in a market damage award stems from the problem of accurately measuring the seller's incidental damages. A lost profit remedy, however, requires the seller to prove its costs of acquiring and selling the good, and the buyer to prove the costs the seller saved by not having to deliver the good. Both of these costs are systematically more difficult to verify than the seller's incidental resale expenses and the market price. Typically, courts have difficulty assessing the costs the seller saved by not having to deliver the good to the buyer and therefore underestimate those savings. Lost profits awards thus typically overcompensate the seller by failing to reduce the award by the total costs seller saved because of the breach.

The Code and the common law therefore limit the seller to market damages in ordinary circumstances. A lost profits award is available only if the seller can show that only a lost profits award, and not market damages, can fully compensate it for the loss caused by the breach. In theory, the seller can do this by demonstrating that it is a "lost volume" seller. Like any seller, a volume seller might be able respond to the buyer's breach by reselling the good to another buyer. But when a volume seller makes a resale it does not replace the breached sale. Thus, when a buyer breaches a contract with a volume seller, it reduces the total volume of goods sold by that seller and the seller loses the profit it would have made from the additional sale. In such a case, market damages fail to provide appropriate compensation to the seller. In this case, the argument goes, a lost profits award is the only means available for fully compensating the lost volume seller.

Contracts scholarship has identified two difficulties with the lost volume justification for awarding a seller lost profits instead of market damages. First, scholars have argued that basic principles of economics prove that many so-called "volume" sellers face constraints that, in effect, limit them to selling a fixed supply of goods. Even if goods are in theory infinite in supply, these sellers' marginal costs increase (and/or marginal revenues decrease) with additional sales. Therefore, a volume seller must be able to show that it would have made the resale in addition to the sale it made to the breaching buyer *and would have captured the full resulting profit.* In that case, the seller would be entitled to its lost profits. But the second point scholars have made is that even if the seller hasn't reached the quantity beyond which it is unprofitable to sell more goods, it will, for all practical purposes, rarely be true that a seller can prove that it would have made the sales both to the breaching buyer *and* to the buyer to whom it resold the goods. This is because a buyer that regrets its contract will then also resell the goods (e.g., by simply assigning its sales contract) to another buyer who otherwise might have purchased the good from the seller. In other words, if buyers who purchase from volume sellers and then regret their purchase were required to pay lost profits awards, rather than market damages, they would respond by not breaching and instead taking delivery of the goods and reselling them to another buyer, thereby depriving the seller of an additional sale. The seller can't prevent its own buyers from reselling and therefore can't prove that the buyers to whom it resold goods would have bought the good from the seller even if the buyer hadn't breached. In short, while the volume seller does suffer some loss in attempting to conclude a sale with the breaching buyer, there is little reason to believe that this loss will equal the entire expected profits from the breached contract.

What the volume seller *should* recover is an award of incidental damages under UCC § 2-710 equal to *all of* the incurred selling costs attributable to the breached contract. Unfortunately, courts have tended to limit incidental damages to the seller's *post-breach* reliance costs. As a consequence, *pre-breach* selling costs (e.g., advertising, promotion and sales staff) are generally not recoverable as incidental damages even when breach causes them to increase. Under these circumstances, a traditional market damages recovery will not fully protect the seller's expectancy.[18]

The fact that the standard ways of measuring damages (whether market damages or lost profits) will tend to either under-compensate or over-compensate a volume seller clarifies the function of the default damage rule in contracts with volume sellers. Market damages and lost profits provide alternative ways of allocating the risk of cancellation by the buyer. To see how, suppose a seller decides to market a product for which many consumers are likely to change their minds before delivery. The seller can choose either to market the product at a higher price but with a generous cancellation policy, or at a lower price with a harsh cancellation policy, perhaps including a pre-paid non-refundable deposit. Common observation tells us that in many industries (such as soft goods), sellers offer a product that includes a free right of cancellation or return. In others, non-refundable deposits are commonplace. Thus, whether a given volume seller would have chosen to give a buyer an option to walk away from the deal and at what price the option would be offered simply cannot be determined a priori. And, in any event, the termination provision any seller chooses is unlikely to have much to do with compensating the seller for the lost sale.

Robert Scott and George Triantis argue in *Embedded Options and the Case Against Compensation in Contract Law*, 104 COLUM. L. REV. 1428 (2004), that the legal default rules governing these cancellation or termination rights should be separated from the compensation principle of contract damages. Given that merchant sellers typically draft consumer contracts, the legal rule might better impose on the seller, as the drafter of the contract, the obligation to provide explicitly for termination rights. They propose, therefore, that absent a specific agreement regarding termination rights (such as the requirement of a pre-paid non-refundable deposit), the default rule should give consumer buyers free options: the right to walk away from the executory exchange, but to specifically hold the merchant seller to the deal. This proposal requires courts to craft a set of associated rules governing the timing of the buyer's decision whether or not to exercise her option to terminate. The authors suggest that a convenient analogy exists with the

---

[18] *See, e.g., Nobs Chemical, U.S.A., Inc. v. Koppers Co.*, 616 F.2d 212, 216 (5th Cir. 1980); *Harlow & Jones, Inc. v. Advance Steel Co.*, 424 F. Supp. 770 (E.D. Mich. 1976); *see also Industrial Circuits Co. v. Terminal Communications, Inc.*, 26 N.C. App. 536, 216 S.E.2d 919 (1975).

buyer's right to reject defective goods under the UCC. Section 2-602 provides that a rejecting buyer must exercise the right of rejection within a reasonable time, cannot thereafter exercise ownership inconsistent with the seller's rights and must hold the rejected goods for the seller with reasonable care. Applying a similar standard to the terminating buyer would protect both the consumer buyer's option and the seller's interest in the underlying goods or services.

[2] Damages as to Accepted Goods

CARLSON v. RYSAVY
Supreme Court of South Dakota
262 N.W.2d 27 (1978)

MORGAN, J.

This is an action for breach of warranty against a dealer and the manufacturer of a double-wide modular home. The plaintiffs, Dale Carlson and La Vona Carlson (Carlsons), commenced the action against the dealer, Donald Rysavy, d/b/a Don's Mobile Homes (Rysavy) of Winner, South Dakota, and the manufacturer, Town & Country Mobile Homes, Inc. (Town & Country). In addition to his answer, the dealer Rysavy counterclaimed against the plaintiffs for an unpaid furniture bill in the amount of $900, and cross-claimed against the defendant Town & Country, alleging that Town & Country was statutorily liable for any costs, losses, and damages which might be recovered against defendant Rysavy, including legal expenses not to exceed $1,500. The jury returned three verdicts. The first, in favor of defendant Rysavy on the claim by the Carlsons; the second, against the defendant Town & Country, and in favor of the Carlsons, in the amount of $9,000; and the third, against the defendant Town & Country, and in favor of defendant Rysavy on his cross-claim, in the amount of $1,100. Judgment was entered on the verdicts and defendant Town & Country's motion for remittitur or new trial was denied, from which judgment and denial of motions the defendant Town & Country appeals. We affirm the judgment in favor of respondents Carlsons and reverse the judgment in favor of Rysavy on the cross-claim and remand for further proceedings.

We first examine the assignments of error raised by the defendant Town & Country with respect to the principal action as commenced by the Carlsons.

The first point argued by the appellant is that the court erred in admitting testimony as to alleged defects raised for the first time at the trial, which defects were not included in any notice given to the appellant, nor were not enumerated in the plaintiffs' complaint, nor were they found in the answers to the appellant's interrogatories. The record discloses that the purchase of the mobile home from Rysavy was made after the plaintiffs had viewed a model or pilot home constructed at the Town & Country plant at Canton, South Dakota. A similar home, with modifications not pertinent to any of the issues in this appeal, was to be delivered and set up at the plaintiffs' site at Sturgis, South Dakota. Mr. Carlson testified that he had inspected the pilot or model home with specific interest in type of siding, insulation, paneling, etc., and that he was told that the home's insulation consisted of 33/4th inch fiberglass batting, and that the roof and floor of the mobile home had sufficient insulation to meet all state specifications required for an electric heating furnace.

Upon delivery of the modular home Mr. Carlson noticed some apparent defects, which he noted on the delivery receipt returned to Town & Country, the most important of which was the fact that there were no heating ducts or tubing in the floor of the home, no hot water heater delivered, wind and water damage from transportation, and the center I-beams were bent and misshaped. Throughout the ensuing few months the Carlsons were faced with many problems. The two halves could not be bolted together due to the crooked I-beams. In response to continuous telephone calls and inquiries Town & Country finally sent a serviceman, who hired a local welder to force the I-beams together by means of C-clamps and to weld them. The serviceman failed to bring the right size heat tubes, however, he assured the plaintiffs he would return with the right size, which he never did. Mr. Carlson finally had to drive to Winner, pick up the right size, and install them himself. As time progressed and the weather became colder other problems became evident. Pipes froze, temperature in the home with the furnace running at full capacity would only reach 50/d, water leaked around the doors and the door frame, and paneling bulged. Upon the suggestion of Rysavy, the Carlsons, late in February of 1975, sent a list of twenty-one defects to Mr. Rysavy for forwarding to Town & Country. There is no dispute that this list was forwarded. In March of 1975, upon investigation, the Carlsons learned that the home was inadequately insulated under the standards for electric furnaces and accordingly hired a local contractor to insulate the home properly. During this process Mr. Carlson discovered that his modular home did not have 3/8th plywood sheeting under the siding, as the modular home they viewed in Canton did, but rather had a cardboard-type substance called Foam core. During all this period, except for dispatching the serviceman in August of 1974, appellant ignored the plaintiffs' complaints.

The requirement for notice is codified at [UCC § 2-607(3)] and requires that the buyer must, within a reasonable time after he discovers or should have discovered any breach, notify the seller of breach or be barred from any remedy.

The commentaries to the 1962 official text, comment 4 at page 167, points out that "the rule . . . is designed to defeat commercial bad faith, not to deprive a good faith consumer of his remedy." Further, "the content of the notification need merely be sufficient to let the seller know that the transaction is still troublesome and must be watched. There is no reason to require that the notification . . . must include a clear statement of all of the objections that will be relied on by the buyer."

The record discloses that the plaintiffs gave notice to Town & Country that the transaction was troublesome. We find no difficulty in holding that the notice given in this case was more than adequate, and Town & Country's utter failure to respond beyond the initial dispatch of a repairman to pull the framework back together leaves them little room to complain. Furthermore, with respect to the two items of which they particularly complained, that is, as to the floor and the roof, the record clearly shows that the condition of the rafters was newly discovered shortly prior to the trial; that counsel for Town & Country and Town & Country's expert were both present at the time it was discovered, and that Town & Country's expert was examined directly during the course of the trial regarding the matter. Town &

Country made no motion indicating surprise or asking for any continuances. We find no error in the trial court's ruling on admissibility of that evidence.

The next issue, and easily the most troublesome one, is what is the proper measure of damages?

The provisions of the Uniform Commercial Code, with respect to the buyer's remedies when he accepts the goods and does not reject or revoke his acceptance, but sues for damages because the accepted goods are not as warranted, are codified under the provisions of [UCC §§ 2-714 and 2-715]. In our opinion these have to be read as a whole. The statutory scheme, as it appears from examining all of the statutes, is that (1) where the buyer has accepted the goods and given notification he may recover damages as determined in any manner which is reasonable; (2) the measure of damages is the difference at the time and place of acceptance between the value of the goods accepted and the value they would have had if they had been as warranted, unless special circumstances show proximate damages of a different amount; and (3) in a proper case incidental and consequential damages may also be recovered.

The duality of standards between [UCC § 2-714(1)] and [UCC § 2-714(2)] is taken from precode law and presumably courts will continue to interpret the more specific rule of [UCC § 2-714(2)] as governing where applicable. Thus defects relating to the goods, their quality or their title (rather than to the manner of their delivery) will invoke the "formula" of the latter section, looking to a difference in value and not in price. There is no code definition of value application to [UCC § 2-714(2)]. The general definition of value in [UCC § 1-201(44)] obviously has no relevance here since it looks to the characteristics of an entirely different transaction.

The value criterion in [UCC § 2-714(2)] is confusing because it serves two very different functions. One use of value is to measure the utility of the defective goods received. Value also serves to define the other component in the compensation equation, the value of the goods as warranted, with which the goods as delivered are to be compared. It is noteworthy that the authors of the Uniform Code did not use market price as the measure of damages as they did in the case of buyer's damages for nondelivery or repudiation, [UCC § 2-713(1)]; or seller's damages for nonacceptance or repudiation by buyer, [UCC § 2-708(1)]. The confusion is deepened when we note that the courts and the writers continually interchange value and market value.

[UCC § 1-102(1)] provides that the [UCC] shall be liberally construed and applied to promote its underlying purposes and policies which are set out to be: (1) to simplify, clarify and modernize the law governing commercial transactions; (2) to permit the continued expansion of commercial practices through custom, usage and agreement of the parties; and (3) to make uniform the law among the various jurisdictions.

[UCC § 1-106(1)] directs that the remedies provided shall be liberally administered to the end that the aggrieved party may be put in as good a position as if the other party had fully performed. [UCC § 2-714(2)] cautions us to measure damages at the time and place for acceptance.

Town & Country contends, and it is generally held, that a useful objective measurement of the difference in value as is and as warranted is the cost of repair. However, there are many cases in which the injury will be irreparable and therefore the cost of repairs will not serve as a yardstick of the buyer's damage. In such cases the court will have to determine by some other measure the value of the goods as warranted and the value of the goods as accepted.

As the authors in White & Summers noted:

> In sum, the general application of the [UCC § 2-714(2)] formula offers a variety of difficult factual problems but few questions that are unique or legally difficult. In many cases the court can refer to the cost of repair in order to estimate the difference in value of the goods as warranted and as delivered. In other cases it will have to cast about for the usual and almost invariably unsatisfactory evidence of market value.

As this Court has recently ruled in the case of Fredrick v. Dreyer v. Falcon Coach Company, Inc., S.D., 257 N.W.2d 835, "fair market value is the usual standard upon which testimony as to damages in such cases is based." We distinguish this case from *Fredrick* because Carlson stated that, while he did not know the market value, he did testify to a substantial value of $5,000 based on the value of the appliances, which value was affirmed by his expert witness. Carlson's opinion was not a backhanded estimate, as that of Fredrick's, and the opinion evidence of his expert was more certain than that in *Fredrick*.

With respect to the value of the goods as warranted, contract price offers strong evidence of such value, although not conclusive.

Viewing the record, we hold that, while there was evidence of a considerable amount of repairs to some of the major discrepancies in construction, many others have not and cannot be adequately repaired so as to place the plaintiffs in as good a position as if Town & Country had fully performed. Therefore, the measure of damages contended for by Town & Country, the cost of repairs, will not serve as a proper yardstick of the buyers' damages, and the trial court did not err in submitting the case to the jury on the difference in value formula.

In this vein we find the Court of Appeals of Michigan holding, in a case involving a similarly inadequately constructed mobile home, that:

> This verdict and judgment does not shock this court nearly so much as the conduct of the defendants in this case. Rather, the sum of $9,000.00 is fair compensation for a life lived in fear, cold and discomfort occasioned by the calculated and deliberate inaction of these defendants breaching the warranties and leading to the plaintiffs' default in contract payments owed to the financing bank and guaranteed by the FHA.

. . . Thus, we affirm the judgment in favor of the respondents Carlsons, and against the appellant Town & Country, and we reverse the judgment in favor of the defendant Rysavy and against the appellant Town & Country and remand the same for further proceedings in accordance with our opinion.

NOTES

1. *The Structure of Sections 2-714 and 2-715.* Section 2-714 includes two damage formulae to be applied in different situations. Subsection (1), governing damages "for any non-conformity of tender," is generally understood to apply to problems not related to the quality of the merchandise, such as a damaging tardy tender. Subsection (2) is understood to apply to problems of defective merchandise which the buyer nonetheless elects to keep. This classification structure, together with § 2-715, allows the courts wide latitude in measuring damages in the case of accepted goods. Consider, for example, the following facts:

(a)   your client purchases automatic car wash equipment for $67,000,

(b)   the unit continually breaks down costing your client $35,500 in repairs,

(c)   the equipment fails to wash cars effectively, leaving customers dissatisfied,

(d)   your client's finger is badly broken due to a defect in the equipment, causing your client pain and the loss of two weeks wages, and

(e)   your client is able to resell the unit for $5,500.

The court in *Auto-Teria, Inc. v. Ahern*, 170 Ind. App. 84, 352 N.E.2d 774 (1976), granted damages on three separate bases. First, the court held that the personal injury was compensable under §§ 2-714(3) and 2-715(2)(b). Second, the court granted value-based damages under § 2-714(2), using the contract price as "competent evidence" of the equipment's value as warranted and the resale (scrap) price as the value of the equipment as accepted. Finally, the court permitted the buyers to recover for "lost profits, repairs, and costs of pacifying dissatisfied patrons" under §§ 2-714(3) and 2-715.

Suppose that a clause in the contract stated that the seller would not be liable for any consequential damages as defined in §§ 2-714(3) and 2-715. Could the buyer's attorney successfully argue that "lost profits, repairs, and costs of pacifying dissatisfied patrons" were direct damages, recoverable under § 2-714(1)?

2. *Measuring "the Difference in Value."* The *Carlson* court concluded that the value the buyer has lost because of the defect may be measured in two ways: by the cost to repair and by the diminution in value based on a comparison of the goods as tendered and the goods as warranted. In *Soo L. R. Co. v. Fruehauf Corp.*, 547 F.2d 1365 (8th Cir. 1977), the court did not limit the buyer's recovery to cost to repair since it would not have completely restored the goods to the value which they would have had if built in conformity with the contracts. The remaining diminution in value was also recoverable.

Can a plaintiff buyer who has accepted the goods ever recover more than the contract price? The answer appears to be yes. In *Chatlos Systems, Inc. v. National Cash Register Corp.*, 670 F.2d 1304 (3d Cir. 1982), the Third Circuit, applying UCC § 2-714(2), upheld an award to Chatlos of $201,826.50, despite the fact that the contract set the price at $46,020, when National Cash Register ("NCR") delivered a computer system that did not perform as warranted. According to the majority, NCR had not simply warranted a specific NCR computer model, "but an NCR computer system with specified capabilities." *Id.* at 1306. Chatlos' expert testified that building a computer with those capabilities would cost over $200,000. In coming to this number, the expert pieced together parts from various manufacturers, creating a hypothetical computer that could not be bought on the market. The dissent criticized this approach to damages:

> There are a number of major flaws in the plaintiff's attempt to prove damages in excess of the contract price. I commence with an analysis of plaintiff's basic theory. Chatlos presented its case under a theory that although, as a sophisticated purchaser, it bargained for several months before arriving at a decision on the computer system it required and the price of $46,020, it is entitled, because of the breach of warranty, to damages predicated on a considerably more expensive system. Stated another way, even if it bargained for a cheap system, i.e., one whose low cost reflects its inferior quality, because that system did not perform as bargained for, it is now entitled to damages measured by the value of a system which, although capable of performing the identical functions as the NCR 399, is of far superior quality and accordingly more expensive.
>
> The purpose of [UCC § 2-714] is to put the buyer in the same position he would have been in if there had been no breach. See UCC § 1-106(1). The remedies for a breach of warranty were intended to compensate the buyer for his loss; they were not intended to give the purchaser a windfall or treasure trove. The buyer may not receive more than it bargained for; it may not obtain the value of a superior computer system which it did not purchase even though such a system can perform all of the functions the inferior system was designed to serve. . . ."

Id. at 1309, 1310, 1312.

Do you agree with the *Chatlos* decision? Is there any principled reason why the "value as warranted" should be limited to the contract price? What if the defendant's expert testifies that a system with those specifications would only have a value of $20,000? Should that be the upper bound on the plaintiff's recovery?

3.   *Other Issues With Measuring "Value."* In *Tarter v. MonArk Boat Co.*, 430 F. Supp. 1290 (E.D. Mo. 1977), the court found that the cost of repairs ($37,000) provided a more accurate measure of the difference between the value of a boat as accepted and as warranted than did the plaintiff's testimony that the value of the boat was $80,000 as accepted and was $160,000 as warranted.

What about cases in which the cost of repairs exceeds the value of the goods as warranted? In *R. Clinton Constr. Co. v. Bryant & Reaves, Inc.*, 442 F. Supp. 838 (N.D. Miss. 1977), the court permitted the plaintiff to recover the purchase price of antifreeze which had been rendered valueless by the inclusion of a harmful chloride solution. Conversely, an Alabama court held that the "measure of damages due to injury to personal property which is a total loss after accident . . . is reasonable market value before accident, less salvage value after." *Winston Industries, Inc. v. Stuyvesant Ins. Co.*, 55 Ala. App. 525, 317 So. 2d 493 (1975).

As the cases illustrate, direct proof of market values is often unavailable. Is the contract price of the goods an acceptable surrogate for the value as warranted at the time and place of acceptance? Remember that, at best, the contract price reflects the market price for a forward contract at the date of contracting. This price represents the best estimate of what the market price at the time of acceptance is likely to be. In many cases, however, the contract price will vary unpredictably from the market price. Therefore, it seems that the aggrieved buyer should be permitted to prove that the value of the goods as warranted exceeds the contract price, thereby protecting the benefit of his bargain. Alternatively, where the defaulting seller has made a "good" bargain, § 2-714(2) should authorize a court to protect his expectancy interest as well.[19] On the other hand, was the court in *Chatlos* correct in sustaining an award based on expert testimony that a properly functioning computer system would have been worth more than four times the contract price?

4.   *Breach of Warranty of Title and § 2-714.* When a seller falsely claims title (ownership) of a good, and thus the right to sell it, does § 2-714 provide a remedy to the buyer when the real owner asserts their right to the good? Most courts have said yes. This raises an interesting problem: Buyers who lose a good through repossession by its original owners often claim the actual value of the good at acceptance was zero, since the seller did not have the legal right to transfer the good. Courts frequently reject this claim as granting a windfall to the buyer, who would receive the entire contract price in damages but still enjoyed use of the good for a period of time after delivery and before the true owner asserted her rights. Consider the case of *Metalcraft, Inc. v. Pratt*, 500 A.2d 329 (Md. Ct. Spec. App. 1985). Metalcraft purchased a set of molding equipment from Pratt, some of which belonged to other companies. When these companies asserted their ownership rights, Metalcraft sued Pratt for damages, claiming the value of the equipment was zero when transferred and thus that damages should be the entire contract price. The court considered this claim:

> There is no doubt that the language of § 2-714(2) can be read as Metalcraft reads it; indeed, it seems to say precisely what Metalcraft claims it does. At least one other court has construed it that way. In *Murdock v. Godwin*, 154 Ga. App. 824, 269 S.E.2d 905 (1980) Godwin, in April 1974, purchased a car from Murdock. There was a warranty of title. The car turned out to have been stolen. The police seized it in February 1977 and Godwin never saw it again. He sued Murdock and recovered the purchase price of the car (its value as it had been warranted less zero- its value at acceptance). On appeal, Murdock claimed that the purchase price should have been reduced by the value of Godwin's almost three years' use of the vehicle. The Georgia Court of Appeals rejected this argument, quoting the Georgia version of § 2-714(2). . . .
>
> [However], [w]e hold that there are special circumstances here which take the case out of the ordinary § 2-714(2) rule. This, too, is an issue that other jurisdictions have addressed. With the sole exception of Georgia, all have found special circumstances to exist in breach of warranty of title cases. The special circumstances have arisen because, *e.g.*, the buyer of a stolen car had use and possession of it for some period of time without notice of any title defect, because the goods in question had been stolen, and because

---

[19] For further discussion, see David W. Barnes, *The Meaning of Value in Contract Damages and Contract Theory*, 46 Am. U. L. Rev. 1 (1996).

a unique chattel was involved. [footnotes omitted]. Two of those factors are involved here. Metalcraft had use and possession of the patterns for varying periods of time before it had knowledge of any title defects. And the patterns were unique; they were specially designed to produce castings to particular specifications.

Id. at 335–36.

The Maryland appeals court thus rejected Metalcraft's claim that the value of the patterns at acceptance was zero, and instead assessed the actual value of the patterns as the value of Metalcraft's use of them from delivery until non-possession by the true owners. Damages were then the contract price minus whatever this "use" value turned out to be.

Consider the language of § 2-714. Does the "special circumstances" clause allow courts to exercise too much discretion, and thus harm predictability of verdicts? If it does, is there a way to modify the section to resolve the issue discussed in *Metalcraft*, without leaving such substantial discretion to the courts?

C. LIMITATIONS ON COMPENSATION

Although many difficult questions arise when courts attempt to determine what recovery will be truly compensatory in particular cases, the expectation damages default rule is remarkably robust. As we learned in Chapter 1, however, in specific contexts contract law limits a promisee's right to recover full compensation even though the promisor has concededly breached the contract. These limitations are typically described in terms of the promisee's obligation: 1) to establish her losses from the breach with reasonable certainty; 2) to ensure that at the time of contracting the promisor has reason to foresee any special or unusual consequences that might enhance the promisee's losses from breach; and 3) to take cost-justified steps to mitigate (or avoid aggravating) the promisor's losses under the contract. In each case, begin by asking whether the particular limitation can be justified in instrumental terms. Since both parties collectively bear the costs of contracting failure (the promisor bears the risk and the promisee pays the risk premium as part of the contract price), it follows that most parties would, *ex ante*, prefer contract default rules that worked to minimize the joint costs of contracting. The question in each of these instances is to determine first whether this cost minimizing principle justifies the three main limitations on compensation and, second, whether that principle adequately explains the cases that deny full compensation for breach. We begin in this part with the classic limitations — certainty, foreseeability, and mitigation — that the common law implies as default rules and then consider, finally, the freedom of the parties to opt out of the compensation principle by agreeing to a contract term that limits damages to a predetermined "liquidated" amount.

[1]   The Certainty Limitation

DREWS CO. v. LEDWITH-WOLFE ASSOCIATES, INC.
Supreme Court of South Carolina
371 S.E.2d 532 (1988)

HARWELL, J.

This case involves the breach of a construction contract. We affirm the trial court's refusal to grant a new trial, but reverse the jury's award of lost profits.

FACTS

The Drews Company, Inc. ("Contractor") contracted to renovate a building owned by Ledwith-Wolfe Associates, Inc. ("Owner"). Owner intended to convert the building into a restaurant. From its inception, the project was plagued by construction delays, work change orders, and general disagreement over the quality of work performed. Contractor eventually pulled its workers off the project. Contractor later filed, then sued to foreclose, a mechanic's lien for labor and materials used in renovating the building. Owner counterclaimed, alleging Contractor breached the contract and forced Owner to rework part of the job. Owner also claimed that Contractor's delays in performance caused Owner to lose profits from the restaurant.

The jury returned an $18,000 verdict for Contractor on its complaint. The jury awarded Owner $22,895 on its counterclaim for re-doing and completing the work and $14,000 in lost profits caused by Contractor's delays. The trial judge denied Contractor's new trial motion and awarded Owner attorney's fees and costs pursuant to S.C. Code Ann. § 29-5-10 (Supp.1987) (mechanics' liens).

B.

Contractor's next exception presents this Court with an opportunity to address a legal issue unsettled in South Carolina: Does the "new business rule" operate to automatically preclude the recovery of lost profits by a new business or enterprise? We hold that it does not.

1. Lost Profits In South Carolina

We begin our analysis of the lost profits issue by recognizing an elementary principle of contract law. The purpose of an award of damages for breach is "to give compensation, that is, to put the plaintiff in as good a position as he would have been in had the contract been performed." 11 S. Williston, A Treatise on the Law of Contracts, § 1338 (3d ed. 1968). The proper measure of that compensation, then, "is the loss actually suffered by the contractee as the result of the breach." *South Carolina Finance Corp. v. West Side Finance Co.*, 236 S.C. 109, 122 (1960).

"Profits" have been defined as "the net pecuniary gain from a transaction, the gross pecuniary gains diminished by the cost of obtaining them."

Restatement of Contracts § 331, Comment B (1932). Profits lost by a business as the result of a contractual breach have long been recognized as a species of recoverable consequential damages in this state. The issue is more difficult, however, when a new or unestablished business is the aggrieved party seeking projected lost profits as damages.

The new business rule as a per se rule of nonrecoverability of lost profits was firmly established in this state in *Standard Supply Co. v. Carter & Harris*, 81 S.C. 181, 187, 62 S.E. 150, 152 (1907): "When a business is in contemplation, but not established or not in actual operation, profit merely hoped for is too uncertain and conjectural to be considered." *McMeekin v. Southern Ry. Co.*, 82 S.C. 468, 64 S.E. 413 (1909), like *Standard Supply Co.*, involved profits allegedly lost when a carrier failed to deliver machinery necessary for a new mill enterprise. The Court adhered to a strict application of the rule, stating that "[t]he plaintiff's business had not been launched, and therefore he could not recover profits he expected to make." *Id.* at 473

Modern cases, however, reflect the willingness of this Court and our Court of Appeals to view the new business rule as a rule of evidentiary sufficiency rather than an automatic bar to recovery of lost profits by a new business. [footnotes omitted] These cases have so eroded the new business rule as an absolute bar to recovery of lost profits that the rigid *Standard Supply Co.* rule is no longer good law.

2. A Multi-Jurisdictional Trend

South Carolina has not been alone in developing its evidentiary view of the new business rule. Numerous authorities and commentators have tracked a similar trend nationwide: "Courts are now taking the position that the distinction between established businesses and new ones is a distinction that goes to the weight of the evidence and not a rule that automatically precludes recovery of profits by a new business." D. Dobbs, Handbook on the Law of Remedies, § 3.3, at 155 (1973). *See* R. Dunn, Recovery of Damages for Lost Profits, § 4.2 (3d ed. 1987) (trend of modern cases plainly toward replacing old rule of law with rule of evidence — reasonable certainty). Moreover, application of the rule in this manner has been applauded as fairer than mechanical application of the old rule.

In light of the facts before us, we find particularly persuasive several cases involving lost profits flowing from breaches of contracts to construct and/or lease buildings for the operation of new business ventures. *See, e.g., Chung v. Kaonohi Center Co.*, 62 Haw. 594, 618 P.2d 283 (1980) (rejecting per se nonrecoverability version of new business rule in favor of "reasonable certainty" evidentiary standard; lost profits award upheld for breach of contract to lease space for new restaurant); *Welch v. U.S. Bancorp Realty and Mortgage*, 286 Or. 673, 596 P.2d 947 (1979) (breach of contract to advance funds for residential and commercial development on land tract; "reasonable certainty" standard applied). We believe South Carolina should now unequivocally join those jurisdictions applying the new business rule as a rule of evidentiary sufficiency and not as an automatic preclusion to recovery of lost profits by a new business or enterprise.

3. The Standard for Entitlement to Lost Profits

The same standards that have for years governed lost profits awards in South Carolina will apply with equal force to cases where damages are sought for a new business or enterprise. First, profits must have been prevented or lost "as a natural consequence of" the breach of contract.

The second requirement is foreseeability; a breaching party is liable for those damages, including lost profits, "which may reasonably be supposed to have been within the contemplation of the parties at the time the contract was made as a probable result of the breach of it." *National Tire & Rubber Co. v. Hoover*, 128 S.C. 344, 348, 122 S.E. 858, 859 (1924).

The crucial requirement in lost profits determinations is that they be "established with reasonable certainty, for recovery cannot be had for profits that are conjectural or speculative." *South Carolina Finance Corp., supra*, at 122, 113 S.E.2d at 336. "The proof must pass the realm of conjecture, speculation, or opinion not founded on facts, and must consist of actual facts from which a reasonably accurate conclusion regarding the cause and the amount of the loss can be logically and rationally drawn." 22 Am. Jur. 2d *Damages* § 641 (1988).

Numerous proof techniques have been discussed and accepted in different factual scenarios. *See, e.g., Upjohn v. Rachelle Laboratories, Inc.*, 661 F.2d 1105, 1114 (6th Cir. 1981) (proof of future lost profits based on marketing forecasts by employees specializing in economic forecasting); *Petty v. Weyerhaeuser Co., supra* (skating rink's projected revenues compared to those of another arena in a nearby town); *see also Restatement (Second) of Contracts* § 352, at 146 (1981) (proof of lost profits "may be established with reasonable certainty with the aid of expert testimony, economic and financial data, market surveys and analyses, business records of similar enterprises, and the like."); Note, *supra*, 48 Ohio St. L.J. at 872-3 (means of proving prospective profits include: (1) "yardstick" method of comparison with profit performance of business similar in size, nature, and location; (2) comparison with profit history of plaintiff's successor, where applicable; (3) comparison of similar businesses owned by plaintiff himself, and (4) use of economic and financial data and expert testimony). While the factual contexts in which new business/lost profits cases arise will undoubtedly vary, these methods of proof and the "reasonable certainty" requirement bear an inherent flexibility facilitating the just assessment of profits lost to a new business due to contractual breach.

4. Application of the Standard to the Present Facts

Applying this standard to the facts before us, we find that Owner's proof failed to clear the "reasonable certainty" hurdle. Owner's projections of the profits lost by the restaurant because of the breach were based on nothing more than a sheet of paper reflecting the gross profits the restaurant made in the first 11 months of operation after construction was completed. These figures were not supplemented with corresponding figures for overhead or operating expenditures, but only with Owner's testimony that he "would expect at least a third of that [gross figure] to be" net profit. Owner's expectations, unsupported by any particular standard or fixed method for establishing net profits, were wholly insufficient to provide the jury with a basis for calculating profits lost with reasonable certainty.

The trial judge erred in failing to rule that, as a matter of law, Owner's proof was insufficient to merit submission to the jury. The $14,000 award of lost profits must therefore be reversed.

Affirmed in part; reversed in part.

NOTES

1. ***Reconciling the Cases.*** Is *Drews Company* consistent with *Freund v. Washington Square Press*, Chapter 1, *supra*? Inability to prove damages with sufficient certainty to gain recovery is a risk knowable at the time of contracting, isn't it? Why didn't these parties specify what the recovery would be? Are you confident that such a specification will be honored?

2. ***When Are Lost Profits Too Speculative?*** *Drews Company* represents the dominant trend among American courts in permitting the award of "lost profits" damages for new enterprises provided that the damages are proved with "reasonable certainty." Traditionally, courts in the United States had adhered to a *per se* rule prohibiting the recovery of lost profits by new businesses on the grounds that the damages were too speculative and uncertain. As courts continue to adopt and employ the more flexible "reasonable certainty" standard discussed in *Drews Company*, however, there has been a predictable increase in the variability of facts found sufficient to satisfy the test of "reasonable certainty." Consider the following:

In *Texas Instruments v. Teletron Energy Management*, 877 S.W.2d 276 (Tex. 1994), the Texas Supreme Court rejected a request by Teletron for "lost profits" damages due to Texas Instrument's breach of contract. Texas Instruments had contracted with Teletron to produce an innovative type of thermostat, using technology never before employed. After numerous attempts, Texas Instruments admitted they were unable to manufacture the new technology, and Teletron sued for breach of contract. The court reversed the lower court's award of lost profit damages because the product's market success was too speculative given the new technology.

In *Smith v. Penbridge Assocs.*, 655 A.2d 1015 (Pa. Super. Ct. 1995), a Pennsylvania couple sued a Michigan emu farm that sold them two male emus after guaranteeing they were a "proven breeding pair." The couple only realized the Michigan farm's mistake when no eggs were produced in the first breeding period after their return to Pennsylvania. The couple requested lost profits damages based on the estimated number of eggs that would have been produced had the emu pair included both a male and female. Though the court acknowledged that emu farming was a new enterprise in Pennsylvania, and thus the number of chicks that might have been born in the first breeding season was speculative, it granted lost profits recovery.

In *Gilroy v. American Broadcasting Co.*, 58 A.D.2d 533 (N.Y. App. Div. 1977), a screenwriter sued ABC for stealing a character he planned to use in two mystery novels. The court held that ABC had breached their contract with the writer regarding permissible uses of his literary property, but reversed the trial court's awarding of lost profits damages. The trial court had permitted evidence to go to the jury demonstrating that the plaintiff-writer would write two mystery novels a year for 15 years, and that these novels would receive certain sales and reprints. The jury then awarded the plaintiff the expected royalties from these future books. The appeals court reduced the damages because it considered these "lost profits" damages too speculative.

Considering these cases, can you answer the question as to when lost profit recovery is too speculative? Does the "reasonable certainty" standard permit the courts too much discretion in deciding lost profits cases?

3. *Recovering the Value of Lost "Good Will."* If a seller fails to timely deliver goods intended for resale, or if the goods are defective, the buyer's reputation may suffer as a result. Historically, courts were resistant to allowing recovery for lost good will:

> Our research fails to reveal any judicial authority in Pennsylvania which sustains, under the Sales Act, a recovery for a loss of good will occasioned either by nondelivery or by the delivery of defective goods. As this Court stated in Michelin Tire Co. v. Schulz, 295 Pa. 140, 144: "so far as appears, the tires in question were all used by defendant's customers and paid for, so he lost nothing thereon. What he claims is that, because the tires were less durable than recommended, he lost customers, which otherwise he would have retained and whose business would have netted him a profit. . . . This is entirely too speculative and not the proper measure of damages.". . . . We are in agreement with the statement of the Court in Armstrong Rubber Co. v. Griffith, 2 Cir., 43 F.2d 689, 691, that: "If the plaintiff here can recover for loss of good will, it is difficult to see what limits are to be set to the recovery of such damages in any case where defective goods are sold (or where goods are not delivered) and the vendee loses customers. Indeed, if such were the holding, damages which the parties never contemplated would seem to be involved in every contract of sale."

Harry Rubin & Sons, Inc. v. Consolidated Pipe Co., 396 Pa. 506, 512–13, 153 A.2d 472, 476–77 (1959).

Today, however, courts are evenly split on the right to recover for good will losses. The Pennsylvania Supreme Court, in a case overturning *Harry Rubin*, discussed the reasons for the modern trend:

> Thirdly, we must address whether good will damages are too speculative to permit recovery . . . Although we disallowed good will damages in [*Harry Rubin* and other cases], they are not recent. They were written in a time when business was conducted on a more simple basis, where market studies and economic forecasting were unexplored sciences.

> We are now in an era in which computers, economic forecasting, sophisticated marketing studies and demographic studies are widely used and accepted. As such, we believe that the rationale for precluding prospective profits under the rubric of "too speculative" ignores the realities of the marketplace and the science of modern economics. We believe that claims

for prospective profits should not be barred *ab initio.* Rather, plaintiffs should be given an opportunity to set forth and attempt to prove their damages.

AM/PM Franchise Ass'n v. Atlantic Richfield Co., 526 Pa. 110, 128, 584 A.2d 915, 924–25 (1990)

Redgrave v. Boston Symphony Orchestra, Inc., 855 F.2d 888 (1st Cir. 1988) is another example of the modern trend. There, the actress Vanessa Redgrave sued the Boston Symphony Orchestra (BSO) for wrongfully terminating her contract to narrate certain concerts for the BSO amid widespread publicity that she was an active supporter of the Palestine Liberation Organization. Ms. Redgrave claimed that "a significant number of movie and theater offers that she would ordinarily have received in the years 1982 and following were in fact not offered to her as a result of the BSO's cancellation in April 1982." *Id.* at 892. The jury found for Ms. Redgrave and awarded her $100,000 in consequential damages based on the harm caused her reputation by BSO's breach. Though acknowledging the general rule against allowing damages for harm to reputation, the appeals court permitted the verdict to stand, though the $100,000 figure was reduced to $12,000. The court held that:

> a plaintiff may receive consequential damages if the plaintiff proves with sufficient evidence that a breach of contract proximately caused the loss of identifiable professional opportunities. This type of claim is sufficiently different from a nonspecific allegation of damage to reputation that it appropriately falls outside the general rule that reputation damages are not an acceptable form of contract damage.

Id. at 894.

The court found that Ms. Redgrave's lost profits due to the BSO breach were not unduly speculative and could "reasonably be presumed to have been within the contemplation of the parties when they entered the contract." *Id.* at 893.

4. ***Problem.*** Tess, the Wonder Dog, has become somewhat notorious in Charlottesville, so much so that the local pet store announced a "Tess-lookalike" contest. The grand prize to the owner of the dog looking the most like Tess was $1,000. Anyone wanting their dog to be a contestant needed to appear at the pet store at 10 a.m. on the Saturday of the contest. Adam, a Vassar College student home on holiday, brought his dog, Lucy. Lucy and two other dogs made it to the finals. This required them to spend most of the day at the pet store. Two hours before the final judging between Lucy and the two other dogs, Tess growled at the pet store owner, and she canceled the contest. If the pet store is liable to Adam, what is the appropriate remedy?

[2]   Foreseeability

HADLEY v. BAXENDALE
Court of Exchequer
9 Exch. 341, 156 Eng. Rep. 145 (1854)

See p. 120, *supra*.

SPANG INDUSTRIES, INC., FT. PITT BRIDGE DIV. v. AETNA CASUALTY & SURETY CO.
United States Court of Appeals, Second Circuit
512 F.2d 365 (1975)

MULLIGAN, C.J.

Torrington Construction Co., Inc. (Torrington), a Connecticut corporation, was the successful bidder with the New York State Department of Transportation for a highway reconstruction contract covering 4.47 miles of road in Washington County, New York. Before submitting its bid, Torrington received an oral quotation from Spang Industries, Inc., Fort Pitt Bridge Division (Fort Pitt), a Pennsylvania corporation, for the fabrication, furnishing and erection of some 240 tons of structural steel at a unit price of 27.5 cents per pound; the steel was to be utilized to construct a 270 foot long, double span bridge over the Battenkill River as part of the highway reconstruction. The quotation was confirmed in a letter from Fort Pitt to Torrington dated September 5, 1969, which stated in part: "Delivery to be mutually agreed upon." On November 3, 1969, Torrington, in response to a request from Fort Pitt, advised that its requirements for delivery and erection of the steel would be late June, 1970. On November 12, 1969, Fort Pitt notified Torrington that it was tentatively scheduling delivery in accordance with these requirements. On January 7, 1970, Fort Pitt wrote to Torrington asking if the June, 1970 erection date was still valid; Torrington responded affirmatively on January 13, 1970. However, on January 29, 1970, Fort Pitt advised that it was engaged in an extensive expansion program and that "(d)ue to unforeseen delays caused by weather, deliveries from suppliers, etc., it is our opinion that the June date cannot be met." On February 2, 1970, Torrington sent a letter requesting that Fort Pitt give a delivery date and, receiving no response, wrote again on May 12, 1970 requesting a written confirmation of the date of delivery and threatening to cancel out if the date was not reasonably close to the originally scheduled date. On May 20, 1970, Fort Pitt responded and promised that the structural steel would be shipped early in August, 1970.

Although some 25 tons of small steel parts were shipped on August 21, 1970, the first girders and other heavy structural steel were not shipped until August 24, 26, 27, 31 and September 2 and 4, 1970. . . . Not until September 16 was there enough steel delivered to the job site to permit Syracuse to commence erection. The work was completed on October 8, 1970 and the bridge was ready to receive its concrete deck on October 28, 1970. Because of contract specifications set by the State requiring that concrete be poured at temperatures of 40° Fahrenheit and above, Torrington had to get special permission from the State's supervising engineer to pour the concrete on October 28, 1970, when the temperature was at 32°.

Since the job site was in northern New York near the Vermont border and the danger of freezing temperatures was imminent, the pouring of the concrete was performed on a crash basis in one day, until 1 a. m. the following morning, which entailed extra costs for Torrington in the form of overtime pay, extra equipment and the protection of the concrete during the pouring process.

In July, 1971, Fort Pitt instituted an action against Aetna Casualty and Surety Co., which had posted a general contractor's labor and material bond, seeking to recover the balance due on the subcontract. . . . In the interim, Torrington had commenced suit in New York Supreme Court, Washington County, seeking damages in the sum of $23,290.81 alleged to be caused by Fort Pitt's delay in furnishing the steel. Fort Pitt then removed the case to the United States District Court for the Northern District of New York [and] . . . on September 12, 1973, Judge Holden filed his findings of fact and conclusions of law in which he held that Fort Pitt had breached its contract by its delayed delivery and that Torrington was entitled to damages in the amount of $7,653.57. He further held that Fort Pitt was entitled to recover from Torrington on the counterclaim the sum of $23,290.12, which was the balance due on its contract price plus interest, less the $7,653.57 damages sustained by Torrington. He directed that judgment be entered for Fort Pitt against Torrington and Aetna on their joint and several liability for $15,636.55 with interest from November 12, 1970.

Fort Pitt on this appeal does not take issue with any of the findings of fact of the court below but contends that the recovery by Torrington of its increased expenses constitutes special damages which were not reasonably within the contemplation of the parties when they entered into the contract.

While the damages awarded Torrington are relatively modest ($7,653.57) in comparison with the subcontract price ($132,274.37), Fort Pitt urges that an affirmance of the award will do violence to the rule of Hadley v. Baxendale, 156 Eng. Rep. 145 (Ex. 1854), and create a precedent which will have a severe impact on the business of all subcontractors and suppliers.

While it is evident that the function of the award of damages for a breach of contract is to put the plaintiff in the same position he would have been in had there been no breach, Hadley v. Baxendale limits the recovery to those injuries which the parties could reasonably have anticipated at the time the contract was entered into. If the damages suffered do not usually flow from the breach, then it must be established that the special circumstances giving rise to them should reasonably have been anticipated at the time the contract was made.

There can be no question but that Hadley v. Baxendale represents the law in New York and in the United States generally. [footnotes omitted] There is no dispute between the parties on this appeal as to the continuing viability of Hadley v. Baxendale and its formulation of the rule respecting special damages, and this court has no intention of challenging or questioning its principles. . . .

The gist of Fort Pitt's argument is that, when it entered into the subcontract to fabricate, furnish and erect the steel in September, 1969, it had received a copy of the specifications which indicated that the total work was to be completed by December 15, 1971. It could not reasonably have anticipated that Torrington would so expedite the work that steel delivery would be called for in 1970 rather than 1971. Whatever knowledge Fort Pitt received after the contract was entered into, it argues, cannot expand its liability, since it is essential under Hadley v. Baxendale and its Yankee progeny that the notice of the facts which would give rise to special damages in case of breach be given at or before the time the contract was made. The principle urged cannot be disputed. We do not, however, agree that any violence to the doctrine was done here.

Fort Pitt also knew from the same specifications that Torrington was to commence the work on October 1, 1969. The Fort Pitt letter of September 5, 1969, which constitutes the agreement between the parties, specifically provides: "Delivery to be mutually agreed upon." On November 3, 1969, Torrington, responding to Fort Pitt's inquiry, gave "late June 1970" as its required delivery date and, on November 12, 1969, Fort Pitt stated that it was tentatively scheduling delivery for that time. Thus, at the time when the parties, pursuant to their initial agreement, fixed the date for performance which is crucial here, Fort Pitt knew that a June, 1970 delivery was required. It would be a strained and unpalatable interpretation of Hadley v. Baxendale to now hold that, although the parties left to further agreement the time for delivery, the supplier could reasonably rely upon a 1971 delivery date rather than one the parties later fixed. The behavior of Fort Pitt was totally inconsistent with the posture it now assumes. In November, 1969, it did not quarrel with the date set or seek to avoid the contract. It was not until late January, 1970 that Fort Pitt advised Torrington that, due to unforeseen delays and its expansion program, it could not meet the June date. None of its reasons for late delivery was deemed excusable according to the findings below, and this conclusion is not challenged here. It was not until five months later, on May 20, 1970, after Torrington had threatened to cancel, that Fort Pitt set another date for delivery (early August, 1970) which it again failed to meet, as was found below and not disputed on this appeal.

We conclude that, when the parties entered into a contract which, by its terms, provides that the time of performance is to be fixed at a later date, the knowledge of the consequences of a failure to perform is to be imputed to the defaulting party as of the time the parties agreed upon the date of performance. This comports, in our view, with both the logic and the spirit of Hadley v. Baxendale. Whether the agreement was initially valid despite its indefiniteness or only became valid when a material term was agreed upon is not relevant. At the time Fort Pitt did become committed to a delivery date, it was aware that a June, 1970 performance was required by virtue of its own acceptance. There was no unilateral distortion of the agreement rendering Fort Pitt liable to an extent not theretofore contemplated.

Having proceeded thus far, we do not think it follows automatically that Torrington is entitled to recover the damages it seeks here; further consideration of the facts before us is warranted. Fort Pitt maintains that, under the Hadley v. Baxendale rubric, the damages flowing from its conceded breach are "special" or "consequential" and were not reasonably to be contemplated by the parties. Since Torrington has not proved any "general" or "direct" damages, Fort Pitt urges that the contractor is entitled to nothing. We cannot agree. It is commonplace that parties to a contract normally address themselves to its performance and not to its breach or the consequences that will ensue if there is a default. As the New York Court of Appeals long ago stated:

> [A] more precise statement of this rule is, that a party is liable for all the direct damages which both parties to the contract would have contemplated as flowing from its breach, if at the time they entered into it they had bestowed proper attention upon the subject, and had been fully informed of the facts. (This) may properly be called the fiction of law. . . .

Leonard v. New York, Albany & Buffalo Electro-Magnetic Telegraph Co., 41 N.Y. 544, 567 (1870).[20]

It is also pertinent to note that the rule does not require that the direct damages must necessarily follow, but only that they are likely to follow; as Lord Justice Asquith commented in Victoria Laundry, Ltd. v. Newman Industries, Ltd., (1949) 2 K.B. 528, 540, are they "on the cards"? We believe there that the damages sought to be recovered were also "in the cards."

It must be taken as a reasonable assumption that, when the delivery date of June, 1970 was set, Torrington planned the bridge erection within a reasonable time thereafter. It is normal construction procedure that the erection of the steel girders would be followed by the installation of a poured concrete platform and whatever railings or super-structure the platform would require. Fort Pitt was an experienced bridge fabricator supplying contractors and the sequence of the work is hardly arcane. Moreover, any delay beyond June or August would assuredly have jeopardized the pouring of the concrete and have forced the postponement of the work until the spring. The work here, as was well known to Fort Pitt, was to be performed in northern New York near the Vermont border. The court below found that continuing freezing weather would have forced the pouring to be delayed until June, 1971. Had Torrington refused delivery or had it been compelled to delay the completion of the work until the spring of 1971, the potential damage claim would have been substantial. Instead, in a good faith effort to mitigate damages, Torrington embarked upon the crash program we have described. It appears to us that this eventuality should have reasonably been anticipated by Fort Pitt as it was experienced in the trade and was supplying bridge steel in northern climes on a project requiring a concrete roadway.

Torrington's recovery under the circumstances is not substantial or cataclysmic from Fort Pitt's point of view. It represents the expenses of unloading steel from the gondola due to Fort Pitt's admitted failure to notify its erection subcontractor, Syracuse Rigging, that the steel had been shipped, plus the costs of premium time, extra equipment and the cost of protecting the work, all occasioned by the realities Torrington faced in the wake of Fort Pitt's breach. In fact, Torrington's original

---

[20] [3] A second fiction, added as an embellishment to *Hadley v. Baxendale* by Mr. Justice Holmes as federal common law in *Globe Ref. Co. v. Landa Cotton Oil Co.*, 190 U.S. 540, 23 S.Ct. 754, 47 L.Ed. 1171 (1903), would require not only knowledge of the special circumstances but a tacit agreement on the part of the party sought to be charged to accept the liability imposed by the notice. This second test has generally been rejected by the courts and commentators. [footnotes omitted].

claim of $23,290.81 was whittled down by the court below because of Torrington's failure to establish that its supervisory costs, overhead and certain equipment costs were directly attributable to the delay in delivery of the steel.

In this case, serious or catastrophic injury was avoided by prompt, effective and reasonable mitigation at modest cost. Had Torrington not acted, had it been forced to wait until the following spring to complete the entire job and then sued to recover the profits it would have made had there been performance by Fort Pitt according to the terms of its agreement, then we might well have an approximate setting for a classical Hadley v. Baxendale controversy. As this case comes to us, it hardly presents that situation. We therefore affirm the judgment below permitting Torrington to offset its damages against the contract price.

[The court then ruled that the trial court erred in its calculation of interest on the award.]

Affirmed in part, reversed in part and remanded. No costs.

NOTES

1. ***Foreseeability of Business Purposes.*** *Spang Industries* illustrates that an actual meeting of the minds is not necessary to charge the promisor with responsibility for extended consequential damages. That is, the decision clearly does not rest on the rationale that the parties explicitly or even tacitly agreed that the seller would assume the risk of tardy delivery. Do you think most sellers of goods or services realize the extent of their liability and charge commensurately? Note the UCC treatment of this branch of the *Hadley* rule: Section 2-715(2)(a) includes among the buyer's consequential damages "any loss resulting from the general or particular requirements and needs of which the seller at the time of contracting has *reason to know* and which could not reasonably be prevented by cover or otherwise" (emphasis supplied). In *Cricket Alley Corp. v. Data Terminal Systems, Inc.*, 732 P.2d 719 (Kan. 1987), the court held that the additional labor costs occasioned by the failure of the DTS computerized cash registers to communicate, as warranted, with Cricket Alley's main computer system were "general needs" of the buyer that did not have to be communicated to the seller at the time of contracting. The court explained:

> DTS computerized cash registers are expensive and sophisticated pieces of equipment and the market for them lies largely in the more complex retail establishments. The "mom and pop" grocery store operation is, obviously, not the prime market for such products. The submission of data from the cash registers to the mainline computer on sales, payrolls, inventory, etc. is a common feature of such equipment and the failure of the cash registers to do so would foreseeably create additional labor costs for the afflicted retail merchants. The additional labor costs sought by plaintiff, herein, as consequential damages are not attributable to any unique features of plaintiff's business. We conclude that consequential damages as an element of plaintiff's damages were properly submitted to the jury herein.

Id. at 725.

2. *Foreseeable Damages and Lost Profits.* Recent court decisions tend to include damages for lost profits among reasonably foreseeable damages.[21] Why does the modern view diverge from that which prevailed in the 1850s? Has there been a substantive change in the commercial world since *Hadley* was decided or does the modern view simply rectify a deficiency in the original rule?

The tendency of modern courts to include lost profits as reasonably foreseeable damages raises the question of how these profits are to be established in court. On this point, see *Cook Assocs. v. Warnick*, 664 P.2d 1161 (Utah 1983) (a new business established lost profits with sufficient certainty to merit recovery under UCC § 2-715(2)); *Albin Elevator Co. v. Pavlica*, 649 P.2d 187 (Wyo. 1982) (lost profits are a proper element of damages for breach of warranty but plaintiff's proof insufficient to establish them). The *Albin Elevator* resolution is one often seen despite the change to the modern view. Does the modern rule guarantee the success of the promisee's business? Who bears the burden of proof on this issue?

3. *Can Consequential Damages Be Disclaimed?* In *Western Industries, Inc. v. Newcor Canada, Ltd.*, 739 F.2d 1198 (7th Cir. 1984), Western purchased several custom-built welding machines from Newcor that failed to work correctly soon after delivery. Western sued for actual and consequential damages and was awarded $1.3 million by the jury. On appeal, Newcor claimed that consequential damages were disclaimed in the contract because it is "the custom of the specialty welding machine trade not to give a disappointed buyer his consequential damages but just to allow him either to return the machines and get his money back . . . or keep the machines and get the purchase price reduced." *Id.* at 1201. Writing for the Seventh Circuit, Judge Posner reversed and remanded the case for further proceedings on the question of trade custom in the specialty welding industry. Judge Posner explained that if sufficient evidence was produced on remand demonstrating that trade custom in the welding industry called for waiving consequential damages due to seller's breach, Western's damage award should be reduced.

Compare *Western Industries* to *Golden Reward Mining Co. v. Jervis B. Webb Co.*, 772 F. Supp. 1118 (D.S.D. 1991), in which the U.S. District Court for South Dakota considered whether an express disclaimer of liability for consequential damages was unconscionable. Here, Golden Reward purchased from Webb a custom-built reclaimer machine used for mining gold. The contract provided that the exclusive remedy for breach by seller was either "repair or replacement," and also included a "limitation of remedy" provision that prohibited recovery of consequential damages. In concluding that the disclaimer was not unconscionable, the court stated that it would "not interfere with what is simply a bargained-for allocation of risk." *Id.* at 1125. Focusing on the instant facts, the court then explained the benefits of allowing corporations to bargain around liability for consequential damages:

> Certainly, Webb would not consider building this reclaimer if the reclaim-er's potential breakdown might ultimately generate liability for an incalcu-

---

[21] Representative cases include *Compania Embotelladora Del Pacifico, S.A. v. Pepsi Cola Co.*, 650 F. Supp. 2d 314 (S.D.N.Y. 2009); *Horizons, Inc. v. Avco Corp.*, 714 F.2d 862 (8th Cir. 1983); and *United California Bank v. Eastern Mountain Sports, Inc.*, 546 F. Supp. 945 (D. Mass. 1982).

lable amount of gold. Both parties realized, at the time of negotiations, that this was a prototypical machine, designed and built to achieve a production result heretofore unknown to both parties. No doubt, Golden Reward realized that to encourage successfully Webb's participation in this project, the fear of consequential damages in a volatile precious metals market must be removed. By the same token, Webb demanded only a warranty which encouraged innovation — without the fear of financial paralysis if projected, but yet untested, production goals were not met. A contract, under these circumstances, which omits a clause prohibiting recovery of consequential damages would, perhaps, be more surprising than one which did not.

Id.

In its conclusion, the district court in *Golden Reward* refers to the parties before it as "large commercial entities." *Id.* Do you think the results in both *Western Industries* and *Golden Reward* would be different if the parties involved included consumers, rather than corporations? (*See* UCC § 2-719(3).) Why should the enforceability of a clause opting out of the general default rule governing consequential damages depend on the status of the parties?

In his article *Beyond Foreseeability: Consequential Damages in the Law of Contract*, 18 J. LEGAL STUD. 105 (1989), Professor Richard Epstein argued that results such as that in *Golden Reward* should be encouraged in the legal community since the awarding of consequential damages for seller's breach is often overcompensatory. Epstein contended that the relaxation of the *Hadley* foreseeability test in our modern legal system is a mistake, evidenced by the proliferation of consequential damages waivers employed in the commercial world. Epstein argued for a return to the "nineteenth-century view that depended on a theory of tacit assumption of risk." *Id.* at 138. At the least, the judicial tendency to narrowly construe contractual damage limitations should be modified, allowing negotiating parties greater freedom to "contract out" of default rules such as consequential damages.

4. *Are Consequential Damages for Emotional Distress Foreseeable?* In *Valentine v. General American Credit, Inc.*, 420 Mich. 256, 362 N.W.2d 628 (1984), an employee sued her employer for damages due to wrongful termination, asserting that the service contract entitled her to peace of mind and job security, and thus that its wrongful termination resulted in emotional distress for which she deserved compensation. The Supreme Court of Michigan denied recovery for emotional distress, stating that "the general rule, with few exceptions, is to uniformly deny recovery for mental distress damages although they are foreseeable within the rule of *Hadley v. Baxendale*." *Id.* at 260. The court concluded by discussing when emotional distress damages might be recoverable:

An employment contract will indeed often have a personal element. Employment is an important aspect of most persons' lives, and the breach of an employment contract may result in emotional distress. The primary purpose in forming such contracts, however, is economic and not to secure the protection of personal interests. The psychic satisfaction of employment is secondary. Mental distress damages for breach of contract have not been awarded where there is a market standard by which damages can be adequately determined. Valentine's monetary loss can be estimated with reasonable certainty according to the terms of the contract and the market for, or market value of, her service.

Id. at 263.

When will a breach of contract action result in recovery for mental distress? Consider the case of *Allen v. Jones*, 104 Cal. App. 3d 207 (1980):

> Plaintiff sued defendants, individually and as a partnership doing business under the name of Miller Jones Valley Mortuary, to recover damages for mental distress suffered upon learning that the cremated remains of plaintiff's brother, which defendants had undertaken to ship to Illinois, were lost in transit . . . [T]he rule has developed that damages for mental suffering or injury to reputation are generally not recoverable in an action for breach of contract. [footnotes omitted] There are, however, certain contracts which so affect the vital concerns of the individual that severe mental distress is a foreseeable result of breach. For many years, our courts have recognized that damages for mental distress may be recovered for breach of a contract of this nature. [However,] [t]o date all the cases in this state in which mental distress damages have been awarded for breach of contract have been cases in which the mental distress caused physical illness, and it is not clear whether mental distress damages alone can ever support an action for breach of contract in this state.

Id. at 209–13.

The court in *Allen* did not answer its own question, concluding that the plaintiff had pleaded an action in tort as well as contract and allowing recovery against defendants for their negligence. Does a rule that ties a contract remedy for mental distress to physical illness make sense? When, if at all, should a plaintiff be permitted to recover for emotional suffering caused by a breach of contract?

5. *Modern Applications of the Rule.* The rule of *Hadley v. Baxendale* continues to be deployed in new ways in the modern commercial world. For example, in *Lewis v. Mobil Oil Corp.*, 438 F.2d 500 (8th Cir. 1971), the plaintiff, after purchasing a hydraulic system for his sawmill business, relied on the defendant to select and provide the proper hydraulic fluid for the equipment. The local Mobil dealer, who was familiar with the plaintiff's operation, apparently made an incorrect selection. Subsequently, another Mobil representative misdiagnosed the problem, causing the plaintiff to needlessly purchase new equipment. Finally, after approximately two-and-a-half years, the proper lubricant was suggested and the problems rectified.

The jury found the defendant in breach of an implied warranty of fitness under § 2-315 of the Code and that this breach caused the plaintiff's misfortunes. On the issue of damages, the appellate court affirmed the jury's award of lost profits under § 2-715, holding that lost profits are foreseeable "if they are proximately caused by and are the natural result of the breach." *Id.* at 510.

The plaintiff also advanced a novel claim under the *Hadley* doctrine. He contended that the defendant's breach had caused him to needlessly purchase extra equipment that in turn jeopardized his financial situation. As a result, he was undercapitalized and could finance his operations at only 50 to 60% of full profitability. He asked for a recovery of lost profits based on 100% capacity performance. How should this claim have been answered?

[3]   Duty to Mitigate

ROCKINGHAM COUNTY v. LUTEN BRIDGE CO.
Circuit Court of Appeals, Fourth Circuit
35 F.2d 301 (1929)

[The plaintiff contracted on January 7, 1924 with the defendant Rockingham County Board of Commissioners to build a bridge in a remote part of the county. The contract award engendered considerable controversy which resulted in one of the board members who had voted to award the contract resigning and two others, who had similarly voted, refusing to attend further meetings. The resignee was replaced and the board (minus the two non-attending members) was reconstituted as a three man tribunal. On February 21, 1924, the reconstituted board voted to rescind the earlier action. As of this vote, the plaintiff had incurred costs of about $1900. The plaintiff was notified of the board's action shortly thereafter, but chose instead to consider the board in breach of the contract and continue work on the bridge.

Plaintiff filed suit on November 24, 1924, alleging damage incurred due to work on the bridge through November 3, 1924 of $18,301.07. The trial judge directed verdict in accordance with this claim. The defendant appealed the award, alleging that the plaintiff's failure to mitigate by continuing work on the bridge after the county rescinded (albeit wrongfully) the contract, resulted in excess damages that should have been denied.]

PARKER, J.

Coming, then, to the third question — i.e., as to the measure of plaintiff's recovery — we do not think that, after the county had given notice, while the contract was still executory, that it did not desire the bridge built and would not pay for it, plaintiff could proceed to build it and recover the contract price. It is true that the county had no right to rescind the contract, and the notice given plaintiff amounted to a breach on its part; but, after plaintiff had received notice of the breach, it was its duty to do nothing to increase the damages flowing therefrom. If A enters into a binding contract to build a house for B, B, of course, has no right to rescind the contract without A's consent. But if, before the house is built, he decides that he does not want it, and notifies A to that effect, A has no right to proceed with the building and thus pile up damages. His remedy is to treat the contract as broken when he receives the notice, and sue for the recovery of such damages, as he may have sustained from the breach, including any profit which he would have realized upon performance, as well as any other losses which may have resulted to him. In the case at bar, the county decided not to build the road of which the bridge was to be a part, and did not build it. The bridge, built in the midst of the forest, is of no value to the county because of this change of circumstances. When, therefore, the county gave notice to the plaintiff that it would not proceed with the project, plaintiff should have desisted from further work. It had no right thus to pile up damages by proceeding with the erection of a useless bridge.

The contrary view was expressed by Lord Cockburn in Frost v. Knight, L.R. 7 Ex. 111, but, as pointed out by Prof. Williston (*Williston on Contracts*, vol. 3, p. 2347), it is not in harmony with the decisions in this country. The American rule and the reasons supporting it are well stated by Prof. Williston as follows:

> There is a line of cases running back to 1845 which holds that, after an absolute repudiation or refusal to perform by one party to a contract, the other party cannot continue to perform and recover damages based on full performance. This rule is only a particular application of the general rule of damages that a plaintiff cannot hold a defendant liable for damages which need not have been incurred; or, as it is often stated, the plaintiff must, so far as he can without loss to himself, mitigate the damages caused by the defendant's wrongful act. The application of this rule to the matter in question is obvious. If a man engages to have work done, and afterwards repudiates his contract before the work has been begun or when it has been only partially done, it is inflicting damage on the defendant without benefit to the plaintiff to allow the latter to insist on proceeding with the contract. The work may be useless to the defendant, and yet he would be forced to pay the full contract price. On the other hand, the plaintiff is interested only in the profit he will make out of the contract. If he receives this it is equally advantageous for him to use his time otherwise.

The leading case on the subject in this country is the New York case of Clark v. Marsiglia, 1 Denio (N.Y.) 317, 43 Am. Dec. 670. In that case defendant had employed plaintiff to paint certain pictures for him, but countermanded the order before the work was finished. Plaintiff, however, went on and completed the work and sued for the contract price. In reversing a judgment for plaintiff, the court said:

> The plaintiff was allowed to recover as though there had been no countermand of the order; and in this the court erred. The defendant, by requiring the plaintiff to stop work upon the paintings, violated his contract, and thereby incurred a liability to pay such damages as the plaintiff should sustain. Such damages would include a recompense for the labor done and materials used, and such further sum in damages as might, upon legal principles, be assessed for the breach of the contract; but the plaintiff had no right, by obstinately persisting in the work, to make the penalty upon the defendant greater than it would otherwise have been.

And the rule as established by the great weight of authority in America is summed up in the following statement, which is quoted with approval by the Supreme Court of North Carolina in the recent case of Novelty Advertising Co. v. Farmers' Mut. Tobacco Warehouse Co., 186 N.C. 197, 119 S.E. 196, 198:

> While a contract is executory a party has the power to stop performance on the other side by an explicit direction to that effect, subjecting himself to

such damages as will compensate the other party for being stopped in the performance on his part at that stage in the execution of the contract. The party thus forbidden cannot afterwards go on and thereby increase the damages, and then recover such damages from the other party. The legal right of either party to violate, abandon, or renounce his contract, on the usual terms of compensation to the other for the damages which the law recognizes and allows, subject to the jurisdiction of equity to decree specific performance in proper cases, is universally recognized and acted upon. . . .

We have carefully considered the cases . . . upon which plaintiff relies; but we do not think that they are at all in point. . . . In the opinions in all of these some language was used which lends support to plaintiff's position, but in none of them was the point involved which is involved here, viz. whether, in application of the rule which requires that the party to a contract who is not in default do nothing to aggravate the damages arising from breach, he should not desist from performance of an executory contract for the erection of a structure when notified of the other party's repudiation, instead of piling up damages by proceeding with the work. As stated above, we think that reason and authority require that this question be answered in the affirmative. It follows that there was error in directing a verdict for plaintiff for the full amount of its claim. The measure of plaintiff's damage, upon its appearing that notice was duly given not to build the bridge, is an amount sufficient to compensate plaintiff for labor and materials expended and expense incurred in the part performance of the contract, prior to its repudiation, plus the profit which would have been realized if it had been carried out in accordance with its terms.

Our conclusion, on the whole case, is that there was error in failing to strike out the answer of Pruitt, Pratt, and McCollum, and in admitting same as evidence against the county, in excluding the testimony offered by the county to which we have referred, and in directing a verdict for plaintiff. The judgment below will accordingly be reversed, and the case remanded for a new trial.

Reversed.

PARKER v. TWENTIETH CENTURY-FOX FILM CORP.
Supreme Court of California
3 Cal. 3d 176, 89 Cal. Rptr. 737, 474 P.2d 689 (1970)

Burke, J.

Defendant Twentieth Century-Fox Film Corporation appeals from a summary judgment granting to plaintiff [Shirley MacLaine] the recovery of agreed compensation under a written contract for her services as an actress in a motion picture. As will appear, we have concluded that the trial court correctly ruled in plaintiff's favor and that the judgment should be affirmed.

Plaintiff is well known as an actress, and in the contract between plaintiff and defendant is sometimes referred to as the "Artist." Under the contract, dated August 6, 1965, plaintiff was to play the female lead in defendant's contemplated production of a motion picture entitled "Bloomer Girl." The contract provided that defendant would pay plaintiff a minimum "guaranteed compensation" of $53,571.42 per week for 14 weeks commencing May 23, 1966, for a total of $750,000. Prior to May 1966 defendant decided not to produce the picture and by a letter dated April 4, 1966, it notified plaintiff of that decision and that it would not "comply with our obligations to you under" the written contract.

By the same letter and with the professed purpose "to avoid any damage to you," defendant instead offered to employ plaintiff as the leading actress in another film tentatively entitled "Big Country, Big Man" (hereinafter, "Big Country"). The compensation offered was identical, as were 31 of the 34 numbered provisions or articles of the original contract.[22] Unlike "Bloomer Girl," however, which was to have been a musical production, "Big Country" was a dramatic "western type" movie. "Bloomer Girl" was to have been filmed in California; "Big Country" was to be produced in Australia. Also, certain terms in the proffered contract varied from those of the original.[23] Plaintiff was given one week within which to accept; she did not and the offer lapsed. Plaintiff then commenced this action seeking recovery of the agreed guaranteed compensation.

The complaint sets forth two causes of action. The first is for money due under the contract; the second, based upon the same allegations as the first, is for damages resulting from defendant's breach of contract. Defendant in its answer admits the existence and validity of the contract, that plaintiff complied with all the conditions, covenants and promises and stood ready to complete the performance, and that defendant breached and "anticipatorily repudiated" the contract. It denies, however, that any money is due to plaintiff either under the contract or as a result of its breach, and pleads as an affirmative defense to both causes of action plaintiff's

---

[22] [1] Among the identical provisions was the following found in the last paragraph of Article 2 of the original contract: "We [defendant] shall not be obligated to utilize your [plaintiff's] services in or in connection with the Photoplay hereunder, our sole obligation, subject to the terms and conditions of this Agreement, being to pay you the guaranteed compensation herein provided for."

[23] [2] Article 29 of the original contract specified that plaintiff approved the director already chosen for "Bloomer Girl" and that in case he failed to act as director plaintiff was to have approval rights of any substitute director. Article 31 provided that plaintiff was to have the right of approval of the "Bloomer Girl" dance director, and Article 32 gave her the right of approval of the screenplay. Defendant's letter of April 4 to plaintiff, which contained both defendant's notice of breach of the "Bloomer Girl" contract and offer of the lead in "Big Country," eliminated or impaired each of those rights. It read in part as follows: "The terms and conditions of our offer of employment are identical to those set forth in the "BLOOMER GIRL" Agreement, Articles 1 through 34 and Exhibit A to the Agreement, except as follows:

"1. Article 31 of said Agreement will not be included in any contract of employment regarding "BIG COUNTRY, BIG MAN" as it is not a musical and it thus will not need a dance director.

"2. In the "BLOOMER GIRL" agreement, in Articles 29 and 32, you were given certain director and screenplay approvals and you had preapproved certain matters. Since there simply is insufficient time to negotiate with you regarding your choice of director and regarding the screenplay and since you already expressed an interest in performing the role in "BIG COUNTRY, BIG MAN," we must exclude from our offer of employment in "BIG COUNTRY, BIG MAN" any approval rights as are contained in said Articles 29 and 32; however, we shall consult with you respecting the director to be selected to direct the photoplay and will further consult with you with respect to the screenplay and any revisions or changes therein, provided, however, that if we fail to agree . . . the decision of . . . (defendant) with respect to the selection of a director and to revisions and changes in the said screenplay shall be binding upon the parties to said agreement."

allegedly deliberate failure to mitigate damages, asserting that she unreasonably refused to accept its offer of the leading role in "Big Country."

Plaintiff moved for summary judgment under Code of Civil Procedure section 437c, the motion was granted, and summary judgment for $750,000 plus interest was entered in plaintiff's favor. This appeal by defendant followed. . . .

The general rule is that the measure of recovery by a wrongfully discharged employee is the amount of salary agreed upon for the period of service, less the amount which the employer affirmatively proves the employee has earned or with reasonable effort might have earned from other employment. However, before projected earnings from other employment opportunities not sought or accepted by the discharged employee can be applied in mitigation, the employer must show that the other employment was comparable, or substantially similar, to that of which the employee has been deprived; the employee's rejection of or failure to seek other available employment of a different or inferior kind may not be resorted to in order to mitigate damages.

In the present case defendant has raised no issue of *reasonableness of efforts* by plaintiff to obtain other employment; the sole issue is whether plaintiff's refusal of defendant's substitute offer of "Big Country" may be used in mitigation. Nor, if the "Big Country" offer was of employment different or inferior when compared with the original "Bloomer Girl" employment, is there an issue as to whether or not plaintiff acted reasonably in refusing the substitute offer. Despite defendant's arguments to the contrary, no case cited or which our research has discovered holds or suggests that reasonableness is an element of a wrongfully discharged employee's option to reject, or fail to seek, different or inferior employment lest the possible earnings therefrom be charged against him in mitigation of damages.[24]

Applying the foregoing rules to the record in the present case, with all intendments in favor of the party opposing the summary judgment motion — here, defendant — it is clear that the trial court correctly ruled that plaintiff's failure to accept defendant's tendered substitute employment could not be applied in mitigation of damages because the offer of the "Big Country" lead was of employment both different and inferior, and that no factual dispute was presented on that issue. The mere circumstance that "Bloomer Girl" was to be a musical review calling upon plaintiff's talents as a dancer as well as an actress, and was to be produced in the City of Los Angeles, whereas "Big Country" was a straight dramatic role in a "Western Type" story taking place in an opal mine in Australia, demonstrates the difference in kind between the two employments; the female lead as a dramatic actress in a western style motion picture can by no stretch of imagination be considered the equivalent of or substantially similar to the lead in a song-and-dance production.

Additionally, the substitute "Big Country" offer proposed to eliminate or impair the director and screenplay approvals accorded to plaintiff under the original "Bloomer Girl" contract (see fn. 2, *ante*), and thus constituted an offer of inferior

---

24 [5] Instead, in each case the reasonableness referred to was that of the *efforts* of the employee to obtain other employment that was not different or inferior; his right to reject the latter was declared as an unqualified rule of law.

employment. No expertise or judicial notice is required in order to hold that the deprivation or infringement of an employee's rights held under an original employment contract converts the available "other employment" relied upon by the employer to mitigate damages, into inferior employment which the employee need not seek or accept.

Statements found in affidavits submitted by defendant in opposition to plaintiff's summary judgment motion, to the effect that the "Big Country" offer was not of employment different from or inferior to that under the "Bloomer Girl" contract, merely repeat the allegations of defendant's answer to the complaint in this action, constitute only conclusionary assertions with respect to undisputed facts, and do not give rise to a triable factual issue so as to defeat the motion for summary judgment.

In view of the determination that defendant failed to present any facts showing the existence of a factual issue with respect to its sole defense — plaintiff's rejection of its substitute employment offer in mitigation of damages — we need not consider plaintiff's further contention that for various reasons, including the provisions of the original contract set forth in footnote 1, *ante*, plaintiff was excused from attempting to mitigate damages.

The judgment is affirmed.

SULLIVAN, C.J. (dissenting).

The basic question in this case is whether or not plaintiff acted reasonably in rejecting defendant's offer of alternate employment. The answer depends upon whether that offer (starring in "Big Country, Big Man") was an offer of work that was substantially similar to her former employment (starring in "Bloomer Girl") or of work that was of a different or inferior kind. To my mind this is a factual issue which the trial court should not have determined on a motion for summary judgment. The majority have not only repeated this error but have compounded it by applying the rules governing mitigation of damages in the employer-employee context in a misleading fashion. Accordingly, I respectfully dissent.

The familiar rule requiring a plaintiff in a tort or contract action to mitigate damages embodies notions of fairness and socially responsible behavior which are fundamental to our jurisprudence. Most broadly stated, it precludes the recovery of damages which, through the exercise of due diligence, could have been avoided. Thus, in essence, it is a rule requiring reasonable conduct in commercial affairs. This general principle governs the obligations of an employee after his employer has wrongfully repudiated or terminated the employment contract. Rather than permitting the employee simply to remain idle during the balance of the contract period, the law requires him to make a reasonable effort to secure other employment.[25] He is not obliged, however, to seek or accept any and all types of work which

---

[25] [1] The issue is generally discussed in terms of a duty on the part of the employee to minimize loss. The practice is long-established and there is little reason to change despite Judge Cardozo's observation of its subtle inaccuracy. "The servant is free to accept employment or reject it according to his uncensored pleasure. What is meant by the supposed duty is merely this: That if he unreasonably reject, he will not be heard to say that the loss of wages from then on shall be deemed the jural consequence of the earlier discharge. He has broken the chain of causation, and loss resulting to him thereafter is

may be available. Only work which is in the same field and which is of the same quality need be accepted.[26]

Over the years the courts have employed various phrases to define the type of employment which the employee, upon his wrongful discharge, is under an obligation to accept. Thus in California alone it has been held that he must accept employment which is "substantially similar."

For reasons which are unexplained, the majority cite several of these cases yet select from among the various judicial formulations which contain one particular phrase, "Not of a different or inferior kind," with which to analyze this case. I have discovered no historical or theoretical reason to adopt this phrase, which is simply a negative restatement of the affirmative standards set out in the above cases, as the exclusive standard. Indeed, its emergence is an example of the dubious phenomenon of the law responding not to rational judicial choice or changing social conditions, but to unrecognized changes in the language of opinions or legal treatises. However, the phrase is a serviceable one and my concern is not with its use as the standard but rather with what I consider its distortion.

The relevant language excuses acceptance only of employment which is of a *different kind*. It has never been the law that the mere existence of *differences between two jobs in the same field* is sufficient, as a matter of law, to excuse an employee wrongfully discharged from one from accepting the other in order to mitigate damages. Such an approach would effectively eliminate any obligation of an employee to attempt to minimize damage arising from a wrongful discharge. The only alternative job offer an employee would be required to accept would be an offer of his former job by his former employer.

Although the majority appear to hold that there was a difference "in kind" between the employment offered plaintiff in "Bloomer Girl" and that offered in "Big Country," an examination of the opinion makes crystal clear that the majority merely point out differences between the two *films* (an obvious circumstance) and then apodically assert that these constitute a difference in the *kind of employment*. The entire rationale of the majority boils down to this: that the *"mere circumstances"* that "Bloomer Girl" was to be a musical review while "Big Country" was a straight drama "demonstrates the difference in kind" since a female lead in a western is not "the equivalent of or substantially similar to" a lead in a musical. This is merely attempting to prove the proposition by repeating it. It shows that the vehicles for the display of the star's talents are different but it does not prove that her employment as a star in such vehicles is of necessity different in kind and either inferior or superior.

I believe that the approach taken by the majority (a superficial listing of differences with no attempt to assess their significance) may subvert a valuable

---

suffered through his own act." (McClelland v. Climax Hosiery Mills (1930) 252 N.Y. 347, 359, 169 N.E. 605, 609, concurring opinion).

[26] [2] This qualification of the rule seems to reflect the simple and humane attitude that it is too severe to demand of a person that he attempt to find and perform work for which he has no training or experience. Many of the older cases hold that one need not accept work in an inferior rank or position nor work which is more menial or arduous. This suggests that the rule may have had its origin in the bourgeois fear of resubmergence in lower economic classes.

legal doctrine.[27] The inquiry in cases such as this should not be whether differences between the two jobs exist (there will always be differences) but whether the differences which are present are substantial enough to constitute differences in the *kind* of employment or, alternatively, whether they render the substitute work employment of an *inferior kind*.

It seems to me that *this* inquiry involves, in the instant case at least, factual determinations which are improper on a motion for summary judgment. Resolving whether or not one job is substantially similar to another or whether, on the other hand, it is of a different or inferior kind, will often (as here) require a critical appraisal of the similarities and differences between them in light of the importance of these differences to the employee. This necessitates a weighing of the evidence, and it is precisely this undertaking which is forbidden on summary judgment.

This is not to say that summary judgment would never be available in an action by an employee in which the employer raises the defense of failure to mitigate damages. No case has come to my attention, however, in which summary judgment has been granted on the issue of whether an employee was obliged to accept available alternate employment. Nevertheless, there may well be cases in which the substitute employment is so manifestly of a dissimilar or inferior sort, the declarations of the plaintiff so complete and those of the defendant so conclusionary and inadequate that no factual issues exist for which a trial is required. This, however, is not such a case. . . .

I believe that the judgment should be reversed so that the issue of whether or not the offer of the lead role in "Big Country, Big Man" was of employment comparable to that of the lead role in "Bloomer Girl" may be determined at trial.

NOTES

1. ***Dealing with the Breacher.*** Suppose there is an unequivocal breach by the promisor, who then offers "to mitigate the promisee's loss" by offering a substitute contract. What arguments are there that of all the substitute contracts in the world, this is the only one that the promisee need not accept in mitigation? Now suppose that the breach is not unequivocal — the promisor and the promisee disagree on the meaning of the contract terms. The promisee would like to treat this as a contract breach situation, and the promisor tenders what he considers to be "performance." What ought the promisee to do?

Most courts have declined to impose any duty on the promisee to deal with the breacher, even where the breacher offers the best option in mitigation.[28] Particu-

---

[27] [5] The values of the doctrine of mitigation of damages in this context are that it minimizes the unnecessary personal and social (e.g., nonproductive use of labor, litigation) costs of contractual failure. If a wrongfully discharged employee can, through his own action and without suffering financial or psychological loss in the process, reduce the damages accruing from the breach of contract, the most sensible policy is to require him to do so. I fear the majority opinion will encourage precisely opposite conduct.

[28] *See, e.g., Everett v. Emmons Coal Mining Co.*, 289 F. 686 (6th Cir. 1923) (nonbreaching buyer has no duty to mitigate by providing bond rather than by paying on credit); *Theis v. DuPont, Glore Forgan, Inc.*, 212 Kan. 301, 510 P.2d 1212 (1973) (where one broker in commodity trading firm had traded in

larly in cases where the breach occurs in a market with close substitute performances, courts rarely penalize the promisee for failing to accept a substitute performance. As the market for substitute performance thins, however, the judicial decisions become increasingly less uniform. A number of courts have held that a promisee should accept a new offer from the promisor on similar terms whenever no close, substitute transaction is available. *See, e.g., Henrici v. South Feather Land & Water Co.,* 170 P. 1135 (Cal. 1918) (landowner required to pay additional charge for water services rather than permit crops to be lost). On the other hand, courts have not imposed a duty to deal if the new offer appears to be strategically motivated.

How would you characterize the market context in *Parker*? Was the studio's offer one that should be taken at face value? Would it matter to you if you knew that *Bloomer Girl* was not just a generic musical comedy, but rather traced the lives of Amelia Bloomer and Evelina Applegate (the role assigned to MacLaine) who were 19th century feminists and activists for racial equality?

2.   *Exceptions to Mitigation.* *Luten Bridge* illustrates the rule that, when one party repudiates a contract, it is the duty of the other party to stop performance so as to mitigate damages. This rule is subject to some exceptions, however:

> The reason for this rule is twofold: Ordinarily a plaintiff is interested only in the profit he will make from his contract, and if he receives this he obtains the full benefit of his bargain; on the other hand, performance by the plaintiff might be useless to the defendant, although he would have to pay the entire contract price if the plaintiff were permitted to perform, and this would inflict damage on the defendant without benefit to the plaintiff. If these reasons are not present, the rule is not applied. For example, where the plaintiff is not interested solely in profit from the agreement but must proceed with the work in order to fulfill contract obligations to others, or where refraining from performance might involve closing a factory, damages may be inadequate and the plaintiff may have a right to continue performance. It has likewise been held that where a contractor has started work and has reached a point where it would be impracticable to attempt to make a reasonable estimate of damages, or where to complete the work will diminish damages or at least not enhance them, the contractor may go forward and complete performance. In the Restatement of Contracts, Comment a on section 336, it is said that 'It is not reasonable to expect the plaintiff to avoid harm if at the time for action it appears that the attempt may cause other serious harm. He need not enter into other risky contracts, incur unreasonable inconvenience or expense, disorganize his business, or put himself in a humiliating position or in one involving loss of honor and respect.'

> The general rule is also subject to the jurisdiction of equity to order specific performance of the contract, and, apparently in recognition of this principle, it has been held that in cases where damages will not afford adequate

---

disregard of principal's orders, principal had no duty to deal with another broker from same firm even though that might reduce damages).

compensation and where specific performance will lie, the plaintiff may continue to perform, in spite of a notice to stop, and thereafter recover on the basis of his continued performance. . . ."

Bomberger v. McKelvey, 35 Cal. 2d 607, 614–15, 220 P.2d 729, 733–34 (1950).

These exceptions can lead to arguably inefficient outcomes. In *Bomberger*, McKelvey bought a lot from Bomberger and agreed to pay $3,500 for Bomberger to demolish the existing building on the lot. Bomberger was allowed to salvage parts from the building. Bomberger planned to use the parts to build a new home for the current tenant in the building. This second contract was understood to be a requisite condition to the formation of the original contract between McKelvey and Bomberger. Due to delays in its construction plans for the lot, McKelvey ordered Bomberger to not proceed with the demolition. Bomberger ignored the order, demolishing the building in order to salvage parts that, due to wartime shortages, could not be obtained elsewhere for three months. The demolished building was worth approximately $26,000 and generated $300 in monthly rent, while replacing the salvageable parts would have cost $540, plus the expenses of a three-month delay., The Supreme Court of California awarded Bomberger the contract price, despite the discrepancy between the lost value of the demolished building and the cost to Bomberger of a three-month delay. Did the court get it right, or does its application of the rule cause more social harm than good? *See* Mark P. Gergen, *A Theory of Self-Help Remedies in Contract*, 89 B.U. L. Rev. 1397, 1408 (2009). After discussing *Bomberger* and other examples, Professor Gergen argues that the mitigation doctrine is riddled with so many exceptions that the *Luten Bridge* decision should be seen as the exception, not the rule.

For another exception to the mitigation doctrine, consider UCC § 2-704. When a buyer breaches a contract and the contracted-for goods are unfinished, a seller may complete the manufacture of the goods "for the purposes of avoiding loss and of effective realization." UCC § 2-704(2). The seller is to exercise "reasonable commercial judgment" in making this decision, and he will not be awarded damages if it was clear that completing the goods would increase damages. *See* UCC § 2-704 cmt. 2. Why this exception for goods? What justifies treating a bridge to nowhere and a halfway-built recliner differently?

3. ***Mitigation in Personal Service Contracts.*** What are the parties' incentives when an employer breaches a personal service contract? Suppose that, following the studio's breach, Shirley MacLaine had gone to work as an investment banker and earned twice as much as she expected to earn from "Bloomer Girl." Would her salary be credited to the studio's "account"? Suppose, instead that in order to prepare herself for possible future parts in the movies, she goes to work as a department store salesperson at a salary of $150 per week? What effect would this have on her breach of contract action? Would you give a different answer if she went to work as a department store salesperson in order to feed herself?

Professor Victor Goldberg has criticized the *Parker* court's decision as a judicial misconstruction of the contract's plain meaning and the parties' clear *ex ante* intentions.[29] Goldberg suggests that the California Supreme Court ignored the easy and obvious solution to MacLaine's dispute with Twentieth Century Fox: enforcing Fox's contractual obligation as expressly specified in the contract. He points to the contract's "pay-or-play" provision, which provided that Fox "shall not be obligated to utilize your services in or in connection with the Photoplay hereunder, our sole obligation, subject to the terms and conditions of the Agreement, being to pay you the guaranteed compensation provided for." 1998 WIS. L. REV. AT 1055. By the terms of this provision, the studio purchased the option to use MacLaine in the film (the price of the option being the fixed compensation), and she promised to be available during the specified time period and to forego other roles that might be offered her. Indeed, she did turn down one role with a fixed compensation of $1 million. Moreover, the court failed to note that the $750,000 fixed fee was only a portion of her compensation; it was to be offset against 10% of the gross.

Goldberg asserts, then, that the California courts misinterpreted the contract by focusing on the question of mitigating damages, an issue which the clear language of the contract rendered moot. The "pay-or-play" clause meant MacLaine did not have to mitigate the damages at all, since her $750,000 was guaranteed the moment the parties signed the contract. Even if she had taken the "different and inferior" alternative employment offered by Fox, MacLaine would still be entitled to her compensation from "Bloomer Girl" under the contract's express provisions.

4. *Calculating the Mitigation Offset.* Courts often deal with the difficult issue of assessing how much a damage award should be reduced by mitigation efforts of the plaintiff. *Kearsage Computer v. Acme Staple Co.*, 116 N.H. 705, 366 A.2d 467 (1976), illustrates the issues a court must consider when calculating the mitigation offset to a damage award. Kearsage performed electronic data processing for Acme under a one-year contract, which Acme wrongfully terminated. On appeal to the New Hampshire Supreme Court, Acme argued that Kearsage's damage award of $12,313.22 should be reduced by the expenses Kearsage saved due to the breach and by the new business Kearsage generated following the breach. The court first rejected Acme's claim for a reduction based on saved expenses, concluding that any variable expenses Kearsage's three employees saved due to Acme's breach were nominal. The court ruled that all other costs, including labor, space and equipment rental, and other overhead expenses, were fixed and did not change significantly after Acme's breach. The court then rejected Acme's second claim for a mitigation offset due to new business accepted after the breach:

> After Acme terminated the contract, Kearsage increased its efforts to secure new business. Acme's position is that at least some of the income from the new business should mitigate the damages. The general rule is that gains made by the injured party on other transactions after the breach are never to be deducted from damages that are otherwise recoverable, unless such gains could not have been made, had there been no breach. . . . In contrast, no deduction is allowed if the plaintiff sells to a third party a product that can be produced on demand. The theory is that the second sale would have occurred even if the defendant did not breach

---

[29] *See* Victor Goldberg, *Bloomer Girl Revisited or How to Frame an Unmade Picture*, 1998 WIS. L. REV. 1051; *see also* VICTOR GOLDBERG, FRAMING CONTRACT LAW: AN ECONOMIC PERSPECTIVE 279–309 (2007).

his contract. . . . The law presumes that they can accept a virtually unlimited amount of business so that income generated from accounts acquired after the breach does not mitigate the plaintiff's damages. . . . We hold that in the absence of evidence to the contrary a data processing contract does not involve personal services to such an extent that when the provider of such services seeks new business after a breach of contract, the income from such new business mitigates the damages owed him by the breaching party.

Id. at 709–10.

What if a wrongfully discharged employee mitigates by taking a substantially similar position, and then is fired for bad conduct at the new job? Will a court still count the new job as mitigation and thus decrease the employee's damages from the original wrongful termination? A California Court of Appeals thought so:

> The parties have not cited nor has our independent research revealed any cases analyzing what is meant by the duty to mitigate in the context of an employee who, after finding and accepting comparable employment, loses the position because of his or her own conduct. . . . However, when one considers the basic principles underlying the mitigation rule, it is manifest that a jury, in deciding the reasonableness of a wrongfully discharged employee's efforts to mitigate damages, may properly take into account that employee's failure to retain comparable employment once it has been secured. The crux of the mitigation rule is that while the compensation to which the employee would have been entitled for the unexpired period of the contract affords a prima facie measure of damages, the employee's "actual damage is the amount of money he [or she] was out of pocket *by reason of the wrongful discharge.*" [footnotes omitted, emphasis original]. Therefore, in those instances where the jury determines the employee was fired from a substantially similar position for cause, any amount the employee with reasonable effort could have earned by retaining that employment should be deducted for the amount of damages which otherwise would have been awarded to the employee under the terms of the original employment agreement.

Stanchfield v. Hamer Toyota, Inc., 37 Cal. App. 4th 1495, 1502–03, 44 Cal. Rptr. 2d 565, 568 (1995).

In *Stanchfield*, the employee was wrongfully terminated from a "for cause" employment contract, which means that the employer was required to state a good reason for the termination. At trial, the court concluded that Stanchfield's second job could mitigate the original employer's damages, even though his second job was "at will," meaning the employer could fire him for any or no reason. Given the *Parker* court's conclusion that a "different and inferior" position offered a wrongfully terminated employee will not offset the damage award, is this correct?

[4] Liquidated Damages

The doctrines requiring that damage claims be reasonably certain, foreseeable and mitigated represent classic common law limitations on the plaintiff's right to recover full compensatory damages. We turn now to a final method of limiting a defaulting promisor's liability for fully compensatory damages. Assume the parties agree at the time of contracting that damages for breach will be limited according to a prescribed formula. Subsequently, following a breach by the promisor, the promisee sues for full consequential damages, claiming that the clause liquidating damages is not enforceable. How would you predict that a court will respond to such a claim? Your first reaction might be to ask whether or not the promisee was a consumer, and whether the contract passed the tests of informed, voluntary consent that we examined in Chapter 5. Assume that you determine that both parties were large business firms and that the contract was negotiated over time with competent legal counsel on both sides. At that point, you might be tempted to conclude that — just as with any freely negotiated opt out from the standard default rules — the limited damages clause should be fully enforceable. Before you reach this conclusion, however, consider the following cases.

LAKE RIVER CORP. v. CARBORUNDUM CO.
United States Court of Appeals, Seventh Circuit
769 F.2d 1284 (1985)

POSNER, J.

This diversity suit between Lake River Corporation and Carborundum Company requires us to consider questions of Illinois commercial law, and in particular to explore the fuzzy line between penalty clauses and liquidated-damages clauses.

Carborundum manufactures "Ferro Carbo," an abrasive powder used in making steel. To serve its midwestern customers better, Carborundum made a contract with Lake River by which the latter agreed to provide distribution services in its warehouse in Illinois. Lake River would receive Ferro Carbo in bulk from Carborundum, "bag" it, and ship the bagged product to Carborundum's customers. The Ferro Carbo would remain Carborundum's property until delivered to the customers.

Carborundum insisted that Lake River install a new bagging system to handle the contract. In order to be sure of being able to recover the cost of the new system ($89,000) and make a profit of 20 percent of the contract price, Lake River insisted on the following minimum-quantity guarantee:

> In consideration of the special equipment (i.e., the new bagging system) to be acquired and furnished by LAKE-RIVER for handling the product, CARBORUNDUM shall, during the initial three-year term of this Agreement, ship to LAKE-RIVER for bagging a minimum quantity of (22,500 tons). If, at the end of the three-year term, this minimum quantity shall not have been shipped, LAKE-RIVER shall invoice CARBORUNDUM at the then prevailing rates for the difference between the quantity bagged and the minimum guaranteed.

If Carborundum had shipped the full minimum quantity that it guaranteed, it would have owed Lake River roughly $533,000 under the contract.

After the contract was signed in 1979, the demand for domestic steel, and with it the demand for Ferro Carbo, plummeted, and Carborundum failed to ship the guaranteed amount. When the contract expired late in 1982, Carborundum had shipped only 12,000 of the 22,500 tons it had guaranteed. Lake River had bagged the 12,000 tons and had billed Carborundum for this bagging, and Carborundum had paid, but by virtue of the formula in the minimum-guarantee clause Carborundum still owed Lake River $241,000 — the contract price of $533,000 if the full amount of Ferro Carbo had been shipped, minus what Carborundum had paid for the bagging of the quantity it had shipped.

When Lake River demanded payment of this amount, Carborundum refused, on the ground that the formula imposed a penalty. At the time, Lake River had in its warehouse 500 tons of bagged Ferro Carbo, having a market value of $269,000, which it refused to release unless Carborundum paid the $241,000 due under the formula. Lake River did offer to sell the bagged product and place the proceeds in escrow until its dispute with Carborundum over the enforceability of the formula was resolved, but Carborundum rejected the offer and trucked in bagged Ferro Carbo from the East to serve its customers in Illinois, at an additional cost of $31,000.

Lake River brought this suit for $241,000, which it claims as liquidated damages. Carborundum counterclaimed for the value of the bagged Ferro Carbo when Lake River impounded it and the additional cost of serving the customers affected by the impounding. The theory of the counterclaim is that the impounding was a conversion, and not as Lake River contends the assertion of a lien. The district judge, after a bench trial, gave judgment for both parties. Carborundum ended up roughly $42,000 to the good: $269,000 + $31,000 – $241,000 – $17,000, the last figure representing prejudgment interest on Lake River's damages. (We have rounded off all dollar figures to the nearest thousand.) Both parties have appealed.

The only issue that is not one of damages is whether Lake River had a valid lien on the bagged Ferro Carbo that it refused to ship to Carborundum's customers — that, indeed, it holds in its warehouse to this day. Although Ferro Carbo does not deteriorate with age, the domestic steel industry remains in the doldrums and the product is worth less than it was in 1982 when Lake River first withheld it. If Lake River did not have a valid lien on the product, then it converted it, and must pay Carborundum the $269,000 that the Ferro Carbo was worth back then.

It might seem that if the minimum-guarantee clause was a penalty clause and hence unenforceable, the lien could not be valid, and therefore that we should discuss the penalty issue first. But this is not correct. If the contractual specification of damages is invalid, Lake River still is entitled to any actual damages caused by Carborundum's breach of contract in failing to deliver the minimum amount of Ferro Carbo called for by the contract. The issue is whether an entitlement to damages, large or small, entitles the victim of the breach to assert a lien on goods that are in its possession though they belong to the other party.

Lake River has not been very specific about the type of lien it asserts. We think it best described as a form of artisan's lien, the "lien of the bailee, who does work upon or adds materials to chattels. . . ." Restatement of Security § 61, comment on clause (a), at p. 165 (1941). Lake River was the bailee of the Ferro Carbo that Carborundum delivered to it, and it did work on the Ferro Carbo — bagging it, and also storing it (storage is a service, too). If Carborundum had refused to pay for the services that Lake River performed on the Ferro Carbo delivered to it, then Lake River would have had a lien on the Ferro Carbo in its possession, to coerce payment. But in fact, when Lake River impounded the bagged Ferro Carbo, Carborundum had paid in full for all bagging and storage services that Lake River had performed on Ferro Carbo shipped to it by Carborundum. The purpose of impounding was to put pressure on Carborundum to pay for services not performed, Carborundum having failed to ship the Ferro Carbo on which those services would have been performed.

Unlike a contractor who, having done the work contracted for without having been paid, may find himself in a box, owing his employees or suppliers money he does not have — money he was counting on from his customer — Lake River was the victim of a breach of a portion of the contract that remained entirely unexecuted on either side. Carborundum had not shipped the other 10,500 tons, as promised; but on the other hand Lake River had not had to bag those 10,500 tons, as it had promised. It is not as if Lake River had bagged those tons, incurring heavy costs that it expected to recoup from Carborundum, and then Carborundum had said, "Sorry, we won't pay you; go ahead and sue us."

The hardest issue in the case is whether the formula in the minimum-guarantee clause imposes a penalty for breach of contract or is merely an effort to liquidate damages. Deep as the hostility to penalty clauses runs in the common law, see Lloyd, *Penalties and Forfeitures*, 29 Harv. L. Rev. 117 (1915), we still might be inclined to question, if we thought ourselves free to do so, whether a modern court should refuse to enforce a penalty clause where the signator is a substantial corporation, well able to avoid improvident commitments. Penalty clauses provide an earnest of performance. The clause here enhanced Carborundum's credibility in promising to ship the minimum amount guaranteed by showing that it was willing to pay the full contract price even if it failed to ship anything. On the other side it can be pointed out that by raising the cost of a breach of contract to the contract breaker, a penalty clause increases the risk to his other creditors; increases (what is the same thing and more, because bankruptcy imposes "deadweight" social costs) the risk of bankruptcy; and could amplify the business cycle by increasing the number of bankruptcies in bad times, which is when contracts are most likely to be broken. But since little effort is made to prevent businessmen from assuming risks, these reasons are no better than makeweights.

A better argument is that a penalty clause may discourage efficient as well as inefficient breaches of contract. Suppose a breach would cost the promisee $12,000 in actual damages but would yield the promisor $20,000 in additional profits. Then there would be a net social gain from breach. After being fully compensated for his loss the promisee would be no worse off than if the contract had been performed, while the promisor would be better off by $8,000.

But now suppose the contract contains a penalty clause under which the promisor if he breaks his promise must pay the promisee $25,000. The promisor will be discouraged from breaking the contract, since $25,000, the penalty, is greater than $20,000, the profits of the breach; and a transaction that would have increased value will be forgone.

On this view, since compensatory damages should be sufficient to deter inefficient breaches (that is, breaches that cost the victim more than the gain to the contract breaker), penal damages could have no effect other than to deter some efficient breaches. But this overlooks the earlier point that the willingness to agree to a penalty clause is a way of making the promisor and his promise credible and may therefore be essential to inducing some value-maximizing contracts to be made. It also overlooks the more important point that the parties (always assuming they are fully competent) will, in deciding whether to include a penalty clause in their contract, weigh the gains against the costs — costs that include the possibility of discouraging an efficient breach somewhere down the road — and will include the clause only if the benefits exceed those costs as well as all other costs.

On this view the refusal to enforce penalty clauses is (at best) paternalistic — and it seems odd that courts should display parental solicitude for large corporations. But however this may be, we must be on guard to avoid importing our own ideas of sound public policy into an area where our proper judicial role is more than usually deferential. The responsibility for making innovations in the common law of Illinois rests with the courts of Illinois, and not with the federal courts in Illinois. And like every other state, Illinois, untroubled by academic skepticism of the wisdom of refusing to enforce penalty clauses against sophisticated promisors, see, e.g., Charles J. Goetz & Robert E. Scott, *Liquidated Damages, Penalties and the Just Compensation Principle*, 77 Colum. L. Rev. 554 (1977), continues steadfastly to insist on the distinction between penalties and liquidated damages. See, e.g., Stride v. 120 West Madison Bldg. Corp., 132 Ill. App. 3d 601, 605-06 (1985). To be valid under Illinois law a liquidation of damages must be a reasonable estimate at the time of contracting of the likely damages from breach, and the need for estimation at that time must be shown by reference to the likely difficulty of measuring the actual damages from a breach of contract after the breach occurs. If damages would be easy to determine then, or if the estimate greatly exceeds a reasonable upper estimate of what the damages are likely to be, it is a penalty.

The distinction between a penalty and liquidated damages is not an easy one to draw in practice but we are required to draw it and can give only limited weight to the district court's determination. Whether a provision for damages is a penalty clause or a liquidated-damages clause is a question of law rather than fact, and unlike some courts of appeals we do not treat a determination by a federal district judge of an issue of state law as if it were a finding of fact, and reverse only if persuaded that clear error has occurred, though we give his determination respectful consideration.

Mindful that Illinois courts resolve doubtful cases in favor of classification as a penalty, see, e.g., Stride v. 120 West Madison Bldg. Corp., *supra*, we conclude that the damage formula in this case is a penalty and not a liquidation of damages, because it is designed always to assure Lake River more than its actual damages. The formula — full contract price minus the amount already invoiced to Carborundum — is invariant to the gravity of the breach. When a contract specifies a single sum in damages for any and all breaches even though it is apparent that all are not of the same gravity, the specification is not a reasonable effort to estimate damages; and when in addition the fixed sum greatly exceeds the actual damages likely to be inflicted by a minor breach, its character as a penalty becomes unmistakable. This case is within the gravitational field of these principles even though the minimum-guarantee clause does not fix a single sum as damages.

Suppose to begin with that the breach occurs the day after Lake River buys its new bagging system for $89,000 and before Carborundum ships any Ferro Carbo. Carborundum would owe Lake River $533,000. Since Lake River would have incurred at that point a total cost of only $89,000, its net gain from the breach would be $444,000. This is more than four times the profit of $107,000 (20 percent of the contract price of $533,000) that Lake River expected to make from the contract if it had been performed: a huge windfall.

Next suppose (as actually happened here) that breach occurs when 55 percent of the Ferro Carbo has been shipped. Lake River would already have received $293,000 from Carborundum. To see what its costs then would have been (as estimated at the time of contracting), first subtract Lake River's anticipated profit on the contract of $107,000 from the total contract price of $533,000. The difference — Lake River's total cost of performance — is $426,000. Of this, $89,000 is the cost of the new bagging system, a fixed cost. The rest ($426,000 – $89,000 = $337,000) presumably consists of variable costs that are roughly proportional to the amount of Ferro Carbo bagged; there is no indication of any other fixed costs. Assume, therefore, that if Lake River bagged 55 percent of the contractually agreed quantity, it incurred in doing so 55 percent of its variable costs, or $185,000. When this is added to the cost of the new bagging system, assumed for the moment to be worthless except in connection with the contract, the total cost of performance to Lake River is $274,000. Hence a breach that occurred after 55 percent of contractual performance was complete would be expected to yield Lake River a modest profit of $19,000 ($293,000 – $274,000). But now add the "liquidated damages" of $241,000 that Lake River claims, and the result is a total gain from the breach of $260,000, which is almost two and a half times the profit that Lake River expected to gain if there was no breach. And this ignores any use value or salvage value of the new bagging system, which is the property of Lake River — though admittedly it also ignores the time value of money; Lake River paid $89,000 for that system before receiving any revenue from the contract.

To complete the picture, assume that the breach had not occurred till performance was 90 percent complete. Then the "liquidated damages" clause would not be so one-sided, but it would be one-sided. Carborundum would have paid $480,000 for bagging. Against this, Lake River would have incurred its fixed cost of $89,000 plus 90 percent of its variable costs of $337,000, or $303,000. Its total costs would thus be $392,000, and its net profit $88,000. But on top of this it would be entitled to "liquidated damages" of $53,000, for a total profit of $141,000 — more than 30 percent more than its expected profit of $107,000 if there was no breach.

The reason for these results is that most of the costs to Lake River of performing the contract are saved if the contract is broken, and this saving is not reflected in the damage formula. As a result, at whatever point in the life of the contract a breach occurs, the damage formula gives Lake River more than its lost profits from the breach — dramatically more if the breach occurs at the beginning of the contract; tapering off at the end, it is true. Still, over the interval between the beginning of Lake River's performance and nearly the end, the clause could be expected to generate profits ranging from 400 percent of the expected contract profits to 130 percent of those profits. And this is on the assumption that the bagging system has no value apart from the contract. If it were worth only $20,000 to Lake River, the range would be 434 percent to 150 percent.

Lake River argues that it would never get as much as the formula suggests, because it would be required to mitigate its damages. This is a dubious argument on several grounds. First, mitigation of damages is a doctrine of the law of court-assessed damages, while the point of a liquidated-damages clause is to substitute party assessment; and that point is blunted, and the certainty that liquidated-damages clauses are designed to give the process of assessing damages impaired, if a defendant can force the plaintiff to take less than the damages specified in the clause, on the ground that the plaintiff could have avoided some of them. It would seem therefore that the clause in this case should be read to eliminate any duty of mitigation, that what Lake River is doing is attempting to rewrite the clause to make it more reasonable, and that since actually the clause is designed to give Lake River the full damages it would incur from breach (and more) even if it made no effort to find a substitute use for the equipment that it bought to perform the contract, this is just one more piece of evidence that it is a penalty clause rather than a liquidated-damages clause.

But in any event mitigation would not mitigate the penal character of this clause. If Carborundum did not ship the guaranteed minimum quantity, the reason was likely to be — the reason was — that the steel industry had fallen on hard times and the demand for Ferro Carbo was therefore down. In these circumstances Lake River would have little prospect of finding a substitute contract that would yield it significant profits to set off against the full contract price, which is the method by which it proposes to take account of mitigation. At argument Lake River suggested that it might at least have been able to sell the new bagging equipment to someone for something, and the figure $40,000 was proposed. If the breach occurred on the first day when performance under the contract was due and Lake River promptly sold the bagging equipment for $40,000, its liquidated damages would fall to $493,000. But by the same token its costs would fall to $49,000. Its profit would still be $444,000, which as we said was more than 400 percent of its expected profit on the contract. The penal component would be unaffected.

With the penalty clause in this case compare the liquidated-damages clause in Arduini v. Board of Education, *supra*, which is representative of such clauses upheld in Illinois. The plaintiff was a public school teacher whose contract provided that if he resigned before the end of the school year he would be docked 4 percent of his salary. This was a modest fraction of the contract price. And the cost to the school of an untimely resignation would be difficult to measure. Since that cost would be greater the more senior and experienced the teacher was, the fact that the liquidated damages would be greater the higher the teacher's salary did not make the clause arbitrary.

Even the fact that the liquidated damages were the same whether the teacher resigned at the beginning, the middle, or the end of the school year was not arbitrary, for it was unclear how the amount of actual damages would vary with the time of resignation. Although one might think that the earlier the teacher resigned the greater the damage to the school would be, the school might find it easier to hire a replacement for the whole year or a great part of it than to bring in a replacement at the last minute to grade the exams left behind by the resigning teacher. Here, in contrast, it is apparent from the face of the contract that the damages provided for by the "liquidated damages" clause are grossly disproportionate to any probable loss and penalize some breaches much more heavily than others regardless of relative cost.

We do not mean by this discussion to cast a cloud of doubt over the "take or pay" clauses that are a common feature of contracts between natural gas pipeline companies and their customers. Such clauses require the customer, in consideration of the pipeline's extending its line to his premises, to take a certain amount of gas at a specified price — and if he fails to take it to pay the full price anyway. The resemblance to the minimum-guarantee clause in the present case is obvious, but perhaps quite superficial. Neither party has mentioned take-or-pay clauses, and we can find no case where such a clause was even challenged as a penalty clause — though in one case it was argued that such a clause made the damages unreasonably low. See National Fuel Gas Distribution Corp. v. Pennsylvania Public Utility Comm'n, 76 Pa. Commw. 102, 126-27 n. 8 (1983). If, as appears not to be the case here but would often be the case in supplying natural gas, a supplier's fixed costs were a very large fraction of his total costs, a take-or-pay clause might well be a reasonable liquidation of damages. In the limit, if all the supplier's costs were incurred before he began supplying the customer, the contract revenues would be an excellent measure of the damages from breach. But in this case, the supplier (Lake River, viewed as a supplier of bagging services to Carborundum) incurred only a fraction of its costs before performance began, and the interruption of performance generated a considerable cost saving that is not reflected in the damage formula.

The fact that the damage formula is invalid does not deprive Lake River of a remedy. The parties did not contract explicitly with reference to the measure of damages if the agreed-on damage formula was invalidated, but all this means is that the victim of the breach is entitled to his common law damages. See, e.g., Restatement, Second, Contracts § 356, comment a (1981). In this case that would be the unpaid contract price of $241,000 minus the costs that Lake River saved by not having to complete the contract (the variable costs on the other 45 percent of the Ferro Carbo that it never had to bag). The case must be remanded to the district judge to fix these damages.

The judgment of the district court is affirmed in part and reversed in part, and the case is returned to that court to redetermine both parties' damages in accordance with the principles in this opinion. The parties may present additional evidence on remand, and shall bear their own costs in this court.

CALIFORNIA & HAWAIIAN SUGAR CO. v. SUN SHIP, INC.
United States Court of Appeals for the Ninth Circuit
794 F.2d 1433 (1986)

NOONAN, J.

BACKGROUND

C and H is an agricultural cooperative owned by fourteen sugar plantations in Hawaii. Its business consists in transporting raw sugar — the crushed cane in the form of coarse brown crystal — to its refinery in Crockett, California. Roughly one million tons a year of sugar are harvested in Hawaii. A small portion is refined there; the bulk goes to Crockett. The refined sugar — the white stuff — is sold by C and H to groceries for home consumption and to the soft drink and cereal companies that are its industrial customers.

To conduct its business, C and H has an imperative need for assured carriage for the raw sugar from the islands. Sugar is a seasonal crop, with 70 percent of the harvest occurring between April and October, while almost nothing is harvestable during December and January. Consequently, transportation must not only be available, but seasonably available. Storage capacity in Hawaii accommodates not more than a quarter of the crop. Left stored on the ground or left unharvested, sugar suffers the loss of sucrose and goes to waste. Shipping ready and able to carry the raw sugar is a priority for C and H.

In 1979 C and H was notified that Matson Navigation Company, which had been supplying the bulk of the necessary shipping, was withdrawing its services as of January 1981. While C and H had some ships at its disposal, it found a pressing need for a large new vessel, to be in service at the height of the sugar season in 1981. It decided to commission the building of a kind of hybrid — a tug of catamaran design with two hulls and, joined to the tug, a barge with a wedge which would lock between the two pontoons of the tug, producing an "integrated tug barge." In Hawaiian, the barge and the entire vessel were each described as a Mocababoo or push boat.

C and H relied on the architectural advice of the New York firm, J.J. Henry. It solicited bids from shipyards, indicating as an essential term a "preferred delivery date" of June 1981. It decided to accept Sun's offer to build the barge and Halter's offer to build the tug.

In the fall of 1979 C and H entered into negotiations with Sun on the precise terms of the contract. Each company was represented by a vice-president with managerial responsibility in the area of negotiation; each company had a team of negotiators; each company had the advice of counsel in drafting the agreement that was signed on November 14, 1979. This agreement was entitled "Contract for the Construction of One Oceangoing Barge for California and Hawaiian Sugar Company By Sun Ship, Inc." The "Whereas" clause of the contract identified C and H as the Purchaser, and Sun as the Contractor; it identified "one non-self-propelled oceangoing barge" as the Vessel that Purchaser was buying from Contractor. Article

I provided that Contractor would deliver the Vessel on June 30, 1981. The contract price was $25,405,000.

Under Article I of the agreement, Sun was entitled to an extension of the delivery date for the usual types of force majeure and for "unavailability of the Tug to Contractor for joining to the Vessel, where it is determined that Contractor has complied with all obligations under the Interface Agreement." (The Interface Agreement, executed the same day between C and H, Sun, and Halter provided that Sun would connect the barge with the tug.) Article 17 "Delivery" provided that "the Vessel shall be offered for delivery fully and completely connected with the Tug." Article 8, "Liquidated Damages for Delay in Delivery" provided that if "Delivery of the Vessel" was not made on "the Delivery Date" of June 30, 1981, Sun would pay C and H "as per-day liquidated damages, and not as a penalty" a sum described as "a reasonable measure of the damages" — $17,000 per day.

On the same date C and H entered into an agreement with Halter to purchase "one oceangoing catamaran tug boat" for $20,350,000. The tug (the "Vessel" of that contract) was to be delivered on April 30, 1981 at Sun's shipyard. Liquidated damages of $10,000 per day were provided for Halter's failure to deliver.

Halter did not complete the tug until July 15, 1982. Sun did not complete the barge until March 16, 1982. Tug and barge were finally connected under C and H's direction in mid-July 1982 and christened the Moku Pahu. C and H settled its claim against Halter. Although Sun paid C and H $17,000 per day from June 30, 1981 until January 10, 1982, it ultimately denied liability for any damages, and this lawsuit resulted.

ANALYSIS

Sun contends that its obligation was to deliver the barge connected to the tug on the delivery date of June 30, 1981 and that only the failure to deliver the integrated hybrid would have triggered the liquidated damage clause. It is true that Article 17 creates some ambiguity by specifying that the Vessel is to be "offered for delivery completely connected with the Tug." The case of the barge being ready while the tug was not, is not explicitly considered. Nonetheless, the meaning of "Vessel" is completely unambiguous. From the "Whereas" clause to the articles of the agreement dealing with insurance, liens, and title, "the Vessel" is the barge. It would require the court to rewrite the contract to find that "the Vessel" in Article 8 on liquidated damages does not mean the barge. The article takes effect on failure to deliver "the Vessel" — that is, the barge.

Sun contends, however, that on such a reading of the contract, the $17,000 per day is a penalty, not to be enforced by the court. The barge, Sun points out, was useless to C and H without the tug. Unconnected, the barge was worse than useless — it was an expensive liability. C and H did not want the barge by itself. To get $17,000 per day as "damages" for failure to provide an unwanted and unusable craft is, Sun says, to exact a penalty. C and H seeks to be "paid according to the tenour of the bond"; it "craves the law." And if C and H sticks to the letter of the bond, it must like Shylock end by losing; a court of justice will not be so vindictive. Breach of contract entitles the wronged party only to fair compensation.

Seductive as Sun's argument is, it does not carry the day. Represented by sophisticated representatives, C and H and Sun reached the agreement that $17,000 a day was the reasonable measure of the loss C and H would suffer if the barge was not ready. Of course they assumed that the tug would be ready. But in reasonable anticipation of the damages that would occur if the tug was ready and the barge was not, Article 8 was adopted. As the parties foresaw the situation, C and H would have a tug waiting connection but no barge and so no shipping. The anticipated damages were what might be expected if C and H could not transport the Hawaiian sugar crop at the height of the season. Those damages were clearly before both parties. As Joe Kleschick, Sun's chief negotiator, testified, he had "a vision" of a "mountain of sugar piling up in Hawaii" — a vision that C and H conjured up in negotiating the damage clause. Given the anticipated impact on C and H's raw sugar and on C and H's ability to meet the demands of its grocery and industrial customers if the sugar could not be transported, liquidated damages of $17,000 a day were completely reasonable.

The situation as it developed was different from the anticipation. The barge was not ready but neither was the tug. C and H was in fact able to find other shipping. The crop did not rot. The customers were not left sugarless. Sun argues that, measured by the actual damages suffered, the liquidated damages were penal.

We look to Pennsylvania law for guidance. Although no Pennsylvania case is squarely on point, it is probable that Pennsylvania would interpret the contract as a sale of goods governed by the Uniform Commercial Code. *Belmont Industries, Inc. v. Bechtel Corp.*, 425 F. Supp. 524, 527 (E.D.Pa.1976). The governing statute provides that liquidated damages are considered reasonable "in the light of anticipated or actual harm." UCC 2-718(1).

The choice of the disjunctive appears to be deliberate. The language chosen is in harmony with the Restatement (Second) of Contracts § 356 (1979), which permits liquidated damages in the light of the anticipated or actual loss caused by the breach and the difficulties of proof of loss. Section 356, Comment b declares explicitly: "Furthermore, the amount fixed is reasonable to the extent that it approximates the loss anticipated at the time of the making of the contract, even though it may not approximate the actual loss."

Despite the statutory disjunctive and the Restatement's apparent blessing of it, the question is not settled by these authorities which must be read in the light of common law principles already established and accepted in Pennsylvania. Prior to the adoption of the Uniform Commercial Code, Pennsylvania enforced liquidated damage clauses that its courts labeled as nonpenal, but equitable considerations relating to the actual harm incurred were taken into account along with the difficulty of proving damages if a liquidated damage clause was rejected, e.g., *Emery v. Boyle*, 200 Pa. 249, 49 A. 779 (1901). We do not believe that the *UCC* overrode this line of reasoning. Indeed, in a lower court case, decided after the *UCC*'s enactment, it was stated that if liquidated damages appear unreasonable in light of the harm suffered, "the contractual provision will be voided as a penalty." *Unit Vending Corp. v. Tobin Enterprises*, 194 Pa. Super. 470, 473, 168 A.2d 750, 751 (1961). That case, however, is not on all fours with our case. . . . The case, however, does show that Pennsylvania courts, like courts elsewhere, attempt to interpret the governing statute humanely and equitably.

The Restatement § 356 Comment b, after accepting anticipated damages as a measure, goes on to say that if the difficulty of proof of loss is slight, then actual damage may be the measure of reasonableness: "If, to take an extreme case, it is clear that no loss at all has occurred, a provision fixing a substantial sum as damages is unenforceable. See Illustration 4." Illustration 4 is a case of a contractor, A, agreeing to build B's race track by a specific date and to pay B $1,000 a day for every day's delay. A delays a month, but B does not get permission to operate the track for that month, so B suffers no loss. In that event, the Restatement characterizes the $1,000 per day as an unenforceable penalty. Sun contends that it is in the position of A: no actual loss was suffered by C and H because C and H had no tug to mate with the barge.

This argument restates in a new form Sun's basic contention that the liquidated damage clause was meant to operate only if the integrated tug barge was not delivered. If Illustration 4 is the present case, Sun is home scot-free. The Restatement, however, deals with a case where the defaulting contractor was alone in his default. We deal with a case of concurrent defaults. If we were to be so literal-minded as to follow the Restatement here, we would have to conclude that because both parties were in default, C and H suffered no damage until one party performed. Not until the barge was ready in March 1982 could C and H hold Halter for damages, and then only for the period after that date. The continued default of both parties would operate to take each of them off the hook. That cannot be the law.

We conclude, therefore, that in this case of concurrent causation each defaulting contractor is liable for the breach and for the substantial damages which the joint breach occasions. Sun is a substantial cause of the damages flowing from the lack of the integrated tug; Sun cannot be absolved by the absence of the tug.

Sun has a final argument. Even on the assumption that it is liable as a substantial cause of the breach of contract, Sun contends that the actual damages suffered by C and H for lack of the integrated tug boat were slight. Actual damages were found by the district court to consist of "interest on progress payments, unfavorable terms of conversion to long-term financing, and additional labor expense." No dollar amount was determined by the district court in finding that these damages "bore a reasonable relationship to the amount liquidated in the Barge Contract."

The dollar value of the damages found by the district judge is, to judge from C and H's own computation, as follows:

Additional Construction Interest	$1,486,000
Added Payments to J.J. Henry	161,000
Added Vessel Operating Expenses	73,000
C and H Employee Costs	109,000
	$1,829,000

But "actual damages" have no meaning if the actual savings of C and H due to the nondelivery of the integrated tug barge are not subtracted. It was clearly erroneous for the district judge to exclude these savings from his finding. These savings, again according to C and H's own computation, were:

Transportation Savings	$525,000
Lay-up Costs	$936,000
	$1,461,000

The net actual damages suffered by C and H were $368,000. As a matter of law, Sun contends that the liquidated damages are unreasonably disproportionate to the net actual damages.

Litigation has blurred the line between a proper and a penal clause, and the distinction is "not an easy one to draw in practice." *Lake River Corp. v. Carborundum Co.*, 769 F.2d 1284, 1290 (7th Cir. 1985) (per Posner, J.). But the desire of courts to avoid the enforcement of penalties should not obscure common law principles followed in Pennsylvania. Contracts are contracts because they contain enforceable promises, and absent some overriding public policy, those promises are to be enforced. "Where each of the parties is content to take the risk of its turning out in a particular way" why should one "be released from the contract, if there were no misrepresentation or other want of fair dealing?" *Ashcom v. Smith*, 2 Pen. & W. 211, 218-219 (Pa. 1830) (per Gibson, C.J.). Promising to pay damages of a fixed amount, the parties normally have a much better sense of what damages can occur. Courts must be reluctant to override their judgment. Where damages are real but difficult to prove, injustice will be done the injured party if the court substitutes the requirements of judicial proof for the parties' own informed agreement as to what is a reasonable measure of damages. Pennsylvania acknowledges that a seller is bound to pay consequential damages if the seller had reason to know of the buyer's special circumstances. The liquidated damage clause here functions in lieu of a court's determination of the consequential damages suffered by C and H.

These principles inform a leading common law case in the field, *Clydebank Engineering & Shipbuilding Co. v. Yzquierdo y Castaneda*, 1905 A.C. 6. The defendant shipyard had agreed to pay 500 pounds per week per vessel for delay in the delivery of four torpedo boat destroyers to the Spanish Navy in 1897. The shipyard pointed out that had the destroyers been delivered on schedule they would have been sunk with the rest of the Spanish Navy by the Americans in 1898. The House of Lords found the defense unpersuasive. To prove damages the whole administration of the Spanish Navy would have had to have been investigated. The House of Lords refused to undertake such a difficult investigation when the parties had made an honest effort in advance to set in monetary terms what the lack of the destroyers would mean to Spain.

C and H is not the Spanish Navy, but the exact damages caused its manifold operations by lack of the integrated tug boat are equally difficult of ascertainment. C and H claimed that it suffered $3,732,000 in lost charter revenues. Testimony supported the claim, but the district court made no finding as to whether the claim was proved or unproved. The district court did find that the loss of charter revenues had not been anticipated by the parties. But that finding has no bearing on whether the loss occurred. Within the general risk of heavy losses forecast by both parties when they agreed to $17,000 per day damages, a particular type of loss was pointed to by C and H as having happened.

Proof of this loss is difficult — as difficult, perhaps, as proof of loss would have been if the sugar crop had been delivered late because shipping was missing. Whatever the loss, the parties had promised each other that $17,000 per day was a reasonable measure. The court must decline to substitute the requirements of judicial proof for the parties' own conclusion. The Moku Pahu, available on June 30, 1981, was a great prize, capable of multiple employments and enlarging the uses of the entire C and H fleet. When sophisticated parties with bargaining parity have agreed what lack of this prize would mean, and it is now difficult to measure what the lack did mean, the court will uphold the parties' bargain. C and H is entitled to keep the liquidated damages of $3,298,000 it has already received and to receive additional liquidated damages of $1,105,000 with interest thereon, less setoffs determined by the district court. . . .

AFFIRMED.

NOTES

1. *Was Posner Wrong?* According to Professor Victor Goldberg, yes. He believes Judge Posner failed to recognize the functions that the minimum quantity clause served:

> Lake River provided a valuable service by standing ready to bag Carborundum's product. The minimum quantity/minimum payment served two functions (in addition to providing consideration). First, given that Carborundum would have been free to take its business to a lower-cost provider during the three years, the minimum payment drastically reduced the incentive to do so. In effect the clause set the price on the first 22,500 tons at $0. Only for quantities greater than the minimum would Carborundum find it potentially profitable to shop.
>
> Second, it priced the service Lake River provided. Carborundum paid for three years' worth of access to Lake River's bagging facilities at a predetermined pricing formula and that is what it received. It could decide whether to exercise its option (that is, use the facilities) after it learned more about market conditions. The price of that flexibility has nothing to do with damage estimates. The flexibility had value to Carborundum and it was costly to provide for Lake River. The price, like that for other services, would fall somewhere between the expected value to the former and the expected cost of the latter. The price was not quoted explicitly. The higher the minimum, the greater the implicit price of the flexibility. Perhaps Carborundum paid too much for the flexibility, but there is no reason to second-guess the consideration paid for provision of a valuable service."

Victor P. Goldberg, *Cleaning Up Lake River*, 3 Va. L. & Bus. Rev. 427, 440–41 (2008)

Goldberg argues that, when the terms are understood as such, the minimum quantity clause is not a penalty or a liquidated damages clause. Rather, the clause "was a key factor in defining the obligation and in pricing the service." *Id.* at 429. Even if one sees it as a liquidated damages clause, then the added services Goldberg identifies show that it is not a penalty. Do you agree with his analysis?

2. *A Judicial Shift on Liquidated Damages?* Have courts begun to change their outlook on the enforceability of liquidated damages clauses?[30] Compare *C & H Sugar Co. v. Sun Ship* to *Massman Const. Co. v. City Council of Greenville*, 147 F.2d 925 (5th Cir. 1945). In *Massman Construction*, the Fifth Circuit was confronted with a situation substantially similar to the concurrent breach issue in *Sun Ship*. The City of Greenville hired a bridge-builder to construct a bridge across the Mississippi River, and included in the contract a liquidated damages provision that required the builder to pay the City $250 a day for each day delivery of the bridge was late. The bridge-builder was late in delivering the bridge, but argued that the liquidated damages clause was a penalty since Arkansas, the state on the other side of the river, had not completed a road to connect to the new bridge anyway. Similar to Sun Ship's defense above, the bridge-builder claimed that the City suffered no real damages since delay in operating the bridge was inevitable given Arkansas' failure to construct a connecting road. Unlike the result in *Sun Ship*, the Fifth Circuit agreed with the builder and reversed an award of liquidated damages. Can *Sun Ship* be better understood, therefore, as signaling an increased willingness on the part of courts to enforce liquidated damages provisions between sophisticated parties?

3. *Deposit Forfeiture and Liquidated Damages.* Litigation is common in real property transactions when a seller retains a defaulting buyer's deposit as liquidated damages. Buyers often attempt to characterize the deposit forfeiture as an unenforceable penalty and seek to prove this by demonstrating the property's appreciation, suggesting that the seller was benefited by the buyer's breach. Modern courts sometimes decline to accept buyers' arguments in these situations. Consider *Lind Bldg. Corp. v. Pacific Bellevue Dev.*, 55 Wash. App. 70, 776 P.2d 977 (1989). Lind contracted to purchase a tract of land from Bellevue for $4,144,085, paying a deposit of $20,000 in September of 1983. Lind encountered financing difficulties that required four separate extensions of the contract, and Bellevue demanded additional deposits from Lind for every extension. By May 6, 1984, when Bellevue declared the contract breached, Lind had transferred $250,000 in deposits, which Bellevue retained as liquidated damages.

On June 5, 1984, Bellevue sold the property to a third party for $5,150,000. Lind sued Bellevue for recovery of its down payments, contending that the liquidated damages clause was an unenforceable penalty. The Washington appeals court agreed, and concluded as follows:

> There are three reasons the liquidated damages clause in this case is unenforceable. The amount of $250,000 came into existence for reasons

---

[30] There has been considerable scholarly debate on the utility of liquidated damages provisions in recent years. Many of these articles have been critical of the continuing reluctance of courts freely to enforce liquidated damages clauses. *See, e.g.*, Alan Schwartz, *The Myth That Promisees Prefer Supracompensatory Remedies: An Analysis of Contracting for Damage Measures*, 100 YALE L.J. 369 (1990); Lewis Kornhauser, *An Introduction to the Economic Analysis of Contract Remedies*, 57 U. COLO. L. REV. 683 (1986); Kenneth W. Clarkson, Roger L. Miller & Timothy Muris, *Liquidated Damages v. Penalties: Sense or Nonsense?*, 1978 WIS. L. REV. 351; Charles J. Goetz & Robert E. Scott, *Liquidated Damages, Penalties, and the Just Compensation Puzzle*, 77 COLUM. L. REV. 554 (1977). *But see* Samuel Rea, *Efficiency Implications of Penalties and Liquidated Damages*, 13 J. LEGAL STUD. 147 (1984) (arguing that non-enforcement of penalty clauses promotes efficiency).

unrelated to a provision calling for liquidated damages and, therefore, does not represent an effort by the parties to make a reasonable forecast of anticipated damages. The second reason is that, there being no actual substantial damages, the requirement of the rule that the amount of liquidated damages be reasonable in the light of the anticipated or actual loss cannot be satisfied. Thirdly, calculation of the amounts [Bellevue] claims represent losses due to Lind's default are not difficult of ascertainment or proof.

Id. at 77–78, 776 P.2d at 981–982.

Essay: An Economic Analysis of Liquidated Damages

In their article on liquidated damages cited in *Lake River*,[31] Professors Goetz and Scott note the historic antagonism of courts towards liquidated damages clauses.[32] They argue that there are benign reasons for employing such clauses and that courts should therefore give them effect on a much wider basis. The following excerpt summarizes their arguments.

> Facing [the] conventional damage measure, contracting parties have incentives to negotiate liquidated damages clauses whenever the costs of negotiating are less than the expected costs resulting from reliance on the standard damage rule for breach. There are two primary factors which might induce the decision to negotiate: (1) The expected damages are readily calculable, but the parties determine that advance stipulation will save litigation or settlement costs; (2) The expected damages are uncertain or difficult to establish and the parties wish to allocate anticipated risks. Of course, these factors may be present singly or in combination.
>
> Pre-breach agreements will not be legally enforceable, however, unless two requirements coincide. First, the agreement must be a reasonable forecast of just compensation for the anticipated harm that would be caused by the breach. Second, the possible damages which might result from the breach must be uncertain and difficult to estimate. However, liquidated damages provisions have seldom been voided solely because the damages were easy to estimate. Instead, courts have considered the degree of uncertainty an influential factor in determining the reasonableness of the estimate. If the conditions inducing damage agreements are viewed on a continuum, the application of the penalty rule becomes clearer: as the uncertainty facing the contracting parties increases, so does their latitude in stipulating post-breach damages.[33]

---

[31] Charles J. Goetz & Robert E. Scott, *Liquidated Damages, Penalties and the Just Compensation Principle: Some Notes on an Enforcement Model and a Theory of Efficient Breach*, 77 COLUM. L. REV. 554 (1977).

[32] Clauses providing for specific performance as the remedy for breach have also fared poorly in the courts. *See Stokes v. Moore*, 262 Ala. 59 (1955).

[33] It appears that the drafters of the Uniform Commercial Code have tacitly adopted this approach. Section 2-718(1) of the UCC allows parties to liquidate damages for breach as long as the amount stipulated is "reasonable." The reasonableness of a particular amount is determined, in part, by the

The threat of subsequent review clearly increases the costs of negotiating a damages clause relative to relying on the standard damages rule. Are these costs accompanied by counterbalancing advantages? The traditional justification for post-breach inquiry is prevention of "unjust" punishment to the breacher, i.e. compensation exceeding the harm actually caused. This justification has been expressed in two distinct forms. One basis for invalidation is the presumption of unfairness: liquidated damage provisions are unreasonable — a penalty — whenever the stipulated sum is so disproportionate to provable damages as to require the inference that the agreement must have been effected by fraud, oppression, or mistake. The other major basis for invalidating agreed remedies is that, since the courts set damages based upon the principle of just compensation, parties should not be allowed to recover more than just compensation from the courts through a privately concocted alternative arrangement, even one fairly negotiated.

The common theme of these decisions is that a disproportion between the stipulated and the anticipated damage justifies an inference of overcompensation. In turn, overcompensation implies either bargaining unfairness or an objectionable *in terrorem* agreement to secure performance. This line of reasoning suggests two benefits which may be expected from the current rule invalidating penalties. First, the cost of identifying unfairness may be reduced by a standard rule-of-thumb based on disproportion. Second, an enforceable *in terrorem* clause might discourage promisors from breaching and reallocating resources where changed circumstances would ordinarily create efficiency gains from this behavior. Inducing performance under these conditions is a misallocation which prevents the net social gain that would result from nonperformance.

As the efficient damages model demonstrates, however, this analysis incorrectly assumes that, rather than negotiating out of the penalty, the promisor who is subject to an *in terrorem* clause will inevitably undertake an inefficient performance. In addition, there is no basis for the apparent assumption that the premium placed by the promisee on performance is valueless. Indeed, the market paradigm on which the compensation standard is based requires a contrary presumption: a promisee has a recognizable utility in certain *in terrorem* provisions and this utility is frequently reflected in willingness to pay a price for such clauses.

Goetz & Scott, 77 Colum. L. Rev. at 556.

"difficulties of proof of loss" from the breach. While it might be argued that the UCC rule approximates the common law uncertainty requirement, . . . it appears that a change has been made. The language of UCC § 2-718 itself treats "uncertainty" as merely one factor, and not even a required one, of many to be considered in determining reasonableness. In addition to uncertainty, courts have also been influenced by the relationship between the stipulated amount and the provable harm actually caused by the breach. Although a number of courts have refused to enforce agreements because of the absence of provable losses upon breach, many cases have held that actual loss is irrelevant except as it permits inferences concerning the reasonableness of the agreements viewed *ex ante*.

D.　BIBLIOGRAPHY AND SUGGESTED READING

David W. Barnes, *The Meaning of Value in Contract Damages and Contract Theory*, 46 AM. U. L. REV. 1 (1996).

David W. Barnes & Deborah Zalesne, *A Unifying Theory of Contract Damage Rules*, 55 SYRACUSE L. REV. 495 (2005).

David W. Barnes & Deborah Zalesne, *The Shadow Code*, 56 S.C. L. REV. 93 (2004).

Robert Birmingham, *Breach of Contract, Damage Measures, and Economic Efficiency*, 24 RUTGERS L. REV. 273 (1970).

John Breen, L.L. Fuller & William R. Perdue, Jr., *The Lost Volume Seller and Lost Profits Under UCC 2-708(2): A Conceptual and Linguistic Critique*, 50 U. MIAMI L. REV. 779 (1996).

Curtis Bridgeman, *Corrective Justice in Contract Law: Is There a Case for Punitive Damages?*, 56 VAND. L. REV. 237 (2003).

Robert Childres & Robert Burgess, *Seller's Remedies: The Primacy of UCC 2-708(2)*, 48 N.Y.U. L. REV. 833 (1973).

Robert Childres & Jack Garamella, *The Law of Restitution and the Reliance Interest in Contract*, 64 NW. U. L. REV. 433 (1969).

Kenneth W. Clarkson, Roger L. Miller & Timothy J. Muris, *Liquidated Damages v. Penalties: Sense or Nonsense?*, 1978 WIS. L. REV. 351.

Robert Cooter & Melvin A. Eisenberg, *Damages for Breach of Contract*, 73 CAL. L. REV. 1434 (1985).

Arthur Corbin, *The Right of a Defaulting Vendee to the Restitution of Installments Paid*, 40 YALE L.J. 1013 (1931).

Richard Craswell, *Against Fuller and Perdue*, 67 U. CHI. L. REV. 99 (2000).

Richard Craswell, *Contract Remedies, Renegotiation, and the Theory of Efficient Breach*, 61 S. CAL. L. REV. 629 (1988).

Richard Craswell, *Performance, Reliance, and One-Sided Information*, 18 J. LEGAL STUD. 365 (1989).

Stephen Daniels & Joanne Martin, *Myth and Reality in Punitive Damages*, 75 MINN. L. REV. 1 (1990).

William Dodge, *The Case for Punitive Damages in Contracts*, 48 DUKE L.J. 629 (1999).

Aaron S. Edlin & Alan Schwartz, *Optimal Penalties in Contracts*, 78 CHI.-KENT L. REV. 33 (2003).

Melvin A. Eisenberg & Brett H. McDonnell, *Expectation Damages and the Theory of Overreliance*, 54 HASTINGS L.J. 1335 (2003).

Richard Epstein, *Beyond Foreseeability: Consequential Damages in the Law of Contract*, 18 J. LEGAL STUD. 105 (1989).

E. Allan Farnsworth, *The Past of Promise: An Historical Introduction to Contract*, 69 COLUM. L. REV. 576 (1969).

Daniel Friedmann, *The Efficient Breach Fallacy*, 18 J. LEGAL STUD. 1 (1989).

Daniel Friedmann, *Restitution of Benefits Obtained Through the Appropriation of Property or the Commission of a Wrong*, 80 COLUM. L. REV. 504 (1980).

Lon Fuller & William R. Perdue, *The Reliance Interest in Contract Damages*, 46 YALE L.J. 52 (1936).

Mark P. Gergen, *A Theory of Self-Help Remedies in Contract*, 89 B.U. L. REV. 1397 (2009).

Charles J. Goetz & Robert E. Scott, *Liquidated Damages, Penalties and the Just Compensation Principle*, 77 COLUM. L. REV. 554 (1977).

Charles J. Goetz & Robert E. Scott, *Measuring Sellers' Damages: The Lost-Profits Puzzle*, 31 STAN. L. REV. 323 (1979).

Victor Goldberg, *Bloomer Girl Revisited or How to Frame an Unmade Picture*, 1998 WIS. L. REV. 1051.

Victor Goldberg, *An Economic Analysis of the Lost-Volume Retail Seller*, 57 S. CAL. L. REV. 283 (1984).

VICTOR GOLDBERG, FRAMING CONTRACT LAW: AN ECONOMIC PERSPECTIVE (2007).

Victor Goldberg, *Emotional Distress Damages and Breach of Contract: A New Approach*, 20 U.C. DAVIS L. REV. 57 (1986).

Victor Goldberg, *Cleaning Up Lake River*, 3 VA. L. & BUS. REV. 427, 440–41 (2008).

Robert Harris, *A Radical Restatement of the Law of Seller's Damages: Sales Act and Commercial Code Results Compared*, 18 STAN. L. REV. 66 (1965).

Calvin R. House, *Good Faith Rejection and Specific Performance in Publishing Contracts: Safeguarding the Author's Reasonable Expectations*, 51 BROOK. L. REV. 95 (1984).

Louis Kornhauser, *An Introduction to the Economic Analysis of Contract Remedies*, 57 U. COLO. L. REV. 683 (1986).

Saul Levmore, *Obligation or Restitution for Best Efforts*, 67 S. CAL. L. REV. 1411 (1994).

Saul Levmore, *Explaining Restitution*, 71 VA. L. REV. 65 (1985).

Richard B. Lillich, *The Malpractice Statute of Limitations in New York and Other Jurisdictions*, 47 CORNELL L.Q. 339 (1962).

Peter Linzer, *On the Amorality of Contract Remedies — Efficiency, Equity, and the Second Restatement*, 81 COLUM. L. REV. 111 (1981).

Daniel Markovits & Alan Schwartz, *The Myth of Efficient Breach: New Defenses of the Expectation Interest*, 97 VA. L. REV. 1939 (2011).

Henry Mather, *Restitution as a Remedy for Breach of Contract: The Case of the*

Partially Performing Seller, 92 YALE L.J. 14 (1982).

Daniel W. Matthews, *Should the Doctrine of Lost Volume Seller Be Retained?*, 51 U. MIAMI L. REV. 1195 (1997).

Judith Maute, Peevyhouse v. Garland Coal & Mining Co. *Revisited: The Ballad of Willie and Lucille*, 89 Nw. U. L. REV. 1341 (1995).

Timothy Muris, *Cost of Completion or Diminution in Market Value: The Relevance of Subjective Value*, 12 J. LEGAL STUD. 379 (1983).

Ian R. Macneil, *Efficient Breach of Contract: Circles in the Sky*, 68 VA. L. REV. 947 (1982).

Phillip R. Kaplan, Note, *A Critique of the Penalty Limitation on Liquidated Damages*, 50 S. CAL. L. REV. 1055 (1977).

Nathan B. Oman, *Specific Performance and the Thirteenth Amendment*, 93 MINN. L. REV. 2020 (2009).

Edwin Patterson, *The Apportionment of Business Risks Through Legal Devices*, 24 COLUM. L. REV. 335 (1924).

Edwin Patterson, *The Scope of Restitution and Unjust Enrichment*, 1 Mo. L. REV. 223 (1936).

Ellen Peters, *Remedies for Breach of Contract Relating to the Sale of Goods Under the Uniform Commercial Code: A Roadmap for Article Two*, 73 YALE L.J. 199 (1963).

George Priest, *Breach and Remedy for the Tender of Nonconforming Goods Under the Uniform Commercial Code: An Economic Approach*, 91 HARV. L. REV. 960 (1978).

Samuel Rea, *Efficiency Implications of Penalties and Liquidated Damages*, 13 J. LEGAL STUD. 147 (1984).

David Rice, *Exemplary Damages in Private Consumer Actions*, 55 IOWA L. REV. 307 (1969).

Alan Schwartz, *Price Discrimination with Contract Terms: The Lost-Volume Problem*, 12 AM. L. & ECON. REV. 394 (2010).

Alan Schwartz & Robert Scott, *Market Damages, Efficient Contracting, and the Economic Waste Fallacy*, 108 COLUM. L. REV. 1610 (2008).

Alan Schwartz, *The Myth That Promisees Prefer Supracompensatory Remedies: An Analysis of Contracting for Damage Measures*, 100 YALE L.J. 376 (1990).

Robert E. Scott, *The Case for Market Damages: Revisiting the Lost Profits Puzzle*, 57 U. CHI. L. REV. 1155 (1990).

Robert E. Scott & George G. Triantis, *Embedded Options and the Case Against Compensation In Contract Law*, 104 COLUM. L. REV. 1428 (2004).

Warren Seavey, *Problems in Restitution*, 7 OKLA. L. REV. 257 (1954).

John A. Sebert, *Punitive and Nonpecuniary Damage in Actions Based Upon*

Contract: Toward Achieving the Objective of Full Compensation, 33 UCLA L. REV. 1565 (1986).

John A. Sebert, *Remedies Under Article Two of the Uniform Commercial Code: An Agenda for Review*, 130 U. PA. L. REV. 360 (1981).

Anthony J. Sebok, *Punitive Damages: From Myth to Theory*, 92 IOWA L. REV. 957 (2007).

Morris Shanker, *The Case for a Literal Reading of UCC Section 2-708(2)*, 24 CASE W. RES. L. REV. 697 (1973).

David Simon & Gerald A. Novack, *Limiting the Buyer's Market Damage to Lost Profits: A Challenge to the Enforceability of Market Contracts*, 92 HARV. L. REV. 1395 (1979).

Timothy Sullivan, *Punitive Damages in the Law of Contract: The Reality and the Illusion of Legal Change*, 61 MINN. L. REV. 207 (1977).

George G. Triantis & Alexander J. Triantis, *Timing Problems in Contract Breach Decisions*, 41 J.L. & ECON. 163 (1998).

Thomas Ulen, *The Efficiency of Specific Performance: Toward a Unified Theory of Contract Remedies*, 83 MICH. L. REV. 341 (1984).

Wade, *Restitution of Benefits Acquired Through Illegal Transactions*, 95 U. PA. L. REV. 261 (1947).

Ernest J. Weinrib, *Punishment and Disgorgement as Contract Remedies*, 78 CHI.-KENT L. REV. 55 (2003).

Edward Yorio, *In Defense of Money Damages for Breach of Contract*, 82 COLUM. L. REV. 1365 (1982).

Chapter 11

THIRD-PARTY RIGHTS

A. AN INTRODUCTION TO THIRD-PARTY BENEFICIARIES

Most of contract law concerns the facilitation and regulation of relationships between two parties. Normally, even though the contract performance may benefit others, third parties cannot enforce a contract between a promisor and promisee. Thus, for example, a favorable contract for the sale of a million dollars in electronic parts may benefit the employees of both the buyer and the seller, yet they cannot recover damages for breach. The central purpose of the law of third-party beneficiaries is to identify the circumstances that justify a departure from this general rule.[1]

The law of third-party beneficiaries thus relaxes a central assumption of contract law that a contract has consequences only for the parties themselves and does not have external effects on others. In Chapter 5 we saw that the law declines to enforce certain contracts — such as those that are illegal or violate public policy — because the contracts in question create negative externalities. The justification for non-enforcement in these instances is based on the fact that whenever the contracting parties do not internalize the costs of their promissory acts we can no longer assume that the resulting exchange enhances social welfare. In a sense, then, third-party beneficiary law deals with the converse situation: how should the law treat promises that create positive externalities? Here the key questions are: When and to what extent can a third party who receives an external benefit from a promise made to another sue to enforce the promise? And, if the third party can enforce the promise, can the promisee also sue to enforce? If so, is the promisor liable to *both* the promisee and the third-party beneficiary? Consider the following cases and notes and then formulate your answers to these core questions.

LAWRENCE v. FOX
Court of Appeals of New York
20 N.Y. 268 (1859)

Appeal from the Superior Court of the city of Buffalo. On the trial before Mr. Justice Masten it appeared by the evidence of a bystander, that one Holly, in November, 1857, at the request of the defendant, loaned and advanced to him $300, stating at the time that he owed that sum to the plaintiff for money borrowed of him, and had agreed to pay it to him the then next day; that the defendant in

---

[1] *See generally* E. Allan Farnsworth, Contracts 709–10 (1982).

961

consideration thereof, at the time of receiving the money, promised to pay it to the plaintiff the then next day. Upon this state of facts the defendant moved for a nonsuit, upon three several grounds, *viz.*: That there was no proof tending to show that Holly was indebted to the plaintiff; that the agreement by the defendant with Holly to pay the plaintiff was void for want of consideration, and that there was no privity between the plaintiff and defendant. The court overruled the motion, and the counsel for the defendant excepted. The cause was then submitted to the jury, and they found a verdict for the plaintiff for the amount of the loan and interest, $344.66, upon which judgment was entered; from which the defendant appealed to the Superior Court, at general term, where the judgment was affirmed, and the defendant appealed to this court. The cause was submitted on printed arguments.

GRAY, J.

The first objection raised on the trial amounts to this: That the evidence of the person present, who heard the declarations of Holly giving directions as to the payment of the money he was then advancing to the defendant, was mere hearsay and therefore not competent. Had the plaintiff sued Holly for this sum of money no objection to the competency of this evidence would have been thought of; and if the defendant had performed his promise by paying the sum loaned to him to the plaintiff, and Holly had afterwards sued him for its recovery, and this evidence had been offered by the defendant, it would doubtless have been received without an objection from any source. All the defendant had the right to demand in this case was evidence which, as between Holly and the plaintiff was competent to establish the relation between them of debtor and creditor. For that purpose the evidence was clearly competent; it covered the whole ground and warranted the verdict of the jury.

But it is claimed that notwithstanding this promise was established by competent evidence, it was void for the want of consideration. It is now more than a quarter of a century since it was settled by the Supreme Court of this State — in an able and pains-taking opinion by the late Chief Justice Savage, in which the authorities were fully examined and carefully analyzed — that a promise in all material respects like the one under consideration was valid; and the judgment of that court was unanimously affirmed by the Court for the Correction of Errors. (Farley v. Cleaveland, 4 Cow., 432; same case in error, 9 *id.*, 639). In that case one Moon owed Farley and sold to Cleaveland a quantity of hay, in consideration of which Cleaveland promised to pay Moon's debt to Farley; and the decision in favor of Farley's right to recover was placed upon the ground that the hay received by Cleaveland from Moon was a valid consideration for Cleaveland's promise to pay Farley, and that the subsisting liability of Moon to pay Farley was no objection to the recovery. The fact that the money advanced by Holly to the defendant was a loan to him for a day, and that it thereby became the property of the defendant, seemed to impress the defendant's counsel with the idea that because the defendant's promise was not a trust fund placed by the plaintiff in the defendant's hands, out of which he was to realize money as from the sale of a chattel or the collection of a debt, the promise although made for the benefit of the plaintiff could not enure to his benefit. The hay which Cleaveland delivered to Moon was not to be paid to Farley, but the debt incurred by Cleaveland for the purchase of the hay, like the debt incurred by the defendant for money borrowed, was what was to be paid. That case has been often referred to by the courts of this State, and has never been doubted as sound authority for the principle upheld by it. (Barker v. Buklin, 2 Denio, 45; Hudson Canal Company v. The Westchester Bank, 4 *id.*, 97.) It puts to rest the objection that the defendant's promise was void for want of consideration. The report of that case shows that the promise was not only made to Moon but to the plaintiff Farley.

In this case the promise was made to Holly and not expressly to the plaintiff; and this difference between the two cases presents the question, raised by the defendant's objection, as to the want of privity between the plaintiff and defendant. As early as 1806 it was announced by the Supreme Court of this State, upon what was then regarded as the settled law of England, "That where one person makes a promise to another for the benefit of a third person, that third person may maintain an action upon it." Schermerhorn v. Vanderheyden (1 Johns. R., 140), has often been re-asserted by our courts and never departed. This question was subsequently, and in a case quite recent, again the subject of consideration by the Supreme Court, when it was held, that in declaring upon a promise, made to the debtor by a third party to pay the creditor of the debtor, founded upon a consideration advanced by the debtor, it was unnecessary to aver a promise to the creditor; for the reason that upon proof of a promise made to the debtor to pay the creditor, a promise to the creditor would be implied. And in support of this proposition, in no respect distinguishable from the one now under consideration, the case of Schermerhorn v. Vanderheyden, with many intermediate cases in our courts, were cited, in which the doctrine of that case was not only approved but affirmed. (The Delaware and Hudson Canal Company v. The Westchester County Bank, 4 Denio, 97.) The same principle is adjudged in several cases in Massachusetts. I will refer to but few of them. (Arnold v. Lyman, 17 Mass., 400; Hall v. Marston, *id.*, 575; Brewer v. Dyer, 7 Cush., 337, 340.) In Hall v. Marston the court says: "It seems to have been well settled that if A promises B for a valuable consideration to pay C, the latter may maintain assumpsit for the money;" and in Brewer v. Dyer, the recovery was upheld, as the court said, "upon the principle of law *long recognized and clearly established*, that when one person, for a valuable consideration, engages with another, by a simple contract, to do some act for the benefit of a third, the latter, who would enjoy the benefit of the act, may maintain an action for the breach of such engagement; that it does not rest upon the ground of any actual or supposed relationship between the parties as some of the earlier cases would seem to indicate, but upon the broader and more satisfactory basis, that the law operating on the act of the parties creates the duty, establishes a privity, and implies the promise and obligation on which the action is founded."

There is a more recent case decided by the same court, to which the defendant has referred and claims that it at least impairs the force of the former cases as authority. It is the case of Mellen v. Whipple (1 Gray, 317). In that case one Rollins made his note for $500, payable to Ellis and Mayo, or order, and to secure its payment mortgaged to the payees a certain lot of ground, and then sold and conveyed the mortgaged premises to the defendant, by deed in which it was stated that the "granted premises were subject to a mortgage for $500, which mortgage, with the note for which it was given, the said Whipple is to assume and cancel." The deed thus made was accepted by Whipple, the mortgage was afterwards duly assigned, and the note indorsed by Ellis and Mayo to the plaintiff's intestate. After Whipple received the deed he paid to the mortgagees and their assigns the interest upon the mortgage and note for a time, and upon refusing to continue his payments was sued by the plaintiff as administratrix of the assignee of the mortgage and note. The court held that the stipulation in the deed that Whipple should pay the mortgage and note was a matter exclusively between the two parties to the deed; that the sale by Rollins of the equity of redemption did not lessen the plaintiff's security, and that as nothing had been put into the defendant's hands for the purpose of meeting the plaintiff's claim on Rollins, there was no consideration to support an express promise, much less an implied one, that Whipple should pay Mellen the amount of the note. This is all that was decided in that case, and the substance of the reasons assigned for the decision; and whether the case was rightly disposed of or not, it has not in its facts any analogy to the case before us, nor do the reasons assigned for the decision bear in any degree upon the question we are now considering.

But it is urged that because the defendant was not in any sense a trustee of the property of Holly for the benefit of the plaintiff, the law will not imply a promise. I agree that many of the cases where a promise was implied were cases of trusts, created for the benefit of the promiser. The case of Felton v. Dickinson (10 Mass., 189, 190), and others that might be cited are of that class; but concede them all to have been cases of trusts, and it proves nothing against the application of the rule to this case. The duty of the trustee to pay the *cestuis que trust*, according to the terms of the trust, implies his promise to the latter to do so. In this case the defendant, upon ample consideration received from Holly, promised Holly to pay his debt to the plaintiff; the consideration received and the promise to Holly made it as plainly his duty to pay the plaintiff as if the money had been remitted to him for that purpose, and as well implied a promise to do so as if he had been made a trustee of property to be converted into cash with which to pay. The fact that a breach of the duty imposed in the one case may be visited, and justly, with more serious consequences than in the other, by no means disproves the payment to be a duty in both. The principle illustrated by the example so frequently quoted (which concisely states the case in hand) "that a promise made to one for the benefit of another, he for whose benefit it is made may bring an action for its breach," has been applied to trust cases, not because it was exclusively applicable to those cases, but because it was a principle of law, and as such applicable to those cases.

It was also insisted that Holly could have discharged the defendant from his promise, though it was intended by both parties for the benefit of the plaintiff, and therefore the plaintiff was not entitled to maintain this suit for the recovery of a demand over which he had no control. It is enough that the plaintiff did not release the defendant from his promise, and whether he could or not is a question not now necessarily involved; but if it was, I think it would be found difficult to maintain the right of Holly to discharge a judgment recovered by the plaintiff upon confession or otherwise, for the breach of the defendant's promise; and if he could not, how could he discharge the suit before judgment, or the promise before suit, made as it was for the plaintiff's benefit and in accordance with legal presumption accepted by him (Berky v. Taylor, 5 Hill, 577–584, et seq.), until his dissent was shown.

The cases cited, and especially that of Farley v. Cleaveland, establish the validity of a parol promise; it stands then upon the footing of a written one. Suppose the defendant had given his note in which, for value received of Holly, he had promised to pay the plaintiff and the plaintiff had accepted the promise, retaining Holly's liability. Very clearly Holly could not have discharged that promise, be the right to release the defendant as it may. No one can doubt that he owes the sum of money demanded of him, or that in accordance with his promise it was his duty to have paid it to the plaintiff; nor can it be doubted that whatever may be the diversity of opinion elsewhere, the adjudications in this State, from a very early period, approved by experience, have established the defendant's liability; if, therefore, it could be shown that a more strict and technically accurate application of the rules applied, would lead to a different result (which I by no means concede), the effort should not be made in the face of manifest justice.

The judgment should be affirmed.

JOHNSON, C. J., and DENIO, J., were of opinion that the promise was to be regarded as made to the plaintiff through the medium of his agent, whose action he could ratify when it came to his knowledge, though taken without his being privy thereto.

COMSTOCK, J. (dissenting).

The plaintiff had nothing to do with the promise on which he brought this action. It was not made to him, nor did the consideration proceed from him. If he can maintain the suit, it is because an anomaly has found its way into the law on this subject. In general, there must be privity of contract. The party who sues upon a promise must be the promisee, or he must have some legal interest in the undertaking. In this case, it is plain that Holly, who loaned the money to the defendant, and to whom the promise in question was made, could at any time have claimed that it should be performed to himself personally. He had lent the money to the defendant, and at the same time directed the latter to pay the sum to the plaintiff. This direction he could countermand, and if he had done so, manifestly the defendant's promise to pay according to the direction would have ceased to exist.

The plaintiff would receive a benefit by a complete execution of the arrangement, but the arrangement itself was between other parties, and was under their exclusive control. If the defendant had paid the money to Holly, his debt would have been discharged thereby. So Holly might have released the demand or assigned it to another person, or the parties might have annulled the promise now in question, and designated some other creditor of Holly as the party to whom the money should be paid. It has never been claimed, that in a case thus situated, the right of a third person to sue upon the promise rested on any sound principle of law. We are to inquire whether the rule has been so established by positive authority.

The cases which have sometimes been supposed to have a bearing on this question, are quite numerous. In some of them, the dicta of judges, delivered upon very slight consideration, have been referred to as the decisions of the courts. Thus, in Schermerhorn v. Vanderheyden (1 Johns., 140), the court is reported as saying, "We are of opinion, that where one person makes a promise to another, for the benefit of a third person, that third person may maintain an action on such promise." This remark was made on the authority of Dalton v. Poole (Vent., 318, 332), decided in England nearly two hundred years ago. It was, however, but a mere remark, as the case was determined against the plaintiff on another ground. Yet this decision has often been referred to as authority for similar observations in later cases.

In another class of cases, which have been sometimes supposed to favor the doctrine, the promise was made to the person who brought the suit, while the consideration proceeded from another; the question considered being, whether the promise was void by the statute of frauds. . . .

The cases in which some trust was involved are also frequently referred to as authority for the doctrine now in question, but they do not sustain it. If A delivers money or property to B, which the latter accepts upon a trust for the benefit of C, the latter can enforce the trust by an appropriate action for that purpose. (Berly v. Taylor, 5 Hill, 577.) If the trust be of money, I think the beneficiary may assent to it and bring the action for money had and received to his use. If it be of something else than money, the trustee must account for it according to the terms of the trust, and upon principles of equity. There is some authority even for saying that an express promise founded on the possession of a trust fund may be enforced by an action at law in the name of the beneficiary, although it was made to the creator of the trust. Thus, in Comyn's Digest (Action on the case upon Assumpsit, B. 15), it is laid down that if a man promise a pig of lead to A, and his executor give lead to make a pig to B, who assumes to deliver it to A, an assumpsit lies by A against him. The case of The Delaware and Hudson Canal Company v. The Westchester County Bank (4 Denio, 97), involved a trust because the defendants had received from a third party a bill of exchange under an agreement that they would endeavor to collect it, and would pay over the proceeds when collected to the plaintiff's. A fund received under such an agreement does not belong to the person who receives it. He must account for it specifically; and perhaps there is no gross violation of principle in permitting the equitable owner of it to sue upon an express promise to pay it over. Having a specific interest in the thing, the undertaking to account for it may be regarded as in some sense made with him through the author of the trust. But further than this we cannot go without violating plain rules of law. In the case before us there was nothing in the nature of a trust or agency. The defendant borrowed the money of Holly and received it as his own. The plaintiff had no right in the fund, legal or equitable. The promise to repay the money created an obligation in favor of the lender to whom it was made and not in favor of any one else.

NOTES

1. *The "Missing" Case of* **Lawrence v. Holly.** At the time of contracting, if Holly and Fox had thought about the issue, would they have specified that Lawrence could enforce the contract?

Why didn't Lawrence sue Holly? Such an action clearly would have been the more traditional route. After all, Lawrence had a contractual relationship with Holly, who was obligated to repay the $300 he owed Lawrence. Why not enforce the debt contract against Holly and let Holly pursue the crafty Fox? In an article on the evolution of third-party beneficiaries, Professor Anthony Waters suggests that the $300 in question represented a gambling debt, so that a direct suit was not a practical alternative. *See* Anthony Jon Waters, *The Property in the Promise: A Study of the Third Party Beneficiary Rule*, 98 HARV. L. REV. 1109, 1127 (1985).

2.   *Third Parties and the Hypothetical Bargain.* Professor Melvin Eisenberg uses a hypothetical bargain analysis as one way of explaining why the courts, as a general rule, do not allow all third-party beneficiaries of contracts to sue for enforcement:[2]

> For example, suppose Martial is a manufacturer of specialty toy soldiers, and Access is a toy distributor. Martial purchases special paint for her soldiers from Color, and employs skilled workers on an hourly basis. At a time when Martial would have otherwise had to idle her plant for lack of business, Access places a large order for highly detailed Civil War toy soldiers to take advantage of a special surge of interest in that war. Access plans to resell the toy soldiers to large retailers, including Toys "R" Us. Martial designs the soldiers and draws engineering plans for the necessary dies and then enters into a contract with Diemaker, who agrees to produce the dies. At the time the contract is made, Diemaker knows that Martial requires the dies to fill her contract with Access, that Access plans to resell to Toys "R" Us and other retailers, and that Martial has no other business in prospect.
>
> In breach of his contract, Diemaker fails to deliver the dies. As a result, Martial, in turn, is in breach of her contract with Access and also is forced to idle her plant for six weeks, until new orders begin to come in. Access and Toys "R" Us sue Diemaker for their lost profits on resale of the toy soldiers. Color sues Diemaker for lost profits on sales of paint. Martial's workers sue Diemaker for their lost wages. Access, Toys "R" Us, Color, and the workers are all third-party beneficiaries of the contract between Diemaker and Martial, but intuitively it seems clear that none of these beneficiaries should be able to bring suit against Diemaker.
>
> The source of the intuition lies in considerations that might be thought of as remedial, that is, considerations concerning the promisor's liability and the impact of that liability on the contracting parties. In the hypothetical, Martial is entitled to expectation damages against Diemaker as a result of Diemaker's breach, and these damages would be measured in large part by Martial's lost profits. It can be assumed that the prospect of such damages affected the price Diemaker charged. If Martial had initially agreed to forgo expectation damages in the event of Diemaker's breach, Diemaker presumably would have agreed to a lower price. If Martial did not agree to forgo those damages, presumably that was partly because she wanted full compensation if Diemaker breached, and partly because she would have viewed the contract with Diemaker as unreliable if the contract was not backed by the sanction of expectation damages.

---

[2] Melvin A. Eisenberg, *Third-Party Beneficiaries*, 92 COLUM. L. REV. 1358 (1992).

Suppose now that the parties had directly addressed the issue of the third parties' rights. If Diemaker was to be exposed to liability to the third parties, as well as liability to Martial, Diemaker would certainly have demanded a higher price from Martial. Martial, however, would almost certainly have been unwilling to pay that higher price, because she would receive little or no corresponding benefit in return. We can therefore be fairly confident that if Martial and Diemaker had directly addressed the issue, they would have agreed that the third parties should not be able to enforce the contract. Accordingly, if the interests of the contracting parties, Martial and Diemaker, are measured by what they would have agreed to if they had addressed the issue, allowing the third parties in the hypothetical to enforce the contract would conflict with those interests.

92 COLUM. L. REV. at 1374–76.

Several courts have explicitly addressed the concerns raised by Eisenberg regarding the possible negative effects of over-enforcing third party contract rights. Judge Posner recently discussed this problem and suggested that the solution lay in the test devised by the drafters of the Restatement (Second) (discussed in more depth in Section B[2], Note 4, *infra*).

The rule allowing someone who is not a party to a contract to sue under it as a "beneficiary" is a relative novelty in the common law (the analogous right of a trust's beneficiary is equitable in origin), and at first glance invites practical as well as conceptual objections. Contracts often benefit persons besides the signatories, and a breach harms them. To allow all of these injured beneficiaries to sue would expose contract promisors to enormous potential liabilities, even for involuntary breaches (which many breaches of contracts are), and would be inconsistent with the limitations that tort law imposes on remote liability. . . . And how can there be a meeting of the minds between a party and a nonparty? But these puzzles dissipate when attention is shifted to the intentions of the contracting parties. The parties may for their own purposes want to confer a power of enforcing their contract upon a third party. If they make this intention adequately clear in the contract, the concept of freedom of contract becomes a compelling ground for allowing the third party to enforce the contract.

Vidimos, Inc. v. Laser Lab, 99 F.3d 217, 219–20 (7th Cir. 1996).

When reviewing the following materials, ask yourself whether Judge Posner's optimism is justified. Can a simple "intent to benefit" criterion adequately discriminate between those cases where enforcement by third parties is appropriate and those where enforcement would impose excessive sanctions for breach? Does the "intent to benefit" criterion enhance parties' freedom to contract as they wish (as Posner believes), or is it an overly vague standard that grants courts too much discretion to choose between worthy and unworthy third party beneficiaries (as others have argued)?

B.   INTENDED AND INCIDENTAL BENEFICIARIES

Read Restatement (Second) § 302. As the Restatement language suggests, contract law implements the "intent" criterion in two steps. The ultimate step is to distinguish between those beneficiaries who the contracting parties intend to give rights of enforcement and those whose benefits are merely "incidental" to the purpose of the contract. The latter have no standing to enforce rights under the contract. *See* § 302(2). In order to be considered an "intended" beneficiary, the law traditionally asks two preliminary questions: did the promisee have a specific intent to make a gift of the promisor's performance to the third party (the so-called "donee beneficiary" cases) *or* does the promised benefit to the third party satisfy an obligation of the promisee to pay money to the third party (the so-called "creditor" beneficiary cases)? In the cases that follow we evaluate each of these questions in turn.

[1]   The "Donee Beneficiary" Cases

SEAVER v. RANSOM
Court of Appeals of New York
224 N.Y. 233, 120 N.E. 639 (1918)

POUND, J.

Judge Beman and his wife were advanced in years. Mrs. Beman was about to die. She had a small estate, consisting of a house and a lot in Malone and little else. Judge Beman drew his wife's will according to her instructions. It gave $1,000 to plaintiff, $500 to one sister, plaintiff's mother, and $100 each to another sister and her son, the use of the house to her husband for life, and remainder to the American Society for the Prevention of Cruelty to Animals. She named her husband as residuary legatee and executor. Plaintiff was her niece, 34 years old, in ill health, sometimes a member of the Beman household. When the will was read to Mrs. Beman, she said that it was not as she wanted it. She wanted to leave the house to plaintiff. She had no other objections to the will, but her strength was waning, and, although the judge offered to write another will for her, she said she was afraid she would not hold out long enough to enable her to sign it. So the judge said, if she would sign the will, he would leave plaintiff enough in his will to make up the difference. He avouched the promise by his uplifted hand with all solemnity and his wife then executed the will. When he came to die, it was found that his will made no provision for the plaintiff.

The action was brought, and plaintiff recovered judgment in the trial court, on the theory that Beman had obtained property from his wife and induced her to execute the will in form prepared by him by his promise to give plaintiff $6,000, the value of the house, and that thereby equity impressed his property with a trust in favor of plaintiff. Where a legatee promises the testator that he will use property given him by the will for a particular purpose, a trust arises. Beman received nothing under his wife's will but the use of the house in Malone for life. Equity compels the application of property thus obtained to the purpose of the testator, but equity cannot so impress a trust, except on property obtained by the promise. Beman was bound by his promise, but no property was bound by it; no trust in plaintiff's favor can be spelled out.

An action on the contract for damages, or to make the executors trustees for performance, stands on different grounds. The Appellate Division properly passed to the consideration of the question whether the judgment could stand upon the promise made to the wife, upon a valid consideration, for the sole benefit of plaintiff. The judgment of the trial court was affirmed by a return to the general doctrine laid down in the great case of Lawrence v. Fox, 20 N.Y. 168, which has since been limited as herein indicated.

Contracts for the benefit of third persons have been the prolific source of judicial and academic discussion. Williston, *Contracts for the Benefit of a Third Person*, 15 Harvard Law Review, 767; Corbin, *Contracts for the Benefit of Third Persons*, 27 Yale Law Journal, 1008. The general rule, both in law and equity was that privity between a plaintiff and a defendant is necessary to the maintenance of an action on the contract. The consideration must be furnished by the party to whom the promise was made. The contract cannot be enforced against the third party, and therefore it cannot be enforced by him.

On the other hand, the right of the beneficiary to sue on a contract made expressly for his benefit has been fully recognized in many American jurisdictions, either by judicial decision or by legislation, and is said to be "the prevailing rule in this country." Hendrick v. Lindsay, 93 U.S. 143; Lehow v. Simonton, 3 Colo. 346. It has been said that "the establishment of this doctrine has been gradual and is a victory of practical utility over theory, of equity over technical subtlety." *Brantly on Contracts* (2d Ed.) p. 253. The reasons for this view are that it is just and practical to permit the person for whose benefit the contract is made to enforce it against one whose duty it is to pay. Other jurisdictions will adhere to the present English rule.

In New York the right of the beneficiary to sue on contracts made for his benefit is not clearly or simply defined. It is at present confined: First. To cases where there is a pecuniary obligation running from the promisee to the beneficiary, "a legal right founded upon some obligation of the promisee, in the third party, to adopt and claim the promise as made for his benefit." Secondly. To cases where the contract is made for the benefit of the wife, affianced wife, or child of a party to the contract. The close relationship cases go back to the early King's Bench Case (1677), long since repudiated in England, of Dutton v. Poole, 2 Lev. 211. The natural and moral duty of the husband or parent to provide for the future of wife or child sustains the action on the contract made for their benefit. "This is the farthest the cases in this state have gone," says Cullen, J., in the marriage settlement case of Borland v. Welch, 162 N.Y. 104, 110.

The right of the third party is also upheld in, thirdly, the public contract cases, where the municipality seeks to protect its inhabitants by covenants for their benefit; and, fourthly, the cases where, at the request of a party to the contract, the promise runs directly to the beneficiary although he does not furnish the consideration. It may be safely said that a general rule sustaining recovery at the suit of the third party would include but few classes of cases not included in these groups, either categorically or in principle.

The desire for the childless aunt to make provision for a beloved and favorite niece differs imperceptibly in law or in equity from the moral duty of the parent to make testamentary provision for a child. The contract was made for the plaintiff's benefit. She alone is substantially damaged by its breach. The representatives of the wife's estate have no interest in enforcing it specifically. It is said in Buchanan v. Tilden [, 158 N.Y. 109,] that the common law imposes moral and legal obligations upon the husband and the parent not measured by the necessaries of life. It was, however, the love and affection or the moral sense of the husband and the parent that imposed such obligations in the cases cited, rather than any common-law duty of husband and parent to wife and child. If plaintiff had been a child of Mrs. Beman, legal obligation would have required no testamentary provision for her, yet the child could have enforced a covenant in her favor identical with the covenant of Judge Beman in this case. The constraining power of conscience is not regulated by the degree of relationship alone. The dependent or faithful niece may have a stronger claim than the affluent or unworthy son. No sensible theory of moral obligation denies arbitrarily to the former what would be conceded to the latter. We might consistently either refuse or allow the claim of both, but I cannot reconcile a decision in favor of the wife in Buchanan v. Tilden, based on the moral obligations arising out of near relationship, with a decision against the niece here on the ground that the relationship is too remote for equity's ken. No controlling authority depends upon so absolute a rule. In Sullivan v. Sullivan, [161 N.Y. 554], the grandniece lost in a litigation with the aunt's estate, founded on a certificate of deposit payable to the aunt "or in case of her death to her niece"; but what was said in that case of the relations of plaintiff's intestate and defendant does not control here, any more than what was said in Durnherr v. Rau, *supra*, on the relation of husband and wife, and the inadequacy of mere moral duty, as distinguished from legal or equitable obligation, controlled the decision in Buchanan v. Tilden. Borland v. Welch, *supra*, deals only with the rights of volunteers under a marriage settlement not made for the benefit of collaterals. . . .

But, on principle, a sound conclusion may be reached. If Mrs. Beman had left her husband the house on condition that he pay the plaintiff $6,000, and he had accepted the devise, he would have become personally liable to pay the legacy, and plaintiff could have recovered in an action at law against him, whatever the value of the house. That would be because the testatrix had in substance bequeathed the promise to plaintiff, and not because close relationship or moral obligation sustained the contract. The distinction between an implied promise to a testator for the benefit of a third party to pay a legacy and an unqualified promise on a valuable consideration to make provision for the third party by will is discernible, but not obvious. The tendency of American authority is to sustain the gift in all such cases and to permit the donee beneficiary to recover on the contract. The equities are with the plaintiff, and they may be enforced in this action, whether it be regarded as an action for damages or an action for specific performance to convert the defendants into trustees for plaintiff's benefit under the agreement.

The judgment should be affirmed, with costs.

DRAKE v. DRAKE
Supreme Court of New York, Appellate Division
89 A.D.2d 207, 455 N.Y.S.2d 420 (1982)

DOERR, J.

The question presented on this appeal is whether a child of the parties to a separation agreement has standing as a third party beneficiary, to enforce the terms of the agreement insofar as it relates to periodic support payments. Under the facts of this case we hold that she may not.

In 1963 plaintiff's parents, Winifred B. Drake and Richard E. Drake, entered into a separation agreement later incorporated, but not merged, in a divorce decree. The agreement required the husband to make periodic payments to the wife for the support of five children, whose custody remained in the wife, according to a fixed schedule tied to the husband's then earnings. The agreement also provided for escalated payments of child support as the husband's earnings increased. Payments were to continue until each child reached the age of 21 years, died, became self-supporting, or married and were to be reduced according to a fixed schedule upon the happening of the expressed contingency. Plaintiff is the only child who has not reached the age of 21 years and is presently a full-time college student.

Defendant made the required fixed payments throughout the intervening years, but never made any escalated payments under the agreement and was never called upon by the wife in any judicial proceeding to make such payments. In February 1981, while still a high school senior, plaintiff moved from her mother's house to that of a friend and requested defendant to send the support payments directly to her. Upon learning that plaintiff no longer resided with her mother, defendant concluded that she was emancipated and ceased making any support payments. Plaintiff thereupon learned for the first time of the terms of her parents' separation agreement, including the escalation clause, and commenced the instant action seeking back payments for the preceding six years, escalated to reflect defendant's earnings which were now substantially greater than in 1963. She also sought an order directing defendant to make support payments to her as required by the agreement until she reaches the age of 21, marries, dies, or becomes self-supporting.

On cross-motions for summary judgment Special Term held that plaintiff could not recover sums due prior to the commencement of the action, but that she may recover sums falling due thereafter, including sums due pursuant to the escalation clause in the agreement. Both parties appeal.

The issue here is concerned with the contractual rights of the parties insofar as they flow from the separation agreement of plaintiff's parents and is not to be confused with a child's statutory rights to be supported by its parents.

It is familiar law that a contract entered into between two parties may be enforced by a third party if the contracting parties intended the contract for the third party's direct benefit. Where performance is rendered directly to the third party, it is presumed that the contract was for his benefit. It is not enough that the contract benefit the third party incidentally; the agreement must express an intent to assume a duty directly to the third party. In ascertaining the rights of an asserted third party beneficiary, the intention of the promisee is of primary importance, since the promisee procured the promise by furnishing the consideration therefor.

Applying these principles to separation agreements, New York courts long ago concluded that a child could not enforce the support provisions of the agreement, although it could enforce other provisions, such as a promise to set up a trust fund. The seminal case is Kendall v. Kendall, 193 N.Y.S. 661). In *Kendall* the child, relying on her parents' separation agreement, sued her father in two separate lawsuits (1) to recover monthly arrearages (*Kendall I*) and (2) to require him to set up a trust fund (*Kendall II*). The Appellate Division held that the child could enforce the trust fund provision, since she was the sole beneficiary of it, but that she could not enforce the support provisions of the agreement. The court reasoned that the support money was payable to the mother, who had discretion in how the money was spent. Unlike the trust fund, which benefitted the daughter exclusively, payment of the support money was an obligation running to the child's mother. Therefore, the court concluded that the mother was the proper party to enforce the support provision of her contract. This distinction has been recognized repeatedly (see Ben Ami v. Ben Ami,191 N.Y.S.2d 369, affd. 203 N.Y.S.2d 924 [dismissing a complaint seeking enforcement of monthly support, but without prejudice to a suit seeking to enforce other provisions of the agreement relating to life insurance policies; the court noted "There is no occasion to depart from the controlling principle that a separation agreement between parents providing for payment to another for the support and maintenance of the children may not, in the ordinary case, be enforced by the children"]; Magrill v. Magrill, 184 N.Y.S.2d 516 [dismissing a cause of action by a child against the father for support based on the separation agreement, noting that the cause of action vests in the mother and that children have no direct interest in the money paid to the mother even though it be wholly or partly for their benefit]; but see Weiss v. Weiss, 81 N.Y.S.2d 197, [child permitted to enforce support provisions; issue of standing not discussed]).

In 1966 the Court of Appeals decided what has become the leading case on this issue. In Forman v. Forman, 17 N.Y.2d 274, 270 N.Y.S.2d 586 the court addressed at length the standing of a child to enforce his parents' separation agreement. The question of periodic support was not at issue in *Forman*, since the mother had breached the separation agreement by moving the children out of state. The Court of Appeals noted that the Forman children "concede" that they could not enforce the support provisions. Instead, the Forman children sought specific performance of their father's promise to make them equal and irrevocable beneficiaries of a life insurance policy in the face amount of $10,000. The Court of Appeals, citing *Kendall I*, not[ed] that the general rule in New York is that ordinarily "children for whose support a provision is made in a separation agreement between their parents, payable to the mother, are usually not able to enforce the agreement directly in an action against their father . . . [since] such a suit ordinarily should be maintained by the mother" (Forman v. Forman, *supra*, p. 280, 270 N.Y.S.2d 586). The court then approved of this general rule, noting that "there are probably good enough policy reasons to hold to the usual rule that it is preferable to have a mother, who is a direct party to a separation agreement and to whom payments for the support of infant children in her custody are to be made, enforce it" (Forman v. Forman, *supra*, p. 280, 270 N.Y.S.2d 586). The court then held, however, that in some cases children should have standing as third party beneficiaries to enforce the agreement. The court stated:

> But children are often the actual third party beneficiaries of provisions in separation agreements between the parents; and in cases of disability of one kind or another of one spouse to enforce his own legal rights against the other, some procedural facility for enforcement should be available to the children. This would usually apply to rights other than periodical support; but cases could arise, no doubt, where even periodical support might have to be enforceable by infants themselves. We ought not by a general rule of abnegation foreclose ourselves completely from allowing a remedy that may become appropriate, effective and just.

Thus, the rule that comes out of *Forman* is that in some cases children should be granted third party beneficiary status, although such status will usually apply to promises other than periodic support. However, the door has been left ajar for them to enforce the "incidental" benefits of periodic support upon a proper showing of status to do so. None has been shown in this case.

Since *Forman* was decided, there have been several cases in which children have sought to enforce their parents' separation agreements. These cases fall into two categories: promises to provide educational expenses and promises to provide for a child in a will or policy of life insurance. In both kinds of cases, the child has uniformly been granted standing as a third party beneficiary. Significantly, there has been only one case in which a child sought to enforce the periodic support provisions of the separation agreement, and that attempt was denied. The court noted that "[a]n action by children for support payable to a parent pursuant to a separation agreement or decree does not accrue due to a breach unless there are unusual circumstances" (March v. Rumish, 191 N.Y.S.2d 369, affd. 203 N.Y.S.2d 924; and Forman v. Forman, 270 N.Y.S.2d 586).

From this may be distilled a simply stated general rule in New York that, barring unusual circumstances, children have no standing to enforce the periodic support provisions of their parents' separation agreement, although they may enforce other specific provisions of the agreement clearly made exclusively for their benefit, such as a promise to pay college tuition or to make the child a beneficiary of a life insurance policy. The distinction drawn comports with the rules of law applicable to third party beneficiaries and further is rooted in considerations of public policy designed to promote familial harmony and foster the parent-child relationship. A parent's contractual promise to pay support is made with a view toward his statutory duty of support. This duty ceases when the adult child refuses to heed the parent's reasonable restrictions and leaves the custodial home.

We have no doubt that circumstances may arise, such as death or disability, or outright refusal of a contracting parent to seek enforcement of periodic support provisions for a child, which would give a child the necessary standing to enforce the agreement. Such circumstances would have to be pleaded and proved and all necessary parties joined in the action. In such an event it is to be noted that any waiver of past due periodic support payments effectuated by the failure of the mother to compel enforcement will effectively bind the mother as to such payments, and such waiver is effective against the beneficiary. Such waiver of past due support, however, is no bar from asserting future claims for support asserted by the promisee to the agreement or by the child upon a proper showing of standing.

For the reasons stated herein the order of Special Term should be modified by striking the second and third ordering paragraphs and by dismissing the complaint *in toto* and as modified affirmed.

NOTES

1. *"Direct Benefit."* As *Seaver* indicates, courts in the aftermath of *Lawrence v. Fox* were hesitant to interpret that ruling too broadly. For the most part, courts continued to rely on the traditional legal categories. Thus, where the third-party plaintiff was a spouse or a child, the courts generally permitted third-party enforcement on the grounds that the promises were based on the "natural and moral duty of the spouse or parent to provide for the future of [his] wife or child." As Professor Melvin Eisenberg notes, however, *Seaver* was an important, albeit veiled, step away from these categories:

> In form, *Seaver* looked backward to classical contract law. Classical contract law tended either to deny the right of a third-party beneficiary to enforce a contract, or, at best, to allow enforcement only by third parties who fell within specific, well-defined, and standardized categories — most prominently, third parties to whom the promisee owed a preexisting legal obligation. *Seaver*, too, only allowed enforcement by a third-party beneficiary to whom the promisee owed a preexisting obligation, although the concept of obligation was expanded to include moral obligation.

> In substance, however, *Seaver* looked forward to modern contract law. The recognition of prior moral obligations as a basis for enforceability was inherently much more expansive, less standardized, and more openly dependent on social propositions than was the earlier restriction to preexisting legal obligations. And recognition of this large new class set the stage for the creation of a general principle that could both explain and go beyond the specific instances. Thus, the ruling in *Seaver*, although tied to classical contract law in form, in substance bore the seeds of the modern expansion of the law governing third-party beneficiaries.

Melvin A. Eisenberg, *Third-Party Beneficiaries*, 92 Colum. L. Rev. 1358, 1372–73 (1992).

Many modern cases reflect the departure from strict categorization. For example, in *Detroit Inst. of Arts Founders Soc'y v. Rose*, 127 F. Supp. 2d 117 (D.C. Conn. 2001), the court held that the Detroit Arts Institute (DIA) was a third party beneficiary of a contract between Rufus Rose, the puppeteer who made and operated the puppets on the long-running children's show "Howdy Doody," and NBC, the television network that owned the rights to the television show. Under the terms of the contract, NBC agreed to pay Rufus Rose $35,000 for maintaining care of the puppet and Rose agreed that Howdy Doody be given to the DIA. The DIA brought suit claiming it was a third party beneficiary of this contract. The court agreed, holding that:

> Two parties may enter into a contract to benefit a third party beneficiary who is then entitled to enforce contractual obligations without being a party to the contract and thus may sue the obligor for breach. To be valid, there need not be express language in the contract creating a direct obligation to the third party beneficiary. However, a contract can only result in an obligation to a third party if both parties to the contract intended to created a direct obligation from the promisor to the third party. In other words, the fact a third party may gain an incidental benefit is not enough to support third-party beneficiary status. The intent of the parties is to be "determined from the terms of the contract read in light of the circumstances attending the making of the contract, including the motives and the purposes of the parties. . . ."

> The three letters show that the parties intended not only to resolve their past dispute over these charges, but also to resolve how the puppets would be handled in the future. This was an essential part of the agreement between Rufus Rose and NBC, not merely an afterthought or a separate topic from the contract. The three letters also show that NBC was committed to assuring that Howdy Doody be given to the DIA. There was a special significance and status of Howdy Doody, and the letters recognize it and deal with it.

Id. at 129–32.

2. ***The Child Support Cases.*** Clearly, the contract between Judge Beman and his wife was entered into primarily to benefit a third party, Mrs. Beman's favorite niece. Yet nearly 70 years later, the same court held that a separation agreement which provided for periodic child support payments was not meant to directly benefit the child. Do you still have faith in the direct benefit test? In *Drake*, the court finds comfort in the fact that the mother can still maintain an action against the father. Is this a good reason for denying the child third-party beneficiary status? Do you find persuasive the court's distinction between cases in which children have been permitted to enforce their parents' separation agreements and cases in which they have not?

At the time of contracting, if they had thought about the issue would the parties in *Seaver* have specified that Marion (the niece) could enforce the contract? What about the contracting parties in *Drake*?

3. ***Attorney Liability to Third Party Beneficiaries.*** The *Seaver* situation (a promise to effect a testamentary bequest in favor of a third party) results in many suits by third party plaintiffs when the promise is not fulfilled. In many of these cases, the promise is made by an attorney to the testator as part of an agreement to provide professional services (i.e., drafting a will) for a fee. Thereafter, the intended beneficiaries sue the attorney whose allegedly erroneous drafting deprived them of the testamentary bequest. Historically, such an action did not lie because the testamentary beneficiary lacked privity with the lawyer, whose sole duty was to the now-deceased client. Thus, unless the executor of the decedent's estate

voluntarily fulfilled the decedent's promise or was willing to sue the attorney for breach of contract or malpractice, the beneficiary lacked any recourse. There has been a gradual relaxation of the strict privity requirement over the past century, however, and an increasing minority of jurisdictions now permit a third party beneficiary to sue the attorney when a drafting error deprives the beneficiary of a promised bequest or devise. *See* Barbara Walker, Note: *Attorney's Liability to Third Parties for Malpractice: The Growing Acceptance of Liability in the Absence of Privity*, 21 Washburn L.J. 48, 56 (1981).

As in other areas of contract law, the trend away from strict privity requirements has blurred the line between contract and tort, with courts employing both negligence and third-party beneficiary theories in awarding damages to third-party plaintiffs. In *Hale v. Groce*, 304 Or. 281, 744 P.2d 1289 (1987), the Oregon Supreme Court addressed this issue in a case involving an attorney whose drafting error prevented the plaintiff from receiving her promised inheritance. The court recited the old rule requiring privity of contract, but then stated that "[s]ince 1900, many courts have reconsidered that proposition, some preferring a contract analysis, some negligence, and at least one 'a definite maybe.'" 744 P.2d at 1291.

After surveying the confused and varying judicial results on third party suits against attorneys, the court concluded:

> We agree that the beneficiary in these cases is not only a plausible but a classic "intended" third-party beneficiary of the lawyer's promise to his client. . . . The promise, of course, was not that the lawyer would pay the plaintiff the stipulated sum, and it is too late for the lawyer to perform the promise that he did make, but this does not preclude an action for damages for the nonperformance. In principle, such an action is available to one in plaintiff's position.

Id. at 1292.

[2] The "Creditor Beneficiary" Cases

HAMILL v. MARYLAND CAS. CO.
United States Court of Appeals, Tenth Circuit
209 F.2d 338 (1954)

Murrah, J.

This is an appeal from a judgment of the District Court of New Mexico in favor of appellee, Maryland Casualty Company, on a contract between appellant, Don Hamill and the Gunnell Construction Company.

The pertinent facts are briefly to the effect the Gunnells were engaged in the general construction business. Appellant, Hamill, was a merchant in Las Cruces, New Mexico. To stabilize their financial condition by providing necessary working capital pending completion and final acceptance of construction projects, the Gunnells prevailed upon Hamill to enter into a contract dated May 4, 1951. As inartistically drawn by the Gunnells, the contract provided that Hamill would advance 10 per cent of any contracts awarded the Gunnell Construction Company and approved by Hamill, in consideration of 10 per cent of the net profits realized on any such contracts. The amount of the advances under the contract were to be evidenced by notes of Gunnell payable to Hamill and attached to the contract.

While this contract was in force, and with the approval of Hamill, Gunnell entered into a contract with the Board of Regents of a New Mexico state college for the construction of a physical science laboratory annex. The contract was for the total amount of $30,723.00, and the Maryland Casualty Company issued its conventional performance bond. While the Gunnell-Hamill contract was in force, and with Hamill's approval, the Gunnells contracted to construct an addition to the La Mesa Elementary School in Dona Ana County, New Mexico, for the total sum of $25,538.41. When Gunnell made application to Maryland for a performance bond, it was informed by Maryland's local agent that Gunnell's working capital was insufficient to justify the issuance of the bond. Whereupon, one of the Gunnells submitted the Hamill contract, apparently to strengthen the company's financial stability. When the local bondwriting agent submitted the contract to the general agent in El Paso, Texas, a new contract was drafted and returned to the local agent, who gave it to the Gunnells for execution, with the explanation that the obligations of the parties under the first contract were not sufficiently clear. In the revised contract, Hamill agreed to advance, as additional operating capital to be used in the performance of contracts awarded to the Gunnells with his approval, 10 per cent of the contract price; and the Gunnells agreed that upon final completion and acceptance of the contract, the payment of all bills and expenses, and the collection of the final amount due on the contract, it would return to Hamill the amount advanced in connection with the contract, plus 10 per cent of the net profits realized from its performance. It was further agreed that the amounts advanced by Hamill on any contract would be evidenced by a promissory note due and payable only upon final completion and acceptance of the contract and the final payment thereon. The latter contract, dated May 18, 1951, was submitted to Hamill by one of the Gunnells with the explanation that the bonding company wanted a clarification of the first contract, and that the latter contract had been drafted for that purpose. Hamill executed the contract without scrutinizing it, and a copy was submitted to the El Paso office by the local agent, after which the performance bond for the La Mesa project was executed.

During the construction of the two projects, Hamill advanced approximately $15,000 to enable Gunnell to "complete his job and get paid for it." After the projects were completed and the last payment received, Gunnell informed Hamill that they were in "financial difficulty"; that they "had more bills than they had money." Hamill replied, "according to our agreement, you are supposed to repay me," and one of the Gunnells answered, "Well, under the terms of the agreement we will pay you." On the next day Hamill presented his notes for amounts advanced and they were paid. Upon completion of the college project, there was $9,691.15 in unpaid bills for labor and material, and $11,229.30 unpaid bills on the La Mesa School project.

To discharge its obligation on the performance bonds, Maryland paid the outstanding claims and brought this suit against Gunnell and Hamill jointly to recover such sums. The complaint, in two counts, alleged the execution of the performance bond, the indemnity agreement, the Gunnell-Hamill contracts and the payment of the outstanding bills on each project. The demand was for judgment against Gunnell and Hamill jointly on each count for the amounts paid by Maryland to discharge the performance bond. The suit was prosecuted apparently on the theory that Gunnell and Hamill were partners and jointly liable to indemnify Maryland.

The trial court rejected the partnership theory in its entirety. It found, however, that the performance bond for the La Mesa School project was furnished by Maryland in reliance upon Hamill's last agreement with Gunnell to advance 10 per cent of the contract price in the amount of $2,553.81; that in pursuance of the agreement, Hamill did advance 10 per cent of the contract price on the La Mesa School project; and that "before all of the bills were paid on the said building the defendant Gunnell repaid to the defendant, Don Hamill, out of proceeds from the La Mesa School contract, the said sum of $2,553.81, contrary to the provisions of said agreement of May 18, 1951, which said repayment was made to the defendant, Don Hamill, prior to September 15, 1951."

Apparently proceeding on the theory that having relied upon the Gunnell-Hamill contract in the issuance of its performance bond, Maryland became a third party beneficiary and entitled to sue for its breach; and having further found that Hamill breached the contract by demanding and receiving payment before the bills were paid, the court rendered judgment for Maryland for 10 per cent of the contract price advanced by Hamill on the La Mesa School project in the total sum of $2,553.81. Since Maryland admittedly did not reply upon the Gunnell-Hamill contract in the issuance of the performance bond on the college project, the court denied any relief against Hamill on the first cause of action.

Hamill has appealed from the judgment on the second cause of action, contending that Maryland, not being a party to the Gunnell-Hamill contract, cannot maintain this suit upon it.

Of course Maryland may recover upon any theory legally sustainable under established facts regardless of the demand in the pleadings. And, New Mexico, where this contract was made and sought to be enforced, recognizes the now well established rule to the effect that a third party may sue and recover upon a valid contract in which he has a beneficial interest, whether designated therein as beneficiary or not.

The intent to benefit the third person is generally said to be controlling, and it is to be gathered from a construction of the contract in the light of the surrounding circumstances. The third party may be (a) a donee beneficiary, (b) a creditor beneficiary, or (c) an incidental beneficiary, Restatement of Contracts § 133; either a donee or creditor beneficiary may recover §§ 135 and 136; but an incidental beneficiary may not, § 147.

The manifest purpose or motive for the contract was benefit to the parties. Gunnell sought financial stability for his business, and Hamill profits from his investment. But, "motive and intent are not synonymous. . . . Intent, in its legal sense, is quite distinct from motive. It is defined as the purpose to use a particular means to effect a certain result. Motive is the reason which leads the mind to desire that result." See James Stewart & Co. v. Law, 149 Tex. 392. Moreover, Mr. Williston says, "There is no requirement of a mutual intent, as to right of enforcement, on the part of the contracting parties; instead, it is the intent or purpose of the promisee who pays for the promise that has been generally looked upon as governing . . . if an intent can legitimately be found to give a third party a right, the intent should be given effect." Williston § 356A. It has been said that so long as the contract necessarily and directly benefits the third party, he may enforce it. Byram Lbr. & Supply Co. v. Page, 109 Conn. 256. Otherwise stated, if the "performance of the promise will satisfy an actual or supposed or asserted duty of the promisee to the beneficiary," he is a creditor beneficiary and may enforce the promise. See §§ 133(b) and 136(1)(a) Restatement Contracts; Williston, § 361. The beneficiary's right is of course limited by the terms of the promise. See Williston § 364A.

Fairly interpreted, Hamill's agreement with Gunnell to advance 10 per cent of the contract price, to be repaid only after the completion of the contract and the payment of all bills, constituted a contingent promise to pay the expenses incident to the performance of the contract to the extent of 10 per cent of the contract price. This promise was an available asset to Gunnell on which Maryland relied when it executed the performance bond. If Maryland had furnished labor and materials on the project, Hamill would have undoubtedly been obligated to the extent of 10 per cent of the contract price to Maryland and all others similarly situated. We think the liability is not different where Maryland furnished a bond to guarantee payment of the bills and did pay them in performance thereof. If Hamill had not received repayment of his advances before the bills were paid, the amount of such advances would have been subjected to the satisfaction of the bills and Maryland would have been thus benefitted. When Maryland issued its performance bond in reliance upon Hamill's contingent promise, it thereby acquired a vested beneficial interest in the performance of the promise, and that interest could not be defeated or impaired by a subsequent rescission. Whether Maryland may be called a creditor beneficiary of Hamill's promise or subrogee of the third party beneficiary labor and material claimants, its right to recover is equally plain.

The judgment is affirmed.

PIERCE ASSOCIATES, INC. v. NEMOURS FOUNDATION
United States Court of Appeals, Third Circuit
865 F.2d 530 (1988)

I. *The Parties and the Proceedings*

The Nemours Foundation ("Nemours") owns the Alfred I. duPont Institute Children's Hospital in Wilmington, Delaware. In January 1980 Nemours entered into a general contract with Gilbane Building Company ("Gilbane") for completion of the interior of the Hospital. The Aetna Casualty & Surety Company ("Aetna") became surety on a performance bond which named Gilbane as principal and Nemours as obligee.[3]

---

[3] Like the donee beneficiary cases, the so-called "creditor beneficiary" cases account for a significant percentage of third-party litigation. Many of these cases involve complex construction contracts, which are even more difficult to sort through when a surety steps in. Basically, a surety is "one who undertakes

Gilbane entered into a number of subcontracts, including a $35.9 million fixed-price subcontract with Pierce Associates, Inc. ("Pierce") pursuant to which Pierce agreed to perform the mechanical work on the project (the heating, ventilation, air-conditioning, plumbing and fire-protection systems). Federal Insurance Company ("Federal") became surety on a performance bond which named Pierce as principal and Gilbane as obligee.

Disputes arose about performance under the general contract and under the subcontracts, and complex multi-party litigation ensued. During pretrial proceedings there were various changes in the parties' positions and realignments of adversaries which resulted in a trial at which Nemours and its general contractor Gilbane (joined by its surety Aetna) were plaintiffs seeking damages against Gilbane's subcontractor Pierce and Pierce's surety Federal.

After a 79 day trial the jury found in favor of Nemours and Gilbane on all their claims against Pierce and Federal and found against Pierce on its counterclaims. On September 15, 1986 final judgment was entered awarding $26,017,411 in damages and pre-judgment interest to Nemours and $3,018,372 in damages and pre-judgment interest to Gilbane. . . .

We conclude as follows: (i) The award of $19,045,982 in favor of Nemours against Pierce must be reversed for the reason that Nemours has neither a contract claim nor a negligence claim against Pierce. (ii) The award of $19,045,982 in favor of Nemours against Federal must be reversed for the reason that Federal's liability is dependent upon and derivative of Pierce's liability. (iii) The award of $2,066,699 for contract damages in favor of Gilbane and against Pierce and Federal will be reversed to the extent it represents delay liquidated damages and affirmed to the extent it represents recovery of $269,699 in back charges. . . .

II. *The Background*

These appeals do not challenge the sufficiency of the evidence. Rather, they challenge the legal sufficiency of the claims submitted to the jury and concern legal rulings of the trial court. The facts upon which these rulings were based are not in dispute.

As recited above, in January 1980 Nemours entered into a general contract with Gilbane to complete the interior of its Children's Hospital. This contract includes the American Institute of Architects' "General Conditions of the Contract of Construction" (1976 ed.) (the "AIA General Conditions"). Article 1.1.2 of the AIA General conditions states:

---

to pay money or do any other act in event that his principal fails therein." *In re Brock*, 312 Pa. 92, 166 A. 785 (1933). In most construction contracts, the owner requires the general contractor to furnish a performance bond and/or a payment bond, which are usually "covered" by a surety company. Performance bonds, which are promises to pay conditioned to be void on performance, are intended to insure the owner against the contractor's failure to complete the contract. Payment bonds, on the other hand, are conditioned to be void once the contractor has paid all subcontractors, laborers, and materialmen. [*Eds.*]

Nothing contained in the Contract Documents shall create any contractual relationship between the Owner [Nemours] or the Architect and any Subcontractor or Sub-subcontractor.

Gilbane in turn entered into a number of subcontracts. The largest was its $35.9 million fixed-price subcontract with Pierce, executed in June 1980 which called for Pierce to perform the mechanical work on the project. Gilbane entered into other subcontracts including a $19.7 million subcontract with Dynalectric Company ("Dynalectric") for electrical work and an $8.6 million subcontract with Honeywell, Inc. ("Honeywell") for installation of the building management systems.

Section 1 of the Gilbane-Pierce subcontract provided that Pierce would "furnish all materials and perform all work as described in Section 2 hereof for Phase 5B: A.I. duPont Institute for the Nemours Foundation Hospital Building . . . all in accordance with the Drawings and Specifications . . . and subject in every detail to the supervision and satisfaction of [Gilbane] and of [Nemours] or his duly authorized representative."

The subcontract provided in Section 6 that "[Pierce] agrees to be bound to [Gilbane] by the terms and conditions of this Agreement, the Drawings and Specifications, the General Contract and the General Conditions for construction . . . , and to assume toward [Gilbane] all the obligations and responsibilities that [Gilbane], by these documents, assumes toward [Nemours]." The General Conditions, of course, contained the provision that nothing contained in the "Contract Documents" shall create any contractual relationship between Nemours and any subcontractor.

A number of provisions in the subcontract, particularly those found in Section 7, imposed upon Pierce specific obligations vis-a-vis Nemours. For example: Section 7(a) requires Pierce to "furnish Shop Drawings, Erection Drawings, Details, Samples, etc.," for Nemours' approval. Section 7(b) bestowed upon Nemours the right to agree on lump sum pricing of changes to Pierce's work. Section 7(c) gave Nemours the right to inspect and condemn Pierce's work and required Pierce to "make good" the condemned work at its own expense. Section 7(e) required Pierce to "indemnify and save harmless" Nemours from any expenses, liability or loss arising from patent, copyright or trademark infringement.

After the terms of the GilbanePierce subcontract were agreed upon, Gilbane sent it to Nemours for approval. By letter dated September 9, 1980 Nemours approved the subcontract and also stated, "[b]y this approval, The Nemours Foundation does not waive, and expressly reserves all of its rights and remedies under said contract and nothing herein shall be deemed or construed to create any contractual relationship between The Nemours Foundation and said subcontractor." At the foot of the letter Gilbane executed the following: "Receipt and Acceptance acknowledged this 19th day of September, 1980."

Pursuant to the requirements of the subcontract Pierce furnished Gilbane a performance bond naming Pierce as principal, Federal as surety and Gilbane as obligee. Two provisions are pertinent to the present case. The bond provides, "No right of action shall accrue on this bond to or for the use of any person or corporation other than the Obligee named herein or the heirs, executors, administrators or successors of the Obligee." Immediately after that provision there appears the following: "Provided, however, that this Performance Bond issued on behalf of the named Principal may not be assigned to any party other than the Owner, The Nemours Foundation, without the consent of the Sureties." The bond was never assigned to Nemours.

Gilbane and its subcontractors commenced performance under their respective contracts. Serious delays ensued, the causes of which were the subject of vigorous disagreement. The delays and disputes over contract plans and specifications, design revisions, job progress schedules, progress payments and change orders resulted in Nemours withholding payments. In response, in April 1983 Pierce suspended performance under the subcontract. Although the other subcontractors asserted claims against Gilbane and Nemours, they stayed on the job.

To meet the situation created by Pierce's abandonment of the job, Nemours hired contractors to correct and finish Pierce's work under the direction of Turner Construction Company ("Turner"). Gilbane and its other subcontractors coordinated with Turner and the completion contractors to finish the Hospital. Substantial completion took place by December 1984 twenty-one months late.

Not surprisingly, litigation ensued. [Gilbane originally filed a complaint against Nemours, and Nemours filed an action against Pierce. After a very complicated litigation process, the two parties settled. In the settlement agreement, Gilbane promised to cooperate with Nemours in its action against Pierce, "to seek commitments from its subcontractors in their settlement agreements to cooperate with Nemours in a similar fashion, and to refrain from settling with Pierce or Federal without Nemours' written consent."]

In order to reflect the realignment of the parties resulting from the settlement, the district court designated Nemours and Gilbane as co-plaintiffs and Pierce and Federal as the defendants. On November 4, 1985 the district court denied Pierce's motion to dismiss Nemours' claim seeking indemnification for the $3,375,000 which Nemours had paid in settlement.

A trial by jury commenced on March 31, 1986. The results are reflected in the final judgment described in Part I above.

III. *Third Party Beneficiary Claims*

It must first be determined whether the district court erred as a matter of law by holding that Nemours was a third party beneficiary of the Gilbane-Pierce subcontract. [footnote omitted] Since this issue involves only a question of law the standard of review is plenary. This being a diversity of citizenship case brought pursuant to 28 U.S.C. § 1332, this and the other substantive issues are controlled by Delaware law.

"It is well settled in Delaware that a third-party may recover on a contract made for his benefit. . . . But in order for there to be a third party beneficiary, the contracting parties must intend to confer the benefit." *Ins. Co. of North America v. Waterhouse*, 424 A.2d 675, 679 (Del. Super. 1980). The intent to confer a third party beneficiary benefit is to be determined from the language of the contract.

Thus in the present case an intent to confer third party beneficiary status on Nemours must be gleaned from the language of the Gilbane-Pierce subcontract. The language of a contract, however, cannot be divorced from the context in which it was written. Here, we are dealing with a general contract and a subcontract in the construction industry.

Typically when major construction is involved an owner has neither the desire nor the ability to negotiate with and supervise the multitude of trades and skills required to complete a project. Consequently an owner will engage a general contractor. The general contractor will retain, coordinate and supervise subcontractors. The owner looks to the general contractor, not the subcontractors, both for performance of the total construction project and for any damages or other relief if there is a default in performance. Performance and the payment of damages are normally assured by the bond of a surety on which the general contractor is principal and the owner is the obligee.

The general contractor, in turn, who is responsible for the performance of the subcontractors, has a right of action against any subcontractor which defaults. Performance and payment of damages by a subcontractor are normally assured by the bond of a surety on which the subcontractor is principal and the general contractor is the obligee.

Thus the typical owner is insulated from the subcontractors both during the course of construction and during the pursuit of remedies in the event of a default. Conversely, the subcontractors are insulated from the owner. The owner deals with and, if necessary, sues the general contractor, and the general contractor deals with and, if necessary, sues the subcontractors.

These typical construction contract relationships have long been recognized . . .

These typical construction relationships are also recognized in Delaware law. In Cannon the Delaware Supreme Court referred to the "buffer zone" which a general contract creates between the owner and a subcontractor, although in that case it found that the language of the subcontract evidenced an intent to extinguish the buffer zone. 336 A.2d at 216.

There is nothing to prevent a departure from the typical pattern, and, as was the case in *Cannon*, a contractor and subcontractor may agree to confer upon an owner rights which are enforceable directly against the subcontractor. However, an intent to do so must be found in the contract documents. Thus in the present case it must be determined whether the Gilbane-Pierce subcontract evidences an intent on the part of both Pierce and Gilbane to depart from the typical owner-general contractor and general contractor-subcontractor relationships to confer upon Nemours a direct right of action against Pierce.

The overall structure of the contractual relationships in this case falls into the traditional mold. Nemours as owner entered into a general contract with Gilbane. Gilbane's obligations were assured by a performance bond issued by Aetna. Gilbane entered into a number of subcontracts, including the one with Pierce. Each subcontractor's obligations were assured by a performance bond, a performance bond issued by Federal in the case of Pierce. If indeed Gilbane intended that the subcontract create an obligation running directly from Pierce to Nemours, it is curious that it accepted (in fact, prescribed) a performance bond which provided that no right of action would accrue on it to or for the use of any person other than Gilbane.

The language of the Gilbane-Pierce subcontract suggests that Gilbane and Pierce contemplated that Pierce was to be obligated to Gilbane, not to Nemours.

The subcontract is between Pierce, as subcontractor, and Gilbane as the contractor. Section 6 specified Gilbane as the entity to which Pierce was to be responsible: "The *Subcontractor* agrees to be bound to the *Contractor* by the terms and conditions of the Agreement . . . and to assume toward the *Contractor* all the obligations and responsibilities that the *Contractor*, by these documents, assumes toward the *Owner*." (Emphasis added.)

Section 7(f) of the subcontract provides that if Pierce fails to perform, Gilbane may provide labor, equipment or materials or may terminate Pierce and complete the work itself. Section 38E of the Special conditions provides that the *subcontractor's* payment and performance bond shall name *Gilbane* as obligee.

Exhibit A to the general contract, which of course is evidence of Gilbane's intent, provides that "[t]he *Contractor* shall have sole and *total responsibility* for completing the [general] contract . . . and is responsible to the *Owner* for the full, proper, and timely performance of all work under the contract." (Emphasis added.) Article 4.3.2 of the General Conditions provides that "[t]he *Contractor* shall be responsible to the *Owner* for the acts and omissions of his employees, *Subcontractors* and their agents and employees. . . ." (Emphasis added.)

Of significance is the incorporation of the standard AIA General Conditions of the Contract for Construction into both the general contract and the subcontract. Article 1.1.2 of the General Conditions provides:

> Nothing contained in the Contract Documents shall create any contractual relationship between the Owner or the Architect and any Subcontractor or Sub-subcontractor.

Nemours urges that in light of the definition of "Contract Documents" in Article 1.1.1, the Article 1.1.2 language serves only to preclude the general contract from creating a contractual relationship between Nemours as owner and Pierce as subcontractor but does not preclude the subcontract from creating such a relationship. Article 1.1.2 provides that "[n]othing contained in the *Contract Documents* shall create any contractual relationship between the Owner . . . and any Subcontractor. . . ." (Emphasis added.) As defined in Article 1.1.1, however, "Contract Documents" does not include the subcontract and, therefore, Nemours argues, there is no prohibition against the subcontract creating a third party beneficiary relationship between Nemours and Pierce.

If the Article 1.1.2 language appeared only in the general contract, Nemours' argument might be persuasive. However, there was repeated incorporation of the General Conditions and its Article 1.1.2 language into the subcontract.

At page 1A of the subcontract it is provided that all work thereunder shall be in accordance with "General Conditions of the Contract for Construction, in (sic) Specifications, (AIA Document A201 — 1976 Edition)". In Section 6, referred to above, Pierce as subcontractor agrees to be bound by the General Contract and the General Conditions for Construction. Section 7(g) provides that "[t]he Terms and Provisions herein contained and the General Conditions For Construction (AIA Document A201 — 1976 Edition) . . . shall supersede all previous communications, representations, or agreements, either oral or written, between the parties hereto with respect to the subject matter hereof."

This repeated incorporation of the General Conditions and its Article 1.1.2 no contractual relationship language is a strong indication of an intent on Gilbane's and Pierce's part to maintain the separate owner-general contractor and general contractor-subcontractor relationships.

No Delaware court appears to have construed general contracts or subcontracts which contain Article 1.1.2 of the AIA General Conditions or comparable language. Decisions in other jurisdictions, however, have held that this provision (or like language) prevents an owner from maintaining a breach of contract action against a subcontractor on a third party beneficiary theory, or prevents a subcontractor from maintaining a breach of contract action against an owner on such a theory. Thus the buffer is preserved by Article 1.1.2 or its equivalent. . . .

Nemours' principal argument in support of its third party beneficiary theory is that the Gilbane-Pierce subcontract contains numerous provisions which evidence an intent that Nemours be benefitted by Pierce's performance. The description of Pierce's work in Section 1 provides that it shall be subject to the supervision and satisfaction of the contractor and the owner. There are a number of other provisions which impose obligations on Pierce vis-a-vis Nemours, such as an obligation to furnish Shop Drawings, Erection Drawings, etc. for Nemours' approval, the requirement that Pierce indemnify and save harmless Nemours from any expense, liability or loss arising from patent, copyright or trademark infringement.

In every construction subcontract the owner is the one which ultimately benefits from its performance. However, this does not create a third party beneficiary relationship.

Nemours relies heavily on *Oliver B. Cannon & Sons, Inc. v. Dorr-Oliver, Inc., supra,* in which the court held that in the circumstances of that case the various provisions of the subcontract benefitting the owner demonstrated an intent by the parties to the subcontract that the owner be a third party beneficiary of the subcontract. The result in that case turned on the ascertainment of the parties' intent. What distinguishes the present case from *Cannon* is Pierce's and Gilbane's expressed intent that there be no third party beneficiary relationship between Pierce and Nemours. For the same reason *Sears, Roebuck and Co. v. Jardel Co.,* 421 F.2d 1048 (3d Cir. 1970) (applying Pennsylvania substantive law) is inapplicable.

Until the execution of the settlement agreement between Nemours and Gilbane, the actions of all three parties affirmed the absence of a contractual relationship between subcontractor and owner. In its September 9, 1980 letter to Gilbane approving the Gilbane-Pierce subcontract, Nemours wrote "nothing herein shall be deemed or construed to create any contractual relationship between The Nemours Foundation and said subcontractor [Pierce]." During the period when disputes about performance of the contract had developed Nemours looked to Gilbane and

Gilbane alone with respect to completion of Pierce's work under the subcontract. The manner in which the contract litigation was instituted and initially prosecuted and defended evidenced the understanding of Nemours, Gilbane and Pierce that no contractual relationship existed between Nemours and Pierce.

We conclude that the subcontract does not manifest an intent by Pierce and Gilbane to confer third party beneficiary status upon Nemours. In fact, the subcontract evidences an intent to preclude such a status. Nemours and Gilbane were but two of three parties in a relationship carefully structured by contract (the general contract and the subcontract). Pierce was the third party in that relationship. By means of the settlement agreement Nemours and Gilbane, in effect, sought to change that relationship to give Nemours a previously non-existent direct cause of action against Pierce. Without Pierce's participation that was not possible. Contractual rights cannot be so casually disregarded.

Thus to the extent that the judgment of the trial court rests upon Nemours' third party beneficiary claim it must be reversed.

SLOVITER, CIRCUIT JUDGE, dissenting.

Although I am in agreement with a substantial portion of the majority opinion in this complex appeal, I respectfully dissent because I disagree with the conclusion that under Delaware law the owner, Nemours, could not be considered to be a third party beneficiary of the subcontract for purposes of bringing suit for damages sustained when Pierce, the subcontractor, walked off the job. The effect of the majority's decision is that while Nemours had a substantial dispute with general contractor, Gilbane, over performance and payment, which resulted in litigation, Nemours was nonetheless required either to depend on Gilbane to file and process Nemours' claim for damages against Pierce or to sue Gilbane for what the jury found was Pierce's unjustifiable refusal to perform.

As the majority recognizes, this court sitting in diversity is bound to apply Delaware law. Because I believe that a fair reading of the applicable Delaware case law supports the inference that Pierce and Gilbane intended to benefit Nemours, I conclude that Nemours could maintain a third party beneficiary suit against Pierce.

The majority correctly points out that under Delaware law the right to sue on a contract as a third party beneficiary is a function of the contracting parties' intent to confer a benefit on the third party. As I read Delaware case law, contractual provisions in a subcontract such as those in the Gilbane-Pierce subcontract are sufficient to permit an inference of intent to benefit the owner. *See Oliver B. Cannon & Sons, Inc. v. Dorr-Oliver, Inc.*, 336 A.2d 211, 215-16 (Del. 1975). . . .

Factors referred to in these cases as significant were that the subcontracts in question identified the owner, specified that work was to be done on the owner's premises, and contained provisions whereby the subcontractor undertook to indemnify the owner against certain losses arising out of the execution of the subcontractor's work. *Cannon*, 312 A.2d at 327-28 & nn. 4-5 (Del. Super. Ct.). . . . Additionally the Delaware Supreme Court, in affirming the Superior Court's decision in *Cannon*, cited the existence of a warranty for defective workmanship running from the subcontractor to the owner. *Cannon*, 336 A.2d at 216 (Del.).

Because the Gilbane-Pierce contract contains equivalent provisions, I believe that there was sufficient evidence under Delaware law to find that Gilbane and Pierce intended to make Nemours a beneficiary of the subcontract.

The majority declines to follow the *Cannon* courts' rationale on the grounds that there is other evidence which negates the inferences of intent which are permissible under those decisions. To the extent the majority relies on evidence gleaned from sources other than the Gilbane-Pierce contract itself, such as statements by Nemours to the effect that there was no contractual relation between it and Pierce, the majority deviates from the acknowledged Delaware requirement that the intent to create a third party beneficiary must be ascertained from the language of the contract itself. *See Cannon*, 336 A.2d at 215 (Del.); *Royal Indemnity Co. v. Alexander Industries, Inc.*, 211 A.2d 919, 920 (Del. 1965).

The majority's conclusion that Pierce and Gilbane did not intend to benefit Nemours rests primarily on the incorporation of Article 1.1.2 of the AIA General Conditions of the Contract for Construction from the Nemours-Gilbane contract into the Gilbane-Pierce contract. That clause, which states that nothing contained in the "Contract Documents" shall create any contractual relationship between the Owner and a Subcontractor, clearly expresses Nemours' intent not to confer third party rights on *Pierce*. The "Contract Documents" as defined in the Nemours-Gilbane contract in which Article 1.1.2 is embedded do not include the Gilbane-Pierce contract; the Gilbane-Pierce contract does not expressly preclude the formation of contractual relations between Pierce and Nemours. I am willing to assume *arguendo* that the relationship established by the scheme of incorporated provisions precluded the Owner and Subcontractor from asserting contractual claims against each other arising in the ordinary course of the construction, such as claims for additional payment due or failure to follow the contract specifications, and required that such claims be funneled through the prime contractor. I believe, however, that Delaware would require a more explicit preclusion of Nemours' right to sue the subcontractor for total failure of performance than the mere inclusion of this standard clause in the form contract, particularly in light of the indemnity and warranty provisions in the Gilbane-Pierce contract that were designed to benefit Nemours. Therefore I would affirm the district court's ruling that this case could proceed to the jury on a third party beneficiary theory.

NOTES

1. ***Construction Contract Relationships.*** As discussed in *Nemours*, construction contracts generally are structured so that owners deal directly with general contractors, who then deal directly with subcontractors. Usually there is no direct connection between the owner of the site and subcontractors working on the project, which precludes litigation between owners and subs and between tenants of the owner and the general contractor. In some extraordinary circumstances, however, courts have given non-parties the ability to sue as third-party beneficiaries. Consider the case of *Kmart Corp. v. Balfour Beatty, Inc.*, 994 F. Supp. 634 (1998). Balfour (BBI) was hired to build a shopping center in the Virgin Islands, contracting with the owner of the proposed site. Kmart was to be the principal tenant of the new shopping center, and the contract between BBI and the owner

provided Kmart with numerous powers of approval and review of the construction as it proceeded. Due to delays and mistakes on the part of BBI, Kmart initiated an action for breach of contract claiming that it was a third party beneficiary of the contract between BBI and the owner. After reviewing the case law, the court concluded as follows:

> Just as the Maryland court had no difficulty finding the tenant was a third party beneficiary to the construction contract, so does this Court find that KMART was a third party beneficiary of the construction contract between BBI and [the Owner]. The contractual duty of performance owed by BBI to its promisee, [the Owner], would satisfy [the Owner's] duty to its beneficiary, KMART. KMART, then, is a third party beneficiary to the construction contract between BBI and [the Owner.]

Can you reconcile *Nemours* with *Kmart Corp.*? Nemours received similar powers of approval and review over the work of Pierce, the subcontractor. Moreover, it would seem that Nemours as owner of the site would even more directly benefit from Pierce's work than the tenant Kmart would from BBI's, but one court held that Kmart had standing to sue as a third-party beneficiary, and the other held that Nemours did not. Does this make sense?

2. *Intent*. The Restatement (Second) emphasizes intent to benefit the third party as a controlling factor. See Restatement (Second) § 302. Professor Eisenberg illustrates the alternative meanings of "intent":[4]

> First, "intent" can refer either to the parties' actual subjective intent or to an intent that is objectively manifested. Second, "intent" can refer either to acting with a motive to achieve a given result, or to choosing a course of action with knowledge that a given result is likely to follow from the action, even if the actor is indifferent about achieving the result or indeed would prefer to avoid it.
>
> . . . .
>
> Third, "intent" can refer either to the end an actor seeks to achieve or to the means that an actor uses to achieve an end. For example, suppose that *A*, a country at war, stages a bombing raid on the civilian population of its enemy, *B*. The end that *A* seeks to achieve by the raid may be to kill *B*'s civilians (perhaps in retribution for the killing of *A*'s civilians) or to induce *B*'s surrender. Although in the first case killing civilians is intended as an end, and in the second it is intended as a means, in both cases it could be said that *A* intended to kill civilians.
>
> Courts that use the intent-to-benefit test often fail to make clear what they mean by "intent" in the context of this test. Certainly, the test could not be satisfied merely by knowledge that performance of the contract will benefit the third party. By definition, in every case involving a third-party beneficiary the third party will benefit from performance of the contract, and normally the contracting parties will know with substantial certainty that this benefit will result. Accordingly, if the intent-to-benefit test was

---

[4] Melvin A. Eisenberg, *Third-Party Beneficiaries*, 92 Colum. L. Rev. 1358 (1992).

satisfied merely by knowledge that performance would benefit the third party, every third-party beneficiary could enforce a contract. Many or most courts that use the test avoid this problem by effectively treating the issue as whether the contracting parties, or the promisee, had a subjective motive to confer a benefit on the third party as an end.

Indeed, unless the intent-to-benefit test has this meaning, it is largely empty. If the intent-to-benefit test is satisfied by objective intent, it provides no guidance on the issue the test, as so formulated, makes critical: How is it to be determined, as an objective matter, why in some contracts whose performance will benefit a third party, the benefit is objectively "intended" within the meaning of the test, while in other contracts whose performance will benefit a third party, the benefit is not so "intended"?

Perhaps to ameliorate these difficulties, some courts patch additional formal requirements onto the intent-to-benefit test. For example, some cases impose a requirement that an intent to benefit the third party be "clear," "express," or "definite," and some require that an intent to benefit the third party be found in the language of the contract itself. . . . [B]oth types of requirement are difficult or impossible to apply meaningfully and consistently, and are not so applied in fact.

Id. at 1378–80.

Eisenberg would replace the intent test with the following:

A third-party beneficiary should have power to enforce a contract if, but only if:

(I) allowing the beneficiary to enforce the contract is a necessary or important means of effectuating the contracting parties' performance objectives, as manifested in the contract read in the light of surrounding circumstances; or

(II) allowing the beneficiary to enforce the contract is supported by reasons of policy or morality independent of contract law and would not conflict with the contracting parties' performance objectives.

Id. at 1385.

Orna Paglin has argued that court use of both an intention criterion (as demonstrated in *Nemours*) and a reliance criterion (as demonstrated in *Hamill*) tends to subvert the contracting parties' true objectives. She contends that classical contract principles emphasizing the consensual nature of liability between contracting parties (meaning the parties voluntarily accept certain levels of liability should they breach) are threatened by third-party beneficiary theories:

Several factors may account for the change of what is essentially a consensual liability field into an imposed liability field. First, third party beneficiary disputes, which involve three parties, are prone to the invocation of such standards of liability as foreseeability. Second, the attempt of the courts to adhere to the notion of consensual liability by means of the intention criterion leads to serious interpretative and evidentiary difficulties. Third, courts are tempted to use third party beneficiary law as a tool for implementing desired social and economic policies, even when to do so thwarts the parties' intentions.

The imposition of liability in the field of third party beneficiaries assumes various, sometimes intricate forms. For example, when the search for the parties' intention is complicated by definitional or evidentiary difficulties, courts frequently engage in the process of supplementation; they employ public policy considerations to resolve the dispute. Yet this process is sometimes disguised as a quest for the parties' intention. Hence, courts may allude to the intention criterion even when the true rationale for their decisions has nothing to do with this criterion. Only rarely do the courts admit that they police the parties' agreements in order to carry out social or economic policies.

Another way to impose liability in the field of third party beneficiaries is through the application of the reliance doctrine. Like its antecedent, the intention criterion, the reliance doctrine is used as a facade for other approaches, such as a utilitarian form of market approach. Only rarely is the reliance doctrine examined on its own merits and even then it is prone to a formalistic application which may lead to arbitrary results. There are distinct reasons, however, for the use of these two disguises. While the intention criterion is used as a disguise in an attempt to adhere to the notion of consensual liability, the reliance doctrine is used as a disguise in an attempt to avoid a shift from doctrinal to non-doctrinal analysis. . . .

The increasing tension between classical principles of contract law, such as the importance of a bargain and of consensual liability, and regulative tendencies in this field, suggests that the contracting parties and the courts may find themselves involved in a continuous contest: The parties may try to disclaim liability to third parties and the courts may try to police their agreements whenever the protection of third parties' interests seems desirable.

Orna S. Paglin, *Criteria for Recognition of Third Party Beneficiaries' Rights*, 24 New Eng. L. Rev. 63, 111–12 (1989).

3.   *The Intention Criterion and Contractual Ambiguity.* In ascertaining the "intention" of the contracting parties, courts often resort to the facts and circumstances surrounding the making of the contract whenever the document's terms are themselves ambiguous. Ambiguity is a term of art, generally defined by the courts as "when the words used to express the meaning and intention of the parties are insufficient in the sense the contract may be understood to reach two or more possible meanings." *Wolfgang v. Mid-America MotorSports*, 111 F.3d 1515, 1524 (1997) (quoting *Fasse v. Lower Heating & Air Conditioning, Inc.*, 736 P.2d 930, 933 (Kan. 1987)). Thus, third-party plaintiffs often argue that the express terms of a contract are unclear in order to present contextual evidence of an intent to benefit third parties. Similarly, defendants will claim ambiguity in order to admit extrinsic evidence rebutting any intention to benefit third parties. In many cases, extrinsic evidence may indeed be necessary to determine the intent of the contracting parties regarding third-party beneficiaries. As we have seen in other contexts, however, the risk of imposing non-bargained-for liability increases once courts employ evidence beyond the explicit contractual language.

4. ***Modification of Third-Party Rights by the Original Parties.*** Once a contract has been made for the benefit of a third party, can the original contracting parties alter the rights or benefits conferred on the third party? This question turns on when, according to the courts, the benefits conferred on a third party "vest," which describes when the right or benefit of the third party is no longer alienable or revocable without the third party's assent. Under certain circumstances, the parties to the contract *can* agree to alter or even eliminate the benefit originally intended for a third party, though as we shall see, the concept of when a third party's benefit "vests" has changed over time. Consider the following:

In *Robson v. Robson*, 514 F. Supp. 99 (N.D. Ill. 1981), the defendant had contracted with his son to provide for the disposition of their fifty percent interests in the family business. The contract stated that in the event of the death of either father or son, the surviving party would receive the decedent's fifty percent interest in the company, and would provide $500 a month to the decedent's wife. A few years after this agreement was signed, the son and his wife filed for divorce proceedings, and the son learned he had cancer. The son died before the divorce proceedings were completed. Two days before his death, and in the presence of three witnesses, the son crossed through the section of the agreement providing $500 a month to his wife. The wife sued as a third-party beneficiary of the contract between father and son, arguing that the alteration of the document was invalid. In rejecting the wife's claim, the court held that she was a third-party beneficiary of the agreement, but went on to say:

> The more difficult question, and the one that as far as our research discloses, has never been faced by an Illinois court, is whether contracting parties may discharge, rescind, or revoke the benefit promised to a third-party donee beneficiary prior to the vesting of the beneficiary's rights, where the beneficiary has not detrimentally relied upon receiving the benefit. Although some authorities have stated that the promisor in a third-party beneficiary contract has no right to deprive the beneficiary of his vested rights therein, . . . these authorities have no bearing on the case at bar because they fail to distinguish between creditor beneficiaries . . . and donee beneficiaries (at issue in the instant case), and because plaintiff's rights in the instant case had not vested at the time the contracting parties attempted to discharge [plaintiff's] interest. [Citations omitted.]

Id. at 102. The *Robson* court limited its holding to donee beneficiaries, but the Illinois Supreme Court (following the majority trend among the states) expanded the modification rule to all third party beneficiaries a few years later:

> *Bay* established the rule in Illinois that third-party beneficiary rights vest immediately and cannot be altered or extinguished through a later agreement of the original parties to the contract, unless the beneficiary assents.

> Englhaupt urges us to replace the *Bay* rule with the "modern view" as set forth in section 311 of the second Restatement. Section 311, entitled

"Variation of a Duty to a Beneficiary," stands in direct contrast to *Bay.* It provides that, in the absence of language in a contract making the rights of a third party beneficiary irrevocable, the parties to the contract "retain power to discharge or modify the duty by subsequent agreement," without the third-party beneficiary's assent, at any time until the third party beneficiary, without notice of the discharge or modification, materially changes position in justifiable reliance on the promise, brings suit on the promise or manifests assent to the promise at the request of the promisor or promisee.

Section 311 now represents the majority view on the subject of vesting. [citations omitted] In contrast, the immediate vesting rule as set forth in *Bay* represents the minority view, followed by only a handful of states. [citations omitted]. . . . Englehaupt maintains that we should adopt section 311. He asserts that section 311 represents the majority rule on vesting because it better conforms to modern commercial practices and general principles of contract law. According to Englhaupt, parties should remain free to modify or discharge their contracts as they see fit, without the assent of a third-party beneficiary, subject only to the three exceptions provided for in section 311.

Finding Englehaupt's arguments persuasive, we hereby adopt the vesting rule set forth in section 311 of the Second Restatement.

Olson v. Etheridge, 177 Ill. 2d 396, 408–10, 686 N.E.2d 563, 568–69 (1997).

5. *Express Denials of Third-Party Beneficiaries.* Will a provision expressly denying the contracting parties' intention to benefit any third parties be recognized by the courts? Generally, the answer is yes. In a contract between two private parties, an unambiguous statement rejecting the empowerment of any third parties usually is sufficient to disclaim liability to third parties benefited by the contract. *See, e.g., Hossain v. Rauscher Pierce Refsnes,* 97 F. Supp. 2d 1237 (D. Kan. 2000) (cases cited therein).

The same is true of government contracts. In *Aristil v. Housing Auth.,* 54 F. Supp. 2d 1289 (M.D. Fla. 1999), residents of a housing project sued the local housing authority as third-party beneficiaries of the Authority's Annual Contributions Contract (ACC) with the U.S. Department of Housing and Urban Development (HUD). The ACC requires the Housing Authority to provide "safe and decent" housing to residents, and the plaintiffs alleged that the Authority violated this provision. The Housing Authority moved to dismiss the third-party beneficiary claim because any intention to empower third party-beneficiaries had been expressly denied in the contract. The court agreed, stating that "[s]ection twenty-one (21) of the ACC explicitly states that '[e]xcept as to bondholders . . . nothing in this ACC shall be construed as creating any right of any third party to enforce any provision of the ACC or to assert any claim against HUD or the [Housing Authority].'" *Id.* at 1296.

Should this ruling be cause for concern? In similar cases, plaintiffs have argued that, if third-party beneficiaries cannot legally enforce government contracts, there is no one else with enough incentive to take the government to court. Thus, the interests of the beneficiaries — the people that the government's contract is purported to serve — are not protected. *See Johnson v. City of Detroit*, 446 F.3d 614, 623 (6th Cir. 2006). Is there merit to this argument?

C. SPECIAL APPLICATIONS

H. R. MOCH CO. v. RENSSELAER WATER CO.
Court of Appeals of New York
247 N.Y. 160, 159 N.E. 896 (1928)

CARDOZO, J.

The defendant, a waterworks company under the laws of this state, made a contract with the city of Rensselaer for the supply of water during a term of years. Water was to be furnished to the city for sewer flushing and street sprinkling; for service to schools and public buildings; and for service at fire hydrants, the latter service at the rate of $42.50 a year for each hydrant. Water was to be furnished to private takers within the city at their homes and factories and other industries at reasonable rates, not exceeding a stated schedule. While this contract was in force, a building caught fire. The flames, spreading to the plaintiff's warehouse near by, destroyed it and its contents. The defendant, according to the complaint, was promptly notified of the fire, "but omitted and neglected after such notice, to supply or furnish sufficient or adequate quantity of water, with adequate pressure to stay, suppress, or extinguish the fire before it reached the warehouse of the plaintiff, although the pressure and supply which the defendant was equipped to supply and furnish, and had agreed by said contract to supply and furnish, was adequate and sufficient to prevent the spread of the fire to and the destruction of the plaintiff's warehouse and its contents." By reason of the failure of the defendant to "fulfill the provisions of the contract between it and the city of Rensselaer," the plaintiff is said to have suffered damage, for which judgment is demanded. A motion, in the nature of a demurrer, to dismiss the complaint, was denied at Special Term. The Appellate Division reversed by a divided court.

Liability in the plaintiff's argument is placed on one or other of three grounds. The complaint, we are told, is to be viewed as stating: (1) A cause of action for breach of contract within Lawrence v. Fox, 20 N.Y. 268; (2) a cause of action for a common-law tort, within MacPherson v. Buick Motor Co., 217 N.Y. 382; or (3) a cause of action for the breach of a statutory duty. These several grounds of liability will be considered in succession.

We think the action is not maintainable as one for breach of contract.

No legal duty rests upon a city to supply its inhabitants with protection against fire. That being so, a member of the public may not maintain an action under Lawrence v. Fox against one contracting with the city to furnish water at the hydrants, unless an intention appears that the promisor is to be answerable to individual members of the public as well as to the city for any loss ensuing from the failure to fulfill the promise. No such intention is discernible here. On the contrary, the contract is significantly divided into two branches: One a promise to the city for the benefit of the city in its corporate capacity, in which branch is included the service at the hydrants; and the other a promise to the city for the benefit of private takers, in which branch is included the service at their homes and factories. In a broad sense it is true that every city contract, not improvident or wasteful, is for the benefit of the public. More than this, however, must be shown to give a right of action to a member of the public not formally a party. The benefit, as it is sometimes said, must be one that is not merely incidental and secondary. It must be primary and immediate in such a sense and to such a degree as to bespeak the assumption of a duty to make reparation directly to the individual members of the public if the benefit is lost. The field of obligation would be expanded beyond reasonable limits if less than this were to be demanded as a condition of liability. A promisor undertakes to supply fuel for heating a public building. He is not liable for breach of contract to a visitor who finds the building without fuel, and thus contracts a cold. The list of illustrations can be indefinitely extended. The carrier of the mails under contract with the government is not answerable to the merchant who has lost the benefit of a bargain through negligent delay. The householder is without a remedy against manufacturers of hose and engines, though prompt performance of their contracts would have stayed the ravages of fire. "The law does not spread its protection so far." Robins Dry Dock & Repair Co. v. Flint, 275 U.S. 303.

So with the case at hand. By the vast preponderance of authority, a contract between a city and a water company to furnish water at the city hydrants has in view a benefit to the public that is incidental rather than immediate, an assumption of duty to the city and not to its inhabitants. Such is the ruling of the Supreme Court of the United States. German Alliance Ins. Co. v. Homewater Supply Co., 226 U.S. 220. Such has been the ruling in this state, though the question is still open in this court. Such with few exceptions has been the ruling in other jurisdictions. The diligence of counsel has brought together decisions to that effect from 26 states. Only a few states have held otherwise. An intention to assume an obligation of indefinite extension to every member of the public is seen to be the more improbable when we recall the crushing burden that the obligation would impose. The consequences invited would bear no reasonable proportion to those attached by law to defaults not greatly different. A wrongdoer who by negligence sets fire to a building is liable in damages to the owner where the fire has its origin, but not to other owners who are injured when it spreads. The rule in our state is settled to that effect, whether wisely or unwisely. If the plaintiff is to prevail, one who negligently omits to supply sufficient pressure to extinguish a fire started by another assumes an obligation to pay the ensuing damage, though the whole city is laid low. A promisor will not be deemed to have had in mind the assumption of a risk so overwhelming for any trivial reward.

The cases that have applied the rule of Lawrence v. Fox to contracts made by a city for the benefit of the public are not at war with this conclusion. Through them all there runs as a unifying principle the presence of an intention to compensate the individual members of the public in the event of a default. For example, in Pond v. New Rochelle Water Co., 183 N.Y. 330, the contract with the city fixed a schedule of rates to be supplied, not to public buildings, but to private takers at their homes. In Matter of International R. Co. v. Rann, 224 N.Y. 83, 85, the contract was by street railroads to carry passengers for a stated fare. In Smyth v. City of New York, 203

N.Y. 106, and Rigney v. New York Cent. & H.R.R. Co., 217 N.Y. 31, covenants were made by contractors upon public works, not merely to indemnify the city, but to assume its liabilities. These and like cases come within the third group stated in the comprehensive opinion in Seaver v. Ransom, 224 N.Y. 233, 238. The municipality was contracting in behalf of its inhabitants by covenants intended to be enforced by any of them severally as occasion should arise.

[The court also held that the action was not maintainable as one for a common-law tort or as one for breach of a statutory duty.]

KLAMATH WATER USERS PROTECTIVE ASSOCIATION v. PATTERSON
United States Court of Appeals, Ninth Circuit
204 F.3d 1206 (1999)

TASHIMA, CIRCUIT JUDGE:

This appeal involves a basic contract issue: whether the Klamath Water Users Protective Association and other irrigators in the Klamath Basin (collectively, the "Irrigators") are third-party beneficiaries to a 1956 contract (the "Contract") between the United States Bureau of Reclamation ("Reclamation" or "United States") and the California Oregon Power Company ("Copco") that governs the management of the Link River Dam (the "Dam") in the Klamath Basin (the "Project"). We hold that they are not. The district court concluded that the Irrigators do not have third-party beneficiary water rights under the Contract. It granted a declaratory judgment to Reclamation and PacifiCorp, Copco's successor in interest that now operates and maintains the Dam under the Contract, holding that PacifiCorp is not liable to the Irrigators for implementing Reclamation's water allocation decisions for the Project. See Klamath Water Users Ass'n v. Patterson, 15 F. Supp. 2d 990, 997 (D. Or. 1998) ("*Klamath*"). We have jurisdiction under 28 U.S.C. § 1291, and we affirm.

I. Background

The Project, located within the Upper Klamath and Lost River Basins in Oregon and California, was authorized by Congress in 1905 pursuant to the Reclamation Act of 1902. In 1905, in accordance with state water law and the Reclamation Act, the United States appropriated all available water rights in the Klamath River and Lost River and their tributaries in Oregon and began constructing a series of water diversion projects.

In 1917, the United States and Copco entered into an agreement under which Copco would construct the Dam and then convey it to the United States. In return, Copco and the United States entered into a fifty-year contract (1917-1967) that gave Copco the right to operate the Dam. The Contract was amended in 1920 and 1930, and was renewed in 1956 for an additional fifty years (1956-2006). The United States and Copco are the only named parties to the Contract. The Contract, as renewed in 1956, remains in effect and is the subject of controversy here. The Contract states that it was entered into pursuant to the Reclamation Act and "acts of Congress relating to the preservation and development of fish and wildlife resources."

The parties do not dispute that the Dam was built to help the United States satisfy its contractual obligations to water users in the basin, including the Irrigators. However, the project served other federal purposes, such as impounding water to flood the adjacent wildlife refuges. Copco's interest related primarily to controlling the flow of water to the Copco-owned hydroelectric facilities downstream from the Dam.

Operation of the Dam is also subject to the requirements of federal statutes, such as the Endangered Species Act ("ESA.") The coho salmon of the lower Klamath River has been listed as threatened, and two species of sucker fish, the Lost River and shortnose suckers, located in and around the Project, are listed as endangered. In 1992, the United States Fish and Wildlife Service issued a Biological Opinion that required certain minimum elevations for Upper Klamath Lake to avoid jeopardizing these protected species. In addition, the Secretary of the Interior has recognized that a number of Oregon tribes, including the Klamath, Yurok and Hoopa Valley tribes (the "Tribes"), hold fishing and water treaty rights in the basin.

In recognition of the federal government's various obligations related to the Project, Reclamation initiated a public process to establish a new operating plan for the Dam. For the next several years, Reclamation intends to issue one- year interim plans while formulating a long term plan for water distribution. Pursuant to this policy, in April, 1997, Reclamation circulated to interested parties a draft of its proposed 1997 interim plan for the Project. In May, 1997, Reclamation issued its final 1997 interim plan. Soon thereafter,

PacifiCorp stated it would not implement the plan because the required flow levels would force it to violate its Federal Energy Regulatory Commission ("FERC") license. PacifiCorp's FERC license required FERC flows[5] in September at 1,300 cubic feet per second ("cfs"), while Reclamation's 1997 plan allowed for only 1,000 cfs.

Reclamation and PacifiCorp agreed upon a short-term modification to the Contract. The modification directed PacifiCorp to implement the 1997 plan, contingent upon FERC concurrence. The Irrigators were not included in the negotiations that led to this modification.

The Irrigators filed this action claiming, among other things, breach of the Contract based on their alleged third-party beneficiary status. In response, PacifiCorp filed a counterclaim, seeking a declaration of rights with respect to the Irrigators' standing under the Contract. The parties then filed cross-motions for summary judgment.

The district court denied the Irrigators' motion for summary judgment and granted PacifiCorp's and Reclamation's motions for summary judgment on Pacifi-Corp's counterclaim. *See Klamath*, 15 F. Supp. 2d at 997. The Irrigators appeal.

---

[5] [1] "FERC" flows refer to certain minimum flows for fish downstream. A FERC license regulates FERC flows.

II. Discussion

The Irrigators argue that under the plain language of the Contract, they are third-party beneficiaries and thus entitled to enforce the Contract's existing terms. We review the district court's grant of summary judgment de novo. *See Tri-State Dev. v. Johnston*, 160 F.3d 528, 529 (9th Cir. 1998). Because the facts are not in dispute, the only question we must decide is whether the district court correctly applied the relevant law in concluding that the Irrigators are not third-party beneficiaries under the Contract . . . Federal law controls the interpretation of a contract entered pursuant to federal law when the United States is a party. For guidance, we look to general principles for interpreting contracts. Before a third party can recover under a contract, it must show that the contract was made for its direct benefit — that it is an intended beneficiary of the contract. *See Williams v. Fenix & Scisson, Inc.*, 608 F.2d 1205, 1208 (9th Cir. 1979). A written contract must be read as a whole and every part interpreted with reference to the whole, with preference given to reasonable interpretations. Contract terms are to be given their ordinary meaning, and when the terms of a contract are clear, the intent of the parties must be ascertained from the contract itself. Whenever possible, the plain language of the contract should be considered first. The fact that the parties dispute a contract's meaning does not establish that the contract is ambiguous; it is only ambiguous if reasonable people could find its terms susceptible to more than one interpretation.

When distinguishing between intended and incidental beneficiaries, the Restatement of Contracts explains:

> (1) Unless otherwise agreed between promisor and promisee, a beneficiary of a promise is an intended beneficiary if recognition of a right to performance in the beneficiary is appropriate to effectuate the intention of the parties and . . . (b) the circumstances indicate that the promisee intends to give the beneficiary the benefit of the promised performance.

> (2) An incidental beneficiary is a beneficiary who is not an intended beneficiary. Restatement (Second) of Contracts § 302 (1979) ("Restatement").

To sue as a third-party beneficiary of a contract, the third party must show that the contract reflects the express or implied intention of the parties to the contract to benefit the third party.[6] The intended beneficiary need not be specifically or individually identified in the contract, but must fall within a class clearly intended by the parties to benefit from the contract. One way to ascertain such intent is to ask whether the beneficiary would be reasonable in relying on the promise as manifesting an intention to confer a right on him or her. *See* Restatement § 302(1)(b) cmt. d.

Parties that benefit from a government contract are generally assumed to be incidental beneficiaries, and may not enforce the contract absent a clear intent to

---

[6] [2] A promisor owes a duty of performance to any intended beneficiary of the promise, and "the intended beneficiary may enforce the duty," Restatement § 304, whereas an incidental beneficiary acquires "no right against the promisor or the promisee." *Id.* § 315.

the contrary. *See* Restatement § 313(2). "Government contracts often benefit the public, but individual members of the public are treated as incidental beneficiaries unless a different intention is manifested." *Id.* cmt. a.

The Irrigators derive their alleged intended beneficiary status from Articles 2 and 6 of the Contract. Article 2 provides, in pertinent part:

> Copco shall operate and maintain for a period of fifty (50) years from the effective date hereof . . . Link River Dam, hereby constructed by Copco and transferred to the United States pursuant to the agreement of February 24, 1917. Copco may regulate the water level of Upper Klamath Lake between the elevations 4143.3 and 4137. . . . *Provided,* that the Contracting Officer from time to time may specify a higher minimum elevation than 4137 if in his opinion such must be maintained in order to protect the irrigation and reclamation requirements of Project Land. . . .

Article 6 provides in pertinent part:

> Nothing in this agreement shall curtail or in anywise be construed as curtailing the rights of the United States to Klamath Water or to the lands along or under the margin of Upper Klamath Lake. No Klamath Water shall be used by Copco when it may be needed or required by the United States or any irrigation or drainage district, person, or association obtaining water from the United States for use for domestic, municipal, and irrigation purposes on Project Land: *Provided,* That nothing in this agreement shall curtail or interfere with the water rights of Copco having a priority earlier than May 19, 1905. . . .

The plain language of the Contract is sufficient to rebut the contention that the Irrigators are intended third-party beneficiaries. Neither Article 2 nor Article 6 illustrates an intention of Copco or the United States to grant the Irrigators enforceable rights. The Irrigators argue that the language of Article 2 contains such an intention because it allows Copco to go below the minimum elevation level only "in order to protect the irrigation and reclamation requirements of Project Land." This sentence, however, does not manifest an intention to give third-party beneficiary rights to the Irrigators; rather, it grants discretion to the United States, through the person of the Contracting Officer, to enforce the Contract by taking control of the Dam.

The Irrigators also invoke Article 6 to prove their intended beneficiary status. They rely on the phrase stating that Copco may not use water "when it may be needed or required by the United States or any irrigation or drainage district, person, or association obtaining water from the United States for use for domestic, municipal, and irrigation purposes on Project Land." This phrase, however, simply preserves the United States' ultimate control over the Dam and its operations. It does not confer rights on the Irrigators. *See Norse v. Henry Holt & Co.,* 991 F.2d 563, 568 (9th Cir. 1993) (holding that contract provisions preventing interference with existing rights do not turn holders of such rights into third-party beneficiaries).

Additionally, the recitation of constituencies whose interest bear on a government contract does not grant these incidental beneficiaries enforceable rights.

Vague, hortatory pronouncements in the Contract, by themselves, are insufficient to support the Irrigators' claims that the United States and Copco intended to assume a direct contractual obligation to every domestic, municipal, or irrigation water user.

Examination of the contract as a whole illustrates that it was intended to benefit only the contracting parties. Article 15 provides:

> This contract binds and inures to the benefit of the parties hereto, their successors and assigns, including without limitation any water users' organization or similar group which may succeed either by assignment or by operation of law to the rights of the United States hereunder.

This language clearly evinces the intent of the parties to limit intended beneficiaries to the contracting parties. The language "any water user's organization or similar group" does not give the Irrigators any rights besides those of incidental beneficiaries, because they have not succeeded, either by assignment or operation of law, to the rights of the United States. Although the Contract operates to the Irrigators' benefit by impounding irrigation water, and was undoubtedly entered into with the Irrigators in mind, to allow them intended third-party beneficiary status would open the door to all users receiving a benefit from the Project achieving similar status, a result not intended by the Contract. Accordingly, we hold that the Irrigators are not intended third-party beneficiaries.

III. Conclusion

Under the plain language of the 1956 Contract between Copco and Reclamation, the Irrigators do not possess third-party beneficiary water rights. Accordingly, the district court's grant of summary judgment to Reclamation and PacifiCorp is

AFFIRMED.

NOTES

1.   ***Contracts Between Government and Private Parties: The* Moch *Legacy.*** *Moch* stands for the proposition that, absent an explicit declaration of intent to benefit the general public, individual members of the public cannot sue as third-party beneficiaries of a contract between the government and a private party. This holding has been challenged over the years, though it remains persuasive authority and is still the law in New York. Most criticisms of *Moch* have focused on Cardozo's dismissal of the plaintiff's tort claim. For instance, in *Doyle v. South Pittsburgh Water Co.*, 414 Pa. 199, 199 A.2d 875 (1964), the Supreme Court of Pennsylvania held for the plaintiffs in a case factually similar to *Moch.* The court expressly concurred with Justice Cardozo's dismissal of the contract claim by members of the public claiming to be third-party beneficiaries, instead finding the water company negligent and thus liable in tort. Consider the court's analysis:

> The appellee here also depends for non-liability on the case of *Moch Co. v. Rensselaer Water Co.*, 247 N.Y. 160, 159 N.E. 896, where the Court's opinion was also written by Justice Cardozo. In that case, the plaintiff's property was destroyed because the defendant water company failed to supply an

adequate water supply with sufficient pressure to extinguish the fire, even thought the plaintiff had notified the water company of the fire. The Court held that there was no liability. It is to be particularly noted in that case that in its complaint the plaintiff alleged that the water company failed to *"fulfill the provisions of the contract between it and the city of Rensselaer."* (Emphasis supplied). Here again the claim, entirely different from the one at bar, was predicated on a contract with the involved municipality. No breach of duty to use reasonable care in the erection, operation and maintenance of the water system was alleged or relied upon. Under these facts, which, of course, are distinguishable from the case at bar, Justice Cardozo held there was no action *ex contractu* and no action *ex delictu* or a common law tort. . . . It must be stated, with some regret, that at this point Homer nodded. . . . [for Cardozo] contradicted what he said in the MacPherson case. [Disagreeing with Cardozo, the court permitted plaintiff's tort claim to proceed to trial, though rejecting any standing for breach of contract.]

414 Pa. at 212–13.

2.   *Insurance Beneficiaries.* In *Franklin Cas. Ins. Co. v. Jones*, 362 P.2d 964 (Okla. 1961), the Supreme Court of Oklahoma denied a physician's action to recover for medical services rendered to a passenger injured in insured's car. Although insured had standard medical payment coverage, the court found that Dr. Jones was not a proper party plaintiff:

> The general rule is that an action may not be maintained on a contract on the theory that it was made for the benefit of the plaintiff, a third party, merely because such third party would be incidentally benefitted by the performance of the contract. He must be a party to the consideration, or the contract must have been entered into for his benefit, and he must have some legal or equitable interest in its performance. . . .

Id. at 966.

On the other hand, the government, as a third-party beneficiary, was found entitled to collect the cost of medical care for an insured veteran to the extent of the veteran's insurance coverage in a factually similar case in Louisiana. *See United States v. Automobile Club Ins. Co.*, 522 F.2d 1 (5th Cir. 1975).

3.   *Third Parties and Binding Contract Conditions.* If a contract between two parties benefits a third party, but without the third party's knowledge, is the third party *limited* by the terms of that contract as well as benefited? Generally, the answer is yes. Most courts hold that a third party is limited to the terms of a contract made for its benefit. This rule fosters some interesting litigation. Usually, the defendant-promisor attempts to *deny* third-party beneficiary status so as to deprive the plaintiff of standing to sue. Sometimes, however, the defendant also may attempt to *compel* the court to designate the plaintiff as a third-party beneficiary if the contractual provisions work to the defendant's benefit.

In *Peter's Clothiers v. National Guardian Sec. Servs. Corp.*, 994 F. Supp. 1343 (D. Kan. 1998), Peter's Clothiers requested additional security measures from its landlord, Kessinger/Hunter, who then contracted with National Guardian for a new security system. The contract between Kessinger/Hunter and National Guardian included an express limitation of National Guardian's liability for robberies occurring after installation of the system. A few months following the installation, Peter's was robbed of $100,000 worth of merchandise.

Peter's sued National Guardian, alleging negligence and breach of an implied warranty of workmanlike performance with respect to the design and installation of the security system. Peter's did not assert its status as a third-party beneficiary of the contract between National Guardian and the landlord for either claim. National Guardian responded by moving for summary judgment, contending that Peter's was a third-party beneficiary of its contract with Kessinger/Hunter and therefore limited by the express terms of the contract to a maximum recovery of $1,972.24. The court considered this claim and Peter's rebuttal:

> Peter's claims that it was not a third-party beneficiary to the contract because it was not aware that the contract existed and because Kessinger/Hunter did not intend that Peter's should have any rights under the contract. The court disagrees. It is undisputed that the purpose of the contract was to upgrade and monitor the security system protecting Peter's Overland Park store. Agents of Peter's met with National Guardian and selected the various components that were to comprise the upgraded system. Furthermore, when the system was in need of repair, National Guardian, as required by the contract, went to Peter's store and made any necessary adjustments to the system. These facts show that National Guardian, Kessinger/Hunter, and Peter's all recognized Peter's was a third-party beneficiary of the contract and that Peter's accepted the benefits that flowed from the contract. . . . Because Peter's has accepted the benefits of the contract, its action is subject to the applicable provisions of the original contract signed by Kessinger/Hunter and National Guardian.

Id. at 1347. The court then limited plaintiff's recovery to the maximum allowed under the contract, or $1,972.24.

4. ***Contracts Between Governments?*** In *Kwan v. United States*, 84 F. Supp. 2d 613 (E.D. Pa. 2000), Korean veterans of the Vietnam War filed a class-action suit against the United States. The veterans claimed to be third-party beneficiaries of the Brown Commitment, an agreement between the U.S. and Korea in which the U.S. promised to compensate Korean soldiers who died or were injured fighting for the U.S. in the Vietnam conflict. Most of the veterans alleged that they were still suffering from the effects of exposure to Agent Orange, a chemical used by the American military in the war, and that the U.S. government should pay for their medical expenses. The court rejected this argument, reciting the well-recognized rule that third parties may not sue on an agreement between two sovereign states:

> By characterizing the Brown Commitment as a contract to which the individual plaintiffs are third-party beneficiaries, the individual plaintiffs are patently attempting to make an impermissible end run around the law regarding derivative standing with respect to agreements between sovereign nations.

Id. at 618–19. The court held, however, that the individual parties would have standing to maintain an action if the Republic of Korea were to join them as a plaintiff or authorize the lawsuit in some other manner. Since Korea had not, the complaint was dismissed. *Id.* at 624.

5.   *The Limits of Third-Party Beneficiary Theory.* Because third-party beneficiary law is grounded on a flexible conception of party intent that delegates broad discretion to courts, third-party claims often are based on novel theories of contractual relations. Consider the following:

In *Bain v. Gillispie*, 357 N.W.2d 47 (Iowa Ct. App. 1984), John and Karen Gillispie appealed a lower court ruling denying their status as third-party beneficiaries of a contract between James Bain, a college basketball referee, and the Big 10, the conference in which he refereed. The Gillispies had claimed that Mr. Bain made a bad call in the last seconds of an Iowa-Purdue game that resulted in free throws for Purdue, which then won the game. Since the Gillispies owned a novelty store in Iowa City selling University of Iowa memorabilia, they claimed Mr. Bain's bad call had breached his contract with the Big 10, resulting in their loss of income by eliminating Iowa from the Big 10's championship. Are the Gillispie's third-party beneficiaries of the contract between the Big 10 and Bain?

In *Storts v. Hardee's Food Sys.*, 919 F. Supp. 1513 (D. Kan. 1996), Tammy Stort sued Hardee's after being abducted from the parking lot of a Hardee's restaurant on the Kansas Turnpike. Stort claimed to be a third-party beneficiary of the Turnpike's lease agreement with Hardee's, which required certain maintenance, repairs, and levels of safety and service by Hardee's. Plaintiff argued that the contractual duties imposed on Hardee's a higher standard of care than the negligence standard, and thus in situations such as this, the public should be able to sue Hardee's as third-party beneficiaries of the Turnpike lease contract. (Ms. Stort probably sued on the contract rather than in tort because the statute of limitations had run for any claim of negligence against Hardee's.) Is Ms. Stort a third-party beneficiary to the Turnpike-Hardee's contract?

In *Dushkin v. Desai*, 18 F. Supp. 2d 117 (D. Mass. 1998), Desai, a yoga-guru, was sued by his disciples for breaching his contract with the corporation that operated their meditation compound. Desai started the compound for yoga meditation and exercise, and advocated that his followers adopt a life of celibacy, poverty, and contemplation. The corporation that ran the compound contracted with Desai to retain his services as guru to the disciples who lived at the complex and to the thousands of visitors arriving each year. In a shocking 1994 disclosure, however, Desai admitted to having sexual relations with many of his female disciples and to conducting a for-profit business with many of those who lived at the complex. The remaining disciples then initiated the breach of contract action against Desai, claiming that they were third-party beneficiaries of the contract with the corporation that operated the compound. The disciples alleged that Desai's profiteering and carousing had violated provisions of the contract and asked for contract damages. Are the disciples third-party beneficiaries of the guru's contract with the corporation?

In *Bain*, the court rejected the Gillispies' argument, holding that individual members of the public with no connection to the Big 10 could not be third-party beneficiaries of Big 10 contracts. In *Storts*, the court found that Hardee's and the Turnpike Authority had not intended to create any contract duties greater than those under existing Kansas law. The court dismissed the suit for lack of standing for third-party beneficiary plaintiffs. In *Desai*, the court held that the plaintiffs *were* third-party beneficiaries of the contract, though it also found no provisions within the contract explicitly stating the type of behaviors that were forbidden the guru. Finding that there was no breach of contract, the court dismissed the case.

6. ***Problem.*** Evans, an elderly, wealthy individual, hired Scott, a young, practicing attorney, to prepare his last will and testament. Evans wished to make Noble the beneficiary of a trust in which she would receive 15% of his entire fortune. Scott, in violation of instructions and a breach of his contract, negligently prepared the will so that Noble's provision was legally invalid due to the rule against perpetuities. Subsequently, Noble was forced to settle her claim with Evans' blood relatives, Dwight and Linda, and received an amount $75,000 less than the sum which she would have received had Scott done an adequate job. Noble, as third-party beneficiary, sues Scott. What result?[7]

D.   ASSIGNMENT AND DELEGATION

An executory contract is a valuable property right, and, as with most such rights, it is (within certain limitations) transferable to third parties. When a promisee transfers the benefits that are due under an executory contract, the resulting relationship is called an *assignment*. Although the early common law courts viewed assignments with suspicion, contract *rights* today are freely transferable except where the assignment would materially alter the risks or obligations of the other party, or otherwise violate public policy. *See, e.g.*, UCC § 2-210. In general, the rights of the assignee are governed by a hallmark rule of property law: One cannot transfer greater rights than one has (embodied in the Latin maxim *nemo dat quod non habet*). Thus, the assignee is subject to any claims or defenses arising from the contract that the promisor could have raised against the promisee-assignor. These defenses would include failure of consideration, breach of warranty, mistake, fraud, duress, etc. Furthermore, if the promisor satisfies her contractual duty to the promisee-assignor before she has received notice of the assignment, she is then discharged from any responsibility to the assignee.

Assume, instead of the *promisee* assigning his rights under an executory contract, the *promisor* attempts to transfer her obligations and duties under the contract to a third party. In this case, the resulting relationship is a *delegation* of the duty of performance. Not surprisingly, it is more difficult to delegate contractual duties than it is to assign contractual rights. A performance cannot be delegated where it depends upon the personal characteristics or skill of the promisor or, if for other reasons, the promisee has a "substantial interest" in obtaining the performance of the original promisor or in having that party control the performance. *See, e.g.*, Restatement (Second) § 318(2). Thus, for example, neither a sculptor who agrees to cast a statue or an author who contracts to write a book on contracts can

---

[7] This problem is based loosely on *Lucas v. Hamm*, 56 Cal. 2d 583, 15 Cal. Rptr. 821, 364 P.2d 685 (1961).

delegate their performances, even if the delegated performance would be, by any objective measure, superior to the contractual performance. Moreover, even if an attempted delegation is effective by its terms, it does not relieve the promisor from her contractual duty. Rather, the effective delegation serves to discharge the promisor once the performance has been properly supplied by the delegate.

The law of assignments and delegation will form an important part of your study of corporations, secured transactions, and other commercial relationships involving third parties. For purposes of this brief introduction, however, it is important to see how these transfers of contract rights and duties work in two different settings: (1) the transfer of both rights and duties under an executory contract (such as the sale of a business) and (2) the assignment of contract rights as security for a debt (an important part of commercial financing). We consider each of these in turn.

CRANE ICE CREAM CO. v. TERMINAL FREEZING & HEATING CO.
Court of Appeals of Maryland
147 Md. 588, 128 A. 280 (1925)

Action by the Crane Ice Cream Company against the Terminal Freezing & Heating Company. Demurrer to the declaration was sustained, and from the judgment entered thereon against plaintiff, it appeals. Judgment affirmed.

Parke, J.

The appellee and one W. C. Frederick entered into a contract for the delivery of ice by the appellee to Frederick, and, before the expiration of the contract, Frederick executed an assignment of the contract to the appellant; and on the refusal of the appellee to deliver ice to the assignee it brought an action on the contract against the appellee to recover damages for the alleged breach. . . .

The contract imposed upon the appellee the liability to sell and deliver to Frederick such quantities of ice as he might use in his business as an ice cream manufacturer to the extent of 250 tons per week, at and for the price of $3.25 a ton of 2,000 pounds on the loading platform of Frederick. The contractual rights of the appellee were (a) to be paid on every Tuesday during the continuation of the contract, for all ice purchased by Frederick during the week ending at midnight upon the next preceding Saturday; (b) to require Frederick not to buy or accept any ice from any other source than the appellee, except in excess of the weekly maximum of 250 tons. . . .

Before the first year of the second term of the contract had expired Frederick, without the consent or knowledge of the appellee, executed and delivered to the appellant, for a valuable consideration, a written assignment dated February 15, 1921, of the modified agreement between him and the appellee. The attempted transfer of the contract was a part of the transaction between Frederick and the appellant whereby the appellant acquired by purchase the plant, equipment, rights, and credits, choses in action, "good will, trade, custom, patronage, rights, contracts," and other assets of Frederick's ice cream business which had been established and conducted by him in Baltimore. The purchaser took full possession and continued the former business carried on by Frederick. It was then and is now a corporation "engaged in the ice cream business upon a large and extensive scale in the city of Philadelphia, as well as in the city of Baltimore, and state of Maryland," and had a large capitalization, ample resources, and credit to meet any of its obligations "and all and singular the terms and provisions" of the contract; and it was prepared to pay cash for all ice deliverable under contract.

As soon as the appellee learned of this purported assignment and the absorption of the business of Frederick by the appellant, it notified Frederick that the contract was at an end, and declined to deliver any ice to the appellant. Until the day of the assignment the obligations of both original parties had been fully performed and discharged. . . .

The basic facts upon which the question for solution depends must be sought in the effect of the attempted assignment of this executory bilateral contract on both the rights and the liabilities of the contracting parties, as every bilateral contract includes both rights and duties on each side while both sides remain executory. *Williston on Contracts*, sec. 407. If the assignment of rights and the assignment of duties by Frederick are separated, they fall into these two divisions: (1) The rights of the assignor were (a) to take no ice, if the assignor used none in his business, but if he did (b) to require the appellee to deliver, on the loading platform of the assignor, all the ice he might need in his business to the extent of 250 tons a week, and (c) to buy any ice he might need in excess of the weekly 250 tons from any other person; and (2) the liabilities of the assignor were (a) to pay to the appellee on every Tuesday during the continuance of the contract the stipulated price for all ice purchased and weighed by the assignor during the week ending at midnight upon the next preceding Saturday, and (b) not directly or indirectly, during the existence of this agreement, to buy or accept any ice from any other person, firm, or corporation than the said Terminal Freezing & Heating Company, except such amounts as might be in excess of the weekly limit of 250 tons.

Whether the attempted assignment of these rights, or the attempted delegation of these duties must fail because the rights or duties are of too personal a character, is a question of construction to be resolved from the nature of the contract and the express or presumed intention of the parties. *Williston on Contracts*, sec. 431.

The contract was made by a corporation with an individual, William C. Frederick, an ice cream manufacturer, with whom the corporation had dealt for 3 years, before it executed a renewal contract for a second like period. The character, credit, and resources of Frederick had been tried and tested by the appellee before it renewed the contract. Not only had his ability to pay as agreed been established, but his fidelity to his obligation not to buy or accept any ice from any other source up to 250 tons a week had been ascertained. In addition, the appellee had not asked in the beginning, nor on entering into the second period of the contract, for Frederick to undertake to buy a specific quantity of ice or even to take any. Frederick simply engaged himself during a definite term to accept and pay for such quantities of ice as he might use in his business to the extent of 250 tons a week. If he used no ice in his business, he was under no obligation to pay for a pound. In any week, the quantity could vary from zero to 250 tons, and its weekly fluctuation, throughout the life of the contract, could irregularly range between these limits. The weekly payment might be nothing or as much as $812.50; and for every week a credit was extended to the eighth day from the beginning of every week's delivery. From the time of the beginning of every weekly delivery of the ice to the date of the payment therefor the title to the ice was in the purchaser, and the seller had no security for its payment except in the integrity and solvency of Frederick. The performances, therefore, were not concurrent, but the performance of the nonassigning party to the contract was to precede the payments by the assignor.

When it is also considered that the ice was to be supplied and paid for, according to its weight on the loading platform of Frederick, at an unvarying price without any reference either to the quantity used, or to the fluctuations in the cost of production or to market changes in the selling price, throughout 3 years, the conclusion is inevitable that the inducement for the appellee to enter into the original contract and into the renewal lay outside the bare terms of the contract, but was implicit in them, and was the appellee's reliance upon its knowledge of an average quantity of ice consumed, and probably to be needed, in the usual course of Frederick's business, at all times throughout the year, and its confidence in the stability of his enterprise, in his competency in commercial affairs, in his probity, personal judgment, and in his continuing financial responsibility. The contract itself emphasized the personal equation by specifying that the ice was to be bought for "use in his business as an ice cream manufacturer," and was to be paid for according to its weight "on the loading platform of the said W. C. Frederick."

When Frederick went out of business as an ice cream manufacturer, and turned over his plant and everything constituting his business to the appellant, it was no longer his business, or his loading platform, or subject to his care, control, or maintenance, but it was the business of a stranger, whose skill, competency, and requirements of ice were altogether different from those of Frederick. The assignor had his simple plant in Baltimore. The assignee, in its purchase, simply added another unit to its ice cream business which it had been, and is now, carrying on "upon a large and extensive scale in the city of Philadelphia and state of Pennsylvania, as well as in the city of Baltimore and state of Maryland." The appellee knew that Frederick could not carry on his business without ice wherewith to manufacture ice cream at his plant for his trade. It also was familiar with the quantities of ice he would require, from time to time, in his business at his plant in Baltimore, and it consequently could make its other commitments for ice with this knowledge as a basis.

The appellant, on the other hand, might wholly supply its increased trade acquired in the purchase of Frederick's business with its ice cream produced upon a large and extensive scale by its manufactory in Philadelphia, which would result in no ice being bought by the assignee of the appellee, and so the appellee would be deprived of the benefit of its contract by the introduction of a different personal relation or element which was never contemplated by the original contracting parties. Again, should the price of ice be relatively high in Philadelphia in comparison with the stipulated price, the assignee could run its business in Baltimore and furnish its patrons, or a portion of them, in Philadelphia with its product from the weekly maximum consumption of 250 tons of ice throughout the year. There can be no denial that the uniform delivery of the maximum quantity of 250 tons a week would be a consequence not within the normal scope of the contract, and would impose a greater liability on the appellee than was anticipated. 7 *Halsbury's Laws of England*, sec. 1015, p. 501. . . .

While a party to a contract may as a general rule assign all his beneficial rights, except where a personal relation is involved, his liability under the contract is not assignable *inter vivos*, because any one who is bound to any performance whatever or who owes money cannot by any act of his own, or by any act in agreement with any other person than his creditor or the one to whom his performance is due, cast off his own liability and substitute another's liability. If this were not true, obligors could free themselves of their obligations by the simple expedient of assigning them. A further ground for the rule, is that, not only is a party entitled to know to whom he must look for the satisfaction of his rights under the contract, but in the familiar words of Lord Denman in Humble v. Hunter, 12 Q.B. 317, "you have a right to the benefit you contemplate from the character, credit, and substance of the person with whom you contract." For these reasons it has been uniformly held that a man cannot assign his liabilities under a contract, but one who is bound so as to bear an unescapable liability may delegate the performance of his obligation to another, if the liability be of such a nature that its performance by another will be substantially the same thing as performance by the promisor himself. In such circumstances the performance of the third party is the act of the promisor, who remains liable under the contract and answerable in damages if the performance be not in strict fulfillment of the contract. . . .

However, the analysis of the facts on this appeal leaves no room for doubt that the case at bar falls into the category of those assignments where an attempt is made both to transfer the rights and to delegate the duties of the assignor under an executory bilateral contract whose terms and the circumstances make plain that the personal qualification and action of the assignor, with respect to both his benefits and burdens under the contract, were essential inducements in the formation of the contract, and further, that the assignment was a repudiation of any future liability of the assignor. The attempted assignment before us altered the conditions and obligations of the undertaking. The appellee would here be obliged not only to perform the subsequent stipulations of the contract for the benefit of a stranger and in conformity with his will, but also to accept the performance of the stranger in place of that of the assignor with whom it contracted, and upon whose personal integrity, capacity, and management in the course of a particular business he must be assumed to have relied by reason of the very nature of the provisions of the contract and of the circumstances of the contracting parties. . . .

Judgment affirmed.

EVENING NEWS ASSO. v. PETERSON
United States District Court, District of Columbia
477 F. Supp. 77 (1979)

PARKER, J.

The question presented in this litigation is whether a contract of employment between an employee and the owner and licensee of a television station, providing for the employee's services as a newscaster-anchorman, was assigned when the station was sold and acquired by a new owner and licensee.

Plaintiff Evening News Association (Evening News) a Michigan Corporation, acquired station WDVM-TV (Channel 9) a District of Columbia television station from Post-Newsweek Stations, Inc. (Post-Newsweek) in June of 1978. At that time, the defendant Gordon Peterson was and had been employed for several years as a newscaster-anchorman by Post-Newsweek. This defendant is a citizen of the State of Maryland. The plaintiff claims that Peterson's employment contract was assignable without the latter's consent, was indeed assigned, and thus otherwise enforceable. The defendant contends, however, that his Post-Newsweek contract required him to perform unique and unusual services and because of the personal relationship he had with Post-Newsweek the contract was not assignable.

Mr. Peterson was employed by the plaintiff for more than one year after the acquisition and received the compensation and all benefits provided by the Post-Newsweek contract. In early August, 1979, he tendered his resignation to the plaintiff. At that time the defendant had negotiated an employment contract with a third television station located in the District of Columbia, a competitor of the plaintiff. The Evening News then sued Peterson, seeking a declaration of the rights and legal relations of the parties under the contract and permanent injunctive relief against the defendant.

Following an accelerated briefing schedule and an expedited bench trial on the merits, the Court concludes that the contract was assignable and that Evening News is entitled to appropriate permanent injunctive relief against the defendant Gordon Peterson.

FINDINGS OF FACT

The defendant was employed by Post-Newsweek Stations, Inc. from 1969 to 1978. During that period he negotiated several employment contracts. Post-Newsweek had a license to operate television station WTOP-TV (Channel 9) in the District of Columbia. In June of 1978, following approval by the Federal Communications Commission, Post-Newsweek sold its operating license to Evening News and Channel 9 was then designated WDVM-TV. A June 26, 1978, Bill of Sale and Assignment and Instrument of Assumption and Indemnity between the two provided in pertinent part:

> PNS has granted, bargained, sold, conveyed and assigned to ENA, . . . all
> the property of PNS . . . including, . . . all right, title and interest, legal or
> equitable, of PNS in, to and under all agreements, contracts and commitments listed in Schedule A hereto. . . .

When Evening News acquired the station, Peterson's Post-Newsweek employment contract, dated July 1, 1977, was included in the Bill of Sale and Assignment. The contract was for a three-year term ending June 30, 1980, and could be extended for two additional one-year terms, at the option of Post-Newsweek. . . .

As compensation the defendant was to receive a designated salary which increased each year from 1977 through the fifth (option) year. Post-Newsweek was also obligated to provide additional benefits including term life insurance valued at his 1977 base salary, disability insurance, an annual clothing allowance and benefits to which he was entitled as provided in an underlying collective bargaining agreement with the American Federation of Television and Radio Artists.

There was no express provision in the 1977 contract concerning its assignability or nonassignability. However, it contained the following integration clause:

> This agreement contains the entire understanding of the parties . . . and this agreement cannot be altered or modified except in a writing signed by both parties.

A.

Aside from the various undisputed documents and exhibits admitted into evidence, there were sharp conflicts in testimony concerning various events and what was said and done by the parties and their representatives, both before and after the Evening News' acquisition. As trier of fact, having heard and seen the several witnesses testify and after assessing and determining their credibility, the Court makes the following additional findings.

The defendant's duties, obligations and performance under the 1977 contract did not change in any significant way after the Evening News' acquisition. In addition, the Evening News met all of its required contract obligations to the defendant and its performance after acquisition in June, 1978, was not materially different from that of Post-Newsweek.

Mr. Peterson testified that he had "almost a family relationship" with James Snyder, News Director, and John Baker, Executive Producer, for Post-Newsweek, which permitted and promoted a free exchange of ideas, frank expressions of dissent and criticism and open lines of communication. These men left Channel 9 when Post-Newsweek relinquished its license, and they have since been replaced by Evening News personnel. According to Mr. Peterson, the close relationship and rapport which existed between him and them was an important factor as he viewed the contract; these relationships made the contract in his view nonassignable and indeed their absence at the Evening News prevented defendant from contributing his full efforts. Even if Mr. Peterson's contentions are accepted, it should be noted that he contracted with the Post-Newsweek corporation and not with the News Director and Executive Producer of that corporation. Indeed, the 1977 contract makes no reference to either officer, except to provide that vacations should be scheduled and coordinated through the News Director. Had the defendant intended to condition his performance on his continued ability to work with Snyder and Baker, one would have expected the contract to reflect that condition.

The close, intimate and personal relationship which Mr. Peterson points to as characterizing his association with Post-Newsweek and its personnel, was highly subjective and was supported only by his testimony. The Court cannot find that Peterson contracted with Post-Newsweek in 1977 to work with particular individuals or because of a special policy-making role he had been selected to perform in the newsroom. For the fourteen-month period of Peterson's employment at the Evening News, there is no showing that he was in any way circumscribed, limited in his work or otherwise disadvantaged in his performance. Nor is there any credible evidence that the News Director or other top personnel of Evening News were rigid, inflexible, warded off any of Mr. Peterson's criticisms or even that at any time he gave suggestions and criticisms which were ignored or rejected. Finally, the Court does not find that

Post-Newsweek contracted with Peterson because of any peculiarly unique qualities or because of a relationship of personal confidence with him.

B.

In his direct testimony, Mr. Peterson expressed a degree of disappointment because of Evening News' failure to keep apace with advances in technology and to seize opportunities for live in-depth coverage of current events. He characterized the plaintiff's news coverage as "less aggressive" than what he had experienced with Post-Newsweek.

On cross-examination, however, he was shown an exhibit comparing the broadcast of special assignments reported and produced by him for two one-year periods, one before and one after the June, 1978 acquisition. While he admitted to its accuracy with some reservation, the exhibit clearly showed that a comparable number of such assignments of similar quality, were broadcast within the two years. He also conceded that for the same period Evening News received two Peabody awards, an award for best editorials, and a number of Emmy awards for public affairs exceeding those received in prior years by Post-Newsweek. Finally, he acknowledged that Channel 9 still maintained the highest ratings for audience viewing among the television stations in the Washington, D.C. market area.

A great amount of testimony was generated as to when Peterson learned of the Evening News' acquisition and what then occurred relative to the assignment of the contract. The testimony on this issue was conflicting, largely cumulative and as now viewed, over-emphasized by the parties. The Court finds that the defendant gained first knowledge of a possible sale and transfer of the station in December, 1977. At that time, the president of Post-Newsweek publicly announced to the station's employees, including Peterson, that an agreement in principle had been reached, subject to approval by the Federal Communications Commission. At no time from December, 1977, until December, 1978, did the defendant or his attorney ever indicate or venture an opinion that the contract was not assignable. Indeed, through at least April, 1979, the defendant's attorney made representations that assignment of the contract presented no problem to his client.

In summary, the Court finds that the performance required of Mr. Peterson under the 1977 contract was (1) not based upon a personal relationship or one of special confidence between him and Post-Newsweek or its employees, and (2) was not changed in any material way by the assignment to the Evening News.

CONCLUSIONS OF LAW

A.

The distinction between the assignment of a right to receive services and the obligation to provide them is critical in this proceeding. This is so because duties under a personal services contract involving special skill or ability are generally not delegable by the one obligated to perform, absent the consent of the other party. The issue, however, is not whether the personal services Peterson is to perform are delegable but whether Post-Newsweek's right to receive them is assignable.

Contract rights as a general rule are assignable. Munchak Corp. v. Cunningham, 457 F.2d 721 (4th Cir. 1972); 4A. Corbin, Contracts § 865 (1951); Restatement (First) of Contracts § 151 (1932). This rule, however, is subject to exception where the assignment would vary materially the duty of the obligor, increase materially the burden of risk imposed by the contract, or impair materially the obligor's chance of obtaining return performance. Corbin § 868; Restatement § 152. There has been no showing, however, that the services required of Peterson by the Post-Newsweek contract have changed in any material way since the Evening News entered the picture. Both before and after, he anchored the same news programs. Similarly he has had essentially the same number of special assignments since the transfer as before. Any additional policy-making role that he formerly enjoyed and is now denied was neither a condition of his contract nor factually supported by other than his own subjective testimony.

The general rule of assignability is also subject to exception where the contract calls for the rendition of personal services based on a relationship of confidence between the parties. Munchak, 457 F.2d at 725. As Corbin has explained this limitation on assignment:

> In almost all cases where a "contract" is said to be non-assignable because it is "personal," what is meant is not that the contractor's right is not assignable, but that the performance required by his duty is a personal performance and that an attempt to perform by a substituted person would not discharge the contractor's duty.

Corbin § 865.

In Munchak, the Court concluded that a basketball player's personal services contract could be assigned by the owner of the club to a new owner, despite a contractual prohibition on assignment to another club, on the basis that the services were to the club. The Court found it "inconceivable" that the player's services "could be affected by the personalities of successive corporate owners." 457 F.2d at 725. The policy against the assignment of personal service contracts, as the Court noted, "is to prohibit an assignment of a contract in which the obligor undertakes to serve only the original obligee." 457 F.2d at 726.

Given the silence of the contract on assignability, its merger clause, and the usual rule that contract rights are assignable, the Court cannot but conclude on the facts of this case that defendant's contract was assignable. Mr. Peterson's contract with Post-Newsweek gives no hint that he was to perform as other than a newscaster-anchorman for their stations. Nor is there any hint that he was to work with particular Post-Newsweek employees or was assured a policy-making role in concert with any given employees. Defendant's employer was a corporation, and it was for Post-Newsweek Stations, Inc. that he contracted to perform. The corporation's duties under the contract did not involve the rendition of personal services to defendant; essentially they were to compensate him. Nor does the contract give any suggestion of a relation of special confidence between the two or that defendant was expected to serve the Post-Newsweek stations only so long as the latter had the license for them.

B.

As noted, the 1977 contract contained a clause providing that the entire understanding between the parties was contained within the four corners of the agreement. The contract contains no provision relating to assignment. The defendant's counsel asserts, however, that an ambiguity exists and he therefore seeks to introduce certain exhibits and other extrinsic evidence for purposes of explaining and discerning the intentions of the parties. Specifically, he seeks to introduce four documents: an earlier 1973 contract; a draft of a proposed 1974 contract; the final 1974 contract; and a letter of 1975 from the president of Post-Newsweek to the defendant. The Court reserved decision on admissibility of the exhibits and now rules that they are inadmissible for the purposes intended by the defendant. The 1977 contract makes no reference to any prior agreements, to any negotiations between the parties, or specifically to the four proffered exhibits. To make use of them to show the intention of the parties in 1977, or to show what happened in past contract negotiations, simply asks too much.

The Court does not share the defendant's belief that silence on the issue of assignability creates ambiguity, and he fails to provide any legal authority to warrant such an inference. An unsupported assertion that ambiguity exists is insufficient to give a different meaning to a contract when there is in fact no contractual provision. For the Court to accept the defendant's exhibits in an effort to explain the parties' intent would modify and enlarge the provisions of the agreement and bestow upon the defendant an advantage which he did not originally have.

The contract before the Court, as the agreement in [Clayman v. Goodman Properties, Inc., 518 F.2d 1026, 1033, 171 U.S. App. D.C. 88, 95 (D.C. Cir. 1973)], contains a merger clause stating that the contract embodies the final and exclusive understanding of the parties. Such a stipulation is given full effect in this jurisdiction absent the Court's finding of any ambiguity in the contract.

C.

Plaintiff's argument that defendant has waived any objection to the assignment by accepting the contract benefits and continuing to perform for the Evening News for over a year has perhaps some merit. If defendant has doubts about assignability, he should have voiced them when he learned of the planned transfer or at least at the time of transfer. His continued performance without reservation followed by the unanticipated tender of his resignation did disadvantage Evening News in terms of finding a possible replacement for him and possibly in lost revenues. The Court, however, concludes that the contract was assignable in the first instance and thus it is not necessary to determine whether defendant's continued performance constitutes a waiver of objection to the assignment.

During the course of this trial Edwin W. Pfeiffer, an executive officer of WDVM-TV, testified that Mr. Peterson allegedly stated "if the Judge decides I should stay, I will stay." Assuming that he did not overstate Mr. Peterson's position and that Mr. Peterson was quoted in appropriate context, the television audience of the Washington, D.C. metropolitan area should anticipate his timely reappearance as news anchorman for station WDVM-TV. Of course, the avenue of appeal is always available.

An order consistent with this Memorandum Opinion will be entered. Counsel for the plaintiff shall submit immediately an appropriate order.

NOTES

1. **Delegation and the UCC.** To what extent is delegation of performance more easily effected under the UCC? Read § 2-210 and Comment 4. Does the addition of a specific provision on insecurity in § 2-609 ameliorate the concerns that underlie the legal restraints on delegation? Given the uncertainty over the proper application of § 2-609, is the optimism expressed in § 2-210, Comment 4 justified?

2. **Personal Service Contracts.** *Crane Ice Cream* was decided in 1925 and represents the traditional view prohibiting the assignment of rights or delegation of obligations in contracts deemed "personal" in nature. Indeed, courts and commentators have so clearly developed this conception of the law of assignments over the past century that personal service contracts are often termed "per se non-assignable" today. *See, e.g., Sally Beauty Co. v. Nexxus Products Co.*, 801 F.2d 1001, 1008 (7th Cir. 1986). The "personal service" criterion has not been without its critics, however. The criterion frequently is challenged as unnecessarily restrictive, and many courts have adopted a narrower view of those relationships that are "personal" and thus cannot be assigned or delegated. As demonstrated by the preceding cases, the varying perceptions of "personal" service contracts often leads to confusing and conflicting jurisprudence.

In *Macke Co. v. Pizza of Gaithersburg, Inc.*, 259 Md. 479, 270 A.2d 645 (1970), the Maryland Court of Appeals reached the opposite result from *Crane*, although the facts of the case were substantially similar. Pizza contracted with the Virginia Coffee Service for installation and maintenance of cold drink vending machines at its six pizza parlors. Soon after, Macke purchased Virginia Coffee Service. Pizza then attempted to terminate its contract with Virginia Coffee, now assigned to Macke, claiming the Virginia Coffee contract was based on Pizza's personal relationship with Virginia Coffee's president and his flexible way of conducting business. Pizza further asserted that it had dealt with Macke before, but chose Virginia Coffee because it was disappointed with Macke's performance. The Maryland Court of Appeals held in *Macke* that the Pizza-Virginia Coffee contract was not so personal in nature to be non-assignable. Considering *Crane* and *Macke* together, if you practiced law in Maryland, how would you explain to a client when a contract is "too personal" to assign or delegate?

Professor Dimatteo asserts that this result is symptomatic of the assignment/delegation case law, which shows no "consistent underlying jurisprudence that a practicing lawyer can look to in preparing his arguments on assignability." Larry A. Dimatteo, *Depersonalization of Personal Service Contracts: The Search for a Modern Approach to Assignability*, 27 AKRON L. REV. 407 (1994). Dimatteo contends that the per se rule of nonassignability is an outdated concept no longer applicable in the modern commercial world:

> The world has changed since the adoption of the per se rule of nonassignability. In the past almost all contracts were of a personal nature. They involved mostly one-on-one dealing for the sale of goods and services. The nature of relational contracts has changed dramatically over the last fifty to one hundred years. In the age of large corporations, mega-sized law firms, the large size of financial stakes, and the length and sophistication of today's contracts, the per se rule is out of touch with the reality of the times.
>
> At the same time relational contracts have expanded in scope, they have also in some areas become more fungible or standardized. Thus, many transactions considered strictly personal in the past have become more transactional in nature and more akin to a sale of goods.

Id. at 439.

Professor Dimatteo concludes by calling for elimination of the "per se nonassignable" test, to be replaced by a presumption of assignability unless the "obligee gives a 'good faith' reason for not consenting to an assignment." *Id.* at 439. Is this proposal an improvement on the per se nonassignability test? Did the Pizza Shops in *Macke* have a "good faith" reason for rejecting the assignment to Macke? Did the Crane Ice Cream Company have a "good faith" reason for protesting the assignment to Terminal Freezing and Heating?

3. ***"Assignment of the Contract" under the UCC.*** The drafters of UCC § 2-210(4) altered the traditional meaning of "assignment of the contract," and provided some anxiety for drafting attorneys. An assignment traditionally described the transfer of *rights* under a contract, while the term delegation was required for a transfer of *obligations*. Section 2-210(4) eliminates this distinction to some extent, providing that the phrase "assignment of 'the contract'" is sufficient to confer both rights *and* obligations on the assignee, "unless the language or the circumstances . . . indicate the contrary." UCC § 2-210(4). In *P/T, Ltd. II v. Friendly Mobile Manor, Inc.*, 79 Md. App. 227, 237–39, 556 A.2d 694, 699–700 (1989), the court discussed this shift:

> We believe that the UCC rule, like the common law rule, merely creates a presumption as to the intentions of the parties to the assignment. [citations omitted.] Under the common law, by the great weight of authority, the assignee of rights, benefits, or privileges under a contract did not become responsible for the assignor's duties unless he expressly assumed performance of those duties. In other words, in the absence of an express manifestation of intention to accept the assignor's duties along with his

rights and benefits, the assignee is presumed not to assume those duties, and they remain the obligation of the assignor. The UCC, however, provides that duties as well as rights pass under the assignment unless there are circumstances or language to the contrary. Thus, absent a clear manifestation of contrary intent, the assignee of a contract for the sale of goods takes the assignor's burdens along with his benefits because the law presumes that to be the intent of the parties.

There is, at least historically, a logical basis for the distinction. Originally, assignments of contracts were either not permitted or were frowned upon. When A contracts with B, he bargains for B's performance, not C's. But if the contract is one of performance of service by A in exchange for payment of money by B, it is of little consequence to B whether he pays the money to A or C, provided he gets what he bargained for, A's performance. Correspondingly, so long as he is paid for his work, it little matters to A whether he performs the same duties for the benefit of B or C. Consequently, the law came to accept the notion of assignment of benefits while still rejecting the proposition that one could assign his duties, i.e., foist off on the promisee someone else's work, craftsmanship, reliability, skill, etc., in place of his own. Most contracts for sales of goods, however, involve obligations that can be performed by C just as well as A or B. Unless the goods are unique, they may be supplied by C as well as B; unless A is relying on B's credit, payment by C should be just as satisfactory as payment by B. And if the contract is of such peculiar nature that substitution of C for B would be prejudicial to A, A may by appropriate contract provision prevent the assignment of either benefits or duties.

4. *Assignments of Future Rights.* Can an assignor transfer expected future profits to an assignee? Generally, the answer is yes, although assignments of future rights are sometimes restricted by statute and public policy. *See* Restatement (Second) § 321; Restatement (Second), Statutory Note to Chapter 15. Courts generally permit the assignment of future rights not yet realized by the assignor. Consider the case of *Speelman v. Pascal*, 10 N.Y.2d 313, 178 N.E.2d 723 (1961). Gabriel Pascal, a theatrical producer, received the rights to produce a musical play and motion picture based on George Bernard Shaw's play "Pygmalion" in 1952. In 1954, Mr. Pascal signed an agreement with Ms. Kingman, assigning a certain percentage of his royalties from the expected production of the musical and movie, which he was to entitle "My Fair Lady." A few months later Mr. Pascal died. As the success and profits of "My Fair Lady" grew, his estate refused to honor the agreement with Ms. Kingman, claiming the assignment of future rights was void. The New York Court of Appeals disagreed:

> The only real question is as to whether the 1954 letter above quoted operated to transfer to plaintiff an enforcible (sic) right to the described percentages of the royalties to accrue to Pascal on the production of a stage or film version of a musical play based on "Pygmalion." We see no reason why this letter does not have that effect. It is true that at the time of delivery of the letter there was no musical stage or film play in existence but Pascal, who owned and was conducting negotiations to realize on the stage and film rights, could grant to another a share of the moneys to

accrue from the use of those rights by others. There are many instances of courts enforcing assignments of rights to sums which were expected thereafter to become due to the assignor.

10 N.Y.2d at 318, 178 N.E.2d at 725.

A more difficult situation for many courts, and one frequently regulated by state and federal statutes, is a future wage assignment by an employee. An employee who assigns future wages to cover a debt often assigns only part of his future wages, which raises additional issues for the courts. In *Space Coast Credit Union v. Walt Disney World Co.*, 483 So. 2d 35 (1986), a Disney employee assigned a portion of his monthly paycheck to the plaintiff-credit union for payment of a debt. The employee authorized Disney to pay the credit union directly, but Disney refused, prompting an action by the credit union for enforcement of the assignment. Consider the court's conclusion:

> Florida prohibits voluntary wage assignments to secure a loan made under the Florida Consumer Finance Act, but this is not such a transaction. Further, Florida impliedly recognizes that voluntary wage assignments may exist, since it taxes such assignments under the provision of its excise tax on documents statute.
>
> We think given the Florida statutes on this subject matter, voluntary wage assignments exist under Florida's common law, as they do in other jurisdictions. At common law, wage assignments are treated as any other chose in action, and the general law of assignments applies, except when changed by statute.
>
> However, it is also well-established that if the assignment is partial only, it cannot be enforced against the debtor, or employer, without his consent, or the joinder in an equitable proceeding of all persons entitled to the various parts of the debt. Neither event occurred in this case. . . . The rationale for this rule is that the debtor, here the employer, should not be subjected to multiple suits or claims not contemplated by the original assigned contract. The debtor's objection to a partial assignment may be asserted as in this case, by a rejection of the claim and an absence of proof of consent; or a showing of hardship on the part of the debtor-employer, in complying with the partial assignment. Since it is clearly established in this case that Walt Disney World did not consent to this partial wage assignment, it was entitled to ignore it, and to pay [the employee] pursuant to its original employment under his contract of employment.

Id. at 36.

The assignment in *Space Coast* required Disney to transfer only 20 dollars a month from the employee's paycheck to the credit union. Given the court's opinion, is it clear why Disney litigated this case over such a small claim?

5.   *Contract Terms Expressly Prohibiting Assignment and Delegation.* The right to assign and (within limits to delegate) are default rules of contract law. Thus, as with any default rules, express contractual provisions prohibiting an assignment of rights under a contract are generally effective, although (as with other efforts to opt out of default rules such as warranty disclaimers) such provisions are strictly construed by courts. The UCC and Restatement (Second) illustrate the modern trend to strictly construe contract terms restricting or prohibiting assignment and delegation. A clause that forbids the assignment of "the contract" should be construed as "barring only the delegation to the assignee of the assignor's performance," unless circumstances indicate to the contrary. UCC § 2-210(3); RESTATEMENT (SECOND) OF CONTRACTS § 322(1).

When considering express contractual prohibitions on assignment and delegation, courts have had to confront the tension between two different doctrinal claims: the "freedom of assignability" and the "freedom of contract." In *Allhusen v. Caristo Const. Corp.*, 303 N.Y. 446, 103 N.E.2d 891 (1952), the New York Court of Appeals was asked to interpret a contract clause declaring that any attempted "assignment . . . shall be void." 303 N.Y. at 451, 103 N.E.2d at 892. Consider the court's analysis:

> In the light of the foregoing, we think it is reasonably clear that, while the courts have striven to uphold freedom of assignability, they have not failed to recognize the concept of freedom to contract. In large measure they agree that, where appropriate language is used, assignments of money due under contracts may be prohibited. When "clear language" is used, and the "plainest words . . . have been chosen", parties may "limit the freedom of alienation of rights and prohibit the assignment." *State Bank v. Central Mercantile Bank*, 248 N.Y. 428 at 435, 162 N.E. 475 at 477. We have now before us a clause embodying clear, definite and appropriate language, which may be construed in no other way but that any attempted assignment of either the contract or any rights created thereunder shall be "void as against the obligor. One would have to do violence to the language here employed to hold that it is merely an agreement by the subcontractor not to assign. The objectivity of the language precludes such a construction. We are therefore compelled to conclude that this prohibitory clause is a valid and effective restriction of the right to assign. . . . Such a holding is not violative of public policy. . . . Plaintiff's claimed rights arise out of the very contract embodying the provision now sought to be invalidated. . . . No sound reason appears why an assignee should remain unaffected by a provision in the very contract which gave life to the claim he asserts.

303 N.Y. at 452, 103 N.E.2d at 893.

Allhusen represents the traditional view on express contractual limits on assignability, a view that uses "freedom of contract" reasoning to enforce contractual opt outs that prohibit assignment. Presumably influenced by the Restatement (Second) and the UCC, however, some modern courts have restricted parties' ability to prohibit the assignment or delegation of the contract, especially in the case of the assignment of rights under the contract. In *Larese v. Creamland Dairies, Inc.*, 767 F.2d 716 (10th Cir. 1985), the Tenth Circuit considered language restricting a franchisee's ability to assign a contract with his franchisor. The franchise agreement provided that the franchisee "shall not assign, transfer or sublet this franchise, without the prior written consent of [Creamland] and Baskins Robbins, any such unauthorized assignment . . . being null and without effect." *Id.* at 717. When the franchisee sought permission to assign the franchise to another party, the franchisors refused to grant permission, giving no reasons for their refusal. The franchisee sued on the grounds that any refusal to allow assignment must be reasonable. The court agreed and held that, absent an explicit grant to the franchisor of an absolute right to refuse to consent to assignment, the franchisor "did not have the right to withhold consent unreasonably." *Id.* at 718.

In *Wonsey v. Life Ins. Co. of N. Am.*, 32 F. Supp. 2d 939 (E.D. Mich. 1998), the court adopted the Restatement and UCC approaches favoring strict construction of nonassignability clauses. Chad Wonsey was severely injured in a car accident when he was six years old. In 1983, Wonsey's parents entered into a settlement agreement with the defendant-insurer providing future payments to Wonsey according to an agreed upon schedule. Included in the settlement agreement was a clause prohibiting assignment of these future payments, which stated: "it is understood and agreed that the Insurance Company of America (ICA) shall be the owner of the aforesaid annuity policy and the Plaintiffs should have: (1) no right to change the beneficiary of the policy . . . [and] (5) no right to assign the policy." *Id.* at 940. In 1998, Wonsey attempted to assign three of his future payments under the settlement agreement to a third party, which ICA rejected. Wonsey then filed a motion for declaratory judgment, seeking a court order allowing the assignments. The court concluded as follows:

> As the latest Restatement makes clear, the modern trend with respect to contractual prohibitions on assignments is to interpret these clauses narrowly, as barring only the delegation of duties, and not necessarily as precluding the assignment of rights from assignor to assignee. The rationale behind these cases is derived from the implicit recognition that the obligor, the party obligated to perform, would not suffer any harm by a mere assignment of payments under a contract. Harm to obligor would result, however, in cases involving personal service contracts or other situations where the duties owed the parties may change depending on the identity of the assignee. . . .

> The instant case does not involve a situation where significant harm would result to the defendant . . . by the proposed assignment of rights to future payments. Nor is this a situation involving a delegation of duties under a personal services contract. Nonetheless, defendants strenuously argue that when a beneficiary of a structured settlement agreement decides to sell all or a number of his future payments, "it requires a complicated review process" and that "defendants [would be required] to review substantial paperwork, and [to] determine if the assignment appears to be legal . . . and/or whether any guarantees or releases provided by the assignor . . . are satisfactory to fully and completely protect [defendants]." The Court is not persuaded. The reasons asserted by defendants in objecting to the proposed assignment do not appear to amount to substantial harm or actual prejudice to defendants' interests, but merely center upon the necessary administrative tasks associated with the assignment's implementation. As such, defendants have not submitted sufficient reasons to justify disregarding the modern trend of upholding assignments in the face of contractual anti-assignment clauses.

Id. at 943.

Consider once again *Space Coast Credit Union v. Walt Disney World Company* in Note 4, *supra.* Do you think that Disney had the same concerns regarding the assignment in *Space Coast* as the Life Insurance Company of America had in *Wonsey*? Did the *Wonsey* court simply ignore the problem of a partial assignment of future rights? Are these two cases reconcilable?

6. *Assignability of Warranties.* In *Gold'n Plump Poultry, Inc. v. Simmons Engineering Co.*, 805 F.2d 1312 (8th Cir. 1986), the Eighth Circuit addressed the issue of assignability of warranties. Armour Food Company, which owned a chicken processing plant, purchased two chicken processing machines from Simmons Engineering. Simmons warranted that the machines would operate properly or Armour was entitled to a refund of all monies paid for the equipment. Soon after this warranty was issued, Armour sold the plant and equipment "as is" to Gold'n Plump, who immediately encountered problems with Simmons' chicken-processing machines. After an attempted modification of the machines, Gold'n Plump concluded that they were useless and requested a refund of the purchase price based on Simmons' warranty to Armour. Simmons refused, and Gold'n Plump sought relief in the courts. The court responded as follows:

> Gold'n Plump asserts that the plant sale agreement provided for assignment of Armour's warranty rights against Simmons.
>
> The Minnesota UCC [§ 2-210] authorizes such an assignment of contract rights. However, a subsequent purchaser of a warranted article is not automatically entitled to a cause of action against the original seller for breach of warranty. There must be a contract of assignment of rights to entitle the subsequent purchaser to this cause of action. . . . An assignment generally requires the underlying elements of a valid contract, including intent. . . .
>
> There is no evidence in the record of intent to assign Armour's warranty rights against Simmons. The mere sale of the plant did not create a warranty assignment. Although the sales agreement specifically listed certain of Armour's rights against third parties as assigned to Gold'n Plump, it made no reference to rights against Simmons. The omission of this assignment clearly indicates that Gold'n Plump did not intend to reserve a right of direct action against Simmons. We note further that the parties negotiating the plant sale agreement were fully aware of the problems with the venter-opener machines. Accordingly, we affirm the district court's conclusion of no valid assignment.

Id. at 1316–17.

The court concluded that no valid assignment of the warranty rights occurred in *Gold'n Plump* because there was no explicit discussion of Simmons' warranty in the contract between Armour and Gold'n Plump. Assuming these parties had made explicit their intention to assign Simmons' warranty, would the assignment be effective? Would an assignment here "materially change the duty of the obligor [Simmons], or materially increase the burden or risk imposed on him by his contract . . . or materially reduce its value to him"? Restatement (Second) of Contracts

§ 317(2)(a). *See also* UCC § 2-210(2) Alternatively, could Simmons reject an explicit assignment of the warranty by claiming that their warranty was based on the long and "personal" nature of their relationship with Armour, which they lack with Gold'n Plump?

E.   NOVATION

An effective delegation does not discharge a promisor until the contractual performance is provided by the delegate. A discharge may result, however, if the parties enter into a novation. A novation is a three-party agreement in which the delegate agrees to perform the contractual duty to the promisee in consideration for the promisee's agreement to presently discharge the promisor. Novations are commonly employed in the sale of a business or of other continuing obligations. Consider, for example, the following case.

ROSENBERGER v. SON, INC.
Supreme Court of North Dakota
491 N.W.2d 71 (1992)

ERICKSTAD, J.

Harold Rosenberg and Gladys E. Rosenberg (Rosenbergs) appeal two district court decisions granting summary judgment in favor of Son, Inc., and Mary Pratt. We reverse and remand for further proceedings.

On February 8, 1980, Pratt entered into a contract for the sale of a business with the Rosenbergs, agreeing to purchase the Rosenbergs' Dairy Queen located in the City Center Mall in Grand Forks. The terms of the sales contract for the franchise, inventory, and equipment were a purchase price totaling $62,000, a $10,000 down payment, and $52,000 due in quarterly payments at 10 percent interest over a 15-year-period. The sales contract also contained a provision denying the buyer a right to prepayment for the first five years of the contract.

Mary Pratt assigned her rights and delegated her duties under the sales contract to Son, Inc., on October 1, 1982. The assignment agreement contained a "Consent To Assignment" clause which was signed by the Rosenbergs on October 14, 1982.[8] The assignment agreement also included a "save harmless" clause in which Son, Inc., promised to indemnify Pratt. [footnote omitted]. Subsequent to this transaction, Mary Pratt moved to Arizona and had no further knowledge of, or involvement with, the Dairy Queen business. Also following the assignment, the Dairy Queen was moved from the City Center Mall to the corner of DeMers and North Fifth Street in Grand Forks.

The sales contract was then assigned by Son, Inc., to Merit, Corporation (Merit) on June 1, 1984. This assignment agreement did not contain a consent clause for the

---

[8] [2] The language of the consent clause was very brief and direct. In full, it read: "The undersigned, Harold Rosenberg and Gladys E. Rosenberg, sellers in the above described Contract of Sale, do hereby consent to the above assignment."

Rosenbergs to sign. However, the Rosenbergs had knowledge of the assignment and apparently acquiesced. They accepted a large prepayment from Merit, reducing the principal balance due to $25,000. Following this assignment, Merit pledged the inventory and equipment of the Dairy Queen as collateral for a loan from Valley Bank and Trust of Grand Forks.

Payments from Merit to the Rosenbergs continued until June of 1988, at which time the payments ceased, leaving an unpaid principal balance of $17,326.24 plus interest. The Rosenbergs attempted collection of the balance from Merit, but the collection efforts were precluded when Merit filed bankruptcy. The business assets pledged as collateral for the loan from Valley Bank and Trust of Grand Forks were repossessed. The Rosenbergs brought this action for collection of the outstanding debt against Son, Inc., and Mary Pratt.

We disagree with the trial court's analysis and decision to grant summary judgment.

It is a well-established principle in the law of contracts that a contracting party cannot escape its liability on the contract by merely assigning its duties and rights under the contract to a third party. This principle is codified in Section 41-02-17(1), N.D.C.C.:

> "*Delegation of performance — Assignment of rights.*
>
> 1. A party may perform his duty through a delegate unless otherwise agreed or unless the other party has a substantial interest in having his original promisor perform or control the acts required by the contract. *No delegation of performance relieves the party delegating of any duty to perform or any liability for breach* [Emphasis added]."

Professor Corbin explained this point succinctly in his treatise on contract law.

> "An assignment is an expression of intention by the assignor that his duty shall immediately pass to the assignee. Many a debtor wishes that by such an expression he could get rid of his debts. Any debtor can express such an intention, but it is not operative to produce such a hoped-for result. It does not cause society to relax its compulsion against him and direct it toward the assignee as his substitute. In spite of such an 'assignment,' the debtor's duty remains absolutely unchanged. The performance required by a duty can often be delegated; but by such a delegation the duty itself is not escaped."

4 Corbin on Contracts § 866 at 452.

This rule of law applies to all categories of contracts, including contracts for the sale or lease of real property, service contracts, and contracts for the sale of goods, which is present in the facts of this case. "In the case of a contract for the sale of goods, the assignment and delegation may be by the buyer as well as by the seller. The buyer's assignment of his right to the goods and his delegation of the duty to pay the price are both effective; but he himself remains bound to pay the price just as before. If the assignee contracts with the assignor to pay the price, the seller can maintain suit for the price against the assignee also, as a creditor beneficiary of the assumption contract; *the seller has merely obtained a new and additional security.*"

Id. at 454-455 (emphasis added) (footnotes omitted).

Thus, when Pratt entered into the "assignment agreement" with Son, Inc., a simple assignment alone was insufficient to release her from any further liability on the contract. *See Jedco Development Co., Inc. v. Bertsch*, 441 N.W.2d 664 (N.D.1989) (lessee is not relieved of this obligation to pay rent merely because he had assigned lease with lessor's consent absent a novation); *Brooks v. Hayes*, 133 Wis.2d 228, 395 N.W.2d 167 (1986) (party delegating duties under contract is not relieved of responsibility for fulfilling an obligation or liability in the event of a breach). *See also* Restatement (Second) of Contracts § 318; 6A C.J.S. *Assignments* § 97 at 753; 6 Am.Jur.2d *Assignments* § 110; 67 Am.Jur.2d *Sales* § 383 at 649.

It is not, however, a legal impossibility for a contracting party to rid itself of an obligation under a contract. It may seek the approval of the other original party for release, and substitute a new party in its place. In such an instance, the transaction is no longer called an assignment; instead, it is called a novation. If a novation occurs in this manner, it must be clear from the terms of the agreement that a novation is intended by all parties involved. "An obligor is discharged by the substitution of a new obligor only if the contract so provides or if the obligee makes a binding manifestation of assent, forming a novation." Restatement (Second) of Contracts § 318 cmt. d. Therefore, both original parties to the contract must intend and mutually assent to the discharge of the obligor from any further liability on the original contract.

It is evident from the express language of the assignment agreement between Pratt and Son, Inc., that only an assignment was intended, not a novation.[9] The agreement made no mention of discharging Pratt from any further liability on the contract. To the contrary, the latter part of the agreement contained an indemnity clause holding Pratt harmless in the event of a breach by Son, Inc. Thus, it is apparent that Pratt contemplated being held ultimately responsible for performance of the obligation.

Furthermore, the agreement was between Pratt and Son, Inc.; they were the parties signing the agreement, not the Rosenbergs. An agreement between Pratt and Son, Inc., cannot unilaterally affect the Rosenbergs' rights under the contract.

As mentioned earlier, the Rosenbergs did sign a consent to the assignment at the bottom of the agreement. However, by merely consenting to the assignment, the Rosenbergs did not consent to a discharge of the principal obligor — Pratt. Nothing in the language of the consent clause supports such an allegation. A creditor is free to consent to an assignment without releasing the original obligor.

> "Where the obligee consents to the delegation, the consent itself does not release the obligor from liability for breach of contract. More than the obligee's consent to a delegation of performance is needed to release the obligor from liability for breach of contract. For the obligor to be released from liability, the obligee must agree to the release. If there is an agreement between the obligor, obligee and a third party by which the third party agrees to be substituted for the obligor and the obligee assents

---

[9] [8] The agreement itself was titled "ASSIGNMENT OF CONTRACT FOR SALE." . . .

thereto, the obligor is released from liability and the third person takes the place of the obligor. Such an agreement is known as a novation." Brooks v. Hayes, 395 N.W.2d at 174.

See also Jedco Development Co., Inc. v. Bertsch, 441 N.W.2d at 666 ("a lessee is not relieved of his obligation to pay rent merely because he has assigned the lease with the lessor's consent . . . rather, the lessor must intend to release the lessee"). Thus, the express language of the agreement and intent of the parties at the time the assignment was made did not contemplate a novation by releasing Pratt and substituting Son, Inc., in her stead.

Without thoroughly acknowledging the above principles and their importance, the trial court concluded that once Pratt assigned her contract she became a guarantor on the contract. The trial court proceeded to apply North Dakota guaranty statutes and guaranty case law to Pratt, and exonerated her under that authority. We do not believe that the trial court appropriately applied the law.

As stressed above, a party assigning its rights and delegating its duties is still a party to the original contract. An assignment will not extinguish the relationship and obligations between the two original contracting parties. However, an assignment does result in the assignor having a surety relationship, albeit involuntary, with the assignee, but not with the other original contracting party.

> "A common instance of involuntary suretyship, *at least as between the principal and surety themselves*, occurs where one party to a contract [Son, Inc.], as a part of the agreement, assumes an indebtedness owing by the other [Pratt] to a third person [the Rosenbergs], the one assuming the indebtedness becoming the principal [Son, Inc.], and the former debtor a surety [Pratt]." 72 C.J.S. *Principal and Surety* § 35 (emphasis added).

Therefore, in the present facts, Pratt enjoyed a surety position as to Son, Inc., but remained a principal on the contract with the Rosenbergs. The inquiry as to Pratt's liability does not end at this juncture. Pursuant to guaranty law, the trial court released Pratt from any liability on the contract due to the changes or alterations which took place following her assignment to Son, Inc. While it is true that Pratt cannot be forced to answer on the contract irrespective of events occurring subsequent to her assignment, it is also true that she cannot be exonerated for *every* type of alteration or change that may develop.

> "The buyer can assign his right to the goods or land and can delegate performance of his duty to pay the price. He himself remains bound as before by his duty to pay that price. But observe that he remains bound 'as before'; the assignee and the seller cannot, by agreement or by waiver, make it the assignor's duty to pay a different price or on different conditions. If the seller is willing to make such a change, he must trust to the assignee alone. It has been held that, if a tender of delivery by a certain time is a condition precedent to the buyer's duty to pay, the assignee of the buyer has no power to waive this condition, and substantial delay by the seller will prevent his getting judgment against the assignor for the price. If the assignee has contracted to pay the price, his waiver of the condition

will be effective in a suit against him, but it will not be allowed to prejudice the position of the assignor, who now occupies substantially the position of surety."

4 Corbin on Contracts § 866 at 458-459.

The trial court decided pursuant to guaranty statutes, Section 22-01-15, N.D.C.C., and case law, *Tri-Continental Leasing Corp. v. Gunter*, 472 N.W.2d 437, that any alteration in the underlying obligation resulted in a release of Pratt on the contract. It appears that an assignor occupies a much different position from that of a guarantor; not every type of alteration is sufficient to warrant discharge of the assignor. As suggested by Professor Corbin, the alteration must "prejudice the position of the assignor." 4 Corbin on Contracts § 866 at 459.

> "Accordingly, unless the other contracting party has consented to release him, the assignor remains bound by his obligations under the contract and is liable to the other party if the assignee defaults,. . . . However, the assignor is responsible only for the obligation which he originally contracted to assume, and the assignee cannot, without the assignor's knowledge, *increase the burden*."

6A C.J.S. *Assignments* § 97 at 753-754 (emphasis added).

Further authority for this principle is found in *Jedco*, 441 N.W.2d 664. The facts in *Jedco* involved an assignment of the lease of a building, to which the lessor consented. Various changes occurred following the assignment of the lease. When the assignee defaulted, the lessor sued the assignor for uncollected rental payments. This Court reversed the summary judgment of the trial court, which judgment was in favor of the assignor, and remanded for further proceedings. Justice VandeWalle, speaking for the Court, said:

> "Thus, if the lessor and assignee materially change the terms of the lease as it existed between the lessor and assignor, a new tenancy relationship is established and the assignor is released from his obligations under the original lease. This rule of law is qualified, however, in that: 'The [assignor] is not discharged, however, by *variations which inure to his benefit.* Nor is the [assignor] discharged by agreements between lessor and assignee which may increase the liability of the [assignor], but which are permitted by the terms of the original lease, to the benefits of which the assignee is entitled.' *Walker v. Rednalloh Co.*, 299 Mass. 591, 595-596, 13 N.E.2d 394, 397 (1938)."

Jedco, 441 N.W.2d at 667 (emphasis added). See also Boswell v. Lyon, 401 N.E.2d 735 (Ind.1980) (subsequent assignments do not relieve the assignor of any liability on the contract because it is not a change in the time or manner of payment).

If the changes in the obligation prejudicially affect the assignor, a new agreement has been formed between the assignee and the other original contracting party. More concisely, a novation has occurred and the assignor's original obligation has been discharged. This is consistent with our previous decisions and statutory authority. *See* Section 9-13-09, N.D.C.C. Although we have previously determined that the terms of the assignment agreement between Pratt and Son, Inc., did not contemplate a novation, there are additional methods of making a novation besides doing so in the express terms of an agreement. In Jedco, we held that:

> "The intent to create a novation may be shown not only by the terms of the agreement itself, but also by the character of the transaction and by the facts and circumstances surrounding the transaction. *Cane River Shopping Center v. Monsour*, [443 So.2d 602 (La.Ct.App.1983)]."

441 N.W.2d at 666.

The question of whether or not there has been a novation is a question of fact, as decided by this Court in *Herb Hill Ins., Inc. v. Radtke*, 380 N.W.2d 651. "[T]he question of whether or not there has been a novation is a question of fact if the evidence is such that reasonable persons can draw more than one conclusion." Id. at 654. [citations omitted].

The trial court should not have granted summary judgment on the basis of guaranty law. First of all, guaranty law does not apply to contract assignments without more. Further, there are questions of fact remaining as to the result of the changes in the contract. These issues were not addressed by the trial court. In reversing and remanding in *Jedco*, we said:

> "We cannot determine as a matter of law that the assignment was intended to be a novation which resulted in a release of [the assignor's] liability under the lease. Because there are different inferences to be drawn from the undisputed facts, reasonable persons could draw more than one conclusion in this case. Therefore, the summary judgment is reversed and the case is remanded for further proceedings." 441 N.W.2d at 668.

We must do the same in this case. Thus, we reverse the summary judgment and remand for further proceedings.

NOTES

1. *Continuing Obligations in Assignment Law.* In *Rosenberger*, the court held that Ms. Pratt would still be liable to the Rosenbergs if her subsequent transfer of rights and obligations to Son, Inc. only amounted to an assignment, and not a novation. Thus, even though she had no connection with the operation or subsequent transfers of the Dairy Queen after 1982, Ms. Pratt might still be liable for the outstanding debt owed the Rosenbergs in 1992.

Compare this conclusion to *Allianz Life Ins. Co. of N. Am. v. Riedl*, 264 Ga. 395, 444 S.E.2d 736 (1994). In *Riedl*, the Georgia Supreme Court considered the question of whether an insured, having assigned their right to payment under a medical insurance policy to a medical provider, could still sue their insurer for payment. The court held that once an assignor had transferred their right to payment in a contract with the obligor, the assignor also had transferred their substantive right to enforce the contract, in this case Riedl's insurance policy with the defendant insurer. After assignment, only the assignee can maintain an action on the contract against the obligor.

2. *The Equities of Assignment and Delegation.* *Rosenberger* raises an interesting question regarding the equities between assignment and delegation. It is well-accepted, for example, that a delegation of the assignor's duties does not discharge the assignor of ultimate responsibility for those duties, unless the parties explicitly agree to discharge the assignor of any future liability (i.e., grant the assignor a novation). *See* RESTATEMENT (SECOND) CONTRACTS § 318(3); UCC § 2-210(1). The Supreme Court of North Dakota thus concluded that, absent the parties' intention to make Ms. Pratt's assignment of the Dairy Queen to Son, Inc. a novation, Ms. Pratt would remain liable to the Rosenbergs. On the other hand, an assignment by the assignor extinguishes the assignor's right to enforce the contract herself, leaving sole power of enforcement to the assignee. *See* RESTATEMENT (SECOND) CONTRACTS § 317 (1). *Riedl* demonstrates this principle, since Riedl's assignment of his right to payment also eliminated his ability to sue the obligor, his insurer, for that payment. Considering *Rosenberger* together with *Riedl* thus demonstrates that an assignor remains liable on the original contract should her assignee default, but also loses the power to enforce her rights under the contract should the assignee fail to assert them. Can you think of a policy rationale for this inequitable distribution of post-assignment rights and obligations? Considering this situation, how easy do you think it would be to obtain a novation as an assignor?

F.   BIBLIOGRAPHY AND SUGGESTED READING

Arthur Corbin, *Contracts for the Benefit of Third Persons*, 27 YALE L.J. 1008 (1918).

Larry A. Dimatteo, *Depersonalization of Personal Service Contracts: The Search for a Modern Approach to Assignability*, 27 AKRON L. REV. 407 (1994).

Melvin A. Eisenberg, *Third-Party Beneficiaries*, 92 COLUM. L. REV. 1358 (1992).

William R. Jones, *Legal Protection of Third Party Beneficiaries: On Opening Courthouse Doors*, 46 U. CIN. L. REV. 313 (1977).

Peter Karsten, *The "Discovery" of Law by English and American Jurists of the Seventeenth, Eighteenth, and Nineteenth Centuries: Third-Party Beneficiary Contracts as a Test Case*, 9 LAW & HIST. REV. 327 (1991).

Barbara Walker, Note, *Attorney's Liability to Third Parties for Malpractice: The Growing Acceptance of Liability in the Absence of Privity*, 21 WASHBURN L.J. 48 (1981).

William H. Page, *The Power of the Contracting Parties to Alter a Contract for Rendering Performance to a Third Person*, 12 WIS. L. REV. 141 (1937).

Orna Paglin, *Criteria for Recognition of Third Party Beneficiaries' Rights*, 24 N. ENG. L. REV. 63 (1989).

Harry G. Prince, *Perfecting the Third Party Beneficiary Standing Rule Under Section 302 of the Restatement (Second) of Contracts*, 25 B.C. L. REV. 919, 973–90 (1984).

Anthony Jon Waters, *The Property in the Promise: A Study of the Third Party Beneficiary Rule*, 98 HARV. L. REV. 1109 (1985).

Samuel Williston, *Contracts for the Benefit of a Third Person*, 15 Harv. L. Rev. 767 (1902).

John Wladis, *The Contract Formation Sections of the Proposed Revisions to U.C.C. Article 2*, 54 Smu L. Rev. 997 (2001).

TABLE OF CASES

[References are to pages.]

[References are to pages.]

[References are to pages.]

[References are to pages.]

[References are to pages.]

[References are to pages.]

[References are to pages.]

[References are to pages.]

[References are to pages.]

T

U

[References are to pages.]

INDEX

[References are to chapters and sections.]

[References are to chapters and sections.]

[References are to chapters and sections.]

[References are to chapters and sections.]